A significantly expanded range of issues and international sweep. Cutting edge stuff – original and challenging essays reaching way beyond the useful overview of the field that the title *Handbook* conjures up.

David Brown, *Emeritus Professor, Law Faculty,*
University of NSW, Sydney, Australia

An impressive collection of essays addressing some of the key issues in prison research and practice which are currently engaging policy makers, academics and practitioners alike. This is a considerable achievement for the editors – Yvonne Jewkes, Jamie Bennett and Ben Crewe, who have brought together leading authorities in the field to write about these issues in a fresh and engaging way. If you only buy one textbook on prisons this year, make sure that it is this one.

Dr Sharon Shalev, *Centre for Criminology,*
University of Oxford, UK

The arrival of this second edition of the *Handbook on Prisons* could not be more timely. Mass incarceration, perhaps the most significant social fact of our time, is both expanding and transforming on a global basis. The new volume brings the world's leading experts on penology and punishment and society together and forges a comprehensive platform of historical, theoretical, and problem centered frameworks to analyze the present conjuncture.

Jonathan S. Simon, *Adrian A. Kragen Professor of Law; Director of the*
Center for the Study of Law and Society, UC Berkeley, USA

Handbook on Prisons

The second edition of the *Handbook on Prisons* provides a completely revised and updated collection of essays on a wide range of topics concerning prisons and imprisonment. Bringing together three of the leading prison scholars in the UK as editors, this new volume builds on the success of the first edition and reveals the range and depth of prison scholarship around the world.

The *Handbook* not only contains chapters written by those who have established and developed prison research, but also features contributions from ex-prisoners, prison governors and ex-governors, prison inspectors and others who have worked with prisoners in a wide range of professional capacities. This second edition includes several completely new chapters on topics as diverse as prison design, technology in prisons, the high security estate, therapeutic communities, prisons and desistance, supermax and solitary confinement, plus a brand-new section on international perspectives. The *Handbook* aims to convey the reality of imprisonment, and to reflect the main issues and debates surrounding prisons and prisoners, while also providing novel ways of thinking about familiar penal problems and enhancing our theoretical understanding of imprisonment.

The *Handbook on Prisons, Second edition* is a key text for students taking courses in prisons, penology, criminal justice, criminology and related subjects, and is also an essential reference for academics and practitioners working in the prison service, or in related agencies, who need up-to-date knowledge of thinking on prisons and imprisonment.

Yvonne Jewkes is Professor of Criminology at the University of Brighton. She is editor of the first *Handbook on Prisons* (2007), author of *Captive Audience: Media, Masculinity and Power in Prisons* (2002), and series editor (with Ben Crewe and Thomas Ugelvik) of *Palgrave Studies in Prisons and Penology*. Professor Jewkes's publications on prison architecture include (with Philip Hancock) 'Penal Aesthetics and the Pains of Imprisonment', *Punishment & Society*; (with Dominique Moran) 'The paradox of the "green" prison: sustaining the environment or sustaining the penal complex?', *Theoretical Criminology*; and 'The Aesthetics and Anaesthetics of Prison Architecture', in J. Simon et al., *Architecture and Justice* (2013).

Ben Crewe is Deputy Director of the Prisons Research Centre at the Institute of Criminology, University of Cambridge. Dr Crewe has published widely on prisons and imprisonment, and is on the editorial board of the *British Journal of Criminology*. His current research is on prisoners serving very long sentences from an early age.

Jamie Bennett has been a prison manager since 1996 and is currently Governor of HMP Grendon and Spring Hill. Dr Bennett is also a Research Associate at the University of Oxford and has edited *Prison Service Journal* since 2004. He has written widely on prisons and was awarded a PhD at the University of Edinburgh.

...book on Prisons

Second edition

Edited by
Yvonne Jewkes, Ben Crewe and
Jamie Bennett

 Routledge
Taylor & Francis Group

LONDON AND NEW YORK

Second edition published 2016
by Routledge
2 Park Square, Milton Park, Abingdon, Oxon OX14 4RN

and by Routledge
711 Third Avenue, New York, NY 10017

Routledge is an imprint of the Taylor & Francis Group, an informa business

British Library Cataloguing in Publication Data
A catalogue record for this book is available from the British Library

Library of Congress Cataloging in Publication Data
Handbook on prisons / edited by Yvonne Jewkes, Ben Crewe and Jamie Bennett. – Second edition.
        pages cm
    1. Prisons–Great Britain. 2. Prison administration–Great Britain. 3. Prisoners–Great Britain. 4. Imprisonment–Great Britain. I. Jewkes, Yvonne, 1966- II. Crewe, Ben. III. Bennett, Jamie.
        HV9647.H38 2016
        365'.941–dc23
                2015025831

ISBN: 978-0-415-74565-9 (hbk)
ISBN: 978-0-415-74566-6 (pbk)
ISBN: 978-1-315-79777-9 (ebk)

Typeset in Bembo
by Taylor & Francis Books

MIX
Paper from
responsible sources
FSC® C013056
www.fsc.org

Printed and bound in Great Britain by
TJ International Ltd, Padstow, Cornwall

Contents

List of illustrations	xi
Acknowledgement	xiii
List of contributors	xiv
Abbreviations	xvii

Introduction   1
YVONNE JEWKES, BEN CREWE AND JAMIE BENNETT

PART I
Prisons in context   **5**

1 Prisons in context   7
ANDREW COYLE

2 Prison histories, 1770s–1950s: Continuities and contradictions   24
HELEN JOHNSTON

3 The aims of imprisonment   39
IAN O'DONNELL

4 The politics of imprisonment   55
RICHARD SPARKS, JESSICA BIRD AND LOUISE BRANGAN

5 The sociology of imprisonment   77
BEN CREWE

6 Prison expansionism   101
DEBORAH H. DRAKE

7 Prison design and carceral space   114
DOMINIQUE MORAN, YVONNE JEWKES AND JENNIFER TURNER

8 Prison managerialism: Global change and local cultures in the working lives of prison managers   131
JAMIE BENNETT

PART II
Prison controversies 147

9 Private prisons 149
JOHN RYNNE AND RICHARD HARDING

10 Segregation and supermax confinement: An ethical evaluation 169
DEREK S. JEFFREYS

11 Mental health in prisons 187
ALICE MILLS AND KATHLEEN KENDALL

12 Drug misuse in prison 205
MICHAEL WHEATLEY

13 Suicide, distress and the quality of prison life 224
ALISON LIEBLING AND AMY LUDLOW

14 Sex offenders in prison 246
RUTH E. MANN

15 The prison officer 265
HELEN ARNOLD

16 Prisons and technology: General lessons from the American context 284
ROBERT JOHNSON AND KATIE HAIL-JARES

PART III
International perspectives on imprisonment 307

17 Punishment and political economy 309
ESTER MASSA

18 Prisons and human rights 324
PETER BENNETT

19 An international overview of the initiatives to accommodate
Indigenous prisoners 340
ELIZABETH GRANT

20 Ironies of American imprisonment: From capitalizing on prisons to
capital punishment 359
MICHAEL WELCH

21 Houses for the poor: Continental European prisons 375
VINCENZO RUGGIERO

22 Prisons as welfare institutions?: Punishment and the Nordic model 388
THOMAS UGELVIK

23 Australasian prisons   403
    CLAIRE SPIVAKOVSKY

24 Prisons in Africa   423
    ANDREW M. JEFFERSON AND TOMAS MAX MARTIN

25 Asian prisons: Colonial pasts, neo-liberal futures and subversive sites   441
    MAHUYA BANDYOPADHYAY

26 Latin American prisons   460
    SACHA DARKE AND MARIA LÚCIA KARAM

PART IV
The penal spectrum   **475**

27 High security prisons in England and Wales: Principles and practice   477
    ALISON LIEBLING

28 Therapeutic communities   497
    ALISA STEVENS

29 Older age, harder time: Ageing and imprisonment   514
    NATALIE MANN

30 Young people and prison   529
    ROB ALLEN

31 Doing gendered time: The harms of women's incarceration   549
    LINDA MOORE AND PHIL SCRATON

32 Race, ethnicity, multiculture and prison life   568
    ROD EARLE

33 The prisoner: Inside and out   586
    JASON WARR

PART V
Beyond the prison   **605**

34 Prisons and desistance   607
    FERGUS MCNEILL AND MARGUERITE SCHINKEL

35 Social injustice and collateral damage: The families and children of prisoners   622
    RACHEL CONDRY, ANNA KOTOVA AND SHONA MINSON

36 Inspecting the prison   641
    NICK HARDWICK

37 Researching the prison   659
    YVONNE JEWKES AND SERENA WRIGHT

38 Representing the prison   677
    EAMONN CARRABINE

39 Imprisonment in a global world: Rethinking penal power   698
    MARY BOSWORTH, INÊS HASSELBERG AND SARAH TURNBULL

40 Campaigning for and campaigning against prisons: Excavating and
    reaffirming the case for prison abolition   712
    MICK RYAN AND JOE SIM

    Index   734

Illustrations

Figures

13.1 Modelling overall distress GHQ-12 and suicide rates   236
13.2 Distress and well-being in prison   237
13.3 Prison quality and prison suicide: a testable working model   238
14.1 Reconviction rates by index offence, 2005–12   247
17.1 Incarceration rates in the USA and Italy (1850–2006), per 100,000   319
24.1 Prison population rate per 100,000 in Africa, 2014   427
24.2 Occupancy level in African prisons, 2014 (%)   428
24.3 Pre-trial detainees in African prisons, 2014 (%)   429
38.1 Het Rasp-Huys   680
38.2 The Representations of the several Fetters, Irons, & Ingines of Torture that were taken from the Marshalsea Prison   683
38.3 The Gaols Committee of the House of Commons   684
38.4 The Chapel, Pentonville, 1862   687
38.5 Newgate Prison   689
38.6 PAR55771 – USA. Huntsville, Texas. 1968   692
38.7 LON92615 – South Africa. Beaufort West. 2006   694

Tables

6.1 Selected imprisonment rates per 100,000 population in 2003 and 2013, and percentage change   102
13.1 Percentage frequency of imported vulnerability per prison   227
13.2 Difference between groups of prisoners in level of distress   235
13.3 Correlation between institutional suicide rates and distress variables (n=12)   235
14.1 Reoffending rates by risk band for RM2000 and OSP   248
14.2 Recent systematic reviews of sex offender treatment effectiveness   258
15.1 EQ factor scores for prison officers   276
15.2 EQ subscale scores for prison officers   276
22.1 Nordic prison systems: key figures   390
22.2 New arrivals in the Nordic Correctional Services, relative to population   390
23.1 Australia's imprisonment rate, 1970–2013   404
23.2 Number of unsentenced prisoners in Australia, 2003–13   405

23.3 Percentage of sentenced male prisoners in Australia by most serious
       offence, 2003–13   406
23.4 Percentage of sentenced female prisoners in Australia by most serious
       offence, 2003–13   406
23.5 Percentage of Indigenous people in Australian prisons 2003–13   407
23.6 Pacific islands of Australasia prison statistics   412

Box

3.1   A miscellany of aims   42

Acknowledgement

Thanks go to Helen Fair, the *Prison Service Journal*, Amsterdam City Archives, The British Library Board, The National Portrait Gallery, Mary Evans Picture Library, Danny Lyon, Magnum Photos, Mikhael Subotzky and Taylor & Francis for their kind permission to reproduce previously published material in this book.

Contributors

Rob Allen, Justice and Prisons, UK.

Helen Arnold, University Campus Suffolk, UK.

Mahuya Bandyopadhyay, Tata Institute of Social Sciences, India.

Jamie Bennett, HMP Grendon and Spring Hill, UK.

Peter Bennett, former Governor of HMP Grendon and Spring Hill and former Director of International Centre for Prison Studies, UK.

Jessica Bird, University of Edinburgh, UK.

Mary Bosworth, University of Oxford, UK.

Louise Brangan, University of Edinburgh, UK.

Eamonn Carrabine, University of Essex, UK.

Rachel Condry, University of Oxford, UK.

Andrew Coyle, University of Essex, UK.

Ben Crewe, University of Cambridge, UK.

Sacha Darke, University of Westminster, UK.

Deborah H. Drake, The Open University, UK.

Rod Earle, The Open University, UK.

Elizabeth Grant, University of Adelaide, Australia.

Katie Hail-Jares, American University, USA.

Richard Harding, University of Western Australia, Australia.

Nick Hardwick, HM Chief Inspector of Prisons, England and Wales.

Inês Hasselberg, University of Oxford, UK.

Andrew M. Jefferson, DIGNITY – Danish Institute Against Torture, Denmark.

Derek S. Jeffreys, University of Wisconsin, USA.

Yvonne Jewkes, University of Brighton, UK.

Robert Johnson, American University, USA.

Helen Johnston, University of Hull, UK.

Maria Lúcia Karam, Carioca Institute of Criminology, Brazil.

Kathleen Kendall, University of Southampton, UK.

Anna Kotova, University of Oxford, UK.

Alison Liebling, University of Cambridge, UK.

Amy Ludlow, University of Cambridge, UK.

Fergus McNeill, University of Glasgow, UK.

Natalie Mann, Anglia Ruskin University, UK.

Ruth E. Mann, National Offender Management Service, England and Wales.

Tomas Max Martin, Danish Institute for Human Rights, Denmark.

Ester Massa, University of Winchester, UK.

Alice Mills, University of Auckland, New Zealand.

Shona Minson, University of Oxford, UK.

Linda Moore, University of Ulster, UK.

Dominique Moran, University of Birmingham, UK.

Ian O'Donnell, University College Dublin, Republic of Ireland.

Vincenzo Ruggiero, University of Middlesex, UK.

Mick Ryan, University of Greenwich, UK.

John Rynne, Griffith University Brisbane, Australia.

Marguerite Schinkel, University of Glasgow, UK.

Phil Scraton, Queen's University Belfast, UK.

Joe Sim, Liverpool John Moores University, UK.

Richard Sparks, University of Edinburgh, UK.

Claire Spivakovsky, Monash University Melbourne, Australia.

Alisa Stevens, University of Southampton, UK.

Sarah Turnbull, University of Oxford, UK.

Jennifer Turner, University of Leicester, UK.

Thomas Ugelvik, University of Tromso, Norway.

Jason Warr, University of Lincoln, UK.

Michael Welch, Rutgers University, USA.

Michael Wheatley, National Offender Management Service, England and Wales.

Serena Wright, University of Cambridge, UK.

Abbreviations

ACA	American Correctional Association
ACCT	Assessment, Care in Custody and Teamwork
ACM	Australian Correctional Management
BFM	Buildings and Facilities Management
BOSS	Body Orifice Security Scanning
CCA	Corrections Corporation of America
CHE	Community Homes with Education
CIES	Correctional Institution Environment Scale
C of C	Community of Communities
CPT	(European) Committee for the Prevention of Torture and Inhuman or Degrading Treatment or Punishment
CQC	Care Quality Commission
CRC	Control Review Committee
CRC	Community Rehabilitation Company
CRE	Commission for Racial Equality
CSAAP	Correctional Services Accreditation and Advisory Panel
CSC	Close Supervision Centre
CSC	Correctional Service Canada
D&B	Design & Build
DCMF	Design, Construct, Manage and Finance
DFID	Department for International Development
DoH	Department of Health
DSPD	Dangerous and Severe Personality Disorder
DTO	Detention and Training Order
DYOI	Detention in a Young Offender Institution
ECHR	European Convention on Human Rights
EQ	emotional intelligence
EU	European Union
FBP	Federal Bureau of Prisons
FCC	Federal Communications Commission
FCO	Foreign and Commonwealth Office
GHQ	General Health Questionnaire
GP	general practitioner
HC Deb	House of Commons Debate
HIPP	Health in Prisons Programme

HL Deb	House of Lords Debate
HMCIP	Her Majesty's Chief Inspector of Prisons
HMIC	Her Majesty's Inspectorate of Constabulary
HMIP	Her Majesty's Inspectorate of Prisons
HMPS	Her Majesty's Prison Service
ICCPR	International Covenant on Civil and Political Rights
ICESCR	International Covenant on Economic, Social and Cultural Rights
ICPS	International Centre for Prison Studies
ICRC	International Committee of the Red Cross
IEP	incentive and earned privilege
IMB	Independent Monitoring Board
IPP	indeterminate imprisonment for public protection
IRA	Irish Republican Army
IRC	immigration removal centre
JE	Joint Enterprise
KPI	key performance indicator
KPT	key performance target
LASCH	Local Authority Secure Children's Home
LASH	Local Authority Secure Home
LWOP	life without parole
MDT	mandatory drug testing
MHIRT	mental health in-reach team
M&M	Manage & Maintain
MMPR	Minimizing and Managing Physical Restraint
MoJ	Ministry of Justice
MQPL	measuring the quality of prison life
NACRO	National Association for the Care and Resettlement of Offenders
NGO	non-governmental organization
NHS	National Health Service
NIHRC	Northern Ireland Human Rights Commission
NOMS	National Offender Management Service
NPM	National Preventive Mechanism
NPM	new public management
NPS	novel psychoactive substances
OASys	Offender Assessment System
ONS	Office for National Statistics
OPCAT	Optional Protocol to the United Nations Convention against Torture and Other Cruel, Inhuman or Degrading Treatment or Punishment
OPDP	offender personality disorder pathway
OSP	OASys Sexual Predictor
PCT	Primary Care Trust
PFI	Private Finance Initiative
PIPE	psychologically informed planned environment
POA	Prison Officers Association
PPI	Prison Policy Institute
PPO	Prison and Probation Ombudsman
PPP	public–private partnership

PRC	Prisons Research Centre
PROP	Preservation of the Rights of Prisoners
PRS	Prison Rating System
PRT	Prison Reform Trust
PRT	Prison Review Team
PSO	Prison Service Order
RAB	Restraint Advisory Board
RAP	Radical Alternatives to Prison
RNR	Risk, Need and Responsivity
ROTL	release on temporary licence
RRF	Returns and Reintegration Fund
SCH	Secure Children's Home
SEU	Social Exclusion Unit
SMART	Systematic Monitoring and Analysing of Race Equality Template
SMI	severe mental illness
SOP	standard operating procedure
SOV	special operating vehicle
SPV	special purpose vehicle
SPT	Sub-committee on Prevention of Torture
STC	Secure Training Centre
STO	Secure Training Order
TBI	traumatic brain injury
TC	therapeutic community
TUPE	(European) Transfer Undertaking Protection of Employment
UDHR	Universal Declaration of Human Rights
UKBA	UK Border Authority
UN	United Nations
VPU	Vulnerable Prisoner Unit
WHO	World Health Organization
YJB	Youth Justice Board
YOI	Young Offender Institution

Introduction

Yvonne Jewkes, Ben Crewe and Jamie Bennett

As we send this second edition of the *Handbook on Prisons* to print, it is inevitable that we reflect on the state of imprisonment in the nine years since the first edition came out. It is tempting to see the last decade as another chapter of unmitigated failure in the history of punishment. Between the end of 2006 and the end of 2013 the global prison population increased from 9.25 million to 10.2 million (Walmsley 2007, 2013). As the World Prison Population List (www.apcca.org/uploads/10th_Edition_2013.pdf) shows, prisoner numbers are growing in all five continents and most of the countries represented in this volume imprison more people today than they did when the *Handbook* first came out. There are, of course, exceptions, and the picture of incarceration is not entirely bleak. Even the league table leader, the USA, has seen a small drop in its prison population – from 738 to 716 per 100,000 of the general population – and, while this might barely seem noteworthy given the size and scale of the total numbers of people that America locks up, some of the most significant decreases have been in conservative states such as Texas and Arkansas. Optimists might highlight the fact that such decreases have been occurring year-on-year since 2010 and that, although initially driven by necessity in an economic recession, the decline has subsequently been attributed to a softening of public punitiveness and a redirection of public spending priorities from crime to health and education. One scholar, Natasha Frost, has gone so far as to say 'This is the beginning of the end of mass incarceration' (quoted in *The New York Times*, 23 July 2013).

Of course, any criminology student will immediately want to look behind these figures and examine who is more, or less, likely to be sentenced to custody, what kinds of offences no longer carry a prison sentence that previously did, and what kinds of prison conditions are experienced by those left in the system. Like its predecessor, this second edition of the *Handbook* aims to look behind the statistics and try to convey some of the realities of imprisonment as they are shaped by those in power and experienced by those with relatively little power. Indeed, this second edition is even more wide ranging and ambitious than the first edition, with an additional ten chapters, including a new section on international perspectives, to reflect the growth of high-quality scholarship on prisons across the world and to encourage thinking about imprisonment in a global context. Contributors to the *Handbook* have also gone beyond thinking about the prison as a bounded institution (that is, bounded by time, space or place) and considered, in myriad ways, how the present and the past intertwine, the importance of viewing any country's incarcerated population heterogeneously, the extent to which the 'effects' of prison are felt far beyond its physical walls, and how 'imprisonment' has spread into other areas of state practice.

Once again we have gathered together many of the leading scholars in penology and asked them to reflect on the main issues and debates surrounding prisons and prisoners while providing new ways of thinking about familiar penal problems and enhancing our theoretical understanding of imprisonment. However, this second edition should not be regarded as a straightforward 'replacement' of the first edition and, in many ways, they can be read alongside each other. Of course, some aspects of the penal landscape have changed since 2007, yet much of the content of the first *Handbook on Prisons* remains pertinent and it contains chapters on topics that, for various reasons, could not be included in this second edition. However, like its forerunner, this second volume reveals the range and depth of current knowledge about prisons, combining contributions from many of those who have established and developed prison research over the last half-century and who continue to shape it in its current phase, with more recent entrants to prison studies who are building on this tradition and breaking new ground. The volume also contains contributions from prison governors, ex-governors, non-academic specialists, and from a chief inspector of prisons in England and Wales.

The *Handbook* is divided into five parts, each of which is distinctive in its focus, yet interrelated in many of the themes and issues raised. The first part considers the prison in its comparative and historical context. It looks at the birth of the modern prison and considers changing aims and rationales for imprisonment over the last three centuries. The chapters individually and collectively address many important questions concerning the purpose, aims and understandings of imprisonment. How important are historical contexts and continuities for our understanding of the current penal landscape? How have philosophies of punishment changed and what can they tell us about what prisons are for? How should philosophical aims be reconciled with performance measures and targets? What drives prison expansionism? Why do some countries have very high prison populations while others maintain low rates of incarceration? Why do imprisonment rates not always correlate with crime rates? To what extent does the architecture and design of prisons indicate what goes on within their walls? What impact does space and place have on the lives of a prison's occupants? How are prisons managed?

The second part of the *Handbook* reflects on some of the controversies that have dominated penal discussions over many years. By their very nature controversial, prisons are suffused with contentious policies and practices and this section of the *Handbook* looks at some of them. How can prisons achieve a balance between custody and care, decency and austerity? What has been the impact of the introduction of private sector punishment provision? On what grounds, and with what effects, is solitary confinement imposed upon prisoners? What is the mental health profile of the prison population? What role do drugs play in the lives of prisoners? What are the causes of and solutions to prisoner suicide and self-harm? How are sex offenders imprisoned and treated, with what results? Who are prison officers, what do they do, and what constitutes 'good' prison officer work? What is the role and use of technology in prisons?

Part III discusses international perspectives on imprisonment, exploring the role of the states and the political contexts within which imprisonment is located. The task of this section includes describing the practices of imprisonment in different states. What is the rate of imprisonment in different countries? What are the characteristic practices and cultures of those institutions? How does the use of imprisonment reflect the relationship between political economy, the state and the prison in different jurisdictions? Collectively, the chapters invite comparative and critical reflections. What practices are replicated and repeated across states? In what ways do countries vary in their practices, and why? Are certain practices to be considered more equitable or effective than others? What can be learned or transferred through international dialogue? As a whole, the chapters also raise broader questions about criminal justice in an age of globalization. Each jurisdiction has its own unique story to tell about the interplay between global trends and historically rooted local cultures. These stories reveal issues not only about the technicalities and everyday practices of imprisonment, but also about global and national power structures that criminal justice systems reflect and sustain.

The fourth part of the volume looks at some of the prisoners who make up the prison population and discusses some of the issues affecting them as they enter, experience and leave custody. How do prisons differ? What is imprisonment like, and what determines the prisoner experience? What are the characteristics of late modern penality? Why have the concepts of risk and dangerousness become synonymous with prison populations? Why has the issue of 'public protection' overtaken debates about prisoner welfare? What is a 'therapeutic' prison? Why are there now so many older prisoners and what are the particular demands on the prison service in accommodating these prisoners? Might there be alternative forms of punishment that could be implemented which would be less damaging to vulnerable groups and more effective in reducing offending?

The fifth and final part of the *Handbook on Prisons* is entitled 'Beyond the prison', and it brings together contributions that have an external dimension. What is done to ease the transition from prison to community? What is the relationship between prisons and desistance from crime? Why do many prisoners' families feel they have been condemned to serve a 'second sentence'? Who scrutinizes what goes on inside prisons? Why is independent inspection important? What does academic research add to our knowledge and what are the issues that first-time prison researchers need to think about before they enter the field? How have prisons been represented in art and literature and how do these representations inform public debate about punishment? Why has penality spread to other kinds of institutions? Do we need prisons at all?

It is these questions and topics that shape the parameters within which the authors who have contributed to the *Handbook on Prisons* offer their expertise. First, though, Andrew Coyle offers his reflections on how prisons have changed over the course of his professional life. As Emeritus Professor and Director of the International Centre for Prison Studies at King's College London, an ex-prison governor, and a visitor to many countries' prisons, Coyle's memories and observations provide a fascinating, personal insight into some of the issues that will be discussed in greater detail in later chapters. Entering prison for the first time as an assistant governor in 1973, he remembers the sights and smells that greeted him, recalls the structure of the prison day, and reminds us of the casual brutality that marked the system in the 1970s before independent inspection and monitoring was introduced to hold prison staff and managers to account. Underlying Coyle's chapter are the questions, 'what can we learn from the past?' and 'what can we learn from each other?' Viewing 21st-century prison systems in historical and global perspectives, he suggests, not only encourages reflection on the continuities that speak to the permanence of the prison but also raises questions about the social values that underpin our treatment of offenders. As such, Chapter 1 of the *Handbook on Prisons* is a thought-provoking and timely prologue to the chapters that follow.

Bibliography

Walmsley, R. (2007) *World Prison Population List*, seventh edn, London: International Centre for Prison Studies, www.prisonstudies.org/sites/default/files/resources/downloads/world-prison-pop-seventh.pdf.

Walmsley, R. (2013) *World Prison Population List*, tenth edn, London: International Centre for Prison Studies, www.apcca.org/uploads/10th_Edition_2013.pdf.

Part I

Prisons in context

Chapter 1

Prisons in context

Andrew Coyle

Introduction

This chapter provides a personal overview of some features of imprisonment over the last 40 years. In the early 1970s the world was quite different in many relevant respects. The colonial empires of European countries were being dismantled to be replaced by newly independent countries, and the Cold War was a major part of our political lives. Prisons and labour colonies throughout the Soviet Union and neighbouring countries held well over 1 million men and women in virtual slavery, and the very existence of many of these places of detention was a state secret. In the United Kingdom the world of prisons was also largely hidden from public view and a number of prisons were places of brutality and inhumanity. Within a few years the first cracks began to appear in that closed world. In 1975 the European Court of Human Rights reached its first decision in a case concerning a prisoner in the United Kingdom (Golder v United Kingdom [1975] 1 EHRR 524). In this case the Court concluded that the refusal of the UK authorities to allow a prisoner access to a solicitor constituted a violation of European Convention on Human Rights Article 6 (right to a fair and public hearing within a reasonable time by an independent and impartial tribunal) and Article 8 (right to respect for private and family life, home and correspondence). The Council of Europe Committee for the Prevention of Torture and Inhuman or Degrading Treatment or Punishment (CPT) began its work in 1990 when it visited Denmark, Turkey, the United Kingdom, Malta and Austria. In respect of the United Kingdom the CPT reached a damning conclusion about conditions in Brixton, Leeds and Wandsworth Prisons:

> The CPT's delegation found that the conditions of detention in the three male local prisons visited were very poor. In each of the three prisons there was a pernicious combination of overcrowding, inadequate regime activities, lack of integral sanitation and poor hygiene. In short, the overall environment in which the prisoners had to lead their lives amounted, in the CPT's opinion, to inhuman and degrading treatment.
>
> (Council of Europe 1991)

This report was published shortly after I became governor of Brixton Prison. The Optional Protocol to the United Nations Convention against Torture and Other Cruel, Inhuman or Degrading Treatment or Punishment entered into force in 2006 and led to the establishment of an international inspection system for places of detention in countries that have ratified the Protocol. All of these developments are discussed in greater detail elsewhere in this volume.

There are now over 10.2 million men, women and children in prison in the world (Walmsley 2013) – a number which would have been beyond belief 40 years ago – and in many countries the conditions and environment within prisons have changed dramatically. The overview in this chapter is intended to provide a context for the succeeding contributions which deal with specific issues relating to imprisonment. It invites the reader to consider the nature of imprisonment in the first two decades of the 21st century and whether the prison as now constituted is fit for its purpose.

As it was then

I entered the world of prisons in 1973 when I was appointed as one of the first assistant governors in Edinburgh Prison (Coyle 1994). Until that point the management structure in prisons in Scotland, as in the rest of the United Kingdom, had been very simple, with a single governor, assisted in larger prisons by a deputy governor. The vast majority of staff were 'discipline officers' of various grades, led by a chief officer. Other groups of uniformed officers with varying or no specialized training were responsible for the prison 'hospital', the industrial and working units, maintenance, catering and administration.

The prisoners' day was structured and predictable. It began with cell doors being unlocked around 7.00am, leading to the infamous 'slopping out' parade with a procession of prisoners rushing to the 'arches' or 'recesses', each carrying a brimming chamber pot which was emptied into or around the toilets and slop basins. Each prisoner also had a bottle or jug which he filled with water from the same sink before heading back to his cell. The lucky or experienced prisoners made use of the toilets in the vicinity. The stench pervaded the whole prison and was no respecter of persons. As a new assistant governor and one of the few people who wore civilian clothes, I quickly learned that the suits which I wore to work had to be kept separate from all my other clothes at home and be cleaned regularly to minimize the prison smell that saturated them.

Prisoners were then locked in their cells for a short period while they shaved and washed the best they could with the water that they had brought back, after which they went to one of four dining rooms for breakfast. They then went directly to their work parties. Some of the work was relatively sophisticated and required a degree of skill: printing, bookbinding, carpentry. At the other end of the spectrum there was work that was basically monotonous and unskilled. In those days prisons still had contracts with what was then the Post Office to make and repair hemp mailbags. The most unpopular work was in the salvage party, stripping out redundant copper and other wiring. The prisoners allocated to this work were generally those who had no skills and little ability to learn, by and large men on the merry-go-round of short sentences for repetitive low-level offences. A small number of prisoners were employed on general maintenance in the prison, working alongside prison officer tradesmen, in the prison kitchen or on general cleaning duties. At the end of the morning the men returned to their cells for a numbers count before going on to the dining rooms for lunch, after which there was a one-hour period of exercise in the open air, although in reality there was not much exercise and most prisoners spent the time walking around the yard in small groups. It was then back to the work parties until it was time for the evening meal, usually served around 4.00pm. Following a short period locked in cells while numbers were checked, there was evening recreation, spent in the accommodation halls, playing table games, watching the communal television or cleaning their cells. By 9.00pm all prisoners were locked in their cells until the following morning.

Prisoners on remand or unsentenced were held in an accommodation hall separate from sentenced prisoners and were not required to work. This meant that they spent most of each day locked in their cells, apart from meal and exercise times. They were also entitled to a short daily visit from family or close friends and to see lawyers or other persons in connection with their cases.

In the early 1970s there were no full-time teachers, social workers or other specialists in the prison. Criminal justice social workers (who were the Scottish equivalent of probation officers) visited to prepare reports on remand prisoners when requested to do so by the court, as did psychiatrists and psychologists, and also to report, if required, on prisoners who were being considered for early release. There was a welfare officer who was employed by the prison and who acted as a conduit between prisoners and their families when asked to do so, and who might liaise on behalf of a prisoner with authorities, for example, in respect of housing tenancies. The prison chaplain was a key figure in terms of prisoners' access to external support. If a prisoner wished for educational support he applied to the chaplain who would decide whether the man would have access to the small number of ad hoc people who came into the prison to provide this. The chaplain also coordinated volunteer visitors who befriended individual prisoners. In 1974 a qualified full-time education officer was appointed in Edinburgh Prison, the first such appointment in any Scottish prison.

The primary task of the new group of assistant governors that I joined in 1973 was to organize and oversee the writing of reports on prisoners who were to be considered for early release under the new parole arrangements which had recently been introduced following the Murder (Abolition of the Death Penalty) Act 1965 and the consequent legislation in the Criminal Justice Act 1967. In those days a prisoner serving a sentence of more than 18 months became eligible for early release after serving 12 months or one third of the sentence, whichever was longer. Most prisoners who were serving life sentences became eligible for release after they had completed about nine years in prison, and the preparation of reports and documentation had to begin some 18 months before that date. Prisoners serving indeterminate and other long sentences now serve much longer periods before being considered for early release.

One undoubtedly positive change in the last 40 years has been the increase in transparency in prisons. Prisons used to be described as the last great secretive institutions in modern society because of the shortage of information about what happened within them. Given the reach of modern communications it is no longer possible to prevent much of what happens in prisons from coming into the public domain. The publication of regular reports from HM Inspectorate of Prisons and the work of Independent Monitoring Boards (IMBs) in each prison has also brought much of what goes on inside prisons in England and Wales into the public spotlight. A changed public climate as to what is and is not acceptable behaviour on the part of public servants has resulted in significant changes in the behaviour of many staff. For example, it is hard to imagine that today there might be such a sequence of events as surrounded the death of Barry Prosser in Birmingham Prison in 1980. These were summarized in a statement by the Home Office minister of state to the House of Commons on 1 July 1982:

Mr. Prosser was found dead in his cell in the hospital wing of Birmingham prison in the early morning of 19 August 1980. The post mortem which was held that afternoon revealed the full and horrifying extent of Mr. Prosser's injuries. The pathologist's report was that Mr. Prosser had extensive bruising all over his body. His stomach, his oesophagus and one of his lungs had been ruptured, and the pathologist thought that the cause of death was a blow, probably by a heavy weight. The inquest into Mr. Prosser's death was held in April 1981. It lasted for seven days and heard the evidence of nearly 50 witnesses ... At the end of the proceedings, the jury returned a verdict that Mr. Prosser had been unlawfully killed.

The minister then moved on to deal with some of the recommendations that the coroner had made. His comment on the last of these recommendations is a reminder of how weak management of staff was in those days:

The coroner's final recommendation was that hospital officers should submit a report if they had to use force on a prisoner ... We recognise that when, in the proper execution of his duties, an officer has to use physical force, there is always the possibility that there will later be a complaint by a prisoner or an inquiry into the incident. Thus, we issued instructions last year reminding staff that, as a safeguard, each prison officer, including any hospital officer or nurse involved in such an incident, should write a brief factual report to the governor in addition to making any other record. Some concern was expressed by the Prison Officers Association about this instruction and it advised its branches not to comply with it.

(HC Deb 1982: 1130–1132)

The final sentence of the minister's statement includes a damning indictment of the mores of the time within the Prison Service. A mentally ill prisoner had been 'unlawfully killed' in a punishment cell. A coroner made what today would be considered a straightforward and entirely proper recommendation that prison staff should in future submit a report whenever force had to be used on a prisoner. The Home Office issued an instruction that this should be done. The Prison Officers Association took issue with this and instructed their members not to comply with the instruction. The minister appeared to accept this as an end to the matter. There is little doubt that the behaviour and reaction of the successors of all those involved – staff, management, trade unions and ministers – would be quite different today.

As it is now

Conditions

Physical conditions in prisons have improved significantly in a number of respects. The daily degradation of hundreds of prisoners carrying foetid chamber pots along landings to stinking slop sinks is thankfully long gone. In his seminal 1991 report following riots at Strangeways and other prisons, the then Lord Justice Woolf described this practice as an uncivilized and degrading process, which destroyed the morale of prisoners and staff (Woolf 1991: 24). Woolf had recommended that ministers should set a timetable to provide access to sanitation for all prisoners not later than February 1996. In April of that year, Prisons Minister Ann Widdecombe travelled to Leeds Prison to witness, in the words of *The Independent* newspaper (13 April 1996), the last plastic pot being discarded as slopping out came to an end in prisons in England and Wales.

It soon became clear that the much-heralded end to slopping out was not all that it might seem. In 2004 the chief inspector of prisons found that there was still slopping out in a women's prison (Lewis 2006) and in 2010 the National Council for Independent Monitoring Boards published a report on the difficulties that some prisoners had in getting regular access to toilet facilities. The haste to abolish collective slopping out had meant that what had been implemented in many cases fell far below what would be considered decent. In his introduction to the IMB report, its president described the arrangements in the following terms:

> Like many who will read this report I had assumed that following the acceptance of Lord Woolf's recommendations slopping out was a thing of the past. Only when the annual reports of IMBs became part of my staple reading diet did I realise that it had been replaced by a situation in which – as IMBs constantly report – two men will be living, eating and spending most of the day in what is in effect their shared lavatory.
>
> (National Council for Independent Monitoring Boards 2010: 2)

This comment indirectly draws attention to another feature of prison life that has become increasingly prevalent: the fact that many prisoners now spend the bulk of each day locked in their cells with little or nothing to do. This has been the situation in England and Wales for many years as far as the 20% of prisoners who are not sentenced are concerned, but shortage of work, training or educational opportunities now means that many convicted prisoners are left in their cells each day. Independent commentators, including successive HM chief inspectors of prisons and local IMBs, have regularly raised concerns about these matters over the years. Speaking to the BBC in July 2014, Chief Inspector Nick Hardwick issued a warning in unusually stark terms:

> We are seeing a lot more prisons that are not meeting acceptable standards ... There is a danger of the politicians over-analysing the figures and miss[ing] what is under their noses on the wings ... people being held in deplorable conditions who are suicidal, they don't have anything to do and they don't have anyone to talk to.
>
> (BBC *Newsnight* 2014)

Speaking on the same programme, the chief executive officer of the National Offender Management Service (NOMS) acknowledged that there had been 'some deterioration' in standards in prisons, with additional pressures arising over the previous six months, including an increase in prisoner numbers (among them, more remand prisoners and sex offenders, who present particular challenges, than anticipated) and fewer staff than were needed. Some 23% of prisoners were sharing cells designed for one prisoner. He went on to confirm that there had been a 25% reduction in spending over 'the spending review period' and that in order to eliminate overcrowding he would require an increase in budget of £900 million which was not going to materialize.

There have been many other improvements in prisons since the early 1970s. Prisons are undoubtedly managed in a much more efficient manner now, although as the quotations above demonstrate, that does not of itself imply an improvement in decency and humanity. Increased efficiency can sometimes lead to an excessive emphasis on how things are done rather than on what is being done, which results in an attention to detail that misses the reality, as noted by the chief inspector.

Violence

The gratuitous violence that went unremarked in some prisons in the United Kingdom 30 or so years ago would not be tolerated today. This is not the case in some other countries. Prisons in Latin America are marked by unbelievable levels of violence. I have visited prisons in Brazil where staff will only enter the areas where prisoners live if they have a heavily armed escort. In Venezuela some years ago I was accompanied on a visit to the main prison in Caracas by the deputy director of the national prison service. He reluctantly took me into an accommodation block. The gate to each unit was manned by a prisoner throughout each 24-hour cycle. His task was to ensure that no prisoner from another gang was able to enter the unit. If he was found asleep at his post he would face instant death at the hands of his own gang members. The toilet areas were the dirtiest I had ever seen, with detritus lying almost a metre deep. The deputy director told me that prisoners kept the area in this state so that guns and other weapons could be hidden there, and he pointed out wires sticking out at various points, explaining that these were attached to the weapons which could be recovered when needed. He also pointed out loose bricks in the walls and told me that weapons and cell phones were being kept there. Numbers of prisoners followed us everywhere and the director spoke quite openly about all of this in front of them.

This scenario is a far cry from anything that might be seen in the United Kingdom yet there is little room for complacency. Following an inspection of Feltham Young Offenders' Institution in March 2013, the chief inspector of prisons reported that:

> Levels of violence at Feltham were too high, resulting in high levels of adjudications and use of force. Some of the incidents were serious and sometimes involved gangs attacking single prisoners. Many prisoners had felt unsafe at some time and/or victimised. The unprecedented and illegitimate use of batons at Feltham B was emblematic of this problem and the broader weakness of effective relationships between staff and prisoners.
>
> (HM Inspectorate of Prisons 2013b: 16)

In January 2013 the chief inspector had inspected the part of Feltham that held children and young people between the ages of 15 and 17 years. He was every bit as concerned about what he discovered there:

> We had serious concerns about the safety of young people held at Feltham A. Many told us they were frightened at the time of the inspection, and that they had little confidence in staff to keep them safe. Gang-related graffiti was endemic. There was an average of almost two fights or assaults every day. Some of these were very serious and involved groups of young people in very violent, pre-meditated attacks on a single individual with a risk of very serious injury resulting.
>
> (HM Inspectorate of Prisons 2013a)

In an interview with *The Independent* newspaper he commented further: 'It was a very disturbing place. If you were a parent with a child in Feltham you would be right to be terrified. It would be very hard not to join a gang in Feltham.' Responding to the chief inspector's report, the chief executive of NOMS acknowledged the depth of the problem: 'All the gangs in London meet in Feltham. There are fewer young people in prisons but the ones who are there are troubled, difficult and challenging' (Peachey 2013).

These problems are not peculiar to Feltham; they are also to be found in adult prisons. In Oakwood Prison in the West Midlands, 'a huge and structurally impressive facility capable of holding more than 1,600 category C prisoners' which opened in April 2010, the chief inspector found that:

> Too many prisoners felt unsafe and indicators of levels of violence were high, although we had no confidence in the quality of recorded data or in the structures and arrangements to reduce violence. Even the designated units meant to protect those declared vulnerable were not working effectively and too many prisoners on these units also felt unsafe. Levels of self-harm, some linked to day-to-day frustrations as well as perceived victimisation, were high but again processes to support those in crisis were not good enough.
>
> (HM Inspectorate of Prisons 2013c)

Number of prisoners

One of the most outstanding changes over the last 40 years has been the growth in the number of people being held in prison. In 1973 the average number of people in prison in Scotland was just over 4,600, of whom 180 were women (Scottish Executive 2006). I well remember the concern that was expressed in 1986 when the figure broke through the 5,000 mark, a level of imprisonment that had never before been experienced in Scotland. There was less public discussion when it broke through the 6,000 mark in 2003. In mid-2014 there were 8,200 people in Scottish prisons, of whom 420 were women. The story in England and Wales has been a similar one. In 1973 there were 35,700 people in prison (Home Office 1984), and a few years later Home Secretary Roy Jenkins expressed great concern at the prospect that the prison population might eventually reach 45,000 (HL Deb 2009). In mid-2014 there were 85,500 people in prison in England and Wales, of whom almost 4,000 were women (Ministry of Justice 2014b).

The growth in the number of prisoners has been influenced in the main not by any increase in the number of offences and crimes, nor by increased detection rates but, as observed by a recent report from the British Academy (2014), by changes in penal policy. The British Academy report notes that courts are now much more likely than they were in the past to sentence offenders to prison, that prison sentences have been getting longer and that there has also been a steady increase in the number of prisoners serving life or indeterminate sentences. One might add to this the fact that the proportion of prisoners being granted conditional early release has reduced, as has the period of the early release.

The United Kingdom does not stand alone in this matter. I first visited federal prisons in the USA in 1984, when they held a total of 45,000 prisoners. In mid-2014 they held 216,000. Commenting on the massive rise in the number of incarcerated Americans in the late 20th century, Timothy Lynch, director of The Cato Institute's project on criminal justice, observed:

America's criminal justice system is going to make history this month as the number of incarcerated people surpasses 2 million for the first time. To appreciate why this is such an extraordinary moment, one needs to put the 2-million-prisoner factoid into context. It took more than 200 years for America to hold 1 million prisoners all at once. And yet we have managed to incarcerate the second million in only the past 10 years.

(Lynch 2000)

By any measure these are extraordinary increases in respect of an institution that involves a significant degree of human suffering as well as a massive input of public resources. There are now signs that this trend is being reversed. The prison population in the USA has shown a consistent reduction since 2010 (US Department of Justice 2013), with the greatest reduction occurring in some of the largest state prison systems. California has accounted for over half of the decrease in the entire state prison population.

During an extended period in which prison populations in the UK have risen consistently, a number of other European countries have shown quite different patterns. The Netherlands provides an example of how changes in government policies can push rates of imprisonment higher or lower. In 1992 the country had one of the lowest rates, with a prison population of 7,397. By 1995 this had increased to 11,886 and it continued to increase annually until it peaked in 2004 at 20,075, almost three times higher than it had been 12 years previously. Since then the number of prisoners has fallen year-on-year, and in 2013 it stood at 12,638 (World Prison Brief 2014c). Throughout this period, near-neighbour Denmark retained a remarkably stable and relatively small prison population, moving from 3,597 in 1992 to 4,091 in 2013 (World Prison Brief 2014a). In Germany there were 57,448 prisoners in 1992; the figure rose to 81,166 in 2004 but in 2013 it had fallen back to 62,632 (World Prison Brief 2014b) – this for a country of over 80 million inhabitants, compared with 85,582 prisoners in England and Wales with a population of just over 57 million.

There is very little evidence from any country that crime levels are affected for better or for worse by variations in levels of imprisonment. Instead, social scientists have gathered evidence which demonstrates that rates of imprisonment are influenced by socio-economic structures and levels of social trust. Where these are strong and there is a consensual rather than a confrontational approach among politicians on these matters, the use of imprisonment tends to be lower. Where the opposite is the case, the use of imprisonment is more likely to be high and increasing.[1]

The prisoners

Other chapters in this volume deal in detail with issues relating to specific groups of prisoners. The underlying message from these contributions is that prisoners are not a homogeneous group, identified solely by the fact of their imprisonment. In this contextual chapter two groups are worthy of mention.

In many countries a significant proportion of those in prison are awaiting trial or other court process. In India, for example, two thirds of all prisoners fall into this category. In Scotland almost one fifth of prisoners are on some type of remand, while in England and Wales 10% of prisoners have not been convicted. Despite this fact, they are held in the care of the NOMS, where their treatment gives only limited recognition to the fact that they are legally innocent. In many cases their treatment is even more restricted because of reduced access to a variety of facilities in the prison, including education and work.

The second group that is of particular importance in England and Wales includes all of those who are serving indeterminate sentences. Almost 15% of all prisoners are serving life imprisonment or an Extended Determinate Sentence (Ministry of Justice 2014a). The history of this latter group demonstrates the unforeseen consequences of legislation. The Criminal Justice Act of 2003 introduced imprisonment for public protection (IPP), a new sentence designed to be used for serious sexual and violent offenders. The government indicated that it expected the prison population to increase by around 900 as a result of this provision. In fact there were 6,000 such prisoners in 2012 when the government abolished IPP and replaced it with the Extended Determinate Sentence. Some 5,500 prisoners are still in prison under the IPP legislation (Prison Reform Trust 2014). Speaking to the BBC in March 2014, former Home Secretary David Blunkett, who had introduced the IPP legislation, acknowledged that '[t]he consequence of bringing that Act in has led, in some cases, to an injustice and I regret that' (Conway 2014). That injustice is still being suffered by the prisoners involved.

Learning from our past

Before attempting any prediction of what the future might hold for prisons in the UK, it is worth considering what we might learn from past experience. In my travels to the prisons of the world I am frequently struck by the consistent lack of institutional memory; many prison systems appear to be institutionally incapable of learning from past successes or failures. They will frequently fail to develop existing examples of effective practice, either because they do not register them for what they are, or they are unaware of them, or because the examples do not conform to mainstream thinking. In England and Wales an example of unwillingness to learn from success is Grendon Prison, which has consistently performed well in terms of what are considered sound operational indicators: the positive management of men who have been difficult if not unmanageable in other secure settings and rates of successful resettlement of men who are released. Yet after more than 50 years of existence, Grendon continues to be regarded as experimental and unique because it simply does not fit in with the public rhetoric about how a prison should operate.

In the same jurisdiction the treatment of young offenders provides an example of the inability to learn from the past. In the early 20th century the English Prison Commission introduced a new type of institution for young offenders which was based on the public school system. Accommodation units were described as 'houses'; the persons in charge of the units were known as 'housemasters' and often recruited from a public school background; each unit had a mature female prison officer who was known as 'matron'. Sir Alexander Paterson described the institutions in the following way:

> A Borstal Institution is a training school for adolescent offenders, based on educational principles, pursuing educational methods. To be sent there is a punishment, for the training involves a very considerable loss of liberty, but to stay there is to have a chance to learn the right way of life, and to develop the good there is in each.
>
> (Paterson 1934: 13)

The borstal system lasted for 75 years. This is not the place to embark on an assessment of its merits or demerits but the system came to an end because it had outlasted its time. Fast forward to 2014 and the Ministry of Justice announced its intention to build a 'secure college', led by a 'head teacher or principal' and housing up to 320 young men aged between 12 and 17.

> The Government is introducing a new model of youth custody, the Secure College, which will improve outcomes and reduce cost. Education will be firmly at the heart of the Secure College, with other services designed around and intended to support innovative and intensive education delivery.
>
> (Ministry of Justice 2014c: 2)

In 1934 Alexander Paterson had pleaded for an alternative name for borstals, given to the first such institution after the Kent village in which it was located. Eighty years later his plea was heard; they are to be recreated as secure colleges.

These two examples are from England and Wales, but one could identify similar examples from many other countries. It could be argued that this demonstrates a systemic failure to update a concept of imprisonment that is rooted in the 18th and 19th centuries. This concept is founded in the very buildings that go to make up the prison. Architecture is very important for communicating a sense of purpose to any institution, a subject dealt with in this volume (Chapter 7) and by Jewkes (2013). It has been said that if Charles Dickens were to return to Pentonville Prison in London today he would immediately recognize its wings and landings. The same might be said if Tolstoy were to return to Butyrka Prison in Moscow, or Victor Hugo to La Santé in Paris. In the 1960s and early 1970s in the UK there was an attempt to alter the structure of prisons by building accommodation blocks with hotel-like corridors, but in recent decades there has been a return to what is basically the older panopticon style which fits best with the surveillance model of imprisonment. In other words the mindset of what prisons should be and even what they should look like has changed little in the last 200 years.

Learning from others

I have had the privilege of visiting prison systems all over the world, usually at the invitation of national governments or of international bodies such as the United Nations (UN) or regional bodies such as the Council of Europe, the Organization of American States or the African Commission on Human and Peoples' Rights. My involvement has often coincided with periods of traumatic political upheaval or radical legislative change which have led to fundamental changes within prison systems on an unprecedented scale. A common thread that ran through events in many of these countries was that after the collapse of a totalitarian system or after a democratic change of government, one of the priorities was general reform of the justice system and specifically reform of the prison system which had frequently been the epitome of the worst excesses of the former regime. This was the case in Russia, which I first visited in 1992, at a time when the democratic future of the country was not at all clear. Despite the continuing struggle for the political soul of the country, the authorities were determined to begin the process of reform of the infamous Gulag system. I continued to visit Russian prisons regularly for over ten years, sometimes assisting the Ministry of the Interior and later the Ministry of

Justice in their reform efforts, at other times with intergovernmental bodies such as the Council of Europe and the Organization for Security and Co-operation in Europe. In 1998 and 1999 I was an expert member of the first two missions of the CPT to the Russian Federation, when we inspected infamous prisons including Butyrka in Moscow and Kresty in St Petersburg and travelled beyond the Urals to Chelyabinsk, which had been a transport hub in Soviet times for prisoners being exiled to the Siberian Gulag. In 1998 the number of prisoners in Russia was estimated at over 1 million. In mid-2014 it stood at 670,000, a significant reduction but still one of the highest rates in the world (World Prison Brief 2014d).

At the beginning of 1995 I worked with the UN Centre for Human Rights in providing advice to the new government that had replaced the Khmer Rouge in Cambodia. The prison in Siem Reap, a few kilometres from the monastery of Angkor Wat, remained much as it had been in French colonial times and the new administration had little idea as to how it should be managed. At that time there were 2,600 prisoners in the country and I still have a copy of my report in which I cautioned about the danger that the introduction of a Western model of imprisonment which took no account of local traditions might lead to a vastly inflated prison population. In mid-2014 the number of prisoners had indeed increased almost six-fold to 14,500, while the population of the country had risen by 75%.

Also in 1995, in the company of the reforming commissioner of prisons for Uganda, I was invited to visit prisons and to speak to prison staff in South Africa. Our main discussions were held in the staff training school in Kroonstad in the Orange Free State. The school was still known as the John Vorster Training Centre; his bust was in the main foyer and his photograph hung in the senior staff mess. We were met by General Sitole, the first black provincial commissioner, who had previously been a schoolmaster in Soweto. The commissioner of the Department of Corrections told us that he was determined to correct the racial imbalance at senior level and expected that within five years 70% of the senior staff would be black. Reality moved rather more quickly than the commissioner had anticipated. Within a very short period he had retired and the whole cadre of senior staff had been replaced.

All of these experiences and others have helped me to identify two key issues that require attention if prisons are to deliver their stated aims. They apply in all countries, including the UK.

Political will

The first is political will. Prisons are not as a matter of course a high priority for most governments. They do not interest the public in the way that health, education or the economy do. Imprisonment is something that happens to 'other people' and those other people are generally regarded as undeserving of sympathy. Experience in many countries demonstrates that if there is no government will for prison reform then it will be unlikely to make any headway. I recollect hearing a commissioner of prisons at a regional conference in Eastern Africa a decade ago encouraging politicians to take an interest in ensuring that there were decent and humane conditions inside prisons and quoting the example of a vice-president of one country who had refused to allow prisoners to have mattresses and later was subject to his own rule when he was sent to prison for corruption. That was a case of using whatever argument would best win the day in a particular situation. It is probably not one that could be advanced in many countries.

The Dominican Republic provides an interesting example, which I have observed at first-hand over several years, of how determined political will can lead to dramatic change in a manner appropriate to the local situation. In common with many countries in the region, the history of prisons in the Dominican Republic has been one of gross overcrowding, chronic shortage of resources for basic human needs, and lack of proper budgetary arrangements. There was no proper prison administration, with half of the prisons being under military control and the remainder in the charge of the police. In 2003 a new attorney-general who had the president's political support decided to take action. Having taken advice, he decided that rather than continue nugatory attempts to reform the existing prison system he should set about creating a new one to replace it. The key to any decent prison system is the quality of the staff, particularly those who interact directly with prisoners, and the attorney-general decided to base the reforms on that premise. His first and most crucial action was to find the right person to develop and lead the New Model, as it came to be called. Roberto Santana, a nationally distinguished educator and former rector of the University of Santo Domingo, took up the challenge. Santana, who had in the past been a prisoner under the dictatorship, appointed a former director of the capital's largest prison as his deputy. One of his first moves was to establish a National Penitentiary School. He recruited several of his previous colleagues in the world of education, administration and professional development as tutors in the school, alongside some carefully chosen men and women with previous experience of working in prisons. He then set about selecting a completely new cadre of students to be trained for work in prisons, all of whom were young and highly motivated. One requirement was that they should have no previous experience in either the police or the military. They were trained for a full academic year and on graduation in 2004 they went as a group to staff the first of the New Model prisons. The same practice has continued over the past decade, with new prisons being opened as each new cohort of staff matriculated. Roberto Santana has brought all his skills as an educator to bear in the New Model system which provides decent living conditions for prisoners and humane treatment by staff. Education has a high priority and the target is that by the time they are released, all prisoners will be literate. Official sources claim that only 5% of persons from the new prisons have been convicted of further crimes within three years of release. Because of shortage of resources the government has continued to develop the new system on a gradual basis, and in 2014 over half of the country's prisons were part of the New Model.

The 'Nuevo Modelo' has attracted regional and international attention. The director of the United National Latin American Institute commented: 'What's remarkable about the Dominican Republic's example is that it has taken place in a country that has the same socio-economic conditions as other Latin American countries. Before when I would go to a government and say, "Look at what they're doing in Switzerland" they'd say, "That's a different world". But now I can say, "Look at the Dominican Republic"' (Fieser 2014).

Not all problems have been solved. In the ten years since the New Model was launched the number of prisoners in the country has risen from 13,500 to 25,500, largely as a result of harsher sentencing practices. This confirms the fact that it is very difficult to effect reform of a prison system in isolation from wider developments in criminal justice. Despite this, the message from the Dominican Republic is clear. A determined senior government minister rose above the political pressures of the day and adopted a radical strategy for change. He identified a person who was capable of achieving the desired change, agreed with him a plan of action and then gave him operational authority to deliver that change with full political support and no operational interference. Successive governments of different political persuasions have maintained that position and the benefits of this are now becoming clear. There are examples of similar positive reforms stemming from a political consensus in a number of other countries. Finland is an obvious example within Europe as it determined to move away from the historical influence of the former Soviet Union to align itself with its Scandinavian neighbours in respect of the restricted contribution that prisons have to play in contributing to their countries' safety and security.

Leadership

The second key issue is leadership. I saw the importance of this in Poland, which I visited several times in the 1990s. After the collapse of communism in 1989 the new democratic government invited Pavel Moczydlowski, professor of sociology in Warsaw University, to lead the Polish prison administration. For several years thereafter Moczydlowski led a radical reform of the former system (Moczydlowski and Rzeplinski 1990; Moczydlowski 1992). His leadership had a number of essential elements. In the first case he and his senior staff had a clear vision of what they wanted to achieve, which was to introduce a culture in which prisoners were treated decently and humanely by staff and in which they were to be given the opportunity to maintain and develop links with family and friends. The new leadership was confident that they could implement this without placing public security in danger and without sacrificing good order in prisons. They replaced the bureaucratic centralized structure with a lean regional structure. In the early years they spent a great deal of time visiting prisons and explaining their vision to both staff and prisoners. Moczydlowski told me that by his estimation, one in five members of staff never quite shook off the old mentality. He adopted a pragmatic and sympathetic response to them by making clear that dissent was not an option while making great efforts to support them through the transition process. For the small number who found this impossible he arranged early retirement. He also spent considerable time ensuring that the prisoners were aware that along with the new rights to which they were entitled came a responsibility to behave positively.

Throughout this period of change the senior prison administrators made sure that they retained the confidence of their new government ministers. They asked for and received operational autonomy but regularly explained to the politicians what they were attempting to achieve and how they could contribute to public stability. Finally, they explained the changes to the media and to local community groups and were given their support. As the changes took hold, the prison system then became more open to the press and to the public. Non-governmental organizations, church and other groups began to come into the prisons regularly.

For a few years during the last decade of the 20th century the Polish prison system shone as a beacon. As a model of how a decent and humane prison system might operate it was an example not only to other countries in Central and Eastern Europe, but also for those in the West. As both the prison system and the country were drawn into the orbit of Western Europe and its regional structures, the new vision for prisons became submerged in the complicated target-driven cultures so favoured in the West and models of centralized management all but obliterated the regional partnerships that had been introduced in the early 1990s (Coyle 2002).

An important function of leadership in the prison environment is to set the requisite ethical standards and to ensure that they are observed by all staff. Without a strong ethical context the circumstances in which one group of people has considerable power over another can easily degenerate into an abuse of that power. The world was shocked a few years ago when it saw the photographs of abuse of prisoners by American soldiers in Abu Ghraib prison in Iraq. What was particularly disturbing was that several of those involved were part-time soldiers and had been employed in civilian life as prison officers in the USA. They knew that what they were doing was wrong but they had lost their moral compass and had ceased to see the prisoners for whom they were responsible as human beings. The story of what went wrong in Abu Ghraib in 2003 is recounted from the perspective of some of the staff involved in Morris and Gourevitch (2009). The title of their book is a reference to the standard operating procedures (SOP) that are part and parcel of the daily life of prison staff in the USA – procedures that specify every detail of what staff must do in every conceivable situation. Prison staff in Abu Ghraib did not have any such procedures, a fact which was not lost on at least one of them:

> An orthodox SOP leaves nothing to the imagination, and as Ambuhl settled into her job, it occurred to her that the absence of a code was the code at Abu Ghraib. 'They couldn't say that we broke the rules because there were no rules', she said. 'Our mission was to help Military Intelligence, and nobody ever said, "This is your SOP". But that was in a sense what it became, because our job was to stress out the detainees, and help facilitate information to the interrogators, and save the lives of other soldiers out there.'
>
> (Morris and Gourevitch 2009: 92)

One lesson to be drawn from the terrible pictures from Abu Ghraib is that those who work in prisons or are responsible for prisons must repeatedly ask themselves the question, 'Is what we are doing the right thing to do?' This ethos must pervade the whole management process from the top down. It must also go beyond the prison administration to politicians and government officials who have ultimate responsibility for prison systems.

In the early 1970s junior assistant governors in the UK would from time to time ruminate on the profession that they had entered and the demands it made of them. One way of formulating the discussion was to consider at what point one might have to decide that what one was being asked to do was personally unacceptable. In those days, relatively soon after the abolition of the death penalty, there was a consensus that if ever hanging were to be reintroduced, the requirement on a governor to supervise an execution would be the Rubicon that could not be crossed and which would lead to resignation. One wonders what might trigger the Rubicon moment of today.

Conclusion

So 40 years after I first entered prison, what am I to conclude? I have always recognized that for the foreseeable future there will be no alternative other than imprisonment for some offenders. When I was governor of Peterhead Prison in the late 1980s, the prison held a cohort of young men who had all been involved in serious criminal acts both in their communities and while serving their sentences. There was no doubt that prison was the proper location for them at that point. My task and that of all staff was to hold them in custody as decently and humanely as possible – a task which was relatively simple in theory but extremely complex in practice. Throughout the early and mid-1990s I was governor of Brixton Prison. During my early years Brixton held a small number of prisoners who required very high security but the majority of the prisoners in my charge did not come into that category. Brixton at that time could better have been described, as could many prisons today, as a place of asylum in the proper sense of that word, a place of safety for the mentally ill, for the drug and alcohol addicted and for the wide spectrum of men who for one reason or another find it difficult to secure the accommodation, employment and support that would enable them to live a full life in society. These men often operate under the radar of the institutions of society that deal with health, with accommodation, with employment and similar matters. They only come above the institutional radar when they commit or are accused of committing an offence, and the part of the radar that picks them up is the criminal justice system. Prisons provide singularly inappropriate environments for dealing with these persons other than in exceptional circumstances.

As this chapter has demonstrated, there have undoubtedly been significant changes in prisons in a number of countries over the last 40 years. At the same time the nature of imprisonment itself has become increasingly restrictive, with large numbers of prisoners being held in conditions of maximum security, often with little or no justification. This situation has grown steadily over the last 30 years as Derek Jeffreys describes in his chapter, and has accelerated since 2001 as countries respond to perceived threats of terrorism. The justification for this has been, as Prime Minister Tony Blair said in 2005 when talking about those who 'meddle with extremism', 'Let no one be in any doubt. The rules of the game have changed' (Jeffery 2005). The reality is somewhat different. The events in Abu Ghraib prison in Iraq in 2003 and the continuing events in Guantanamo are not evidence that the principles on which good prison management should operate are no longer applicable. Instead, they are evidence that little has been learned from experiences such as those of the UK with republican and loyalist prisoners in Northern Ireland in the 1970s and 1980s, and those of Turkey more recently with PKK (Kurdistan Workers' Party) and other prisoners.

The increased use of imprisonment is also a reflection of new insecurities in a changing world order. As inequality increases between nations and within nations, governments are making greater use of criminal justice systems to deal with social and economic problems. In the decade from 1997 there were over 50 new major pieces of Home Office legislation with criminal justice implications (Faulkner 2010), and more than 1,000 new offences for which a person could be given a prison sentence were created (Johnston 2009). The increased use of imprisonment has been a direct consequence of this expanded reach of criminal justice. This in turn has placed an intolerable burden on prisons as they struggle to provide minimally decent living conditions for men and women who have myriad personal, social and health problems that cannot be resolved within the high walls and fences of a prison.

Successive governments have concluded that the answer to the failure of prisons to rehabilitate those who are sent there is to send more people to prison and to send them there for longer periods, while at the same time berating those who work in prisons for not doing more to ensure that those who leave prison do not break the law again after they return to the community. That is rather like blaming the surgeon who mends a skier's broken leg for the fact that the person later returns to the slopes and breaks his or her leg again. In recent years prison systems throughout Europe have become much more efficient in their processes, but being more efficient is of little moment if what is being done is itself the wrong thing. The result is merely that one ends up doing the wrong thing better, but it remains wrong. The prison services of the UK generally do what they do well; they do what they are asked to do. Yet the question remains, are they being asked to do the right thing?

A recent report from the British Academy (2014: 17) recognized the sterility of merely rehearsing arguments about costs and benefits in respect of the use of imprisonment. Instead it pointed to the need:

> to develop a different kind of argument, one that appeals not to empirical evidence about the effects of imprisonment but to a set of fundamental social and political values – liberty, autonomy, solidarity, dignity, inclusion and security – that penal policy should support and uphold rather than undermine. Such values should guide our treatment of all citizens, including those convicted of criminal offences: we should behave towards offenders not as outsiders who have no stake in society and its values but as citizens whose treatment must reflect the fundamental values of our society.

The report concluded that it is 'very hard to see how our current use of imprisonment could be said to reflect these social values'.

This is a challenge that merits a response.

Note

1 See for example, Lappi-Seppälä 2008.

Bibliography

BBC Newsnight (2014) 9 July.

British Academy (2014) *A presumption against imprisonment: Social order and social values*, London: British Academy.

Conway, Z. (2014) 'David Blunkett "regrets injustices" of indeterminate sentences', *BBC News* website, 13 March.

Council of Europe (1991) *Report to the United Kingdom government on the visit to the United Kingdom carried out by the European Committee for the Prevention of Torture and Inhuman or Degrading Treatment or Punishment from 29 July 1990 to 10 August 1990*, Strasbourg: Council of Europe.

Coyle, A. (1994) *The prisons we deserve*, London: Harper Collins.

Coyle, A. (2002) *Managing prisons in a time of change*, London: International Centre for Prison Studies.

Faulkner, D. (2010) *Criminal justice and government at a time of austerity*, London: Criminal Justice Alliance.

Fieser, E. (2014) 'Dominican Republic's more humane prison model', *Reuters* website, 22 May.

HC Deb (1982) 01 July, vol. 26, cc1130–1136.

HL Deb (2009) 27 April, vol. 710, col. 32.

HM Inspectorate of Prisons (2013a) *Report on an unannounced inspection of HMP/YOI Feltham (Feltham A – children and young people) 21–25 January 2013*, London: HMIP.

HM Inspectorate of Prisons (2013b) *Report on an unannounced full follow-up inspection of HMP/YOI Feltham (Feltham B – young adults) 18–22 March 2013*, London: HMIP.

HM Inspectorate of Prisons (2013c) *Report on an unannounced inspection of HMP Oakwood 10–21 June 2013*, London: HMIP.

Home Office (1984) *Prison statistics England and Wales 1983*, London: HMSO.

Jeffery, S. (2005) 'The rules of the game are changing', *The Guardian* website, 5 August.

Jewkes, Y. (2013) 'Penal aesthetics and the pains of imprisonment', in J. Simon, N. Temple and R. Tobe (eds) *Architecture and justice: Judicial meanings in the public realm*, Farnham: Ashgate.

Johnston, P. (2009) 'Why is Labour so keen to imprison us?', *Telegraph* website, 4 January.

Lappi-Seppälä, T. (2008) 'Trust, welfare and political culture: Explaining differences in national penal policies', *Crime and Justice* 37(1).

Lewis, P. (2006) 'End "degrading" slopping out, says prison watchdog', *The Guardian*, 1 June.

Lynch, T. (2000) 'All locked up', *The Washington Post*, 20 February.

Ministry of Justice (2014a) *Offender management statistics: Quarterly Bulletin October to December 2013*, London: MoJ.

Ministry of Justice (2014b) *Prison population bulletin: Weekly 27 June 2014*, London: MoJ.

Ministry of Justice (2014c) *Criminal Justice and Courts Bill. Fact sheet: Secure colleges*, London: MoJ.

Moczydlowski, P. (1992) *The hidden life of Polish prisons*, Indianapolis: Indiana University Press.

Moczydlowski, P. and Rzeplinski, A. (1990) *Collective protests in penal institutions*, Oslo: University of Oslo.

Morris, E. and Gourevitch, P. (2009) *Standard operating procedure: A war story*, Basingstoke: Picador.

National Council for Independent Monitoring Boards (2010) *Slopping out? A report on the lack of in-cell sanitation in Her Majesty's Prisons in England and Wales*, London: National Council for Independent Monitoring Boards.

Paterson, A. (1934) 'Introduction', in S. Barman, *The English Borstal system*, London: P.S. King & Son Ltd.

Peachey, P. (2013) 'Gang violence "out of control" in Feltham prison', *The Independent*, 10 July.

Prison Reform Trust (2014) *Prison: The facts – Bromley Briefings Summer 2014*, London: PRT.

Scottish Executive (2006) *High level summary of equality statistics: Key trends for Scotland 2006*, Edinburgh: Scottish Government.

US Department of Justice (2013) *Prisoners in 2012 – Advance counts*, Washington, DC: USDOJ.

Walmsley, R. (2013) *World prison population list*, tenth edn, London: International Centre for Prison Studies.

Woolf, L.J. (1991) *Prison Disturbances April 1990: Report of an Inquiry by the Rt Hon. Lord Justice Woolf (Parts I and II) and His Honour Stephen Tumim (Part II)* (The Woolf Report), London: HMSO.

World Prison Brief (2014a) *Country page: Denmark*, www.prisonstudies.org/country/denmark (accessed 28 July 2014).

World Prison Brief (2014b) *Country page: Germany*, www.prisonstudies.org/country/germany (accessed 28 July 2014).

World Prison Brief (2014c) *Country page: Netherlands*, www.prisonstudies.org/country/netherlands (accessed 28 July 2014).

World Prison Brief (2014d) *Country page: Russian Federation*, www.prisonstudies.org/country/russian-federation (accessed 28 July 2014).

Chapter 2

Prison histories, 1770s–1950s

Continuities and contradictions

Helen Johnston

> A fearful man, all in coarse grey, with a great iron on his leg. A man with no hat, and with broken shoes, and with an old rag tied round his head. A man who had been soaked in water, and smothered in mud, and lamed by stones, and cut by flints, and stung by nettles, and torn by briars; who limped, and shivered, and glared and growled; whose teeth chattered in his head as he seized me by the chin.
>
> (Dickens 1881: 2)

The above description is one of the most famous 19th-century fictional criminal creations, Magwitch – the escaped convict, loose on the Kent moors, who terrifies the young boy Pip into stealing food and equipment to aid his flight. The image evoked by Dickens has endured in the popular imagination: when people think of prison history, they tend to think of the convict prisoner, the dangerous, long-term criminal, clothed in the broad arrowed uniform, put to long hours of hard labour in the mid-Victorian prison. Along with the convict, they often have a vision of Victorian prison architecture: long brick wings with small windows, stemming from a central hub, rows of cells on three or four levels stretching out as far as the eye can see (Jewkes and Johnston 2007). In the popular imagination, then, prison history often evokes a particular moment in the history of imprisonment – the mid-Victorian prison and the Victorian convict. In this chapter, we will examine the realities of this image. As we shall see, this archetype lasted for two or three generations, but imprisonment has a much longer history before then and an important one since. Whilst the image of the Victorian prison and prisoner may be an enduring one in our popular culture, it was a relatively short period in the much longer story of the emergence and history of imprisonment.

So, why and how would the prison emerge as one of the main forms of punishment by the mid-19th century? Once we had decided on the prison as a form of punishment, what should we 'do' with people during their time confined within? These are the questions that permeate the use of imprisonment since at least the 18th century and remain at the heart of penal policy and criminal justice discussion in the 21st century. As the chapter will demonstrate, this narrative is not just one story of progressive change across hundreds of years of humanity; the modern prison, since its conception, has been a site of contest and discussion; an environment of experiment and a source of continued debate between administrators, prison staff, prisoners, academic scholars and the public about its role and legitimacy within society, and its effects, results and consequences.

The mid-Victorian prison: deterrence and bureaucratic administration, 1850–95

By the mid-19th century, the prison existed in the form in which we recognize it today: large, austere prisons holding hundreds of people; timetabled, organized institutions, populated by uniformed inmates, staffed by officers and experts. Though the prison was not a Victorian creation, the mid-Victorians fashioned the institution to such a degree that it has had an enduring effect not only on our collective imagination but also on many current aspects of the penal estate, particularly the buildings themselves which continue to house thousands of prisoners every day (Jewkes and Johnston 2007). However, we must also be aware that whilst we might be familiar with this image of the prison, the realities of mid-Victorian confinement were born of the questions raised by, and responses to, the problems of crime and punishment as they saw them at that time.

By the 1850s there were two systems of imprisonment in operation on the British mainland. Local prisons were operated by local authorities and held prisoners who were sentenced to short periods of incarceration, usually periods of up to two years. The government had experimented with two large prisons, Millbank and Pentonville, which will be discussed in the next section, but with the demise of the transportation of offenders to Australia they were faced with a much greater problem: how were they to deal with offenders who would otherwise have been banished overseas? By the 1850s, transportation was already contentious and on the decline. In the 1830s, at the height of the system, around 5,000 convicts were sent to Australia, but from 1840 the colonists in New South Wales and (from 1853) Van Diemen's Land, refused to accept any more. Subsequently, only Western Australia was willing to take convicts and whilst this continued until the last ship sailed in 1867, prisoners were sent in much smaller numbers – just under 10,000 men in total in the last 14 years. This was but a small fraction of the 160,000 convicts sent to the Antipodes between the discovery and establishment of the colony at Botany Bay in 1787 and the end of the system (Shaw 1998; Godfrey and Cox 2008; Maxwell-Stewart 2010; Johnston 2015).

The government set down plans to accommodate prisoners at home. Instead of sending offenders overseas they would be imprisoned in a government-run system called the convict prison system. In convict prisons, inmates would undergo a sentence of long-term incarceration called 'penal servitude', initially set at four years; one year to be served in separate confinement and three years on the public works, followed by release on licence (Tomlinson 1981). Early release from convict prisons on licence was gained through remission earned inside prison and, broadly speaking, this continued a practice that had operated in Australia to help encourage convicts to establish themselves within the colony (Johnston and Godfrey 2013a; Cox et al. 2014). Transportation as a sentence was abolished by the second Penal Servitude Act 1857, though the ability to send convicts overseas was retained. Once fully established (some convict prisons had to be built or adapted), the system operated across a range of prisons, all in London and the South of England. Millbank and Pentonville were used for the initial part of the sentence when convicts were placed in separate confinement (in Scotland, the government used cells at Perth prison); then convicts were sent to the public works. At Brixton, Chatham, Chattenden, Dartmoor, Parkhurst, Portsmouth, Portland and Borstal prisons, convicts were put to labour, building docks and sea defences, working in quarries and excavations, reclaiming moorland or farming. Female prisoners were sent to Brixton and

Parkhurst in the early years of the system but when it was more established they underwent separation at Millbank and were then sent to Fulham Refuge (although called a refuge it was a convict prison) or Woking prison, where they worked in the laundry or were set to needlework and knitting (Tomlinson 1981; Johnston 2015).

The mid-Victorian prison was developed in a climate of fear and anxiety about crime and the penal system. From the mid-1850s and into the 1860s, these fears contributed to the way in which the mid-Victorians responded to crime and shaped the prison and its regime. From the early 19th century onwards, social and legal reformers, investigators and journalists, as well as magistrates and politicians, had increasingly drawn attention to the problem of crime, collecting evidence, statistics and documenting material, identifying the supposed 'criminal classes' with a view to addressing crime and its causes. Whether or not the 'criminal classes' actually existed is a point of debate, but at the very least the Victorian public believed they existed and the consequences of these views for the criminal justice system, rather than the reality of their existence, are of greater importance for our purposes (McGowen 1990; Emsley 2010; Johnston 2015). In addition, by this time the early Victorian 'reformatory' prison project was regarded as a failure and fears that the 'criminal classes' would swamp British society were considerable. These anxieties were compounded by a moral panic about garrotting (violent street crime) in 1856 and again in 1862 (Davis 1980; Sindall 1990) and, as noted above, by the end of transportation (Bartrip 1981; Smith 1982). The vision evoked by the escaped convict, Magwitch, who had broken free from the confines of the hulks (decommissioned warships moored on the coast, where convicts sentenced to transportation were housed until they set sail), gripped the public imagination and, writing in 1861, Dickens drew on the fears and anxieties that were apparent in British society at this time.

The consequences of the failed reformatory prison project, the end of transportation, fears about the criminal classes and the release of convicts at home resulted in a shift towards a more deterrent penal philosophy from the 1850s and 1860s onwards. Ushered in by two government committees – the Carnarvon Committee on prison discipline and the Penal Servitude Commission, both held in 1863 – the subsequent legislation, the Penal Servitude Act 1864 and the Prisons Act 1865, implemented more severity and a deterrence-based penal philosophy in convict and local prisons which would dominate the system until at least the end of the 19th century. The Penal Servitude Act set a minimum five-year sentence and mandatory seven years for those who had previously undergone penal servitude. The stages of the sentence remained the same: separate confinement, followed by labour on public works and then the possibility of release on licence. The daily regime also used a system of marks or progressive stages under which a small amelioration in conditions could be gained through obtaining and maintaining 'marks' (these could be removed as a punishment or the convict could be placed back a stage) (Johnston 2015).

Similarly, in the local prison system, a policy based on 'hard labour, hard board, hard fare' predominated. This regime asserted deterrence through long hours of hard labour, sparse living conditions and a minimal diet – just enough to endure the hours of labour, but monotonous and bland to ensure it did not attract any potential entrants to the prison from the workhouse or the vagrant community. Uniformity in the local prisons had been continually urged by the central prison administrators and by the prison inspectors; the Prisons Act 1865 continued this policy, tying funding grants to local authorities from the Treasury to prisons that met the required standards. The Act also adopted the term 'local prisons' to distinguish these prisons from the government-controlled convict system. The government finally gained control of the local prisons in 1878. The Prison Act 1877 had transferred the control of all local prisons from April 1878 to the newly formed Prison Commission under the leadership of Edmund Du Cane, who became chairman of both prison systems, having been director of the Convict Prisons since 1869. The marks system and progressive stages as used in convict prisons were also implemented into the local prison regimes, although, as McConville (1995) has observed, for many local prisoners the use of progressive stages was pretty futile. The overwhelming majority of those who were sent to prison were sentenced to short periods (most under one month) and therefore would spend all of their time at the most severe stage no matter how well behaved or industrious they were. The main problem with this was not so much the short sentence, which though undoubtedly harsh could be got through, but the cumulative effect of multiple short sentences at this severity. Such experiences were common for a certain proportion of local prisoners who were repeatedly sent to prison for short terms and whose recidivism, by the latter decades of the century, would be viewed as increasingly problematic (McConville 1998b, 1995; Johnston and Godfrey 2013b).

Whilst the image of the mid-Victorian prison has been an enduring one, the convict like Magwitch was not the common prison experience; instead, it was the short-term prisoner, serving a period of seven or 14 days in a local prison, who was common among those sentenced to imprisonment. As we shall see later in this chapter, the severity of the late-Victorian prison was increasingly called into question by the end of the 19th century. The move to the deterrent system described above came from the demise of the reformatory project of the late 18th and early 19th centuries and it is to this period, often referred to as the one in which the birth of the modern prison occurred, that we shall now turn.

Prison reform, 1770s–1850s

It is a modern idea that people can be changed or altered by imprisonment and this section will examine the evolution of this idea in the period of 'prison reform', from the 1770s to the early 19th century. Whilst this period is important, we should not overlook the fact that prisons have existed for hundreds and hundreds of years, back to at least the Middle Ages and before. They were used to detain people before trial; they were also used as a punishment, and formed part of a much greater range of different possible penalties that made up the state apparatus of punishment.

It was not until the end of the 18th and into the early 19th centuries that a major transformation took place with regard to the use and purpose of imprisonment. During the 18th century prisons existed in two main forms: gaols, and houses of correction or bridewells. Although legally distinct, in practice the two forms often blurred. In theory, gaols held those people who were to be detained before trial, or sentencing, those awaiting removal to the hulks for transportation overseas (from 1718 onwards to America, then from 1787 to Australia), or those awaiting the death sentence. Gaols also held people who were in debt, until their creditors could be satisfied, though they were not subject to the same rules as criminal prisoners, having greater freedoms. Houses of correction or bridewells (so called as in England in 1555 the then king gave up Bridewell Palace to house the poor and disorderly and put them to work) were probably the first prisons in the sense that their aim was corrective or to teach habits of industry. They were used from at least the mid–16th century onwards and existed in various forms across Europe (similar examples include the *rasphuis* in Germany, *spinhuis* in Holland) and detained vagrants, the idle and disorderly poor as well as petty offenders (Spierenburg 1991; Innes 1987). As the centuries wore on, in England at least, some of the original aims had fallen by the wayside, and in many boroughs and counties the gaols and houses of correction were largely indistinguishable. All prisons at this time were maintained and operated by local authorities through the Quarter Sessions courts or the borough authorities. The government did not have any involvement in prisons, except for the maintenance of hulks and through contracts with those shipping sentenced convicts abroad.

In the decades leading up to the 1770s, serious offenders tended to be dealt with either by the death sentence (carried out in public) or through transportation. Lesser offences were dealt with through the imposition of fines, or the use of other public punishments, such as whipping or the pillory, or offenders may have been given a short sentence of imprisonment. A crime wave in the 1750s, or at least a perceived crime wave, had drawn increased attention to the use of the death penalty. Commentators felt that those sent to the gallows died a debauched, drunken death, playing to the crowd with long dying speeches, or that the crowd observing sympathized with the offender. If crime rates were increasing and crimes occurred at executions then this seemed to be evidence that the populace was undeterred by the spectacle of public execution or the state's message of punishment. One suggestion put in place by the Murder Act 1752 was that the bodies of murderers be given over for medical dissection after execution. The destruction of the dead body by the anatomists would add more terror to public execution and act as a greater deterrence; the practice stood against the view that bodies should remain whole to ensure that the soul passed into the afterlife. This Act resulted in struggles for the condemned's body after executions: sometimes families and friends mistakenly believed that their loved ones would be anatomized; in other instances, supporters of the offenders would try to retrieve bodies before the surgeon's assistants, to take them and bury them appropriately (see Linebaugh 1975).

There was also growing concern by the later 18th century that the death penalty was not always used appropriately. By this time, whilst thousands of people were sentenced to death for a range of offences, it was not necessarily the case that the execution would actually be carried out. The 'Bloody Code' refers to the large number of statutes that made up the laws of capital punishment, over 200 different Acts of Parliament. On the face of it, this seems a huge number of capital crimes, but the law was not consolidated, as it was by the early 19th century, so every offence would have a separate Act, unlike later when offences were all grouped together in criminal law – for example, as thefts or violence.

Those offenders processed by the criminal justice system for a capital offence did not always end up at the gallows due to the operation of various mechanisms in the legal system (Hay 1975). For example, offenders would plead for Royal Mercy or claim 'benefit of clergy' (reading a passage from the Bible) to receive a lesser sentence, and from 1718 on, the alternative sentence of transportation became more common. It was also possible that during the trial the offence would be manipulated by the judge or jury towards clemency. For example, the judge could use a very strict interpretation of the law to diminish the charge, or the jury might lower the value of the goods stolen, to avoid having to impose the death penalty. Theft of goods worth more than five shillings was a capital offence, so the jury might find the offender guilty but only of stealing goods worth four shillings and sixpence, therefore avoiding the death sentence. From the Transportation Act 1718 onwards, transportation to America was increasingly used as an alternative to capital punishment, and as a sentence in its own right. Around 30,000 people were banished to America, but transportation was used much more extensively from the 1780s onwards after the discovery of Australia.

The American War of Independence put paid to the transportation of offenders to the former colony in the 1770s, and whilst the government held out for the resumption of the practice, it did not come. At least in part to address this, the government passed the Penitentiary Act 1779 with the intention of building two penitentiaries, one for men and one for women, where offenders would be held before they were sent overseas. The committee that proposed this penitentiary, made up of William Blackstone, William Eden and John Howard, envisaged this penitentiary in a new way: prisoners would not just be held or detained, but would be changed or altered by their imprisonment; they would 'do penance' for their crimes. In the end, the penitentiary was never built, although the proposed scheme is well known as Jeremy Bentham submitted his plan for a panopticon prison to the government tender (Semple 1993). The panopticon, or 'Inspection House', is one of the most famous architectural prison designs. The original design embraced principles of surveillance and observation. The building stood six storeys high in a circular formation with a central guard tower. All cells faced the central tower and therefore the prisoners housed in them were observable at all times. A simple method to induce conformity, the panoptic power of prison was in the maximization of inspection and surveillance; the prisoners never knew when they were being observed.

Whilst government-level involvement with prisons had stalled, at the local level there was far more activity and this was where 'prison reform' was really taking place. Prior to his involvement in the penitentiary committee, John Howard had been an influential campaigner for change in the disorderly and unhealthy prisons he had seen as sheriff of Bedford. Howard undertook a survey of prisons across the country, published as *The State of the Prisons* in 1777. Howard was dismayed to discover the unhealthy and ill prisoners, the mixed population (male and female, tried and untried, serious and petty offenders, young and old), the poor management, lack of sanitation and water, as well as discovering the fees the prisoners paid for food, lodgings, the prison 'tap' (alcohol), and for admittance and other sundries. Those with money or family to assist them may have been able to endure such conditions for a time, but those in poverty had no means of subsistence or support. Howard also found prisoners who had completed their sentences but were unable to pay the discharge fee and obtain their release. His investigation and campaign was to have a considerable influence on county magistrates across the country as well as on the government. He fell short of accusing the magistracy of 'cruelty', aware that the gaols and houses of correction were in their hands, instead noting 'the inattention, of sheriffs, and gentlemen' … 'the cause of this distress is, that many prisons are scantily supplied, and some almost totally destitute of the necessaries of life' (Howard 1929 [1777]: 1).

The Gaol Fees Abolition Act was passed in 1815 and for the most part this abolished the entrepreneurial aspects of imprisonment, setting down the appointment of paid gaolers and replacing fees paid by prisoners with basic maintenance to be provided by the authorities. The passing of the Act was a significant success for Howard, but perhaps even more successful had been his ability to draw other magistrates and county gentlemen to his cause. Howard (and other reformers, including Elizabeth Fry) moved in distinguished social circles, and social, family and religious connections were prominent with the emerging industrialists, entrepreneurs, bankers, medical men and philanthropists of the early 19th century (Ignatieff 1978). This resulted in the rebuilding of over 45 prisons across the country in the latter decades of the 18th century (Evans 1982) and widespread recognition for Howard; for example, streets where new county or borough prisons were built were named after him, or busts of the reformer, like the one above the prison gatehouse at Shrewsbury prison, opened in 1793, were constructed in his honour (Johnston 2015).

There were certainly a great many improvements in prisons during this period. Greater awareness about hygiene and the necessary prevention of diseases like 'gaol fever' and smallpox had motivated many magistrates to embrace more sanitary prison conditions, but Howard was not just concerned about physical health and he castigated the lack of progress on 'that still more important object, the reformation of morals in our prisons' (Howard 1791: 233, cited in Forsythe 1987: 16). Further recognition of the influence of John Howard and of reformer Elizabeth Fry came in the Gaols Act passed in 1823, which implemented a system of classified association: prisoners would be held in different wards or wings of prisons according to their status (e.g. untried, felon, misdemeanant, debtor) and their sex. Howard had noted the unregulated nature of imprisonment in his campaigns but the plight of female prisoners had been the main cause for Fry (1827) since she had started visiting Newgate prison in 1813.

In 1810 the government revisited the idea of the penitentiary and the Holford Committee recommended the establishment of a government prison, which came to fruition in 1816 when Millbank Penitentiary opened in London. By this time, transportation to Australia had been under way for 30 years, but the idea that convicts may be held in prison before they were sent abroad was revisited in the rationale for Millbank. The first government penitentiary would incorporate some of the new penitential ideals: not only would the prisoner be employed, but s/he would be reformed and improved through the use of seclusion and religious education. The experiment was relatively short lived, however. Millbank was criticized for its huge cost, only inflated by the poor marshland location on which it was built as well as difficulties with staff shortages and corruption. In addition, there were problems with physical illness and disease which caused the prison to be temporarily abandoned, but these were only compounded by allegations that the isolation and solitude inflicted on prisoners were more than their mental health could endure (McConville 1981; Wilson 2002). By the early 1840s, Millbank was a convict depot and the prison administrators' aspirations for a new 'model' prison had turned to Pentonville prison.

By the 1820s and 1830s, the moral reform of prisoners had become the most significant part of discussion and just how the reform of prisoners was to be achieved was dominated by the debate between two prison regimes: the separate system and the silent system. Both systems were first used in America – the silent system in New York at Auburn and Sing Sing prisons, and the separate system in Philadelphia at the Eastern Penitentiary and Walnut Street prison. Both systems were based on the idea of the prevention of communication between prisoners, which, it was thought, would prevent the spread of moral corruption or pollution inside prison walls. The separate system sought to achieve these goals through the use of isolation and religious and moral influence;

prisoners would be placed alone in individual cells, where they would spend all of their time, only being allowed out for exercise or to attend chapel, and only to be visited by the staff or the chaplain. The silent system would achieve the same goals through the implementation of complete silence; prisoners would be held together in large work-rooms during the day and in cells at night, but communication between them would be prevented at all times.

William Crawford, one of the first prison inspectors, appointed in 1835, had been a keen supporter of the separate system and had visited and reported on the system in operation in the USA (Crawford 1834). Along with Reverend Whitworth Russell (also a prison inspector), he lobbied for the use of the separate system in England and ultimately its implementation was regularized by the Prisons Act 1839. The changes in the prison system from the 1830s onwards also reflected greater government involvement in prisons; whilst the state only maintained the hulks and Millbank Penitentiary at this time, they were keen to impose greater control and uniformity on the mass of local prisons that were spread across the country. One way in which this was to be achieved was through the use of the prison inspectors, established by the Prisons Act 1835. The country was divided into districts, each having at least one inspector who would regularly visit all of the prisons in that region. As the century progressed, the inspectors were used to impose greater uniformity on the local prisons; policies and the implementation of prison practices were increasingly tied to funding from central government. In theory, from 1839 onwards, all local prisons would operate the separate system of imprisonment and would adhere to the same practices and policies within prison walls. In practice, local prisons remained diverse for much of this period and into the 1850s and 1860s, and regimes, diets, hard labour and other practices all varied according to the size and population of local prisons, the willingness or interest of the local magistrates to spend money on prisons in their areas, as well as local views about how to treat the prisoners (for examples, see DeLacy 1986; Forsythe 1983; Saunders 1986; Ireland 2007; Johnston 2015).

The failure of Millbank led to a new government focus. At first the gaze fell on Parkhurst prison, which had opened in 1838 to hold juvenile offenders under the separate system. Parkhurst, unlike Millbank, was deemed a success, at least by the administrators, and this encouraged them to seek out a new project for the application of the separate system to adult offenders. This second experiment was Pentonville prison, which opened in 1842, built on the Caledonian Road in London, to hold 520 prisoners. If the use of the separate system was not in question before Pentonville opened, it certainly was after the initial months of the operation of the regime. Newspapers and commentators cautioned against the severity of the prison regime, the long hours of isolation and deprivation and their effects on the mental health of the inmates. Subsequently, prisoners were removed from Pentonville due to insanity and other nervous illnesses caused or exacerbated by the solitary conditions, and the periods of separation were reduced from 18 to 12 and then to nine months (Ignatieff 1978; Johnston 2006). Conversely, Pentonville's regime was also criticized for not being severe enough; critics argued that despite the use of face masks and the specially constructed cells, prisoners did recognize and even communicate with each other. The idea of this method of 'reform' and what this meant in practice was increasingly called into question, as was the religious and moral thread of the separate system that was central to its operation. Not only was the regime either too soft or not strict enough, it was also argued that the chaplains and governors were duped into believing prisoners who claimed that they had been changed by the system.

By the late 1840s and into the 1850s, the cumulative effect of this criticism led to increasing calls for a more deterrent prison regime. The architectural aspects of the separate system remained but the reformatory project had been undermined; instead, the isolation of the separate cell would be fashioned into a new deterrent philosophy of the mid-Victorian prison and would dominate the prison system until at least the end of the 19th century (Henriques 1972; Johnston 2006).

The emergence of the modern prison and into the 20th century: the demise of Du Cane, decarceration and two World Wars, 1895–1945

As we have seen, the modern prison emerged in the late 18th and beginning of the 19th centuries. The contrast between the unregulated gaols and bridewells of the 18th century and the timetabled, orderly and functional prisons of the early Victorian period is marked (McGowen 1998). By this time the prison embraced some central features that would determine its use and existence in the following generations and which continue today. As noted above, the reformed prisons were healthier, more orderly and better regulated than the gaols of the past, and traditional interpretations of this change have observed this as a progressive change in which reformers such as Howard and Fry are celebrated for bringing about the end to barbaric and neglectful practices of the past (Webb and Webb 1963; Stockdale 1977; Whiting 1977; Radzinowicz and Hood 1990). Other commentators have questioned the motives of reformers. Unwilling to take the philanthropy and benevolence of reformers at face value, they have examined the unintended consequences of reforms that have resulted in more severe practices or stricter discipline (Ignatieff 1978; Platt 1969; Rothman 1990). Authors such as Foucault (1991), Cohen (1985), Cohen and Scull (1983), Melossi and Pavarini (1981) and Ignatieff (1978) have revised the traditional account of such changes, and all see the prison as emerging alongside other institutions of modern society, such as the school, hospital and asylum, which all share similar disciplinary features and operate as part of a state apparatus of social control. The Marxist accounts of Rusche and Kirchheimer (1939) and Melossi and Pavarini (1981) see the emergence of the prison alongside the development of capitalist society: necessary to instil habits of industry and discipline on the labouring masses.

Foucault (1991) observes the central features of the new prison as: functioning to transform the behaviour of the individual; to classify and categorize prisoners according not only to their offence but also their age, mental health, background; to adapt punishment according to the progress of the prisoner; and to provide both work and education to socialize the individual and for the benefit of wider society. All these processes are overseen by specialist staff and experts and are followed up by measures of supervision after imprisonment to maintain or complete the rehabilitation of the prisoner. Rather than the displays of torture and bodily punishments carried out in public in the past, the new prison inflicts punishment through the internal prison regime with the objective of changing the behaviour of the offender, not just avenging the crime (Foucault 1991). Others have observed these changes in punishment and the rise of the disciplinary prison over a longer period of time, and considered its emergence alongside wider civilizing processes (Spierenburg 1991, 2005; Pratt 2002; Smith 2008).

By the 1890s, the deterrent regimes in prisons established at mid-century were being increasingly called into question. There were a number of concerns, not least the severity of prison regimes. Despite the administrators' best efforts, the full force of the regime could not be applied uniformly to all prisoners; some groups needed to be protected due to their age or infirmity. Second, even for those prisoners subject to the most deterrent regimes, questions began to be asked about the appropriateness of these methods; critics complained that there was simply no hope of reformation in the crushing prison regime. Third, the administration and operation of the system was too bureaucratic and Edmund Du Cane, who had led both prison systems from 1877 onwards, was viewed as having far too much power and control, while systems of accountability were distinctly lacking (Bailey 1997; Harding 1988; Nellis 1996; Pratt 2004). It was the case that under Du Cane's leadership both convict and local prison populations had fallen; the daily average in the convict system had more than halved from 10,880 to 4,770 between 1879 and 1894, and in the local system it had also fallen, by about one-third from 20,833 to 13,850. However, other factors could have influenced this decline, including a drop in recorded crime, a reduction in the length of penal servitude in 1891 from five to three years, as well as an increased use of non-custodial sentences for some offenders (Bailey 1997). In addition, whilst the average population was declining, recidivism rates were increasing and this was a considerable area of concern (Johnston and Godfrey 2013b).

Criticism of the prison system and the regimes within came from a number of sources. Prisoner memoirs in the preceding decades had called the system into question (Pratt 2002), but in 1894 a series of articles appeared in the *Daily Chronicle* which drew widespread attention. The series, entitled 'Our Dark Places', was thought to have been written by Reverend William D. Morrison, then the chaplain of Wandsworth prison. The 'special commissioner' focused on the autocratic authority of Du Cane, the military character of the system, the discontent of staff, as well as the effects of solitary confinement, overcrowding and recidivism. Calling for the appointment of a Royal Commission, the author concluded that the 'local prison system stands confessed a vast and appalling failure. It cannot be patched from within; it must be remedied from without' (Anonymous 1894).

This media attention was shortly followed by the high-profile criminal trial of Oscar Wilde and his subsequent sentence of two years' imprisonment with hard labour for offences under the Criminal Law Amendment Act 1885 (relating to homosexual practices). Further to the trial, Wilde published a scathing attack on the prison system, written under his cell number pseudonym 'C.3.3', and entitled *The Ballad of Reading Gaol* (1898). By this time, criticism of the system was impossible to ignore and the government had already appointed a departmental committee to examine the prison system, led by Herbert Gladstone.

The Gladstone Committee (1895) acknowledged many of the problems with the severity of the prison regimes but stopped short of a complete shift, instead wishing to promote a balance between deterrence and reform. Hard labour was replaced with 'productive labour', prisoners could work in association (though often this was still in silence), the provision of education was acknowledged as an important aspect of reform and, importantly, remission of sentence was introduced to local prisons from the Prison Act 1898 onwards, as was greater support for prisoners on their release.

David Garland (1985) has argued that this period, between 1895 and 1914, was when the modern 'penal-welfare' complex was established. Changes affected the whole penal system rather than just prisons and were influenced by the ideas emanating from the positivist school of criminological thought which located the sources of criminality within the environment and in family, including physical traits and hereditary, as opposed to individual morality, which had dominated such discussions in the preceding centuries. Undoubtedly the early 20th century was an important time. With changes in the wider penal system that would have a dramatic effect on the prison system and particularly on the prison population levels, it was a 'truly extraordinary period in our penal history' (Wilson 2014: 89). The development of probation from 1907; the establishment of borstal institutions for young offenders; changes in sentencing practice, particularly allowing increased time to pay court fines and alternative disposals for first offenders; diversion for the mentally ill and those under 16 years old – all contributed to a declining population. In 1908 the daily average population had been 22,000 (over 200,000 receptions to prisons; three out of four of these for non-indictable offences or defaulting on fines); by 1938 it was just over 11,000, which constituted the smallest prison population in Europe (Rutherford 1984; Wilson 2014).

Behind prison walls, though, internal regimes were marked by continuity rather than change. The deterrent and severe practices of the latter 19th century, particularly the use of separation and silence, continued to be the norm for most prisoners who experienced the penal system into the 1920s and 1930s (Forsythe 1990; Bailey 1997; Brown 2013; Johnston 2008). Winston Churchill had become Home Secretary in 1910 and whilst his tenure is often associated with his famous speech on the 'treatment of crime and criminals' as an indicator of the 'civilization' of a country, this image belies some of the more contradictory elements of his penal policy and the bleak and oppressive nature of the prison system (Bennett 2008). For example, despite some reduction in the use of separate confinement for convicts, its use continued for most prisoners until 1931, as did criticism of the rigid and deterrent, 'machine-like' operation of the system. This was most notably demonstrated by the unofficial inquiry into the prison system, *English Prisons Today*, published in 1922 and compiled by two ex-prisoners (conscientious objectors to the First World War), Stephen Hobhouse and A. Fenner Brockway. In the same year, Alexander Paterson became a prison commissioner, and although he was never chairman, his influence was important and his view that people should be sent to prison '*as* punishment rather than *for* punishment' (Ruck 1951: 23) is a well-cited liberal sentiment. This period is often described as 'the golden age of prison reform', but as we have seen with other periods of prison history, it was also a contested and contradictory time, and regimes were slow to change. The period also encompassed the largest prison disturbance in English prison history, at Dartmoor in 1932 (Brown 2013; Wilson 2014; Forsythe 1990).

Inside the prison system during the two World Wars, 1914–18 and 1939–45

One hundred years after the outbreak of the First World War we are commemorating and remembering the great sacrifice and loss of life during this period. Both World Wars would have a significant impact on the prison system and remain largely hidden and undocumented periods within the history of our penal system. Although both wars would have a significant impact on the prison system, they would do so for different reasons. It is perhaps the case that the lasting effect of the devastation and loss of life across Europe in the First World War helped to sustain a more reformative and rehabilitative philosophy inside prisons in the 1920s and 1930s, but this also occurred within a broader period of decarceration that had begun at the turn of the 20th century (Rutherford 1984; Wilson 2014). The Second World War had a physical impact on the prison system, with air raids and bombings destroying the buildings, but the crime rate and the prison population began to rise during the early 1940s, which would have a different lasting effect.

The prison population during the First World War dropped quite significantly, though it may already have been on the decline anyway. A smaller prison population (particularly in the convict system) had made the authorities more open to the possibilities of different regimes and the comparative easing of some of the more deterrent aspects inside prisons that had continued from the Du Cane era. At least in the convict prisons, by the 1920s conditions were beginning to ameliorate, though they took longer to come to bear in the local prison system. The number of sentenced prisoners diminished by over 50,000 during 1915–16. Home Secretary Chuter Ede proclaimed that the criminals of England, like the rest of the population, had patriotically signed up, but others claimed that petty crimes had increased (stealing food, rationing coupons, looting), and moreover those imprisoned during this period were more likely to be 'physically or mentally weaker' (Jewkes and Johnston 2011; *The Times*, 26 September 1916).

The Second World War would be a different experience for the prison system to operate within. Once again a significant proportion of prison staff were called up to regiments and large numbers of auxiliary staff were called in to operate prisons alongside the remaining staff. However, this period would present new challenges of air raids, bombings, rationing and restrictions not felt in the same way during the First World War. When air raids and bombings began in 1940, the borstal institutions at Borstal, Feltham and Portland were the first to be hit, and by September, air raids had resulted in the bombings of four London prisons in the first few weeks of attacks. A large incendiary device hit Pentonville prison on 10 May 1941, resulting in the deaths of 17 people – staff and their families, and prisoners. The air raids also affected many prisons outside London, notably HMP Walton in Liverpool, Bristol and Hull (though Hull had been closed as a precaution in 1939). HMP Walton was hit by three bombs in September 1940, resulting in loss of life and destruction of parts of the prison. In April and May 1941, incendiary devices again hit Walton, starting fires, and even greater devastation occurred when consecutive nights of Luftwaffe air raids resulted in the deaths of 22 prisoners killed on 3 May when eight direct hits engulfed the prison (Jewkes and Johnston 2011; RCP and DCP 1945).

In addition to the destruction of the buildings during the Second World War, the prison population had also begun to rise, increasing by 50% between 1938 and 1946. After the end of the war this resulted in a new building programme under which 17 new prisons and borstals were established (Soothill 2007). Some parts of pre-war penal policy were continued; the most significant were proposals for 'open' prisons, which had stalled in Parliament in 1938. The first open prison, New Hall, Wakefield, had been established in 1936 and a growing acknowledgement in the 1920s and 1930s, that prisoners could be held in different security settings rather than just within the secure perimeters of the local or convict prison, was put into practice (McConville 1998b). Lionel Fox had become chairman of the Prison Commission in 1942 and oversaw the post-war building programme. Askham Grange in Yorkshire became the first open prison for women and received prisoners in 1946, and penal servitude as a sentence was abolished in 1948. The prison system remained under the Prison Commission until 1963 but by this time indictable crime had reached an all-time high (Morris 1989), and some of the advances from before the war were overtaken. The Prisons Act 1952 consolidated a large number of pieces of prison legislation from the 19th century onwards and remains the central Act for the governance of prisons today.

Bibliography

Anonymous (1894) 'Our Dark Places', *The Daily Chronicle*, 29 January.

Bailey, V. (1997) 'English Prisons, Penal Culture, and the Abatement of Imprisonment, 1895–1922', *Journal of British Studies* 36: 285–324.

Bartrip, P. (1981) 'Public Opinion and Law Enforcement: The Ticket of Leave Scares in Mid-Victorian Britain', in V. Bailey (ed.) *Policing and Punishment in Nineteenth Century Britain*, London: Croom Helm.

Bennett, J. (2008) 'The Man, the Machine and the Myths: Reconsidering Winston Churchill's Prison Reforms', in H. Johnston (ed.) *Punishment and Control in Historical Perspective*, Basingstoke: Palgrave Macmillan.

Brown, A. (2013) *Inter-war Penal Policy and Crime in England: The Dartmoor Convict Prison Riot, 1932*, Basingstoke: Palgrave Macmillan.

Cohen, S. (1985) *Visions of Social Control*, London: Polity.

Cohen, S. and Scull, A. (eds) (1983) *Social Control and the State*, London: Martin Robertson.

Cox, D.J., Godfrey, B., Johnston, H. and Turner, J. (2014) 'On Licence: Understanding Punishment, Recidivism and Desistance in Penal Policy, 1853–1945', in V. Miller and J. Campbell (eds) *Transnational Penal Cultures*, Abingdon: Routledge.

Crawford, W. (1834) *Report of William Crawford Esq., on the Penitentiaries of the United States*, (593), Vol. XLVI.349, Parliamentary Papers, London: Home Office.

Davis, J. (1980) 'The London Garrotting Panic of 1862: A Moral Panic and the Creation of a Criminal Class in Mid-Victorian England', in V.A.C. Gatrell, B. Lenman and G. Parker (eds) *Crime and the Law*, London: Europa.

DeLacy, M. (1986) *Prison Reform in Lancashire 1700–1850*, Stanford, CA: Stanford University Press.

Dickens, C. (1881 [1861]) *Great Expectations: The Works of Charles Dickens in Thirty Volumes*, Volume XII, London: Chapman & Hall Limited.

Emsley, C. (2010) *Crime and Society in England, 1750–1900*, fourth edn, Harlow: Longman.

Evans, R. (1982) *The Fabrication of Virtue: English Prison Architecture, 1750–1840*, Cambridge: Cambridge University Press.

Forsythe, B. (1995) 'The Garland Thesis and the Origins of Modern English Prison Discipline: 1835 to 1939', *The Howard Journal* 34(3): 259–273.

Forsythe, W.J. (1983) *A System of Discipline: Exeter Borough Prison, 1819–1863*, Exeter: Exeter University Press.

Forsythe, W.J. (1987) *The Reform of Prisoners, 1830–1900*, London: Croom Helm.

Forsythe, W.J. (1990) *Penal Discipline, Reformatory Projects and the English Prison Commission 1895–1939*, Exeter: Exeter University Press.

Foucault, M. (1991) *Discipline and Punish – The Birth of the Prison*, London: Penguin.

Fry, E. (1827) *Observations on the Visiting, Superintending, and Government of Female Prisoners*, London: John and Arthur Arch.

Garland, D. (1985) *Punishment and Welfare*, Aldershot: Gower.

Garland, D. (2002) *The Culture of Control: Crime and Social Order in Contemporary Society*, Oxford: Oxford University Press.

Gatrell, V.A.C. (1994) *The Hanging Tree*, Oxford: Oxford University Press.

Gladstone Committee (1895) *Report from the Departmental Committee on Prisons*, (C.7702), Vol. LVI, London: Home Office.

Godfrey, B. and Cox, D. (2008) 'The "Last Fleet": Crime, Reformation and Punishment in Western Australia', *Australian and New Zealand Journal of Criminology* 41(2): 236–258.

Harding, C. (1988) 'The Inevitable End of a Discredited System? The Origins of the Gladstone Committee Report on Prisons, 1895', *The Historical Journal* 31(3): 591–608.

Hay, D. (1975) 'Property, Authority and the Criminal Law', in D. Hay, P. Linebaugh, J.G. Rule, E.P. Thompson and C. Winslow (eds) *Albion's Fatal Tree*, London: Allen Lane.

Henriques, U.R.Q. (1972) 'The Rise and Decline of the Separate System of Prison Discipline', *Past and Present* 54: 61–93.

Hobhouse, S. and Brockway, A.F. (1922) *English Prisons To-day*, London: Longmans, Green and Co.

Howard, J. (1929 [1777]) *The State of the Prisons*, London: Dent.

Ignatieff, M. (1978) *A Just Measure of Pain*, London: Macmillan.

Ignatieff, M. (1983) 'State, Civil Society and Total Institutions: A Critique of Recent Social Histories of Punishment', in S. Cohen and A. Scull (eds) *Social Control and the State*, London: Martin Robertson.

Innes, J. (1987) 'Prisons for the Poor: English Bridewells, 1555–1800', in F. Snyder and D. Hay (eds) *Labour, Law and Crime: An Historical Perspective*, London: Tavistock.

Ireland, R.W. (2007) *'A Want of Order and Good Discipline': Rules, Discretion and the Victorian Prison*, Cardiff: University of Wales Press.

Jewkes, Y. and Johnston, H. (2007) 'The Evolution of Prison Architecture', in Y. Jewkes (ed.) *Handbook on Prisons*, Cullompton: Willan.

Jewkes, Y. and Johnston, H. (2011) 'The English Prison During the First and Second World Wars: Hidden Lived Experiences of War', *Prison Service Journal* 198: 47–51.

Johnston, H. (2006) '"Buried Alive": Representations of the Separate System in Victorian England', in P. Mason (ed.) *Captured by the Media: Prison Discourse in Popular Culture*, Cullompton: Willan.

Johnston, H. (2008) 'Reclaiming the Criminal: The Role and Training of Prison Officers in England, 1877–1914', *Howard Journal of Criminal Justice* 47(3): 297–312.

Johnston, H. (2015) *Crime in England, 1815–1880: Experiencing the Criminal Justice System*, Abingdon: Routledge.

Johnston, H. and Godfrey, B. (2013a) *'The Costs of Imprisonment: A Longitudinal Study'*, ESRC End of Award Report, RES-062-23-3102, Swindon: ESRC.

Johnston, H. and Godfrey, B. (2013b) 'Counterblast: The Perennial Problem of Short Prison Sentences', *Howard Journal of Criminal Justice* 52(4): 433–437.

Linebaugh, P. (1975) 'The Tyburn Riot against the Surgeons', in D. Hay et al. (eds) *Albion's Fatal Tree*, London: Pantheon Books.

McConville, S. (1981) *A History of Prison Administration, 1750–1877*, London: Routledge & Kegan Paul.

McConville, S. (1995) *English Local Prisons: Next Only to Death, 1860–1900*, London: Routledge.

McConville, S. (1998a) 'The Victorian Prison: England, 1865–1965', in N. Morris and D.J. Rothman (eds) *The Oxford History of the Prison: The Practice of Punishment in Western Society*, Oxford: Oxford University Press.

McConville, S. (1998b) 'Local Justice: The Jail', in N. Morris and D.J. Rothman (eds) *The Oxford History of the Prison: The Practice of Punishment in Western Society*, Oxford: Oxford University Press.

McGowen, R. (1990) 'Getting to Know the Criminal Class in Nineteenth-Century England', *Nineteenth Century Contexts* 14(1): 33–54.

McGowen, R. (1998) 'The Well-Ordered Prison: England, 1780–1865', in N. Morris and D.J. Rothman (eds) *The Oxford History of the Prison: The Practice of Punishment in Western Society*, Oxford: Oxford University Press.

Maxwell-Stewart, H. (2010) 'Convict Transportation from Britain and Ireland', *History Compass* 8(11): 1221–1242.

Melossi, D. and Pavarini, M. (1981) *The Prison and the Factory: Origins of the Penitentiary System*, London: Macmillan.

Morris, T. (1989) *Crime and Criminal Justice Since 1945*, Oxford: Basil Blackwell.

Nellis, M. (1996) 'John Galsworthy's Justice', *British Journal of Criminology* 36(1): 61–84.

Platt, A. (1969) *The Child Savers*, Chicago, IL: Chicago University Press.

Pratt, J. (2002) *Punishment and Civilisation*, London: Sage.

Pratt, J. (2004) 'The Acceptable Prison: Official Discourse, Truth and Legitimacy in the Nineteenth Century', in G. Gilligan and J. Pratt (eds) *Crime, Truth and Justice: Official Inquiry, Discourse, Knowledge*, Cullompton: Willan, 71–88.

Radzinowicz, L. and Hood, R. (1990) *A History of the English Criminal Law and its Administration from 1750. Volume 5: The Emergence of Penal Policy*, London: Stevens.

RCP and DCP (1945) *Report of the Commissioners of Prisons and Directors of Convict Prisons for the Years 1939–1941*, Parliamentary Papers, Cmd. 6820.

Rothman, D.J. (1990) *The Discovery of the Asylum*, second edn, Boston, MA: Little, Brown & Co.

Ruck, S.K. (ed.) (1951) *Paterson on Prisons*, London: Frederick Muller.

Rusche, G. and Kirchheimer, O. (1939) *Punishment and Social Structure*, New York: Columbia University Press.

Rutherford, A. (1984) *Prisons and the Process of Justice: The Reductionist Challenge*, London: Heinemann.

Saunders, J. (1986) 'Warwickshire Magistrates and Prison Reform, 1840–1875', *Midland History* XI: 79–99.

Semple, J. (1993) *Bentham's Prison: A Study of the Panopticon Penitentiary*, Oxford: Clarendon.

Shaw, A.G.L. (1998) *Convicts and the Colonies*, Dublin: Irish Historical Press.

Sim, J. (1990) *Medical Power in Prisons*, Milton Keynes: Open University Press.

Sindall, R.S. (1990) *Street Violence in the Nineteenth Century: Media Panic or Real Danger?* Leicester: Leicester University Press.

Smith, D. (1982) 'The Demise of Transportation: Mid-Victorian Penal Policy', *Criminal Justice History* 3: 21–45.

Smith, P. (2008) *Punishment and Culture*, Chicago, IL: Chicago University Press.

Soothill, K. (2007) 'Prison Histories and Competing Audiences, 1776–1966', in Y. Jewkes (ed.) *Handbook on Prisons*, Cullompton: Willan.

Spierenburg, P. (1991) *The Prison Experience: Disciplinary Institutions and their Inmates in Early Modern Europe*, New Brunswick, NJ: Rutgers University Press.

Spierenburg, P. (2005) 'The Origins of the Prison', in C. Emsley (ed.) *The Persistent Prison: Problems, Images and Alternatives*, London: Francis Boutle.

Stockdale, E. (1977) *A Study of Bedford Prison, 1660–1877*, Chichester: Phillimore.

Thomas, J.E. (1972) *The English Prison Officer since 1850*, London: Routledge & Kegan Paul.

Tomlinson, M.H. (1981) 'Penal Servitude 1846–1865: A System in Evolution', in V. Bailey (ed.) *Policing and Punishment in Nineteenth-Century Britain*, London: Croom Helm.

Webb, S. and Webb, B. (1963) *English Prisons Under Local Government*, London: Longmans Green.

Whiting, J.R.S. (1977) *Prison Reform in Gloucestershire*, London: Phillimore.

Wilde, O. (2002 [1898]) *De Profundis, The Ballad of Reading Gaol and Other Writings*, London: Wordsworth.

Wilson, D. (2002) 'Millbank, The Panopticon and their Victorian Audiences', *The Howard Journal* 41(4): 364–381.

Wilson, D. (2014) *Pain and Retribution*, London: Reaktion Books.

Chapter 3

The aims of imprisonment

Ian O'Donnell

Introduction

The stated aims of imprisonment became markedly less ambitious when the confidence that characterized the 19th-century reform movement was displaced by a realization that places of confinement – no matter how well designed or humanely intentioned – could never 'grind rogues honest and idle men industrious'. Today the emphasis is on risk reduction and performance management; lofty aspirations have been trumped by narrow measures of target delivery. In an attempt to find principled common ground upon which to advance the debate, a new formulation is offered in this chapter, namely: the aim of imprisonment is to reconstitute the prisoner's spatiotemporal world without causing avoidable collateral damage. It is argued that this minimalist statement provides a foundation upon which to build prison regimes that are oriented towards the future and acknowledge that all prisoners, no matter what they have done, possess the capacity to redirect their lives. Devoid of hope, imprisonment is pointless pain:

> II. [T]he supreme aim of prison discipline is the reformation of criminals, not the infliction of vindictive suffering ...
>
> XIV. The prisoner's self-respect should be cultivated to the utmost ... There is no greater mistake in the whole compass of penal discipline, than its studied imposition of degradation as part of punishment. Such imposition destroys every better impulse and aspiration. It crushes the weak, irritates the strong, and indisposes all to submission and reform. It is trampling where we ought to raise ...
>
> XXII. The state has not discharged its whole duty to the criminal when it has punished him, nor even when it has reformed him. Having raised him up, it has the further duty to aid in holding him up.
> (Principles promulgated by the congress of the National Prison Association held in Cincinnati, Ohio, in October 1870, cited in Wines 1871: 541–7)

Antecedents

Two hundred years ago the aims of imprisonment were clear, namely: (i) to contain debtors until what was owed was paid; (ii) to detain accused persons pending trial; (iii) to hold convicted persons pending the execution of the sentence of the court (e.g. corporal or capital punishment, or transportation); (iv) to punish offenders for periods so brief that ascribing to them a purpose other than incapacitation seems somewhat grandiose – little can really be expected of prison terms that are completed in a matter of days or weeks; (v) to profit gaolers.

The focus of the debate about the aims of imprisonment was sharpened by the stuttering emergence, across Europe and the USA, of a penal philosophy that stressed the importance of reflective solitude as an engine for reform. This coincided with, and was given impetus by, the discovery of architectural solutions to the problem of unauthorized prisoner communication which meant that prisons could be designed to enforce silent separation, something that had not previously been possible. For a time in the early 19th century there was a close alignment between broadly agreed aims (i.e. reformation underpinned by deterrence), the technologies required to deliver them (e.g. timetables, surveillance, diet, cellular accommodation), the associated regimes (whether congregate and silent – the Auburn system, or separate – the Pennsylvania system), and administrative imperatives (e.g. uniformity, hierarchy, security, micro-regulation). This cohesion is evident in the adoption of the Pennsylvania system of prison discipline across much of Europe. Prison chaplains enthusiastically propounded the merits of this approach and their assertive writings, assured tone and assumed universality of appeal have few parallels today. The rival Auburn system, which thrived in the USA, was characterized by a lower level of confidence in the individual prisoner's capacity to reform and the maintenance of silence required the frequent use of the whip (for a review and reappraisal of these competing paradigms, see O'Donnell 2014: Chapters 1, 2; see also Chapter 2 of this volume).

Adding urgency to the debate in the UK was the shift in temporal parameters that accompanied the ending of transportation. If men and women were to be incarcerated for years, some thought had to be given to why, as well as to how and where. The Penal Servitude Acts of 1853 and 1857 played an important, but often overlooked, role in this regard. Prior to their enactment the primary aim of the prison was to hold convicts for a fixed period of time in order to ready them for a new life in the colonies (minor offenders, debtors and those on remand continued to be sent to local gaols for brief periods). When the option of transportation was withdrawn, men and women faced the prospect of spending years behind bars on home soil, something that had not previously been contemplated. This stretching of time horizons forced a reappraisal of penal purposes at a juncture when the optimism that had breathed life into the separate system was waning. Consequently the emphasis shifted away from the prison cell as a crucible for personal transformation and it became, for a time, a place of unyielding discipline, of hard labour, hard fare and a hard bed. While the clarity of purpose may have dulled somewhat, the technologies, regimes and administrative imperatives remained largely unchanged. Rupturing the link between what was desired and how this was to be delivered had lasting ramifications. Subsequent waves of hope and despair occurred within a built environment that was slow to change, and against a background where discipline was pursued as an end in itself, untethered from a reformative ethic.

The confidence of the early reformers evaporated when it became apparent that new prison designs, and the muscular Christianity espoused by their advocates, were insufficient to the task of inspiring wholesale cognitive, spiritual and behavioural change. A truncated version of the 37 principles espoused by the National Prison Association in the USA in 1870 – three of which were quoted at the start of this chapter – was adopted by the International Penitentiary Congress in London two years later (Wines 1873: 177–8).

Despite initial enthusiasm, these eloquently phrased and ebulliently expressed aspirations soon came to be seen as disconnected from the realities of imprisonment, however noble the sentiments they embodied.

Thinking about aims requires consideration of how they have changed over time. The disappearance of benevolent intent meant that imprisonment felt different to those forced to endure its strictures. Despite the harshness of the silent and separate systems, and concern about the adverse mental health implications of regimes that required the termination of meaningful human relationships, their champions wished to force change upon the prisoner so that when he or she re-entered society it was on mutually beneficial terms. Bentham (1843: 226) described the panopticon prison as 'a mill for grinding rogues honest and idle men industrious', a description that might equally be applied to prisons of the late 19th century when the hope that penal treatment could bring the prisoner closer to God, and into harmony with his law-abiding fellows, proved to be misplaced. However grim Bentham's philosophy might appear, it is a world away from grinding without purpose.

Contrast the use of solitary confinement in Eastern State Penitentiary in Philadelphia, or Pentonville prison in London, or any of their numerous imitators in the 1800s, with the 20th-century manifestation of penal solitude in the supermax (see Chapter 10). There are two important distinctions for present purposes. The first is the absence of any pretence that prolonged isolation is for the good of the prisoner. The second is that for a significant cohort of those so detained, there is no prospect of eventual release, no 'fold' to return to. Supermax custody defines prisoners by their criminal conduct, is pessimistic (at worst) or disinterested (at best) about the possibility of personal change, and its advocates have no compunction about administering a kind of treatment that would be adjudged harsh and degrading by anything but the most elastic of standards. Modern technology allows a studied indifference to be paid to prisoners; they command less personal attention than did their 19th-century predecessors and this reinforces their status not only as morally repugnant but also as socially redundant.

I do not wish to suggest that the past was an unproblematically better place, but simply to advert to the fact that there was a singularity of purpose (especially among the proponents of the Pennsylvania system), and an irrepressible confidence that the stated aims could be delivered that, to a great extent, has disappeared from the discourse. When the first wave of penal optimism receded it was replaced by a lurch to harsh – and hopeless – discipline. In Priestley's (1999: 119) words, 'the darkness closed in around the Victorian prisoner'. However, confidence returned eventually, a rehabilitative ethic came to dominate, and there was renewed emphasis on the individual prisoner's capacity to change in a pro-social direction. The disappointing results of empirical studies and the hasty and erroneous conclusion that nothing worked when it came to prisoner rehabilitation caused a fresh reappraisal of the aims of imprisonment. The wheel of penal change completed another revolution. The emergence in recent decades of cognitive behavioural programmes, along with more sophisticated approaches to programme design and better measurement of effects, has renewed confidence in the potential for imprisonment to catalyse meaningful personal change and to improve community safety. As expectations and the associated aims have risen and fallen, the distance between the opposite ends of the spectrum of penal treatment has reduced considerably. When cognitive behaviourism is supplanted by a new approach, it is likely that the impact on prison regimes will be modest.

Official formulations

So what are the expressed aims of imprisonment today? Box 3.1 presents a selection of official declarations of purpose. This is by no means a representative sample, being biased towards (but not limited to) Anglophone jurisdictions. Nonetheless, the selected mission statements give a flavour of contemporary priorities and indicate the range of public messages that prison systems strive to convey. There are noteworthy omissions. Imprisonment in some parts of the world has been designed to serve the interests of the ruling class, unapologetically and unambiguously, through the suppression of political dissent or the control of prisoners' minds. While forced re-education through labour was abolished in 2013, the aims of imprisonment in China are said to still include political indoctrination (laogai.org, accessed 20 May 2014). The prison systems of many African countries are severely overcrowded, poorly resourced, and controlled by their inmate populations (e.g. Jefferson and Martin 2014; see also Chapter 24). In these circumstances to aim for much more than perimeter security, the avoidance of malnutrition, the containment of infectious diseases and the preservation of bodily integrity, may be to aim unfeasibly high.

Accepting the inevitably limited generalizability of the analysis, it is suggested that examining a range of countries avoids the pitfall of adopting an unreflectively ethnocentric approach and proceeding on the basis that an examination of, for instance, the situation in England and Wales, is necessarily of cross-national significance (the Council of Europe and the United Nations have published detailed sets of prison rules that address the purposes of imprisonment but constraints of space preclude analysis of their contents and how they have been revised over time). With these caveats in mind, what can be learned from the official pronouncements of a cross-section of prison services in developed countries?

Box 3.1 A miscellany of aims

Ireland

'Providing safe and secure custody, dignity of care and rehabilitation to prisoners for safer communities' (www.irishprisons.ie/index.php/about-us/mission-statement).

Scotland

'We will be recognised as a leader in offender management services for prisoners, that help reduce re-offending and offer value for money for the taxpayer. We will maintain secure custody and good order; and we will care for offenders with humanity and provide them with appropriate opportunities' (www.sps.gov.uk/AboutUs/aims-of-the-sps.aspx).

England and Wales

'Her Majesty's Prison Service serves the public by keeping in custody those committed by the courts. Our duty is to look after them with humanity and help them lead law-abiding and useful lives in custody and after release' (www.justice.gov.uk/about/hmps).

Finland

'The goals of the Criminal Sanctions Agency are to contribute to the security in society by maintaining a lawful and safe system of enforcement of sanctions and reduce recidivism and endeavour to break social exclusion that also reproduces crime' (www.rikosseuraamus.fi/en/index/criminalsanctionsagency/goalsvaluesandprinciples.html).

Sweden

'Our vision is that spending time in the prison and probation system will bring about change, not simply provide secure custody. We want to encourage our clients to live a better life after serving their sentence' (www.kriminalvarden.se/sv/Other-languages/).

Canada

'The Correctional Service of Canada, as part of the criminal justice system and respecting the rule of law, contributes to public safety by actively encouraging and assisting offenders to become law-abiding citizens, while exercising reasonable, safe, secure and humane control' (www.csc-scc.gc.ca/hist/mission-eng.shtml).

New Zealand

'The Department of Corrections works to make New Zealand a better, safer place by protecting the public from those who can cause harm and reducing re-offending' (www.corrections.govt.nz/about_us.html).

USA (Federal Bureau of Prisons)

'It is the mission of the Federal Bureau of Prisons to protect society by confining offenders in the controlled environments of prisons and community-based facilities that are safe, humane, cost-efficient, and appropriately secure, and that provide work and other self-improvement opportunities to assist offenders in becoming law-abiding citizens' (www.bop.gov/about/agency/agency_pillars.jsp).

(All website addresses correct as of 20 May 2014)

Most official statements mention post-release behaviour or public protection. It is a high expectation to have of any institution that it would continue to be influential even when no longer part of an individual's life, but an enduring impact is commonly demanded of the prison. Mission statements tend to be silent on the needs of particular prisoner groupings, such as persons on remand, women, juveniles, foreign nationals and those sentenced to die behind bars (whether having received the death penalty, a sentence of life without parole or a determinate sentence that exceeds their life expectancy). These groups may pose particular challenges and require bespoke aims.

Official formulas tend not to mention staff or victims, although both of these con-
stituencies are name-checked in the mission statements of several US states, such as
Oklahoma ('Our mission is to protect the public, to protect the employee, to protect the
offender'; www.ok.gov/doc/About_Us/Agency_Mission/index.html, accessed 20 May
2014) and Texas ('The mission of the Texas Department of Criminal Justice is to provide
public safety, promote positive change in offender behavior, reintegrate offenders into
society, and assist victims of crime'; www.tdcj.state.tx.us/index.html, accessed 20 May
2014). Some mention value for money (e.g. Scotland, US Federal Bureau of Prisons).
Others stress dignity (e.g. Ireland). Finland refers to tackling social exclusion in order to
reduce the likelihood of future crime. Sweden connects prison and probation treatment.
Canada draws attention to the rule of law. None mentions the saving of prisoners' souls,
which was a pressing concern for those who defined the aims of imprisonment in previous eras. While a religious dimension is largely absent from the official discourse, it
continues to resonate among prisoners, who have long found comfort, and a higher
purpose, in the tenets of Christianity and, more recently and in increasing numbers, in
Islam (Pew Forum on Religion and Public Life 2012). In this way their individual and
collective aims are facilitated by prison systems that will not always share them.

Mission statements are accompanied by targets, the achievement of which is considered to indicate progress towards realizing the mission. These targets and the associated
tasks are specified with varying degrees of precision. If they are to be of value they must
be amenable to reliable measurement, but if they are too narrowly defined they lose
contact with the worlds they are supposed to shape and become empty signifiers.

Thinking in terms of aims inclines us towards the adoption of an instrumental
approach which emphasizes what works (and at what cost) as opposed to what is right
(and for whom). It frames problems so that they are susceptible to technical solutions and
thereby closes off potentially fruitful lines of enquiry. It risks prioritizing means over
ends. Such a focus has a seductive appeal in that it offers the possibility of demonstrable
progress, however faltering it may prove to be. It privileges calculating and comparing.
However, it deflects attention from the ethics of imprisonment and the place of prison in
society. As Garland (1991: 117) expressed it:

> [P]enal measures and institutions have social determinants that have little to do with
> the need for law and order, social effects that go well beyond the business of crime
> control, and a symbolic significance that routinely engages a wide population,
> making it inappropriate to think of them in purely instrumental terms.

An instrumental view of the prison might examine its impact in terms of reducing crime
and incapacitating offenders. This in turn lends itself to questions regarding efficiency and
economy, the design of attainable targets, and performance monitoring; it is the dominant perspective in corrections today. It could be argued that there has been a further
shift away from the objective of crime control – the results of recidivism studies have
dented confidence that it is achievable – and towards the management of prison populations, almost regardless of any post-release effects. The emphasis has narrowed from
having an impact on the world outside to ensuring the smooth running of the prisoner
society. There is an associated shift from outcomes to outputs. For example, rather than
aiming to reduce reoffending, the target becomes the completion rate for offending
behaviour programmes.

While managerial approaches are fraught with difficulty in complex human environments such as prisons, especially when management imperatives become disconnected from a broader sense of purpose, it would be incorrect to suggest that precise measurements and ulterior motives are incompatible. The 18th- and 19th-century prison reformers were great counters and calibrators. They did not deviate from the timetable. They devised dietary scales that ensured prisoners' appetites were never sated while starvation was kept at bay (just). They tallied the number of times the crank had been turned and the treadwheel spun and adjusted the resistance so that these pointless exercises brought prisoners to the brink of exhaustion but did not render them unfit for the next day's exertions. However, all of this counting and checking and rule enforcement was aligned with clear aims, at least in the early years – namely, the prevention of contagion (whether of physical diseases or criminal beliefs), the assertion of a principle of less eligibility, and the promotion of deterrence and reformation as two sides of the same providential coin. This overarching purpose and the accompanying belief that time apart would prompt self-examination ensured a firmness of resolve even when fears surfaced regarding the deleterious consequences of the new arrangements. When full-throttled confidence was supplanted by uncertainty, then scepticism, and finally pessimism, the counting continued but to no apparent end.

Attempting a new definition

Are there any grounds for consensus when it comes to formulating the aims of imprisonment? One aim around which it is likely that wide agreement could be secured is that prisons should have a null effect. In other words, strenuous efforts should be made to ensure that their occupants are no worse off at the end of their sentences than at the beginning. After all, they have been sent there *as* punishment not *for* punishment. If we define 'worse off' in terms of harm endured as well as risk posed, the corollary is that prisoners must be safe, that their bodily integrity must not be compromised. There will always be some observers who are careless as to the consequences of incarceration for the prisoner society, who would not be concerned if prisoners wreaked havoc on each other, but even those espousing such a view would desire that staff were not caught in the cross-fire and that communities were not endangered when prisoners were released. Imprisonment is associated with a range of unavoidable harms such as the rupturing of community and family ties and the diminution of career prospects. The goal for the prison system must be to anticipate these harms and soften their impact while not adding to them.

Another aim around which it would be possible to generate consensus is that imprisonment should involve the deprivation of liberty. This is vitiated when prisoners escape. Even at open prisons, where perimeter security is largely non-existent, the retention of prisoners is a sine qua non. While prisoners can often influence the duration and conditions of their confinement through their behaviour, they cannot administer their sentences according to personal priorities and proclivities.

Imprisonment necessitates the loss of time. Courts award punishments measured in units of time and the point of any prison system is to ensure that they are served. The removal of sovereignty over time is an aim of imprisonment the effects of which cannot be dodged. The prisoner must march to a new disciplinary cadence and while liberty can at least be restored, lost time cannot be. This is something of which prisoners are acutely aware and against which they marshal whatever resources are at their disposal (O'Donnell 2014: Chapter 10). This allows us to posit the following definition. Stripped to its undeniable essentials, the aim of imprisonment is to reconstitute the prisoner's spatio-temporal world without causing avoidable collateral damage. A statement of intent along these lines would seem appropriate to prison systems everywhere and it is difficult to imagine that it would meet with principled resistance. Although minimalist, it acts as a foundation upon which to layer additional, and always subsidiary, aims. It has the twin virtues of clarity and parsimony.

The Irish political prisoner Michael Davitt (1885: 180) described hope as the 'all-sustaining prison virtue'. Devoid of hope, imprisonment is pointless pain. This is degrading for all concerned. If the carceral experience can be imbued with the possibility of something better this will redound to our collective advantage. By definition, hope is slippery, elusive and difficult to operationalize. It cannot be weighed or measured. Nonetheless, there is a need to orientate prison treatment towards the future so that prisoners' capacity to change their lives for the better is acknowledged. There is some-thing to be said for striving towards a worthwhile goal even if it remains somewhat inchoate. There is something to be said, also, for accepting that prisoners are not entirely defined by their pasts. Like all of us, their life stories can be re-narrated and later chapters can be very different in style and substance from earlier ones. Hope is the state of remaining open to this possibility.

There are clear parallels here with the debate about 'humane containment' versus 'positive custody' that took place in England and Wales in the late 1970s and early 1980s. There was a concern that to allow the former concept to act as an organizing principle for prison regimes was to require staff to work in a moral vacuum and to expect too little of prisoners (see Bottoms 1990). Such an approach, it was believed, would be damaging because it would strip the prison experience of a wider sense of purpose. Undergirding my cautiously expressed aim is the firm belief that improved behaviour is a welcome bonus and should always be hoped for and worked towards.

Accepting the desire for a null effect as a starting place, what does this mean? The first implication is that prisoners must be at least as safe as an equivalent group in the com-munity. The evidence suggests that when it comes to lethal violence they are (Mumola 2005; Sattar 2001); when it comes to sexual victimization they may not be, especially in the USA (O'Donnell 2004); and when it comes to routine victimization not enough is known. It cannot be gainsaid that assault, theft and robbery are common in prisons (Edgar et al. 2012), but whether they are significantly more hazardous environments than the areas of urban deprivation from which many prisoners are drawn, and the domestic environments in which they dwell, we cannot be certain. Without doubt, prisoners should be safe from the predations of staff. Regrettably, they are not (Kaiser and Stan-now 2013). This is an important difference from community life, where it does not appear that offenders face the threat of being sexually violated by authority figures to whom they report.

The second dimension of the null effect relates to post-release behaviour. Does imprisonment place society at elevated risk? There are three possible answers to this question. First, that risk is unchanged but put in abeyance. Such an outcome may dis-appoint but it is consistent with the achievement of a null effect. Second, that risk is reduced and the community to which the prisoner returns is safer as a result. This may be a consequence of deterrence, rehabilitation, ageing, the removal of suitable targets, or some other process, and it is an improvement on a null effect. Third, that risk is elevated and the prison has failed to meet its most basic aim.

As Box 3.1 shows, prison systems everywhere strive to exceed the modest baseline of neutral spatio-temporal reorientation. Key personnel desire that prisons are secure, safe and humane places for both inmates and staff. They are alive to the potential for prisons to entrench disadvantage. They seek an extramural impact in terms of community protection and, while reluctant to take responsibility for changing the lives of those in their charge, wish to equip prisoners with the tools necessary for self-improvement should they be motivated to learn how to use them. How aims are implemented is influenced by the values and beliefs held by those who are required to give effect to them (e.g. Rutherford 1994) and, significantly, by the relationships between staff and prisoners (Liebling, with Arnold 2004).

A constriction of ambition

It could be argued that there has been shrinkage over time in the breadth of ambition associated with the expressed aims of imprisonment. There has been a shift from the articulation of nebulous aspirations to the specification of tasks that can be measured and targets that are associated with the successful completion of these tasks. Partly this constriction of ambition was brought about by the disappointing results of penal practice; prisoners all too rarely repaid the brimming confidence of the reformers with good behaviour after release. Partly it reflects the encroachment of new ideas about performance management and a sense that the prison should not be immune from the chastening effects of the 'three Es' of economy, efficiency and effectiveness. Partly it is a logical extension of the squeezing out of the person that accompanies advanced bureaucratization when the rule book comes to dictate the terms of engagement (O'Donnell 2011).

It is entirely reasonable, of course, to adopt aims that can be operationalized, but it is important not to lose sight of the fact that what is measured is never more than a proxy for what is important. Performance measures and targets should flow from aims, and regularly be reconciled with them. If the measurement fails, this does not imply that the aim should be jettisoned. Aims that are narrowly focused, uniformly applicable, unfreighted by ideology or complex sentiment, and amenable to quantification appeal to the managerial mind (it is a bonus if they are disconnected from the world outside the prison walls). They have the undoubted advantage of precision, however poorly they grip the complexities of prison life. However, like the metrics that accompany them, they are guilty of offering false hope regarding the potential of ever more precise measurement to capture – or to catalyse – meaningful change. The instrumental approach can efface its alternatives, with aims collapsing into metrics and measurement becoming an end in itself. In this way a sense of purpose can become detached from the day-to-day organization of prison life. The many things that prisons aim to do, and the resources that are devoted to ensure that they are done – quantifiably – eclipse the overarching sense of purpose that might otherwise attend the enterprise. Seeing the completion rate of an offending behaviour course as indicative of anything else is fraught with difficulty.

Modern mission statements, like those included in Box 3.1, are characterized by the qualified nature of their claims. They aid to encourage and to provide opportunities rather than to reform and to cultivate self-respect. Such caution is understandable given the limited positive effects of imprisonment and the reluctance to make claims that will not be supported, but it is more difficult to generate enthusiasm around a mission statement that is descriptive and unambitious than one which suggests the possibility of personal transformation or institutional triumph against the odds. The flipside of extravagant aims is the pessimism that follows when they are not realized (or when the realization dawns that they never will be). The aims embedded within, and emanating from, modern mission statements are predominantly intramural ones: to provide safety, security and order; to ensure compliance with disciplinary codes; to monitor participation in appropriate programmes; and to remain within budget.

Aims have been progressively narrowed, management techniques have become increasingly sophisticated, and the attempt to connect these manifold measures to something that unites and elaborates them is missing. It could be said that today's 'aims' reflect imperatives that relate to the smooth running of the institution rather than the transformation of the prisoner (and, as a corollary, the improvement of society), but what happens when aims conflict and there is no larger sense of purpose that might help to resolve such conflicts? The difficulty with a piecemeal approach is that it reflects a particular view of the prisoner, who is seen in a disaggregated way, rather than as a whole person, whose needs and drives, strengths and weaknesses, history, character and potential, require attention. My minimalist definition of aims does not overcome these difficulties but it remains open to the manifold possibilities associated with human development and maturation.

The prison in society

The aims of prisons cannot be divorced from the characteristics of the societies in which they take root. Local legislative and policy contexts, together with societal values and community sentiment, play a critical role.

Mathiesen (1974: 76–78) argued that imprisonment remained dominant in advanced capitalist countries such as those in Box 3.1 because it served several social functions. The first of these was *expurgatory*: the prison acted as a repository for unproductive members of society who threatened social order. The second was a *power-draining* function: the capacity to resist is reduced through incarceration and oppositional voices become muffled behind prison walls. The third was a *diverting* function: the use of imprisonment, largely targeted at petty offenders, distracts attention from the really damaging crimes of the powerful. The fourth was a *symbolic* function: by turning prisoners into scapegoats, other citizens are reassured of their moral rectitude. Some years later he added a fifth, which he described as an *action* function: by building prisons and legislating for longer sentences the state conveys an impression that something is being done, that decisive action is being taken (Mathiesen 1990: 138).

It would be going too far to equate Mathiesen's social functions with the aims of imprisonment. The value of his critique is that it alerts us to some of the ancillary impacts of imprisonment and the need to place the prison in its national environment to understand what it does and what it might be expected to do. More recently, there have been several attempts to relate cross-national imprisonment rates to varieties of welfare state regime. The earliest of these was probably Kilcommins et al. (2004: 278), who found that 'countries with well-developed, universalistic, generous welfare regimes tend to have lower prison populations than those with low levels of welfare provision'. Box 3.1

comprises a mixture of social democratic (Finland and Sweden) and liberal (USA, Canada, New Zealand, Scotland, Ireland, England and Wales) countries, and it is not surprising that the aims of imprisonment differ according to welfare arrangements. As might be expected, the social democratic mission statements are outward looking and inclusive (e.g. Finland), while the liberal countries prioritize values of cost effectiveness (e.g. USA) and public protection (e.g. New Zealand). The fact that a cursory glance at prison service mission statements raises issues around national political and social priorities demonstrates the importance of viewing prisons in context.

Even if the social functions of imprisonment are seldom spelled out by the architects, administrators and subjects of the system, they remain important. Examining the role of prison in society allows for the possibility that the institution may 'succeed' in some respects just as it 'fails' in others. Indeed, a failure for one observer may be a success for another as the same outcome can lend itself to a variety of interpretations. The prison might 'fail' when it comes to reducing recidivism but 'succeed' in expressing popular revulsion at certain forms of misconduct. Some effects may be welcomed even if they are not aimed for.

The delivery of aims requires the allocation of resources. When Ireland's economy was booming, a commitment was made to expand the prison system with little thought given to the necessity or the wider ramifications; this is an instance of Mathiesen's 'action function' at work. A deep recession caused a change of direction (O'Donnell 2011). Prosaically, then, economic imperatives can have implications for the aims of imprisonment and the role of the prison vis-à-vis other sanctions and measures. This phenomenon is not confined to Ireland. Webster and Doob (2014) have argued that reductions in the prison population in Alberta in the mid-1990s were driven by budget cuts, but given added traction by core Canadian values rooted in the belief that imprisonment plays a minor role in crime control and should be used sparingly.

Garland (1991: 115) suggested that the sociology of punishment offered an analytical framework that was superior to 'the punishment-as-crime-control' or 'punishment-as-moral-problem' approaches of penological studies. This shift of focus downplays concerns about the rationales and effects of punishment and promotes thinking about the social functions that punishment discharges and the relationships between prisons and other institutions. This is a necessary element of any analysis of the prison, which can then be considered from a variety of perspectives, each of which speaks to its possible functions. For example, a Durkheimian might look at imprisonment as enhancing social solidarity and reinforcing social boundaries; a Marxist might prioritize issues of class domination and the need to siphon off surplus labour or to exploit captive populations; a Foucauldian might locate the prison within a broader carceral archipelago, as an instance of a more general disciplinary strategy with surveillance as a route to docility; an Eliasian might emphasize the prison's role in pushing punishment behind the scenes as characterizing a civilizing process. As Garland (1991) noted, and as many chapters in this volume attest, the penal system is not only instrumental in purpose, but also has a cultural style and an historical tradition, which shape the ways in which objectives are pursued.

The value of situating the prison, historically, as but one of a range of sites of social control has largely disappeared from contemporary debate. However, when reinserted, the implications for understanding are profound. As O'Sullivan and O'Donnell (2012: 1–41) have shown, the prison's move to centre stage has occurred against a background where aggregate levels of what these authors term 'coercive confinement' have dropped steeply.

The beneficiaries of this waning culture of control have been numerous women and children whose lives are no longer interrupted by involuntary detention in custodial settings such as psychiatric hospitals, reformatory and industrial schools, mother and baby homes, and Magdalen asylums, places that were experienced as punitive, whatever their expressed rationales. Understanding the aims of imprisonment, therefore, requires consideration of the rise and fall of other modes of incarceration and how these trajectories relate to shifts in family structures, economic opportunities, political priorities and moral imperatives (O'Sullivan and O'Donnell 2012: 250–294). Thinking in terms of coercive confinement allows us to see the prison with fresh eyes. It leads us away from approaches that are rooted in singular interpretations and makes it impossible to consider the prison outside the historical and cultural context that it has shaped and been shaped by. It allows us to draw on the richness of a variety of theoretical traditions and to explore points of convergence and divergence.

What I am attempting to do in this chapter is to keep in sight the social dimensions of punishment as manifest in the prison and to shake off the constraints of an approach that is equated with an examination of instrumental utility. To consider the aims of imprisonment requires loosening the prison-crime nexus and exploring where the prison fits more generally, and why. Absent such contextualization, any attempt at explanation falls short. As this chapter is limited to the aims of 'imprisonment' in particular rather than addressing the aims of 'coercive confinement' more generally, I am relieved of this explanatory burden, but it must be acknowledged that without this wider view, the full picture cannot be painted.

Fragmentation

When it comes to formulating the aims of imprisonment it is necessary to consider who has standing in the debate. Who can speak and who is heard? When multiple voices are raised are they cacophonous or in harmony?

It seems reasonable to suggest that the debate about the prison's role attracts a greater variety of contributors than heretofore. No longer is it restricted to a stratum of legislators and policymakers who had much in common including gender, race, age, social class background and level of educational attainment, and for whom arriving at a consensus was often relatively unproblematic, especially in a context where a high level of public trust could be assumed and crime was not a pressing concern. The situation today is far more fragmented, with numerous actors clamouring to express a view. It is possible that this multiplicity of viewpoints has contributed to a narrowing of ambition and a retrenchment of official aims in order to find a position that excites, at worst, manageable opposition.

The views of legislators may collide with those of judges and prison administrators. Policies and laws may conflict. Communities may wish to have a say, either through the politicians they elect or more directly, on particular issues. Victim organizations have grown in significance, sometimes representing a particular class of victims, sometimes standing for victims (or survivors) in general. Specific victims can act as lightning rods for concerted action. They are often young, vulnerable and horribly violated and may lend their names to legislative initiatives. Prisoners may wish to contribute to the debate and they are sometimes given a voice through organizations like KRUM (in Sweden), KROM (in Norway), KRIM (in Denmark), Preservation of the Rights of Prisoners (in the UK), and the Prisoners' Rights Organisation (in Ireland). Such bodies seldom endure. Even among prisoner organizations there can be dissent and division with little tolerance for certain categories of offender, such as those who commit sex crimes against children (while never mainstream, paedophile support groups had a higher profile in the past; O'Donnell and Milner 2007: 9–15).

Sometimes ex-prisoners can play an important role in creating fresh thinking about the role of imprisonment. Winston Churchill was held captive briefly in a Boer prison and Nelson Mandela spent more than a quarter of a century in custody. While their African experiences were dramatically different, each offered an informed and compassionate voice to the debate about penal reform. Academic commentators, often drawn from the swelling ranks of professional criminologists, sometimes contribute their perspectives in various public forums.

Penal reform bodies also have something to contribute to the debate about aims. The preamble to the 1787 constitution of the Philadelphia Society for Alleviating the Miseries of Public Prisons, which remains in existence as the Pennsylvania Prison Society, set out a number of underlying principles (Anonymous 1987: 1–2), which when read from a distance of almost 230 years, are seen to have lost little of their cogency, even if they have faded from view in many policy contexts. They stress the common humanity of those who find themselves on either side of the law. They express a deep scepticism about the effects of harsh punishment and offer an optimistic view of the human capacity to change direction. They are strongly echoed in the 1870 principles that open this chapter, and are heard more faintly today. These principles are:

- Prisons are 'public' institutions and the public should be concerned about their objectives and their effectiveness.
- Criminals are human beings and not made less so by the commission of crimes.
- It is legitimate to punish those who commit crimes.
- Harsh and degrading treatment tends to increase crime.
- Ways of turning law breakers into law-abiding citizens can be found.
- Society benefits from a system that 'reforms' criminals.

In addition to prisoners, policymakers, victims and reformers of various hues, there is another group that seeks to play a role in determining the aims of imprisonment. This comprises the shareholders in companies that build and manage prisons. In some jurisdictions they are becoming influential.

Where prison privatization exists (largely, it must be said, in the common law world), this brings in its wake an additional – and novel – aim of imprisonment, namely, the creation of shareholder value out of human suffering. Under such funding arrangements, profitability is an essential goal of imprisonment. The wheel has completed another revolution here as the entrepreneurial (and exploitative) gaoler was a much-maligned feature of the pre-reform prison. Today prison managers do not benefit to the immediate financial detriment of prisoners, but the companies that employ them, and their shareholders, have a vested interest in keeping the stock price high. The imperatives of the market also play a role when it comes to selecting appropriate locations for building new prisons, as the construction and operation of these facilities are believed to provide a vital economic stimulus to economically depressed rural communities (a belief that would appear to be exaggerated, according to King et al. 2003).

Oscar Wilde (1891: 301, emphasis in original) lamented in his essay, 'The Soul of Man under Socialism', published several years before his imprisonment, that the sickening lesson of history is not 'the crimes that the wicked have committed, but ... the punishments that the good have inflicted; *and a community is infinitely more brutalised by the habitual employment of punishment, than it is by the occasional occurrence of crime*'. While there is no end to human ingenuity when it comes to inflicting pain, what is novel about today's arrangements is that investors can benefit from its infliction. In the past gaolers made a comfortable living through the extraction of fees from those in their 'care', but they lived in close proximity to the degradation that generated their livelihoods. Recent developments have led to the disturbing scenario whereby shareholders may never set foot in prisons but can grow rich from their existence. The financial imperative has returned with a twist: those who receive the dividends are distanced from the pain that turns their profit.

A final area characterized by novel challenges relates to prisoners serving sentences of life without parole (LWOP) or determinate sentences that exceed their life expectancy. For these prisoners the issues are starkly drawn. When release is no longer a possibility, thinking of the aims of imprisonment in terms of potential societal benefits is highly problematic. What can be expected of a prison system where, for some, the prospects of eventual community return have been obliterated? Looking at LWOP prisoners specifically, there were more of them in Angola prison in Louisiana in the early 21st century – 3,660 according to Ridgeway (2011: 48) – than there were across the entirety of the USA at the end of the 19th century (2,766 in 1890 out of 70,295 prisoners who had been sentenced and for whom further particulars were available; Department of the Interior, Census Office 1896: 199). This prison now has a hospice as well as a more traditional death row. In the former, death is certain and comes soon after arrival there. In the latter, execution is far from inevitable and the wait for it, in maximum-security conditions, is long and fraught. The aim in both places is bleak: to prevent premature death.

Conclusion

There are obvious challenges associated with attempting to define the aims of imprisonment in a way that will take account of the prison's relationship to other carceral institutions, its historical trajectory, the need to accommodate a variety of stakeholder perspectives, and pragmatic considerations around the specification of targets and tasks that are derived from the aims but can still be meaningfully related to them. One way forward is to adopt a minimalist statement of aims such as that set out in this chapter – to reconstitute the prisoner's spatio-temporal world without causing avoidable collateral damage – and to insist that its articulation occurs in a context that is optimistic about the individual's capacity to seize control of, and redirect, his or her life. The degree to which such insistence will be effective will vary by time and place, but it chimes with the mission statements of modern prison services such as those summarized in Box 3.1. What an attitude of hope means for the practical operation of prison regimes is similarly variable but the point is that keeping it firmly in view means that the debate about aims will be regularly resuscitated. It would be regrettable if the search for aims that can be easily and reliably translated into practice was at the expense of necessarily imprecise sentiments about dignity, the cultivation of self-respect and the releasing of human potential.

Bibliography

Anonymous (1987) 'Introduction', *The Prison Journal* 67: 1–37.

Bentham, J. (1843) *The Works of Jeremy Bentham published under the Superintendence of his Executor, John Bowring, Vol. X (Memoirs Part I and Correspondence)*, Edinburgh: William Tait.

Bottoms, A.E. (1990) 'The aims of imprisonment', in D. Garland (ed.) *Justice, Guilt and Forgiveness in the Penal System, Occasional Paper No. 18*, Edinburgh: University of Edinburgh Centre for Theology and Public Issues, 3–36.

Davitt, M. (1885) *Leaves from a Prison Diary, or Lectures to a Solitary Audience*, Vol. 1, London: Chapman and Hall.

Department of the Interior, Census Office (1896) *Report on Crime, Pauperism, and Benevolence in the United States at the Eleventh Census: 1890, Part I Analysis*, Washington, DC: Government Printing Office.

Edgar, K., O'Donnell, I. and Martin, C. (2012 [2003]) *Prison Violence: The Dynamics of Conflict, Fear and Power*, London: Routledge.

Garland, D. (1991) 'Sociological perspectives on punishment', in M. Tonry (ed.) *Crime and Justice: A Review of Research*, Vol. 14, Chicago, IL: University of Chicago Press, 115–165.

Jefferson, A.M. and Martin, T.M. (eds) (2014) 'Everyday prison governance in Africa', *Prison Service Journal* (Special Edition) 212 (March).

Kaiser, D. and Stannow, L. (2013) 'The shame of our prisons: New evidence', *New York Review of Books* 60(16) (24 October).

Kilcommins, S., O'Donnell, I., O'Sullivan, E. and Vaughan, B. (2004) *Crime, Punishment and the Search for Order in Ireland*, Dublin: Institute of Public Administration.

King, R.S., Mauer, M. and Huling, T. (2003) *Big Prisons, Small Towns: Prison Economics in Rural America*, Washington, DC: The Sentencing Project.

Liebling, A., with Arnold, H. (2004) *Prisons and their Moral Performance: A Study of Values, Quality, and Prison Life*, Oxford: Oxford University Press.

Mathiesen, T. (1974) *The Politics of Abolition*, Scandinavian Studies in Criminology No. 4, London: Martin Robertson.

Mathiesen, T. (1990) *Prison on Trial: A Critical Assessment*, London: Sage.

Mumola, C.J. (2005) *Suicide and Homicide in State Prisons and Local Jails, Bureau of Justice Statistics Special Report*, Washington, DC: US Department of Justice.

O'Donnell, I. (2004) 'Prison rape in context', *British Journal of Criminology* 44: 241–255.

O'Donnell, I. (2011) 'Criminology, bureaucracy and unfinished business', in M. Bosworth and C. Hoyle (eds) *What is Criminology?* Oxford: Oxford University Press, 488–501.

O'Donnell, I. (2014) *Prisoners, Solitude, and Time*, Oxford: Oxford University Press.

O'Donnell, I. and Milner, C. (2007) *Child Pornography: Crime, Computers and Society*, Cullompton: Willan.

O'Sullivan, E. and O'Donnell, I. (eds) (2012) *Coercive Confinement in Ireland: Patients, Prisoners and Penitents*, Manchester: Manchester University Press.

Pew Forum on Religion and Public Life (2012) *Religion in Prisons: A 50-State Survey of Prison Chaplains*, Washington, DC: Pew Research Center.

Priestley, P. (1999 [1985]) *Victorian Prison Lives: English Prison Biography 1830–1914*, London: Pimlico.

Ridgeway, J. (2011) 'God's own warden', *Mother Jones*, July/August: 44–51.

Rutherford, A. (1994) *Criminal Justice and the Pursuit of Decency*, Winchester: Waterside Press.

Sattar, G. (2001) *Rates and Causes of Death among Prisoners and Offenders under Community Supervision*, Home Office Research Study 231, London: Home Office Research, Development and Statistics Directorate.

Webster, C.M. and Doob, A.N. (2014) 'Penal reform "Canadian style": Fiscal responsibility and decarceration in Alberta, Canada', *Punishment and Society* 16: 3–31.

Wilde, O. (1891) 'The soul of man under socialism', *Fortnightly Review* XLIX: 292–319.

Wines, E.C. (ed.) (1871) Transactions of the National Congress on Penitentiary and Reformatory Discipline, held at Cincinnati, Ohio, 12–18 October 1870, Albany, NY: The Argus Company.

Wines, E.C. (1873) *Report on the International Penitentiary Congress of London, held 3–13 July 1872*, Washington, DC: Government Printing Office.

Chapter 4

The politics of imprisonment

Richard Sparks, Jessica Bird and Louise Brangan

Introduction

Prisons are not always and everywhere equally politically controversial, although they have provoked periodic moral and ideological argument since their inception in something like recognizably modern form in the 18th century. Sometimes – though given the often fevered condition of penal politics in Britain and the USA before and since the turn of the century it is sometimes hard to recall this – they slip well below the radar of political contention for long periods. Indeed, it has historically been a frequent lament of prison reformers and penal practitioners that politicians, journalists and the general public are characteristically not very interested in prisons unless and until things go sharply and visibly wrong. The adage 'there are no votes in prisons' expresses the frustrations implicit in this view, alongside a sense that there is little natural sympathy for prisoners – and perhaps not for their custodians either – in most quarters.

As we shall see, the idea that there are no votes in prisons has become, in some senses, rather misleading, albeit generally in the opposite sense from the one originally intended. Over the last quarter of a century a series of questions about who goes (or should go) to prison, for how long, under which conditions, and when or whether and under what circumstances they should be released have become persistent topics in media commentary and political competition. Perhaps then there *are* votes in prisons after all, but not for the prisoners, nor usually much in sympathy with their cause. This politicization of imprisonment has had sharp consequences for the scale of the prison enterprise and for the conditions under which prisoners and prison staff live or work. Indeed, for many involved in the penal system as practitioners or reformers, their most earnest hope has often been that they drop out of sight again long enough for the passions that have been stoked around them to cool off, even if this seems a somewhat modest and defensive aspiration compared with the crusading zeal of earlier generations.

In this respect the effects of the politics of imprisonment are felt across the whole range of issues addressed in this book. They influence the numbers of people sent to prison, including the representation there of specific groups such as the very young, the very old, women and members of ethnic, political or religious minorities. Questions of security and control have often been behind-the-scenes issues – the very thing we delegate to professionals to sort out quietly behind prison walls. Indeed, as Garland (1990: 183–185) points out, this tendency to sequester and professionalize penal problems has been part and parcel of what is (or just possibly was) *modern* about 'penological modernism'. However, sometimes, episodically, these problems instead find a place in the foreground of politics and when this happens they generate anxieties, calls for accountability and the placing of blame.

Similarly, how we treat prisoners whilst incarcerated is a question that slips in and out of the focus of public attention. Throughout the modern history of imprisonment, how prisoners are to be fed, what work they should be expected to do and for what pay, how many baths, letters or visits they should receive, what educational opportunities should be made available to them, how they should access medical services, whether they should be permitted to vote in elections (Uggen and Manza 2002; Behan and O'Donnell 2008; Mauer 2010) are all questions that (along with many others) have persistently exercised the minds of prison administrators, prison reformers and lobby groups, but only more occasionally breached the threshold of visibility as questions of public controversy. Yet when these issues do enter public discourse they are often debated with real intensity. Finally, for now, the question of when prisoners should be released, following what preparation, on whose authority, under what level of supervision, following what form of assessment of the risks they may present to the public, is nowadays perhaps the most contentious question of all.

Many such issues arise elsewhere in this volume and are dealt with in specific detail by other authors. Rather than duplicate any of those discussions, our purpose in this chapter is to offer some sense of context and to suggest some common threads in what might otherwise appear to be an inventory of discrete and isolated issues. We will attempt to draw out some of what is at stake in debates over the scale, character and purposes of imprisonment and to suggest some reasons why, in some Western countries though not all or not equally, the arguments over those issues have taken a peculiarly complex and intense form.

Prisons seem to be amongst the most paradoxical as well as contentious of institutions. At times they have been seen as sites of optimism and experiment, as prototypes for new ways of organizing and disciplining societies and treating or spiritually improving people. Some early prison advocates spoke of them in terms that we find scarcely credible now. Consider here the aspirations of the inspectors of the Eastern State Penitentiary in Philadelphia (a key institution in the development of modern imprisonment), who regarded the prison as '[t]he beautiful gate of the Temple', through which the inmate might pass 'by a peaceful end to Heaven' (quoted in Sykes 1958: 132). Yet there has also been a longstanding anxiety concerning the oppressive and brutalizing potentialities of incarceration, and about the limitations on the prison's real capacity to effect positive change. Hence the celebrated remark of Sir Godfrey Lushington in evidence to the Gladstone Committee in 1895: 'I regard as unfavourable to reformation the status of a prisoner throughout his whole career … the unfavourable features … are inseparable from prison life' (cited in Stern 1987: 48). One could multiply examples on both sides almost indefinitely.

We should therefore not find contemporary evidence of ambivalence, uncertainty and dispute about prisons and their proper role or scale unduly surprising, since these debates have long antecedents. Commentators as diverse as Fyodor Dostoyevsky and Winston Churchill have at different times come quite separately to the conclusion that the condition of a society's penal institutions provides a measure of its magnanimity or meanness, its self-assurance or anxiety – its 'mood and temper', as Churchill put it. At least since the political and intellectual revolutions of the later 18th century, and with them the idea of subjecting human institutions to disciplined study for the purposes of their improvement, the urge to examine and to compare penal systems and institutions has been evident (Scharff Smith 2004). This was at the basis of John Howard's arduous journeys through the prisons of Britain and Europe in the 1770s. It animated the writings home from the USA of French intellectuals like La Rochefoucauld-Liancourt in the 1790s and Beaumont and de Tocqueville in the 1830s. In the fervent excitement of revolutionary France, Mirabeau articulated the dream of 'a special kind of prison, for which humanity need not blush'. Suffice to note that reactionaries, revolutionists and reformers have all at some point sensed a connection between the ways in which their societies punished and the moral or political character and constitution of the times.

In England and Wales in the 1980s and 1990s, for example, the mantra became that prisons should be 'decent but austere'. It may be doubted whether the authors of such expressions had much idea how often that thought had been framed before. Throughout the modern history of imprisonment the need to make prisons aversive has jostled against the imperative not to allow them to become so dreadful as to shame the society to which they belong. The requirement that prisons punish sufficiently has stood in chronic tension with the aspiration that they reform, educate or rehabilitate. Committees of learned and conscientious people have repeatedly convened in order to seek to reconcile these disparate demands, to declare minimum standards, restate missions and so on. Current controversies, debates and scandals demand contemporary explanation and understanding. At the same time we need to grasp the ways in which these recall or indeed reproduce enduring perplexities. For example, in an earlier paper, Sparks (1996) tried to show how the language of 'austerity' (in the USA the favoured terminology has been 'no-frills prisons', perhaps by analogy with 'no-frills' budget airlines) reiterated themes known to 18th- and 19th-century observers as the 'doctrine of less eligibility'. This principle asserted that the conditions of life in prisons must be set lower than those of the labouring poor, or risk both sacrificing the prison's deterrent effect on the lower orders and insulting the honest worker (see further, Radzinowicz and Hood 1986; Wiener 1990). Consider the following example:

CONS TV ENOUGH TO MAKE YOU SICK
It's cheaper than hospital
Fury erupted last night as it emerged prisoners can watch TV in their cells for £1 A WEEK – but NHS patients have to pay £3.50 A DAY ...
MSP Michael Matheson stormed: 'It is simply outrageous that patients pay so much more than cons.'

(*The Scottish Sun*, 20 March 2006: 1)[1]

Prime Minister David Cameron's celebrated declaration on the floor of the House of Commons on 3 November 2010 that the idea of anyone in prison being entitled to vote in elections made him feel 'physically ill' was one of the more graphic recurrences of a principle of less eligibility in recent times. It was also a catalyst for increasing tension between the UK government and the European Court of Human Rights, as well as the senior judiciary in both England and Wales, and Scotland. The story of the controversies around prisoners' voting rights in the UK remains to be told as fully as it deserves. The point here is that the less eligibility question is a chronic one that also continues to have acute episodes, aggravated by certain emblematic issues. Hermann Mannheim's judgement as long ago as 1939 in *The Dilemma of Penal Reform* that it was 'the *Leitmotif* of all prison administration down to the present time' hardly seems to have been rendered obsolete by subsequent experience.

Prison, for the inhabitants of modern societies, is a paradigmatic punishment. It is the most severe, the one that is always called for in cases of serious crime when public sentiment – at least as filtered and articulated by the popular press – finds other penalties inadequate and unsatisfying. It is the one in which political capital is invested, the one that is supposed *ipso facto* to 'work'. Yet it is also the one that, however much public support there appears to be for greater stringency and severity, can on occasion become brutalizing and dangerous to a point that no one expressly supports. Thus prisons commonly become the subject of scandal for being too lax, too undisciplined and too comfortable; for 'coddling' prisoners and providing them with levels of material comfort that are not universally available to more deserving people outside, as in the example above. Conversely they can also become scandalous – albeit perhaps less frequently – for failing to protect or properly care for their inmates (especially those who are young or otherwise vulnerable), or for imposing invasive or oppressive searching or other procedures, especially on prisoners whose condition elicits some degree of sympathy. In Britain in the mid-1990s, for example, the widely reported practice of requiring female prisoners to give birth while handcuffed to their hospital beds was roundly condemned, including in such predominantly conservative quarters as the *Daily Mail*, and aroused a widespread sense of unease and distaste. The issue was an indicative one to the extent that although it occurred during one of the most heated periods in recent penal politics – one in which the virtues of more stringent prison regimes (and of sending more people to prison) were widely touted in some quarters – it exposed the outer boundary of acceptability in general public sensibilities. Similar dynamics can be identified in respect of a range of issues, including access to adequate sanitation, protection in the face of bullying, and deaths in custody. In the UK the death in Feltham Young Offenders' Institution in 2000 of Zahid Mubarek at the hands of a profoundly disturbed and openly racist cellmate was perhaps the single most shocking and widely reported failure of care in that period (see in particular House of Commons 2006).

These sightings are important in a number of respects. They provide contemporary extensions and developments of arguments and ambivalences about the nature of prisons as institutions that echo throughout their modern history. Prisons are places of humane aspiration (Wiener 1990) *and* sites of struggle, abuse and neglect. They are places of secrecy and discretionary power *and* they are proving grounds for social experimentation and administrative improvement. Latterly, much social analysis emphasizes the pressure in political discourse and moral enterprise towards retrenchment, the reinvention of austerity (Sparks 1996; Simon 2000; Wacquant 2001) and populism (Pratt 2006). Yet this can be to overlook the gradual and uneven encroachment of law into prison administration (Feeley and Rubin 1998) and perhaps more especially the extension of human rights standards and concerns with convention compliance into a range of aspects of prison life (e.g. Morgan and Evans 1998; Van Zyl Smit and Snacken 2009).

Prisons are, literally and metaphorically, concrete. Many other penalties, such as fines or orders for community supervision of one sort or another, are difficult for most of us to visualize. Prisons, on the other hand, are physical places; the iconographies and typologies they summon are, and must be, explicitly *situated* within particular kinds of carceral environments. Typically chilling images of traditional, monolithic prisons are widely used as motifs across a variety of media, marshalling a series of hackneyed associations about what prisons are 'like' and what kinds of people live and work there. Many of their names – Dartmoor, Spandau, San Quentin, Alcatraz, Abu Ghraib – have an emotive and even, to use a somewhat overworked term, iconic resonance.

Prisons also have a place in our literary and cinematic traditions that other modern penalties do not have. The figures or types that we associate with them – the hard man, the wronged innocent, the stool pigeon, the crazed killer, the fugitive, the reforming warden, the officious guard – occupy a distinct position in our cultural imagination. Imbued with metaphor and hyperbole, the physicality of prisons produces melodrama: prisons are reliably popular sources of primetime entertainment. This is salient for political analyses to the extent that (i) the rhetoric mobilized by political elites is responsive to public penal expectations that are at least partially informed by these cultural depictions, and (ii) the physical shape and aesthetics of prisons, particularly as they are currently designed and/or adapted, materially illustrate the coalescence of, and tensions between, shifting penal strategies. It is perhaps small wonder, then, that many public discussions about punishment, however misleadingly, reduce or circle back to questions of imprisonment. The prison is in this sense a longstanding cultural resource. It can be brought back into focus periodically, and issued with a fresh mandate and fresh set of objectives.

Yet, because it is to this extent a culturally important idea, and one heavy with history, it is also complex and ambiguous. Prisons seem capable of offering the answer to every penal question, and yet always open to being seen as failing. For these reason prisons are 'political' in broad as well as narrow senses. How many people should go to prison and what prisons should be like are questions that excite us and divide us politically. The uses we make of them and the conditions we consider acceptable within them are issues that provide clues to our social organization and values in ways that go beyond the obvious, the immediate and the conscious.

For these reasons the politics of imprisonment is inherently more than a matter of numbers, crucial as these are (see below). Given the powerful expansionary pressures on some prison systems in recent years it is all too easy to become preoccupied with large numbers, and the strain these place on all involved, to the exclusion of other matters. However, the question of the politics of imprisonment leads us in other directions as well. It directs attention also to the issues of the form, character and level of prison regimes. It asks, for example, why in some countries at some times prisoners have been entitled to vote and in others not; why in some places prisoners are encouraged to pursue higher education and in others forbidden from doing so; why in some systems prisoners are enabled to have intimate contact with their families, whilst in others the merest touch is strictly prohibited, and so on. These sorts of questions allow us to ask not just how much imprisonment but also of what kind, and to what purpose? It seems very important, in light of the number of people in prison, the extreme dependency of prisoners on prison authorities and the all-encompassing nature of the penalty, to focus on the politics of imprisonment in its institutional aspect closely and in detail (Liebling 2004). Whether imprisonment is or can be a legitimate penalty, executed in a legitimate manner, seems a persistent question and one that arises in new forms in each successive period. Yet it is also clear that the politics of imprisonment is also a special case of the wider societal politics of security and order, and it is to this larger dimension that we now turn.

What do we want prisons to do?

Imprisonment is by no means the most usual or characteristic penalty for most contemporary criminal justice systems. In general the everyday business of the courts more commonly concludes in some form of financial penalty or non-custodial supervision. Of course, much controversy centres on the boundary cases, especially offences that sometimes do receive a prison sentence and sometimes do not. Many participants and onlookers have strong feelings about whether those convicted of particular offences should go to prison, and for how long. The point here is just that whilst marginal differences in custody rates and sentence lengths matter greatly to those involved and have a powerful impact on the workload of the prison system, those numbers almost always relate to a minority of convictions, and a very small minority of all crimes. Yet such cautionary notes tend to be overlooked in the heat of political rhetoric, once the scale and character of imprisonment has become contentious. Whether to imprison and when or whether to release have latterly tended to dominate public discussion of criminal justice, often to the exclusion of other issues and other possibilities. Why should this be so? Why has it been so, admittedly with some variations in intensity and salience, for a quite extended period? Why did the heat of that discussion nevertheless increase so sharply, especially during the 1990s and the first decade of the 21st century?

It might now be argued – indeed it is very important to our argument – that this salience is not necessarily a permanent condition. It is not something that is equally evident in all times and places. Indeed we think that it may now be possible to suggest, however tentatively, that the predominance (though demonstrably not the drama) of imprisonment as a foreground political issue has on the whole begun to subside again, or at least has receded somewhat in the last few years from its high-water mark in the 1990s and early 2000s. If so this would on some accounts seem puzzling. In the context of global recession with the attending range of insecurities felt at international, national and individual levels – contributing to a haemorrhaging of state legitimacy and support – we might expect the sphere of criminal justice, and imprisonment more specifically, to be vigorously remobilized within the political discourse. We might expect deep and widespread economic insecurity to reactivate imprisonment as a 'live' issue, such that it has repeatedly proven popular and effective as a means of reasserting state control by (isolating and then) assuaging general public anxieties. However, beginning in the last decade other sites and targets of insecurity appear more politically expedient. The effect of this movement, we suggest, has been a gradual relegation, if not quite a wholesale depoliticization, of imprisonment as a key battleground upon which political contests are fought. It is not enough to argue that penal politics increases and decreases in intensity on the basis of some sort of loose 'cyclical' pattern. On the other hand it is quite clear that its heat is capable of being both raised and lowered by influences that originate elsewhere in the broader political economy, and the effects of those oscillations on the culture and practice of incarceration, and its alternatives, demand to be understood.

In almost all economically advanced countries imprisonment represents the apex of the criminal justice system. The obvious, though partial, exception is the USA where – in some states – capital punishment persists. Yet even there imprisonment is a gigantic enterprise by comparison with the actual level of capital sentencing, let alone of executions, however symbolically potent and emotive the latter may be.

We call for prisons both to be of practical utility and to furnish punishments that we find meaningful and emotionally satisfying. David Garland has argued that we are today living out the consequences of a 'crisis of penal modernism' (Garland 1990: 4). Whereas some intellectuals and *fonctionnaires* have thought it possible to subject punishment entirely to the demands of rational administration, it has in part escaped such domestication. What results is a chronic tension. For Garland:

> There are two contrasting visions at work in contemporary criminal justice – the passionate, morally-toned desire to punish and the administrative, rationalistic, normalizing concern to manage. These visions clash in many important respects, but both are deeply embedded within the [modern] social practice of punishing.
>
> (Garland 1990: 180)

This seems a good starting point. It acknowledges what some critical perspectives too readily deny, namely that punishment really is practically involved, however failingly, in attempts to control crime and govern social existence. However, at the same time Garland gives full recognition to the tendency of punishment to exceed the bounds of the practical and to become enmeshed in the flux of culture and politics, including sometimes in the most exorbitantly emotive forms of demagogic posturing. Such a position suggests the possibility at least of unpicking some important puzzles. Principal among these is that whilst in broad terms all advanced capitalist countries (including that outlier of penal severity the USA) have developed recognizably similar arrays of penal measures and techniques, they differ markedly in terms of penal range (a term that we explore further below) and in the centrality of questions of punishment to their electoral politics and cultural conflicts. If we begin to examine such questions empirically we may thereby start to clarify a central paradox, namely that whereas some features of the penal realm seem both rather durable and quite widely diffused across national boundaries, others are currently highly unstable and prone to sudden and often quite jagged changes of direction. Garland (1995) again anticipates this issue pointedly when he distinguishes between the 'relatively fixed infrastructure of penal techniques and apparatuses' on the one hand, and on the other those 'mobile strategies that determine aims and priorities'.

We can capture some of these shifts of strategy in the following terms (see Sparks 2001, for a more detailed analysis):

- *Changes in the 'mode of calculation'*. Here we encounter debates about risk and prediction, and the uses of cost–benefit arithmetic to argue the utility of particular penal strategies. One important possibility is that the current prominence of *incapacitation* as a rationale for imprisonment in the advanced liberal societies (and for more intensive forms of non-custodial supervision) stems rather directly from the invention of new techniques for calculating the frequency and prevalence of offending. The implication is that the penal system is entirely a regulatory instrument – a kind of social sluice gate whose optimal rate of flow can in principle be rationally determined. This perspective has certainly had its influential intellectual proponents in recent years. A related question concerns how the state itself has shifted its posture in respect of punishment. Is it the case that the state has on the one hand divested itself of some of its former obligations towards its offending citizens (specifically the expectation that it will 'treat', 'rehabilitate' or 'resettle') and on the other undertaken an enhanced role in the management of the risks presented by that fraction of its subjects regarded as inherently and incorrigibly troublesome? If so, in what sense do these shifts flow from larger changes in the dominant economic and political principles of those societies?

- *Changes in the 'mode of representation'.* How and why, in some countries much more than in others, is punishment invoked in response to allegations of social crisis or emergency? Under what conditions does it take a central position in political rhetoric, and what kinds of rhetoric are these? Are there special moments (when certain kinds of anxiety or resentment are felt especially acutely, or the tolerance of the public especially strained) when the time is ripe for politicians and demagogues to turn the penal question to their own advantage? Are there countervailing forces that produce or reflect equally passionate though more tolerant public sensibilities – those which are exploited with similarly calculated enthusiasm by political elites?

Although these two sets of issues look very distinct they are rarely encountered separately in empirical reality. Rather, they are two aspects of a complex formation – a duality rather than a dualism. Thus, for example, even if a certain set of bloodless and dispassionate calculations in some sense underpinned the increasing frequency and length of prison sentences for drugs offences in several Western countries in the latter decades of the 20th century, it is also true that in its public aspect that strategy came vested in all the ancient, drastic and dramatic language of warfare – the 'war on drugs'. If we wish to understand precisely why the attempt to intervene in illegal drug markets so often terminates in imprisonment *rather than in other varieties of risk management or 'harm reduction'* then it would seem important to grasp what it means to be at war – wars are special times and they call for special measures.

In other words, even if risk calculations become predominant within the procedures and decisions of the agents of the penal apparatus, there is no morally neutral or politically anodyne position from which to begin. Nowadays, cultural contests about the proper scale and purposes of punishing take place increasingly on the terrain of risk. In looking more closely at the ambiguities implied in that term, we edge closer again to the central perplexities of the contemporary penal realm. First, however, we need some sense of the *scale* of that domain and of the historical and international dimensions on which it has varied. Only then can we begin to reach towards explanation (what features of the contemporary scene seem to produce penal populations and regimes of these kinds?) or intervention (are we fated to go on in this way or can we plausibly imagine and create other futures for punishment?).

Why are so many people in prison, or so few?

It is commonly agreed in the social sciences that thinking comparatively about problems is a good thing. There is rather less agreement about how to go about it or indeed about precisely what comparison is for. It can indeed be argued that *all* serious and imaginative social inquiry is in a broad sense comparative – whether the terms of comparison involve placing our present local circumstances in a longer *historical* perspective (how differently did our own predecessors think about this?) or whether they involve a similar displacement in terms of *contemporary* differences of place and culture.

There may be pressing reasons why we should wish to subject our experience of penality to this kind of intellectual discipline. The penal practices characteristic of our own current contexts confront us as obdurate and embedded realities. Yet these are also dynamic systems, subject at times to rapid and seemingly uncontrolled growth and change and to the push and pull of successive fashions and projects. Our politicians and newspaper headlines often urgently insist that there is no morally or practically viable alternative to this or that course of action with regard to the sentencing, supervision or release of offenders. Even if we have vague misgivings about this, without a more cosmopolitan perspective we have little prospect of rationally appraising these assertions, let alone contesting their claims or arguing for other possibilities.

Notwithstanding both pronounced and more subtle comparative differences, the politics of imprisonment within most advanced Western societies shares a common tone of inherent conservatism. The assumed necessity and appropriateness of prison as a state sanction, in whatever particular form and to whatever specific degree, is presupposed. Political arguments tend to converge around ideological contests between 'tough' and 'tougher' policy agendas, whilst narratives that fundamentally challenge the inevitability of prison are typically and pejoratively consigned to the radical fringes. Where we do find evidence of more apparently nuanced political rhetoric, that which attempts to integrate rehabilitative goals with those of straightforward punitiveness, it does little to dislodge the primacy of imprisonment per se. Foucauldian undertones of not (only) *more* punishment but *better* punishment persist. In the UK, Home Secretary Theresa May exemplified this impulse with the following public statement:

> ... prison works but it must be made to work better. The key for members of the public is that they want criminals to be punished. They want them to be taken off the streets. They also want people who come out of prison to go straight.
>
> (*Daily Telegraph*, 10 March 2010)

It should be noted, however, that within a wider international frame, an historically embedded attachment to imprisonment is not taken as read in every locality. In some developing countries, for example, 'there is no indigenous concept of imprisonment'; indeed, the idea of the institutional and civic separation of lawbreakers from their communities is understood as 'culturally odd' (Coyle 2004).

Nevertheless, punishment is amongst the defining activities of the nation-state. It is a core feature of the state's sovereign power, and stands close to the heart of its claim to exercise legitimate authority; and the political and cultural dynamics of punishment remain sharply different in distinct national contexts. In advanced capitalism, however, we can no longer presume that nation-states are sharply bounded and separate entities which we can simply line up and compare one with another. Contemporary states are intrinsically permeable to the movement of capital and technology. Both the problems of economic management and those of social regulation and ordering that confront them with their most acute political difficulties increasingly exceed their capacity to control. In particular, the very crime problems that demand visible and authoritative action from national governments either literally transgress their borders (as is the case with drugs markets or the illegal movement of people, money, arms and other commodities), or else seem so deeply woven into the opportunity structures, the routine activities and transactions and the ceaseless consumption and flows of popular culture of their citizens as to escape them from below. In this sense the nation-state is doubly in jeopardy – 'hollowed out' from without by economic globalization and from within by the barely controllable complexity of the social formations over which they preside in their increasingly impotent magnificence.

All of this has profound and complicated consequences for the politics of punishment in the advanced capitalist countries. In the first place globalization does not produce homogeneity. The penal cultures of the different nation-states remain in some degree distinctive, structured by their diverse legal and political traditions and the exigencies of their domestic crime problems and priorities. Furthermore, the clamour from anxious and uneasy citizens for reassurance and protection by the state arises with differing degrees of insistence, and this seems more prone to being translated into a demand for reassurance *through state punishment* in some national contexts than in others. It remains essential to grasp these differences and to think through their implications.

Yet nowhere is immune. At the level of the individual, it may be argued, concerns about crime take their place among what Anthony Giddens (1991) terms the 'anxieties that press in on everyone' in late modernity. For Giddens, '[t]he risk climate of modernity is unsettling for everyone; no-one escapes', and one response to the disruptions and uncertainties of the modern world is the growth of moral fundamentalisms – of which the demand for traditional and stringent forms of punishment may be one form. At the level of the nation-state the picture is also complex.

Contemporary states are subject to penal trends and influences of diverse kinds. First, they are signatories to international treaties and agreements on human rights, migration, extradition and other matters. Some of these, for example the European Convention on Human Rights, and (although its legal force is less clear) the Council of Europe's European Prison Rules, expressly seek to regulate and in some degree harmonize penal practice. As a European reform project, some commentators have suggested that efforts to 'humanize' imprisonment through the development and implementation of objective standards has ostensibly instituted 'evolving standards of decency' (Van Zyl Smit 2006). The performance of national governments in these matters is also monitored by non-governmental organizations of various kinds, some of which (such as Amnesty International and Human Rights Watch) are themselves transnational in scope. Though laudable, we might be cautious about the unintended political consequences of these movements such that they may to some degree perversely enable the penal expansionist project. To the extent that ethical standards and external monitoring systems provide guidance for prison administrators, effectively contributing to less abhorrent conditions and practices, imprisonment is rendered more publicly acceptable and therefore more resistant to fundamental challenge.

Second, there is routine exchange of information and expertise through governmental, commercial and intellectual networks. One key sphere in which this applies is the growth of an international market in private correctional services, whose major players increasingly have global reach and interests. Yet something similar also applies to the transfer of criminological and penological *knowledge* as such. Ideas, techniques, slogans and catch-words (such as 'risk assessment', 'selective incapacitation', 'truth in sentencing' and 'zero tolerance') scurry around the world with accelerating rapidity. This has some curious and as yet uncertain consequences. An appealing idea adapted from Maori traditional practices (the family group conference pioneered in New Zealand, the central totem of the 'restorative justice' movement) is abruptly wrenched away from its original context and experimentally applied in Oxfordshire or Manitoba. Global mass media ensure that instantaneous exchange of news and imagery infiltrates popular culture and everyday life as well. Unsuccessful eleventh-hour pleas for a stay of execution in the southern USA arouse more outrage and sorrow in Italy than in the communities clustering around the prison walls. The effect of these borrowings and influences is by no means uniform, as this ad hoc list suggests. They compound the feeling that punishment is a major political question, but that its forms may be varied if not outright contradictory.

Third, therefore, the receptiveness of both policymakers and publics to some of these globally available themes and images varies widely but probably not in accidental ways. One dimension of this variation in recent decades may be the degree of exposure of the political cultures and policy networks of different states to the influence of 'New Right' political thought. Until very recently the primary laboratories for this political experiment have been the UK and the USA, and here penal politics since the late 1970s has been especially volatile and expansive in nature.

Most international and historical comparisons of prison systems have remained concerned with fluctuations in certain 'headline' figures, notably the absolute size of prison populations or their size expressed as a rate per 100,000 inhabitants of a given country. These numbers remain of compelling interest, of course, and they are now more readily available for more countries in more detail than ever before (Walmsley 2005). Yet, even quite cursory examination of the numbers reveals their striking diversity, and the faintness of any relationship between their variations and the crime trends of their respective nation-states. Various authorities have challenged the assumption of a neat or simple relationship between crime and incarceration. Tonry provides a lucid summary:

> Put crisply, at a societal level crime does not cause punishment. Imprisonment rates and severity of punishment move independently from changes in crime rates, patterns and trends. Governments decide how much punishment they want, and these decisions are in no simple way related to crime rates, patterns and trends. This can be seen by comparing crime and punishment trends in Finland, Germany and the United States between 1960 and 1990. The trends are close to identical ... yet the U.S. imprisonment rate quadrupled in that period. The Finnish rate fell by 60 percent and the German rate was broadly stable.
>
> (Tonry 2004: 14)

Overall crime rates and imprisonment rates show no simple correspondence. This is true over extended time scales, for example for the USA in the 1960s (crime rose, imprisonment fell) and for Australia in the 1970s (ditto). As Zimring and Hawkins report for California, a state whose incarcerated population tripled during the 1980s, the majority of the increased imprisonment was not directly related to either increases in crime or changes in population; in fact, most crime levels in 1990 were close to their 1980 rates. Furthermore, they say, the kinds of crime associated with much of California's prison expansion, e.g. drug offences, housebreaking and theft, are:

> precisely the offences that flood the criminal justice systems of every major Western democracy. We think that the sorts of policy shifts observed in California could

double the prison population of any country in Western Europe experiencing no change in the volume or character of crime.

(Zimring and Hawkins 1994: 92)

The data reported by Zimring and Hawkins are of historical interest now, but their argument remains a pressingly contemporary one. The 'policy shifts' they have in mind here are changes in discretionary law enforcement and sentencing rather than being centrally directed or statutorily required. They are, as Zimring and Hawkins put it, 'more a matter of sentiment than legislation'. The shifts in question include a disproportionate increase in the numbers imprisoned for lesser property offences (they report a 565% increase in the number of persons imprisoned for the various categories of theft). Meanwhile, although there is some evidence from survey data of a *decline* in illicit drug use in the USA throughout the 1980s, the number of persons arrested for drugs offences continued to increase sharply for some time afterwards, and so did the proportion of those imprisoned following conviction. In fact, the number of males in Californian prisons for drugs offences increased *15-fold* during the 1980s. This followed the national shift in the mid-1980s towards a widely publicized, symbolically powerful and punitively oriented 'war on drugs' as a primary way in which the USA was to address its problems of addiction. Such accelerations in imprisonment do not now have, and have never had, equal impact throughout the population. In the USA (and elsewhere) the 'war' has primarily been directed at street-level drug markets and it has drawn its combatants from among particular people and places. For this reason among others the prison population, like the 'ghetto underclass' that supplies so many of its personnel, consists increasingly and disproportionately of black and Hispanic people.

This recognition of an explanatory gap between crime and imprisonment is, however, the beginning of a political analysis rather than its conclusion. It raises an open question of what other cultural, economic and political pressures influence the scale of imprisonment, and of which ideological principles or moral assumptions predispose us to believe that imprisonment is a primary way of addressing our crime problems.

As Zimring and Hawkins comment, it would appear that given sufficiently great changes in the 'penal climate' or political culture of a society, its prison population may have an 'open ended capacity for change' and there is a significant puzzle for political sociology here. Yet recent research exploring these very questions has offered a more hopeful reading of punitive and expansionist penal politics. Comparative reflection has demonstrated that the resilience (for both good and bad) of local political factors remains fundamental in exposing that seemingly identical penal policy outcomes may have grown out of markedly different political cultures, illustrating that penal policy, within the UK at least, may no longer be moving lockstep towards increasingly punitive political uses of incarceration. As we have seen above, convicted prisoners have been denied the right to vote across the UK. The issue has generated much heat and exposed human rights legislation to vitriol in England and Wales. Contrastingly, in Scotland the debate that preceded the ban on prisoner voting during this same period was much more measured and politicians displayed less embedded commitment to denying prisoners the franchise (Howard League Scotland 2013).

Despite the alluring appearance of commonality between jurisdictions that are in various political and cultural ways very close, understanding the politics of imprisonment would benefit from casting the comparative light upon the less visible penal political practices, values and norms as well as policy outcomes (Brangan 2014). In moving beyond and below the headline numbers we may, therefore, want to consider and compare what politicians and those in the policymaking process are '*actually* trying to do' (Nelken 2009: 307, emphasis in original).

Comparatively highlighting the different political trajectories and phenomena that shape punishment could recast generally accepted narratives concerning how and why the uses and practice of imprisonment vary across different times and places. The gloss of Nordic exceptionalism has been recently challenged as being more troublingly paradoxical, with distinctly exclusionary policies existing in tandem with more widely known welfare-orientated practices (Barker 2013). Barker (2009) has also told the less-discussed story of American penal politics – one which is markedly more complex, variegated and, essentially, hopeful. Politics, and consequently penal strategies, are shaped by the degree and character of democratic engagement. Somewhat counter-intuitively, Barker's argument maintains that greater democratic engagement can actually foster fewer, rather than more, retributive penal cultures. Further complicating matters is the 2011 US Supreme Court's dramatic and 'remarkable decision' (Simon 2014) which has set in motion a decarceration agenda in California's prisons. It could be that matters of penal politics are more divergent and less embedded than previously feared.

Punishment and the 'New Right'

The term 'New Right' is an umbrella that encompasses a broad and internally differentiated social movement. Under that umbrella have marched libertarians, liberals, conservatives and outright reactionaries of many stripes. What unites these diverse strands of opinion is a vigorous critique of the outcomes of the economic interventionism and welfare provision that characterized the post-World War II 'settlements' of many Western countries. For some, whom we may see as being primarily *neo-liberals*, the key result has been economic inefficiency. The suppression of market freedoms for political purposes diminishes competitiveness, multiplies tax burdens and discourages entrepreneurship – all perverse outcomes of good intentions. For others, primarily *neo-conservative* in orientation, the greatest detriment has been moral. The interventionism of the 'nanny state' promotes dependency rather than personal responsibility, and engages in a wrongful transfer of authority from families and local communities to the state. The result is again perverse – a moral climate of permissiveness, agnosticism, mushy pluralism and hedonism. Where these streams of thinking primarily flow together, therefore, is in the critique of the over-ambition of the state and the resulting inflation of the public sector.

Space entirely precludes an adequate summary of these positions which have generated a massive literature of both advocacy and criticism. These are after all, initially in the USA and UK and latterly in varying degrees across the developed and developing worlds, the most influential political and economic intellectual movements of our times. Here we can deal only with their strictly *penological* consequences. These are themselves complex and can be rendered here only in summary, and doubtless contentious, form.

Governments influenced by the New Right have characteristically assumed power partly on the strength of an allegation of social and economic 'crisis' of the 'welfare state'. In the United Kingdom in 1979 Margaret Thatcher successfully seized the initiative by representing the accumulation of problems of the Keynesian welfare state as a twin crisis of 'ungovernability' and uncompetitiveness. 'Law and order' was a key token of ungovernability, and her project promised nothing less than the 'restoration of freedom under law'. The state was to withdraw from those tasks that it performed badly (micro-managing economic and social activity whilst profligately wasting public monies) in order to focus on its essential and legitimate tasks – sound money, free trade, defence and the maintenance of 'law and order'. Countries in which governments have adopted similar positions have in this sense experienced a hiatus – a self-conscious discontinuity from a discredited past – in their recent history. The politics of law and order, and the associated naming of enemies, have been part and parcel of representing that moment as a quasi-revolutionary one. Amongst Western countries the USA and UK have perhaps experi-enced this revivalism of state authority (what Mrs Thatcher memorably called the 'smack of firm government') in combination with a neo-liberal emphasis on the free play of market forces most forcefully, especially during the 1980s and early 1990s. Elsewhere in the world, perhaps especially in the countries of the former Soviet bloc – most obviously Russia itself – other and more drastic social and political transformations have also had far-reaching penological effects. The picture is complex. Suffice to note that the advent of liberal free-market economic reforms has by no means automatically heralded a new liberalism in the penal realm, especially in those countries where the state itself seems menaced by the very disorders and upheavals that the political transitions have unleashed. These have in some cases included alarm about newly virulent forms of criminality (the rise of the Russian 'mafia', the extraordinary murder rates in parts of South Africa); and such alarm frequently finds its political expression in nationalist and fundamentalist political movements and in nostalgia for the ordered world of the *anciens régimes*. In many of these very different circumstances an association can be seen between an alle-gation of political or social crisis and the demand for 'law and order', crystallized in the intensification of state punishment.

In this context, where anxieties associated with a 'risk climate' have been exacerbated by the recent fallout from global economic instability, and where public confidence in state authority has been correspondingly undermined, it is surprising when we encounter a reduction rather than an amplification of the rhetorical function of penality. The now entrenched 'public protection' agenda is instead presently finding new or reimagined expression within discourses of immigration, terrorism and national security, between which tenuous connections is typically drawn. Discussion surrounding the limits and purpose of the welfare state is also feeding into these discourses, conceptualized on the grounds of intensifying resource constraints, in turn provoking urgent questions about how resources should be fairly distributed. The named enemies are changing as a result; narratives of the undeserving *criminal* 'other' are being both displaced by and conflated with those of the undeserving *foreign* 'other'. Traditional factions of the New Right, such that they now dominate mainstream politics, appear to be exploiting this particular site of public concern, forced to adopt increasingly tough stances by the insurgent popularity of parties running on narrow platforms of controlled immigration and national isolationism.

Amongst the mistakes of social democracy, for thinkers of the New Right, were its tendency to assume the malleability and even perfectibility of human nature. Neo-liberalism, by contrast, is a 'politics of imperfection'. People's behaviour can be guided (by the early inculcation of a proper respect for authority and a love of family and country) and they have a legitimate and socially necessary desire to enrich themselves. However, they cannot fundamentally be changed. They are whatever their upbringing and personal dispositions make them. It follows that it makes little sense (other than with the partial exception of the very young) to counsel, treat, coddle or blandish those who misbehave. In order that people learn to govern their own conduct they must be treated as personally responsible for it (hence eligible for retributive punishment). At the same time, insofar as their motivations (and certainly those of the less respectable) are fundamentally economic and self-interested, the law must ensure that the incentives to compliant behaviour outweigh the attractions of offending. Since only the latter is directly under its control, its proper business focuses on setting the level of sanctions sufficiently high (hence a principle of rational deterrence). Those who demonstrate a persistent failure to comply must be incapacitated or effectively supervised. There is thus a preference not only for robustness in determining *levels* of penalties, but also for those *justifications* for punishing that favour a certain implied account of human motivation.

'Good governance' is a key theme of neo-liberalism, but the best government, according to the world view of the New Right, is limited in its scale and objectives. We do not live in state-governed societies. The over-reach of government during the era of welfarism encroached upon personal freedom and inhibited responsibility, impeded competitiveness and perversely undermined the authority of the state. The attempt to use taxation and state institutions for redistributive purposes – and thereby to impose artificial egalitarian restraints on natural hierarchies of talent and application – is the single most foolish, and ultimately immoral, of these errors. Redistributive social policy illegitimately transfers wealth from its creators to the unproductive, non-contributing members of society. Not only is this wrong in itself but it may also constrain the performance of the economy as a whole and, moreover, let those at the bottom off the hook of attempting to better their own lot; and anyway, the intensifying demands of international competition in a globalizing economy make the strategy unsustainable. International capital will simply flee those countries in which tax burdens are aversive; entrepreneurs will not take risks without the possibility of sufficient dividends; and the prize of prosperity flows towards those economies whose social costs are kept in check.

For all these reasons neo-liberal economic and political strategy is more tolerant of inequality than were its predecessor *state regimes* (Hay 1996). Ultimately, it is asserted, the bloat and inefficiency of welfarism has its most detrimental consequences on those at the bottom of the heap. In softening the impact of inequality it tends to maintain the poor in their poverty: it provides a 'handout' where it should at most offer a 'hand up'. In so doing it transfers responsibility away from individuals and families and onto state agencies. The perverse result is an undermining of the personal virtues of thrift and prudence and the preparedness to accept the burden and challenge of responsibility for shaping one's own destiny. In place of these we get 'dependency', apathy, fecklessness and the assumption that the world 'owes us a living', which in turn sap the very forms of individual self-government and familial solidarity that provide the basis for social order and the restraint of crime. In certain locations, it is asserted, this decadence has taken hold. Young women see no moral or practical inhibition against lone motherhood. Young men lose sight of the notion of the dignity of labour or the pride of supporting their family. Instead they become feral, wayward, hedonistic and impulsive. They serially father children and then abandon them. They mistreat their women, but they are in any case unmarriageable. Their lives are a mixture of swagger and drift. They do little well, not even crime. They do and deal drugs, joy-ride, burgle and rob with the same intermittent abandon that they do everything else. They are not in the classic sense 'underprivileged', and their lifestyle is a mockery of the term 'working class'. They have become 'the underclass'.

In New Right political thought the misguided generosity of the welfare state and the moral vapidity of liberal 'permissiveness', with its refusal to countenance the necessity of social discipline, condemnation and punishment, have conspired to produce this disaster. Meanwhile, law-abiding citizens, fearing victimization or hearing disturbing rumours through the mass media about the alien and predatory free-riders in their midst, look upon this spectacle with understandable dismay. The idea of a social, and more especially a redistributive, approach to the problem has become threadbare and politically unsayable – the degrees of sympathy, fellow-feeling or confidence that would make it plausible are ideologically precluded. Conversely, as Tonry (2004) has suggested, penal strategies that were formerly unthinkable can become mainstream.

Yet at the same time there is the assurance, both in political rhetoric and from certain serviceable quarters of criminological knowledge, that the threat resides in persons and places that can be identified. Perhaps then those who stand beyond the pale of recuperation can at least be *known*, and their behaviour predicted. To this extent the political demands upon the state become simpler and clearer and they focus more sharply on its specifically *penal* capacities. The state must use its knowledge to predict effectively. It must manage the risks it discovers (preferably without overburdening taxpayers) in ways that do not reflect badly on its competence. It must be unambiguous in its allocation of punishments and rewards, or face damage to its own legitimacy. It must therefore be plausible in its 'vocabulary of motives', speaking over the heads of sceptics, doubters, liberals and permissives directly to the motivations and dispositions of offenders themselves. It may correct where it can, deter whom it cannot otherwise correct and incapacitate all who show themselves impervious. Only under these conditions will it ride the tiger of its crime problems without severe damage to its authority. In these respects the two faces of punishment (the managerial and the emotive) and the two dimensions of risk (the mode of calculation and the mode of representation) remain integral to the position of the state in advanced capitalism, whatever other roles and responsibilities it divests, delegates or denies.

Two faces of risk: calculation and representation

The problem of risk arises wherever institutions and individuals encounter a need to weigh the possibility of harm or loss against desired outcomes and thus to institute practices that will manage or reduce their risks. Put in this way the question of risk sounds like a very rational, calculable and practical matter. Indeed, for many purposes it is. In many organizations and systems (and in the bodies of knowledge that inform how those organizations work) planning for and predicting risk are core activities. We can easily think of a list of such activities that are integral to contemporary social organization – weather forecasting, insurance, road safety, air traffic control, immunization, routine health screening for common cancers or circulatory illnesses, water purity, cashless transactions and 'smart cards', sell-by dates on food packaging, the inspection of restaurant premises by environmental health officers, fire safety regulations and so on. The list could be extended almost indefinitely. In many contemporary intellectual disciplines (in economics and in some branches of psychology, for example) behaviour under risk has become the very criterion of what it means to act rationally. Risk in this sense refers not simply to an 'amount' of danger to which one is exposed but rather to ways of assessing and deciding about undesirable things. One of the distinctive features of the late 20th century is that as well as creating or discovering many risks (from the management of nuclear waste to the carcinogenic properties of sunshine), it has invented and institutionalized many ingenious and refined ways of predicting and coping with them (actuarial tables, psychological profiles, manuals of professional good practice, prison architectures, and so on). The 'best' systems are for us those that build in the 'smartest' ways of anticipating and rectifying their own possible failures. These combinations of risk generation and risk management lead some social commentators to characterize our contemporary social reality as a 'risk society'.

It would be amazing if the domain of crime and punishment were untouched by such developments, and there are indeed grounds for thinking that this is not the case, but what would be the signs of such influence, and what consequences ought we to expect? One of the more provocative responses to such questions is offered by Malcolm Feeley and Jonathan Simon, who argue that we are witnessing the emergence of a 'new penology', one that is less concerned either to 'do justice' as traditionally understood or indeed to look to the welfare and correction of the erring citizen but rather which confines itself to managing the degrees of risk that certain *categories* of offender present. Feeley and Simon argue that although these changes are 'incremental' and 'emergent', they herald a shift in the very aims and purposes of penality. Whereas older penologies were concerned with individual culpability, specific deterrence or clinical dangerousness:

> [i]n contrast the new penology is markedly less concerned with responsibility, fault, moral sensibility, diagnosis, or intervention and treatment of the individual offender. Rather it is concerned with techniques to identify, classify and manage groupings sorted by dangerousness. The task is managerial, not transformative.
>
> (Feeley and Simon 1992)

Perhaps it is possible to overstate the newness of some of these sightings. Utilitarian calculation has played a prominent role in penal practice at least since Jeremy Bentham formulated the principles of rational deterrence in the late 18th century. The hyper-rational physical design of his panopticon represents a concrete statement of this. Conversely it is hard to argue that the impassioned reactions of anger, resentment, censure and fear have actually departed the field of penal politics. Nor have they, and here our argument starts to draw towards completion. We have spoken above of the Janus-faced nature of punishment, in its governmental and passionate aspects. We have pointed to some influences from contemporary social and political ideology (especially those views associated with the so-called New Right) in accentuating the prominence of the penal in the maintenance of social order. Now we have briefly alluded to the ways in which risk-based reasoning increasingly pervades our institutions including, it is argued, those of the penal system. The outstanding question is: what sorts of hybrids arise when these diverse and ostensibly disparate influences conjoin?

First, we should simply expect to continue to see a certain amount of diversity. In any given period certain sets of ideas may predominate, but other and sometimes incompatible views (survivals from the past, or else intimations of a somewhat different possible future) also circulate. So, for example, in the present penal practices centring on the anticipation of future risk seem ascendant, but they are accompanied by a different emphasis – to some extent a counter-movement – that favours a language of 'shaming', 'reintegration' and 'restoration'.

Second, the risk arithmetic is also very much accompanied by the emotionally vivid rhetoric of politicians promising firmness, protectiveness and the old-fashioned satisfactions of justice. Both these (falsely dichotomous) logics of 'justice' and 'reintegration' are particularly well articulated through the aesthetics of prison buildings, where the politics of imprisonment is materially and symbolically translated into its design. As both rationally planned and emotionally evocative artefacts, prison buildings perfectly express the ubiquity and fetishizing of risk thinking. At the same time, a politically expedient rhetoric is vociferously employed to describe these 'new and improved' designs, intended to signal strengthened security and appropriate austerity but, crucially, within a progressive context of humane care. On those grounds, where imprisonment does feature within mainstream political discourse, the trends in prison design mirror the trends in penal–political representation. Behind a less visually daunting exterior, the assumed punitive bloodlust of public opinion, real or imagined, continues to be indulged by reference to larger buildings, higher walls, sturdier hardware and the prevalence of advanced surveillance technologies. A vote-winning message of severity is sent. Simultaneously, the gleaming, sterile edifices, the presence of green space and the absence of ostentatious symbols of captivity – bars, locks, heavy gates, etc. – offer a sanitized image, appealing to extant public sensibilities towards moderation and 'smarter' punishment, or at least against brutal authoritarianism. To whatever precise depth or scale tolerant attitudes might now prevail in Western societies, political efforts to mollify public punitiveness have become increasingly moderate in line with generally more restrained and legitimacy-seeking legal and civic cultures.

However, dramatic and sometimes harrowing stories of newspapers and 'reality television' shows detailing the latest horror to befall somebody's daughter, son, spouse, parent, still permeate popular culture, sustaining the emotive heat of punitive attitudes. So far as crime and punishment are concerned the professional practice of the criminal justice process may increasingly tend to prioritize risk management, but we the public continue to inhabit an environment of story and symbol. As Mary Douglas (1992) has argued, risk does not 'unload its ancient moral freight'. Instead this ostensibly very modern diction has 'fallen into antique mode'. It is for this reason that we have argued throughout this essay that we need to understand punishment both in terms of *calculation* and of *representation*. This may strike some people as unduly abstract, but it is not. It is real in its consequences. It means that how we picture to ourselves those whose past actions we deplore or whose future ones we fear determines what we feel entitled to do to them.

Here we rejoin the question of how risk-calculation and New Right political thinking meet and cross-fertilize. Increasingly, we suggest, we are encouraged to hold two convictions, somewhat in tension with one another but both very current. The first is that we have the ability to predict what people will do. The second is that we each make our own luck. The first conviction gives us permission to hold or supervise people not primarily on grounds of justice or censure but against the expectation that they will incorrigibly reoffend. The second conviction allows us to disclaim interest in the personal or social circumstances that preceded the offence and licenses us to feel that whatever hardships they incur as a result are ones that they have brought on their own heads. Insofar as our ways of calculating about and of representing the offender tend to reduce him or her to a cipher, a mere bearer of a certain quotient of risk, it is unsurprising if our characteristic disposition towards him or her comprises some combination of fear, contempt and indifference. As Sean McConville pithily puts it:

The essence of incapacitation is that the offender lies beyond human intervention and influence, whether measured by susceptibility to deterrence or reform, or expiation through suffering ...

... Containment means that we can't be bothered to engage the offender: 'It is too much trouble, too unreliable, and might make civic demands which I have neither the time nor the inclination to meet.' The offender becomes a commodity or waste product.

(McConville 1998: 5)

In this respect, and others, the state of the penal realm reflects a rather dismal picture of the way we live now. There is a certain moral flatness, punctuated by bursts of outrage and indignation; an uneasy oscillation between the technocracy of risk management and the archaism of the mass media hue and cry. Are these the best visions of social order that market society offers? There is no shortage of evidence that urges this gloomy conclusion, but many reasons for wishing to resist its inevitability.

In the USA the 'natural experiment' in prison expansion has been running now for some 30 years, but its scale and ferocity appear to have begun to abate somewhat. In some places courts have indicated that the modest objectives they mandate (such as prison systems maintaining adequate medical records) may not be achievable in the face of overwhelming numbers and chronic crowding (Simon 2014). Eventually, even with the weight of ideological support that mass imprisonment has received, a sustained secular trend of declining crime rates begins to make what the American criminologist Barry Krisberg (1984) once called a penal policy 'fashioned on an anvil of fear' less compelling and perhaps less emotionally necessary.

For these reasons, following several decades in which the tone of the most persuasive forms of commentary on penal politics in many Western countries has become ever more despondent and dismayed, there might now be some slender grounds for cautious hopefulness. An increasingly society-defining shift that may in time have valuable penological consequences, especially with regard to popular modes of representation, is the democratization and diversification of the 'mass media'. The ever burgeoning electronic mediascape is fast becoming a key conduit for political discourse; it continues to emasculate traditional media forms, disrupting narrative orthodoxies regarding crime and punishment, and providing multiple platforms for alternative stories, critiques and passions. More conspicuous now than at any other time are pockets of citizens' groups campaigning, lobbying and petitioning for change in the penal arena, with some notable successes in terms of policy, if not full legislative reform. Moreover, the responsivity and speed at which such efforts can be coordinated across geographies and cultures should give policymakers sufficient pause, though it is still too nascent a shift to determine how (whether?) and to what degree this might produce a genuinely heterogeneous and more optimistic penological civic climate, with attending consequences for the politics of imprisonment (and indeed for penal policy and practice).

Concluding remarks

This chapter began by raising some persistent questions about what prisons are, have been, or could be like in terms of shifting social evaluations of appropriate conditions and services. It moved on to rehearse some well-known issues about imprisonment rates, especially where these have shown a marked upward pressure, sometimes to spectacular levels, in recent times. Finally it sketched some features of recent political discourse — with some generic features, but very much more pronounced in some countries than in others — that have favoured the more 'robust' handling of offenders. One aspect of this has been a confluence between approaches emphasizing risk management (often favouring the greater use of imprisonment on grounds of incapacitation) and more populist forces, invoking a heightened emotional language of fear, anger and indignation. Populism — in the sense of a direct appeal to powerful emotions, over the heads of dubious experts and vested interests — has become a much more marked feature of penal politics in many countries in the last couple of decades than it appears to have been in the preceding ones (Pratt 2006). Moreover there appears to be a trend towards the conflation of what are arguably distinct sources of trouble or anxiety under the name of 'security' (Sparks 2006; Ericson 2006), with the cumulative result of a greater requirement for supervision, detention and incarceration.

What may be less apparent is whether there is any necessary connection between the questions of regimes and conditions on the one hand and those of punishment numbers or levels on the other. Those who have taken an interest in the vagaries of the doctrine of less eligibility historically (cf. Sparks 1996) would tend to suggest that these issues are in fact quite closely connected. Not only do rising prison populations increase workload and spread resources more thinly but also the pressures within a given political culture that may favour greater levels of incarceration tend to favour a firmer and less indulgent style of handling as well (see Melossi 1993). Where offenders are viewed as more numerous, more threatening, more undeserving, less corrigible and, perhaps, less akin to ourselves, then priorities accordingly tend to refocus on deterrence and secure confinement. Certainly some of the most refined empirical reports we have on the practice and experience of imprisonment today (Liebling 2004) envisage a quite direct relationship between the vagaries of wider societal sensibilities about punishment, and the conduct and delivery of penal regimes as such.

We should not leave the argument at this dispiriting point, tempting as this is from the point of view of recent experience. First we should recall, as sketched above, that the gradual entrenchment of human rights standards in prison regimes has proceeded, even in the face of rising populations and the strain on prison space and regimes that they bring in train. Many professionals are determined to maintain prison regimes that are purposive and morally defensible, a task that the confusions of penal purpose and the over-politicization of the penal realm make ever more difficult. We tend to do a disservice to the seriousness and perseverance of many of those involved — as practitioners as well as external critics — if we overlook these matters. The vocational commitments that Carlen (2001: 460) characterizes as 'penal probity' remain highly significant, and all too easily slighted in generalized commentary.

Neither is it clear that either public anxiety or public commitment to a robust sense of justice necessarily produces an unlimited vindictiveness. There is growing recent evidence that what we commonly term 'public opinion' is considerably more complex, and more open to argument and persuasion than many commentators have tended to allow. A number of researchers have recently suggested that broad-brush generalizations concerning 'populist punitiveness' are not always empirically convincing (for example Brown 2006). There is also a danger that some dismal projections are just insufficiently aware of comparative data showing that some economically advanced countries have succeeded in stabilizing their prison populations, and even in some instances reducing them. In this respect the exceptional nature of the American case, and latterly the intensification of penal politics in certain other countries such as the UK and New Zealand, has tended to obscure divergent examples from which different lessons might be drawn. That suggests that some aspects of the *politics* involved in 'the politics of imprisonment' are considerably more local and more culturally specific, and in these senses potentially more alterable and less deterministic, than is sometimes acknowledged.

Our ways of writing about these issues, some observers now argue, are inflected by what has come to be called a 'criminology of catastrophe' that overlooks counter-examples, and asserts changes in the nature of prevailing sensibilities that do not always stand up to close scrutiny (O'Malley 2000; Hutchinson 2006). We do not have good grounds in extrapolating from the experience of the last couple of decades, and on the basis of the two or three most widely known examples, for presupposing that things must continue to evolve on the same template forever. It remains more appropriate to see prisons as sites of moral anxiety and ideological dispute (which they have always been) rather than the inevitable outcome of a singular viewpoint that happens to predominate now.

Note

1 It may be that Mr Matheson's primary concern was indeed with the cost of television to NHS patients, rather than with its provision to prisoners. Since, in November 2014, Mr Matheson was appointed cabinet secretary for justice in the Scottish government, one rather hopes so.

Bibliography

Barker, V. (2009) *The Politics of Imprisonment: How the Democratic Process Shapes the Way America Punishes Offenders*, New York: Oxford University Press.

Barker, V. (2013) 'Nordic Exceptionalism Revisited: Explaining the Paradox of a Janus-faced Penal Regime', *Theoretical Criminology* 17(1): 3–23.

Behan, C. and O'Donnell, I. (2008) 'Prisoners, Politics and the Polls: Enfranchisement and the Burden of Responsibility', *British Journal of Criminology* 48(3): 319–336.

Brangan, L. (2014) *Plenary Address to the COST Offender Supervision in Europe Conference, Valletta, Malta: Understanding Penality: A Comparative Political Perspective*, 27 March.

Carlen, P. (2001) 'Death and the Triumph of Governance? Lessons from the Scottish Women's Prison', *Punishment and Society* 3: 459–471.

Coyle, A. (2003) 'Prison Reform Efforts around the World: The Role of Prison Administrators', *Pace Law Review* 24(2): 825–835, digitalcommons.pace.edu/cgi/viewcontent.cgi?article=1217&context=plr.

Douglas, M. (1992) *Risk and Blame*, London: Routledge.

Ericson, R. (2006) *Crime in an Insecure World*, Cambridge: Polity Press.

Feeley, M. and Rubin, E. (1998) *Judicial Policy Making and the Modern State: How the Courts Reformed America's Prisons*, Cambridge: Cambridge University Press.

Feeley, M. and Simon, J. (1992) 'The New Penology: Notes on the Emerging Strategy of Corrections and its Implications', *Criminology* 30(4): 449–475.

Garland, D. (1990) *Punishment and Modern Society*, Oxford: Oxford University Press.

Garland, D. (1995) 'Penal Modernism and Postmodernism', in S. Cohen and T. Blomberg (eds) *Punishment and Social Control*, New York: Aldine de Gruyter.

Hay, C. (1996) *Re-stating Social and Political Change*, Buckingham: Open University Press.

Hough, M., Jacobson, J. and Millie, A. (2003) *The Decision to Imprison: Sentencing and the Prison Population*, London: Prison Reform Trust.

House of Commons (2006) *Report of the Zahid Mubarek Inquiry (Keith Report), HC 1082- I*, London: The Stationery Office.

Hutchinson, S. (2006) 'Countering Catastrophic Criminology: Reform, Punishment and the Modern Liberal Compromise', *Punishment & Society* 8(4): 443–467.

Krisberg, B. (1984) 'Distorted by Fear: The Make-believe War on Crime', *Social Justice* 21(3): 38–34.

Liebling, A. (2004) *Prisons and their Moral Performance*, Oxford: Oxford University Press.

McConville, S. (1997) 'An Historic Folly?', *Criminal Justice Matters* 30: 4–5.

Mannheim, H. (1939) *The Dilemma of Penal Reform*, London: Allen and Unwin.

Mauer, M. (2010) 'Voting Behind Bars: An Argument for Voting by Prisoners', *Howard Law Journal* 54(3): 549–566.

Melossi, D. (1993) 'Gazette of Morality and Social Whip: Punishment, Hegemony and the Case of the USA, 1970–1992', *Social & Legal Studies* 2(3): 259–279.

Morgan, R. and Evans, M. (1998) *Preventing Torture*, Oxford: Oxford University Press.

Nelken, D. (2009) 'Comparative Criminal Justice: Beyond Ethnocentrism and Relativism', *European Journal of Criminology* 6(4): 291–311.

O'Malley, P. (2000) 'Criminologies of Catastrophe: Understanding Criminal Justice on the Edge of the New Millennium', *Australian and New Zealand Journal of Criminology* 37(3): 323–343.

Pratt, J. (2006) *Penal Populism*, London: Routledge.

Radzinowicz, L. and Hood, R. (1986) *A History of English Criminal Law. Volume 5, The Emergence of Penal Policy*, London: Stevens & Sons.

Scharff-Smith, P. (2004) 'A Religious Technology of the Self: Rationality and Religion in the Rise of the Modern Penitentiary', *Punishment & Society* 6(2): 195–220.

Simon, J. (2000) 'From the Big House to the Warehouse: Rethinking Prisons and State Government in the 20th Century', *Punishment & Society* 2(2): 213–234.

Simon, J. (2014) *Mass Incarceration on Trial: A Remarkable Court Decision and the Future of Prisons in America*, New York: The New Press.

Sparks, R. (1996) 'Penal Austerity: The Doctrine of Less Eligibility Reborn?', in R. Matthews and P. Francis (eds) *Prisons 2000*, London: Macmillan.

Sparks, R. (2001) 'Degrees of Estrangement: The Cultural Theory of Risk and Comparative Penology', *Theoretical Criminology* 5(2): 159–176.

Sparks, R. (2006) 'Everyday Anxieties and States of Emergency: Statecraft and Spectatorship in the New Politics of Insecurity', in S. Armstrong and L. McAra (eds) *Perspectives on Punishment*, Oxford: Oxford University Press.

Stern, V. (1987) *Bricks of Shame: Britain's Prisons*, London: Penguin.

Tombs, J. (2004) *A Unique Punishment: Sentencing and the Prison Population in Scotland*, Edinburgh: Scottish Consortium on Crime and Criminal Justice.

Tonry, M. (2004) *Thinking About Crime: Sense and Sensibility in American Penal Culture*, Oxford: Oxford University Press.

Uggen, C. and Manza, J. (2002) 'Democratic Contraction: Political Consequences of Felon Disenfranchisement in the United States', *American Sociological Review* 67: 777–803.

Van Zyl Smit, D. (2006) 'Humanising Imprisonment: A European Project', *European Journal of Criminal Policy Research* 12: 107–120.

Van Zyl Smit, D. and Snacken, S. (2009) *Principles of European Prison Law and Policy*, Oxford: Oxford University Press.

Wacquant, L. (2001) 'Deadly Symbiosis: When Ghetto and Prison Meet and Mesh', *Punishment & Society* 3(1): 95–133.

Walmsley, R. (2005) *World Prison Population List*, sixth edn, London: International Centre for Prison Studies.

Wiener, M. (1990) *Reconstructing the Criminal: Culture, Law and Policy, 1830–1914*, Cambridge: Cambridge University Press.

Zimring, F. and Hawkins, G. (1994) 'The Growth of Imprisonment in California', *British Journal of Criminology* (special issue 'Prisons in context'): 83–96.

Chapter 5

The sociology of imprisonment

Ben Crewe

Introduction

It is because of the prison's social role and function that studies of its interior life always hold more than abstract or intrinsic interest. At the same time, the prison's distinctive qualities – pain, deprivation, inequalities of power, social compression – are such that its inner world provides particularly striking illustrations of a range of social phenomena. There are few other environments in which the relationship between constraint and agency can be so clearly observed, in which the consequences of power and power-lessness are so vividly manifested, and in which groups with divergent values and interests are put into such close proximity. Few other social contexts expose so barely the terms of friendship, conflict, loyalty and alienation, make questions of order and stability so germane, or bring into such sharp relief the qualities and capacities of humanity and inhumanity. Such issues will be returned to throughout this chapter, following a detailed exposition of Sykes's *The Society of Captives*, which will provide the basis for discussion of a range of debates, concepts and concerns. The chapter's main focus will be the inner world of the prison rather than its broader social and political functions.[1] However, in elaborating the debate about how prison culture is best explained, the chapter will explore the relationship between the prison and its external environment as well as its interior features.

The 'society of captives'

Although Sykes was by no means the first person to provide an academic account of the prison, *The Society of Captives* (1958) is commonly cited as the field's seminal text (Sparks et al. 1996; see Reisig 2001). Sykes regarded the prison as emblematic of systems of domination, such as concentration camps and labour colonies, and saw its study as a means of exploring the nature, consequences and potential limits of totalitarian control. With the US prison system having seen a spate of disturbances in the period preceding the study, including two riots in the maximum security facility in New Jersey where Sykes undertook his fieldwork, questions about penal order and disorder were particularly salient. He also recognized the intrinsic value of understanding prison life, at a time when changes in the aims and means of incarceration had been introduced with little understanding of how ambitions to control and rehabilitate prisoners might be hindered or supported by what went on, day to day, between prisoners: their everyday social life and culture.

The Society of Captives carries two, connected arguments, the first of which relates to power and institutional order. Sykes argued that the total dominance over prisoners that the prison ostensibly possessed was, on closer inspection, something of a fiction. The number of violations of the prison's regulations indicated how often institutional dominance was compromised, and illustrated the incessant nature of the struggle to maintain control. Sykes provided a number of reasons why order was far from guaranteed. Prisoners had no 'internal sense of duty' to comply: even if, at one level, they recognized the legitimacy of their confinement, in their daily behaviour they lacked intrinsic – i.e. moral or 'normative' – motivation to conform to the prison's demands. In theory, the prison could simply coerce prisoners into obedience through force. However, as Sykes pointed out, this was an inefficient and dangerous way to get things done: prisoners outnumbered officers, and violence could easily spiral out of control. Rewards and punishments were, likewise, much less effective than might be expected. Given the prison's conditions – Sykes argued – the latter could do little to worsen the prisoners' circumstances, whilst the former were not powerful enough to motivate prisoners positively.

There were also reasons why prison officers struggled to maintain formal boundaries and apply rules. First, it was difficult to remain aloof from prisoners when one worked with them all day and might identify with them, or even grudgingly admire them. Second, officers were surprisingly dependent on those they guarded. Prisoners carried out everyday functions and minor chores (delivering mail, checking cells, cooking and washing clothing), and if they withheld their services, this not only interfered with the smooth running of the wing, but was also taken to reflect the competence of the staff responsible. Officers were also aware that if riots did occur, their personal safety might depend on how they had used their apparently limitless power.

Sykes considered these defects in the prison's supremacy – 'cracks in the monolith' (Sykes 1958: 53) – to be virtually intrinsic to prison organizations, and to lead to a number of compromises between the prison officials and prisoners. 'In effect, the guard buys compliance or obedience in certain areas at the cost of tolerating disobedience elsewhere' (ibid.: 57); that is, officers ignored minor infractions in order to keep the peace and successfully undertake their daily tasks. As well as turning a blind eye to some activity, they also induced compliance through the provision of unofficial rewards and information to inmate leaders (e.g. extra food or coffee, warnings about upcoming searches, good jobs or cells), who in turn distributed these privileges within the inmate population. This informal arrangement was crucial for the maintenance of order. First, it directly relieved some of the tensions and deficits of imprisonment. Second, by sweetening them into compliance, it kept in check those prisoners who might otherwise 'cause trouble'. Third, it reinforced the power and status of inmate leaders – men who had a stake in institutional calm and were committed to inmate solidarity (see below). For Sykes, disorder was likely to occur if this relationship of negotiation and compromise was broken – if the rules were too strictly enforced, or the informal power of dominant prisoners were to be eroded, leading to a disintegration of the normal bonds and hierarchies between prisoners. To summarize at this point, then – and we will return shortly – order was *negotiated*, and it functioned *through* the inmate hierarchy, via those men at the apex of the prisoner community.

It is through the figure of the inmate leader that Sykes links his theory of order to his other primary argument, which is about the role and function of the 'inmate code': the set of norms and values that prisoners publicly espoused as a guide to behaviour. Sykes outlined five chief tenets of this code, crudely summarized as follows: 'don't interfere with other inmates' interests, or 'never rat [grass] on a con'; don't lose your calm, or 'play it cool and do your own time' (Sykes and Messinger 1960: 8); don't exploit or steal from other prisoners; don't be weak, or 'be tough; be a man'; and don't ever side with or show respect for the institution and its staff. This normative system had been described before (see particularly Clemmer 1958 [1940]). However, Sykes sought to explain both its origins and its functions. Noting that this was a 'strikingly pervasive value system', which could be found among apparently diverse prison populations and regimes (Sykes and Messinger 1960: 5), he reasoned that the roots of the code lay in the fundamental properties of imprisonment.

These properties were identified as the 'pains of imprisonment': those deprivations beyond the loss of liberty that defined the experience of incarceration and had a profound effect on the prisoner's self-image. These included various forms of moral condemnation, and the deprivations of goods and services, heterosexual relations, autonomy and personal security. Sykes and Messinger argued that the inmate code could be explained as a mechanism for alleviating these pains. If prisoners developed a positive shared identity, if they were loyal and respectful towards each other, if they shared their goods, caused no unnecessary frictions, kept their promises, showed courage and fortitude, and remained in staunch opposition to the prison administration, they could collectively deflect the moral censure of lawful society and mitigate many of the practical and psychological problems of incarceration.

Sykes (1995: 82) was explicit in stating that this code was 'an ideal rather than a description of how inmates behaved'. It was a set of norms to which prisoners pledged allegiance, but which most did not actually follow. In response to the pains and deprivations that they encountered, the majority of prisoners acted in ways that were 'alienative' rather than cooperative. Indeed, Sykes claimed that the various labels ('argot roles') used within the prisoner community were organized around different kinds of deviation from the central value system. There were terms for prisoners who profited from others ('merchants') or threatened them with force ('gorillas'), informed on their peers ('rats'), were insufficiently masculine ('punks' and 'fags'), or caused unnecessary friction with officers ('ballbusters'). All prisoners had good reason to espouse the code and demand that others conform to it – for there was no benefit in encouraging others to be exploitative or disloyal, even if one was oneself – but only one prisoner type embodied its doctrine. In doing so, this prisoner – the 'real man' – generated admiration among the inmate body, for he personified its collective ideals.

Real men could act as intermediaries between prisoners and officers because they stood up for the former and derided the latter without needlessly provoking incidents or pushing officers too far. They walked 'the delicate line between rejection of the officials and cooperation' (Sykes 1958: 126). Crucially, too, their commitment to the inmate code meant that they served to assist the prison officials. Although they exemplified a value system that appeared 'anti-institutional', by encouraging other prisoners to curb hostilities against each other and to protest against the prison only if really necessary, they were central figures in ensuring institutional stability. As Clemmer had noted, the code contained admonitions to 'do one's own time' – to limit social bonds and activity – which were 'the exact counterparts of the official admonitions' (Clemmer 1958: ix). Through both material and cultural means – the distribution of favours, and the dissemination of a value system that discouraged in-group antagonism and helped relieve the deprivations of imprisonment – real men prevented the prisoner community from exploding into unrest *and* from disintegrating into a state of rampant exploitation. In short, then, it had a double function: as a collective coping mechanism for prisoners, and a vital source of institutional order.

Sykes's work merits this lengthy elaboration because it covers and connects a number of key issues in prison sociology: the relationship between the prison and the outside world; the everyday culture of prison life; the pains of imprisonment; adaptation, hierarchy and social relationships; and questions of power, order and resistance. The sociology of imprisonment is by no means limited to these concerns, but it is to these areas that we now turn.

The prison, inmate culture and the outside world

The clearest theoretical contribution of *The Society of Captives* was its assertion that inmate culture was determined by the inherent deprivations of prison life. Sykes made some comments about the influence of personality factors on inmate adaptation, and some references to the influence of outside society on the prison's inner world, but these were tentative and tokenistic. It is tempting to speculate that Sykes deliberately underplayed the relevance of external factors in order to shore up the theoretical simplicity of his case. It is also important to note that at the time of his writing, prisons were more socially isolated, more 'total' institutions than they are today: without the same avenues to the outside world that telephones and televisions now provide. Still, Sykes clearly conceptualized prison culture as something determined by the inherent deficits of incarceration, consistent across spatial boundaries (i.e. regardless of a prison's location), and distinctive to the penal environment. Each of these claims has been developed and challenged in subsequent work.

In his classic (1961) text, *Asylums*, Goffman drew upon Sykes to make the case that the prison was just one of a range of 'total institutions' which shared certain functions and characteristics. Goffman defined a total institution as 'a place of residence and work where a large number of like-situated individuals, cut off from the wider society for an appreciable period of time, together lead an enclosed, formally administered round of life' (Goffman 1961: 11), a definition which therefore included mental hospitals, monasteries, boarding schools and navy ships. Like Sykes, Goffman presented the prison – and all other total institutions – as a social system that was largely autonomous from the outside world. Indeed, this autonomy was critical to its ambition to reconstruct and rehabilitate the inmate. Goffman listed practices such as the removal of personal possessions, the assignment of numbers or uniforms, the shaving of hair and the banning of normal contact with the outside world as ways of stripping inmates of their prior identities, and creating a ritual break with their past. Total institutions sought to rebuild the identities of their inhabitants by limiting their physical and psychological autonomy (regulating basic tasks such as washing and spending money; placing curbs on personal movement; withholding information), at the same time as providing a new set of rules, relationships and rewards around which identity could be reconstituted. Issues that were minor and taken for granted in the outside world – a jar of coffee, the right to smoke – became levers around which behaviour could be refocused.

Just as Sykes highlighted how imprisonment engendered a profound attack on the inmate's self-identity, Goffman's concern was the struggle of the individual to maintain self-integrity in the face of persistent attack from social rituals and institutions. Despite being socially and physically sequestered from the outside world, inmates were rarely obliterated or overwhelmed by institutional imperatives. Invariably, they sought some control over the environment, and retained some kind of independent self-concept, resulting in a range of 'secondary adaptations' to the prison's restricted social environment (see below). The resulting culture was one in which institutional and individual objectives existed in tension, and it was coloured appropriately by a preoccupation with the self. This was manifested in a generalized sadness about the inmate's lowly status or in a narrative about his (or her) social demise; and by a tendency for inmates to immerse themselves in 'removal activities' (education, exercise, card playing, fantasy) that created a space between themselves and the institution.

Although Goffman's focus was individual rather than collective adaptation, like Sykes he located the resources for adjustment as lying inside the institution. He conceived of the inmate as an individual cut off from wider social ties and stripped of pre-prison characteristics, and gave no meaningful description of how personality factors or cultural orientations influenced prison conduct. It is for this reason that Goffman is generally identified with Sykes as a proponent of 'deprivation' or 'indigenous' theory, which focuses on prison-specific variables in explaining inmate culture and behaviour. The opposing view is normally ascribed to Irwin and Cressey, who resurrected Clemmer's (1958: xv) earlier observation that the 'penitentiary is not a closed culture'. Although they acknowledged that inmate society was a 'response to problems of imprisonment', they questioned 'the emphasis given to the notion that solutions to these problems are found within the prison' (Irwin and Cressey 1962: 145). Rather, they argued, prisoners 'imported' into the prison characteristics and orientations from the external community, and adapted in ways that *maintained* or were consistent with these pre-existing selves. The inmate code was by no means distinctive to the prison, but was a version of criminal cultures existing beyond the prison.

More specifically, Irwin and Cressey regarded inmate culture as the outcome of three distinctive subcultures imported into the penal institution. The first was a 'thief culture', carried by professional and serious criminals, emphasizing reliability, loyalty, coolness in the face of provocation and 'moral courage'. Thieves were oriented to criminal life rather than the prison world itself, and aimed to serve their sentences as smoothly as possible, seeking out occasional luxuries to make life easier. The second was a 'convict subculture', carried by prisoners whom Irwin (1970) subsequently labelled 'state-raised youth'. These were men with long records of confinement in juvenile institutions, who were socialized within these individualistic, exploitative and manipulative cultures. Convicts actively sought status and influence within the prison – this being the world they knew – and were likely to be involved in the prison's illicit activities as a means to these ends. The third, more marginal, subculture was the 'legitimate' value system held by 'straight' prisoners, with anti-criminal attitudes, who generally conformed to institutional goals and acted in accordance with conventional, lawful principles. Prison culture as a whole was 'an adjustment or accommodation of these three systems within the official administrative system of deprivation and control' (Irwin and Cressey 1962: 153).

The importation-deprivation debate has continued to provide the primary framework for discussions of prison social life and culture, but has advanced in a number of directions. The notion that there was any such thing as 'The Prison', with stable properties and consistent characteristics, was challenged by a number of studies which showed how much variety existed between different regimes, populations and even a prison's physical design (see Chapter 7, this volume). As was broadly consistent with Sykes's model, custody-oriented establishments generated more oppositional cultures than treatment-based facilities. Studies of women's prisons found very different inmate social systems from those described in men's establishments, raising further questions about whether prisons could be said to have 'intrinsic' features at all (Ward and Kassebaum 1965; Giallombardo 1966). Meanwhile, Mathiesen's (1965) account of a Norwegian treatment-oriented establishment described a prisoner community with little cohesive behaviour, little faith in the effectiveness of norms promoting solidarity, a flat inmate hierarchy, no apparent ban on contact with prison staff, and no 'honourable' inmate identity (the latter features apparently reflecting Norway's relatively undeveloped criminal culture). Lacking peer solidarity or a positive collective identity, prisoners developed alternative means of coping from those identified by Sykes, primarily oriented around accusations that power holders were deviating from their own established norms or those rooted in broader notions of justice. Thus, a value system emphasizing opposition to the institution and solidarity to one's peers did not appear to be the only functional responses to the pains of imprisonment.

The picture of prison life in Jacobs's (1977) *Stateville* bore even less resemblance to Sykes's account, and its analysis represented an advanced challenge to indigenous theories of prison culture. Instead of a single normative code, Jacobs found a prisoner community that was fragmented into mutually antagonistic, ethnically defined gangs, with codes of loyalty that stretched little beyond in-group members. Significantly, these gangs had emerged on the streets of Chicago, from where their values and leadership structures had in effect been *transplanted* into the prison. Jacobs (1974: 399) contrasted Goffman's description of the 'role-stripping' of new prisoners with what he observed as a 'home-coming ceremony', whereby new entrants were greeted and looked after by affiliates from the streets. Here, then, external identities defined and were reinforced by the prison's social structure. Moreover, it was the gang system, rather than informal negotiation with prison officials, that buffered many prisoners from the pains of prison life by providing a sense of collective identity as well as social and economic support.

Stateville was significant not only in capturing the transformation of the prison's social organization, but in explicitly identifying the macro-mechanisms that rendered it historically mutable. While Irwin and Cressey had illustrated the permeability of the prison to external cultures and dispositions, Jacobs showed how its social life and administration were moulded by wider social, political and legal conditions. Prisoner expectations had been raised by expanded notions of rights and 'citizenship', and these expectations were validated by court interventions that secured for them a growing range of entitlements. Meanwhile, the politicization of ethnic-minority prisoners reflected political cultures outside the institution. For Jacobs, such changes represented 'the movement of the prison's place in society from the periphery towards the center' (Jacobs 1977: 6). The prison could no longer insulate itself from the trends and values of the outside world, and from demands for its inhabitants to be treated as normal citizens.

This description of the prison's rationale and societal location has not been without criticism. Although long-term patterns suggest that prisons have been subject to certain kinds of 'civilizing' processes, the coercive turn within prison management (as embodied by the 'supermax' prison in the USA), the contracting out of imprisonment to the private sector, and the potency of law-and-order politics in both the USA and Western

Europe indicate a more complex configuration of the prison-society relationship. First, then, while the prison – and crime control more generally – has become central to political discourse (Simon 2007), it has done so in a way that reassures the 'respectable' classes of their difference from the 'criminal class', and has little compunction about treating the latter in ways that are highly punitive (Christie 1981). Some scholars have characterized the 'extra-penological' role of the prison as the primary means of managing and neutralizing the American underclass, with money drained from welfare into penal services in the interests of neo-liberalism (Wacquant 2001). Clearly, the prison has multiple functions beyond its technical ends (Garland 2001) – indeed, judged by its primary aims, it is an astonishing failure. Symbolically, it serves to represent state authority and reinforce moral boundaries and sentiments (Durkheim 1933); at the level of political economy, it acts as an instrument of class domination and a means of maintaining social order (Rusche and Kirchheimer 1939). As feminist scholars have also highlighted (Carlen 1983; Howe 1994), often drawing on the work of Foucault (1977), the prison may be emblematic of a web of social control strategies that regulate and discipline women throughout society: within the family, relationships, by the state and in terms of general definitions of femininity. Here then, the conceptual distinction between the prison and the outside world begins to crumble.

Second, privatization could be seen as a de-coupling of the prison from the state, especially in the USA, where regulation practices are less stringent than in the UK. Further, private companies form part of the bloc of interest groups whose political lobbying reinforces the momentum for mass incarceration: thus, the penal body now feeds into political life, as well as vice versa. Third, imprisonment rates in the USA (and, to a more limited extent, in Western Europe) are such that the prison and its culture can no longer be seen as mere reflections of or appendages to a separate, external world. Imprisonment has become a 'shaping institution for whole sectors of the population' (Garland 2001: 2), stripping some communities of young men, disenfranchising them from the political process, and creating generational spirals of criminality. In some areas of the USA (and other countries, to a lesser degree), incarceration is not just a normal social expectation and experience, but a source and requirement for status. For Loic Wacquant (2000, 2001), the prison and the ghetto are now barely distinguishable. The ghetto has been swamped by criminal justice agencies, and deserted by non-state, civic agencies. Meanwhile, the 'warehouse' prison has little purpose beyond containment and control. Like the ghetto, it merely quarantines its inhabitants from the rest of the social body. Both prison and ghetto are characterized by racial cleavages, enforced idleness, and by cultures of suspicion, distrust and violence. Wacquant argues that street culture is no longer simply imported into the prison – as Jacobs described – but has itself been deeply imprinted by norms and values from the prison that have been re-exported and integrated over many years.[2] In such respects, the separation of these cultural domains may be fatuous, and the importation-deprivation debate appears somewhat obsolete.

It is important to maintain some distinction between theories of prison culture and empirical accounts of its terms and influences. A multitude of quantitative studies have shown that the relationship between pre-prison variables and in-prison behaviour is complex and variable, and that activities such as drug taking and homosexuality have both imported and indigenous components (Zamble and Porporino 1988). The prison's inner world is best seen as a *distorted* and *adapted* version of social life and culture outside. However, for reasons discussed below, studies that would more sharply illuminate the complex interplay between imported factors and the imperatives generated by the prison remain uncommon. At the structural level, few scholars now seek to explain the role or function of the prison through a single theoretical lens (be it derived from Marx, Durkheim, Talcott Parsons or Foucault). Rather, it is generally accepted that the values and sensibilities that shape the broad purposes and practices of imprisonment derive from multiple sources, and are realized in practice in complex and messy ways.

David Garland (2001) has provided the most recognized account of this kind, arguing that on both sides of the Atlantic, penal welfarism has been replaced by a 'culture of control', one element of which is the emergence of more coercive and punitive penal sanctions, and the reinvention of the prison. Such broad characterizations tend to be over-schematic. As Liebling (with Arnold 2004) has shown, Garland's narrative cannot explain some of the countervailing tendencies in UK imprisonment, such as the re-emergence of rehabilitative ambitions, and the advancement of a 'decency agenda'. Such discourses are promoted and undermined by powerful individuals (e.g. ministers, Prison Service heads) and unanticipated events (e.g. riots, escapes, high-profile crimes), significantly altering the general climate of incarceration, in ways that have a demonstrable impact on the degree to which prisons feel decent or distressing. Since some prisons are evidently more respectful or safe than others, it is also clear that management styles, staff cultures and institutional histories mediate the ways that penal values and sensibilities are translated into material practices (see also Kruttschnitt and Gartner 2005). Thus, through the messages that prison staff receive and instantiate about the moral status of prisoners and the boundaries of acceptable behaviour, the prison experience is sensitive to both the macro- and micro-politics of imprisonment.

Prison adaptation and socialization

Sykes noted that the roles taken up by prisoners were not static, and that many prisoners moved between different roles over the course of their sentence. However, he provided no account of how or why this might happen and did little to develop the concept of 'prisonization', a term that captures the *dynamic* process of prisoner socialization. Clemmer had defined prisonization as the 'taking on in greater or lesser degree of the folkways, mores, customs and general culture of the penitentiary' (Clemmer 1958: 299). He argued that the degree to which a prisoner became assimilated into prison culture depended on a range of factors, including personality, demographic characteristics, and relationships within and outside the prison. The implications for rehabilitation were gloomy. Prisoners who became socialized into prison culture had 'no chance of being salvaged' (ibid.: 313). If rehabilitation occurred, it did so *in spite* of the influence of prison culture, and it happened to those prisoners who were the least oriented to criminal subcultures in the first place. However, such conclusions relied on the assumption that socialization into the norms of imprisonment simply deepened over time. By exploring prisoner attitudes at different sentence stages, Wheeler (1961) showed this supposition to be faulty. Prisonization took the shape of a 'U-curve': it was in the middle stage of a sentence that prisoner values most closely conformed to the inmate code. As prisoners anticipated release back into the community, these values shifted back to the more 'conventional' norms with which they initially entered the prison community.

To some degree, Wheeler's findings supported Sykes's theorization of the inmate code as a problem-solving mechanism (and Goffman's belief that inmates were able to readjust to non-institutional life relatively quickly). It was when prisoners were furthest from the outside community, i.e. when the pains of imprisonment were most acute, that they were most dependent on the prisoner society and the code was most potent. Subsequent work has confirmed that there are particular stages of a sentence at which prisoners feel most isolated and distressed, albeit generally earlier than Wheeler suggested (Liebling 1999), and that sentence length has a considerable impact on adaptation (Sapsford 1983). Prison behaviour of various kinds can be plotted against time served, and certainly many prisoners report that they deliberately curb illicit activities as they approach release and have more to lose from such exploits (Crewe 2009).

However, as Sykes's work illustrated, there is no single pattern of adjustment to prison life. A comprehensive – though static – typology of adaptations can be provided by combining the frameworks presented by Merton (1938) and Goffman (1961). First, then, some prisoners 'withdraw', 'retreat' or 'regress', focusing on little beyond immediate events around themselves. Often these prisoners are former drug addicts, whose mission is simply to get themselves 'back on track' (Crewe 2009). Retreatism might also include what would be considered maladaptations, such as self-isolation and repeated self-mutilation (Liebling 1992), but could also incorporate the obsessive bodybuilding that some prisoners take up, or the deep absorption into art or education that allows others some mental escape from institutional life (Cohen and Taylor 1972; Boyle 1984).

Second, some prisoners rebel against the prison, attempting escapes, engaging in concerted physical resistance, or 'campaigning' against prison practices and conditions. In the UK, such activities tend to be concentrated within higher-security establishments, where long sentences generate profound frustration, and where prisoners themselves may be more anti-authoritarian, or sufficiently resourceful to orchestrate effective campaigns against the system. As some scholars have suggested, however, resistance is not limited to these prisoners, or to its more spectacular and confrontational manifestations. Power is not simply held by the powerful, to be directly confronted and seized. It flows throughout the social body, through surveillance, petty rules and assumptions about 'appropriate behaviour' (Foucault 1977). Resistance therefore occurs through everyday, minor acts of subversion (backstage jokes, the use of in-group language, stealing from prison supplies) and through assertions of identity ('as a mother ...'; 'as a black woman ...') that contest and recast the meanings, directives and restrictions imposed by the institution. Ugelvik (2014) highlights a set of creative practices, including forms of improvised cooking and the transformation of cells into private spaces, which enable prisoners to reclaim some sense of masculinity, individuality and moral status. These forms of micro-resistance – which make use of the body as a tool of violence, a site of representation (e.g. through modes of dress or make-up), or an object of desecration and destruction (e.g. dirty protests; self-harm) – may be particularly common when prisoners have little collective organization.

A third kind of adaptation is represented by 'conformity' (Merton 1938), 'colonization' or 'conversion' (Goffman 1961), where prisoners appear relatively satisfied with their existence in prison, where they internalize official views of themselves, and where they comply with sincerity and enthusiasm to the demands of the system. This category includes the 'centre-men' and 'straights' described in the early ethnographies – men who identified with conventional values prior to imprisonment. It also incorporates those 'gleaners' whom Irwin (1970) described as seeking change and self-improvement through official programmes and structures. Some researchers have implied that this adaptation is uncommon or superficial, because it means prisoners discarding anti-social values or accepting their inferior moral status (Morris and Morris 1963; Carrabine 2005). In fact, there are an increasing number of drug addicts entering prison who compare it favourably to life on the streets on drugs, and whose shame and self-loathing lead them to act as model inmates, desperate to prove their moral reformation (Crewe 2005b, 2009).

Fourth, there are prisoners who fit into the category of 'innovators' that Merton described as accepting official objectives but rejecting the institutional means of attaining them. Mathiesen (1965) identified this 'censoriousness' as the primary response among prisoners in his study of a Norwegian prison: criticism of those in power for not conforming to their own stated rules and standards, or for acting in ways that would be considered unjust within a broader moral framework. These strategies – which can be seen as a form of resistance – are significant because, rather than representing a stance of normative opposition (as Sykes described), they accept the norms of the officials. Mathiesen argued that, in this respect, they derive from a position of weakness and social atomization: a lack of other, more collective means of challenging the regime. At the same time, they may be highly effective ways of contesting the terms of one's incarceration, and blurring the moral divide between prisoners and their state custodians.

The majority of prisoners find ways of coping with imprisonment that do not involve either extreme resistance or complete acquiescence, and which combine the strategies and adjustments described above. Whether described as 'playing it cool', 'ritualism' or 'doing time', this involves supporting other prisoners, albeit within limits, showing little enthusiasm for the regime, and seeking to make the prison experience as comfortable as possible, while trying to avoid trouble. Some prisoners – perhaps a sixth category – will also seek to *manipulate* the system (Morris and Morris 1963; King and Elliott 1977; Crewe 2009), using their prison experience to exploit rules, work 'angles' and perform desired behaviour to prison officials whilst flouting it elsewhere. Most prisoners want to 'do their time and get out' (Carrabine 2004), but how they choose to do so – whether they get involved in trade, or the accumulation of status – depends on peer obligations, criminal and institutional careers, family loyalties, economic and psychological needs within prison, and future hopes whose inter-relationships remain under-researched. Certainly though, prisoners do not just 'undergo' imprisonment as passive agents of prisonization and socialization, as much of the early literature seems to imply. Rather, as Cohen and Taylor (1972) emphasized, they are often highly conscious of their social predicament and are strategic in the choices they make about how to address it.

It is also clear that imprisonment is considerably more painful for some prisoners than for others (Liebling 1992), and that prisoner *sub-groups* experience and adapt to the prison environment in different ways. In part, as the next section illustrates, this relates to aspects of social organization within and outside the prison. However, it also indicates the different psychological preoccupations that prisoners import into the environment, and the ways in which institutions address their populations. Evidence from the USA has suggested that the concerns of black prisoners are focused on issues of freedom, autonomy, disrespect and discrimination, while white prisoners are more likely to fear for their physical safety and experience prison as a loss to self-esteem (Toch 1977). In the UK, black prisoners feel lower levels of respect, humanity and fairness than other prisoners (Cheliotis and Liebling 2006), while the prison system has been described as 'institutionally thoughtless' about the needs of the old and disabled, to whom it is not primarily oriented (Crawley 2005; Chapter 29, this volume).

Research consistently reports that for female prisoners, the rupturing of ties to children and intimate others, and the possibility of being in prison during one's fertile years, are particularly painful dimensions of imprisonment (Walker and Worrall 2000). Female prisoners also express greater concern than male prisoners about privacy, intimate intrusions, personal health and autonomy, and those dynamics of penal power that can evoke memories of abuse (Carlen 1998; Zaitzow and Thomas 2003). Such concerns reflect, and are exacerbated by, the nature of women's imprisonment. Female prisoners are often incarcerated at great distance from their homes, while the regimes to which they are subjected are generally more petty and infantilizing (as well as domesticated and medicated) than those in men's prisons (Carlen 1998). These higher expectations about the personal behaviour of female prisoners are emblematic of the discourses of 'normal femininity' that are embedded in the practices and philosophies of women's incarceration (Bosworth 1999; Carlen 1983, 1988), and which amplify the gendered dimensions of collective adaptation that are described within the section that follows.

Social relations and everyday culture

Sykes did not claim that the prisoner world was defined by inmate cohesion or actual solidarity. However, by describing a society with a single normative framework, and by providing only passing reference to social and ethnic cleavages within this community, he portrayed prisoners as unified by some kind of common purpose. This may have reflected the nature of the 'Big House' prison, in which prisoners were subjected to a stupefying regime, rigid timetabling and highly authoritarian staffing, and yet were allowed to develop a relatively self-contained world, which they managed with little interference from the authorities (Irwin and Austin 1997; Irwin 2005). In such a context – and given Sykes's interest in systemic order and equilibrium – communal objectives and collective functions may well have appeared more significant than social divisions and interpersonal relationships.

Other accounts of the prison, both during the Big House era and in later periods, have explored the nature of social relations *within* the prisoner community. Generally, they have emphasized conflict, 'disorganization' and sub-group rivalry as much as collective organization. Clemmer (1958) described a tiered hierarchy of elite, middle-class and lower-status prisoners. The latter – around 40% of prisoners – tended to be solitary, being civil to others but not close or cooperative. Higher-status prisoners were more sociable, mixing within their class either in 'semi-primary' groups, sharing luxuries and information, or in smaller cliques, where resources were shared and members thought collectively. Subsequent accounts of prison life have depicted similar patterns of loosely structured, interlocking social groups, with little formal organization or leadership, based upon locality, religion, age, lifestyle and criminal identity (Irwin 2005; Crewe 2005a, 2009). Such groups offer forms of material and social support, and physical backing if required, while also providing networks for trade and avenues for settling disputes. As Clemmer noted, though, loyalties are generally limited and groups rarely display genuine cohesion (Mathiesen 1965; though see McEvoy 2000). Prisoners tend to differentiate between acquaintances, with whom relationships are transient, instrumental and defensive (often based on self-interest and fear of exploitation rather than affection and admiration), and a very small number of trusted friends, often known prior to the sentence. For most prisoners, then, the prisoner community is 'an atomized world', characterized more by 'trickery and dishonesty' than by 'sympathy and cooperation' (Clemmer 1958: 297).

Whether race was a significant factor in the Big House era is difficult to know. Jacobs (1983) suggests that, given the discriminatory values of white prisoners and officials, black prisoners were probably excluded from certain roles within the prison and were unlikely to be as committed to the inmate code as whites.[3] In any case, over the two decades that followed the publication of Sykes's work, any notion of a single solidarity culture among prisoners in the USA was obliterated as racial and ethnic conflict became the dominant feature of American prisons. By the 1950s, black Muslims had begun to preach their racial superiority, rejecting the notion of inmate equality (Jacobs 1983). In the years that followed, as prisons became more open to the outside world, and as the percentage of non-white inmates began to rise, racial and ethnic differences were amplified. Prisoners started to organize themselves into ethnically homogeneous cliques, with separate informal economies. Ethnic co-mingling became more limited. When there was enthusiasm for a more rehabilitative regime (Irwin 2005), and while the numerical dominance of white prisoners counterbalanced the greater solidarity of black prisoners, peace and tolerance prevailed. By the 1970s, the changes described in *Stateville* had eroded this social accord. Informal segregation had hardened into factional conflict, both between and within ethnic groups, and violent gangs from the streets began to dominate the prisoner social world. The norms of these gangs stressed intense in-group allegiance while encouraging the exploitation of non-members (Jacobs 1977; Irwin 1980). Unaffiliated prisoners either had to 'prove themselves' worthy of membership, usually through violence, or withdraw from the prison's public culture. As gang members and state-raised youth took over the prison social world, random violence, robbery and sexual predation became everyday facts of life, turning the prison into 'an unstable and violent social jungle' (Johnson 1987: 74).

Recent work suggests that although race remains the primary axis of social life in American prisons, and informal segregation persists, 'the intensity and importance of racial identities and gang affiliations has diminished somewhat' (Irwin 2005: 86). To a large degree, this social 'détente' (Irwin 2005) is explained by the emergence of the supermax prison, which has allowed for the segregation of violent and gang-affiliated prisoners, and which stands as a potent threat to those who want to remain in more humane conditions. Here then, prison culture has been moulded by a particular form of administrative control. Most European societies have had neither the gang culture nor the racial cleavages whose importation into prison have led to so many problems in the USA (Morgan 2002). In UK prisons, despite fairly widespread prejudice and frequent verbal skirmishes, race relations have historically tended to be relatively harmonious (Genders and Player 1989). Black and Muslim prisoners are more cohesive than whites – and this can generate envy and hostility from white prisoners, who consider themselves somewhat marginalized – but their solidarity functions primarily in defensive, self-supporting ways rather than as a means of achieving collective power. Prisoners are loosely self-segregating, but such groupings reflect shared cultural backgrounds rather than racial hostility or political assertions of ethnic difference. In most establishments, prisoners mix across ethnic lines, espouse 'a desire to see themselves and others simply as human beings, not defined by their race or ethnicity' (Phillips 2012: 86), and publicly express norms of multicultural liberalism.

One reason for this culture of 'multicultural conviviality' (Phillips 2012: 124) is that many prisoners are raised in diverse inner-city areas, and socialize naturally in ethnically heterogeneous groups both inside and outside prison. Indeed, in most UK establishments, locality is at least as important as ethnicity in defining prisoners' loyalties. Alliances and networks are normally founded on hometown contacts, such that groups from large urban centres tend to be dominant in a prison's informal economy – without normally seeking wider control of the prison's public spaces. Occasionally such groups come into conflict with each other over trade and collective reputation; more often, disputes stem from relatively minor disagreements between individuals. On the whole though – as in the USA, prior to racial Balkanization (Irwin 2005) – the social world is balanced by a multitude of cliques and social clusters which are relatively fluid and interconnected (see also Sparks et al. 1996).

In England and Wales, the starkest exception to this picture can be found in some high security establishments, where the social world is much more sharply defined by the increasing collective power of Muslim prisoners. Liebling et al. (2012) describe considerable tension between the growing Muslim population and other prisoner groups (see also Liebling and Arnold 2012). Importantly, they argue that the appeal of Islam is to some degree institutionally determined: in a culture of violent insecurity and lengthening sentences, Islam – like other faith systems – offers valuable forms of fraternity, safety, hope and meaning. Muslim prisoners, who in previous decades were considered highly compliant (Genders and Player 1989), have become the most challenging and oppositional members of the prisoner community, in part because of suspicion and cultural distance between them and prison staff.

In all penal jurisdictions, certain criminal offences appear to generate status and stigma (Winfree et al. 2002). Thus, sex offenders are widely reviled by other prisoners, while armed robbers, terrorists, high-level drug dealers and organized, professional criminals are given a certain amount of kudos.[4] As Morgan (2002) notes, though, such labels are problematic: drug addicts committing small-scale post office robberies to fund their habits have little social standing; spouse murderers and contract killers generate very different levels of fear and status among other prisoners; and while terrorists and 'faces' (prisoners with reputations) are given 'respect', this tends to be based upon fear as much as admiration. Many petty criminals are as morally judgemental about serious, violent offenders and the activities of drug dealers as these more powerful prisoners are socially judgemental about them (Crewe 2009).

Meanwhile, although certain offences almost categorically lead to stigma, few in themselves 'carry an automatic bonus of prestige' (Morris and Morris 1963: 226). Status and power are also associated with certain kinds of acts and attributes (Clemmer 1958; King and Elliott 1977). Low status tends to be assigned to prisoners who are unintelligent, provincial, cowardly, mentally unstable, poor copers, criminally naïve, or who inform on others. Prisoners who are unpredictably violent or uncompromisingly hostile are given little credibility, but their aggression allows them to carve out a certain degree of social space and autonomy. Those who are intelligent, charismatic, strong, and criminally mature, who are faithful to inmate values and who do not subordinate themselves to officials, tend to generate respect (Clemmer 1958; Sykes 1958; Irwin 2005).

These terms appear to have changed little since the early ethnographies, yet the precise nature of the prisoner hierarchy is related to the prison's institutional properties and to changes in the external world. Many UK prisoners report a decline in the currency of violence since prisons introduced anti-bullying strategies and challenged cultures of staff brutality. In the current system of England and Wales, it is significant that status and stigma are so closely bound up with the drugs economy. Since its widespread presence in the prison system from the late 1980s, heroin's economic potency, and the desire it generates, has made it a major source of power in the prisoner world, albeit in a form that is somewhat ephemeral and is different from respect (Crewe 2005b). In contrast, heroin users are stigmatized and disrespected. Their consumption indicates weakness and dependency, and is associated with a range of behaviours – such as stealing and manipulation – that constitute serious breaches of the prisoner value system. It remains to be seen how the recent influx of legal highs into the prison system, particularly synthetic cannabinoids, might reshape these kinds of hierarchies and social relations.

The nature of power is also defined by an establishment's security status. In medium security conditions, where prisoners are in sight of release, few seek to impose their power upon others for fear of what they might lose. Although a distinction between 'lads' and 'idiots' is apparent, on the whole, interpersonal power is granted rather than actively sought out, and has implications rather than ends: it means being safe from violence, receiving a certain amount of recognition, and having the capacity to intervene in wing issues and disputes, but it is rarely imposed upon others directly or for its own sake (also see Sparks et al. 1996: 177–178).

Like the prisoner hierarchy, the inmate code is more complex than basic maxims suggest, and while showing continuity with early formulations, has been responsive to changes in the nature of prison life. First, then, there is no simple consensus on its terms. Prisoners may agree that informing is generally wrong, but many believe that it is justified in extreme circumstances, for example if a prisoner or staff member is going to be seriously assaulted. Likewise, while some prisoners consider charging others for small favours or demanding interest on loans to be shrewd, others regard it as exploitative. Second, there is considerable variance between its form, not only across the prison estate, but also within individual establishments (Sparks et al. 1996). The therapeutic prison, HMP Grendon, exhibits a culture without conventional norms about not informing on or disclosing to others, distrusting staff and publicly denigrating sex offenders (Genders and Player 1989; Stevens 2013). In Young Offender Institutes, the ritual humiliation of vulnerable prisoners is legitimated by norms that revile weakness. Violence and victimization are rife (Edgar et al. 2003; HMCIP 2001). By contrast, in adult prisons, although weakness is disdained, its exploitation is not celebrated.

Additionally, the code is subject to change, both in its content and its primary functions. Early theorists recognized that there was considerable disparity between the solidarity that prisoners verbally demanded, and the individualistic behaviour that many of them actually exhibited. Clemmer suggested that code violations were most likely to occur among prisoners with loyalties to people both within and outside the institution. In Sykes's formulation, verbal allegiance to the code was virtually unanimous, but was based on markedly different motivations. 'True believers' (Sykes and Messinger 1960: 18) were normatively committed to its values; other prisoners were more pragmatic, supporting it to stop themselves being exploited ('believers without passion'), or asserting it disingenuously to protect their violations from being reported. Nevertheless, writers agreed that the code was universally acknowledged, and that without it, the prisoner world would be all the more conflictual and unpredictable. It provided a common source of identity and self-respect, promoted mutual aid, and reduced the degree to which less respected prisoners were exploited. By the 1970s, as the prisoner community factionalized, normative consensus likewise splintered (Jacobs 1977; Irwin 2005).

Skarbek (2014) argues that as prison populations expanded, more first-time prisoners entered the system and prisons become more crowded, the system of norms (a reputation-based system) was no longer able to govern prisoner behaviour effectively. Gang culture emerged because it was a more effective mechanism for protecting property, enforcing informal agreements and arbitrating disputes. Soon, though, the ideals of toughness and machismo that had formerly served as a collective mechanism for coping with the prison experience became sources of exploitation; aggression supplanted fortitude as the basis of admiration. Meanwhile, the informal economy functioned less to cushion prisoners against the prison's daily deprivations than as a wellspring of profit, power and exploitation. White-collar criminals and white prisoners who refused to join neo-Nazi counter-gangs developed a code that illustrated the new, defensive terms of prison survival: 'Don't gamble, don't mess with drugs, don't mess with homosexuals, don't steal, don't borrow or lend' (Hassine 1999: 42).

Notwithstanding the variations and complexities sketched out above, a number of commentators have remarked that the cultures of men's prisons appear deeply inscribed by discourses of masculinity, the celebration of violence and toughness, the stigmatization of weakness and femininity, and fraternal codes of in-group loyalty (e.g. Sim 1994; Carrabine and Longhurst 1998; Sabo et al. 2001). Sykes's (1958) description of the manner in which, in the absence of normal gender relations, male prisoners seek to demonstrate their masculinity through the 'secondary proof of manhood', remains an elegant summary of what has now become prevailing wisdom about the culture of men's prisons. As Newton (1994) argues, the prison breeds hyper-masculinity by taking men who already lack conventional means of establishing masculine status, besieging them with further threats to their gender identities, and thus encouraging them to shore up anxieties about weakness and dependency through the hardening of stereotypically male traits, in particular those that demonstrate power over the self and others. Prison rape has been taken as the ultimate symbol of this dynamic (Scacco 1975). Although sexual coercion is relatively uncommon in UK prisons (O'Donnell 2004), in some jurisdictions it appears endemic, and is saturated with gendered (and racial) meanings, creating a surrogate gender hierarchy. Typically, the man who rapes another man is not considered homosexual. Rather, his actions are taken to indicate dominance and masculine power, while the victim is irrevocably stigmatized and emasculated − often expected to carry out 'female' duties, such as housekeeping, on behalf of the aggressor. Those men who choose to take up a homosexual role within the prison's sexual subculture are less reviled than those who have the passive, 'feminine' role forced upon them. Correspondingly, within the prisoner hierarchy, respect seems to correlate with crimes and behaviours that entail the imposition of will and self-definition upon others: armed robbery, terrorism and the willingness to 'go all the way', regardless of risk. Discourses of masculinity − mutual interest in sports, shared notions of 'giving your word' − may also serve to lubricate relationships between male prisoners and staff (Carrabine and Longhurst 1998).

However, these mechanisms are complex and, in the UK at least, prisons do not exhibit a homogeneous culture of ruthless and uncompromising machismo, nor are their emotional cultures uniform (Crewe et al. 2014). In relating to female officers, male prisoners are just as liable to use discourses of charm, chivalry and the 'good son' as those of sexism to confirm their masculine identities. There is a danger that by focusing on the 'hyper-masculinity' of men's prisons, we portray the prisoner world as a lawless jungle, without moral baselines. Such representations ignore the banal kindness that characterizes prison life alongside all its depredations. These everyday details of the prison have tended to be documented within the margins of other studies. They have highlighted: the importance to prisoners of clothing and body maintenance; the performative nature of public discourse in prison, based around embellished tales of past behaviour and the street, cynical pronouncements about criminal justice and 'the man', and often grandiose plans for the future (Irwin 1985); the private stories of personal demise and shame (Goffman 1961); the surprising punitiveness of many prisoners (Winfree et al. 2002); the 'mind games' played out on the landings between prisoners and staff (McDermott and King 1988); the combination of wariness, opportunism and improvisation that characterizes the 'rabble mentality' (Irwin 1985); the raw, 'pungent argot [language] of the dispossessed' (Sykes and Messinger 1960: 11); and the wit of prison humour, with its wry appreciation of the surreal (Morris and Morris 1963). Highlighting such dimensions is important in humanizing a world that is often portrayed to be completely alien and inhumane.

Formulations that equate prison culture with masculinity are also troubled by findings that reveal the presence of coercion, violence and sexual exploitation in women's prisons. In general, however, the cultures of women's prisons have differed from men's establishments: being less tense and predatory (Zaitzow and Thomas 2003), harbouring higher rates of distress and self-harm (Liebling 1992; see Chapter 31, this volume), and lacking such strong norms of general solidarity. At the level of social structure, in women's prisons in the USA, race operates as a subtext in daily life rather than as its defining axis (Owen 1998). Many of the roles identified in the early ethnographies of men's facilities, such as the 'politician', 'tough' and 'merchant', have not been found in women's prisons. Rather, their social worlds have been organized through same-sex relationships and pseudo-family units, which seem to provide important forms of intimacy and the kinds of emotional roles that imprisonment threatens (Ward and Kassebaum 1965; Giallombardo 1966). Relative to men's prisons, then, collective adaptations function to provide emotional as much as social and economic support, while sex serves as a basis for comfort rather than power.

At the same time, it is important not to overstate the uniqueness of women's prison adaptations. 'Homegirl' networks of friendships and acquaintances from outside the prison are similar to the kinds of social lattices that shape the affiliations of male prisoners (Owen 1998). Furthermore, it is clear that the nature of social life in women's prisons is influenced by the degree to which the regime is itself gendered. In their comparison of adaptations in two women's prisons in California, Kruttschnitt and Gartner (2005) found little evidence of racial tension, and intimate relationships between women were common, indicating some continuities with older studies that emphasized the distinctive social lives of men's and women's prisons. However, women in the more restricted, gender-neutral prison were more likely to be distrustful of other prisoners and staff, to self-isolate and to report emotional distress than those in the prison that had retained more traditional assumptions about femininity and women's criminality. Research of this kind alerts us to the danger of ascribing all aspects of prison culture to the imported gender identities of prisoners without paying sufficient attention to the role of the institution itself in reproducing certain kinds of gendered roles and behaviours. In relation to men, this means attributing cultures of violence and aggression to aspects of the administration – harsh regimes, hostile staff cultures, etc. – as well as to the characters of prisoners themselves.

Power, order and resistance

Some comments have already been offered on individual forms of resistance, but power is also exercised by prisoners at a collective level, most obviously in the form of riots, but also in everyday attempts to push back against the imposition of institutional power. As Sykes (1958) suggested, one basis of collective power is a shared set of values generated by common predicament – what might be referred to as structural solidarity – and the bargaining power that this provides. Collective power might also stem from values imported from networks and organizations located outside the prison (Jacobs 1977). Most notably, political convictions appear to be among the only adhesives that can bind prisoners into organized and purposeful collective action, particularly when reinforced through support in a wider social or ideological community. McEvoy (2000) describes how shared commitments to political ends among paramilitary prisoners in Northern Ireland provided both the will and solidarity that enabled them to sustain long-term hunger strikes and dirty protests. Meanwhile, the power of these prisoners was bolstered by the strength of the paramilitary organizations within Northern Irish society, and their ability to intimidate prison staff. Polite but persistent requests over relatively small matters were underwritten by threats to the safety of staff members' families, allowing para-military factions to establish control incrementally not only over prisoners' cells and landings, but other public spaces within the institution. The ability of individual prisoners to instigate legal interventions that apply collectively to prisoners is another potent source of collective power, one that can be engaged in with complete moral legitimacy. Like-wise, the appeal to collective, moral norms can be a powerful means of holding the authorities to account (Mathiesen 1965).

The ways that prisoners assert and resist power are defined to a significant degree by the ways it is imposed upon them. Imprisonment restricts normal means of coping (alcohol, drugs, friendship), and provides alternative means of exercising agency. In Foucault's terms, 'where there is power, there is resistance, and yet, or rather consequently, this resistance is never in a position of exteriority in relation to power' (Foucault 1978: 95). Equally, prison institutions deploy power with forms of resistance in mind – primarily, that is, to achieve *order*. Order in prison is an issue of particular interest given the obstacles to its accomplishment that seem inherent in the penal situation. For Sykes, then, the pragmatic trade-off between rulers and rules was a *necessary* accommodation. Subsequent writers continued to explore how order was achieved through the values and hierarchy of the inmate community, stressing the combination of solidarity ('don't exploit others') and anomie ('but do your own time …') that made the code such an effective source of stability, and the conservatism of prisoner leaders keen to maintain the status quo. However, by the time of *Stateville*, with gangs less inclined towards negotiation, and less in need of its benefits, powerful prisoners were undermining rather than contributing to institutional stability. Liebling and colleagues' recent (2012) research in the UK suggests that similar processes may be occurring in high security prisons, with Muslim prisoners less inclined than the 'old-school' gangsters of the past to negotiate with the authorities.

Of course, order had never been achieved through informal accommodation alone. It is also clear that Sykes's theory rested on a number of flawed assumptions. One tenet of his argument was that the rewards and punishments offered by prison officials had little persuasive influence. Yet there is plentiful evidence that the opposite is the case, and that prisoners can be motivated a great deal not only by the prospect of freedom (early release, home leave), but also by 'details' whose significance is amplified in the spartan context of the prison (extra spending money, in-cell televisions). In the UK, the introduction of the incentives and earned privileges (IEP) scheme in 1995 was explicitly guided by the assumption that prisoners were more likely to comply when good behaviour brought material benefits (Liebling et al. 1997). Such rational choice models of prisoner behaviour are flawed: many prisoners are not 'rational choice' thinkers, and resent being addressed by a 'carrot and stick' approach to behaviour modification, especially if it is implemented unfairly. Nonetheless, by easing the material deficits of imprisonment through formal channels (rather than leaving them to be filled by informal arrangements between prisoners), prison officials have reduced both the need for peer solidarity and the basis of collective identification. Prisoners do not share the same predicament, and focus on individual rather than collective concerns. Prospects and living standards can be more easily enhanced through compliance rather than collective action, while the material improvements on offer directly reduce the feelings of deprivation that can inflame group unrest.

Second, it is not the case that prisoners will inevitably lack any 'inner moral compulsion to obey' (Sykes 1958: 48). Few prisoners dispute the right of the state to imprison them and some 'enthusiasts' place themselves on the same moral plane as the institution, expressing shame about their previous behaviour and identifying themselves as fundamentally non-criminal people (Crewe 2009). More importantly, the degree to which prisoners submit to a regime depends partly on *how* their imprisonment is delivered, and whether it conforms to broad principles of justice. Prisoners recognize the difference between treatment that is fair, humane and respectful, or brutal, inconsistent and dehumanizing (Sparks et al. 1996; Liebling, with Arnold 2004). These differentials are critical, for even when prisoners dislike the outcomes of institutional practices, they are more likely to comply with them and accept the prison's authority if decisions and treatment can be justified in terms of the values, beliefs and expectations that prisoners hold. Here, then, the interface between officers and prisoners is critical. Prisoners will make normative judgements about an establishment according to its material provisions – decent cells, access to telephones – and whether its systems deliver fair procedures and consistent outcomes. However, as frontline representatives of the prison, it is officers whose everyday behaviour comes to embody the perceived legitimacy of the institution. It is at the level of staff–prisoner relations that the prison's everyday moral climate is determined, and its pains cushioned and crystallized.

Third, although, as Sykes suggested, physical force remains a dangerous and inefficient way of running a prison with complex institutional tasks, it is by no means impossible to generate order through highly coercive and controlled regimes. In the USA, supermax prisons do this by separating prisoners from each other, minimizing contact between prisoners and staff, and employing stringent measures of restraint (e.g. handcuffs, leg irons) whenever dealing with prisoners. These organizations are a world away from the Big House, in which prisoners mixed relatively freely and were integrated into the daily maintenance of the establishment. In the UK, although very few prisoners exist in supermax-style conditions, situational control measures introduced since the widespread disturbances of 1990 – smaller wings, fewer communal areas, more surveillance – have placed greater limits upon movement, association and potential disorder. As Foucault (1977) highlighted, the use of timetabling and spatial organization is a key means by which prisons – and other state institutions such as schools and hospitals – regulate and discipline their members.

The achievement of control via architecture and restraint contributes to a fourth source of order: fatalistic resignation or 'dull compulsion'. For many prisoners, the sheer power imbalance within the prison, the stultifying routine, and the constant symbolic reminders of powerlessness (security cameras, barbed wire, etc.) lead to a feeling that nothing much can be done about one's current predicament. This distinction between power that is accepted as legitimate and power that is taken for granted is crucial. Not least, it would be a mistake to interpret the absence of open resistance as an indication of normative consent. As analysis of the Strangeways riot implies (Carrabine 2004), if the only thing preventing insurrection is acquiescence to the apparent inevitability of the situation, once this impression is shattered, a disturbance might very rapidly spread.

There is a great deal of variation in the degree to which prisons achieve order, and the means by which they do so. Supermax prisons come close to embodying a control–coercion model of order, while democratic–therapeutic prisons such as Barlinnie and Grendon have achieved high levels of legitimacy, even when dealing with difficult prisoners (see Boyle 1984; Sparks et al. 1996; Stevens 2013). On the whole, though, most establishments rely on a combination of techniques to achieve stability, and cannot be characterized according to a simple model of coercion or consent. In the UK, in recent years, situational control measures and the IEP scheme have co-existed alongside efforts to boost legitimacy through improved physical conditions, and attempts to humanely recondition staff cultures. Meanwhile, prisoners are increasingly encouraged to self-govern and assume responsibility for the terms of their own incarceration, in a way that represents neither direct coercion nor autonomous consent (Garland 1997; Liebling, with Arnold 2004; Crewe 2009). They participate in defining their own sentence plans, but have no option to refuse one; they are motivated to address their offending behaviour, with the knowledge that there are implications in not doing so for their release date; and they are aware that to gain 'enhanced' status, passive obedience is insufficient. Through a discourse of threats and opportunities, then, they are channelled and stimulated into producing institutionally desirable behaviour.

Different ways of accomplishing order have different effects. Sparks et al. (1996) have demonstrated how an apparently more 'liberal' and legitimate prison might harbour more backstage violence than one that appears more authoritarian. However, everyday violence differs significantly from the breakdown of order, which is more likely to occur in less legitimate regimes, where prisoners feel a profound 'lack of justice' (Woolf 1991: para. 9.24).[5] While riots have multifaceted roots, recent theories suggest that they tend to occur when widespread prisoner grievances exist alongside administrative confusion and disorganization (Useem and Kimball 1989). However, if these were the only conditions necessary to provoke major disturbances, they would happen far more frequently than they do. To understand why riots occur in particular times and places, we need to theorize the pleasures and triggers of disruptive activity, and explore the mechanisms by which disorder spreads.

Sykes's claim that unrest occurred when the informal power of inmate leaders was undermined was simplistic, but there remains much of value in his analysis of the role of the prisoner community in securing order. First, the prisoner hierarchy is influenced by the deficits of prison life. By shaping these deficits, institutions can mould the adaptations that prisoners are required to make and the currency within the prisoner community of violence, trade and manipulation. Second, where overseen judiciously, the capacity of prisoners to self-govern can be harnessed to positive effect. Prisoners themselves can reduce levels of alienation and can benefit from being placed in roles that allow them to take responsibility and mentor their peers. In turn, prison officials may not want *too much* solidarity among prisoners, but nor do they want the prisoner community to fragment into clusters of mutually hostile, untrusting individuals. The shape of the inmate body – the nature of leadership, the balance of different prisoner groups, levels of trust and friendship – can contribute positively or negatively to order. Finally, even if negotiation no longer seems the most effective means of securing order, prisons *are* systems of cooperation, where staff and prisoners have many common interests and values, and where these values contribute in significant ways to legitimacy, well-being and order. In the USA, DiIulio (1987) has argued, with great influence, that the informal accommodation approved by Sykes was a disastrous surrender of authority whose resulting lawlessness was inevitable. However, a prison that relies on rules and restrictions, at the cost of relationships and consensus, might produce stability at the price of pain and social resentment.

Conclusion

The sociology of prison life covers a vast landscape, but has been mapped selectively and sporadically. Meaningful comparisons between the inner social world of prisons in different jurisdictions are made difficult by the scarcity of comparative ethnographic studies. One reason why, in the USA, studies of the prisoner society have become less common is that the relationship between policymakers and the penological community has changed. At the time of Sykes's study, social science was regarded as having a key role in forging a more ordered and successful penal system (see Chapter 37, this volume). Now, such optimism about the state's ability to manage society through informed governance of its social institutions has receded, and there is less interest in prison social life as an object of study and intervention. In the era of the 'warehouse prison' and the supermax, prisoners are to be stored, contained and processed: their values, adaptations and social relationships are somewhat irrelevant to prison managers. There are more risks than gains in allowing researchers to document this world and, at a time when the prison population is exploding, prison ethnography is 'not merely an endangered species but a virtually extinct one' (Wacquant 2002: 385).

In the UK and some other European countries – notably, Belgium and Norway – prison research seems to be undergoing something of a revival, and the links between policymakers and academics remain relatively strong. There are dangers that research findings become simplistically co-opted into managerial agendas, and that attempts to reform the prison serve to legitimate its use as a substitute for broader social policy and welfare provision, but the dangers of leaving the prison's culture and social dynamics uncharted are surely greater. This is not only to document what prisons are like and how they are experienced, but to help address questions about their social roles and consequences – what they should and should not be for, and what claims can be made for them. Likewise, prisons are more than just abstract systems, and their study should continue to illustrate not only the humanity of prisoners, but the more universal aspects of humanity – distress, endurance, adaptation and social organization – that the prison's special conditions make visible.

Notes

1 Since discussions of prison staff can be found elsewhere in this volume, although the chapter will highlight how institutional factors influence the prison's inner world, it will not dwell on issues such as staff practices or the effects of the prison on its workers.
2 Beyond the ghetto, prison culture has penetrated the mainstream through rap music, clothing (e.g. baggy, belt-less trousers), tattoos, slang, and a range of body gestures that register the perverse kudos of incarceration among those people least likely to experience it.
3 Sykes (1956) noted that 38% of his sample were black, but said little else about race. Writing some years later (Sykes 1995), he explained that researchers at the time assumed that the experiences of white and black prisoners were the same, and that being white also made it more difficult to undertake research among black prisoners.
4 In most UK prisons, sex offenders are housed separately from other prisoners, but continue to function in the moral hierarchy of mainstream prisoners as examples of what they distinguish themselves from.
5 There is insufficient space here to explore the causes of interpersonal violence, but see Edgar et al. (2003) for a symbolic interactionist analysis, and Gambetta (2005) and Kaminski (2004) for innovative discussions based upon behavioural and game theory.

Bibliography

Bosworth, M. (1999) *Engendering Resistance: Agency and Power in Women's Prisons*, Aldershot: Dartmouth.
Boyle, J. (1984) *The Pain of Confinement*, Edinburgh: Canongate.
Bukstel, L. and Kilman, P. (1980) 'Psychological Effects of Imprisonment on Confined Individuals', *Psychological Bulletin* 88: 469–493.
Carlen, P. (1983) *Women's Imprisonment: A Study in Social Control*, London: Routledge & Kegan Paul.
Carlen, P. (1998) *Sledgehammer: Women's Imprisonment at the Millennium*, Basingstoke: Macmillan.
Carrabine, E. (2004) *Power, Discourse and Resistance: A Genealogy of the Strangeways Prison Riot*, Dartmouth: Ashgate.
Carrabine, E. (2005) 'Prison Riots, Social Order and the Problem of Legitimacy', *British Journal of Criminology* 45: 896–913.
Carrabine, E. and Longhurst, B. (1998) 'Gender and Prison Organisation: Some Comments on Masculinities and Prison Management', *The Howard Journal* 37(2): 161–176.
Cheliotis, L. and Liebling, A. (2006) 'Race Matters in British Prisons', *British Journal of Criminology* 46(2): 286–317.
Christie, N. (1981) *Limits to Pain*, Oxford: Martin Robertson.
Clemmer, D. (1958 [1940]) *The Prison Community*, second edn, New York: Holt, Rinehart and Winston.
Cohen, S. and Taylor, L. (1972) *Psychological Survival: The Experience of Long-Term Imprisonment*, Harmondsworth: Penguin.
Crawley, E. (2005) 'Institutional Thoughtlessness in Prisons and its Impacts on the Day-to-Day Prison', *Journal of Contemporary Criminal Justice* 21: 350–363.
Crewe, B. (2005a) 'Codes and Conventions: The Terms and Conditions of Contemporary Inmate Values', in A. Liebling and S. Maruna (eds) *The Effects of Imprisonment*, Cullompton: Willan, 177–208.
Crewe, B. (2005b) 'The Prisoner Society in the Era of Hard Drugs', *Punishment and Society* 7(4): 457–481.

Crewe, B. (2009) *The Prisoner Society: Power, Adaptation and Social Life in an English Prison*, Oxford: Oxford University Press, Clarendon.

Crewe, B., Bennett, P., Smith, A. and Warr, J. (2014) 'The Emotional Geography of Prison Life', *Theoretical Criminology* 18(1): 56–74.

DiIulio, J. (1987) *Governing Prisons: A Comparative Study of Correctional Management*, New York: The Free Press.

Durkheim, E. (1933) *The Division of Labour in Society*, New York: The Free Press.

Edgar, K., O'Donnell, I. and Martin, C. (2003) *Prison Violence: The Dynamics of Conflict, Fear and Power*, Cullompton: Willan.

Foucault, M. (1977) *Discipline and Punish: The Birth of the Prison*, Harmondsworth: Penguin.

Foucault, M. (1978) *The History of Sexuality*, Vol. I, trans. Robert Hurley, New York: Pantheon.

Foucault, M. (1991) 'Governmentality', in G. Burchell, C. Gordon and P. Miller (eds) *The Foucault Effect*, Hemel Hempstead: Harvester Wheatsheaf, 87–104.

Gambetta, D. (2005) 'Why Prisoners Fight', in *Crimes and Signs: Cracking the Codes of the Underworld*, Princeton, NJ: Princeton University Press.

Garland, D. (1997) '"Governmentality" and the Problem of Crime: Foucault, Sociology, Criminology', *Theoretical Criminology* 1: 173–214.

Garland, D. (2001) *The Culture of Control: Crime and Social Order in Contemporary Society*, Oxford: Oxford University Press.

Genders, E. and Player, E. (1989) *Race Relations in Prisons*, Oxford: Oxford University Press.

Giallombardo, R. (1966) *Society of Women: A Study of a Women's Prison*, New York: John Wiley.

Goffman, E. (1961) *Asylums: Essays on the Social Situation of Mental Patients and Other Inmates*, Harmondsworth: Penguin.

Hassine, V. (1999) *Life Without Parole: Living in Prison Today*, Los Angeles, CA: Roxbury Publishing Company.

HMCIP (HM Chief Inspector of Prisons) (2001) *HM YOI and Remand Centre Feltham*, London: Home Office.

Howe, A. (1994) *Punish and Critique: Towards a Feminist Analysis of Penality*, London and New York: Routledge.

Irwin, J. (1970) *The Felon*, Englewood Cliffs, NJ: Prentice Hall.

Irwin, J. (1980) *Prisons in Turmoil*, Chicago, IL: Little, Brown.

Irwin, J. (1985) *The Jail*, Oakland, CA: University of California Press.

Irwin, J. (2005) *The Warehouse Prison: Disposal of the New Dangerous Classes*, Los Angeles, CA: Roxbury.

Irwin, J. and Austin, J. (1997) *It's About Time: American's Imprisonment Binge*, second edn, Belmont, CA: Wadsworth.

Irwin, J. and Cressey, D.R. (1962) 'Thieves, Convicts and the Inmate Culture', *Social Problems* 10: 142–155.

Jacobs, J. (1974) 'Street Gangs Behind Bars', *Social Problems* 21(3): 395–409.

Jacobs, J. (1977) *Stateville: The Penitentiary in Mass Society*, Chicago, IL: University of Chicago Press.

Jacobs, J. (1983) *New Perspectives on Prisons and Imprisonment*, Ithaca, NY: Cornell University Press.

Johnson, R. (1987) *Hard Time: Understanding and Reforming the Prison*, Pacific Grove, CA: Brooks/Cole Publishing.

Kaminski, C. (2004) *Games Prisoners Play: The Tragicomic Worlds of Polish Prison*, Princeton, NJ: Princeton University Press.

King, R. and Elliott, K. (1977) *Albany: Birth of a Prison – End of an Era*, London: Routledge & Kegan Paul.

Kruttschnitt, C. and Gartner, R. (2005) *Marking Time in the Golden State: Women's Imprisonment in California*, Cambridge: Cambridge University Press.

Liebling, A. (1992) *Suicides in Prison*, London: Routledge Press.

Liebling, A. (1999) 'Prison Suicide and Prisoner Coping', in M. Tonry and J. Petersilia (eds) *Crime and Justice: A Review of Research*, Vol. 26, Chicago, IL: University of Chicago Press, 283–360.

Liebling, A., with Arnold, H. (2004) *Prisons and their Moral Performance: A Study of Values, Quality, and Prison Life*, Oxford: Clarendon Press.

Liebling, A. and Arnold, H. (2012) 'Social Relationships between Prisoners in a Maximum Security Prison: Violence, Faith, and the Declining Nature of Trust', *Journal of Criminal Justice* 40: 413–424.

Liebling, A., Arnold, H. and Straub, C. (2012) *An Exploration of Staff-Prisoner Relationships at HMP Whitemoor: Twelve Years On*, London: Ministry of Justice.

Liebling, A., Muir, G., Rose, G. and Bottoms, A.E. (1997) 'An Evaluation of Incentives and Earned Privileges: Final Report to the Prison Service', unpublished report to the Home Office, London.

McDermott, K. and King, R. (1988) 'Mind Games: Where the Action is in Prisons', *British Journal of Criminology* 28(3): 357–377.

McEvoy, K. (2000) *Paramilitary Imprisonment in Northern Ireland*, Oxford: Clarendon Press.

Mathiesen, T. (1965) *The Defences of the Weak: A Sociological Study of a Norwegian Correctional Institution*, London: Tavistock.

Merton, R. (1938) 'Social Structure and Anomie', *American Sociological Review* 3: 672–682.

Morgan, R. (2002) 'Imprisonment: A Brief History, the Contemporary Scene, and Likely Prospects', in M. Maguire, R. Morgan and R. Reiner (eds) *The Oxford Handbook of Criminology*, Oxford: Oxford University Press.

Morris, P. and Morris, T. (1963) *Pentonville: A Sociological Study of an English Prison*, London: Routledge & Kegan Paul.

Newton, C. (1994) 'Gender Theory and Prison Sociology: Using Theories of Masculinities to Interpret the Sociology of Prisons for Men', *The Howard Journal* 33(3): 193–202.

O'Donnell, I. (2004) 'Prison Rape in Context', *British Journal of Criminology* 44: 241–255.

Owen, B. (1998) *In the Mix: Struggle and Survival in a Women's Prison*, Albany: State University of New York Press.

Phillips, C. (2012) *The Multicultural Prison: Ethnicity, Masculinity, and Social Relations*, Oxford: Oxford University Press.

Reisig, M.D. (2001) 'The Champion, Contender, and Challenger: Top Ranked Books in Prison Studies', *The Prison Journal* 81(3): 389–407.

Rusche, G. and Kirchheimer, O. (1939) *Punishment and Social Structure*, New York: Russell and Russell.

Sabo, D., Kupers, T. and London, W. (eds) (2001) *Prison Masculinities*, Philadelphia, PA: Temple University Press.

Sapsford, R.J. (1983) *Life-sentence Prisoners: Reaction, Response and Change*, Milton Keynes: Open University Press.

Scacco, A. (1975) *Rape in Prison*, Springfield, IL: Charles C. Thomas.

Sim, J. (1994) 'Tougher than the Rest? Men in Prison', in T. Newburn and E. Stanko (eds) *Just Boys Doing Business*, London: Routledge.

Simon, J. (2007) *Governing Through Crime: How the War on Crime Transformed American Democracy and Created a Culture of Fear*, Oxford: Oxford University Press.

Skarbek, D. (2014) *The Social Order of the Underworld: How Prison Gangs Govern the American Penal System*, Oxford: Oxford University Press.

Sparks, R., Bottoms, A. and Hay, W. (1996) *Prisons and the Problem of Order*, Oxford: Clarendon Press.

Stevens, A. (2013) *Offender Rehabilitation and Therapeutic Communities: Enabling Change the TC Way*, Abingdon: Routledge.

Sykes, G. (1956) 'Men, Merchants and Toughs: A Study of Reactions to Imprisonment', *Social Problems*: 130–138.

Sykes, G. (1958) *The Society of Captives: A Study of a Maximum-Security Prison*, Princeton, NJ: Princeton University Press.

Sykes, G. (1995) 'The Structural-functional Perspective on Imprisonment', in T. Blomberg and S. Cohen (eds) *Punishment and Social Control: Essays in Honor of Sheldon L. Messinger*, New York: Aldine de Gruyter.

Sykes, G. and Messinger, S. (1960) 'The Inmate Social System', in R.A. Cloward et al. (eds) *Theoretical Studies in the Social Organization of the Prison*, New York: Social Science Research Council, 5–19.

Toch, H. (1977) *Living in Prison: The Ecology of Survival*, New York: The Free Press.

Ugelvik, T. (2014) *Power and Resistance in Prison: Doing Time, Doing Freedom*, Basingstoke: Palgrave Macmillan.

Useem, B. and Kimball, P. (1989) *States of Siege: US Prison Riots, 1971–1986*, Oxford: Oxford University Press.

Wacquant, L. (2000) 'The New "Peculiar Institution": On the Prison as Surrogate Ghetto', *Theoretical Criminology* 4(3): 377–389.

Wacquant, L. (2001) 'Deadly Symbiosis: Where Ghetto and Prison Meet and Merge', *Punishment and Society* 3(1): 95–133.

Wacquant, L. (2002) 'The Curious Eclipse of Prison Ethnography in the Age of Mass Incarceration', *Ethnography* 3(4): 371–398.

Walker, S. and Worrall, A. (2000) 'Life as a Woman: The Gendered Pains of Indeterminate Imprisonment', *Prison Service Journal* 132: 27–37.

Ward, D.A. and Kassebaum, G. (1965) *Women's Prison: Sex and Social Structure*, Chicago, IL: Aldine.

Wheeler, S. (1961) 'Socialization in Correctional Communities', *American Sociological Review* 26: 697–712.

Winfree, T., Newbold, G. and Tubb III, H. (2002) 'Prisoner Perspectives on Inmate Culture in New Mexico and New Zealand: A Descriptive Case Study', *The Prison Journal* 82(2): 213–233.

Woolf, L.J. (1991) *Prison Disturbances April 1990: Report of an Inquiry by the Rt Hon. Lord Justice Woolf (Parts I and II) and His Honour Stephen Tumim (Part II)* (The Woolf Report), London: HMSO.

Zaitzow, B. and Thomas, T. (eds) (2003) *Women in Prison: Gender and Social Control*, Boulder, CO: Lynne Rienner Publishers.

Zamble, E. and Porporino, F.J. (1988) *Coping, Behaviour and Adaptation in Prisons Inmates*, Secaucus, NJ: Springer-Verlag.

Chapter 6

Prison expansionism

Deborah H. Drake

Introduction

> The prison has become a looming presence in our society to an extent unparalleled in our history – or that of any other industrial democracy. Short of major wars, mass incarceration has been the most thoroughly implemented government social program of our time. And as with other government programs, it is reasonable to ask what we have gotten in return.
>
> (Currie 2013: 18)

The above quotation, expressed by American criminologist, Elliott Currie, in 1998, sums up the role that the prison has come to play in many countries around the world. According to the tenth edition of the *World Prison Population List* (Walmsley 2013), there are more than 10.2 million people living in custodial settings, either as detainees/remand or sentenced prisoners. The number of people imprisoned is growing on five continents. Walmsley states:

> In the 15 years since the first edition of the World Prison Population List the estimated world prison population has increased by some 25–30% but at the same time the world population has risen by over 20%. The world prison population rate has risen by about 6% from 136 per 100,000 of the world population to the current rate of 144.
>
> (Walmsley 2013: 1)

The prison has, increasingly, become an automatic policy response to an ever growing range of social issues and problems. There appears to be a growing consensus that imprisonment is an acceptable measure not only as a response to street, interpersonal and property crime, but also to activities not straightforwardly defined as 'criminal', such as mental illness, homelessness, public drunkenness, squatting, young people congregating or misclaiming benefits (Wacquant 2001; Rodger 2008; Squires 2008). The prison is a well-entrenched feature of national and international crime control strategies and is poised to play an ever greater role in both local and global social control agendas and security strategies.

This chapter examines the phenomenon of *prison expansionism*. It does so by first considering trends of imprisonment, demonstrating that despite differences within and between countries in the use of the prison, there is a continuing convergence of prison responses. These trends, however, are juxtaposed against the uncertain relationship between prison use and crime trends. It is argued that little conclusive evidence supports the use of imprisonment for the purpose of reducing crime rates. Moreover, it is suggested that questions need to be asked about the function of prisons in society and the extent to which they fulfil any of their imagined purposes. To this end, the chapter considers the purported uses of the prison alongside theorizations of its actual uses and functions. The chapter concludes by considering the problems of both prison and penal expansionism, questioning the logic and potential consequences of governing social policy problems with a chronically failing criminal justice response.

Imprisonment trends

The prison is one of the most widespread criminal justice sanctions in the world. However, attempting to measure rates and trends of imprisonment for international comparison is an inexact and potentially misleading exercise. There are differing conventions from country to country on who is counted in official prison figures and who is not. For example, remand prisoners, detained young people, or psychiatric patients might be included in the general adult prisoner population in some countries, but not in others. Thus, available statistics on prisoner numbers need to be considered and interpreted cautiously. At the same time, however, some attempt to examine general trends in rates of imprisonment over time can provide a useful overview of changes in prison populations.

Examination of a selection of imprisonment rates from 2003 and 2013 in North America, Europe and Australasia suggests differing trends and rates of change. Table 6.1 demonstrates some of the variations between different nations in the use of the prison. Whilst some countries show considerable increases between 2003 and 2013 (e.g. New

Table 6.1 Selected imprisonment rates per 100,000 population in 2003 and 2013, and percentage change

Country	2003	2013	% change
USA	701	716	+2.1
Russia	606	475	−21.6
New Zealand	155	192	+23.8
England and Wales	141	148	+4.9
Spain	138	147	+6.5
Australia	115	130	+13.0
Canada	116	118	+1.7
France	93	98	+5.3
Switzerland	68	82	+20.5
Netherlands	100	82	−18.0
Germany	98	79	−19.3
Denmark	64	73	+14.0
Sweden	73	67	−8.2
Finland	70	58	−17.1

Source: Walmsley 2003, 2013.

Zealand, Australia, Switzerland), others reveal a downward trend (Russia, the Netherlands, Germany). In addition to these broad comparisons, differences within countries are also worth noting. For example, the world 'leader' of imprisonment, the USA (716/100,000 in 2013), has considerable within-country variation in the use of the prison. Barker (2009: 4) argues that criminal justice policymaking and implementation in the USA is a subnational responsibility and thus individual states utilize the prison and other penal sanctions differently. She draws attention to 'gross disparities' in imprisonment rates in the USA, with Louisiana imprisoning over 800 people per 100,000, Texas and Mississippi at around 700, and Maine and Minnesota at 159 and 181, respectively (ibid.: 4). She argues:

> American penal sanctioning is fragmented, multidimensional, and often contradictory. It is an odd mix of policies and practices that are ad hoc, reactive to current events, and sometimes the result of long-term planning. The reality of American penal sanctioning is much more complicated, uneven, and obscure than the discussion of national trends allows.
>
> (Barker 2009: 6)

Barker's (2009) detailed work on the USA adds credence to the assertion that the use of punishment varies between different societies and within different societies at different times. However, taking account of the complexities of comparative measurement and despite both within and between country variations, it is widely agreed that the use of the prison has been on the increase over the last 20 years (Cavadino and Dignan 2006; Lappi-Seppälä 2012; Scott 2013; Walmsley 2013). In some respects, this increase is to be expected, given the rise of the world population, but there are numerous examples of where the increase of the prison population outstrips the growth of the general population. There have been particularly sharp rises in the prison populations in Latin America over the last 20 years, with Brazil seeing a 380% increase, Colombia a 322% increase, and a 158% increase in Mexico (Allen 2013: 3). Thus, whilst there are clear differences in the 'consumption' of punishment (Simon 2010), the use of the prison as a form of punishment and as a tool for crime and social control is continuing without challenge or question.

Prisons and crime control

The political justification and common sense purpose of prisons is that they play an integral role in keeping people safe from those amongst the general population who have proven their dangerousness or who have transgressed property laws or other laws that have been deemed important for maintaining social order, safety and security. Prisons are also widely believed to serve five other purposes (or some combination thereof): general prevention (deterrence from committing a crime in the first place); deterrence (from future offending); incapacitation; rehabilitation; and the delivery of justice (often seen to be operationalized though punishment). The difficulty is that there is, to date, no definitive evidence that prisons effectively fulfil any of these purposes in practice (Mathiesen 2000).

The most damning evidence for the use of the prison is the problematic and seemingly spurious relationship between crime rates and imprisonment rates. One of the reasons that the weakness of the crime–imprisonment relationship has been under-considered by criminologists and policymakers alike is that there are methodological difficulties in equating crime rates with imprisonment rates, especially when attempting national or international comparisons. As with imprisonment rates, official crime rates between jurisdictions are rarely recorded on a 'like-for-like' basis. Moreover, official crime rates might differ quite substantially from rates of victimization, which means that there is not a sufficiently accurate way to measure the true extent of property or interpersonal crime within a given country. Additionally, the impact that imprisonment may or may not have on a given type of crime is not well understood or easy to examine. National statistics often do not publish matched data on prisoner populations by recorded crime and sentence length, which are figures that would be required in order to examine effects of imprisonment in relation to particular crimes (Aebi and Kuhn 2000). Based, however, on the crime rate figures that are available, no clear relationship between crime rates and imprisonment rates is in evidence.

A number of detailed research studies have illustrated that correlations between crime rates and imprisonment rates are weak (Young and Brown 1993: 23–33; Beckett and Western 2001: 49–50). The Council of Europe has long concluded that there is no relationship between crime and prison rates, arguing that: 'high overall crime rates do not necessarily induce high prison rates and vice versa' (Council of Europe 2003: 193). Furthermore, Lappi-Seppälä (2008: 340), who has examined associations between crime and imprisonment rates cross-sectionally and over time, has argued that:

> It is possible to reduce the number of prisoners during times when crime rates are increasing (Finland 1980–90 and Austria 1985–90). It is also possible to increase the imprisonment rates during times when crime rates are stable (Netherlands 1985–2000) and to maintain both of them as stable (Denmark 1985–95, France 1985–2005). And it has been possible to increase imprisonment rates when crime rates were falling (England during most of the 1990s, New Zealand 1995–2005, and the United States 1990–2005).

These discontinuities between crime and prison rates are also found between different legal jurisdictions within countries, such as the USA. Barker (2009: 4) acknowledges that sometimes high imprisonment rates correlate with high crime rates within given states in the USA, but some states with low crime rates have high imprisonment rates.

To look more closely at the way it is assumed that prisons work, it is helpful to consider the role of the prison as a deterrent – either in a general and preventative sense (i.e. as an ominous threat that prevents people from law breaking in the first place) or as a specific, consequential effect (i.e. to teach people a retrospective 'lesson' that will keep them from engaging in further law breaking in the future). The notion that prison 'works' as a deterrent seems to be 'just common-sense', particularly when viewed from a utilitarian, rational or cost–benefit perspective. However, with respect to both general deterrence and specific deterrence, Scott (2013: 12) persuasively argues that 'not only is it actually impossible to determine if deterrence has a positive effect (we cannot measure what does not happen) but what evidence we do have – recidivism rates – overwhelmingly indicates that prison does not prevent "crime"'.

Some of the most conclusive evidence on the spuriousness between the use of the prison and crime reduction (specific deterrence) has been revealed through detailed studies at jurisdictional levels. For example, Spohn and Holleran (2002) examined the question of whether imprisonment rates reduced the likelihood of reoffending amongst people convicted of a felony in Jackson County, Missouri. Their study revealed robust evidence that people given a prison sentence reoffended more often and more quickly than people given a probation order. Likewise, comparisons of youth imprisonment practices and percentages of young people imprisoned for offences classified as murder, violent crime, property crime and drug offences, in California and Texas between 1995 and 2005, show no impact on rates of crime in relation to imprisonment rates (Males et al. 2007).

Other frequently cited reasons for the importance of prison as a crime control tool are their role in the delivery of justice, rehabilitative ambitions and their incapacitation effect. With respect to the delivery of justice, there are some firmly held philosophical arguments that favour the importance of the prison as a symbolic means of formally denouncing an activity that is collectively viewed by society as wrong. It has long been argued that prisons provide a necessary social function as places of blame and punishment (Durkheim 1997 [1893]). However, as with many of the other beliefs about the prison, the extent to which prisons really fulfil this function is not sufficiently evidenced in practice. Whilst the use of the prison may offer some form of symbolic comfort to victims of crime, members of the general public or to various newspaper and tabloid journalists, these symbolic effects must be weighed up against the tangible and actual effects and social costs of imprisonment (see Drake 2012; Currie 2013). Furthermore, and with respect to rehabilitation, it is highly questionable whether an institution fundamentally founded on principles of punishment and less eligibility can ever provide a genuinely rehabilitative or restorative function (Mathiesen 2000; Sim 2009; Drake 2012).

The incapacitation function of prison, it might be argued, can hold some value as a last resort safety measure for a person who may pose imminent danger (Gilligan 2001). However, the vast majority of people in prison are not 'imminently' dangerous. Most people in prison are from socially disadvantaged, impoverished backgrounds and the majority of them are convicted for acquisitive or drug-related crimes (Reiman and Leighton 2010). Moreover, the need temporarily to hold a person in secure conditions for their own safety or the safety of others need not include a punishment dimension. Indeed, the rationale of utilizing prisons as places of 'secure containment' has been called into question on the grounds that they are fundamentally violent places that perpetrate and exacerbate harm, rather than ameliorating or reversing it (Gilligan 2001; Kupers 2006; Drake 2012).

It would seem that none of the supposed purposes and functions of the prison translate into the common sense outcomes that people expect or want. The above discussed 'mythologies' of the prison are, in some respects, perpetuated through a kind of thought trickery, rooted in a variety of moral beliefs and long-held philosophical theories about what 'should be done' to prevent or to respond to transgressive acts. However, as psychiatrist James Gilligan has argued, we have been conducting a:

> great social experiment to test the hypothesis that we could prevent violence by defining it as a crime … and then punishing those who commit it with more violence of our own (which we define as justice). Three thousand years is long enough to test any hypothesis, and the results of this experiment have been in for some time now.
>
> (Gilligan 2001: 745)

The persistence of prisons, despite the evidence

Given the lack of evidence that prisons fulfil any of their expected functions or purposes, what accounts for their persistent and expanding use? As might be expected, the social and political conditions that support prison expansionism are not well understood. Cavadino and Dignan (2006) have argued that efforts to explain either variations in imprisonment rates or the spread in prison use have proven a difficult task. They suggest, however, that there are general associations between political economies, income inequalities and punishment, and thus it has been found that social and economic factors are the strongest predictors of both rates of crime and imprisonment rates. These linkages and interconnections have been systematically studied and revealed in a large number of research studies.

Drawing on longitudinal data, Sutton (2000) identified strong correlations between social and political factors and crime rates. His research (ibid.: 376–377) found that independent of changes in crime rates, prison numbers decline when employment rates increase, declines in welfare spending are associated with growths in imprisonment rates, right-wing governments, and that conservative politics are associated with increased prisoner numbers. These results have been confirmed in a variety of subsequent studies, where correlations between uses of imprisonment and particular political economic and labour market conditions have been found (Cavadino and Dignan 2006; Downes and Hansen 2006; Lacey 2008; Lappi-Seppälä 2008; Pratt 2008a, 2008b; Snacken 2010). The sum total of this body of work consistently reveals that trends in penal severity and prison excess or parsimony are closely associated with public sentiments, welfare provision, income distribution, political structures and legal cultures.

The above findings, taken alongside the continued failures of the prison, seem to suggest that ideology (i.e. ideas that distort reality to justify the status quo) and a specific ideology of imprisonment (i.e. that 'prison works') are significant drivers behind prison expansionism. Importantly, it must be recognized that the use of imprisonment requires the belief that the wilful exclusion, segregation or exile of certain members of society is an appropriate response when certain socially censured acts are committed. It might be argued, then, that the increasing dominance of the prison as a crime control tool must be indicative of increasing political and societal commitments to these exclusionary methods as a means of managing social problems. With respect to the use of the prison as an exclusionary device, prisons become places where societies seem symbolically to censure and actively segregate those social members who are not fully participating in social life or are engaging in activities that attract social condemnation. The choice of imprisonment over other sanctions suggests, in some respects, a weakening of state commitments to understanding and solving the social causes of crime and opting instead for a simple, symbolic response. Arguments that have been put forward by Jonathan Simon (2009), in his 'governing through crime' thesis, suggest that the social consequences of an increasingly unequal and divided society are, to some extent, obscured and deflected by an increasing focus by government on problems of crime. Simon's arguments are particularly apropos in Western, capitalist, neo-liberal/liberal market economies wherein governments have withdrawn their commitment to welfarist concerns that included a more directive approach to managing economic inequalities. Directing public attention towards issues of crime and punishment serves a useful government function, as Scott (2013: 311) argues, in that it:

not only demonstrates strength but can also become an invaluable mechanism through which politicians in liberal market economies can mystify and direct attention away from the growing gap between the rich and the poor and the radical retrenchment and penal reorientation of social welfare provision.

Whilst the work of Simon and other theorists such as Garland (2001) and Wacquant (2001) provides a useful blueprint for understanding the political drivers for prison expansionism in developed, Western democracies, their arguments cannot provide a clear explanation for global trends in penal excess. It might be argued, however, that the reliance on imprisonment in Western democracies as the social and economic policy of choice for a range of social ills is symbolically important beyond sovereign borders too. Prisons researchers working in developing countries have noted the tendency for particular justice practices and reforms – especially those associated with the use of imprisonment – to be exported (or imported) to the 'global South'. Andrew Jefferson, discussing the issues of human rights and penal norms in Africa, has argued that justice sector reform has become integral to development aid policy as a part of 'state building projects'. In countries emerging from war (he gives the example of Sierra Leone since 2002) or moving from authoritarian rule to democracy (he cites Nigeria since 1999), criminal justice systems are targeted for two major reasons:

> Firstly, because an accountable justice system is necessary to ensure the rule of law is followed. Secondly, the state security apparatus, including prisons and the police, has often been used as a repressive tool of the state pre-transition to democracy. Thus, in a new dispensation the old security institutions are seen as illegitimate and in need of transformation.
>
> (Jefferson 2007: 33; see also Chapter 24, this volume)

The role of the prison as a seemingly legitimate means to signal effective 'state building' in developing or conflict-ridden nations is all the more troubling, given the 'fiasco' of the prison to fulfil its own purposes (Mathiesen 2000: 141), as discussed earlier in this chapter. In addition, as De Giorgi (2007) has argued, the links between the use of the prison and particular forms of market capitalism as applied within a global context have the capacity to assist in 'configuring a paradigm of global less eligibility,' which extends the relationship between social structure and punishment 'well beyond borders' (ibid.: 18). The potential danger of a paradigm of global less eligibility can be brought into fuller view by looking closely at the linkages between social structure, political economy and patterns of punishment. As Reiman and Leighton (2010: 187) argue, 'when the poor individual is found guilty of a crime, the criminal justice system acquits the society of its responsibility not only for crime *but for poverty as well*' (emphasis in original).

Social and economic structures and prison expansionism

In an interview conducted by Avery F. Gordon with professor and prison activist Angela Y. Davis, published in the journal *Race and Class*, Davis notes that imprisonment has become the first, not last, resort for many social problems that blight the lives of those in poverty; problems that become 'conveniently grouped together under the category "crime" and by the automatic attribution of criminal behaviour to people of colour' (Gordon

1999: 146–147). She goes on to say that homelessness, unemployment, drug addiction and illiteracy are just some of the problems that disappear from public view when the individuals contending with them are incarcerated. Prisons thus perform a 'feat of magic', except that:

> Prisons do not disappear problems, they disappear human beings and the practice of disappearing vast numbers of people from poor, immigrant and racially marginalised communities literally has become big business.
>
> (Gordon 1999: 146–147)

Whilst the linkages between social structure, political economy and the use of imprisonment have long been recognized (Rusche and Kirchheimer 1968), the importance of the problem of disproportionality in prisons and the corporatization of imprisonment have received comparatively less attention. Each will be considered briefly in turn.

There are dominant social structures that support exclusion, confinement and ostracism as appropriate reactions to certain social problems. It might be argued that a society that favours the use of the prison is one that:

- is primarily or at least foundationally oriented around the interests of more affluent social members (middle or upper classes);
- has heavily prescribed gender roles, where the economic, social and political status of women is subordinated (and unequal) to the status of men;
- sees black, minority ethnic or immigrant groups disproportionately occupying economic, social and political margins.

To begin with the final point in the above list, the disproportionate over-representation of black, minority ethnic or immigrant groups in marginalized economic, social and political positions is mirrored by their over-representation in prison populations (see Chapter 32, this volume). Warde (2013) provides a compelling comparison of black male disproportionality in the criminal justice systems of the USA, Canada and England. Each of these countries shows a grossly disproportionate number of black men occupying prison places, particularly when compared with their numbers in free society. Warde's work suggests a common pattern of differential selection and processing in various criminal justice practices that results in disproportionate numbers of young black men being policed, arrested, convicted and imprisoned. He argues that criminal justice processes are systemically drawn along and reinforce colour lines as well as lines of economic disadvantage. Likewise, both Angela Davis (in Gordon 1999) and Loïc Wacquant (2001) argue that the fundamental role of the prison is, quite clearly, to contain and control the poorest classes – many of whom are also people of colour. Wacquant argues:

> The increasingly tight meshing of the hyperghetto with the carceral system suggests that … lower-class African Americans now dwell, not in a society with prisons as their white compatriots do, but in *the first genuine prison society* of history.
>
> (Wacquant 2001: 120–121, emphasis in original)

The writing and work of Bryan Stevenson, professor of law at New York University and executive director of the Equal Justice Initiative, takes these ideas even further. In a widely publicized article in *Smithsonian Magazine*, written by Chris Hedges, Stevenson argues that mass incarceration defines American society in the way that slavery once did (see also Stevenson and Friedman 1994). In this article, paraphrasing Stevenson's arguments, Hedges observes that one in every three black men in their twenties is in prison, on probation or parole, or bound in some other way to the criminal justice system. This, he says, has far-reaching social consequences:

> Once again families are broken apart ... huge numbers of black men are disenfranchised, because of their criminal records ... people are locked out of the political and economic system. Once again we harbor within our midst black outcasts, pariahs. As poet Yusef Komunyakaa said: 'The cell block has replaced the auction block.'
>
> (Hedges 2012: 4)

Other minority groups are similarly marginalized, economically excluded and subsequently confined in other liberal market-based countries around the world. Individuals from migrant and/or minority ethnic groups are often relegated to impoverished and disadvantaged social positions, primarily due to precarious employment prospects and a highly insecure labour market. Prison systems in the UK and Europe reveal over-representations of foreign nationals and other 'irregular migrant' groups who are excluded from any form of social welfare support (Scott 2013). It is important to recognize also that black and ethnic minority groups are not only more likely to occupy marginalized groups and become caught up in the criminal justice system, but they are also amongst the least likely to have their voices heard as victims of crime.

With respect to the other two points listed above which identify the dominant social structures that support exclusion and confinement as solutions to social problems, it is important to recognize the foundations on which criminal law and criminal justice are built. Barbara Hudson (2006) has argued that criminal law in most Western societies fundamentally reflects the positioning of the dominant white, affluent, adult male. She states: 'it is he whose behaviour law has in mind when it constructs its proscriptions and remedies; and it is this subject who constructs the law' (ibid.: 30). The consequences of these inherent biases in criminal law and, consequently, in the apparatus of criminal justice processing is that prisons were established almost exclusively to focus on harms or crimes perpetrated by poor men and only exceptionally on crimes of the powerful. Moreover, neither criminal law nor the criminal justice system was designed to protect women, children or members of minority ethnic or sexuality groups from the harms they may suffer as a result of their vulnerability and voicelessness (e.g. children and paedophilia or trafficking), gender (e.g. rape, domestic violence, trafficking), or ethnicity and sexuality (e.g. hate crimes). As some of these forms of harm are becoming more recognized, they have begun to be processed through criminal justice systems. Prisons therefore are, increasingly, relied upon to absorb growing numbers of people convicted of sexual or hate-based offences. The difficulty is not that these offences are now becoming better recognized, it is the fact that the prison is, increasingly, the only means by which problems associated with social and economic structure are being dealt with. Thus, as with the other interpersonal or acquisitive crimes for which the prison has long been the (failing) solution, there is little hope of permanently solving or even significantly reducing the occurrence of crimes associated with the social inequalities that are drawn along the lines of age, gender, 'race' or sexuality.

As set out at the start of this chapter, the prolific and increasing use of the prison has meant, in many jurisdictions, ever growing prisoner numbers. Large prisoner populations coupled with continued political commitment to liberal market models of economic development have meant that prisons and punishment – like other traditionally state-run institutions – have become areas for private economic investment and growth. Again, the USA leads the way with the most intricate development of private prison expansionism and the creation of what Davis (in Gordon 1999) and others (Wehr and Aseltine 2013) have characterized as a 'prison industrial complex', whereby private capital has become enmeshed in the delivery of punishment in a variety of ways and consequently (because of their considerable profit potential) has become increasingly central to the US economy.

The prison system in England and Wales includes the highest number of prison places run by private companies in Europe. As of March 2014, 13,449 people or 16% of the prisoner population were held in private prisons in England and Wales. This contrasts with 8.7% of the total US prison population housed by private sector prisons (Bromley Briefings 2014; see also Chapter 9, this volume). A number of major corporations are involved in what has become known as the 'security industry' and shares in these companies are traded on the stock market. Geo Group, Serco and G4S are all privately run 'security firms' which build, operate and manage prisons. Human suffering, first in the forms of poverty and crime and then in their proffered solutions – prisons and punishment – has become a 'big business, growth industry'. The development of a privatized market for prisons and punishment is surely implicated in the continuing growth and spread of prison expansionism. On the emergence of the private prison industry, Leighton (1995: 390) has argued that it creates 'large numbers of people who have a vested financial interest in having a large and increasing incarceration rate'. Likewise, in their seminal book, now in its tenth edition (2012), Reiman and Leighton (2010: 177) write that their work fundamentally attempts to show 'how the *rich get richer* WHILE *the poor get prison*, but the privatization movement points to a new phrase in which *the rich get richer* BECAUSE *the poor get prison!*' (emphasis in original).

Conclusion

One of the key arguments made in this chapter is that the rise and spread in the use of the prison is highly associated with government decisions to withdraw from a welfare-based approach to solving social problems. Over several years, governments in the USA and England and Wales (particularly, but some other European countries too) have been increasingly choosing to manage a range of social problems through the control and regulation imposed by criminal justice policy as opposed to welfare-based social policies. This has, increasingly, become the case for governments from both the left and the right wherein even when left-leaning governments are in power, their seemingly welfare-based policies, which might purport to address problems of inequality, are in practice oriented towards control, surveillance and ultimately criminalization (Dixon and Gadd 2006).

It is evident that penal measures are more frequently being called upon as means of *prevention* as well as the *response* to a wide range of issues that were once dealt with through informal means or through regulatory mechanisms or welfare-based policies. For example, breaches of immigration rules, benefits claimant regulations and a seemingly ever-increasing array of activities that are deemed 'anti-social' now fall within the purview of the criminal justice system. Punitive measures have permeated a number of different social institutions and this reflects a trend towards a more endemic and widespread 'penal culture' that extends well beyond the prison, thus contributing not just to prison expansionism, but *penal expansionism*.

The continued use of the prison and penal measures to solve social problems obscures a number of important and pressing social issues. The first, as the chapter has illustrated, is that there is little evidence that prisons fulfil any of their expected functions or purposes. In addition, their failure provides robust evidence that taking a punishing approach when attempting to resolve a social conflict is the reaction least likely to resolve the problem and, indeed, the evidence suggests that it serves to exacerbate it (Gilligan 2001). The second issue that is obscured is the fact that criminal law and its corresponding penal sanctions tend to focus on the social problems and conflicts that emerge between individuals and thus pertain to interpersonal harms and property crimes. Corporate and state crimes are left largely unacknowledged by the criminal justice system due to an overemphasis and seeming obsession by the media and politicians to focus almost exclusively on populations labelled 'problematic' or on certain types of harm. The ways in which social, economic and political structures might perpetuate inequalities, injustices or perpetrate socially harmful activities remain invisible. This is not to say, however, that imprisonment or other penal measures would be an appropriate response to state or corporate representatives who engage in harmful activities either. The danger, of course, is that if crimes of the powerful began to be more frequently recognized then their transgressions would be dealt with by the same failing system that is currently deployed. The difficulty here fundamentally lies in foregrounding of individual factors *to the exclusion of* contextual or structural factors as an explanation for transgression. Locating problems of crime or social harm within individuals obviates the capacity to view the roles of power, politics and economics in the way the social world and its regulatory and legal frameworks are constructed. Penal and criminal justice policies that dismiss the role of social structure either in the way 'crime' is defined or in the way it is prosecuted, and instead locate the sources of crime more firmly within individuals, contribute to the mythology surrounding prisons that prevents more critical public engagement with the question Elliott Currie asks in the quotation that opened this chapter: What have we got in return?

Bibliography

Aebi, M.F. and Kuhn, A. (2000) 'Influences on the Prisoner Rate: Number of Entries into Prison, Length of Sentences and Crime Rate', *European Journal on Crime Policy and Research* 8(1): 65–75.

Allen, R. (2013) *The Use and Practice of Imprisonment: Current Trends and Future Challenges*, Vienna: Penal Reform International.

Barker, V. (2009) *The Politics of Imprisonment: How the Democratic Process Shapes the Way America Punishes Offenders*, Oxford: Oxford University Press.

Beckett, K. and Western, B. (2001) 'Governing Social Marginality: Welfare, Incarceration and the Transformation of State Policy', *Punishment and Society* 3(1): 43–59.

Bromley Briefings (2014) *Prison: The Facts*, London: Prison Reform Trust.

Cavadino, M. and Dignan, J. (2006) 'Penal Policy and Political Economy', *Criminology and Criminal Justice* 6(4): 435–456.

Council of Europe (2003) *European Sourcebook of Crime and Justice Statistics*, second edn, The Hague: Wetenschappelijk Onderzoek-en Documentatiecentrum.

Currie, E. (2013) *Crime and Punishment in America*, New York: Henry Holt and Company.

De Giorgi, A. (2007) 'Rethinking the Political Economy of Punishment', *Criminal Justice Matters* 70(1), Winter: 17–18.

Dixon, B. and Gadd, D. (2006) 'Getting the Message? New Labour and the Criminalization of Hate', *Criminology and Criminal Justice* 6(3): 309–328.

Downes, D. and Hansen, K. (2006) 'Welfare and Punishment in Comparative Context', in S. Armstrong and L. McAra (eds) *Perspectives on Punishment: The Contours of Control*, Oxford: Oxford University Press.

Drake, D.H. (2012) *Prisons, Punishment and the Pursuit of Security*, Basingstoke: Palgrave.

Durkheim, E. (1997 [1893]) *The Division of Labor in Society*, New York: Free Press.

Garland, D. (2001) *The Culture of Control: Crime and Social Order in Contemporary Society*, Oxford: Oxford University Press.

Gilligan, J. (2001) *Preventing Violence*, London: Thames and Hudson.

Gordon, A.F. (1999) 'Globalism and the Prison Industrial Complex: An Interview with Angela Davis', *Race and Class* 40(2/3): 145–157.

Hedges, C. (2012) 'Why Mass Incarceration Defines Us as a Society', *Smithsonian Magazine*, December, www.smithsonianmag.com/people-places/why-mass-incarceration-defines-us-as-a -society-135793245/?no-ist (accessed 11 May 2014).

Hudson, B. (2006) 'Beyond White Man's Justice: Race, Gender and Justice in Late Modernity', *Theoretical Criminology* 10(1): 29–47.

Jefferson, A.M. (2007) 'The Political Economy of Rights: Exporting Penal Norms to Africa', *Criminal Justice Matters* 70(1): 33–34.

Kupers, T.A. (2006) 'How to Create Madness in Prison', in D. Jones (ed.) *Humane Prisons*, Oxford: Radcliffe Publishing.

Lacey, N. (2008) *The Prisoners' Dilemma: Political Economy and Punishment in Contemporary Democracies*, Hamlyn Lectures 2007, Cambridge: Cambridge University Press.

Lappi-Seppälä, T. (2007) 'Penal Policy in Scandinavia', in M. Tonry (ed.) *Crime, Punishment and Politics in Comparative Perspective, Crime and Justice: A Review of the Research 36*, Chicago, IL: Chicago University Press, 217–296.

Lappi-Seppälä, T. (2008) 'Trust, Welfare and Political Culture: Explaining Difference in National Penal Policies', in M. Tonry (ed.) *Crime, Punishment and Politics in Comparative Perspective, Crime and Justice: A Review of the Research 37*, Chicago, IL: Chicago University Press, 313–387.

Lappi-Seppälä, T. (2012) 'Explaining National Differences in the Use of Imprisonment', in S. Snacken and E. Dumortier (eds) *Resisting Punitiveness in Europe?*, London: Routledge, 35–72.

Leighton, P. (1995) 'Industrialized Social Control', *Peace Review: A Journal of Social Justice*, Special Issue 7(3–4): 387–392.

Males, M., Stahlkopf, C. and Macallair, D. (2007) *Crime Rates and Youth Incarceration in Texas and California Compared: Public Safety or Public Waste?* Centre on Crime and Criminal Justice, www.jdaihelpdesk.org/Research%20and%20Resources/Crime%20Rates%20and%20Youth%20 Incarceration%20in%20Texas%20and%20California%20Compared.pdf (accessed 22 June 2014).

Mathiesen, T. (2000) *Prison on Trial*, second edn, Winchester: Waterside Press.

Pratt, J. (2008a) 'Scandinavian Exceptionalism in an Era of Penal Excess Part I: The Nature and Roots of Scandinavian Exceptionalism', *British Journal of Criminology* 48(2): 119–137.

Pratt, J. (2008b) 'Scandinavian Exceptionalism in an Era of Penal Excess Part II: Does Scandinavian Exceptionalism Have a Future?', *British Journal of Criminology* 48(3): 275–292.

Reiman, J. and Leighton, P. (2010) *The Rich Get Richer and the Poor Get Prison: Ideology, Class and Criminal Justice*, ninth edn, Boston, MA: Allyn and Bacon.

Rodger, J.J. (2008) *Criminalising Social Policy: Anti-Social Behaviour and Welfare in a De-Civilised Society*, Cullompton: Willan.

Rusche, G. and Kirchheimer, O. (1968) *Punishment and Social Structure*, New York: Russell and Russell.

Scott, D. (ed.) (2013) *Why Prison?* Cambridge: Cambridge University Press.

Sim, J. (2009) *Punishment and Prisons: Power and the Carceral State*, London: Sage.

Simon, J. (2009) *Governing through Crime: How the War on Crime Transformed American Democracy and Created a Culture of Fear*, Oxford: Oxford University Press.

Simon, J. (2010) 'Do these Prisons Make me Look Fat?: Moderating the USA's Consumption of Punishment', *Theoretical Criminology* 14(3): 257–272.

Snacken, S. (2010) 'Resisting Punitiveness in Europe?', *Theoretical Criminology* 14(3): 273–292.

Spohn, C. and Holleran, D. (2002) 'The Effect of Imprisonment on Recidivism Rates of Felony Offenders: A Focus on Drug Offenders', *Criminology* 40(2): 329–358.

Squires, P. (ed.) (2008) *ASBO Nation: The Criminalisation of Nuisance*, Bristol: The Policy Press.

Stevenson, B.A. and Friedman, R.E. (1994) 'Deliberate Indifference: Judicial Tolerance of Racial Bias in Criminal Justice', *Washington and Lee Law Review* 51(2): 509–527.

Sutton, J.R. (2000) 'Imprisonment and Social Classification in Five Common-Law Democracies, 1955–1985', *The American Journal of Sociology* 106(2): 350–386.

Wacquant, L. (2001) 'The Penalisation of Poverty and the Rise of Neoliberalism', *European Journal on Criminal Policy and Research* 9(4): 401–412.

Walmsley, R. (2003) *World Prison Population List*, fourth edn, London: International Centre for Prison Studies.

Walmsley, R. (2013) *World Prison Population List*, tenth edn, London: International Centre for Prison Studies.

Warde, B. (2013) 'Black Male Disproportionality in the Criminal Justice Systems of the USA, Canada and England: A Comparative Analysis of Incarceration', *Journal of African American Studies* 17: 461–479.

Wehr, K. and Aseltine, E. (2013) *Beyond the Prison Industrial Complex: Crime and Incarceration in the 21st Century*, New York: Routledge.

Young, W. and Brown, M. (1993) 'Cross-National Comparisons of Imprisonment', in M. Tonry (ed.) *Crime and Justice: A Review of the Research 17*, Chicago, IL: Chicago University Press, 1–49.

Chapter 7

Prison design and carceral space

Dominique Moran, Yvonne Jewkes and Jennifer Turner

Introduction

Prison design is crucial to the relationship between the 'carceral' and the state, in that it is the process which determines, in large part, how the goals of a criminal justice system are materially expressed (Moran 2015). With this in mind, this chapter takes forward the notion of prison buildings as coded, scripted entities, exploring the design of prisons and the intentions behind their operation in terms of the imperatives of states and their criminal justice systems. It pursues the notion that the design of carceral space has a significant role to play in understanding the extent to which the aims of a carceral system are translated into experiences of imprisonment.

Drawing on scholarship at the intersection between criminology and carceral geography (Moran 2015), the chapter begins by briefly tracing the history and significance of prison design, with a focus on the UK. It suggests that prison buildings can be read, and are experienced, as symbolic of the relationship between the 'carceral' and a punitive state – in terms of who prisoners 'are' and what they represent in the minds of those involved in producing the buildings in which to incarcerate them. Outlining the policy context for current UK prison building, the chapter then sketches out the processes involved in the construction of new-build prisons and the imperatives that shape their design; it briefly draws out contrasts between the UK and other penal regimes; and it suggests that both the intentions behind their design and the lived experience of the resulting prisons are worthy of further interrogation.

Prison design

> [J]ails and prisons represent more than just warehouses of bed space for arrested or convicted men and women. They are more complicated environments than just good or bad, comfortable or not. The design of a jail or prison is critically related to the philosophy of the institution, or maybe even of the entire criminal justice system. It is the physical manifestation of a society's goals and approaches for dealing with arrested and/or convicted men and women, and it is a stage for acting out plans and programs for their addressing their future.
>
> (Wener 2012: 7)

As this quote suggests, prison design is about more than accommodating and securing populations from whom society needs to be protected – although these two functions are themselves challenging and complex. The design of a prison reflects the penal philosophy of the prevailing social system; its ideas about what prison is 'for' and what it is considered to 'do'; and the messages about the purpose of imprisonment that it wants to communicate to prisoners, potential offenders and to society at large. As comparative criminology points out, offending behaviour is sanctioned in different ways in different places. Punishment and crime are argued to have very little to do with one another, with imprisonment rates 'to a great degree a function of criminal justice and social policies that either encourage or discourage the use of incarceration' (Aebi and Kuhn 2000: 66, cited in Von Hofer 2003: 23; see also Tonry 2004; and Chapters 4 and 6, this volume), rather than a function of the number of crimes that are committed. Imprisonment is not inevitable, therefore; rather it is a conscious choice about the appropriate response to offending behaviour, and the purpose of that response – in terms of the prevailing understanding of what it is that prison is intended to achieve – both for society as a whole, and for offenders themselves (Moran 2015).

The following statement, made to *The Guardian* newspaper by the then UK Home Secretary Theresa May, neatly sums up the intentions of imprisonment in the UK, as expressed by politicians to the electorate:

> Prison works but it must be made to work better. The key for members of the public is that they want criminals to be punished. They want them to be taken off the streets. They also want criminals who come out of prison to go straight. What our system is failing to do at the moment is to deliver that for the public. And that's what we want to do.
>
> (*The Guardian*, 14 December 2010; see Travis 2010: n.p.)

The notion that 'prison works' is of course highly contentious, as numerous contributions to this volume attest, but in her statement the home secretary communicated three 'aims' of imprisonment: to remove ('taking them off the streets'); to punish; and to rehabilitate ('going straight'). These aims characterize most prison systems, albeit the extent to which prison can achieve all, or indeed any, of these ends is highly debatable; and the balance *between* them – both as stated in public discourse, and as manifest and experienced in the criminal justice system itself – can vary widely (see Chapter 3). Just as prison design has yet to be foregrounded in academic literature, it also seems strangely largely disconnected from public discourses of imprisonment, despite being an integral part of prison commissioning and the expansion of the carceral estate.[1]

Whereas the USA and Western Europe are highly incarcerative (or perhaps hypercarcerative), other countries are by contrast *decarcerative* – actively deploying different techniques and sanctions to decrease their prison populations. This divergence reflects a different underlying principle of imprisonment. For example, a 'less eligibility' principle informs much prison policy in the USA and Western Europe, based on an understanding that prisoners should 'suffer' in prison, not only through the loss of freedom but also by virtue of prison conditions, which should be of a worse standard than those available to the poorest free workers. In other contexts, such as in Finland, prison conditions are intended to correspond as closely as possible to general living conditions in society (Ministry of Justice of Finland 1975). Penalties for offences are implemented in such a way that they do not unduly interfere with prisoners' participation in society, but as far as possible, promote it. The intention here is neither to oversimplify nor to romanticize the 'penal exceptionalism' of the Nordic countries (Pratt and Eriksson 2012; Ugelvik and

Dullum 2012; Shammas 2014), but rather to point out that both the different philoso-phies of imprisonment, and the different relative prison populations that these deliver, require and enable different intentions to be translated into the built form of prisons.

With regard to Anglophone penal 'excess' rather than Nordic 'exceptionalism', as Theresa May's comments suggested, prisons must not only deliver a punished offender, but must do so in a way that satisfies the 'assumed punitiveness' of the public (Frost 2010; Garland 2001; Greer and Jewkes 2005; Hancock 2004; Young 2003) – those whose apparent desire is for 'prisoners to be punished'. To these ends, prisons are subject to a new government-imposed 'public acceptability test' which, although devised to provide a check on educational and constructive activities that prisoners are permitted to undertake while serving their sentences (following negative media coverage of a comedy course at HMP Whitemoor), also impacts on ideas around what prisons should look like and feel like. UK prisons today must both punish and *be seen* to punish, as well as removing offenders from society in order to deliver some form of rehabilitation that reduces their future likelihood of reoffending. Although as UK prison architecture has evolved, there has been no transparent, linear translation of 'punishment' into prison design, the interplay between philosophies of punishment and theories of prison design has resulted in preferred types of building thought capable of accomplishing the prevailing goals of imprisonment – which themselves have changed over time as penal philosophies have ebbed and flowed (Johnston 2000; Jewkes and Johnston 2007).

A comprehensive survey of the history of UK prison design and the interrelationships between the various influences that have affected it (considered in detail by Brodie et al. 1999, 2002; and Fairweather and McConville 2000) was discussed in depth by Jewkes and Johnston in the first edition of this *Handbook* (2007), and is beyond the scope of this chapter. However, considering prison buildings as scripted expressions of political–eco-nomic imperatives allows the aesthetics of prison buildings to be viewed as imbued with cultural symbolism (Moran and Jewkes 2015). Although when focusing on the UK carceral estate there is no 'typical' prison, for the majority, exterior architectural features render them instantly recognizable, within that cultural context, as places of detention and punishment. Mid-19th-century prisons, for example, were built to resemble fortified castles (e.g. HMP Leeds 1847), or gothic monasteries (e.g. Strangeways, 1868), and exterior facades communicated the perils of offending and the retributive power of the state. The 20th century gradually saw a more utilitarian style reject the decorative aes-thetic, communicating an ideal of modern, 'rational' justice and authority (Hancock and Jewkes 2011). In the 1960s and 1970s, new prisons such as Gartree and Long Lartin, whilst still communicating authority and efficiency, echoed the austere, functional styles of high, progressive modernism (ibid.). By the end of the 20th century, UK prison architecture demanded higher walls, tighter perimeters and heightened surveillance in response to earlier escapes, riots and security breaches,[2] and in parallel with the rise of 'new punitiveness' in wider criminal justice policy. The evolution of prison architecture has at various points been intended to communicate a message about the nature of the imprisoning state and the legitimacy of its power to imprison, with the 'audience' for the various messages of this architecture being the inmate who receives the punishment handed down by the state, and society at large to whom imprisonment as punishment must be legitimated (Moran and Jewkes 2015).

Research into prison design

As early as the 1930s, architectural researchers pointed out the importance of prison design in shaping the experience of incarceration. In 1931, Robert Davison, former director of research for the *Architectural Record*, published a caustic article that castigated both US prison commissioners – for lack of knowledge about what they wanted new prisons to achieve – and penologists – for being 'surprisingly insensitive to the enormous importance of the building in the treatment of the prisoner' (Davison 1931: 39). Recognizing that the design of prisons seemed to be a blind spot for the criminal justice system, he advocated that it was the job of the architect, even though they could 'scarcely be expected to be a penal expert', to indicate the 'necessity for a prolonged and careful study of this problem', and for 'thorough research in [prison] building' (ibid.).

Despite the subsequent expansion of the penal estate and the immense investment in prison building in the UK and elsewhere, prison design has received remarkably little academic attention, and Davison's 'prolonged and careful study' is still to materialize. In the early 1960s, interest in new prison architecture and design reached its peak when a special issue of *British Journal of Criminology* was devoted to the topic. In subsequent decades, however, criminological interest in this subject seems to have waned; academic commentary on prison design has been sparse and its focus has been largely historical rather than contemporary, tracing the 18th- and 19th-century 'birth of the prison' (e.g. Johnston 2000). The dearth of scholarship on this topic is remarkable since the voices of prisoners, reflecting their experiences of incarceration in media such as autobiographies and poetry, speak vividly of prison design and its effects on the lived experience of incarceration (e.g. Boyle 1977, 1984; Hassine 2010; McWatters 2013). However, whilst criminological prison research has long been dominated by Sykes's (1958) notion of the 'pains of imprisonment', recent work has started to consider new and different ways of understanding the experience of incarceration, which lend themselves more readily to dialogue with the notions of carceral space and prison design. Encompassing discourses of legitimacy and non-legitimacy (Sparks et al. 1996); security (Drake 2012); therapy (Stevens 2012); compliance and neo-paternalism (Liebling, with Arnold 2004; Crewe 2009); quality of life and healthy prisons (Liebling 2002; Liebling, with Arnold 2004); normalization (Jewkes 2002); the depth, weight and tightness of imprisonment (Crewe 2009); the resurgence of the doctrine of less eligibility (White 2008); and public acceptability (Liebling, with Arnold 2004), these studies hint at, if not fully articulate, a relationship between these notions and aspects of prison design.

The late 1980s saw a fleeting interest in prison design and prisoner well-being emerge within environmental psychology, with research identifying a link between physical environment and social climate (Houston et al. 1988), and finding that prison architecture that creates overcrowded conditions causes significant stress to inmates (Schaeffer et al. 1988). Although Canter (1987: 227) argued that a 'systematic, scientific evaluation of the successes and failures' of prison design was urgently required in order to explore this relationship further, no such evaluation has taken place. What is more, in the intervening period, research in environmental psychology has tended to focus its attention chiefly on negative prisoner behaviours and the risk factors that are perceived to contribute towards them; for example, focusing on 'hard' prevention techniques for prison suicide, such as developing cell designs with no ligature points from which prisoners can hang themselves. In other words, focus has shifted away from a concern for social climate, towards the designing-out of risk of physical harm from prisoners' destructive behaviour through environmental modification, and by maximizing control on the part of the prison authorities (Tartaro 2003; Krames and Flett 2002). Recent attempts have been made to establish a broad-brush link between different architectural types and elements of prisoner behaviour – for example, in the USA between prison layouts (as determined by satellite imagery) and 'misconduct' on the part of inmates (Morris and Worrall 2010), and in the Netherlands between prison design and prisoner perceptions of interactions with prison staff (Beijersbergen et al. 2014). These are tantalizing studies, although their quantitative methodologies preclude further explication of the means by which any such linkages take form.

Despite, then, guarded transdisciplinary recognition that the design of carceral spaces has a direct effect on prisoner behaviour and control (Foucault 1979; Alford 2000), the lived environment of prisons, including its potential for positive experience, has been relatively overlooked. Moreover, the dominance of psychological methodologies in extant research on the prison environment has delivered rather a narrow range of largely quantitative studies, based on, for example: urine tests to determine stress responses (Schaeffer et al. 1988); the deployment of suicide or misconduct statistics as a proxy for stress, towards which the physical environment might (or might not) be a contributory factor (Tartaro 2003; Morris and Worrall 2010); and true/false questionnaire responses as part of the Correctional Institution Environment Scale (CIES), which lacks an explicit environmental dimension, simply being used to measure 'well-being' in different institutions (Houston et al. 1988). At the other end of the methodological spectrum, in his work with prisoner poetry, McWatters adds to understandings of how prison space is actually experienced by those for whom 'it is an ordinary space of daily life' (McWatters 2013: 199), describing carceral space as 'more plastic, fluid and manifold than totalizing notions permit' (ibid.: 200), and arguing in support of efforts to expand the imaginary of lived spaces of incarceration.

Having recognized that the carceral environment 'matters' to prisoners' experiences, and having demonstrated it to some degree using a variety of methodologies, without exception, these studies call for a more nuanced investigation of the impact of design on those using and occupying prison spaces.

The policy context of prison design

Globally, the imprisonment of offenders takes place within a framework of primary international covenants and conventions, such as the Convention Against Torture and Other Cruel, Inhuman or Degrading Treatment or Punishment, which is intended to guarantee proper treatment for those in detention under all circumstances. Driven by a concern for the humane treatment of those detained, these conventions do not extend to prescriptions about the exact nature of prison buildings, in terms either of their outward appearance and architectural style, or internal configuration.

Contemporary UK penal architecture reflects government reports commissioned within this policy context, which have transformed prison security and with it prisoners' quality of life (Liebling 2002; Liebling et al. 2011; Drake 2012; see also Chapter 13, this volume). A preoccupation with 'hardening' the prison environment to design-out risk through environmental modification coincided with the UK Prison Service becoming an executive agency in 1993, and with the early 1990s enabling of private contracts for the design, construction, management and finance of penal institutions. An approach to prison control based on a balance between situational and social control has arguably swung towards an understanding of the situational dependence of behaviour, 'creating safe situations rather than creating safe individuals' (Wortley 2002: 4).

In recent years, UK prison new-builds have been driven by logics of cost, efficiency and security. However, there is also a need to comply with HM Prison Service Orders about the specification of prison accommodation, which lay out 'measurable standards' that can be 'applied consistently across the estate' in order to enable the prison service to provide 'decent living conditions for all prisoners' (HMPS 2001: 1). In this context, prison exteriors have tended to adopt a bland, presumably cheap, unassuming and uniform style with vast expanses of brick, few, small windows and no unnecessary decoration (Jewkes 2013). Internally, the imperative in spending the Ministry of Justice's approximate £300 million annual capital budget is to deploy indestructible materials to create custodial environments with no ligature points so that prisoners cannot physically harm themselves or others (RICS 2012). For example, one of the most recent UK prison new-builds, constructed as a part of the 'custodial architecture' portfolios of a specialist building contractor, was described as 'very operationally efficient' with 'a modern custodial aesthetic'.[3] Advertising their 'Custodial and Emergency Services' project capabilities, the contractor, whilst conceding the need for a prison building to 'have a positive impact' and to be 'safe, non-threatening, secure and aesthetically pleasing', highlighted the imperative for 'value for money [to] be carefully balanced against the need for robustness and security'. Their experience and expertise in this area was described as bringing 'efficiencies at the design stage' including the kind of modified environments that create safe situations (Wortley 2002), such as 'designing ligature free environments by incorporating junctions and fixing details within structural walls and floors' (Pick Everard n.d.: n.p.).

Nineteenth-century prison buildings still in service are usually considered the least desirable environments within the UK penal estate, but while these Victorian 'houses of correction' ensured inmates' restricted economy of space, light and colour, imprisoning psychologically as well as physically, it has yet to be established empirically whether 'old' always means 'bad' or whether the kind of 'contemporary' prison described above necessarily equates to 'progressive' or 'humanitarian' (Hancock and Jewkes 2011; Moran and Jewkes 2015). For example, within a year of reopening in 1983, the 'new' Holloway Prison was criticized by the UK Prisons Inspectorate as engendering a form of torture that could result in acute mental illness. Levels of self-harm, suicide and distress were high, and vandalism, barricading of cells, floods, arson and violence against other prisoners and staff were common (Medlicott 2008). Among interior layouts recently advocated to manage problems like these is the 'new generation' campus-style arrangement of discrete housing units connected by outdoor space and flexible planning and design. Such prisons have experienced different levels of success. Although prison architecture may reflect underlying penal philosophies, the ways in which it is experienced depend heavily on local contingencies and on the human subjectivity of the habitation of buildings. For example, Feltham and Lancaster Farms Young Offenders' Institutions have been perceived differently on issues such as bullying, self-harm and suicide. Lancaster Farms has been held up as a shining example of commitment and care, whilst Feltham's reputation is coloured by years of damning reports and a high-profile murder (Jewkes and Johnston 2007).

The 'new punitiveness', discussed earlier with regard to the relationship between the carceral and the state, comes clearly into view when considering the prison estate. Latterly, it has expanded to accommodate those imprisoned under circumstances of increasing (and, increasingly, indeterminate) prison sentences, more punitive prison sanctions, and more austere and spartan prison conditions, operating to a greater or lesser extent in various contexts (Pratt et al. 2011; Hallsworth and Lea 2011; Lynch 2011; Snacken 2010). This hardening of penal sensibilities is coupled in the UK and elsewhere with more severe sentencing policies (Criminal Justice Act 2003); the fetishizing of risk and security within and outside the penal estate; and a rising prison population (which, in England and Wales, has grown by 30% since 2001 and stood at 85,414 in June 2014). All of this makes questions of prison design and the lived experience of carceral space particularly pertinent. Although chronic overcrowding, high rates of drug use, mental illness, self-harm and suicide and recidivism and its associated financial and social costs, mar the UK system, absconds from closed prisons have fallen dramatically, due in part to prison design: prison walls are higher, prison space is sequestered through zoning, and CCTV cameras and other technologies proliferate.

In the USA, perceived public endorsement for rigorous and unpleasant conditions has also resulted in new prisons being built with 'a level of security above "high security"' and internal routines not seen for 150 years (Johnston 2000: 4). Morin (2013: 381) has argued that the 'latest punitive phase' in the USA neither simply *eliminates*, as in the pre-modern spectacle, nor *creates* the docile, rehabilitated bodies of the modern panopticon. Rather, she argued that the late-modern prison 'produces only fear, terror, violence, and death' (see Chapter 3 of this volume). In support of this view, Victor Hassine, a 'lifer' who committed suicide after serving 28 years in various correctional facilities in the USA, comments on the 'fear-suffused environments' he endured, and writes:

> To fully understand the prison experience requires a personal awareness of how bricks, mortar, steel, and the endless enforcement of rules and regulations animate a prison into a living, breathing entity designed to manipulate its inhabitants … Prison designers and managers have developed a precise and universal alphabet of fear that is carefully assembled and arranged – bricks, steel, uniforms, colors, odors, shapes, and management style – to effectively control the conduct of whole prison populations.
>
> (Hassine 2010: 7)

Carceral geography and prison design

Recent work within carceral geography has addressed the significance of carceral space (Moran et al. 2013; Moran 2015), recognizing space as more than the surface where social practices take place (Gregory and Urry 1985; Lefebvre 1991; Massey 1994). Although geographers understand that space can affect the ways people act within it and are increasingly applying this perspective to carceral spaces, Siserman (2012) points out that studies of prisons as buildings and environments where the behaviour of inmates can be dramatically changed, and which investigate how this might happen, remain scarce. Commentaries within architectural geographies and cultural geographies have argued for the importance of considering buildings in a number of connected ways (e.g. Kraftl 2010; Jacobs and Merriman 2011; Rose et al. 2010; Jacobs 2006; Kraftl and Adey 2008):

as everyday spaces in which people spend a significant proportion of their lives; as expressions of political–economic imperatives that code them with 'signs, symbols and referents for dominant socio-cultural discourses or moralities' (Kraftl 2010: 402); and in terms of perspectives that emphasize materiality and affect.

A representationalist focus on prison buildings as sites of meaning, symbolic of intentions and imperatives is itself arguably underdeveloped in prison scholarship. However, there is the potential to go beyond the symbolic meaning of prison buildings to consider the 'inhabitation' (Jacobs and Merriman 2011: 213) in terms of the dynamic encounters between these buildings and their constituent elements and spaces, design, planners, inhabitants, workers, visitors, and so on. Like any other buildings, prisons are sites in which myriad users and things come into contact with one another in numerous complex, planned, spontaneous and unexpected ways, and where the encounters are both embodied and multi-sensory, and resonant of the power structures that exist both within and beyond the prison building, and which shape its inhabitation.

Recent developments in both prison architecture and design (albeit outwith the context of the 'new punitiveness') and criminological research into prison aesthetics and 'anaesthetics' (Jewkes 2013) echo Kraftl and Adey's suggestion that one function of buildings can be an attempt to stabilize affect, 'to generate the possibility of pre-circumscribed situations, and to engender certain forms of practice, through the design and planning of buildings, including aspects such as form and atmosphere' (Kraftl and Adey 2008: 228). In their work, they found that certain generic expressions of affect evoked certain kinds of inhabitation, materialized via buildings in their 'potential capacities to affect their inhabitants in certain ways' (ibid.). In other parts of the world – in which the 'new punitiveness' of the USA, UK and elsewhere has not taken hold – prison designers have focused on the rehabilitative function of imprisonment, and have experimented with progressive and highly stylized forms of penal architecture. There, internal prison spaces exhibit soft furnishings, colour zoning, maximum exploitation of natural light, displays of art and sculpture, and views of nature through vista windows without bars.

For example, in designing a planned women's prison in Iceland, the project team from OOIIO Architecture intended:

> to design a prison that doesn't look like a prison, forgetting about dark spaces, small cells, and ugly grey concrete walls ... we based the building design on natural light, open spaces, and natural green materials like peat, grass and flowers.
>
> (OOIIO Architecture 2012: n.p.)

Instead of designing one large building (like a 'typical repressive old prison'), they decided to break it into several 'human-scale, connected' pavilions, which must be efficient and functional to enable the spatial separation of prisoners, but must also have 'natural light and exterior views, to increase the feeling of freedom'. The architects also had an eye to the speed and ease of construction, and to the eco standards of the building, planning to draw upon Icelandic vernacular architecture to insulate the building. With a facade constructed from peat-filled cages planted with local flowers and grasses, they intended to deliver a building 'that changes with the seasons', making prison life 'less monotonous and more human and natural related' (OOIIO Architecture 2012: n.p.).

This kind of design of new prisons in Norway, Iceland and Denmark arguably plays up and enhances certain generic expressions of affect connected to openness, flexibility and 'humane' treatment. It evokes certain kinds of inhabitation that encourage personal and intellectual creativity, and even a lightness and vividness of experience (Hancock and Jewkes 2011). Away from this Nordic context, however, what drives the building of new prisons in the UK, and how much do we know about it?

Building new prisons in the UK

Kraftl and Adey (2008: 228) called for further research into the ways in which architectural forms try to manipulate and create possibilities, and into how those affects are experienced and negotiated in practice, via the notion of inhabitation. Attending to the processes of architectural design and construction reveals the multiple political, affective and material ways in which prison buildings are designed and constituted. These in turn play a part in constructing the affectual potentialities of prison buildings that are negotiated in and through practices of inhabitation.

The design process is, as Wener noted, 'the wedge that forces the system to think through its approach and review, restate, or redevelop its philosophy of criminal justice' (Wener 2012: 7). Embedded within this process is the conscious and intentional design of carceral spaces, in response to contingent policy imperatives and in the context of local budgetary constraints. In the UK, the contemporary process of designing and building new prisons now rests upon a complex and varied framework with an intricate network of individuals, companies and capital, and is driven primarily by concerns for security, cost and efficiency – concerns which materially shape the buildings themselves.

Since the recommendation of the 1987 Select Committee on Home Affairs report that the Home Office should enable private companies to tender for the management of prisons, the landscape of UK prison construction has shifted considerably. The 1990 Criminal Justice Bill provided enabling legislation for prison privatization, and Section 84 of the Criminal Justice Act 1991 allowed for the private running of new prisons. These 'Manage & Maintain' (M&M) contracts involved the then Ministry of Prisons leasing prisons to private operators contracted to run them, and maintain their buildings and infrastructure, for 15 years. The Conservative government's introduction in 1992 of the Private Finance Initiative (PFI) enabled 'public–private partnerships' (PPPs) to fund public infrastructure projects with private capital, and the 1994 Criminal Justice and Public Order Act allowed for the private *provision* as well as the operation and maintenance of prisons. Following a tendering process in which the public sector was barred from participating, Group 4 (now G4S) was awarded a contract to manage HMP Wolds, a newly built remand prison that opened in April 1992. What started as an 'experiment', however, soon became routine policy (Panchamia 2012) and, in 1997, the incoming New Labour government adopted PFI. HMP Altcourse in Liverpool, and HMP Parc at Bridgend in Wales, became the first PFI builds under Labour in England and Wales, respectively.

Now known as Design, Construct, Manage and Finance (DCMF) contracts, PFI builds involve private sector finance for the construction of new prisons, as well as providing their custodial services. A consortium of financiers, constructors and a facilities operator form a special purpose vehicle (SPV) or special operating vehicle (SOV), which, in a PFI, carries the profit or loss from the venture. The secretary of state contracts with the SPV which, in turn, subcontracts the immediate construction to a Design and Build Contractor (D&B), and the long-term operation of the prison to a Buildings and Facilities Management company (BFM), typically for 25 years. In some cases in the UK, prisons are still built and run using public funds, whereas others may be publicly financed, but operated by private companies under M&M contracts. Recent examples of these generic types of construction in the UK include HMP Oakwood (opened 2012 – M&M) in Staffordshire, HMP Thameside (2012 – DCMF) in London, and HMP Grampian (2014 – public funds and publicly run) in northern Scotland.

In terms of the build process itself, contractors that have had previous success delivering prisons on time and within budget tend to be commissioned for subsequent projects. At HMP Thameside, for example:

> Skanska brought together its in-house expertise in construction, piling, structural and civil design, and the installation of mechanical and electrical services to deliver the project. It also built on its experience from similar projects, such as the HMP Dovegate project in Staffordshire.
>
> (Skanska 2012: 1)

Experience is important, therefore, but so is cost. In the case of the planned prison HMP North Wales, four main contractors were in competition: Carillion, Interserve, Lend Lease and Kier. Lend Lease's award of the contract in May 2014 perhaps rewarded a projected build cost of £212 million, 15% below the government's original planned budget of £250 million, as well as a commitment to spend £50 million with small and medium-sized enterprises, and £30 million with local businesses. For a government eager to stimulate local economic activity and development, Lend Lease's plan to recruit 50% of the site workforce from the local area, including around 100 apprenticeships (Morby 2014) may also have increased the attractiveness of their bid. The cost of operation is also critical. HMP Oakwood, for example, accommodates up to 2,000 prisoners relatively cheaply (at £13,200 per inmate per year, compared with the England and Wales average of £21,600 per year for Category C prisoners and £31,300 for all prisoners). The G4S-run facility has been lauded as a 'model' prison by the secretary of state for justice.

In terms of the built form of new prisons, cost concerns – in relation to both building materials and build duration – heavily influence the fabric of the resulting facility. In order to reduce both the build time and the on-site workforce, off-site pre-fabrication is preferred. HMP Oakwood, for example, consists of 12 precast buildings, including four, four-storey house blocks, and entry and facilities buildings. These buildings were quickly assembled on site from precast concrete panels with window grilles, sanitary provisions and drainage pre-installed. At HMP Thameside, Skanska coordinated a similar process of the delivery of off-site precast concrete components, the use of which facilitated swift construction on the small and confined site, allowing some buildings to be handed over 14 weeks early (Skanska 2012: 1). In prison building, time is money. Whilst HMP Grampian was under construction, prisoners from closed prisons at Aberdeen and Peterhead had to be held elsewhere (Premier Construction 2014). Finishing on time and on budget meant that they could be rehoused quickly, with minimal additional cost, security worries or disruption to their sentence planning.

The pre-eminence of financial considerations shapes a government procurement process that is arguably engineered towards the most cost-effective solution. In a prevailing climate of cuts to justice spending, contractors who have delivered previous projects on time and on budget are well placed to win subsequent tenders. This has two implications. First, breaking into the marketplace as a new SPV/D&B company is difficult, as newcomers face considerable disadvantages. Second, and connectedly, alternative or experimental prison designs that deviate from a 'tried and tested' template amenable to precast construction and on-site assembly may simply be priced out of the market. This often, and perhaps understandably, results in contractors sticking to designs whose construction costs and build times they can confidently predict, in order to bid competitively for new contracts. What this effectively means is that new prisons tend to be virtually identical to other recently built prisons (Jewkes and Moran 2014), with architectural aesthetics taking a back seat, and innovation limited to efficiency of build, rather than creativity of design.

Discussion

In addition to the conscious and intentional meanings attached to carceral spaces (relating to cost, reliability, security and so on) that are embedded in the procurement and contracting processes outlined above, research on emotional geographies of prisons (Crewe et al. 2013) highlights the more subtle ways in which architecture and design communicate the aims and techniques of penal authority. We have argued elsewhere that the large, bland prison warehouses that are now built in the contemporary UK may communicate a particular message about society's attitudes to prisoners (Jewkes and Moran 2014; Jewkes 2015; Jewkes, Moran and Slee 2016). The nondescript external appearance of new-build prisons could be regarded as a visual metaphor for the loss of public empathy for the excluded offender, where 'municipal' architecture enables us to turn a blind eye to the plight of the confined. Although such a benign facade might suggest a benevolent regime, it has recently been argued that concerns for security within many countries' penal systems have risen to such a level of prominence that they eclipse almost every other consideration, including what it means to be human (Drake 2012). In this context, the benign exterior can mask a sterile, 'mean-spirited', assembly line quality (Hassine 2010: 125).

The penal philosophies and imperatives underpinning the design of newly commissioned and newly built facilities thus shape the relationship between space, meaning and power, and have an undeniable impact on the experience of imprisonment and on the behaviour of those who occupy and move through carceral spaces. The 'dynamic encounters' (Jacobs and Merriman 2011: 213) that occur between the inhabitants of prison buildings, the technologies operational within them, and the buildings themselves, are critical to understanding their inhabitation. Criminologists recognize that prisoners constantly 'manage' issues of self and identity and adapt socially under intense and inescapable duress; and the kinds of encounters between prisoners and prison staff that are encouraged by, or which are even possible within, differently designed prison buildings are worthy of investigation. 'Dynamic security', in which prison staff are encouraged to develop good relationships with prisoners through direct contact and conversation, is no longer possible in many new-build prisons where staff are physically separated from prisoners.

Where surveillance technologies enhance the observation of carceral space, some prisoners may value CCTV as a means of protecting their personal safety and for its capacity to provide evidence of bullying and assaults. However, these technologies also reinforce the absence of privacy and create additional stresses for both prisoners and staff (Liebling et al. 2011). The utilization of surveillance and monitoring technologies in prisons as workplaces has inevitably brought prison employees under closer scrutiny from their managers (Townsend and Bennett 2003; Ball 2010), and it is argued that the notion of trust, once regarded as essential to prison management-staff relationships, has been undermined by surveillance systems that ensure that 'correct' organizational procedures are followed. Increasingly, prisons routinely monitor everyone passing through them via an interface of technology and corporeality, encouraging flexibility of movement while retaining high levels of security. For example, cameras wirelessly transmit digital images, which are then screened for unusual objects and atypical movements; biometric and electronic monitoring of prisoners and visitors allow the tracking of bodies within in the prison; listening devices monitor the spectral content of sound to spot illicit use of mobile phones or early signs of aggressive behaviour; and prison officers' Blackberry-style devices enable immediate reports to be relayed to Security (OIS 2008; cited in Hancock and Jewkes 2011).

Whereas Morin's (2013) work suggested that like the UK, the USA is experiencing a trend towards increasingly severe and restrictive prison designs, elsewhere, prison buildings are being designed with different intentions in terms of the manipulation and creation of possibilities. In north-west Europe, decarcerative policies deliver smaller numbers of prisoners, and for these smaller prison populations the use of surveillance technologies facilitates 'humane', open-plan, 'progressive' prisons with a greater degree of movement among and between inmates and staff, and a wider range of possible encounters. Here, new-build prisons are not only the result of experimentation with progressive and highly stylized forms of penal architecture, but they also have internal prison spaces that explore more open, flexible and normalized spatial planning than is the norm in the UK. Among the design features to be found in these new prisons are: soft furnishings replacing hard fixtures and fittings; zoning different parts of the prison through colour coding and use of psychologically effective colour schemes; attention to the maximum exploitation of natural light and/or artificial light that mimics daylight; greater access to outdoor spaces with trees, planting and water features; the incorporation of differing levels, horizons and building materials to ward off boredom and monotony; and displays of art and sculpture (Hancock and Jewkes 2011; Moran and Jewkes 2015). This kind of strategic application of architectural and aesthetic principles to the design of new prisons in, for example, Norway, Iceland and Denmark, has been found to encourage personal and intellectual creativity, and even a lightness and vividness of experience (Hancock and Jewkes 2011), in contrast to the depth, weight and tightness commonly associated with imprisonment (Crewe 2011) and its material darkness, even hellishness (Wacquant 2002; Jewkes 2014, 2015).

Even in the Nordic countries, however, prison design may not be straightforwardly humane and positive – or may at least have perverse consequences. For example, although the appearance of these prison buildings – in terms of their natural materials, large windows and natural light – conveys a sense of ease and relaxation, it arguably replicates and perhaps enhances some of the issues of privacy, identity management and presentation of self-identity in more obviously 'restrictive' settings. Meanwhile, Shammas (2014: 104) has called for attention to be paid to the 'pains of freedom' inherent in Norway's more 'humane' prisons. There is some evidence that technology-assisted, decentralized, podular designs approximate 'normality' by providing safer and more comfortable living environments, and removing security gates, bars and grilles, enabling prison officers to be more than 'turn-keys' (Spens 1994), but as Hancock and Jewkes (2011) have argued, there has been scant official or scholarly discussion of other potential uses of technology, such as the identification of abuse or aggressive behaviour by prison officers (either to prisoners or their colleagues), the surveillance of staff smuggling contraband into the prison or behaving in ways disapproved of by prison authorities. Similarly, there is little debate about the moral and ethical implications of near-constant surveillance of prisoners and officers, or the difficulties in establishing trust when basic standards of privacy are compromised. The use of technologies could exacerbate complex horizontal and vertical relationships between prison inmates, officers, managers and ministers. Everyone who moves within and through these 'hyper-organizational spaces' (Zhang et al. 2008) is not only enmeshed in a surveillance assemblage that forces them to manage their own presentation of self within the regulative framework of the institution, but is further encouraged to watch while knowingly being watched. Although lack of privacy has long been recognized as a 'pain of imprisonment' for inmates, for prison staff the new panopticism is a novel form of control (Hancock and Jewkes 2011).

Conclusion

With Wener's (2012: 7) proposition that 'the design of a jail or prison is critically related to the philosophy of the institution, or maybe even of the entire criminal justice system', a better understanding of prison design could in turn enable a better understanding of the lived experience of carceral spaces – a central theme of recent research in carceral geography. Geographers have made valuable contributions to understanding how, even within the most restrictive conditions of confinement, prisoners employ effective spatial tactics within surveilled space, create individual and collective means of resistance to carceral regimes, and succeed in appropriating and personalizing carceral spaces (Moran and Jewkes 2015). Yet, the majority of research to date has tended to focus on inmate responses to, and adaptations of, the physical spaces of incarceration, rather than drawing attention to the processes that led those spaces to *be* as they are, and what this means for the ends prison buildings serve for the state that creates them. Missing from this work is a consideration of the ways in which punitive philosophies are manifest in prison commissioning and construction, and subsequently in prison buildings themselves.

The challenge, therefore, is to start to address *why* those spaces are as they are, and to interrogate the intentions behind their design. Returning to Davison's (1931) condemnation of US prison design, research needs to illuminate further the commissioning process, to uncover what it is that architects are asked to draw, contractors to build and facilities managers to maintain, and how those demands are articulated and addressed. Davison argued that prison authorities would 'never get the most out of their architects until specifications are presented not in terms of definite plans and materials, but in terms of performance' (ibid.: 33). He called for commissioners not to request cell blocks, but sleeping places; not to demand mechanical ventilation, but instead to require good air for every prisoner. Then, he concluded, 'let the solution be worked out. In many instances the result will be astonishing. It will not resemble the present jail at all' (ibid.: 34). Designing a prison based on the requirements of the building, rather than simply accepting and replicating what has been built before, was for him the key to delivering 'better' prisons.

Pursuing these questions could enable us not only to better understand the experience of incarceration, but also to open the design process itself to scrutiny and reflection (Moran and Jewkes 2015; Jewkes and Moran 2014).[4] Wener (2012: 7) argued that prison environments represent both an 'overt' agenda that provides measurable quantities of space for accommodation, training, therapy, education and so on, and also a 'covert' agenda that reflects what or who inmates 'are' in the minds of planners, designers, and those who commission them to design and build prisons. Opening a space for the articulation of this 'covert' agenda could contribute positively to the ongoing debate over the expansion of the penal estate.

Notes

1 In the UK, a former home secretary recalled that he was never asked to adjudicate on matters of prison design, rating 'the prison designs of much of the post-war period' as 'shoddy, expensive and just a little inhuman' (Hurd 2000: xiii–xiv).
2 1990s security breaches included prisoner rooftop protests at Strangeways in 1990 and escapes from Whitemoor and Parkhurst prisons in 1994.
3 David Nisbet, partner at Pick Everard (see Pick Everard 2012: n.p.).
4 To these ends, the authors are currently conducting a three-year research study. Taking a lead from Victor Hassine's biographical writings on his experience as a prisoner in the US system, the project is entitled 'Fear-suffused environments or potential to rehabilitate? Prison architecture, design and technology and the lived experience of carceral spaces' (ESRC Standard Grant ES/K011081/1).

Bibliography

Adey, P. (2008) 'Airports, mobility and the affective architecture of affective control', *Geoforum* 39: 438–451.

Aebi, M.F. and Kuhn, A. (2000) 'Influences on the prisoner rate: Number of entries into prison, length of sentences and crime rate', *European Journal on Criminal Policy and Research* 8(1): 65–75.

Alford, C.F. (2000) 'What would it matter if everything Foucault said about prison were wrong? Discipline and Punish after twenty years', *Theory and Society* 29(1): 125–146.

Allen, J. (2006) 'Ambient power: Berlin's Potsdamer Platz and the seductive logic of public spaces', *Urban Studies* 43: 441–455.

Ball, K.S. (2010) 'Workplace surveillance: An overview', *Labor History* 51(1): 87–106.

Beijersbergen, K.A., Dirkzwager, A.J.E., Van der Laan, P.H. and Nieuwbeerta, P. (2014) 'A social building? Prison architecture and staff-prisoner relationships', *Crime & Delinquency*, DOI: 10.1177/0011128714530657.

Boyle, J. (1977) *A Sense of Freedom*, London: Pan.

Boyle, J. (1984) *The Pain of Confinement*, Edinburgh: Canongate.

Brodie, A., Croom, J. and Davies, J.O. (1999) *Behind Bars: The Hidden Architecture of England's Prisons*, London: English Heritage.

Brodie, A., Croom, J. and Davies, J.O. (2002) *English Prisons: An Architectural History*, London: English Heritage.

Canter, D. (1987) 'Implications for "new generation" prisons of existing psychological research into prison design and use', in A.E. Bottoms and R. Light (eds) *Problems of Long-term Imprisonment*, Aldershot: Gower.

Crewe, B. (2009) *The Prisoner Society: Power, Adaption, and Social Life in an English Prison*, Oxford: Oxford University Press.

Crewe, B. (2011) 'Depth, weight, tightness: Revisiting the pains of imprisonment', *Punishment and Society* 13(5): 509–529.

Crewe, B., Warr, J., Bennett, P. and Smith, A. (2013) 'The emotional geography of prison life', *Theoretical Criminology*, DOI: 1362480613497778.

Davison, R.L. (1931) 'Prison architecture', *Annals of the American Academy of Political and Social Science* 157: 33–39.

Drake, D. (2012) *Prisons, Punishment and the Pursuit of Security*, London: Palgrave Macmillan.

Fairweather, L. and McConville, S. (eds) (2000) *Prison Architecture: Policy, Design, and Experience*, Oxford: Elsevier.

Foucault, M. (1979) *Discipline and Punish: The Birth of the Prison*, New York: Vintage.

Frost, N.A. (2010) 'Beyond public opinion polls: Punitive public sentiment and criminal justice policy', *Sociology Compass* 4(3): 156–168.

Garland, D. (2001) *The Culture of Control*, Oxford: Oxford University Press.

Great Britain (1991) *Criminal Justice Act 1991*, London: The Stationery Office, www.legislation.gov.uk/ukpga/1991/53/contents (accessed 4 July 2014).

Great Britain (1994) *Criminal Justice and Public Order Act 1994*, London: The Stationery Office, www.legislation.gov.uk/ukpga/1994/33/contents (accessed 4 July 2014).

Great Britain (2003) *Criminal Justice Act 2003*, London: The Stationery Office, www.legislation.gov.uk/ukpga/2003/44/contents (accessed 4 July 2014).

Greer, C. and Jewkes, Y. (2005) 'Extremes of otherness: media images of social exclusion', *Social Justice* 32(1): 20–31.

Gregory, D. and Urry, J. (eds) (1985) *Social Relations and Spatial Structures*, London: Macmillan.

Hallsworth, S. and Lea, J. (2011) 'Reconstructing Leviathan: Emerging contours of the security state', *Theoretical Criminology* 15(2): 141–157.

Hancock, L. (2004) 'Criminal justice, public opinion, fear and popular politics', in J. Muncie and D. Wilson (eds) *The Cavendish Student Handbook of Criminal Justice and Criminology*, London: Cavendish.

Hancock, P. and Jewkes, Y. (2011) 'Architectures of incarceration: The spatial pains of imprisonment', *Punishment and Society* 13(5): 611–629.

Hassine, V. (2010) *Life Without Parole: Living and Dying in Prison Today*, New York: Oxford University Press.

HMPS (HM Prison Service) (2001) *Prison Service Order 1900: Certified Prisoner Accommodation*, London: HMPS.

Houston, J.G., Gibbons, D.C. and Jones, J.F. (1988) 'Physical environment and jail social climate', *Crime & Delinquency* 34(4): 449–466.

Hurd, D. (2000) *Memoirs*, London: Little, Brown.

Jacobs, J.M. (2006) 'A geography of big things', *Cultural Geographies* 13(1): 1–27.

Jacobs, J.M. and Merriman, P. (2011) 'Practising architectures', *Social & Cultural Geography* 12(3): 211–222.

Jewkes, Y. (2002) *Captive Audience: Media, Masculinity and Power in Prisons*, London: Routledge.

Jewkes, Y. (2013) 'On carceral space and agency', in D. Moran, N. Gill and D. Conlon (eds) *Carceral Spaces: Mobility and Agency in Imprisonment and Migrant Detention*, Farnham: Ashgate.

Jewkes, Y. (2015) 'Fear-suffused hell-holes: The architecture of extreme punishment', in K. Reiter and A. Koenig (eds) *Extraordinary Punishment: An Empirical Look at Administrative Black Holes in the United States, the United Kingdom, and Canada*, London: Palgrave.

Jewkes, Y. and Johnston, H. (2007) 'The evolution of prison architecture', in Y. Jewkes (ed.) *Handbook on Prisons*, London: Routledge.

Jewkes, Y. and Moran, D. (2014) 'Should prison architecture be brutal, bland or beautiful?', *Scottish Justice Matters* 2(1): 8–11.

Jewkes, Y., Moran, D. and Slee, E. (2016) 'The visual retreat of the prison: non-places for non-people', in M. Brown and E. Carrabine (eds) *The Routledge Handbook of Visual Criminology*, London: Routledge.

Johnston, N. (2000) *Forms of Constraint: A History of Prison Architecture*, Urbana, IL: University of Illinois Press.

Kraftl, P. (2010) 'Geographies of architecture: The multiple lives of buildings', *Geography Compass* 4(5): 402–415.

Kraftl, P. and Adey, P. (2008) 'Architecture/affect/inhabitation: Geographies of being-in buildings', *Annals of the Association of American Geographers* 98(1): 213–231.

Krames, L. and Flett, G.L. (2002) *The Perceived Characteristics of Holding Cell Environments: Report of a Pilot Study*, Regina: Canadian Police Research Centre.

Leech, M. (2005) *The Prisons Handbook*, Manchester: MLA Press.

Lefèbvre, H. (1991) *The Production of Space*, Oxford: Blackwell.

Liebling, A. (2002) *Suicides in Prison*, London: Routledge.

Liebling, A., with Arnold, H. (2004) *Prisons and their Moral Performance: A Study of Values, Quality, and Prison Life*, Oxford: Oxford University Press.

Liebling, A., Arnold, H. and Straub, C. (2011) *An Exploration of Staff-Prisoner Relationships at HMP Whitemoor: Twelve Years On*, London: MoJ.

Lynch, M. (2011) 'Mass incarceration, legal change, and locale', *Criminology & Public Policy* 10(3): 673–698.

McWatters, M. (2013) 'Poetic testimonies of incarceration: Towards a vision of prison as manifold space', in D. Moran, N. Gill and D. Conlon (eds) *Carceral Spaces: Mobility and Agency in Imprisonment and Migrant Detention*, Farnham: Ashgate.

Massey, D. (1994) *Space, Place and Gender*, Cambridge: Polity Press.

Medlicott, D. (2008) 'Women in prison', in Y. Jewkes and J. Bennett (eds) *Dictionary of Prisons and Punishment*, London: Routledge.

Ministry of Justice of Finland (1975) *Statute on Prison Administration*, Helsinki: Ministry of Justice.

Moran, D. (2015) *Carceral Geography: Spaces and Practices of Incarceration*, Farnham: Ashgate.

Moran, D., Gill, N. and Conlon, D. (eds) (2013) *Carceral Spaces: Mobility and Agency in Imprisonment and Migrant Detention*, Farnham: Ashgate.

Moran, D. and Jewkes, Y. (2015) 'Linking the carceral and the punitive state: Researching prison architecture, design, technology and the lived experience of carceral space', *Annales de la Geographie*.

Morby, A. (2014) 'Lend Lease wins £212m Wrexham super prison', *Construction Enquirer*, www.constructionenquirer.com/2014/05/30/lend-lease-wins-212m-wrexham-super-prison/ (accessed 19 June 2014).

Morin, K.M. (2013) '"Security here is not safe": Violence, punishment, and space in the contemporary US penitentiary', *Environment and Planning D: Society and Space* 31(3): 381–399.

Morris, R.G. and Worrall, J.L. (2010) 'Prison architecture and inmate misconduct: A multilevel assessment', *Crime & Delinquency*, DOI: 10.1177/0011128710386204.

OIS (Offender Information Services) (2008) *Prison Technology Strategy, Version 0.8*, London: NOMS.

OOIIO Architecture (2012) 'Female prison in Iceland', *OOIIO Architecture* website, plusmood.com/2012/06/female-prison-in-iceland-ooiio-architecture/ (accessed 2 February 2014).

Panchamia, N. (2012) *Competition in Prisons*, London: Institute for Government, www.instituteforgovernment.org.uk/sites/default/files/publications/Prisons%20briefing%20final.pdf (accessed 22 July 2014).

Pick Everard (2012) 'Pick Everard completes UK's largest public funded prison project', *Pick Everard* website, www.pickeverard.co.uk/news/2012/Pick-Everard-completes-UKs-largest-public-funded-prison-project.html (accessed 4 February 2014).

Pick Everard (n.d.) 'Custodial and emergency services', *Pick Everard* website, www.pickeverard.co.uk/custodial-emergency-services/index.html (accessed 3 February 2014).

Pratt, J., Brown, D., Brown, M., Hallsworth, S. and Morrison, W. (eds) (2011) *The New Punitiveness: Trends, Theories, Perspectives*, Oxford: Routledge.

Pratt, J. and Eriksson, A. (2012) *Contrasts in Punishment: An Explanation of Anglophone Excess and Nordic Exceptionalism*, London: Routledge.

Premier Construction (2014) 'Unveiling HMP and YOI Grampian', *Premier Construction* website, premierconstructionnews.com/2014/02/25/unveiling-hmp-and-yoi-grampian/ (accessed 19 June 2014).

RICS (Royal Institute of Chartered Surveyors) (2012) *Modus: The Security Issue* 22(11).

Rose, G., Degen, M. and Basdas, B. (2010) 'More on "big things": Building events and feelings', *Transactions of the Institute of British Geographers* 35: 334–349.

Schaeffer, M.A., Baum, A., Paulus, P.B. and Gaes, G.G. (1988) 'Architecturally mediated effects of social density in prison', *Environment and Behavior* 20(1): 3–20.

Shammas, V.L. (2014) 'The pains of freedom: Assessing the ambiguity of Scandinavian penal exceptionalism on Norway's Prison Island', *Punishment & Society* 16(1): 104–123.

Siserman, C. (2012) *Reconsidering the Environmental Space of Prisons: A Step Further towards Criminal Reform*, Santa Cruz, CA: GRIN Verlag.

Skanska (2012) 'Case study 98 HMP Thameside', *Skanska* website, skanska-sustainability-case-s tudies.com/HMP-Thameside-UK (accessed 16 June 2014).

Snacken, S. (2010) 'Resisting punitiveness in Europe?', *Theoretical Criminology* 14(3): 273–292.

Sparks, R., Bottoms, A. and Hay, W. (1996) *Prisons and the Problem of Order*, Oxford: Clarendon Press.

Spens, I. (ed.) (1994) *Architecture of Incarceration*, London: Academy Editions.

Stevens, A. (2012) *Offender Rehabilitation and Therapeutic Communities: Enabling Change the TC Way*, London: Routledge.

Sykes, G.M. (1958) *The Society of Captives: A Study of a Maximum Security Prison*, Princeton, NJ: Princeton University Press.

Tartaro, C. (2003) 'Suicide and the jail environment: An evaluation of three types of institutions', *Environment and Behavior* 35(5): 605–620.

Tonry, M. (2004) *Thinking about Crime: Sense and Sensibility in American Penal Culture*, Oxford: Oxford University Press.

Townsend, A.M. and Bennett, J.T. (2003) 'Privacy, technology and conflict: Emerging issues and action in workplace privacy', *Journal of Labor Research* 24(2): 195–205.

Travis, A. (2010) 'Prison works, says Theresa May', *The Guardian* online, www.theguardian.com/p olitics/2010/dec/14/prison-works-says-theresa-may (accessed 3 July 2014).

Ugelvik, T. and Dullum, J. (eds) (2012) *Penal Exceptionalism? Nordic Prison Policy and Practice*, London: Routledge.

Von Hofer, H. (2003) 'Prison populations as political constructs: The case of Finland, Holland and Sweden', *Journal of Scandinavian Studies in Criminology and Crime Prevention* 4(1): 21–38.

Wacquant, L. (2002) 'The curious eclipse of prison ethnography in the age of mass incarceration', *Ethnography* 3(4): 371–397.

Wener, R.E. (2012) *The Environmental Psychology of Prisons and Jails: Creating Humane Spaces in Secure Settings*, Cambridge: Cambridge University Press.

White, A.A. (2008) 'Concept of less eligibility and the social function of prison violence in class societies', *The Buffalo Law Review* 56: 737.

Wortley, R. (2002) *Situational Prison Control: Crime Prevention in Correctional Institutions*, Cambridge: Cambridge University Press.

Young, J. (2003) 'Searching for a new criminology of everyday life: A review of the "culture of control"', *British Journal of Criminology* 43(1): 228–243.

Zhang, Z., Spicer, A. and Hancock, P. (2008) 'Hyper-organizational space in the work of JG Ballard', *Organization* 15(6): 889–910.

Chapter 8

Prison managerialism

Global change and local cultures in the working lives of prison managers

Jamie Bennett

Introduction

The role of prison managers is frequently elevated in discussions about prisons. One study cited half a dozen official and academic publications that attest to the central importance of the prison governor (Bryans 2007: 2). However, no individual or organization sits in isolation and any consideration of prison managers has to be situated in a broader social context. This chapter attempts to provide an overview of how the work of prison managers has been theorized and discussed historically, but also attempts to provide an exploration of their contemporary working lives, drawing in part upon ethnographic research conducted in England and Wales. This is intended to illuminate the various pressures and tensions that shape their work, in particular, global trends that push in from the outside and influences that are drawn from within, including local cultures and practices, and how they are negotiated.

The chapter opens by discussing the ways in which the working world of prison managers has previously been described, which have alternatively focused on the polar extremes, either emphasizing the empowered agency of prison managers or their conformity to the constraints placed upon them by global changes in organizational practice, including the development of managerialism. It is argued that these binary accounts are no longer adequate to describe the work of prison managers in late modernity. The second section goes on to provide the theoretical framework for a new way of thinking about prison managers, which locates them as agents attempting to navigate the tensions of the embedded local cultures of prisons and prison management, and the development of global practices in public management. From this perspective, local and global forces are a duality, with prison managers both enabled and constrained by these pressures, attempting to sustain a balance between them. The chapter then provides an empirical illustration of everyday practice, drawing upon an ethnographic study of prison managers. This particularly focuses on how two performance measures are interpreted, practised and understood by prison managers, illuminating how both global and local forces shape and intersect in their thinking and behaviour.

Thinking about prison management

Prison managers have previously been discussed in ways that emphasize two polar extremes. On the one hand, there is a body of work that describes prison management and prison occupational cultures as distinct, rooted in local history and practice. On the other, there is a more recent body of work which suggests that the forces of globalization, particularly the growth of managerialism, including the importation of commercial practices into public management, have had a profound impact on the occupational culture, constraining prison managers and homogenizing their practice. These two strands will be briefly elucidated.

Prison managers as local practitioners

Prison staff, in particular both prison officers (e.g. Crawley 2004; Liebling et al. 2011) and prison managers (e.g. Bryans and Wilson 2000) have been described in ways that emphasize localized and idiosyncratic aspects of their practice. However, this has been in contrasting and apparently mutually exclusive ways. For prison officers, research has generally described occupational culture as a homogeneous set of practices, shaping and constraining the behaviour and attitudes of those concerned. For prison managers, occupational culture has been described as heterogeneous and as empowering them to act with agency.

Prison officers have been discussed as a distinct group, studied in their own right and distinguished from managers or other professions working in prisons. From this work, three major elements can be drawn that characterize the 'traditional' prison officer occupational culture, just as classic studies on police officers have identified an enduring culture (see Loftus 2011). The first element of this culture is *insularity* – that prison officers have an internal focus, strong bonds of solidarity with colleagues and are cut off professionally and socially from those outside prisons. The second element is *staff–prisoner relationships*, where it has been argued that there is broad consensus about what constitutes the 'right' relationships with prisoners (or at least what are the 'wrong' sorts). This is a hierarchical relationship that emphasizes a professional and social distance. The third element is *machismo* – the 'traditional male qualities of dominance, authoritativeness and aggressiveness' (Crawley and Crawley 2008: 141) or what Sim (2009: 145) describes as 'untrammelled, corrosive masculinity'. These three features create the basis of an occupational culture or 'working personality' (Skolnick 1966; Crawley 2004; Liebling 2007). Such cultures can be deeply embedded, for example it has been argued that police officer culture has largely endured despite social and political changes (Loftus 2011).

Although earlier research has emphasized the coherence of this culture and the homogeneous nature of the group, recent work has provided some corrective, suggesting that prison officer culture is not monolithic but can vary in its precise dimensions within and between prisons, and that individuals do act with a degree of discretion and choice (Crawley 2004; Liebling et al. 2011). Nevertheless, the work described generally traces a distinct, local or 'traditional' occupational culture.

In contrast, the research on prison managers has emphasized diversity rather than homogeneity. These accounts suggest that prison managers shape the social climate of the institutions they command. It has even been suggested that prison management as an occupation is 'sui generis' or unique (Bryans and Wilson 2000) and that there is a distinct 'prison management competence' that is different from any other leadership role (Bryans 2000). This distinctiveness was described by Wilson (2000: 12) in the following terms:

> To work as a [prison manager], you had to understand prisoners, and be able to manipulate prison life to push it forward. This was not so much about

management – or to further managerial ends – but to fashion and re-shape an essentially punitive structure into one that was positive and optimistic.

It seems here to be implied that the occupational culture of prison officers forms part of the 'punitive structure'. This depiction of prison managers suggests that they are distinct from – even perhaps in conflict with – other groups within the prison as well as from managers in other organizations. The idea being presented here is that it is prison managers who are the heroic guardians and agents of moral progression in prisons.

Other research on the practice of prison managers has suggested that they do not act uniformly but instead there is a diversity of values and approaches. In his ethnographic study of American prison managers, DiIulio (1991: 54) concludes that 'there is no one theory of organizational leadership ... and certainly no management formula that guarantees success' (see also DiIulio 1987). Instead, it has been suggested that there is a range of values, motivations and approaches. Two important studies of criminal justice managers in the UK reflect this idea, namely Rutherford (1993) and Bryans (2007). Rutherford (1993: 26) suggests that criminal justice management is 'an arena characterized by competing ideologies'. Based on interviews with 28 managers, he argues that there are three clusters of values or 'credos' that shape individual practice: humanity, punitiveness and expedient managerialism. More recently, Bryans (2007) conducted interviews with 42 governors in the late 1990s and from this identified four ideal types of prison governor: 'general managers' (focus on performance management and their own career); 'chief officers' (work their way through the ranks and adopt an approach based upon their operational experience); 'liberal idealists' (concerned with the morality of imprisonment, have an academic background); and 'conforming mavericks' (individualists who develop innovative practices whilst also achieving the majority of conventional targets).

Together, these works foreground the distinctiveness of prisons from other organizations, and of prison managers from prison officers. They also suggest that prison managers act with significant agency and are participants in value-driven field struggles. However, these are approaches that raise a number of problems. The first is that emphasizing the distinctive, local features of prisons and prison management, overlooks those aspects that are consistent with other organizations, including the influence of global trends such as managerialism. The second is that emphasizing the distinctiveness of prison managers from other staff, particularly prison officers and prison officer culture, ignores the ways in which there may be intersections and links created through dialectical relationships and how prison managers may be shaped and constrained by this. In other words, both global and local structures retreat to the background in these studies. The emphasis on diversity is also exaggerated by the creation of ideal types, which neatly but artificially construct imaginary figures that may not exist so distinctly in reality. Instead, complexity is lost in favour of an idealized image of the prison manager as heroic agent.

Prison manager as agent/subject of global change

A second approach to understanding prison managers presents their working lives as being fundamentally transformed by the rise of managerialism. It has been suggested that as a reflection of the globalization of consumer capitalism, a hegemonic form of management now dominates contemporary organizations, particularly in the developed

Western world (Parker 2002). This includes a movement towards larger organizations with hierarchical structures that attempt to monitor and control the behaviour of employees through target setting and the use of information technology. It also encompasses the use of human resource management techniques such as recruitment, reward, appraisal, development, communication and consultation in order to shape the ways that employees think about their work, enlisting them as corporate citizens. Underpinning managerialism is a set of values that place emphasis upon economic rationality and the commodification of workers as efficient units of production.

This particular description of managerialism draws out three significant and interlinked developments. The first relates to changes in organizational structures and practices. The second is a set of normative changes that provide ways of thinking about and legitimizing organizational practice. The third is the important, but sometimes overlooked, aspect of how managerialist practices seek to shape the agency of workers, penetrating deep into their ways of thinking and being. Each of these three elements will be briefly elaborated below.

It has been argued that globalized capitalism has led to altered structures of work characterized by increased fluidity and insecurity (Giddens 1991; Beck 1992; Bauman 2000). This has included greater mobility of capital; the replacement of the job for life with short-term, sub-contracted and part-time employment; rapidly changing technology and skills; and the replacement of the work place with decentred home and mobile working (Sennett 2004). Linked but distinct changes have also been noted in the public sector, including the development of commercial competition for the delivery of public services, and within state-operated organizations the introduction of practices imported from the commercial sector, including increased financial control and the use of performance monitoring (Hood 1991; Pollitt 1993; Ferlie et al. 1996; Greener 2013).

The normative changes that have occurred have seen these emerging practices legitimized by reference to the market, including the need for 'efficiency' and 'competitiveness'. This has also seeped into the public sector so that there has been the 'introduction and promotion of short-term, cost-benefits thinking within the public sector' and 'the language of economics, efficiency and technological solutions is … favoured at the expense of more normative, long-term … policy debates' (Aas 2013: 156).

In terms of agency, there are a number of ways in which the processes of managerialism seek to permeate the subjectivity of workers. The use of human resources techniques such as training and development, consultation and engagement, and communication are often deployed in order to enlist workers into seeing their own interests and that of the organization as intertwined and strengthening their capacity to advance the interests of the organization (Rose 1999). As well as this deployment of soft power in order to responsibilize workers (Garland 2001), organizations also deploy methods of control and surveillance. In particular, the development and expansion of methods of monitoring, including audits, targets and technology, are used to provide 'management at a distance' (O'Malley 2004) where successive layers of workers exercise control so as to align employees' actions, behaviours and thinking with centralized objectives. It has been suggested that such technologies of surveillance also induce self-regulation in actors (Foucault 1977; Rose 1999).

Applying this to prison managers, it has been suggested that they have become homogenized, moulded and reshaped by a new set of expectations. In English and Welsh prisons, the development of managerial practices included the opening of a commercial market for prison services, the importation of techniques including performance targets, and professionalization of managers in fields including finance and human resources. The development of performance measurement has been the most extensive and important development in that process, reshaping modes of practice and thinking, rather than the development of commercial competition, which has remained limited (Armstrong 2007).

Initially, there was resistance to managerialism from managers themselves (Wilson 1995; Godfrey 1996) and unions (Bennett and Wahidin 2008). However, by the turn of the century, Bryans (2007: 63) noted that:

> More recently, Governors have been required to adopt a more managerial ethos. Prisons have to be managed in a more passionless and bureaucratic manner. Efficiency and compliance have become the administratively defined goals. Governors are increasingly seen as general managers and held to account for the total operation of their prisons, through more comprehensive line management.

This description suggests that this has been a disciplinary process in which reluctant prison managers have been 'required' to change through tight accountability through performance measurement. However, the idea that the growth of managerialism as exclusively a top-down process forced upon unwilling professionals is not tenable. Some managers willingly embrace managerialist techniques, finding them empowering. For example, a former director-general of the National Offender Management Service described managerialism as making it easier to get things done and turning the good intentions of liberal predecessors into reality (Wheatley 2005), whilst his successor (Spurr and Bennett 2008) has argued that performance measures are a means to achieve good works and that compliance is a way of managing risk, avoiding disasters such as the escapes that occurred in the 1990s (Woodcock 1994; Learmont 1995), or the racist murder of Zahid Mubarek (Keith 2006).

Whilst some managers were compelled to conform and others willingly did so, for the majority there are more subtle processes through which they have become embroiled in managerialism. Some of these changes relate to structures of prison management. In his study of managers' use of discretion, Cheliotis (2006: 316) describes that these changes have been reinforced by social processes, or what he calls the:

> three basic managerial forces that, together, serve subtly to rigidify the nature and scope of criminal justice work, and to mould professionals into patterns of conformity to systematic goals, while also playing attention to the human consequences of these forces.

First, there is an increasingly hierarchical division of labour, particularly between headquarters and establishments, so that establishments are focused on service delivery rather than engaging in wider cultural, moral or strategic development. Second, there is intensive inter- and intra-agency competition, fuelled by commercial competition and publicly available performance information. Third is the breeding of a new, up-and-coming generation of blasé professionals who are less concerned about moral aspects of imprisonment and see their work as a general management role.

For many workers, these changes have brought about not only a shift in how they work but also how they think and feel about it, reflecting contemporary organizational practice where 'the management of subjectivity has become a central task of the modern organization' (Rose 1999: 2). This development of self-regulation, along with the accumulation of surveillance through performance monitoring, facilitates the process of 'management at a distance' (O'Malley 2004).

These works collectively present a picture of managerialism sweeping through and reconstructing the practice of prison management. From this perspective, prison management has become less distinct, with localism and idiosyncrasy excluded in favour of a more rigid, consistent and predictable form. However, this also raises a number of problems. First, this presents a picture of a process that has attained a degree of domination and control that is virtually complete. Is it realistic to suggest that managerial practices cover every situation and circumstance that can be produced in a complex institution like a prison? Do responses not vary at different times and places? Is it realistic to suggest that individuals are so tightly controlled as to have such little choice and discretion in their actions? Finally, is it realistic to suggest that ubiquitous, deeply held and longstanding local features such as occupational cultures could be so completely eliminated in such a relatively short period of time? It is therefore argued that although there is a trend of growing managerialism as both a set of practices and a set of emotional and cognitive responses to the working environment, the works described above push this too far and give insufficient account of the complexities of individuals, cultures and variations of time and place.

Rethinking prison management in late modernity

So far, two distinct perspectives have been presented, one that sees prison management as a set of localized practices and cultures and a second that has been recast in the shape of globalized managerialism. The work of Giddens (1984, 1991) can be usefully drawn upon to question the assumptions that underpin this previous work, and to propose a new way ahead. This involves moving away from the inherent dualisms and instead exploring these dynamic inter-relationships as dualities: globalism and localism, agency and structure. In common with Giddens, such an approach is interested in how structures are both constraining and enabling; how individuals are not only subject to rules and structures but are also participants in their creation, maintenance and adaptation; the dialectics between the holders of power and the subjects of it; and the duality between the local and the global.

Those who argue that managerialism has transformed prison management are advancing a strong version of globalization, which has swept all before it and has not only replaced existing practices and cultures but has also captured the agency and subjectivity of workers. In this version, the relationship between local cultures and globalization is set up as a competitive binary, which 'encourages us to believe that the local and the global are pitted against each other in some sort of battle for survival or supremacy which the former will inevitably lose' (Kennedy 2010: 141–142).

Increasingly, such a version of globalization has come under criticism. From a structural perspective, it has been argued that the case for the transformation in organizational practice has been exaggerated and instead traditional structures have persevered, for example long-term employment has remained the norm, and capital is less mobile than has often been suggested (Doogan 2009). From a normative perspective, it has also been argued that the dominance and legitimation of global capitalism has been overstated and that the significance of deeply entrenched local cultures and practices has been underplayed. From this perspective, the local is:

> ubiquitous and commonplace … It absorbs, diverts and distracts us. It surrounds and envelops us, filling our lives with huge volumes of detail, information, attachments, pressures, expectations and demands, patterns, routines, responsibilities, pleasures, desires but also familiar routes and spacial-social niches … The ordinariness of the local and its powerful centripetal tendencies and attraction, pulling us inwards, affects everyone to a greater or lesser extent and usually the former.
>
> (Kennedy 2010: 7)

It has therefore been argued that the inter-relationship between local and global forces is better described as a 'dialectical phenomenon' (Giddens 1991: 32) involving a dualistic, dynamic exchange.

In addition, the strong case for globalization may provide insufficient attention to the role of agency. Giddens has argued that:

> modernity radically alters the nature of day-to-day social life and affects the most personal aspects of our experience. Modernity must be understood on an institutional level; yet the transmutations introduced by modern institutions interlace in a direct way with individual life and therefore with the self.
>
> (Giddens 1991: 1)

It is therefore suggested that individuals are directly drawn into, implicated and affected by the circumstances of late modernity. This has been contextualized in the everyday world by Kennedy, who has argued that understanding globality and social change is not solely a matter of tracing broad macro-developments, but is equally about understanding the role of individuals as 'micro actors':

> It is ordinary people in their everyday lives who cope with and sometimes react to the global forces penetrating their particular life spaces – threats to jobs, the casualization of work, the effects of climate change or the stresses of living in a multicultural city – even though they do not always understand or interpret them as global forces.
>
> (Kennedy 2010: 13)

The nature of late modernity and globalization shapes the broader context but also intersects with individual agency. Individuals are micro actors who interpret, adapt, implement, resist, ignore and facilitate the changes. These changes not only occur in the actions of individuals, but also in their sense of identity and self.

This approach attempts to re-emphasize the duality of agency and structure in the development of globalized practices such as managerialism (Giddens 1984). There are particular forms of organizational structure and practices that have developed, underpinned by a particular set of ideologies, and those practices and structures are deployed in an attempt to mould the agency of individual actors. However, it would be unrealistic to suggest that those changes are uniformly implemented, or that they sweep away all that has gone before in a hostile takeover of culture and practice, and it would also be inadequate to argue that individuals are automatons whose souls are simply captured and controlled by these forces. Instead, an approach is being proposed which considers the ways in which globalized developments interplay with both local cultures and practices and with individual agency. Such an approach offers a more realistic and more complex approach to understanding the nature of late modernity.

It is within this context that prison management can be reconsidered and reframed. Sensitivity to the dualities inherent in late modernity can be detected in some wider studies. For example, in their study of order in prisons, Sparks et al. (1996: 136–137) argued that 'power is not untrammelled' but instead there is a process of negotiation between different players and that prison management involves '"balancing" or walking tightropes ... reconciling competing priorities and concerns in the face of different kinds of constraint'. This starts to reveal some of the complex tensions that prison managers have to navigate.

Two particular writers, namely Pat Carlen (2001, 2002) and Leonidas Cheliotis (2006), have developed research on prison managers that directly addresses issues of agency and structure. Carlen's work in women's prisons attempts to present performance measurement and managerialism as essentially dysfunctional but also illustrates how managers respond to this, for example by choosing between different measures, ignoring others and emphasizing what they consider important. Similarly, Cheliotis (2006) uses decision making regarding temporary release in order to illustrate how managers engage in acts of resistance. He argues that individuals negotiate a position between revolutionary resistance and blind conformity, and that they are sophisticated consumers able to discern between competing messages and make choices about what they do. Cheliotis argues that this use of agency can be humanizing. These studies start to reveal the ways in which structure and agency are inter-related.

These studies draw out a number of features that reflect work on the wider world of work. In particular, they challenge the idea that managerialism has a complete and dominating role in practice and subjectivity. They highlight the inchoate and incomplete nature of monitoring and control and also attempt to rediscover and reclaim the role of agency. However, one element that is given insufficient attention in these studies is the importance of localized values and cultures, including prison management and prison officer cultures. Most importantly, Sparks et al. (1996) illuminate the dualities inherent in prison management and the need to balance and make sense of competing tensions and pressures. A new approach to the study of prison managers is being proposed which builds upon these dualities. From this perspective, prison management is not a set of rigid managerialist prescriptions or untrammelled individualism, but is instead a complex set of negotiations. In this sense prison managers are being seen as micro actors entangled within and attempting to make sense of the dialectical relationship between global and local (Giddens 1991; Kennedy 2010).

Late modern prison management in practice

As has been described above, the trend towards managerialism has had a role in the shaping of the contemporary prison and the practice of prison managers but this also has to be situated within the particular local culture and account for the role of agency. This section sets out to explore these dynamics within the working lives of prison managers. It will do so by considering and contrasting two particular performance measures: key performance targets (KPTs) and 'measuring the quality of prison life' (MQPL).

This section draws upon empirical research of prison managers conducted in two medium security prisons in 2007 and 2008 (Bennett 2015). This was ethnographic in nature and included 60 days of observation of and 60 semi-structured interviews with prison managers at all levels from governors to uniformed managers (senior officers and principal officers), and also encompassed non-operational managers including those responsible for finance, human resources, offender management, psychology, and learning and skills. The quotes and observations below are drawn from both field notes and interviews.

Key performance targets

Quantitative measures are the most visible form of performance management and as such they have a particular resonance in discussions regarding managerialism; they are the performance measurement *par excellence*. They were introduced to prisons in the early 1990s, imported from the commercial sector by then Director-General Derek Lewis (1997). During the period of the study, there were approximately 45 KPTs, although only approximately 40 would be relevant to each prison. These covered five categories: 'Decency & Health' (such as suicide and self-harm audit score, time unlocked); 'Organisational Efficiency & Effectiveness' (such as completion of staff appraisals, timely responses to prisoner complaints and public correspondence); 'Regimes' (such as purposeful activity and the attainment of qualifications by prisoners); 'Safety' (such as assaults and accidents); and 'Security' (such as escapes, breach of temporary release and completion of searches). These were drawn together into a single measure known as the 'weighted scorecard', which enabled prisons to be ranked in a 'league table' (Wagstaffe 2002).

These measures had a high visibility, being discussed at all levels in formal and informal meetings. They were subject to regular senior management scrutiny. Managers described how KPTs exercised a powerful role within their working lives, conveying both their pervasiveness and the depth to which they penetrated, becoming an all-embracing, continuous and conscious presence. Such measures were often referred to as fundamental to the practice of prison management: 'they underpin everything we do', 'they're my bread and butter', and 'they are our core business'. In general, managers felt these measures had a dominating presence.

The reach and power of KPTs, however, was not uniform but instead varied. One reason for this was differing levels of competence. Some managers were better than others at reading and using such measures. Their impact also varied depending upon the number of targets that groups or individuals held and the difficulty of achieving them. For example, some managers had few targets and they were easily achieved as there were sufficient staff resources allocated and the practice was routinized, whilst others were more difficult to sustain and required cross-department cooperation. The role of KPTs in the manager's working life also varied with a person's place within the hierarchy, so more senior staff including governor grades generally saw them as having a dominating role, whilst others felt the pressure less intensely.

Managers complied with key performance targets for a number of reasons. Many saw them as having an instrumental value in improving managerial effectiveness, providing a rational basis for management action. This was a source of empowerment for managers; a means through which their skills could be applied. These measures were also seen as having some normative value or moral benefit by enabling progressive change, for example by advancing improvements in services for prisoners. Many also considered that KPTs were backed up by a punitive mechanism. Many believed that if they did not achieve targets they would get 'hammered', be given 'a kicking', get 'our arses kicked' or 'it would come back on me'. The language used is in itself not insignificant, reflecting as it does a particular form of aggressive masculinity. In reality, managers who did not succeed in meeting targets were not dismissed, managed as poor performers or treated in harsh ways, and indeed many would have their reasons for non-attainment which would usually be accepted as legitimate. However, managers were concerned about this and felt that the experience of accounting for non-compliance was uncomfortable and that this caused them anxiety about the security of their position, reputation and future career.

In contrast, success brought with it a sense of personal attainment and the prospect of rewards and enhanced reputation or career prospects. Interestingly, there was also a sense in which managers absorbed the attainment of these targets within their own sense of identity. Many were unswerving in their desire to attain targets, using phrases such as 'you don't miss a KPT, you just don't do it', and 'I guard them with my life'. Sometimes this commitment was expressed in ways that appeared extreme. For example, one manager described how he found it 'devastating' that he had failed to meet a target despite the fact that this failure was caused by a large increase in the prisoner population. Another manager said that the thought of not meeting a target 'makes me feel ill thinking about it', whilst a third described that they had been burned out and had become 'fraggled' as a result of chasing a target in difficult circumstances. These intense physiological feelings were elicited by the drive that these individuals had regarding targets.

Most managers were not slavishly uncritical of output measurement and indeed many were conscious of their limitations. First, they recognized that targets did not always reflect what was important but instead were incomplete and opportunistic (see Smith and Goddard 2002). Second, they were described as inflexible; for example, measures were not altered to reflect changed resources or contexts. Third, it was claimed that these measures did not take account of quality but were only concerned with quantity. Fourth, managers were conscious of deliberate gaming and manipulation of figures, which in some cases was chronic (Carlen 2002; HMCIP 2008). Although many managers were aware of these limitations, their criticisms were largely reserved for the back room or for occasional comment in open forum; it did not prevent them engaging in the pursuit of targets, either because they saw it overall as desirable or simply as a necessity in the contemporary prison.

The attainment of KPTs was embraced, albeit unevenly and not uncritically, by prison managers as a fundamental aspect of their role. This not only absorbed their time and energy, but also seeped into how they thought about themselves and their working world.

Measuring the quality of prison life

In 2002, HM Prison Service launched a drive to improve 'decency' in prisons. This reflected a broader move within public management to incorporate the values of customer service and the experience of individual service users (Greener 2013). At the time this was emerging, a tool was being developed at the University of Cambridge described as 'measuring the quality of prison life' (MQPL) (Liebling, with Arnold 2004). Subsequently, this tool was adapted and developed as a means of assessing prison performance. An evaluation of each prison is conducted every two years, involving surveys of a random representative sample of 10–15% of the prisoner population followed by a series of focus groups. A report is produced, summarizing the results and providing comparative data. It is for managers to decide how to respond as there is no formal requirement to do so.

The most striking feature of managers' views of MQPL in the study was how little they knew about it. Many had only a vague understanding of what it was or how it was conducted. It was the least visible and least understood of all the performance measures. Those who were aware of it generally described it as a measure of 'prisoners' perceptions' and considered that it related to issues of 'respect', 'decency' and 'staff–prisoner relationships'. Some saw this as having value as a measure of 'the feel of the place', as a tool to assess and manage prisons, and a means by which the views of prisoners could be elicited and considered. Some also valued the independence of the measure. Academic commentators have responded positively to MQPL, describing it as a sophisticated measure (Van Zyl Smit 2005) that can promote a human rights approach (Harding 2005). On a more instrumental level, some managers stated that they paid attention to MQPL because senior echelons in the Prison Service took account of it in forming a view about individual prisons.

Managers were often sceptical of MQPL. Some felt that the nature of imprisonment militated against honest appraisal by prisoners. For example, one manager said:

> [P]risoners will say things that are not really the way they are, it will be their perception and maybe they're getting a lot better conditions, things are maybe a lot better than they are portraying … That worries me sometimes, you never get a true picture from them. Prisoners will be prisoners and they will complain to complain.

These comments indicated a concern that the measure served the interests of prisoners, painting a partial and untruthful picture. They also described that prisoners will inevitably be critical due to some ingrained pathology, described as 'prisoners will be prisoners'. This was elaborated by other managers who suggested: 'You ask any prisoner, he's going to moan because he's in prison'; and, 'you have to take them with a pinch of salt'.

Many managers also argued that the methodology was unreliable as it provided a disproportionate voice to 'a small minority of prisoners' who had been 'rubbed … up the wrong way' or were taking the opportunity of 'a good place for them to have a go'. From this perspective, '[u]nfortunately prisoners, they do tell lies …' For example, one manager stated:

> MQPL I find that frustrating because that's a prisoner's perspective of what's going on but there's nothing in there, as far as I can see, that addresses any vindictive actions that a prisoner might take, some prisoners might say something and half a dozen prisoners say something completely different and radical, perhaps because they've got an axe to grind.

Other managers also claimed that it was the luck of the draw as to who was selected to take part and therefore an unstable, unpredictable measure:

> It can be extremely subjective because they will come in and pick up a percentage of the jail … they could come in this week and find one set of results and come in

next week and find a completely different set ... It's good luck or bad luck as to which prisoners they select randomly from a computer. It's just how it goes.

These views about MQPL revealed that it was a controversial measure. This was partly due to a lack of understanding about research methodologies such as sampling. What also underpinned the scepticism was a cultural response to the foregrounding of the interests and voice of prisoners. This was represented by managers as an unreliable source of information. Of course, such views revealed more deep-seated perceptions of prisoners and their appropriate position. The scepticism commonly pathologized prisoners as untrustworthy and delegitimized them as a focus of concern and instead suggested that they should be the silent, passive and powerless subjects.

In terms of how MQPL was followed up and its effects, it was seen by many as having a limited impact. Managers described that the report would be read, discussed and published, but there would not be rigorous analysis and follow-up:

It seemed more like another paper exercise ... You send them back, you get some feedback sent out or published on the intranet and its end of story.

The only exception was that one manager suggested that as with other reports, if there was a particularly good or bad assessment, it would have an impact but beyond these polar outcomes it was often seen as marginal. There were several reasons given for this. The first was that the MQPL report was complicated and difficult to interpret and turn into clear action (Bennett 2007). Managers described how they were presented with 'all these graphs and charts' which they struggled to understand. The reports were composed of myriad statistical information using means and standard deviations. However, for many prison managers, in comparison with the simplicity of KPTs, MQPL appeared to be extraordinarily complex. The reports also did not immediately lend themselves to practical action. The report would reflect what prisoners had said, what their perspectives were and how they rated aspects of the prison, but it did not identify specific issues that shaped this perception or any changes that could be made in order to improve. This meant that they were of limited practical application without further analysis and action planning.

Overall, MQPL had a limited effect on the prison. This was partly a function of its complexity as a measure but it was also as a result of the cultural response to it being based on prisoners' views.

Conclusion: *prison* managerialism

This chapter has explored the complex lived experience of globalized change, using the example of the development of managerialism in prisons in England and Wales. This final section attempts to draw the themes and issues together.

The case of prisons has illustrated that managerialism has indeed had a deep and profound impact on the organization and individuals. Whilst the creation of a full commercial market has not come about, the importation of practices such as performance measurement has had an effect. Personal and organizational resources have been deployed towards the attainment of targets and this was a dominating concern of many managers. This also had an effect upon how they felt about themselves and their work.

The managerialist approach has been given depth and intensity not only through the development of technological apparatus, but through the absorption of these approaches within the *habitus* (Bourdieu 1977) of prison managers so that they have come to exercise a degree of self-government and self-control. Managers experienced the development of performance measurement as both constraining, inasmuch as it placed limits upon their own actions, and also enabling, inasmuch as it was a means to exercise control over their subordinates. Through this chain of power and control, 'management at a distance' (O'Malley 2004) was realized.

However, it is important that these developments are not presented or viewed as a 'fantasy of total control' (O'Neill 2002). Managers were conscious of the limitations, they understood that such monitoring did not address all of their work or indeed all of the important aspects of it and they were capable of gaming the system. Although the managerialist project has had a significant impact, it is incomplete or inchoate: there is not a panoptic form of surveillance and managers have not been turned into automatons.

The spread of globalized practices, such as managerialism, has interacted with other forces that play a powerful role in working lives, in particular local cultures. As can be seen in prisons, this interconnectedness can be uneven and complex; it can be the source of both conflict and mutual reinforcement. The contrasting views and responses by prison managers to KPTs and MQPL can be used in order to illustrate this. The relatively positive reception afforded to KPTs can be accounted for in relation to risk, uncertainty and order. The emergence of performance management provides a means through which the complex tasks of prison management can be simplified and controlled. It provides a means of managing risk or at least presenting the appearance of doing so (O'Malley 2004). The harder, qualitative measures are also more amenable to management action. They are clearer and more predictable, and managers can influence results. In contrast, those measures based upon structured judgement and prisoner perceptions are more unpredictable and unmanageable. The measures themselves therefore differ in the degree to which they are perceived as intrinsically risky for managers and to which they could provide a means through which managers could control risk. The simplification and certainty provided by KPTs helps to explain their attraction to prison managers as it provides them with meaning and control. However, what they also do is provide a set of tools that enable the reaffirmation of organizational hierarchy through monitoring, feedback and the allocation of resources, whilst also aligning the interests of workers with that of the organization, creating a shared sense of purpose. KPTs therefore address both global and local concerns, playing with the grain of a hierarchical and highly controlled total institution (Goffman 1961), with a quasi-military command and control structure (Thomas 1972). In contrast, MQPL was received more problematically, in particular because the attention paid to prisoners' needs and views acted to spoil the identity (Goffman 1963) of the measure in the eyes of some managers. This related to a traditional cultural view of prisoners, who have been seen within the occupational group as being subservient and cast as the 'other' (Sim 2009). This went against the local organizational culture and MQPL therefore had an uncomfortable reception. The cultural context was important in understanding the differences in how measures were understood and practised.

These conflicts, accommodations and intersections did not take place in an abstract way, but instead, this was a lived experience involving prison managers themselves. It was they, as micro actors, who had to make sense of the various pressures playing upon them, including local culture, global change and their own individual sense of values and beliefs. They were often in a position of having to navigate and negotiate between the competing demands. They were not only subjects of the inter-relatedness of global and local forces, but had an active role in this dialectical process.

Rather than talking about prison management or managerialism, it is more appropriate to refer to 'prison managerialism'. At the most general level this term attempts to capture the inter-relationship of the forces of managerialism and prison occupational culture. The term is intended to convey an acknowledgement of the influence of global change, whilst also recognizing that this is mediated through local cultures and individual actors.

Bibliography

Aas, K. (2013) *Globalization and Crime*, second edn, London: Sage.

Armstrong, S. (2007) 'What Good are Markets in Punishment?', *Prison Service Journal* 172: 12–16.

Bauman, Z. (2000) *Liquid Modernity*, Cambridge: Polity Press.

Beck, U. (1992) *Risk Society: Towards a New Modernity*, London: Sage.

Bennett, J. (2007) 'Measuring Order and Control in HM Prison Service', in Y. Jewkes (ed.) *Handbook on Prisons*, Cullompton: Willan, 518–542.

Bennett, J. (2015) *The Working Lives of Prison Managers: Global Change, Local Culture and Individual Agency in the Late Modern Prison*, Basingstoke: Palgrave Macmillan.

Bennett, J. and Wahidin, A. (2008) 'Industrial Relations in Prisons', in J. Bennett, B. Crewe and A. Wahidin (eds) *Understanding Prison Staff*, Cullompton: Willan, 117–133.

Bourdieu, P. (1977) *Outline of a Theory of Practice*, Cambridge: Cambridge University Press.

Bryans, S. (2000) 'Governing Prisons: An Analysis of who is Governing Prisons and the Competencies they Require to Govern Effectively', *The Howard Journal of Criminal Justice* 30(1): 14–29.

Bryans, S. (2007) *Prison Governors: Managing Prisons in a Time of Change*, Cullompton: Willan.

Bryans, S. and Wilson, D. (2000) *The Prison Governor: Theory and Practice*, second edn, Leyhill: Prison Service Journal.

Carlen, P. (2001) 'Death and the Triumph of Governance? Lessons from the Scottish Women's Prison', *Punishment and Society* 3(4): 459–471.

Carlen, P. (2002) 'Governing the Governors: Telling Tales of Managers, Mandarins and Mavericks', *Criminal Justice* 2(1): 27–49.

Cheliotis, L. (2006) 'How Iron is the Iron Cage of New Penology? The Role of Human Agency in the Implementation of Criminal Justice Policy', *Punishment and Society* 8(3): 313–340.

Crawley, E. (2004) *Doing Prison Work: The Public and Private Lives of Prison Officers*, Cullompton: Willan.

Crawley, E. and Crawley, P. (2008) 'Understanding Prison Officers: Culture, Cohesion and Conflict', in J. Bennett, B. Crewe and A. Wahidin (eds) *Understanding Prison Staff*, Cullompton: Willan, 134–152.

DiIulio, J. (1987) *Governing Prisons: A Comparative Study of Correctional Management*, New York: The Free Press.

DiIulio, J. (1991) *No Escape: The Future of American Corrections*, New York: Basic Books.

Doogan, K. (2009) *New Capitalism? The Transformation of Work*, Cambridge: Polity Press.

Ferlie, E., Pettigrew, A., Ashburner, L. and Fitzgerald, L. (1996) *The New Public Management in Action*, Oxford: Oxford University Press.

Foucault, M. (1977) *Discipline and Punish: The Birth of the Prison*, London: Allen Lane.

Garland, D. (2001) *The Culture of Control: Crime and Social Order in Contemporary Society*, Oxford: Oxford University Press.

Giddens, A. (1984) *The Constitution of Society: Outline of the Theory of Structuration*, Cambridge: Polity Press.

Giddens, A. (1991) *Modernity and Self-identity: Self and Society in the Late Modern Age*, Cambridge: Polity Press.

Godfrey, D. (1996) 'The Morale of Prison Governors: Some Reflections', *Prison Service Journal* 104: 12–14.

Goffman, E. (1961) *Asylums*, London: Penguin.

Goffman, E. (1963) *Stigma*, Englewood Cliffs, NJ: Prentice Hall.

Greener, I. (2013) *Public Management*, second edn, Basingstoke: Palgrave Macmillan.

Harding, R. (2005) 'Book Reviews: *Prisons and their Moral Performance: A Study in Values, Quality and Prison Life*, Alison Liebling. Clarendon Studies in Criminology, Oxford University Press 2004', *Punishment and Society* 7: 222–224.

HMCIP (HM Chief Inspector of Prisons) (2008) *Time Out of Cell: A Short Thematic Review*, London: HMCIP.

Hood, C. (1991) 'A Public Management for All Seasons', *Public Administration* 69: 3–19.

Keith, B. (2006) *Report of the Zahid Mubarek Inquiry*, London: The Stationery Office.

Kennedy, P. (2010) *Local Lives and Global Transformations: Towards World Society*, Basingstoke: Palgrave Macmillan.

Learmont, J. (1995) *Review of Prison Service Security in England and Wales and the Escape from Parkhurst Prison on Tuesday 3 January 1995*, London: HMSO.

Lewis, D. (1997) *Hidden Agendas: Politics, Law and Disorder*, London: Hamish Hamilton.

Liebling, A. (2007) 'Why Prison Staff Culture Matters', in J. Byrne, D. Hummer and F. Taxman (eds) *The Culture of Prison Violence*, Upper Saddle River, NJ: Prentice Hall, 105–122.

Liebling, A., with Arnold, H. (2004) *Prisons and their Moral Performance: A Study of Values, Quality and Prison Life*, Oxford: Clarendon Press.

Liebling, A., Price, D. and Shefer, G. (2011) *The Prison Officer*, second edn, Abingdon: Willan.

Loftus, B. (2011) *Police Culture in a Changing World*, Oxford: Oxford University Press.

O'Malley, P. (2004) *Risk, Uncertainty and Government*, London: The GlassHouse Press.

O'Neill, O. (2002) 'Reith Lectures: A Question of Trust', www.bbc.co.uk/radio4/features/the-reith-lectures/transcripts/2000/ (accessed 19 May 2013).

Parker, M. (2002) *Against Management: Organization in the Age of Managerialism*, Cambridge: Polity Press.

Pollitt, C. (1993) *Managerialism and the Public Services: Cuts or Cultural Change in the 1990s?* Oxford: Blackwell.

Rose, N. (1999) *Governing the Soul: The Shaping of the Private Self*, second edn, London: Free Association Books.

Rutherford, A. (1993) *Criminal Justice and the Pursuit of Decency*, Oxford: Oxford University Press.

Sennett, R. (2004) *The Culture of the New Capitalism*, New Haven, CT: Yale University Press.

Sim, J. (2009) *Punishment and Prisons: Power and the Carceral State*, London: Sage.

Skolnick, J. (1966) *Justice without Trial*, New York: Wiley.

Smith, P. and Goddard, M. (2002) 'Performance Management and Operational Research: A Marriage Made in Heaven?' *Journal of the Operational Research Society* 53(3): 247–255.

Sparks, R., Bottoms, A. and Hay, W. (1996) *Prisons and the Problem of Order*, Oxford: Clarendon Press.

Spurr, M. and Bennett, J. (2008) 'The Interview: Michael Spurr', *Prison Service Journal* 177: 54–61.

Thomas, J. (1972) *The English Prison Officer Since 1850: A Study in Conflict*, London: Routledge & Kegan Paul.

Van Zyl Smit, D. (2005) 'Reviews: *Prisons and their Moral Performance*. By Alison Liebling assisted by Helen Arnold (Oxford: Clarendon Studies in Criminology, Oxford University Press 2004)', *British Journal of Criminology* 45: 765–767.

Wagstaffe, S. (2002) 'There is Measure in all Things', *Prison Service Journal* 141: 2–4.

Wheatley, P. (2005) 'Managerialism in the Prison Service', *Prison Service Journal* 161: 33–34.

Wilson, D. (1995) 'Against the Culture of Management', *Prison Service Journal* 98: 7–9.

Wilson, D. (2000) 'Whatever Happened to "The Governor"', *Criminal Justice Matters* 40: 11–12.

Woodcock, J. (1994) *Report of an Inquiry into the Escape of Six Prisoners from the Special Secure Unit at Whitemoor Prison in Cambridgeshire on Friday 9 September 1994*, London: HMSO.

Part II

Prison controversies

Chapter 9

Private prisons

John Rynne and Richard Harding

Delivery of custodial services for profit is not a new concept, with evidence of private people profiting from punishment even in Ancient Greece (D'Amico 2010). As early as 1625, prison administrators in Hamburg and Bremen were paid *per diem* rates based on prisoner type, with the most profitable prisoner, *losamenten*, detained for being a troublesome family member. Wealthy families could pay the *oeconomus* to feed and provide basic prison accommodation until the family was satisfied their behaviour had improved or money ran out (Spierenburg 2007). England's influential prisoner reformer, Jeremy Bentham (1791: 19–58), proposed a fee for service contract for his panopticon prison model, and was an avid promoter of prisons operated on a for-profit basis.

The literature on private prisons and its controversies is voluminous. Often the research is atheoretical and repetitive, without making any substantial contributions to understanding the impact of prison (Volokh 2014). For example, comparative studies focused on proving private or public superior effectiveness and efficiency over the other are replete. A range of limiting data access factors makes absolute claims as to the efficiency or cost-effectiveness of one sector over the other nearly impossible. The following summarizes factors that have influenced the global introduction of private prisons as well as limiting factors in their growth.

A current definition of private or contract prisons is where the state partially or wholly purchases, via tender, contracts for custodial services (Harding 2001). Based on this definition, the following chapter summarizes the growth of private prisons, international variations in contractual approaches and consequences of private sector entry into the custodial component of the criminal justice system.

Background

Australia also had an active role in early custodial privatization. The first fleet of convicts (1788) transported to Australia was of ships contracted by the British government at a cost of £20,000 (Hughes 1987). When in Australia, the private sector was substantially involved from 1788 to 1849, when convict labourers were assigned to free settlers who then became responsible for their feeding, clothing and accommodation (Shaw 1966). Similarly, in the USA following the Civil War, prisoners (the majority of whom were black) provided a cheap and ready answer to rebuilding the country (DiIulio 1990). Prisoner leasing was established as a replacement for slavery, with prisoners virtually owned by contractors (Mancini 1996). With minimal state involvement, apart from some profit sharing, contractors sought to maximize profits from a prisoner leasing system that was not surprisingly indifferent to basic prisoner rights and rehabilitation. Consequently, the system was soon corrupted through unrestricted profit taking (Mancini 1996). A variation to private enterprise prisoner leasing was the consignment of prisoners from state-run prisons to work in factories or participate in piece-rate work, where despite being held in state institutions, workplace conditions were appalling and human rights abuse common (Smith and Morn 2001).

Since the mid-19th century, the administration of justice, including prisons, has been considered a core or intrinsic function of government (DiIulio 1990; Feeley 2014; Moyle 2000; Shichor 1995). A common feature of privatization history was that the State failed to maintain its sovereign obligations by abrogating punishment responsibilities to commercial entities (Dolovich 2005; Feeley 2014; Gilbert 2001; Harding 2012; Ryan and Ward 1989). With minimal government oversight, commercial potential was maximized at the expense of prisoners' basic human rights or rehabilitation opportunities. A great deal of discussion regarding the appropriateness of private prisons therefore revolves around the legitimacy, effectiveness and efficiency compared with the public sector; the maximization of profit as opposed to the delivery of high-quality services; the potential contribution to net widening to ensure full prisons as opposed to improving recidivism; and generally the issue of accountability for standards.

Overview

Privatization has now spread to a wide range of custodial services – juvenile detention, custodial transport, court security and immigration detention. Across the globe, the delivery of custodial services by non-government providers occurs in various forms including the financing and construction of prisons; the management, staffing and operation of prisons; or the provision of ancillary services (e.g. prisoner healthcare, rehabilitation and education programmes) (Kyle 2013; Mennicken 2013; Volokh 2014). In France the notion of *prisons semi-privées* refers to private sector provision of prison services other than custodial services, whereas in the UK privatization usually refers to the full package of services required in a prison, though with the paradoxical situation that often the non-custodial services are contracted in from the non-government sector or even some other part of the government sector (such as the Education Department).

The modern era of privatization commenced in 1984 with Corrections Corporation of America being awarded a contract to fully own and operate a detention centre in Houston, by the US Immigration and Naturalization Service (Mattera et al. 2003). This shift to the private sector marked the global emergence of contract prisons. Commencing in the US states, private prisons then followed with Borallon in Queensland, Australia (1990), the Wolds in England (1992),[1] HMP Kilmarnock in Scotland (1999), Koraal Specht prison, Curaçao, Netherlands Antilles (1999), Auckland Central Remand Prison, New Zealand (2000), Central North Correctional Centre, Ontario, Canada (2001), and Manguang prison, Bloemfontein, South Africa (2001) (Begg 2003; Goyer 2001; Harding 2001; Moore et al. 2003; Prison Privatization Report International 2000).

There are 12 countries that have contracted adult custodial facilities. The majority of these are in the USA (137,220 people representing 8.7% of the total US prison population; US Department of Justice 2013).[2] Rates of incarceration in private prisons vary from Australia (19%) (Productivity Commission 2013), through Scotland (17%), England and Wales (14%), New Zealand (11%) to South Africa (4%) (Mason 2013).

Catalysts of privatization

There is substantial variation across jurisdictions for introducing private prisons. Harding (2001) proposes six catalysts that drove corrections agencies across the world to reintroduce private prisons. These catalysts are: (i) exponential increases in incarcerated populations; (ii) overcrowding leading in the USA to Federal Court intervention; (iii) legal and political inhibitions upon capital expenditure by governments; (iv) concern about recurrent costs; (v) growing impatience with the perceived obstructionism of unionized labour; and (vi) in some jurisdictions, though not the USA, some concern for regime improvement (Harding 2001: 269). Hakim and Blackstone (2013) propose that the sole reasons for contracting US prisons are financial, revolving around cost savings and reducing capital expenditure and limiting exposure to litigation.

Expanding prisoner populations

The increase in world prison populations over the last 40 years is well documented. While decreasing slightly over recent years (Glaze and Herbermann 2013), the world's leader in incarceration, the USA, has seen a 92% increase in its prison population, from 773,919 in 1990 to 2.2 million (including those held in jails) in 2013 (The Sentencing Project 2014). In that same period, Australian prisoner numbers increased by 115%, from 14,305 to 30,775 (Australian Bureau of Statistics 2013), while the UK prisoner population increased by 86.5%, from 44,975 to 83,842 (Berman and Dar 2013).

Overcrowding and judicial orders

A corollary of these rapidly expanding prison populations was an increase in the dysfunctional behaviours associated with prison overcrowding (i.e. increased prisoner suicide, self-harm and declining health) (Goffman 1961; Haney 1997; James et al. 1997; Ruback and Innes 1988; Sykes 1958). In the USA, prisoners and prisoner support groups responded to these failing institutions with legal action undertaken to improve conditions, for example Section 1983 of the US Code (Hanson and Daley 1994), under which prisoners were permitted to sue state correctional officials when the conditions of confinement contravened constitutional rights under the Eighth Amendment of the Bill of Rights. Where the standards of physical security, adequate medical treatment and freedom of religious expression were not appropriate, they were deemed to be 'cruel and unusual' punishment (Hanson and Daley 1994; Marquart and Crouch 1985), and consequently court orders or consent decrees were issued requiring the facilities to be improved or otherwise closed (McDonald et al. 1998a, 1998b). Some US state prison systems continue to operate under such court-ordered sanctions, and/or comply with court orders in ways which transfer the problem rather than fixing the cause, for example reducing overcrowded prisons by transferring to county-based facilities (i.e. jails) or to spare prison beds in out-of-state (usually private) prisons (Hakim and Blackstone 2013; Lofstrom et al. 2012).

The consequences of overcrowding and deplorable conditions were also experienced by prisoners in the UK (Woolf 1991), as well as Australia (Harding 1997). In the UK, the majority of prison infrastructure, comprising Victorian-era prisons, was not capable of providing safe and secure accommodation, while ancillary services like prisoner programmes, training or work were limited. The consequences were long hours of idleness and associated interpersonal trauma (James et al. 1997). In Australia, the state prison system was characterized by decaying and inadequate infrastructure coupled with increasing prison populations which exacerbated prisoners' vulnerability to poor health, self-harm and limited opportunity or commitment to deal with factors contributing to recidivism (Kennedy 1988; Kirby 2000; Longland 1985; Nagle 1978). While prison authorities in Australia and the UK were not under court orders to improve prison conditions (as in the USA), similar reform pressure was created by repeated criticism in independent reviews or enquiries (Kennedy 1988; Longland 1985; Nagle 1978; Woolf 1991).

Political influences

The sentencing changes of the late 1980s saw increases in carceral pressure across most modern jurisdictions. Politically populist approaches espousing longer and harsher prison sentences combined with social restructuring (e.g. de-institutionalization of the mentally ill) required innovative responses to overcrowded prisons (Caplow and Simon 1999; Hinds 2002; Logan 1990; Scottish Executive 2002; Shichor and Sechrest 2002).

Coalescing with conservative and punitive approaches to crime and prison sentences was substantial reform to the management and operation of the public sector (Hancock 1998; Pollitt and Bouckaert 2000; Raine and Willson 1997). The economic rationalization of President Regan's neo-liberalism (Sinden 2003), Prime Minister Thatcher's 'New Right' or 'Free Market' ideology (Lane 2001; Rutherford 1990), and in Australia the proliferation of government-owned corporations in the 1980s and the national competition policy reforms (Davis and Wood 1998; Hilmer and Taperell 1993) stimulated efficiency and effectiveness in public sector gains via decreasing administrative bureaucracy and altering management approaches.

Driven by the profit motive, private prisons appeared to offer a service delivery that improved on the previous 200 years of custodial operations (Austin and Coventry 2001; Harding 1997). It was proposed that private sector efficiency, achieved through public–private partnership (PPP), or private finance initiatives (PFI), would provide the model on which to reform the public sector (Carter 2001; Domberger and Jensen 1997; Osborne and Gaebler 1992; Sachdev 2001).

Inhibitions to increased capital expenditure

Prison overcrowding and the need for new infrastructure in an era of tight fiscal control meant governments, restrained from further borrowing that would increase the public debt, sought innovative solutions. Private prisons appeared as an alternative means to maximize taxpayer expense through innovative accounting practices. For example, prison construction costs could be spread across the life of the contract rather than paid in one year as per traditional government-owned procurement contracts (Logan 1990; McDonald 1990).

Compared with the public sector, private sector procurement enabled efficient prison construction and completions (Austin and Coventry 2001; Mattera et al. 2003; Segal and Moore 2002). For example, research suggests that in the USA private sector construction takes approximately half the time of the public sector (Austin and Coventry 2001).

Reducing recurrent costs

Privatization proponents argued that the private sector would ensure more effective and efficient prison operation than the public sector (Austin and Coventry 2001). Innovation in staffing strategies, prison design and construction, and technological advances would all combine to reduce costs and improve performance (House of Commons Committee of Public Accounts 2003).

To justify private provision over the public sector, in some instances the private sector was required to demonstrate operational savings. For example, the following savings are mandated by some US states: Kentucky (10%), Mississippi (10%), Ohio (5%) and Texas (10%) (Hakim and Blackstone 2013). In Florida, at least 7% savings (compared with the public sector) are necessary to be awarded a contract (McDonald et al. 1998a). In instances where contracts require mandated savings, it is likely that value-for-money considerations have less influence in determining the successful tender.[3]

Service delivery reform

In the UK and Australia, a review of the numerous external and internal investigations since 1980 indicated that along with service delivery, prison organizational cultures were dysfunctional (Johnston 1991; Kennedy 1988; Longland 1985; Nagle 1978; Woolf 1991). In the UK and Australia, and to a lesser extent the USA, prison privatization was initiated as an organizational development catalyst (Harding 2001; McDonald 1999; Sturgess 2003). While governments, academics, prison administrators and some sections of the public were no longer prepared to maintain custodial models based on punishment and retribution in deplorable conditions, an array of reasons such as prison officer resistance meant that organizational reform and work practice change following those reviews were limited (Queensland Prison Service 1986). In line with Schein's (1990) proposal that positive organizational development (that is, strategic reform) requires a critical incident to replace entrenched behavioural norms which sustain resilient organizational cultures, privatization provided an avenue through which to address entrenched prison regimes (DiPiano 1995). Thus, privatization was a planned process initiated as a strategy to change organizational culture, environment and climate (Harding 1997, 2001; Saylor 1984; Schein 1990), the outcomes of which would include improvements in the quality of service delivery.

The global spread of private prisons

Discussion to date has focused primarily on the USA, Australia and the UK as these countries shared the greatest commitment to private prisons. The spread of private prisons goes beyond these countries to include Brazil, Chile, France, Germany, Holland (Dutch East Indies), Japan, South Africa and Peru (Mason 2013). While the reasons for introducing private prisons into these latter countries are similar to those identified above, the style of privatization or its delivery method vary considerably depending on the country and its ongoing experience with privatization (Macaulay 2013).

The model of privatization in France, Germany and Holland is as described by Harding (2001: 274), 'semi-privée'. In this approach, custodial functions remain with the state while support services (e.g. prisoner programmes and food preparation) are tendered through contracts. In France, a mixed model has been developed where the private sector builds the institutions and the public sector maintains operational responsibility (Cabral and Saussier 2013; Kenter and Prior 2012; Vagg 1994). The 'semi-privée' approach is particularly popular, with 50% of all French prisoners in 2012 estimated as being held in these types of prisons (Cabral and Saussier 2013).

In South Africa, the newly installed post-apartheid government was confronted by an overcrowded and violent correctional system in disarray with a large percentage of the prison population suffering HIV infection (Goyer 2001). In response, amendments to the Corrective Services Act were made in 1998 to allow prison privatization. Poor planning and procurement processes meant that contracts for the first two private prisons were let prior to criteria for affordability, value for money and risk management processes being established as government policy (Prison Task Team 2002). Consequently, these prisons operate as well as, if not better than, the public sector but at extraordinary cost. While accounting for approximately 5% of the total Department of Corrective Services budget (Du Plessis 2012), G4S, the Bloemfontein prison operator, has reported returns on investment as high as 29.9% and GEO at Louis Trichardt also recorded a 25% profit margin (Du Plessis 2012). Despite attempting to renegotiate, the South African government has found itself locked in for the remainder of the 25-year contract, amidst allegations of prisoner torture and brutality at the Bloemfontein Manguang prison, including the unapproved administering of anti-psychotic drugs and electroshock therapy and a recent hostage-taking incident (Azzakanni 2013). Unsurprisingly, the South African government has indicated that the foreseeable future of private prisons is limited, even in relation to ancillary services such as food provision (Portfolio Committee on Correctional Services 2012).

Israel (under its 2004 Prisons Ordinance Amendment Law (Amendment 28)) and Costa Rica in 2005 (Macaulay 2013) had both approved private prisons. In each case, the relevant Supreme Court later forced the decisions to be reversed. In Israel's case, this was on the basis that private prisons breached Basic Law provisions as they relate to rights to life, to personal liberty and human dignity (Feeley 2014; Harding 2012; Resnik 2013). Similar reasons were also indicated in Costa Rica.

New Zealand's first private prison, the Auckland Central Remand Prison, opened in 2000 with the contract awarded to Australian Correctional Management (ACM) (Mason 2013). However, in 2004 the Corrections Act was amended by the left-wing Labor government to extinguish extension of any private prison contract. In another political, ideologically driven change, in 2008 the conservative government introduced the Corrections (Contract Management of Prisons) Amendment Act 2009, allowing competitive tendering and private sector operation of prisons (Chan 2010; Kenter and Prior 2012). Serco was subsequently successful in the re-tender of the remand centre, which was packaged into a larger contract for the Mount Eden Correctional Facility in 2012 (Mason 2013). Serco has also been successful in tendering for New Zealand's second DCMF (design, construct, manage and finance) contract for the Men's Corrections Facility at Wiri that was due to open in 2015.

The Brazilian approach to private sector prisons rests between the French and the US approaches. The state retains ownership of the facility while the private sector operates internal security, food, health, education and facilities. All external security and senior management roles (i.e. warden, deputy warden and security manager) are retained by the public sector (Cabral and Saussier 2013).

Have private prisons delivered the anticipated outcomes?

Despite international variations in models of privatization, the overarching goal of private prisons was to invoke service delivery reform. Driven by market forces and competition, private prisons were to model a new approach to custodial service delivery that transferred it from an input-only public sector model to effective and efficient outcome delivery achieved through innovation in input, process and outputs (Volokh 2014). Given the controversy around private prisons and the subsequent plethora of academic research and general exposure, and also the 30-year time lapse since the reinvention of private prisons, it would be assumed that how successfully or otherwise these goals have been delivered would be clearly evident. However, this is not the case. In particular, methodological problems associated with comparative studies have made it difficult, if not impossible, to compare the public and private sectors in terms of outcomes.

Cost effectiveness

Many government and academic studies have focused on determining recurrent cost efficiencies through privatization, usually through cross-sector comparisons. However, comparing public and private prisons to determine effectiveness and efficiency is highly problematic due to issues such as ability to access data and cross-sector accounting differences (Arizona Department of Corrections 2011; Association of Private Correctional and Treatment Organizations 2003; Austin and Coventry 2001; Criminal Justice Policy Council 2001; Edwards 1996; Gaes et al. 2004; Guppy 2003; Hakim and Blackstone 2013; Hamburger 1994; Home Affairs Committee 1997; Inspector of Custodial Services 2003; Kenny and Gilroy 2013; McDonald et al. 1998a; Moore 1998; Nelson 1998; Park 2000; Perrone and Pratt 2003; Sturgess 2003; Woodbridge 1999). Cross-sector efficiency comparisons are further complicated when specific corrections costs, as opposed to commercial issues, are considered. For example, public sector prisons are frequently older than private sector prisons, thus increasing the cost of the former (Gaes 2012). Other operational complications include prisoners' security level, prison population, gender, age and health. Controlling for these variables across sectors requires centralized data management (Perrone and Pratt 2003). Like all good science, iterative prison efficiency research is progressing along a continuum in the development of sophisticated economic and accounting models towards delivering valid and reliable cross-sector comparisons, and with each iteration, the real cost of prison, public and private, becomes more evident.

The next section briefly reviews the development of private sector-driven efficiency research, focusing on the USA and the UK, as the majority of efficiency research has been conducted in these countries.

The USA

Meta-analyses of cross-sector comparisons demonstrate the inconsistencies found within efficiency research. Lundahl et al.'s (2009) meta-analysis of 12 studies indicated that cost efficiencies were not certain from private sector prisons. Similarly, Pratt and Maahs (1999), in a review of 33 cost evaluations, concluded that private sector management of correctional services was 'unlikely' (ibid.: 368) to reduce the cost on the public purse.

However, they also indicated that through privatization 'specific policy alternatives may result in modest cost savings' (ibid.: 367). Included in 'specific policy alternatives' were lower infrastructure costs, for example. Therefore, despite acknowledging that the private sector reduced infrastructure costs, they did not consider that this saving flowed to overall cost reduction.

Segal and Moore (2002) overviewed 28 cost analysis studies comparing private and public prisons. The conclusion of this overview was that the private sector attained significant savings in 22 of the 28 prisons. However, this study summarized each of the previous 28 studies and lacks the methodological rigour required to support its conclusions. Perrone and Pratt (2003: 315), in analysing the methodological characteristics of studies comparing cost effectiveness in the public and private prisons, propose that the median *per diem* cost difference between public and private prisons was that the latter was US$3.40 less expensive. However, they caution interpretation of the result for reasons previously identified.

The mandated ongoing evaluation of private prisons operating under contract to the US Federal Bureau of Prisons (FBP) utilizes cost-efficiency research that controls for many of the problems previously indicated. Results indicate no significant differences in operational costs between the private and public sector (Nelson 1998, 2005); however, comparisons are made between Federally operated prisons and one private prison only (Taft Correctional Institution).

There are few studies available for state-based comparisons of public and private sector prisons. Of those available, the results appear consistent with FBP research. For example, the 2010 biennial comparison of cross-sector performance by the Arizona Department of Corrections (2011) indicates that the daily per capita cost for public sector minimum security beds was $46.59 and private sector $46.56, and for medium custody $48.42 and $53.02, respectively. That is, the minimum security unit costs were on par while for medium security the public sector was more financially efficient. Kenny and Gilroy (2013) criticize this review, however, for several reasons, including poor or no consideration of such things as capital assets and liabilities, prisoner and employee healthcare costs, taxes paid by private correctional companies, and differences in programming.

The most recent and rigorous comparative cost analysis by Hakim and Blackstone (2013) identifies the private sector as more efficient than the public. Advancing the avoidable and unavoidable cost considerations identified by Gaes et al. (2004), Hakim and Blackstone include measures previously not dealt with, such as short- (underfunded pension costs and retiree healthcare costs) and long-run costs (depreciation, and government principal and interest on bonds used to fund prisons) (Hakim and Blackstone 2013: 2). While including only eight private prisons, private sector prisons were more efficient on long-run costs by 12% to 58%.

The UK

The methodological difficulties highlighted also impacted on the robust comparative research conducted by the UK Home Office for 1997/98 and 1998/99. The Home Office was in the fortunate position of being the overseer of the criminal justice system, yet also at arm's length in all correctional services purchases and regulation (Harding 1997). Accordingly, it was not bound by commercial-in-confidence restrictions and had access to all public funding details. In its initial comparative studies, the Home Office established that private prisons offered greater savings than the public, although in the second year the cross-sector differential had reduced (Park 2000; Woodbridge 1999). On average, the cost savings for the four years from 1994/95 to 1997/98 from private prisons were estimated at 12.5% (Tanner 2013).

Significant advances in actually determining the cost and effectiveness of public and private prisons have been made in the UK. System-wide contestability and centralized data reporting in the Ministry of Justice bring this jurisdiction closest to making definitive statements regarding comparative assessments. For example, the annual report on costs per prisoner 2012/13 indicates costs as follows: public sector prisons £34,507, PFI prisons £38,936, and private sector operated and managed prisons £24,483 (National Offender Management Service 2013a). Greatest efficiency appears in the latter. However, the data table includes a footnote indicating that unit costs cannot be directly comparable as PFI prisons include interest costs, and private prisons include health and education costs.

Correctional effectiveness

The privatization of prisons was, in some jurisdictions, proposed as the means to enable reform of public sector prisons. In some instances, public sector prisons were characterized by dysfunctional and intractable organizational cultures and social climates and largely unconcerned by day-to-day service efficiencies. Prison research tends to interchange measures of organizational culture and social climate as indicators of prison quality; however, there are distinctions between these, with the former referring to overall philosophy and condition of an organization that shapes the attitudes, perceptions, motivation, goals and behaviours of the staff, whereas climate refers to perceptions of the organization at an operational level, such as ability to be a big supporter of new ideas and demonstrate openness to change. In addition to culture and climate, assessment of prison effectiveness frequently includes evaluations of logistical effectiveness of service delivery – that is, how well the prison conducts day-to-day operational matters. Organizational culture and social climate are typically assessed via surveys, with a rich history of high-quality survey-based prison research in organizational culture and climate having developed over the last 20 years (Day et al. 2011; Liebling 2004; Moos 1975; Saylor et al. 1996; Toch 1985).

As with the cost comparison studies, there is a substantial literature on cross-sector quality comparison studies. However, the value of this research varies according to philosophical bias, data access and research methods (Association of Private Correctional and Treatment Organizations 2003; Camp 1998; Camp et al. 2002; Lanza-Kaduce et al. 2000; Liebling et al. 2011; McDonald et al. 1998a; Moyle 2000; Perrone and Pratt 2003; Sturgess 2003). Comparison variables are typically either objective measures taken from organizational records, such as out-of-cell hours, quality of healthcare, escapes, recidivism, assault and death rates, or subjective measures of prison quality taken from officer and/or prisoner surveys. The next section reviews this comparative research by country.

The USA

One of the first and most influential studies grounded in sound methodology was Logan's (1992) comparison of the Corrections Corporation of America-owned and -operated

New Mexico Women's Correction Facility with state and federal prisons for women. Logan's prison quality index based on eight factors determined by 333 separate performance measures indicated the one private prison performed better than two public sector comparator prisons on six of the eight factors. On this basis, Logan suggested private prisons outperform public sector in the level of service delivery.

The FBP has been particularly active in the mandated ongoing evaluation of private prisons performance, with the most cogent research comparing Taft Correctional Institution with three public operated facilities. To summarize the ongoing evaluations, there are primarily no differences between the public prisons and privately operated Taft Institution (Camp et al. 2001; Gaes et al. 2004; Nelson 2005), particularly with regard to prisoner perceptions of quality (Camp et al. 2001). While high-quality research, the primary criticism of the Bureau of Prisons analysis is that it appears only to include Taft as a comparator and not any of the other 13 private prisons in the federal system. Research by Makarios and Maahs (2012) using census data from federal and state prisons for cross-sector comparisons on the quality of confinement supports FBP findings, however, showing a general similarity across sectors with regard to quality.

The UK

Of all countries to introduce private prisons, the UK is the most advanced in developing system-wide performance measures that provide accurate evaluations of prison quality. The UK National Audit Office (2003) report into PFI provides a detailed account of objective private prison performance data.[4] The report highlights private sector performance deficits leading to substantial financial penalties, particularly at two prisons: Parc, totalling £862,500 across three years of operations since 1997, and Altcourse, totalling £337,000 across three years of operations also since 1997. The best PFI prisons were identified as outperforming most public prisons, but the lowest performing PFI prisons were 'among the worst in the prison estate' (ibid.: 7). An interesting finding of the review was that regardless of sector, prisons that were strong in regime (e.g. prisoner programmes and work) and decency factors performed not as well in safety and security factors.

The current model of comparative evaluation, the Prison Rating System (PRS), ranks each of the 134 prisons including the 14 private institutions on a four-point rating scale according to performance on 27 performance indicators (National Offender Management Service 2013b). The 2012/13 rankings indicated that two private prisons rated as one, the lowest possible, and two prisons rated a two, while one scored the highest rank of four. In comparison, one public institution scored the lowest rank and ten rated the next rank of two.

Interpretation of the PRS data by Reform, a UK-based think tank for improved public sector service delivery and economic prosperity, suggests that the private sector provides superior performance to the public sector prisons (Mason 2013). The Reform analysis is selective, however. For example, of the 12 prisons included in the analysis, all were reported as outperforming the public sector in one of the four domain areas (i.e. resource management and operational effectiveness); seven out of 12 outperformed the public sector in the decency and reoffending domains; and five out of 12 in the fourth domain, public protection. Apart from not explaining why 15 as opposed to the 14 PRS private prisons were included, the Reform analysis excludes three private prisons, two of which scored the lowest possible overall rating, on the basis that they either commenced operation during the review period or at the end of the measurement period. Future PRS data will clarify the situation.

The NOMS findings are supported by other empirical research comparing public and private facilities on aspects of prison quality assessed through the prison quality instrument, measuring the quality of prison life (MQPL) (Crewe et al. 2011; Hulley et al. 2012; Liebling 2004; Liebling et al. 2011). Findings from this research indicate that there are cross-sector differences in the prison officer culture that have positive and negative performance impacts. It appears that, rather than sector, institutional differences warrant more attention for determining prison quality.

Australia

The only major Australian review to date that attempted to determine regime impacts was that conducted by the NSW Department of Corrective Services on Junee prison. To identify innovative work practice and provide public/private comparisons, annual comparative studies were initiated in 1994 wherein objective and subjective data were collected on operational processes such as healthcare, programmes, occupational health and safety, staffing, incidents and training. The studies found that ACM's organizational culture was conducive to immediately providing a prisoner management model based on positive officer/prisoner interaction and case management, which was distinct from the existing public sector culture (Bowery 1994). In the fourth and final year of the study, Bowery (1999) suggested that this positive culture had become entrenched in the centre, as a large percentage of the original staff had been retained. Objective data indicated that in some areas (e.g. offences in custody and assaults on officers) Junee did not perform as well as similar public sector prisons, yet in other areas (e.g. prisoner-on-prisoner assaults and prisoner self-harm incidents) they performed better. Overall, the accumulated data suggest that despite performance fluctuations in both sectors, Junee at that time operated at least as well as its public sector comparators (Bowery 1999).

In Western Australia an autonomous prisons inspectorate was established in 2000 as a direct response to the decision to privatize Acacia Prison. Since that time there have been five full inspections, creating, in effect, a running commentary on the evolution of performance that has been mostly positive in tone. The most recent assessment (2014) noted that while there had been some slippage since the very high standard achieved in 2011, Acacia Prison was still performing to a good standard, concluding that 'the 13-year history [of Acacia Prison] shows that the private sector, like the public sector, is quite capable of operating very good prisons' (www.oics.wa.gov.au, Report 90, p. xi). The other interesting aspect of this report is that costs were fairly rigorously assessed, with Acacia coming in at A$150 per prisoner, per day and the public sector across the board coming in at A$320.

Brazil

Research on the effectiveness of privatization outside the USA, Australia and the UK is limited. As an indication of the international growth of privatization outside the Anglophone countries, there is, however, a recent analysis of outsourcing in the Brazilian prison system (Cabral et al. 2013). Through analysing qualitative and quantitative data for the private-hybrid model and state-run prisons between 1999 and 2006, it was identified that the private sector did not reduce the quality of the overall prison service or lack of probity. In some cases, the private sector outperformed state-operated prisons on security and order and was more efficient in delivering a higher ratio for the number of release orders to the number of legal appointments (Cabral et al. 2013). It was proposed that the key mechanism driving the results of the private sector was the presence of public supervisors to oversee operations.

Recidivism

A primary measure of prison effectiveness should be its capacity to reduce recidivism. Recidivism research appears to follow the same pattern identified for cost effectiveness and prison quality research, where initial studies indicate private prisons as being more effective than the public sector counterparts. However, with time, the outcome seems either neutral or to be reversed. In part, some of the differential can be explained through improvements in research methods. For example, while comparative recidivism studies between the private and public prisons are an attractive option, in the UK and Australia it is common practice for prisoners to be frequently transferred between prisons during the period of their sentence, which undermines the effectiveness of comparative analysis. Thus, some comparative recidivism research in the USA has been challenged for failure to control for time spent in particular prisons, the importance of the prisoner's experience in the exit prison, and a failure to select prisoner cohorts so as to be able to compare like with like (Bales et al. 2005; Duwe and Clark 2013; Farabee and Knight 2002; Lanza-Kaduce et al. 2000; Spivak and Sharp 2008).

Initial research on cross-sector recidivism outcomes in Florida indicated that private prisons were more effective than a public sector counterpart in recidivism and seriousness of subsequent offences (Lanza-Kaduce et al. 1999). Subsequent Florida research, however, reached different outcomes. Bales et al. (2005) found no significant differences in recidivism rates between the public and private prison systems using larger case sizes and multiple methods of private prison exposure. Spivak and Sharp (2008) identified that Oklahoma inmates from private prison groups had a greater hazard of recidivism than their public sector counterparts. Further, the longer periods spent in an Oklahoma private prison, the greater the hazard of recidivism. Finally, Duwe and Clark (2013) compared recidivism in inmates from Minnesota's public and private prisons, reporting that inmates from private prisons were at significantly greater risk of recidivism in eight of the 20 that the regression models tested. These researchers propose that the significant differences were attributable to the reduced visitation and prison programmes that are often found in US private prisons compared with the public system. However, this variable was not tested and was offered only as a possibility.

Recidivism rates are published by prison for England and Wales (Ministry of Justice 2013). Accordingly, while it is possible for raw data comparisons to be made between private and public prisons, such comparisons do not control for inter-prison variables. Based on the Ministry of Justice data, Tanner (2013) proposes private prisons outperform public sector prisons by as much as 10%. However, given the lack of methodological rigour, this conclusion should be treated with caution.

Some big issues for the future

The State must remain responsible for the prisoners sentenced under its authority

Contracting out the management of prisons and prisoners is not the same as contracting out of legal responsibility. In the end, the State owes prisoners a duty of care and should be ensuring that its prison system is managed decently, purposefully and with hope. Sometimes the ways in which private arrangements have been structured muddy that fact. A notable example relates to the notion – exemplified by past US experience – of exporting prisoners from one state to prisons, often privately managed ones, in other states. In practical day-to-day terms, these arrangements stretch the chain of legal responsibility to breaking point.

Such arrangements are not confined to private sector relations, however. There are examples of European prison systems exporting prisoners. For example, the Dutch prison system, having excess capacity, has leased a prison at Tilburg to the Belgian Prison Service, causing some confusion as to who is responsible for what. These sorts of arrangements – public or private – should be watched intensely and, preferably, prohibited.

The corporate structure of the private operators should be kept under review

Most of the leading private prison operators are global general service companies. They may be contracted, for example, to provide public transport services or hospital logistics or general security at military installations or remote mining site services for staff. This is broadly the case with the private prison companies Serco, G4S and Sodexo. For these companies, the provision of custodial services represents a tiny percentage of their overall business. It is also the case that, usually, this business activity provides quite a poor return on capital in comparison with some of their other activities.

A problem, at least in Australia, has been that when a custodial contract is available that offers a large return, the global company in question – invariably controlled from overseas – may take on that task without full regard to the local demands, conditions and capacity to carry it out without risk to routine custodial operations. This has been the case with regard to immigration detention arrangements. The government, lacking any direct capacity to carry out this task, is in effect a supplicant to the private sector to get this service provided at all. The profits have been enormous. Yet it is evident that the companies that have taken on these services have each, in turn, suffered a reputation risk.[5] It is also possible that to some extent their ability to manage their core custodial services with their normal efficiency and to their customary standards has been undermined.[6]

Contracting skills

Historically, and as has been confirmed recently, the contracting skills of the governments that purchase custodial services have been quite poor (Ludlow 2014). In the early days conditions were typically so generic as to be unenforceable – 'to provide suitable education programmes', for example. Another weakness was long contracts (such as 25 years), unless there was some clear basis for terminating the arrangement, whereas the prudent approach would be to permit contract extensions at regular intervals on the condition that performance met the expected standard. Recent research has identified other contract difficulties with government's incapacity to effectively use the contract procurement process to purchase innovation (Ludlow 2014).

In later years some jurisdictions have become so prescriptive as to get in the way of the very innovation and freshness that privatization was intended to foster. However, recent improvements include the notion of folding 'payment by results' into the contract, and also at the bidding stage the notion of 'interactive bidding' so that the purchaser and the provider can explore before contract their mutual understanding of what each wishes to achieve.

Nevertheless, governments by and large lack sufficient skills to develop and manage major contracts, of any kind, in an optimum manner. This may be endemic to the nature of government and the qualities that public servants require for the bulk of their work, but it is a factor that needs to be constantly borne in mind.

The not-for-profit NGO sector

Increasingly the non-governmental organization (NGO) sector has become involved in correctional work over the years. In the USA it has from the outset been dominant in the contracting out of juvenile services, sometimes including the custodial function itself. Public sector prisons increasingly rely on services from the NGO sector, be they recreational, programmatic, spiritual, medical or educational. That pattern has now become familiar with private sector prisons. Indeed, recent contracting arrangements (for example, regarding Wandoo Young Adult Prison in Western Australia) require that the private sector bidder nominate a primary NGO provider of ancillary services. It can be anticipated that the private sector arrangements will increasingly work on the premise that NGO not-for-profit providers will also be involved in service delivery.

The future

Governments of all persuasions are increasingly stressed in their efforts to provide the range of social, educational, health, welfare and justice services that citizens have come to expect. Each of these areas has seen, over recent years, a marked increase in private sector participation. It can be expected that custodial services generally, and prison services in particular, will continue to rely upon some degree of private sector input, whether by way of direct management or by way of non-custodial contributions to the total custodial situation. Regardless of discussions about core state functions and the like, the economic and governmental imperative is such that these services are here to stay and are likely, if anything, gradually to increase.

Notes

1 In this research the UK refers to England and Wales.
2 The USA distinguishes between prisons and jails, and 8.7% refers to the proportion of the prison population. If reference is made to the whole incarcerated adult population, the figure of those held in privately managed custodial facilities is about 6%.
3 In Australia about half of new contracts have been awarded to a consortium that is not the cheapest bidder. A notable example was the first contract awarded in Western Australia (for the prison now known as Acacia), where the successful bidder was the most expensive of the four

shortlisted bidders but was judged to be offering the best correctional value for money (Personal information from author Harding who was a member of the Government Tender Committee).

4 In the UK, two models of private sector involvement in custodial corrections service delivery exist. Private Finance Initiative prisons are private sector prisons usually with DCMF contracts. Private sector management-only contracts also exist.

5 In Australia successively in 2003 GEO (then known as ACM) and in 2009 G4S lost their immigration detention contracts with the Commonwealth government following periods of disturbance at the mainland immigration detention centres. These disturbances had attracted wide media attention as well as adverse reports by various monitoring bodies including the Australian Human Rights Commission.

6 Serco Asia-Pacific took over the principal immigration detention contract responsibility in 2009. At the time of doing so, there were only about 600 people in immigration detention, but within a short time this had increased to almost 6,000. This number far exceeded the number of ordinary prisoners that Serco had been managing in Australia and New Zealand. To an observer, it has been apparent that the logistics of training new staff and of switching experienced staff across the two systems has caused strain on the primary function of prison management.

Bibliography

Arizona Department of Corrections (2011) *Biennial Comparison of 'Private Versus Public Provision of Services' Required per A.R.S 41-1609.01(K)(M)*, Phoenix, Arizona.

Association of Private Correctional and Treatment Organizations (2003) *Correctional public-private partnership outcomes*, Centerville, UT.

Austin, J. and Coventry, G. (2001) *Emerging issues on private prisons*, Washington, DC: US Department of Justice, Office of Justice Programs, Bureau of Justice Assistance.

Australian Bureau of Statistics (2013) *Prisoners in Australia*, Canberra: Australian Bureau of Statistics.

Azzakanni, R. (2013) 'South Africa: Private Prisons a No-No, Says Committee', allafrica.com/stories/201311071490.html.

Bales, W.D., Bedard, L.E., Quinn, S.T., Ensley, D.T. and Holley, G.P. (2005) 'Recidivism of Public and private state prison inmates in Florida', *Criminology & Public Policy* 4(1): 57–82.

Begg, J. (2003) 'Prison privatization: Developments in South Africa', in A. Coyle, A. Campbell and R. Neufeld (eds) *Capitalist Punishment: Prison privatization and human rights*, London: Zed Books.

Bentham, J. (1791) *Panopticon, Or The Inspection House*, Volume 2, Lausanne: University of Lausanne.

Berman, G. and Dar, A. (2013) *Prison Population Statistics*, London: House of Commons Library.

Bowery, M. (1994) *Junee: One year out – Research Publication No. 29*, Sydney: NSW Department of Corrective Services.

Bowery, M. (1999) *Junee: A four-year review – Research Publication No. 42*, Sydney: NSW Department of Corrective Services.

Cabral, S., Lazzarini, S.G. and Azevedo, P.F. (2013) 'Private entrepreneurs in public services: A longitudinal examination of outsourcing and statization of prisons', *Strategic Entrepreneurship Journal* 7(1): 6–25.

Cabral, S. and Saussier, S. (2013) 'Organizing Prisons through public-private partnerships: A cross-country investigation', *BAR: Brazilian Administration Review* 10(1): 100–120.

Camp, S.D. (1998) *Assessing the Effects of Organizational Commitment and Job Satisfaction on Turnover: An event history approach*, Washington, DC: Federal Bureau of Prisons, Office of Research and Evaluation.

Camp, S.D., Gaes, G.G., Klein-Saffran, J., Daggett, M.S. and Saylor, W.G. (2001) *Assessing Prison Performance from the Inmates' View: Comparing private and public prisons*, Washington, DC: Federal Bureau of Prisons, Office of Research and Evaluation.

Camp, S.D., Gaes, G.G. and Saylor, W.G. (2002) 'Quality of prison operation in the US federal sector. A comparison with a private prison', *Punishment and Society* 4(1): 27–53.

Caplow, T. and Simon, J. (1999) 'Understanding prison policy and population trends', in M. Tonry and J. Petersilia (eds) *Prisons*, Chicago, IL: University of Chicago Press, 63–120.

Carter, P. (2001) *Review of PFI and Market Testing in the Prison Service*, London: Prison Reform Trust.

Chan, E. (2010) 'Prisons for Profit: The Corrections (Contract Management of Prisons) Amendment Act 2009', *Auckland UL Rev.* 16: 303.

Crewe, B., Liebling, A. and Hulley, S. (2011) 'Staff culture, use of authority and prisoner quality of life in public and private sector prisons', *Australian & New Zealand Journal of Criminology* 44(1): 94–115.

Criminal Justice Policy Council (2001) *Limes to Limes: Comparing the operational costs of juvenile and adult correctional programs in Texas*, Austin, TX: Criminal Justice Policy Council.

D'Amico, D.J. (2010) 'The prison in economics: private and public incarceration in Ancient Greece', *Public Choice* 145(3–4): 461–482.

Davis, G. and Wood, T. (1998) 'Is there a future for contracting in the Australian public sector', *Australian Journal of Public Administration* 57(4): 85–97.

Day, A., Casey, S., Vess, J. and Huisy, G. (2011) *Assessing the Social Climate of Prisons*, Canberra: Criminology Research Council.

DiIulio, J.J. (1990) 'The duty to govern: A critical perspective on the private management of prisons and jails', in D. McDonald (ed.) *Private Prisons and the Public Interest*, New Brunswick, NJ: Rutgers University Press, 155–178.

DiPiano, J.G. (1995) 'Private prisons: Can they work? Panopticon in the twenty-first century', *New England Journal of Criminal and Civil Confinement* 21(1): 171–202.

Dolovich, S. (2005) 'State punishment and private prisons', *Duke Law Journal*: 437–546.

Domberger, S. and Jensen, P. (1997) 'Contracting out by the public sector: Theory, evidence, prospects', *Oxford Review of Economic Policy* 13(4): 67–78.

Du Plessis, C. (2012) *How the Private Prisons Were Barred*, Pinelands, South Africa: Open Society Foundation for South Africa.

Duwe, G. and Clark, V. (2013) 'The effects of private prison confinement on offender recidivism evidence from Minnesota', *Criminal Justice Review* 38(3): 375–394.

Edwards, G. (1996) 'Public crime, private punishment: Prison privatization in Queensland', *International Journal of Social Economics* 23(4/5/6): 391–408.

Farabee, D. and Knight, K. (2002) *A Comparison of Public and Private Prisons in Florida: During-and post-prison performance indicators*, Los Angeles, CA: Query Research.

Feeley, M.M. (2014) 'The unconvincing case against private prisons', *Indiana Law Journal* 89(4): 1401–1436.

Gaes, G.G. (2012) *The current status of prison privatization research on American prisons*, PhD, Florida State University.

Gaes, G.G., Camp, S.D., Nelson, J. and Saylor, W.G. (2004) *Measuring Prison Performance: Government Privatization and Accountability*, Walnut Creek, CA: AltaMira Press.

Gilbert, M.J. (2001) 'How much is too much privatization in criminal justice', in D. Shichor and M.J. Gilbert (eds) *Privatization in Criminal Justice: Past, present, and future*, Cincinnati, OH: Anderson Publishing Co., 41–80.

Glaze, L.E. and Herbermann, E.J. (2013) 'Correctional populations in the United States, 2012', www.bjs.gov/content/pub/pdf/cpus12.pdf.

Goffman, E. (1961) *The Inmate World Asylums: Essays on the social situation of mental patients and other inmates*, Harmondsworth: Penguin, 23–72.

Goyer, K.C. (2001) *Prison Privatization in South Africa: Issues, challenges and opportunities*, Monograph 64, Pretoria: Institute of Strategic Studies.

Guppy, P. (2003) *Private Prisons and the Public Interest: Improving quality and cost reduction through competition*, Washington, DC: Washington Policy Institute.

Hakim, S. and Blackstone, E.A. (2013) *Cost Analysis of Public and Contractor-Operated Prisons*, Working Paper, Economics, Trans., Philadelphia, PA: Temple University.

Hamburger, K. (1994) 'Prison breaks-out from old system', *Directions in Government* 8(8): 14–15.

Hancock, L. (1998) 'Contractualism, privatisation and justice: Citizenship, the State and managing risk', *Australian Journal of Public Administration* 57(4): 118–127.

Haney, C. (1997) 'Psychology and the limits to prison pain: Confronting the coming crisis in Eighth Amendment Law', *Psychology, Public Policy, and Law* 3(4): 499–588.

Hanson, R.A. and Daley, H.W.K. (1994) *Challenging the Conditions of Prisons and Jails*, Washington, DC: US Department of Justice, Office of Justice Programs.

Harding, R.W. (1997) *Private Prisons and Public Accountability*, Buckingham: Open University Press.

Harding, R.W. (2001) 'Private prisons', in M. Tonry (ed.) *Crime and Justice: A review of research*, Vol. 28, Chicago, IL: Chicago University Press, 626–655.

Harding, R.W. (2012) 'State monopoly of "permitted violation of human rights": The decision of the Supreme Court of Israel prohibiting the private operation and management of prisons', *Punishment & Society* 14(2): 131–146.

Hilmer, F.M. and Taperell, G. (1993) *National Competition Policy: Report of the independent committee of inquiry into competition policy in Australia*, Canberra: Australian Government Publishing Service.

Hinds, L.R. (2002) *Law and order: The politics of get tough crime control*, unpublished doctoral dissertation, Brisbane: Griffith University.

Home Affairs Committee (1997) *Second Report, the Management of the Prison Service (public and private)*, London: Home Affairs Committee.

House of Commons Committee of Public Accounts (2003) *The Operational Performance of PFI Prisons, HC904*, London: House of Commons Committee of Public Accounts.

Hughes, R. (1987) *The Fatal Shore*, London: Collins.

Hulley, S., Liebling, A. and Crewe, B. (2012) 'Respect in prisons: Prisoners' experiences of respect in public and private sector prisons', *Criminology and Criminal Justice* 12(1): 3–23.

Inspector of Custodial Services (2003) *Report of an Announced Inspection of Acacia Prison March 2003*, Perth: Office of the Inspector of Custodial Services.

James, A., Bottomley, K., Liebling, A. and Clare, E. (1997) *Privatizing Prisons: Rhetoric and reality*, London: Sage Publications Ltd.

Johnston, E. (1991) *Report of the Royal Commission into Aboriginal Deaths in Custody*, Canberra: Australian Government Publication Service.

Kennedy, J.J. (1988) *Commission of Review into Corrective Services in Queensland, Final Report*, Queensland: Government Printer.

Kenny, H. and Gilroy, L. (2013) *The Challenge of Comparing Public and Private Correctional Costs*, Washington, DC: Reason Foundation.

Kenter, R.C. and Prior, S.V. (2012) 'The globalization of private prisons', in B.E. Price II and J.C. Morris (eds) *Prison Privatization: The many facets of a controversial industry*, Vol. 1, Santa Barbara, CA: Praeger, 87–105.

Kirby, P. (2000) *Report of the Independent Investigation into the Management and Operations of Victoria's Private Prisons*, Melbourne: State Government of Victoria.

Kyle, P.H. (2013) 'Contracting for performance: Restructuring the private prison market', *Wm. & Mary L. Rev.* 54: 2087–2087.

Lane, J.E. (2001) 'From long-term to short-term contracting', *Public Administration* 79(1): 29–47.

Lanza-Kaduce, L., Parker, K.F. and Thomas, C.W. (1999) 'A comparative recidivism analysis of releasees from private and public prisons', *Crime & Delinquency* 45(1): 28–47.

Lanza-Kaduce, L., Parker, K.F. and Thomas, C.W. (2000) 'The devil in the details: The case against the case study of private prisons, criminological research, and conflict of interest', *Crime and Delinquency* 46(1): 92–136.

Liebling, A. (2004) *Prisons and their Moral Performance*, Oxford: Oxford University Press.

Liebling, A., Hulley, S. and Crewe, B. (2011) 'Conceptualising and measuring the quality of prison life', *The Sage Handbook of Criminological Research Methods*, London: Sage, 358.

Lofstrom, M., Petersilia, J. and Raphael, S. (2012) *Evaluating the Effects of California's Correction to Realignment on Public Safety*, San Francisco, CA: Public Policy Institute of California.

Logan, C. (1990) *Private Prisons: Cons and pros*, New York: Oxford University Press.

Logan, C. (1992) 'Well kept: Comparing quality of confinement in a public and a private prison', *Journal of Criminal Law and Criminology* 83(3): 577–613.

Longland, D. (1985) *Enquiry into the Management Practices Operating at H.M. Prison Brisbane*, Brisbane.

Ludlow, A. (2014) 'Transforming rehabilitation: What lessons might be learned from prison privatisation?' *European Journal of Probation* 6(1): 67–81.

Lundahl, B.W., Kunz, C., Brownell, C., Harris, N. and Van Vleet, R. (2009) 'Prison privatization: A meta-analysis of cost and quality of confinement indicators', *Research on Social Work Practice* 19(4): 383–394.

Macaulay, F. (2013) 'Modes of prison administration, control and governmentality in Latin America: Adoption, adaptation and hybridity', *Conflict, Security & Development* 13(4): 361–392.

McDonald, D.C. (1990) *Private Prisons and the Public Interest*, New Brunswick, NJ: Rutgers University Press.

McDonald, D.C. (1999) 'Performance issues', paper presented at the Private Prison Workshop, Institute of Criminal Justice, Minneapolis: University of Minnesota.

McDonald, D.C., Fournier, E., Russell-Einhorn, M. and Crawford, S. (1998a) *Private Prisons in the United States: An assessment of current practice*, Cambridge, MA: Adt Associates Inc.

McDonald, D.C., Fournier, E., Russell-Einhorn, M. and Crawford, S. (1998b) 'Private prisons in the United States: An assessment of current practice', in D.C. McDonald, E. Fournier, M. Russell-Einhorn and S. Crawford (eds) *Private Prisons in the United States: An assessment of current practice*, Cambridge, MA: Adt Associates Inc.

Makarios, M.D. and Maahs, J. (2012) 'Is private time quality time? A national private-public comparison of prison quality', *The Prison Journal* 92(3): 336–357.

Mancini, M.J. (1996) *One Dies, Get Another: Convict leasing in the American south, 1866–1928*, Columbia, SC: University of South Carolina Press.

Marquart, J.W. and Crouch, B.M. (1985) 'Judicial reform and prisoner control: The impact of Ruiz v. Estelle on a Texas penitentiary', *Law and Society Review* 19(4): 557–586.

Mason, C. (2013) *International Growth Trends in Prison Privatization*, Washington, DC: The Sentencing Project.

Mattera, P., Khan, M. and Nathan, S. (2003) *Corrections Corporation of America: A critical look at its first twenty years*, Charlotte, NC: Grassroots Leadership.

Mennicken, A. (2013) '"Too big to fail and too big to succeed": Accounting and privatisation in the Prison Service of England and Wales', *Financial Accountability & Management* 29(2): 206–226.

Ministry of Justice (2013) *Proven Re-offending Statistics Quarterly Bulletin April 2010 to March 2011*, England and Wales Ministry of Justice, London: Statistics Bulletin.

Moore, A. (1998) *Private Prisons: Quality corrections at a lower cost*, Los Angeles, CA: Reason Public Policy Institute.

Moore, D., Burton, K.L. and Hannah-Moffat, K. (2003) '"Get tough" efficiency: Human rights, correctional restructuring and prison privatization in Ontario, Canada', in A. Coyle, A. Campbell and R. Neufeld (eds) *Capitalist Punishment: Prison privatization and human rights*, London: Zed Books.

Moos, R. (1975) *Evaluating Correctional and Community Settings*, New York: John Wiley and Sons.

Moyle, P. (2000) *Profiting from Punishment: Private prisons in Australia; reform or regression?* Annandale: Pluto Press Australia Limited.

Nagle, J.F. (1978) *Report of the Royal Commission into New South Wales Prisons*, Sydney: NSW Government Printer.

National Audit Office (2003) *The Operational Performance of PFI prisons*, London: Report by the Comptroller and Auditor General HC 700.

National Offender Management Service (2013a) *National Offender Management Service Annual Report and Accounts 2012–2013, Management Information Addendum Ministry of Justice Information Release*, London: UK Ministry of Justice.

National Offender Management Service (2013b) *National Offender Management Service Prison Annual Performance Ratings 2012/13 Ministry of Justice Information Release*, London: UK Ministry of Justice.

Nelson, J. (1998) 'Comparing public and private prison costs', in D.C. McDonald, E. Fournier, M. Russell-Einhorn and S. Crawford (eds) *Private Prisons in the United States: An assessment of current practice*, Cambridge, MA: Adt Associates Inc.

Nelson, J. (2005) *Competition in Corrections: Comparing public and private sector operations*, Arlington, VA: The CNA Corporation.

Osborne, D. and Gaebler, T. (1992) *Reinventing Government: How the entrepreneurial spirit is transforming the public sector*, New York: Plume/Penguin.

Park, I. (2000) *Review of Comparative Costs and Performance of Privately and Publicly Operated Prisons 1998–1999*, London: Home Office, Research, Development and Statistics Directorate.

Perrone, D. and Pratt, T.C. (2003) 'Comparing the quality of confinement and cost-effectiveness of public versus private prisons: What we know, why we do not know more, and where to go from here', *The Prison Journal* 83(3): 301–322.

Pollitt, C. and Bouckaert, G. (2000) *Public Management Reform: A comparative analysis*, Oxford: Oxford University Press.

Portfolio Committee on Correctional Services (2012) 'Prison Food Services Should Be Kept Inhouse – Committee', press release, www.parliament.gov.za/live/content.php?Item_ID=2007&Revision=en/0&SearchStart=0.

Pratt, T.C. and Maahs, J. (1999) 'Are private prisons more cost-effective than public prisons? A meta-analysis of evaluation research studies', *Crime and Delinquency* 45(3): 358–371.

Prison Privatization Report International (2000) No. 37 September/October, www.psiru.org/justice/ppriarchive/ppri37-09-00.asp (accessed 2 January 2003).

Prison Task Team (2002) *Technical Review of the Public-Private Partnership Prisons Contracts for the PPP Prisons Task Team*, South Africa.

Productivity Commission (2013) *Report on Government Services 2013*, Canberra: Steering Committee for the Review of Commonwealth/State Service Provision.

Queensland Prison Service (1986) *Progress Report: Management practices operating at HM Prison Brisbane*, Brisbane: Queensland Prison Service.

Raine, J.W. and Willson, M.J. (1997) 'Beyond managerialism in criminal justice', *The Howard Journal* 36(1): 80–95.

Resnik, J. (2013) 'Globalization(s), privatization(s), constitutionalization, and statization: Icons and experiences of sovereignty in the 21st century', *International Journal of Constitutional Law* 11(1): 162–199.

Ruback, R.B. and Innes, C. (1988) 'The relevance and irrelevance of psychological research: The example of prison crowding', *American Psychologist* 43(9): 683–693.

Rutherford, A. (1990) 'British penal policy and the idea of prison privatization', in D. McDonald (ed.) *Private Prisons and the Public Interest*, New Brunswick, NJ: Rutgers University Press, 42–65.

Ryan, M. and Ward, T. (1989) *Privatisation and the Penal System: The American experience and the debate in Britain*, Milton Keyes: Open University Press.

Sachdev, S. (2001) *Contracting Culture from CCT to PPPs: The private provision of public services and its impact on employment relations*, Kingston upon Thames: Kingston University.

Saylor, W.G. (1984) *Surveying Prison Environments*, Washington, DC: Federal Bureau of Prisons.

Saylor, W.G., Gilman, E.G. and Camp, S.D. (1996) *Prison Social Climate Survey: Reliability and validity analyses of the work environment constructs*, Washington, DC: Federal Bureau of Prisons, Office of Research and Evaluation.

Schein, E.H. (1990) 'Organizational culture', *American Psychologist* 45(2): 109–119.

Scottish Executive (2002) *Consultation Paper on the Future of the Scottish Prison Estate*, Edinburgh: Scottish Executive.

Segal, G.F. and Moore, A. (2002) *Weighing the Watchmen: Evaluating the costs and benefits of outsourcing correctional services. Part I: Employing a best-value approach to procurement. Part II: Reviewing the literature on cost and quality comparisons*, Los Angeles, CA: Reason Public Policy Institute.

The Sentencing Project (2014) 'Trends in U.S. Corrections. Fact Sheet: Trends in U.S. Corrections', sentencingproject.org/doc/publications/inc_Trends_in_Corrections_Fact_sheet.pdf.

Shaw, A.G.L. (1966) *Convicts and the Colonies: A study of penal transportation from Great Britain and Ireland to Australia and other parts of the British Empire*, London: Faber and Faber.

Shichor, D. (1995) *Punishment for Profit: Private prisons/public concerns*, Thousand Oaks, CA: Sage Publications Inc.

Shichor, D. and Sechrest, D.K. (2002) 'Privatization and flexibility: Legal and practical aspects of interjurisdictional transfer of prisoners', *The Prison Journal* 82(3): 386–407.

Sinden, J. (2003) 'The problem of prison privatization: The US experience', in A. Coyle, A. Campbell and R. Neufeld (eds) *Capitalist Punishment: Prison privatization and human rights*, London: Zed Books, 39–47.

Smith, B.A. and Morn, F.T. (2001) 'The history of privatization in criminal justice', in D. Shichor and M.J. Gilbert (eds) *Privatization in Criminal Justice: Past, present, and future*, Cincinnati, OH: Anderson Publishing Co., 3–22.

Spierenburg, P. (2007) *The Prison Experience: Disciplinary institutions and their inmates in early modern Europe*, New Brunswick, NJ: Rutgers University Press.

Spivak, A.L. and Sharp, S.F. (2008) 'Inmate recidivism as a measure of private prison performance', *Crime & Delinquency* 54(3): 482–508.

Sturgess, G. (2003) *Competition: A catalyst for change in the prison service*, London: Confederation of British Industry.

Sykes, G.M. (1958) *The Society of Captives: A study of a maximum security prison*, Princeton, NJ: Princeton University Press.

Tanner, W. (2013) *The Case for Private Prisons: Reform Ideas*, second edn, London: Reform.

Toch, H. (1985) 'Social climate and prison violence', in M.C. Braswell, S. Dillingham and R.H. Montgomery (eds) *Prison Violence in America*, Lexington, KY: Anderson Publishing Co., 37–46.

US Department of Justice (2013) 'Prisoners in 2012', www.bjs.gov/index.cfm?ty=pbdetail&iid=4842 (accessed 22 January 2014).

Vagg, J. (1994) *Prison Systems: A comparative study of accountability in England, France, Germany, and the Netherlands*, Oxford: Oxford University Press.

Volokh, A. (2014) 'Prison accountability and performance measures', *Emory Law Journal* 63.

Woodbridge, J. (1999) *Review of Comparative Costs and Performance of Privately and Publicly Operated Prisons 1997–1998*, London: Home Office, Research, Development and Statistics Directorate.

Woolf, L.J. (1991) *Prison Disturbances April 1990: Report of an Inquiry by the Rt Hon. Lord Justice Woolf (Parts I and II) and His Honour Stephen Tumim (Part II) (The Woolf Report)*, London: HMSO.

Chapter 10

Segregation and supermax confinement

An ethical evaluation

Derek S. Jeffreys

> We do not believe it necessary to take time, to-day, to argue the barbarous and futile nature of long-enduring solitary confinement without labor.
>
> (O.F. Lewis 1922: 83)

Introduction

The last few decades in the USA saw a return to retributive conceptions of criminal punishment. Beginning in the 1970s, social scientists began attacking the idea of rehabilitation. They questioned whether penal sanctions actually rehabilitate (Wilson 2013; DiIulio 1990; Martinson 1974; Von Hirsh 1976). Philosophers began arguing that the purpose of punishment is to give criminals what they deserve. These academic debates were accompanied by a renewed public fury at crime. The USA witnessed the rise of a powerful victims' rights movement that shaped public policy.[1] It also embraced draconian sentencing, launched a 'war on drugs' and embarked on an imprisonment binge that produced an enormous carceral state. Today, the American public shows little interest in rehabilitating offenders and seems content to embrace a purely retributive approach to them.

Supermax confinement symbolizes this retributive stance. The USA has developed a sophisticated and punitive way of dealing with disobedient inmates. They are isolated in small cells either within jails and prisons or inside specially constructed 'supermax' facilities. Officials use technology to completely control their lives. Their confinement is also marked by its duration; inmates can remain in solitary confinement for years or even decades. This brutal and damaging form of solitary confinement seeks to break an inmate's will and force him to conform to institutional rules. Today, we seem to have completely rejected O.F. Lewis's confident moral conviction that solitary confinement is a barbarous form of punishment.

In this chapter, I explore the ethical justification for using supermax confinement, focusing particularly on retributive views of punishment. First, I briefly discuss the definition of punishment, noting some standard philosophical justifications for it. Second, I explore a defense of retribution based on punishment and fairness. Some philosophers maintain that punishment prevents offenders from taking unfair advantage over law-abiding citizens. Third, turning to supermax imprisonment, I trace its historical development, emphasizing how it emerged as a tool for maintaining prison order. Fourth, I define supermax imprisonment, emphasizing how it includes not only supermax facilities, but also segregation units in jails and prisons. Fifth, citing psychological and other evidence, I discuss how supermax imprisonment damages the person. Returning to retributive justifications of punishment, I maintain that the fairness account of retribution cannot justify supermax confinement. Finally, looking to the future, I suggest that although the USA may be moving away from supermax incarceration, we see disturbing signs that it endures.

Defining punishment

How does punishment differ from taxation? When an angry mob attacks a sex offender does it punish him? To respond to such questions, philosophers generally link punishment to authority. Some hold that it occurs only when an authority enacts laws and legal procedures (Hart 1968). However, this institutional approach ignores non-legal contexts in which punishment occurs, such as parents punishing children and teachers punishing students. To encompass these cases, we should hold that punishment involves some authority without specifying its nature. Punishment also differs from other social practices because it is an intentional act. We do not say that we accidentally punished someone. This distinguishes punishment from accidents and natural occurrences like disease and hurricanes. We might attribute them to divine or demonic causality, but this would only acknowledge the close connection between intention and punishment.

Punishment also inflicts deprivation on a person. We might ask someone to apologize if he wrongs another. We might also request that he compensate his victim. However, these acts may involve no deprivation. A criminal, for example, might see compensation as the price of doing business rather than as punishment. Historically, political communities differ on the means they use to inflict deprivation. They have embraced torture, public humiliation, imprisonment and many other practices. Among historians, we find considerable debate about the development of punishment methods (Foucault 1995; Spierenburg 2008; McKelvey 1993). Some see in modernity a progressive move away from physical punishment toward the psychological kind, while others reject this historical account. Regardless of how we understand punishment's history, its diverse forms involve some kind of deprivation.

By themselves, deprivation and authority are insufficient for distinguishing punishment from other social practices. For example, if I receive a heavy tax bill, an authority intentionally deprives me of income, but I should not see it as punishment. Likewise, if I serve in the military, I suffer many deprivations at the hands of authorities, but they are not all punishment. To constitute punishment, we need an alleged or real offense. Some philosophers argue that an actual violation is a necessary feature of punishment (Quinton 1969). However, we can easily imagine situations where someone receives punishment for an alleged offense. For example, in the early 1990s, the so-called Central Park Five, a group of five young men in New York City, were convicted of raping a woman in Central Park. Years later, their convictions were overturned after a rapist came forward and admitted that he committed the crime (Burns 2012). These men were punished even though they were innocent of a crime. Thus, we are better off arguing that punishment occurs because of an alleged or real offense.

Finally, as Joel Feinberg pointed out years ago, punishment also includes moral disapproval of behavior (Feinberg 1970). Wisconsin may deprive me of income by imposing taxes on me, but I cannot see them as punishment because they imply no moral disapproval (unless, of course, we are talking about so-called sin taxes, which smokers and others might see as punishment). I might get drafted into the Army, but the deprivations I suffer in basic training do not necessarily express moral condemnation. In contrast, punishment expresses values or emotions of a negative kind. For instance, it would be strange if a judge were to sentence someone to death, while simultaneously declaring that she approved of his criminal act. We would rightfully be surprised at her statement.

To summarize, punishment involves an authority that intentionally inflicts deprivation on someone for a real or alleged offense that carries moral disapproval.

Punishment and justification

Not all social practices demand the same kind of ethical justification. I might want to explain to my wife why I spend hours watching golf on television. Yet, within general ethical parameters, most people would be comfortable allowing me to spend my free time as I wish. Few would say the same of the decision to imprison someone. Punishment requires ethical justification because it intentionally inflicts deprivation on another. Additionally, it usually includes acts that we normally condemn; attacks on someone's physical integrity, forced confinement and removal of personal property. Finally, punishment profoundly affects people and their families. Some never recover from it, retaining physical or emotional scars from their experience of punishment for years. For these reasons, punishment requires strong ethical justification.

Twentieth-century philosophers and legal theorists offer useful conceptual tools for thinking about punishment's ethical justification. For example, H.L.A. Hart once distinguished between diverse questions we can ask about punishment (Hart 1968). We can consider its general justification. What is its goal? Why do we punish people at all? We can also ask about punishment's distribution. Who should be punished? For example, is it appropriate to punish those with mental illness? Finally, we can discuss the severity of punishment. Should we execute murderers? What exactly is cruel and unusual punishment?

When discussing punishment's general justification, we can further differentiate between forward- and backward-looking justifications. Backward-looking ones focus on something that happened in the past. They include retributive views that see punishment as giving offenders what they deserve, or metaphysical accounts (not popular today) that posit that punishment annuls a past criminal act. Forward-looking justifications of punishment look to the future. We punish because we want to bring about some future state of affairs. We might want to rehabilitate criminals, bringing them away from their criminal habits toward some ideal of citizenship. Or we might want to deter offenders from committing further criminal acts (special deterrence) or deter others from emulating them (general deterrence).[2]

Some philosophers and jurists maintain that forward- and backward-looking justifications are incompatible, but others mix them creatively. Twentieth-century philosophers argued fiercely about whether we should justify punishment solely on the grounds of its positive or negative consequences. However, the last part of the century saw attempts to deny a strict separation between forward- and backward-looking justifications of punishment. They emphasize one of these justifications, but recognize the importance of the side they de-emphasize. For example, some theorists discuss the expressive function of punishment (Feinberg 1970; Hampton 1988; Duff 1986; Jeffreys 2013). It holds that punishment expresses emotions and values. It corrects a past offense, but also aims at expressing values to the offender and a community. The expressive view thus incorporates both forward- and backward-looking elements.

Retribution

With these general comments about the ethical justification of punishment in mind, let me turn to retributive conceptions. They come in several varieties, but retributivists generally embrace the idea that we punish people primarily because they have committed an offense (Dolinko 1991). We do not punish to rehabilitate or deter offenders from future wrongdoings. They have committed an offense and deserve to be punished, and their offense alone justifies punishing them.

Retributive theories have always faced challenging questions about desert, suffering and authority. For example, why do we deserve deprivation if we commit an offense? Why is the state its appropriate dispenser? Many people feel that those who harm them should suffer, but for others, this impulse lacks rational justification. It seems like an atavistic reaction that civilized people should resist and eliminate.

Retributivists respond to the demand for justification in several ways. Some hold that we have a basic intuition that wrongdoers deserve to suffer. We all have intuitions, they hold, and the retributivist is justified in holding hers as a 'primitive' upon which to build a theory of punishment. The retributive intuition appears early in life and in many diverse societies, and produces powerful emotions. Recent philosophical work on the emotions has emphasized their cognitive content. Rather than mere sensations, emotions involve beliefs, judgments and values (Nussbaum 2001). Naturally, they can include distorted values or be inappropriately intense. However, they can also be rational and appropriate. Among others, Jeffrie Murphy and Michael Moore have developed this kind of argument (Moore 2010; Murphy 2003).[3] They hold that we are rationally justified in holding the retributive intuition.

Sometimes, defenders of retribution use evolutionary theory to support it. The urge to make offenders suffer for harming others, they maintain, is a defensive emotional reaction natural to human beings and other animals. Retributive emotions constitute a part of our psychological makeup that we cannot eliminate. Any attempt to do so would be unsuccessful, and would yield psychologically deleterious consequences. It would also likely produce hypocrisy, with those claiming to eliminate retribution displaying retributive emotions themselves. In short, retribution is a natural and justifiable reaction that needs no philosophical justification (Mackie 1982)

Many philosophers find this appeal to intuition problematic. Yes, we have diverse intuitions, but philosophy should move beyond them and provide a rational ground for punishment. Evolution has bequeathed to us many problematic behaviors and emotions, but we need not accept them all. Moreover, what happens if you have an intuition that I lack? How can we rationally discuss and resolve our differences? Appealing to intuition thus seems like an inadequate way of legitimizing retribution.

Retribution and fairness

To respond to this challenge, some philosophers buttress the retributive intuition with arguments about fairness. They maintain that human society requires norms and practices that define obligations and limit harms to others. Through this system we learn self-restraint, understanding that we cannot exercise our wills in whichever way we please. We also recognize that self-restraint requires a sacrifice, and often constitutes a burden. Finally, we all realize that we benefit from the self-restraint required by any system of benefits and burdens. No society has a perfect balance of benefits and burdens, but modern democratic societies achieve a relatively just one.[4]

Given this background, we can justify the retributive intuition by describing what happens when someone takes unfair advantage of others. Suppose I refuse to pay taxes, using what would be my tax bill to entertain myself. In evading the law, I gain an unfair advantage over other taxpayers. Naturally, they feel I have done something wrong, and think I deserve to suffer deprivation for my offense. Fairness requires an equal distribution of burdens and benefits, and I have claimed an unequal share of them.

What precisely do I gain when I break the law? Some retributive theorists focus on what I materially achieve by flouting laws. This leads them into complex discussions of how to calculate unfair advantages (for one example, see Hirsch 1992). John Finnis, I think, provides a more useful way of thinking about unfairness. Yes, I gain extra income through tax evasion, but the unfairness lies in the perverse exercise of my will. The unfairness occurs not only when I gain something that others lack, but earlier, when I indulged a wrongful self-preference. I accord myself excessive freedom (Finnis 2011).

Punishment seeks to restore the imbalance created by the offender. Using deprivation, the community subjects the offender's will to the restraint he failed to exercise. Punishment corrects the offender's will and allows others to continue to participate in a system that burdens them. Through his perverse exercise of will, he elevates himself above others, and the state uses deprivation to restore equality.

Do we really need deprivation to restore a balance of burdens and benefits? Retributive theorists grant that compensation and penance may help re-establish this balance. By itself, however, compensation restores only what the offender has gained (e.g. back taxes). It fails to restore the moral order she disrupted through a perverse exercise of will. The deprivation she receives restores this order. Concretely, it indicates that her will has been restrained. Ideally, forgiveness might also substitute for punishment, but many offenders are unwilling to take the steps necessary to achieve it. They continue to exercise their freedom inordinately, and we thus need deprivation to correct this perversion.

Finnis makes an additional point that is integral to a retributive conception of punishment. Crimes damage individual victims who deserve compensation or restitution. However, they also damage a community because an offense produces an inequality 'relative to all the offender's fellows in the community against whose law, and so whose common good, the offence offends' (Finnis 2011: 175, emphasis in the original). Punishment ensures that those who remain law abiding suffer no disadvantage when criminals perversely exercise their freedom. It cannot negate the crime itself, but it removes the offender's advantage.

Some retributivists add a final element to their theory, the explicit or implicit consent of citizens. Those who participate in a fair system of burdens and benefits recognize that it requires self-restraint. To ensure it, they also understand that punishment is sometimes necessary. Even if they never explicitly agree to participate in this system, their participation in social life indicates an implicit acceptance of punishment. To support this argument, philosophers usually draw on some variant of social contract theory (see

Morris 1968). Through their acts, citizens endorse a fair system of benefits and burdens, and acknowledge punishment's central role in sustaining it.

Critics of the fairness version of retributivism maintain that it only explains certain crimes (Duff 1986; Hampton 1988). Fairness arguments apply well to property and financial crimes, where offenders seek unfair advantage in a distribution of resources. In these cases, we can reasonably suppose that most of us are tempted to act unfairly. Punishment corrects those who succumb to this temptation, and gives us all reason to continue participating in a system of property allocation. However, as Jean Hampton points out, the fairness account of retribution falls short when we think about crimes like rape (Hampton 1988). It is implausible to think that we are all tempted to rape others in order to take advantage of a system of self-restraint. Some crimes are so horrible that few people are tempted to commit them. In such cases, arguments about fairness and punishment falter because they apply only to a select few who are willing to commit heinous acts.

To summarize, for some retributivists the retributive intuitive is no mere primitive that we use to theorize about punishment. Instead, it expresses our justifiable sense of unfairness that arises when someone disrupts a balance of benefits and burdens. The notion of fairness bolsters our intuition that offenders should suffer when they break the law.

The retributive turn and supermax confinement

Turning to solitary confinement, it emerged in the early days of the penitentiary in nineteenth-century Britain and the USA. It was designed to transform inmates by producing pangs of conscience and a moral transformation. However, as many historians have detailed, solitary confinement soon produced numerous psychological problems and drove some inmates mad (Ignatieff 1978; Rothman 1990; Lewis 1922). For these and other reasons, prisons in the USA and Britain soon abandoned solitary confinement as a primary instrument of punishment. They reserved it for recalcitrant inmates. They were placed in dark, filthy cells and placed on dietary restrictions. In some cases, time in isolation deeply damaged inmates. However, with some exceptions, twentieth-century US prisons tended to limit solitary sentences to short periods of time.

US penal policy began to change in the 1970s. Facing a growing prison population, officials began experimenting with solitary confinement as a way to deal with disorder and political dissent (Kerness 2013; Kurshan 2013). The most significant change came at the federal prison in Marion, Illinois. Opened in 1963, Marion replaced Alcatraz as the location for recalcitrant inmates in federal and state prisons. Penal officials concentrated them in one location in the hope that they could control them. Marion became an experimental institution, where officials pioneered different forms of behavior modification.

At Marion, prison overcrowding, inmate activism and official brutality produced a volatile mix. In the late 1970s, disorder increased, and things came to a head in 1983. Inmates brutally murdered two corrections officers and an inmate. Responding to this violence, authorities initiated a lockdown. Inmates were confined to their cells all day and night, and their movement outside of them was severely restricted. Education and other opportunities disappeared, and inmates reported significant staff brutality (Griffin 1993; Gomez 2006).

What distinguished the Marion lockdown from others was not only its conditions, but also its legal aftermath. Inmates and their allies protested the constitutionality of the lockdown but it endured for years. Legal challenges wound their way through the courts, but eventually the US Supreme Court declined to hear them. Penal authorities took this legal victory as validation for their tactics at Marion, and thus began the era of the new supermax confinement (Kurshan 2013).

After Marion, officials throughout the USA embraced solitary confinement. Federal, state and local authorities constructed a host of new institutions and units similar to the Marion facility. Some became known as 'supermax' prisons – stand-alone prisons designed specifically to isolate inmates. In the late 1980s and 1990s, Arizona, California and other states opened supermax prisons. In 1994, the federal government opened its supermax in Florence, Colorado, to house convicted terrorists and notorious criminals. By 2004, at least 44 US states had built supermax facilities (Shalev 2009).

Scholars and reporters who discuss supermax prisons often overlook what also occurred in prisons and jails. In the 1990s and 2000s, they built new 'segregation' units designed to isolate inmates. Sometimes capable of housing hundreds of inmates, they reproduce conditions in the supermax facilities. Gradually, the USA built an enormous solitary confinement system. Scholars have difficulty determining the exact number of inmates living in solitary confinement. Departments of Correction refuse to release information and researchers cannot gain access to segregation units and supermax prisons. Despite these difficulties, researchers estimate that 50,000–80,000 people live in solitary confinement (New York State Bar Association Committee on International Human Rights 2011).

Defining solitary confinement

Those operating prisons often deny that they use solitary confinement. They mask their practices with strange euphemisms like 'administrative segregation', 'seg' or 'the Bing'. Despite these diverse names, contemporary solitary confinement arrangements exhibit certain common characteristics. A 1999 Department of Justice report held that a supermax facility is:

> [A] freestanding facility, or a distinct unit within a freestanding facility, that provides for the management and secure control of inmates who have been officially designated as exhibiting violent or seriously disruptive behavior while incarcerated. Such inmates have been determined to be a threat to safety and security in high-security facilities and their behavior can only be controlled by separation, restricted movement, and direct limited access to staff and other inmates.
>
> (US Department of Justice and National Institute of Corrections 1999)

In both supermax prisons and segregation units, inmates generally live in their cells for at least 23 hours a day. If released for exercise or showering, they do so alone. Exercise often occurs in a single cage and showering where no one is present. Inmates are observed through cameras, and when they are done, they are returned to their cells (Shalev 2009; Jeffreys 2013).

Conditions in solitary confinement

What is life like in contemporary solitary confinement? Supermax confinement generally marries technology and isolation (Shalev 2009).[5] Architecturally, supermax prisons are often located in remote areas of a state so as to ensure greater control over inmates. Remote location reduces inmate contact with the world outside prison, and minimizes escape possibilities. Within prisons and jails, segregation units often appear in a remote part of the facility. They might be up on a hill or in a basement. Technology enables corrections officials to minimize contact with inmates. In many facilities, officials open and close cells from a distance with the help of computers. When released for showers or exercise, inmates make no contact with corrections officials or other inmates. If they have visitors, they leave their cells in shackles, and may be subjected to body cavity searches. Often, they can see visitors only at a distance through videoconferencing.

Life within a solitary cell is grim and monotonous. Inmates are fed through slots in their doors. Environmental uniformity is the rule; cells are painted in drab colors and inmates are allowed no wall decorations. In some units, lights remain on continually, and in others cameras monitor inmates. Officials control every aspect of an inmate's life. Television, radio and books are considered privileges, and access to them depends on an inmate's behavior. Inmates have little or no educational opportunities, and in many prisons they cannot participate in religious services. If and when they receive chaplain or medical visits, corrections officers monitor them. The atmosphere in segregation is one of stifling control.

Inmates in solitary who resist authorities are met with overwhelming and dramatic violence. Jails and prisons employ 'extraction teams' – groups of corrections officers trained to crush dissenters. Equipped with shields and body armor, they carry weapons like chemical agents, mace and rubber bullets. They first order the inmate to cooperate. Inmates sometimes throw feces or other substances at the officers or simply refuse to leave their cell. Officers may throw chemical agents into the cell. Officers then open the cell door and rush the inmate. A violent struggle often ensues, and inmates and officers can be injured. Five or six officers use whatever force necessary to end this conflict. At the end of the day, the inmate cannot prevail in his resistance, and will eventually be forced to obey orders. The result, however, is that segregation units are sites of continual violence and conflict between corrections officers and inmates (for a good account of cell extractions, see Goode 2014).

Who lives in solitary?

In addition to violent, grim and monotonous conditions, contemporary solitary confinement is also marked by arbitrary procedures. Jails and prison officials, rather than judges, generally decide whom to isolate and how long isolation will last. They claim to employ due process, but inmates rarely prevail when contesting a decision to send them to isolation. If there is a conflict between an officer and an inmate, officials will often side with the officer. Inmates can end up in segregation for a host of reasons. Some are violent and dangerous and cannot function around others. However, most inmates find themselves in segregation for relatively minor offenses. These can include insubordination, failure to follow orders, possession of contraband, writing subversive essays and a host of minor rules violations. For example, New York City's enormous jail, Rikers Island, maintains a large population of inmates in solitary. They can end up in isolation for a hundred offenses, but they are not informed of all of them (Law 2014). Such arbitrary procedures exist in many US jails and prisons.

Sentences in solitary vary widely in duration. For minor offenses, inmates can be isolated for weeks or months. For more serious ones, they can serve years in isolation. Those who are officially labeled gang members may live in permanent isolation, which they can only escape by renouncing their gang membership at great risk to their lives (Reiter 2012). Others commit additional offenses while in segregation, and receive more time in isolation. Some inmates end up serving decades in solitary confinement. Although their sentences may be reviewed occasionally, they have little hope of ever exiting segregation. In general, US isolation policies are draconian in nature, aimed at crushing dissent and disobedience.

Breaking the will: solitary and the person

What happens to a person enduring this kind of punishment? For almost two centuries, we have known about solitary confinement's deleterious effects on the person. Nineteenth-century British and American prison officials reported them in great detail. They realized that solitary confinement failed to redeem convicts, and many judicial and penal authorities came to see it as a destructive form of punishment. For example, discussing solitary confinement in the famous Auburn prison in New York State, Gershom Powers commented that 'a number of convicts became insane while in solitude; one was so desperate that he sprang from his cell, when the door was opened, and threw himself from the gallery upon the pavement, which nearly killed him, and he undoubtedly would have destroyed his life instantly, had an intervening stovepipe not broken the force of his fall. Another beat and mangled his head against the walls of his cell until he destroyed his eyes' (quoted in Lewis 1922: 82). Multiple testimonies from wardens and inmates testify to the destructive character of solitary confinement.

What our ancestors learned through hard experience was rediscovered by psychiatrists and psychologists studying contemporary solitary confinement. Among others, Stuart Grassian, Terry Kupers, Craig Haney and Peter Scharff Smith have documented how isolation damages people (Grassian 2006; Kupers 2006; Haney 2003; and Smith 2006). After a few weeks alone, a person begins to develop psychological symptoms that impede his functioning. They can include hypersensitivity to external stimuli, panic attacks, difficulties concentrating, intrusive thoughts, problems with memory, impulse control problems and paranoia. Many also report that they continue to display these negative psychological effects long after they are released.

The psychological effects of solitary confinement appear even more prominently in inmates suffering from mental illness. US jails and prisons have become *de facto* mental institutions, holding those who cannot find mental healthcare elsewhere. Many of these inmates have difficulty adjusting to prison life, and are overrepresented in segregation. They often disobey rules or lash out at corrections officers and other inmates. Their behavior in segregation leads to additional time in isolation. Isolation exacerbates their illness, and gradually, some inmates withdraw into themselves, engage in self-mutilation or commit suicide. For those with mental illness, solitary confinement is deeply damaging.

Solitary and the self

In addition to empirically measurable psychological effects, solitary also damages a person's sense of self. Through imagination and intellectual curiosity, people can transcend their circumstances. They can conceive of goals that guide their behavior. Solitary confinement gradually undermines this capacity to transcend an environment. Environmental uniformity, relentless monotony and continual hostility from corrections staff narrow a person's relationship to his environment. Inmates report experiencing difficulties in thinking of anything except their confinement. They struggle to think about life outside prison, long for something positive in the future or try to devote themselves to political or religious ideals. Some extraordinary people survive by cultivating these ideals. However, they do so in spite of circumstances that drive them toward a narrow conception of their existence.

These conditions also undermine a person's self-identity. By acting and relating to others, we develop a sense of ourselves that endures in time. We gradually actualize a narrative of our lives. Solitary confinement fractures such narratives. Inmates often describe how they struggle to relate coherently to their past. They talk only to themselves or shout at others. Segregation units are filled with screaming and cursing inmates. This constant din makes it difficult for people to compose themselves or to think clearly. Irregular sleep and a loss of a sense of time contribute to listlessness and a sense of meaninglessness. Inmates report that they struggle to recognize themselves in mirrors. Slowly and relentlessly, they feel their identities disintegrate (Jeffreys 2013; O'Donnell 2014).

By recognizing this loss of a coherent self and a capacity for transcendence, we better understand solitary's deleterious effects on the person. Social scientists and medical personnel document psychological damage, but isolation's attack on the person goes beyond what they can measure. Inmate testimony, literary accounts and the experiences of those working with inmates all testify to how solitary confinement damages a person's inner life. After a short period alone, human beings experience terrible inner suffering and a loss of their sense of self (Rhodes 2004; Bauer 2012). When crafting penal policy, we need to carefully take into account such real but sometimes intangible damage to the person.[6]

Deterrence and segregation

Although some penal authorities acknowledge this damage, they defend the use of solitary confinement by appealing to deterrence. They maintain that punitive segregation is an essential tool for maintaining order within prisons and jails. They further assert that segregation deters inmates from repeating destructive behavior. It also promotes general deterrence because the prospect of segregation will make inmates think twice before breaking rules. Officials make empirical claims about segregation. They also insist that it reduces institutional violence by removing violent inmates from the general population. Prison officials also hold that solitary confinement reduces gang activity. For example, the California prison system used it extensively to respond to sophisticated gangs within its institutions. It isolates gang leaders from others, and maintained that this practice reduced the power of gangs (Shalev 2009). In sum, many prison officials justify using segregation by citing its deterrent effects and noting how it reduces violence and gang activity.

Philosophically, deterrence as a justification of punishment confronts a number of conceptual challenges (see Duff 1986: Chapter 6). However, even if these did not exist, we simply lack the evidence necessary to argue for the deterrent power of solitary confinement. Too often, those operating prisons make unfounded empirical claims or appeal to common sense or experience. For example, how do we know that solitary confinement deters inmates from breaking rules? Wardens often use it against inmates with mental illness who have difficulty following rules. In their cases, solitary confinement only exacerbates mental illness. With other inmates, solitary may simply embitter them, leading them to commit further acts of violence and disruption. Similar questions arise about the argument that solitary confinement reduces gang influence. As Sharon Shalev notes, in some cases removing a gang leader may create additional violence as others struggle to gain power in the gang (Shalev 2009). Power vacuums can create considerable unrest in a prison.

The few scholarly studies we do have of segregation lend little support to the idea that it serves as a deterrent. For example, almost a decade ago, Jesenia M. Pizzaro, Vanja M. K. Stenius and Travis C. Pratt evaluated the claim that solitary confinement reduces institutional violence. They concluded that we have little empirical evidence to sustain it (Pizzaro et al. 2004). Others like Daniel P. Mears supported this conclusion (Mears 2006). More recently, the New York Civil Liberties Union published a study of solitary confinement in New York State (New York Civil Liberties Union 2014). It found little evidence that it improved institutional safety. In fact, the report maintained that segregation often damages inmates with mental illness who then create further disruption in the prison. In many cases, inmates in solitary are released immediately back to their communities, and are totally unprepared for life outside a prison or jail. We thus have little empirical evidence to support the deterrent power of solitary confinement.

Retribution and segregation

Although some corrections officials make arguments about segregation and deterrence, others talk about retribution. When I speak to them, they often tell me that inmates *deserve* to be isolated because they committed terrible crimes or cannot function with others. Bad behavior yields bad consequences. Those in solitary bring their suffering on themselves, and cannot legitimately claim to be unjustly punished.

We can buttress this common argument by returning to the question of fairness. Outside prison, those who commit heinous crimes display a perverse disregard for others. They exercise their freedom without concern for the lives of others. For such people, solitary confinement is a fit punishment. It corrects their errant will, and indicates to others that society will not tolerate outrageous and immoral exercises of freedom.

Inside a prison, we might talk about fairness within the 'society of captives' (to use Gresham Sykes's (1958) famous phrase). Prisons house people who have been unable to live by society's rules, but this does not mean that prisons are lawless environments. Like all societies, the prison requires its members to comply with minimal social norms. Prison inmates are always trying to circumvent them, and authorities have an obligation to maintain minimal order. Segregation and supermax confinement serve this goal by correcting the perverse will of those claiming excessive freedom.

Let me offer an example to illustrate this point. Violence against corrections officers is an ever-present danger in many prisons. Inmates may be angered at officers who demean them. They may become deeply frustrated at their degrading condition and the continual need to follow orders. In such cases, they may lash out violently against their captors.

Such an attack, however, would constitute a perverse exercise of will, unavailable to the many inmates who just want to do their time quietly and safely. The violent inmate gains an unfair advantage over them, and undermines the minimal restraint all inmates must show. By placing him in segregation, prison officials correct his perverse act of will. On the retributive view, he deserves isolation because of his inordinate exercise of freedom.

An inadequate justification

To those familiar with our segregation policies, philosophical defenses of retribution have an air of unreality about them. Theorists talk about well-ordered societies, fairness and relatively just social structures. Such discussions bear little relation to the brutal conditions we find in segregation and supermax units. In the world of penal institutions, the enormous gap between theory and reality challenges anyone interested in philosophical justifications of punishment.

In particular, segregation policies diverge widely from concepts of fairness. The fairness defense of retribution presupposes a relatively fair balance of burdens and benefits. On its account, 'a system of law must be justified to those who are subject to it, by showing that it secures a fair distribution of benefits and burdens' (Duff 1986: 209). We may debate whether US society in general fits this description, but segregation confinement falls far short of it. Except in rare cases of terrorism, judges make no decisions about whether to isolate an inmate. Instead, such decisions are administrative ones, and are often hidden from the public. Inmates violating rules undergo disciplinary hearings consisting of corrections officers, security directors or wardens. They have no lawyers or legal representatives of any kind. Evidence from confidential informants may be used against them, but for security reasons they have no access to their accusers and can know almost nothing about the evidence against them. We have little empirical evidence about how often inmates prevail when they contest disciplinary charges. However, the odds are stacked against them because they lack the legal or administrative resources to defend themselves.

The unfairness of this procedure is compounded by the presence of large numbers of inmates with mental illness in segregation. Over the last two decades, human rights and legal organizations have repeatedly drawn attention to their plight. In state after state, county jail after county jail, and federal facility after federal facility, mentally ill inmates live in segregation units. Unable to cope with the restrictions and subject to brutal violence from staff and inmates, they live in isolation. For example, the US Department of Justice recently concluded that the Rikers Island jail in New York City exhibited a pattern of brutality against adolescent inmates that violated their constitutional rights (US Department of Justice 2014). A culture of brutality prevailed that included excessive use of segregation and violence against inmates with mental illness. Similarly, a recent Amnesty International report about solitary confinement in the federal prison system found grossly negligent treatment of inmates with mental illness (Amnesty International 2014). Many lack adequate medication or therapy and their conditions worsen. Penal institutions throughout the USA use segregation to control people who are unable to adapt to prison life. In no way can we say that these inmates operate in a system that fairly balances burdens and benefits. On the contrary, they live in a punitive environment that makes little attempt to help them deal with their illness.

Most significantly, although individual wardens, corrections officers, teachers and others often act fairly toward inmates, fairness is not the main goal driving correctional institutions. Systemically, as many scholars have demonstrated, security concerns dominate custodial institutions (Goffman 1961; Rothman 1990; Spillane 2014). When therapeutic goals or attempts to develop fair policies emerge, they often clash with security needs. In this clash, security concerns usually prevail, often despite the best intentions and efforts of prison workers. Today's penal institutions aim to incapacitate inmates, crush dissent and ensure public safety. They show little interest in developing a fair system of burdens and benefits, and US public opinion tends to support this punitive incarceration.

When facing these realities, the fairness defense of retribution collapses. We cannot plausibly claim that inmates who disobey institutional rules take unfair advantage of others in a relatively just system. We certainly cannot say that inmates would voluntarily accept brutal segregation if they were to choose punishment under ideal circumstances! Some of them have committed violent acts against staff and inmates, but the wrongness of their acts has little to do with a mythical system of burdens and benefits. Most inmates are simply swept up in a confusing system of minor rules offenses, while still others cannot adhere to rules because of mental illness. All of these inmates live in oppressive conditions that bear little resemblance to ideals of justice (for a good discussion of the gap between theory and reality in the philosophy of punishment, see Duff 1986).

Prospects for the future

Given this failure of retributive theory, one would think that solitary confinement would lack legitimacy and gradually disappear. However, for years penal authorities have hidden jails and prisons from public view. Scholars and journalists have difficulties visiting them, and rarely get access to segregation units. For example, few reporters have ever been inside the Federal Supermax in Florence, Colorado. With little or no information about the conditions inside penal institutions, many Americans cannot make moral judgments about them.

In the last decade, however, this situation has changed, particularly as the financial costs of supermax confinement have become clearer. Major newspapers like *The New York Times* have highlighted the horrors of solitary confinement. A host of smaller news outlets have followed suit, devoting long stories to the subject. Prominent journalists and ex-wardens have spoken out against solitary confinement. Gradually, people are gaining information about the horrors of isolation, and many are appalled by what they have learned.

Most importantly, state governments have altered their segregation and supermax policies. Some have focused on juvenile offenders and those suffering from mental illness. Courts have intervened to demand that prisons evaluate an inmate's mental health before she is consigned to segregation. Some state prisons have limited the time those with mental illness can be in segregation. States like New York and Maine have prevented juvenile offenders from spending excessive time in isolation. Others like Mississippi and Illinois has closed their supermax facilities altogether, transferring inmates to maximum security facilities. All these developments provide hope for a change in US penal policy.

Unfortunately, other developments render it difficult to be confident that the USA is moving in a positive direction. For example, the federal government has undertaken reviews of its segregation policies, and examined the plight of those with mental illness.

However, it also plans to open another federal supermax within a few years (Casella and Ridgeway 2013). Reports indicate that in this proposed prison, many inmates will live in harsh isolation. Similarly, the large jails in Los Angeles, New York and Chicago continue to face allegations of brutality against inmates in segregation. Finally, segregation continues to exist in many of the over 3,000 jails in the USA. Millions of people find themselves in these jails, and can disappear into segregation with little fanfare. Given the size and decentralized character of US corrections policy, it will take years or even decades to reverse a policy based on brutal isolation.

Conclusion

If we read literature on incarceration in the 1960s and 1970s, we might have thought retribution theories of punishment were an endangered species. Philosophers and opinion writers proclaimed that retribution was a barbaric remnant of a bygone era. Critics proclaimed the end of the prison, and heralded a new age of dealing with society's deviants in a humane way. For complex political and social reasons, this optimism soon disappeared, replaced by the harsh and punitive attitudes that now exist in the USA. For many Americans, retribution constitutes the sole reason to punish. They justify the incarceration of millions of people by claiming not only that it brings safety, but also that it gives criminals what they deserve.

This retributive attitude is expressed in the explosive growth of supermax and segregation confinement. Designed to break the will of inmates and destroy any resistance, modern solitary confinement makes little claim to benefit inmates. Instead, its architects and defenders make broad claims about deterrence and safety without any evidence to support them. More often, they simply assert that those who are isolated deserve to be alone. They are the 'worst of the worst', who refuse to live by institutional rules, and have no legitimate reason to complain once they suffer the consequences of their disruptive behavior.

In this essay, I have challenged this retributive justification of supermax incarceration. Despite its critics, the retributive approach to punishment retains a powerful appeal and strong philosophical credentials. I have examined only one justification for it, the appeal to fairness that has appeared in philosophy during the last few decades. I find it one of the more interesting ways of defending retributivism, but believe it cannot legitimize supermax confinement. Assuming a relatively fair balance of burdens and benefits in society, it insists that punishment restores this balance by humbling the will of the offender who takes unfair advantage of others. Such a defense of retribution bears little relation to what happens in contemporary penal institutions. Segregation policies involve an unfair distribution of burdens and benefits. With little or no due process, inmates find themselves isolated for months or years. Subjected to a continual assault on their personalities, they gradually deteriorate psychologically and physically.

In his famous treatise, *The Prince*, Machiavelli remarks that 'many have pictured republics and principalities that have never been seen or known to exist in reality; for there is such a gap between how one lives and how one should live that one who neglects what is being done for what should be done will learn his destruction rather than his preservation' (Machiavelli 1964: Chapter 15). I often think of this compelling passage when reading philosophical defenses of retribution. Philosophers have an obligation to discuss the ideal conditions under which punishment is justified. However, they should recall the enormous gap that exists between theory and reality in the penal arena. Our current system of isolating tens of thousands of human beings in terrible isolation bears no relationship to the imaginary republics where fairness guides public policy. For years, supermax and segregation policies were hidden from a public all too willing to ignore them. Today, many Americans have learned about the financial and moral costs of solitary confinement. States and municipalities are revisiting their penal policies. These developments provide hope that we can reverse our irrational and destructive retributivism.

Selected further reading

For good discussions of the history of solitary confinement, see David J. Rothman's seminal book (1971) *The Discovery of the Asylum: Social order and disorder in the new republic*, and Michael Ignatieff's fascinating study (1978) *A Just Measure of Pain: The penitentiary in the industrial revolution, 1750–1850*. For a remarkable account of the effects of solitary confinement in 19th-century British prisons, see Harry Mayhew and John Binny (1862) *The Criminal Prisons of London and Scenes of Prison Life*.

For a good account of the development of the Marion prison, see Nancy Kurshan (2013) *Out of Control: A fifteen-year battle against control unit prisons*. For a first-hand account of the effects of solitary confinement at Marion, see Eddie Griffin (1993) 'Breaking Men's Minds: Behavior Control and Human Experimentation at the Federal Prison in Marion'.

Anthropologist Lorna Rhodes offers a thoughtful discussion of the effects of solitary confinement in her book (2004) *Total Confinement: Madness and reason in the maximum security prison*. Colin Dayan has written two eloquent books that discuss solitary, see (2011) *The Law Is a White Dog: How legal rituals make and unmake persons* and (2007) *The Story of Cruel and Unusual*.

Notes

1 For an excellent discussion of the US victims' rights movement, see Gottschalk (2006: Chapters 5 and 6).
2 For older anthologies of philosophical articles about punishment, see Acton (1969) and Murphy (1995). For more recent philosophical studies of punishment see Boonin (2008) and Ellis (2012).
3 In the latter part of his career, Murphy has expressed reservations about the retributive justification for punishment, but he still reluctantly adheres to it. For his later discussion, see Murphy (2006).
4 In this section, I rehearse elements of Herbert Morris's well-known argument about punishment; see Morris (1968).
5 I have learned a great deal from Sharon Shalev's (2009) work, which I use extensively in this chapter.
6 I provide philosophical justifications for my account of transcendence and the self in two books (Jeffreys 2009, 2013). In these volumes, I consider how torture and solitary confinement affect human spirituality.

Bibliography

Acton, H.B. (ed.) (1969) *The Philosophy of Punishment: A collection of papers*, New York: Macmillan.
Amnesty International (2014) 'Entombed: Isolation in the U.S. Prison System', solitarywatch.com/wp-content/uploads/2014/07/Entombed-Report-Final-Web-15072014-1.pdf.

Bauer, Shane (2012) 'Solitary in Iran nearly broke me. Then I went inside America's Prisons', *Mother Jones*, November/December, www.motherjones.com/politics/2012/10/solitary-confi nement-shane-bauer.

Boonin, David (2008) *The Problem of Punishment*, Cambridge: Cambridge University Press.

Burns, Sarah (2012) *The Central Park Five: The untold story behind one of New York City's most infamous crimes*, New York: Vintage Press.

Casella, Jean and Ridgeway, James (2013) 'Obama's 2014 budget confirms plans for "ADX Thomson", new federal supermax prison', *Solitary Watch*, 13 April, solitarywatch.com/2013/04/ 13/obamas-2014-budget-confirms-plans-for-adx- thomson-new-federal-supermax-prison/.

Dayan, Colin (2007) *The Story of Cruel and Unusual*, with a Preface by Jeremy Waldron, Cambridge, MA: The MIT Press.

Dayan, Colin (2011) *The Law is a White Dog: How legal rituals make and unmake persons*, Princeton, NJ: Princeton University Press.

DiIulio, John J. (1990) *Governing Prisons*, New York: Free Press.

Dolinko, David (1991) 'Some thoughts about retributivism', *Ethics* 101 (April): 537–559.

Duff, Antony (1986) *Trials and Punishments*, Cambridge: Cambridge University Press.

Ellis, Anthony (2012) *The Philosophy of Punishment*, Exeter: Imprint Academic.

Feinberg, Joel (1970) 'The expressive function of punishment', in Joel Feinberg (ed.) *Doing and Deserving: Essays in the theory of responsibility*, Princeton, NJ: Princeton University Press, 95–118.

Finnis, John (2011) 'Retribution: Punishment's Formative Aim', in *Human Rights and Common Good. Collected Essays Volume III*, 167–180.

Foucault, Michel (1995) *Discipline and Punish: The birth of the prison*, trans. Allan Sheridan, New York: Vintage.

Goffman, Erving (1961) *Asylums: Essays on the social situation of mental patients and other inmates*, New York: Anchor Press.

Gomez, A.E. (2006) 'Resisting living death at Marion Federal Penitentiary, 1972', *Radical History Review* 96 (Fall): 58–84.

Goode, Ericka (2014) 'When cell door opens, tough tactics and risk', *The New York Times*, 14 July, www.nytimes.com/2014/07/29/us/when-cell-door-opens-tough-tactics-and-risk.html?hp&action= click&pgtype=Homepage&version=HpSumSmallMediaHigh&module=second-column-region&reg ion=top-news&WT.nav=top-news&_r=0 (accessed 11 September 2014).

Gottschalk, Maria (2006) *The Prison and the Gallows: The politics of mass incarceration in America*, Cambridge: Cambridge University Press.

Grassian, Stuart (2006) 'Psychiatric effects of solitary confinement', *Journal of Law and Policy* 22: 325–380.

Griffin, Eddie (1993) 'Breaking men's minds: behavior control and human experimentation at the federal prison in Marion', *Journal of Prisoners on Prisons* 4(2): 1–8.

Hampton, Jean (1988) 'The retributive idea', in Jeffrie G. Murphy and Jean Hampton (eds) *Forgiveness and Mercy*, Cambridge: Cambridge University Press, 111–161.

Haney, Craig W. (2003) 'Mental issues in long-term solitary and "supermax" confinement', *Crime and Delinquency* 43: 124–156, cad.sagepub.com/content/49/1/124.full.pdf+html.

Hart, H.L.A. (1968) 'Prolegomenon to the principles of punishment', in *Punishment and Responsibility: Essays in the philosophy of law*, New York: Oxford University Press, 1–27.

Ignatieff, Michael (1978) *A Just Measure of Pain: The penitentiary in the industrial revolution, 1750–1850*, New York: Pantheon Books.

Jeffreys, Derek S. (2009) *Spirituality and the Ethics of Torture*, New York: Palgrave Macmillan.

Jeffreys, Derek S. (2013) *Spirituality in Dark Places: The ethics of solitary confinement*, New York: Palgrave Macmillan.

Kerness, Bonnie (2013) 'The hidden history of solitary confinement in New Jersey's control units', *Solitary Watch*, March, solitarywatch.com/2013/03/13/the-hidden-history-of-solitary-confinem ent-in-new-jerseys-control-units/.

Kupers, Terry (2006) 'How to create madness in prison', in David Jones (ed.) *Humane Prisons*, Oxford: Radcliffe Publishing, 47–59.

Kurshan, Nancy (2013) *Out of Control: A fifteen-year battle against control unit prisons*, San Francisco, CA: Freedom Archives.

Law, Victoria (2014) 'Teens in isolation: state advisers to the U.S. Civil Rights Commission hold briefing on juvenile solitary confinement in New York', *Solitary Watch*, 14 July, solitarywatch. com/2014/07/14/teens-isolation-state-advisory-committee-u-s-human-rights-commission-holds-briefing-juvenile-solitary-confinement-new-york/#more-13137/.

Lewis, O.F. (1922) *The Development of American Prisons and Prison Customs, 1776–1845*, New York: Prison Association of New York.

Machiavelli, Niccolò (1964) *The Prince*, trans. Mark Musa, New York: St Martin's Press.

McKelvey, Blake (1993) *American Prisons: A history of good intentions*, Monclair, NJ: Patterson Smith.

Mackie, John L. (1982) 'Morality and the retributive emotions', *Criminal Justice Ethics* 1(1): 3–10.

Martinson, Robert (1974) 'What works – questions and answers about prison reform', *The Public Interest* 10: 22–54.

Mayhew, Harry and Binny, John (1862) *The Criminal Prisons of London and Scenes of Prison Life*, London: Griffin, Bohn, and Company.

Mears, Daniel P. (2006) 'Evaluating the effectiveness of supermax prisons', *Urban Institute Research Report*, March, www.urban.org/UploadedPDF/411326_supermax_prisons.pdf.

Moore, Michael S. (2010) 'The moral worth of retribution', in *Placing Blame: A general theory of the criminal law*, Oxford: Oxford University Press, 104–152.

Morris, Herbert (1968) 'Persons and punishment', *The Monist* 52: 475–501.

Murphy, Jeffrie G. (ed.) (1995) *Punishment and Rehabilitation*, third edn, Belmont, CA: Wadsworth Publishing.

Murphy, Jeffrie G. (2003) 'Two cheers for vindictiveness', in Jeffrie G. Murphy (ed.) *Getting Even: Forgiveness and its limits*, Oxford: Oxford University Press, 17–26.

Murphy, Jeffrie G. (2006) 'Legal moralism and retribution revisited', *Proceedings and Addresses of the American Philosophical Association* 80(2): 45–62.

New York Civil Liberties Union (2014) *Boxed In: The true cost of extreme isolation in New York's prisons*.

New York State Bar Association Committee on International Human Rights (2011) 'Supermax Confinement in U.S. Prisons', September, www2.nycbar.org/pdf/report/uploads/20072165-theBrutalityofSupermaxConfinement.pdf.

Nussbaum, Martha C. (2001) *Upheavals of Thought: The intelligence of emotions*, Cambridge: Cambridge University Press.

O'Donnell, Ian (2014) *Prisoners, Solitude and Time*, Clarendon Studies in Criminology, Oxford: Oxford University Press.

Pizzaro, Jesenia M., Stenius, Vanja M.K. and Pratt, Travis C. (2006) 'Supermax prisons: myths, realities, and the politics of punishment in American society', *Criminal Justice Policy Review* 17 (1): 6–21, www.sagepub.com/stohrstudy/articles/11/Pizarro.pdf.

Quinton, Anthony M. (1969) 'On punishment', in H.B. Acton (ed.) *The Philosophy of Punishment: A collection of papers*, New York: Macmillan, 55–65.

Reiter, K. (2012) 'Parole, snitch or die: California's supermax prisons and prisoners, 1987–2007', *Punishment & Society* 14(5): 530–563.

Rhodes, Lorna A. (2004) *Total Confinement: Madness and reason in the maximum security prison*, Berkeley, CA: University of California Press.

Rothman, David J. (1971) *The Discovery of the Asylum: Social order and disorder in the new republic*, Boston, MA: Little, Brown.

Rothman, David J. (1990) *Conscience and Convenience: The asylum and its alternative in progressive America*, Boston, MA: Little, Brown.

Shalev, Sharon (2009) *Supermax: Controlling risk through solitary confinement*, Cullompton: Willan.

Smith, Peter Scharff (2006) 'The effects of solitary confinement on prison inmates: a brief history and review of the literature', *Crime and Justice* 34(1): 441–528, www.jstor.org/stable/10.1086/500626.

Spierenburg, Pieter (2008) *The Spectacle of Suffering: Executions and the evolution repression from a pre-industrial metropolis to the European experience*, Cambridge: Cambridge University Press.

Spillane, Joseph (2014) *Coxsackie: The life and death of prison reform*, Baltimore, MD: Johns Hopkins University Press.

Sykes, Gresham M. (1958) *The Society of Captives: A study of a maximum security prison*, Princeton, NJ: Princeton University Press.

US Department of Justice (2014) August, www.justice.gov/usao/nys/pressreleases/August14/RikersReportPR/SDNY%20Rikers%20Report.pdf.

US Department of Justice and National Institute of Corrections (1999) 'Supermax prisons: overview and general considerations, National Institute of Corrections', January, static.nicic.gov/Library/014937.pdf.

Von Hirsch, Andrew (1976) *Doing Justice: The choice of punishments*, New York: Hill and Wang.

Von Hirsch, Andrew (1992) 'Proportionality in the philosophy of punishment', *Crime and Justice* 16: 55–98.

Wilson, James Q. (2013) *Thinking about Crime*, revised edn with a new Foreword by Charles Murray, New York: Basic Books.

Chapter 11

Mental health in prisons

Alice Mills and Kathleen Kendall[1]

Introduction

High levels of mental health problems amongst prison populations are a global issue, with research showing that prisoners have substantially higher rates of mental disorder than the general population. Imprisonment itself is a stressful experience, entailing separation from family and friends, living at close quarters with other prisoners, and a lack of constructive activity. Prisons are hostile environments where people experience fear, intimidation, psychological and physical damage, and suicide rates in prison are thought to be at least three times higher than in the community (Fazel et al. 2011). Despite substantial recognition that those with mental health problems should not be sent to prison, high levels of mental disorder in prison show no sign of abating, and mental health therefore remains a salient topic for anyone concerned with prisoners and imprisonment.

Definitions of mental health problems can differ substantially and they are variously referred to as 'mental disorders', 'mental illnesses', 'psychiatric disorders' or 'neurological disorders'. These terms are often used interchangeably, although the term mental disorder is arguably the broadest and the most used. The World Health Organization (WHO 2014) defines mental disorders as comprising 'a broad range of problems … generally characterized by some combination of abnormal thoughts, emotions, behaviour and relationships with others. Examples are schizophrenia, depression, intellectual disabilities and disorders due to drug abuse'. Mental health problems amongst prisoners are often complex and bound up with a combination of other issues including substance misuse, personality disorder, brain injury, intellectual disabilities, histories of trauma, loss and abuse, chaotic lifestyles and social exclusion, many of which are substantially more likely to be present in the prison population than the general population (Durcan 2006). Prisoners bring with them a high degree of 'imported vulnerability' (Bradley 2009) and the prison environment and regime may create or exacerbate mental distress.

In the last 15 years or so, the literature on prisoner mental health has grown considerably. The vast majority of this has been authored by mental healthcare professionals or those concerned with psychiatry as a field of academic study and has tended to focus on the prevalence of mental health problems in prison and appropriate models of care, with little attention paid to the constraints and impositions of the prison environment and the exercise of penal power. The challenges of providing mental healthcare in an environment that prioritizes containment, discipline and control have merited generally no more than a tokenistic mention. Accordingly, in this chapter, we briefly examine international research on the level of mental health needs in prison and models of mental health treatment provision before moving on to discuss some of the key critical issues regarding the interface between confinement and mental health. These include the notion of 'healthy' prisons, personality disorders, issues of risk and whether so-called 'equivalent' care can ever be provided in the prison setting. We illustrate some of these topics by drawing on a small qualitative study of mental health in-reach services in a local prison[2] in England. The study involved six focus groups and 48 qualitative interviews with mental health service users, other prisoners, mental health treatment staff, and other personnel working in the prison. We argue that despite substantial improvements in mental healthcare, prison remains an unsuitable place for treatment. Until a shift occurs away from the whole confinement project, high numbers of prisoners with mental health problems will remain a feature of prison life.

Prevalence of mental health problems amongst prisoners

Statistics regarding the prevalence of mental health problems in prisons vary considerably according to the research tools employed, whether the research is conducted by clinical or lay interviewers, the cultural interpretation of mental health symptoms in different jurisdictions, and the range of mental health problems measured. Some studies include a broad range of mental health and mental health-related conditions, including substance misuse and personality disorders. For example, the most comprehensive study of prison mental health in England and Wales found that approximately 90% of prisoners experienced one of the five categories of psychiatric disorder studied (Singleton et al. 1998)[3] – four times the corresponding rate in the wider community (Brooker et al. 2008). Some 70% of prisoners had two or more of these problems (Singleton et al. 1998). Studies of severe mental illness (SMI), which includes conditions such as major depression, bipolar disorder, schizophrenia and other forms of psychosis, give a better idea of the proportion of prisoners who might be expected to receive specialist mental healthcare. In a systematic review of 81 studies from 24 countries, Fazel and Seewald (2012) found a prevalence of psychosis of 3.6% in male prisoners and 3.9% in female prisoners. The corresponding figures for major depression were 10.2% and 14.1%. In the USA, prisons are seen as '*de facto*' psychiatric hospitals because there are more mentally ill people in prison than in state hospitals across the country (Daniel 2007), an issue which can be attributed to the low tolerance shown towards disorderly public behaviour in the 1990s (Young 2004).

As indicated by the figures above, female prisoners are more likely to suffer from mental health problems than male prisoners. Additionally, women in prison have high rates of suicide and self-harm (WHO Regional Office for Europe 2009), with female prisoners more than three times as likely to self-harm than men (NHS Commissioning Board 2013). Explanations for the higher prevalence of mental health needs among women include the 'multiplicity of disadvantage and damage' (Medlicott 2007: 250) that women prisoners experience before they enter prison, including high rates of domestic violence, sexual abuse, bereavement and teenage pregnancy (Corston 2007; O'Brien et al. 2001), with self-medication often used as a coping strategy (Mills et al. 2012). Women may experience the pains of imprisonment more intensely than men, due to their abuse histories and because they are more likely to be the primary carers of their children, yet are held further away from their families due to the limited number of prisons for women.

The prevalence of mental disorder is higher among young offenders and juveniles, with 80% suffering from two or more psychiatric disorders[4] (Lader et al. 2000). A meta-analysis of 25 surveys involving young people aged 10–19 found similar rates of psychosis as for adults, but levels of major depression for young females were substantially higher than their adult counterparts (Fazel et al. 2008). Children and young people in the justice system are thought to be at least three times as likely to have mental health problems as those in the community (NHS Commissioning Board 2013). The steadily growing number of older people behind bars has been of considerable concern in recent years (HMIP 2004; Kapoor et al. 2013; Potter et al. 2007). Rates of depressive illness amongst older prisoners have been found to be five times greater than those found in young adult prisoners or a matched community sample (Fazel et al. 2001), although prison mental healthcare tends to be aimed at a younger, more vocal population (HMIP 2004).

Research evidence suggests there is either little difference between the prevalence of mental disorders in minority ethnic groups, including indigenous populations, and the majority population in prisons (Durey et al. 2014; HMIP 2007; Simpson et al. 2003), or that minority ethnic groups have lower prevalence rates of mental illness. For example, in the USA in 2005, 61% of Caucasian prisoners reported any mental health problem in comparison with 54% of African American inmates and 44% of Hispanic inmates (James and Glaze 2006). This is somewhat surprising given their over-representation in prison systems (Durey et al. 2014; Primm et al. 2005; Prins et al. 2012; Simpson et al. 2003), factors of social disadvantage and social exclusion to which these groups are disproportionately subject, and in the case of Indigenous groups, the enduring legacy of colonization (Durey et al. 2014), which are all commonly associated with mental disorders. This may reflect their lack of prior contact with mental health services which some research uses as an imperfect proxy measure for current mental illness (Prins et al. 2012).

The offender pathway: diversion away from prison

There is a general consensus amongst academics, penal reform groups and professional bodies that prison is an unsuitable place for mental health treatment[5] and that those with severe mental illness should be kept out of prison, particularly if they have committed non-violent offences. Police or court diversion schemes operate to divert mentally disordered offenders away from the criminal justice system or to recommend a more suitable criminal justice disposal than imprisonment. For example, in New Zealand, mental health nurses perform initial assessments on persons appearing before the courts who appear unwell. Referrals to this service can be made by the presiding judges, lawyers, police prosecutors and even the family of the accused (Brinded 2000). In England and Wales the provision of such schemes has traditionally been highly patchy (Bradley 2009). The Bradley Report (2009) therefore recommended the establishment of Criminal Justice Mental Health Teams to provide diversion and liaison services for those with mental health problems in the criminal justice system. Five years later, a pilot scheme to introduce such services in ten areas of the UK was announced (DoH 2014). Such teams are to be based in police custody suites to enable the screening and identification of individuals with mental health problems or learning disabilities at the beginning of the so-called 'offender pathway', and will provide information to the police and prosecutors to inform charging and prosecution decisions (Bradley 2009; DoH 2014). It remains to be seen what impact these services will have on mental health in prisons, particularly as their effectiveness, and that of other diversionary measures such as mental health courts,[6] is likely to depend on the availability of scarce community mental health resources.

Mental healthcare provision in prisons

Models of prison mental healthcare

Broadly speaking there are three main models of prison mental healthcare provision, although a mix of models is often used, particularly in federal systems. First, mental healthcare in prisons may be the responsibility of, and provided by, the prison itself. In such instances healthcare may be part of the disciplinary mechanism of the power operating within the prison. Until the mid-2000s, healthcare in public prisons in England and Wales was the responsibility of the Prison Service and was repeatedly criticized for being inadequate and substandard (Birmingham et al. 1996; Smith 2000), and more concerned with control and custody than care (Coggan and Walker 1982; Sim 1990, 2002). Allegations were also made that prisoners were used as test subjects for experimental medication (Sim 1990), and that psychotropic medication was administrated to control recalcitrant prisoners (Coggan and Walker 1982; Sim 1990, 2002).

In countries such as Belgium and Lithuania, treatment for mentally ill offenders suffering from an acute psychotic episode is provided solely in prison psychiatric units (Dressing and Salize 2009). The WHO and the International Committee of the Red Cross (ICRC) (2005: 2) are highly critical of such facilities as they have low release rates and potentially leave individuals with a 'severe and persistent' stigma. Furthermore, operating outside the health departments responsible for healthcare standards may lead to substandard care and human rights violations (WHO and ICRC 2005).

Second, a 'hybrid' model may be used whereby the general responsibility for psychiatric services lies with the prison administration or justice ministry, which commissions healthcare agencies outside the prison to provide services such as outpatient clinics. In some instances, for example in Canada, this role is taken in partnership with regional health ministries, or, as in New Zealand, prison authorities may be responsible for primary mental healthcare services with health authorities responsible for specialist secondary mental health services (Wakem and McGee 2012). Even though the provider is not directly employed by prison services, Mullen et al. (2000) caution that as the clients, they may believe that health providers should have a primary duty to them. Decisions regarding treatment may therefore be made in the interests of the institution, rather than the patient, and healthcare budgets may be reduced if custody budgets are over-committed (Wakem and McGee 2012).

Finally, mental healthcare treatment in prisons may be the responsibility of agencies outside the prison, usually national or local health authorities. This model is perceived as likely to improve access to care and allow for more effective transition to services in the community after release from prison (Dressing and Salize 2009; Simpson et al. 2013). From 1964, calls began for prison healthcare services in England and Wales to be taken over by the National Health Service (NHS) to ensure equivalence of care with that of the general population (Coggan and Walker 1982; Gunn et al. 1991; HMIP 1996; Reed and Lyne 1997). Since 2006 administrative authority for prison healthcare has lain with the Department of Health,[7] as is the case in a small number of other jurisdictions such as France and Iceland (Dressing and Salize 2009), although health authorities became responsible for providing secondary mental healthcare in prisons a few years previously. In 2002, multi-disciplinary mental health in-reach services, commissioned by local healthcare agencies, were introduced to provide the same range and quality of care to prisoners with severe mental illness as community mental health services do to patients in the community. They were also intended to improve continuity of care between prison and community services and speed up arrangements for transferring the most seriously ill prisoners to community facilities (DoH et al. 2001). In-reach services are now provided by a variety of public, private and third sector organizations. The quality and efficacy of healthcare in English prisons is thought to have improved considerably since the transfer of responsibility for healthcare services to local health authorities, and prisoners receiving in-reach services are often extremely positive about the care that they receive (Durcan 2008; HMIP 2007; Mills and Kendall 2010). As will be discussed later in this chapter, mental health in-reach teams (MHIRTs) have, however, struggled to conform to the principle of equivalence in the prison setting.

Accessing treatment in prison

In order to receive any mental healthcare, prisoners' mental health problems must first be identified. However, Brooker et al. (2002) estimate that reception screening only picks up 25–33% of prisoners with serious mental illness. Reception is a time of substantial stress and anxiety for prisoners and screening is often rushed, may not take place in private or be carried out by a qualified mental health professional, or may be overly concerned with risk assessment (Seddon 2007). Prisoners may be reluctant to reveal mental health difficulties for fear it will stigmatize them as 'weak', or will lead to detrimental treatment. If they do reveal such difficulties, prisoners need to be believed by healthcare professionals or prison staff, who may feel that the prisoner is malingering or attempting to 'blag' the system (Sim 2002). Prison officers can identify mental health problems amongst prisoners on prison wings, and in England and Wales mental health awareness training for prison officers has been rolled out (DoH 2009) for this purpose. However, Birmingham (2004) suggests that they may tolerate symptoms unless prisoners' behaviour infringes prison rules or causes a problem to the prison regime, so a prisoner who is quietly psychotic, for example, is likely to be overlooked.

Even where mental health needs have been detected, they may go untreated. An evaluation of prison mental health in-reach services in England and Wales found that only 25% of prisoners with severe mental illness were assessed by in-reach services and just 13% received treatment (Senior et al. 2013). In the USA only one in three state prisoners and one in six jail inmates with a mental health problem have been found to have received treatment in prison (James and Glaze 2006). Some prisoners may refuse psychiatric care due to concerns about reputation, confidentiality or the restrictions it may place on their daily life (Simpson et al. 2013). Certain groups are less likely to have their treatment needs met than others. Those with a dual diagnosis of substance misuse and mental illness may be excluded from psychiatric services due to their substance misuse and excluded from substance misuse treatment due to their mental health issues (Bradley 2009). Prisoners from minority ethnic groups are substantially less likely to receive treatment for their mental health problems, either in the community or during imprisonment (HMIP 2007; Prins et al. 2012; Simpson et al. 2003). Some groups may not recognize the symptoms experienced as mental health-related or may feel that admitting such symptoms would be a source of substantial stigma (Prins et al. 2012), for example in African American or Latino communities (Kapoor et al. 2013). Alternatively they may express symptoms of mental disorder differently, which is then prone to mis-interpretation by clinicians from other backgrounds (Peters et al. 2008), reflecting a lack of cultural competence on the part of mental health professionals during screening pro-cesses when 'unwarranted judgement or erroneous assumptions are made about people on the basis of their race or ethnicity' (Prins et al. 2012: 636). This has led to calls for more culturally competent services and staff to meet the needs of minority ethnic groups (Auditor-General 2008; Kapoor et al. 2013; Primm et al. 2005; Simpson et al. 2003).

Transfer from prison to community mental healthcare

Prisoners with severe mental illness can be transferred to a secure mental health institu-tion in the community, particularly in those jurisdictions such as England and Wales and New Zealand which do not allow compulsory mental health treatment in prisons. However, such transfers can be delayed or even blocked for several reasons, including disputes between doctors as to the diagnosis or severity of mental disorders, lack of beds at the appropriate security level and the reluctance of community psychiatric staff to accept patients who may be perceived as difficult or even 'undeserving' (Bradley 2009; Mullen et al. 2000; Wakem and McGee 2012). In England and Wales, measures have been introduced to expedite such transfers in 14 days (DoH 2009), but delays remain and prisoners may still be waiting a significant length of time. Forrester et al. (2009), for example, found that just 20% of prisoners in two London prisons were transferred in a month or less, with the average wait in one of the prisons being 102 days. In the next section, we further problematize some of the issues surrounding mental healthcare in prisons by considering the broader social, political and cultural contexts within which they are situated.

Critical issues and mental health in prisons

Equivalence of care in the prison environment

The principle of prisoners receiving care equivalent to that available in the community enjoys a broad consensus amongst international human rights and health organizations (Lines 2006). For example, the United Nations Basic Principles for the Treatment of Prisoners (1990: para. 9) states: 'Prisoners shall have access to the health services available in the country without discrimination on the grounds of their legal situation.' Many jurisdictions have enshrined the principle of equivalence into their own laws and guide-lines (Australian Health Ministers' Advisory Council Mental Health Standing Committee 2006; Niveau 2007; US Department of Justice 2001; Wakem and McGee 2012). How-ever, despite these good intentions, prisoners do not receive equivalent mental health-care, and services in England and Wales, particularly MHIRTs, can be used to illustrate this. First, MHIRTs and other services have undoubtedly struggled to meet the high demand for their services (HMIP 2007), not least because the prison population has risen substantially since they were first introduced in 2002. Given the extent and severity of psychiatric morbidity in prisons, to offer an equivalent service to a community mental health team, a typical men's prison of 550 prisoners would require 11 full-time equivalent practitioners (Boardman and Parsonage 2007), over twice the current average of five per MHIRT (Brooker and Gojkovic 2009). Per capita spending on prison mental healthcare would also have to increase substantially (Brooker et al. 2008).

Second, despite the high levels of trauma experienced by the prison population, access to psychological therapies in prisons is highly limited. Due to staff recruitment and retention difficulties, few MHIRTs are fully multidisciplinary with teams being overwhelmingly dominated by psychiatric nurses (Shaw et al. 2008) and medication being the main form of treatment. In our qualitative research study of an MHIRT in England, the provision of therapy was also hindered by high prisoner turnover as mental health staff were reluctant to 'open up a can of worms' (MHIRT staff 3) through therapy that could then be damaging if prisoners were moved or released without warning.

Third, although many mental health problems experienced by prisoners are moderate and could be safely treated by primary mental healthcare (Bradley 2009), such services are lacking in prisons. Many GPs who work in prisons lack specialist training in complex mental health needs (Bradley 2009; HMIP 2007; Wakem and McGee 2012), and primary mental health nurses are often withdrawn from their specialist roles to cover more generic duties. Consequently, MHIRTs that were originally intended to focus on those with SMI (DoH et al. 2001) have accepted prisoners with primary level problems onto their caseloads (Bradley 2009). Research has found that 60% of prisoners on MHIRT caseloads did not have a current diagnosis of SMI, although 41% of these prisoners had a personality disorder and 34% had minor mental illness (Bradley 2009). This 'mission creep' (Steel et al. 2007: 373) may elucidate why so few of those with severe mental illness receive treatment from MHIRTs. The Bradley (2009) Report therefore called for the refocusing of MHIRTs on providing services for those with SMI, however, presentations of SMI are rarely straightforward but are often bound up with complex issues of personality disorder and substance misuse (Brooker 2006).

Finally, and most significantly, the goal of providing equivalent mental healthcare is likely to be substantially hindered by the constraints of the prison environment and regime which may require substantial adaptations to the organization of care (Niveau 2007). Despite improvements in mental health services, prisons are not designed to be therapeutic institutions. They are instead places of punishment and confinement which prioritize security, control and discipline. Healthcare is not seen as a core business activity (Mullen et al. 2000; National Health Committee 2010) and mental health is given little priority unless it challenges the running and security of an establishment (Durcan 2006). Concerns about security can seriously encumber the provision of mental health services, particularly for prisoners with mental health problems who are classified as high risk, and located in solitary confinement to manage their perceived difficult behaviour, as is often the case in the USA (Exworthy et al. 2012). In our research, an occupational therapist in the MHIRT could not run group work sessions in the healthcare centre because of a lack of staff needed to let high-risk prisoners out of their cells ensuring that 'those who are more seriously mentally ill, who are deemed to be more of a security risk, are not able to get out' (MHIRT staff 4) and engage in activity that may be beneficial to their mental health.

The prison priorities of security and control may mean that prison staff and management view behaviour exhibited by those with mental health problems as disciplinary problems, marking them out as high risk and potentially perpetuating 'an over-reliance on punishment instead of treatment in dealing with these individuals and their behaviour' (Correctional Association of New York 2011: 1). Sim (1990: 2002) has suggested that healthcare culture within prisons is permeated with custodial and masculinist discursive practices. Those who subscribe to these practices may be irritated by staff who place the interests of the prisoner before the smooth running of the prison (Mullen et al. 2000), and may hinder the implementation of treatment plans (Kapoor et al. 2013), particularly as prison staff can act as a filter between prisoners and healthcare services (Ross et al. 2011). The team leader of the MHIRT in our research described mental health staff as being 'at the officers' mercy', because they were required to escort prisoners to mental health appointments, a job which was often cancelled if other tasks in the prison took priority or in times of staff shortage. MHIRT members were often placed under pressure to conform to traditional custodial ideologies which constructed prisoners as 'less eligible subjects whose criminality has placed them beyond the contractual pale of respectable society' (Sim 2002: 317). When faced with such pressure, healthcare staff may adopt the practices and attitudes of the custodial culture in order to survive (DoH and HM Prison Service 1999; Ross et al. 2011). These informal networks of power in the prison created substantial levels of stress and dissatisfaction among MHIRT members; however, the team felt able to resist such attitudes by proactively aligning themselves and their work with the NHS, its culture and standards of care.

Additionally, inherent tensions are likely to arise between the custodial role of prisons and the delivery of high-quality equivalent healthcare, not least because the practice of imprisonment is likely to be 'fundamentally disempowering for inmates' (National Health Committee 2010: 101) and detrimental to their health (Niveau 2007). Whilst some inmates may perceive imprisonment as a welcome respite from difficult and chaotic lives on the outside and as an opportunity to improve their mental and physical health (Crewe 2005; Douglas et al. 2009; Woodall et al. 2013), there is a substantial body of research demonstrating the physical and psychological harms of imprisonment (Birmingham 2003; Bradley 2009; Corston 2007; Durcan 2008; Haney 2006; Liebling 1992). In our own research, prisoners expressed how a number of different aspects of imprisonment, including safety concerns, worries about family and life outside, and the uncertainty of life inside, could be detrimental to their mental health, with the lack of constructive activity and the amount of time prisoners spent 'banged up' in their cells being the most frequently mentioned:

> If you're incarcerated in here for a length of time, it's gonna have some kind of effect on your head isn't it? Being locked up in a cell for 22 hours a day doesn't really stimulate your mind. It makes you bang your fucking head against the wall.
>
> (Prisoner, Focus Group B)

> Being locked away all the time doesn't help ... you've too much time to think ...
>
> (Prisoner K)

Recent public sector cuts and reductions in the prison 'core day' have further limited the time prisoners spend out of cell engaged in constructive activities. Prisons therefore 'epitomise the antithesis of a healthy setting' (de Viggiani 2007: 115). Forensic psychiatrist John Gunn similarly states, 'It's [prison] meant to be a place where to put it very crudely you damage people's health. Punishment almost by definition is damaging people' (cited in Seddon 2007: 130). Furthermore, as Cunneen et al. (2013: 96) note, 'Even if prison services provide the best programmes and health care possible, being imprisoned and having a criminal record disadvantages the already disadvantaged'. Upon release, prisoners may face unemployment, debt, homelessness, the collapse of relationships and the loss of children. These issues can create or worsen mental health problems, contribute to substance use and lead to further contact with criminal justice and mental health systems. MHIRTs tend to adhere to an individualistic medical model of mental health which does not seek to address structural factors or the consequences of imprisonment which may contribute to complex mental health problems, such as poor access to housing. Organizations responsible for prisoners' mental health tend to work in silos (Bradley 2009; HMIP 2007), and in our research links between the MHIRT and other services in the prison, notably drug treatment and resettlement, were derisory, with little active engagement on either side, often due to concerns about information sharing, despite a desperate need for a holistic approach to mental health.

Increasingly, equivalence is viewed not only as unachievable but also undesirable within the prison setting. Equivalent care suggests that community mental health services represent a gold standard against which prison mental health services should be measured. This shrouds huge problems and inequalities within community provision, particularly in jurisdictions, such as the USA, where access to care may be better in prison, and the inadequacies of community mental health services can be illustrated by prisoners' long histories of transcarceration (Mills and Kendall 2010; Niveau 2007). Additionally, the notion of equivalence cannot adequately address the high and complex levels of multiple need in the prison population (Durcan 2008) as it seeks to 'impose standardisation of the inherently dissimilar' (Exworthy et al. 2011: 201). As Lines (2006) argues, through the act of incarceration, states have a responsibility to provide healthcare that protects the well-being of prisoners. Considering the intense, severe and complex health needs of prison populations, that the conditions of imprisonment may worsen prisoners' health, and prisoners' reliance on the prison authority for healthcare provision, providing only equivalent care in prisons frequently does not protect prisoners' health and falls short of states' human rights obligations.[8] Rather than equivalence of care, healthcare in prisons should seek to achieve equivalence of outcome. Far from seeing prisoners as 'less eligible' for healthcare services, this may entail providing services of substantially higher standard and scope than in the community (Lines 2006). However, as Seddon (2007) notes, to frame the idea of equivalence in terms of prisoners' rights to high-quality healthcare ignores the fact that prisoners are punishable subjects and healthcare may be implicated in punishment and control of prisoners.

Healthy prisons?

In 1995, the WHO European Region introduced its 'Health in Prisons Programme' (HIPP) to promote prison health among its member states as part of a larger WHO initiative to encourage 'healthy settings' through interventions that emphasize the specific contexts within which people carry out their everyday activities (WHO n.d.). In theory, this approach considers how the organizational, social and physical settings in which people are situated hinder or help their health. As such, it offers the possibility of moving beyond interventions simply targeting individuals toward holistic measures that address socio-political and economic structures, including power (Poland et al. 2009). Unfortunately, the model's progressive potential has not been borne out in practice (Woodall et al. 2013). The healthy settings orientation has been interpreted narrowly as 'using the strengths of the settings to encourage healthy choices and allow choice through healthy policies' (Gatherer et al. 2009: 86). Prisons are touted as being therapeutic as they are perceived to offer opportunities for engaging with hard-to-reach and typically unhealthy populations that would otherwise not receive healthcare. Recent WHO guidance on prison health promotion states that '[p]risoners' attitudes to health should be assessed and encouraged, and help given to change unhealthy behaviour such as tobacco use, substance abuse and alcohol abuse' (Gatherer et al. 2014: 4). Health promotion is thus reduced to behavioural change.

Health promotion is not a value-free enterprise but instead reflects neo-liberal ideals (Lupton 1995). While there are many variations of neo-liberalism, the term typically refers to the notion that unregulated, open and competitive markets, free from state interference, will bring prosperity and contentment. Underpinning this logic are the core values of individual responsibility, competition, privatization, consumerism, cost-effectiveness and efficiency. In holding individuals responsible for both the cause and treatment of health problems, while drawing attention away from the broader social structures contributing to them, the HIPP strategy described above and other health promotion strategies knit neo-liberal ideology and logic together with penality. Neo-liberal ideals also inform penal policy and practice more widely (Cunneen et al. 2013; Kemshall 2002; O'Malley 2009; Wacquant 2009, 2010), including the government of prisoners with mental health problems (Seddon 2007). The emphasis is on changing unhealthy behaviour by providing prisoners with opportunities to make better choices, rather than challenging the prison setting. Ill health, including poor mental health, can therefore be blamed on prisoners themselves for not taking up what is on offer to them.

Neo-liberalism and risk

Although proponents of neo-liberalism contend that governments should not interfere in citizens' lives, there has been increased state involvement and spending in some spheres, notably immigration control, the military and the prison industrial complex (Pollack 2010). Reforms inspired by neo-liberalism, including the erosion of the welfare state and cuts to mental health services, have been shown to be associated with greater poverty and poorer physical and mental health (Coburn 2004; Hansen et al. 2014; Navarro 2007), pushing greater numbers of people toward engaging in illicit activities for survival and creating a vacuum to be filled by the criminal justice system under the guise of therapeutic services. Neo-liberalism has intensified both the abandonment and containment of society's most vulnerable and marginalized populations (Horan 2010). Yet not all individuals with mental health problems are equally liable to encounter the criminal justice system. It is the most destitute and racialized whose chances of incarceration are heightened. These groups often do not have access to conventional advocacy and support, and they are furthermore perceived to be highly dangerous and risky. As such, they are regarded as 'suitable penal subjects' (Cunneen et al. 2013: 91).

While the concept of risk has been present in penal and mental health practices since the late 18th century, it has become an increasingly central feature of neo-liberal governance (O'Malley 2009). Risk practices are especially evident in the management of prisoners with mental health problems. The protection of the public, not the care of the patient, is the primary function of forensic services (Mason and Mercer 1999). As such, psychiatrists, psychologists and other mental healthcare workers conduct assessments in order to predict, control and manage the risk inmates pose to other people, to the order of the institution and to themselves. However, risk is fluid and can be merged with other governing practices, such as rehabilitation, to create hybrid technologies or assemblages (O'Malley 2009; Maurutto and Hannah-Moffat 2006). In this way, risk assessments can claim to fulfil both therapeutic and disciplinary roles. It is unsurprising therefore that the most common forms of mental healthcare intervention experienced by prisoners are mental health assessment and monitoring (Durcan 2008). In Anglo-Welsh prisons, MHIRTs have been co-opted into risk assessment and management (for example, to assess the risk of self-harm). This is particularly the case in local remand prisons, where their work may be dominated by such demands, as we found in our study, illustrated by the following quotes from MHIRT members:

> We seem to just do lots of assessments and bare minimum really of therapeutic work.
>
> (MHIRT staff 3)

> I think it's fair to say that the kind of therapeutic stuff isn't that huge at the moment because of constraints on both our time and the facilities in prison. But it's certainly one-to-one assessments and risk assessment.
>
> (MHIRT staff 1)

Such risk management practices are integral to the control and disciplinary regime of the prison and to the larger socio-legal apparatus (Carlen 1986).

Personality disorder

The knotty issue of risk is most apparent in the category of personality disorder, and Dangerous Severe Personality Disorder in particular. Broadly speaking, personality disorder can be understood as a psychiatric construct denoting 'enduring dysfunctions of personality' (Pickersgill 2012: 30). It is thought to be largely unchangeable and fundamental to who a person is. Until recently, mental health professionals generally perceived individuals with personality disorders to be a nuisance, untreatable and not proper subjects for their attention. One study, aptly titled 'Personality Disorder: The Patients Psychiatrists Dislike', found that people with the label were often excluded from health services and unpopular with practitioners (Lewis and Appleby 1988).

The relationship between personality disorders and crime rose to public attention in the UK following the very high-profile case of Michael Stone, who was found guilty of killing Lin Russell and her six-year-old daughter Megan in 1998. Before the murder, Stone had served three prison sentences and had been labelled as a psychopath. Although the Mental Health Act (1983) in place at the time recognized psychopathy as a mental disorder, individuals given the label could not be involuntarily detained because it was understood to be an untreatable condition. Therefore, although there was concern before the homicide about Stone's potential for future violence, he could not be kept in custody (Corbett and Westwood 2005; Pickersgill 2012). The case, and the heavy media coverage around it, prompted vigorous campaigns for changes to the law, and in 2000 the UK government proposed the removal of the treatability clause and the introduction of a new condition called Dangerous and Severe Personality Disorder (DSPD). A number of psychiatrists and other mental health professionals spoke out against the plan on ethical, practical and empirical grounds (Mental Health Alliance 2005). Nonetheless, the new Mental Health Act was passed in 2007 and the treatability requirement was abolished. In its place, the Act simply requires that 'appropriate medical treatment is available', and individuals can now be detained against their will if this criterion is met. In preparation for the change in law, in 2005 four centres designed to research, assess and manage DSPD were opened (Corbett and Westwood 2005; Pickersgill 2012). Two, based inside high security hospitals, have since closed down, while the two prison-based units remain operational. Resources and funding for DSPD are currently being disinvested and redirected towards interventions for personality disorders. The example of DSPD demonstrates how, in response to a perceived social problem, notions of risk and danger were fused to create a new category of people. It also shows how panic over 'moral monsters' can fade. In this way, DSPD can be understood as a 'moral invention' (Seddon 2007).

Conclusion: mental health and dividing practices

Despite a general consensus that those with severe mental illness should not be imprisoned, and the implementation of various diversionary measures, penal institutions continue to contain high levels of individuals with mental health problems. Seddon (2007: 157) argues that this 'should not be viewed as the result of an aberration or a malfunctioning of systems, but rather as an intrinsic element of the whole project of using institutional confinement'. For Seddon, the purpose of confinement is to provide a means of excluding and managing people considered to be 'deviant' because of their perceived dangerousness or vulnerability. In this sense, the incarceration of people with mental health problems is a dividing practice (Foucault 1982).

However, who is considered to be dangerous and/or vulnerable and the means of their exclusion changes over time and place. Notions of threat and vulnerability and what to do about them are not value-free or self-evident but instead are informed by the broader political, social and economic context. In current times, neo-liberal policies, practices and logic have contributed to the casting out and criminalization of increasingly large numbers of people. Particular groups including racialized populations, the poor and women and individuals with mental health problems and cognitive disabilities have been especially subjected to the intensification of penality and, of course, there is significant overlap between these groups (Cunneen et al. 2013).

Efforts to reduce the high levels of prisoners with mental health problems through improved mental health services and diversion and transfer schemes like those proposed by the Bradley Report (2009) simply tinker at the edges without getting to the root of the problem (Seddon 2007). Although there have been substantial efforts to develop and improve mental health services in England and Wales, driven by the desire to provide equivalent opportunities for prisoners to engage with mental health treatment, prisons are not therapeutic institutions. By virtue of being situated in the penal environment, mental health services cannot subjugate the effects of imprisonment and, despite being provided by agencies outside the prison itself, such services have instead found themselves co-opted into the tasks of risk assessment and management.

To fundamentally tackle the issue of mental health in prison, what is therefore required are more radical solutions involving alternatives to confinement which embody values of justice, humility and compassion. A concept that may be helpful in guiding us toward such a vision is 'intelligent kindness', defined as 'something that is generated by an intellectual and emotional understanding that *self-interest and the interests of others are bound together*' (Ballatt and Campling 2011: 5). The notion of intelligent kindness suggests that we address social problems through practices that recognize our interdependence and bond us rather than by those that divide us and exclude the poor and most vulnerable. To do this, it is necessary to abandon the confinement project. The resources pumped into the carceral state can then be redirected toward community programmes and activities which tackle poverty and encourage us to value and care for one another. As a prisoner in our study explained, actions rooted in kindness and connection with others can bring change:

> The main thing is with [the] support that I have … everyone really came together … people that I have contact with everyday. They were very helpful. I was quite taken back by that. In the end I said, I feel quite guilty that so many people actually see the value of my life when I don't see it. So that's one of the reasons why I've changed.
>
> (Prisoner A)

Notes

1 The authors would like to thank Luke Birmingham and David Morton for their contributions to the research on which this chapter is based.
2 Local prisons are those located close to centres of population and the courts they serve. They accommodate those on remand, short-sentence prisoners and those at the beginning of their sentence.
3 Psychosis, neurotic disorders, personality disorders, hazardous drinking and drug dependency.
4 From psychosis, neurotic disorders, personality disorders, hazardous drinking and drug dependency.
5 See, for example, the Trenčín Statement which states that acceptance is needed that 'penal institutions are seldom, if ever, able to treat and care for seriously and acutely mentally ill prisoners' (WHO Regional Office for Europe 2008).
6 Mental health courts are based on the principles of therapeutic justice and attempt to meet the social and treatment needs of those who enter the court. See Petrila (2013) for an overview of mental health courts in the USA.
7 Prior to 2013, local Primary Care Trusts (PCTs) were responsible for commissioning healthcare services in England and Wales. In 2013, this became the responsibility of NHS England through ten 'Health and Justice' commissioning teams (NHS England 2014).
8 For example, case law of the European Convention on Human Rights suggests states have a positive obligation to prevent the occurrence of inhuman or degrading treatment by providing effective protective healthcare (Lines 2006).

Bibliography

Auditor-General (2008) *Mental Health Services for Prisoners*, Wellington: Office of the Auditor-General.

Australian Health Ministers' Advisory Council Mental Health Standing Committee (2006) 'National statement of principles for forensic mental health', www.health.gov.au/internet/mhsc/publish ing.nsf/Content/EA8277CBEE4D16B2CA257A5A0081C323/$File/forens.pdf (accessed 6 July 2014).

Ballatt, J. and Campling, P. (2011) *Intelligent Kindness: Reforming the culture of healthcare*, London: RCPsych Publications.

Birmingham, L. (2003) 'The mental health of prisoners', *Advances in Psychiatric Treatment* 9: 191–201.

Birmingham, L. (2004) 'Mental disorder and prisons', *Psychiatric Bulletin* 28: 393–397.

Birmingham, L., Mason, D. and Grubin, D. (1996) 'Prevalence of mental disorder in remand prisoners', *British Medical Journal* 313: 1521–1524.

Boardman, J. and Parsonage, M. (2007) *Delivering the Government's Mental Health Policies: Services, staffing and costs*, London: Sainsbury Centre for Mental Health.

Bradley, L. (2009) *The Bradley Report*, London: Department of Health.

Brinded, P.M.J. (2000) 'Forensic psychiatry in New Zealand', *International Journal of Law and Psychiatry* 23: 453–465.

Brooker, C. (2006) 'The contribution of education and training to the development of appropriate mental health service provision for those in contact with the offender health system', *Journal of Mental Health Workforce Development* 1: 2–4.

Brooker, C., Duggan, S., Fox, C., Mills, A. and Parsonage, M. (2008) *Short Changed: Spending on Prison Mental Health Care*, London: Sainsbury Centre for Mental Health.

Brooker, C. and Gojkovic, D. (2009) 'The second national survey of mental health in-reach services in prisons', *Journal of Forensic Psychiatry and Psychology* 20: S11–28.

Brooker, C., Repper, J., Beverley, C., Ferriter, M. and Brewer, N. (2002) *Mental Health Services and Prisoners*, Sheffield: University of Sheffield School of Health and Related Research.

Carlen, P. (1986) 'Psychiatry in prisons: Promises, premises, practices and politics', in P. Miller and N. Rose (eds) *The Power of Psychiatry*, Cambridge: Cambridge University Press.

Coburn, D. (2004) 'Beyond the income inequality hypothesis: Class, neo-liberalism, and health inequalities', *Social Science and Medicine* 58: 41–56.

Coggan, G. and Walker, M. (1982) *Frightened for My Life: An account of deaths in British prisons*, Glasgow: Fontana.

Corbett, K. and Westwood, T. (2005) 'Dangerous and severe personality disorder: A psychiatric manifestation of the risk society', *Critical Public Health* 15: 121–133.

Correctional Association of New York (2011) *Testimony by Jack Beck, Director, Prison Visiting Project*, New York: Assembly's Corrections and Mental Health Committees Prison Mental Health Services and Suicides.

Corston, J. (2007) *The Corston Report: A review of women with particular vulnerabilities in the criminal justice system*, London: Home Office.

Crewe, B. (2005) 'Prisoner society in the era of hard drugs', *Punishment and Society* 7: 457–481.

Cunneen, C., Baldry, E., Brown, D., Brown, M., Schwartz, M. and Steel, A. (2013) *Penal Culture and Hyperincarceration: The Revival of the Prison*, Farnham: Ashgate.

Daniel, A.E. (2007) 'Care of the mentally ill in prisons: Challenges and solutions', *Journal of the American Academy of Psychiatry and the Law Online* 35: 406–410.

de Viggiani, N. (2007) 'Unhealthy prisons: Exploring structural determinants of prison health', *Sociology of Health and Illness* 29: 115–135.

DoH (Department of Health) (2009) *Improving Health, Supporting Justice*, London: Department of Health.

DoH (Department of Health) (2014) 'Extra funding for mental health nurses to be based at police stations and courts across the country', www.gov.uk/government/news/extra-funding-for-menta l-health-nurses-to-be-based-at-police-stations-and-courts-across-the-country (accessed 6 July 2014).

DoH (Department of Health) and HM Prison Service (1999) *The Future Organisation of Prison Healthcare*, London: Department of Health.

DoH (Department of Health), HM Prison Service and National Assembly for Wales (2001) *Changing the Outlook: A Strategy for Developing and Modernising Mental Health Services in Prisons*, London: Department of Health.

Douglas, N., Plugge, E. and Fitzpatrick, R. (2009) 'The impact of imprisonment on health: What do women prisoners say?', *Journal of Epidemiology and Community Health* 63: 749–754.

Dressing, H. and Salize, H.-J. (2009) 'Pathways to psychiatric care in European prison systems', *Behavioral Sciences and the Law* 27: 801–810.

Durcan, G. (2006) 'Equivalent to what? Mental health care in Britain's prisons', *Journal of Mental Health Workforce Development* 1: 36–44.

Durcan, G. (2008) *From the Inside: Experiences of prison mental health care*, London: Sainsbury Centre for Mental Health.

Durey, A., Wynaden, D., Barr, L. and Ali, M. (2014) 'Improving forensic mental health care for Aboriginal Australians: Challenges and opportunities', *International Journal of Mental Health Nursing* 23: 195–202.

Exworthy, T., Samele, C., Urquia, N. and Forrester, A. (2012) 'Asserting prisoners' right to health: Beyond equivalence', *Psychiatric Services* 63: 270–275.

Exworthy, T., Wilson, S. and Forrester, A. (2011) 'Beyond equivalence: Prisoners' right to health', *The Psychiatrist* 35: 201–202.

Fazel, S., Doll, H. and Langstrom, N. (2008) 'Mental disorders among adolescents in juvenile detention and correctional facilities: A systematic review and metaregression analysis of 25 surveys', *Journal of American Academy of Child and Adolescent Psychiatry* 47: 1010–1019.

Fazel, S., Grann, M., Kling, B. and Hawton, K. (2011) 'Prison suicide in 12 countries: An ecological study of 861 suicides during 2003–2007', *Social Psychiatry and Psychiatric Epidemiology* 46: 191–195.

Fazel, S., Hope, T., O'Donnell, I. and Jacoby, R. (2001) 'Hidden psychiatric morbidity in elderly prisoners', *British Journal of Psychiatry* 179: 535–539.

Fazel, S. and Seewald, K. (2012) 'Severe mental illness in 33,588 prisoners worldwide: Systematic review and meta-regression analysis', *British Journal of Psychiatry* 2000: 364–373.

Forrester, A., Henderson, C., Wilson, S., Cumming, I., Spyrou, M. and Parrott, J. (2009) 'A suitable waiting room? Hospital transfer outcomes and delays from two London prisons', *Psychiatric Bulletin* 33: 409–412.

Foucault, M. (1982) 'Afterword: The subject of power', in H. Dreyfus and P. Rabinow (eds) *Michel Foucault: Beyond Structuralism and Hermeneutics*, second edn, Abingdon: Routledge.

Gatherer, A., Enggist, S. and Møller, L. (2014) 'The essentials about prisons and health', in S. Enggist, L. Møller, G. Galea and C. Udeson (eds) *Prisons and Health*, Copenhagen: WHO Regional Office for Europe.

Gatherer, A., Møller, L. and Hayton, P. (2009) 'Achieving sustainable improvement in the health of women in prisons: The Approach of the WHO Health in Prisons Project', in D. Hatton and A. Fisher (eds) *Women Prisoners and Health Justice*, Oxford: Radcliffe Publishing.

Gunn, J., Maden, A. and Swinton, M. (1991) *Mentally Disordered Prisoners*, London: Home Office.

Haney, C. (2006) *Reforming Punishment: Psychological Limits to the Pains of Imprisonment*, Washington, DC: American Psychological Association.

Hansen, H., Bourgois, P. and Drucker, E. (2014) 'Pathologizing poverty: New forms of diagnosis, disability and structural stigma under welfare reform', *Social Science and Medicine* 103: 76–83.

HMIP (HM Inspectorate of Prisons) (1996) *Patient or Prisoner: A New Strategy for Healthcare in Prisons*, London: Home Office.

HMIP (HM Inspectorate of Prisons) (2004) *'No Problems – Old and Quiet': Older Prisoners in England and Wales*, London: HM Inspectorate of Prisons.

HMIP (HM Inspectorate of Prisons) (2007) *The Mental Health of Prisoners: A thematic review of the care and support of prisoners with mental health needs*, London: HM Inspectorate of Prisons.

Horan, L. (2010) *Against a Better Prison: Gender Responsiveness and the changing terrain of abolition*, BA thesis, Wesleyan University.

James, D.J. and Glaze, L.E. (2006) 'Mental health problems of prison and jail inmates', US Department of Justice, www.bjs.gov/content/pub/pdf/mhppji.pdf (accessed 6 July 2014).

Kapoor, R., Dike, C., Burns, C., Carvalho, V. and Griffith, E.E.H. (2013) 'Cultural competence in correctional mental health', *International Journal of Law and Psychiatry* 36: 273–280.

Kemshall, H. (2002) 'Effective practice in probation: An example of "advanced liberal" responsibilisation', *Howard Journal of Criminal Justice* 41: 41–58.

Lader, D., Singleton, N. and Meltzer, H. (2000) *Psychiatric Morbidity among Young Offenders in England and Wales*, London: Office for National Statistics.

Lewis, G. and Appleby, L. (1988) 'Personality disorder: The patients psychiatrists dislike', *British Journal of Psychiatry* 153: 44–49.

Liebling, A. (1992) *Suicides in Prison*, London: Routledge.

Lines, R. (2006) 'From equivalence of standards to equivalence of objectives: The entitlement of prisoners to health care standards higher than those outside prisons', *International Journal of Prisoner Health* 2: 269–280.

Lupton, D. (1995) *The Imperative of Health*, London: Sage.

Mason, T. and Mercer, D. (1999) *A Sociology of the Mentally Disordered Offender*, Abingdon: Routledge.

Maurutto, P. and Hannah-Moffat, K. (2006) 'Assembling risk and restructuring penal control', *British Journal of Criminology* 46: 438–454.

Medlicott, D. (2007) 'Women in prison', in Y. Jewkes (ed.) *Handbook on Prisons*, first edn, Cullompton: Willan.

Mental Health Alliance (2005) 'Towards a better Mental Health Act', www.mentalhealthalliance. org.uk/pre2007/documents/AGENDA2.pdf (accessed 8 July 2014).

Mills, A. and Kendall, K. (2010) 'Therapy and mental health in-reach teams', in J. Harvey and K. Smedley (eds) *Psychological Therapy in Prisons and Other Secure Settings*, Abingdon: Routledge.

Mills, A., Kendall, K., Lathlean, J. and Steel, J. (2012) 'Researching the mental health needs of women in prison: Problems and pitfalls', in M. Malloch and G. McIvor (eds) *Women, Punishment and Social Justice: Human Rights and Penal Practices*, London: Routledge.

Mullen, P.E., Briggs, S., Dalton, T. and Burt, M. (2000) 'Forensic mental health services in Australia', *International Journal of Law and Psychiatry* 23: 433–452.

National Health Committee (2010) *Health in Justice Kia Piki te Ora, Kia Tika!*, Wellington: Ministry of Health.

Navarro, V. (2007) 'Neoliberalism as a class ideology; or the political causes of the growth of inequalities', *International Journal of Health Services* 37: 47–62.

NHS Commissioning Board (2013) *Securing Excellence in Commissioning for Offender Health*, London: Department of Health.

NHS England (2014) 'Health and justice commissioning intentions 2014/2015', www.england. nhs.uk/wp-content/uploads/2014/05/hlth-just-comms-intent.pdf (accessed 24 June 2014).

Niveau, G. (2007) 'Relevance and limits of the principle of "equivalence of care" in prison medicine', *Journal of Medical Ethics* 33: 610–613.

O'Brien, M., Mortimer, L., Singleton, N. and Meltzer, H. (2001) *Psychiatric Morbidity Amongst Women Prisoners in England and Wales*, London: Office for National Statistics.

O'Malley, P. (2009) *Neoliberalism and Risk in Criminology, Legal Studies Research Paper No. 09/83*, Sydney: Sydney Law School, The University of Sydney.

Peters, R.H., Bartoi, M.G. and Sherman, P.B. (2008) *Screening and Assessment of Co-occurring Disorders in the Justice System*, Delmar, NY: Center for Mental Health Services National GAINS Center.

Petrila, J. (2013) 'Mental health courts may work, but does it matter if they do?', in R.L. Weiner and E.M. Brank (eds) *Problem Solving Courts: Social science and legal perspectives*, New York: Springer.

Pickersgill, M. (2012) 'How personality became treatable: The mutual constitution of clinical knowledge and mental health law', *Social Studies of Science* 43: 30–53.

Poland, B., Krupa, G. and McCall, D. (2009) 'Health promotion: An analytic framework to guide intervention design and implementation', *Health Promotion Practice* 10: 505–516.

Pollack, S. (2010) 'Labeling Clients "Risky": Social work and the neo-liberal welfare state', *British Journal of Social Work* 40(4): 1263–1278.

Potter, E., Cashin, A., Chenoweth, L. and Jeon, Y.-H. (2007) 'The healthcare of older inmates in the correctional setting', *International Journal of Prisoner Health* 3: 204–213.

Primm, A.B., Osher, F.C. and Gomez, M.B. (2005) 'Race and ethnicity, mental health services and cultural competence in the criminal justice system: Are we ready to change?', *Community Mental Health Journal* 41: 557–569.

Prins, S.J., Osher, F.C., Steadman, H.J., Clark Robbins, P. and Case, B. (2012) 'Exploring racial disparities in the brief jail mental health screen', *Criminal Justice and Behavior* 39: 635–645.

Reed, J. and Lyne, M. (1997) 'The quality of health care in prison: Results of a year's programme of semi structured inspections', *British Medical Journal* 315: 1420–1424.

Ross, M.W., Liebling, A. and Tait, S. (2011) 'The relationships of prison climate to health service in correctional environments: Inmate health care measurement, satisfaction and access in prisons', *Howard Journal of Criminal Justice* 50: 262–274.

Seddon, T. (2007) *Punishment and Madness: Governing Prisoners with Mental Health Problems*, Abingdon: Glasshouse.

Senior, J., Birmingham, L., Harty, M.A., Hassan, L., Hayes, A.J., Kendall, K., King, C., Lathlean, J., Lowthian, C., Mills, A., Webb, R., Thornicroft, G. and Shaw, J. (2013) 'Identification and management of prisoners with severe psychiatric illness by specialist mental health services', *Psychological Medicine* 43: 1511–1520.

Shaw, J., Birmingham, L., Brooker, C., Harty, M., Kendall, K., Lathlean, J., Lowthian, C., Mills, A., Senior, J. and Thornicroft, G. (2008) *A National Evaluation of Prison Mental Health In-Reach Services*, unpublished final research report to the National Institute for Health Research.

Sim, J. (1990) *Medical Power in Prisons*, Milton Keynes: Open University Press.

Sim, J. (2002) 'The future of prison health care: A critical analysis', *Critical Social Policy* 22: 300–323.

Simpson, A.I.F., Brinded, P.M., Fairley, N., Laidlaw, T.M. and Malcolm, F. (2003) 'Does ethnicity affect need for mental health services among New Zealand prisoners?', *Australian and New Zealand Journal of Psychiatry* 37: 728–734.

Simpson, A.I.F., McMaster, J.J. and Cohen, S.N. (2013) 'Challenges for Canada in meeting the needs of persons with serious mental illness in prison', *Journal of the American Academy of Psychiatry and Law* 41: 501–509.

Singleton, N., Meltzer, H. and Gatward, R. (1998) *Psychiatric Morbidity among Prisoners*, London: Office for National Statistics.

Smith, C. (2000) '"Healthy prisons": A contradiction in terms?', *Howard Journal of Criminal Justice* 39: 339–353.

Steel, J., Thornicroft, G., Birmingham, L., Brooker, C., Mills, A., Harty, M. and Shaw, J. (2007) 'Prison mental health in-reach services', *British Journal of Psychiatry* 190: 373–374.

United Nations (1990) 'Basic principles for the treatment of prisoners', www.ohchr.org/EN/Pro fessionalInterest/Pages/BasicPrinciplesTreatmentOfPrisoners.aspx (accessed 27 June 2014).

US Department of Justice (2001) *Correctional Health Care: Guidelines for the Management of an Adequate Delivery System*, Washington, DC: US Department of Justice, National Institute of Corrections.

Wacquant, W. (2009) *Prisons of Poverty*, Minneapolis: University of Minnesota Press.

Wacquant, W. (2010) 'Crafting the neoliberal state: Workfare, prisonfare, and social insecurity', *Sociological Forum* 25: 197–220.

Wakem, B. and McGee, D. (2012) *Investigation of the Department of Corrections in Relation to the Provision, Access and Availability of Prisoner Health Services*, Wellington: Office of the Ombudsman.

WHO (World Health Organization) (n.d.) 'Health promoting prisons', www.who.int/healthy_settings/types/prisons/en/ (accessed 1 July 2014).

WHO (World Health Organization) (2014) 'Mental disorders', www.who.int/topics/mental_disorders/en/ (accessed 6 July 2014).

WHO and ICRC (International Committee of the Red Cross) (2005) 'Mental health in prisons', www.euro.who.int/__data/assets/pdf_file/0007/98989/WHO_ICRC_InfoSht_MNH_Prisons.pdf (accessed 17 June 2014).

WHO Regional Office for Europe (2008) *Trenčín Statement on Prisons and Mental Health*, Copenhagen: World Health Organization.

WHO Regional Office for Europe (2009) *Women's Health in Prison: Correcting gender inequality in health*, Copenhagen: World Health Organization.

Woodall, J., Dixey, R. and South, J. (2013) 'Control and choice in English prisons: Developing health-promoting prisons', *Health Promotion International*, advance access, published online 10 April 2013, doi: 10.1093/heapro/dat019.

Young, J. (2004) 'Crime and the dialectics of inclusion/exclusion: Some comments on Yar and Penna', *British Journal of Criminology* 44: 550–561.

Chapter 12

Drug misuse in prison

Michael Wheatley

Throughout the world, large numbers of drug users are imprisoned. This chapter describes why people take drugs, estimates the prevalence and incidence of drug use among prisoners, explores the relationship between drug misuse and imprisonment, describes an explanatory model of drug misuse in prison, and then discusses policy and commissioning responses to help address the issue, and considers emerging issues in relation to this topic. The chapter is based primarily on the English prison system, and on male prisoners.

Why take drugs?

Drug use occurs in almost every society: statistically, it is the person who does not take drugs who is abnormal (Gossop 2013). However, the use of certain drugs has very different meanings in different cultures and countries (Westermeyer 1995). Gossop (2013) provides a framework to help understand and explain why people take drugs, proposing three separate, but intrinsically linked, rationales for taking drugs: their pharmacological effects (physiological reactions); the psychology of the user (intrinsic beliefs); and the social situation (environmental relationships) in which drug taking occurs. As drug users are a diverse group of people, each person's rationale for taking a drug will be different, as will be their subjective experience of drug consumption.

Drugs can be broadly divided into four categories, based on their pharmacological properties: depressants, pain reducers, stimulants and hallucinogens (DrugScope 2004). Drugs that *depress* the central nervous system by slowing down messages travelling from the brain to the body (e.g. cannabis, tranquillizers, solvents or gases) help relieve tension and anxiety, promote relaxation and sedation, impair the efficiency of mental and physical functioning, and often decrease self-control or reduce inhibitions. *Pain reducers*, such as opiates, opioids or narcotic analgesics (e.g. heroin, methadone, buprenorphine or fentanyl) help decrease sensitivity, and emotional reaction, to pain, discomfort and anxiety. *Stimulant drugs* (e.g. cocaine, crack, amphetamine, caffeine or tobacco) increase alertness, diminish fatigue, delay sleep and promote vigilance and the ability to perform physical tasks over a long period. Finally, *hallucinogens* (e.g. LSD, magic mushrooms, phencyclidine – PCP) alter perceptual function which can heighten appreciation of sensory experiences, provoke perceptual or visual distortions and feelings of dissociation and insight. An individual's needs often determine the choice of drug used: if relaxation and sleep are desired, depressants are more likely to be used, whilst stimulants might be used where confidence is needed.

Psychological factors, which are often underestimated, can affect how an individual reacts to and experiences a particular drug: 'taking a drug is not a psychologically neutral event' (Gossop 2013: 26). Early experimenters with drugs may be alarmed by their physical and psychological experiences and fear for their well-being. More regular users, however, may define the same experiences as extremely pleasurable, as they have learned how to interpret and enjoy the effects; individuals shape their beliefs and expectations with positive outcome expectancies such as euphoria, relaxation, mood elevation and pain relief. The development and reinforcement of these outcomes can lead to dependency, especially when the positive outcome expectancy outweighs any negative outcomes. These expectancies can be strong enough to alter the response to the pharmacological effects of a drug. Studies have shown that users can react as if they are intoxicated, even when no psychoactive agents have been taken at all: the placebo effect (Gossop 2007).

Gossop (2013: 47) describes how the pharmacological effects and psychological expectations of drug use can also be shaped by social factors such as relationships with others and the world in general:

> The way we think about drugs reflects our understanding of the social world around us, and as a result of the social context influences three central aspects of drug taking. It influences what is defined as a drug and what is not; it influences the way a person behaves after taking a drug; it influences their subjective experience of the drug effects. We cannot hope to understand the complexities of drug taking by studying either the drugs or those who take them in isolation from the social context. The social context influences which drugs we take, how we respond to them and when and where we take them.

In sum, people use drugs for a variety of reasons. Experience of drugs is dependent on the type of drug used, the beliefs and expectations held and the social context within which they are consumed.

The prevalence and incidence of drug misuse among prisoners

The relationship between drug misuse and offending has been well established (see Bean 2008). Several studies have found that drug use appears to intensify, motivate and perpetuate a range of offending behaviours (Allen 2005). Ramsey (2003) reported that 55% of new prison receptions declared committing offences due to their drug taking (the need for money to buy drugs was commonly cited).

Numerous studies have consistently reported that approximately 50–70% of prisoners had misused drugs in the 12 months prior to imprisonment (Singleton et al. 1998; Swann and James 1998; Burrows et al. 2001; Weekes 2002; Ramsey 2003; Metribian et al. 2004; Stewart 2008; Information Services Division (Scotland) 2012; Light et al. 2013). According to the Home Affairs Committee (2012: section 6, para. 184), 51% of prisoners report being drug dependent. From the drug misusing population seeking help in prison, May (2005) reported that 93% had used drugs in the 30 days before imprisonment; at this time, heroin, crack cocaine and cannabis were the most frequently used drugs (Penfold et al. 2005). Of those receiving treatment in prison in 2014, the main drugs of choice reported to staff were heroin (35%), alcohol (26%), cannabis (14%), cocaine

(7%) and crack (6%) (Cooper 2014). Cannabis is still the most commonly reported illicit drug used in Scotland, England and Wales, and Northern Ireland (Fraser 2014).

These data give treatment providers some idea of the potential prevalence of drug use, and the proportion of the overall prison population found to have a drug-related issue, which can then determine *what* treatments need to be provided, such as opiate substitution therapy or alcohol withdrawal symptomatic relief. However, it is also important to consider prisoner churn or throughput as this determines the incidence or *how much* of a particular treatment intervention may be required. For example, data from 2009 described the national average prison churn rate as three (HM Government 2010). If a prison of 1,000 prisoners had a 60% prevalence of substance misuse, approximately 600 people would be present at any one time, and if 35% were heroin dependent this could mean 210 people wanting opiate substitution therapy. However, a prison churn rate of three would mean that 3,000 people will pass through the prison gate annually, increasing the potential incidence of drug misuse to 1,800 people per year, thereby helping determine that drug teams should plan to deploy sufficient resources to provide for approximately 630 opiate substitution therapy treatment presentations in one year. However, prevalence and incidence can only be estimated; drug misuse is concealed by prisoners for a variety of reasons and obtaining an accurate assessment of prevalence and incidence is virtually impossible. Individuals may also not wish to engage with a particular service for a variety of reasons and therefore the demand for actual service provision may be less. Calculating and configuring the quantity of service provision in prisons is both complex and challenging, especially with a changing prison population.

The relationship between drug misuse and imprisonment

The Social Exclusion Unit (2002) reported that most prisoners enter prison with a history of drug and alcohol misuse. Goffman (1968) had also observed this and described inmates coming into an institution with a 'presenting culture' derived from their 'home world'. Liebling (1992, 1999) argued that the propensity for misusing drugs and alcohol prior to imprisonment is evidence of poorer coping, increases vulnerability to suicide, can contribute towards social isolation from the wider community and may promote poor interaction with others. These 'imported vulnerabilities' (Maruna and Liebling 2005), when combined with a low trust, overcrowded, stressful and often hostile environment (Edgar et al. 2002; Liebling, with Arnold 2004; Stöver and Weilandt 2007; HMIP 2014), can encourage drug-seeking behaviours in prison.

Although each person entering prison imports aspects of their culture from the outside, inmates are also likely to experience 'prisonization' whereby, to some extent, they suffer the loss of many of their previous roles and identities, and come to adopt the inmate subculture of the institution (Carroll 1974, 1982; Clemmer 2001; Crewe 2004, 2009). Once in the prison, encountering the pains of imprisonment – the deprivation of liberty, goods and services, relationships, autonomy and security (Sykes 1958: 63–83), as well as the deprivation of normal contact with family members, particularly children (Stohr and Mays 1993; Gray et al. 1995; Stohr and Walsh 2012) – may lead to prisoners engaging in activities which function to alleviate these pains.

Importation and deprivation factors together may play a part in drug-seeking behaviours in prison. It is therefore critical to understand the relationship between drug misuse and prisons (Swann and James 1998).

An explanatory model

Evidence suggests five possible explanations for drug misuse in prison. These should be seen as potentially complementary rather than mutually exclusive. Drug misuse can serve a variety of purposes for any individual over a period of time.

Self-medication

Self-medication involves the use of medicinal products to treat self-recognized disorders or symptoms, or the intermittent or continued use of a medication prescribed by a doctor for chronic or recurring diseases or symptoms (WHO 2000). Drug misuse in prison could therefore be a compensatory means to modulate physical pain and treat distressing psychological states. Different drugs produce different effects, therefore prisoners choose the drug that will best manage their specific type of physical, psychological or psychiatric distress and help them achieve emotional stability (Khantzian et al. 1974; Khantzian 1997, 1999). The choice of drug is usually the result of an interaction between the psychopharmacologic properties of the drug and the affective states from which the user was seeking relief (Khantzian 1985). The self-medication hypothesis promotes that drug misuse relieves '[h]uman psychological suffering in susceptible individuals and that there is a considerable degree of psychopharmacological specificity in an individual's preferred drug' (Khantzian 2003: 47).

Keene (1997: 32) found that self-medication as a form of coping was emphasized by many inmates, with some reporting the calming, soothing effect of drugs in the prison environment: 'I think that all prisoners should have a little medication to help with the trauma of prison life'; 'it gets rid of your worries and certain drugs help you to sleep at night'. Sleep deprivation, headaches, depression and anxiety are problems frequently managed by self-medication. Research on drug-related choices in prison has found that cannabis and opiates are often selected to aid relaxation, to help users stop worrying about problems and to relieve boredom (Boys et al. 1999, 2000, 2001, 2002; Cope 2003). Crewe (2004: 12) found from his research into prison drug culture that the appeal of heroin was discussed in terms of sanctuary, diversion and relief: 'it brings the walls down', 'it's like being wrapped up in cotton wool', 'every single weight on your shoulders just seems to disappear', and 'it would take the walls away'. Hough (1996: 8) described a coping or self-medication model as an explanation of how 'drug taking is seen as a palliative to the poor quality of economic and social life'.

Time management

Drug misuse in prison can also help pass or 'kill' time (Larner and Tefferteller 1964; Dorn and South 1987; Cope 2003). Cohen and Taylor (1976: 26) refer to this as 'mindscaping', whereby prisoners, unable to change their physical surroundings and structural inequalities, seek to 'slip away' from their reality thereby affecting their perception of time.

Time and imprisonment are inextricably linked because 'time is the basic structuring dimension in prison life for both prisoners and the staff' (Sparks et al. 1996: 350). In prison, time is predominantly externally controlled by judges, governors and other prison staff, who exert and maintain control (Adams 1990). In order to cope with the situation, prisoners can only manipulate how they experience time (as they have little opportunity in reality to change their sentence). A common way to do this 'symbolically' is to suspend time through sleeping (Meisenhelder 1985). Suspending time means that whilst hours pass from day to day, prisoners do not construct their sentences as impacting negatively on their physical development, ageing and maturation, thereby limiting the perceived deteriorating effects of long-term imprisonment (see Cohen and Taylor 1976). Drugs, particularly cannabis and heroin, are frequently used to promote sleep and relaxation (Crewe 2004) making the passage of time seem effortless. In other words, sleeping becomes more than resting: it offers inmates a way to control, repress and suspend time (Cope 2003). A prisoner's attraction to cannabis and opiates must therefore be understood in the context of their pharmacological and psychological effects on the pains of imprisonment and the symbolic management of time.

A social network

The relationships and networks that are forged to enable drug misuse in prison can often reduce a prisoner's sense of isolation and can give the impression of being connected to a wider social group or community. Connection to this network can foster solidarity and a sense of belonging, while contributing towards the rationale for drug misuse. Tompkins et al. (2007) found that the use of drugs in prison was frequently influenced by other prisoners; being in prison at the same time as drug-using friends or sharing a cell with someone using drugs could promote drug taking. However, these relationships may be fragile and unstable, since many prisoners regard their peers within these social networks as 'associates' rather than friends (Crewe 2005).

Acquiring and enhancing status

The status model originates from opportunity theory – an approach to explaining criminal behaviour where crime is regarded as a function of the characteristics of situations where opportunities to benefit from an illegal act become apparent (McLaughlin and Muncie 2001). Preble and Casey (1969) reported that drug takers and dealers could obtain status and satisfaction from the daily hustle of drug acquisition and supply, where control, wealth and knowledge were publicly exhibited within the prison's sub-culture. Sociological analysis shows that prisoners organize themselves through a constructed status hierarchy, determined by the perceptions that others have of them. Status can therefore be conferred on an individual for participating in the prison's drug culture. Hough (1996) described a positive social and economic payoff from drug misuse in subcultures that respect anti-authoritarian, macho, risk-taking and entrepreneurial activities. These subcultures are often observed in prisons. Courtenay and Sabo (2001) describe how drug dealing is considered a high-risk endeavour which derives intense respect from peers. Drug dealers can therefore occupy an elevated position in the prison pecking order, not out of admiration, but recognition and kudos for being able to organize the importation of drugs into the prison and the money made, items acquired and services obtained in the process. This form of status is rooted in the drug supply and in the financial power that drug transactions engender. The ability to import and distribute drugs symbolizes 'nerve', system rejection, ambition and connections to organize drug networks outside the prison. This is often referred to as 'powder power' (Crewe 2005).

Economic incentives and rewards

Drug dealing and supply facilitate a drug economy in a prison. Financial gain as well as status and power are linked to this economy, especially where prisoners are influenced to use drugs so that their vulnerabilities can then be exploited by others for financial gain – for example, a new prisoner being offered illicit painkillers to help promote sleep, then being classified by his dealer as being 'in debt' and charged an extortionate price as repayment or pressurized to behave in a particular way, not of their own choosing. As already mentioned, drug dealers can often occupy an elevated position in the prison pecking order. In interviews with drug dealers in prison, Crewe (2006) found that many wanted to maintain a lifestyle of relative comfort and status that they had experienced in the community. Drug dealing was a 'job', a way of making money or getting goods; illicit drug supply can be a lucrative business, especially as substances can be worth up to three or four times their street value (Crewe 2005). Furthermore, the gains from the drugs economy may often be enhanced precisely because they are made in breach of the official rules.

How imprisonment discourages drug misuse

Imprisonment can be an opportunity not to use drugs for a range of personal or structural reasons (Advisory Council on the Misuse of Drugs 1996; Tompkins et al. 2007). Researchers have found many factors that discourage drug use and promote self-change, such as personal illness or accident, hitting 'rock bottom', the drug-related death of another person, legal or financial problems, loss of employment or loss of an important relationship or marriage (see Saunders and Kershaw 1979; Tuckfield 1981; Willie 1983). As Crewe (2004: 11) notes, '[i]mprisonment can often be an opportunity or a relief from the chaos, misery and immorality of their lives outside'. Swann and James (1998: 262) asked prisoners why their drug-taking behaviour stopped in prison and many respondents made reference to the salutary impact imprisonment had upon them. Comments included: 'being placed in prison woke me up from a dream world', and 'now there is much more incentive for me to stop. Look where it got me.' Fountain et al. (2004) also found that drug taking in prison could stigmatize and induce feelings of shame, or even fear, and could therefore deter drug seeking and misuse.

Furthermore, Sherwan et al. (1994) suggest that drug use in prison is reduced because of the highly controlled, regulated environment with physical security measures such as the perimeter wall, surveillance and searching, which help to restrict supply.

Strategic and treatment responses to drug misuse in prisons

Imprisonment is an opportune time to intervene and promote major lifestyle changes to reduce reoffending and promote health (Lipton 1995; WHO 2014). An effective substance misuse service is therefore a key strategic priority for any government and for the National Offender Management Service (NOMS). The NOMS drug strategy (Home Office 2008) aimed to reduce demand and harm associated with problematic drug use through effective treatment interventions and by curtailing the supply of illicit drugs into and around prisons. This strategy built the foundation of much of the service provision available today. However, there have been many developments in the last decade, and particularly the last four years, in the policy and commissioning landscape, that have special relevance to drug misuse in prisons. Three particular events have impacted on service provision within prisons.

First, Lord Patel chaired a review of and published a report on drug treatment and interventions in prisons (Department of Health 2010). The review group took a fresh look, in England, at service provision and the continuity of care for people on release from prison. The review group liaised with government officials in Scotland and Wales who subsequently introduced their own policy responses. The aim of the report was not to 'reinvent the wheel' but to build on the successes of preceding strategies, research and reviews. The Patel Report made six strategic recommendations to strengthen service provision, such as developing a cross-government strategy, establishing national outcomes, redesigning commissioning systems, improving service delivery, engaging service users and carers, and widening links between criminal justice and health and social care systems (Department of Health 2010: 13). The Patel Report informed a new drug strategy in 2010 for adults aged over 18 in England.

The second important event was the publication of a new Drug Strategy in 2010 promoting reducing demand, restricting supply and building recovery (HM Government 2010). This strategy holds the government accountable for reducing illicit and other harmful drug use and emphasized an ambition to increase the numbers of people recovering from drug dependence, including alcohol, prescription and over-the-counter medicines. It made clear that individuals should be considered responsible, held accountable for their actions and work with those who are there to support them in addressing drug dependency. What it did not do was define by how much drug use should be reduced, and how many drug users should recover. The strategy represented a fundamental shift in policy because it was more concise, promoted localism, abandoned target-driven approaches and emphasized the concept of recovery.

At this point, a definition of 'recovery' is needed, particularly since it can mean different things to different people (White et al. 2006). It is therefore useful to think of recovery as a process containing numerous features. The consensus statement lists some of the key features (UKDPC 2008: 5) and describes a helpful vision of recovery, saying: 'The process of recovery from problematic substance use is characterised by voluntary-sustained control over substance use which maximises health and wellbeing and participation in the rights, roles and responsibilities of society' (UKDPC 2008: 6).

A third important event that changed the commissioning landscape in prisons was the implementation of the Health and Social Care Act 2012, which prompted significant restructuring of health services in England. This had particular relevance to prisons because it created an independent single National Health Service (NHS) commissioning organization – NHS England – with specific responsibilities for commissioning 'services and facilities for people in prison and other places of detention' from April 2013 (NHS 2013). Mandated by the Department of Health, NHS England is responsible for commissioning nearly all health services, including substance misuse in English prisons, thereby effectively completing the transfer of responsibility for prison healthcare to the NHS, a process which began in 2003. The NOMS and prison managers now have a duty of care to facilitate and enable health services in prison as well as restricting supply through various interdiction initiatives. The National Partnership Agreement (NOMS 2015) describes this arrangement in more detail.

Reducing demand: treatment to manage and promote recovery

The Patel Report (Department of Health 2010: 115) described a consensus amongst commissioners and drug treatment providers that interventions should be evidence based, but acknowledged an absence of high-quality research addressing the effectiveness of drug treatment in prisons. Most of the studies on effectiveness were either from community settings or were international, and might not necessarily translate to the English prison system. The review group therefore undertook a systematic review of available research in order to assess the efficacy of various treatment modalities principally delivered to people in prison. To be included in the systematic review, the research studies had to meet specific standards of academic rigour. Treatment modalities were then scored and mapped against three treatment outcomes defined by the Patel review group – reduced drug use, reduced use in prison and reduced reoffending (see Department of Health 2010: appendix B, 142). Six interventions showed the most promise in generating the treatment outcomes: opioid substitution therapy, children and family support, high-intensity programmes, enhancing life skills, therapeutic communities, and intensive support upon release.

Pharmaceutical and psychosocial interventions in prisons

A range of pharmaceutical interventions are available in all prisons to clinically manage drug and alcohol dependency and associated health issues. This service, largely involving medicines such as methadone, buprenorphine and disulfiram, had been developed since 2000, informed by Department of Health guidance on drug misuse and dependence (Department of Health 1999) and a prison service order related to clinical services for substance misusers (HM Prison Service 2000).

To strengthen service provision and target resources, all prisons, especially local and remand establishments, were mandated to offer evidence-based clinical services to manage drug dependence alongside psychosocial rehabilitation and education opportunities from around 2006 onwards, informed by specific guidance documents (Department of Health 2006, 2007; NICE 2007). This resulted in the creation of the Integrated Drug Treatment System as described in a dedicated prison service instruction (NOMS 2010).

Psychosocial interventions were recommended as a core component of the pharmaceutical clinical services on offer in prisons. Numerous guidance documents related to psychosocial interventions were produced to strengthen service provision (see 'Recovery Resources', at www.nta.nhs.uk/recovery-resources.aspx).

Service provision varies from region to region because of the local NHS England commissioning arrangements and different ways of working. It is therefore not possible to describe what psychosocial provision is available in each prison. However, commissioners are encouraged to include several key components into service delivery arrangements informed by other academic disciplines such as criminology or psychology, to establish a more balanced approach to treating dependency and promoting recovery. As described by Weekes et al. (2013), based on research into what works with offenders who misuse substances, the components include: interventions based on social learning and a cognitive behavioural approach; adherence to risk–needs–responsivity principles; matching problem severity with intensity of intervention; the incorporation of motivational enhancement techniques; demonstration of therapeutic integrity; the inclusion of a maintenance and aftercare component; and use of pharmaceutical treatments such as opiate substitution therapy. Aftercare or throughcare is particularly important as research has indicated that the duration of care is often more important than the amount of care (Crits-Christoph and Sidiqueland 1996; Moos et al. 2000). The process of change does not end on the final day of treatment. Integrating these components into service provision helps strengthen delivery and improve effectiveness.

Restricting supply: interdiction to support and promote recovery

Restricting the supply of drugs into prison is not an easy or straightforward task (NOMS 2009). Prisons are small communities with a steady daily flow, both in and out, of people, goods and services. Penfold et al. (2005), reiterated by Blakey (2008), describes a number of routes for illicit drugs to get into prison, including over the perimeter wall (or fence), mail and parcels, reception and remand prisoners, visitors and staff. The use of each route and the traffic flowing along it will alter according to time and place. If one route is disrupted or closed, then more pressure will be placed on the others. Blakey (2008: 6) noted that disrupting the entry of drugs in those circumstances is much more complex than popular wisdom would suggest.

Weaknesses in prison design, operational practice and systems can work against restricting the supply of drugs into prisons: many of these challenges can be overcome by introducing structural improvements and by supporting the efforts of appropriately trained staff collectively to stifle drug availability. These interdiction efforts are described in the *Supply Reduction Good Practice Guide* (NOMS 2009). This guide calls upon three key principles to restrict drug supply in prisons: deterrence, detection and disruption. Deterrence measures include the use of leaflets, posters and media displays during the entry process that explain the consequences attached to illicit drug supply, such as banning or restricting contact during visits. Low-level fixed furniture in visiting rooms can also stifle supply, as can security patrols by staff, especially when with drug detection dogs. If visitors, contractors or staff are not deterred, a variety of detection technologies can be deployed to stifle trafficking. These technologies include Trace Detection (Ion) Scanners, X-ray machines, CCTV surveillance, searching on entry and exit (body, property and accommodation) including the use of drug detecting dogs, the use of PIN technology to facilitate only pre-approved phone calls, random phone conversation monitoring and Body Orifice Security Scanning ('BOSS') chairs to detect illicit concealed phones or metal items. To complement deterrence and detection, activity disruption techniques can be deployed, based on collaborative efforts involving security and criminal justice organizations using gathered intelligence (see Pearson and Hobbs 2001). The subsequent actions include using only approved suppliers of items to prisoners, and transferring prisoners to other prisons to break up supply activities.

Mandatory drug testing (MDT) results have often been cited as a measure of the success of tackling drug problems in prisons (see Matthews 2008 for a description of MDT). The Ministry of Justice uses the proportion of prisoners detected testing positive under the random MDT programme as a proxy measure to demonstrate the effectiveness of both treatment and interdiction interventions. The incidence of sampled prisoners testing positive for controlled drugs has fallen significantly, from 24.4% in 1996/97 to 7.1% in 2010/11, representing a decline of 71% in the proportion of prisoners testing positive

(Home Affairs Committee 2012). However, it has been argued that MDT statistics are not necessarily reliable indicators of levels of supply, drug use or the success of disrupting methods in individual prisons (Singleton et al. 2005; Penfold et al. 2005: 36)

Overall, drug interdiction tools are capable of detecting drugs. What remains unclear is how each technique or combination of interdiction interventions yields most effective results. Analysis and comparisons are difficult because of often inconsistent collection and data presentation. Difficulties in acquiring accurate baseline data also make it challenging to determine the overall effect of any single interdiction method. To address this problem, studies on the efficacy of drug interdiction practices need to include a standardized method of tracing all searches and uses of detection tools (Dastouri et al. 2012). In addition, all of the methods described above are only effective if deployed correctly, applied consistently and implemented collectively by competent members of staff who are aware of the limitations of each intervention when reviewing the overall picture. Penfold et al. (2005) also suggest that if supply reduction measures are to have a positive impact, they must be revised and implemented with a view to balancing enhanced security with effective treatment in order to create the right context within which recovery can flourish.

Building recovery capital: a strengths-based approach to recovery

One of the best predictors of sustained recovery is an individual's 'recovery capital' – the resources necessary to start and sustain recovery from drug and alcohol dependence (Best and Laudet 2010). Recovery capital has four components (Cloud and Granfield 2009): *social* capital (support received and obligations resulting from relationships with family, partners, children, friends and peers); *physical* capital (money and a safe place to live); *human* capital (including skills, a job, and physical and mental health); and *cultural* capital (personally held values, beliefs and attitudes). Best and Laudet (2010) suggest that recovery capital also includes 'community recovery capital' as an index of the level of support available to a person in recovery, such as mutual aid groups, local treatment services, or more broadly housing, education and employment opportunities. The Drug Strategy 2010 advocates support services from cross-government agencies working with individuals to develop and draw on this capital to inform personal recovery journeys (Home Office 2010: 19).

Community and mutual aid groups are frequently integrated into treatment systems with the aim of complementing statutory provision, enhancing social integration and well-being as well as being an important way to promote direct service user involvement. The national drug strategy 2010 states that '[a]ctive promotion and support of local mutual aid networks such as Alcoholics and Narcotics Anonymous will be essential', and mutual aid has been promoted by many organizations such as the National Institute of Health and Care Excellence (NICE 2007, 2012), the Recovery Orientated Drug Treatment Expert Group (National Treatment Agency 2012a) and the Advisory Council on the Misuse of Drugs (2013). Public Health England (2013a) describes mutual aid as the social, emotional and informational support provided by, and to, members of a group at every stage of recovery. The most common mutual aid groups in England include 12-step self-help fellowships such as Alcoholics Anonymous (AA), Narcotics Anonymous (NA), Cocaine Anonymous (CA) and Al-Anon. Also increasing in popularity are cognitive behavioural-orientated groups such as UK SMART Recovery. However, it is important to match an individual with the right intervention and while mutual aid should be offered as an option, it may not appeal to all clients (National Treatment Agency 2012b)

Another important aspect of an integrated recovery-orientated system is creating opportunities for peer support. Service users are often most motivated to start on their individual recovery journey by seeing the progress made by their peers (National Treatment Agency 2012b). In this sense, recovery can be seen to be contagious. Recovery support is often promoted informally by people whose credentials rest on a personal understanding of the situation, making them 'experts by experience'. The growth of peer support is said to come from the failure of addiction treatment to provide a continuum of care that is accessible, affordable and capable of helping people with the most severe and complex problems move from brief recovery initiation to stable, long-term recovery (White 2009). Peer-based support and professional-based interventions should not antagonize each other or compete for superiority. Both approaches can be complementary, can help establish a seamless system of long-term recovery support, and can help counter the over-emphasis on traditional, medical models of treatment.

New challenges: the rise of novel psychoactive substances and prescription medicine misuse

The 1980s and 1990s saw a significant increase in reported drug use, but the general picture has changed since 2000, following the stabilization and decline of illicit drug use ranging from heroin to cannabis (DrugScope 2014). However, the period since 2008 has seen what appears to be a significant increase, in both interest and probable misuse, of a new range of psychoactive drugs and the misuse of prescribed medicines.

Novel psychoactive substances (NPS) are not a new phenomenon. NPS can occur naturally but many are synthesized from patented substances (often from the 1970s or earlier) and have only recently had their chemistry or process of synthesis slightly modified to produce effects similar to known illicit drugs. The United Nations Office on Drugs and Crime report (UNODC 2013) identifies six main groups of drugs in the NPS market: synthetic cannabinoids (e.g. Spice, Black Mamba); synthetic cathinones (amphetamine-like stimulants such as mephedrone); ketamine (rapid-acting general anaesthetic); phenethylamines (psychoactive stimulants such as benzofury); piperazines (ecstasy-like e.g. benzylpiperazine); and plant-based substances (e.g. the amphetamine-like Khat and the 'hallucinogenic', Salvia Divinorum).

Many NPS fall outside international drug control conventions. This is why sometimes they are referred to as 'legal highs'. NPS manufacturers circumvent legal and marketing drug controls by labelling products 'not for human consumption', and they are often sold as plant food, bath salts, cleaning solutions or incense with 'risk of harm if consumed' written on the product packaging. Over the last decade NPS have become increasingly popular through distribution networks like high street 'head shops' and various technological advances such as the Internet 'dark web', the portion of the World Wide Web content that is not indexed by standard search engines and contains websites that use anonymity tools to hide IP addresses. These networks make information sharing and supply easier.

The European Monitoring Centre for Drugs and Drug Addiction (EMCDDA) reported that a record number of 81 substances were detected for the first time in

Europe in 2013, up from 73 substances in 2012, 49 in 2011, 41 in 2010 and 24 in 2009. In total, over 300 NPS had been identified, by member states, by mid-2013 (EMCDDA 2014a). However, this figure may reflect increasing efforts and capability to detect NPS as well as the emergence of new compounds. It appears that 'the world is witnessing an alarming new drug problem … NPS are proliferating at an unprecedented rate and posing a significant public health challenge' (UNODC 2014: 2). Evidence from national surveys describes the use of NPS amongst the general adult population (those aged 16–59) as relatively low compared with the use of other illicit drugs. However, use amongst younger age groups and some sub-sections of the population is higher. In the UK, the most robust estimates of NPS use in the general population come from the national crime surveys 2012/13, which report that in Scotland 0.5% of all adults had tried any NPS, mephedrone being the most common (Scottish Government 2014). In England and Wales in 2013/14, of adults aged 16–59, 0.6% had taken mephedrone, 2.3% nitrous oxide and 0.5% salvia (Home Office 2014); in Northern Ireland, in 2010/11, NPS prevalence was 3.5% (National Advisory Council on Drugs 2012: 63).

There is a growing body of clinical evidence demonstrating the potential acute and persistent risks to health associated with NPS use (Winstock et al. 2011; Winstock and Barratt 2013; Hermanns-Clausen et al. 2011; Corkery et al. 2013). Health problems include: users frequently being hospitalized following overdose; severe intoxication causing psychotic states and unpredictable behaviours, sudden increases in body temperature, heart rate, hallucinations and vomiting; confusion leading to aggression and violence; and intense 'comedowns' that can cause users to feel suicidal (DrugScope 2014: 11).

The prevalence of NPS use in prison is not currently known. However, incidents are frequently reported. The HM Inspectorate of Prisons for England and Wales (HMIP) reported that 'the increased availability in prisons of NPS was a source of debt and associated bullying and a threat to health' (HMIP 2014: 9). The report describes the negative physical effects related to ingesting 'Spice' (the prison term frequently used to describe NPS) as including fast and irregular heart rate, decreased blood pressure, occasional dizziness and, in some cases, short-term loss of consciousness as well as vomiting, seizures and loss of motor control. Psychological effects can include paranoia, increased anxiety and hallucinations. HMIP (2014) concluded that whilst Spice in prison may not be widespread, it can have consequences for the security of the prison and the safety of other prisoners as well as potential damage to the users. Spice and Black Mamba were cited as causes for concern in 14 (37%) of the adult male prisons inspected, highlighting the need for staff and prisoners to be given accurate and up-to-date information on the acute health dangers associated with NPS.

HMIP (2014) also commented on the continuing diversion and misuse of prescription medication as a dangerous new trend. In the reporting year 2013/14, diverted medication (that taken by someone other than for whom it was prescribed) was reported as an issue in 19 (50%) of adult male prisons fully inspected in England and Wales. This concern is not only held by HMIP. The 2010 Drug Strategy (Home Office 2010) considered dependency on all drugs including prescription-only medicines and over-the-counter medicines. The strategy advocated that local responses to drug misuse and dependence are expected to cover addiction to medicines too.

Prisoners may use prescription medicines as a supplement or alternative to illicit drugs, to sell as well as to help cope with genuine or perceived physical or psychological symptoms (Public Health England 2013b). Prisoners may also be more likely than the general population to suffer from conditions such as insomnia, anxiety and pain which lead them to seek medicines liable to misuse. Additionally prisoners may claim to have these conditions as a way of obtaining medicines for personal misuse or as currency to trade for other things in prison. Prescription medicines therefore require careful management within a prison – for example, not allowing high-risk tradable medication to be kept 'in-possession', supervising consumption of controlled drugs at point of supply, changing choice and form of preparation where risk is evident (Royal College of General Practitioners 2011), and having prison officers supervise the medicine queues to minimize the risk of medication being diverted.

Conclusion

Essentially, the national drug strategy, mirrored within prisons, attempts to address drug misuse by restricting the supply of drugs susceptible to misuse, reducing the demand for psychoactive substances frequently linked to problematic dependency, and promoting sustainable recovery. This approach supports drug users becoming drug free and choosing recovery as a new way of life.

To achieve this, drug users require support from competent people, enlightened with the necessary knowledge and skills to help. A balanced and holistic approach is required, with sufficient flexibility to respond to individual changing need. Medically orientated pharmaceutical interventions will be necessary to reduce the pain and discomfort associated with long-term drug use and stabilize individuals in such a way as to cope with the chores of everyday life. New skills to build recovery capital need to be encouraged through psychosocial interventions in whatever format is best for the individual. Personal strengths such as social skills, craving management, managing the negative influence of others, emotional regulation, goal setting and prevention relapses are essential protective factors in recovery promotion. Individuals need to harness and keep hope levels high as well as minimize pain. A one-size-fits-all intervention is therefore unlikely to have an impact. Treatment needs have to be tailored to the individual and delivered over a time period when change can be consolidated. This will vary from person to person.

Community and societal support is a critical success factor in sustainable recovery. Prevention and treatment interventions are highly dependent upon the living environment and social context within which a person must exist. It is therefore essential that society stops viewing drug use as a moral or personal failing and explores elements of the social context of a drug user and to address these in order to reduce the susceptibility to misuse drugs. Reducing social exclusion by promoting inclusion will support recovery.

Having built recovery capital and community support, individual recovery is not about avoiding the 'troubled person' of the past but building a new positive identity filled with elements that stimulate, interest, promote and sustain a new lifestyle. This takes time. Support is often required after many of the professionals have long gone, hence the importance of tapping into long-term peer and community support.

Finally, a question often asked is, when is a person's recovery complete? There is no easy answer. However, William L. White (2013) helps address the issue of 'when does recovery today predict recovery for life?' He investigated all the scientific evidence and concluded that the point of durability seems to be reached at four to five years of continuous recovery. White (2013) found that around 15% of those who reach the five-year point re-experience active addiction within their lifetime (for opiate users this percentage increases to around 25%). This means that if the five-year recovery benchmark is reached, the risk of again meeting the diagnostic criteria for a substance use disorder is similar to the risk for such a diagnosis within the general population. White (2013) suggests that this benchmark is approached with caution, as it is not an assurance of invulnerability. Instead he believes that it marks the point at which a much greater force is needed to destabilize recovery. For this reason, it might be argued that all people treated for addiction should be afforded support over a five-year post-treatment period similar to that which is often afforded to patients diagnosed with conditions such as cancer. What an interesting concept.

Bibliography

Adams, B. (1990) *Time and Social Theory*, Cambridge: Polity Press.

Advisory Council on the Misuse of Drugs (1996) *Drug misuse and the prison system – an integrated approach*, London: HMSO.

Advisory Council on the Misuse of Drugs (2013) *What Recovery Outcomes does the Evidence Tell us we Can Expect. Second report of the Recovery Committee*, www.gov.uk/government/uploads/system/uploads/attachment_data/file/262629/Second_report_of_the_Recovery_Committee.pdf (accessed 12 April 2015).

Allen, J.P. (2005) 'The links between heroin, crack cocaine and crime', *British Journal of Criminology* 45: 355–372.

Bean, P. (2008) *Drug and Crime*, Cullompton: Willan.

Best, D. and Laudet, A.B. (2010) 'The potential of recovery capital', RSA Projects Online, www.thersa.org/discover/publications-and-articles/reports/the-potential-of-recovery-capital/Download (accessed 14 April 2015).

Blakey, D. (2008) 'Disrupting the supply of illicit drugs into prisons', www.drugscope.org.uk/Resources/Drugscope/Documents/PDF/Good%20Practice/blakeyreport.pdf (accessed 14 April 2015).

Boys, A., Farrall, P., Beddington, T., Brugha, J., Coid, R., Jenkins, G., Lewis, J., Marsden, H., Singleton, N. and Taylor, C. (2002) 'Drug use and initiation in prison: Results from a national prison survey in England and Wales', *Addiction* 97: 1551–1560.

Boys, A., Fountain, J., Marsden, J., Griffiths, P., Stillwell, G. and Strang, J. (2000) *Drug decisions: A qualitative study of young people, drugs and alcohol*, London: Health Education Authority.

Boys, A., Marsden, J., Fountain, J., Griffiths, P., Stillwell, G. and Strang, J. (1999) 'What influences young people's use of drugs? A qualitative study of decision making', *Drugs: Education, Prevention and Policy* 6: 373–389.

Boys, A., Marsden, J. and Strang, J. (2001) 'Understanding reasons for drug use amongst young people: A functional perspective', *Health Education Research* 16: 457–469.

Burrows, J., Clarke, A., Davison, T., Tarling, R. and Webb, S. (2001) *Research into the Nature and Effectiveness of Drug Throughcare*, Occasional Paper 68, London: Home Office.

Carroll, L. (1974) *Hacks, Blacks and Cons: Race relations in a max security prison*, Lexington, MA: Lexington Books.

Clemmer, D. (2001) 'The prison community', in E.J. Latessa, A. Holsinger, J.W. Marquart and J.R. Sorensen (eds) *Correctional Contexts: Contemporary and classical readings*, second edn, Los Angeles, CA: Roxbury, 83–87.

Cloud, W. and Granfield, W. (2009) 'Conceptualising recovery capital: Expansion of a theoretical construct', *Substance Use and Misuse* 42(12/13): 1971–1986.

Cohen, S. and Taylor, L. (1976) *Escape Attempts: The theory and practice of resistance to everyday life*, London: Allen Lance.

Cooper, A. (2014) *National Drug Treatment Monitoring System – 2014 Statistics*, unpublished presentation, London: Public Health England.

Cope, N. (2003) 'It's no time or high time: Young offenders experiences of time and drug use in prison', *Howard Journal* 42: 158–175.

Corkery, J., Elliot, S., Schifano, F., Corazza, O. and Ghodse, A.H. (2013) 'MDAI (5,6-methyle-nedioxy-2-aminoindane; 6,7-dihydro-5H-cyclopental[f] [1,3]benzodioxol-6-amine; 'sparkle'; 'mindy') toxicity: A brief overview and update', *Human Psychopharmacology* 28(4): 345–355.

Courtenay, W.H. and Sabo, D. (2001) 'Preventive health strategies for me in prison', in D. Sabo, T.A. Kupers and W. London (eds) *Prison Masculinities*, Philadelphia, PA: Temple University Press.

Crewe, B. (2004) 'The drugs economy and the prisoner society', www.perrielectures.org.uk/wp-content/uploads/2012/03/PerrieSpurrCreweWyne (accessed 24 March 2015).

Crewe, B. (2005) 'Prisoner society in the era of hard drugs', *Punishment and Society* 7: 457–481.

Crewe, B. (2006) 'Prison dealing and the ethnographic lens', *Howard Journal* 45: 347–368.

Crewe, B. (2009) *The Prisoner Society: Power, adaptation and social life in an English prison*, Oxford: Oxford University Press.

Crits-Christoph, P. and Sidiqueland, L. (1996) 'Psychosocial treatment for drug abuse: Selected review and recommendations for national health care', *Arch Gen Psychiatry* 53: 749–756.

Dastouri, S., Johnson, S. and Moser, A. (2012) *Drug Detection Strategies: International practices within correctional settings, research report, R258*, Ottawa, ON: Correctional Service Canada, www.csc-scc.gc.ca/005/008/092/005008-0258-eng.pdf (accessed 14 April 2015).

Department of Health (1999) 'Drug misuse and dependence – Guidelines on clinical management', www.dldocs.stir.ac.uk/documents/clinical.pdf (accessed 10 April 2015).

Department of Health (2006) 'Clinical management of drug dependence in the adult prison setting including psychosocial treatment as a core part', www.nta.nhs.uk/uploads/clinicalmanagementof drugdependenceintheadultprisonsetting-incamendmentatpara7.7.pdf (accessed 14 April 2015).

Department of Health (2007) 'Drug misuse and dependence: UK guidelines on clinical management', www.nta.nhs.uk/uploads.clinlcal_guidelines_2007.pdf (accessed 10 April 2015).

Department of Health (2010) 'The Patel Report – Prison drug treatment strategy review group: Reducing drug-related crime and rehabilitating offenders – recovery and rehabilitation for drug users in prison and on release: Recommendations for action', www.gov.uk/government/uploa ds/system/uploads/attachment_data/file/216012/dh_119850.pdf (accessed 10 April 2015).

Dorn, N. and South, N. (1987) *A Land Fit for Heroin? Drug policies, prevention and practice*, Basingstoke: Macmillan.

DrugScope (2004) *Druglink Guide to Drugs: A guide to the non-medical use of drugs in the UK*, London: DrugScope.

DrugScope (2014) 'Business as usual? A status report on new psychoactive substances (NPS) and 'club drugs' in the UK', www.drugscope.org.uk/Resources/Drugscope/Documents/PDF/ Policy/BusinessAsUsual.pdf (accessed 12 April 2015).

Edgar, K., O'Donnell, I. and Martin, C. (2002) *Prison Violent: The dynamics of conflict, fear and power*, Cullompton: Willan.

EMCDDA (European Monitoring Centre for Drugs and Drug Addiction) (2014a) 'European drug report: Trends and developments 2014', www.emcdda.europa.eu/publications/edr/trends-deve lopments/2014 (accessed 12 April 2015).

EMCDDA (European Monitoring Centre for Drugs and Drug Addiction) (2014b) 'Report on the risk assessment of ketamine in the framework of the joint action on new synthetic drugs', www.emcdda.europa.eu/html.cfm/index33341EN.html.

Fountain, J., Roy, A., Anitha, S., Davies, K., Bashford, J. and Patel, K. (2004) *The Delivery of Prison Drug Services in England and Wales, with a Focus on Black and Minority Ethnic Prisoners, Report by the Centre of Ethnicity and Health*, University of Central Lancashire (unpublished).

Fraser, F. (2014) 'New psychoactive substances – Evidence review. Scottish Government social research', www.scotland.gov.uk/Resource/0045/00457682.pdf (accessed 14 April 2015).

Goffman, E. (1968) *Asylums*, Harmondsworth: Penguin.

Gossop, M. (2013) *Living with Drugs*, seventh edn, Farnham: Ashgate.

Gray, T., Mays, C.L. and Stohr, M.K. (1995) 'Inmate needs and programming in exclusively women's jails', *The Prison Journal* 75(2): 186–202.

Hermanns-Clausen, M., Kneisel, S., Szabo, B. and Auwarter, V. (2011) 'Acute toxicity due to the confirmed consumption of synthetic cannabinoids: clinical and laboratory findings', *Addiction* 108: 534–544.

HM Government (2010) 'Safety in custody statistics – Churn rate, prison population turnover', www.gov.uk/government/uploads/syste3m/uploads.attachment_data/file/218403/saftey-custody-assaults-statistics-0710.xls (accessed 28 March 2015).

HMIP (HM Inspectorate of Prisons) (2014) 'HM Inspector of Prisons for England and Wales annual report 2013–2014', www.justiceinspectorates.gov.uk/hmiprisons/wp-content/uploads/sites/4/2014/10/HMIP-AR_2013-14.pdf (accessed 14 April 2015).

HM Prison Service (2000) 'Clinical services for substance misusers', www.justice.gov.uk/downloads/offenders/psipso/pso/PSO_3550_clinical_services.doc (accessed 10 April 2015).

Home Affairs Committee (2012) 'Drugs: Breaking the cycle: Ninth report of session 2012–2013', www.publications.parliament.uk/pa/cm201213/cmselect/cmhaff/184/184.pdf (accessed 14 April 2015).

Home Office (2008) 'Drugs: Protecting families and communities', webarchive.nationalarchives.gov.uk/20100419081707/http://drugs.homeoffice.gov.uk/publication-search/drug-strategy/drug-strategy-20082835.pdf?view=Binary (accessed 10 April 2015).

Home Office (2010) *Drug Strategy 2010: Reducing demand, restricting supply, building recovery: Supporting people to live a drug free life*, London: HM Government, www.gov.uk/government/uploads/system/uploads/attachment_data/file/118336/drug-strategy-2010.pdf (accessed 10 April 2015).

Home Office (2014) 'Drug misuse: Findings from the 2013 to 2014 crime survey for England and Wales', www.sps.gov.uk/Publications/Publications-3696.aspx (accessed 25 October 2014).

Hough, M. (1996) *Drug Misusers and the Criminal Justice System: A review of the literature*, Drugs Prevention Initiative Paper 15, London: Home Office.

Information Services Division (Scotland) (2012) 'Drug misuse statistics Scotland 2011', www.isdscotland.org/Health-Topics/Drugs-and-Alcohol-Misuse/Publications/2012-02-28/2012-02-28-dmss2011-report.pdf (accessed 12 April 2015).

Keene, J. (1997) 'Drug misuse in prisons: Views from inside – a qualitative study of prison staff and inmates', *Howard Journal* 36: 28–41.

Khantzian, E.J. (1985) 'The self medication hypothesis of addictive disorders: Focus on heroin and dependence', *Am J Psychiatry* 142: 1259–1264.

Khantzian, E.J. (1997) 'The self medication hypothesis of drug use disorders: A reconsideration and recent applications', *Harvard Review of Psychiatry* 4: 231–244.

Khantzian, E.J. (1999) *Treating Addiction as a Human Process*, Northvale, NJ: Jason Aronson.

Khantzian, E.J. (2003) 'The self medication hypothesis revised: The dually diagnosed patient', *Primary Psychiatry* 10(47–48): 53–54.

Khantzian, E.J., Mack, J.F. and Schatzberg, A.F. (1974) 'Heroin use as an attempt to cope: Clinical observations', *Am J Psychiatry* 131: 160–164.

Larner, J. and Tefferteller, R. (1964) *The Addict in the Street*, Harmondsworth: Penguin Books.

Liebling, A. (1992) *Suicides in Prison*, London: Routledge.

Liebling, A. (1999) 'Prison suicides and coping', in M. Tonry and J. Petersilia (eds) *Prison, Crime and Justice Review of Research*, Vol. 26, Chicago, IL: University of Chicago Press.

Liebling, A., with Arnold, H. (2004) *Prisons and their Moral Performance*, Oxford: Oxford University Press.

Light, M., Grant, E. and Hopkins, K. (2013) *Gender Differences in Substance Misuse and Mental Health amongst Prisoners. Results from the surveying prisoner crime reduction (SPCR) longitudinal cohort study of prisoners*, Ministry of Justice Analytical Services, www.gov.uk/government/uploads/system/uploads/attachment_data/file/220060/gender-substance-misuse-mental-health-prisoners.pdf (accessed 14 April 2015).

Lipton, D.S. (1995) *The Effectiveness of Treatment for Drug Abusers under Criminal Justice Supervision*, National Institute of Justice Research Report, www.ncjrs.gov/pdffiles/drugsupr.pdf (accessed 14 April 2015).

McLaughlin, E. and Muncie, J. (2001) *The Sage Dictionary of Criminology*, London: Sage.

Maruna, S. and Liebling, A. (2005) *The Effects of Imprisonment*, Cullompton: Willan.

Matthews, S. (2008) 'Mandatory drug testing', in Y. Jewkes and J. Bennett (eds) *Dictionary of prisons and punishment*, Cullumpton: Willan.

May, C. (2005) *The CARAT Drug Service in Prisons: Findings from the research database*, Home Office Research Findings 262, London: Home Office.

Meisenhelder, T. (1985) 'An essay on time and the phenomenology of imprisonment', *Deviant Behaviour* 6: 39–56.

Metribian, N., Martin, A., Madden, P., Stimson, G.V., Acejais, C. and Fotopoulou, M. (2004) *An Evaluation of Drug and Alcohol Detoxification Programmes in Three High Security Prisons in England: Final report*, unpublished report, London: HM Prison Service.

Moos, R., Finney, J.W., Federman, B. and Suchinsky, R. (2000) 'Speciality mental health care improves patients' outcomes: Findings from a nationwide program to monitor the quality of care for patients with substance use disorders', *J Stud Alcohol* 61: 704–713.

National Advisory Council on Drugs (2012) 'Drug use in Ireland and Northern Ireland 2010–11', www.dhsspsni/gov/uk/bulletin_2.pdf (accessed 12 April 2015).

National Treatment Agency (2012a) 'Medications in recovery – Re-orientating drug dependence treatment', www.nta.nhs.uk/uploads/medications-in-recovery-main-report3.pdf (accessed 14 April 2015).

National Treatment Agency (2012b) 'Building recovery in communities: A summary of the responses to the consultation', www.nta.nhs.uk/uploads/bricresponsefinal17052012.pdf (accessed 12 April 2015).

NHS (2013) 'Securing Excellence in Commissioning for Offender Health', www.england.nhs.uk/wp-content/uploads/2013/03/offender-commissioning.pdf (accessed 14 April 2015).

NICE (National Institute for Health and Care Excellence) (2007) 'Drug misuse – psychosocial interventions: NICE clinical guidelines 51', www.nice.org.uk/guidance/cg51 (accessed 10 April 2015).

NICE (National Institute for Health and Care Excellence) (2012) 'Quality Standard for drug use disorders (NICE Quality Standard 23)', www.nice.org.uk/guidance/qs23 (accessed 14 April 2015).

NOMS (National Offender Management Service) (2009) 'Prison drug supply reduction – A good practice guide', www.whatdotheyknow.com/request/70601/response/180218/attach/4/Prison%20Drug%20Supply%20Reduction%20Practice%20Guide.pdf (accessed 12 April 2015).

NOMS (National Offender Management Service) (2010) 'Integrated drug treatment system', www.justice.gov.uk/downloads/offenders/psipso/psi-2010/psi_2010_45_IDTS.doc (accessed 10 April 2015).

NOMS (National Offender Management Service) (2015) 'The national partnership agreement between: The National Offender Management Service, National Health Service England and Public Health England for the co-commissioning of health services in prisons in England 2015–2016', www.justice.gov.uk/downloads/about/noms/work-with-partners/national_partnership_agreement_commissioning-delivery-healthcare-prisons2015.pdf (accessed 10 April 2015).

Pearson, G. and Hobbs, R. (2001) *Middle market drug distribution*, Home Office Research Study 227, London: Home Office, core.ac.uk/download/pdf/94137.pdf (accessed 14 April 2015).

Penfold, C., Turnbull, P.J. and Webster, R. (2005) 'Tackling prison drug markets: An exploratory qualitative study', Home Office online report 39/05, www.drugscope.org.uk/Resources/Drugscope/Documents/PDF/Good%20Practice/prisonmarkets.pdf (accessed 12 April 2015).

Preble, E. and Casey, J.J. (1969) 'Taking care of business', *International Journal of Addictions* 4: 1–24.

Public Health England (2013a) 'A briefing on the evidence-based drug and alcohol treatment guidance recommendations on mutual aid', www.nta.nhs.uk/mutualaidbriefing.aspx (accessed 12 April 2015).

Public Health England (2013b) 'Commissioning treatment for dependence on prescription and over the counter medicines: A guide for NHS and local authority commissioners', www.nta.nhs.uk/uploads/pheatmcommissioningguide.pdf (accessed 14 April 2015).

Ramsey, M. (ed.) (2003) *Prisoners' drug use and treatment: Seven research studies*, Home Office Research Study 267, London: Home Office.

Royal College of General Practitioners (2011) *Safer prescribing in prisons: Guidance for clinicians*, RCGP Secure Environments Group, www.rcgp.org.uk/clinical-and-research/clinical-resources/%7E/media/106D28C849364D4CB2CB5A75A4E0849F.ashx (accessed 10 April 2015).

Saunders, W.M. and Kershaw, P.W. (1979) 'Spontaneous remission from alcoholism – A community study', *British Journal of Addiction* 74: 251–265.

Scottish Government (2014) 'Scottish crime and justice survey 2012/13: Drug use', www.gov.scot/Resource/0045/00455131.pdf (accessed 12 April 2015).

Sherwan, D., Gemmell, M. and Davies, J.B. (1994) 'Prison as a modifier of drug using behaviour', *Addiction Research and Theory* 2(2): 203–215.

Singleton, N., Meltzer, H., Gatward, R., Coid, J. and Deasy, D. (1998) *Psychiatric Morbidity among Prisoners in England and Wales*, London: HMSO.

Singleton, N., Pendry, E., Simpson, T., Goddard, E., Farrell, M., Marsden, J. and Taylor, C. (2005) *The Impact and Effectiveness of Mandatory Drug Testing in Prisons*, Home Office Research Findings 223, London: Home Office.

Social Exclusion Unit (2002) 'Reducing reoffending by ex-prisoners: Report by the social exclusion unit', www.bristol.ac.uk/poverty/downloads/keyofficialdocuments/Reducing%20Reoffending.pdf (accessed 12 April 2015).

Sparks, R., Bottoms, A.E. and Hay, W. (1996) *Prisons and the Problem of Order*, Oxford: Clarendon Press.

Stewart, D. (2008) *The Problems and Needs of Newly Sentenced Prisoners: Results from a national survey*, Ministry of Justice Research Series 16/08, London: Ministry of Justice.

Stohr, M.K. and Mays, G.L. (1993) *Women's jails: An investigation of offenders, staff, administration, and programming*, Washington, DC: National Institute of Corrections.

Stohr, M.K. and Walsh, A. (2012) *Corrections: The essentials*, Thousand Oaks, CA: Sage.

Stöver, H. and Weilandt, C. (2007) 'Drug use and drug services in prison', in L. Møller, H. Stöver, R. Jürgens, A. Gatherer and H. Nikogosian (eds) *Health in Prisons*, Copenhagen: WHO, 85–112.

Swann, R. and James, P. (1998) 'The effect of the prison environment upon inmate drug taking behaviour', *Howard Journal* 37: 252–265.

Sykes, G. (1958) *The Society of Captives: A study of a maximum security prison*, Princeton, NJ: Princeton University Press.

Tompkins, C.N.E., Neale, J., Sheard, L. and Wright, N.M.J. (2007) 'Experiences of prison amongst injecting drug users in England: A qualitative study', *International Journal of Prisoner Health* 3(3): 189–203.

Tuckfield, B.S. (1981) 'Spontaneous remission in alcoholics', *J Stud Alcohol* 42: 626–641.

UKDPC (UK Drug Policy Commission) (2008) 'The UK Drug Policy Commission recovery consensus group: A vision of recovery', www.ukdpc/org.uk/wp-content?uploads/Policy%20report%20-%20A%20vision%20of%20recovery_%20UKDPC%20recovery%20consensus%20group.pdf (accessed 28 March 2015).

UNODC (United Nations Office on Drugs and Crime) (2013) 'The challenge of new psychoactive substances', www.unodc.org/documents/scientific/NPS_2013_SMART.pdf (accessed 12 April 2015).

UNODC (United Nations Office on Drugs and Crime) (2014) 'NPS: New psychoactive substances', www.unodc.org/documents/scientific/NPS_leaflet_2014.EN.pdf (accessed 12 April 2015).

Weekes, J.R. (2002) *Assessment and Treatment of Forensic Clinical Populations*, Invited paper presented at the 10th British Drug Workers Conference, Manchester, UK, unpublished.

Weekes, J.R., Moser, A.E., Wheatley, M. and Matheson, F.I. (2013) 'What works in reducing substance-related offending?' in L.A. Craig, L. Dixon and T.A. Gannon (eds) *What Works in Offender Rehabilitation: An evidence based approach to assessment and treatment*, London: John Wiley and Sons.

Westermeyer, J. (1995) 'Cultural aspects of substance abuse and alcoholism', *Psychiatric Clinics of North America* 18: 589–605.

White, W.L. (2009) 'Peer-based addiction recovery support – history, theory, practice and scientific evaluation', www.drugslibrary.stir.ac.uk/documents/PeerRecoverySupportMonograph2009.pdf (accessed 12 April 2015).

White, W.L. (2013) 'Recovery durability: The 5-year set point', www.williamwhitepapers.com/blog/2013/07/recovery-durability-the-5-year-set-point.html (accessed 10 April 2015).

White, W. and Kurtz, E. (2006) *The varieties of recovery experience*, Chicago, IL: Great Lakes Addictions Technology Transfer Centre, www.naadac.org/assets/1959/whitewkurtze2006_the_varieties_of_recovery_experience.pdf (accessed 14 April 2015).

White, W.L., Kurtz, E. and Sanders, M. (2006) 'Recovery Management', www.nattc.org/recoveryresourc/docs/RecMgmt.pdf (accessed 14 April 2015).

WHO (World Health Organization) (2000) 'Guidelines for the regulatory assessment of medicinal products for use in self medication', apps.who.int/iris/bitstream/10665/66154/1/WHO_EDM_QSM_00.1_eng.pdf (accessed 14 April 2015).

WHO (World Health Organization) (2014) 'Prisons and health', www.gov.uk/government/uploads/system/uploads/attchment_data/file/2789123/2014-01-15_Enablers_Specification_P2_3.pdf.

Willie, R. (1983) 'Processes of recovery from heroin dependence: Relationship to treatment, social changes and drug use', *Journal of Drug Issues* 13: 333–342.

Winstock, A. and Barratt, M.J. (2013) 'The 12 month prevalence and nature of adverse experiences resulting in emergency presentations associated with the use of synthetic cannabinoids products', *Hum Psychopharmacology* 28: 390–393.

Winstock, A., Mitchelson, L., Ramsey, J., Davies, S., Puchnarewicz, M. and Marsden, J. (2011) 'Mephedrone use, subjective effects and health risks', *Addiction* 106: 1991–1996.

Chapter 13

Suicide, distress and the quality of prison life

Alison Liebling and Amy Ludlow[1]

[Prison Service Order 2700] brings existing policy in line with the direction of the Prison Service's targeted but holistic approach to suicide prevention ... and the broader context (decency, safety, the concept of the healthy prison) ... Governors should ensure that ... the guiding principle in management of the reception and first night processes is the Prison Service's duty of care to prisoners ... Even if the prisoner appears to be using self-harm as a means of gaining something, it is still a desperate act and the prisoner should be helped to find constructive ways to meet the underlying need ... Supervision of the suicidal should be active, involving supportive contact rather than mere observation.

(Prison Service 2003: 2–11)

A decent society is one whose institutions do not humiliate people.

(Margalit 1996: 1)

Introduction

Research into prison suicide can tell us a great deal about prisons, and the nature of the prisoner population, highlighting, for example, prisoners' extreme vulnerability to suicide. Imprisonment causes an 'additional strain', to which identifiable groups of prisoners are especially susceptible, yet literature on adjustment to imprisonment rarely mentions suicide. Most theories of prison suicide take insufficient account of the differential nature of the prison experience. A significant contribution to prisoner distress, and therefore to suicide risk, is made by uneven experiences of unfairness, disrespect and lack of safety in prison. As Margalit argues above, a decent society is one whose institutions do not humiliate people. The role of prison staff, of all kinds, is critical in making prisons 'survivable' (see Liebling and Tait 2006).

In this chapter, we reflect upon some important suicide prevention efforts made by the Prison Service in England and Wales between 2004 and 2014 (e.g. Prison Service Order 2700 above), and consider some of the increased risks that have appeared recently (Prisons and Probation Ombudsman 2014). We argue that findings from studies of suicide risk and its prevention provide a detailed empirical development of the theoretical claims made by legitimacy scholars. This evidence suggests that the experience of fairness and safety in prison, which are experienced as a kind of trust in the environment, have significant emotional consequences for prisoners. We suggest that existing policy reflects good suicide prevention principles but an 'enabling' moral climate is critical to its sound implementation. The use of imprisonment, and the resourcing and organization of prisons, also require analysis in any explanation of increased suicide rates, and in prevention efforts.

Policy background in England and Wales

There have been numerous policy initiatives aimed at reducing the suicide rate in prisons in England and Wales, including the *Caring for the Suicidal in Custody* strategy launched in 1994. This was regarded at the time as a carefully researched and 'fundamentally sound' document (HMCIP 1999: 3), which required joint responsibility between healthcare and discipline staff for prisoners at risk. Following the 1994 strategy, the role of The Samaritans was developed in prisons and 'Listener Schemes' were introduced, whereby prisoners, trained by The Samaritans, support their fellow prisoners (see Davies 1994; Power et al. 2003). At the heart of this strategy was a collective approach, 'which encouraged supportive relationships' (HMCIP 1999: 46).

The 1994 strategy suffered from major problems of implementation (HMCIP 1999). Several important aspects of the policy were never fully put into operation, so that there was little 'ownership of the strategy by senior managers', case reviews were infrequent, staff were insufficiently trained, and there were no quality checks on 'vital documentation' (HMCIP 1999). In January 1999, a working group was set up by the World Health Organization to review suicide policy in prisons and make improvements. In July 1999, the group produced a White Paper, *Saving Lives: Our Healthier Nation*, which aimed to 'reduce the death rate from suicides and undetermined death by at least a fifth by 2010 – saving up to 4,000 lives in total' (Home Office 1999: 59).

The notion of 'collective responsibility' from the 1994 strategy was taken further in a Thematic Review carried out by HM Chief Inspector of Prisons for England and Wales in 1998/99: *Suicide is Everyone's Concern*. The review outlined the broader objective of developing 'healthy prisons': institutions 'in which prisoners and staff are able to live and work in a way that promotes their well-being' (HMCIP 1999: 59).[2] The 'test' of a healthy prison included that:

- The weakest prisoners feel safe.
- All prisoners are treated with respect as individuals.
- All prisoners are busily occupied, are expected to improve themselves and given the opportunity to do so.
- All prisoners can strengthen links with their families and prepare for release.

(HMCIP 1999: 60)

In April 2001, the Prison Service's new Safer Custody Group proposed a three-year strategy (the Safer Locals Programme), whereby 'an all-round pro-active approach will be developed which encourages a supportive culture in prisons based on good staff–prisoner relationships, a constructive regime and a physically safe environment' (Safer Custody Group 2002). It was the broadest, most generously resourced and most determined strategy to date. The strategy aimed 'to raise the standards of prisoner care and make prisons safer places in which to live and work' (Narey 2002a, 2002b). The programme was supported by a team in Prison Service Headquarters, The Samaritans, and a wide range of prison interest groups. It involved, *inter alia*, providing full-time suicide prevention coordinators in high-risk local prisons, developing new screening procedures, improving mental health support, and improving drug detoxification and treatment procedures. There was particular emphasis on the first phase of custody, with newly built (or converted) first night centres.

The new Safer Locals Programme was piloted in six prisons (Feltham, Winchester, Leeds, Eastwood Park, Wandsworth and Birmingham). Significant related interventions also took place elsewhere, as other establishments learned from a well-supported national initiative. A Cambridge Institute of Criminology research team evaluated the strategy. The team found that, where fully implemented, the strategy both reduced distress and managed distress more effectively. 'It was focused on the right areas of prison life (entry into custody, care, and safety) in the right kind of establishments (high turnover, at a time of maximum risk)' (Liebling et al. 2005: 28). In October 2007, the Prison Service introduced the Assessment, Care in Custody and Teamwork procedure (ACCT), alongside a requirement for staff to carry ligature cut-down tools and for most prisons to have 'safer' cells (cells that have minimal ligature points). ACCT is described as a 'necessarily prescriptive' 'prisoner-centred, flexible care-planning system which, when used effectively, can reduce risk' (NOMS 2011: 26). Since 2004, all deaths in prison custody have been investigated by the Prisons and Probation Ombudsman with a view to lesson learning. These have been important developments.

The causes of prison suicide: what do we know?

The rate of prison suicide in England and Wales is high, like elsewhere, but was significantly lowered during 2005–11 (see e.g. Shaw et al. 2013). The rate has increased since 2012 (Ministry of Justice 2014: table 2). Explanations for high rates of suicide in prison include: (i) population size, turnover and overcrowding; (ii) the vulnerability of the prison population (e.g. offenders being drawn from increasingly high-risk groups in the community); (iii) the underestimated and varied pains of imprisonment; and (iv) problems relating to prison life and management (e.g. less time out of cell and lower staffing levels).

Although substantial international interest exists in the study of suicides in prison, there are few systematic attempts to investigate which aspects of the prison experience might be most relevant to suicides and suicide attempts. Theories of prison suicide include *importation* models (that is, prisoners bring with them elevated suicide risk; e.g. Home Office 1984, 1986, 2001; Zamble and Quinsey 1997), *deprivation* models (that is, suicide is caused by prison-induced distress; e.g. Kennedy 1984; Backett 1988), and *combined* models (that is, prisons expose already vulnerable populations to additional risk; e.g. Toch 1975; Hatty and Walker 1986; Liebling 1995). Considerable evidence exists to support the third, combined model, although importation and deprivation factors seem to play different roles in different types of prison suicide (Liebling 1999). The specification of 'prison-induced distress' in research is often vague. Although there is a well-known 'prison effects' literature, surprisingly little of it considers distress or suicide, as its main focus is reconviction. There is a rich 'prison sociology' literature, which tells us much about the generalized pains of imprisonment (e.g. Sykes 1958), but which is striking for its avoidance of individual differences between types of prison or the topic of suicide (for a review see Liebling 1992).

Individual vulnerability factors

Imported vulnerability makes an important contribution to prison suicide rates. A measure of imported vulnerability developed by Liebling et al. (2005) (which includes previous suicide attempts, psychiatric treatment, self-harm and drug misuse) showed that levels vary significantly between establishments, even of the same type (see Table 13.1). Populations from geographical areas with high psychiatric morbidity, drug dependence and prior suicide attempts bring more suicide risk into prison with them than populations from 'less risky' parts of the country.

The earliest studies of prison suicide in the UK were carried out by prison medical officers, who began the search for a 'suicidal inmate profile' in their capacity as medical inspectors of prisons (see Gover 1880; Smalley 1911; Goring 1913; Topp 1979; Liebling 1992; Liebling and Ward 1995). This approach set the tone for most future studies of prison suicide, which have been retrospective profile accounts in search of medical knowledge based on small numbers of prisoners (e.g. Hankoff 1980; Danto 1973; and see Liebling and Ward 1995). These early studies observed that prison suicide accounted for a disproportionate number of deaths, and argued that the demographic profile of the prison population could explain this. Prison chaplains were held to possess greater knowledge than most about prisoners' possible motivations for suicide. The chaplain at Clerkenwell prison considered that: 'Suicide, like every other kind of sin, crime and misery, was caused by intemperance, impurity, laziness, and bad temper, and nothing else' (Liebling and Ward 1995: 124). Attempted suicide was punished as a crime, so that some prisoners were serving sentences because of attempted suicide in the community. Attempted suicide was also a prison disciplinary offence. Growth in the power of prison medical officers contributed to the creation of an important assumption, which was enshrined in suicide prevention procedures and reflected in most studies, that suicide was a medical–psychiatric problem.

Table 13.1 Percentage frequency of imported vulnerability per prison

Percentage of prisoners in each establishment	Attempted suicide	Psychiatric treatment	Self-harm	Drug misuse	All three indicators (suicide, psych treat, self-harm)	All four indicators
Winchester	25.0	22.0	16.0	41.0	9.0	8.0
Lewes	25.2	28.87	12.5	45.2	5.8	4.8
Eastwood Park	38.8	35.9	16.7	58.3	13.6	10.7
Styal	36.0	37.0	17.0	53.5	13.9	11.9
Leeds	12.3	22.8	9.6	57.0	5.3	3.5
Liverpool	11.9	21.4	6.0	55.6	2.5	1.7
Wandsworth	18.7	24.1	12.3	42.6	7.4	4.6
Manchester	13.1	20.4	7.1	38.4	5.1	4.0
Feltham	12.3	15.0	10.6	31.3	3.5	2.6
Glen Parva	8.4	17.6	7.6	47.1	3.4	2.5
Swansea	17.9	27.1	10.3	62.7	5.9	1.7
Forest Bank	6.9	18.8	6.9	48.5	4.0	3.0

Source: see Liebling et al. 2005.

Note: based on samples of 100 randomly selected prisoners in each prison.

Prison suicides 'represent a profile which is distinct from the population of suicides generally, but little different from that of the general prison population' (Hankoff 1980: 166; Fazel et al. 2008). Studies conclude overall that suicide is most common among males who are on remand at the time of death, that a third have a history of in-patient psychiatric treatment, that lifers are over-represented, that most have previous convictions and that 40% have been seen by a doctor in the week preceding death (Topp 1979; Backett 1987; Dooley 1990a; Fazel et al. 2008). Many completed suicides have injured themselves before (often in custody) and many have serious drug or alcohol problems (Topp 1979; Backett 1987; Dooley 1990a; Lloyd 1990; Liebling 1992; Power et al. 2003; Shaw et al. 2004; Fazel et al. 2008). A history of psychiatric treatment is less likely among prison suicides than among suicides in the community (Backett 1987, 1988). Only one-third of prison suicides are found to have a psychiatric history, as opposed to 80–90% of suicides in the general community (Backett 1987; Dooley 1990a; see also Fazel et al. 2013). A high proportion are found to have psychological and emotional difficulties falling short of a formal psychiatric diagnosis, such as alcohol or drug problems, personality disorders or borderline personality disorders, self-reported anxiety and depression (Skegg and Cox 1993; Shaw et al. 2004; Rivlin et al. 2010). This suggests that suicide prevention strategies that treat suicide as an exclusively medical or psychiatric problem are likely to prove ineffective.

Prison suicides are found to be younger than suicides in the community, reflecting the relatively young age profile of the prison population. The proportion of female suicides in prison is found to be proportionate to their numbers in the population (see Liebling 1994 and further below). Ethnic minorities are represented in the prison suicide statistics proportionate to their numbers in the prison population in the UK (they are vastly over-represented in custody). Isolation from relationships, or a breakdown in communication, is more important to suicide risk than marital status (Fazel et al. 2008). Offence history may be related to prison suicide, but research results are contradictory. A recent study in France by Duthé et al. (2013) found higher suicide risk among those accused or convicted of violent crimes, as did Fazel et al. (2008). Prison Service Instruction 64/2011 considers that individuals accused or convicted of violent offences, especially against family members, have especially high risks of suicide (NOMS 2011: 18; see also Prisons and Probation Ombudsman 2014: 23). Ludlow et al. (2015) reported a belief among prison staff that suicide risk was higher where an individual's offence had a 'domestic' component. This was reflected in some suicide prevention policies at individual establishments (Ludlow et al. 2015: 40, 56).

Situational vulnerability factors

Over time, it has become clear that *situational* factors are easier to identify, and may be more informative, than *individual* factors in the prediction of suicide in prison, as is the case with absconders from prison (Clarke and Martin 1971; Banks et al. 1975; Laycock 1977; Liebling 1992). Most suicides occur by hanging, and at night. A slightly disproportionate number occur at the weekend, during the summer months (when staffing and activity levels are low), and during the early stages of custody (both before and after trial). A disproportionate number of suicides occur in secluded locations, such as healthcare centres and segregation units, and in single cells (Fazel et al. 2008). Overcrowding may exacerbate problems that contribute to suicide risk among the vulnerable, such as lack of access to medical and other specialist care, increased misconduct and assault rates, lack of time spent in activity, lack of clothing and food, feelings of helplessness, and rapidly changing hierarchies among prisoners (see Liebling 1992; Rabe 2012). A senior psychiatrist asked to investigate a series of young prisoner suicides in Scotland's Glenochil prison in 1985 concluded that prison suicide 'is not a psychiatric problem, it's a management problem' (Scottish Home and Health Department 1985).

Motivations for prison suicide appear to be fear and loss: fear of other prisoners, of the consequences of one's crime, of imprisonment, and the loss of a significant relationship. Shame, guilt, and psychiatric disorder play a role, but seem to be less relevant for the younger sentenced prisoner (Liebling 1992; Ludlow et al. 2015). The most common emotions in suicides in the community are hopelessness, intense anguish, depression or 'ennui' (see Beck et al. 1974; also Maltsberger and Goldblatt 1996). Prison-induced distress may be seen as a continuum that contributes to suicide, particularly if a threshold is exceeded (Backett 1987). Where this threshold lies will depend on the coping skills and resources of particular prisoners (which may be lower among younger prisoners; Ludlow et al. 2015), as well as the competence of establishment staff in managing distress. Repeated disruptions to prison life (through e.g. transfers, relocations, cell changes) may be as damaging as one particularly stressful experience (see in relation to women, Mackenzie et al. 2003).

One of the most consistent findings of research is that a disproportionate number of suicides occur amongst remand prisoners and/or early in custody (Topp 1979; Backett 1987; Dooley 1990a; Lloyd 1990; Liebling 1992; Fazel et al. 2008). The large number of receptions, especially at local prisons, means that a high number of prisoners are exposed to risk during what is an extremely stressful stage. Studies suggest that the disproportionate rate of suicides during the remand period is in part due to the greater number of prisoners exposed to risk (Crighton and Towl 1997). Other factors contribute to an excess, however. These include the stressful and unstable nature of early confinement, the tension and uncertainty of the pre-trial phase, the proximity of the offence, overcrowding and staff shortages, fear of other prisoners, and the high proportion of mentally disordered prisoners on remand. Alcohol and drug dependence play an important role, particularly amongst those suicides that occur within the first 24 hours of reception into custody (see, for example, Danto 1973; Flaherty 1980; Hayes and Rowan 1988; and Copeland 1989).

Suicide among younger prisoners

In the UK, suicides amongst prisoners under 21 years old (or under 24, in some studies) have been a recurring cause for concern. Studies have linked these suicides particularly to bullying, inactivity, lack of contact with families, and volatility, which results in an especially complex relationship between violence and vulnerability among younger prisoners (Grindrod and Black 1989; Liebling 1992; Davies 1994; Ludlow et al. 2015). A group of 31 prison suicides under age 21 were identified in a study of all prison suicides occurring in England and Wales between 1972 and 1987, and a comparison was made with the general pool of prisoner suicides (see Dooley 1990a for original study, and Liebling 1992 for analysis). The following results were found: young prisoner suicides were more likely to cluster in particular establishments (partly because young prisoners are more likely to be accommodated in separate establishments or wings; partly because young prisoners may be more susceptible to intimidation – see Lester and Danto 1993;

Cheng et al. 2014; Ludlow et al. 2015). They were more likely to be charged with, or convicted of, property offences. They were likely to be serving slightly shorter terms and to end their lives within one month or at most one year of reception into custody. They were less likely to have received psychiatric treatment (13% as opposed to a third of all prison suicides) and were slightly more likely to have injured themselves before. They were slightly more likely to die between midnight and 8.00am. Almost half of these suicides were attributed to prison pressures (Liebling 1992).

Several studies support the argument that the under-21 age group may have a different susceptibility to suicide in prison (Flaherty 1980, 1983; also Grindrod and Black 1989; Home Office 1990; Scottish Home and Health Department 1985; Hawton and James 2005). Their offences are less serious, their suicide attempts more frequent and, within an establishment, such attempts are more likely to occur in clusters. Their need for support is intense, and their reactions to distress impulsive. Young prisoners may be particularly susceptible to threats or attacks from others, having few of the resources and skills necessary to avert such behaviour (Ludlow et al. 2015). Rates of bullying and victimization in young offender establishments and in prisons that accommodate young offenders are high, and may be increasing (Johnson 1978; McGurk and McDougal 1986; Shine et al. 1990). The young offender with a history of convictions for property offences who is single, with no job or family support, with a history of self-injury stands out as a distinct type of prison suicide (e.g. Hatty and Walker 1986). However, the term 'young' can apply in this context to prisoners up to the age of about 26–28, as many studies suggest that this highly situational susceptibility does not end at age 21 (Liebling 1992; Liebling and Krarup 1993; Ludlow et al. 2015; see also Hatty and Walker 1986).

Suicide and gender

The rate of suicide amongst women prisoners is underestimated in research (Liebling 1994; Sandler and Coles 2008). Few official publications about suicides in prison include women, and most studies argue that one of the most important risk factors associated with suicide both in prison and in the community is being male (Home Office 1986). In fact, women in prison outnumber men in terms of the number of incidents of self-injury per head of population. Although the suicide rate by women prisoners may be subject to large fluctuations because of small statistical numbers (Cookson and Williams 1990; Fazel and Benning 2009), the suicide rate for women prisoners is as high as the suicide rate for male prisoners. It may, in fact, be higher since apparent suicides by women prisoners may be less likely to receive suicide verdicts at inquests (Dooley 1990b; Liebling 1994). They may instead attract verdicts such as 'misadventure', 'accidental' or 'open', as a result of (gendered) assumptions of low intent. This is unexpected, given the disproportionate male to female ratio for suicides in the community (suicides by men outnumber suicides by women by a factor of 2.5 to 1; see e.g. Stephens 1987; Lester and Gatto 1989; Rutter and Smith 1995; Mackenzie et al. 2003). That the suicide rates for male and female prisoners are similar requires explanation. There are two possibilities:

1 Greater vulnerability of the female prison population

The female prison population differs from the male prison population in important respects: a higher proportion of women are on remand; women tend to be serving shorter sentences and are less recidivist; a far higher proportion of women prisoners are drawn from ethnic minorities, their average age is higher, and they have fewer previous convictions (Morgan 1997: 1155). Women prisoners are more likely to have received in-patient psychiatric care. They are far more likely to have been sexually abused or experienced violence at home (Liebling 1992; Fazel and Benning 2009; and see Loucks 1998). There is some evidence that the female prison population has a higher level of borderline psychiatric disorder (Völlm and Dolan 2009), although this finding may be compounded by labelling: women attract higher levels of psychiatric attention and their behaviour is pathologized (see e.g. Allen 1987; for critique see e.g. Brickman 2004). High levels of sexual and physical abuse may render the female prisoner population especially vulnerable – they may be especially vulnerable to 'control' (Mackenzie et al. 2003).[3] This raises the second possibility – that the experience of imprisonment for women is qualitatively different.

2 Specific impact of imprisonment upon women

There may be gender-specific effects of custody upon women, particularly amongst women with dependent children (Corston 2007; Walmsley et al. 1992). Suicide by women prisoners tends to be linked to the removal of children into care; or the use of drugs and its consequences for the future of the child (Liebling 1994; Mackenzie et al. 2003; INQUEST 2014).

In his 1992 study of *Women and Attempted Suicide*, Jack argues that women may be more predisposed to feelings of learned helplessness than men. Women were found to be more driven by present feelings (such as feeling lonely or unwanted) than with feelings about the past (such as shame or failure). Other studies show that women are more likely to suffer from depression, lack of self-worth, and from a low sense of their 'locus of control' (ability to affect their environment; see Jack 1992; Mackenzie et al. 2003). Coid's detailed study of women self-injurers in Holloway prison described a progressive build-up of symptoms of anxiety, dysphoria (unpleasant depressed feelings), irritability and feelings of emptiness prior to self-harm. Some 12% said they were intending to kill themselves when they self-harmed. The remainder described wanting to relieve tension, anger and feelings of depression (Wilkins and Coid 1991; Coid et al. 1992). Situational triggers may include cancellations of parole or home leave, receiving distressing or incomplete news, removal of a cellmate, an unwanted transfer, or problems with children and contact with family. Women who injure themselves often become involved in disciplinary infractions in prison (Mackenzie et al. 2003) and are more likely to have received psychiatric treatment and to have injured themselves before (Liebling 1992).

It is possible that there are some special problems of prison management and culture in women's prisons. Rock and Hannah-Moffatt suggest that the tensions between therapeutic, medical and disciplinary penal ideologies may be especially acute in women's prisons (Rock 1996; Hannah-Moffatt 2001; see also Howe 1994). This is an under-researched area.

Types of suicidal prisoner rather than a single profile

There are useful lessons to be learned from the search for a profile of the suicidal prisoner. However, there are flaws in the 'single profile' approach. It may be more helpful to regard prison suicides as heterogeneous – consisting of different types (e.g. lifers, the psychiatrically ill, and younger prisoners who cope poorly with imprisonment; Liebling 1999), with different offence and demographic profiles, and different histories and motivations. For example, long-sentence prisoner suicides (which include a high proportion of domestic homicide cases, and which may include, for the purposes of this category, prisoners on remand but facing life or long sentences) tend to be older than average. Some take their lives significantly later during their sentences. Links have long been established between domestic homicide and suicide before arrest (West 1967). Including this group of prison suicides in a general profile may distort the profile towards violent offences and longer sentences. Removing them and treating them as a distinct group enables a slightly different criminal justice profile to be described for other types of prison suicide. The psychiatrically ill may constitute another 'separate' group. It is well established that there is a strong association between psychiatric illness and suicide (e.g. Sainsbury 1988). There is an established link between the closure of psychiatric institutions and increases in suicides in prison amongst this population (Skegg and Cox 1993). These suicides tend to be older than the average prison population, of no fixed abode, and to feel alienated and helpless (see Liebling 1999: Table 4). Finally, there are vulnerable prisoners, or 'poor copers'. This group resembles other prisoners most closely. They are arguably the most preventable group, despite being the most difficult to identify. The vulnerable constitute the most numerous group of prison suicides and the significance of the immediate prison situation may be most acute in these cases. More of this group have attempted suicide or injured themselves before.

The relationship between suicide and self-harm

> It is like the blood is doing the crying for me … It's not a cry for help. It's a cry of pain.
>
> (Liebling 1997: 191)

> I wanted someone to stop me. But no-one stopped me. So I carried on.
>
> (Liebling 1997: 191)

No fully reliable figures on attempted suicide and self-injury exist, either in prison or in the community, although the situation has improved considerably. Reporting can be haphazard (Tumim 1990; Ludlow et al. 2015), despite increased emphasis on its importance (especially through the ACCT procedure). No consensus exists as to what constitutes a 'genuine' suicide attempt. In a 2015 study by Ludlow et al., staff reflected upon the challenge of categorizing the behaviour of prisoners who make 'rational choices' to die (e.g. by refusing medical treatment for serious illness) or who injure themselves as a way to manage or express emotion.[4] There also may be factors that discourage staff from raising the relevant forms every time an incident occurs: the time and manpower required to manage incidents and follow them up through formal channels, perceptions of deficiencies in expertise and complexity in the use of official procedures, limited information about the prisoner concerned that makes it difficult to assess risk, a wish to keep incidents out of Safer Custody figures, or a disbelief in the seriousness of the behaviour (it is 'just attention seeking': see Ludlow et al. 2015). As a consequence of these limitations, there are difficulties in relying upon statistical information alone when trying to assess the incidence of self-harm and attempted suicide in prison.

Attempted suicide and self-injury have typically been treated as separate phenomena in the community, having a limited association with completed suicide. This is despite evidence that such a separation is artificial (Stengel 1971; Kreitman 1977; Morgan 1979), and follow-up studies of suicide attempts showing up to 30 times greater risk of suicide than the general population (e.g. Hawton et al. 1993). Several studies have been carried out on attempted suicide and self-harm in prison (e.g. Liebling 1992; Liebling and Krarup 1993; Inch et al. 1995; Snow 2002; Humber et al. 2013; Hawton et al. 2014). Studies of suicides and suicide attempts in prison often seek differences between populations who engage in these supposedly distinct behaviours (e.g. Phillips 1986; Griffiths 1990). The causes of the two behaviours are in fact found to be similar. Acts of self-injury, like suicide attempts and suicides, are associated with feelings of 'melancholy tinged with self-contempt' (Cooper 1971), depression, self-doubt and the search for relief (Toch 1975; Liebling 1992; Snow 2002; Kenning et al. 2010). The populations involved overlap considerably: half of all those who die by suicide in prison have injured themselves before – one-third in prison (Dooley 1990a). In the controlled environment of the prison, many potentially lethal suicide attempts are prevented by chance intervention (e.g. staff having 'a feeling' or encountering prisoners on a wing: Ludlow et al. 2015).

The relationship between suicide and self-harm is complex and has been over-simplified in research (see Paykel et al. 1974). Self-injury and suicide can be seen as 'expressions of a common suicidal process' (Goldney and Burvil 1980: 2; Humber et al. 2013; Hawton et al. 2014). As Stengel has argued, suicide attempts can have an 'appeal function' (Stengel 1971). If there is no response to a prisoner's 'last ditch' effort to change an unbearable environment, suicide may be extremely likely. It may be useful, then, to see suicide – both in action and intent – as a continuum.[5] Self-injury may be the first overt symptom of a level of distress only steps away from a final act of despair (see Liebling 1992: 59–67; Humber et al. 2013; Hawton et al. 2014). The continuities between suicide and self-harm (particularly in terms of motivation, causes and prevention) may be more important than their differences. Both may be reactive rather than purposive (or 'manipulative'; Shaw 2002), and may be impulsive rather than planned (Liebling 1992). It is important to inquire why the behaviour occurred rather than what it was intended to achieve (Wicks 1974; Shaw 2002). If staff respond, and provide support and solutions, prisoners may be diverted from the destructive route on which they are setting out (see e.g. Shepherd 1991).

Understanding prison life and its relationship to prisoner distress

Recent prison scholars, informed by theorists of justice, have argued that fairness or legitimacy is empirically related to willing compliance and the reproduction of order (Bottoms 1999: 254–257). Sparks and Bottoms define legitimacy as encompassing 'considerations of fairness and respect' (Sparks and Bottoms 1995: 59). Fair actions are described as 'justifiable, comprehensible and consistent' (Bottoms and Sparks 1997: 22). Relationships, or how you are treated, are central to perceptions of fairness (Bottoms and Rose 1998).

There are important links between the literature on prison legitimacy and prisoner well-being. Demeaning and careless treatment is delegitimating, and causes non-compliance, or 'righteous anger'. As Sparks and Bottoms argue, convincingly, 'every instance of brutality in prisons, every casual racist joke and demeaning remark, every ignored petition, every unwarranted bureaucratic delay, every inedible meal, every arbitrary decision to segregate or transfer without giving clear and well-founded reasons, every petty mis-carriage of justice, every futile and inactive period of time – is delegitimating' (Sparks and Bottoms 1995: 60). We argue that delegitimating experiences, or feelings of injustice, are also distressing. Many autobiographical and qualitative studies of prison life suggest that lack of respect and fairness are frustrating and painful. Empirical studies show that these experiences are linked to elevated levels of distress, and higher rates of suicide (Liebling et al. 2005). These findings challenge the position of those who argue that prison life has little effect on the psychological well-being of prisoners overall (e.g. Walker 1987; Zamble and Porporino 1988). They provide an important and empowering narrative to prison staff and managers: that organizational culture and staff practices can make a difference.

Distress in prison and its relationship to suicide rates

In a 12-prison study of suicide prevention carried out by Liebling and colleagues, distress was measured using the General Health Questionnaire (GHQ-12),[6] and a 'prison distress' measure that encompassed hopelessness, depression, stress and coping difficulties.

Levels of distress in prison were found to be extremely high. The average score on the GHQ-12 across the ten 'high-risk' establishments in the study (where a score of 12 or 13 is the standard threshold indicating significant illness), was 16.78. Mean scores varied significantly between establishments (from 11.99 at one prison, to 18.87 at another). At 11 of the 12 establishments, the mean score was above the threshold used in most studies to indicate treatable illness. Some of the differences in levels of distress (here, anxiety and depression) were related to circumstances, so as Table 13.2 shows, the highest levels of distress were found among the unsentenced (18.82 > 14.86, p<.001), unemployed prisoners (17.99 > 15.27, p<.001), first-time prisoners (17.23 > 15.87, p<.01), and those who were 'first time in this prison' (16.85 > 15.54, p<.05). The highest levels of distress on entry into prison were found among those with the highest levels of imported vulnerability (4.05 > 3.43, p<.001),[7] women (3.97 > 3.44, p<.001), unsentenced prisoners (3.64 > 3.45, p<.001), black and Asian prisoners (3.66 > 3.50, p<.05), and those who were 'first time in this prison' (3.44 > 3.25, p<.05). The highest levels of imported vulnerability were found among women prisoners (2.47 > 1.93, p<.001), those who were repeatedly coming back to prison (2.13 > 1.76, p<.001), often to the same prison (2.18 > 2.02, p<.05), and white prisoners (2.10 > 1.70, p<.001). The most vulnerable prisoners reported the lowest levels of perceived physical safety (p<.001), family contact (p<.001) and personal development (p<.05), and the highest levels of drug use (p<.01).

In other words, we found evidence of the combined model: that the prison interacts with the person and exposes already vulnerable populations to additional risk. We also found evidence to support the 'slow and gradual amelioration' described by Clemmer and others (Clemmer 1958; Sapsford 1983): that is, that levels of distress and dissatisfaction decline over time, with particularly high levels throughout the first month (see also Harvey 2007).[8]

Institutional suicide rates over five periods (two short, three long) were calculated for each prison. Table 13.3 shows the results from a multi-level analysis. Hopelessness and depression, GHQ-12, 'overall distress' and a single item, 'I have thought about suicide in this prison', were significantly related to most (in the case of GHQ-12, all) of the

Table 13.2 Difference between groups of prisoners in level of distress

	Mean score	Mean score	Difference
Anxiety and depression (GHQ)			
Unsentenced v sentenced prisoners	18.82	14.86	*p<.001*
Unemployed v employed prisoners	17.99	15.27	*p<.001*
First time v experienced prisoners	16.85	15.54	*p<.05*
First time in this prison v rest	16.85	15.54	*p<.05*
Distress on entry			
High imported vulnerability v rest	4.05	3.43	*p<.001*
Women v men	3.97	3.44	*p<.001*
Unsentenced v sentenced prisoners	3.64	3.45	*p<.001*
Black and Asian prisoners v rest	3.66	3.50	*p<.05*
First time in this prison v rest	3.44	3.25	*p.<05*
Imported vulnerability	2.47	1.93	*p<.001*
Women v men	2.13	1.76	*p<.001*
Experienced prisoners v rest	2.10	1.70	*p<.001*
White prisoners v rest	2.10	1.70	*p<.001*

Table 13.3 Correlation between institutional suicide rates and distress variables (n=12)

Variables		Rate I 1995–2001	Rate II 2000–01	Rate III 1998–2002	Rate IV 2001–02	Rate V 1995–2002
Hopelessness	Pearson Correlation	.43	.67	.43	.07	.40
	Sig. (2-tailed)	.16	.02★	.16	.82	.20
Coping difficulties	Pearson Correlation	.41	.74	.66	.60	.63
	Sig. (2-tailed)	.18	.01★★	.02★	.04★	.03★
Stress	Pearson Correlation	.36	.61	.55	.30	.45
	Sig. (2-tailed)	.25	.03★	.06	.35	.14
Distress on entry into custody	Pearson Correlation	.16	.69	.48	.33	.42
	Sig. (2-tailed)	.62	.01★	.12	.30	.18
Depression	Pearson Correlation	.44	.74	.69	.60	.66
	Sig. (2-tailed)	.15	.01★★	.01★	.04★	.02★
New coping difficulties	Pearson Correlation	.33	.68	.55	.55	.51
	Sig. (2-tailed)	.30	.02★	.06	.07	.09
Hopelessness and depression	Pearson Correlation	.52	.81	.73	.60	.70
	Sig. (2-tailed)	.09	.00★★	.01★★	.04★	.01★
GHQ-12	Pearson Correlation	.66	.62	.78	.66	.76
	Sig. (2-tailed)	.02★	.03★	.00★★	.02★	.00★★
Distress (overall)	Pearson Correlation	.45	.77	.66	.48	.61
	Sig. (2-tailed)	.15	.00★★	.02★	.11	.04★
Item 25 'thought of suicide'	Pearson Correlation	.49	.66	.75	.68	.71
	Sig. (2-tailed)	.11	.02★	.01★★	.02★	.01★

Note: *p <.01 **p<.01

institutional suicide rates. The other results for these dimensions were in the right direction and approached significance.[9] These results show a statistically significant relationship between individual distress and institutional suicide rates. Distress is therefore a good measure of suicide risk.

The survey used in the study included detailed measures of aspects of the prison environment relevant to the care of individual prisoners, as well as the broader measures of 'moral performance' (Liebling, with Arnold 2004). An exploration of the relationships between the dimensions in the study, controlling for establishment variation as well as population differences, resulted in the conceptual model shown in Figure 13.1.

Using the GHQ-12 measure of anxiety and depression as the dependent variable in a stepwise regression, the four measures of the prison environment that contributed most directly to suicide risk were perceptions of safety, personal development, family contact and dignity.[10] Frustration, high levels of drug use, poor relationships with staff, low levels of support on entry into prison, low levels of individual care, and lack of activities aimed at personal development or addressing offending behaviour were significantly correlated with high levels of distress. Reconceptualizing suicide prevention as 'the promotion of well-being', rather than the avoidance of suicide (the aspiration of policy and practice), was proposed as an important way of linking the quality of life in prison to better outcomes (see Figure 13.2). Most aspects of 'enabling environments' (fairness, relationships, care, confident staff and so on) also make for good suicide prevention policy. A concern with promoting well-being, or human flourishing, might be highly relevant to both suicide prevention and reducing reoffending (see e.g. Ward and Mann 2003; Ward and Stewart 2003).[11]

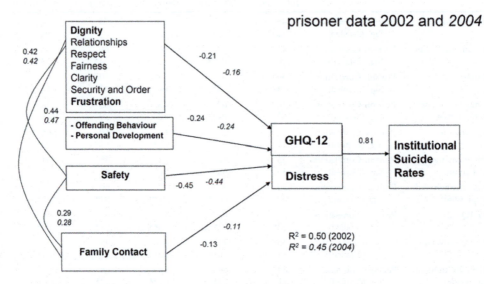

Figure 13.1 Modelling overall distress GHQ-12 and suicide rates

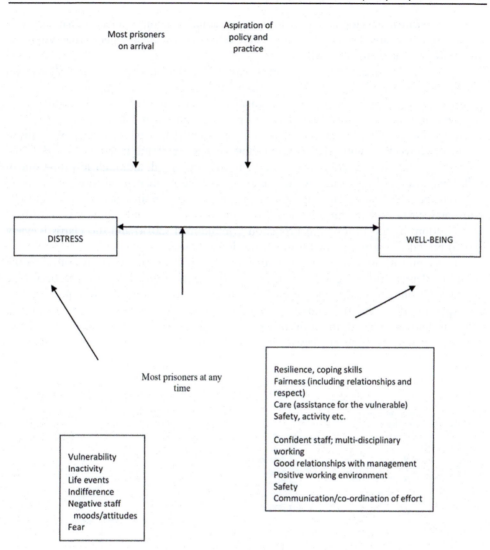

Figure 13.2 Distress and well-being in prison

Conclusion

> Human beings are creatures capable of feeling pain and suffering not only as a result of physically painful acts but also as a result of acts with symbolic meaning.
>
> (Margalit 1996: 84–85)

As Haney argues, the prison is a high-threat, low-control environment (Haney 1997; see also Goffman 1961; Goodstein 1979). De Zuleuta has suggested that 'an unpleasant but predictable world is preferable to a chaotic one' (De Zuleuta 1993: 90). Much has been learned about the importance of the prison environment, and the role of staff in the prevention of suicide. Distress is lower in safe prisons that treat prisoners with dignity, promote personal development and facilitate meaningful family contact. That sustained reductions in the rate of suicides in prison were achieved post-2005 suggests that systematic efforts to prevent them can work.

Rapid population growth, major organizational change, decreased predictability and safety, and 'the withdrawal of care and kindness from prison landings' (senior manager, personal communication) may have precipitated a reverse in 2012–14 and beyond in the welcome and sustained downward trend in prison suicides that followed the 2001 Safer Custody strategy. The rise has included an even higher than typical number of deaths in the first two weeks in custody. Causes of these changes are being investigated at the time of writing, and attempts are being made to reverse the trend, although less time out of cell, lower staffing levels, and curtailed regimes may be permanent features of the new, benchmarked landscape. The capacity of prison staff to identify and best manage self-harm and suicide risk within this new landscape may be reduced (Ludlow et al. 2015). Investigations by the Prisons and Probation Ombudsman (2014) and the Harris Review (2015) provide a starting point for much-needed analysis.

The account in this chapter suggests that an 'enabling' moral climate is critical to the sound implementation of good existing suicide prevention principles and practices. The use of imprisonment, and the resourcing and organization of prisons, also require analysis in explanations of the rise and in prevention efforts. A tentative model, integrating research findings related to both prisoners and staff, might start with Figure 13.3. Detailed exploration of specific aspects of prison regimes and suicide prevention strategies is also needed.

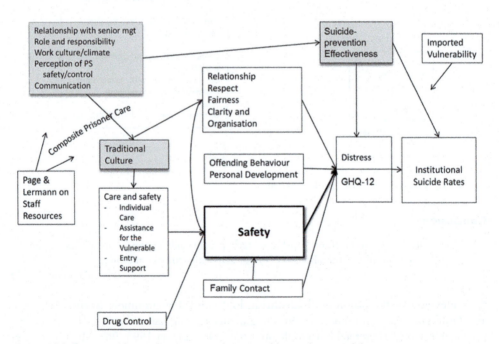

Figure 13.3 Prison quality and prison suicide: a testable working model

Notes

1 We are grateful to Linda Durie, Sarah Tait, Joel Harvey, Annick Stiles, Bethany Schmidt, Thomas Akoensi and Gerry Rose for their invaluable assistance in the various projects drawn on in this chapter.

2 A Response to the Chief Inspector's 1999 Report was produced by the Royal College of Psychiatrists, *Suicide in Prisons* (2002). One of the conclusions of this report was that 'all prisons need an enhanced psychiatric and substance misuse service' (Royal College of Psychiatrists 2002: 5).

3 It is surprising, given what is known about the abuse backgrounds of many women, that questions of fairness, and uses of authority and power and their effects, are rarely studied in relation to women in prison (see Liebling 2009).

4 Few studies seek to understand deliberate self-harm as a response to, and expression of, pain, which may occur well within the boundaries of 'normal mental health' (though see normalizing feminist critiques of self-harm as poor coping in e.g. Crowe 1996; Pembroke 2007).

5 Though persistent self-harm may merit distinctive analysis.

6 Several studies have confirmed that the 12-item GHQ can be used as a short screening instrument for psychological disorders and minor (non-psychotic) psychiatric disorders. It produces comparable results to longer versions (Goldberg et al. 1997). Its brevity makes it attractive for use in busy settings, and where it forms part of a broader survey. The results from GHQ studies have been shown to be unaffected by gender, age and educational level (Goldberg et al. 1997). This method is particularly suited to comparing levels of anxiety and depression within and between populations (Banks et al. 1980).

7 For overall distress, and imported vulnerability, a five-point scale was used, where higher is more distressed/vulnerable.

8 Prisoners attributed their distress to continuing stressful life events (such as bereavement and relationship breakdown), frustration, shock and fear, lack of clarity and uncertainty about the rules, drug withdrawal, lack of support for major problems, lack of appropriate healthcare, indifference and lack of respect from staff, and worries about family.

9 Some of our measures of distress (like stress and coping difficulties) are less directly related to suicide risk than others. However, individual-level data on levels of distress can serve as an important indicator of institutional suicide risk. This avoids the methodological problem of assuming a clear overlap between prisoners who have self-harmed and suicide risk (see Liebling 1992).

10 The conceptual model was estimated using multiple regression. The objective was to build a model in which levels of distress were predicted by other variables, whether directly or indirectly. In order to control for establishment-level effects, dummy variables were created for the prisons (11 dummy variables, with one establishment as the reference group). The dummy variables were entered into the model as predictors prior to adding any other explanatory variables. This ensured that the influence of prison-level variables would be removed. The dependent variable 'GHQ score' was predicted from a number of 'quality of prison life' predictors, such as respect, relationships and fairness. A forward stepwise regression method was used in order to select the predictor variables from the set of 17 which would account for the most variance. Forward variable selection enters the variables into the model one at a time based on whether the variable contributes significantly. Using collinearity diagnostics, a cut-off point was determined so that the variables included in the model did not show high levels of multicollinearity. Multicollinearity means that predictor variables are highly correlated and this is unfavourable because it suggests that the similar constructs are being measured and that variables are to a certain degree redundant. Condition indices were inspected and a condition index greater than 15 was seen to indicate a possible problem with collinearity. Once the predictor(s) of distress had been determined, the next step was to examine which variables would in turn explain variance in the predictors of distress. This was again estimated using a forward stepwise regression method. Imported vulnerability measures contributed between 8 and 15% of the explained variance in distress. Prison quality measures contributed between 34 and 46% of the explained variance in distress. Together, these concepts accounted for 38–53% of the explained variance in distress.

11 In the Good Lives Model of offender rehabilitation (a strengths-based model) emphasis is placed on increasing the individual's capacity to live a more fulfilling life, to seek primary goods (such as mastery experiences, autonomy, freedom from emotional turmoil and relatedness) via socially acceptable ways, and to achieve high levels of well-being. The model stresses the promotion of welfare as well as the reduction of risk (Ward and Mann 2003). As Margalit says, 'respecting humans means never giving up on anyone, since all people are capable of living dramatically differently from the way they have lived so far' (Margalit 1996: 71).

Bibliography

Allen, H. (1987) *Justice Unbalanced: Gender, psychiatry and judicial decisions*, Milton Keynes: Open University Press.

Backett, S. (1987) 'Suicides in Scottish prisons', *British Journal of Psychiatry* 151: 218–221.

Backett, S. (1988) 'Suicide and stress in prison', in S. Backett, J. McNeil and A. Yellowlees (eds) *Imprisonment Today*, London: Macmillan.

Banks, C., Mayhew, P. and Sapsford, R. (1975) *Absconding from Open Prisons*, Home Office Research Studies, Vol. 26, London: HMSO.

Banks, M.H., Clegg, C.W., Jackson, P.R., Kemp, N.J., Stafford, E.M. and Wall, T.D. (1980) 'The use of the general health questionnaire as an indicator of mental health in occupational studies', *Journal of Occupational Psychology* 53: 187–194.

Beck, A.T., Weissman, A., Lester, D. and Trexler, L. (1974) 'The measurement of pessimism: the hopelessness scale', *Journal of Clinical and Consulting Psychology* 42: 861–865.

Bottoms, A.E. (1999) 'Interpersonal violence and social order in prisons', in M. Tonry and J. Petersilia (eds) *Prisons, Crime and Justice: A Review of Research*, Vol. 26, Chicago, IL: University of Chicago Press, 205–282.

Bottoms, A.E. and Rose, G. (1998) 'The importance of staff-prisoner relationships: results from a study in three male prisons', in D. Price and A. Liebling (eds) *Staff–Prisoner Relationships: A Review of the Literature*, unpublished report submitted to the Prison Service.

Bottoms, A.E. and Sparks, R. (1997) 'How is order in prisons maintained?' in A. Liebling (ed.) *Security, Justice and Order in Prison: Developing Perspectives*, Cambridge: Cambridge University Press.

Brickman, B.J. (2004) 'Delicate cutters: gendered self-mutilation and attractive flesh in medical discourse', *Body and Society* 10(4): 87–111.

Cheng, Q., Li, H., Silenzio, V. and Caine, E.D. (2014) 'Suicide contagion: a systematic review of definitions and research utility', *PLoS One* 26 9(9): e108724.

Clarke, R.V.G. and Martin, D.N. (1971) *Absconding from Approved Schools*, Home Office Research Studies, Vol. 12, London: HMSO.

Clemmer, D. (1958) *The Prison Community*, New York: Holt, Rinehart and Winston.

Coid, J., Wilkins, J., Coid, B. and Everitt, B. (1992) 'Self-mutilation in female remanded prisoners. II. A cluster analytic approach towards identification of a behavioural syndrome', *Criminal Behaviour and Mental Health* 2: 1–14.

Cookson, H.M. and Williams, M. (1990) *Assessing the Statistical Significance of Rare Events*, Directorate of Psychological Services Report, ser. 1, no. 33, London: Home Office.

Cooper, H. (1971) 'Self-Mutilation by Peruvian prisoners', *International Journal of Offender Therapy and Comparative Criminology* 15(3): 180–188.

Copeland, A. (1989) 'Fatal suicidal hangings among prisoners in jail', *Medicine Science and the Law* 29: 341–345.

Corston, J. (2007) *The Corston Report: A report by Baroness Jean Corston of a review of women with particular vulnerabilities in the criminal justice dystem*, London: Home Office.

Crighton, D. and Towl, G. (1997) 'Self-inflicted deaths in prisons in England and Wales: an analysis of the data for 1988–90 and 1994–95', in G. Towl (ed.) *Suicide and Self-Injury in Prisons:*

Research Directions in the 1990s, Issues in Criminological and Legal Psychology no. 28, Leicester: British Psychological Society.

Crowe, M. (1996) 'Cutting up: signifying the unspeakable', *Australia and New Zealand Journal of Mental Health Nursing* 5: 103–111.

Danto, B. (1973) *In Jail House Blues: Studies of suicidal behavior in jail and prison*, Orchard Lake, MI: Epic Publications.

Davies, B. (1994) 'The Swansea listener scheme: views from prison landings', *Howard Journal* 33 (2): 125–136.

De Zuleuta, F. (1993) *From Pain to Violence: The traumatic roots of destructiveness*, London: Whurr.

Dooley, E. (1990a) 'Prison suicide in England and Wales, 1972–1987', *British Journal of Psychiatry* 156: 40–45.

Dooley, E. (1990b) 'Non-natural deaths in prison', *British Journal of Criminology* 30: 229–234.

Duthé, G., Kensey, A. and Shon, J. (2013) 'Suicide among male prisoners in France: a prospective population-based study', *Forensic Science International* 233: 273–277.

Fazel, S. and Benning, R. (2009) 'Suicide in female prisoners in England and Wales, 1978–2004', *British Journal of Psychiatry* 194(2): 183–184.

Fazel, S., Cartwright, J., Noman-Nott, A. and Hawton, K. (2008) 'Suicide in prisoners: a systematic review of risk factors', *Journal of Clinical Psychiatry* 69(11): 1721–1731.

Fazel, S., Wolf, A. and Geddes, J.R. (2013) 'Suicide in prisoners with bipolar disorder and other psychiatric disorders: a systematic review', *Bipolar Disorders* 15(5): 491–495.

Flaherty, M.G. (1980) *An Assessment of the National Incidence of Juvenile Suicide in Adult Jails, Lock-ups and Juvenile Detention Centres*, Urbana-Champaign: University of Illinois Press.

Flaherty, M.G. (1983) *The National Incidence of Juvenile Suicide in Adult Jails, Lock-ups and Juvenile Detention Centres*, Urbana-Champaign: University of Illinois Press.

Goffman, E. (1961) 'On the characteristics of total institutions', in D.R. Cressey (ed.) *The Prison: Studies in Institutional Organisation and Change*, New York: Holt, Rinehart and Winston.

Goldberg, D.P., Gater, R., Sartorius, N., Ustin, T.B., Piccinelli, M., Gureje, O. and Rutter, C. (1997) 'The validity of two versions of the GHQ in the WHO study of mental illness in general health care', *Psychological Medicine* 27: 191–197.

Goldney, R.D. and Burvil, P.W. (1980) 'Trends in suicidal behaviour and its management', *Australian and New Zealand Journal of Psychiatry* 14: 1–15.

Goodstein, L. (1979) 'Inmate adjustment to prison and the transition to community life', *Journal of Research in Crime and Delinquency* 16(2): 246–272.

Goring, C. (1913) *The English Convict: A statistical study*, London: HMSO.

Gover, R.M. (1880) 'Notes by the medical inspector', in *Prison Commission Annual Report 1880*, Appendix No. 19, London: HMSO.

Griffiths, A.W. (1990) 'Correlates of suicidal history in male prisoners', *Medicine, Science and the Law* 30(3): 217–218.

Grindrod, H. and Black, G. (1989) *Suicides at Leeds Prison: An enquiry into the deaths of five teenagers during 1988/9*, London: Howard League for Penal Reform.

Haney, C. (1997) 'Psychology and the limits to prison pain: confronting the coming crisis in the Eighth Amendment Law', *Psychology, Public Policy and Law* 3(4): 499–588.

Hankoff, L.D. (1980) 'Prisoner suicide', *International Journal of Offender Therapy and Comparative Criminology* 24(2): 162–166.

Hannah-Moffatt, K. (2001) *Punishment in Disguise: Penal governance and federal imprisonment of women in Canada*, Toronto: University of Toronto Press.

Harris Review (2015) *Independent Review into Self-inflicted Deaths in NOMS Custody of 18–24 Year Olds*, London: Ministry of Justice.

Harvey, J. (2007) *Young Men in Prison: Surviving and adapting to life inside*, Abingdon: Willan Publishing.

Hatty, S.E. and Walker, J.R. (1986) *A National Study of Deaths in Australian Prisons*, Canberra: Australian Centre of Criminology.

Hawton, K., Fagg, J., Platt, S. and Hawkins, M. (1993) 'Factors associated with suicide following parasuicide in young people', *British Medical Journal* 306: 1641–1644.

Hawton, K. and James, A. (2005) 'Suicide and deliberate self-harm in young people', *The BMJ* 330: 891–894.

Hawton, K., Linsell, L., Adeniji, T., Sarlaslan, A. and Fazel, S. (2014) 'Self-harm in prisons in England and Wales: sn epidemiological study of prevalence, risk factors, clustering and subsequent suicide', *The Lancet* 383(9923): 1147–1154.

Hayes, L. and Rowan, J. (1988) *National Study of Jail Suicides: Seven Years Later*, Baltimore, MD: National Center on Institutions and Alternatives.

HMCIP (HM Chief Inspector of Prisons) (1999) *Suicide is Everyone's Concern: A thematic review by HM Chief Inspector of Prisons for England and Wales*, London: Home Office.

Home Office (1984) *Suicides in Prison: Report by HM Chief Inspector of Prisons*, London: Home Office.

Home Office (1986) *Report of the Working Group on Suicide Prevention*, London: HMSO.

Home Office (1990) *Report on a Review by Her Majesty's Chief Inspector of Prisons for England and Wales of Suicide and Self-Harm in Prison Service Establishments in England and Wales*, London: HMSO.

Home Office (1999) *White Paper Saving Lives: Our healthier nation*, London: HMSO.

Home Office (2001) *Rates and Causes of Death among Prisoners and Offenders under Community Supervision*, London: HMSO.

Howe, A. (1994) *Punish and Critique: Towards a feminist analysis of penality*, London: Routledge.

Humber, N., Webb, R., Piper, M., Appleby, L. and Shaw, J. (2013) 'A national case-control study of risk factors for suicide among prisoners in England and Wales', *Social Psychiatry and Psychiatric Epidemiology* 48(7): 1177–1185.

Inch, H., Rowlands, P. and Soliman, A. (1995) 'Deliberate self-harm in a young offenders' institution', *The Journal of Forensic Psychiatry* 61: 161–171.

INQUEST (2014) 'Preventing the deaths of women in prison: the need for an slternative spproach', inquest.org.uk/pdf/briefings/Jan2014_updated_INQUEST_Preventing_deaths_of_women_in_prison.pdf.

Jack, R. (1992) *Women and Attempted Suicide*, Hillsdale: Lawrence Erlbaum Associates.

Johnson, R. (1978) 'Youth in crisis: dimensions of self-destructive conduct among adolescent prisoners', *Adolescence* 1(51): 461–482.

Kennedy, D.B. (1984) 'A theory of suicide while in police custody', *Journal of Police Science and Administration* 12(2): 191–200.

Kenning, C., Cooper, J., Short, V., Abel, K. and Chew-Graham, C. (2010) 'Prison staff and women prisoners' views of self-harm: their implications for service delivery and development: a qualitative study', *Criminal Behaviour and Mental Health* 20(4): 274–284.

Kreitman, N. (ed.) (1977) *Parasuicide*, London: Wiley.

Laycock, G.K. (1977) *Absconding from Borstals*, Home Office Research Study, Vol. 41, London: HMSO.

Lester, D. and Danto, B. (1993) *Suicide Behind Bars: Prediction and Prevention*, Philadelphia, PA: Charles Press.

Lester, D. and Gatto, J. (1989) 'Self-destructive tendencies and depression as predictors of suicidal ideation in teenagers', *Journal of Adolescence* 12: 221–223.

Liebling, A. (1992) *Suicides in Prison*, London: Routledge.

Liebling, A. (1994) 'Suicides amongst women prisoners', *Howard Journal* 33(1): 1–9.

Liebling, A. (1995) 'Vulnerability and prison suicide', *British Journal of Criminology* 35(2): 173–187.

Liebling, A. (1997) 'Risk and prison suicide', in H. Kemshall and J. Pritchard (eds) *Good Practice in Risk Assessment and Risk Management 2: Protection, rights and responsibilities*, London: Jessica Kingsley Publishers, 188–204.

Liebling, A. (1999) 'Prison suicide and prisoner coping', *Prisons, Crime and Justice: An Annual Review of Research* 26 (ed. M. Tonry and J. Petersilia): 283–360.

Liebling, A. (2009) 'Women in prison prefer legitimacy to sex', *British Society of Criminology Newsletter* 63: 19–23.

Liebling, A., with Arnold, H. (2004) *Prisons and their Moral Performance: A study of values, quality and prison life*, Clarendon Studies in Criminology, Oxford: Oxford University Press.

Liebling, A. and Krarup, H. (1993) *Suicide Attempts in Male Prisons*, London: Home Office.

Liebling, A. and Tait, S. (2006) 'Improving staff–prisoner relationships', in G.E. Dear (ed.) *Preventing Suicide and Other Self-harm in Prison*, London: Palgrave-Macmillan, 103–117.

Liebling, A., Tait, S., Durie, L., Stiles, A. and Harvey, J. (2005) *An Evaluation of the Safer Locals Programme*, London: Home Office.

Liebling, A. and Ward, T. (1995) 'Prison doctors and prison suicide research', in R. Cresse, W. F. Bynum and J. Bearn (eds) *The Health of Prisoners: Historical essays*, Atlanta, GA: Editions Rodopi.

Lloyd, C. (1990) *Suicide and Self-injury in Prison: A literature review*, Research Study No. 115, London: Home Office.

Loucks, N. (1998) *HMP Cornton Vale: Research into drugs and alcohol, violence and bullying, suicide and self-injury, and backgrounds of abuse*, Occasional Paper No. 1, Edinburgh: Scottish Prison Service.

Lucas, J.R. (1980) *On Justice*, Oxford: Clarendon Press.

Ludlow, A., Schmidt, B., Akoensi, T., Liebling, A., Giacomantonio, C. and Sutherland, A. (2015) '*Self-inflicted Deaths in NOMS*': *Custody amongst 18–24 Year Olds: Staff experience, knowledge and views*, study commissioned by Harris Review.

McGurk, B.J. and McDougal, C. (1986) *The Prevention of Bullying among Incarcerated Delinquents*, DPS Report, ser. 11, no. 114, London: Directorate of Psychology Services.

Mackenzie, N., Oram, C. and Borrill, J. (2003) 'Self-inflicted deaths of women in custody', *British Journal of Forensic Practice* 5(1): 27–35.

Maltsberger, J.T. and Goldblatt, M.J. (1996) *Essential Papers on Suicide*, New York: New York University Press.

Margalit, A. (1996) *The Decent Society*, Cambridge, MA: Harvard University Press.

Ministry of Justice (2014) *Safety in Custody Statistics England and Wales: Deaths in custody to September 2014*, London: Ministry of Justice.

Morgan, H.G. (1979) *Deathwishes: The understanding and management of deliberate self-harm*, Chichester: Wiley.

Morgan, R. (1997) 'Imprisonment: current concerns and a brief history', in M. MacGuire, R. Morgan and R. Reiner (eds) *The Oxford Handbook of Criminology*, Oxford: Oxford University Press.

Narey, M. (2002a) 'Prevention programme leads to drop in prison suicides', Prison Service website, www.hmprisonservice.gov.uk (accessed 7 January 2002).

Narey, M. (2002b) *Speech to the Prison Service Conference 2002*.

NOMS (National Offender Management Service) (2011) *Prison Service Instruction PSI 64/2011 Management of Prisoners at Risk of Harm to Self, to Others and from Others (Safer Custody)*, London: Ministry of Justice.

Paykel, E.S., Myers, J.K. and Lindenthal, J.J. (1974) 'Suicidal feelings in the general population: a prevalence study', *British Journal of Psychiatry* 124: 460–469.

Pembroke, L.R. (2007) 'Harm minimisation: limiting the damage of self-injury', in S. Warner and H. Spandler (eds) *Beyond Fear and Control: Working with young people who self-harm*, Herefordshire: PCCS Books.

Phillips, M. (1986) *Suicide and Attempted Suicide in Brixton Prison*, London: Directorate of Psychological Services Report.

Power, K., Swanson, V., Luke, R., Jackson, C. and Biggam, F. (2003) *Act and Care: Evaluation of the revised SPS suicide risk management strategy*, Occasional Paper Series 01/2002, Anxiety and Stress Research Centre, University of Stirling.

Prison Service (2003) *Order 2700 Suicide and Self-harm Prevention*, London: Prison Service.

Prisons and Probation Ombudsman (2014) *Learning from PPO Investigations: Risk factors in self-inflicted deaths in prisons*, London: PPO.

Rabe, K. (2012) 'Prison structure, inmate mortality and suicide risk in Europe', *International Journal of Law and Psychiatry* 35(3): 222–230.

Rivlin, A., Hawton, K., Marzano, L. and Fazel, S. (2010) 'Psychiatric disorders in male prisoners who made near-lethal suicide attempts: case-control study', *British Journal of Psychiatry* 197(4): 313–319.

Rock, P. (1996) *Reconstructing a Women's Prison: The Holloway Redevelopment Project, 1968–88*, New York: Clarendon Press.

Royal College of Psychiatrists (2002) *Suicide in Prison, Council Report CR99*, London: Royal College of Psychiatrists.

Rutter, H. and Smith, D. (1995) *Psychosocial Problems in Young People: Time trends and their causes*, Chichester: Wiley & Sons.

Safer Custody Group (2002) *Safer Custody Report for 2001: Self-inflicted deaths in prison service custody*, London: HM Prison Service.

Sainsbury, R. (1988) 'Suicide prevention: an overview', in H.G. Morgan (ed.) *The Clinical Management of Suicide Risk*, London: Royal Society of Medicine Press.

Sandler, M. and Coles, D. (2008) *Dying on the Inside: Examining women's deaths in prison*, London: INQUEST.

Sapsford, R. (1983) *Life Sentence Prisoners*, Milton Keynes: Open University Press.

Scottish Home and Health Department (1985) *Report of the Review of Suicide Precautions at H.M. Detention Centre and Young Offenders Institution Glenochil*, Edinburgh: HMSO.

Shaw, J., Baker, D., Hunt, I., Moloney, A. and Appleby, L. (2004) 'Suicide by prisoners: national clinical survey', *British Journal of Psychiatry* 184(3): 263–267.

Shaw, J., Wainwright, V., Webb, R., Appleby, L., Piper, M., Rees, J. and Elder, R. (2013) *National Study of Self-inflicted Deaths by Prisoners 2008–2010*, University of Manchester.

Shaw, S.N. (2002) 'Shifting conversations on girls' and women's self-injury: an analysis of the clinical literature in historical context', *Feminism & Psychology* 12(2): 191–219.

Shepherd, S. (1991) *A Brief Group Cognitive-Behavioural Intervention for Anxiety and Depression with Young Offenders in Custody*, MSc thesis, Birkbeck College, London.

Shine, J., Wilson, R. and Hammond, D. (1990) 'Understanding and controlling violence in a long-term young offender institution', in N.L. Fludger and I.R. Simmons (eds) *Proceedings from Psychologists Conference 1989, Directorate of Psychological Services Report 1/34*, London: Home Office, Prison Department.

Skegg, K. and Cox, B. (1993) 'Suicide in custody – occurrence in Maori and non-Maori New Zealanders', *New Zealand Medical Journal* 106(948): 1–3.

Smalley, H. (1911) 'Report by the medical inspector', in *Report by the Prison Commissioners*, London: HMSO.

Smyth, N.J., Ivanoff, A. and Jang, S.J. (1994) 'Changes in psychological maladaptation among inmate parasuicides', *Criminal Justice and Behavior* 21: 357–365.

Snow, L. (2002) 'Prisoners' motives for self-injury and attempted suicide', *British Journal of Forensic Practice* 4(4): 18–29.

Sparks, R. and Bottoms, A.E. (1995) 'Legitimacy and order in prisons', *British Journal of Sociology* 46 (1): 45–62.

Stengel, E. (1971) 'Suicide in Prison: The gesture and the risk', *Prison Service Journal* 2: 13–14.

Stephens, J. (1987) 'Cheap thrills and humble pie: the sdolescence of female suicide attempters', *Suicide and Life-Threatening Behaviour* 12(2): 107–118.

Sykes, G. (1958) *The Society of Captives*, Princeton, NJ: Princeton University Press.

Toch, H. (1975) *Men in Crisis: Human breakdowns in prisons*, New York: Aldine.

Topp, D.O. (1979) 'Suicide in prison', *British Journal of Criminology* 143: 24–27.

Towl, G. (1999) 'Self-inflicted deaths in prisons in England and Wales from 1988 to 1996', in G. Towl, M. McHugh and D. Jones (eds) *Suicides in Prisons: Research, policy and practice*, Brighton: Pavilion Publishing.

Tumim, S. (1990) *Report of a Review by Her Majesty's Chief Inspector of Prisons for England and Wales of Suicide and Self-Harm in Prison Service Establishments in England and Wales*, London: HM Stationery Office.

Völlm, B. and Dolan, M. (2009) 'Self-harm among UK female prisoners: a cross-sectional study', *Journal of Forensic Psychiatry and Psychology* 20(5): 741–751.

Walker, N. (1987) 'The unwanted effects of long-term imprisonment', in A.E. Bottoms and R. Light (eds) *Problems of Long-term Imprisonment*, Gower: Aldershot.

Walmsley, R., Howard, L. and White, S. (1992) *The National Prison Survey 1991: Main findings*, London: HM Stationery Office.

Ward, T. and Mann, R. (2003) 'Good lives and the rehabilitation of sex offenders: a positive approach to treatment', in A. Linley and S. Joseph (eds) *Positive Psychology in Practice*, Hoboken, NJ: John Wiley and Sons.

Ward, T. and Stewart, C.A. (2003) 'Criminogenic needs and human needs: a theoretical model', *Psychology, Crime, and Law* 9: 125–143.

West, D. (1967) *Murder Followed by Suicide: An inquiry carried out for the Institute of Criminology*, Cambridge, MA: Harvard University Press.

Wicks, R.J. (1974) 'Suicidal manipulators in the penal setting', *Chitty's Law Journal* 22(7): 249–250.

Wilkins, J. and Coid, J. (1991) 'Self-mutilation in female remanded prisoners. An indicator of severe pathology', *Criminal Behaviour and Mental Health* 1: 247–267.

Zamble, E. and Porporino, F.J. (1988) *Coping, Behavior, and Adaptation in Prison Inmates*, New York and Berlin: Springer-Verlag.

Zamble, E. and Quinsey, V.L. (1997) *The Criminal Recidivism Process*, Cambridge: Cambridge University Press.

Chapter 14

Sex offenders in prison

Ruth E. Mann

Introduction

Sex offenders warrant special consideration in a book about prisons because in many ways they have a unique experience of imprisonment. They are also a population for whom prison authorities have to make special provisions. In this chapter, primarily based on research from England and Wales, and referring to male sex offenders aged over 18, I will discuss some of the reasons why sex offenders have become a separate subgroup within the prison population; how their experiences are different; and why they present particular dilemmas for prison managers and policymakers.

Criminal justice systems are becoming increasingly committed to evidence-based policymaking. In the case of sex offenders, however, it can be hard to cut a swathe through the understandable public outrage about sex offending to reach an unbiased evidence position. Indeed, realistically, policymaking cannot always be purely evidence based. Public policy must also be acceptable to the public and thus issues other than academic evidence must be taken into account. Furthermore, this chapter will demonstrate that there are many aspects of sex offender management where limited or no evidence exists, or where the evidence is so inconsistent that it is not possible to draw confident conclusions about the best policy to implement.

The number and proportion of sex offenders in prison is rising

In 1981, there were just 1,110 convicted sex offenders in prison, making up 4% of the prison population. By 1990, when national structured treatment programmes were first introduced, the number had risen to over 3,000, and the proportion to 7% (Sampson 1994). In 2000, the proportion of sex offenders in prison reached 10%, and by the end of September 2014 sex offenders made up 16% of the prison population, with the total figure at 11,119 (Ministry of Justice 2014a).

In the *Story of the Prison Population 2003–2012*, the Ministry of Justice (2013) for England and Wales describes and accounts for the major changes to the size and nature of the prison population since the turn of the century. Over this period, the prison population almost doubled, rising to over 86,000. The growth was due to both a larger number of people being sentenced to prison, and an increase in the length of prison sentences. In particular, the number of sex offenders increased dramatically during this period, with an increase of 31% between 2004 and 2011 as a result of the Sexual Offences Act 2003. The average sentence length for sex offenders also increased during this period by over 13 months. Indeed, in just one year, from 2012 to 2013, the average custodial sentence length for sexual offenders rose from 54.5 months to 59.1 months (Ministry of Justice 2014c). The Prison Service has never before had to handle so many sex offenders, and has had to find the resources for assessing and managing them from within existing budgets, which have themselves been subject to reductions as part of a pattern of wider extensive savings required from public service organizations.

In this chapter I will focus on three issues that are of particular interest to the management of sex offenders in prison: the nature of their risk, the hostility that they face because of the nature of their offending, and the uncertainty about what constitutes effective treatment.

Sex offenders present a paradox of an extremely low likelihood of reoffending but a high risk of harm

Compared with all offender types other than those convicted of fraud, sex offenders have lower reconviction rates (Ministry of Justice 2014b). In the 12 months ending September 2012, 13.2% of convicted adult sex offenders committed a proven reoffence within one year (note this figure is *any* reoffence, not *sexual* reoffences; comparable data are not available on sexual offence outcomes alone). This compares with, for example, a 20% reoffending rate for people convicted of violent reoffending, 35% for people convicted of robbery, and 41% for people convicted of theft. Reoffending rates have remained fairly stable for most offending types including sexual offending, with the exception of robbery where the rate has decreased (see Figure 14.1).

Ministry of Justice reoffending rates, however, do not specify the nature of reoffending. When trying to understand the risk presented by sexual offenders, the rate of further

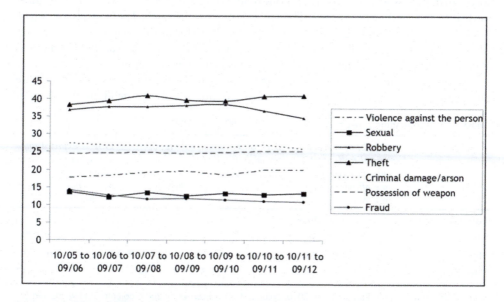

Figure 14.1 Reconviction rates by index offence, 2005–12
(Data drawn from Ministry of Justice 2014b)

proven *sexual* offences is of particular interest. These rates can be estimated from studies of sexual recidivism prediction tools. For instance, Barnett, Wakeling and Howard (2010) published a validation study of the prediction tool Risk Matrix 2000, which is the tool currently used across prison, probation and police in England and Wales to assess the likelihood of sexual reconviction for convicted sex offenders. In this study, with a total sample size of almost 5,000 sexual offenders, the authors reported an overall sexual reoffending rate of 2.2% (95% confidence interval 1.8–2.7) after two years following release from prison, rising to 5.5% after four years (although the sample was much smaller for the longer follow-up). The sample for this study, however, was probably not entirely representative of all sexual offenders released from prison, because it was restricted only to sex offenders who had completed a treatment programme or who had a full Offender Assessment System (OASys) assessment.

Howard and Barnett (2014) described sexual reoffending rates for an even larger and more representative sample of almost 15,000 sex offenders in a validation study of a new sexual offending prediction tool, the OASys Sexual Predictor (OSP). Howard and Barnett reported reoffending rates, over an average of 37.3 months, for four types of sexual reoffending as follows: contact sexual offending against an adult 1.1%, contact sexual offending against a child 0.7%, paraphilic offending (offences related to unusual sexual interests such as voyeurism, exhibitionism or bestiality) 1.1%, and convictions for possessing indecent images 0.8%.

Studies such as the RM2000 and OSP validations also confirm that it is possible to place sex offenders reliably into bands that reflect different levels of likelihood of reoffending. The advantage of this sort of grouping is that it helps both policymakers and practitioners decide how to allocate scarce resources. If the average sexual reoffending rate is 2% after two years, banding can identify the offenders whose predicted rate is lower than this, as well as some for whom reoffending is much more likely. For example, both RM2000 and OSP allocate offenders to one of four bands. These bands are usually referred to as 'risk bands' but it should be noted that risk in this usage means only *likelihood* of reoffending, and does not take account of any differences in expected harmfulness. Reoffending rates (actual for RM2000, predicted for OSP) are shown in Table 14.1.

Sex offenders are often believed to have very high reoffending rates. Yet the figures above show that, on average, sex offenders do not usually reoffend in the short to

Table 14.1 Reoffending rates by risk band for RM2000 and OSP

Risk band	RM2000 – actual sexual reoffending after two years (% of sex offenders in this risk band)	RM2000 – actual sexual reoffending after five years*	RM2000 – actual sexual reoffending after 19 years*	OSP – expected contact sexual reoffending after two years (% of sex offenders in this risk band)
Low	0.6 (17%)	0.7	8.0	0.4 (26%)
Medium	1.5 (50%)	2.8	18.1	1.0 (37%)
High	3.3 (26%)	9.0	40.5	2.0 (29%)
Very high	7.2 (7%)	27.3	60.0	4.6 (8%)

Source: Columns 2 and 3: Barnett et al. 2010; column 4: Thornton et al. 2003; column 5: Howard and Barnett 2014.

Note: * Caution: small sample size.

medium term (under five years). Note that OSP outcomes are not directly comparable with RM2000 outcomes but are presented alongside in order to illustrate their different approaches. First, the predicted reoffending rates for OSP are lower than reoffending rates found with RM2000 because OSP is optimized to predict contact sexual reoffending, which occurs at a lower frequency than non-contact sexual offending such as exhibitionism. Second, the rates in this table are estimated rates for OSP, but actual rates for RM2000. Taking these differences into account, it is possible to conclude that only a small percentage of convicted sex offenders (less than 10%) are at any appreciable risk of further proven sexual reoffending within two years of release from prison. Furthermore, it is apparent that the separation between the risk bands becomes more evident as time passes, and the conventional labels for risk bands make most sense only when the long-term reoffending rates are considered. That is, one might not consider that a 7% reoffending rate after two years warrants the label 'very high risk', but this seems a more acceptable label if the sexual reoffending rate is 60% after 19 years.

Hanson (2014) has argued that some sex offenders present such an extremely low risk of sexual reoffending that policymakers should question the need to direct specialized treatment resources towards them. Hanson argued that where the risk of sexual (re)offending is no greater for a convicted sex offender than it is for a member of the general population, or for a convicted non-sex offender, it is illogical to treat the offender as if he is at special risk of further sexual offending. Indeed, to build on Hanson's argument, it may actually be damaging to do so. There is some evidence to suggest that not only do low-risk sex offenders not benefit from intensive treatment programmes, but that such programmes can actually be iatrogenic for this group, resulting in higher reconviction rates (Wakeling et al. 2012; Lovins et al. 2009). It could be, for instance, that placing a low-risk offender into a treatment programme changes his self-identity, so that he begins to label himself as more deviant than he actually is. Additionally or alternatively, it could be that where low-risk offenders are mixed with higher-risk offenders in a treatment programme there is a deviancy training effect (Dodge et al. 2006), where low-risk offenders begin to see more deviant behaviour as normative or even desirable.

Sex offenders therefore present a paradox for criminal justice policymakers. They are very unlikely to reoffend but the nature of their offending is a matter of considerable public concern: sex offending is both highly traumatic and highly politicized. It would not be appropriate for policymakers to ignore the potential for harm in this group, but on the other hand, it is also inappropriate to spend public funds on services that are counterproductive, no matter how intuitive and appealing they seem.

Sex offenders experience imprisonment differently

It is no secret that sex offenders in prison suffer both verbal and physical abuse from other non-sex offender prisoners. In a study conducted during the 1960s, Priestley (1980) described what he called the 'scapegoating' of sex offenders in prison; placing them at the bottom of the hierarchy of offenders, with no 'claim to ties of affinity [with other prisoners], either of motive or of common hardship' (ibid.: 17). Priestley described a wide range of ways in which sex offenders were identified, targeted and shunned by other prisoners. In 1994, Sampson documented a similar range of forms of abuse directed at sex offenders by other prisoners, including persistent use of abusive labels such as 'nonce' and 'beast', food and drink being adulterated with insects and bodily fluids, and physical and sexual violence. Sampson also recorded how sex offenders have been particularly targeted during episodes of riot and disorder, such as the Strangeways riot in April 1990 when one remand prisoner, accused of sexual offences, was so badly beaten that he died in hospital. In their 2013 report (of a study actually conducted in 2002), Mann, Webster, Wakeling and Keylock found that 63% of their sex offender sample reported having had experiences in prison because of the nature of their conviction that led to them feeling unsafe. Their experiences included being belittled and humiliated by staff, being verbally abused by other prisoners, and being subjected to physical violence.

Sex offenders in prisons in England and Wales, and many other jurisdictions, face two options in terms of their location. They can opt to be located in a Vulnerable Prisoner Unit (VPU) where their fellow prisoners are also sex offenders or other prisoners deemed vulnerable for reasons such as poor coping or debt. Or they can remain on 'normal location', where their fellow prisoners are rarely sex offenders. For those who opt for normal location, they can survive either by lying about their crime and claiming to be a non-sex offender, by denying their guilt, or by 'fronting it out' (Sampson 1994) using bodily strength and physical aggression to protect themselves.

VPUs (also sometimes called Rule 43 Units, after the prison rule that allows prisoners to opt to be held separately from others for their own protection) originate from the mid-1960s (Priestley 1980). Previously, prisoners seeking protection from others were held in complete isolation, but in 1965 a wing at Strangeways prison in Manchester experimented by holding a number of sex offenders together and allowing them to mix with each other. However, because the prisoners on this wing were still exposed to taunts and threats from other prisoners during movement about the prison, a decision was taken to set aside a whole prison for this population and, consequently, in 1966 the sex offenders from Manchester were transferred to Shepton Mallet, where they formed approximately two thirds of the prison's population (the other third comprised informers). Priestley's research, conducted in Shepton Mallet during the late 1960s, showed that to some extent the experiment was successful. At least sex offenders were no longer expected to serve their sentences in complete isolation: 'Clearly, so far as the Forty Threes themselves are concerned, places like Shepton Mallet and Reading and Gloucester are preferable to being left in a helpless "diaspora" in local prisons around the country' (Priestley 1980: 145). Furthermore, the grouping of sex offenders in one place enabled people in more welfare-oriented staff roles to begin to identify patterns in offending behaviour: an opportunity which over time has developed into the rich field of research that exists today.

However, despite these advantages, Priestley considered that sex offender units were simply another way to scapegoat sex offenders, which in some ways enabled the hostility against them to be expressed more systematically. These sorts of concerns were shared by Sampson (1994), who repeated a chief inspector of prisons' view that the segregation of sex offenders constituted a 'prejudice against the weak and inadequate' (Prison Reform Trust 1989).

Priestley (1980) correctly predicted that the practice of segregating sex offenders to separate prisons would increase. Sex offenders continue to this day to be mainly located in separate units. At the end of 2014, six prisons in England and Wales held a population almost entirely of sex offenders. Nine further prisons had capacity to hold over 400 sex offenders each, and a further 20 prisons had capacity to hold between 150 and 400 sex offenders each. Hence, sex offenders in prison in England and Wales are mainly residing together in units or prisons where they are separated from prisoners convicted of non-sex offences. The risks and benefits of such separate units have been the subject of intense discussion for many years. Some of the arguments for and against such units are summarized below.

Disadvantages of locating sex offenders in segregated prison units

In 1994, Sampson, then deputy director of the Prison Reform Trust, argued that VPUs provided more restricted regimes to main location prison wings, and that this policy exacerbated the danger that sex offenders present:

> The endless hours many of them will spend in their cells leaves them little to think about other than their offences, and little to do other than to masturbate to their fantasies.
> (Sampson 1994: 92)

Furthermore, Sampson was concerned that there is a danger that when large numbers of sex offenders are held in prison together, this will foster networking, where prisoners make plans to meet after release and share future victims or commit sexual offences together:

> Rule 43 ... inevitably fosters the development of rings of sexual abusers. Some sex offenders have reported that paedophile information is freely exchanged in prison and that the court transcripts of sexual abuse cases are circulated as pornography.
> (Sampson 1994: 92)

However, 20 years on, not all of Sampson's criticisms have been borne out. For example, although few research studies have examined networking among sex offenders in prison, the studies that do exist have uncovered only limited evidence. For example, Smallbone and Wortley (2000) surveyed 182 Australian child molesters in prison. Within the wide scope of this survey, they asked six questions about the extent to which participants had taken part in conversations with other sexual offenders that might enhance their offending capacity. They found 'some evidence of problematic prison-based networking activity' (ibid.: 32) but 'exchange of information in prison was reported generally to be low' (ibid.: xiv). About one-third of intra-familial and extra-familial child molesters had spoken to others in prison about child sexual offending outside a treatment context (which does not necessarily imply networking). For those child molesters who had abused *both* inside and outside the family, this rose to two thirds. Some 4% of intra-familial offenders and 6% of extra-familial offenders had had other inmates ask them about how to access child pornography. This rose to 11% for those who had abused both inside and outside the family. Some 3% of intra-familial and 6% of extra-familial offenders had been provided with information about child pornography. This rose to 11% for those who had abused both inside and outside the family. None of the intra-familial and 4% of the extra-familial offenders had been provided with information about how to access a child for sexual abuse (the activity closest in definition to networking). This rose to 18% for those who had abused both inside and outside the family. None of the intra-familial, 10% of the extra-familial and 7% of the mixed offenders had been provided with information about clubs or organizations that distribute child pornography. Lastly, 1% of the intra-familial, none of the extra-familial and 11% of the mixed offenders had been provided with information about Internet sites concerned with child pornography.

Smallbone (personal communication) has commented that he concluded from this study that networking in prison was a lesser issue than popular belief would have it. However, he did raise a different concern: that another possible risk for sex offenders living together in a separate prison regime is that of sexual victimization taking place between prisoners. This possibility was not tested in the Smallbone and Wortley study.

Another angle from which networking could be established would be to examine the extent to which known co-offending involves offenders who met in prison. This avenue of exploration has not identified any examples of prison networking. For instance, Roxell's (2011) study of co-offending after imprisonment in Sweden identified no examples of sexual co-offenders. In the 1980s, "child sex rings" were popularly thought to be started by men who had met in prison, but Wild and Wynne's (1986) analysis of child sex rings in Leeds found only three rings that were led by two perpetrators; none of these perpetrators had met in prison. (In one case the perpetrators were brothers, in another they were neighbours, and in the third they had met in a pub.)

If anything, research into sex offender units in prison has identified an unwritten rule among inmates not to share offence information. Priestley (1980) described the prevailing approach on sex offender units as 'pluralistic ignorance of each other's misdeed' (ibid.: 67). Ievins and Crewe (2015), in their interviews with 22 sex offenders in a therapeutic prison in England, reached the same conclusion: the sex offenders in their sample actively avoided finding out what each other had done, because ignorance of crime details made it easier to accept people at face value, which was a necessary part of living together in sufficient harmony.

The extent of networking among imprisoned sex offenders may therefore be lower than feared, although research is very limited, and it is possible that the sensitivity of the topic means that conclusive research findings are difficult to achieve.

Another potential disadvantage of segregated units involves the way in which staff view the prisoners for whom they are responsible. Where prison units do not have a strong rehabilitative purpose, staff could hold prejudiced or hostile attitudes about sex offenders which may lead to systematic, unofficially sanctioned, poor treatment of prisoners. This was certainly the case in the first ever sex offender units (Priestley 1980), where staff were affronted to find that sex offenders were allowed normal prison privileges, and 'seemed afraid that the taint of the Rule might rub off on them; blighting their occupational futures and even wreaking havoc with their manhood' (ibid.: 111–112). In response, the staff routinely ensured that sex offenders' identities were made available to non-sex offenders, and turned a blind eye to violence, bullying and extortion.

Indeed, there are several studies that indicate that prison officers hold ambivalent, detached or punitive attitudes to sex offenders. For instance, Weekes, Pelletier and Beaudette (1995) found that correctional officers in Canada considered sex offenders to have many more negative characteristics than non-sex offenders, including being more dangerous, harmful, irrational, weak and aggressive. Furthermore, men who had offended against children were considered more immoral and mentally ill than men who had offended against adults. Mann et al. (2013), in their study of sex offenders in prison who refused treatment programmes, found that in some cases, prisoners had been offered a treatment place by a member of staff who did not provide any information about the nature of treatment, or who did not discuss the relevance of treatment to their individual needs, or worse, who made 'derogatory offers' (ibid.: 201).

Segregated units, therefore, are certainly not wholeheartedly advantageous options. The main drawbacks that have been identified are systematic ill treatment and an increased opportunity for networking. While the evidence for networking is limited, there is a stronger indication that staff who work with sex offenders may struggle to align the requirement that they treat prisoners professionally with the knowledge that wider society, both inside and outside prison gates, deplores sexual offenders.

Advantages of segregated units

A major argument for the value of the segregated approach is that such units confer a greater sense of safety for sex offenders, and this enables them to devote cognitive resources towards rehabilitation rather than survival. Some larger sex offender units have explicitly adopted a rehabilitative ethos, emphasizing to prisoners that the purpose of their time in prison is to plan and prepare to desist from offending after release. Blagden, Winder and Hames (2015) described the rehabilitative culture at one such prison from the viewpoint of staff and prisoners. The staff and prisoners were united in their perception that the purpose of this particular prison was to rehabilitate, a goal that they believed was achieved mainly through participation in offence-focused treatment programmes. All prisoner participants in the study felt safe in the prison and their sense of safety contributed to them being able to address other aspects of themselves (e.g. those related to their offending behaviour), which previously they did not have the 'headspace' to deal with. The reduction in anxiety about their physical safety gave participants more cognitive capacity to contemplate psychological change. The prisoners in this study also felt that staff provided validation of their behaviour changes and treated them as human beings. Both staff and prisoners reported 'incremental implicit theories' of behaviour change – that is, the belief that people can change criminal behaviour rather than the belief that criminality is a fixed trait. There were some differences between prisoners and staff: staff evaluated the prison as more safe and therapeutic than prisoners (mirroring findings in the wider prison climate research), and scored lower than prisoners on a measure of attitudes to sex offenders (Hogue 1994), although their scores were still among the highest found in the literature.

Ievins and Crewe (2015) interviewed 22 sex offenders in the same treatment-oriented prison as that studied by Blagden et al. Their participants confirmed the greater sense of safety that they experienced in this prison compared with the prisons they had lived in previously: 'Whether they had been on mainstream wings or on a VPU, interviewees recounted frequent and frightening experiences of violence, fear and victimisation in their previous institutions. In comparison, coming to Whatton felt like a "ton weight lifted off your shoulders"' (ibid.: 10).

Both Blagden et al.'s and Ievins and Crewe's studies took place in a fairly unique rehabilitative regime and, as such, their findings do not necessarily generalize to prison sex offender units that are not so focused on rehabilitation. We cannot be sure that sex offenders in all segregated units would feel as safe as they reported feeling in these two studies, nor that they would use 'headspace' to reflect upon their identities and offending behaviour.

In conclusion, there seem to be some benefits to sex offender units in prison that were not foreseen by Sampson (1994). These include principally the opportunity to create safer conditions, where sex offenders are not subject to abuse or humiliation, and can therefore devote 'headspace' to rehabilitation work. However, these features are not automatically found in sex offender units. The research that has taken place in HMP Whatton suggests that it takes time, effort and leadership to ensure that all staff and prisoners buy into the idea of a fully rehabilitative prison environment. Even when this is largely achieved, undercurrents of hierarchy and mutual distrust will remain (Ievins and Crewe 2015). When a sex offender unit does not have a clear rehabilitative ethos, it may still feel like a safer environment than an integrated location, but mistrust between prisoners may be stronger and staff, if not trained to work with sex offenders, may communicate hostile or other anti-rehabilitative attitudes.

Experiences of sex offenders in integrated units or prisons

There has been even less research into the experiences of sex offenders in integrated prisons. In a US study, Schwaebe (2005) described the strategies employed by sex offenders trying to survive within an 'integrated' regime (i.e. a regime where sex offenders and non-sex offenders were mixed). This study revealed that fellow inmates play a more significant role in prisoners' lives than do staff. Between prisoners, the force of inmate cohesion (solidarity, loyalty) is opposed by the force of inmate alienation (distrust, exploitation, harm). Of the two, alienation is a stronger force (Cordilia 1983) and sex offenders are a particularly vulnerable sub-population. It was clear that the sexual offenders in Schwaebe's study were highly aware of how stigmatized and unsafe they were. Their descriptions of their relationships with other prisoners frequently returned to the metaphor of 'predator and prey'. They reported learning quickly that they needed survival strategies. Three main strategies were described.

The first major survival strategy was to deny one's offending. The second was to establish a reputation as someone able to defend himself and who is prepared to use violence. This strategy was sometimes extended to becoming the harasser – shaming or exploiting others for being sex offenders – and in doing so, 'pass' as a non-sex offender. The third strategy involved engaging the protection of others, usually through paying extortion fees, although this strategy was seen as less desirable because debts could snowball fast. Schwaebe found that these strategies were employed even when sex offenders constitute the numerical majority, such is the force of the alienation associated with being a sexual offender, at the bottom of the pecking order of criminality.

Schwaebe's participants were all sex offenders participating in a sex offender treatment programme. They further described the delicate balance they had to achieve between surviving the daily life of prison using the strategies above, and meeting the requirements of treatment which involved disclosing details of their offending in the presence of other group members who, outside treatment, were engaged in exactly the same survival strategies. The contradictory requirements of denial outside the group and truthfulness inside the group are, presumably, not conducive to rehabilitation.

Denial: a response to the stigma of being a sex offender in prison?

The studies reviewed so far indicate rather clearly that sex offenders in prison are stigmatized by the nature of their crime. It is perhaps unsurprising, therefore, that a common mechanism for avoiding the stigma is to deny having committed the offence at all

(Blagden et al. 2011). To take this stance on one's offending can be termed 'categorical denial' and should be differentiated from minimization of offending (although the mechanisms underlying minimization may also include shame and stigma). Categorical denial is thought to be a more common state of affairs for prisoners convicted of sex offences than for other types of offender. The limited available evidence suggests that about one-third of imprisoned sex offenders categorically deny the offending (Hood et al. 2002; Kennedy and Grubin 1992). (Of course, the term 'in denial' implicitly communicates that all prisoners are guilty. While miscarriages of justice do occur, however, and without intending to diminish their awful implications for a prisoner when they do occur, it is unlikely that the extent of denial found in sex offenders is mainly down to false convictions.)

The 'problem' of denial among sex offenders has taxed the authorities for years. Official statements from bodies such as the Parole Board state that denial is not a barrier to release. Furthermore, denial does not seem to increase the risk of reoffending, despite intuitive assumptions otherwise, although research into denial and recidivism is complicated by overly broad definitions of both. Mann, Hanson and Thornton (2010), in their meta-analytic review of risk factors for sexual recidivism, categorized denial as 'unsupported with interesting exceptions'. This category included risk factors where 'the overall effect from meta-analysis is small and the confidence interval (CI) included zero, but where at least one large, credible study has found a significant effect, or where a significant effect has been found for subgroups of sexual offenders' (ibid.: 196). Denial was categorized in this way on the grounds that meta-analysis has not found that denial is associated with recidivism overall but some studies have found varied effects for subgroups of sex offenders. Mann et al. concluded that denial may contribute to recidivism risk in some ways for some people, but that this was certainly not true for everybody:

> It is likely that some aspects of denial are genuinely protective, [where] some offenders can be distancing themselves from their prior misdeeds ... Denial also can be criminogenic when it is motivated by the crass desire to avoid punishment or by a failure to recognize their transgression as sexual crimes.
>
> (Mann et al. 2010: 205–206)

However, categorical denial can frustrate staff (Blagden et al. 2011), impede psychological assessment and reduce engagement in rehabilitative activities. Many treatment programmes require participants to describe and analyse their offending patterns – requirements which cannot be met by categorical deniers. As a result, deniers do not 'fit' the usual pathway expected of sex offenders in prison, and their lack of fit can often be interpreted as a failure to reduce risk, or even a sign of increased risk.

Two responses to the 'problem' of denial have been reported in the literature. One approach is to attempt to persuade deniers to abandon their denial. A handful of studies have reported on programmes designed to achieve this aim, claiming some success at encouraging deniers to admit their offences (e.g. O'Donohue and Letourneau 1993; Schlank and Shaw 1996). Another response is to redesign the treatment approach to enable deniers to participate. Marshall and colleagues (e.g. Marshall et al. 2001) have been strong proponents of this approach, and their persistence in reporting successful engagement with deniers has strongly influenced recent thinking in the field of sex offender assessment and treatment.

There are also concerns that sex offenders 'in denial' will corrupt those who admit their offending, for instance by swaying the norm of a sex offender unit towards denial, which could reduce the numbers of sex offenders willing to engage in treatment. Consequently, over the years there have been occasional suggestions that some vulnerable prisoner units could be dedicated to deniers, allowing those prisoners who admit their offending to congregate in prisons that have a more rehabilitative ethos. However, the arguments for mixing deniers with admitters seem stronger than the arguments for holding them separately. First, a small-scale but enlightening study with sex offenders who had 'exited denial' indicated that deniers were encouraged to admit their offending by seeing that others around them did so without incurring greater hostility or rejection (Lord and Willmot 2004). Second, Marshall's work as above has encouraged criminal justice agencies to move away from traditional offence-oriented treatment programmes. His questioning of the accepted approach to treatment has inspired in-depth evidence reviews, which have found the basis of the offence-oriented approach to be more intuitive than empirical (e.g. Ware and Mann 2012; Mann and Barnett 2013). Removing the aspects of treatment programmes that require participants to describe their offending and 'take responsibility' for it would enable deniers and admitters to be treated together, reducing the extent to which denial is assumed to be problematic. As an added benefit, 'denial-friendly' programmes may also be more attractive to admitters, especially that group of admitters who currently refuse treatment programmes (Mann et al. 2012).

The impact of treatment programmes for sex offenders on reoffending has not been consistently established

Many jurisdictions provide treatment programmes in prisons designed to reduce recidivism in sexual offenders. In England and Wales, there has been a national treatment strategy since 1991, involving different intensities of treatment according to level of risk. The England and Wales programme, like most other prison programmes, is based on the cognitive-behavioural model, meaning that it aims to develop both *cognitions* and *behavioural skills* that should assist people in desisting from offending.

Over the last 30 years, the typical approach to sex offender treatment has evolved from the confrontational approach of the 1980s, as exemplified by Salter (1988), to an approach that pays more attention to the quality of therapeutic relationships (Marshall et al. 2003), focuses more on enhancing strengths rather than addressing deficits (Marshall et al. 2005), and most recently, pays less attention to notions of taking responsibility for the offence (Ware and Mann 2012) and developing victim empathy (Mann and Barnett 2013). We have also learned considerably more about the 'criminogenic needs' of sex offenders – that is, the factors associated with higher rates of recidivism that should form the focus of treatment programmes (Mann et al. 2010).

Despite these apparent advances, the impact of sex offender treatment programmes is still uncertain. The findings are so ambiguous that it is possible to interpret them positively or negatively, and one of the difficulties with the treatment outcome literature is that both interpretations have been strongly argued (e.g. Crighton and Towl 2007; Ho and Ross 2012; Mann et al. 2012; Marshall and Marshall 2010).

Four recent systematic reviews of treatment impact (Hanson et al. 2009; Dennis et al. 2012; Långström et al. 2013; and Schmucker and Losel 2015) continue this ambiguity to a certain extent, but overall point to a more disappointing effect for treatment than treatment providers hoped for. These four reviews adopted slightly different inclusion and outcome criteria (as set out in Table 14.2), which may explain the different conclusions of each study, but some patterns are also evident. In terms of treatment effectiveness, Hanson et al. found that sexual and general recidivism rates for treated sexual offenders were lower than for comparisons. However, they also stated that '[r]eviewers confining themselves to the better-quality, published studies, could reasonably conclude that there is no evidence that treatment reduces sexual offence recidivism' (Hanson et al. 2009: 881), and that it is certainly true that not all interventions reduce recidivism. For example, they found that more recent treatments were more effective than older treatments, and that programmes which adhered to all three of the Risk, Need and Responsivity (RNR) principles had consistently large effects, whereas programmes adhering to none of these principles had consistently low effects.

Långström et al. (2013: 4) emphasized the 'remarkable lack of quality research studies', concluding that, for adult offenders, there was insufficient evidence to determine if cognitive-behavioural treatment worked, and no evidence on which to determine if other psychological approaches, or a pharmacological approach, were effective.

Dennis et al. (2012: 2) shared the same concerns, stating that 'the inescapable conclusion is the need for further randomised controlled trials', and that without such evidence, 'society is lured into a false sense of security in the belief that once the individual has been treated, their risk of reoffending is reduced. Current available evidence does not support this belief'.

The reviews differed in their findings in relation to treatment setting. Hanson et al. found similar effects for treatment in prison as for other settings, but Schmucker and Losel found otherwise, with prison-based treatment failing to achieve a significant impact. Schmucker and Losel commented that their finding accorded with the general 'what works' literature (e.g. Andrews and Bonta 2010; Losel 2012), as well as with previous sex offender treatment reviews (e.g. Aos et al. 2006; Hall 1995).

Why are prison programmes less effective? Schmucker and Losel suggested that poorer outcomes in prison may occur because treatment in groups causes a contamination effect, or because prison settings do not enable transfer of learning to the real world, or because any treatment gains may be overshadowed by subsequent difficulties in resettlement. Some of the problems reviewed earlier in this chapter, such as inadequate rehabilitative cultures and hostile attitudes of prison staff to sex offenders, may also contribute to poorer outcomes from prison treatment programmes.

The finding that the prison setting is less conducive to effective treatment also accords with Parhar et al.'s (2008) meta-analysis of whether coerciveness affects treatment impact. Although this meta-analysis was not specific to sex offender treatment, it compared crime-related rehabilitation programmes more generally in prison and community settings according to their level of coerciveness. The outcome of the meta-analysis indicated that treatment programmes in prison were only effective when they were fully voluntary, whereas programmes delivered in community settings were effective at all levels of compulsion, including fully mandated programmes. Furthermore, the best effect in the prison setting – fully voluntary programmes – was only as good as the weakest effect in the community setting – fully mandated programmes.

Taken together, the four studies summarized in Table 14.2 indicate that it is a real challenge to deliver effective rehabilitation programmes in a prison setting for sex offenders. However, it seems unlikely that attempts to work with prisoners to reduce

Table 14.2 Recent systematic reviews of sex offender treatment effectiveness

Review	Number of studies in review	Inclusion criterion – population	Inclusion criterion – study design	Inclusion criterion – outcome variables	Differentiated outcomes for prison settings?
Hanson et al. 2009	23	Adolescents or adults convicted of sexually motivated offences against an identifiable victim	Outcome studies rated as good or weak according to a rating system. Accepted weaker studies than Dennis et al. and Långström et al., but all included studies had to have a comparison group	Recidivism outcome, including re-arrest, non-Criminal Justice System-recorded reoffending such as child protection records, and self-reported recidivism. Both general and sexual recidivism	10 of the 23 studies were in institutions, 11 in the community, two in both. Outcomes were analysed by setting: no difference in effect for institution or community
Dennis et al. 2012	10	Adults who have sexually offended or are at risk of offending	Randomized controlled trials	Any (three studies had outcomes not now considered criminogenic). Primary outcome was recidivism; secondary outcomes included cognitive distortions, sexual urges, anxiety and anger	Two of the ten studies were conducted in prisons. The majority were conducted in secure hospital settings. No analysis by setting
Långström et al. 2013	8	Sexual abusers of children (adults, adolescents, and children with sexual behaviour problems)	Randomized controlled trials and prospective observational studies	Broad reoffending criteria – convictions, arrests, breaches and self-reported offending	Three of the eight studies were reported as involving incarcerated populations. Analysis did not examine for differences between settings
Schmucker and Losel 2015	28	Males convicted of a sexual offence or who had committed acts of illegal sexual behaviour that would have led to conviction if prosecuted	Studies with equivalent treatment and control groups	Official measures of sexual recidivism from charges to incarceration but excluding self-reported offending and clinical outcomes	In comparison with treatment in the community and in hospitals, treatment in prison did not reveal a significant effect

reoffending rates are going to be abandoned. Not only does the public clearly expect imprisonment to have a rehabilitative effect, but many sex offenders are subject to parole board decisions in order to get released, and the parole board's prime concern is whether risk has been reduced. Were prisons not to offer any means of demonstrating risk reduction, they would be likely to be found to be failing in their public duty. Hence, a more productive response to research findings of weak effectiveness for prison programmes is to seek to understand what impeded the outcome. This is likely to be a combination of programme design (does the programme contain the right components?), implementation (is implementation faithful to the design?) and inadequacies in the supporting context for the programme (do other aspects of the prison context undermine the messages of the treatment programme, as suggested by Schwaebe 2005, and Mann 2009?).

The recent systematic reviews suggest that further advances are needed in order to provide effective sex offender treatment programmes in prison. First, programme content should be reviewed to ensure it is in line with the recommendations from the four systematic reviews, which were remarkably consistent:

> In practice, it is likely that both pharmacological and psychological therapies will need to be used in unison in order to obtain the greatest benefit.
>
> (Dennis et al. 2012: 28)

> The most ethically defensible position would be to assess the presence of treatable risk factors ... and offer individualised treatment. Ensure that the model complies with the risk, need and responsivity principles.
>
> (Långström et al. 2013: 6)

> Attention to the need principle would motivate the largest changes in the interventions given to sexual offenders ... Consequently it would be beneficial for treatment providers to carefully review their programmes to ensure that the treatment targets emphasised are those empirically linked to sexual recidivism.
>
> (Hanson et al. 2009: 886)

> Cognitive-behavioral and multisystemic treatment had larger effects than other approaches. In addition, studies with small samples, high-risk offenders, more individualized treatment, and good descriptive validity revealed better effects.
>
> (Schmucker and Losel 2014: 2)

These quotations emphasize that the most effective approach to sex offender treatment should be to combine psychological treatment with medical treatment, ensure that treatment is delivered in a flexible and individualized way, focus on higher-risk offenders, and ensure that the issues addressed are empirically associated with recidivism. Really, these recommendations do little more than strongly remind treatment providers of the importance of the Risk, Need and Responsivity principles (Andrews and Bonta 2010).

It is also important to understand the views that sex offenders themselves hold about the value of treatment programmes. On the one hand, many sex offenders report considerable benefits from attending programmes (e.g. Wakeling et al. 2005). On the other hand, a Canadian study reported that almost 50% of sex offenders did not express a desire for treatment (Langevin 2006), although this kind of survey has not been replicated in the UK. While sex offenders do report benefits from treatment, the benefits they report seem, curiously, to be in relation to the areas of treatment thought to be least evidence based, namely 'taking responsibility for offending' and 'victim empathy' (Levenson et al. 2009; Levenson et al. 2010; Wakeling et al. 2005). It is possible that sex offenders simply report benefits in the areas they perceive to be most important to treatment providers, either because they believe this is what people want to hear, or because these parts of treatment are delivered with the most enthusiasm and therefore have the greatest subjective impact (Mann and Barnett 2013). Indeed, treatment participants may be unaware of the aspects of a programme that benefit them the most – what Wilson (2011) calls the 'Don't Ask – Can't Tell' principle. Also important, particularly in understanding treatment take-up and refusal rates, is to identify what sex offenders know and believe about treatment programmes at the point when they are referred. To this end, Mann et al. (2010) asked 101 sex offenders across eight prisons what they understood about the effectiveness of treatment and what they believed would be the side effects of attending a treatment programme. Their findings confirmed that many sex offenders, particularly those who had refused treatment, did not feel informed about the nature, aims and effectiveness of treatment, felt that they saw negative changes in people who attended treatment, and felt that their status in prison would be diminished if they attended a treatment programme.

Conclusions: sex offenders in prison

Sex offenders face considerable public hostility and this stigma permeates throughout decision making about incarceration. If one were to accept a pure position that resources should follow risk (of reoffending), then sex offender treatment programmes would not exist, because the reoffending rates for this type of offending are very low. However, likelihood of reoffending is not the only consideration. The harm caused by sexual offending raises its profile and places more responsibility on prison authorities to provide effective solutions.

In this chapter I have argued that sex offenders in prison present many paradoxes. Often thought of as a high-risk type of offender, research indicates that sex offences are much more rarely repeated than thought. Whilst it is usually assumed that the general public seeks a punitive response to sex offenders, evidence suggests this type of response would be counterproductive, potentially increasing the intensity of many risk factors for recidivism such as loneliness, isolation, and hostility towards others. There is also no clear best answer to the question of whether sex offenders should be separated from other types of offender, or integrated, whilst they are in prison. For their safety, sex offenders in prisons tend not to be integrated with non-sex offenders, and the sense of increased safety they feel when separated from 'mainstream prisoners' seems to assist rehabilitation. However, separating them can further stigmatize them. Other risks of segregation, such as the danger of networking, may not be as endemic as feared, but research is difficult to conduct in such a sensitive area.

The evidence in support of prison treatment remains mixed, and this again presents a challenge for policymakers and prison staff. There is a public expectation that prison will rehabilitate sex offenders, but research suggests this is more difficult than might be assumed. This is not necessarily because sex offenders are resistant to rehabilitation (although some clearly are; Webster 2005), but also because the low base rate of sexual recidivism makes it hard to detect a treatment effect if one exists. Furthermore, the content of many treatment programmes may not be fully evidence based. Many programmes focus on encouraging participants to take responsibility for their offending and acquire better victim empathy. The rationale for such treatment components is anecdotal rather than empirical, and I have argued elsewhere (Maruna and Mann 2006; Mann and

Barnett 2013; Ware and Mann 2012) that better theory and evidence are needed to justify the time that is often spent in programmes on addressing these targets. Another part
of the case against the effectiveness of prison programmes might be that the prison context, being typically hostile to sexual offenders, limits the extent to which an individual
can safely embark upon psychological change (Schwaebe 1995). While critics of psychological
treatment abound (e.g. Ho 2015), evidence for alternative models is scarce, and so the
way forward seems likely to be one of small steps of change rather than an entirely new
model. It is likely, for example, that insights from the emerging ersearch field of desistance from sex offending will prompt adjustments to the widely accepted RNR approach.

This chapter has attempted to set out some of the issues faced by those charged with
protecting the public against further offending by people with convictions for sexual
offences. The harmful, indeed often shocking, nature of sex offending dominates public
discourse about the people who have committed this type of crime, and often also scientific discourse as well. Sex offenders have low recidivism rates, but in resource and
management terms they are given considerable attention by criminal justice policymakers. The safe, effective and efficient management of sex offenders in prison requires
that frontline and policy staff thread their way through a complex maze of morals, public
opinion, tradition and evidence. Yet, despite the existence of several international
research journals and professional organizations devoted to understanding sex offending,
we still have insufficient knowledge about the opportunities and threats presented by a
prison sentence for those convicted of sexual offending.

Bibliography

Andrews, D.A. and Bonta, J. (2010) *The Psychology of Criminal Conduct*, Abingdon: Routledge.
Aos, S., Miller, H.G. and Drake, E. (2006) *Evidence-based Adult Corrections Programs: What works and what does not*, Washington, DC: Washington State Institute for Public Policy.
Barnett, G.D., Wakeling, H.C. and Howard, P.D. (2010) 'An examination of the predictive validity of the Risk Matrix 2000 in England and Wales', *Sexual Abuse: A Journal of Research and Treatment*, 1079063210384274.
Blagden, N., Winder, B., Gregson, M. and Thorne, K. (2013) 'Working with denial in convicted sexual offenders: A qualitative analysis of treatment professionals' views and experiences and their implications for practice', *International Journal of Offender Therapy and Comparative Criminology* 57(3): 332–356.
Blagden, N., Winder, B. and Hames, C. (2015, in press) '"They treat us like human beings". Experiencing a therapeutic sex offenders' prison: Impact on prisoners and staff and implications for treatment', *International Journal of Offender Therapy and Comparative Criminology*.
Blagden, N.J., Winder, B., Thorne, K. and Gregson, M. (2011) '"No-one in the world would ever wanna speak to me again": An interpretative phenomenological analysis into convicted sexual offenders' accounts and experiences of maintaining and leaving denial', *Psychology, Crime & Law* 17(7): 563–585.
Cordilia, A. (1983) *The making of an inmate: Prison as a way of life*, Rochester, VT: Schenkman.
Crighton, D. and Towl, G. (2007) 'Experimental interventions with sex offenders: A brief review of their efficacy', *Evidence Based Mental Health* 10(2): 35–37.
Dennis, J.A., Khan, O., Ferriter, M., Huband, N., Powney, M.J. and Duggan, C. (2012) 'Psychological interventions for adults who have sexually offended or are at risk of offending', *Cochrane Database Syst Rev* 12.
Dodge, K.A., Dishion, T.J. and Lansford, J.E. (2006) *Deviant peer influences in programs for youth*, New York: Guilford Press.

Hall, G. C. N. (1995) 'Sexual offenders recidivism revisited: a meta-analysis of recent treatment studies' *Journal of Consulting and Clinical Psychology* 63(5): 802.

Hanson, R.K. (2014) *Developing Non-arbitrary Categories for Sexual Offender Risk Communication: Construct validity and the quantification of 'riskiness'*, Workshop presented at the 13th Conference of the International Association for the Treatment of Sexual Offenders, September, Porto, Portugal.

Hanson, R.K., Bourgon, G., Helmus, L. and Hodgson, S. (2009) 'The principles of effective correctional treatment also apply to sexual offenders: A meta-analysis', *Criminal Justice and Behavior* 36(9): 865–891.

Ho, D.K. and Ross, C.C. (2012) 'Cognitive behaviour therapy for sex offenders. Too good to be true?' *Criminal Behaviour and Mental Health* 22(1): 1–6.

Ho, D.K. and Ross, C.C. (2015) 'Ineffective Treatment of Sex Offenders Fails Victims' *BMJ: British Medical Journal* 350: h199.

Hogue, T.E. (1994) 'Training multi-disciplinary teams to work with sex offenders: Effects on staff attitudes', *Psychology, Crime and Law* 1(3): 227–235.

Hood, R., Shute, S., Feilzer, M. and Wilcox, A. (2002) 'Sex offenders emerging from long-term imprisonment. A study of their long-term reconviction rates and of Parole Board members' judgements of their risk', *British Journal of Criminology* 42(2): 371–394.

Howard, P.D. and Barnett, G. (2014) 'Development of a new sexual reoffending predictor', in R. Moore (ed.) *A compendium of research and analysis on the Offender Assessment System (OASys) 2009–2013*, London: Ministry of Justice.

Ievins, A. and Crewe, B. (2015, in press) '"Nobody's better than you, nobody's worse than you": Moral community among prisoners convicted of sexual offences', *Punishment and Society*.

Kennedy, H.G. and Grubin, D.H. (1992) 'Patterns of denial in sex offenders', *Psychological Medicine* 22(01): 191–196.

Langevin, R. (2006) 'Acceptance and completion of treatment among sex offenders', *International Journal of Offender Therapy and Comparative Criminology* 50(4): 402–417.

Långström, N., Enebrink, P., Laurén, E.M., Lindblom, J., Werkö, S. and Hanson, R.K. (2013) 'Preventing sexual abusers of children from reoffending: Systematic review of medical and psychological interventions', *BMJ: British Medical Journal* 347.

Levenson, J.S., Macgowan, M.J., Morin, J.W. and Cotter, L.P. (2009) 'Perceptions of sex offenders about treatment: Satisfaction and engagement in group therapy', *Sexual Abuse: A Journal of Research and Treatment* 21(1): 35–56.

Levenson, J.S., Prescott, D.S. and D'Amora, D.A. (2010) 'Sex offender treatment consumer satisfaction and engagement in therapy', *International Journal of Offender Therapy and Comparative Criminology* 54(3): 307–326.

Lord, A. and Willmot, P. (2004) 'The process of overcoming denial in sexual offenders', *Journal of Sexual Aggression* 10(1): 51–61.

Lösel, F. (2012) 'Offender Treatment and Rehabilitation: What works', in M. Maguire, R. Morgan and R. Reiner(eds) *The Oxford Handbook of Criminology*, Oxford: Oxford University Press, 986–1016.

Lovins, B., Lowenkamp, C.T. and Latessa, E.J. (2009) 'Applying the risk principle to sex offenders: Can treatment make some sex offenders worse?' *The Prison Journal* 89(3): 344–357.

Mann, R.E. (2009) 'Getting the context right for sex offender treatment', in D. Prescott (ed.) *Building motivation for change in sexual offenders*, Brandon, VT: Safer Society Press.

Mann, R.E. and Barnett, G. (2013) 'Victim empathy intervention with sexual offenders: Rehabilitation, punishment or correctional quackery?' *Sexual Abuse: A Journal of Research and Treatment* 25: 282–301.

Mann, R.E., Carter, A.J. and Wakeling, H.C. (2012) 'In defence of NOMS' point of view on sex offending treatment: A reply to Ho and Ross', *Criminal Behaviour and Mental Health* 22: 7–10.

Mann, R.E., Hanson, R.K. and Thornton, D. (2010) 'Assessing risk for sexual recidivism: Some proposals on the nature of psychologically meaningful risk factors', *Sexual Abuse: A Journal of Research and Treatment* 22: 172–190.

Mann, R.E., Webster, S.D., Wakeling, H.C. and Keylock, H. (2013) 'Why do sex offenders refuse treatment?' *Journal of Sexual Aggression* 19(2): 191–206.

Marshall, W.L., Fernandez, Y.M., Serran, G.A., Mulloy, R., Thornton, D., Mann, R.E. and Anderson, D. (2003) 'Process variables in the treatment of sexual offenders: A review of the relevant literature', *Aggression and Violent Behavior: A Review Journal* 8: 205–234.

Marshall, W.L. and Marshall, L.E. (2010) 'Can treatment be effective with sexual offenders or does it do harm? A response to Hanson (2010) and Rice (2010)', *Sexual Offender Treatment* 5(2).

Marshall, W.L., Thornton, D., Marshall, L.E., Fernandez, Y.M. and Mann, R.E. (2001) 'Treatment of sexual offenders who are in categorical denial: A pilot project', *Sexual Abuse: A Journal of Research and Treatment* 13: 205–215.

Marshall, W.L., Ward, T., Mann, R.E., Moulden, H., Fernandez, Y.M., Serran, G. and Marshall, L. (2005) 'Working positively with sexual offenders: Maximising the effectiveness of treatment', *Journal of Interpersonal Violence* 20: 1096–1114.

Maruna, S. and Mann, R.E. (2006) 'A fundamental attribution error? Rethinking cognitive distortions', *Legal and Criminological Psychology* 11: 155–177.

Ministry of Justice (2013) 'Story of the prison population 1993–2012 England and Wales', www. gov.uk.

Ministry of Justice (2014a) *Offender Management Atatistics Bulletin, England and Wales. Quarterly April–June 2014*, London: Ministry of Justice, www.gov.uk.

Ministry of Justice (2014b) *Proven Reoffending Statistics Quarterly Bulletin. October 2011–September 2012*, London: Ministry of Justice, www.gov.uk.

Ministry of Justice (2014c) *Criminal Justice Statistics 2013*, London: Ministry of Justice, www.gov. uk.

O'Donohue, W. and Letourneau, E. (1993) 'A brief group treatment for the modification of denial in child sexual abusers: Outcome and follow-up', *Child Abuse & Neglect* 17(2): 299–304.

Parhar, K.K., Wormith, J.S., Derkzen, D.M. and Beauregard, A.M. (2008) 'Offender coercion in treatment: A meta-analysis of effectiveness', *Criminal Justice and Behavior* 35(9): 1109–1135.

Priestley, P. (1980) *Community of Scapegoats: The segregation of sex offenders and informers in prison*, Oxford: Pergamon Press.

Prison Reform Trust (1989) *Sex Offenders in Prison*, London: Prison Reform Trust.

Roxell, L. (2011) 'Co-offending among prison inmates', *The Prison Journal* 91(3): 366–389.

Salter, A. (1988) *Treating Child Sex Offenders and Victims: A practical guide*, London: Sage.

Sampson, A. (1994) *Acts of Abuse: Sex offenders and the criminal justice system*, London: Routledge.

Schlank, A.M. and Shaw, T. (1996) 'Treating sexual offenders who deny their guilt: A pilot study', *Sexual Abuse: A Journal of Research and Treatment* 8(1): 17–23.

Schmucker, M. and Losel, F. (2015, in press) 'The effects of sexual offender treatment: An international meta-analysis of sound quality evaluations'.

Schwaebe, C. (2005) 'Learning to pass: sex offenders' strategies for establishing a viable identity in the prison general population', *International Journal of Offender Therapy and Comparative Criminology* 49(6): 614–625.

Smallbone, S. and Wortley, R.K. (2000) *Child Sexual Abuse in Queensland: Offender characteristics and modus operandi*, Queensland Crime Commission and Queensland Police Service.

Thornton, D., Mann, R., Webster, S., Blud, L., Travers, R., Friendship, C. and Erikson, M. (2003) 'Distinguishing and combining risks for sexual and violent recidivism', in R. Prentky, E. Janus, M. Seto and A.W. Burgess (eds) *Understanding and Managing Sexually Coercive Behaviour: Annals of the New York Academy of Science*, 989: 225–235.

Wakeling, H., Mann, R.E. and Carter, A.J. (2012) 'Are there any benefits in treating low risk sexual offenders?' *The Howard Journal of Criminal Justice* 51: 286–299.

Wakeling, H., Webster, S.D. and Mann, R.E. (2005) 'Sexual offenders' treatment experiences: A qualitative and quantitative investigation', *Journal of Sexual Aggression* 11: 171–186.

Ware, J. and Mann, R.E. (2012) 'How should "acceptance of responsibility" be addressed in sexual offending treatment programmes?' *Aggression and Violent Behavior* 17: 279–288.

Webster, S.D. (2005) 'Pathways to sexual offense recidivism following treatment: An examination of the Ward and Hudson self-regulation model of relapse', *Journal of Interpersonal Violence* 20(10): 1175–1196.

Weekes, J.R., Pelletier, G. and Beaudette, D. (1995) 'Correctional officers: How do they perceive sex offenders?' *International Journal of Offender Therapy and Comparative Criminology* 39(1): 55–61.

Wild, N.J. and Wynne, J.M. (1986) 'Child sex rings', *British Medical Journal* 293: 183–185.

Wilson, T.D. (2011) *Redirect: The surprising new science of psychological change*, London: Hachette.

Chapter 15

The prison officer

Helen Arnold

No longer can it be argued that the prison officer is abjectly neglected within research on prison life or that accounts of prison officer work are 'sociologically impoverished and deeply misleading' (Arnold et al. 2007: 471). Whilst much prison research remains focused on prisoners and their experience of imprisonment, the gap has narrowed in recent years with notable contributions describing and contextualizing the work of officers both in England and Wales and internationally (see for example the special issue of the *European Journal of Criminology*, November 2011; Crewe et al. 2011; Lerman and Page 2012; Scott 2012; and Jefferson 2007, 2014). It may not yet be possible to paint a complete and inclusive portrait of the prison officer or to submit an unqualified 'clear and viable vision of what being a prison officer means' (Hay and Sparks 1991: 7), but certainly more is known than previously about who prison officers are, what they do, and the centrality of their work within prisons. Prison officers are perhaps no longer the 'invisible ghosts of penality' (Liebling 2000: 337), and have been exposed as key regulators of the quality and purpose of confinement.

Despite the continuing materialization of prison officers within the literature, however, there are some aspects of their work that remain in the shadows. 'Talk', the use of discretion, the use of power and authority, the art of peacekeeping, the furnishing of care, emotion management and working personalities are all important components of the prison officer role; however, what it *means* to be a prison officer and to what extent these elements of the job are performed depend on, and therefore require a closer examination of, the more intrapersonal and psychological attributes of the prison officer – their self-conception as an officer, their sense of meaning and purpose, and their motivations, coping mechanisms, values, stresses and emotions. Understanding these facets will help our comprehension of how prison officer conduct embodies the prison regime (Liebling and Price 1999), and will identify the ways in which officers contribute to the moral climate and stated aims of imprisonment.

This chapter will, first, outline the nature and landscape of prison officer work. Second, it will describe the process of occupational socialization and the origins of an occupational identity in the context of prison officer selection and training. Based on prison officer testimonies, the third section will examine the ways in which officers conceptualize their job and find meaning and purpose within it. The fourth section will address the question of what makes a good prison officer, and will focus in particular on the emotional nature of prison work and the importance to the role of emotional intelligence. The final section of the chapter discusses in detail the use of humour as a coping technique. The chapter will end with some concluding comments and some suggestions for future research.

The nature of prison officer work

Since Gilbert's (1997: 50) claim that 'it is difficult to define what corrections officers do', a number of empirical studies have set out to redress this gap in penological knowledge (see further Crawley 2004; Arnold 2005; Tait 2011; Liebling et al. 2011). Prison work has been characterized as 'low visibility', and yet 'highly skilled' (Liebling and Price 1999), as 'complex' and 'varied' (Arnold et al. 2007), and as 'testing and specialised' (Liebling et al. 2011): as stated by Sparks et al. (1996: 60), prison sociology can no 'longer rest content with a depiction of the guards as merely shadowy figures, peripheral to the main action, who are just there as an inertial and conservative influence'. It is difficult to argue against the proposition that the prison officer performs a crucial role in the operation and administration of a prison: the modern prison officer is far from merely a turnkey or warder (see House of Commons Justice Committee 2009; *Prison Service Journal* 168, November 2006). Whilst maintaining security is undoubtedly a fundamental, unequivocal and significant aspect of any officer's job, officers are not just simply concerned with keeping prisoners securely in custody.

Scott (2006: 15), based on the work of Lombardo (1989: 61–66), suggests that the custodial tasks of an officer can be divided into four categories or functions: security, supervision, service and policing. These categories all suggest practical, rather than relational, characteristics of the job. Whilst acknowledging that undertaking a policing function is more complex than it may appear, and that the use of personal authority is 'the most significant strategy in the maintenance of penal order'[1] (Scott 2006: 17), Scott also proposes that 'the day of a prison officer is mainly interspersed with monotonous routines and long hours of boredom' (ibid.: 15). He states:

> The daily caretaking duties of the residential officer are largely mundane, such as unlocking prisoners, checking locks, bolts and bars, carrying out roll checks, dealing with prisoner requests or disciplinary offences, serving meals, supplying toilet rolls, changing the laundry, delivering the post, playing pool, watching television, reading the newspaper, talking with officers and prisoners, or drinking tea.
>
> (Scott 2006: 15)

Similarly, Bryans (2001: 156–157) states that although attempts have been made to enlarge and enrich the prison officer's job, they:

> are still required to do the basic routine custodial work: they continue to do the locking and unlocking, walking the landings and serving meals to prisoners. The systematic approach to these tasks ensures security and control in prison establishments and thus will remain a key part of prison officers' work.

Other scholars, however, have provided more nuanced accounts of officer work that intimate the importance of relationships and interpersonal interactions, of 'human service', decision making, and the use of power and authority. They have also suggested that these interactions are key determinants of order, control and rehabilitation, and the overall quality of life that prisoners experience. Liebling and Price (1999: 86), for example, stated that: 'Staff were gatekeepers, agents of criminal justice, peacemakers, instruments of change, and deliverers and interpreters of policy.' As well as being guardians, advocates and managers of prisoners, Liebling and Price noted that officers facilitated and mediated access to highly valued services, goods, activities and specialists, contact with families, and opportunities to progress. Moreover, officers' *approach* to their role set the tone on a wing, and affected outcomes for, and relationships between, prisoners. The role, self-concept and competence of prison officers shaped the prison experience and the quality of prison life in highly significant ways, and determined to a large extent the legitimacy of the experience in the eyes of prisoners. Crawley (2004: 95) claimed that 'in addition to their primarily custodial tasks ... the modern prison officer is also expected to change prisoners' behaviours and outlooks and to provide him or her with care'. This highlights the key relational dimensions of the prison officer role. The much-cited excerpt from the Home Office Control Review Committee report remains pertinent in any consideration of the role of the prison officer:[2]

> At the end of the day, nothing else that we can say will be as important as the general proposition that *relations between staff and prisoners are at the heart of the whole prison system* and that control and security flow from getting that relationship right. Prisons cannot be run by coercion: they depend on staff having a firm, confident and humane approach that enables them to maintain close contact with prisoners without abrasive confrontation.
>
> (Home Office 1984: para. 16)

As the two ever-present groups within a prison, and those who have the most frequent contact, a relationship – whether good or bad – will exist in some form between uniformed staff and prisoners.[3] It is not only control and security that result from this relationship but other responsibilities such as the provision of safety, well-being, care, support, and assisting prisoners in their rehabilitation.[4] The role of the officer 'as a key figure in reducing reoffending' (House of Commons 2009) relates in part to endorsing, validating, encouraging and facilitating more formal rehabilitative mechanisms, for example by helping in the delivery of accredited offending behaviour programmes or assisting the provision of education, training and pre-release courses. Yet officers contribute to rehabilitation in more subtle forms, as discussed below. As well as an illustration of the varied and complex nature of the work of a prison officer, the multifarious roles that have been attributed to the prison officer also belie their status as 'being in a (care-based) relationship' with those in their charge. Officers act 'in loco parentis', as mentors, counsellors, teachers, social workers, comedians, psychologists and police officers (Crawley 2004: 95). This range of roles is indicative both of the many personal qualities deemed apposite to do the job (as discussed below) and of the various means by which officers can have a positive influence on the lives of offenders. As advocated by a previous Chief Inspector of Prisons, '[p]risoners are people, not merely offenders; and the turning points in their lives are usually people, not just programmes or plans' (Owers 2006: 26).

The prison officer has increasingly been seen as a role model for prisoners, as an agent of change who, through his or her encounters with prisoners, has the opportunity to exhibit and promote pro-social behaviours and values. Trotter (2009: 142) argues that '[p]ro-social modelling is increasingly becoming recognised as a key skill in the supervision of offenders', and while he refers in the main to the work of probation officers, the relevance to the role of the prison officer is clear, particularly since their often enduring relationships with prisoners give them considerable opportunity to model and express views that support law-abiding lifestyles. Officers also have the opportunity to reinforce and reward pro-social actions, views and comments made by prisoners, including those that express a desire and belief in change, through 'setting an example' in their language, behaviours and attitudes (Arnold and Barnett-Page 2006).

Peacekeeping and maintaining order is another key role of the prison officer: 'what the guards do, and the manner in which they do it, is central to an understanding of "what type of order" (Young 1987: 99) the prison seeks to impose and its chances of "success" constructing it' (Sparks et al. 1996: 60). In their policing role, officers have a number of different power bases, or policing styles, and the different types of power available may be more or less successful in helping them to gain or maintain order (Hepburn 1985): too much power of the wrong sort can generate resistance and the full enforcement of the rules can undermine legitimacy and order (Liebling and Price 2001). Although the role of the prison officer is imbued with a legal power, officers tend to reject this mode of power, and the use of force or coercion, in favour of exercising more informal power and personal, rather than legal, authority. This can be described as a form of peacekeeping, whereby prison officers 'under-use their power to create a peaceful and safe environment' (Scott 2006: 14). So, rather than imposing the law, and enforcing rules to the letter, the prison officer uses his or her discretion to decide which rules to apply (often tacitly, using humour for example) and negotiates a series of accommodations with prisoners in order to maintain a reasonable and functioning social order and smooth the flow of prison life (Liebling and Price 2001). The best officers use informal strategies, are willing but not over-eager to use force, and use their discretion in order to get things done (Liebling and Price 2001). In doing so, officers 'perform the delicate art of peacekeeping' which is 'accomplished and re-accomplished through the diligent and skilled building of relationships with prisoners through talk and the under-use of the officer's powers' (Scott 2006: 17). As claimed by Reiner (1997: 997), then, prison work, like police work, sometimes requires 'the law' or 'rule enforcement' to be subordinated to the 'craft of governing social order'. To quote Liebling:

> What is distinctive about the work of prison officers is, first, the centrality of often enduring relationships to their work and, second, the harmonizing of welfare and discipline, or care and power. Prison officers negotiate their authority on a day-to-day basis with a sceptical and complex audience, through interaction and in a context in which enforcing all the rules 'by the book' would be impossible. This is an extremely tricky and inherently unstable business.
>
> (Liebling 2011: 485)

Thus, there is far more to prison officer work than 'common sense', the term that officers themselves often use to describe it. The nature of prison work is highly skilled, based on experience, fine judgement and the development of exceptionally good informal working strategies (Liebling 2009, cited in House of Commons Justice Committee 2009). In making their decisions, officers draw on unconscious but experience-laden knowledge, what Giddens (1984) calls 'practical consciousness'. Using the metaphor provided by Hay and Sparks (1991: 3): 'Like a footballer who can score a wonderful goal but not really describe how he did it, prison officers sometimes exercise social skills of great refinement and complexity without dwelling upon or articulating what they are doing.' The term 'jailcraft', which is often used to describe such skills, tends to underplay both the personal qualities and the key psychological and emotional components of the prison officer role, which the remainder of this chapter will discuss.

Occupational socialization and identity

Whilst the academic lens has increasingly focused on what prison officers *do*, there remains limited knowledge as to their values, beliefs, motivations and personality characteristics. For example, police research has suggested that recruits are more authoritarian, dogmatic and conservative than the general population (Colman and Gorman 1982) but there are no equivalent studies of prison officers. Given this lack of knowledge, it is difficult to ascertain the extent to which the collective occupational identity of prison officers originates in the imported characteristics of those people who are attracted to the job, or in forms of occupational socialization. The typical prison officer has been described as white British, male, aged between 30 and 40, and with around ten years of experience (Liebling and Price 2001). The vast majority of new officers have very little, if any, experience of working with offenders or in the criminal justice system; fewer prison officers enter the job from a background in the armed forces than in the past; more new entrant officers have completed further or higher education; and new entrant prison officers come from an extensive array of previous occupations. Many join as a result of recommendations from friends or family who suggest that they have the 'right' kind of personality, or as a result of changes in personal circumstances: for example, relocation, redundancy, or dissatisfaction with their current job. For others, the job of a prison officer captures a specific interest in working with offenders in the secure setting of a prison (see Arnold et al. 2007).

Overall, new officers join the service for two primary reasons: economic pragmatism and 'self–other actualization'. Economic pragmatism relates to the appealing terms and conditions of employment such as pay, job security, promotion prospects, pension, shift patterns, and locale. 'Self–other actualization' refers to the potential for personal growth and development and the opportunity to influence the personal growth and development of prisoners; it is about fulfilment and reflects a desire to make a difference. Regardless of their reasons, new officers seem to share a sense of self-efficacy: a belief that they have what it takes to do the job, to rise to the challenges presented to them and to accomplish the tasks required, even if they are unsure as to what these challenges and tasks are. However, there is little evidence that at the outset, prison officers constitute a homogeneous group in terms of temperament, personality or character.

There is a disparity in content and focus between prison officer selection, assessment and recruitment procedures and the entry-level training course for new recruits (see Crawley 2004; Arnold 2008; and Arnold et al. 2007, for more detailed descriptions of the recruitment process and the training course). Whilst the former processes are designed to evaluate a range of interpersonal, reasoning, leadership, teamwork and problem-solving skills (such as listening, assertiveness and resolving conflict), prison officer training tends to prioritize the security, supervisory and policing tasks of the officer's roles. The bulk of initial training is spent learning about either the practical tasks of maintaining security (such as searching and conducting roll checks) or the physical task of restraining prisoners safely and appropriately. When interpersonal skills are promoted, often they are done so in connection with the responsibility to maintain security – as part of the process of 'dynamic security' (Dunbar 1985). It can be argued, then, that in the early stages of occupational socialization, new officers are indoctrinated into a role that stresses security as the critical occupational value.

At the same time, acculturation during training involves becoming sensitized to the informal norms and values of the occupational culture. In particular, the focus on security leads to two outcomes that are central to the officer's occupational identity: loyalty and solidarity, and cynicism (distrust). The process of learning the complex and colleague-dependent techniques of Control and Restraint bonds and unites new officers more than any other aspect of the training course, providing a sense of cohesion and 'esprit de corps'. Meanwhile, the prominence of the theme of security reinforces the notion that relationships with prisoners are procedural and instrumental, promoting social distance and constructing prisoners as dangerous, difficult to manage, untrustworthy, violent, manipulative and disingenuous (Arnold 2008).

These two factors help to cement a kind of 'all for one and one for all' mentality, involving intense peer solidarity. This is expressed in terms of an unfailing willingness to 'be there' for other officers and to cover their back. Crawley and Crawley (2008: 138) suggest that prison officer solidarity is 'perhaps the most significant cultural norm prison officers are expected to observe', and arises directly from a sense of social isolation (including the sense of being 'the forgotten service'). Kauffman argues that the commitment to rushing to the scene of an incident 'is the most important positive responsibility of any officer: it is the norm on which officer solidarity is based, the foundation of their sense of brotherhood'. 'Always go to the aid of an officer in distress' is first on a list that constitutes an officer code (Kauffman 1988: 86). Officers who do not conform to this principle of conduct are considered a burden and a liability. The retelling of episodes where officers have dealt with particularly significant events of concerted indiscipline, use of force, or emergencies creates a form of collective meaning and esteem, and thus reinforces the importance of peer loyalty and solidarity.

Prison officers' insularity also stems from being socialized into a view that in order to maintain security it is prudent to be mistrustful of prisoners. As a result of undergoing training, as well as becoming more assertive, self-assured and confident, new officers also report becoming more observant, alert and watchful, more cynical, suspicious and mistrustful of people (Arnold 2005). They also develop a number of fears and concerns, particularly in terms of facing aggression, being assaulted, dealing with conflict and becoming 'conditioned' (manipulated by prisoners). The result is that a degree of fear is seen to be necessary in order to facilitate security, and that maintaining boundaries and emotional distance is imperative in order to minimize the possibility that the prison's security might be compromised. This results in over-caution, personal detachment and some aversion towards engaging with prisoners in more informal and proactive ways, or in ways that extend beyond meeting their basic needs (Arnold 2008). At the end of the training period, then, whilst most officers feel they have yet to become a 'proper' prison officer, it is possible to identify the beginnings of an occupational culture based in values such as security, protection, loyalty and mistrust. However, many officers retain their expectation that they are there to help prisoners, to care for them. The focus on security provides the foundation on which they are able to develop their own working personality (see Scott 2012; Crawley 2004) and to (learn to) practise and understand ways of making a difference.

Motivation, meaning and purpose

Over the last 40 years, since the emergence of the 'so-called rehabilitative ideal' (Bottoms 1990: 4), discussions of the prison officer role have inclined towards issues of role conflict where there has been an assumed incompatibility between security and reformative 'treatment' or rehabilitation. If the tasks of a prison officer are constructed dia-grammatically as a stratified pyramid (much like Maslow's 1954 'Hierarchy of Needs' model of human motivation; see also Lombardo 1989), at the base of this 'role hierarchy' would lie security (e.g. preventing escapes; upholding order and control). From initial training onwards, officers see security as their core purpose which logically underpins and facilitates other aspects of their role. Delivering the regime, providing domestic services, ensuring prisoners' entitlements and needs are identified and met, offering practical and emotional support, assisting prisoners through their sentence, and treating prisoners with decency, are all significant tasks but ones contingent upon the establishment and maintenance of security.[5]

> Everybody's main responsibility as a discipline officer is security, keeping them locked up. I don't think you'll get a different answer from anybody. Security will always be the number one priority. It's drummed into you from day one; security is the main objective, always has been.

For prison officers, the definition of security stretches to include safety: to provide a safe environment for both staff and prisoners. Officers refer to their 'duty of care' as a responsibility to keep prisoners alive and protect them from coming to harm (either from themselves or other prisoners). It is in this way that officers feel they 'look after' and care *for* prisoners (not *about* them) and treat them with humanity.

> The aim of the job is security really ... there's a humane way of doing it, and we have a duty of care ... they've been judged in court and their punishment is having their liberty taken away, and it's our job to make sure from a security point of view that they stay in here, they stay secure, they're not a threat to the public, and they're all still here at the end of the day, alive and kicking ... for as long as their sentence is. We don't want to lose anybody in prison, the aim is, security-wise, to keep them secure, keep them safe, keep them alive and that's what we all want to see.

However, there are times when the core operational tasks of an officer make evident a tension between security and care:

> On the night shift what do you do? On your wing there might be 20 or 25 pris-oners on an 'at risk' form and you have to check each of them regularly, like every 15 minutes, and you have to do the pegging[6] too and there isn't time in an hour to do both so it's pegging versus self-harm risks, you have to choose sometimes between either security or preservation of life.

Research on the occupational orientation of officers has reported that rehabilitation programmes are generally supported (Farkas 1999), that 'beliefs are less punitive than could be expected from the literature' (Shamir and Drory 1981: 233), and that 'most officers seek to enrich their work through a human services or rehabilitative orientation' (Cullen et al. 1989: 40). Despite the overriding task of security, there is a notable congruence between prison officers' talk of their responsibilities and the expectation formulated in the current Prison Service 'Statement of Purpose' (dating from 1988) that both custody and rehabilitation are the necessary objectives of prison.[7] The assimilation of the statement of purpose into the everyday lexicon of prison officers, which begins on the first day of entry-level training, accounts for the recurrence of what can be termed 'mission statement speak' when officers are asked to describe their job.

Prison officers, prisoners and managers recognize the numerous 'hats' that officers don in pursuit of security and control (custodian, supervisor, negotiator, peacekeeper, rule enforcer, disciplinarian), compared with those that reflect care and support (teacher, counsellor, mentor, parent, role model, provider). It requires balance and skill to adopt the appropriate persona depending on the presenting circumstances, and the myriad and sometimes conflicting role expectations can lead to role ambiguity. This ambiguity can result in a reversion to the 'basics' (or the 'bread and butter') of the job: security, regime delivery and (instrumental) relationships for dynamic security reasons. Officers find a sense of 'security in security'. They resort to a clear, actionable, short-term goal: reaching the end of the day without any major incidents, without any escapes, and without anybody coming to harm. Defaulting in this way to the rational minimum of keeping people in custody (securely and safely) provides clarity and coherence during times of uncertainty.

As new officers acclimatize to the realities of working life, their initial optimism can become subsumed by pragmatism and a sceptical attitude towards the efficacy of imprisonment in rehabilitating prisoners (Arnold 2005: 408). Officers frequently quote estimated reoffending rates and statistics, and, in local prisons in particular, they find visible 'proof' that prison fails in one of its aims by the fact that they repeatedly 'see the same faces' coming through the gates (see also Chan 2003). However, 'good' and experienced officers reflect on and redefine their sense of meaning at various points through their career, 'scaling down' their ambitions and finding value and fulfilment in less 'global' definitions of 'making a difference'. That is, they see their potential to influence prisoners' behaviours, attitudes or future prospects, and make efforts to address their immediate and tangible problems by providing practical help (such as allowing a phone call that would put a prisoner's mind at ease), listening and offering direction or, for example, giving educational assistance to an illiterate prisoner:

> I collected this bloke's silver [food] tray one day and he said 'Look at this!' and he showed me a children's book – only 25 pages, and he said 'I read that! I've read that!' Nothing else happened you know but 'this sentence I've learned to read that book'. I was fucking choked; I still get choked about that.

In these ways officers not only encourage and support prisoners' personal development but actively generate and deliver it. When officers discern the (often comparatively modest) results of their efforts they gain a sense of value from small ways of 'making a difference'.

The good prison officer: the role of emotional intelligence

Previous research has found that there exists a consensus amongst officers, managers and prisoners as to the characteristics and qualities of good, or role model, prison officers (Liebling and Price 2001; Arnold et al. 2007). The good prison officer is skilled at using their authority and discretion and at communicating known and consistent boundaries to prisoners; they have 'moral fibre', a 'professional orientation', an optimistic but realistic outlook, and understand the painfulness of imprisonment; they are confident, enthusiastic, discerning and are neither over-eager nor reluctant to use force (Liebling et al. 2011: 52–53). Crawley (2004) highlights the fact that the 'good' officer has confidence, powers of persuasion, and the ability to say 'no' to prisoners; they are assertive, good at listening and communicating, patient, mentally tough, operate in a fair and professional manner, and have a good sense of humour.

In addition, doctoral research by the author found that the 'best' officers have probity (honesty and personal integrity), moral values and reasoning, equanimity and composure, self-confidence and assuredness. They have empathy for the prisoner situation and demonstrate an understanding of human behaviour, motivations and individual needs. They are able to recognize the pains and frustrations of imprisonment and the impact that these may have for prisoners. They are capable of showing care and compassion whilst also treating prisoners in a firm, fair and consistent manner. They are able to adapt quickly to changing circumstances, structure the expectations of others, act with professionalism and have a sense of humour. They are resilient, sanguine, tolerant and reliable, vigilant, prudent, perceptive, non-confrontational and non-judgemental. They find the right 'line' when establishing and maintaining boundaries with prisoners, are authoritative without being authoritarian, are skilled communicators – they use 'straight talk' rather than formal sanctions when possible – and are undaunted by the use of force when it is necessary. They are self-reflexive and insightful about the impact of their own behaviour on others, and recognize their own strengths and weaknesses.

While this list of qualities is somewhat exhaustive, one of the key qualities of good officers is their competency in selecting the right skill or 'tool' for the particular person or situation. It is also important for the prison officer to leave behind any lasting, especially negative, feelings and attitudes before being able to deal appropriately with the next, and to achieve the right balance in their use of certain attributes. For example, too little empathy can result in a lack of 'duty of care', role detachment, the neglect of prisoners' emotional, psychological and material welfare, and unprofessional conduct. On the other hand, too much empathy can result in inconsistent boundaries and emotional over-involvement, lower levels of resilience and an inability to 'switch off' (something that officers consider vital in being able to cope with the demands of the job).

This highlights the importance of having a mix of officers with different skills. Many of the core characteristics of being a good officer are part of a good officer's underlying personality. At the same time, there are different conceptions of the 'ideal' officer, and more than one way of being a good officer. Within a residential wing, for example, some officers may have a tendency towards a counselling role, based on a working style involving compassion and care; others may gravitate towards a facilitator role, with a focus on regime delivery and meeting the daily needs of prisoners; and some may be more inclined towards rule enforcement, challenging behaviour and maintaining good order and control. What is important is that officers are supported in establishing a working personality that is authentic, compatible with their dominant skill set, and which helps establish a sense of purpose in their work.

Emotions in prison work

That prisons are emotional places has been recognized in previous research (Crawley 2004: 43). Crawley, for example, has claimed that 'the emotions generated by prison work are many and varied' (ibid.: 131), and that the job of a prison officer is an emotionally demanding one that requires 'often significant engagement in emotion work and the employment of a range of emotion work strategies' (ibid.: xii). Using Hochschild's (1983: 7) concept of emotional labour ('the management of feeling to create a publicly observable facial and bodily display', or the ways in which people manage their emotions while at work), Crawley suggests that 'becoming a prison officer is inextricably tied up with the management of certain emotions', such as anxiety, stress, sympathy, fear and anger. Officers are expected to remain emotionally detached and to present an image of authoritative confidence and indifference, even if this means masking 'how they really feel during certain types of interactions with certain prisoners' (Crawley 2004: 141). Crawley argues that 'staff-prisoner interactions and relationships are often emotionally charged, not least because the degree of intimacy involved in working with prisoners is relatively high' (ibid.: 131) and that emotion management has two dimensions: the emotions expressed by prisoners and the emotions that the prison generates within officers themselves (ibid.: 132). Emotional expression is constrained by the 'feeling rules' of the organization, such that some emotions are deemed more acceptable to disclose than others; those who transgress these 'rules' 'risk presenting themselves as unreliable, untrustworthy or simply unsuitable employees' (ibid.: 56).

Other research (Arnold 2005) has described how working in a prison environment can have negative emotional effects on prison officers and has defined the array of feelings that officers experience and encounter in their daily working lives: whilst anger and frustration were the most frequently cited emotions that officers experienced, they also reported feeling fear, guilt, sadness, anxiety, empathy, pity, relief and uncertainty. Most described themselves as having become hardened, cynical and detached. These processes represent an adaptive and protective defence mechanism which enable officers to cope with potentially traumatizing incidents, such as serious self-harm, suicides, prisoner deaths or violent assaults. Responding to such incidents produced a numbing, desensitizing effect; officers talked of acquiring an immunity and dissociation that kept at bay emotional discomfort. An impression of hardness and lack of emotional display facilitated the effective management of prison incidents and relationships. As one officer said:

> You just can't get too involved, you have to be detached, that's the best word for it. It doesn't mean you're heartless and it does mean you can have sympathy. Like when you deal with a self-harm incident, you have to just focus on getting him sorted and doing the paperwork afterwards. Then you can just carry on and try not to dwell on it – manage and deal with the problem, just go in there and deal with the wound.

Generally, officers are reluctant to acknowledge that they feel emotions or respond in emotional ways to the people and situations they encounter. Instead, emotions are generally denied, minimized, normalized and controlled:

Sometimes you get a bit choked up, you know what I'm saying? It's not for me to share my emotions because I'm a big lump and I shouldn't be showing my emotions but I've been there with them pouring their heart out. Why do you go all wishy-washy when you are watching a film? It's that sort of thing, that sort of emotion. It's not bad to have emotions but I'd hate to have emotions I couldn't control, couldn't hide. I can't function as well if my own personal head is not focused.

Officers often confuse *emotion* with being *emotional* (although both are considered undesirable), find it difficult to name the feelings and emotions they experience (commonly reporting that they 'don't really feel anything'), and believe that having and expressing emotions can cloud their judgement and undermine their authority: 'You can't be emotional; you couldn't do the job if you were.'

Emotional intelligence

Given the centrality of relationships, emotions and emotion management to the work of the prison officer, the construct of emotional intelligence merits further exploration. Emotional intelligence (or 'EQ') denotes the capacity to understand and use emotional information in day-to-day functioning; it largely relates to individual variation in the ability to effectively perceive, understand, integrate, and reflectively manage one's own emotions and those of others. It has been suggested that EQ is a better predictor of success in life than IQ, and can be advantageous in performing well and countering stress. Stein and Book (2000: 14) define EQ as:

A set of skills that enables us to make our way in a complex world – the personal social and survival aspects of overall intelligence … In everyday language emotional intelligence is what we commonly refer to as 'street wise', or that uncommon ability we label 'common sense'.

The doctoral research of the author set out to measure emotional intelligence amongst prison officers as a possible indicator of high job performance. The EQ questionnaire (Bar-On 1996) comprised 133 items or statements to which respondents were required to indicate their agreement or disagreement on a five-point Likert scale, from 'not true of me' to 'true of me'; the items were grouped into five factors and 15 subscales. A score of 100 indicates effective emotional and social functioning; scores greater than 100 indicate enhanced functioning; and scores of less than 100 indicate areas that may be improved. The results are presented below, first for the five factors (Table 15.1), and second for the 15 subscales (Table 15.2), for the total sample of officers (n=96), a sample of high-performing officers (n=22), and a random sample of 'other' officers for comparative purposes (n=22).

The table shows that for the total prison officer sample the highest score was for stress management and the lowest for interpersonal EQ. The sample of high-performing prison officers scored higher than the sample of other officers on each of the five EQ factors. The difference was statistically significant for total EQ and intrapersonal EQ, and was close to significance for interpersonal EQ. These aggregate results indicate that prison officers have adequate or average emotional capacity and typical healthy functioning on all five factors (scores range between 90 and 109); they are particularly able to withstand

Table 15.1 EQ factor scores for prison officers

EQ factors	Total sample	Sample of 'other' officers	Sample of 'high-performing officers'
Total EQ	99.47	94.05	101.86★
Intrapersonal EQ	100.77	94.91	103.82★
Interpersonal EQ	*94.86*	*88.09*	*96.27*
Adaptability EQ	100.60	96.27	100.95
Stress management EQ	**104.43**	**103.09**	**104.77**
General mood EQ	98.17	95.68	100.23

Note: Figures in bold indicate the highest scores for each group; figures in italics indicate the lowest scores for each group. An asterisk indicates a statistically significant score between the high-performing officer sample and the other sample.

Table 15.2 EQ subscale scores for prison officers

EQ subscales	Total sample	Sample of 'other' officers	Sample of 'high-performing officers'
IntRApersonal EQ			
Self-regard	100.93	98.64	102.32
Emotional self-awareness	99.32	93.05	101.82★
Assertiveness	**105.40**	**101.50**	**109.45**
Independence	100.67	95.00	104.32★
Self-actualization	97.84	93.23	97.95
IntERpersonal EQ			
Empathy	*90.96*	*84.73*	*93.09*
Social responsibility	*94.48*	*89.86*	*94.59*
Interpersonal relationships	97.33	*90.86*	98.50
Adaptability			
Reality testing	**101.08**	97.23	103.00
Flexibility	100.72	98.45	99.45
Problem solving	99.64	95.00	99.41
Stress management			
Stress tolerance	**106.73**	**104.59**	**107.45**
Impulse control	100.89	**100.23**	101.27
General mood			
Optimism	*94.58*	93.64	*96.23*
Happiness	**101.68**	98.23	**104.00**

Note: Figures in bold indicate the highest scores for each group; figures in italics indicate the lowest scores for each group. An asterisk indicates a statistically significant score between the high-performing officer sample and the other sample.

stress without 'falling apart' or losing control; are generally calm, rarely impulsive and work well under pressure; they can handle tasks that are stressful or anxiety provoking, or that involve an element of danger. However, the results also indicate that, whilst still within the 'normal' range, they perform less well with regard to social skills, understanding, interacting and relating well to others.

For each of the subscales, the group of officers as a whole again score within the normal and healthy functioning range (90–109). The highest scores were for stress tolerance, assertiveness, happiness and reality testing; the lowest scores were for empathy, social responsibility and optimism. These results suggest that officers have a high degree of self-efficacy; they are able to cope with stress actively and positively, are not reserved or limited by self-consciousness, are realistic, well-grounded and 'tuned into' their environments, good at assessing situations, and are satisfied with their lives. The lower scores suggest, however, that as a group they may lack a sensitivity to others' feelings, may not always be considered a constructive member of their social group, and do not necessarily have a particularly positive outlook. The group of 'other' officers score particularly low on empathy and social responsibility. As suggested in the previous section, the lack of empathy found overall may be explained as a protective mechanism and a functional response to the job.

The sample of 'good' or high-performing officers scored significantly higher than the sample of other officers on two of the subscales: emotional self-awareness and independence. This indicates that they are more able to recognize their emotions and to differentiate between them (to know what they are feeling and why). It also suggests that they are more self-directed, self-reliant and self-controlled in their thinking and actions, are less emotionally dependent and more able to function autonomously. The discrepancy between low optimism and high happiness may be accounted for by the ability to find meaning and purpose; so despite a somewhat pessimistic outlook and a negative view of the future, they are still able to construct and derive pleasure from life.

Prison officer culture: features and functions

Prison officer humour

Alongside loyalty and solidarity, cynicism and emotional detachment, another important aspect of prison officer culture that is deserving of attention is the use of humour. Humour within prisons is ubiquitous; it is central to prison life and the relationships within it, yet represents a glaring omission from the sociological accounts of prison work (although see Crawley 2004; and Nielson 2011). For Crawley (2004: 44), humour functions as 'a strategy for conveying, disguising and managing emotion'; as a means of communicating and integrating members of a group; as a way of establishing and maintaining informal work hierarchies (found in practices such as teasing the new recruit); and as a survival strategy (for new recruits who need to learn to 'give and take' banter with their colleagues). Nielson (2011) provides examples from a Danish prison to illustrate how humorous exchanges between officers and prisoners enable officers to briefly meet prisoners as equals, and to manage relationships without conflict, as well as to express hostility towards their peers.

However, the functions of humour are broader than is often implied. Prison officer humour is multifarious, nuanced and instrumental; it takes many forms but is often typified as 'gallows humour', as 'black', 'sick' or 'dark', and as such displays a pronounced cynicism when there may be nothing intrinsically amusing about its source. It has numerous bases, uses and manifestations (in joke telling, storytelling, practical pranks, gossip, the use of nicknames and general 'banter'). It generates rapport and respect, breaks down (and conversely maintains) barriers and boundaries, resolves and diffuses conflict (as a 'talking-down' tool with recalcitrant prisoners), promotes dynamic security, and helps to achieve compliance, order and control:

> The humour side comes out ... there is a term, which is dynamic security, and that's all about interacting with them and you're going to form relationships and bonds with some of these people and humour is a good way of doing that.
> To try and break the ice, you've got to create humour in a difficult situation. It's a way of diffusing the majority of the situations we come across on a daily basis I guess.

Attempts to make light of some of the more discomforting procedures (such as conducting strip searches or dealing with a first-time prisoner throughout the reception process) are often evident, and can demonstrate affective empathy for the prisoner predicament, alleviate anxiety and reduce potential embarrassment for both officer and prisoner.

Humour is also associated with the more intense and challenging aspects of prison officer work and is particularly prevalent in the aftermath of serious incidents, where its function as a coping mechanism is apparent. To describe a prisoner who has committed suicide by hanging as having received a 'suspended sentence' is a widespread and expected 'joke'.[8]

> There have been ... incidences ... on A Wing where I've answered the bell and there's been a bloke hanging and his cell mate's put the bell on and started kicking the door and we've had to go in and cut them down. You just look at it and I suppose we all sort of, we laugh afterwards because that's the sort of mechanism for relieving the stress and the day to day stuff. We get together and we laugh and we take the piss because that's what we do, that's the way that you deal with it.

Theories of humour as well as studies of other occupational groups (such as nurses, firefighters, coal miners and emergency workers) support the notion that it functions as an emotional 'safety valve' for difficult subjects and feelings (Palmer 1994), particularly in professions that involve exposure to death, suffering and pain, or precarious, dangerous and sensitive situations. Morreall (1987) proposes a 'relief theory', whereby laughter equates to a release of pent-up nervous energy. Critchley (2002: 9) goes further in claiming that a 'joke' says the 'unsayable', and reveals a truth about a situation, or about what hurts or scares people. Zijderveld (1968: 121) claims that through laughter and joking, 'emotional experiences which are hard to express verbally are made collective, and communicative; cognitive dissonances are lifted, and reality is restored'.

So, humour can enhance the performance and social functioning of the occupational group (in fulfilling a shared purpose). As well as facilitating 'adjustment to difficult, arduous and exhausting situations', it also precipitates 'cognitive reframing and social support': it permits a reinterpretation of distressing events that makes negative emotions more manageable (Moran and Massam 1997); it produces a distancing effect that enables emotions to be controlled and therefore situations to be managed more effectively. Participative humour gives meaning (and perspective) to an experience or situation (Gadamer 1975); it creates a sense of belonging and boosts self-esteem (Sanders 2004); it fosters solidarity (Crowe 2008), and strengthens morale (Zijderveld 1983). It unites members of an occupational group and reinstates social veracity. Humour amongst prison officers is a 'shibboleth' – a feature of language that identifies the speaker as being a member (or not) of a particular group or subculture. When prison officers use coded language and private jokes, it establishes group membership, recognition and acceptance. Recurring jokes, and ritual laughter, indicate belonging and help to sustain a group identity.

The function of culture

The core features of prison officer culture discussed here, such as cynicism, emotional detachment, solidarity and humour, are linked in two fundamental ways: first, the seeds of these norms are sown through a process of occupational socialization that begins during prison officers' initial training; second, they are all functionally linked in that they enable prison officers to survive the structural and occupational demands of the job. Although traditionally considered negative, the prison officer sub-culture performs a vital role in protecting officers physically, psychologically and emotionally. This helps to explain the existence and continuity of prison officer sub-culture, and the reasons why attempts to reform it tend to fail.

The components of prison officer culture discussed here are remarkably analogous to other occupations, such as the police and medical professions, which require dealing with people in situations where the psychological, emotional and physical well-being of the worker is potentially threatened. Prison officer sub-culture is not, therefore, completely distinctive. Nor is it undifferentiated. Despite agreement on the dominant features of the prison officer sub-culture, individuals adhere to its characteristics to a greater or lesser degree. Meanwhile, prisons with different functions and populations have distinctive value cultures and emotional climates (see Liebling, with Arnold 2004), and the development of prison officer typologies suggests that, even within a prison, groups of officers conform to different sets of values, beliefs and practices (see for example, Farkas 2000; Gilbert 1997; Kauffman 1988). The existence of both 'types' of officers and 'types' of culture suggests that neither the characteristics of officers nor their sub-culture is homogeneous.

Conclusion

Arguably, there exists less solidarity, loyalty and trust amongst officers now than in the past. Prison officer culture has become more individualized and more about 'watching your own back than others'. The prison officer group has become more fragmented and loyalty is being undermined by pressures and concerns such as fear of disciplinary action for political incorrectness, and different (divisive) conceptions of what it means to do the job in a rapidly changing environment (Liebling et al. 2012). The low trust that characterizes the prison environment has extended to the relationships between officers. That features of prison officer culture such as loyalty and solidarity may be diminished may also mean that other features such as cynicism and emotional detachment have become more pronounced.

The current penological climate, with increasing prison populations, continuing budget cuts and reductions in staff numbers, presents a challenging time for prison officers, who feel they are constantly required to do more with less; this strain can exacerbate the tendency to resort to 'the basics' of the job, can produce a tension between what is practicable and what is possible, and can therefore create a lack of meaning, purpose and identity, not only at the level of the individual but at a cultural one. It is clear from this account that psychological constructs have an important role in explaining and understanding the work of prison officers, but exactly how these internal perceptions relate to specific outward behaviours, how they might either reflect or produce a prison officer culture, and how they might be more or less present at varying points during the career of an officer requires further exploration. Although scholars have commented on some features of prison officer culture, a rigorous, empirical study of culture remains absent from the literature. What is needed is a robust multi-site study that examines the origins, development, reach and continuity of clearly defined features of culture.

Notes

1 Thanks to Jamie Bennett and the *Prison Service Journal* for their kind permission to reproduce these quotes in this chapter.
2 The following quote from Gilbert (1997: 53) makes a similar point: 'it is clear that the direct work product that these officers produce is not security, control or safety but personal interactions between themselves and inmates. The affective nature of these interactions directly influences the level of tension between officers and inmates and indirectly influences the safety, security and control within the prison.'
3 Liebling (2011: 491) makes the distinction between 'good' and 'right' relationships: 'staff-prisoner relationships can be too close or too informal, lacking boundaries and professional distance ... "Right" relationships sat somewhere between formality and informality, closeness and distance, policing by consent and imposing order. They were respectful, but incorporated a "quiet flow of power".'
4 Various job descriptions on recruitment websites and within the NOMS recruitment literature refer not only to security and supervisory duties but to an officer's role in the rehabilitation of offenders which includes motivating prisoners to change, establishing and maintaining 'positive working relationships with prisoners ... in order to effect rehabilitation' (*Prospects*, October 2013); taking an active part in rehabilitation programmes in 'preparing prisoners for release', for example, and in helping prisoners 'reflect on their offending behaviour' (National Careers Service, nationalcareersservice.direct.gov.uk/advice/planning/jobprofiles/Pages/prisonofficer.aspx) (accessed 2012). Previously, on the Prison Service website it was stated that prison officers 'are expected to promote pro social behaviour', and to 'encourage' and provide 'opportunities for prisoners to address their offending behaviour' (September 2012). Current job descriptions found on the Justice website state that 'A career as a Prison Officer isn't about keeping people under lock and key [although security is obviously an important aspect of the role]. It's about understanding challenging behaviour, acting as a role model and providing encouragement and support so prisoners can break free from crime. You'll not only get enormous satisfaction from helping to turn lives around, you'll also be making a valuable contribution to society as a whole' (accessed 7 July 2014).
5 The following quotes are taken from interviews with prison officers that were conducted as part of the author's doctoral research into what makes a good prison officer.
6 'Pegging' is a mandatory security procedure carried out by officers working on night shifts. Pegging devices are located at various points around the prison which an officer must 'tag' at regular intervals as evidence the areas have been patrolled.

7 'Her Majesty's Prison Service serves the public by keeping in custody those committed by the courts. Our duty is to look after them with humanity and help them lead law-abiding and useful lives in custody and after release.'

8 That prison officer humour often has undertones of mockery, derision and sarcasm represents the capacity of humour to be destructive and disparaging. It can therefore be perceived as inappropriate, unprofessional and insensitive (particularly by 'outsiders') and as contributing to the conception of a negative prison officer sub-culture. Whilst the negative connotations of humour should not be ignored, it is arguably the adaptive and ameliorative use of humour by officers that dominates prison life.

Bibliography

Arnold, H. (2005) 'The effects of prison work', in A. Liebling and S. Maruna (eds) *The Effects of Imprisonment*, Cullompton: Willan, 391–420.

Arnold, H. (2008) 'The experience of prison officer training', in J. Bennett, B. Crewe and A. Wahidin (eds) *Understanding Prison Staff*, Cullompton: Willan, 399–418.

Arnold, H. and Barnett-Page, C. (2006) 'Wandsworth staff do jigsaws blindfolded: an evaluation of the Wandsworth saff development course using appreciative inquiry', *Prison Service Journal* 164: 41–45.

Arnold, H., Liebling, A. and Tait, S. (2007) 'Prison officers and prison culture', in Y. Jewkes (ed.) *Handbook on Prisons*, Cullompton: Willan, 471–495.

Bar-On, R. (1996) *The Emotional Quotient Inventory (EQ-i): A test of emotional intelligence*, Toronto: Multi-Health Systems.

Bar-On, R. (2002) *EQ-I BarOn Emotional Quotient Inventory Technical Manual*, New York: MHS.

Bogardus, E.S. (1932) 'Social distance scale', *Sociology and Social Research* 17: 55–62.

Bottoms, A.E. (1990) 'The aims of imprisonment', in D. Garland (ed.) *Justice, Guilt and Forgiveness in the Penal System*, Edinburgh: Centre for Theology and Public Issues, 3–36.

Bryans, S. (2001) 'Prison service staff', in S. Bryans and R. Jones (eds) *Prisons and the Prisoner: An Introduction to the Work of Her Majesty's Prison Service*, London: The Stationery Office, 153–181.

Chan, J.B.L., with Devery, C. and Doran, S. (2003) *Fair Cop: Learning the art of policing*, Toronto: University of Toronto Press.

Colman, A.M. and Gorman, L.P. (1982) 'Conservatism, dogmatism and authoritarianism in British police officers', *Sociology* 16(1): 1–11.

Crawley, E.M. (2004) *Doing Prison Work: The public and private lives of prison officers*, Cullompton: Willan.

Crawley, E. and Crawley, P. (2008) 'Understanding prison officers: culture, cohesion and conflict', in J. Bennett, B. Crewe and A. Wahidin (eds) *Understanding Prison Staff*, Cullompton: Willan, 134–152.

Crewe, B., Liebling, A. and Hulley, S. (2011) 'Staff culture, the use of authority, and prisoner outcomes in public and private prisons', *Australia and New Zealand Journal of Criminology* 44(1): 94–115.

Critchley, S. (2002) *On Humour*, London: Routledge.

Crowe, L. (2008) *Humour and Swearing: Tools for staff that build a culture of camaraderie and resilience against the loss and trauma of a paediatric intensive care unit*, paper presented at the Eighth International Conference on Grief and Bereavement in Contemporary Society.

Cullen, F.T., Lutze, F.E., Link, B.G. and Wolfe, N.T. (1989) 'The correctional orientation of prison guards: do officers support rehabilitation?' *Federal Probation* 53: 33–42.

Dunbar, I. (1985) *A Sense of Direction*, London: Home Office.

Farkas, M.A. (1999) 'Correctional officer attitudes toward inmates and working with inmates in a "get tough" era', *Journal of Criminal Justice* 27(6): 495–506.

Farkas, M.A. (2000) 'A typology of correctional officers', *International Journal of Offender Therapy and Comparative Criminology* 44(4): 431–449.

Gadamer, H.-G. (1975) *Truth and Method*, London: Sheed and Ward.

Garland, D. (1996) 'The limits of the sovereign state: strategies of crime control in contemporary society', *British Journal of Criminology* 36(4): 445–471.

Giddens, A. (1984) *The Constitution of Society*, Cambridge: Polity Press.

Gilbert, M.J. (1997) 'The illusion of structure: a critique of the classical model of organisation and the discretionary power of correctional officers', *Criminal Justice Review* 22(1): 49–64.

Goleman, D. (1995) *Emotional Intelligence: Why it can matter more than IQ*, London: Bloomsbury.

Hay, W. and Sparks, R. (1991) 'What is a prison officer?' *Prison Service Journal* 83: 2–7.

Hepburn, J.R. (1985) 'The exercise of power in coercive organisations: a study of prison guards', *Criminology* 23(1): 145–164.

Hochschild, A. (1979) 'Emotion work, feeling rules and aocial atructure', *American Journal of Sociology* 85: 551–575.

Hochschild, A. (1983) *The Managed Heart*, Berkeley, CA: University of California Press.

Home Office (1979) *Committee of Inquiry into the United Kingdom Prison Service – The May Inquiry (Cmnd 7673)*, London: HMSO.

Home Office (1984) *Managing the Long-Term Prison System: The report of the Control Review Committee*, London: Home Office.

Home Office (1991) *Custody, Care and Justice: The way ahead for the prison service in England and Wales*, London: HMSO.

Home Office (1995) *Review of Prison Service Security in England and Wales – The Learmont Report (Cmnd 3020)*, London: HMSO.

House of Commons Justice Committee (2009) *Role of the Prison Officer, Twelfth Report of Session 2008–2009*, London: The Stationery Office.

Irwin, J. and Cressey, D.R. (1962) 'Thieves, convicts and the inmate culture', *Social Problems* 10: 142–155.

Jefferson, A. (2007) 'Prison officer training and practice in Nigeria: contention, contradiction and re-imagining reform strategies', *Punishment and Society* 9(3): 253–269.

Jefferson, A. (2014) 'Prison officers in Sierra Leone: paradoxical puzzles', *Prison Service Journal* 212: 39–44.

Jiang, S. and Fisher-Giorlando, M. (2002) 'Inmate misconduct: a test of the deprivation, importation, and situational models', *The Prison Journal* 82: 335–358.

Kauffman, K. (1988) *Prison Officers and their World*, Cambridge, MA and London: Harvard University Press.

Lerman, A. and Page, J. (2012) 'The state of the job: an embedded work role perspective on prison officer attitudes', *Punishment and Society* 14(5): 503–529.

Liebling, A. (2000) 'Prison officer, policing and the use of discretion', *Theoretical Criminology* 4(3): 333–357.

Liebling, A., with Arnold, H. (2004) *Prisons and their Moral Performance: A study of values, quality and prison life*, Oxford: Oxford University Press.

Liebling, A., Arnold, H. and Straub, C. (2012) *An Exploration of Staff-Prisoner Relationships at HMP Whitemoor: Twelve years on*, London: NOMS.

Liebling, A. and Price, D. (1999) *An Exploration of Staff-Prisoner Relationships at HMP Whitemoor*, Prison Service Research Report No. 6, London: Prison Service.

Liebling, A. and Price, D. (2001) *The Prison Officer*, Leyhill: Prison Service (and Waterside Press).

Liebling, A., Price, D. and Shefer, G. (2011) *The Prison Officer*, second edn, Cullompton: Willan.

Lombardo, L.X. (1989 [1981]) *Guards Imprisoned: Correctional officers at work*, second edn, New York: Elsevier.

Moran, C. and Massam, M. (1997) 'An evaluation of humour in emergency work', *The Australasian Journal of Disaster and Trauma Work* 3: 26–38.

Morreall, J. (ed.) (1987) *The Philosophy of Laughter and Humour*, Albany: State University of New York Press.

Newell, T. (2002) 'The prison officer as moral agent', *Prison Service Journal* 139: 29–30.

Nielson, M. (2011) 'On humour in prison', *European Journal of Criminology* 8(6): 500–514.

Overell, S. (2008) *Inwardness: The rise of meaningful work*, Provocation Series Vol. 4, No. 2, London: The Work Foundation.

Owers, A. (2006) 'Turnkeys or role models?', *Prison Service Journal* 168: 20–26.

Palmer, J. (1994) *Taking Humour Seriously*, London: Routledge.

Reiner, R. (1997) 'Policing and the police', in R. Maguire, R. Morgan and R. Reiner (eds) *The Oxford Handbook of Criminology*, Oxford: Oxford University Press, 997–1050.

Robertson, R. (2004) *Assessing the Predictive Validity of Emotional Intelligence in Prison Officer Job Performance*, unpublished MSc dissertation, University of Hertfordshire.

Sanders, T. (2004) 'Controllable laughter: managing sex work through humour', *Sociology* 38: 273–291.

Scott, D. (2006) 'The caretakers of punishment: prison officer personal suthority and the rule of law', *Prison Service Journal* 168: 14–19.

Scott, D. (2012) 'Guarding the ghosts of time: working personalities and the prison officer-prisoner relationship', *Prison Service Journal* 201: 18–24.

Shamir, B. and Drory, A. (1981) 'Some correlates of prison guards' beliefs', *Criminal Justice and Behaviour* 8(2): 233–249.

Sparks, R., Bottoms, A.E. and Hay, W. (1996) *Prisons and the Problem of Order*, Oxford: Clarendon Press.

Stein, S.J. and Book, H.E. (2000) *The EQ Edge*, Toronto: MHS.

Sykes, G. (1958) *The Society of Captives*, Princeton, NJ: Princeton University Press.

Tait, S. (2008) 'Care and the prison officer: beyond "turnkeys" and "carebears"', *Prison Service Journal* 180: 3–11.

Tait, S. (2011) 'A typology of prison officer approaches to care', *European Journal of Criminology* 8 (6): 440–454.

Trotter, C. (2009) 'Pro-social modelling', *European Journal of Probation* 1(2): 142–152.

Young, P. (1987) 'The concept of social control and its relevance to the prisons debate', in A.E. Bottoms and R. Light (eds) *Problems of Long-term Imprisonment*, Aldershot: Gower.

Zijderveld, C. (1968) 'Jokes and their relation to social reality', *Social Research* 35: 268–311.

Zijderveld, C. (1983) 'The sociology of humour and laughter', *Current Sociology* 31(3).

Chapter 16

Prisons and technology

General lessons from the American context

Robert Johnson and Katie Hail-Jares[1]

In preparing this chapter, the authors relied on a number of technological innovations to communicate and collaborate. Both sent emails back and forth, checking those emails on their smartphones, and replying while on the go, sometimes by text message. Important contacts were interviewed, primarily by cell phone, to provide their insight on the implementation and innovation of technology within corrections and prisons. Eventually, the final product was typed up (on a rather old laptop), submitted, again via email, to the editors, and prepared for consumption. Indeed, you may be reading this chapter on an e-reader or tablet. The ubiquity of communication technology has become so engrained in our modern world that it is jarring to imagine situations where this technology does not exist. Prisons, notoriously technologically impoverished, are a telling case in point and the focus of this chapter.

In such settings as the prison, the rarity of modern communication technology is notable, prompting me to comment, nearly ten years ago, that inmates were fast becoming 'cavemen in an era of speed-of-light technology' (Johnson 2005: 263). (This metaphor was adopted by Jewkes and Johnston (2009: 132, 135) to suggest commonalities between prisons in America and the UK). Here, I partner with Hail-Jares to assess how prisons have adopted communication technologies and made them available to inmates. Specifically, we ask whether American inmates, captives of a massive and repressive correctional system, are still stuck in the technological version of the Paleolithic Age or whether they are notably more able to keep up with technological innovation and stay in touch with those on the outside. In this chapter, we report on a survey in which we explore how prisons in the USA use communication technology, how much access inmates have in practice, what trends are emerging in the availability and use of technology, and how access to technology entails both benefits and costs to inmates.

Background considerations

Prison inmates are physically and socially isolated from society. Physical isolation sets the scene for several forms of deprivation – the deprivation of freedom, ownership, touch and, to an increasing degree, contact with the world. The social isolation of today's prisons, though less obvious than the walls and bars and cages that hold prisoners apart from society, is striking, particularly since the wider world is increasingly connected via new forms of technology (Johnson 2005: 155; Jewkes 2008: 174; Smith 2012: 454–455). In a world that relies on a host of communication technologies to maintain almost constant communication with others, inmates, especially those serving long or life sentences, are increasingly left behind, to their detriment and ours.

America as a society uses prisons at high rates, resulting in a phenomenon called 'mass incarceration'. This dubious appellation might also apply to the UK, where incarceration rates are high by European standards. Whatever the rate of confinement, and with the notable exception of the Scandinavian countries and perhaps Holland, the masses incarcerated in prisons are meant to be held in austere, isolated conditions as a part of their punishment (Clear 1994: 5; Ferguson 2014: esp. Chapter 6). Citizens are perennially concerned that prisons may provide too many amenities to those convicted of serious, including heinous, crimes (Jewkes 2008: 171; see generally, Johnson 2005). Johnson (2005: 271–273) suggested that the growth in the use of isolated, austere prisons is not merely a desire to inflict punishment on underserving offenders but may stem from jealousy, specifically 'time envy'. Technology has produced an interconnected but also extremely fast-paced life that leaves many citizens feeling harried and pressed for time. Prisoners, by contrast, seem to have time on their hands. Their purported ability to fill that time with appealing activities, such as education, weightlifting, writing and even self-reflection evokes outrage not because these privileges are excessive in themselves, but because they are precisely what *we* in the free world would want for ourselves, if only we had the time. Inmates may yet have time on their hands, but they are increasingly being deprived of meaningful ways to fill it.

Additionally, providing inmates with access to technology is thought to pose security risks (Jewkes 2008: 140). Ostensibly, providing inmates with modern communication technologies would allow them to contact and harass victims or run scams on an unsuspecting public. Periodic scandals, in which inmates secure cell phones and use them to support criminal activity, feed these fears. Yet, as Jewkes (2008: 178) notes, European prisons that implemented email for inmates experienced little or no misuse of the system, suggesting these fears, as a general matter, may be overblown. With careful monitoring, Jewkes suggests, communication technologies may be deployed with minimal risk. The focus on the immediate security risks, though, obscures how technological isolation may actually threaten public safety in the long term (Jewkes 2008: 184). As the in-prison technological isolation intensifies, those incarcerated face more significant obstacles to reentry, particularly in their ability to gain employment in a society increasingly reliant upon such technology. As Jewkes (2008: 185) has observed, with understated irony: 'Certainly, a technologically illiterate prisoner population cannot be regarded as desirable in a fast-moving and technologically advanced society.' Without the necessary modern job skills, ex-offenders are unemployable and may be increasingly likely to return to criminal activity to survive.

Recidivism is not only a matter of job skills; social support is critical as well. Widespread use of communication in prisons could have significant impact on allowing inmates to remain connected to supportive communities, particularly family and friends. Petersilia summarized just how salient such support is to reducing recidivism:

> If prison is judged necessary, then maximum effort should be made to encourage ties with the family and community throughout the prisoner's stay, and prerelease programs should focus on actively connecting the prisoner to the host community … *Every* known study that has been able to examine the relationship between a prisoner's legitimate community ties and recidivism has found that feelings of being

welcome at home and the strength of interpersonal ties outside prison help predict postprison adjustment.

(Petersilia 2003: 246, original emphasis)

Since Petersilia's book was released, new research continues to support these assertions. Bales and Mears (2008) found that Florida inmates who received visits were less likely to recidivate, and that visits had a larger impact on reducing recidivism among men, racial minorities, and individuals with previous criminal records – three groups that traditionally have the highest reoffense rates. Subsequent research has reinforced that family support and visits are protective factors for at-risk groups, particularly inmates with substance abuse and mental illness (Spjeldnes et al. 2012). Yet, despite the consensus among such research, all authors note that most inmates receive no visits at all. In their study, Bales and Mears (2008) found that 58% of inmates received no visits – most often, it seems, because the prisons are distant from the homes of the prisoners' families. Modern communication technologies, such as video conferencing and email, may make maintaining long-distance relationships easier and more affordable for inmates and their families.

It is clear that communication technologies can be beneficial to our comparatively isolated prison populations, but we have a limited understanding of just how much legitimate access inmates have to communication technologies and what benefits accrue in practice. Nor do we have any sense of the downside of increased access to technology; more is not always better in any area of endeavor, presumably including technology. Since Johnson (2005) first wrote about technological isolation, a handful of other articles have addressed inmate access to technology (Jewkes 2002; Jewkes and Johnston 2009; Smith 2012), and established a rich theoretical base for considering inmate access and its consequences. However, as theoretical pieces, the existing literature relies upon limited, anecdotal examples of how technology is made accessible to inmates. These examples seldom represent a systematic, let alone full or complete, picture of how inmates can and do access technology.

Our study and its implications

Despite the easy availability of technology in our modern day-to-day lives, little research has examined the role of technology in inmates' lives, either with respect to their daily lives behind bars or in relation to their communications with the outside world. Historically, the introduction of technology into prisons served the goal of control. Any technological innovation, including something as basic as the radio, became a valued privilege that could be manipulated to produce good behavior among its inmate recipients (Jewkes and Johnston 2009: 140–141). Moreover, the appeal of the radio, and later the television, was such that these devices served as a sort of pacifier; the inmates became captives of the radio and television shows, which filled their time in ways that kept them out of trouble and helped officials maintain order. Television, in particular, has been described as having addictive qualities that promote passivity among habitual viewers. It has been established that the introduction of televisions into San Quentin prison served as an electronic babysitter, of sorts, with the result that inmates were less inclined to read, write or, presumably, riot (Johnson 2005: 264–271). As a result, the number of inmate-authored manuscripts and books held in the prison library dropped by more than half: inmates, it appears, effectively stopped reading and writing in favor of watching television (Johnson 2005: 267). On the other hand, television provides a common medium by which inmates can keep in touch with the general culture and, presumably, have a shared set of topics that can help them maintain their connections with loved ones (see generally, Jewkes 2002). Many of us in the free world spend a fair amount of time watching television and talking about it with others. Prisoners want to remain in that picture, understandably. They may write fewer books, but presumably they have more to talk about with loved ones by virtue of shared exposure to television.

New and more pervasive communication technologies such as email, video conferencing and cell phone service have generally been embraced by scholars as promising ways to humanize prisons by allowing prisoners to maintain contact with the free world and, by implication, remain a part of the lives of their loved ones. Upon release, it is reasonable to suppose that these inmates will be more able to assimilate back into their families and into the larger free society. Yet scholars have provided little or no empirical data on the availability of such communicative technologies in prisons, let alone their effects on the lives of inmates, in or after incarceration. Peter Scharff Smith sums up this dilemma in his review of inmate access to the Internet in European prisons systems, noting:

> Although, to my knowledge, no prison system allows prisoners free internet access, there are local examples (at least in some jurisdictions) where limited access to [information and communication technologies] has been granted to some prisoners. However, it is very difficult to get an overview of the situation since research in this area is very scarce. Unsurprisingly, the overall picture seems to be one of lack of access or very limited access.
>
> (Smith 2012: 457)

Smith (2012: 457) goes on to note that in their review of prisons in the UK, Johnston and Jewkes found limited access to such technologies. In 2009, just seven UK prisons offered Internet access of some sort, and nearly three times as many provided e-learning facilities where incarcerated persons could learn basic keyboarding or have access to shared computer kiosks. Other national systems reviewed by Smith (2012: 457–459), including Dutch, French and Scandinavian prisons, typically provided much more access to the Internet and computers overall. Still, the actual usage and effects of communication technologies in these more open penal regimes remains the subject of speculation and anecdote, not empirical research.

When Smith (2012: 458) turns his focus on American prisons, the picture is unremittingly bleak. He notes only one example of innovative Internet access, the Massachusetts Institute for Technology's (MIT) Between the Bars blog platform hosted by the MIT Center for Civil Media. Through the program, inmates (including those on death row) can send, via letter, journal entries which MIT students then blog online. As a result, the stories of incarcerated men and women are able to reach a vast number of web browsers. Today, the platform hosts over 5,000 blogs, relying upon a manual process of turning written word into typed text on webpages. Though innovative, taking the Between the Bars project as an example of American inmate access to technology presents an incomplete picture.

A survey commissioned by the American Correctional Association in 2009 shows a more technologically accessible prison system than was understood to be the case in earlier work and speculation. Forty-nine state systems responded to the survey

(Anonymous 2009).[2] A majority of states used communicative technologies (most often some form of video conferencing) to facilitate inmate care, arraignment and release via parole boards. Additionally, 38 states provided inmates with opportunities to use computers in some aspect of their work in prison industries, such as learning computer-assisted drafting (CAD), call center support, or publishing. Overall, though, as Smith predicted, actual inmate access to computers and other communicative technologies was sharply restricted. Only ten states allowed video conferencing for inmates,[3] nine provided personal computers for inmate use, six allowed inmates to send or receive emails, and just four provided inmates with access to the Internet.[4] Moreover, access to these technologies was routinely limited by an array of factors. For example, video visitations were typically limited to inmates who were either in segregation (and therefore not allowed contact visits) or in states with large geographical areas and remote prisons, rendering face-to-face visits quite rare (including, for example, Alaska, Arizona and New Mexico). Email systems relied on a closed platform, which limited access (see the next section for more information on this matter), and Internet access was almost always limited to offenders who were a few months from release, with use restricted to job searches. The 2009 survey, then, suggests that some American inmates, like their European counterparts, did have access to various technologies, but that their access was almost always extremely limited in practice.

In 2014, we sought to update the American Correctional Association's (ACA) survey and to supplement findings with follow-up interviews to determine if there had been any significant changes in the uses of technology in the past several years. We sent out a survey to each of the 50 states (the District of Columbia and federal system were not included), and interviewed seven tech providers and correctional administrators, and 107 inmates. Of the 38 states that responded, it is telling that none had rolled back inmates' email privileges. It was not long ago that the very idea of email in prison seemed outlandish; though still comparatively rare, prison email appears to be here to stay in many states. In fact, our survey indicated that at least 15 systems now allowed inmates to send, receive, or send and receive email messages; some mix of these communication options was planned or pending in one more state. No states offering email access had withdrawn that access since the original ACA survey.

The story of video visits is a bit more complicated. Overall, video visits had expanded. In the 38 states that responded to our survey, 14 either had implemented video visitations or had pending programs. However, one state – Arizona – had repealed video visitations. A second – Louisiana – had piloted a video visitation program after the ACA survey in 2009 but abandoned full-scale implementation. In these two cases, inconvenience to family members led to the limited use and ultimate demise of video visitation. As a general matter, though, the 2014 survey suggests that American prisons are providing inmates with more opportunities to engage with and use communicative technologies.

Drawing upon these survey results and accompanying interviews with corrections administrators, inmates, and technology developers, we were able to examine empirically the way that the implementation of communicative technologies – specifically email, video visitation and cell phones – has affected inmates, their families, and correctional officers. Some technologies, such as email, have had an overwhelmingly positive impact on all involved. Other forms, such as video visits, have received more tepid approval (from all parties) and appear to require further improvements before being fully embraced. Finally, still other technologies, particularly cell phones, illustrate how inmates and administrators often clash in their attempts to balance public safety with affordability. We conclude by discussing future trends in prison-based technology innovation and persistent challenges for correctional systems.

The good: OMail

Perhaps unlike European prisons, communication technologies were ushered into the American prison systems by private companies seeking profit. Access to email – or, as it is called in many American states 'OMail' (offender mail) – is provided to state systems by for-profit contractors. This for-profit model, rather than the Between the Bars non-profit alternative noted earlier, has served as the impetus for bringing technology into American prisons and expanding its uses.

The term email is a bit of a misnomer for the system used by most American prisons. Inmates often do not have access to the broader Internet and do not have an email address, per se. Instead, they rely upon closed-circuit kiosks set up around the prison. If an inmate wants to send a message, he or she logs into the platform and sends an invitation to family members and friends. Recipients can choose to accept or block the inmate-initiated request.[5] This initial request is the only message that actually goes to an outside recipient's email. After that, to either accept or block the request, individuals (on both sides of the fence) must log into a third-party platform to read and send messages.

Delivery of these messages varies by state. In some states, inmates may check their OMail at their convenience by logging into computer kiosks in their units. In other states, inmates can purchase a small MP3 device (resembling an iPod both in form and function), which allows them to read new messages. In yet other states, the messages are printed by correctional officers and hand delivered to inmates, sort of in-prison express mail service. In all scenarios, messages are delayed and thus are not instantaneous, like email as we in the free world understand the term. Another primary difference is that there is a fee per sent message. The fee is usually borne by the writer, requiring inmates to load money into their account in order to send messages, and of course requiring the system to be able to accommodate these transactions. Receiving a message does not cost anything.[6]

Today, most of the closed-platform email systems used in prisons are operated by two contractors, J-Pay and ATG. ATG started developing the technology in 1998. Originally, ATG was unsure how its technology would be accepted, not just by the broader public, but by corrections. One executive recalled that in 2002, he broached the subject at a meeting with the directors of state and federal departments of corrections. The response was a unanimous sentiment that 'no one [was] going to do email for inmates'. Still, ATG persisted in the software's development, and by 2004, at a subsequent meeting of state and federal correctional officials, the federal government agreed to pilot the technology. The lack of public outcry – and even more so, the support, however tepid, from the public – over OMail's introduction was a surprise. The initial reception of OMail foreshadowed a commercial success for ATG. On an average day, the OMail system now delivers over 700,000 messages. By the end of 2015, ATG estimated that 500,000 inmates would be using their system to send and receive email. The introduction of easily accessible inmate computer kiosks has also led to more streamlined communication internally within the prisons. In Iowa, for example, inmates can now use the broader 'OffNet' system (a sort of Internet that only casts its net inside the prison) to access their individual commissary accounts, send money to family members outside the institution, sign up for classes, send a note to staff (informally called a 'kite'), read the weekly newsletter, or even add people to their visiting lists. All of these internal services are free of charge for inmates once they log into the portal.

ATG executives acknowledge the commercial success of OMail, and are just as quick to assert that OMail is an example of the ways that businesses can serve a broader social good. First, they note that the wider array of services, such as those mentioned above, actually work to empower inmates by making them more self-sufficient and less dependent on prison staff. Prior paper-based systems relied on inmates to turn in paper request forms to staff members, who gave the forms to counselors, who in turn completed the task. This process was frequently marred with delays. Now in prisons where an OffNet system is used, inmates can proactively do many of these same tasks themselves. In response, prisons have been able to streamline the approval process. Promoting self-sufficiency among inmates encourages them to make decisions on their own and may help to reduce the uncertainty and anxiety many inmates, and especially long-term inmates, face when released (see generally, Irwin 1970, 2009). OMail also adds to the few inexpensive options available for prisoners to maintain communication with their families, one of the best predictors of parole success, as noted earlier (Petersilia 2003: 246). Indeed, ATG executives noted that several older inmates favored OMail because it allowed them to establish or reestablish relationships with younger children and grandchildren who were more comfortable with such electronic systems of communication.

Currently, the cost to send a message via ATG's service ranges from 5 cents all the way up to 30 cents. Nationwide, ATG executives estimated that the highest cost for sending an OMail message was 50 cents (charged by a competitor). While the pricing scheme seems comparable – or even favorable – to regular mail, critics note that the cost per word is likely higher. The system currently caps correspondence at 13,000 characters or two printed pages, whichever comes first. Thus, the true comparison, critics continue, should not be made on the cost per message, but cost per word. To send a ten-page letter, an inmate could either purchase one stamp (for approximately 50 cents) or send five messages, costing as much as US$2.50 in total. The trade-off, supporters argue, is speed. Whereas it can take up to a week for a local letter to work its way in or out of a correctional facility, OMail messages are typically delivered within 24 hours. Inmates, such as Tom,[7] generally seem willing to make that trade:

> I still write a lot of letters, more on OMail now. I have thirteen people on my [writing] list and at least eight of them I write to once a week using OMail. [Compared with regular mail] OMail is a good way to do it. It's cheaper. And it's a lot faster. I like it though. I mean, no matter how old you are, you still want that paper letter when they do mail call, you want something personal to read. But I like OMail.

As Tom explains, that prison's shift to OMail allowed him to increase the frequency of his correspondence. The trade-off of not receiving a physical letter is lessened by how quickly letters are exchanged. Later in the same interview, Tom went on to note that before OMail was implemented, letters could take up to a week to travel back and forth through prison. Now, that same correspondence took less than 24 hours.

Inmate advocacy groups have criticized electronic-based communication, suggesting it may stifle some forms of artistic expression. Sending drawings and other inmate art via OMail is not possible. Though supporters of OMail note that such missives could still be sent via regular mail, the Prison Policy Institute (PPI) noted in a recent letter to the Federal Communications Commission (FCC) that they found some jails and prisons moving toward an all-email format for correspondence (Wagner and Sakala 2013). Our own state-by-state survey, though, did not find these one-communication-fits-all policies at the statewide level, suggesting that such decisions are made by individual facilities (most likely, as the PPI report indicates, by county jails). Similarly, ATG executives identified that the company did not include exclusivity clauses in their contracts. Such clauses, as we discuss later, limit the other forms of communication available to inmates in exchange for technology services.

Interestingly, at their core, such debates about the costs and benefits of communication technologies are similar to those happening outside prison. Other scholars have noted how our reliance on electronic forms of communication has eroded more personal forms of correspondence in favor of instantaneous delivery. Instead of writing letters, people now email. Instead of calling, they now text. Instead of protesting, they now tweet. Robert Putnum (2000), among others, has noted how although people today are increasingly connected by technology, the technologies that enable such connections have degraded the quality of relationships, making them shallower, or less intimate (Bloom and Bloom 2013). Until the introduction of OMail, inmates were essentially the last group of people in our society still engaged in lengthy written correspondences. During in-prison interviews, one incarcerated man indicated he wrote to nearly 20 friends weekly. Though the same respondent was enthusiastic about the introduction of OMail, his letters are no longer physical objects, but temporary data files. A degree of loss will happen, and even less will be known about the lives of inmates and their loved ones because of lost information that might otherwise be available to ethnographers or historians.

At the same time that information on the lives of inmates may be lost to outsiders, more potentially security-related information about inmates is available to correctional officials. As Smith (2012: 473–474) noted in his article, the most common argument against inmate access to communicative technology is public safety. OMail systems are closed and secure. Ultimately, that security is the primary appeal of such closed email platforms. One prison administrator, noting increased 'control' and 'oversight' of inmate communications, summed up the benefits:

> This system actually allows a little more security than the snail [regular] mail. We can search by keyword. Whereas with snail mail, we scan it, then it goes out, and we never see it again. Here, we have around 200 words, and we can even modify it to look for those words without proper context. So it gives us a lot more possibilities to monitor than just mail. And we can also go back and look at emails from a month, or more than a month ago, and look at all of that. It's just like with the telephone. All of that is recorded. And if one of those keywords comes up, it is held and not sent until a staff member releases it. And usually, ninety, ninety-nine times out of one hundred, there is nothing to it. But it gives us a little more control and a little more oversight than the snail mail. And you know, [inmates] can send anyone a letter. Whereas, again, with this system, the person who is receiving the email has to approve the [inmate's] request.

There is also an added safety benefit conferred by the immaterial nature of electronic correspondence: '[A]nything we can do to reduce the amount of materials, literally physically material, coming and going into the facility, reduces the potential for contraband.' Reducing contraband, theoretically, increases the safety of the prison as a whole and reduces illegal activity therein.

In many ways, corrections-based email platforms are the poster child for how communicative technologies can be successfully introduced into prisons. Such platforms are widely lauded by inmates and administrators for convenience and their rehabilitative promise. Administrators prefer the ability to streamline functions such as monitoring incoming correspondence and reducing the physical introduction of contraband. Inmates prefer the speed of delivery, self-sufficiency, and the ability to maintain connections with family members who are less likely to call or write. Although criticisms do exist, they are largely concerned with affordability, a concern that the creators of the technology share as well. As such, compared with other forms of communicative technology, corrections-based email seems poised to be widely adopted in the future.

The bad: video conferencing

Compared with corrections-based email, video conferencing has a less linear history of implementation within American prisons. Nearly all the states that responded to our survey (36 of 38) used video conferencing to facilitate some type of administrative function. None of the responding states had eliminated the use of video conferencing since 2009, and one state had added it. Thirty-one states used video conferencing to provide telemedicine services. These services primarily related to mental health treatment – the single largest use of video conferencing – offering inmates a way to visit with a psychiatrist or psychologist who was not on site. Parole board hearings comprised the second most common form of video conferencing and were found in 30 states. Finally, pre-trial arraignment was conducted via video conferencing in 23 states.[8] A number of states reported having video conferencing capabilities, but the actual use was much lower, frequently due to the request of the partnering agency (such as the court, parole board or psychiatrist).

Yet while these states had widespread administrative usage of video conferencing, video visitation for inmates appears to have stagnated since the original ACA survey. Video visitation relies upon video conferencing systems, similar to Skype, to allow inmates to visit with their friends and family members. Of the states that responded to our survey, 14 now offered some form of video visitation in 2014, and the program was pending in two more.[9] This number does not indicate an increase over 2009; indeed, in that year, 11 states were offering video visitation, with the program pending in two more. These numbers hint at how complicated the introduction of video visitation throughout the USA has been. Two states – Arizona and Alaska – implemented video visitation in 2009, primarily to facilitate visits for inmates who were sent out of state. Once these inmates returned to in-state incarceration, approximately a year later, the programs were discontinued. Another state – Louisiana – piloted a video visitation after 2009, but found it was too rarely used to be cost effective. The state ended the pilot program prior to the 2014 survey.

We found that similar to the administrative use of video conferencing, video visitation happens more in theory than in practice. Very few systems provided video visitation as it is envisioned by Securus Technology, one of the largest providers of the service nationwide:

> Securus Video Visitation is a web-based video visitation system that allows you to securely communicate with your Friends & Family members or clients from your home, office, or anywhere equipped with a PC, internet access, and webcam. [The system] provides you with a convenient alternative to traveling to correctional facilities for on-site visitations … It provides a simple to use, secure and safe form of communication that reduces the need for travel. It also helps by eliminating the amount of time wasted waiting in long lines. Save time, [s]top traveling, [and] [j]ust connect.

Instead, over half the states indicated they had the capabilities to conduct video visitation, but offered it only for inmates in solitary confinement or protective segregation, to enable visits from children, or provided the service only at certain facilities.

While Securus stresses the mobile nature of visiting for family and friends (that it can be done in the comfort of their own homes), that was seldom true in correctional facilities. The more common practice was for the video visitation system to be set up in the prison visiting room during periods specially designated as electronic visiting hours. The system still required staffing, as many administrators pointed out, but did serve a number of unique situations. In Minnesota, for example, video visitation is being considered as a way to connect Native American inmates with family members who still live in the state's northern reservation. Other states, though, were reluctant to allow family members to initiate visits from home. Louisiana struggled with how to enforce visitor decorum outside the confines of the prison visiting room:

> We tried. We piloted [video visitation]. [W]e had families that had to go to a certain location, but it didn't really catch on … At the time, and currently, we [didn't] have the staff to monitor it, especially from unrestricted locations, like [visitors'] houses. So we instead allowed for families to go to churches [in major locations] like New Orleans. We were concerned about people doing inappropriate things [during the video visit], and we thought, well maybe in a church people wouldn't do crazy things […] Now I think if families could use it from home, it would probably be utilized more. But as it was, [visitors] had to go to a location, and [inmates had to] schedule a time, and it just wasn't used.

This administrator acknowledged that the home-based visiting service may work best, but reiterated that current staffing levels did not support that option. Other systems dealt with the same issue in similar ways. Both Arizona and Alaska identified staffing costs as the primary reasons for discontinuing their programs as well, despite, like Minnesota, having a large geographic area that was not conducive to face-to-face visitation.

Though the trend shows more state prisons moving towards video visitation, more county jails have done so. Securus currently provides services to 105 jail facilities in 33 states – almost all county jails. The services do cost. In most institutions, Securus charges $5 for 20 minutes of visiting. A typical two-hour visit (the limit at many correctional facilities) would cost $30. Again, the company notes that the convenience of video visits outweighs the cost, and that many jails provide more availability for video visiting than in-person visits.

Perhaps the more serious costs of video visitation are a byproduct of the service contracts. The PPI, in a 2013 letter to the FCC, noted that in a number of new contracts, counties were required to cease offering any in-person contact visits, and instead only provide onsite video conferencing, which was fee-based (Wagner and Sakala 2013). For example, Securus' contract with the Shawnee County, Kansas jail explicitly instructs that the county will 'eliminate all face-to-face visitation through glass or otherwise at the Facility and will utilize video visitation for all non-professional on-site visitors' (ibid.: 2). The PPI found similar clauses in other contracts, and noted that the exclusive use of video conferencing had often continued, despite public opposition (ibid.). In contrast, supporters of video visitations point to the cost savings and the role that video visitations can play in increasing family visits.

A revealing debate about these matters unfolded in Washington, DC. In 2012, the city eliminated all in-person visits in favor of video visitations. The visits are free, but officials estimated the program would save as much as $420,000 annually in personnel costs. Additionally, video visits could reduce recidivism by prompting more visits from family and friends, administrators contended, since the switch immediately doubled the jail's visiting capacity to 400 visits per day (Austermuhle 2012; DC DOC 2012; Hermann 2012; WP Editorial Board 2012a, 2012b). Visits are onsite only, with inmates participating in one computer lab and visitors in another. The labs are housed in different buildings. The plan was immediately met by opposition, despite the projected savings. Two *Washington Post* editorials (WP Editorial Board 2012a, 2012b) decried the decision, concluding: '[T]he option of in-person visitation should be restored, at least as an alternative to video visits [...], [i]n the meantime, the D.C. jail owes the public an explanation for heaping an even greater burden on those who already suffer enough.' Similarly, at City Council hearings, residents noted how the video visits were of poor technical quality and were not a substitute for in-person visits. One mother explained that before, during in-person visits, she felt reassured in being able to view her son. By seeing him, she was able to check his body for new scratches or scars, read his body language, and pick up on his mood. 'He doesn't know that, but that's what I'd be doing ... I can't really do that if he's just sitting there and all I see is his face. You can't really do that on a monitor' (Emmanuel 2012). Shortly after this hearing, several City Council members introduced a bill to restore in-person visiting. The bill was tabled.

While video visitation has garnered much attention from prisoner rights advocates and administrators, both related to its costs and exclusive contract agreements, the use of video conferencing in administrative policies has, by comparison, received almost no attention. Inmates, though, frequently share the same concerns about such video conferencing as their families and advocates share about video visiting. The lack of personal contact with individuals who are prescribing, treating or making legal decisions is distracting, many inmates noted. Carl, an incarcerated man in Iowa, summed up the sentiments of many inmates interviewed about the state's use of video conferencing to facilitate parole hearings:

> I think [the parole board hearings] should go back to face to face [...] It's more of a personal meeting that way. It's not just them staring at you over a monitor or a TV screen. [The parole board members are] actually seeing the [inmate] in-person. And

I think you can read facial expressions and get cues off of their voice way better in person than you can over the [video conferencing system] ... So you might be able to understand emotions and stuff like that way better if you're face to face than if you're over a TV screen.

By bringing the inmate and the parole board face to face, parole board members (or judges or medical doctors) had to directly observe, if not acknowledge, the humanity of the inmate. This desire for face-to-face communication was repeatedly expressed. Inmates were routinely frustrated by how their attempts to connect on a personal level with the professionals they encountered were stymied by poor connections or resolution. One evocative story, relayed by a lawyer, involved an African-American woman who was applying for commutation of her life sentence. In preparation, the woman spent many hours doing her make-up, braiding her hair and arranging her appearance for the hearing. Once on the video conferencing screen, though, the system's poor resolution failed to pick up any of this detail. Instead, cameras failed to differentiate the contours and shading of her skin, making her appear monochrome and emotionless on the screen. The woman's entire effort to convey how seriously she had prepared for this encounter was pixelated.

The concerns and benefits associated with video visitation and conferencing expand upon those seen with corrections-based email – the erosion of personal connections as a byproduct of technologically mediated contact. While many of the arguments – both in favor and against – are the same for these two types of technology, they are more intensely expressed in the disagreements over video visitation, in particular. Since contractors providing this technology have actively sought to limit or end in-person visits, the potential deprivation of *real* human contact faced by inmates is greater. Similarly, prison administrators themselves seem sharply divided on the use of these practices. On the one hand, administrators recognized the money saved and potential opportunities to expand visiting, but they also acknowledged that the technology did not seem quite ready to take the place of face-to-face contact. None of the administrators we interviewed talked about video visitation as the only option, but like email, viewed it as a part of a wider buffet of options for increasing inmate contact with their support systems. Conversely, inmates, their families and their supporters expressed considerable reservations about the systems, both in terms of their often considerable technical shortcomings and in terms of the intrinsic limits of mediated contact, especially when direct contact seems readily available as an option. As one family member, interviewed in a Spokane, Washington area jail, noted: 'With all the technology today on smartphones and everything it's all clear, it's high definition. You know [the video visitation system is] like slow moving, there's kind of delays and it's not like you're right there – I mean I'm in the same building as them, I don't see why I shouldn't be able to see them' (Robinson 2013).

The ugly: cell phones

In American prisons, the introduction of technology has largely been predicated upon its promised cost savings. OMail popularity, particularly among inmates, stems from its affordability, followed closely by the fact that the system is easy to use. Corrections administrators noted how the program saved money in the long term by reducing the staff hours needed to search traditional mail for contraband. The implementation of video visitations has similarly been driven by its promise to reduce staff hours. Less successfully, such companies often market themselves by emphasizing how at-home video visitation can actually save inmates' families money over the long run (when compared with in-person visits). With respect to both OMail and video visitation, the cost savings for the state have been a primary motivation for introducing these technologies. However, the state is not the only party interested in cutting costs. Inmates and their families have routinely searched for alternatives to the daily, often considerable, costs associated with incarceration. Cell phones have emerged as one popular, if illicit, way to save money.

Among technologies adding to the burdens faced by the families of inmates, prison telephone costs are perhaps the most well documented. Prison telephone price gouging has drawn considerable condemnation from many corners. Researchers have argued that such arrangements limit families' ability to stay connected (George 2010; Hasine 2010; Rose and Clear 2006). A 2005 editorial from the *New York Daily News* called upon the state to end such exploitative practices and illustrated just how lucrative such contracts are:

> The arrangement drains an estimated $20 million a year from mostly low-income families in a handful of inner-city neighborhoods ... New York families have to cough up a flat fee of $3 per call plus 16 cents a minute – the highest rates of any prison system in America and more than twice the 7 cents a minute paid by federal prison inmates. About half a million calls come out of state prisons every month and more than 9 million minutes of talk time get billed [...] A slice of the proceeds ends up with MCI, the company with monopoly control over phone service in the state's 70 prisons – but more than 57% of the fees go to the state.
>
> (Louis 2005)[10]

Based upon the math provided in this editorial, a local family that called their incarcerated loved one for a minimum of an hour each week would end up paying over $50 per month.[11] The incentives offered to states in such phone contracts create a perverse incentive for corrections. Prison administrators readily acknowledge the high costs, but also point out that the money drawn from such contracts is commonly used to fund rehabilitative programming for inmates (programming which would otherwise be the victim due to budget constraints).

In an outside world where the price of communication is dropping, the high prices of phone conversations in prisons are particularly frustrating for inmates and their families. The result, these same administrators note, is the proliferation of illicit cell phone use:

> [L]ike everyone else, we're fighting the influx of cell phone. We can have one [cell] phone, with thirty inmates who all have their own SIM cards. And most of the conversations are not around doing anything wrong or security breaches, but because it is cheaper. The conversations are cheaper. The calling is nationwide and there is only one monthly fee. So it is a lot cheaper.

Proliferation, indeed, may be a modest term for the growth in illegal cell phone seizures. In 2008, Texas authorities seized over 600 phones – 26 from inmates on the state's death row, a notoriously restrictive environment (AAS Editorial Staff 2008; see generally, Johnson and Davies 2014; Latson 2008). In 2012, Texas state authorities announced they had confiscated over 900 cell phones (New 2013). Yet that growth is dwarfed by the explosion seen in other states, such as California. In 2009, California reported it had seized more than 2,800 phones, doubled from the year before (Associated Press 2011). A year later, authorities reported they had seized nearly 11,000 phones (Severson and Brown 2011).

Prison administrators have responded to the flood of contraband cell phones with a number of countermeasures. Since 2008, states have petitioned the FCC to make prisons an exception to the 1934 federal law that makes it illegal to jam phone signals. The FCC has fought against this change, arguing that jamming technologies could affect the cell phone usage of non-incarcerated people in the same areas (Associated Press 2008c, 2008e; Kinnard 2008a, 2008b; MTRN Editorial Staff 2009; n.a. 2008c; n.a. 2009; Ward 2008). In response, states have invested in other technologies to thwart cell phone use. The most effective – and expensive – are systems that do not block the signal, but render unregistered cell phones unusable (Kinnard 2008a; Severson and Brown 2011). When a prisoner using an unregistered phone attempts to call out, he or she is told that the phone has not been approved and the device is no longer usable. However, these systems are extremely costly. Coverage must be purchased for each housing unit. As a result, such systems are only in place in a few prisons in a few states, including Texas and Mississippi. Other states have relied upon less expensive but also less precise methods, including handheld detectors, which can locate a cell phone once it is turned on, and cell phone sniffer dogs that are trained to fix on the phone's lithium battery (Associated Press 2008a; Binetti 2008; Gresko 2008; n.a. 2008b).

As the number of cell phones in prison swells, more and more attention is being paid to how these phones find their way into prisons. Most cell phones are smuggled in by family members or guards (AAS Editorial Staff 2008; Associated Press 2007, 2008b, 2008c, 2008e; Hopkins 2007; Marimow and Wagner 2013; MTRN Editorial Staff 2009; Severson and Brown 2011). A correctional officer who decides to smuggle in a cell phone can make as much as $2,000 per phone, a lucrative prospect, especially in states where salaries are low. States have struggled with how to prevent smuggling. In some states, such as North Dakota, state legislatures have made it a felony to provide an inmate with a cell phone. Other states, including Kentucky and Texas, have prosecuted correctional officers under federal statutes for selling cell phones (Hopkins 2007; n.a. 2007). Other states have seen their attempts to prevent smuggling stymied. When the California legislature proposed that correctional officers be required to go through a metal detector prior to beginning work, the union opposed it. The provision was later dropped (Associated Press 2011; Kahn 2011). In other countries, inmates have creatively worked around guards, when bribery has not worked. Some phones – no one knows how many – are smuggled in by inmates, who are inventive in matters relating to treasured contraband. A recent news report noted that at a Brazilian prison, gangs were sending cell phones in on the backs of pigeons, making these birds the communication carriers of choice in these institutions (n.a. 2008a).

Perhaps the most convincing countermeasure to inmate access to cell phones has been public fear. A recent article in Ohio's *The Plain Dealer* summed up the sentiment expressed in most coverage:

No good can come from inmates having cell phones … It is a huge security issue. Inmates can plan attacks, smuggling and escapes. They can use them to run their various crimes and businesses. They can use them to videotape. Doing that [video-taping] on the outside is fine, but prisoners can use that to extort various people on the inside.

(Caniglia 2013)

Though these fears are often overstated, as noted earlier, there is some truth to this concern, at least in isolated instances. A case in point: during the summer of 2013, Tavon White, a leader of the Black Guerrilla Family gang, used a cell phone to orchestrate a money-laundering ring while incarcerated in Maryland's Baltimore County jail (Marimow and Wagner 2013). White also purchased cars, fathered children with five female correctional officers, and paid off other correctional officers and inmates using stolen prepaid debit cards – arranging nearly all of these purchases and activities through his cell phones. Years earlier, in the summer of 2007, a drug dealer and gang member, Patrick Albert Byers, Jr, was alleged to have used a smuggled cell phone to arrange the murder of a key witness from the same jail (Bishop 2009).

Other inmates, such as convicted Kansas murderer John Manard, have planned their escapes from prison with the aid of a cell phone (Associated Press 2008e). Even closely monitored inmates, such as California serial killer Charles Manson, have been able to access cell phones. Guards found two separate phones in Manson's cell in the state's Special Housing Unit – the first in 2009 and the second in 2011. The phones' records indicated that Manson had called people in more than seven states, including as far away as British Columbia (Associated Press 2011).

The illicit cell phone activities of Texas death row inmate Richard Lee Tabler garnered even more media attention than those of Manson (Latson 2008). During the 2008 session, state Senator John Whitmore received a call from Tabler. Tabler, who had been convicted of double homicide in 2004, was making the call from Texas' death row. In the phone call, he threatened Whitmore's daughters, and included information he had received about the girls from the Internet. Once seized, officials learned that the phone, which had been smuggled in by a prison guard, had been passed around death row. Tabler and nine other inmates had used the phone to place over 2,800 calls in just 30 days (Latson 2008). These facts were widely reported, appearing in newspaper articles around the country (AAS Editorial Staff 2008; Kinnard 2008b). Less well reported, though, was Tabler's motivation. Tabler had been seeking a swift execution since his convictions, including asking his attorney to waive his appeals. Following the seizure of his cell phone, and the arrest of his mother (who bought the phone and paid for the monthly plan), Tabler attempted to commit suicide. He later confessed to making the threats in an effort to hasten his own death (Graczk 2012; Latson 2008; TV KEYE News 2009). Instead, Tabler was moved to a psychiatric unit and is still awaiting execution. Similarly, there were few reports about the other calls placed on the cell phone – likely because they were not particularly sinister. The other members of Texas' death row did call fellow gang members, but the majority of calls were to family members, friends, and death penalty opponents (Latson 2008).

In the myriad stories of frightening abuses such as those involving inmates like Tabler, Manson or White, the question of why cell phone use is so pervasive and resistant to control is obscured. Prevention programs and detection devices have primarily focused on locating cell phones or interrupting commerce. Time and time again, the why – as in, why do inmates want access to cell phones and why are they willing to risk punishment to get them? – has been ignored. The evidence suggests that most of the calls made by inmates are less about ordering hits or making threats, and more about maintaining contact with the outside world. Take, for example, the story of how Georgia inmates orchestrated a non-violent strike using cell phones:

> A counterfeiter at a Georgia state prison ticks off the remaining days of his three-year sentence on his Facebook page. He has 91 digital 'friends'. Like many of his fellow inmates, he plays the online games FarmVille and Street Wars. He does it all on a Samsung smart phone … And he used the same phone to help organize a short nonviolent strike among inmates at several Georgia prisons last month. The Georgia prison strike, for instance, was about things prisoners often complain about: They are not paid for their labor. Visitation rules are too strict. Meals are bad […] Inmates punched in text messages and assembled e-mail lists to coordinate simultaneous protests, including work stoppages, with inmates at other prisons. Under pseudonyms, they shared hour-by-hour updates with followers on Facebook and Twitter. They communicated with their advocates, conducted news media interviews and monitored coverage of the strike.
>
> (Severson and Brown 2011: A4)

Like the Texas death row inmates, cell phone access allowed Georgia inmates to blur the line between prison and the outside world, maintain contact with loved ones and the larger world, and expose what was happening inside the prison walls.

Numbers also back up the implication that most cell phones are not used for criminal purposes. After Mississippi installed the new managed access technology, where only approved numbers can call out, the system intercepted 643,388 calls and texts made by the prison's 3,000 inmates during the first 120 days (Severson and Brown 2011). That is a staggering amount, and yet, in the year leading up to the system's implementation, we could not find one high-profile crime orchestrated by inmate cell phone use. It is entirely possible that crimes were not discovered, but the more likely explanation is simply that little or no crime was committed with the aid of cell phones. As the prison administrator we interviewed at the beginning of this chapter suggested, perhaps inmate cell phone use is not motivated by a desire to commit crime but instead by a desire to stay in touch.

New prospects, old problems and an uncertain future

In this chapter, we provided a broad, descriptive overview of the communicative technologies used by American prisons. We also examined how some of the more popular – and problematic – types of technology were adopted in contemporary American prisons and what challenges or benefits accompanied their use. (Many of the issues we address are germane to the prison systems of other countries, notably England and Wales, though the details may differ. See e.g., Jewkes and Johnston 2009.) Our three case studies, focusing on the introduction of OMail, video conferencing and visitation, and illicit cell phone use, all indicate that today's inmates are better connected than ever before. Though incarcerated, American inmates are increasingly being given more access to more communicative technologies. These technologies allow inmates to stay better connected during their imprisonment than in years past, but it is a mistake to conclude that today's inmates are connected in ways comparable to free citizens.

One need only stroll a college campus to see the students seemingly fixated on smartphones, watching the small screens of their devices rather than watching where they are walking, even as they move amid a group of fellow students who are equally absorbed in another world – a world formed by almost continuous use of technology in everyday life in the free world. Prisoners are largely cut off from this world of 24–7 technology. Given the pace of technological change in the free world, it is unclear whether inmates are keeping up with technology or merely falling behind less rapidly than in times past.

If we were writing this chapter with an inmate co-author, for example, we would find that the communications available to us to reach that inmate in a timely fashion would likely be limited and cumbersome. One of us is, in fact, writing a book with an inmate. She is held in a clean, well-ordered modern prison but has no access to OMail (though this is coming, she is told), no access to a cell phone (legitimate or illegitimate), limited opportunities to make expensive phone calls (though the cost is dropping), and limits on the contents of letters she receives (seven pages is the maximum). She is not buried alive (though she may beg to differ). We write, talk, occasionally visit face-to-face, but the barriers to working together, let alone to expressing support, are profound. To be sure, every step forward in the availability of technology examined in this chapter is critically important to inmates, their families and the larger society, but these advances are painfully limited in objective, comparative terms.

The progress that has occurred in access to communication technology in prison has been accompanied by ethical trade-offs. As prisons and jails rely on technologies that bolster staff control, the results often mean inmates have less in-person contact with others, while having more access to electronic means of support. The long-term impacts of these trade-offs are uncertain. To take one example, let us consider the value of keeping in touch with one's family. While many studies have reaffirmed the importance of family involvement as means to improve in-prison behavior and reduce recidivism, we are unaware of any studies that examine how this relationship might be affected by video visits and other contacts mediated by technology. Does a screen-to-screen session with a family member equate to a face-to-face session? Equating all types of family contact with family support may be a mistake. In the midst of this shift to more accessible communication technology – a shift we applaud – we nevertheless encourage prison systems and researchers to examine how variables such as family support are affected by technology. One might, as well, examine the effects of other technologies on relationships, from OMail through licit and illicit cell phone use. If a prisoner's emotional life is mediated by screens or communication devices of one sort or another, is that an emotional life that will sustain and ideally help prepare the prisoner for reentry into society? As more and more technological access is made available in prison, this question will grow in importance.

Additionally, although inmates are better connected, we continue to note that their access to communicative technology is largely defined for them. Inmates and their families have limited input into what technologies they are exposed to or expected to use, and often they use these technologies under supervision and subject to later review by the authorities. Prison officials jealously guard their control of technology. Indeed, the strongest negative reactions we document from officials with respect to technology are in response to illegal cell phone use: not because of a disproportionate number of vicious crimes associated with their use, but because prison administrators lack control of this technology and cannot record and monitor its usage. With cell phones, inmates are able to narrate their own lives, plan their own responses and, yes, exercise bad decision making.

The bottom line is that communicative technology has the potential to empower inmates to become self-sufficient. Prison officials generally resist things that promote self-sufficiency among inmates; autonomy, on its face, conflicts with the conformity sought in prison regimes (see generally, Johnson 2002). However, self-sufficiency is the gold standard in corrections; if we are to rehabilitate, we must produce people able to manage their own lives. American prison officials might thus want to continue experimenting with cell phone access and the relatively unfettered autonomy such use permits, as prisons in the United Kingdom are now doing. There, prisons are experimenting with 'in-cell phones'. The phones, which are landlines, allow inmates to call out to pre-approved numbers, at their own leisure. Costs are minimal – as is screening. Although calls can be recorded, officials note that over 80% are not. Inmates have no restrictions on the duration of the call or how frequently the calls are placed. Officials have already reported that the in-cell phones have increased overall prison safety (by reducing arguments over communal phones), encouraged family contact, and reduced the number of illicit cell phones brought into the facility (Johnson 2013; Saul 2013).

As a practical matter, prisoners almost certainly will never live in the open-access technological world of free citizens, but they may appear to do so, and this appearance may blur the line between prisons and the free world as we now understand it. Inmates who are able to keep up with their loved ones on Facebook or via text message are physically removed from loved ones but not really absent. What, then, are the pains of imprisonment for them?

In an earlier work, Johnson (2005) hypothesized that free citizens may resent in-prison programming not because of vindictiveness, but because of jealousy over the seeming availability of free time in prison. That free time is an illusion – free time in a cage, even a gilded cage, is an oxymoron – but one that haunts some citizens, who lead a fast-paced life and perhaps understandably imagine that the controlled existence of the prison is a kind of vacation from the pressures of everyday life in the real world, with its variety, rapidity and often dog-eat-dog competitiveness. As prisons become more wired, our reaction to the experience of imprisonment may change, too. In a prison environment in which everyone is both 'off the grid' (in the sense that they are free from the pressures of work, raising a family, etc.) and yet seemingly engaged with others (able to savor Facebook exchanges and communal video games, for instance), free citizens may find more grounds for resentment. If citizens come to feel that we cannot tell who is incarcerated by the fact of their physical absence from society, we may see a growing public opposition to the availability of communication technology behind bars and a desire to make sure prisoners serve hard time in the very different world that is the old-fashioned, technologically impaired prison. The perception that technology makes prisoners free from the rigors of confinement would be mistaken, the resulting policies regressive and ill advised. However, should there be a backlash against prison technology, it would be neither the first nor the last time corrections found itself at a crossroads and took a wrong turn.

Notes

1 The authors gratefully acknowledge the research support provided by American University undergraduate students Lia Gargano, Nora Kirk, Christine Kowlessar and Courtney Belme. Each produced a thoughtful compilation and review of newspaper articles on technology in corrections published over the last ten years. In addition, each student reviewed the 2009 American Correctional Association survey of technology in corrections and produced state profiles that were used as a benchmark for the 2013–14 survey reported in this chapter. Lia Gargano also worked on the citations for this chapter.

2 Illinois was the only state not to respond to the survey. Five Canadian systems (Manitoba, New Brunswick, Newfoundland, Nova Scotia and Ontario) responded as well.

3 Video visitations were pending in four more states.

4 These findings were generally shared with the Canadian system. None of the reporting Canadian systems allowed inmates to send or receive email, or to access the Internet. Video visitations were pending in one system.

5 Family and friends can also initiate the request. In this case, the scenario is merely reversed and the inmate is asked if they want to add the individual to their approved contact list.

6 The one exception is that some states will charge the incarcerated recipient a printing cost, particularly if the message is printed off and delivered to the inmate.

7 All names attributed to incarcerated individuals, in keeping with American University's IRB protocols, are pseudonyms.

8 Includes one state – Arizona – where video conferencing is used for Federal Court mediations.

9 Video visitation was pending in Tennessee in 2009. The state was unable to participate in the 2014 survey and asked that their 2009 responses be used. Therefore, it is unclear what happened with the video visitation program.

10 The rates quoted here are actually quite low by 2013 standards. Recent discussions on the inmate family online forum PrisonTalk noted that the local per minute rate for Texas families was 26¢ per minute and 43¢ per minute for long-distance calls – still less than half of the 89¢ per minute cost of long-distance calls in Georgia. In February 2014 the FCC capped long-distance rates at 25¢ per minute nationwide, or a maximum of $3.75 for a 15-minute collect call. Local calling rates were not capped.

11 This calculation, of course, assumes a working telephone system that does not routinely disconnect on the speakers and no additional fees. In fact, the realities of such a glitch-free system are countered by inmates' own narratives, and the narratives of their families. Forums such as PrisonTalk are filled with pages of threads detailing phone problems in each state. Contributors frequently bemoan not only the frustrations of trying to connect with loved ones, but the additional costs, including multiple connection fees during one conversation, or the $9.95 'convenience fee' charged by some companies for adding money with a credit card. Since no incentive exists to fix such issues, either for the state or the telephone company, family members note, they are seldom addressed.

Bibliography

AAS Editorial Staff (2008) 'Can you find it now?' *Austin American-Statesman*, 20 November, www.factiva.com.

Anonymous (2009) 'Computer use for/by inmates', *Corrections Compendium* 34(2): 24–31.

Associated Press (2007) 'Fugitive extradited back to New Mexico', *The Associated Press Newswires*, 9 March, www.factiva.com.

Associated Press (2008a) 'Cell phone sniffing dogs added to NJ prisons', *Associated Press Newswires*, 16 November, www.factiva.com.

Associated Press (2008b) 'Guard accused of smuggling cell phone to inmate', *Associated Press Newswires*, 10 December, www.factiva.com.

Associated Press (2008c) 'Cell phones in use in prisons', *Associated Press Newswires*, 16 December, www.factiva.com.

Associated Press (2008d) 'Families to visit Fla. inmates by video bus', *Associated Press Newswires*, 19 December, www.factiva.com.

Associated Press (2008e) 'Smuggled cell phones concern prisons', *Associated Press Newswires*, 22 December, www.factiva.com.

Associated Press (2011) 'Calif. wants to stop phones used by likes of Manson', *Charleston Gazette*, 15 February: 9B.

Austermuhle, M. (2012) 'D.C. jail video visits prompt complaints', 18 September, dcist.com (accessed 3 June 2014).

Bales, W.D. and Mears, D.P. (2008) 'Inmate social ties and the transition to society: Does visitation reduce recidivism?' *Journal of Research in Crime and Delinquency* 45(1): 287–231.

Binetti, R. (2008) 'Cell phones go to the dogs: Maryland uses phone-finding K-9s to step up security efforts', *Corrections Today*, 1 October, www.factiva.com.

Bishop, T. (2009) 'Murder on call', *The Baltimore Sun*, 26 April, articles.baltimoresun.com (accessed 23 May 2014).

Bloom, L. and Bloom, C. (2013) 'What's missing with our over-reliance on technology?' *Psychology Today*, 10 December, www.psychologytoday.com (accessed 10 June 2014).

Caniglia, J. (2013) 'Ohio prison system sees spike in cell phones behind bars', *The Plain Dealer*, 26 August, www.cleveland.com (accessed 23 May 2014).

Clear, T.R. (1994) *Harm in American Penology: Offenders, victims and their communities*, Albany, NY: State University of New York Press.

DC DOC (2012) 'Video visitations at the DC jail', press release, Issuing agency: District of Columbia Department of Corrections, 30 August, doc.dc.gov (accessed 3 June 2014).

Emmanuel, A. (2012) 'In-person visits fade as jails set up video unit for inmates and families', *The New York Times*, 7 August, www.nytimes.com (accessed 3 June 2014).

Ferguson, R. (2014) *Inferno: An anatomy of American punishment*, Cambridge, MA: Harvard University Press.

George, E. (2010) *A Woman Doing Life: Notes from a prison for women*, London: Oxford University Press.

Graczk, M. (2012) 'Killer who called Texas senator renews death wish', *Austin American-Statesman*, 14 October, www.statesman.com (accessed 25 May 2014).

Gresko, J. (2008) 'Cell-phone sniffling dog to search Florida prisons', *Associated Press Newswires*, 7 October, www.factiva.com.

Hasine, V. (2010) *Life without parole: Living and dying in prison today*, fifth edn, London: Oxford University Press.

Hermann, P. (2012) 'Visiting a detainee in the D.C. jail now done by video', *The Washington Post*, 28 July, www.washingtonpost.com (accessed 14 June 2014).

Hopkins, J. (2007) 'Ex-prison nurse sentenced for giving phone to inmate lover', *McClatchy-Tribune Regional News*, 19 May, www.factiva.com.

Irwin, J. (1970) *The Felon*, Berkeley, CA: University of California Press.

Irwin, J. (2009) *Lifers: Seeking redemption in prison*, New York: Routledge.

Jewkes, Y. (2002) *Captive Audience: Media, masculinity, and power*, Cullompton: Willan.

Jewkes, Y. (2008) 'The role of the Internet in the twenty-first-century prison: insecure technologies in secure spaces', in K.F. Aes (ed.) *Technologies of Insecurity: Surveillance and Securitization of Everyday Life*, Abingdon: Routledge.

Jewkes, Y. and Johnston, H. (2009) 'Cavemen in an era of speed-of-light technology: Historical and contemporary perspectives on communication within prisons', *The Howard Journal of Criminal Justice* 48(2): 132–143.

Johnson, R. (2002) *Hard Time: Understanding and reforming the prison*, Belmont, CA: Wadsworth.

Johnson, R. (2005) 'Brave new prisons: The growing isolation of modern penal institutions', in A. Liebling and S. Maruna (eds) *The Effects of Imprisonment*, Cullompton: Willan, 255–284.

Johnson, R. and Davies, H. (2014) 'Life under sentence of death: Historical and contemporary perspectives', in J.R. Acker, R.M. Bohm and C.S. Lanier (eds) *America's experiment with capital punishment: Reflections on the past, present, and future of the ultimate penal sanction*, third edn, Durham, NC: Carolina Academic Press, 661–685.

Johnson, W. (2013) 'Prisoners should be given in-cell phones, inspector says', *The Telegraph*, 1 March, www.telegraph.co.uk (accessed 25 May 2014).

Kahn, C. (2011) 'Calif. law calls for stricter prison cell phone rules', *All Things Considered*, National Public Radio, 8 February, www.npr.org (accessed 23 June 2014).

Kinnard, M. (2008a) 'SC prisons take on feds over jamming phone signals', *Associated Press Newswires*, 22 October, www.factiva.com.

Kinnard, M. (2008b) 'SC prison hosts cell phone jamming demonstration', *Associated Press Newswires*, 21 November, www.factiva.com.

Latson, J. (2008) 'Two more cell phones confiscated on Texas death row', *Houston Chronicle*, 20 October, www.chron.com (accessed 25 May 2014).

Louis, E. (2005) 'End cell phone ripoff, finally, pols fight to stop MCI from gouging prisoners families', *New York Daily News*, 10 May, www.factiva.com.

Marimow, A.E. and Wagner, J. (2013) '13 corrections officers indicted in Md., accused of aiding gang's drug scheme', *Washington Post*, 23 April, www.washingtonpost.com (accessed 25 May 2014).

MTRN Editorial Staff (2009) 'Editorial: Cell phones in prison – a growing problem', *McClatchy-Tribune Regional News*, 21 July, www.factiva.com.

n.a. (2007) 'Information issued by U.S. attorney's office for the eastern district of Kentucky', *Hindustan Times*, 24 February, www.factiva.com.

n.a. (2008a) 'Brazil: Inmates train pigeons to smuggle drugs into prison', *The Guardian*, 26 June, www.factiva.com.

n.a. (2008b) 'Cell phone sniffling dog helps enforce new law', *US Fed News*, 7 October, www.factiva.com.

n.a. (2008c) 'Citing a violation of federal law, officials cancel test to jam prison cell phones', *Abilene Reporter-News*, 17 December, www.factiva.com.

n.a. (2009) 'Company says cell-jamming will go on without the FCC's approval', *Telecom A.M.*, 20 February, www.factiva.com.

New, B. (2013) 'Texas fighting back against smuggled prison cell phones', *Digital Forensic Investigator*, 2 April, www.dfinews.com (accessed 23 May 2014).

Petersilia, J. (2003) *When Prisoners Come Home: Parole and prisoner reentry*, London: Oxford University Press.

Putnam, R.D. (2000) *Bowling Alone: The collapse and revival of American community*, New York: Simon & Schuster.

Rao, M. (2008) 'Bloods inmates exploiting N.J. jails; a state panel, after 20 months of investigation, found gang crimes freely organized from cells', *The Philadelphia Inquirer*, 19 November, www.factiva.com.

Robinson, J. (2013) 'Inmates' families say they're the ones punished by switch to video visits', *Oregon Public Broadcasting*, 4 June, www.opb.org (accessed 15 June 2014).

Rose, D.R. and Clear, T.R. (2006) 'Incarceration, social capital, and crime: Implications for social disorganization theory', *Criminology* 36(3): 441–480.

Saul, H. (2013) 'Prisoners given in-cell phones and screens', *The Independent*, 12 December, www.independent.co.uk (accessed 25 May 2014).

Severson, K. and Brown, R. (2011) 'Banned, prison cell phones thrive internet-linked devices enable inmates to pursue criminal activities while keeping in touch with kin', *Pittsburgh Post-Gazette*, 3 January: A-4.

Shenoy, R. (2012) 'Minnesota inmates to receive email', *Minnesota Public Radio*, 6 July, www.factiva.com.

Smith, P.S. (2012) 'Imprisonment and internet-access: Human rights, the principle of normalization and the question of prisoners access to digital communications technology', *Nordic Journal of Human Rights* 30(4): 454–482.

Spjeldnes, S., Jung, H., Maguire, L. and Yamatani, H. (2012) 'Positive family social support: Counteracting negative effects of mental illness and substance abuse to reduce jail ex-inmate recidivism rates', *Journal of Human Behavior in the Social Environment* 22(2): 130–147.

TV KEYE News (2009) 'Strip club killer wants to die quickly', 19 October, keyetv.com (accessed 21 May 2014).

Wagner, P. and Sakala, L. (2013) 'Public comment and enclosed exhibits from the Prison Policy Institute to the Federal Communications Commission on the future of correctional communications services', written correspondence, message to: M.H. Dortch (secretary of the FCC), 20 December, Proceeding Number: 12–375, apps.fcc.gov (accessed 15 June 2014).

Ward, M. (2008) 'State: FCC flip-flops on cell jamming test', *Austin American-Statesman*, 17 December, www.factiva.com.

WP Editorial Board (2012a) 'Virtual visits for inmates?' *The Washington Post*, 26 July, www.washingtonpost.com (accessed 15 June 2014).

WP Editorial Board (2012b) 'D.C. prisoners deserve better than flawed video-only visitation policy', *The Washington Post*, 12 August, www.washingtonpost.com (accessed 15 June 2014).

Part III

International perspectives on imprisonment

Chapter 17

Punishment and political economy

Ester Massa[1]

In the opening paragraph of an article written in 1955, Donald Cressey quoted Edwin Sutherland in defining the scope of criminology as 'the study of the processes of making laws, breaking laws, and reacting to the breaking of laws' (Sutherland 1947: 1), pointing out how this very last part was still 'most neglected by sociologist-criminologists, in spite of the fact that the subject matter is intrinsically sociological'.[2] This affirmation shows how, at the time, the sociology of punishment was still considered a new frontier for those criminologists who dared to venture into theoretical speculations beyond just making simple analyses of crime rates and educated guesses about their causes. What is certain, however, is that the concept of crime is very much related to that of punishment, if only for the fact that when we want to discuss the level of crime in a certain area, and maybe compare it with that in another area, we usually refer to official reports, based most of the time on imprisonment rates referring to a certain area in a certain period of time. For several centuries, in fact, imprisonment has been the most common way of administering punishment in modern society. Generally we are led to think that crime and punishment (the penal reaction to crime) are very closely related, being almost a two-faced coin, so much so that when one of the two undergoes a change, the other needs inevitably to follow. Therefore, an increase in crime means also a rise in the official crime rates and, consequently, an increase in imprisonment rates. We will see that this is not always the case.

Crime and punishment are two different concepts pertaining to a single idea, which in turn is not fixed but is a product of the human imagination, and so is changeable and adaptable: law. Crime itself is a concept representing the result of a definition: given by men and women, operating in a certain identifiable place, during a certain historical period. Behaviour which, at a certain time and place, is a crime can be de-penalized later on, whereas some other previously licit behaviour may become a crime because of the choice of a government. Classic examples of this are vagrancy (a crime in the past) and homosexuality (still a crime in some societies, but tolerated and targeted by anti-discrimination campaigns in other countries). Conversely, there are examples of accepted behaviours that turned into crimes: witness offences against the natural environment, as well as the majority of what today are called 'white-collar crimes'. Thus, a certain act is defined as crime by penal law, and penal law is not independent of other social phenomena, representing a social product subject to the same power relations as other social products (more on this in Vanneste 2001). At the same time, punishment, an expression of the criminal law of the moment, can be considered a social construct, depending on the strength of our representations of crime and criminals, or, more accurately, depending on the perception of crime and criminals in the public opinion and law enforcement. As Cressey went on to note:

> A mature sociology of punishment would correlate the variations of punitive reactions to law-breaking with variations in social organization and then would account for the correlation. Thus, the general theoretical problem is not unlike the general theoretical problem of explaining the variation in crime rates. The problem can be summarized by the question: Why does the punitive reaction to crime vary from time to time and from place to place? In dealing with this general question the assumption must be made that societal reactions to crime can be classed as punitive, non-punitive, or partially punitive on a general level, and that techniques or methods of implementing the general reaction need not to be considered. The concern is not with the types of punishment inflicted or with the frequency and severity of the punishment administered, but with the presence or absence of various general modes of responding to criminality in various societies. Preliminary attempts to answer the questions have included cultural, psychoanalytic, and sociological concepts, but the explanations have not been convincing.
>
> (Cressey 1955: 396)

Just as Cressey calls for, this chapter will explore the meaning of the concept of punishment and its relation to society, specifically exploring its ties with political economy. It will narrate how different sociologists and criminologists have so far described the connection between certain aspects of the economic world (along with its policies) and the use of given kinds of punishment – particularly imprisonment – characterized by their levels of punitiveness, as well as by their social function.

The concept of punishment and the role of the prison

As should already be clear from the short introduction to this chapter, the original object of criminology is crime and not punishment, nor is it the criminal policies and strategies of social control connected with the penal system: it is rather the active research and interpretation of the possible causes of deviance and the ways in which deviance and criminality could be governed. The assumed scientific and methodological neutrality the early positivist scholars ascribed to the discipline prevented any possibility of analysing the possible influences that the government, in forging the rules, or the agencies of social control set up to make people obey those rules, could exert on the concept of crime itself or on the ways in which it originated.

At the time, and for several decades afterwards, it was therefore obvious that the discipline's object should be deviation itself and the design of effective strategies for governing deviance and criminality (Pasquino 1980).[3] It is only from the late 1960s to the early 1970s that the epistemological boundaries of the discipline began to be a little blurred, and scholars like David Matza (1969), and later the so-called new criminology, clearly rejected what criminology had symbolized until then and argued for an inescapable influence of state policies and other social factors on the origin and modification of the concepts of crime and the criminal (for example Taylor et al. 1973). Indeed, it was said, whatever approach was chosen to explore them, no strategy could effectively discover the definitive causes of deviance or (ideally) blot them out so as to make crime disappear. From this point onwards, criminology as a discipline should become more focused on examining the policies designed to reduce crime, and in its analysis it should also consider the concept of the various kinds of punishment (those policies were understood as strategies by which to apply sanctions to the criminals and the political choices accompanying those strategies).

It was thus the prison – the embodiment of all the features of the 'modern' technology of punishment – that criminological studies began to turn to as their ideal scenery. The criminology of the 1970s turned its attention to every feature of the prison, from the historical narration of its birth, to the reasons that had made it so suitable for carrying on the punishment of criminals across the centuries (at the expense of other popular forms of punishment), to what ensures its continuing predominance even today.

The analyses of imprisonment carried out over time differ depending on whether the 'quality' or the 'quantity' of this kind of punishment is taken into account (Melossi 1998: xi). To study punishment in its 'qualitative' aspects means, in Sutherland's words, to test the 'consistency' between the core cultural values of a given society and 'the methods of treatment of criminals' (Sutherland 1947: 348). This kind of relation has been studied by scholars like Rusche and Kirchheimer (1939), Foucault (1977), Melossi and Pavarini (1981 [1977]), and Scull (1977). All of them have established a parallelism between the transition from a rural society to the rise of the industrialized capitalist city, and the affirmation of the penitentiary (understood as an enclosed, organized space where criminals are confined for certain periods of time) as the main form of punishment in Western societies.

The two best-known works in this range of studies are perhaps Michel Foucault's *Discipline and Punish* (1977) and Dario Melossi and Massimo Pavarini's *The Prison and the Factory* (1977). Central to both analyses is the notion of *discipline* (Simon 2013). Said notion was applied not only in prison as a way to organize inmates' behaviour, but also within the factory. Through discipline, people in the factory not only should become good workers suited to the needs of production, but should also be forged as new persons, new citizens, much better suited to the new society than the old citizens – ignorant peasants migrating from the country to populate the new, industrialized cities. Having become the organizing principle of the economic and social life of the time, discipline was also exported to all environments (like prisons and asylums) where people were confined en masse (Bentham 1787) and where the time spent could be used to teach a new attitude, submissive and obedient, that would transform the once rebel inmates into docile, useful members of a community to whose growth they could contribute.

On the other hand, to study the *quantity* of punishment means to explore the relations of imprisonment with other fundamental social factors, like our specific focus: political economy.

The first and fundamental contribution to this debate probably lies in Georg Rusche's early ideas, subsequently reworked by Otto Kirchheimer in their well-known *Punishment and Social Structure*, a book that was republished in the 1970s, the same period when criminologists first became interested in studying prisons. In a seminal essay originally written in 1930, Rusche described the criminal justice system as informed by a logic of deterrence, the first and most important function of punishment seeming to be to prevent people from breaking the law. This deterrence works overall on the underclass, the group more prone to commit crimes subject to actual punishment. Rusche, however, also explains that deterrence can be influenced by other factors, especially by the economy and the labour market. Indeed, the threat of punishment becomes effective only when the person it is meant to deter can find some advantage in continuing to abide by the law; in other words, in any given period, living conditions in prison should be less desirable than the conditions of the 'normal' life allotted to the most marginal proletarian stratum. For the marginal man, living in prison should be less 'eligible' than living a poor but licit life.

In this way, Rusche criticized the traditional 'Whig history' of punishment as a progressive line toward more civil, more human ways of punishing, as if the existing criminal justice system were the outcome of a century-long reform tending toward a more egalitarian treatment of inmates. In fact, the principle of lesser eligibility represents, and always has represented, the limit to such evolution. Economic factors became particularly important after the transition from a precapitalist economy to a fully capitalist society, when 'the situation of the proletarian class became a purely economic function' (De Giorgi 2006). By that time, the market, with its laws, had become the only factor defining the situation of the working class, setting what was deemed the fair price of its labour where demand met supply. Prison conditions, also dependent on the laws of the labour market, should change as well: whenever there is a surplus working force, and the unemployed masses would do anything to find sustenance, the threat of the criminal justice system should be particularly cruel, so as to forestall recourse to crime. On the other hand, when there is demand for labour, the prison and punishment in general will serve very different purposes, particularly that of using discipline to forge the 'right worker' for the capitalist society, and persuading the unskilled worker to give up crime and find satisfaction in a life of humble work.

The prison as a means of punishment emerges as the most congenial technology by which to administer sanctions, bringing about a shift from a retributive logic aimed at *destroying* the body – a clear example of this logic can be found in the infamous opening of Foucault's *Discipline and Punish* (Foucault 1977: 3–6) – to a new punitive regime aimed at *preserving* the body and moulding it in such a way that it could be easily exploited by capitalist production (Simon 2013). Once the labour market returns to a condition of balance, and the supply of labour equals or exceeds demand, penal policies will again scale up cruelty, while scaling down living conditions within penitentiaries.

The authors of *Punishment and Social Structure* apply the concept of *lesser eligibility* to historical events from the Middle Ages to the 1930s, making it clear how the birth of the penitentiary was closely bound up with the economic conditions of society at the time, and how it has always been affected by those conditions. The birth of the prison can be traced to the 17th century, when Europe was going through a full-fledged demographic crisis and the scarcity of available workers caused wages to increase. As Rusche predicted, the penal policies of the Western world therefore became less harsh, since all able-bodied men were needed as workers. The consequence was that the first prototype of the prison was indeed more similar to a forced-labour containment camp, at once satisfying the demand for work, keeping beggars out of the streets, and putting a lid on the problem of ever-growing wages. *Workhouses* cropped up in England, the Netherlands and northern Germany, with the aim of controlling the marginal classes and making them productive through discipline. Confinement emerged as supposedly the best way to change attitudes and morality, using a powerful control weapon or (as in Bentham's ideal *panopticon*) a weapon of self-control (Bentham 1787). Having now become the hegemonic form of punishment in the modern world, the treatment of inmates in prisons could therefore be explained through the connection between punishment and the labour market.[4]

In *Discipline and Punish*, Foucault extends this concept to the idea of the complex of rules involved in control, a sizable part of which are the rules that frame a country's political economy. Prison therefore represents only one gear (albeit an important one) in the mechanism based on the new philosophy calling for the State to govern through control, with the aim of transforming unwilling deviants into docile citizens ready to be exploited by capitalists, by applying the very same procedures of discipline used in the factories. At the centre of it all are imprisonment as the main sanction, and prison as the main institution: through confinement in prison, unwilling, wasted bodies are changed into productive entities (Melossi and Pavarini 1981). The role of the prisons therefore changed radically: they are no longer used to exclude part of the population from public life but, on the contrary, they are needed to bring back into the community the people who had been straying from it.

Also proceeding along similar lines is Melossi and Pavarini's *The Prison and the Factory*, an attempt to couple the Marxian approach with the history of the creation and rise of the prison as the central modality of punishment. Central to this explanation is the concept of the transformation of rural masses living off the produce of the earth into urban masses living off the work provided by the factory. In order to enact this transformation, the prospective working class has to go through a sort of a paradox: while freeing themselves from the political and personal serfdom of the Middle Ages, they come to be enslaved once again, in a most subtle way, by the rules of the market and of political economy. Melossi and Pavarini therefore explain the specific role of the prison in the new capitalistic world as that of an institution *ancillary* to the factory. Using the same logic as that of factory discipline, the prison transforms the poor, unemployed peasant into a suitable worker. The procedure followed is to destroy and reconstruct the individual, going through the stages of turning the poor into a criminal, the criminal into an inmate, and the inmate into a proletarian worker fit to withstand the discipline enforced within the factory.

> But once reduced to abstract subject, once his diversity is 'annulled' ... once faced by those material needs which cannot be satisfied independently and thereby rendered dependent on the sovereignty of the administration, ultimately the product of the disciplinary machine has only one possible alternative to his own destruction, to madness: the moral form of subjection, that is the moral form of the proletarian. Better still: the moral form of subjection, that is the moral form of the proletarian is here laid down as the only condition of existence in the sense of being the only way the property-less can survive.
>
> (Melossi and Pavarini 1981: 163)

The prison, finally, is an institution that can subjugate both the body (by depriving it of every means of sustenance and the ability to move) and the soul (driving into the mind the inescapable idea that only by moral submission to the discipline of work will an inmate be able to escape from his current wretched condition). In short, the prison reduces the poor to misery, but at the same time it also supplies the means, both concrete and ideological, by which the inmate can wrest himself from that misery, while also leading him to internalize that the suffering experienced in prison is only the natural consequence of a wayward attitude toward the discipline of work.

Criticisms of 'materialistic criminology'

So far we have discussed how the novelties and labels introduced by critical scholars led criminology to change its perspective, using the Marxist paradigm to explain the historical birth and the predominance of the prison among penal sanctions. However, criticisms have been raised, and some scholars have tried to lead the sociology of punishment along different paths.

Rusche and Kirchheimer's work remains the focus of criticism, in part because it undoubtedly continues to lie at the core of most of the conceptions so far discussed. The general criticism raised in the 1980s and 1990s was that their theory is too 'materialistic' and deterministic, basing all reasoning solely on the mechanisms of the social structure and avoiding any reference to cultural and ideological tools. This criticism has accompanied the two scholars' theory from the outset (see the original reviews of the text in Marshall 1940: 126–127; Riesman 1940: 1299; Burgess 1940: 986). It also resurfaced when the book was plucked out of oblivion in the 1980s, when it was described as one of the most famous books in the sociology of punishment in Garland's *Punishment and Modern Society: A Study in Social Theory*. Garland comments:

> *Punishment and Social Structure* seriously overestimates the effective role of economic forces in shaping penal practice. It grossly understates the importance of ideological and political forces and has little to say about the internal dynamics of penal administration and their role in determining policy. It gives no account of the symbols and social messages conveyed by penal measures to the law-abiding public and hence no sense of the ways in which these symbolic concerns help shape the fabric of penal institutions.
>
> (Garland 1990: 108–109)

Alessandro De Giorgi (2006) highlights how, in Rusche and Kirchheimer's reconstruction as well as in their followers, there seems always to be the old Enlightenment idea of a connection between levels of crimes and levels of punishment, pointing to criminality as a sort of intervening variable between a country's economy and its impact on imprisonment. In other words, economic deprivation, which is usually hardest on the classes in society that are already most disadvantaged, would increasingly push them to commit crimes in order to survive, thus leading to more detention.

As a result of these criticisms, a certain number of scholars have focused their efforts on demonstrating that economic conditions have a direct effect on the number of incarcerations but that this is not connected with actual trends in crime rates. Unemployment has been often used to measure a country's economic condition. The first scholar to try to do this was Ivan Jankovic (1977), who sought to translate Rusche and Kirchheimer's theory of *less eligibility* in empirical terms, thus testing the connection between unemployment and incarceration rates, looking for a positive correlation between imprisonment rates and increasing unemployment in the USA from 1926 to 1974. He was successful, since the two factors seemed to correlate significantly, even controlling for the possible intervening 'crime rates' variable. Unfortunately, it was impossible to determine whether increasing severity of punishment also had a feedback effect on the economy, thus contributing to a 'regulation' of the labour market.

The same empirical analysis was repeated a short time later by David Greenberg, though he focused on both Canada and the USA for the periods 1955–59 and 1960–72, again finding a significant correlation between imprisonment and unemployment, independently of crime rates. However, even more interesting were the results of a second study that Greenberg carried out about Poland, this time running the test on data referring to two different time spans, when the country's political economy went through a dramatic change (Greenberg 1980). Indeed, in the first period (1924–39) Poland was still a capitalist country, while in the second period (1955–76) it had already changed its political economy into a socialist system of production. Greenberg found a significant connection between unemployment and imprisonment during the capitalist period, but nothing significant for the socialist period. This outcome led the author to a couple of conclusions: first, that Rusche and Kirchheimer's theory was verified, as long as it was formulated to explain variations in the economy and punishment in capitalist societies; second, that a very important role in socialist societies was played by other, secondary factors (like, in this case, amnesties, which contributed to breaking the link between unemployment and imprisonment[5]). From this particular finding the author deduced that variation of punishment depended in no small part on political-ideological factors – that is, on factors other than those purely pertaining to the structure of society.

Other scholars have since repeated the research in other contexts, most of the time finding that the relation between imprisonment and unemployment was mediated by other 'qualitative' factors interacting with the labour market and affecting this relationship.[6]

It is also worth mentioning the work by Bruce Western and Katherine Beckett (1999), who instead of focusing on Rusche and Kirchheimer's 'severity' hypothesis (i.e. the *lesser eligibility rule*), concentrate on another aspect of the two scholars' theory, namely, the 'utility' hypothesis (i.e. the 'feedback' effect that the prison policies would have on the economy, contributing to its regulation). In this case the two authors state that incarceration constitutes an integral part of economic policy in the USA, since it represents a very useful way to 'disguise' the real level of unemployment in the country. Entire segments of the population who would have been destined for unemployment (typically the marginal, ethnic, young portion of the population) are 'removed' from the general population by incarceration and the use of ever harsher policies designed to deal with recidivism by securing their permanence within prisons: in this way they disappear from official labour rates, and the incarceration practices and policies therefore contribute to keeping unemployment low. As the two scholars point out, however, in the long run things would take a turn for the worse: people released from prison are bound to be less 'expendable' in the labour market, and so they are bound to contribute to increasing unemployment rates, unless penal policies and sanctions become even harsher, leading to even more imprisonment (something that was happening in the USA in the period of 'mass incarceration').

These studies were replicated outside the USA, not only confirming this relation but also introducing new elements of an ideological and cultural nature.

For instance, Steven Box and Chris Hale (1982), analysing data from the UK, suggested that control agencies share society's common representations and stereotypes about given strata of the population, in general contributing to reproducing the common ideology and maintaining a bourgeois economic and social system. Thierry Godefroy and Bernard Laffargue (1989) found that in France, in periods of economic crisis, the marginal part of the population falls into a 'subproletariat', immediately causing a rise in the sense of insecurity in the country and leading to an increase in institutional punitiveness. In Italy, Dario Melossi (1985) examined the relation between the economy and punishment, this time considering indicators like the average national per capita income to measure the nation's economic prosperity, and prison admission rates as a measure of punitiveness. Melossi did not find any significant relation between the economy and crime rates, and no connection between the economy and prison *conviction* rates either, while a significant link was found between national average income and rates of prison *admission*.

Rusche and Kirchheimer's theory takes a 'cultural turn'

However, advanced capitalist societies were undergoing a serious process of structural transformation, witnessing the crisis of the Fordist-industrial paradigm and the end of the Keynesian welfare state. In a situation moving towards new, globalized forms of production and consumption, in a completely deregulated market, the criminological community began to object to Rusche and Kirchheimer's structuralist paradigm. As Melossi wrote in his introduction to the 2003 edition of *Punishment and Social Structure*, 'Marxism was symbolically burnt at the stake, while honouring the totem pole of "cultural insight"' (Melossi 2003: ix).

As noted, several attempts at exploring the relation between unemployment and imprisonment within a structuralist frame had already led to opening up to the influence of culture, ideology and political change. Criticisms of neo-Marxist criminology, on the grounds of its lack of interest for the cultural, expressive and narrative dimensions of penality, often meant reducing the 'structural dimension', as if 'more culture' in the relation necessarily meant 'less structure'. An interesting attempt to bridge the gap between a purely structural and a purely cultural interpretation of the economy of punishment has recently been offered by Loïc Wacquant (2009) in his analysis of the emergence of what he calls 'an American penal state'. According to Wacquant, changes in the level and kind of imprisonment in the USA over the last 30 years should not be interpreted as the result of a transition from a Fordist-industrial model of production to a post-Fordist model, with the previously stable labour market becoming flexible and deregulated, and the previous inclusive welfare policies being dismantled piece by piece. In his opinion, this interpretation would prevent a deeper and clearer understanding of the evolution of punishment, which needs to be considered as a broader political project: the mass incarceration of the 'surplus' population suits the new American economy, while the troubled time spent by inmates in prison makes way for their transformation into ideal citizens, on a more recent, post-industrial interpretation of discipline. In addition, Wacquant identifies a new, symbolic level in this penal discourse, consisting in a powerful representation of the strength of State power over the poor, dangerous classes, in order to reassure an insecure middle class. Therefore, the punitive turn the Penal State has been giving to the country can not only influence the structural level of society, using punishment to reproduce current capitalist relations, but also extends to the symbolic, ideological level, creating new categories, discourses, and new forms of knowledge (see Wacquant 2009: 295).

The argument is taken even further by Jonathan Simon (2007), who sees the punitive shift in contemporary American penal policies as a reflection of the cultural environment that has characterized the country over the last 20 years, from Nixon's 'war on crime and drugs', to Reagan's and Bush Senior's criminal policies, to the 'war on terror' declared by George W. Bush after 9/11, and so on. The general American attitude emerging from this kind of discourse generated a new paradigm of social governance based on the idea of preventing and neutralizing criminal risk at every level of American society – an activity regarded as a fundamental function of government. It would seem, on Simon's interpretation, that culture has become a driver of structure. However, as De Giorgi (2013) states, 'this reconfiguration of governmental technologies is not disconnected from the deep structural inequalities affecting the social and urban landscape of American Society. The molecular diffusion of the power effects associated with this new model of "governing through crime" does not mean that such effects spread evenly' (De Giorgi 2013: 51).

In fact, Nicola Lacey (2008) argues that economic structure is a central factor if we are to understand the extent to which the punitive turn typical of the contemporary American penal system will unfold. According to Lacey, not all contemporary capitalist democracies have undergone the same radical change in their punitive institutions following the transition to a post-industrial neo-liberal economy. A more significant transition from the social to the penal can certainly be observed in neo-liberal market economies like the USA, and to a lesser extent, the UK. By contrast, the situation is different in social-democratic or corporative countries like those of continental Europe, in which welfare protections have remained in place and the harshness of the penal system has similarly remained relatively stable. The latter's politico-economic and institutional structures (a stable labour market, long-term investment in the public sector, a political system based on coalitions of parties, a judicial system isolated from the distortion of public opinion) seem well suited to resisting the pull of the punitive turn. Therefore, the distinctive punitive character of each society should be defined by the intersection of a materialist, structural, economic approach with an analysis of cultural, institutional and political features.

De Giorgi is right to say that none of these three new perspectives on criminological materialism really seems to contradict Rusche and Kirchheimer's theory or its modern re-propositions, but they do seem to inject into it that symbolic or cultural dimension which has always been pointed out as the theory's biggest flaw. Taken together, these different but complementary perspectives on the role of punishment in society may lead to a new sociology of punishment.

Economic cycles and imprisonment

Out of the Marxist tradition[7] also came the concept of economic cycles, or 'economic waves'. On various accounts of this concept – most notably those put forward by Nikolaj Kondratieff (1935), Joseph Schumpeter (1939), and Ernest Mandel (1980) – the political economy proceeds by long economic cycles of about 50 years. In each cycle, a first phase of economic expansion – marked by decreasing profit, low unemployment and high salaries – is followed by a second phase of contraction in investment, increasing unemployment and decreasing consumption. We have seen that, according to Rusche's hypothesis, periods of economic growth correlate with a decrease in prison population and lenient penal policies. On the contrary, periods of economic crisis – with rising unemployment and falling per capita income and output – bring on punitive penal policies and an increase in the number of prison admissions.

The most extended and representative study was carried out by David Barlow, Melissa Hickman-Barlow, and Theodore Chiricos (1993), who used this long-wave paradigm to explain the economic and penal changes in the USA between 1789 and 1990. The main hypothesis of the study was that in periods of economic recession, the country's penal policies and conditions of imprisonment were made stiffer, so that social and economic elites could regain control of the population and propel a new economic growth, thus beginning a new cycle of prosperity. In the study, the long period taken into account is divided into sub-periods, each corresponding to a long economic cycle. For instance, the last 'cycle', from 1940 to 1990, is divided into: (i) a first wave of prosperity, from 1940 to 1970, in which economic growth and low unemployment correlated with less punitive policies, limited recourse to incarceration, and prison policies aimed at rehabilitation; and (ii) a wave of recession, from about 1970 until the 1990s, during which decreasing profits and rising inflation and unemployment correlated with harsher penal policies, a rise in incarceration rates, and a widespread sense of moral panic (witness 'zero tolerance' and the 'war on drugs'). Barlow and his colleagues did not, however, try to explain what brought about this change in mentality or how cultural values may have had a role in changing penal policies and the attitudes of government agencies. Like Box and Hale (1982) before them, they suggested that a general change of attitude is usually shared by police and the courts.

Dario Melossi has tried to integrate the cultural change paradigm with a Marxian interpretation based on class conflict (Melossi 1978: 81; Melossi 1985: 179–180; Melossi 2008: 230–234; Melossi 2010). In his reconstruction, movements in the cycles can be ascribed to three main actors: workers, entrepreneurs, and the State, the last of which tries to mediate between the other two. While workers try to have their rights recognized and take power away from capitalists, entrepreneurs attempt to limit the freedom and power obtained by workers. Therefore, in periods of prosperity, workers come to be increasingly organized and autonomous, threatening the power of entrepreneurs. This brings about stimuli for innovation on the side of entrepreneurs. New technological advancements transform the older workers into a superfluous and out-dated labour force soon to be replaced by new workers from the lower strata of the population (women, children, immigrants), who are usually younger and less skilled and so less expensive and more adaptable. As the main punitive institution, the prison and its living conditions are just part of a larger structure: as suggested in *The Prison and the Factory*, when the elites react against the workers' 'unexplainable levels of freedom' in an effort to regain power, the prison acts as an 'ancillary' institution to the factory, and through harsher punishment and stricter rules contributes to forging the new worker in line with the times. Later on, when the economy grows and the hegemonic class has firmly regained power, living conditions in prison become less harsh and the prison becomes a place in which to 'reform' criminals rather than punish them. In fact, in this period, punishment becomes less necessary, and there also develops a generally good attitude toward the lowest members of the working class, who are now expected to be able to find employment and make themselves useful to the community. If somebody makes a mistake that really needs to be punished, there is still the expectation that once they get out of prison they will find a regular job – even more evidence (on this view) that this time in prison is necessary to shape these individuals into the ideal workers they ought to embody. In some cases, simple imprisonment is preferred to any alternative sanction that would ease their transition into the labour world.

The only other contemporary scholar who has tried to develop an analysis along these lines is Charlotte Vanneste (2001), who plotted this trend along the longest period for which data were available (approximately from the second half of the 19th century to the end of the 20th) for the case of Belgium. More generally, by reconstructing the literature on long cycles, she identified 'peaks' and 'troughs' – that is, periods of maximum prosperity (after which a downturn begins), followed by periods when the economy bottoms out and begins to pick up – locating the former around 1870, 1920 and 1970, and the latter around 1845, 1895, 1945 and 1995. Developing Vanneste's suggestions, Melossi tried to see whether the data available on incarceration rates for the USA and Italy – the only data we can use as a proxy (however unsatisfactory they may be) for the severity of punishment – can be tested to see if their general trend over the same period follows the economic cycle hypothesis we have been discussing.

Looking at Figure 17.1, it seems pretty clear that this theory is (approximately) verified only for the events of the last two long cycles, which can also be taken as the whole of the 20th century (considering that the first cycle covers the period from 1895 to 1945, and the second the period from 1945 to 1995). By contrast, the theory does not seem a good predictor for imprisonment trends in the 19th century, when there seems to be a substantial stall for the USA, while the two lines seem to follow the same trend for the Italian data. Towards the end of the 20th century, things become quite interesting: while the Italian curve seems to suggest a pretty stable level of incarceration rates, the American curve sees an extraordinary spike. The long cycle could explain this increase in incarceration rates in the last quarter of the century – there seems to be in fact an economic

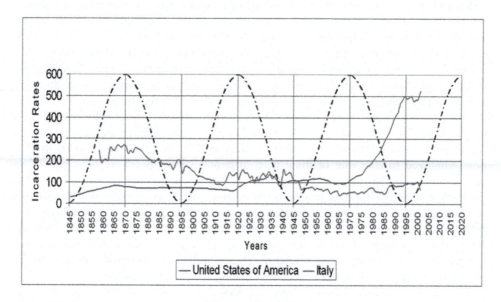

Figure 17.1 Incarceration rates in the USA and Italy (1850–2006), per 100,000
(Melossi 2008: 233)

downtrend from 1970 to the late 1990s, which, consistent with the model, correlates to an increase in the severity of punitive responses. The turn of the century should then mark a change in the direction of imprisonment rates. It is left to see whether the end of mass imprisonment of which some write (Simon 2014) may indeed give the truth to the prediction of our model! In conclusion, if the imprisonment curves are generally predicted by the model, the size and entity of the rates are certainly not predicted. Melossi suggests adding Schumpeter's notion of a 'secular trend' (Schumpeter 1939, 1: 193–219), showing how the curves slope strongly downwards in the Italian case and strongly upwards in the case of the USA (Melossi 2008: 234).

Punishment in a post-Fordist society

The relationship between the political economy and punishment so far discussed has been premised on the assumption of an economy built around the factory as its basic unit. This means that so far we have only considered what we are calling a Fordist kind of society (based on the Fordist model of factory production). What happens when we transition to a *post*-Fordist society? How does the relation between the economy and punishment change with the altering conditions in which people work? Is it possible that some kind of penal practice shaped as factory discipline survives in a society where the factory has ceased to be the main economic paradigm? It is clear that the social function of the prison as an ancillary institution entrusted with remodelling the ideal worker is no longer a possibility, since 'those members of the underclass committed to state prisons no longer provided a coherent target for strategies of integration and normalization' (Simon 1993: 225). In fact, the labour requested in a post-Fordist society is radically different from what the previous prison/factory could deliver through the application of discipline. That is because we are now dealing with work that is increasingly 'immaterial', the outcome of informatization and automation processes that had been under way in growing sectors of production. By comparison with work on the assembly line, the emblem of the disciplined factory worker, the work now carried out in a post-Fordist setting is becoming increasingly cognitive, increasingly consisting in tasks involving the worker manipulating symbols, constructing and deconstructing languages, or inventing and reinventing procedures that are very often anything but repetitive.

This does not mean that the traditional occupations are gone. In fact, there is still need for workers who will satisfy material needs (food, clothing, shelter, house cleaning and the like), and this new crop of workers, usually drawn from the lowest social strata, is now employed to take care of those parts of people's lives that were once part of the private sphere (caring for the young and the elderly, rearing children, and so on). All in all, even if material labour seems to be decreasing, the amount of labour in society is increasing, and even if formal workplaces are fewer than before and unemployment is higher than it once was, the fewer people who work do so longer and harder, some also using what is considered leisure time (in this world, where working increasingly means learning to communicate, even maintaining good public relations with co-workers can be regarded as production of an immaterial good).

The prison, therefore, seems to have definitely lost its old function, since the simple application of factory discipline cannot forge the highly skilled, specialized worker the post-Fordist industry needs, yet the prison is still present as an institution – in fact, it is very much a part of society today. It would be fair to say that in certain places, like the

USA, the prison is more present than at any other moment in history, considering the extraordinary process of 'mass imprisonment' the country has been undergoing (Garland 2001). The only residual function left for the penitentiary seems to be to confine a surplus workforce, or, as Cohen calls the practice, the 'warehousing' of inmates (Cohen 1985), a concept that Feeley and Simon later drew on to elaborate the concept of 'actuarial penology' (Feeley and Simon 1994). What is certain is that since the 1990s, the prison in the USA has acted as a place of confinement, for the purpose of either 'neutralizing' the dangerous classes or serving as a correctional institution, guided by a paternalistic state, with the mandate of imposing restraint and self-control on the inmates. It follows that the prison – once a place where peasants were turned into criminals and criminals into workers – has now been repurposed to carry out an equally important task: to imprison the marginal ethnic strata of the population en masse. This new mandate has a clear disciplining effect, not only on those parts of society it specifically targets (the people who, as Western and Beckett (1999) have argued, are doomed to be imprisoned anyway, just to maintain acceptable levels of unemployment in the country and enable the economy to work) but also other classes. First among them are the parts of the population that exist right next to those who are going to prison: the poor sectors of the population who still have a chance at a legitimate life, and then the middle class, for which the prison acts as a Durkheimian tool, suited to reinforcing social cohesion by scapegoating the marginal classes and labelling them as dangerous.

On the other hand, we must not forget that the prison and its role is closely bound up with the figure of the inmate and the social group of which he or she is part. Originally part of the peasant class or an unskilled worker who finds employment in the new factories, the possible inmate represents what Melossi calls the *canaille*, referring to workers who are not yet conscious of being part of a working class, who pursue narrowly defined individual interests without any sense of mutual solidarity, and who are therefore ready to turn to crime and delinquency when they deem it convenient. As time passes, and the workplace and labour conditions are shared, according to the theory of the cycle, the *canaille* slowly evolves into a working class, with a full-fledged sense of solidarity, thus representing a threat to entrepreneurs. The prison is then again resurrected as a 'training ground for waged work' (Melossi 2008: 241), having at its disposal new marginal people to be trained in the school of factory discipline. Today, the new marginal person is clearly the migrant, who – alone and undocumented – is the perfect candidate to join the contemporary ranks of the *canaille*, at least in Europe (Melossi 2015).

Notes

1 I wish to thank Professor Dario Melossi, for the inspiration, the support and the valuable insights he provided to develop this chapter.
2 See Cressey (1955: 349).
3 See more on this in De Giorgi (2013: 40).
4 The USA, for instance, moved from the Philadelphia penitentiary model, based solely on the principle of solitary confinement, to the Auburn model, which alternated daily labour and nightly confinement. This transition can easily be explained by the need for workers in a period of rapid industrialization. In Europe, over the same period, the surplus of workers made it more attractive to keep a prison model wholly devoted to confinement. See Melossi and Pavarini (1981 [1977]).
5 Of course, this is by no means only a prerogative of socialist countries. Italy and France share this characteristic.

6 For instance, in Wallace's (1980) study, the paradigm was verified only if the institution in question was welfare based, with non-segregative control practices, while in Galster and Scaturo's (1985) study, Rusche and Kirchheimer's theory seemed to find confirmation only for the southern states of the USA, while it was not verified using the data from the USA as a whole (the segmentation of the labour market highlights how the relation between unemployment and incarceration is much more consistent in the lower links of the economic chain, consisting in low-skilled workers, traditionally considered dangerous for the social order, like foreigners and poor youths).
7 And out of confrontations with it, as in the case of Joseph Schumpeter.

Bibliography

Barlow, D.E., Hickman-Barlow, M. and Chiricos, T.G. (1993) 'Long economic cycles and the criminal justice system in the US', *Crime, Law and Social Change* 19: 143–169.

Bentham, J. (1996 [1787]) 'Panopticon', in *The Works of Jeremy Bentham*, New York: Oxford University Press, 37–66.

Box, S. and Hale, C. (1982) 'Economic crisis and the rising prisoner population in England and Wales', *Crime and Social Justice* 17: 20–35.

Burgess, E.W. (1940) 'Book review: *Punishment and Social Structure*, by Georg Rusche and Otto Kirchheimer', *The Yale Law Journal* 49(5): 986.

Cohen, S. (1985) *Visions of Social Control*, Cambridge: Polity Press.

Cressey, D. (1955) 'Hypotheses in sociology of punishment', *Sociology and Social Research* 39: 349–400.

De Giorgi, A. (2006) *Re-thinking the Political Economy of Punishment*, Aldershot: Ashgate.

De Giorgi, A. (2013) 'Punishment and political economy', in J. Simon and R. Sparks (eds) *The Sage Handbook of Punishment and Society*, London: Sage, 40–60.

Feeley, M. and Simon, J. (1994) 'Actuarial justice: the emerging new criminal law', in D. Nelken (ed.) *The Futures of Criminology*, London: Sage.

Foucault, M. (1977) *Discipline and Punish*, New York: Pantheon.

Galster, G.C. and Scaturo, L.A. (1985) 'The US criminal justice system: unemployment and the severity of punishment', *Journal of Research in Crime and Delinquency* 22(2): 163–189.

Garland, D. (1990) *Punishment and Modern Society: A study in social theory*, Oxford: Clarendon Press.

Garland, D. (2001) *Mass Imprisonment: Social causes and consequences*, London: Sage.

Godefroy, T. and Laffargue, B. (1989) 'Economic Cycles and punishment: unemployment and imprisonment. A Time Series Study: France 1920–1985', *Contemporary Crises* 13: 371–404.

Greenberg, D.F. (1977) 'The dynamics of oscillatory punishment processes', *The Journal of Criminal Law and Criminology* 68: 643–651.

Greenberg, D.F. (1980) 'Penal sanctions in Poland: a test of alternative models', *Social Problems* 28 (2): 194–204.

Jankovic, I. (1977) 'Labour market and imprisonment', *Crime and Social Justice* 8: 17–31.

Kondratieff, N.D. (1935) 'The long waves in economic life', *Review of Economic Statistics* 17: 105–115.

Lacey, N. (2008) *The Prisoners' Dilemma: Political economy and punishment in contemporary democracies*, Cambridge: Cambridge University Press.

Mandel, E. (1980) *Long Waves of Capitalist Development: The Marxist interpretation*, New York: Cambridge University Press.

Marshall, T.H. (1940) 'Book Review: *Punishment and social structure*, by Georg Rusche and Otto Kirchheimer', *The Economic Journal* 50(197): 126–127.

Matza, D. (1969) *Becoming Deviant*, Englewood Cliffs, NJ: Prentice Hall.

Melossi, D. (1978) 'Georg Rusche and Otto Kirchheimer: *Punishment and Social Structure*', *Crime and Social Justice* 9: 73–85.

Melossi, D. (1985) 'Punishment and social action: changing vocabularies of punitive motive within a political business cycle', *Current Perspectives in Social Theory* 6: 169–197.

Melossi, D. (ed.) (1998) *The Sociology of Punishment*, Aldershot: Ashgate.

Melossi, D. (2003 [1939]) 'The simple "heuristic maxim" of an "unusual human being"', in G. Rusche and O. Kirchheimer (eds) *Punishment and Social Structure*, New Brunswick, NJ: Transaction, 9–46.

Melossi, D. (2008) *Controlling Crime, Controlling Society*, Cambridge: Polity Press.

Melossi, D. (2010) 'Il diritto della canaglia: teoria del ciclo, migrazioni e diritto', *Studi Sulla Questione Criminale* 5(2): 51–73.

Melossi, D. (2015) *Crime, Punishment and Migration*, London: Sage.

Melossi, D. and Pavarini, M. (1981 [1977]) *The Prison and the Factory*, London: Macmillan.

Pasquino, P. (1980) 'Criminology: the birth of a special savoir', *Ideology & Consciousness* 7: 17–33.

Riesman, D. Jr (1940) 'Book Review: *Punishment and Social Structure*, by Georg Rusche and Otto Kirchheimer', *Columbia Law Review* 40(7): 1299–1301.

Rusche, G. (1930 [1978]) 'Labour market and penal sanction: thoughts on the sociology of punishment', *Social Justice* 10: 2–8.

Rusche, G. and Kirchheimer, O. (2003 [1939]) *Punishment and Social Structure*, New Brunswick, NJ: Transaction.

Schumpeter, J.A. (1939) *Business Cycle*, two vols, New York: McGraw-Hill.

Scull, A. (1977) *Decarceration*, New Brunswick, NJ: Rutgers University Press.

Simon, J. (1993) *Poor Discipline: Parole and the Social Control of the Underclass, 1890–1990*, Chicago, IL: University of Chicago Press.

Simon, J. (2007) *Governing Through Crime: How the war on crime transformed American democracy and created a culture of fear*, New York: Oxford University Press.

Simon, J. (2013) 'Punishment and the political technologies of the body', in J. Simon and R. Sparks (eds) *Sage Handbook of Punishment and Society*, London: Sage.

Simon, J. (2014) *Mass Incarceration on Trial: A remarkable court decision and the future of prisons in America*, New York: The New Press.

Sutherland, E.H. (1947) *Principles of Criminology*, New York: Lippincott.

Taylor, I., Walton, P. and Young, J. (1973) *The New Criminology: For a social theory of deviance*, London: Routledge.

Vanneste, C. (2001) *Les chiffres des prisonnes*, Paris: Editions l'Harmattan.

Wacquant, L. (2009) *Punishing the Poor. The Neoliberal Government of Social Insecurity*, Durham, NC: Duke University Press.

Wallace, D. (1980) 'The political economy of incarceration trends in late US capitalism: 1971–1977', *The Insurgent Sociologist* 11(1): 59–66.

Western, B. and Beckett, K. (1999) 'How unregulated is the US labour market? The penal system as a labour market institution', *American Journal of Sociology* 104(4): 1030–1060.

Chapter 18

Prisons and human rights

Peter Bennett

> No one truly knows a nation until one has been inside its jails.
> A nation should not be judged by how it treats its highest citizens but its lowest ones.
>
> (Nelson Mandela)

I make no excuses for joining the many writers and speechmakers who begin with this quotation. Its inspirational rhetoric captures succinctly what purports to be a universal and indisputable truth. On the one hand it assumes the worth of the individual human being in the face of potential oppression by the state. On the other hand it expresses the grave responsibility of the state to exercise legitimacy through the fair and just treatment of every citizen, a responsibility and a duty that determines its good reputation in the eyes of other states and the world. Nelson Mandela's release from prison has become a symbol of liberation from the shackles of a totalitarian regime, the triumph of democracy over apartheid and of hope for the future of human rights in the person of a prisoner who became a president.

Rendered all the more inspirational coming from the lips of Nelson Mandela, it is one of many variations on a theme of individual and state that has accompanied the rise of humanitarianism, and latterly of the human rights cause, since the 19th century. The treatment of prisoners, those who count among the lowest and the most unpopular, has become a yardstick for judging the progress of civilization. Other well known former prisoners have made similar judgements, including Dostoevsky's 'the degree of civilization in a society can be judged by entering its prisons', and Winston Churchill's 'the mood and temper of the public in regard to the treatment of crime and criminals is one of the most unfailing tests of the civilisation of a society'.[1] So it is that the state becomes subject to the ultimate moral test by the way it treats those subjected to one of its most severe sanctions, the deprivation of liberty with its potential violations of inhuman treatment and torture.

In his eulogy at Mandela's funeral, United Nations Secretary-General Ban Ki-moon urged the world to follow Mandela's inspirational example as one whose 'death has awakened in all of us the flame of human rights and the beacon of hope'. However, for many the storm clouds are gathering and there are fears in this rapidly changing post-modern world that the flame might only be a flicker as hope is tempered by doubt and another more disturbing cliché enters our discourse: 'the end of human rights' (Douzinas 2000). As another millenarian maintains, 'a 150-year experiment in creating global rules to protect and defend individual human beings is coming to an end' (Hopgood 2014). The evidence, according to Hopgood, is all around us, and he goes on to cite the authoritarian pushback against human rights in China and Russia, the introduction of sharia law in Brunei, the resistance to the authority of the International Criminal Court by some African leaders, the extreme conservatism on gay rights throughout Africa, the Middle East, Eastern Europe and as shown by India's Supreme Court. The early promises of the Obama Administration, Hopgood continues, have dimmed as the USA has become associated with the torture and rendition of al-Qaeda suspects, holding detainees without trial at Guantanamo, along with its drone programmes and targeted assassinations. Even as I write, unfolding events in Syria, Iraq and Ukraine threaten to erode further the idea of a universal language of human rights.

Not all observers share Hopgood's and Douzinas's sense of finality, but the 'war on terror', along with the above-mentioned developments, has been a game changer, raising the level of debate as sceptics point out the propensity for the political manipulation of the human rights cause and question the survival of human rights as a framework having universal application. Optimism and pessimism, reassurance and uncertainty, hope and doubt occupy the minds of those who look to the future of a utopian society embodying the principles and ethics of the human rights cause (Kelly 2011).

We are drawn inevitably to these current debates that have arisen partly from the fallout from the 'war on terror' and more generally from shifts in cultural and political alignments in a new and emerging world order. We hear about the judicial reification of human rights and how we are losing sight of its moral and philosophical dimensions (Gearty 2006); the call for *A Universal Declaration of Human Responsibilities* proposed by the Inter-Action Council on 1 September 1997, composed of former presidents and prime ministers from around the world, as a means of balancing freedom with responsibility and reconciling ideologies, beliefs and political views; the political manipulation of human rights as a new form of Western imperialism (Kinzer 2014; Hopgood 2013); the challenges regarding the universalization of human rights and cultural diversity (Ayton-Shenker 1995; Lawson 1998); the failure of the USA to act on genocide (Power 2003); as well as local, highly publicized and controversial issues such as the reluctance of the UK government to follow the authority of the European Court of Human Rights by lifting a blanket ban on prisoners' right to vote. Campaigning groups like Human Rights Watch and Amnesty International have been highly effective in exposing abuses on 'prisoners of conscience' and 'suspected terrorists', but I will resist the temptation to focus principally on these headline issues emerging from major arenas of conflict, among them the fate of 'political prisoners' and 'suspected terrorists', turning instead to the vast numbers of prisoners who make up the 10–11 million of the present, and rapidly rising, world prison population, many of whom are accommodated in poor conditions with few facilities to assist in their social reintegration. The issues surrounding the legitimacy of detention run wide and deep and affect massive numbers, often belonging to marginalized and minority groups, including the poor, the oppressed, the mentally ill, drug and alcohol misusers, and representatives of groups vulnerable to discrimination – those very people whom human rights seek to protect. A high-profile 'political prisoner' associated with a high-profile political cause, Nelson Mandela was nevertheless speaking for the humane treatment of all prisoners.

My concern, then, is with the broader picture. It is more about the wider landscapes, overpopulated by less recognizable figures, yet still worthy of our attention, rather than about people and events in the foreground. For there are questions to be asked and issues to be resolved about the capacity of prisons and prison systems to protect the rights to which all prisoners should be entitled if we are to subscribe to the human rights cause. As places of enforced confinement prisons are by their very function vulnerable to operating in ways that threaten individual rights, especially if they are not adequately resourced, supported and monitored by governments, and managed with due regard for international standards. Governments, policymakers and prison staff have a serious responsibility to ensure the just treatment of those in their care, a responsibility all the more onerous when the powers they exercise remain largely hidden from the gaze of the international community and the world's media. This worsening situation is made more acute by the further erosion of human rights in many countries, and particularly in Western countries, by what has been called the 'new punitiveness'. This tendency, characterized by an increasing emphasis among governments and the public on the punitive as opposed to the reformist dimension of imprisonment, is manifested in a readier resort to imprisonment, increased sentence lengths and a return to more severe, traditional forms of punishment (see Pratt et al. 2005).

Presenting a broad picture is not easy given the vast numbers of prisons, the diversity of administrations, the varying degrees of oversight, the difficulties of accessing reliable information and the sparsity of comparative research. Prisons and prison systems are not only diverse geographically, but also socially and culturally. The familiar description of the prison as a relatively modern invention with its origins in Western Europe and the north-east part of the USA tends to downplay its socio-cultural diversity. However originally conceived and subsequently exported, imposed or imitated in terms of design, function, operation and purpose, prisons have evolved within indigenous systems of justice and institutions for the maintenance of social order. We should therefore avoid the temptation to assume that we fully understand other prison systems because they all have like functions, attributing to them a common diagnosis of their operational failings and suggesting a common remedy for their reform. We should also avoid assuming a simplistic and exaggerated sense of a 'global divide' between the 'West and the rest', the 'rest' often being more open to condemnation in human rights terms and often prompting a resistance to the legal and moral framework promulgated by the 'West'. A readiness to criticize by states whose own practices may be highly questionable can encourage resistance to what has been denigrated as 'human rights imperialism'. The point is that although there are bad prisons, with some countries manifestly worse than others in the way prisoners are treated, it is also the case that prisons may harbour pockets of abuse in all regions and countries of the world. The treatment of prisoners as the test of a civilized country can be a highly subjective judgement: those countries that regard themselves as more civilized than others can also fall short of the standards to which they aspire and be hardly better than those countries they condemn. Critics often point to the USA, which has, as we see below, a greater rate of imprisonment than any other nation, including China and Russia, and yet which routinely asserts itself as an international arbiter of human rights.

There is every reason, therefore, to have concerns about prison standards worldwide and every reason to assert that there is a crisis in prisons which, although manifestly more serious in some countries than others, cannot be reduced simply to a global divide. While it is right to identify the worst offenders, often those countries with totalitarian regimes or which are politically fragile, it is also necessary in a general introduction to human rights and prisons such as this to set out a broad overview which shows that human rights violations in prisons are commonplace and widespread and, disturbingly, are sometimes closer to home than some of us would like to acknowledge.

Human rights and prisons: the legal framework

The language of human rights is typically moral, philosophical and rhetorical, having its roots in the Enlightenment and its early expressions in the American Declaration of Independence (1776) and the French Declaration of the Rights of Man and of the Citizen (1789). However, it is more often than not that governments, policymakers and reformers refer to human rights in the legal sense and as enshrined in the intergovernmental Declarations and Conventions commencing in the aftermath of the atrocities of the Second World War. The Universal Declaration of Human Rights (UDHR), adopted by the United Nations (UN) General Assembly in 1948, if not the urtext of the human rights cause, nevertheless marks the foundation of a new era of human rights in the form of a universal framework based on an international consensus and defining the basic rights to which all individuals are entitled. Of particular relevance to the administration of justice and imprisonment are 'the right to life, liberty and security of the person' (Article 3), the prohibition of 'torture and of cruel, inhuman or degrading treatment or punishment' (Article 5), the prohibition of 'arbitrary arrest, detention or exile' (Article 9), the right to a fair trial (Article 10), 'the right to be presumed innocent until proved guilty' and the prohibition of retroactive penal measures (Article 11).

The declarations of the UDHR were not legally binding, so thereafter work began on preparing conventions, also known as treaties or covenants, framing international laws and standards that could support the implementation of human rights principles. Two covenants were adopted by the UN General Assembly in 1966 and came into force in 1976. The International Covenant on Economic, Social and Cultural Rights (ICESCR) has a special relevance for the minimum standards and well-being of prisoners: Articles 11 and 12 require their fundamental right to adequate food and drinking water. The International Covenant on Civil and Political Rights (ICCPR) also has the status of a treaty for those countries that have ratified it. The ICCPR is of importance for all citizens in safeguarding and promoting rights to life, liberty, fair trial, freedom of conscience, peaceful assembly, and protection from discrimination, arbitrary arrest and imprisonment. It is of particular importance for imprisoned persons whose status renders them vulnerable to human rights violations, their rights being enshrined in Article 10 of the covenant: 'all persons deprived of their liberty shall be treated with humanity and with respect for the inherent dignity of the human person'.

Along with the above conventions which make up the International Bill of Human Rights, there are several other conventions having relevance to detainees. Of particular importance are the Convention on the Elimination of All Forms of Racial Discrimination (1966), the Convention on the Elimination of All Forms of Discrimination Against Women (1979), and the Convention against Torture and Other Cruel, Inhuman or Degrading Treatment or Punishment (1984). The Optional Protocol to the Convention Against Torture, now ratified by 72 countries, with 55 countries having established National Preventive Mechanisms (NPMs), has been particularly influential in promoting the need for oversight and inspection. Unfortunately, ratification in principle is not always matched by commitment in practice: 'the enthusiasm has been limited, mostly, to states in Europe and Latin America, and a large number of countries went down the path of just tagging the respective Ombudsperson's office as an NPM – and ticking the box' (Huber 2014).

There are several international legal documents, or instruments, which further specify the principles contained in the covenants, and which cover the treatment of prisoners and the conditions of their detention. They include the Standard Minimum Rules for the Treatment of Prisoners (1957), the Standard Minimum Rules for the Administration of Juvenile Justice (1985), the Body of Principles for the Protection of All Persons under Any Form of Detention or Imprisonment (1988), and the Basic Principles for the Treatment of Prisoners (1990). In addition, instruments for those charged with working with prisoners include the Code of Conduct for Law Enforcement Officials (1979), the Principles of Medical Ethics Relevant to the Role of Health Personnel, particularly Physicians, in the Protection of Prisoners and Detainees against Torture and Other Cruel, Inhuman or Degrading Treatment or Punishment (1982), and the Basic Principles on the Use of Force and Firearms (1990).

These international standards are supported by regional human rights instruments and courts. In the Americas, the American Convention on Human Rights was established in 1978 and thereafter set up the Inter-American Court of Human Rights and the Inter-American Commission on Human Rights. The African Charter on Human and Peoples' Rights came into force in 1986 and thereafter established the African Commission on Human and Peoples' Rights. In Europe, there is the Convention for the Protection of Human Rights and Fundamental Freedoms (1953), the European Convention for the Prevention of Torture and Inhuman or Degrading Treatment or Punishment (1989), and the European Prison Rules (1987, revised 2006). The European Court of Human Rights is the judicial body that makes judgments on the basis of these conventions. Moreover, the observance of human rights standards in places of detention within the Council of Europe is monitored by the Committee for the Prevention of Torture and Inhuman or Degrading Treatment or Punishment.

I do not have the space here to give details of the considerable corpus of conventions, principles and mechanisms developed at national, regional and international levels, or of the judicial role of bodies like the International Criminal Court, the Inter-American Court of Human Rights or the European Court of Human Rights. Rather, my concern is to provide a general overview of the state of prisons worldwide when measured against international standards, to identify some of the significant abuses, and to explore the relevance and application of human rights principles in developing strategies and methodologies for prison reform. In doing this, I focus attention on what is perhaps the principal challenge to upholding human rights in prisons: the rapidly rising prisoner population and the problems associated with overcrowding.

A global perspective: the *ICPS International Prison News Digest* and the *World Prison Brief*

Despite international efforts to develop a consensus on human rights and a legally binding framework of principles and standards, many of the world's prison systems fall far short of international standards in their treatment of prisoners. We live in an era of human rights but we also live in a world where human rights violations are pervasive, particularly when it comes to conditions accompanying the deprivation of liberty. The daily reports and media articles collated and disseminated by the International Centre for

Prison Studies (ICPS), collated and published bimonthly in the ICPS *Prison Digest*, make for depressing reading.[2] The *Digest* provides no analysis and is restricted to reports and news in the English language, but it does present a useful overview of prison populations, prison health, the treatment of prisoners, prison violence, developments in rehabilitation, sentencing and the law, and prison policy. Take, for example, the following excerpts from the sections on 'Prison Populations' and the 'Treatment of Prisoners' published in the *Digest* for the months of March and April 2014:[3]

> European states are failing to significantly reduce overcrowding in prisons ... according to the newly published Council of Europe Annual Penal Statistics which are based on a survey carried out in 2012. Overcrowding remained a serious problem in 21 prison administrations across Europe.
>
> The Italian House has passed a major reform bill aimed at tackling the serious overcrowding in the country's prisons. The new law makes house arrest or detention in a healthcare facility the primary form of incarceration for lesser crimes ...
>
> The European Committee for the Prevention of Torture has called on authorities in Croatia to improve material conditions in prisons and to reduce overcrowding, notably in the Zagreb County Prison which was 225 per cent over its 400 bed capacity.
>
> Overcrowding remains a problem in Tunisian prisons and preventive detention centres, a report of the UN Office of the High Commissioner for Human Rights concluded. The report noted that overcrowding exceeds 150 per cent of capacity in some prisons ...
>
> Prisoners at Queensland's biggest women's prison claim they are 'starving'. Lawyers said prisoners at Brisbane Women's Correctional Centre were dramatically losing weight ... The prison is reaching capacity and prisoners have been warned that mattresses will be placed on floors to allow three to a cell.
>
> Foreign prisoners in Nicosia Central Prison ... are to be transferred back to their own countries ... while those jailed for misdemeanours will be deported according to the Justice Minister, who announced the move as part of sweeping changes aimed at reducing overcrowding and the problems associated with it ...
>
> United Nations officials have expressed concern at the number of Maori in New Zealand's prisons ... Maori make up more than 50 per cent of the prison population despite comprising around 15 per cent of the general population, while more than 65 per cent of women prisoners are Maori.
>
> Living conditions at Roebourne Regional Prison in Western Australia have been described as 'intolerable and inhumane' in a report by the Inspector of Custodial Services ... The situation is exacerbated by the holding of six prisoners in cells which have been designed for four.
>
> In Canada ... a report by two lawyers from the federal Office of the Correctional Investigator ... highlights the appalling state of a prison housing mainly Inuit prisoners ... some prisoners had to sleep on mattresses on concrete floors due to a lack of beds.
>
> Sanitary conditions at the Sekondi Central Prison in Ghana are deteriorating to the point that all 714 male prisoners currently share only three toilets. Prisoners queue for long hours to use the toilets, a situation which sometimes compels them to defecate on themselves or in plastic bags.

This is a brief and arbitrary selection, but it does throw light on a problem that is current, serious and widespread: poor prisoner conditions, often amounting to human rights violations, and usually caused or exacerbated by congestion. Global trends in prison populations add to this depressing picture. Overcrowding is not an inevitable outcome of the rising prisoner population, but it is very often the case. Indeed, according to a handbook published by the UN Office on Drugs and Crime, 'there is growing recognition that one of the key obstacles to implementing the provisions of the *Standard Minimum Rules for the Treatment of Prisoners (SMR)* is overcrowding in prisons' (UNODC 2013).

The identification of prison populations and population trends by country, region and worldwide has helped considerably in shedding light and provoking debate on the use, and overuse, of imprisonment. The *World Prison Brief*, also a part of the ICPS website, launched in September 2000, gives details of prisoners held in 218 independent countries and dependent territories. It shows the differences in levels of imprisonment across the world and makes possible an estimate of the total world prison population. It also provides information on the proportion of juvenile, women, pre-trial and foreign prisoners, as well as the official capacity of each prison system and its occupancy rate, the latter giving an indication of degrees of overcrowding.[4] The *World Prison Brief* is the only source of comparative data on every prison system in the world and is widely used as an essential reference, regularly cited by governments, non-governmental organizations (NGOs), researchers and the media. The data can be arranged in table form showing countries and their respective prison populations and population rates in a world and regional context. Indeed, the facility to compare countries has often encouraged national administrations to think in more positive terms about their uses of imprisonment and to look to other countries to explore what policies and practices lead to reducing levels of imprisonment in order to stem rising financial and social costs as well as to improve standards. It can be a matter of national pride or national embarrassment to see one's country posted high or low on the world or regional tables for rates of imprisonment, including rates of pre-trial detention, female incarceration and occupancy levels in relation to operational capacity.

Prison systems differ markedly in terms of their rates of imprisonment per 100,000 of the general population, but the statistical evidence in the *World Prison Brief*, and more specifically on the ICPS tenth edition of the *World Prison Population List* (Walmsley 2013), also posted on the ICPS website, reveals disappointing global trends. The numbers of prisoners serving sentences or pre-trial/remand over the last 20 years has seen a massive increase. More than 10.2 million people worldwide were held in penal institutions and, if we include those held in detention camps in China and prison camps in North Korea, the total is more likely to be 11 million. Moreover, prison populations are growing in the five continents. In the 15 years since the first edition of the *World Prison Population List*, the estimated world prison population has increased by some 25–30%, while during the same period the world population has increased by just over 20%. The population rate, the number of prisoners per 100,000 of the general population, has risen by 6%, from 136 per 100,000 to the present rate of 144 per 100,000.

Prison populations vary between different regions of the world and between different parts of the same continent. In Africa, for example, in 2013 the median rate for the Western African countries was 46, whereas for Southern African countries it had risen to 205. In the Americas the median rate for South America was 202, for Caribbean countries 376, and for the USA, which has the highest prison population rate in the world, it was 716 per 100,000. In Asia, the Indian subcontinent was 62, whereas in East Asian countries it was 159.5. In Europe the median rate for Western countries was 98, whereas for countries spanning Europe and Asia, including Russia and Turkey, it was 225 (Walmsley 2013).

Prison populations have been rising in many of the European Union (EU) member states. Taking 1995 figures, followed by figures for 2013, we can see that in some states there have been reductions, such as the Czech Republic (189/154), Estonia (304/238), Finland (64/58), Latvia (374/304), Lithuania (351/329), and Romania (200/155), although these are generally from a figure well above the median for Europe. Some countries with relatively low rates have recorded modest rises or falls, such as Denmark (68/73), France (89/98), Germany (81/79), Luxembourg (114/122), the Netherlands (77/82) and Sweden (66/67). After a rise in recent years, Sweden's population, which had increased between 2000 and 2013, is now beginning to fall rapidly to its 1990s levels. Some countries have seen increases but still remain below 100, including Slovenia (32/66), Ireland (59/88) and Austria (84/98). However, of particular concern are those countries that have registered significant increases, including some of the founding members of the EU: Belgium (74/108), Bulgaria (101/151), Croatia (50/108), Cyprus (31/106), Greece (55/111), Hungary (121/186), Italy (83/106), Malta (53/145), Poland (160/217), Portugal (123/136) and Slovakia (147/187). Perhaps most disappointing of all for Western European countries, are Spain (115/147), and England and Wales (100/148).

A further insight into the growing population is revealed by another ICPS publication in June 2014, the second edition of the *World Pre-Trial/Remand Imprisonment List* (Walmsley 2014), which reports that nearly 3 million people are held in pre-trial detention worldwide, including some 480,000 in the USA, 255,000 in India and an estimated 250,000 in China. Trend data reveal that the pre-trial population rate (the proportion of the national prison populations on pre-trial/remand) has increased in 98 countries and decreased in 80. Moreover, while in the majority of countries (56%) the total prison population of pre-trial/remand is between 10% and 40%, it constitutes more than 40% of the prison population in about half the countries of Africa, the Americas and South-Central and Western Asia. Again, the *World Pre-Trial/Remand Imprisonment List* should be a strong prompt to governments to reduce their pre-trial populations in the interests of good economy, justice and humanity.

Further research by Roy Walmsley shows that in 2013 some 660,000 women were in prison worldwide, about 6.5% of the world's prisoner population, being lowest in African countries and highest in South-Eastern and Central Asia. Of particular note is the trend showing the increase by 40% of women in prison between 2000 and the beginning of 2013, world general population levels having risen by only 16% in the same period. Indeed, the proportion of women within the total world prison population has grown sharply and far greater than men both in terms of total prisoner population and population rates.[5] There is, as yet, insufficient research to explain the reasons for this, although part of the explanation may well be the fallout from the 'war on drugs' and the criminalization of offences relating to drug possession, particularly drug trafficking and the part played by many imprisoned women who have been 'drug mules'.

The figures can never tell the full story, but the fact that prison population rates have been increasing at such a rapid pace should be a matter of grave concern, not only a moral concern or a matter of national embarrassment, but also because it imposes an increasing financial burden on governments having to accommodate such large numbers and to deal with the social disruption arising from a failure adequately to address social reintegration. It is often the case that a rising population leads to increased occupancy rates which exceed the official prison capacity, an occupancy rate above 100% being when available accommodation cannot match the increased demand. The impact of overcrowding on conditions can be highly disruptive and have serious repercussions for the health and well-being of detainees as is apparent from several examples from the *International Prison News Digest* cited above. The lack of sufficient physical space, often accompanied by poor natural light and ventilation, inadequate provision of food and access to fresh drinking water, can lead to a worsening of hygiene standards, tension among prisoners manifested in acts of bullying, disruption and violence, inadequate facilities for sanitation and the spread of communicable diseases. The need to supervise increasing numbers places strains on the provision of work and education, medical care, contact with families and reintegration initiatives. Vulnerable groups, including women, children, those with disabilities and those with mental health problems are more likely to endure deteriorating levels of support, care and protection. Poor working conditions, remuneration and training for insufficient numbers of staff can lead to regimes with an emphasis on punishment, control and security at the expense of prisoner engagement and rehabilitation. Given these pressures, overcrowding becomes an impediment to ensuring the proper treatment of prisoners and the fulfilment of one of the two principal functions of a prison, the first being to keep prisoners securely in custody and the second, 'the essential aim of which shall be their reformation and social rehabilitation ...' (Article 10, the International Covenant on Civil and Political Rights).

Reducing overcrowding: a major challenge for human rights in prisons

The evidence is growing and yet appears to go unheeded by many governments: rising prison populations and population rates do not necessarily reflect rising levels of crime. Trends in each statistical domain do not follow a consistent pattern, while levels of reported crime and victimization are not necessarily reflected in levels of imprisonment. Tapio Lappi-Seppälä (2010) has argued the case convincingly. For example, in Finland, whereas recorded crime increased between 1980 and 2005, the general prison population declined, while in the USA crime trends remained stable and then decreased as imprisonment increased. Between 1975 and 2005 imprisonment increased in the USA six-fold. In the UK, despite falling crime, the prison population continues its inexorable rise. The underlying reasons are complex and call for further research on the economic, social and political factors prevailing in national prison administrations which predispose towards higher or lower rates of incarceration other than crime trends, or the perception of crime trends (see UNODC 2013: 19–27).

Yet it is a widely held assumption routinely promoted by politicians and the media that increasing incarceration rates reflect rising levels of crime in a society, thereby giving credence to claims that increasing resort to imprisonment is necessary because of an increasing need for imprisonment. This assumption, albeit flawed, has the apparent benefit of demonstrating a government's resolve to take firm and decisive action by removing from society those who have committed crimes, or are alleged to have committed crimes, as the most effective remedy for preserving the safety and security of the community. It is little wonder that there is a reticence to address the issue by devising and implementing strategies that will reduce prison population rates. At a conference of the heads of European prison administrations in 2002 some of the speakers put much of the population increase and overcrowding in recent years, especially in the West of Europe, down to a lack of political will and decisions, either consciously or by default, to have higher rates of imprisonment:

> They have done this through the introduction of more punitive legislation or as a result of politicians and the media encouraging judicial authorities to send more people to prison for longer periods of time.[6]

Given political will, supported by a less punitive approach to criminal justice, what might a national strategy for prison reform seek to address? Tackling overcrowding will not be a single objective; rather, it can be an important step towards addressing the wide range of shortfalls in international human rights standards that accompany overcrowding. The strategy will emerge from a comprehensive understanding of penal and criminal justice issues which contribute to overcrowding and which are specific to the country that commits itself to a programme of reform. Otherwise, without a detailed grasp of local circumstances, there is a danger that plans will be implemented explicitly to address the immediate problem with perhaps less thought given to latent, long-term and unintended consequences. One obvious and common solution might be to build new, bigger and better prisons, thereby increasing capacity, reducing overcrowding and improving conditions at a stroke. This has the perceived benefit of rationalizing the prison estate and introducing financial efficiency, for once there has been an outlay on design and construction, new and bigger prisons are often regarded as being more efficient and cheaper to run. The prison administration in England and Wales is currently engaged in a programme of prison building in order to achieve greater efficiency and economy in the use of the prison estate; but not without controversy. The former Lord Chief Justice Woolf (1991: 17) made the point in his report following the 1990 prison riots, notably at Strangeways, when he said that 'jails should not normally hold more than 400 prisoners ... the evidence suggests that if these figures are exceeded, there can be a marked fall-off in all aspects of the performance of a prison'. The rapid increase in population means that, as I write, 28 prisons now hold more than 1,000 prisoners, being 40% of the total prisoner population, with additional plans to build a 'supersize' prison in North Wales, an expansion that raises significant concerns as to the closure of smaller prisons, the accommodation of prisoners further from home, the difficulties of maintaining order and the potential for volatility. Meanwhile, the overcrowding problem, accompanied by staff reductions, is becoming more acute with the chief inspector of prisons announcing on the BBC Radio 4 *Today* programme that:

> men are spending 23 hours a day, two or three to a cell with a shared toilet, locked up in this heat and that is causing huge tensions ... You either have to put in significantly more resources to cope with the numbers ... or you have to reduce the population.[7]

I have observed prison building initiatives in South Africa, Chile and Panama, all of which have high population rates well above the mean. I recently had the opportunity to comment on the implications of a prison building programme in one such country with a rapidly rising prison population with a rate nearly twice the world median of 144 per 100,000, including an exceptionally high rate of pre-trial detainees and an occupancy level of 167%. The government had begun to implement an impressive programme of reform with the worthy and explicit objectives of reducing overcrowding and the high population rate, improving training for prison staff and addressing comprehensively human rights violations. Of particular note was the construction of two new prisons with a total capacity of 6,500 prisoners which, it was envisaged, would inevitably lead to improved conditions by decongesting the country's small and overcrowded traditional prisons.

Having visited one of the traditional prisons and seen one of the new prisons nearing completion, several questions immediately came to mind. What thought has been given to the potential unintended consequences that might arise from creating additional prisoner accommodation? What plans are in place to ensure that additional infrastructure and capacity do not allow the prisoner population to rise rather than to fall? What are the plans for the traditional prisons? Will they no longer be required or will they be refurbished? If the latter, will they be developed to provide less crowded conditions with an emphasis on social integration for lower security prisoners? Will the new, high security prisons also hold prisoners of medium and lower security categories? If so, is it necessary, cost effective and conducive to resettlement to accommodate such prisoners in high security conditions? Is sufficient being done to review the security categories of prisoners to determine their different levels of risk? Perhaps most important of all, what part does the construction of the new prisons play in the implementation of a comprehensive national prison reform plan which anticipates and takes account of potentially negative outcomes? The issues raised by such questions suggest that the solution to improving prison conditions and overcrowding is highly complex and inevitably calls for a wide range of reforms, among them addressing the root causes that predispose towards overcrowding in the countries concerned.

An initial consideration is likely to be a review of sentencing policy consistent with the principle that imprisonment should be used sparingly. There may be opportunities to decriminalize some offences and to make greater use of alternatives to custodial sentences, while also ensuring a proper balance between the rights of offenders, the rights of victims, and concerns for public safety and crime prevention. A range of petty offences could be replaced by fines and other non-custodial alternatives, while the imprisonment of fine defaulters, often contributing to congestion, could also be replaced by non-custodial disposals. Special attention should be given to vulnerable categories: the imprisonment of children is often excessive, with the age of criminal responsibility in many cases being set at too low an age level, and the imprisonment of people with mental health needs is often inappropriate. The sentencing of women, who have responsibilities for family care, might attract stronger mitigating factors. Life sentences could be restricted to those who have committed the most serious crimes, with a right to appeal to a higher jurisdiction, and mandatory minimum sentencing provisions, which can lead to sentences that are disproportionate to the seriousness of the crime committed, could be removed. Pre-trial detention, as we have seen, has reached inordinately high levels in many countries of the world and could be reduced by alternative measures of bail, speeding up the criminal justice process and by simply accepting that many such prisoners do not pose a serious threat to public safety. Sentence lengths, in particular, have been subject to worrying inflation in recent years. In many countries far too little is being done to develop a range of alternatives to prison and to place a greater emphasis on encouraging social integration and desistance from offending. Moreover, custodial sentences for drug-related crime have increased apace with some 70% of prisoners in Indonesia serving sentences for drug-related offences, and more than half of the prison population in the USA (Huber 2014), and yet such long mandatory sentences appear to have little impact on recidivism. Drug dependence is in the main a healthcare problem, many offenders being dependent on drugs who might be better managed by interventions of prevention, care, treatment, support and non-custodial disposals rather than by punishment for use, possession and other low-level drug crimes.

These suggestions are by no means exhaustive. There is an excellent handbook that covers the range of potential options to be considered by countries (UNODC 2013). It is clear that conditions can be improved in many prison administrations by tackling overcrowding. Given a punitive climate, this will depend in the first instance on firm political will to go ahead with developing an implementation plan that is truly comprehensive and which is not so narrow as to focus on simply improving conditions by increasing capacity. A firm resolve will also be necessary to set limits on the numbers of people that countries are prepared to send to prison. In a report on a visit to Hungary in 2001, the European Committee for the Prevention of Torture noted that:

> a number of European States have embarked on extensive programmes of prison building, only to find their prison populations rising in tandem with the increased capacity acquired by their prison estates.[8]

The ensuing strategy will not simply look to solving an overcrowding problem by increasing capacity, while simultaneously improving conditions, but will begin with the presumption that prisons should be reserved for those who are deemed the most serious threat to public safety such that there is no doubt they need to be imprisoned or detained in custody awaiting trial. Lower security accommodation or non-custodial alternatives can be provided for those who are a less serious threat to the community.

Applying international standards in prisons

I should finally mention another and largely invisible dimension of prison reform to which I cannot do full justice in this broad overview. It is one thing to encourage compliance with international standards by legal prescription, inspection and sanction, or by exposing and shaming countries that fail to meet standards, but quite another to secure the translation of principles into practice, a process which requires the willing engagement of prison practitioners and the knowledge of how it can be done. Indeed, my own experience, as well as that of my colleagues, has been that prison staff in many countries of the world are often keen to improve conditions, both for prisoners and themselves, but often feel that they lack the training, the know-how and the resources to do so.

I draw attention to two eminently practical guides which go beyond legal prescription and take the principles as a basis for training prison policymakers, senior government officials, prison managers and their staff. The one is the UNODC manual *Human Rights and Prisons* (2005), and the other is the ICPS handbook *A Human Rights Approach to*

Prison Management (2002, revised 2009). Professor Andrew Coyle, the author of the ICPS handbook, sets out how these principles can be translated into practice, drawing attention to good practices in many prison administrations and stressing throughout the 'importance of managing prisons in an ethical context which respects the humanity of everyone involved ... the concept of human rights is not merely another subject to be added to the curriculum ... rather it suffuses all aspects of good prison management and is integral to it' (Coyle 2009: 9).

Over the past decade the ICPS handbook has been used to assist prison practitioners on how they can best begin to meet international standards by effecting reform from within. Now translated into 18 languages, and having been used as a basis for staff training in many countries of the world, it has proven its worth and continues to be an invaluable resource in bridging the gap between principles and practice, knowledge and know-how, thereby helping to embed human rights principles in all areas of prison management

The key lies in the development of a well-trained, professional staff whose members are recognized within the wider community for the important work they do and who are adequately recompensed. The training, underpinned throughout by attention to international instruments and standards, and based on an acknowledgement of, and respect for, the dignity of every prisoner, will provide staff with the capacity to determine clear and coherent objectives and to implement humane procedures and arrangements that cover all areas of prison management and prisoner supervision. These will include the recognition of the total prohibition of torture, inhuman and degrading treatment; the right to the highest attainable standards of physical and mental health provision; a system of security and control with no more restriction than is necessary for safe custody and a well-ordered community life; the right to a fair disciplinary system; the right to treatment that has the essential aim of reformation and social rehabilitation; the right to communicate with family and friends; the right to make a request or complaint regarding treatment; the right to freedom of thought, conscience and religion; arrangements for regular inspections of the prison by a competent authority; the right to legal representation; along with appropriate provision for the needs of juveniles, women and foreign prisoners. These are some of the principles; training will be directed towards ensuring that they are upheld and embedded in all the procedures, practices and routines of the prison. Indeed, at the level of the prison, small improvements can make a massive difference both for prisoners and practitioners. The provision of ventilation in a hot and humid cell, access to exercise in the fresh air, to education and work, the availability of clean bedding, and the creation of additional sleeping accommodation by the refurbishment of an unused room, all contribute to incremental improvements and can be achieved at relatively little cost. Reform from above will be all the more effective and lasting if supported by staff with the capacity and enthusiasm to undertake reform from within.

The future of human rights as an international paradigm for prison reform

I have described the feelings of ambivalence experienced by many reformers committed to the human rights cause and to prison reform. There is hope and there is doubt. On the one hand, the growth of human rights during the latter half of the 20th century has shone a bright light on matters concerning the deprivation of liberty, along with the responsibility of the state to use imprisonment sparingly, with just cause and with humanity and respect for the inherent dignity of all prisoners. The development of a comprehensive framework of conventions, protocols and standards, subscribed to by most countries, has had a massive impact on encouraging compliance, or the intention to comply, and the implementation of mechanisms of inspection. On the other hand, I have presented an overview of a world where there is increasing resort to the use of imprisonment and an emphasis on 'punitiveness', where overcrowding is widespread and conditions often intolerable. This is not just a matter of concern in those areas of the world where conflict is endemic, arising in the aftermath of the Cold War, 9/11, the 'war on terror' and latterly the Arab Spring. Rather there are prisons in many countries of the world that fail to comply with minimum standards. Little wonder there are doubts about the progress of human rights in general and in prisons in particular.

It is perhaps to be expected that the ascendancy of human rights in an era of mass communication and globalization has made us acutely aware of violations, providing a ready and powerful discourse to judge the respective progress of 'other' nations. The human rights movement as a beacon of hope also casts light on how much there is yet to do in reforming the world's prisons. Yet in spite of all our reservations and doubts, human rights continues to provide a moral objective in terms of an end to suffering and 'dedication to human flourishing' (Gearty 2006: 140), along with a means of achieving it, which remains the best paradigm we have for reform and will continue to be so if it can be adapted and kept free from manipulation by self-serving national interests and become truly relevant for all nations in a changing world order. Human rights will need to free itself from what many perceive as a Western, neo-liberal sense of moral authority and begin to speak for all nations. How human rights can be made more inclusive, but not so inclusive that its fundamental principles are compromised, is a crucial test for governments.

After all, the human rights paradigm is a construct to which we aspire but find difficult to grasp. Well-managed and humane prisons show us how far we have come and how much has been achieved over the years in improving conditions, while prisons that foster abuse are constant reminders of how far we have to go and how much we have failed. The treatment of prisoners with respect and humanity is a measure of a country's progress, but governments will need a steely resolve to keep this in mind when beset by demands to ensure the safety and protection of the public, just as prison staff will need to be patient and determined in their efforts to implement improvements when faced with the immediate challenges of managing highly complex institutions in which conflict is inherent and resources are limited. However, if the human rights cause continues to be developed as a universal paradigm for prison reform, and its principles continue to be translated into practice, then overcrowding in prisons will be regarded increasingly as unacceptable, the prison population should decrease and resources should go to the many who need support in the community and the few who will still need to be kept in conditions of the highest security.

Notes

1 Fyodor Dostoevsky, *The House of the Dead* (1862), translated by Constance Garnett (1961). Winston Churchill was addressing the House of Commons on prison reform when he was home secretary during 1910–11.

2 See the *ICPS International Prison News Digest* collated by Helen Fair, referenced and posted bimonthly on the ICPS website (www.prisonstudies.org).
3 Thanks to Helen Fair at the Institute for Criminal Policy Research, Birkbeck, University of London, for her kind permission to reproduce these quotes from *Digest* in this chapter.
4 See Roy Walmsley, the *World Prison Brief*, ICPS website (ibid.).
5 See *What's New* on the ICPS website (ibid., accessed 10 July 2014).
6 See the *Report of European Committee on Crime Problems*, 13th Conference of Directors of Prison Administration, Strasbourg, November 2002.
7 As reported in *The Guardian*, Saturday 14 June 2014.
8 *Report to the Hungarian Government on the visit to Hungary carried out by the European Committee for the Prevention of Torture and Inhuman or Degrading Treatment or Punishment from 5 to 16 December 1999*, Strasbourg, March 2001.

Bibliography

Ayton-Shenker, D. (1995) 'The challenge of human rights and cultural diversity', United Nations Background Note, United Nations Department of Public Information, March, www.un.org/rights/dpi1627e.htm (accessed 9 July 2014).

Coyle, A. (2009) *A Human Rights Approach to Prison Management: Handbook for prison staff*, London: International Centre for Prison Studies.

Dostoevsky, F. (1961 [1862]) *The House of the Dead*, trans. Constance Garnett, London: Heinemann.

Douzinas, C. (2000) *The End of Human Rights*, Oxford: Hart Publishing.

Gearty, C. (2006) *Can Human Rights Survive?* Cambridge: Cambridge University Press.

Hopgood, S. (2013) *The Endtimes of Human Rights*, Ithaca, NY: Cornell University Press.

Hopgood, S. (2014) 'The end of human rights', *The Washington Post*, 1 March, www.washingtonpost.com/opinions/the-end-of-human-rights/2014/01/03/7f8fa8 (accessed 25 April 2014).

Huber, A. (2014) 'When will the tide turn in prison politics?' *Global Prison Trends*, blog, Human Rights Centre, University of Essex, 11 June, blogs.essex.ac.uk/hrc/2014/06/11 (accessed 11 July 2014).

ICPS (2014) *World Prison Brief*, www.prisonstudies.org.

Kelly, T. (2011) 'The cause of human rights: Doubts about torture, law, and ethics at the United Nations', *Journal of the Royal Anthropological Institute* 17(4): 728–744.

Kinzer, S. (2014) 'Are human rights activists today's warmongers?', *The Boston Globe*, Wednesday 28 May, twincities.com/columnists/ci_25852126 (accessed 9 July 2014).

Lappi-Seppälä, T. (2010) 'Causes of Prison Overcrowding', paper submitted to the Workshop on Strategies to Reduce Overcrowding in Correctional Facilities, 12th United Nations Congress on Crime Prevention and Criminal Justice, Salvador, Brazil, 12–19 April 2010.

Lawson, S. (1998) 'Democracy and the problem of cultural relativism: Normative issues for international politics', *Global Society: Journal of Interdisciplinary International Relations* 12(2): 251–271.

Luban, D. (2002) 'The war on terrorism and the end of human rights', *Philosophy and Public Policy Quarterly* 22(3): 9–14.

Power, S. (2003) *A Problem from Hell: America and the age of genocide*, New York: Harper Collins.

Pratt, J., Brown, D., Brown, M., Hallsworth, S. and Morrison, W. (2005) *The New Punitiveness: Trends, Theories, Perspectives*, Cullompton: Willan.

UNODC (United Nations Office on Drugs and Crime) (2005) *Human Rights and Prisons: Manual on Human Rights training for prison officials*, New York and Geneva: United Nations.

UNODC (United Nations Office on Drugs and Crime) (2013) *Handbook on Strategies to Reduce Overcrowding in Prisons*, Criminal Justice Handbook Series in cooperation with the International Committee of the Red Cross, New York: United Nations.

Walmsley, R. (2013) *World Prison Population List*, tenth edn, London: International Centre for Prison Studies, www.prisonstudies.org.

Walmsley, R. (2014) *World Pre-trial/Remand Imprisonment List*, London: International Centre for Prison Studies, www.prisonstudies.org.

Woolf, L.J. (1991) *Prison Disturbances April 1990: Report of an Inquiry by the Rt Hon. Lord Justice Woolf (Parts I and II) and His Honour Stephen Tumim (Part II)* (The Woolf Report), London: HMSO.

Chapter 19

An international overview of the initiatives to accommodate Indigenous prisoners

Elizabeth Grant

Introduction

The high incarceration rate of people from Indigenous cultures is a worldwide phenomenon. The reasons for overrepresentation vary in detail and multiplicity across different contexts but there are commonalities. The effects of forced colonization are still being experienced in many countries and prison overrepresentation rates are just one indicator of the ongoing trauma and destruction that forced colonization leaves in its wake. There are continuing repercussions of excessive imprisonment. Imprisonment exacerbates the marginalization of Indigenous people, leading to intergenerational trauma, substance abuse, dysfunctional families and communities, higher levels of violence, anger and mistrust of criminal justice systems.

The growing number of Indigenous people in prison systems around the world is of concern. Surviving in the prison can be a difficult task in itself, but the struggle is compounded when one is denied religious and personal freedoms, has different cultural traditions, social norms and domiciliary practices, and is denied access to family, community and country.

This chapter examines the manner in which various countries have sought to accommodate the differing needs of Indigenous prisoners. It outlines the Native American religious practices and ceremonies allowed in US prisons and some of the struggles associated with exercising religious freedoms. The partnerships forged between US correctional agencies and American Indian agencies to allow prisoners to serve time on reservations are also discussed. These experiences are contrasted with the Canadian experience of the establishment of healing lodges and the integration of Aboriginal religious ceremonies into mainstream prisons. Australian experiences have been vastly different and this chapter outlines the various approaches including the recent construction of a prison to meet the needs of Aboriginal prisoners in West Kimberley. In response to the large numbers of Māori imprisoned, New Zealand developed the concept of Māori Focus Units, built on the premise that increased cultural knowledge reduces the criminal behaviour. The Māori Focus Units and Pacific Islander Units present unique responses to incarcerating Indigenous prisoners. Finally, the chapter outlines the establishment of the first prison in Greenland to respond to the needs of the Kalaallit peoples.

The USA

The 2012 Census recorded a population of 2.5 million Native Americans,[1] constituting 1.2% of the total US population. It is estimated that more American Indians[2] are in prison relative to population size than any other ethnic or cultural group in the USA, although it is difficult to get an exact number for those incarcerated.[3] The USA has a bewildering array of places to detain people. There are jails and prisons run by local jurisdictions (cities or counties) which house convicted people serving short sentences and those awaiting trial. Prisons or penitentiaries are run by states or the federal government and house prisoners serving longer sentences. There are also jails and prisons on reservations and in overseas territories, most of which are administered by different entities.

A little over one million American Indians live on one of the 325 reservations (Norris et al. 2012) across the USA. Under federal law, tribal courts have the authority to prosecute members for crimes committed on reservations but cannot sentence offenders to more than three years in prison.[4] The establishment of separate tribal legal structures and prisons has been an attempt to address cultural dislocation and allow reservation self-governance. Tribal jails allow members to be housed within or close to their home community, possibly increasing contact with family and community, while holding offenders accountable to the First Nation concerned. In 2012, a total of 2,364 prisoners were confined in one of the 79 detention facilities on reservations operated by tribal authorities or the Bureau of Indian Affairs. The number of American Indians held in tribal detention centres is rising, increasing by 15% since 2000 (Minton 2013).

There are often greater opportunities for prisoners in tribal prisons to participate in Native American religious practices, such as the wearing of traditional hairstyles, the use and possession of sacred objects, access to traditional religious leaders and ceremonies such as the sweat lodge. Sweat lodges are a salient feature of many Native American traditions and involve ceremonies of prayer, healing and renewal. The structures resemble the womb, with a rounded roof and a single entryway facing either west or east. The dome-like shape of sweat lodges, pervasive across most traditions, is intricately and uniquely significant for different communities. Depending on the Nation, tribal prisons may allow access to traditional religious leaders and have sweat lodges within the grounds. In other circumstances, tribal courts may issue temporary releases for prisoners to participate in sweat lodges and other ceremonies under escort in the community (Luna-Firebaugh 2003).

Operating a separate prison system can be a severe financial burden. The high cost of building, maintaining and staffing tribal prisons has on occasion resulted in substandard conditions. In 2004, inspectors visited 27 sites, noting cases of prisoner neglect and abuse, overcrowding, decrepit and unsafe conditions, and an absence of separate facilities for juveniles (US Department of the Interior, Office of the Inspector General 2004). In 2010, the Tribal Law and Order Act was enacted. It requires tribal agencies to have long-term plans for juvenile detention and allows for the construction of new facilities with standards to be applied to all facilities. The design of new tribal jails is changing as a result and some Nations are recognizing that the use of features such as colours and circular spaces reflects local cultures, provides positive messaging and assists in the reintegration of offenders into the community and culture (Bureau of Justice Assistance 2009). In a number of recently built examples, the natural environment, cultural symbols and representations have been used as therapeutic tools to effect behavioural change. For example, the conceptual design developed for the Ramah Navajo Chapter Adult Detention Center is the shape of a *hooghan* (alt. spelling *hogon*),[5] a Navajo ethnoarchitectural form (Krasnow 2012).

Most American Indians do not live on reservations. In 2010, 92% of American Indians and Alaska Natives lived outside American Indian and Alaska Native designated areas (Norris et al. 2012) and were unlikely to be imprisoned in tribal jails. Many American Indians incarcerated within state or federal systems have had issues with observing religious and cultural practices. The freedom to observe the religion of one's choice is the inherent right of all Americans (Solove 1996), and US prisons are required to accommodate religious beliefs under legislation.[6] Prisoners' religious freedoms, however, are often tempered by budgetary shortfalls, detention philosophies and security concerns.

The long-standing problem of prisoners' religious freedom has been the subject of over 50 lawsuits since 1972. In the 1970s, as the result of extensive litigation, prisons began to recognize and permit American Indian religious practices. In 1985, prisoners in Utah sued the state to provide a sweat lodge claiming that it was an integral practice of their religion (Grobsmith 1994: 162). The state opposed the construction of a sweat lodge based on security concerns. In 1989, the court finally determined that the state of Utah must permit construction of a sweat lodge within the prison grounds and bear the cost as they would for any other religious structure. Unfortunately, this progress was slowed in the late 1980s as a result of several Supreme Court decisions which radically weakened the religious rights of prisoners.[7] In 2003, in Massachusetts, prisoners filed a suit against the state.[8] The American Indian prisoners asserted that their right to free religious exercise was not respected by prison authorities. Traditional items were classified as contraband and American Indians who were not members of recognized tribes were not allowed to participate in spiritual circles. Although lower court rulings on the case favoured the Department of Corrections, settlement was reached with intervention from the Massachusetts Appeals Court.

Other US states negotiate and settle requests for ceremonies and sweat lodges in prison in different ways. In 2002 in Maine, for instance, the state's first prison sweat lodge was approved. A small group of prisoners, known as Kwai Nidobak, or Sacred Feathers, initiated the request for a lodge and other rights pertaining to traditional religious and cultural practices. The process took many years but prisoners are now able to participate in ceremonies, although all the 'items have to be paid for by the inmates' (Stroub 2005).

A number of US prisons have developed or adopted specific cultural/spiritual programmes for the American Indian prisoners. Many authors concur that the most effective approach to rehabilitating Native Americans is re-familiarizing them with the traditional values of their culture, and strengthening cultural values and norms (Albaugh and Anderson 1974; Pedigo 1983). Increasingly, evaluators, treatment personnel and potential clients deplore the Anglo-cultural bias of existing programmes and call for the integration of American Indian forms of healing practices. For example, many prisoners are in prison because of alcohol and/or drug-related offences (Grobsmith 1994: 46) and standard Alcoholics or Narcotics Anonymous programmes are generally rejected by American Indian prisoners (Reed 1990; Grobsmith 1994). The most effective programmes for American Indians with alcohol and drug problems appear to be those integrating traditional Indian activities and elements into their treatment strategies. Programmes such as the United Native Alcohol Program are delivered in some prisons but not universally. Compounding the denial of access to meaningful spiritual opportunities is the related issue of proximity to home communities. With the rise of private prisons, this situation has become particularly exacerbated as multinational corporations locate in the areas with the lowest taxes and wages. Far too often American Indian prisoners are incarcerated hundreds, if not thousands, of miles from their homes and families.

The differing and diverse needs of American Indian prisoners are not consistently recognized across the USA. Tribal jails provide opportunities to establish multi-agency cooperation and collaboration and reduce cultural dislocation but facilities need to be safe, to a standard, and culturally appropriate. American Indians are sentenced at twice the rate of the greater US population for violent and property crimes, and on average receive longer sentences. The types of sentences that can be served in tribal jails are limited and many American Indian people end up in mainstream prisons. Within mainstream jail and prison systems, American Indian people are often subject to abuse when attempting to identify with their culture through the wearing of headbands, using native languages, maintaining braided hair, listening to native music, and securing culturally related educational material. Many prison administrations appear unaware of the central role spirituality plays in the lives of prisoners and deny access to sweat lodge ceremonies, the necessary herbs, items and materials, to traditional spiritual leaders, to traditional foods and the possession of sacred items necessary for ceremonies (Foster 2010).[9] These matters are of importance, as the rights of incarcerated persons are increasingly limited in the face of budgetary shortfalls, increased security measures and detention philosophies. Ironically, religion has always been considered by corrections authorities as a primary rehabilitation tool to return prisoners to society as productive community members.

Canada

Three groups of Aboriginal peoples,[10] the First Nations,[11] the Inuit and the Métis, are officially recognized in Canada. Between and within each group there is considerable linguistic, tribal and cultural diversity. Different groups practise a range of ceremonies and rituals to honour the sacredness of the earth, to commemorate marriages or deaths, for initiations and self-purification (Correctional Service Canada 1990). However diverse, Indigenous people share a commonality in that their societies and cultures have suffered through the processes of colonization. A large proportion of the Canadian Aboriginal population suffers socio-economic disadvantage, with poverty, inadequate educational opportunities, unemployment, poor living conditions, alcohol abuse and domestic violence affecting their lives.

Responsibilities for Canadian prisons are divided between the federal and provincial governments. Convicted offenders sentenced to custody for two years or more are the responsibility of the federal government agency, Correctional Service Canada (CSC), which operates prisons throughout Canada. Persons sentenced to 'two years less a day' and those held on remand are the responsibility of provincial governments and housed in provincial prisons. There are 192 correctional facilities across Canada with 43 institutions (including four Aboriginal healing lodges) under federal jurisdiction. Correctional facilities are identified as either maximum, medium or minimum security. The maximum security facilities have very secure perimeters with prisoner movement highly restricted. Medium security facilities have secure perimeters and prisoner movement is generally less restricted. Canadian minimum security facilities do not generally enclose buildings with fences and prisoner movement is unrestricted most of the day. Multi-level facilities feature two or more of the security levels defined above. Some facilities use the same buildings to accommodate prisoners classified at different security levels, while others use separate structures for each security level.

While Aboriginal people make up about 4% of the Canadian population, in 2013, 23.2% of the federal prisoner population was Aboriginal (First Nation, Métis or Inuit).[12] There were approximately 3,400 Aboriginal offenders in federal penitentiaries, of whom 71% were First Nation people, 24% Métis and 5% Inuit. The Office of the Correctional Investigator estimates that the incarceration rate for Aboriginal adults is ten times higher than the incarceration rate of non-Aboriginal adults (Office of the Correctional Investigator 2013), with a higher over-representation rate for Aboriginal women. In 2012, Aboriginal women accounted for 32.6% of the total female prisoner population. Translated, this means one out of every three women federally incarcerated is of Aboriginal descent (The Public Safety Canada Portfolio Corrections Statistics Committee 2012).

In 1990, the report 'Creating Choices' (Task Force on Federally Sentenced Women 1990) recommended that the needs of women, especially of Aboriginal women, must be addressed. The report called for respectful and dignified prison environments where women could be empowered to make meaningful and responsible choices. The Native Women's Association of Canada proposed the concept of a 'healing lodge', noting that mainstream prisons did not work for Aboriginal offenders. The healing lodge concept was to offer services and programmes reflecting Aboriginal culture in spaces that incorporate Aboriginal peoples' traditions and beliefs. It was proposed that the needs of Aboriginal prisoners would be addressed through Aboriginal teachings, participation in ceremonies, contact with Elders, family and children, and through interaction with nature.

In 1992, the Corrections and Conditional Release Act was revised to state 'that correctional policies, programs and practices respect gender, ethnic, cultural and linguistic differences and be responsive to the special needs of women and Aboriginal peoples'. Sections 79 to 84 of the Act deal with the specifics of CSC's obligations in Aboriginal corrections, discussing the needs of Aboriginal prisoners, including the implementation of programmes, agreements and parole plans, the establishment of advisory committees and Aboriginal prisoners' access to spiritual leaders and Elders to address the needs of Aboriginal prisoners. Section 81 states that CSC may enter into an agreement with an Aboriginal community for the provision of correctional services to Aboriginal offenders.

Healing lodges operate under two different models. The lodges are either funded and operated by CSC, or they are funded by CSC and managed by a partner organization under a section 81 agreement. Canada's first healing lodge, Okimaw Ohci Healing Lodge in the Nekaneet First Nation, Saskatchewan, opened in 1995 and is operated by CSC. This healing lodge was designated for Aboriginal women with minimum or medium security ratings. The design of the healing lodge and building departed radically from that of a traditional prison. The complex is circular with a spiritual lodge where teachings, ceremonies and workshops with Elders take place. Okimaw Ohci contains both single and family residential units, and women prisoners may have their children stay with them. Each unit has a bedroom, a bathroom, a kitchenette dining area and a living room.

Five healing lodges operating under section 81 have since opened across Canada for male Aboriginal offenders. The Stan Daniels Healing Centre (Edmonton, Alberta), the Prince Albert Grand Council Spiritual Healing Lodge (Prince Albert, Saskatchewan), the O-Chi-Chak-Ko-Sipi Healing Lodge (Crane River, Manitoba), the Waseskun Healing

Lodge (St-Alphonse-Rodriguez, Quebec)[13] and the Willow Cree Healing Lodge (Duck Lake, Saskatchewan) have approximately 110 beds in total for male prisoners. The Buffalo Sage Wellness House (Edmonton, Alberta) was opened in 2011 as a minimum and medium security and community residential facility for Aboriginal women on conditional release in the community (Correctional Service Canada 2013). A further three healing lodges were built which are managed by CSC. The Okimaw Ohci Healing Lodge (Maple Creek, Saskatchewan), the Pê Sâkâstêw Centre (Maskwacis, Alberta) and the Kwìkwèxwelhp Healing Village (Harrison Mills, British Columbia) are each designed to reflect Aboriginal world views. In total, the lodges can accommodate approximately 140 male Aboriginal prisoners (Grant 2009).

Aboriginal offenders are more likely to have served previous sentences, are incarcerated more often for violent offences and frequently have gang affiliations (Mann 2009). Many Aboriginal offenders have maximum security ratings and are unable to be accommodated in healing lodges or other minimum security institutions, and so end up in mainstream prisons.

Aboriginal people entering the mainstream prison system are held in mainstream facilities. At most medium and minimum security prisons, there are concerted (although not consistent) attempts to provide facilities for spiritual observance. The presence of sweat lodges and tepees at most prisons is a powerful reminder that Aboriginal prisoners are present in the prison as a distinct and diverse group. In maximum security prisons, participation in regular sweats and other ceremonies provides Aboriginal prisoners with diversions and 'escape' from the highly secure, hardened and regimented prison environments. The presence of Elders and Aboriginal staff and programmes provides important support mechanisms. The ability of Aboriginal prisoners to perform cultural obligations (e.g. carrying a medicine bundle and participating in ceremonies), however, is treated as a privilege and not a right, and varies from prison to prison. Many Aboriginal prisoners become disconnected from family and community while incarcerated. The isolated location of many prisons has an impact on the level of contact Aboriginal prisoners have with their families. Poverty and poor health means that many Aboriginal people are unable to visit imprisoned family members. Prisons are typically located in areas poorly serviced by public transport which makes maintaining contact even more difficult. Numerous initiatives, inquiries, public policy statements and task forces have continued efforts to address the over-representation rate of Aboriginal peoples and the conditions Aboriginal people face whilst in prison (Perreault 2009).

The correctional investigator for Canada reports that the number of Aboriginal people imprisoned has increased 43% in the last five years and there 'is an urgent need for change' (Sapers, cited in Mas 2013). Across Canada, the prisoner population is ageing, has more alcohol and substance addictions and greater mental health issues than ever before. Larger numbers of offenders are being sentenced to federal custody to serve longer sentences. As prisons become more crowded, they become more violent and volatile places. The use of segregation and force interventions is increasing. Due to multiple factors such as systemic discrimination, structural inequality, family, community and cultural breakdown facing Aboriginal people in Canada, there has been a proliferation of Aboriginal youth gangs (Sinclaira and Grekulb 2012) which offer members an opportunity to feel a sense of self-worth and identity. Gang members, most of whom have survived severe trauma in childhood, are committing suicide and killing each other and being incarcerated at alarmingly high rates. Incarcerating gang members does not reduce future criminal behaviour. It has been found that grouping high-risk youth in high security mainstream prisons increases the bonding and leads to even more entrenched anti-social and criminal behaviour (Totten 2009).

The majority of the correctional efforts in Canada have been at developing 'women-focused' and minimum and medium security environments such as healing lodges and other entities. While this may be a crucial factor in rehabilitation, access to healing lodges and many cultural initiatives is limited for many Aboriginal prisoners due to the violent nature of their crimes.

Australia

In the Australian system of government, powers are distributed between the federal government, the states and territories. The states and territories have independent legislative power in all matters not assigned to the federal government. Eight separate state and territory government authorities across Australia operate 94 adult prisons.

Although imprisonment was used as a tool to dispossess Aboriginal people from their land during European settlement, Aboriginal imprisonment rates were low until the 1950s when Aboriginal people migrated from missions and reserves into towns and cities. The rates of Indigenous incarceration increased and have continued to grow steadily ever since. Aboriginal and Torres Strait Islander peoples[14] currently make up 3% of the total Australian population (Australian Bureau of Statistics 2012), while constituting 27% of the total Australian prison population.[15] The growing numbers of Aboriginal people in Australian prisons are a legacy of former government policies (such as forced resettlement, dispossession of land, removal of children and the undermining of Aboriginal social structures). In many areas of Australia, community dysfunction, chronic unemployment, alcohol and substance abuse, and high levels of violence continue to be the norm, despite numerous independent and government inquiries, royal commissions, interventions and programmes to increase the socio-economic position and improve the health status of Aboriginal people.

The landmark Royal Commission into Aboriginal Deaths in Custody (1987–1991) stated that there 'are important cultural differences between Aboriginal and non-Aboriginal detainees for which accommodation can, and should be made in the context of custodial procedures and cell design' (Commonwealth of Australia 1991: 230). It is important to understand that there is considerable diversity in Australian Aboriginal societies, with variations in most aspects (Horton 1994). Aboriginal people live in a variety of circumstances, from residing in urban settings to pursuing traditional lifestyles in remote communities. Most Aboriginal people have cultural obligations and some are subject to Aboriginal Customary Law.[16] There are commonalities between different Aboriginal groups. Family and kin lie at the core of Aboriginal life and may often be the only constant in the lives of Aboriginal people. People generally live with or within close proximity of their extended family. Maintaining connections to one's country[17] is vitally important for well-being for most Aboriginal people. As a result of greater cultural understandings, some correctional agencies have attempted to create prison environments and programmes to better meet the diverse cultural, environmental and criminological needs of Indigenous prisoners.

Some prisons have incorporated separate outdoor areas for cultural gatherings, including building fire pits for the preparation and cooking of traditional foods. One of the major issues facing Aboriginal prisoners is the inability to fulfil cultural obligations by attending family and community funerals. In response, a number of correctional agencies have constructed small shelters to allow prisoners to gather and grieve. For example, Darwin Correctional Centre organized the construction of a bough shelter for prisoners to participate in 'sorry camps'.[18] Similarly, Port Augusta Prison in South Australia erected a gazebo with a small fire pit for a similar purpose (Department for Correctional Services, South Australia 2009). Partaking in cultural activities, however, is a privilege rather than a right.

The Department of Corrective Services, New South Wales moved beyond developing meeting places to establishing a learning and cultural centre outside the walls of the Bathurst Gaol. Girrawaa Creative Works Centre's design was derived from the lace monitor, the totem of the local Wiradjuri people. The site features a men's meeting area abstracted from a traditional ceremony to achieve manhood. The Centre provides for the diverse range of creative endeavours including art, carving, woodwork, theatre and photography.

Indigenous communities and organizations have clearly stated that prisons need to move from being punitive to focusing on the restoration and healing of Indigenous people (Grant 2009a). There is a belief that increased cultural knowledge results in reduced criminal activity. Despite this, Indigenous programmes vary considerably, dependent on the jurisdiction, funding, staffing and political will. Many programmes such as visiting Elders and cultural enrichment packages are delivered periodically. One exception is that most Australian prisons run art programmes or supply art materials to Aboriginal prisoners, and there is generally a large uptake for art and musical programmes. There is a serious need for more Indigenous-specific programmes. Most prisons deliver mainstream education programmes to improve literacy and numeracy outcomes. The uptake of such programmes is often low, as English may be the second or third language for some prisoners and many Aboriginal prisoners are disenchanted from previous experiences of Western education. Prisoners are also often more interested in working to buy necessities in prison. Indigenous prisoners often refuse to enrol in sex offender treatment and anger management programmes as they are seen as culturally inappropriate. Due to the non-completion of such courses, many Aboriginal prisoners are ineligible for parole and end up serving their sentences in their entirety.[19]

Work camps are seen as a way of increasing employment skills, providing meaningful work in a comparatively normalized environment. Camps are generally well suited to Aboriginal offenders who may struggle to cope with imprisonment in standard custodial environments. Correctional agencies with larger Indigenous prison populations have established permanent work camps in regional locations. Western Australia, with the highest rate of Indigenous imprisonment, operates four work camps; the Northern Territory, with a high number of Indigenous prisoners, has established two regional work camps; and Queensland operates 13 work camps. Work camps offer the opportunity to imprison Indigenous people close to their community, potentially reducing the distress of being 'off country' (Office of the Inspector of Custodial Services 2008a: 4). There are constraints to the work camp model for Indigenous prisoners. Unfortunately, many Indigenous prisoners find it difficult to obtain a low security rating and as a result, those who may benefit from being housed in a work camp are often unable to do so.

Some Australian jurisdictions have looked beyond imprisoning Aboriginal people in traditional prison environments. Developments have included correctional environments that emphasize the acquisition of work skills and cultural education and are designed to cater for specific groups. In 2000, the New South Wales Department for Corrective Services opened a separate minimum security facility (Yetta Dhinnakkal) for youthful Aboriginal offenders, housed on a 10,500-hectare sheep farm (Legislative Council of New South Wales 2003). Due to the minimum security rating, only certain categories of prisoner can be placed at the facility. Eight years later, New South Wales opened a second facility to house first-time youthful Indigenous offenders on a 600-hectare cattle station. The establishment of Bugilmah Burube Wullinje Balunda addressed a particular issue faced by many Aboriginal offenders, in that they lack a suitable address while undertaking a community-based court order. Bugilmah Burube Wullinje Balunda has no secure perimeter, is staffed by non-uniformed staff and offers a range of educational and cultural programmes in an attempt to reduce the number of Indigenous men in prison custody. Such initiatives fill a critical gap in the criminal justice system by allowing offenders to serve community-based orders and similar sentences in relatively normalized environments. In most instances, offenders housed at such facilities originate from urban areas and for the period of their sentence they are effectively separated from family and community. While such facilities and intervention programmes may be seen to be more effectively delivered in remote locations, there is a dichotomy in moving young offenders away from family and kin, existing support mechanisms, and 'off country'.

A number of prison agencies have focused on meeting the differing domiciliary and socio-spatial needs of Aboriginal prisoners. Aboriginal prisoners have been found to be less able to tolerate isolation than a person of non-Aboriginal descent. Often Aboriginal prisoners will be housed with other Aboriginal prisoners in shared cells, dormitories or units (Grant and Memmott 2008). There was an incorrect assumption that Aboriginal people had a high tolerance for crowding. Research has indicated that Aboriginal prisoners require accommodation that allows individuals to maintain relationships with family and to live within a specified social group (generally with other people from the same language group) but overcrowded settings cause considerable stress to the Aboriginal prisoner (Grant and Memmott 2008).

Regional prison approaches have been devised to cater for the needs of Aboriginal prisoners. Western Australia has instituted a regional prison policy that wherever possible Aboriginal prisoners serve their sentence near their home country and family and kin to reduce the 'anguish in Aboriginal prisoners' concerns at being held out of their country or under the threat of being sent out of country' (Office of the Inspector of Custodial Services 2008a: 4). The West Kimberley Regional Prison was devised under this strategy. The prison was designed with community consultation to incorporate Indigenous prisoners' cultural, kinship, family and community responsibilities and spiritual connections to land. The prison accommodates 120 male and 30 female prisoners of varying security classifications in separate areas. Accommodation comprises self-care housing units, arranged so that prisoners can be housed according to family ties or language groupings and aligned in radial manner to the direction of their home 'country' (Grant 2013a). Providing 'normalized' self-care cottage accommodation at West Kimberley Regional Prison was a measure to enhance a prisoner's capacity to develop living, communication and negotiation skills required on release. Sleeping arrangements in some housing units are flexible and contain both shared and single rooms and areas for prisoners to sleep outside if they desire.

While there have been a number of initiatives to meet the cultural needs of Aboriginal prisoners, such developments are not consistent across Australia or even within jurisdictions. For example, while Western Australia has developed the award-winning West Kimberley Prison, some Aboriginal prisoners in the same state are imprisoned in overcrowded and decrepit conditions, often in extreme temperatures (Grant et al. 2012).

Australian Aboriginal prisoners have excessively high rates of chronic diseases and mental health issues in comparison with the non-Aboriginal population. Aboriginal prisoners are significantly more likely to have diabetes, asthma, hearing loss, cardiovascular diseases and higher rates of infectious diseases than non-Aboriginal prisoners. Imprisonment often provides Aboriginal prisoners with an environment to improve their health status, if only for a short period of time before they return to dysfunctional communities, overcrowded housing and risk-taking behaviours. Disability is severely under-reported in the Aboriginal communities and while estimates suggest that 50% of the total Aboriginal population live with one or more disabilities, anecdotal evidence is that far greater numbers of people are affected. Increasingly, Aboriginal people with profound or severe physical, intellectual and cognitive disabilities are being imprisoned, often with only other prisoners to provide care and assistance. Alternative humane secure environments are urgently needed for these people.

At this point, Australian correctional agencies appear to be far more likely to consider the cultural, socio-spatial and spiritual needs of Aboriginal people originating from remote areas, rather than those of Aboriginal people formerly living in urban settings. The importance of being connected to country and family is paramount to all Aboriginal prisoners regardless of whether people originate from urban, rural or remote settings. Aboriginal kinship is a cohesive force that binds Aboriginal people together and provides psychological and emotional support. Denying people access to family and country can be soul destroying and perpetuates the cycle of excessive contact with the criminal justice system.

New Zealand (Aotearoa)[20]

The Department of Corrections (Ara Poutama Aotearoa) administers the New Zealand prison system with a mandate of managing offenders in a safe, secure and humane manner, ensuring appropriate compliance and administration of sentences and orders. The New Zealand Corrections Act 2004 includes ombudsmen and justices visiting prisons to maintain a programme of inspections. There are 17 prisons[21] located across New Zealand accommodating over 8,500 sentenced and remand prisoners (Department of Corrections (Ara Poutama Aotearoa) 2014). Of the 16 facilities, 14 are purpose built for men and three for women.

Māori[22] make up approximately 15% of New Zealand's population, with higher numbers of the Māori population living on the North Island. Māori account for over half of the prison population, with the Māori incarceration rate being 175 per 100,000 of the adult population, while the non-Māori incarceration rate is approximately 100 per 100,000 of the adult population (ibid.). The over-representation rates are a result of social and historical factors including the lack of access to services such as healthcare, social support and education, and the effectiveness and cultural appropriateness of services in responding to Māori needs.

New Zealand is a bi-cultural country in which the Treaty of Waitangi[23] has legal status. In recent years, considerable attention has been paid to the quality and responsiveness of services for Māori. In response to the large numbers of Māori imprisoned,

New Zealand Corrections developed the concept of Māori Focus Units. The units are developed on the premise that increased cultural knowledge will reduce criminal behaviour and operate on Māori principles, with the aim of bringing about positive changes in offenders' attitudes and behaviour (Grant 2009). The first Māori Focus Unit opened at Hawkes Bay Prison in 1997. Since then, a further four Māori Focus Units have been established at existing prisons at Waikeria, Tongariro Rangipo, Rimutaka and Wanganui Correctional Centres. Each unit is a stand-alone minimum security unit within an existing prison, housing up to 60 prisoners. The Māori Focus Units are housed in typical prison units (a design idiosyncratic to New Zealand prisons), where cells and ablution blocks are located around three sides of an open courtyard. The entrance, administration, staff facilities, control room and dining spaces are accommodated on the fourth side (Grant 2013).

The Māori Focus Units differ in that they have sacred meeting rooms ('*marae*'), are acculturated with Māori signs and symbols, and act as keeping houses, stages for cultural performances and environments for the revival of cultural practice, language and tradition (Grant 2009). There have been subtle changes to the environment to increase the feeling of living as a *whānau* (family) within the Māori Focus Units. The furniture in the dining rooms is arranged so that the group dines together for each meal. Other areas of the Māori Focus Units have been studiously acculturated to increase programme outcomes. Artefacts are displayed in the reception areas and other areas, and the units often have a garden area where prisoners are encouraged to cultivate traditional foods.

Another development in the New Zealand prison system has been the implementation of a Regional Prison Project. Under this programme, a number of new prisons were constructed across New Zealand to provide an increased standard of secure accommodation, to increase the capacity of the prison system and to allow prisoners to be incarcerated closer to home. Northland Regional Corrections Facility was commissioned in 2005, Auckland Regional Women's Correctional Facility in 2006, and the Otago and Spring Hill Correctional Facilities were both commissioned in 2007.

The prisons within the Regional Prison Project are interesting from a number of perspectives. In developing the project, the department established relationships with Māori communities to design, develop and operate prisons in a manner appropriate for Māori offenders. Communities were engaged in roles as guardians and custodians of the land and local *iwi* [24] representatives were invited to advise on matters relating to cultural and spiritual elements of the design and operation. The projects also used Māori architects to lead the consultation processes, leading to some interesting design developments. One development departing radically from typical New Zealand prisons was Auckland's women's prison.

The Auckland Region Women's Corrections Facility was commissioned in 2006 as New Zealand's first purpose-built women's prison and designed in consultation with local *iwi*. The facility is set on a 47-hectare site with 38 buildings. The facility can house 286 women prisoners in various types of accommodation. High and medium security prisoners are housed in units, while minimum security prisoners are accommodated in living units of ten beds or self-care four-bedroom houses for mothers with babies. The Auckland Region Women's Corrections Facility builds on the Canadian work of normalizing prison environments for women. The prison has courtyards and water features outside interview and visit rooms to reduce stress and increase aesthetic appeal. An innovative colour palette has been used to 'soften' the prison environment. The prison is designed around a Māori sacred site, a low-lying hill, and is the only known example nationally and internationally where such a site has been incorporated into a prison. The prison's plan resembles a stingray, the local Māori totem, which wraps around the sacred hill. Women with high security needs are housed in secure units on the outer side of the spine of the stingray. All services are contained within a curved building (the stingray's spine), low and medium security accommodation is sited inside the spine with views of the sacred hill. The manager of the prison has an uninterrupted view of the sacred hill as it is her/his role to guide the women towards their culture and protect the sacred part of the landscape. At the centre of the site a form of traditional Māori meeting place has been built.

Another project development within the Regional Prison Project was the construction of the Spring Hill Correctional Facility. This prison incorporates a separate unit for prisoners from the Pacific Islands (Vaka Fa'aola, Pacific Focus Unit) and a Māori Focus Unit. The Spring Hill Correctional Facility has specially designed two cultural spaces, the Fale (meeting house) adjacent to the Pacific Focus Unit and a *whare hui*, the Māori meeting place. The perimeter fence follows the contours of the site and allows prisoners a view out to the horizon. The Pacific Islander Focus Unit and the Māori Focus Unit at Spring Hill are 60-bed units built in the form of a figure of eight, with each unit surrounding a courtyard area. The entry and secure officer facilities are housed in the intersection of the '8'. Each prisoner has an individual cell fitted with a toilet and wash basin, and shares shower facilities, dining and recreational areas. The Vaka Fa'aola, Pacific Focus Unit houses prisoners from six Pacific nations (Samoa, Tonga, Cook Islands, Niue, Tokelau and Fiji). While many of the Islander prisoners have had gang affiliations prior to incarceration, it has been noted that gang affiliations are generally 'left at the gate' (Grant 2009). Long-standing historical feuds exist between some Islander groups (e.g. Tongans and Samoans), which on occasion have led to unrest between prisoners, and there have been issues in assuring the safety of young, vulnerable or psychiatrically ill prisoners in the large units.

While New Zealand has been a pioneer in developing separate minimum security environments for Māori and Pacific Islander prisoners, there are considerable constraints in the model. Since the 1960s, many Māori have joined patched gangs such as the Mongrel Mob and Black Power which provide surrogate families to disenfranchised and deracinated youth. Violent crime and drug trafficking are some typical gang activities. Many sentenced Māori gang affiliates have high security ratings and are ineligible or disinclined to be housed in Māori Focus Units. While the cultural units and innovative programmes attempt to reconnect Māori with their families and encourage prisoners to get back in touch with their cultural ancestry, many Māori prisoners are unwilling to undergo the personal journey. Few gang members have family contact and re-establishing that bond is not an easy task. There is also an expectation that prisoners entering Māori and Islander Focus Units remain drug free and participate in cultural and work programmes. Māori leaders who have seen these programmes in operation note that they have little effect unless they connect prisoners with family and the outside world (Al Jazeera 2013).

Greenland (Kalaallit Nunaat)

Greenland's Indigenous peoples, who call themselves Kalaallit or Inuit, constitute around 88% of the Greenlandic population of approximately 56,000 people (Statistics Greenland

2013). Greenlandic society was traditionally based on subsistence hunting. Under the 1953 Danish Constitution, Greenland was incorporated into Denmark as a county and strategies for assimilation were imposed. There was a movement for people to become urbanized wage earners, the Danish language was used for all official matters and Kalaallit were required to go to Denmark for their post-secondary education. Many Kalaallit children grew up in boarding schools in Denmark, often losing their language and cultural ties to Greenland. In the 1970s, a reassertion of Kalaallit cultural identity led to a movement in favour of independence.

In 2008, Greenland voted to become a separate country within the Kingdom of Denmark and assumed the name Kalaallit Nunaat. The administration of the judicial system is one area that has not yet passed to Greenland under the Home Rule scheme (Commission on Greenland's Judicial System 2004). However, offences committed in Greenland come under the Greenlandic Penal Code. The sanctions imposed are unusual in that they are measured against the potential rehabilitative outcomes for the convicted offender (Lauritsen 2012), and are not intended to punish, but to find the 'measure' judged to be most suited to prevent the guilty person from engaging in further crime (Brochmann 2001). There are no minimum or maximum penalties, with sanctions including fines, sentence of supervision, prison and safe custody sentences (otherwise known as indeterminate placement).

Unemployment, industrialization and alcoholism have had a high impact on Greenlandic society. The International Centre for Prison Studies (ICPS) notes the imprisonment rate for Kalaallit was 301 per 100,000 of the adult population (ICPS 2012). Terms of imprisonment are not served in a traditional manner. At this point, all prison places in Greenland are 'open' and mixed gender. The current Nuuk Correction Institution has 60 rooms and most prisoners return home periodically for weekend visits, may be entitled to holidays, and are normally permitted to leave the prison for activities such as medical appointments, educational purposes and personal circumstances.

Greenland does not have psychiatric treatment facilities or a 'closed' institution. Kalaallit sentenced to an indeterminate placement are transferred to Herstedvester Institution outside Copenhagen for psychiatric and psychological care. In 1986, Herstedvester Institution set up a special unit for convicted, non-psychotic[25] Kalaallit sentenced under the Greenlandic criminal code. The unit has 13 mixed gender places and is partially staffed with Greenlandic-speaking staff. The unit consists of prisoners' rooms flanking a central corridor. There are two kitchens to allow the preparation of traditional Greenlandic food in one area (the unusual smell of some of the traditional foods such as seal and reindeer led to complaints) and a lounge. Herstedvester Institution also has an area for Kalaallit to practise Inuit crafts such as the creation of *tupilak* (small wood or bone carvings of supernatural creatures or Arctic animals with pre-Christian origins) (Grant 2009).

The issue of transporting Greenland's most serious offenders over 4,000 kilometres to Denmark has always been problematic. Many prisoners suffer from homesickness and find the transition to Denmark and separation from family very difficult. Most prisoners do not have visitors and miss cultural activities and familiar landscapes. Some Kalaallit prisoners do not speak Danish and communication with Danish correctional staff is difficult. As a result, a new prison (Ny Anstalt) with a capacity of 76 places (40 people within a 'closed' regime) will be constructed in Nuuk by 2018 (Council of Europe 2012), making it possible to repatriate Kalaallit prisoners currently accommodated in

Denmark (Frantzsen 2012). A design competition for the project was held by the Danish authorities in 2009. The Danish Ministry of Justice identified that the new prison needed to accommodate the cultural needs of Kalaallit prisoners, stating that building structure, aesthetics and materials should reflect the culture and traditions of Greenland and a high degree of connection between indoor and outdoor environments together with access to outdoor areas from the living units (Schmidt Hammer Lassen 2013).

Danish architectural firms Schmidt Hammer Lassen, and Friis and Moltke, won the competition with a design comprising five residential blocks. The residential units are designed to bring indoors the experience of natural elements such as daylight, snow, ice, rocks, moss and blue sky. The common areas have been designed with natural views. The design attempts to incorporate a judicious blend of punishment and rehabilitation of prisoners, ensuring zero physical and psychological violence to them (Schmidt Hammer Lassen 2013). The issues of repatriating prisoners currently held in Denmark will be a sensitive task, as many of the prisoners are psychiatrically ill and have been separated from their homeland for considerable periods of time.

Conclusion

Indigenous peoples around the world share long and dismal histories of negative inter-actions with criminal justice legal systems. The imposition of alien ideologies has resulted in disproportionate numbers of Indigenous people being incarcerated. The different world views held by Indigenous and non-Indigenous societies lead to fundamental differences in the way that the philosophy, purpose and practice of criminal justice systems are seen. Disproportionately high numbers of Indigenous people are confined in prisons because of factors such as alcoholism and substance abuse, socio-economic disadvantage, social anomy of living in separate worlds, lack of access to adequate legal representation, and discrimination. The institutionalization of Indigenous people results in the loss of significant human resources, the disintegration of families, the fracturing of relationships, the loss of future employment opportunities and reduced citizenship.

Some countries with Indigenous prisoners face issues not present in others. The issues of dealing with members of gangs in prison in Australia and Greenland are different from the experiences of the USA, New Zealand or Canada. Australian Aboriginal gang membership is not as widespread and the composition and activities of gangs are different. Australian Aboriginal criminal gangs tend to be based on Aboriginal family or kin groups which involve the use of children under the age of criminal responsibility to commit robberies and theft. Once in prison, Australian Aboriginal people are generally compliant if kept as a group, even when incarcerated for serious violent crimes. In Greenland, gang membership is virtually non-existent and hence neither Australia nor Greenland has to face the issues of disenfranchised youth with violent and potentially dangerous behaviours in their prison systems. While all four countries examined here have introduced minimum and medium security cultural units, for countries with groups of Indigenous prisoners connected to gangs, some thought should be given to designing maximum security facilities and programmes to suit disenfranchised gang members in a culturally sensitive manner.

The issues of being away from home and isolated from family and community with a lack of access to cultural activities, religion and traditional foods are common concerns articulated by Indigenous prisoners across the world. If this process is to be reversed, respect for different traditions must be fostered. Importantly, Indigenous prisoners should be kept as close as possible to their families and support systems, and given access to important aspects of their culture to assist people to move away from endlessly recycling through prison systems. Shipping people to faraway prisons that have no vested interest in rehabilitation and the eventual return to prisoners' home communities is a prescription for disaster. It would be far preferable that fewer Indigenous people ended up in prison or less damaging alternatives were implemented; however, while various countries continue to operate in current modes, there is a responsibility to find ways to minimize the damage prisons do to those incarcerated within them. The plight of various Indigenous groups in the prison system is troubling. Across the world, growing numbers of Indigenous prisoners enter prison systems with chronic illnesses, substance abuse problems, learning and cognitive disabilities, and mental illness. Success is dependent on the ability of prison authorities to embrace and respect Indigenous cultural knowledge systems, cultural practices, healing and learning systems, and operate within their philosophies.

Notes

1   The US Census uses self-identification as a means of measuring people as Native American, Aleut or Inuit-Yupik (Gardiner-Garden 2002).
2   There has been considerable debate about the use of 'American Indian' as opposed to 'Native American', 'First Nations' and other terms. The term 'American Indian' is used in this chapter as it is the most common term used by government and advocacy groups. 'Native American' is a broader designation because the US government includes Hawaiians and Samoans in this category (Yellow Bird 2006).
3   A number of US states do not record the ethnicity of Native American prisoners.
4   Criminal jurisdiction in Indian country depends on a number of factors, including the status of the alleged offender and victim, where the crime took place, and the type of offence. The complexity of jurisdictional issues comes under the Major Crimes Act, 18 U.S.C. § 1153, Public Law 83–280 as amended (P.L. 280) other Federal statutes (US Department of the Interior and US Department of Justice 2011).
5   The *hooghan* is one ethnoarchitectural form of the Navajo (Diné) peoples. The structures are constructed with natural materials such as wood and clay, well adapted to the harsh environment of Arizona and New Mexico desert areas and are scale representations of the Navajo universe and form a framework for the performance of Navajo healing ceremonies (Wyman 1975).
6   The Religious Land Use and Institutionalized Persons Act, 2000.
7   For example, *O'Lone v. Estate of Shabazz*, 482 U.S. 342 (1987) and *Turner v. Safley*, 482 U.S. 78 (1987).
8   *Randall Trapp, et al. v. Commissioner DuBois, et al.* Massachusetts Superior Court, US (Worcester, Civil No. 95–0779) Appeals Court, No. 2000-P.
9   Sacred items may include the pipe, mountain tobacco, drum, gourd, sage, cedar, sweet grass, medicine bundles, bags, eagle feather, corn pollen, and other items and materials such as firewood, lava rocks and willow saplings (Foster 2010).
10 The Indian Act, 1951 defines an 'Indian' (meaning American Indian) by ancestry.
11 This chapter uses the terms Aboriginal people, First Peoples and First Nations peoples interchangeably. The descriptor 'Indian' remains in place as the legal term used in the Canadian Constitution but its usage outside such situations may be considered offensive.
12 It is a commonly held view that the available statistics are an underestimate. Ethnicity is determined by self-identification and there is a contentious issue of distinguishing between Status and non-Status Indians, Métis and Inuit offenders.
13 Waseskun Healing Centre operates as a half-way house.

14 In Australia, an Aboriginal or Torres Strait Islander person is defined as a person 'of Aboriginal or Torres Strait Islander ancestry who identifies himself or herself as an Aboriginal person or Torres Strait Islander and is accepted as an indigenous person by members of the indigenous community' (*Aboriginal and Torres Strait Islander Commission (Regional Council Election) Amendment Rules 2002*).

15 There are variations between the number of Aboriginal prisoners in various states and territories. For example, in the Northern Territory 86% of the prison population is identified as being of Aboriginal or Torres Strait Islander descent (Australian Bureau of Statistics 2013).

16 Punishments under Aboriginal Customary Law are still widely accepted in some areas in Australia (e.g. Western and Central Desert Regions). In some instances, Aboriginal offenders are dealt with under the Australian Legal System and return to communities and are dealt punishments under Aboriginal Customary Law (Australian Law Reform Commission 1986).

17 The notion of 'country' is complex and does not just refer to a geographical location or physical features. 'Country' includes all living things and incorporates people, plants and animals, and embraces the seasons, stories and creation spirits. 'Country' is both a place of belonging and a way of believing.

18 A 'sorry camp' is a temporary camp used for mourning rituals during the time following the death of an Aboriginal person.

19 Many Aboriginal prisoners also express the desire to leave prison as 'free men' (Stein 2014).

20 Aotearoa is the accepted Māori name for New Zealand.

21 A new men's prison at Wiri in Manukau was under planning at the time of writing.

22 The Māori Land Act 1993 defines a Māori 'as a person of the Māori race of New Zealand or a descendant of any such person'.

23 The Treaty of Waitangi (1840) is an agreement, in Māori and English, which was made between the British Crown and approximately 540 Māori *rangatira* (chiefs).

24 The term '*iwi*' means 'peoples' or 'nations' in the Māori language.

25 Greenlandic forensic prisoners are housed in a dedicated Greenlandic Unit at Risskow Hospital in Aarhus. A small group of patients on remand are also held at this unit for assessment or treatment during the court process (Grant 2009).

Bibliography

Albaugh, B. and Anderson, P. (1974) 'Peyote in the treatment of alcoholism among American Indians', *American Journal of Psychiatry* 131: 1247–1250.

Al Jazeera (2013) 'Locked up warriors: why does New Zealand have one of the highest rates of incarceration in the developed world?', www.aljazeera.com/programmes/101east/2013/11/locked-up-warriors-201311481133704146.html (accessed 30 June 2014).

Arbour, L. (1996) *Commission of Inquiry into Certain Events at the Prison for Women in Kingston*, Ottawa: Canada Communication Group.

Australian Bureau of Statistics (2012) *Estimates of Aboriginal and Torres Strait Islander Australians*, Canberra: Australian Bureau of Statistics.

Australian Bureau of Statistics (2013) *4517.0 – Prisoners in Australia, 2013*, Canberra: ABS.

Australian Government, Department of Foreign Affairs and Trade (2014) 'About Australia – Legal System', www.dfat.gov.au/facts/legal_system.html (accessed 14 June 2014).

Australian Law Reform Commission (1986) *Recognition of Aboriginal Customary Laws Report 31*, Canberra: Australian Government.

British Broadcasting Corporation (2003) 'Lessons from Danish Prisons', news.bbc.co.uk/2/hi/europe/3036450.stm (accessed 14 June 2014).

Brochmann, H. (2001) *Detention in Greenland. Night-Time Correctional Institutions, Probation and Hostels for Juvenile Offenders as seen by Prisoners and Staff*, Man & Society Series 25, Copenhagen: Danish Polar Center.

Bureau of Justice Assistance (2009) *New Detention & Correctional Facilities Reflect Local Values & Culture*, Washington, DC: The Bureau of Justice Assistance.

Commission on Greenland's Judicial System (2004) *Report on Greenland's Judicial System Report No. 1442/2004*, Copenhagen: Danish Ministry of Justice.

Commonwealth of Australia (1991) *Final Report of the Royal Commission into Aboriginal Deaths in Custody*, Vols 1–5, Canberra: Australian Government Publishing Service.

Correctional Service Canada (1990) 'Aboriginal spirituality: an introduction for the correctional officer in British Columbia', August.

Correctional Service Canada (2013) 'Correctional Service Canada Healing Lodges', Government of Canada, www.csc-scc.gc.ca/aboriginal/002003-2000-eng.shtml (accessed 14 June 2014).

Council of Europe (2012) *Report to the Government of Denmark on the visit to Greenland carried out by the European Committee for the Prevention of Torture and Inhuman or Degrading Treatment or Punishment (CPT) from 25 to 27 September 2012*, Strasbourg: Council of Europe.

Davies, W. and Clow, R. (2009) *American Indian Sovereignty and Law: An Annotated Bibliography*, Lanham, MD: Scarecrow Press.

Department for Correctional Services, South Australia (2009) *'Port Augusta Prison Grieving Shelter – Respecting Cultural Diversity'*, This Month in Corrections, Adelaide: Department for Correctional Services.

Department of Corrections (AraPoutamaAotearoa) (2014) 'Prison Facts and Statistics – March 2014', www.corrections.govt.nz/resources/facts_and_statistics/quarterly_prison_statistics/CP_December_2014.html (accessed 20 June 2014).

Foster, L. (2010) *American Indian Religious and Spiritual Practices in the United States Prison System Submission to the US Periodic Review on Human Rights to the United Nations Human Rights Council*, Albuquerque, New Mexico.

Frantzsen, E. (2012) 'Indefinitely Sentenced to Denmark – The Return to Greenland', *Journal of Scandinavian Studies in Criminology & Crime Prevention* 13 (Supp): 57–68.

Gardiner-Garden, J. (2002) *Defining Aboriginality in Australia Current Issues Brief No. 10*, Canberra: Department of Parliamentary Library.

Glaze, L. (2010) 'Correctional populations in the United States, 2009', *Bureau of Justice Statistics Bulletin* (December).

Grant, E. (2009a) *Report on 2008 Churchill Fellowship to Investigate Correctional Facilities for Indigenous Prisoners New Zealand, Canada & Denmark*, Canberra: Winston Churchill Memorial Trust.

Grant, E. (2009b) 'Prison Environments for Australian Aboriginal Prisoners: A South Australian Case Study', *Australian Indigenous Law Review* 12(2): 66–80.

Grant, E. (2013a) '"Pack 'em, rack 'em and stack 'em": the appropriateness of the use and reuse of shipping containers for prison accommodation', *Australasian Journal of Construction Economics and Building* 13(2): 35–44.

Grant, E. (2013b) 'West Kimberley Regional Prison', *Architecture Australia* 102(4): 74–84.

Grant, E. (2014) 'Approaches to the design and provision of prison accommodation and facilities for Australian indigenous prisoners after the Royal Commission into Aboriginal deaths in custody', *Australian Indigenous Law Review* 77(1): 47–55.

Grant, E., Hansen, A. and Williamson, T. (2012) 'Design issues for prisoner health: thermal Conditions in Australian custodial environments', *World Health Design* 5(3): 80–85.

Grant, E. and Jewkes, Y. (2013) 'More important than guns or grog: the role of television on the health and wellbeing of Australian Aboriginal prisoners', *Current Issues in Criminal Justice* 25(2): 667–683.

Grant, E. and Memmott, P. (2008) 'The case for single cells and alternative ways of viewing custodial accommodation for Australian Aboriginal peoples', *The Flinders Journal of Law Reform* 10 (3): 631–646.

Grobsmith, E. (1994) *Indians in Prison: Incarcerated Native Americans in Nebraska*, Lincoln: University of Nebraska Press.

Hagan, W. (1966) *Indian Police and Judges: Experiments in acculturation and control*, New Haven, CT: Yale University Press.

Hayman, S. (2006) *Imprisoning Our Sisters: The new federal women's prisons in Canada*, Kingston: McGill-Queen's University Press.

Horton, D. (1994) *Unity and Diversity: The history and culture of Aboriginal Australia, 1301.0 – Year Book Australia*, Canberra: Australian Bureau of Statistics.

ICPS (International Centre for Prison Studies) (2012) *World Prison Brief, Greenland*, www.prison studies.org/country/greenland-denmark (accessed 15 June 2014).

Jensen, H. (1992) 'Justice in Greenland', in C. Taylor Griffiths (ed.) *From Self-sufficiency in Northern Justice Issues*, Northern Justice Society, 121–140.

Krasnow, P. (2012) 'Thoughts on planning, programming & designing Indian country detention facilities', paper from Workshop on Planning Alternatives for Correctional Facilities in Indian Country Workshop, Justice Solutions Group (PACIFIC), Correctional News, April.

Lauritsen, A. (2012) 'Greenland's open institution – imprisonment in a land without prison', *Journal of Scandinavian Studies in Criminology & Crime Prevention* 13 (Supp): 47–56.

Legislative Council of New South Wales (2003) *Hansard Transcript Proceedings Thursday 16 October 2003*, Sydney: Parliament of New South Wales.

Luna-Firebaugh, E. (2003) 'Incarcerating ourselves: tribal jails and corrections', *The Prison Journal* 83(1): 51–66.

Mann, M. (2009) *Good Intentions, Disappointing Results: A Progress Report on Federal Aboriginal Corrections*, Ottawa: Office of the Correctional Investigator.

Mas, S. (2013) 'Federal response to Aboriginal corrections report: "dismissive" CSC rejects recommendation to appoint a deputy commissioner for Aboriginal corrections', *CBC News*, 9 March, www.cbc.ca/news/politics/federal-response-to-aboriginal-corrections-report-dismissive-1.1338495 (accessed 30 June 2014).

Minton, T. (2013) 'Jails in Indian country, 2012', *NCJ* 242187, US Department of Justice, www.bjs.gov/index.cfm?ty=pbdetail&iid=4678 (accessed 30 June 2014).

National Indigenous Television (2009) *Balund-A: Wall-less Prison: Tabulam, NSW*, North Sydney: National Indigenous Television.

Norris, T., Vines, P. and Hoeffel, E. (2012) *The American Indian and Alaska Native Population: 2010 Census Briefs*, Washington, DC: US Department of Commerce Economics and Statistics Administration, US Census Bureau.

Office of the Correctional Investigator (2013) 'Backgrounder: Aboriginal offenders – a critical situation', www.oci-bec.gc.ca/cnt/rpt/oth-aut/oth-aut20121022info-eng.aspx (accessed 30 June 2014).

Office of the Inspector of Custodial Services (2003) *Report No. 19: Report of Announced Inspection of Acacia Prison*, Perth: Office of the Inspector of Custodial Services.

Office of the Inspector of Custodial Services (2008a) *Inspection Standards for Aboriginal Prisoners*, Perth: Office of the Inspector of Custodial Services.

Office of the Inspector of Custodial Services (2008b) *Report No. 56: Report of the Short Follow-up Inspection of Broome Regional Prison*, Perth: Office of the Inspector of Custodial Services.

Pedigo, J. (1983) 'Finding the "meaning" of Native American substance abuse: implications for community prevention', *The Personnel and Guidance Journal* (January): 273–277.

Perreault, S. (2009) 'The incarceration of Aboriginal people in adult correctional services', *Juristat, Statistics Canada Catalogue* 29(3).

The Public Safety Canada Portfolio Corrections Statistics Committee (2012) *Corrections and Conditional Release Statistical Overview*, Ottawa: Public Works and Government Services Canada.

Reed, L. (1989) 'The American Indian in the White Man's Prisons: Story of Genocide', *Journal of Prisoners on Prisons* 1(1): 41–56.

Reed, L. (1990) 'Rehabilitation: contrasting cultural perspectives and the composition of Church and State', *Journal of Prisoners on Prisons* 2(2): 3–28.

Ross, J. (2013) 'Introduction to crime, criminal justice and violence in American Indian communities', *American Indians at Risk* 3.

Schmidt Hammer Lassen (2013) 'New correctional facility in Nuuk', shl.dk/eng/#/home/about-architecture/new-correctional-facility-in-nuuk (accessed 30 June 2014).

Sinclaira, R. and Grekulb, J. (2012) 'Aboriginal youth gangs in Canada: (De)constructing an epidemic', *First Peoples Child & Family Review* 1: 8–28.

Solove, D. (1996) 'Faith Profaned: The Religious Freedom Restoration Act and religion in the prisons', *The Yale Law Journal* 106(2): 459–491.

Statistics Greenland (2013) 'Greenland in Figures', www.stat.gl/sae2012/a1a (accessed 30 June 2014).

Stein, G. (2014) 'New Darwin Super Prison Hopes to Rehabilitate Prisoners by Putting them to Work', *ABC Lateline News*, 20 May.

Stroub, J. (2005) *Research Report: Sweat Lodges in American Prisons*, The Pluralism Project, Harvard University, www.pluralism.org/reports/view/103 (accessed 30 June 2014).

Sujan, D. (2008) 'Greenland's Open Prison System', *Radio Netherlands*, www.expatica.com/nl/news/news_focus/Greenland_s-open-prison-system_13264.html (accessed 30 June 2014).

Task Force on Federally Sentenced Women (1990) *Creating Choices: The Report of the Task Force on Federally Sentenced Women*, Ottawa: Correctional Service of Canada.

Totten, M. (2009) 'Aboriginal youth and violent gang involvement in Canada: quality prevention strategies', *IPC Review* 3: 135–156.

UNODC (United Nations Office on Drugs and Crime) (2009) *Handbook on Prisoners with Special Needs, Criminal Justice Handbook Series*, Vienna: United Nations Office on Drugs and Crime.

US Department of the Interior, Office of the Inspector General (2004) *Neither Safe Nor Secure: An Assessment of Indian Detention Facilities*, Washington, DC: Department of the Interior, Office of the Inspector General.

US Department of the Interior and US Department of Justice (2011) *Tribal Law and Order Act (TLOA) Long Term Plan to Build and Enhance Tribal Justice Systems*, Washington, DC: US Department of Justice.

Waldram, J. (1997) *The Way of the Pipe: Aboriginal Spirituality and Symbolic Healing in Canadian Prisons*, Peterborough: Broadview Press.

Wyman, L. (1975) *Blessingway*, Tucson: The University of Arizona Press.

Yellow Bird, M. (2006) *American Indian Politics and the American Political System*, Washington, DC: Rowman & Littlefield Publishers.

Chapter 20

Ironies of American imprisonment
From capitalizing on prisons to capital punishment

Michael Welch

Introduction

The American criminal justice system is rife with contradictions. Among its many problems is mass incarceration, which is grossly expensive and plays little role in reducing crime (Welch 2011). The nation's incarceration rate – 716 per 100,000 – is the highest in the world. Although the USA represents 5% of the world's population, it holds 25% of the world's prisoners. With 2.3 million prisoners under lock and key, the government shells out more than US$24,000 per inmate annually on top of US$5.1 billion in new prison construction and US$60.3 billion in budget expenditures (Bureau of Justice Statistics 2009; Walmsley 2013). Regional patterns throw critical light onto the degrees of punitiveness. Southern states have some of the highest rates of incarceration: for example, Louisiana (867 per 100,000), Mississippi (686), Oklahoma (654). By contrast, in the northeast there is less reliance on imprisonment: Maine (148), Rhode Island (197), Massachusetts (200) (Bureau of Justice Statistics 2009). Despite all the claims of civil rights advances, African-Americans and Latinos are hardest hit by the race to incarcerate, with imprisonment rates of 2,207 and 966, respectively. Whites have an incarceration rate of 380 (Bureau of Justice Statistics 2009; Wagner 2014; see Alexander 2010).

Those disparities are just a few of the glaring paradoxes in the 'land of the free' (Holland 2013). As we shall see, other ironies of imprisonment spill over into institutional violence, healthcare crises, profiteering and the death penalty (Welch 2005). This chapter revisits two of those areas of concern. In the first segment, attention is turned to the ways in which political and corporate elites capitalize on prisons so as to generate profit. Much like other American economic models, such ventures are rarely win–win scenarios. Rather, there are clear winners – businessmen and their stockholders – who cash in on correctional institutions operated by the public or private sector. The losers, of course, are those sentenced to prison since many of them are non-violent offenders who lose their liberty so that politicians can appear to be 'getting tough' on crime – at the taxpayers' expense (Downes 2001; Welch 2011). Those ironies of imprisonment are not mere accidents or flights of fancy; rather, they are deeply embedded in America's predatory economic and political culture.

In the second portion of the critique, capital punishment also is examined from the standpoint of its ironic tendencies. With a brief survey of the deterrence literature, discussion considers the phenomenon of brutalization whereby executions tend to promote lethal violence rather than deter it. So as to create the appearance of humane executions, many states have adopted lethal injection. Paradoxically, that method has produced a host of problems, most notably botched executions in which prisoners are subjected to prolonged suffering. Over the past few years, bungled executions have become more frequent, in part because drug manufacturers have barred their products from being used to put prisoners to death. As those drugs become increasingly scarce, corrections officials have solicited unregulated pharmacies that deliver untested drugs. Defense lawyers argue that their clients are injected with questionable chemicals that produce a degree of pain so high that it violates the US Constitution's Eighth Amendment prohibition on cruel and unusual punishment. So as to deepen our understanding of the ironies of imprisonment, the chapter attends to matters of social and economic inequality in American society.

Capitalizing on prisons

Critical scholarship has consistently revealed that trends in imprisonment are driven more by economics than crime rates (Dunaway et al. 2000; Lynch 2007; White 1999). With that realization in mind, it is crucial to consider two prominent features of the economic-punishment nexus: (i) the tendency in a capitalist system to reduce labor; and (ii) the commercial aspects of the political economy. Together those market forces propel the corrections industry. Under normal conditions of capitalism, the surplus population swells as opportunities for labor are diminished, resulting in unemployment and marginalization. Subsequently, a proportion of the surplus population inevitably becomes snared in the ever widening net of criminal justice in which they serve as raw material for the corrections industry, an enterprise responding to the tenets of a free market economy.

Those mutually reinforcing activities contribute significantly to the economic-punishment nexus which maintains coercive mechanisms of social control. Moreover, the continued reliance on incarceration presents grave threats to democracy and social equality. Nils Christie famously wrote: 'The major dangers of crime in modern societies are not the crimes, but that the fight against them may lead societies towards totalitarian developments' (Christie 1993: 16). In this section, we examine the prison business in light of market forces and escalating incarceration that harms people and a democratic society. Setting the stage for this critical inquiry is an overview of the production of prisoners under capitalism, followed by a close analysis of the corrections industry and its adverse effects.

Production of prisoners

Among the contradictions of capitalism is the economic marginalization of a large segment of society, thus creating a surplus population from which deviance and crime are produced. Because those marginalized are significant in both sheer number and their perceived threat to the social order, the state invests heavily in mechanisms of social control (De Giorgi 2006; Lynch 2007; Welch 2011). Law enforcement and corrections constitute some of the more coercive measures designed to deal with the portion of the surplus population considered a problem. Within the political economy, the criminal justice system functions in ways that protect capitalist relations of production. Given the emergence of the corrections enterprise, it is clear that such operations of social control themselves are engaged in the accumulation of capital. Before identifying the character and composition of the corrections industry, it is fitting that we acknowledge key dimensions of the political economy that contribute to lawlessness, an activity that produces raw materials necessary for the corrections industry: namely, prisoners.

Because large-scale economic marginalization restricts opportunities for legitimate financial survival in a market economy, unlawful enterprises emerge. Perhaps the most widespread underground economy is the illicit drug industry, a form of financial activity (and mood-altering escape from the harsh conditions of poverty) created by the structural inequality of capitalism. Curiously, the selling and consumption of banned drugs has become increasingly criminalized to the extent that vast resources of the state are allocated to control those behaviors. Added measures aimed at prohibiting the drug industry contribute significantly to the ironies of social control (i.e. harsher penalties and mandatory minimum sentences) (Welch 2005).

For instance, even though the drug trade is an outlawed industry, its underground economy conforms to free world, free market, and capitalist principles insofar as costs attached to illegal drugs are contingent upon demand and scarcity. Therefore, reducing the supply merely drives up the price of drugs. That increase in value makes trafficking more profitable, thereby attracting more individuals and groups willing to venture such risks. Wilkins (1991) similarly points out that the cost of illegal substances reflects the risk, not the type or quality of the product. Drug peddlers are not so much selling drugs but – like insurance companies – they are trading in risk.

In sum, the criminalization of drugs, paradoxically, escalates rather than dampens the drug trade. Higher penalties increase the risk of selling drugs, making the activity more lucrative, and in the end, recruiting an endless supply of peddlers who are already marginalized economically. As drug peddlers are apprehended, convicted and incarcerated, they subsequently serve as raw materials for the corrections industry, an economic enterprise considered legitimate by many proponents of a free market (Shelden and Brown 2000; *Social Justice* 2000; Welch 2011).

Corrections in a market economy

Over the past several decades, imprisonment has become big business, and the bitter 'not-in-my-backyard' attacks on prisons have been replaced with welcome mats, such as the one in Canon City (CO) reading 'Corrections Capital of the World'. The mayor of Canon City proudly boasts: 'We have a nice, nonpolluting, recession-proof industry here' (Brooke 2002: 20). In Leavenworth (KS), another community that added a private prison to its already well-stocked corrections arsenal – featuring a federal penitentiary, a state prison and a military stockade – a billboard reads 'How about doin' some TIME in Leavenworth?' Bud Parmer, site acquisition administrator for Florida Department of Corrections, concedes: 'There's a new attitude … small counties want a shot in the arm economically. A prison is a quick way to do it' (Glamser 1996: 3A; Yeoman 2000). Economically strapped towns induce jail and prison construction by offering land, cash incentives, and cut-rate deals on utilities: in return for these accommodations, locales receive jobs and spur other businesses such as department stores, fast-food chains and motels, all of which contribute to the tax base (Kilborn 2001; Martin 2000; Thies 2001).

Prisons are courted not only on Main Street but also on Wall Street, where industrial corrections create a bull market – further evidence that crime does indeed pay. Tremendous growth in the prison population coupled with astonishing increases in expenditures has generated a lucrative market economy with seemingly unlimited opportunities for an array of financial players: entrepreneurs, lenders, investors, contractors, vendors and service providers. The American Jail Association promoted its conference with advertisements reeking of crass commercialism: 'Tap into the Sixty-Five Billion Dollar Local Jails Market' (Donziger 1996). The World Research Group organized a convention in Dallas billed 'Private Correctional Facilities: Private Prisons, Maximize Investment Returns in this Exploding Industry'. Without much hesitation, corporate America has caught the scent of new public money. The Dallas meeting included representatives from AT&T, Merrill Lynch, PricewaterhouseCoopers, and other golden-logo companies (Teephen 1996). The prison industry also has attracted other capitalist heavyweights, including the investment houses of Goldman Sachs and Salomon Smith Barney, which compete to underwrite corrections construction with tax-exempt bonds that do not require voter approval. Defense industry titans Westinghouse Electric, Alliant Techsystems, Inc., and GDE Systems, Inc. (a division of the old General Dynamics) also have entered the financial sphere of criminal justice, not to mention manufacturers of name-brand products currently cashing in on the spending frenzy in corrections. While attending the American Correctional Association's annual meeting, Rod Ryan, representing Dial Corporation, delightedly replied: 'I already sell $100,000 a year of Dial soap to the New York City jails. Just think what a state like Texas would be worth' (Elvin 1994/95: 4; Bates 1999).

A critical look into the financial infrastructure reveals that the private prison industry rests on important forms of investment and stockholdings. Moreover, private correctional companies receive significant capital support from larger corporations and financial institutions. Indeed, that economic backing can be easily traced to institutional stockholders and its volume of shares. For example, Corrections Corporation of America (CCA) lists 114 institutional stockholders that together amount to 28,736,071 shares of stock. RS Investments Wesley Capital MGMT holds the largest number of shares of CCA stock, and 36 institutional stockholders with a total of 9,587,496 shares support Capital Research & MGMT. The GEO Group has 82 institutional stockholders accounting for 9,583,019 shares. Wells Fargo (and Northwest Corporation) holds the most GEO Group stock, followed by Fidelity Management and Research, and Wells Capital MGMT (Welch and Turner 2008: see Dyer 2000; Hall 2004a, 2004b).

The corrections industry operates according to a unique set of economic dynamics insofar as the supply–demand principle operates in reverse. 'More supply brings increased demand. Industry insiders know that there are more than enough inmates to go around' (Adams 1996: 463). That point is particularly significant considering the ongoing production of prisoners in American capitalist society exacerbated by the war on drugs and other tough-on-crime initiatives. Terrence Stevens, an African-American with no previous drug convictions, symbolizes the punitive reality of the campaign against drugs. He was busted for possessing five ounces of cocaine, a violation punishable by 15 years to life under New York's so-called Rockefeller drug law. His prison sentence is the equivalent of that for more serious offenses, including murder and kidnapping, and longer than the minimum terms for armed robbery, manslaughter and rape. The Stevens case invited greater media scrutiny due to his medical condition. As a kid growing up in a housing project in East Harlem, he developed muscular dystrophy. At the time of his arrest, Stevens was confined to a wheelchair and while in prison, he relies on fellow convicts to bathe, dress and lift him onto and off the toilet. Correctional officers appear to ignore his disability. During a routine strip search, he told the guards that he was unable to remove his pants.

For not complying with the order, he was sent to solitary confinement for 40 days. Upon appeal, the disciplinary charge was dropped, but only after he had served the punishment. Ironically, the person who was arrested along with Stevens was not sentenced to prison; rather, he drew probation for testifying against Stevens (Purdy 2000).

In full view of the race to incarcerate, investors are betting that the corrections industry will continue to proliferate because its raw materials – prisoners – are relatively cheap and in constant supply. As we shall discuss in the next segment, a corrections industry that behaves according to market forces also produces serious problems and grave injustices.

Kids for cash

Hillary Transue serves as a brazen example of capitalizing on prisons. In 2007, the 17-year-old built a spoof MySpace page mocking the assistant principal at her high school in Wilkes-Barre, Pennsylvania. She was a stellar student and had never been in trouble; moreover, the webpage stated clearly at the bottom that it was just a joke. Thus, when Hillary appeared in court she had good reason to expect a mere lecture from the judge. To Hillary's surprise, the judge sentenced her to three months at a juvenile detention center on a charge of harassment. As her stunned parents stood by, court officers hand-cuffed Hillary and transported her to jail. 'I felt like I had been thrown into some surreal sort of nightmare. All I wanted to know was how this could be fair and why the judge would do such a thing' said Hillary (Urbina and Hamill 2009: 1). Over time, observers realized that Hillary was just one of thousands of victims of an elaborate 'kids for cash' scheme. In 2009, the judge, Mark A. Ciavarella, Jr, and a judicial colleague, Michael T. Conahan, pleaded guilty to wire fraud and income tax fraud for taking more than $2.6 million in kickbacks to send teenagers to two privately run youth detention centers run by PA Child Care and a sister company, Western PA Child Care.

In laying the groundwork for their corrupt scheme, Judges Conahan and Ciavarella closed the county-run juvenile detention center, arguing that it was in poor condition. Then they claimed to have no choice but to send detained juveniles to the newly con-structed private detention centers. Judge Conahan served as president judge in control of the budget and Judge Ciavarella oversaw the juvenile courts; in 2002, they put in motion the kickback mechanism that would produce millions of personal profit. Judge Conahan secured contracts for the two centers to house juvenile offenders while Judge Ciavarella carried out the sentencing to keep the jails filled. For years, the kickbacks were concealed as payments to a company they controlled in Florida. From 2003 to 2008, more than 5,000 boys and girls, some as young as 11, were torn from their families and sent off to spend months – sometimes years – of confinement and unjust misery. A very short list characterizes the sort of 'crimes' that seem to warrant being locked up:

- A 13-year-old incarcerated for throwing a piece of steak at his mother's boyfriend.
- A 15-year-old for throwing a sandal at her mother.
- An 11-year-old for calling the police after his mother locked him out of the house.
- A 14-year-old, and an 'A' student, was sentenced for writing 'Vote for Michael Jackson' on a few stop signs; while in detention, she suffered a seizure, banging her head so hard she cracked her dental braces.

(Ecenbarger 2014; Smith 2013)

Judge Ciavarella had a well-earned reputation for issuing unusually harsh sentences. Between 2002 and 2006, he ordered detention in one-quarter of his cases, compared with a state rate of one in ten. Still, the corruption did not occur in a vacuum; it was a 'festival of injustice' in which prosecutors, public defenders, teachers and court employees recognized a pattern of cruelty but did nothing. Clay Yeager, the former director of the Office of Juvenile Justice in Pennsylvania, said: 'It's pretty clear those people didn't do their jobs' (Urbina and Hamill 2009: 3). The judge's hearings were especially brief – on average, four minutes. Juvenile probation officers, at Ciavarella's direction, talked kids out of exercising their right to counsel. In 2008, the Juvenile Law Center filed a motion to the State Supreme Court on behalf of more than 500 juveniles who had appeared before the judge without representation; initially, the court rejected the petition, but later reversed its decision.

Family finances figured prominently, feeding a modern-day debtor's prison. 'If parents were unable to pay the costs of detention, their children were sometimes held longer. One teenager's Social Security survivor's check, from his father's death, was garnished to pay the costs' (Smith 2013: 2). In his book, *Kids for Cash*, William Ecenbarger describes the scam as a routine and systematic form of child abuse. In a plea agreement, both judges were sentenced to 87 months in federal prison and forced to resign from the bench and Bar. State law forbids retirement benefits to judges convicted of a felony while in office; therefore, the judges will also lose their pensions. No charges have been filed against executives of the detention centers, but prosecutors continue to investigate the case.

Capital punishment

As we continue to survey the ironies plaguing the American prison system, it is fitting that critical attention be turned to the death penalty. Deterrence is a particularly potent notion shaping public opinion on capital punishment. It is widely believed that executions serve to significantly inhibit other acts of homicide. Critics, however, insist that such a belief is merely a myth, or what Samuel Walker (2001) describes as a crime-control theology, since it rests on faith rather than facts. Refuting that myth, numerous empirical studies fail to support the hypothesis between deterrence and capital punishment (Bohm 1999; Donohue and Wolfers 2005; Peterson and Bailey 1991; Sellin 1967).

The ongoing debate over deterrence and the death penalty began in earnest with the 1975 article by Isaac Ehrlich, an economist who claimed that each execution prevented eight murders. At the time, American society took a dramatic shift toward a conservative law-and-order approach to crime. Supporters of the death penalty celebrated Ehrlich's research. Most notably, the study was cited in the *Gregg* decision in which the US Supreme Court reinstated the death penalty in 1976 (see Yunker 1976).[1] Ehrlich had given deterrence theory a much-needed boost following Zimring and Hawkins's (1973) thorough critique of deterrence propositions. Despite the popularity of Ehrlich's research, its high-level statistical analysis was not immune to methodological problems. Social scientists tested his findings by way of replication: a research procedure by which data are reanalyzed to determine whether previous findings are supported. Ehrlich's research did not pass the test of replication. Several re-evaluations of his data also failed to produce what Ehrlich boasted was a deterrent effect (Bowers and Pierce 1975; Forst 1983; see Bowers et al. 1984).

Not surprisingly, given the enduring popularity of deterrence theory among mainstream economists and criminologists, another round of research returned to the matter of executions (Cloninger and Marchesini 2001; Shepherd 2004). More recently, Land, Teske, and Zheng asked the simple question: 'Does the death penalty save lives?' (2009: 1009). In re-examining claims that many lives are saved through reductions in subsequent homicide rates after executions, Land and his colleagues conclude that those 'findings are not robust enough to model even small changes in specifications that yield dramatically different results' (Land et al. 2009: 1009). Similarly, Donohue and Wolfers report that the death penalty 'is applied so rarely that the number of homicides it can plausibly have caused or deterred cannot be reliably disentangled from the large year-to-year changes in the homicide rate caused by other factors' (Donohue and Wolfers 2005: 794; Fagan et al. 2006). So, is the dispute over deterrence and capital punishment resolved? Hardly. Advocates as well as opponents of the death penalty continue to debate (Berk 2009; Donohue 2009; Kovandzic et al. 2009; Rubin 2009). Among the many issues being raised is a growing concern that, ironically, executions may promote violence rather than suppress it.

Do executions incite violence?

Proponents of deterrence theory argue that publicizing executions is a necessary element of capital punishment. It is through such widespread exposure that the tough law-and-order message of death sentences is conveyed. Over the years, however, a competing perspective has emerged. Brutalization theory suggests that publicized executions do not deter violence; instead, they actually incite violence. To understand the scope of brutalization theory, we move to unpack the main aspects of deterrence theory. Deterrence theory rests on the major assumption that potential killers restrain themselves from committing murder because they identify with the person being executed. That is, potential killers are expected to realize that if they commit murder, they, too, will suffer a similar fate. Publicized executions are thought to reinforce that central idea, thereby curbing future homicides. Similarly, brutalization theory also assumes that members of society identify with executions. Rather than identifying with the condemned, however, it is proposed that some killers identify with the executioner. From that perspective, the message being sent is not so much that killing is wrong; rather, certain persons *deserve* to die. Indeed, executions are sometimes viewed as a 'public service' by some of its supporters, suggesting that society is better off without certain murderers (see Katz 1988).

According to brutalization theory, publicized executions create an alternative identification process that prompts imitation, not deterrence. Considering that dynamic, is it possible in the aftermath of a publicized execution that murder rates might increase? Measuring that phenomenon has been the task of brutalization theorists. In their pioneering work, Bowers and Pierce (1980) hypothesized that some murderers view their victims as comparable to executed offenders. Correspondingly, they found an increase in homicides soon after well-publicized executions – a trend that is reported as evidence of a brutalization, not a deterrent, effect (also see Forst 1983; Phillips 1980; Stack 1987). Bowers and Pierce specify that the brutalization effect has an impact on individuals who are prone to violence, not those who are generally nonviolent. For those accustomed to violence, the publicized execution reinforces the belief that vengeance is justified.

So as to explore the ironies of capital punishment, the brutalization effect has been subjected to additional research. Cochran, Chamlin and Seth (1994: 306) studied the return of capital punishment in Oklahoma and found evidence of a predicted brutalization effect. Cochran and his colleagues took into account various types of murder and discovered that brutalization was more prevalent in stranger homicides in which social ties (or social controls) are much weaker because those persons are not known to one another. Cochran et al. contend that, in general, if inhibitions against the use of lethal violence to resolve confrontations created by 'unworthy' others are reduced by executions, 'such a brutalization effect is most likely to occur in "situated transactions" … where inhibitions against the use of violence are already absent or considerably relaxed' (Cochran et al. 1994: 110). In a widely cited replication, Bailey (1998) confirmed Cochran et al.'s findings. Moreover, that analysis on the different types of murder indicates that the impact of capital punishment in Oklahoma was much more extensive than previously suggested. Bailey emphasized that 'detailed combinations of homicide circumstances and victim offender relationships must be considered, as well as the possibility that the deterrent/brutalization impact of capital punishment may differ for different dimensions of capital punishment' (ibid.: 731–732; see Cochran and Chamlin 2000).

Considerable debate also persists on the issue of whether executions should be televised. Proponents of the death penalty favor televised executions because they maintain that the publicity will have a deterrent effect. Opponents of capital punishment, however, are more diverse in their opinions. Some death penalty abolitionists oppose televised executions because they believe that a brutalization effect might occur. Others favor televised executions so as to display the gruesome realities of the death penalty. Accordingly, such exposure might alter their opinion of executions toward abolition (Leighton 1999).

The ironic case of Jesse Jacobs

As a startling illustration of the ironic value of capital punishment, we turn to 4 January 1995, when Jesse DeWayne Jacobs was put to death by lethal injection in Texas. Because 87 other prisoners have been executed in Texas since the state reinstated the death penalty in 1976, Jacobs's execution looked relatively routine. However, Jacobs's case is complicated by serious problems – most notably, his innocence. Of course, many convicts fight to the finish, proclaiming their innocence, especially when facing the death penalty. However Jacobs's innocence was widely acknowledged, even by the prosecutor who convicted him. As Jacobs was being prepped for lethal injection, he optimistically believed that the courts would intervene at the last moment. Just before Jacobs was put to death, he announced: 'I have news for all of you, there is not going to be an execution. This is premeditated murder by the state of Texas, I am not guilty of this crime' (Hentoff 1995: 22).

Here is how Jacobs's story unfolds. In 1986, Jacobs and his sister Bobbie Jean Hogan were arrested for the fatal shooting of Etta Ann Urdiales. At the time, Hogan was intimately involved with Urdiales's estranged husband. Separate trials were ordered, and Jacobs confessed that he had abducted Urdiales at his sister's request so that these women could have a meeting to sort out their differences. Hogan had hoped to persuade Urdiales to cease contact with her ex-husband and to give up custody of her children. In addition to confessing that he abducted Urdiales, Jacobs initially claimed responsibility for shooting her as well. Although his sister shot Urdiales, Jacobs took the rap because he was already facing life imprisonment for the kidnapping. Moreover, Jacobs had a previous conviction for murder, and at the time of the incident, he was out on parole.

Later, Jacobs reconsidered his confession and decided not to take the blame for his sister. He then told the truth. Jacobs abducted Urdiales and took her to an abandoned farmhouse so that his sister could meet with her. Jacobs left the house to sit on the porch, when he heard gunfire. Quickly returning, Jacobs saw his sister with a gun, and on the floor was a fatally wounded Urdiales. Jacobs explained to the jury that he was unaware that his sister was armed (Hentoff 1995). Nevertheless, the prosecutor insisted that Jacobs, a previously convicted murderer, shot Urdiales to death. The jury concurred, and Jacobs was convicted and sentenced to death.

Seven months later, during the Hogan trial, Peter Speers, the same prosecutor who secured the conviction against Jacobs, presented to the jury a different version of the killing. Curiously, the new version of the incident accurately placed Hogan in the role of the shooter, thereby removing Jacobs as the assailant. Referring to the previous trial, Speers said he had 'changed his mind "about what really happened. And I'm convinced ... that Bobbie Hogan pulled that trigger"' (Hentoff 1995: 22). In the Hogan trial, Speers even went so far as to declare Jacobs innocent. Moreover, since Jacobs was not aware of his sister's intention to shoot Urdiales, he was free from accomplice liability under state law.

Hogan was convicted of involuntary manslaughter and was sentenced to a ten-year prison term. Hogan's conviction and the prosecutor's admission that her brother was falsely imprisoned changed nothing for Jacobs. The state of Texas refused to vacate Jacobs's conviction; nor did he receive legal relief from the court of appeals. Eventually, Jacobs's case reached the US Supreme Court, but it, too, refused to keep him from being executed. In his five-page dissent opinion, Supreme Court Justice John Paul Stevens blamed the state of Texas for the injustice of executing Jacobs (Verhovek 1995). The *Jacobs* case resembles that of *Herrera v. Collins* (1993) in which the US Supreme Court also ruled that 'actual innocence' is not enough to avert execution. In *Herrera*, Justice Harry Blackmun reflected: 'Nothing could be more shocking than to execute a person who is actually innocent', and charged the High Court with coming 'perilously close to murder' (Hoffman 1993: 817; see Sarat 2001).

In the words of Jacobs: 'I have committed a lot of sins in my life ... Maybe I do deserve this. But I am not guilty of this crime' (Verhovek 1995: E-6). Not all observers, however, view Jacobs's execution as tragic. Laurin A. Wollan, Jr, an associate professor of criminology at Florida State University, who advocates the death penalty, concedes that the criminal justice system makes mistakes. Still, 'the value of the death penalty is its rightness vis-à-vis the wrongness of the crime, and that is so valuable that the possibility of the conviction of the innocent, though rare, has to be accepted' (Verhovek 1995: E-6).

Botched executions

Compounding the ironies of capital punishment are executions that do not go smoothly. That difficulty, of course, is as old as executions themselves (King 2009). The adoption of newer – more technologically advanced – methods of capital punishment has not always solved the problem. Ironically, in some cases those practices have made things worse. Compared with hanging, the electric chair was widely considered a more effi-cient, thus a more humane, form of execution (Marquart et al. 1994). However, in 1990 supporters and opponents of the death penalty were reminded just how unstable elec-tricity can be. That year in Florida, Jessie Joseph Tafero (convicted of fatally shooting two law-enforcement officers) was secured to an electric chair, but the wiring failed as fire, smoke and sparks flew from his head. Rather than being put to death instanta-neously, Tafero was set afire. Court filings claim that he was tortured, thereby violating the Eighth Amendment of the US Constitution's ban on cruel and unusual punishment. Lawyers similarly criticized the state's reliance on the 'toaster test', in which a household appliance was used to test the flammability of the sponge, insisting that 'scientific testing is not done with a toaster' (Associated Press 1990: 1). Moreover, attorneys also charged that the corrections officials were not competent to carry out executions without inflicting unnecessary pain.

With the belief that lethal injection was more efficient – thus humane – than the electric chair, many US states began adopting that procedure as their primary method of execution. Botched executions, nonetheless, would persist. In 2009, the execution of Romell Broom was halted after Ohio corrections officials were unable to locate a usable vein to administer lethal injection. Broom (who was convicted of raping and murdering a 14-year-old girl) compliantly cooperated with the execution team for more than two hours as it searched for a possible usable vein. Journalists described the bizarre scene in detail. 'Several times, Broom rolled onto his left side, pointed at veins, straightened tubes or massaged his own arms to help prison staff keep a vein open. He was clearly frustrated as he leaned back on the gurney' (Mackey 2009: 1).

Opponents of capital punishment did not hesitate to condemn the Broom incident. 'The sentence is death, not torture plus death', said Kathleen Soltis, chairwoman of the Cleveland Coalition Against the Death Penalty (Mackey 2009: 2). Defense attorneys argued that proper training of prison officials could have prevented the bungled execu-tion. Court filings contend that Ohio prison officials demonstrated a consistent disregard for their own rules in carrying out executions, including failing to ensure that execution staff members attend required rehearsals and training. 'The state got their chance with Broom', said lawyer Adele Shank, but 'they failed to execute him, and, in the process, they violated his constitutional right to avoid cruel and unusual punishment. So we are arguing it would be further cruelty for them to try again' (Urbina 2014: 1).

In 2014, Arizona corrections officials took nearly two hours to lethally inject Joseph R. Wood III, a procedure that would normally be 10–15 minutes. At issue was a dispute over the effectiveness of the drugs used. While he was gasping on the gurney, Wood's lawyers filed an emergency appeal to a federal district court, to halt the procedure. Moreover, they even phoned US Supreme Court Justice Anthony Kennedy. 'He is still alive', the lawyers said in the district court appeal, filed just after 3:00pm. 'This execution has violated Mr. Wood's Eighth Amendment right to be executed in the absence of cruel and unusual punishment. We respectfully request that this court stop the execution and require that the Department of Corrections use the lifesaving provisions required in its protocol' (Eckholm 2014: 1). Wood expired before the district court responded. Jus-tice Kennedy denied the request to halt the procedure while Wood was still alive. Wood was sentenced for the murder of his estranged girlfriend and her father.

The case of Clayton Lockett has become one of the most closely studied botched executions. In 2014, Lockett (sentenced for shooting a woman and burying her alive) was slated for execution. The morning before the procedure, he became combative and defied being shackled, prompting prison officers to shock him with a Taser. While in the examination room, Lockett slashed his own arm but a physician determined that the wound would not require sutures. That evening, he was strapped to a gurney in the execution chamber where for nearly one hour, a medical technician probed his arms, legs and feet for a usable vein. Eventually a catheter was inserted into his groin, but soon other problems ensued. The window blinds facing the visitors' gallery were closed as the medical team frantically tried to keep the procedure on track. 'With something clearly going terribly wrong, the doctor checked the IV and reported that the blood vein had collapsed, and the drugs had either absorbed into the tissue, leaked out or both' (Eckholm and Schwartz 2014: 2). Due to 'a vein failure in which the chemicals did not make it into the offender', the execution was aborted. Minutes later, Lockett died of a 'massive heart attack' (ibid.: 5). No steps were taken to deliver emergency resuscitation. Many agreed with Madeline Cohen, an attorney who witnessed the execution, who said that Lockett had been 'tortured to death' (Erlanger 2014: 1).

The Lockett incident brought unwanted attention to a procedure that state corrections officials prefer to keep from public scrutiny. Among those who were quick to comment on that particular botched execution were medical practitioners. Anesthesiologists explained that while they occasionally use a femoral vein accessible from the groin when those in the arms and legs are not accessible, the procedure is more complicated and potentially painful. Putting a line in the groin 'is a highly invasive and complex procedure which requires extensive experience, training and credentialing', said Dr Mark Heath, an anesthesiologist at Columbia University (Eckholm and Schwartz 2014: 4). Oklahoma's correctional system is viewed with skepticism because the state does not reveal personnel involved in executions, let alone their credentials. Dr Heath continued: 'There are a number of ways of checking whether a central line is properly placed in a vein, and had those been done they ought to have known ahead of time that the catheter was improperly positioned' (ibid.: 4). Dr Joel Zivot, an anesthesiologist at the Emory University School of Medicine, believes the prison's initial account that the vein had collapsed or blown was almost certainly incorrect: 'The femoral vein is a big vessel. Finding the vein, however, can be tricky. The vein is not visible from the surface, and is near a major artery and nerves. You can't feel it, you can't see it. Without special expertise [and the aid of an ultrasound machine] the failure was not surprising' (ibid.: 4). Among the challenges for lethal injections is the scarcity of medical professionals willing to participate, since both the American Medical Association and the American Society of Anesthesiologists insist that doctors should not take part in executions.

Questions also are raised over the drugs used in lethal injection, since Oklahoma as well as many other states (e.g. Arizona, Georgia, Missouri) conceal their sources, thereby preventing defendants from knowing whether untested combinations may cause suffering barred by the US Constitution. The bungled execution of Lockett has brought legal battles over the state's refusal to disclose where it obtained the drugs. Accidents have become more common as state governments, facing shortages in critical drugs, are trying new drugs and combinations from secret manufacturers (Eckholm and Schwartz 2014: 3). Opponents of the death penalty called for an immediate moratorium on executions in Oklahoma. In the government's 'haste to conduct a science experiment [on two men] behind a veil of secrecy, our state has disgraced itself before the nation and world', said Ryan Kiesel of the American Civil Liberties Union (ibid.: 2).

The issue of secrecy surrounding lethal injection has not gone unnoticed. *The New York Times* published a scathing editorial: 'It is bad enough that the death penalty is barbaric, racist and arbitrary in its application, but it is also becoming less transparent as the dwindling number of death-penalty states work to hide the means by which they kill people' (*The New York Times* 2014: 1). Faced with ethical dilemmas – and negative publicity – many drug manufacturers refuse to supply drugs for use in capital punishment. As a result, states are rushing to replenish their stocks by turning to compounding pharmacies which operate in a largely unregulated market. Prisoners are typically denied basic information about the drugs used to put them to death, and the courts willingly support such secrecy. In 2014, the state of Missouri executed Herbert Smulls for the 1991 murder of a jewelry-store owner. Corrections officials refused to identify the pharmacies involved in manufacturing the execution drugs, a decision upheld by a federal appeals court. The US Court of Appeals for the Eighth Circuit ruled that Smulls had no constitutional claim against the state's execution procedure because he had not demonstrated that the 'risk of severe pain' from the state's intended drug protocol would be substantially greater than a readily available alternative (*The New York Times* 2014: 2).

As a departure from its usual refusal to grant last-minute stays, the US Supreme Court indefinitely halted the execution of Russell Bucklew. Lawyers argued that Bucklew would be subjected to great pain if he were killed by a lethal injection since he had cavernous hemangioma. That vascular disease produced blood vessel deformities and tumors in his face and neck. Medical specialists testified that Bucklew's execution would be prolonged, thus violating the Eighth Amendment ban on cruel and unusual punishment. In court filings, attorneys raised concerns over the compounded drugs used by the state in executions; they claimed the secrecy surrounding the state's execution protocols would further 'increase the risk that he would suffer a torturous death' (Eligon 2014: 2). Bucklew also asked to have his execution filmed, but the request was denied without comment. Bucklew had a long history of violence. He was convicted of killing a man in front of the victim's children in 1996.

In another rare ruling, a Georgia judge in 2014 issued a last-minute stay of execution to an inmate, finding that the state's secrecy law 'makes it impossible' to demonstrate that the drug protocol violates the Eighth Amendment. There, the Drug Enforcement Administration confiscated the state's supply of one lethal-injection drug suspected of having been illegally imported from Britain. In a similar scenario, Louisiana officials attempted to buy drugs from an Oklahoma pharmacy, the Apothecary Shoppe, which is not licensed to distribute drugs in Louisiana. The legal battles over secret execution drugs have become so rampant that legislators are contemplating the return of antiquated methods such as firing squads and electric chairs (*The New York Times* 2014). However, in Tennessee, ten death row prisoners already challenging the state's lethal injection protocol were permitted by a judge to amend their lawsuit to include objections to the electric chair (*The Guardian* 2014).

Perhaps due to the apparent ironies of capital punishment, many states have recently abolished it, including Illinois, Connecticut, Maryland, New Jersey, New Mexico and New York. The Washington State governor declared in 2014 that no executions would take place while he remained in office, following a similar action by the governor of Oregon. In 2013, Colorado's governor issued an indefinite reprieve in the only case on his watch (Baker 2014). President Obama declared in 2014 that the botched execution of Lockett was 'deeply disturbing'. Accordingly, he directed his attorney-general, Eric H.

Holder, Jr, to review how the death penalty is applied in the USA at a time when it has become increasingly debated. While recognizing his support for the death penalty in certain cases, Obama said Americans should 'ask ourselves some difficult and profound questions' about its use (Baker 2014: 1; see Garland 2010).

Conclusion

As this chapter demonstrates, there is no shortage of evidence involving the ironies of imprisonment. In closing, let us consider the case of Oklahoma prisoner Robert Brecheen, who slipped into a self-induced drug stupor. Facing a life-threatening situation, corrections officials rushed him to a nearby hospital where physicians pumped his stomach. His suicide was averted. However, as soon as Brecheen regained consciousness, he was returned to death row so as to keep his execution on schedule. Literally two hours later, Brecheen was prepped in the medical unit and put to death with state-approved drugs. The paradox was obvious. 'This shows the absurdity of the situation. The idea that they're going to stabilize him and bring him back to be executed is plainly outrageous', said the prison chaplain. Even the director of the state's corrections department conceded: 'Certainly there's irony' (*The New York Times* 1995; see Mauro 1999).

Along with a critique of capital punishment, the chapter throws crucial light on a prison apparatus riddled with contradictions. As discussed, profiteering schemes subject non-violent offenders to unnecessary and costly incarceration. Rather than delivering financial dividends that could otherwise be used to improve society, such as educational and healthcare initiatives (both of which have the potential to reduce street crime), efforts to capitalize on prisons merely add to the wealth of the corporate class. When one considers that the economic-punishment nexus is reinforced by a structural pursuit of reducing labor, the future appears dim since growing unemployment contributes to a correctional treadmill. That seemingly endless spending on mass incarceration aimed at those economically marginalized is best captured in the blunt words of Jeffrey Reiman (2001): The rich get richer and the poor get prison.

Note

1 *Gregg v. Georgia*, 428 U.S. 153 (1976).

Bibliography

Adams, K. (1996) 'The bull market in corrections', *The Prison Journal* 76(4): 461–467.

Alexander, M. (2010) *The New Jim Crow: Mass incarceration in the age of colorblindness*, New York: The New Press.

Associated Press (1990) 'Florida execution is called torture', *The New York Times*, 1 June, www. nytimes.com/1990/06/01/us/florida-execution-is-called-torture.html.

Bailey, W.C. (1998) 'Deterrence, brutalization, and the death penalty: Another examination of Oklahoma's return to capital punishment', *Criminology* 36(4): 711–734.

Baker, P. (2014) 'Obama orders policy review on executions', *The New York Times*, 2 May, www. nytimes.com/2014/05/03/us/flawed-oklahoma-execution-deeply-troubling-obama-says.html.

Bates, E. (1999) 'Prisons for profit', in K. Hass and G. Alpert (eds) *The Dilemmas of Corrections*, Prospect Heights, IL: Waveland Press, 592–604.

Berk, R. (2009) 'Can't tell: Comments on "does the death penalty save lives?"', *Criminology & Public Policy* 8(4): 845–852.

Bohm, R.M. (1999) *Deathquest: An Introduction to the theory and practice of capital punishment in the United States*, Cincinnati, OH: Anderson.

Bowers, W.J. and Pierce, G. (1975) 'The illusion of deterrence in Isaac Ehrlich's research on capital punishment', *Yale Law Journal* 85: 187–208.

Bowers, W.J. and Pierce, G. (1980) 'Deterrence or brutalization: What is the effect of executions?', *Crime and Delinquency* 26: 453–484.

Bowers, W.J., with Pierce, G. and McDevitt, J.F. (1984) *Legal Homicide: Death as punishment in America, 1864–1982*, Boston, MA: Northeastern University Press.

Brooke, J. (2002) 'Prisons: A growth industry for some; Colorado County is a grateful host to 7,000 involuntary guests', *The New York Times*, 2 November, A1, A6.

Bureau of Justice Statistics (2009) *Prisoners in 2008*, Washington, DC: US Department of Justice.

Christie, N. (1993) *Crime Control as Industry*, Oslo: Universiteflag.

Cloninger, D. and Marchesini, R. (2001) 'Executions and deterrence: A quasi-controlled group experiment', *Applied Economics* 35: 569–576.

Cochran, J.K., Chamlin, M.B. and Seth, M. (1994) 'Deterrence or brutalization? An impact assessment of Oklahoma's return to capital punishment', *Criminology* 32(1): 107–134.

Cochran, J. and Chamlin, M. (2000) 'Deterrence and brutalization: The dual effects of executions', *Justice Quarterly* 17: 685–706.

De Giorgi, A. (2006) *Re-thinking the Political Economy of Punishment: Perspectives on post-Fordism and penal politics*, Aldershot: Ashgate.

Donohue, J. (2009) 'The impact of the death penalty on murder', *Criminology & Public Policy* 8(4): 795–802.

Donohue, J. and Wolfers, J. (2005) 'Uses and abuses of empirical evidence in the death penalty debate', *Stanford Law Review* 58: 791–845.

Donziger, S. (1996) 'The prison-industrial complex: What's really driving the rush to lock 'em up', *The Washington Post*, 17 March: 24.

Downes, D. (2001) 'The "macho" penal economy: Mass incarceration in the United States – a European perspective', *Punishment and Society* 3(1): 61–80.

Dunaway, R.G., Cullen, F.T., Burton, V.S., Jr and Evans, T.D. (2000) 'The myth of social class and crime revisited: An examination of class and adult criminality', *Criminology* 38(2): 589–632.

Dyer, J. (2000) *The Perpetual Prisoner Machine*, Boulder, CO: Westview Press.

Ecenbarger, W. (2014) *Kids for Cash: Two Judges, Thousands of Children, and a $2.8 Million Kickback Scheme*, New York: The New Press.

Eckholm, E. (2014) 'Arizona takes nearly 2 hours to execute inmate', *The New York Times*, 23 July, www.nytimes.com/2014/07/24/us/arizona-takes-nearly-2-hours-to-execute-inmate.html.

Eckholm, E. and Schwartz, J. (2014) 'Timeline describes frantic scene at Oklahoma execution', *The New York Times*, 1 May, www.nytimes.com/2014/05/02/us/oklahoma-official-calls-for-outside-review-of-botched-execution.html?module=Search&mabReward=relbias%3As%2C%7B%221%22%3A%22RI%3A10%22%7D.

Ehrlich, I. (1975) 'The deterrent effect of capital punishment: A question of life and death', *American Economic Review* 65: 397–417.

Eligon, J. (2014) 'Supreme Court halts Missouri execution and sends case back to Appeals Court', *The New York Times*, 21 May, www.nytimes.com/2014/05/22/us/order-by-supreme-court-halts-missouri-execution.html.

Elvin, J. (1994/95) '"Corrections-industrial complex" expands in U.S.', *The National Prison Project Journal* 10(1): 1–4.

Erlanger, S. (2014) 'Outrage across ideological spectrum in Europe over flawed lethal injection in US', *The New York Times*, 30 April, www.nytimes.com/2014/05/01/us/outrage-across-ideological-spectrum-in-europe-over-flawed-lethal-injection-in-us.html.

Fagan, J., Zimring, F. and Geller, A. (2006) 'Capital homicide and capital punishment: A market share theory of deterrence', *Texas Law Review* 84: 1803–1867.

Forst, B. (1983) 'Capital punishment and deterrence: Conflicting evidence?', *Journal of Criminal Law and Criminology* 74: 927–942.

Garland, D. (2010) *Peculiar Institution: America's Death Penalty in an Age of Abolition*, Cambridge, MA: Harvard University Press.

Glamser, D. (1996) 'Towns now welcome prisons', *USA Today*, 13 March: 3-A.

The Guardian (2014) 'Death row inmates challenge electric chair in Tennessee execution protocol', 19 September, www.theguardian.com/world/2014/sep/19/tennessee-death-row-electric-chair-challenged-inmates-judge.

Hall, L. (2004a) 'Shackles and shareholders: Developments in the business of detentions', *Bender's Immigration Bulletin*, 1 April: 394–404.

Hall, L. (2004b) 'Update to shackles and shareholders: Developments in the business of detentions', *Bender's Immigration Bulletin*, 1 May: 565–570.

Hentoff, N. (1995) 'The Supreme Court approves of a premeditated murder', *The Village Voice*, 7 February: 22–23.

Hoffman, J. (1993) 'Is innocence sufficient? An essay on the United States Supreme Court's continuing problems with federal habeas corpus and the death penalty', *Indiana Law Journal* 68: 817–839.

Holland, J. (2013) 'Land of the free?', billmoyers.com/2013/12/16/land-of-the-free-us-has-5-of-the-worlds-population-and-25-of-its-prisoners/ (accessed 14 October 2014).

Katz, J. (1988) *Seductions of Crime: Moral and Sensual Attraction in Doing Evil*, New York: Basic Books.

Kilborn, P.T. (2001) 'Rural towns turn to prisons to reignite their economies', *The New York Times*, 1 August: A1, A12.

King, G. (2009) *The Execution of Willie Francis: Race, murder and the search for justice in the American South*, New York: Basic Books.

Kovandzic, T., Vieraitis, L. and Boots, D.P. (2009) 'Does the death penalty save lives? New evidence from state panel data, 1977 to 2006', *Criminology & Public Policy* 8(4): 803–844.

Land, K., Teske, R. and Zheng, H. (2009) 'The short-term effects of executions on homicides: Deterrence, displacement, or both?', *Criminology* 47(4): 1009–1043.

Leighton, P.S. (1999) 'Televising executions, primetime "Live"?', *Justice Professional* 12(2): 191–198.

Lynch, M.J. (2007) *Big Prisons, Big Dreams: Crime and the Failure of America's Penal System*, New Brunswick, NJ and London: Rutgers University Press.

Mackey, R. (2009) 'Botched execution described as torture', *The New York Times*, 16 September, thelede.blogs.nytimes.com/2009/09/16/botched-execution-described-astorture/?module=Search&mabReward=relbias%3Ar%2C%7B%221%22%3A%22RI%3A10%22%7D.

Marquart, J.W., Ekland-Olson, S. and Sorensen, J.R. (1994) *The Rope, the Chair, and the Needle: Capital punishment in Texas, 1923–1990*, Austin: University of Texas Press.

Martin, R. (2000) 'Community perceptions about prison construction: Why not in my backyard?', *Prison Journal* 80(3): 265–294.

Mauro, T. (1999) 'Texas executes inmate who tried suicide day earlier', *USA Today*, 9 December: 3A.

The New York Times (1995) 'Revived from overdose, inmate is executed', 12 August: 8.

The New York Times (2014) 'Secrecy behind executions', 29 January, www.nytimes.com/2014/01/30/opinion/secrecy-behind-executions.html.

Peterson, R.D. and Bailey, W.C. (1991) 'Felony murder and capital punishment: An examination of the deterrence question', *Criminology* 29(3): 367–398.

Phillips, D.D. (1980) 'The deterrent effect of capital punishment: Evidence of an old controversy', *American Journal of Sociology* 86: 139–148.

Purdy, M. (2000) 'For paralyzed inmate, rigid drug laws are the crueler trap', *The New York Times*, 16 April: 35.

Reiman, J. (2001) *The Rich Get Richer and the Poor Get Prison: Ideology, class, and criminal justice*, sixth edn, Boston, MA: Allyn & Bacon.

Rubin, P. (2009) 'Don't scrap the death penalty', *Criminology & Public Policy* 8(4): 853–860.

Sarat, A. (2001) *When the State Kills: Capital punishment and the American Condition*, Princeton, NJ: Princeton University Press.

Sellin, T. (1967) *Capital Punishment*, New York: Harper & Row.

Shelden, R.G. and Brown, W. (2000) 'The crime control industry and the management of the surplus population', *Critical Criminology* 9(1–2): 39–62.

Shepherd, J. (2004) 'Murders of passion, execution delays, and the deterrence of capital punishment', *Journal of Legal Studies* 33: 283–321.

Smith, A. (2013) 'Undue process: "Kids for cash" and "the injustice system"', *The New York Times*, 29 March, www.nytimes.com/2013/03/31/books/review/kids-for-cash-and-the-injustice-system.html?pagewanted=all&module=Search&mabReward=relbias%3Ar%2C%7B%221%22%3A%22RI%3A6%22%7D.

Social Justice (2000) Special Issue on Critical Resistance to the Prison-Industrial Complex, 27(3).

Stack, S. (1987) 'Publicized executions and homicide, 1950–1980', *American Sociological Review* 52: 532–540.

Teephen, T. (1996) 'Locking in the profits', *Atlanta Constitution*, 10 December: 21.

Thies, J. (2001) 'The "big house" in a small town: The economic and social impacts of a correctional facility on its host community', *The Justice Professional* 14(2): 221–237.

Urbina, I. (2014) 'Lawyers challenge Ohio on executions', *The New York Times*, 11 January, www.nytimes.com/2010/01/12/us/12ohio.html.

Urbina, I. and Hamill, S. (2009) 'Judges plead guilty in scheme to jail youths for profit', *The New York Times*, 12 February, www.nytimes.com/2009/02/13/us/13judge.html?pagewanted=all&module=Search&mabReward=relbias%3Ar%2C%7B%221%22%3A%22RI%3A6%22%7D.

Verhovek, S.H. (1995) 'When justice shows its darker side', *The New York Times*, 8 January: E-6.

Wagner, P. (2014) 'U.S. incarceration rates by race', Prison Policy Initiative, www.prisonpolicy.org/graphs/raceinc.html (accessed 14 October 2014).

Walker, S. (2001) *Sense and Nonsense About Crime and Drugs: A policy guide*, fifth edn, Belmont, CA: Wadsworth.

Walmsley, R. (2013) *World Prison Population List*, tenth edn, London: International Centre for Prison Studies.

Welch, M. (2005) *Ironies of Imprisonment*, Thousand Oaks, CA and London: Sage.

Welch, M. (2011) *Corrections: A Critical Approach*, third edn, New York and London: Routledge.

Welch, M. and Turner, F. (2008) 'Private corrections, financial infrastructure, and transportation: The new geo-economy of shipping prisoners', in special issue 'Securing the imperium: Criminal justice privatization and neoliberal globalization', *Social Justice: A Journal of Crime, Conflict & World Order* 34(3–4): 56–77.

White, G. (1999) 'Crime and the decline of manufacturing, 1970–1990', *Justice Quarterly* 16(1): 81–98.

Wilkins, L.T. (1991) *Punishment, Crime and Market Forces*, Brookfield, VT: Dartmouth.

Yeoman, B. (2000) 'Steel town: corrections corporation of America is trying to turn Youngstown, Ohio into the private-prison capital of the world', *Mother Jones*, May/June: 39–45.

Yunker, J. (1976) 'Is the death penalty a deterrent to homicide? Some time series evidence', *Journal of Behavioral Economics* 5(1): 1–32.

Zimring, F.E. and Hawkins, G.J. (1973) *Deterrence: The legal threat in crime control*, Chicago, IL: University of Chicago Press.

Zimring, F.E. and Hawkins, G.J. (1986) *Capital Punishment and the American Agenda*, New York: Cambridge University Press.

Chapter 21

Houses for the poor

Continental European prisons

Vincenzo Ruggiero

It would be an act of honesty to rename prison institutions as houses for the poor. The renaming would describe in a nutshell recent developments in penality and incarceration in several European countries, in those where growing punitive harshness is found as well as those apparently displaying no visible growing punitiveness. A proviso, however, should be borne in mind: while the old houses for the poor, established during the course of the eighteenth century in England and Wales, hosted working paupers from whom many parishes expected to earn money, those 'housed' in European institutions today are officially regarded, and by many perceived, as largely unprofitable. One similarity, however, remains between the old and the new houses: they are both the result of philosophies regarding 'poor relief' as a distortion of market freedom. Malthus's complaint that the Poor Laws interfered with the natural laws of supply and demand finds echoes in contemporary advocates of austerity for the disadvantaged and prosperity for those already prospering.

This chapter provides sketches of the use of imprisonment in different continental European countries, identifying the groups that are mainly targeted by penal measures. These are followed by an analysis of the manifest and latent functions of punishment in the countries considered. The countries examined are divided on a purely geographical basis.

North

Scandinavian countries are usually held as examples of parsimony in the use of incarceration. However, in Finland, Norway and particularly in Sweden the number of prisoners rose significantly from the 1970s (currently, the rates of incarceration in the three countries are respectively 75, 66 and 82 per 100,000 population). The increase in Sweden was particularly significant around the turn of the new millennium, although fines still constitute the major penal sanction in the country (Von Hofer and Tham 2013). Rates of imprisonment in this area of Europe are associated with public concerns around violent crime, drug trafficking and illegal migration, but penal moderation and humane prison conditions remain characteristics of the region (Pratt and Ericksson 2012). Scandinavian 'exceptionalism' is said to emerge from the culture of equality prevalent in these countries which is embedded in their social fabrics through the universalism of the welfare state (Pratt 2008). Beyond cultural explanations, however, moderate social inequality has also been indicated as a crucial factor making Scandinavian countries less inclined to adopt the increasing punitiveness characterizing late modern societies (Barry and Leonardsen 2012). Successful rehabilitation programmes are singled out as key tools

for reducing recidivism and hampering criminal careers. Academic and vocational programmes carried out in Swedish prisons, for example, are deemed successful, as are the
provisions of the 1994 Prison Treatment Act, which established the need for prisoners to
be offered a suitable job. Such practices are seen as positive foundations for the offenders'
new lives leading to successful reintegration into society (Pettit and Kroth 2011).

Finland is particularly significant for the long-term decline in prison numbers experienced after the 1990s, while Sweden and Norway show a 'slow creep' in incarceration
rates, particularly relating to foreign nationals (Lappi-Seppälä 2012; Dullum and Ugelvik
2012; Scott 2013). Critics, however, argue that low incarceration rates, like those
observed in Scandinavian countries, do not say much about prison conditions – for
example, they do not account for the numbers of self-inflicted deaths which are relatively high in the institutions of these countries. Moreover, as Mathiesen (2012) has
remarked, they do not illustrate the pain of detention as it is experienced by prisoners. In
Sweden, finally, prison is increasingly becoming the quickest way of dealing with truly
poor citizens, or even with non-citizens, namely migrants devoid of political power and
representation. Von Hofer and Tham (2013: 52) observe: 'These often impoverished
people have nothing of value to offer in the trade: neither in the form of economic or
social capital, nor even in the sense of any meaningful form of electoral support. Thus,
the criminal of today's Sweden has become a true public enemy.'

Research conducted in Scandinavian new generation prisons found that minimum
security and open institutions induce their own specific pains of captivity. Inmates living
in self-managed cottages and enjoying relative freedom of movement are reported to
experience 'prisonization' symptoms similar to those characterizing inmates in closed
institutions: disorientation, anxiety, mental tiredness and fear. Nordic penal regimes
are also seen as Janus faced, with one side relatively mild and benign, and the other
intrusive and oppressive. This duality is associated with the similarly dual nature of the
welfare state, which simultaneously promotes individual well-being while authorizing
disciplinary measures and even violations of basic rights. In Sweden, the welfare state is,
on the one hand, universalistic and egalitarian and, on the other, exclusionary and
essentialist. 'The lack of individual rights and an ethno-cultural conception of citizenship
make certain categories of people such as criminal offenders, criminal aliens, drug offenders and perceived "others", particularly foreign nationals, vulnerable to deprivation and
exclusion' (Barker 2012: 5).

Sweden has been the subject of several reports by the Council of Europe describing it
as a harsher society than people think: 'Swedish law, society and morality can be surprisingly authoritarian' (Neroth 2014: 1). Prison chaplain Birgitta Winberg, who is president of the International Prison Chaplains' Association, also thinks that 'the world has a
rosy view of the country' (ibid.). She described Swedish remand prisons as the worst in
the world, with people kept in isolation before being charged, restricted in their cells for
23 hours a day. In a report published in December 2009, the Council of Europe (2009)
wrote that despite an 'ongoing dialogue' about remand conditions, Sweden had done
little since previous visits and concerns remained valid. The report said its delegates talked
to remand prisoners and that the overwhelming majority had been given no explanation
for the restrictions imposed on them. Many considered that the only reason why they
were being prohibited contact with their family members was to 'break' them. The
health of the accused was found to be severely strained. The report said that many prisoners suffered a lack of concentration, memory disturbance, impaired communication

skills, as well as various physical infirmities. Finally: 'Symptoms of anxiety disorder are commonly seen, post-traumatic stress disorder and depression can develop, and also agitation and self-harm' (ibid.: 34).

Exceptionalism was tragically tested during the summer of 2011, when seven people were killed by a bomb placed in the centre of Oslo and 69 at a youth camp run by the Labour Party. 'The offender was not an immigrant. He was a tall, blond man. He was a very Norwegian-minded Norwegian' (Christie 2011: 1). In Nils Christie's comment, the initial reaction to the atrocity was not inspired by revenge but by an appeal to democratic principles guiding Norwegian society. The Mayor of Oslo promised that the killer would be punished not through a suspension of democracy but an intensification of its ideals of tolerance. Some weeks after the massacre, at the municipal elections, the Mayor of Oslo was re-elected with an extraordinarily large margin. Changing the democratic rules would have meant accepting the killer's victory.

West

When 'contrasting tolerance' in the UK and the Netherlands, the positive aspects of the penal system in the latter country were, in the past, regularly highlighted. Downes (1988) observed better inmate–staff relationships, more lenient regimes, leaner complaint procedures available to prisoners, who also enjoyed the 'one person per cell' right. Currently, there are in the country 128 prisoners per 100,000 population. In the Netherlands, alternatives to custody were introduced in the early 1970s and included activities benefiting the public, which were to become more precise forms of community service by the turn of the decade. The probation service supervising the alternative treatment of offenders was strengthened, but was slowly removed from the social work arena into the sphere of the Ministry of Justice (van Swaaningen 2000). Later, alternatives such as community service orders, educational schemes and electronic monitoring 'became integral parts of the penal system and were reshaped in accordance with the expansionist discourse' (Boone and van Swaaningen 2013: 17).

Between the 1980s and the 1990s, the Netherlands experienced a decline in rehabilitation philosophies and a corresponding growth of the notion of punishment as a measure of social defence (van Swaaningen and de Jonge 1995). How the new punitive philosophy came about is hard to ascertain, although justification for the shift revolves around two readily available variables: public pressure and rising criminality (Boone and Moerings 2007). Imprisonment rates went down from 2005, and then up again after a few years, but fluctuations are explained through structural changes in law enforcement, inconsistent sentencing policies, and new rules for the classification of convicted offenders. The punitive shift has, however, accelerated: non-custodial sentences are no longer intended as lenient alternatives, but as effective forms of social protection, while public discourse on penal issues is increasingly informed by electoral aims. This has resulted in plans for the restructuring of sentencing, with proposals to introduce minimum penalties for every single offence and to exclude specific offenders from the benefits of non-custodial treatment. Campaigns on crime and insecurity tend to embrace any sort of antisocial behaviour, particularly relating to street life, and are principally focused on immigrants. Public debate on crime control, in brief, is 'increasingly defined in terms of "us" – the white Dutch – against "them" – the foreigners who make our society increasingly unpleasant' (Boone and van Swaaningen 2013: 11).

The Dutch rehabilitative stance, if attenuated, has not totally vanished, as proven by the persistence of programmes designed for prisoners returning to the free world and the prevalent use of non-custodial measures for those served with short sentences. Rehabilitation as a general principle, however, seems to be addressed to those who already show signs of social reintegration (white minor offenders), while it is ruled out for those who would genuinely benefit from it (excluded minorities). 'The Dutch attitude, once interpreted as tolerance, has now turned into indifference towards those people who do not belong to us' (Boone and van Swaaningen 2013: 29).

The German criminal justice system was widely criticized during the 1970s for its severity in dealing with political dissent and the actual (and perceived) threat of armed struggle. The special legislation introduced in those years included longer remand periods and solitary confinement for those charged with political violence. It also entailed a widening of power for the police who could cordon off and raid entire urban areas and hold suspects for days without pressing charges (Messner and Ruggiero 1995). By the late 1980s, however, the country managed to reduce the overall size of the prison population, as well as improve conditions in custody. During the course of the 1990s the pendulum swung back again, with the prison population rising, fuelled by public anxiety in the aftermath of unification, but also by the perceived threats of immigration and drug-related crime. It should be noted that the rise took place in the remand population rather than in the prison population as a whole, signalling an attempt by authorities to reassure the public by inflicting some sort of preventive punishment. Fear of crime, therefore, was associated with foreigners, young people and drug users, their visibility and poverty being perceived as precursors of illegal behaviour.

In the new millennium, processes of differential criminalization became more pronounced. Offences reported to the police and police investigations increasingly fell in the domain of illegal conduct typically imputed to marginalized groups. Non-German nationals are over-represented in the prison population (25%), serve comparatively longer sentences and are given fewer non-custodial alternatives. Currently there are 94 prisoners per 100,000 population.

Fines replace prison sentences of up to three months, and their decline is due to the deterioration of economic conditions and failure to pay. Community service is, therefore, more frequently applied to disadvantaged offenders. Probation is available, as is the suspension of a sentence after two thirds of the period has been served, and electronic monitoring was introduced in 2011. 'In brief, probation and conditional sentences make up the bulk of penal measures, while imprisonment, though remaining a crucial form of punishment, is decreasing' (Dollinger and Kretschmann 2013: 143). Despite regional differences, there is no empirical evidence of a general trend towards growing punitiveness in Germany. Punitive tendencies mainly affect particularly stigmatized offenders or particularly vulnerable groups. These are differentially treated throughout the criminal justice process, from public reporting to police investigation, during the judicial phase and, ultimately, at the sentencing stage. The core target of the criminal justice apparatus as a whole is, therefore 'a small group of serious criminals who are seen as highly dangerous and at high risk of recidivism' (ibid.: 150), on the one hand, and traditionally marginalized groups who are deemed incapable to conform, on the other.

The French penal system is said to oscillate between a secular, 'scientific' model born with the Enlightenment and a religious, confessional model aimed at the redemption of offenders (Perrot 1980; Gallo 1995). There are today 85 prisoners per 100,000 population. Only during the 1960s did an 'obsession' with prison security develop, resulting in the identification of a new category of prisoners deemed particularly difficult. The regime imposed on these prisoners 'provided the blueprint for what were eventually to become high security prison institutions' (Gallo 1995: 74). The definition of danger-ousness was applied to professional criminals or those prisoners who challenged the prison regime. Differential treatment followed, whereby inmates were classified on the grounds of their attitude towards the institution. The second half of the 1970s was characterized by a period of reform, with more alternatives to custody being introduced and wider supervisory powers given to the judiciary on issues such as prison treatment and rehabilitation. Many crime prevention projects carried out at the local level in the first half of the 1980s (De Liège 1991) led to a marked decline in the prison population, while the second half of the same decade saw the most ambitious programme to fight crime: the building of new prisons and the expansion of their total capacity.

Over the last three decades or so, the use of imprisonment as a penal measure has remained relatively stable, constituting approximately 20% of all sentences. While fines tend to decline, community service orders observe an ascending trend. Although relative to the use of other sanctions, recourse to prison sentences has hardly increased, 'it has increased significantly in terms of the absolute number of people imprisoned' (Robert 2013: 112). This, accompanied by an increase in the length of sentences handed down and new legislation restricting judicial discretion by mandating minimum sentences for recidivists, led to chronic prison overcrowding. During the first decade of the millen-nium, successive electoral campaigns were fought in the name of security and played to xenophobic and punitive sentiments, producing a very large number of new criminal laws.

The major shift in the composition of prisoners in France regards the percentage of non-French born: well over 30%. The shift, which started in the early 1990s, is due less to the prevalence of conventional offenders among non-nationals than to the stricter regulations introduced in the country with respect to work permits and permits to stay. Non-nationals, therefore, are 'administrative' offenders, *sans-papiers* who keep negotiating and fighting for their presence in France (Ruggiero 2001). Increased powers accorded to law enforcement agencies to carry out identity checks and changes in legislation encouraging the targeting of people with foreign physiognomy were important determinants of the growing incarceration of non-nationals.

East

The prison system in Bulgaria (138 prisoners per 100,000 population) is formed of old correctional facilities, most of which were built during the 1930s. The newest institution was constructed in 1962 and only in 2010 did the government identify an area around Sofia where a new facility with a 2,000 capacity was expected to be built. Bulgarian institutions detain between 8,000 and 9,000 prisoners, and the available space per person measures around 4 square metres. Amnesties are used as a tool to temper overcrowding, although opposition by public opinion has significantly reduced their frequency and effectiveness over recent years. The imprisonment rate grew significantly at the turn of the current millennium, when a serious economic crisis hit the country, but accession to the European Union (EU) required legal renewal and new procedural norms, which resulted in a reduction of custodial sanctions and their average duration (Gounev 2013). Pressure on the country to fight organized crime and corruption, in its turn, caused the reversal of the trend, with custodial measures ascending again and harsher punishments being meted out.

Crime prevention policies and programmes for the reintegration of first-time offenders are insufficient and their impact unknown. Probation has been used since 2005 as the main alternative to custody, and community service, which is loosely regulated, is also applied by the probation service, staffed mainly by former police officers, of whom less than 10% have undergone any professional training. One additional penal sanction available in Bulgaria consists of confiscation of criminal assets.

The prison system is characterized by corruption and a variety of criminal activities, ranging from the smuggling of prohibited objects to mendacious reports about the conduct of prisoners drafted by bribed professionals. The banned objects smuggled in include smartphones which allow offenders to carry out their illicit activities while serving a sentence, while reports relating to good conduct are used to gain regular days of release (Gounev and Bezlov 2012). Drug use in prison is widespread.

Research shows a high degree of impunity for organized criminals and corrupt officials due to procedural loopholes and, conversely, exorbitant harshness inflicted upon socially excluded groups (CSD 2012). 'The treatment of Roma people in the criminal justice system is the most troubling aspect of penal policies and the prison system. Roma are over-represented both in statistics about prosecution and within the prison population' (Gounev 2013: 219).

Poland (210 prisoners per 100,000 population) started its attempts at penal reform during the course of the 1990s, alongside other Eastern European countries (King 1996). Before, as Platek (2013) puts it, it was difficult to distinguish where prison ended, as most people, wherever they happened to be, felt as if they were behind bars. Reform introduced in 1997 stipulated that custody be used as a last resort. However, 'accustomed to harsh, long punishments, we have trouble changing our perspective' (ibid.: 185). In other words, prison in Poland is regarded as 'the' punishment, and despite the possibility of applying fines or probation, imprisonment remains the core provision. Suspended sentences, on the other hand, prove ineffective because they are not accompanied by rehabilitative programmes in the community.

There is a high percentage (25%) of remand prisoners in Polish institutions, a fact regarded by the European Court of Human Rights as a national structural problem. Prisons are overcrowded, detaining twice the number of inmates they should legally hold, and educational or rehabilitative activities can hardly have an impact in such conditions. While in the past inmates worked and made a contribution to state finances, after the transition work was replaced by 'programmes', supposedly aimed at helping prisoners reintegrate into society. Work in houses for the elderly or with children with special needs, work in agriculture and industry are all available on paper. Moreover, programmes for the rehabilitation of alcoholics, drug abusers and sex offenders are also in place. However, 'very few are able to benefit from this rich offer' (Platek 2013: 190).

Around 5,000 people are imprisoned in Poland for drunken driving, most of whom are repeat offenders. Between 5,000 and 7,000 are sentenced to custody for possession of prohibited substances. Prisoners are young and poorly educated, devoid of realistic prospects for employment, and around half have committed property crimes: 'they are the unwanted labour surplus in today's market economy' (Platek 2013: 194). Prisoners serving a sentence for violent offences are about 10% – very few for domestic violence, which is perceived as a family issue. About 2,500 inmates are serving a prison sentence for not paying alimony to their divorced spouses, while foreigners and ethnic minorities only constitute 2% of the prison population. 'This is not because of Polish tolerance, it is rather because there are not many foreigners in Poland' (ibid.: 194). While 80,000 are incarcerated, over 30,000 of those sentenced to custody are not behind bars because they await a place to become vacant before serving their sentence.

The Russian Federation (470 prisoners per 100,000 population) spent the last decade and a half discussing and probing penal reform measures, but political difficulties made their implementation patchy and problematic (McAuley and Macdonald 2007). In 2010, when the remaining pieces of the Gulag system were dismantled, proposals for change aimed at the abolition of labour colonies, the ranking of penal institutions in terms of security and the creation of a single-person-per-cell system (Piacentini 2013). Surveillance technology was seen as paramount, along with the introduction of non-custodial measures, the development of a probation service and, in general, a new emphasis on rehabilitation. Aggregate figures show a decline in the total prison population since 2001, particularly for juveniles, and a marked increase of women in custody. On paper, alternatives offer day release, open institutions and programmes involving local communities, although external entities engaged in such programmes are mainly religious groups (Pallot and Piacentini 2012). Custody, in brief, remains the core of the penal system in the Russian Federation, while post-custodial measures are being developed, including anger-management programmes and projects revolving around cognitive behavioural therapy. With some key figures in the Prison Service publicly supporting Europe-style changes, 'the hoped-for end to the Gulag might just be happening, albeit slowly' (Piacentini 2013: 170).

Violent crime increased significantly during the last decade, particularly racist aggression, leading to condemnation by human rights organizations. According to the United Nations (UN), lack of integration and cohesion in Russian society creates growing marginalization and poverty, with migrants becoming scapegoats. While corruption in the country is rife, affecting all layers of society, and powerful forms of organized and white-collar crime mesh within the institutional apparatus (Rawlinson 2012), the prison population is mainly composed of young, marginalized offenders. Reacting with outrage to criticism from abroad, Russia remains faithful to its past, namely mass incarceration: 'Russia will continue to face urgent questions on how prisons have yet again become tangled in a complex and authoritarian political web' (Piacentini 2013: 179).

South

The prison system in Italy (currently 104 prisoners per 100,000 population) is fostered by a succession of emergencies associated with specific groups of offenders. Such groups are the target of ad hoc pieces of legislation or judicial and executive policies, and demand for their punishment becomes high at particular historical moments (Ruggiero 1995). In Italy, armed robbers, violent political opponents, drug traffickers, organized crime members and migrants have acted as successive emergencies. Prison trends are reflected in this succession of social and institutional alarms augmented by real or imaginary panics, with amnesties used as responses to periodical overcrowding. By the late 1990s the justice system experienced a definitive bifurcation, becoming tolerant with the rich and powerful, and powerful and harsh with the poor. Migrants and drug users became the chosen victims of law and order campaigns, while the variable 'safety' determined who won the elections. Albanians, North Africans, Roma, Romanians, squeegee merchants, the homeless and drug users filled the prisons quickly: 'This changed the Italian penal law to the point that it was no longer facts and offences, but lifestyles and life stories, which were penalized' (Gonnella 2013: 231). Migrants were harshly targeted simply for being illegally present on the Italian territory.

Italian penal institutions are characterized by four distinctive traits. First, the number of non-nationals held in custody (25–30%); second, the number of remand prisoners (almost 40%); third, the number of inmates sentenced for drug-related offences (35%); and fourth, the rate of overcrowding (for each 100 prison places officially available, there are 148 prisoners). A look at the social composition of those processed through the penal system reveals a high degree of selectivity. Custody, for remand or sentenced prisoners, mainly targets the socially and economically disadvantaged. Rules around recidivism, on the other hand, create a situation whereby the same individuals keep entering and exiting the prison system. Another indicator of selectivity is provided by the level of education of those incarcerated: only 1% hold a university degree, while the number of illiterate prisoners is four times higher, and the large majority have only completed primary school.

Alternatives to custody are available and can be applied at any moment of the criminal justice process (Palma 1997). Some completely divert offenders from the prison system, while others apply to offenders who are already serving a sentence. Amnesties, reform on paper, and emergencies suspending reform, aptly describe the vagaries of the penal system in Italy (Gonnella and Marietti 2010). The general climate prevailing in the country affects the number of individuals punished and the nature of the punishment inflicted. 'This, however, does not seem to affect the corrupt elite ruling the country, whose criminality reproduces itself irrespective of the general climate oscillating between harshness and leniency' (Gonnella 2013: 243).

In Spain, after the death of Francisco Franco in 1975, the need and urgency to reform the penal system was intensely felt, but the process of change was met with hard opposition expressed by those social, economic and military forces that fought for a return to the past (Aranda Ocaña and Rivera Beiras 2013). The Spanish Constitution was promulgated in 1978 and a set of principles was established guiding the criminal justice and the penal systems. These affirmed the need for sentencing proportionality, the abolition of capital punishment and torture, and the rehabilitative purpose of custody. Despite the new openings, harsh punitive measures remained in place as a result of growing public alarm addressed to specific groups of offenders, making the reform process uncertain and contradictory. For instance, the old Penal Code, which stood in opposition to the new constitutional principles, was only repealed in 1995. This was also the year when the new Penal Code was ratified, introducing community work as an alternative to custody and probation for prisoners willing to undertake cultural, educational and work activities. At the same time, however, more severe treatment was addressed to offenders deemed particularly dangerous and the maximum sentence was extended to 30 years.

A culture of emergency spread in the penal system leading to what is termed the counter-reform of 2003. This brought the level of the maximum penalty to 40 years' imprisonment, curtailed alternatives to custody for certain categories of offenders, extended remand periods, and ruled the deportation of non-national offenders. This punitive drift gathered momentum when crime rates were falling, and mainly addressed property and drug offenders. Non-nationals in Spanish institutions are around 30% of the total prison population, and conditions for all are such that inmates are unable to benefit

from any educational or rehabilitative programme. Institutions are crammed and cells are shared. The European Court of Human Rights regularly denounces this situation, equating it to inhuman and degrading treatment. Health conditions are dismal, with diseases spreading due to a lack of professional care. What is more disturbing is that harshness in the treatment of offenders goes hand in hand with the economic crisis causing harsher social problems. Spain incarcerates 144 people per 100,000 population.

Greek penal policies seem to be informed by improvisation and inconsistency (Karydis and Koulouris 2013). This is what emerges when two key reports submitted to the parliament, respectively in 1994 and 2011, are examined. The 1994 report (adopted four years later) stressed the ineffectiveness of imprisonment as a correctional tool, remarked on the arbitrariness of the criminal justice system as a whole, and questioned its rehabilitative function. Prison regimes were said to violate elementary human rights and social forms of prevention were encouraged. Critics, however, felt that the report failed to 'consider the structural economic and social inequalities that make prisons continue to detain those whom penal institutions have always confined, namely the poor and dispossessed' (ibid.: 266). Today there are in Greece 120 prisoners per 100,000 population.

The 2011 report provided a list of problems afflicting the Greek prison system, highlighting: overcrowding, the presence of non-national inmates, the prevalence of drug offenders, and widespread corruption within the institutions. The report encouraged the consideration of imprisonment as a last resort and the respect of prisoners' rights and dignity, while work and education were indicated as the key rehabilitative tools. The development of alternatives to custody, including community service, home detention and electronic monitoring, were also proposed. In a contradictory manner, however, while a process of decarceration was apparently advocated in the report, the number of new facilities whose construction was planned exceeded the number of old institutions to be dismantled.

Greece occupies the middle of the punitive ladder among European countries, although the prison population has quadrupled over the last 30 years (Cheliotis and Xenakis 2011). Harsher sentences are the key factor for this, particularly with regard to drug offences, while remand prisoners form almost a third of the total prison population. Irregular migrants 'awaiting deportation after serving a sentence constitute an additional burden for the prison administration' (Karydis and Koulouris 2013: 274). This is a relatively recent development, bringing the current proportion of non-nationals in Greek prisons to around 50% of the total prison population. While the economic crisis and the subsequent austerity measures are poised to cause more unemployment, poverty and exclusion, the international climate encourages both authoritarian and liberal penal policies. In this way, zero tolerance, mass incarceration and degrading conditions in custody coexist with efforts to develop and improve alternatives to custody and humane conditions in prison. 'Penal policies in Greece reflect this contradictory international climate, favoring more use of imprisonment and further restrictions on inmates' fundamental rights – while claiming the exact opposite' (ibid.: 283).

Cultures of punishment

The sketches presented above seem to corroborate the initial statement that prisons in Europe should be renamed houses for the poor. In what follows, an attempt is made to identify the philosophies inspiring these 'houses' and their latent functions.

In the countries considered there are some uniform modalities in the treatment of migrants, non-nationals, ethnic minorities, and young and marginalized people. The harsher punishments inflicted on these groups reveal a process of penal differentiation that has been occurring for decades in most developed countries. Similar uniformity, however, is found in the lack of penal responses against crimes committed by relatively powerful individuals and groups. Such commonalities need some qualification.

It has become by now a common practice to punish individuals who belong to specific groups because of an actuarial calculus indicating them as more likely to offend and reoffend. What is penalized, in most circumstances, is not their actual illegitimate conduct, but their social condition that is deemed conducive to crime. In contexts in which the labour market offers scarce opportunities to migrants and excluded people in general, penalties may be heavier due to the low expectations relating to their current and future participation in the productive process. In such cases, it is their 'indolence' and lack of participation in consumers' markets that are punished, inactivity being perceived as a prerequisite for the adoption of unpredictable conducts, and punishment being deemed an appropriate measure for the exclusion of people from an already crowded labour market. This preventative punishment, in brief, is not aimed at preventing crime, but law-abiding behaviour that would come with work. We can assume, by contrast, that in countries where peripheral areas of employment are still available, punishment, whether more lenient or otherwise, will take on an 'educational' function, training the punished to accept peripheral, badly paid jobs (Ruggiero 2010, 2013).

Trust is a key variable adopted by Mathiesen (2013) to explicate variations in punishment and its intensity. Trusting one's social system means believing that everybody can find a place in it, even those who happen to flout its norms and challenge its values. Punishment, therefore, signals lack of confidence in social arrangements and, conversely, excessive confidence in authorities inflicting it. This excessive confidence in the elite takes the form of leniency for powerful offenders, who paradoxically continue to be trusted even when committing crimes. Trust, however, is also dependent on media power, moral enterprise and anxiety brooding, all elements which end up drawing league tables of dangerousness, designating untrustworthy groups and individuals. In most countries examined above, anxiety associated with economic, political and 'spiritual' difficulties is translated into fear of the other – and the other, whether actually dangerous or not, is subjected to differentiated penal treatment.

This socio-cultural dynamic is questioned by authors who argue that 'changing patterns of punishment lie not in *social* processes but in *state and legal* processes' (Garland 2013: 484). The immediate causes of expanding prison populations and increased punitive measures, in this view, are to be found in specific forms of state action. In brief, legal enactments are deemed crucial for variations in penal outcomes. The leniency shown in the past by the Dutch penal system, for example, can be seen as the result of specific acts performed by state agents and of the professional ideology inspiring them (Downes 1988). Prosecutors and judges held negative views about imprisonment: 'an orientation shaped by their law school education, by their ongoing connections to criminological experts, and by the historical memory of internment under the Nazis' (Garland 2013: 493).

The question remains, however, what type of society the acts performed by state agents are expected to preserve or what type of social characteristics they aim to reproduce.

Inequality, in this respect, is a key characteristic of social systems that can be included in the analysis of penal practices. Let us see how.

State acts performed in societies displaying a large degree of inequality have to be particularly energetic if that degree of inequality is to be maintained (Piketty 2014; Rosanvallon 2014). If penal measures are tools for the perpetuation of the status quo, in other words, more inequality must be turned into harsher penality. This entails an ideological process whereby growing inequality is met with passive consent or even with inoffensive anger 'about so much wealth going to so few' (Starr 2014: 33). Penality, in such cases, aims at making widening economic disparities acceptable and, at the same time, reshaping the very idea of social justice, so that success is highly rewarded and failure heavily penalized. Penality, in brief, has to prevent the dispossessed from thinking of their situation in a collective way, while averting the type of 'reformism of fear' generated by dissent, when governments realize that change is necessary in order to avoid unmanageable conflict. Penal variations, in this sense, are determined less by different socio-economic arrangements (Cavadino and Dignan 2006) than by degrees of inequality.

A related issue pertains to the costs of punishment in situations of budgetary pressure (Lacey 2008; McBride 2013). The financial crash, for instance, may be seen as a lesson teaching us about the costs of unregulated excess, and simultaneously may offer an opportunity to think anew about excessive punishment. Penal moderation might therefore be advocated as a supplement to financial moderation and reform (Loader 2010). Reform campaigners basing their arguments on the necessity to reduce penal expenditure appear to neglect that the elite to which they address their demands embraced a system of waste, where wealth is squandered, dilapidated and the elite itself is prone to destroy what it creates. This practice, as Bataille (1967) would remark, is a characteristic of ruling groups disingenuously displaying a lack of interest in their riches while reproducing the conditions to acquire growing quantities of them. 'Waste' is a good investment if it sustains a penal system that defends privileges, and cannot be measured with the conventional rational calculus applied in common mathematical operations. The 'costs' of penal systems, as argued above, have to be measured through the degree of income differences they are supposed to maintain or exacerbate.

A final thought should be given to the function of punishment when the targets, as in the countries examined, are mainly marginalized, excluded groups. The process of incarceration, with its arbitrariness and differential punitiveness, reproduces the illegal choice presumably embraced by prisoners, thus creating an intelligible cultural continuity between the realm of crime and that of punishment. Prisons, in brief, perpetuate the cognitive structure of offenders prior to imprisonment, who are then more likely to reoffend after being released (Hockey 2012). Moreover, penal action against vulnerable groups does not generate integration or social stability, let alone produce law-abiding citizens. Mass incarceration of the poor causes yet more marginalization, exclusion and community disorganization; it produces criminogenic effects (De Giorgi 2013), destabilizing and tearing apart the very social fabric that it purports to mend.

Bibliography

Aranda Ocaña, M. and Rivera Beiras, I. (2013) 'The Spanish penal and penitentiary system: from the re-socialising objective to the internal governance of prison', in V. Ruggiero and M. Ryan (eds) *Punishment in Europe*, Basingstoke: Palgrave Macmillan.

Barker, V. (2012) 'Nordic exceptionalism revisited: explaining the paradox of a Janus-faced penal regime', *Theoretical Criminology* 17: 5–25.

Barry, M. and Leonardsen, D. (2012) 'Inequality and punitivism in late modern societies', *European Journal of Probation* 4: 46–61.

Bataille, G. (1967) *La part maudite*, Paris: Editions de Minuit.

Boone, M. and Moerings, M. (eds) (2007) *Dutch Prisons*, The Hague: Boom Juridische Uitgevers.

Boone, M. and van Swaaningen, R. (2013) 'Regression to the Mean: Punishment in the Netherlands', in V. Ruggiero and M. Ryan (eds) *Punishment in Europe*, Basingstoke: Palgrave Macmillan.

Cavadino, M. and Dignan, J. (2006) *Penal Systems: A comparative approach*, London: Sage.

CSD (Centre for the Study of Democracy) (2012) *Countering Organized Crime in Bulgaria*, Sofia: CSD.

Cheliotis, L. and Xenakis, S. (eds) (2011) *Crime and Punishment in Contemporary Greece*, Oxford: Peter Lang.

Christie, N. (2011) 'When Atrocities Hit', unpublished paper.

Council of Europe (2009) *Report to the Swedish Government*, Strasbourg: European Committee for the Prevention of Torture and Inhuman or Degrading Treatment or Punishment (CPT).

De Giorgi, A. (2013) 'Crime Up? Decarcerate!', www.socialjusticejournal.org (accessed 5 December 2013).

De Liège, M.P. (1991) 'Social Development and the Prevention of Crime in France', in F. Heidensohn and M. Farrell (eds) *Crime in Europe*, London: Routledge.

Dollinger, B. and Kretschmann, A. (2013) 'Contradictions in German penal practices: the long goodbye from the rehabilitation principle', in V. Ruggiero and M. Ryan (eds) *Punishment in Europe*, Basingstoke: Palgrave Macmillan.

Downes, D. (1988) *Contrasts in Tolerance*, Oxford: Oxford University Press.

Dullum, J. and Ugelvik, T. (2012) 'Exceptional prisons, exceptional societies', in T. Ugelvik and J. Dullum (eds) *Penal Exceptionalism?*, London: Routledge.

Gallo, E. (1995) 'The penal system in France: from correctionalism to managerialism', in V. Ruggiero, M. Ryan and J. Sim (eds) *Western European Penal Systems*, London: Sage.

Garland, D. (2013) 'Penality and the penal state', *Criminology* 51: 475–517.

Gonnella, P. (2013) 'Italy: between amnesties and emergencies', in V. Ruggiero and M. Ryan (eds) *Punishment in Europe: A critical anatomy of penal systems*, Basingstoke: Palgrave Macmillan.

Gonnella, P. and Marietti, S. (2010) *Il carcere spiegato ai ragazzi*, Rome: Il Manifesto Libri.

Gounev, P. (2013) 'Soft and harsh penalties in Bulgaria', in V. Ruggiero and M. Ryan (eds) *Punishment in Europe: A critical anatomy of penal systems*, Basingstoke: Palgrave Macmillan.

Gounev, P. and Bezlov, T. (2012) 'Corruption and criminal markets', in P. Gounev and V. Ruggiero (eds) *Corruption and Organized Crime in Europe*, London: Routledge.

Hockey, D. (2012) 'Analytical reflections on time in custody', *The Howard Journal of Criminal Justice* 51(1): 67–78.

Karydis, V. and Koulouris, N. (2013) 'Greece: prisons are bad but necessary (and expanding), policies are necessary but bad (and declining)', in V. Ruggiero and M. Ryan (eds) *Punishment in Europe: A Critical Anatomy of Penal Systems*, Basingstoke: Palgrave Macmillan.

King, R.D. (1996) 'Prisons in Eastern Europe: some reflections on prison reform in Romania', *The Howard Journal of Criminal Justice* 35: 215–231.

Lacey, N. (2008) *The Prisoners' Dilemma: Political economy and punishment in contemporary democracies*, Cambridge: Cambridge University Press.

Lappi-Seppälä, T. (2012) 'Exploring national differences in the use of imprisonment', in S. Snacken and E. Dumortier (eds) *Resisting Punitiveness in Europe?*, London: Routledge.

Loader, I. (2010) 'For penal moderation. Notes towards a public philosophy of punishment', *Theoretical Criminology* 14: 349–367.

McAuley, M. and Macdonald, M. (2007) 'Russia and youth crime', *British Journal of Criminology* 47: 2–22.

McBride, K. (2013) 'Why prisons? Incarceration and the Great Recession', in D. Scott (ed.) *Why Prisons?*, Cambridge: Cambridge University Press.

Mathiesen, T. (2012) 'Scandinavian exceptionalism in penal matters: reality or wishful thinking?', in T. Ugelvik and J. Dullum (eds) *Penal Exceptionalism?*, London: Routledge.

Mathiesen, T. (2013) 'On Stemming the Tide', in D. Scott (ed.) *Why Prisons?*, Cambridge: Cambridge University Press.

Messner, C. and Ruggiero, V. (1995) 'Germany: the penal system between past and future', in V. Ruggiero, M. Ryan and J. Sim (eds) *Western European Penal Systems*, London: Sage.

Neroth, P. (2014) 'Europe slams Swedish prisons', ieeexpole.ieee.org (accessed 1 May 2014).

Pallot, J. and Piacentini, L. (2012) *Gender, Geography and Punishment: The experience of women in carceral Russia*, Oxford: Oxford University Press.

Palma, M. (ed.) (1997) *Il vaso di Pandora: carcere e pena dopo le riforme*, Rome: Istituto della Enciclopedia Italiana.

Perrot, M. (1980) *L'impossible prison*, Paris: Seuil.

Pettit, M.D. and Kroth, M. (2011) 'Educational services in Swedish prisons: successful programs of academic and vocational teaching', *Criminal Justice Studies* 24: 215–226.

Piacentini, L. (2013) 'The Russian penal system', in V. Ruggiero and M. Ryan (eds) *Punishment in Europe: A critical anatomy of penal systems*, Basingstoke: Palgrave Macmillan.

Piketty, T. (2014) *Capital in the Twenty-First Century*, Cambridge, MA: Harvard University Press.

Platek, M. (2013) 'Poland: the political legacy and penal practice', in V. Ruggiero and M. Ryan (eds) *Punishment in Europe: A critical anatomy of penal systems*, Basingstoke: Palgrave Macmillan.

Pratt, J. (2008) 'Scandinavian exceptionalism in an era of penal excess', *British Journal of Criminology* 48: 119–137.

Pratt, J. and Eriksson, A. (2012) 'In defence of Scandinavian exceptionalism', in T. Ugelvik and J. Dullum (eds) *Penal Exceptionalism?*, London: Routledge.

Rawlinson, P. (2012) 'Corruption, organized crime and the free market in Russia', in P. Gounev and V. Ruggiero (eds) *Corruption and Organized Crime in Europe*, London: Routledge.

Robert, P. (2013), 'The French criminal justice system', in V. Ruggiero and M. Ryan (eds) *Punishment in Europe: A Critical Anatomy of Penal Systems*, Basingstoke: Palgrave Macmillan.

Rosanvallon, P. (2014) *The Society of Equals*, Cambridge, MA: Harvard University Press.

Ruggiero, V. (1995) 'Flexibility and intermittent emergency in the Italian penal system', in V. Ruggiero, M. Ryan and J. Sim (eds) *Western European Penal Systems*, London: Sage.

Ruggiero, V. (2001) *Movements in the City*, New York: Prentice Hall.

Ruggiero, V. (2010) *Penal Abolitionism*, Oxford: Oxford University Press.

Ruggiero, V. (2013) 'Conclusion', in V. Ruggiero and M. Ryan (eds) *Punishment in Europe: A critical anatomy of penal systems*, Basingstoke: Palgrave Macmillan.

Scott, D. (ed.) (2013) *Why Prisons?*, Cambridge: Cambridge University Press.

Starr, P. (2014) 'A different road to a fair society', *New York Review of Books*, 22 May: 33–36.

Ugelvik, T. and Dullum, J. (eds) (2012) *Penal Exceptionalism?*, London: Routledge.

Van Swaaningen, R. (2000) 'Back to the iron cage: the example of the Dutch probation service', in P. Green and A. Rutherford (eds) *Criminal Policy in Transition*, Oxford: Hart.

Van Swaaningen, R. and de Jonge, G. (1995) 'The Dutch prison system and penal policy in the 1990s: from humanitarian paternalism to penal business', in V. Ruggiero, M. Ryan and J. Sim (eds) *Western European Penal Systems*, London: Sage.

Von Hofer, H. and Tham, H. (2013) 'Punishment in Sweden: a changing penal landscape', in V. Ruggiero and M. Ryan (eds) *Punishment in Europe: A critical anatomy of penal aystems*, Basingstoke: Palgrave Macmillan.

Chapter 22

Prisons as welfare institutions?

Punishment and the Nordic model

Thomas Ugelvik[1]

Nordic exceptionalism?

In the field of comparative penology, the Nordic countries – Denmark, Finland, Iceland, Norway and Sweden – are frequently used as an exception to the general rule. As the story goes, these societies are somehow able to resist a current global move towards growing rates of imprisonment and tougher crime control policies. Nordic prisons are seen as beacons of humanity and decency in a world of ever-increasing penal populism. In a much-discussed two-part article, John Pratt (2008a, 2008b) described the Nordic societies as exhibiting a specifically Nordic penal culture, resulting in what he called Scandinavian or Nordic exceptionalism in the penal area;[2] the exceptional qualities, according to Pratt, being consistently low rates of imprisonment and comparatively humane prison conditions.

Imprisonment rates are, in theory at least, simple enough to compare (if, for the time being, we bracket the headaches associated with comparing statistical figures produced by different government agencies in different countries), and several other authors have in fact done so (Cavadino and Dignan 2006; Lacey 2008). The novelty of Pratt's approach was that the question of prison conditions was added to the simple comparison of imprisonment rates.

Pratt's main point is that the prison regimes in two clusters of societies are systematically different. The societies making up what he calls the Anglophone cluster – England, New Zealand and Australia – are more punitive. Their prisons are simple and austere, and their politicians are keen to be seen as credibly 'tough on crime'. The societies making up the Nordic cluster – empirically he is talking about Finland, Norway and Sweden – are more welfare oriented, and their prisons are celebrated either for being relatively safe and humane institutions that provide decent living conditions for prisoners or, depending on whom you ask, notorious for being soft holiday camps for murderers and rapists.

Like imprisonment rates, the quality of prisons and the conditions they provide for prisoners is of course an empirical question. Empirically, 'prison conditions' can be operationalized in a number of different ways. One could focus on more objective aspects of prison life, and ask whether in-cell sanitation facilities are available or count the number of books in the prison library. Or one could choose a more subjective approach and ask prisoners what they think of various aspects of prison life. Is the food tasty? Are the prison officers decent and professional? Do you feel safe here?

The exceptionalism debate has, so far, too often revolved around the question of whether the Nordic prison systems *really* are or are not that exceptional. The discussion has often lacked the appropriate level of specificity. Pratt later expanded on the exceptionalism thesis in several texts co-authored with Anna Eriksson (Pratt and Eriksson 2011a, 2011b, 2012). Much of the debate has taken the less specific argument that can be found in Pratt's original 2008 article as a starting point. Here, the general argument that Nordic prisons and prison systems are more humane and decent than their Anglophone counterparts was largely held up by anecdotal examples. Pratt's descriptions of the Nordic prison conditions, and in particular his choice of examples, have been criticized by Nordic prison scholars (*inter alia* Mathiesen 2012; Smith 2012). According to critics, Pratt was cherry-picking anecdotes to fit his thesis. He could easily have chosen alternative examples to paint a more sombre picture of the Nordic prison systems: more run-down prisons in need of renovation, and a stronger focus on the more problematic aspects of the Nordic penal culture like the frequent use of pre-trial solitary confinement. He has also been criticized for relying too heavily on scripted day visits to a small number of institutions (Minogue 2009).

The very meaning of 'Nordic exceptionalism' has developed through these texts. One might differentiate between a narrow, specific version of the exceptionalism thesis, and a wider, more general and more abstract version. The most specific version can probably be found in Pratt and Eriksson's 2012 book. Here, they operationalize the differences in prison conditions between the two clusters as follows: (i) Nordic prisons tend to be smaller; (ii) officer/inmate relations are better and more egalitarian; (iii) the quality of prison life is better (the quality of the food provided, the hygienic conditions, the amount of personal space and the quality of visiting arrangements are all superior in the Nordic prisons); (iv) prison officers are better trained; and (v) prisoners in the Nordic countries are more likely to be involved in education or vocational training programmes that are more often directed at preparing them for life after release.

At least when seen from a Norwegian perspective, one immediately has to agree that at least two out of the five criteria are accurate. Norwegian prisons are indeed small (even though some of the smallest have been closed or will be in the near future), and the level of training that would-be prison officers have to undergo is impressive compared with training regimes in other jurisdictions. The three remaining aspects – the quality of prison life, officer/inmate relations, and the quality of educational and vocational training programmes – may very well also favour Norwegian prisons, although a more systematic comparative analysis is probably needed before such a conclusion can be made.

In this chapter, I hope to bring the exceptionalism discussion a step forward. It is my thesis that the Nordic systems may be exceptional in another sense: the fact that Nordic prisons and correctional systems are understood as integrated parts of the strong, inclusive and ambitious Nordic welfare states may set them apart from similar institutions and systems elsewhere. Although perhaps not a unique quality that can only be found in the Nordic prison systems and nowhere else, this is certainly not the case in many other jurisdictions, where punishment is regarded as a last resort alternative to, not a part of, the welfare system. My ambition is not to 'solve' the question of exceptionalism once and for all, but to begin an exploration of this alternative framing of the exceptionalism thesis. The main empirical example in the following is Norway, both because the Nordic prison systems and the Nordic societies exhibit important differences, making a single book chapter about all five countries difficult, and because the Norwegian context is the one I know best. I will explore how this welfare-oriented exceptionalism thesis holds up when confronted with recent Norwegian research findings. Where appropriate, I will also draw on research findings from the other Nordic countries. As an introduction, I will first briefly introduce the Norwegian prison and probation system through a selection of key figures from official prison statistics.

Key statistical figures

The Nordic countries all have in common both that they regularly produce comprehensive and advanced prison statistics and that they make versions of them available for the general public. There are even Nordic comparative correctional statistics that are available in English (Kristoffersen 2013).

As Pratt correctly argued, the Nordic correctional systems are small in both absolute and relative terms.[3] The Norwegian prison system had a total capacity of 3,649 prisoners in 2014 – sentenced prisoners and pre-trial detainees combined – spread out across 42 different institutions. The Danish system is somewhat larger in absolute terms, with 4,091 prisoners and 52 institutions, and the Swedish is larger still, with 5,797 prisoners in 79 institutions. Even though they are all relatively small, they are gigantic compared with the Icelandic system. With its 152 prisoners in total, it is one of the smallest correctional systems in Europe (see Table 22.1).

Table 22.1 Nordic prison systems: key figures

	Prison population total	Prison population rate	Number of institutions	Pre-trial detainees, % of total population	Female prisoners, % of total population	Foreign prisoners, % of total population
Denmark	4,091	73	52	33.8	4.6	26.8
Finland	3,134	58	30	19.3	7.2	14.5
Iceland	152	47	5	8.4	3.2	15.8
Norway	3,649	72	42	28.7	5.1	34.0
Sweden	5,797	60	79	24.5	5.8	31.6

Source: ICPS 2014.

Table 22.2 New arrivals in the Nordic Correctional Services, relative to population

	Prison system: new entries in 2012 per 100,000 inhabitants	Probation system: new entries in 2012 per 100,000 inhabitants
Denmark	112	210
Finland	70	85
Iceland	73	127
Norway	147	107
Sweden	99	209

Source: Kristoffersen 2013: 15–19.

Nordic prisons are in general also relatively small institutions. Most Norwegian prisons will have a capacity of between 50 and 100 prisoners. The largest institution in Norway is Oslo prison, with a capacity of only 392 – a size that would make it a small to mid-sized institution in many jurisdictions elsewhere in the world. According to the Norwegian Correctional Services, the special geographical shape of the country and its low population density, combined with an intention to let prisoners serve their sentence close to where they live, makes a relatively large number of relatively small prisons necessary. In Denmark, in contrast, it is possible to go from one end of the country to the other by car or train in a matter of just a few hours. The Danish Correctional Services do not have to take similar considerations, yet they still choose to maintain a relatively large number of relatively small institutions.

The average occupancy rate in the Norwegian system was 96.5% in 2013, giving an average of around 3,670 prisoners in the system at any one time. Based on a national population of 5.1 million, this gives Norway an imprisonment rate of 72 prisoners per 100,000 inhabitants. The Norwegian rate, as is the case in most jurisdictions around Europe and even the world, has gone up, from 58 in 1992 and 61 in 2001, but should still be considered relatively low.

Sweden is an interesting exception to the rule. The Swedish system has shrunk in both absolute and relative numbers in recent years. Through the increased use of community sanctions, the Swedish prison and probation system has succeeded in decreasing the number of prisoners going through the prison system in a year. Sweden has also pioneered the use of home detention with electronic monitoring as an alternative to prison. This development recently resulted in Sweden permanently closing down several of its prisons.

Norway has the largest number of people through its prison system per year of all the Nordic countries, relative to its population. It is in fact the only Nordic country that uses its prison system more than its probation system. Sweden has the most modest use of imprisonment of all three Scandinavian countries.

At the same time, the Norwegian sentencing level is on average relatively low. A total of 13,425 individuals were imprisoned for shorter or longer periods over the course of 2013. Compared with the other Nordic countries, then, a larger number of people pass through the system more quickly. Some 28% of Norwegian prisoners were released within 30 days, 62% within 90 days, and 89% were released within a year. The average time served was only 141 days. At the other end of the spectrum, only 11 individuals were released after serving more than ten years in prison that year. Given that the Norwegian Correctional Services as a matter of principle does not overbook its institutions, and that single-occupancy cells are the norm in high security prisons, there is at any time a waiting list of convicted people waiting to get into prison to serve their prison sentence. The number of verdicts on the waiting list varies quite a bit, but currently consists of around 1,100 verdicts awaiting effectuation. People convicted of serious crimes will of course have to skip this queue; in most cases they will go straight from pre-trial imprisonment to serving their sentence.

Some 28 young offenders under the age of 18 were imprisoned over the course of 2013. The age of criminal responsibility is 15. A recent development is that two special youth prisons – one of which is already operational – will be established to provide these offenders with a prison environment suited to their needs. Some 65% of prisoners were 30 years or older.

In addition to the prisons, the Norwegian correctional system includes 17 probation offices around the country. It is possible to be released from prison on licence having served two-thirds of a prison sentence. Licensees become the responsibility of the probation services for the remaining sentence. They may have to report to the closest probation office at regular times, refrain from the use of alcohol and comply with any other specific conditions that have been imposed on their release.

The probation offices are also responsible for the implementation of community sanctions, the so-called programme for intoxicated drivers, home detention with or without electronic monitoring, and for the writing of pre-sentence reports. A community sentence is imposed by the court and can run from 30 to 420 hours. The probation office in charge of implementing the sentence will establish the contents of the sentence in cooperation with the convict. This may consist of unpaid work as well as other activities that are deemed suitable to prevent reoffending. In 2013, the probation arm of the Norwegian Correctional Services system was responsible for 2,541 community sentences that were initiated in 2013, as well as the 1,877 people serving their sentence entirely in their own homes under a regime of supervision through electronic monitoring.

Norway does not have the death penalty, nor does it have a life sentence. The maximum length of a prison sentence is 21 years. The two exceptions to this rule are a 30-year maximum sentence for genocide, crimes against humanity and some war crimes, and the preventive detention sentence. A small number of prisoners – 84 at the beginning of 2012 – serve a preventive detention order ('*forvaring*'). This type of sentence is given to legally sane (and thus accountable) yet dangerous offenders who typically have been found guilty of serious violent and/or sexual offences. When these sentences are imposed, detainees are given a minimum and maximum sentence length. The minimum sentence length cannot exceed ten years, and the maximum possible preventive detention sentence is 21 years. When the minimum sentence is reached, detainees can start to petition the courts to be released. The courts will decide whether they still pose a likely threat to society. When the maximum sentence is reached, the case automatically goes back to court for a new decision. If the court still believes that the offender poses a threat to society, the sentence can be lengthened by five-year increments, theoretically for the natural life of the offender. Preventive detention may thus work as a *de facto* life sentence, although this has not yet happened, since the sentence was only introduced in 2001.

The *forvaring* sentence has recently been the cause of much international confusion. When terrorist and mass-murderer Anders Behring Breivik was given the maximum *forvaring* sentence, the fact that Breivik might be set free after only ten years, and that 21 years was his 'maximum sentence' was seen as an example of ridiculously low Norwegian sentence levels by many international commentators. Given the potential to prolong the *forvaring* sentence indefinitely, it remains to be seen how many years Breivik will end up serving, but that he will be released after ten years seems highly unlikely at the present time.

Welfare state prisons?

In Norwegian law, a prison sentence is defined as a form of punishment, and thus as a penalty that is supposed to be experienced as an evil by prisoners. However, in the Norwegian Correctional Services' policy documents, a prison sentence is also described as much more than that (Ugelvik 2013). A prison sentence is supposed to quench society's thirst for vengeance, minimizing the need for vendettas and vigilantism. The use of prisons is also seen as a form of communication where the general population is shown what can happen to those who break the law, making crime less attractive. These goals are both seen as important in the Norwegian system, but in the current correctional services policy documents, a prison sentence is first and foremost described as an opportunity, a potential arena for rehabilitation and successful reintegration back into society. Differently put, a spell in prison is supposed to change prisoners in such a way that it is less likely that they will return to the institution in the future. The goal is specified in the following vision statement:

'The goal for all our work is a convict who, when the sentence is served, is:

- Drug-free or has control over his drug use
- Has a suitable place to live
- Can read, write and do basic math
- Will have a chance on the labour market
- Can relate to her/his family, friends and society in general
- Knows how to seek assistance if problems arise after release
- Can live an independent life.'

(MoJ 2008: 105)

The end goal of the entire prison and probation apparatus seen as a whole is defined as 'a safer society for all'.

No prisoner shall serve her or his sentence in a higher security regime than necessary. Differently put, it is a general principle that a prisoner should always be placed in the lowest security regime possible. The so-called principle of normality has a strong standing in the Norwegian system, meaning that all aspects of life inside a prison should resemble life in society outside the prison walls as much as possible, with the obvious exceptions of the security and control measures that are necessary in institutions like prisons. Any deviation from this principle has to be based on an explicit argument.

The punishment element of a prison sentence is supposed to consist solely of the deprivation of liberty for a period specified by the courts. In the Norwegian system, no other individual right has been removed by the prison sentence; a prisoner retains the right to vote in general elections and the right to the various welfare provisions offered by the Norwegian welfare state system, including the right to free healthcare, social services and a secondary education. The general level of the welfare services is high; the country provides citizens with, for example, generous paid parental leave, a general high level of labour market security and a relatively low unemployment rate.

Governments are more or less ambitious when it comes to welfare policies and their intended impacts. The traditional Scandinavian welfare model is comprehensive, institutionalized and universal (Esping-Andersen and Korpi 1987). The welfare schemes are (in principle at least) available to all, irrespective of social or geographical position. The level of what Rugkåsa (2011) has called 'welfare ambitiousness' – the range of responsibilities that the state assumes for the welfare of its citizens and the extensiveness of the welfare system – has been and (to varying degrees) still is second to none. This is certainly the impression one gets from Norwegian Correctional Services policy documents. The

Norwegian government, including its Correctional Services, has high hopes when it comes to the goals of modifying and engineering social conditions in such a way as to create a just and healthy society for all citizens, regardless of background. Compared with many other countries, where welfare-oriented prisons, if they ever truly exist, are things of the past (Garland 1985, 2001), the Norwegian welfare state stretches its safety net wide to include prisoners. Even prisoners are supposed to be the beneficiaries of the welfare state policies; even the prisons are run according to the logic of a universal right to welfare. The Norwegian welfare state runs on need, not merit or social position, and, importantly, all forms of need are legitimate. Welfare aid is yours if and when you need it, regardless of whether you have deserved it in a moral sense. Of course, a system of various controls and incentives are built into the system. You cannot totally refuse to seek employment and then expect to receive unemployment benefits. However, in contrast to earlier regimes and those in operation elsewhere (e.g. according to Prieur (2003) the logics underpinning the British or French systems), there is supposed to be a welfare solution *for everyone*, even for prisoners.

In practice, this is solved through the so-called importation model. Correctional Services imports services such as healthcare, education, and cultural and social services from the external public welfare system on the other side of the wall. The prison healthcare system is thus part of the public healthcare system of Norway; the education department is part of the public school system. The prison librarian is hired by the municipality where the prison is located, and the prison library is part of a national system of public libraries. It should be said that the quality of these public service agencies is higher in Norway, where there is no real tradition for, for example, private hospitals or private schools, than in many other countries. A by-product of this model is that Norwegian prisoners in important ways may be said still to be included in the community outside; they are still acknowledged as citizens with important citizen's rights, even when they are serving a custodial sentence. The prison is part of the society around it. The model also gives these public service institutions regular access to the prison, making the prison accountable to a wide range of potential critics.

The Norwegian government recently established a so-called 'reintegration guarantee', stating that all prisoners shall upon release, if relevant, be offered employment, further education, suitable housing accommodation, medical services, addiction treatment services and debt counselling. The guarantee is political in character and not legal. It represents the intentions of all the various welfare state agencies to cooperate on the common objective that is prisoner rehabilitation and reintegration.

As a preliminary conclusion, the philosophy that prisons are supposed to be places for positive change is coupled in the Norwegian case with a strong welfare state system that is fully integrated into the everyday life of the prison. It all certainly looks good on paper and may very well be exceptional from an international perspective. The goal of the rest of the chapter is to confront the policy document version of the story with recent research findings.

Current trends and recent research findings

In 2002, Wacquant published a paper entitled 'The Curious Eclipse of Prison Ethnography in the Age of Mass Incarceration', often cited since, in which he pointed to the problematic lack of ethnographic field studies of prison settings. At the time when they were most needed, these studies had all but disappeared, according to Wacquant. His lamentations seem almost like an echo of the conclusion of Norwegian criminologist Fridhov in her 1994 review of the Nordic prison research literature. Although she gave her review a more positive spin than Wacquant gave his paper (she concluded that Nordic prison research was 'not entirely absent'), her point was very similar: prison researchers were only in a few exceptional cases actually entering into the institutions they wrote about. Following a few classic studies in the 1950s and 1960s by, *inter alia*, Galtung (1959) and Mathiesen (1965), and with the exception of a few scattered student dissertations, Nordic prison researchers had for decades decided that prison research could best be accomplished from a distance, according to Fridhov. They focused more on constructing a robust external critique of the system (Mathiesen 2006, 2015; Christie 2007), than on empirical engagement with the everyday life behind bars.

This has changed only recently. Over the last ten years or so, prisons in Norway and the other Nordic countries have once again become the object of scholarly attention. In just a few short years, we have gone from knowing very little about the actual everyday life on the wings, to having a number of studies of different kinds of prison regimes to build on.

First, there are now available a few recent studies which in some ways resemble the classics that emerged in the 1950s and 1960s – the kind of comprehensive studies of specific prisons and prison wings as social systems, broadly understood. These studies focus on the social life on the wings, the interaction between prisoners and officers, and the specific (more or less local) culture that permeates the institution. They may often be read as descriptions of the differences between a prison on paper – the institutions as described in laws, regulations and policy documents – and a prison as a specific space where living and breathing people, prisoners and officers alike, try to make the best of the situation they are in.

Ugelvik (2014b), for instance, finds that the prisoners he studied in Oslo prison are often preoccupied with different versions of the common project of turning themselves into something else or something more than just 'prisoners'. Through relentless creative entrepreneurship, they bend rules and 'fool the system', and thus reclaim a sense of both freedom and manhood. One common strategy is the creation and maintenance of alternative ethical systems. To counter the general moral inferiority ascribed them by the fact that they are imprisoned, they recreate themselves as men of high moral fibre through the exclusion of 'immoral others' like sex offenders and police informants.

According to Minke (2012), the rules are enforced even more strictly in Vridsløselille prison in Denmark. Here new arrivals have to show a copy of the official court verdict to the other prisoners before they are accepted by their peers – again to single out and exclude sex offenders and police informants from the prisoner community. These studies may be said to show how a prisoner culture in practice may challenge the implementation of the ideals of the Nordic rehabilitation-oriented welfare state prison.

On the other hand, recent studies of prison recidivism seem to suggest that the Nordic prison systems are doing something right. A study published in 2010 by Graunbøl et al. finds that only 20% of prisoners who were released from Norwegian prisons had reoffended within two years; the lowest recidivism rate in all the Nordic countries. This has been interpreted as a great triumph for the Norwegian Correctional Services. Recidivism is, however, notoriously difficult to measure. Critics have argued that the recidivism rates can be made to look different, depending on different research designs. Andersen and

Skardhamar (2014) show that different designs can give reoffending rates between 9% and 53% from the same Norwegian data set. If we do decide to trust the low figure (the 20% triumph), what, if anything, has actually 'worked' in what way to keep the remaining 80% out of prison, remains unknown. The causes of successful rehabilitation and reintegration remain unidentified to a large degree, and it might be that aspects of the relatively inclusive Norwegian society that prisoners are released back into are more important than anything that goes on behind prison walls. Skardhamar and Telle (2012) find that employment post-release substantially lowers the reoffending risk.

Several studies have specifically looked at the prison as a provider of welfare services in practice. Studies have shown that prisoners have more and more serious health problems, they are more often unemployed, they consume illegal drugs more often, and are more often school drop-outs than the average citizen (Nilsson 2002; Skardhamar 2002; Friestad and Hansen 2004; Thorsen 2004). The prison system is explicitly supposed to target each individual prisoner's problems. When someone is imprisoned in Norway, they are, from the point of view of the prison system, made available for intervention. Around two-thirds of prisoners report illegal drug use in the month prior to incarceration in self-report surveys (Skardhamar 2003; Ødegård 2008). There are several specific drug treatment units in the Norwegian prison system (Mjåland 2014). Opiate-based substitution medication is distributed. This treatment is provided by the regular Norwegian healthcare system. Prison-based drug treatment has increased in all the Nordic countries in recent years (Kolind et al. 2013). Special drug treatment wings, motivational programmes and substitution treatment are all available in the prison system. However, Haugen (2013) shows that the more problematic and counterproductive aspects of prisoner culture can be found even in more purely rehabilitation-oriented regimes, like the drug-treatment wing he studied. Rua's (2012) study of the prison healthcare system in general shows that when conflicts arise between security issues (as seen from the perspective of the prison staff), and individual healthcare issues, the healthcare of the individual may end up being seen as less important.

The marked increase in foreign nationals in prison has also received recent scholarly and political attention. Some 34% of the prisoners in the Norwegian system are currently foreign citizens. The proportion is even higher among the prisoners in pre-trial detention; around two-thirds of detainees are at any time foreign citizens (Ugelvik 2014a). As detailed above, any welfare state organization including a welfare-oriented prison will to a large extent run on the notion of citizens' legal rights to welfare. In most countries, some rights and benefits are reserved for people who possess full citizenship status. This means that individuals who lack citizenship status may be denied the full enjoyment of social, political and civil rights. An important question to ask is whether foreign national prisoners are given the same opportunities and are imprisoned according to the same standards as the Norwegian population. The answer may be complicated, given that some of the 'external' welfare agencies that operate in the prisons may not discriminate between prisoners based on citizenship (e.g. the library service), while others have schemes that are reserved for Norwegian citizens only (e.g. the social services). The increased number of foreign nationals in prison has also led the Norwegian government to focus on return schemes where prisoners are returned – voluntarily or forcefully – to a prison in their country of origin to serve out their sentence there. A recent development elsewhere in Europe is that some countries are opening prison wings on neighbouring soil; notably, Belgium is leasing a prison facility in the Dutch city of Tilburg to cope with its prison-overcrowding problem. The Norwegian government recently approached the Swedish authorities to find out whether a similar deal could be made, given that the Swedish prison system is closing down institutions that are no longer needed. The latest development is that the plan will not come to fruition; a Swedish legal amendment would be necessary to make it possible for Swedish prison officers on Swedish soil to exert penal power on behalf of the Norwegian State. The Norwegian government is, however, considering the possibility of sending prisoners to the Netherlands instead, where there seem to be fewer legal restrictions.

A number of studies have looked at the different kinds of regimes that can be found in the prison systems in the Nordic countries. According to Pratt, Nordic prisons are smaller than prisons in the Anglophone cluster, and they are often more open. In the Norwegian system, the ideal is that prisoners progress through the system from a high-security regime to a low-security prison and (if the sentence is long enough to allow it), finally end up in a half-way house or even serve the remaining sentence in their own homes with an electronic foot bracelet. The logic is gradually to return prisoners to their communities as far as possible while they are already serving their sentence. In open prisons, prisoners will often live in self-organized cottages and enjoy relatively unrestricted freedom of movement on the prison grounds. Employing the measuring the quality of prison life (MQPL) model developed by Liebling and others (Liebling, with Arnold 2004), Johnsen and Granheim (2011) find that the moral performance of Norwegian high-security prisons is not at the standard one might expect, given all the talk of exceptional prison conditions. However, they do find that smaller prisons are better at creating an environment where the prison experience is more constructive and less painful. With this background, it is ironic that several of the smallest prisons have been closed down for economic reasons in recent years. Other studies (Neumann 2012; Shammas 2014) have shown that these open regimes – even though they may be experienced as better in certain ways – produce their own, context-specific 'pains of imprisonment'. According to Shammas (2014), role confusion, anxiety and boundlessness, ambiguity and relative deprivation are among the pains regularly experienced by prisoners in more open prison regimes. A softer and more indirect form of power (Crewe 2011), which nevertheless is experienced as constraining and may be as or even more difficult to cope with than the harder power associated with traditional prison regimes, is common in these institutions. Nordic prisons may be more 'humane' in the sense that the material standard and the living conditions provided are better, but that does not necessarily mean that the prison is experienced as any less prison-like (Neumann 2012).

A few recent studies have also looked at prison officers and their world. Basberg (1999) described in detail how the officers at a large women's prison see their work in terms of a logic of individual care as well as the more familiar logic of control and security. Ibsen (2012) shows how prison officers in a high security Norwegian prison informally create an alternative basis for discipline through the liberal distribution of favours and goods (e.g. extra telephone time), which may then be taken away if prisoners misbehave. Bruhn, Lindberg and Nylander (2011; Nylander et al. 2011) find important subcultural differences between staff in security wings and treatment-oriented wings in the Swedish system: security wing staff are more detached and instrumental in their dealings with prisoners, and their representations of prisoners are more negative and based on an 'us v. them' dichotomy. Staff in the dedicated treatment wings, on the other hand, talk about prisoners in a much more positive and constructive way. Staff in regular prison wings often occupy a sort of middle ground, according to Bruhn, Lindberg and Nylander.

Finally, several studies and reports have directly targeted the prisons as harm-producing institutions. The relatively widespread Norwegian use of pre-trial detention, and in particular the use of solitary confinement pre-trial, has been criticized repeatedly by international agencies like the European Committee for the Prevention of Torture and Inhuman or Degrading Treatment or Punishment (CPT). There is no absolute maximum time limit for pre-trial imprisonment in Norway. The police have to argue for continued imprisonment in front of the court on a regular basis (every four weeks in most cases). The courts decide whether to continue the detention period. In its report following the latest CPT visit to Norway in 2011, it concludes that:

> Given the very harmful effects a solitary confinement regime can have on the prisoner concerned, the CPT wishes once again to express its opinion that the Criminal Procedure Act should stipulate an upper limit on the duration of solitary confinement of remand prisoners by court order.
>
> (CPT 2011: 31)

The CPT also recommends that the Norwegian authorities redouble their efforts to provide more out-of-cell activities for pre-trial detainees held in solitary confinement to counter the adverse effects of such a regime. The CPT criticism of the Norwegian use of solitary confinement has been reiterated and strengthened by scholars (Horn 2011). The destructive effect of solitary confinement in general as well as in the Danish prison system specifically has been discussed extensively by Smith (2006, 2008, 2012). He has also recently published a study of the destructive impact of arrest and imprisonment of a parent on children of prisoners in Denmark (Smith 2014).

Conclusion

The neo-liberal extension of the penal state and the correlative reining-in of the social state described by, *inter alia*, Wacquant (2009) has not yet really happened in Norway. The welfare state is still going strong; in some ways, it is stronger and more multifaceted than ever. Norwegian prisons are not only thought of as a last resort when other forms of welfare state power have failed, however. The prison is also understood as an integral part of the Norwegian welfare state. The ideals of rehabilitation and re-socialization in prison fit hand in glove with the ambitious and generous welfare system of care/control that developed in the years following the Second World War (Hauge 1996), and are still thought of as the main goals of the correctional services (Ugelvik 2011). Whether it is correct to say that Norwegian prisons themselves are welfare institutions or that they should be described as penal institutions with close ties to the welfare state agencies may depend on your perspective. Nevertheless, prisoners in these institutions are given opportunities, resources and living conditions that are not available to prisoners in most other jurisdictions.

Do these facts in themselves make the Norwegian system exceptional? How does it all work in actual practice on the wings? Do prisoners in fact feel embraced by a benevolent and inclusive welfare regime that wants what is best for them? Does the close connection between the Nordic correctional systems and the broader welfare systems really change anything? Does this connection in itself result in more humane institutions? The recent studies referred to in this chapter all show, in different ways, that there are important differences between policy documents and the real-life world of a prison wing. That being said, it should be remembered that the Norwegian prison system (if one puts any faith in such numbers) somehow still produces a relatively low recidivism rate. The question is, perhaps, what is most exceptional: the prisons or the surrounding society with its egalitarian ethos and low employment rate?

Are the Nordic countries less punitive than other societies? Any punitiveness scale should include more than imprisonment rates and the quality of life provided in prison institutions. Advanced welfare states, like the Nordic countries, will often employ other, equally intrusive, but more indirect forms of social control – perhaps even more so than other societies. A low imprisonment society is not necessarily a low social control society, and some of the alternatives to a prison sentence in the Nordic countries have been particularly draconian. From recent Norwegian history we could include, for instance, the aggressive assimilation policies forced upon the indigenous Sami population, as well as the 'treatment' of vagrants in prison-like institutions for years at a time (Olsen 2010). Norwegian history has many examples of the fact that what may be impossible to impose on offenders as a punishment under the rule of law, may still be imposed on clients or patients if rebranded as a form of treatment for their own good.

This conclusion has asked more questions than it has answered. The aim has been to introduce the Nordic correctional systems in general and the Norwegian system in particular, and to provide brief examples of recent relevant research that readers may consult. The focus has admittedly been lopsided in favour of Norway. I invite readers to take up this cue and do their own similar analyses of the other Nordic countries. Seen together, such analyses may form a comparative tapestry that might introduce us, as a collective, to new knowledge about these prison systems that may or may not be seen as exceptions to the general rule.

Notes

1 I would like to thank Jamie Bennett for constructive comments on an earlier version of this chapter. The writing of the chapter has been funded by the European Research Council (ERC Starting Grant).
2 Scandinavia as a geographical area consists of Denmark, Norway and Sweden. Danes, Norwegians and Swedes have a common cultural heritage and can understand each other's languages reasonably well. The Nordic countries also include Iceland and Finland. Although the languages are part of the same linguistic family, most Scandinavians cannot understand Icelandic. Finnish is part of a completely different family of languages, and is, as the proverb goes, as Greek to Scandinavians, even though Greek is actually a closer relative.
3 This statistics section is based on the Norwegian Correctional Services annual statistics (MoJ 2014), Statistics Norway's online prison statistics (SSB 2014), *Correctional Statistics of Denmark, Finland, Iceland, Norway and Sweden 2008–2012* (Kristoffersen 2013) and the International Centre for Prison Studies *World Prison Brief* (ICPS 2014).

Bibliography

Andersen, S.N. and Skardhamar, T. (2014) *Pick a Number: Mapping recidivism measures and their consequences*, Oslo: Statistics Norway.

Basberg, C.E. (1999) *Omsorg i fengsel?* Oslo: Pax.

Bruhn, A., Lindberg, O. and Nylander, P.-Å. (2011) 'A harsher prison climate and a cultural heritage working against it: subcultural divisions among prison officers', in T. Ugelvik and J. Dullum (eds) *Penal Exceptionalism? Nordic prison policy and practice*, London: Routledge.

Cavadino, M. and Dignan, J. (2006) *Penal Systems: A comparative approach*, London: Sage.

Christie, N. (2007) *Limits to Pain*, Eugene, OR: Wipf & Stock.

CPT (2011) *Report to the Norwegian Government on the Visit to Norway Carried out by the European Committee for the Prevention of Torture and Inhuman or Degrading Treatment or Punishment (Cpt) from 18 to 27 May 2011*, Strasbourg: Council of Europe.

Crewe, B. (2011) 'Soft Power in Prison: Implications for staff-prisoner relationships, liberty and legitimacy', *European Journal of Criminology* 8(6): 455–468.

Esping-Andersen, G. and Korpi, W. (1987) 'From poor relief to institutional welfare states: the development of Scandinavian social policy', in R. Erikson (ed.) *The Scandinavian Model: Welfare states and welfare research*, Armonk, NY: Sharpe.

Fridhov, I.M. (1994) *Nordisk fengselsforskning: Ikke helt fraværende*, Oslo: Nordisk Samarbeidsråd for Kriminologi (NSfK).

Friestad, C. and Hansen, I.L.S. (2004) *Levekår blant innsatte*, Oslo: Fafo.

Galtung, J. (1959) *Fengselssamfunnet: Et forsøk på analyse*, Oslo: Universitetsforlaget.

Garland, D. (1985) *Punishment and Welfare: A history of penal strategies*, Aldershot: Gower.

Garland, D. (2001) *The Culture of Control: Crime and social order in contemporary society*, Chicago, IL: University of Chicago Press.

Graunbøl, H.M. et al. (2010) *Retur: En nordisk undersøkelse af recidiv blant klienter i Kriminalforsorgen*, Oslo: KRUS.

Hauge, R. (1996) *Straffens begrunnelser*, Oslo: Universitetsforlaget.

Haugen, S. (2013) *Endringer fra innsiden: Forberedelse til rusbehandling bak fengselsmurene*, Oslo: Gyldendal akademisk.

Horn, T. (2011) 'Hvilken rettspolitisk betydning bør kritikk fra CPT ha for norske regler om isolasjon ved varetektsfengsling?', in O.H. Rønning (ed.) *Med loven mot makta*, Oslo: Novus.

Ibsen, A.Z. (2012) 'Ruling by Favors: Prison Guards' Informal Exercise of Institutional Control', *Law & Social Inquiry* 38(2): 342–363.

ICPS (2014) *World Prison Brief*, London: International Centre for Prison Studies, www.prison studies.org/world-prison-brief (accessed 10 August 2014).

Johnsen, B. and Granheim, P.K. (2011) 'Prison size and the quality of life in Norwegian closed prisons in late modernity', in T. Ugelvik and J. Dullum (eds) *Penal Exceptionalism? Nordic prison policy and practice*, London: Routledge.

Kolind, T., Frank, V.A., Lindberg, O. and Tourunen, J. (2013) 'Prison-based drug treatment in Nordic political discourse: an elastic discursive construct', *European Journal of Criminology* 10(6): 659–674.

Kristoffersen, R. (2013) *Correctional Statistics of Denmark, Finland, Iceland, Norway and Sweden 2008–2012*, Oslo: KRUS, brage.bibsys.no/xmlui/bitstream/handle/11250/160610/9/Kris toffersen_2013.pdf (accessed 3 September 2014).

Lacey, N. (2008) *The Prisoners' Dilemma: Political economy and punishment in contemporary democracies*, Cambridge: Cambridge University Press.

Liebling, A., with Arnold, H. (2004) *Prisons and their Moral Performance: A study of values, quality, and prison life*, Oxford: Oxford University Press.

Mathiesen, T. (1965) *The Defences of the Weak: A sociological study of a Norwegian correctional institution*, London: Tavistock.

Mathiesen, T. (2006) *Prison on Trial*, Winchester: Waterside.

Mathiesen, T. (2012) 'Scandinavian exceptionalism in penal matters: reality or wishful thinking?', in T. Ugelvik and J. Dullum (eds) *Penal Exceptionalism? Nordic prison policy and practice*, London: Routledge.

Mathiesen, T. (2015) *The Politics of Abolition Revisited*, London and New York: Routledge.

Minke, L.K. (2012) *Fængselets indre liv*, København: Jurist- og økonomiforbundets forlag.

Minogue, C. (2009) 'The engaged specific intellectual: resisting unethical prison tourism and the hubris of the objectifying modality of the universalintellectual', *Journal of Prisoners on Prison* 18(1–2): 129–142.

Mjåland, K. (2014) '"A culture of sharing": ddrug exchange in a Norwegian prison', *Punishment & Society* 16(3): 336–352.

MoJ (Ministry of Justice) (2008) *Straff Som Virker – Mindre Kriminalitet – Tryggere Samfunn, St.meld. nr. 37(2007–2008)*, Oslo: Ministry of Justice and the Police.

MoJ (Ministry of Justice) (2014) *Correctional Services Year Statistics*, Oslo: Ministry of Justice and Public Security.

Neumann, C.B. (2012) 'Imprisoning the soul', in T. Ugelvik and J. Dullum (eds) *Penal Exceptionalism? Nordic prison policy and practice*, London: Routledge.

Nilsson, A. (2002) *Fånge i marginalen: Uppväxtvillkor, levnadsförhållanden och återfall i brott bland fångar*, Stockholm: Stockholms universitet.

Nylander, P.-Å., Lindberg, O. and Bruhn, A. (2011) 'Emotional labour and emotional strain among Swedish prison officers', *European Journal of Criminology* 8(6): 469–483.

Ødegård, E. (2008) 'Narkotika- og alkoholproblemer blant innsatte i norske fengsler', *Nordisk alkohol- og narkotikatidsskrift* 25(3): 169–185.

Olsen, S. (2010) *Til Jæderen for å trille tåke: Historien om Opstad tvangsarbeidshus*, Oslo: Scandinavian Academic Press.

Pratt, J. (2008a) 'Scandinavian exceptionalism in an era of penal excess: part I: the nature and roots of Scandinavian exceptionalism', *The British Journal of Criminology* 48(2): 119–137.

Pratt, J. (2008b) 'Scandinavian exceptionalism in an era of penal excess: part II: does Scandinavian exceptionalism have a future?', *The British Journal of Criminology* 48(3): 275–292.

Pratt, J. and Eriksson, A. (2011a) 'In defence of Scandinavian exceptionalism', in T. Ugelvik and J. Dullum (eds) *Penal Exceptionalism? Nordic prison policy and practice*, Abingdon: Routledge.

Pratt, J. and Eriksson, A. (2011b) '"Mr. Larsson is walking out again": the origins and development of Scandinavian prison systems', *Australian and New Zealand Journal of Criminology* 44(1): 7–23.

Pratt, J. and Eriksson, A. (2012) *Contrasts in Punishment: An explanation of Anglophone excess and Nordic exceptionalism*, London: Routledge.

Prieur, A. (2003) 'Senmoderne elendighet: En kommentar om relevansen av Bourdieus bok La Misère du Monde i Norden i dag', *Sosiologisk tidsskrift* 2003(3): 300–322.

Rua, M. (2012) *Hva gjør fengselsleger? En institusjonell etnografi om isolasjon og helse*, Oslo: IKRS.

Rugkåsa, M. (2011) 'Velferdsambisiøsitet sivilisering og normalisering: Statlig velferdspolitikks betydning for forming av borgeres subjektivitet', *Norsk antropologisk tidsskrift* (3–4): 245–255.

Shammas, V.L. (2014) 'The pains of freedom: assessing the ambiguity of Scandinavian penal exceptionalism on Norway's prison island', *Punishment & Society* 16(1): 104–123.

Skardhamar, T. (2002) *Levekår og livssituasjon blant innsatte i norske fengsler*, Oslo: University of Oslo.

Skardhamar, T. (2003) 'Inmate's social background and living conditions', *Journal of Scandinavian Studies in Criminology and Crime Prevention* 4(1): 39–56.

Skardhamar, T. and Telle, K. (2012) 'Post-release employment and recidivism in Norway', *Journal of Quantitative Criminology* 28(4): 629–649.

Smith, P.S. (2006) 'The effects of solitary confinement on prison inmates: a brief history and review of the literature', *Crime and Justice* 34(1): 441–528.

Smith, P.S. (2008) 'Solitary confinement: an introduction to the Istanbul Statement on the use and effects of solitary confinement', *Torture* 18(1): 56–62.

Smith, P.S. (2012) 'A critical look at Scandinavian exceptionalism: welfare state theories, penal populism, and prison conditions in Denmark and Scandinavia', in T. Ugelvik and J. Dullum (ed.) *Penal Exceptionalism? Nordic prison policy and practice*, London: Routledge.

Smith, P.S. (2014) *When the Innocent are Punished: The children of imprisoned parents*, Basingstoke: Palgrave Macmillan.

SSB (2014) *Prison Statistics*, Oslo: Statistics Norway, www.ssb.no/en/sosiale-forhold-og-krimina litet/statistikker/fengsling/ (accessed 3 September 2014).

Thorsen, L.R. (2004) *For mye av ingenting …: Straffedes levekår og sosiale bakgrunn*, Oslo: University of Oslo.

Ugelvik, T. (2011) 'Hva er et fengsel? En analyse av manualen til en sosial teknologi', *Retfærd* 34 (1): 85–100.

Ugelvik, T. (2013) 'Seeing like a welfare state: immigration control, statecraft, and a prison with double vision', in M. Bosworth and K.F. Aas (eds) *Borders of Punishment*, Oxford: Oxford University Press.

Ugelvik, T. (2014a) 'The incarceration of foreigners in European prisons', in S. Pickering and J. Ham (eds) *The Routledge Handbook on Crime and International Migration*, London and New York: Routledge.

Ugelvik, T. (2014b) *Power and Resistance in Prison: Doing time, doing freedom*, London: Palgrave Macmillan.

Wacquant, L.J.D. (2002) 'The curious eclipse of prison ethnography in the age of mass incarceration', *Ethnography* 3(4): 371–397.

Wacquant, L.J.D. (2009) *Punishing the Poor: The neoliberal government of social insecurity*, Durham, NC: Duke University Press.

Chapter 23

Australasian prisons

Claire Spivakovsky

This chapter aims to provide an overview of the use and conditions of imprisonment in Australasian countries. This is no small task. Australasia comprises 14 diverse countries, with its largest, Australia, hosting a population of close to 23 million (ABS 2014), while its neighbour, Tuvalu, only recently reached a peak population of 11,000 (Tuvalu Statistics 2013). Such differences in population size are reflected in prison numbers as well, with Australia reaching its all-time high of 30,775 prisoners in 2013 (ABS 2013a), while Tuvalu reached its grand total of eight (US Department of State 2013). Given these significant differences between Australasian countries, it is important to be clear about the intent and scope of this chapter. The chapter provides a snapshot of the use, extent and position of imprisonment in Australasia's diverse countries. It also provides insight into the major trends and themes of punishment that cut across Australasian countries. To do this, the chapter is organized into two main parts.

The first part of the chapter presents the key similarities and differences among Australasian countries' approaches to imprisonment. Here a statistical picture of the extent and use of imprisonment in major Australasian countries is offered, providing answers to the key questions: How many people are imprisoned? Who are they? What offences bring them there? Once this foundation is established, attention is brought to the role and function of the prison in Australasia. Here the focus is on exploring how changes to the position of imprisonment over the past three or so decades have contributed to growing rates of imprisonment in many Australasian countries.

The second part of the chapter provides a thematic analysis of punishment and prisons in Australasia. Here the common penal trends and themes across Australasian prisons are explored. This part is divided into three main sections. In the first, a commentary on prison conditions in Australasia is provided. Second, the trend of reducing reoffending through offender rehabilitation and risk management is outlined. Finally, insight into a pressing issue facing Australasian prison systems is offered.

Given the broad nature of the task this chapter must perform, it cannot claim to address the nuances of each Australasian country's approach to punishment and imprisonment. Many of these details can, however, be found in Cunneen and colleagues' (2013) book on penal culture in Australia, Pratt's (2013) text on rising imprisonment rates in New Zealand, and Jowitt and Cain's (2010) edited collection on law, society and governance in the Pacific.

The extent, use and position of imprisonment in Australasia

As noted above, Australasia comprises 14 countries which vary significantly in size and population. In order to provide a coherent snapshot of imprisonment in and across these countries, this section proceeds by first considering the extent, use and position of imprisonment in Australasia's largest country, Australia, giving attention to the commonalities and differences among Australia's states and mainland territories; it then continues with a review of imprisonment in Australasia's second largest country, New Zealand, before a final section on imprisonment in the Melanesian, Micronesian and Polynesian Pacific islands of Australasia.

Australia

Australia's imprisonment rate has experienced periods of sizable growth and decline since the 1970s. As Table 23.1 indicates, between 1970 and 1984 there was a steady decrease in the number of adults in Australian prisons, with a rate of 124 per 100,000 of the population recorded in 1970, but only 85.6 per 100,000 by 1984.

Yet, as Table 23.1 further demonstrates, from 1985 onwards, Australia's imprisonment rate has grown rapidly. Indeed, since 1985, the rate of imprisonment in Australia has more than doubled, reaching a peak of 174.7 per 100,000 of the population in 2009, before returning to the slightly lower rate of 170.0 per 100,000 in 2013 (ABS 2009, 2013b).

Table 23.1 Australia's imprisonment rate, 1970–2013

Year	Rate per 100,000
1970	124.0
1973	100.7
1976	93.8
1979	97.6
1981	93.5
1984	85.6
1987	100.8
1990	112.2
1993	119.2
1996	130.9
1999	149.5
2001	153.0
2004	157.2
2007	169.1
2010	172.4
2013	170.0

Source: adapted from Stephens et al. 2012.

Table 23.2 Number of unsentenced prisoners in Australia, 2003–13

Year	2003	2004	2005	2006	2007	2008	2009	2010	2011	2012	2013
No.	4,935	4,935	5,1333	5,581	6,096	6,339	6,393	6,367	6,723	6,870	7,375

Source: adapted from ABS, Prisoners in Australia 'Unsentenced Prisoners' data, 2003–13.

One of the core factors contributing to the growing number of people in Australian prisons is the increasing number of offenders on remand who are being held in custody while awaiting trial or sentence. As Table 23.2 indicates, the number of unsentenced prisoners in Australia has grown from 4,935 to 7,375 in the past decade.

This growth can largely be attributed to the changing position and use of imprisonment in Australia's criminal justice system in this time period.

The position of imprisonment in Australia

In Australia, imprisonment is meant to be reserved for only the most serious offences and dangerous offenders. A custodial sentence is therefore meant to act as the final resort of Australia's criminal justice system. While these broad statements about the position of imprisonment in Australia's criminal justice system have held true since the 1970s, the same cannot be said about the definitions of, or responses to, serious offences or dangerous offenders. Like so many other Western countries, the past 30 years of Australia's criminal justice history have been marked by a series of legislative reforms concerning serious crimes and the management of dangerous offenders. These reforms have had noticeable impact upon Australia's penal landscape, and include changes such as:

- the provision of custodial penalties for a range of non-violent illicit drug offences in the 1980s (see the Controlled Substances Act 1984, and more recently, the Controlled Substances (Serious Drug Offences) Amendment Act 2005);
- the introduction of mandatory sentencing regimes in Western Australia and the Northern Territory in the mid-1990s (see the 1996 and 1997 amendments to the Criminal Code (Western Australia) and Sentencing Act (Northern Territory));
- the amendment of existing Sentencing Acts in the 1990s, and the creation of new 'serious sexual offenders', 'serious violent offenders' and 'serious repeat offender' legislation in the 2000s, which together offer disproportionate and prolonged custodial sentences for 'serious' offences (see for example, Serious Sex Offenders Act (2013) (Northern Territory), or the Criminal Law (Sentencing) (Serious Repeat Offenders) Amendment Bill (2013) (South Australia)); and
- the increasing number of changes to the eligibility criteria for bail regimes, including the introduction of a presumption against bail for certain serious offences, which makes periods of remand more likely (see Cunneen et al. 2013; Steel 2010; Weatherburn et al. 1987).

Tables 23.3 and 23.4 illuminate the effect of these changes on Australia's prison population. Specifically, they reveal the high proportion of both males and females who have received custodial sentences for violent, property and illicit drug offences over the past decade.

Table 23.3 Percentage of sentenced male prisoners in Australia by most serious offence, 2003–13

	Homicide and related offences	*Acts intended to cause injury*	*Sexual assault and related offences*	*Robbery, extortion and related offences*	*Theft and related offences*	*Fraud, deception and related offences*	*Illicit drug offences*
2003	10.3	13.4	12.0	13.4	6.6	2.9	9.5
2004	9.9	13.8	12.1	12.6	6.0	2.8	9.7
2005	10.0	15.0	12.4	11.0	5.5	2.8	9.8
2006	10.2	15.0	13.2	10.4	5.2	2.6	9.9
2007	10.2	15.8	13.4	9.5	4.8	2.6	9.9
2008	10.4	15.9	14.4	9.6	3.7	2.5	9.4
2009	9.6	17.0	14.2	9.5	4.0	2.3	9.8
2010	9.8	17.2	14.4	10.1	3.9	2.3	9.7
2011	10.3	16.5	14.7	10.0	3.5	2.2	10.3
2012	10.2	16.9	14.5	10.1	3.5	2.1	10.7
2013	9.9	17.2	13.5	9.9	3.7	2.0	10.6

Source: adapted from ABS, Prisoners in Australia 'Sentenced Prisoners' data, 2013.

Table 23.4 Percentage of sentenced female prisoners in Australia by most serious offence, 2003–13

	Homicide and related offences	*Acts intended to cause injury*	*Sexual assault and related offences*	*Robbery, extortion and related offences*	*Theft and related offences*	*Fraud, deception and related offences*	*Illicit drug offences*
2003	11.2	11.8	1.1	11.7	11.2	11.7	14.0
2004	10.7	12.3	1.1	7.7	11.9	12.9	14.6
2005	10.5	12.4	1.5	6.5	11.0	14.6	13.4
2006	11.0	13.7	1.5	6.0	10.9	10.4	14.2
2007	10.8	13.2	1.8	6.3	9.6	11.9	14.7
2008	11.2	14.7	1.6	5.7	8.4	12.2	14.6
2009	10.4	13.2	1.8	6.5	10.9	12.9	16.2
2010	10.6	14.6	2.4	6.2	9.3	12.2	17.0
2011	12.3	14.4	2.8	6.8	7.9	11.3	17.1
2012	11.5	14.1	2.3	6.0	8.9	12.3	17.2
2013	10.9	14.8	2.0	6.2	7.7	10.4	17.6

Source: adapted from ABS, Prisoners in Australia 'Sentenced Prisoners' data, 2013).

Yet, while crude figures and overarching explanations such as these provide a useful starting point for understanding the position of imprisonment in Australia, they mask three important issues in Australia's use and extent of imprisonment: the over-representation of Indigenous peoples in Australian prisons, the accelerated growth of Australia's female prison population, and the important inter-jurisdictional differences in Australia's imprisonment rates. These issues are outlined and discussed below.

The over-representation of Indigenous peoples in Australian prisons

Australia's Indigenous populations, the Aboriginal and Torres Strait Islander peoples of Australia, are over-represented in all arms of Australia's criminal justice system, including prisons. Indeed, while Aboriginal and Torres Strait Islander peoples make up 2.5% of Australia's general population, they represent 27% of the adult prisoner population (ABS 2012b, 2013b).

Indigenous peoples' over-representation is by no means a recent issue in Australia's history, however. Finnane and Richards's (2010) archival research, for example, indicates that Aboriginal peoples have been disproportionately represented in Australian prisons since the country's first settlement. Yet, despite this history, the momentum to address the problem of Aboriginal and Torres Strait Islander peoples' over-representation did not begin until the late 1980s and early 1990s. This movement occurred primarily in response to the release of the *Final Report of the Royal Commission into Aboriginal Deaths in Custody*, which indicated that the over-representation of Aboriginal peoples in custody was not only 'totally unacceptable' in its own right, but that this disproportionate treatment would also 'not be tolerated if it occurred in the non-Aboriginal community' (Royal Commission into Aboriginal Deaths in Custody 1991: 6).

The release of this report forced all state and mainland territory governments in Australia to form agreement with their local Indigenous communities about how best to address disadvantage and over-representation in the criminal justice system (see for example *The Victorian Aboriginal Justice Agreement: Phase One* (Department of Justice and Department of Human Services 2004), the *Western Australian Aboriginal Justice Agreement* (Department of Justice et al. 2004) and the *New South Wales Aboriginal Justice Plan* (New South Wales Aboriginal Justice Advisory Council 2003). Yet, little has changed in Australia's rates of Aboriginal and Torres Strait Islander peoples' over-representation since the early 1990s. In fact, as Table 23.5 demonstrates, the percentage of Indigenous people in Australian prisons has steadily increased over the past decade.

Understanding the persistence of Indigenous peoples' over-representation in Australian prisons has polarized Australian criminological scholarship. Scholars such as Weatherburn and colleagues, for example, argue that the rate of Aboriginal and Torres Strait Islander peoples' imprisonment is proportionate to these populations' engagement in crime; that is to say, Indigenous Australians 'commit more serious offences, acquire longer criminal

Table 23.5 Percentage of Indigenous people in Australian prisons 2003–13

Year	2003	2004	2005	2006	2007	2008	2009	2010	2011	2012	2013
%	20	21	22	24	24	24	25	26	26	27	27

Source: adapted from ABS, Prisoners in Australia, 'Aboriginal and Torres Strait Islander Prisoners', 2003–13.

records, and more frequently breach non-custodial sanctions' (Snowball and Weatherburn 2007: 287; Weatherburn 2006; Weatherburn and Fitzgerald 2007; Weatherburn et al. 2003a; Weatherburn et al. 2003b; Weatherburn et al. 2006). Yet, such findings are met with significant criticism from scholars like Cunneen (2006, 2011a, 2011b; Cunneen and McDonald 1997) and Blagg (2008), who propose that the problem instead lies in Australia's racialized approach to governing through crime. Indeed, for these and other scholars, Aboriginal and Torres Strait Islander peoples' over-representation is understood to occur because the markers used to identify and govern risk, dangerousness and seriousness in Australia's criminal justice system are primarily the same markers as those that identify disadvantage, poverty and Indigenous status (see Anthony 2013; Baldry and Cunneen 2014; Cunneen et al. 2013; Spivakovsky 2013). Aboriginal and Torres Strait Islander peoples are not, however, the only population to experience unparalleled entrance into Australia's prison systems.

The accelerated growth of the female prison population

The past few decades have seen the rates of women in prison increase around the world (Chesney-Lind 1991; Moore and Scraton 2014). Australia has followed suit. Indeed, the number of women in Australian prisons has increased by 48% since 2002, compared with an increase of 29% for men over the same time period (ABS 2012c). There appear to be four intersecting factors that contribute to this disproportionate growth.

First, there are differences in the type and nature of offending behaviour between men and women. It is well established that the pathways that bring women into contact with criminal justice systems are often marked by trauma, abuse and repeated institutional contact (Carlen 1983; Carlton and Segrave 2013; Solinger et al. 2010). Such pathways are presented as contributing to a chaotic and vulnerable life, with some women responding to their situation by committing a range of drug, alcohol and other minor offences (Cook and Davies 1999). This pattern of offending behaviour typically results in numerous short-term periods of imprisonment and remand for women, which contributes to the overall number of women entering prisons each year (Carlen 1994; Carlen and Tombs 2006).

However, over the past decade there has also been a steady increase in the number of women in Australia committing violent and serious crimes such as robbery, acts intended to cause injury, and homicide and related offences (Gelb 2003). As previously indicated, both in Australia and around the world, serious and violent offences are increasingly being met with punitive responses such as long prison sentences. Such responses have a strong impact on both the number of people entering the prison each year, and the number who remain in prisons for years at a time. This is the second factor contributing to the accelerated growth of women offenders in Australian prisons: the wide-reaching effects of the global trend towards punitiveness.

The third factor that appears to play a part in the accelerated growth of Australia's female prison population is Australia's racialized trends in imprisonment. That is to say, Aboriginal and Torres Strait Islander women are over-represented in Australian prisons. Indeed, between 2011 and 2012 alone, the rate of Indigenous women's imprisonment increased by 20%, compared with the 3% increase for non-Indigenous women in the same period (ABS 2012a). This disproportionate number has an effect on both the overall rate of women in prison and the growth of female prisoners over time (Baldry and Cunneen 2014; Gelb 2003).

The final factor contributing to the problem are the inter-jurisdictional differences in law and justice in Australia. Given that this problem affects the growth and constitution of all prison populations, not just female prison populations, it is addressed separately below.

The important inter-jurisdictional differences in Australia's imprisonment rates

Australia was settled by the British Crown as a federation. As such, the Commonwealth of Australia is divided into six states and two mainland territories. Under Australia's Constitution, each state and territory has been empowered to make and administer criminal law and justice. This division of judicial power has resulted in significant variations in the use and extent of imprisonment between different jurisdictions. For example, jurisdictions like Western Australia and the Northern Territory have long surpassed the national average rate of imprisonment of 170 per 100,000 of the population, with current rates sitting at 256 per 100,000 for Western Australia and 821 per 100,000 for the Northern Territory (ABS 2013b). Yet at the same time, states like Victoria and Tasmania have fallen short of the national average, only recently having reached their own peak rates of 120 and 118 per 100,000 of the population, respectively (ABS 2013b).

Such inter-jurisdictional differences are reflected in the composition of prison populations as well. For example, while Aboriginal or Torres Strait Islander peoples are over-represented in both the Northern Territory and Victorian prisons, Aboriginal or Torres Strait Islander peoples comprise 86% of the Northern Territory's prison population, whereas in Victoria, this figure is as low as 7% (ABS 2013b). The differences between Aboriginal and Torres Strait Islander imprisonment in the Northern Territory and Victoria can in part be attributed to the general populations of these jurisdictions. Only 1% of Australians live in the Northern Territory, but 30% of those living in the Northern Territory are Aboriginal and Torres Strait Islander peoples (ABS 2011). In contrast, approximately a quarter of Australians live in Victoria, and yet less than 1% are Aboriginal and Torres Strait Islander peoples (ABS 2013c).

Inter-jurisdictional differences can also be seen in the context of female imprisonment rates. Indeed, while the female imprisonment rates in the Northern Territory and Western Australia sit at 129.7 and 47.0 per 100,000 of the population, respectively, Victoria's female imprisonment rate sits at 16.5 per 100,000 and Tasmania's at 18.9 (ABS 2013b). Differences such as these are better explained in terms of the varied responses to reoffending populations. As previously noted, women are one of the key populations to become enmeshed in a cycle of criminal justice contact, often serving numerous short-term sentences. While this history is common among Australian women in prison, the different ways Australian jurisdictions respond to this cycle can lead to variation in prison population. The Northern Territory and Western Australia, for example, are not only known for having more punitive legislation than other parts of Australia (e.g. enforcing mandatory sentencing for a range of minor offences), but also for having harsher responses to parole breaches, and an increased use of remand for repeat offenders (Hogg 1999; O'Malley 2002). Such inter-jurisdictional differences are an important and unique feature of imprisonment in Australia.

New Zealand

New Zealand has one of the highest imprisonment rates in the developed world (Pratt 2013). This rate has been increasing since the mid-1960s, with its growth divided into two key phases. First, from the mid-1960s to the mid-1980s, there was a gradual increase in New Zealand's prison population. Indeed, over this two-decade period, the number of prisoners in New Zealand only increased by approximately 1,000 people (Criminal Justice Policy Group 1998). Since the mid-1980s, however, New Zealand's prison population has grown at an accelerated rate. Indeed, between 1986 and 2010, New Zealand's rate of imprisonment moved from 80 prisoners per 100,000 of the population, to 200 (Department of Corrections 2014; Pratt 2005; Statistics New Zealand 2012).

The significant movement in New Zealand's imprisonment rate has been labelled New Zealand's 'punitive turn' (Pratt and Clark 2005). This 'turn' is marked by a number of punitive legal changes, with the most notable being the recent enactments of the Bail Act 2000, the Parole Act 2002, the Sentencing Act 2002 and the Victims Rights Act 2002. These Acts were developed on the back of a number of other, smaller legislative changes that occurred in the late 1980s and early 1990s, and together they see more offenders remanded in custody, sentenced to longer stays in prison, with greater use of maximum penalties for violent and sexual offenders, and serving longer portions of their sentence in prison due to greater restrictions on parole eligibility (Pratt and Clark 2005; Smith 2006). Indeed, prison statistics from the March 2014 quarter indicate that over 63% of prisoners in New Zealand's prisons have been sentenced for violent or sexual offences (38.7% and 24.9%, respectively), with 12% of all prisoners serving an indeterminate sentence as a result.

Pratt and colleagues highlight a number of factors contributing to New Zealand's punitive turn. Key factors include: New Zealand's turn towards government deregulation in the 1980s and 1990s (Pratt and Clark 2005); the resulting investment of politicians and the public in issues of crime and punishment as a means for finding unification and social cohesion (Pratt 2005); and the subsequent formalization and momentum behind a range of victim movements, pushing for longer prison sentences and harsher responses to crime (Pratt 1995; Pratt and Clark 2005).

Yet, again, while crude imprisonment figures and overarching explanations such as these provide a useful starting point for understanding the position, use and extent of imprisonment in New Zealand, they mask one of the key problems in New Zealand's penal history: the over-representation of Maori offenders.

The over-representation of Maori offenders

Maori make up approximately 14% of New Zealand's general population, and yet represent approximately 50% of New Zealand's prison population (Statistics New Zealand 2014). Maori women make up 60% of the female prison population (Department of Corrections 2007). Such disproportionate figures are, of course, reflected in the rates of imprisonment as well. While the general rate of imprisonment in New Zealand has recently reached its peak of 200 prisoners per 100,000 of the population, the rate of imprisonment for Maori continues to grow, with over 700 Maori per 100,000 of the Maori population being incarcerated (Department of Corrections 2007).

Like Australia, while the over-representation of Maori in New Zealand's prison system is a long-standing issue, it only really began to gain government attention and response in the late 1980s and 1990s. In the case of New Zealand, this attention was prompted by a broader, government-wide move towards a policy of biculturalism, which came on the back of over 40 years of Maori protests for recognition of their rights, customs, lands, language and culture (see Harris 2004). This move to biculturalism required all government departments, including New Zealand's Department of Justice, to review relationships with Maori, and develop a bicultural approach to service delivery which incorporated and valued Maori perspectives and needs alongside those of non-Maori (see Poata-Smith 1996, 1997).

Since the early 1990s, New Zealand's Departments of Justice and Corrections have made several attempts to implement biculturalism in their justice and prison systems (see for example Jackson 1988; McFarlane-Nathan 1999; Patterson 1992). Yet, despite these efforts, the number of Maori entering New Zealand prisons has continued to grow. Indeed, from 1986 to 2013, the number of Maori starting a prison sentence has almost doubled, as has the number of Maori starting a period of custody on remand (Department of Corrections 2013).

New Zealand criminological scholarship offers two main explanations for both Maori offenders' high imprisonment rates and their persistent over-representation in New Zealand's prison system. The first explanation presents these rates as evidence of the problems with New Zealand's approach to biculturalism (Jackson 1988). Tauri, in particular, argues that the attempts of the Departments of Justice and Corrections to offer bicultural services for Maori have amounted to little more than Maori processes and knowledge being co-opted for the purposes of legitimizing unchanged Western practices towards Maori (Tauri 1998, 1999; Tauri and Webb 2011). It is therefore proposed by scholars like Tauri that the number of Maori entering and returning to prison has continued to grow because of the inability of New Zealand's government to develop appropriate bicultural responses.

The second key explanation offered for Maori offenders' high imprisonment rate is concerned with the different movement of Maori and non-Maori through New Zealand's criminal justice system. As the Department of Corrections (2007) recently acknowledged, while more non-Maori were apprehended for violent offences and property offences in the period 1996 to 2004, more Maori were convicted for these offences (Department of Corrections 2007: 20). Maori are also more likely to receive a custodial sentence than Europeans, with 11% to 13% of convicted Maori sent to prison, as opposed to 7% to 9% of Europeans in the period 1996 to 2004 (Department of Corrections 2007: 22). Like Australia, neither the problem of Maori over-representation in New Zealand prisons, nor the discussion surrounding its persistence show any sign of abating.

The Pacific islands of Australasia

The Pacific islands of Australasia include the Melanesian islands of Vanuatu, Solomon Islands, Fiji, Papua New Guinea and New Caledonia; the Micronesian islands of Nauru and Kiribati; and the Polynesian islands of Tonga, French Polynesia, Western Samoa, Tuvalu and the Cook Islands. As Table 23.6 demonstrates, there is great variation in both the rate of imprisonment of these Pacific islands, and their total prison populations.

Table 23.6 Pacific islands of Australasia prison statistics

	World ranking (highest to lowest)	Rate of imprisonment per 100,000	Total prison population
Western Samoa	60	227	430
Fiji	85	172	1,530
Tonga	95	155	163
French Polynesia	101	147	415
New Caledonia	105	144	382
Nauru	109	140	14
Kiribati	112	138	141
Cook Islands	136	109	25
Tuvalu	164	80	8
Vanuatu	170	76	194
Solomon Islands	190	56	326
Papua New Guinea	197	52	3, 863

Source: adapted from International Centre for Prison Studies 2014.

There has been minimal scholarly work produced to explain the use, extent and position of imprisonment among and across these diverse islands. Additionally, few Pacific islands have created a public and accessible face for their correctional service (there is no website for Papua New Guinea's Correctional Service, for example). Of those that have created a public face – Vanuatu and Fiji, for example – minimal information is provided about the operation of their correctional system. As a result, insight into imprisonment in the Pacific islands of Melanesia, Micronesia and Polynesia remains scarce. There is, however, indication that much like Australia and New Zealand, the prison is largely reserved for serious and dangerous offenders (Adinkrah 1995; Hill 2006). There is also indication that like Australia and New Zealand, the prison systems of Pacific islands nations are marked by Australasia's colonial history. Thus, countries like Papua New Guinea and New Caledonia are reported to have struggled to move from traditional, local practices of law and justice, to those of modern Britain or France (Dinnen 1995; Forster 1991; Law and Dinnen 2010; Ottley and Zorn 1983; Toth 1999). Moreover, countries like Fiji are said to be experiencing the legacy of 'protectionist' and strict migration policies which is, at least according to Adinkrah (1995), contributing to the over-representation of Indigenous Fijian people in Fiji prisons. More research into these and other issues of imprisonment in the Pacific islands of Australasia is sorely needed.

Common themes and pressing issues in Australasian prisons

This second part of the chapter provides a thematic analysis of punishment and prisons in Australasia. Here the common penal trends and themes that cut across Australasian countries are explored. This part is divided into three main sections. In the first, a commentary on prison conditions in Australasia is provided. Second, the trend of reducing reoffending through offender rehabilitation and risk management is outlined. Finally, insight into a pressing issue facing Australasian prison systems is offered.

Prison conditions in Australasia

Prison conditions in Australasia are largely linked to the extent, use and position of imprisonment in Australasian countries. That is to say, the decreasing conditions of Australasian prisons over the past three decades appear largely linked to the increasing number of people entering prisons on remand or through custodial sentences over this same time period. Indeed, as this section will demonstrate, most Australasian prisons have struggled to both physically accommodate the increased numbers of people coming into the system, and manage the increased demand such growth places on their services. As a result, both issues of overcrowding and the related consequences of overcrowded conditions have emerged as key problems in Australasian prisons.

For Australia and New Zealand, issues of overcrowding have become a prime issue of concern. This is because the majority of prisons in these countries are operating at or above capacity, and have been doing so for several decades (Harding 1987; Stanley 2011). Australia and New Zealand have responded to this common problem in somewhat divergent ways.

Australia has attempted to address and reduce overcrowding in its prisons by accommodating prisoners elsewhere. Thus, for example, states like Queensland and South Australia have made use of secure facilities such as police watch-houses, or less full prisons in order to accommodate their growing prison numbers (Campbell 2012; Niarchos 2008). In a similar vein, states like Victoria, New South Wales and Western Australia have responded through investment in building new prisons, or new prison accommodation, such as repurposed shipping containers (Victorian Ombudsman 2014). Such approaches to overcrowding have been met with significant criticism, with particular concern raised about the capacity to address the principles of unit management while using repurposed shipping containers, as well as the excessive temperatures such facilities can reach (Grant 2013).

For New Zealand, double bunking has become the preferred method for addressing growing imprisonment numbers. Indeed, from 2009–11 the Department of Corrections increased the number or double-bunked cells by 75%. As a result, by 2011, 1,038 cells were shared by two or more prisoners (Department of Corrections 2012). New Zealand's approach to double bunking has also been met with some criticism, with concerns raised about the excessive temperature of already small prison cells (Human Rights Commission 2009), and the safe placement of prisoners (Stanley 2011), especially those with mental illness (NZPA 2008).

Of course, while issues and concerns about potentially inhumane prison conditions have come to the fore in recent discussions about prison overcrowding, it should be noted that these issues and concerns are situated within a much longer and broader trend in Australia and New Zealand towards punitiveness. Indeed, over the past decade, a number of Australian and New Zealand scholars have raised concerns about the manner in which prisons and prison management in these countries have followed the global trend towards the 'new punitiveness' (see Pratt et al. 2005), with several focusing on the rise of supermax prisons in Australia and New Zealand, and the associated questions these high security prisons raise about the inhumane organization and use of prison space (Brown 2005; Brown and Carlton 2013; Carlton 2006).

While prison overcrowding has emerged as a growing issue for several prison systems in the Pacific islands (Adinkrah 1995; Hill 2006), overcrowding *per se* is not the primary problem affecting prison conditions in the islands. Rather, it is the consequences of overcrowding that are of primary concern. This is because overcrowded prisons exacerbate a number of existing problems with the prison conditions of Pacific island prisons.

As previously noted, the majority of Pacific islands in Australasia have a colonial history. This history has left its mark in many ways, including prison accommodation, with countries like Papua New Guinea, Fiji, Vanuatu and others utilizing prisons and watch-houses built in the colonial era. As can be expected, such buildings have deteriorated over time, and as a result, several have come under scrutiny for being damp, inappropriate and even dangerous (Amnesty International 1998).

The growing number of people entering prisons each year not only compounds the pressures placed on deteriorating prison settings, but further appears to facilitate new concerns. For example, with increasing demand placed on old, typically septic systems, several prisons in the Pacific islands have been reported as overflowing with excrement and urine (Law and Dinnen 2010). Such unsanitary conditions are not only inhumane, but are viewed as having the potential to facilitate the transmission of infectious diseases such as tuberculosis, hepatitis, dysentery and typhoid.

Infectious diseases are already experienced in increased rates within many Pacific island countries and their prisons (Jurgens et al. 2011; Law and Dinnen 2010; Levy 1999). While unsanitary conditions are seen to play a role, so too are other factors such as unsafe sex and unhygienic tattoo practices (Buchanan-Aruwafu 2007). Prison overcrowding has been reported as exacerbating these factors as well. Specifically, it is argued that the inability of Pacific island nations to hire and train sufficient numbers of staff to monitor the health and well-being of the growing number of prison inmates contributes to a range of problematic practices (Law and Dinnen 2010).

Given the strain and complications prison overcrowding poses for the prison sector, considerable attention has been paid to developing approaches that offer any form of redress. One approach that has received significant investment is the practices and programmes associated with reducing reoffending.

Reducing reoffending

Reducing reoffending has become a (if not the) key objective for Australasian correctional systems over the past few decades. Primarily this objective has been approached through the development and delivery of offender rehabilitation programmes. Australasia is not unique in this regard. The past three decades have seen correctional agencies in Canada, the UK and parts of the USA turn to the practice of offender rehabilitation as a means for managing their offender population (see Spivakovsky 2013). This turn comes on the back of an emergent and now expansive body of correctional literature which claims to provide a sound evidence base for the effective classification and treatment of offenders (see Andrews and Bonta 2010 for details). While largely in line with this body of evidence-based practice, there are some differences worth noting among the ways in which Australasian countries have approached the task of reducing reoffending.

Australia and New Zealand have taken similar approaches towards offender rehabilitation. That is to say, both countries approach offender rehabilitation from the perspective of managing the risk of reoffending. In practice, this means two main things occur in Australian and New Zealand prisons under the guise of offender rehabilitation. First, all offenders entering the correctional systems of these countries are subjected to a form of risk assessment. Such assessments are designed both to identify the number and nature of static and dynamic risk factors that offenders possess, and subsequently to classify offenders according to both the risk they pose and the correlating level of intervention they require: low, medium or high (Andrews and Bonta 2010). Second, all correctional programming offered under the guise of offender rehabilitation has a single goal: to reduce and manage offenders' risk of reoffending through the targeted management of both generic risk factors (i.e. factors associated with offending behaviour) and specific risk factors (i.e. factors associated with specific offences or offender populations) (Andrews and Bonta 2010).

In Australia, there is a combined total of over 120 risk-focused offender rehabilitation programmes currently offered across the states and territories. The most common programmes include those that enhance cognitive skills (18 provided across Australia), or target drug and alcohol use (30 provided across Australia) and sex offenders (26 provided across Australia), with some jurisdictions further offering Indigenous- and women-specific programmes (ten each across Australia) (Heseltine et al. 2011). There are also programmes that address violent offenders (11 provided across Australia), domestic violence (nine provided across Australia), anger management (five provided across Australia) and victim awareness (two provided across Australia) (ibid.). Most of these programmes either replicate or adapt offender rehabilitation programmes and practices that have been developed in Canada, the UK and the USA.

While unable to reach the same combined total of rehabilitation programmes as Australia, the New Zealand Department of Corrections provides a somewhat more comprehensive suite of offerings. Indeed, not only does the Department of Corrections provide both offender rehabilitation programmes and dedicated specialist units for rehabilitation, but both programmes and units are built upon research and evaluations conducted by the Department of Corrections into the specific, localized needs of New Zealand's offender populations (see Bakker et al. 1999). As a result, New Zealand's Department of Corrections runs a range of motivational-focused programmes, offence-focused programmes, and drug and alcohol interventions for male, female, Maori, Pasifika and young offenders, as well as Maori Focus Units, Pacific Focus Units, Self-Care Units (for prisoners who have full-time work under the Department's release to work programme), Violence Prevention Units, Specialist Treatment Units (for high risk violent and sex offenders), and the recently added Mothers with Babies Units.

While offender rehabilitation remains a key focus for many of the correctional services in the Pacific islands of Australasia, few appear to share Australia and New Zealand's emphasis on risk management. Instead, the goal of offender rehabilitation has taken a far more vocational and skills-based tone, with an emphasis on preparing offenders for their return and resettlement in society. Thus, for example, Tonga's Prison Department offers programmes in farming, arts and crafts, engineering, carpentry, and 'revival programmes' (Tonga Prisons Department 2014). Vanuatu's Department of Correctional Services offers vocational-based rehabilitation programmes which teach skills such as joinery and construction, art and woodwork, as well as spiritual-based rehabilitation programmes which include both church activities, and learning about *kastom* (traditional practices) from local chiefs (Vanuatu Correctional Services 2013). Fiji's Corrections Service offers educational and vocational rehabilitation programmes, as well as programmes designed to foster parenting skills and address drug and alcohol use (Fiji Corrections Service 2014). There is little information currently available about the operation or outcomes of these countries' rehabilitative efforts. Yet there is indication that these countries are increasingly turning towards the objectives of managing risk (Fiji Corrections Service 2014; Tonga Prisons Department 2014; Vanuatu Correctional Services 2013).

Cognitive impairment: an emergent and pressing issue in Australasian prisons

The purpose of this chapter has been to provide an overview of the use and conditions of imprisonment in Australasia. While it has been difficult, if not impossible, to capture all approaches towards imprisonment and punishment in Australasia over the past 30 or so years, the previous sections of this chapter have provided insight into the key features of Australasian prisons and punishment. There is, however, one final issue that needs to be addressed: the emergent and pressing issue of the disproportionate presence of people with cognitive impairments and/or mental illness in Australasian prison systems.

Over the past decade, a number of Australasian countries have begun to map the nature and prevalence of cognitive impairment and mental illness in their prison population. Doing so has revealed the complex and often co-morbid array of diagnoses present in prison populations. For example, in Australia, approximately 65% of prisoners have sustained a traumatic brain injury (TBI) at some time in their lives (Perkes et al. 2011), with some Australian states higher, such as New South Wales reporting 82% (Schofield et al. 2006). Additionally, a recent survey of Australian prisoners indicates that 31% of prison entrants have received some form of medical intervention for a mental health disorder in their lifetime (AIHW 2012), which is approximately 2.5 times higher than those in the general population (ABS 2010).

Similarly concerning statistics can be found in New Zealand. Barnfield and Leathem's (1998) study, for example, found that 86% of inmates in a New Zealand prison had sustained a TBI at some time in their lives. More recently, a national study of the prevalence of psychiatric disorders in New Zealand prisons revealed that compared with the general population, there is a markedly elevated prevalence of rates of major mental disorders in the prison population, with key concerns being substance misuse, psychotic disorders, major depression, bipolar disorder, obsessive-compulsive disorder and post-traumatic stress disorder (Brinded et al. 2001). Finally, while the majority of the Pacific island nations are yet to provide a statistical account of the problem, the growing number of people with mental illness in prison has been raised as a concern for Tonga, Papua New Guinea, Vanuatu, Fiji and Kiribati (Japan International Cooperation Agency 2002; Roberts 2007).

Of course, it is important to note that the population-based issues facing Australasian prisons are not mutually exclusive. Thus, for example, there is a higher proportion of women with mental health disorders in prison than men (Butler et al. 2006). Moreover, while the rate of TBI among New Zealand's male prisoner population is 64%, it increases by almost 10 percentage points (to 73%) among Maori men in prison (National Health Committee 2010). Such intersections multiply the complexity of issues facing Australasian prison systems at this time.

Australia and New Zealand have taken a multi-pronged approach to addressing the growing number of people entering the prison with cognitive impairments and/or mental illness. Primarily this approach has focused on supporting people with cognitive impairments and/or mental illness during their contact with police (see for example Carswell and Paulin 2008 on the Mental Health Initiative at the Rotorua Police Station in New Zealand), or by implementing court-based processes that might divert people with cognitive impairments and/or mental illness from prison (see for example the Australian state of Victoria's Assessment and Referral Court List). Yet while approaches such as these have the potential to impact upon the number of people with cognitive impairments entering the prison system going forward, they have no effect on the disproportionate number of people with impairments already within the system. These disproportionate figures have been met with questions about both the appropriateness of criminal justice interventions for vulnerable populations (see for example Butler et al. 2005; Lamberti et al. 2001; Prins 2011; Spivakovsky forthcoming), and the capacity of the criminal justice system to reduce the offending behaviour of this population (see for example Abram and Teplin 1991; Corbit 2006; Rock 2001; Rotter and Carr 2011). As such, addressing these disproportionate figures remains a key concern for policymakers, service providers, researchers and the community alike.

Conclusions

The last three decades have been a time of significant change in Australasian prison systems. This chapter has attempted to capture some of the key changes that have occurred, as well as explore some of the core factors contributing to their occurrence. It has offered insight into the growing number of people entering Australasian prisons, as well as the specific populations who appear within these prisons more often. It has also reflected upon the impact such growth has had on the conditions and operation of prisons in Australasia. In doing so, this chapter has located Australasia within the wider penal sphere, and offered new perspective on the localized manifestation and effects of the global trend towards punitiveness and incarceration.

Bibliography

Abram, K. and Teplin, L. (1991) 'Co-occurring disorders among mentally ill jail detainees: Implications for public policy', *American Psychologist* 46(10): 1039–1045.

ABS (Australian Bureau of Statistics) (2009) *Prisoners in Australia, 2009*, Cat. No. 4517, Canberra: ABS.

ABS (Australian Bureau of Statistics) (2010) *National Health Survey: Summary of results, 2007–2008 (Reissue)*, Cat. No. 4364, Canberra: ABS.

ABS (Australian Bureau of Statistics) (2011) *Regional Statistics, Northern Territory, Mar 2011*, Cat. No. 1362.7, Canberra: ABS.

ABS (Australian Bureau of Statistics) (2012a) *Prisoners in Australia, 2012*, Cat. No. 4517, Canberra: ABS.

ABS (Australian Bureau of Statistics) (2012b) *Year Book of Australia, 2012*, Cat. No. 1301.0, Canberra: ABS.

ABS (Australian Bureau of Statistics) (2012c) *Women Prisoners Increasing at a Faster Rate than Men*, Media Release 202/2012, Canberra: ABS.

ABS (Australian Bureau of Statistics) (2013a) *Australian Prisoner Numbers Reach 30,000 for the First Time*, Media Release 219/2013, Canberra: ABS.

ABS (Australian Bureau of Statistics) (2013b) *Prisoners in Australia, 2013*, Cat. No. 4517, Canberra: ABS.

ABS (Australian Bureau of Statistics) (2013c) *Estimates of Aboriginal and Torres Strait Islander Australians, June 2011*, Cat. No. 3238.0.55.00, Canberra: ABS.

ABS (Australian Bureau of Statistics) (2014) *Australian Demographic Statics, Dec 2013*, Cat. No. 3101.0, Canberra: ABS.

Adinkrah, M. (1995) *Crime, Deviance and Delinquency in Fiji*, Suva: Fiji Council of Social Services.

AIHW (Australian Institute of Health and Welfare) (2012) *The Mental Health of Prison Entrants in Australia 2010*, Bulletin no. 104, Cat. No. AUS 158, Canberra: AIHW.

Amnesty International (1998) *Vanuatu: No Safe Place for Prisoners*, AI Index: ASA 44/01/98.

Andrews, D. and Bonta, J. (2010) *The Psychology of Criminal Conduct*, fifth edn, Cincinnati, OH: Anderson Publications.

Anthony, T. (2013) *Indigenous People, Crime and Punishment*, New York: Routledge.

Bakker, L., O'Malley, J. and Riley, D. (1999) *Risk of Reconviction: Statistical Models Predicting Four Types of Re-offending*, Wellington: New Zealand Department of Corrections.

Baldry, E. and Cunneen, C. (2014) 'Imprisoned indigenous women and the shadow of colonial patriarchy', *Australian and New Zealand Journal of Criminology* 47(2): 276–298.

Barnfield, T. and Leathem, J. (1998) 'Incidence and outcomes of traumatic brain injury and substance abuse in a New Zealand prison population', *Brain Injury* 12(6): 455–466.

Blagg, H. (2008) *Crime, Aboriginality and the Decolonisation of Justice*, Annandale: Hawkins Press.

Brinded, P., Simpson, A., Laidlaw, T., Fairley, N. and Malcolm, F. (2001) 'Prevalence of psychiatric disorders in New Zealand prisons: A national study', *Australian and New Zealand Journal of Psychiatry* 35(2): 166–173.

Brown, D. (2005) 'Continuity, rupture, or just more of the "volatile and contradictory"? Glimpses of New South Wales' penal practice behind and through the discursive', in J. Pratt, D. Brown, M. Brown, S. Hallsworth and W. Morrison (eds) *The New Punitiveness: Trends, theories, perspectives*, Cullumpton: Willan.

Brown, D. and Carlton, B. (2013) 'From "Secondary Punishment" to "Supermax": The human costs of high-security regimes in Australia', in J. Ross (ed.) *The Globalization of Supermax Prisons*, New Brunswick, NJ: Rutgers University Press.

Buchanan-Aruwafu, H. (2007) *An Integrated Picture: HIV Risk and Vulnerability in the Pacific – Research Gaps, Priorities and Approaches*, New Caledonia: Secretariat of Pacific Communities.

Butler, T., Allnutt, S., Cain, D., Owens, D. and Muller, C. (2005) 'Mental disorder in the New South Wales prisoner population', *Australian and New Zealand Journal of Psychiatry* 39(5): 407–413.

Butler, T., Andrew, G., Allnutt, S., Sakashita, C., Smith, N. and Basson, J. (2006) 'Mental disorders in Australian prisoners: A comparison with a community sample', *Australian and New Zealand Journal of Psychiatry* 40: 272–276.

Campbell, F. (2012) 'Overcrowding in Queensland prisons', *Indigenous Law Bulletin* 7(28): 12–15.

Carlen, P. (1983) *Women's Imprisonment: A Study in Social Control*, Boston, MA: Routledge.

Carlen, P. (1994) 'Why study women's imprisonment? Or anyone else's?', *British Journal of Criminology* 34: 131–140.

Carlen, P. and Tombs, J. (2006) 'Reconfigurations of penality: The ongoing case of the women's imprisonment and reintegration industries', *Theoretical Criminology* 10(3): 337–360.

Carlton, B. (2006) 'From H Division to Abu Ghraib: Regimes of justification and the historical proliferation of state-inflicted terror and violence in maximum-security', *Social Justice* 33(4): 15–36.

Carlton, B. and Segrave, M. (eds) (2013) *Women Exiting Prison: Critical Essays on Gender, Post-release Support and Survival*, Abingdon: Routledge.

Carswell, S. and Paulin, J. (2008) *Evaluation of the Mental Health Initiative at the Rotorua Police Station*, Wellington: New Zealand Police.

Chesney-Lind, M. (1991) 'Patriarchy, prisons, and jails: A critical look at trends in women's incarceration', *The Prison Journal* 71(1): 51–67.

Cook, S. and Davies, S. (eds) (1999) *Harsh Punishment: International Experiences of Women's Imprisonment*, Indiana: Northeastern University Press.

Corbit, K. (2006) 'Inadequate and inappropriate mental health treatment and minority over-representation in the juvenile justice system', *Hastings Race and Poverty Law Journal* 75(3): 75–94.

Criminal Justice Policy Group (1998) *The Use of Imprisonment in New Zealand*, Wellington: Ministry of Justice.

Cunneen, C. (2006) 'Racism, discrimination and the over-representation of Indigenous people in the criminal justice system: Some conceptual and explanatory issues', *Current Issues in Criminal Justice* 17(3): 329–347.

Cunneen, C. (2011a) 'Indigeneity, sovereignty and the law: Challenging the process of criminalisation', in *University of New South Wales Faculty of Law Research Series*, Paper 11, New South Wales: University of New South Wales.

Cunneen, C. (2011b) 'Punishment: Two decades of penal expansionism and its effects on Indigenous imprisonment', *Australian Indigenous Law Review* 15(1): 8–17.

Cunneen, C., Baldry, E., Brown, D., Schwartz, M., Steel, A. and Brown, M. (2013) *Penal Culture and Hyperincarceration: The Revival of the Prison*, Aldershot: Ashgate.

Cunneen, C. and McDonald, D. (1997) *Keeping Aboriginal and Torres Strait Islander People Out of Custody: An Evaluation of the Implementation of the Recommendations of the Royal Commission in Aboriginal Deaths in Custody*, Canberra: Office of Public Affairs, Aboriginal and Torres Strait Islander Commission.

Department of Corrections (2007) *Over-representation of Maori in the Criminal Justice System: An Exploratory Report*, Wellington: Department of Corrections.

Department of Corrections (2012) *Prisoner Double-bunking: Perceptions and Impacts – Findings from a Two-phase Research Investigation*, Wellington: Department of Corrections.

Department of Corrections (2013) *Trends in the Offender Population*, Wellington: Department of Corrections.

Department of Corrections (2014) *Prison Facts and Statistics – March 2014*, Wellington: Department of Corrections.

Department of Justice, Department for Community Development, Department of Indigenous Affairs, Western Australia Police Service, Aboriginal and Torres Strait Islander Commission, Aboriginal and Torres Strait Islander Services and Aboriginal Legal Service of Western Australia (2004) *Western Australian Aboriginal Justice Agreement*, Perth: Western Australian Department of Justice.

Department of Justice and Department of Human Services (2004) *Victorian Aboriginal Justice Agreement: Phase One*, Melbourne: Victorian Department of Justice.

Dinnen, S. (1995) 'Papua New Guinea in 1994 – The Most Turbulent Year?', *Current Issues in Criminal Justice* 6(3): 395–407.

Fiji Corrections Service (2014) *Rehabilitation Programs*, www.corrections.org.fj/pages.cfm/rehabilitation-programs (accessed 15 August 2014).

Finnane, M. and Richards, J. (2010) 'Aboriginal violence and state response: Histories, policies, legacies in Queensland 1860–1940', *Australian and New Zealand Journal of Criminology* 43(2): 238–262.

Forster, C. (1991) 'French penal policy and the origins of the French presence in New Caledonia', *The Journal of Pacific History* 26(2): 135–150.

Gelb, K. (2003) 'Women in prison: Why is the rate of incarceration increasing?' Paper presented at the conference Evaluation in Crime and Justice: Trends and Methods, www.aic.gov.au/conferences/evaluations/gelb.html (accessed 13 August 2014).

Grant, E. (2013) '"Pack 'em, rack 'em and stack 'em": The appropriateness of the use and reuse of shipping containers for prison accommodation', *Australasian Journal of Construction Economics and Building* 13(2): 35–44.

Harding, R. (1987) 'Prison overcrowding: Correctional policies and political constraints', *Australian and New Zealand Journal of Criminology* 20: 16–32.

Harris, A. (2004) *Hikoi: Forty Years of Māori Protest*, Wellington: Huia Publishers.

Heseltine, K., Day, A. and Sarre, R. (2011) *Prison-based Correctional Offender Rehabilitation Programs: The 2009 National Picture in Australia*, AIC Reports: Research and Public Policy Series no. 112, Canberra: Australian Institute of Criminology.

Hill, G. (2006) 'Prisons in paradise: The correctional service of Tonga', *Corrections Compendium* 31(4): 18–20.

Hogg, R. (1999) 'Mandatory sentencing laws and the symbolic politics of law and order', *University of New South Wales Law Journal* 22(1): 262–266.

Human Rights Commission (2009) *Monitoring Places of Detention: Second Annual Report of Activities under the Optional Protocol to the Convention against Torture (OPCAT) – 1 July 2008 to 30 June 2009*, Wellington: HRC.

International Centre for Prison Studies (2014) 'Highest to Lowest – Prison Population Total', www.prisonstudies.org/highest-to-lowest/prison-population-total (accessed 15 August 2014).

Jackson, M. (1988) *The Māori and the Criminal Justice System He Whaipaanga Hou – A New Perspective: Part 2*, Wellington: New Zealand Department of Justice.

Japan International Cooperation Agency (2002) 'Country Profile on Disability, Kingdom of Tonga', siteresources.worldbank.org/DISABILITY/Resources/Regions/East-Asia-Pacific/JICA_Tonga.pdf (accessed 13 August 2014).

Jowitt, A. and Cain, T. (eds) (2010) *Passage of Change: Law, Society and Governance in the Pacific*, Canberra: ANU ePress.

Jurgens, R., Nowak, M. and Day, M. (2011) 'HIV and incarceration: Prisons and detention', *Journal of the International Aids Society* 14(1): 26–43.

Lamberti, J., Weisman, R., Schwarzkopf, S., Price, N., Ashton, R. and Trompeter, J. (2001) 'The mentally ill in jails and prisons: Towards an integrated model of preventions', *Psychiatric Quarterly* 79(1): 63–77.

Law, G. and Dinnen, S. (2010) 'Prisons and HIV in Papua New Guinea', in V. Luker and S. Dinnen (eds) *Civic Insecurity: Law, Order and HIV in Papua New Guinea*, Canberra: ANU ePress.

Levy, M. (1999) 'Tuberculosis control practices in some prison systems of the Asia-Pacific Region, 1997', *International Journal of Tuberculosis and Lung Disease* 3(9): 769–773.

McFarlane-Nathan, G. (1999) *FReMO Framework for Reducing Māori Offending: How to Achieve Quality in Policy and Services to Reduce Māori Offending and Enhance Māori Aspirations*, Wellington: Psychological Service, New Zealand Department of Corrections.

Moore, L. and Scraton, P. (2014) *The Incarceration of Women: Punishing Bodies, Breaking Spirits*, London: Palgrave Macmillan.

National Health Committee (2010) *Health in Justice: Kia Piki te Ora, Kia Tika! – Improving the Health of Prisoners and their Families and Whānau: He whakapiki i te ora o ngā mauhere me ō rātou whanau*, Wellington: Ministry of Health.

New South Wales Aboriginal Justice Advisory Council (2003) *New South Wales Aboriginal Justice Plan: Beyond Justice 2004–2014*, Sydney: New South Wales Aboriginal Justice Advisory Council.

Niarchos, N. (2008) 'The state of prisons in South Australia: A systemic failure', *Law Society Bulletin* 30(1): 14–18.

NZPA (2008) 'Officers, Mentally Ill in Danger of Prison Overcrowding: Union', 3 December, www.voxy.co.nz/national/officers-mentally-ill-danger-prison-overcrowding-union/5/6086.

O'Malley, P. (2002) 'Globalizing risk? Distinguishing styles of "neo-liberal" criminal justice in Australia and the USA', *Criminology and Criminal Justice* 2(2): 205–222.

Ottley, B. and Zorn, J. (1983) 'Criminal law in Papua New Guinea: Code, custom and the courts in conflict', *The American Journal of Comparative Law* 31(2): 251–300.

Patterson, J. (1992) 'A Māori concept of collective responsibility', in G. Oddie and R. Perret (eds) *Justice, Ethics and New Zealand Society*, Auckland: Oxford University Press.

Perkes, I., Schofield, P., Butler, T. and Hollis, S. (2011) 'Traumatic brain injury rates and sequelae: A comparison of prisoners with a matched community sample in Australia', *Brain Injury* 25: 131–141.

Poata-Smith, E. (1996) 'He pokeke uenuku, tu ai: The evolution of contemporary Māori protest', in P. Spoonley, D. Pearson and C. Macpherson (eds) *Nga Patai: Racism and Ethnic Relations in Aotearoa/New Zealand*, Palmerston North: The Dunmore Press.

Poata-Smith, E. (1997) 'The political economy of inequality between Māori and Pakeha', in C. Rudd and B. Roper (eds) *The Political Economy of New Zealand*, Auckland: Oxford University Press.

Pratt, J. (1995) 'Dangerousness, risk and technologies of power', *Australian and New Zealand Journal of Criminology* 28(1): 3–31.

Pratt, J. (2005) 'The dark side of paradise: Explaining New Zealand's high imprisonment', *British Journal of Criminology* 46(4): 541–560.

Pratt, J. (2013) *A Punitive Society: Falling Crime and Rising Imprisonment in New Zealand*, Wellington: Bridget Williams Books.

Pratt, J., Brown, D., Brown, M., Hallsworth, S. and Morrison, W. (2005) *The New Punitiveness: Trends, theories, perspectives*, Cullumpton: Willan.

Pratt, J. and Clark, M. (2005) 'Penal populism in New Zealand', *Punishment and Society* 7(3): 303–322.

Prins, S. (2011) 'Does transinstitutionalisation explain the overrepresentation of people with serious mental illness in the criminal justice system?', *Community Mental Health Journal* 47: 716–722.

Roberts, G. (2007) 'Masculinity, mental health and violence in Papua New Guinea, Vanuatu, Fiji and Kiribati', *Health Promotion in the Pacific* 14(2): 35–41.

Rock, M. (2001) 'Emerging issues with mentally ill offenders: Causes and social consequences', *Administration and Policy in Mental Health* 28(3): 165–180.

Rotter, M. and Carr, W. (2011) 'Targeting criminal recidivism in mentally ill offenders: Structured clinical approaches', *Community Mental Health Journal* 47: 723–726.

Royal Commission into Aboriginal Deaths in Custody (1991) *Royal Commission into Aboriginal Deaths in Custody Final Report*, Canberra: Australian Government Publishing Service.

Schofield, P., Butler, T., Hollis, S., Smith, N., Lee, S. and Kelso, W. (2006) 'Traumatic brain injury among Australian prisoners: Rates, recurrence and sequelae', *Brain Injury* 20(5): 499–506.

Smith, L. (2006) *Beyond the Holding Tank: Pathways to Rehabilitative and Restorative Prison Policy*, Manukau City: The Salvation Army Social Policy and Parliamentary Unit.

Snowball, L. and Weatherburn, D. (2007) 'Does racial bias in sentencing contribute to Indigenous over-representation in prison?', *The Australian and New Zealand Journal of Criminology* 40(3): 272–290.

Solinger, R., Johnson, P., Raimon, M., Reynolds, T. and Tapia, R. (2010) *Interrupted Life: Experiences of Incarcerated Women in the United States*, Berkeley: University of California Press.

Spivakovsky, C. (2013) *Racialized Correctional Governance: The Mutual Constructions of Race and Criminal Justice*, Surrey: Ashgate.

Spivakovsky, C. (forthcoming) 'From punishment to protection: Containing and controlling the lives of people with disabilities in human rights', *Punishment & Society*.

Stanley, E. (2011) *Human Rights and Prisons: A Review to the Human Rights Commission*, Wellington: New Zealand Human Rights Commission.

Statistics New Zealand (2012) *The Numbers of Justice*, Wellington: Statistics New Zealand.

Statistics New Zealand (2014) *New Zealand's Prison Population*, Wellington: Statistics New Zealand.

Steel, A. (2010) 'Bail in Australia: Legislative introduction and amendment since 1970', in *Australia and New Zealand Critical Criminology Conference Proceedings*, Sydney: University of Sydney.

Stephens, J., Young, C., Steel, A. and Schwartz, M. (2012) *Imprisonment Rates: Statistics and Charts*, Australian Prisons Project, cypp.unsw.edu.au/sites/ypp.unsw.edu.au/files/APP%20-%20Imprisonment%20Rates%20Statistics%20and%20Charts.pdf (accessed 15 August 2014).

Tauri, J. (1998) 'Family group conferencing: A case-study of the indigenisation of New Zealand's justice system', *Current Issues in Criminal Justice* 10(2): 168–182.

Tauri, J. (1999) 'Explaining recent innovations in New Zealand's criminal justice system: Empowering Māori or biculturalising the state?', *Australian and New Zealand Journal of Criminology* 32(2): 153–167.

Tauri, J. and Webb, R. (2011) 'The Waitangi Tribunal and the regulation of Māori protest', *New Zealand Sociology* 26: 21–41.

Tonga Prisons Department (2014) 'Rehabilitation Programs', www.prisons.gov.to/index.php/rehabilitation-programs (accessed 15 August 2014).

Toth, S. (1999) 'Colonisation or incarceration?', *The Journal of Pacific History* 34(1): 59–74.

Tuvalu Statistics (2013) *Tuvalu Statistics at a Glance*, Tuvalu: Tuvalu Central Statistics Division.

US Department of State (2013) *Country Reports on Human Rights Practices for 2013: Tuvalu*, Washington, DC: Bureau of Democracy, Human Rights and Labour.

Vanuatu Correctional Services (2013) 'Rehabilitation', vanuatucorrectionalservices.gov.vu/rehabilitation.html (accessed 15 August 2014).

Victorian Ombudsman (2014) *Investigation into Deaths and Harm in Custody, March 2014, Session 2010–2014*, P.P. No. 310, Melbourne: Victorian Government Printer.

Weatherburn, D. (2006) 'Disadvantage, drugs and gaol: Re-thinking indigenous over-representation in prison', proceedings from the Conference of the Australasian Society on Alcohol and other Drugs, Cairns, 5–8 November.

Weatherburn, D. and Fitzgerald, J. (2007) 'Reducing Aboriginal over-representation in prison: A rejoinder to Chris Cunneen', *Current Issues in Criminal Justice* 18(2): 366–370.

Weatherburn, D., Fitzgerald, J. and Hua, J. (2003a) 'Reducing Aboriginal over-representation in prison', *Australian Journal of Public Administration* 62(3): 65–73.

Weatherburn, D., Lind, B. and Hua, J. (2003b) 'Contact with the New South Wales court and prison systems: The influence of age, indigenous status and gender', in *Crime and Justice Bulletin 78*, Sydney: New South Wales Bureau of Crime Statistics and Research.

Weatherburn, D., Quinn, M. and Rich, G. (1987) 'Drug charges, bail decisions and absconding', *Australian and New Zealand Journal of Criminology* 20(2): 95–109.

Weatherburn, D., Snowball, L. and Hunter, B. (2006) 'The economic and social factors underpinning Indigenous contact with the justice system: Results from the 2002 NATSISS survey', in *Crime and Justice Bulletin 104*, Sydney: New South Wales Bureau of Crime Statistics and Research.

Chapter 24

Prisons in Africa

Andrew M. Jefferson and Tomas Max Martin[1]

Introduction

Prisons in Africa are understudied and therefore often misunderstood. Put less bluntly, prisons in Africa are often approached in a particular way using a particular analytic lens with a strongly normative orientation. As a consequence, the picture is fragmented and blurred. From a social scientific perspective this is unsatisfactory.

In this chapter we will seek to cast some light on what we do and do not know about prisons in Africa. The sections of the chapter will describe the use of imprisonment, prison conditions and the position of imprisonment in the wider criminal justice system in sub-Saharan Africa, and conclude with a brief summary of the trends and themes that we have presented. The chapter serves less as a review of the available literature and more as a discussion of how prisons in Africa might be approached analytically. Our proposal is that there is an increasing need for fine-grained, richly textured social-scientific accounts of prisons *as they are* to complement the multiple accounts (mostly in the form of critical reports of various genres) framed in terms of *how they ought to be*.

As will become evident, prisons in or across Africa vary – often quite dramatically both in terms of use and conditions. Yet there are also similarities. One way of explaining patterns of similarity and difference is to trace local and regional histories of how prisons change and endure. This is beyond the scope of this chapter. However, we will point to *history* (including the role of histories of colonialism) and *development* (including the role and power of the discourse of human rights, good governance and democratization) as two important entry points for context-sensitive analyses of prisons in Africa.

Until recently there has been relatively little literature on prisons in Africa (with few exceptions, see below). What little literature there was contributes to a particular conception of what prisons are – places of squalor, denigration, ill health, poor hygiene and illegitimate violence. That is, they are perceived as failing institutions, embodying deviant states in need of rehabilitation (Jefferson 2005). Much of this literature is so-called 'grey literature' (human rights reports and so on), informed by normative concerns about violations of rights and failure to conform to international standards and norms.

Within the last decade an alternative body of work has emerged which attempts to take prisons in Africa seriously as objects of descriptive, empirical scrutiny. With a field-work-based, ethnographic orientation, this work has aimed for understanding through careful documentation of the texture and grain of everyday dynamics and relations rather than for exposure through exposé. The study of the non-Western prison is a relatively new niche area within prison studies. Studies of prisons in Africa have been central to this development – but not the whole of Africa. An ethnographic orientation calls us to resist the temptation to overgeneralize and we must sound a note of caution even about the overview provided in this chapter. We do not consider the prisons of North Africa around which there is little scholarly work. We limit ourselves to sub-Saharan Africa. However, available knowledge is still scant.

The prisons *we* know best first-hand are in Nigeria, Sierra Leone (West Africa) and Uganda (East Africa). Our studies have focused on prisons in transition. Nigeria was identified as being of particular interest in 2000 because of an apparent shift from authoritarian to democratic rule after decades of more or less continuous military dictatorship. The prisons of Sierra Leone were of particular interest in the wake of the rebel war. Ugandan prisons were approached as illustrative examples of best human rights practice during the equivocal instantiation of liberal democratic reform. Studying prisons during times of transition reminds us that prisons change or mutate even as they endure and persist.[2]

So it is with some hesitation and multiple provisos that we take on a task that we realize may nevertheless be interpreted as an overview of prisons across the African continent. Such an overview is not yet possible. There is a huge diversity across penal establishments in Africa that contemporary social science has so far been unable to capture and to which non-governmental organization (NGO) reports fail to pay due attention. Often basic curiosity is missing and diagnoses and solutions are predictable and unimaginative. For example, the abuses prevalent in prisons in Africa are analysed as caused by ignorance or lack of knowledge; the proposed solution is additional training and better recruitment of personnel. Or incidents of violence and corruption are presented as the bad behaviour of errant 'bad apples' rather than symptoms of dysfunctional and neglected systems. Rarely are prison systems in Africa approached as the 'poisoned orchards' (Gregory 2009) that they seem to be, and the rationales behind these systems and the people populating them are seldom subject to study in their own right. What we see is an epistemological bias (an orientation to other people's ignorance and lack of knowledge) with no epistemological basis (that is no genuine grounding in empirically based knowledge).

What do we know?

Unsurprisingly, there are exceptions to this general lack of prison scholarship in Africa. The most well-studied prisons in sub-Saharan Africa are the South African prisons. There may be a number of reasons for this, including South Africa's rather unique status among African countries, higher levels of urbanization and industrialization, the role of prisons in the maintenance and reproduction of the apartheid regime and the resultant prioritization rather than neglect of the carceral apparatus (cf. Gillespie 2011). The apartheid state needed prisons to assert and maintain control over the non-white population and it did this through financial investment in a relatively sophisticated, security-focused apparatus. Following apartheid's formal demise and the transition to a democracy headed by former iconic Robben Island prisoner Nelson Mandela, it makes sense that critical attention was paid to the prisons sector.

A number of organizations were at the forefront of both reform-oriented advocacy and analysis of prisons in South Africa, for example the Centre for the Study of Violence and Reconciliation (CSVR), the Civil Society Prison Reform Initiative (CSPRI), and the Institute for Security Studies (ISS). Many of the available studies have emanated from scholars and activists associated with these organizations. Oft-present divisions between academia and activism did not really hold in post-apartheid South Africa. University-based scholars also contributed, as illustrated by the work of Professor Dirk Van Zyl Smit, who has been a prolific contributor to both academic debate and policy development within the field of corrections in South Africa.[3]

The literature about South African prisons covers the whole gamut of possible topics featuring discussions of legislation, judicial and civilian oversight (Gallinetti n.d.), prison conditions, overcrowding, health and disease, space and architecture, gangs, violence, sex, survival, prisons as 'risk environments' (Barnett and Whiteside 2002), and reform.[4]

Socio-legal analyses have been complemented by other studies that bring the everyday life of South African prisons into focus. Jonny Steinberg's journalistic account of the 'number gangs' is a great read and offers insights into the constitutive role of violence in South African prisons (Steinberg 2004). Lindegaard and Gear (2014) focus on how (sexual) violence can be a means of surviving prisons. The pronounced and profound role of gangs in South African prisons is also quite unique and more akin to prison systems in Latin America than the rest of sub-Saharan Africa. South Africa is also the only jurisdiction that has so far begun to use electronic monitoring and private prisons (PRI 2014). In the context of a study conducted on the prevalence of HIV/AIDS, Singh describes in passing another way the South African prisons seem exceptional, namely in their constrictive, inhibitive attitude to research (Singh 2007). Such obstacles are one reason for the lacuna in empirical research on everyday life in prisons in Africa. Paradoxically, the more consolidated bureaucratic apparatus around prisons in South Africa seem to make them less amenable to external research than prisons in other African states. It is our experience that with the right degree of patience, obstinacy and perseverance, relatively high levels of access – including opportunities for 'deep hanging out' – can be attained.

Literature on other African countries' prisons is harder to come by, but the field is slowly growing. There exist recent studies of juvenile detention institutions in Ghana (Ayete-Nyampong 2013, 2014); of prison staff in Sierra Leone (Jefferson et al. 2014); prison practice and staff training in Nigeria (Jefferson 2007, 2005); governance and authority in Cameroon (Morelle 2014), the Ivory Coast (Marcis 2014) and Ghana (Akoensi 2014); post-genocide prison life in Rwanda (Tertsakian 2008, 2014); sex and masculinity in Zambia (Egelund 2014); overcrowding in Nigerian prisons (Sale 2014); and disciplinary procedures and bureaucratic quickening through human rights in Uganda (Martin 2014b, 2014a). A wide-ranging volume edited by Jeremy Sarkin on *Human Rights in African Prisons* (2008) offers some insights into prison conditions primarily – as the title suggests – through the lens of human rights.

In addition, three historical works stand out: Bernault's *A History of Prison and Confinement in Africa* (2003a) offers insightful analyses of the origins of the prison in Africa. More specifically Anderson's *Histories of the Hanged* (2005) and Elkins's *Britain's Gulag* (2005) both in different ways document the scope and horror of detention and judicial practices in colonial Kenya. Each of these works contextualizes the prison against a backdrop of socio-political developments and other historical and contemporary forms of confinement.

Jocelyn Alexander is another historian whose work on the political imaginaries of political prisoners in Zimbabwe offers a rare glimpse into the way in which prisons can be catalysts for the formation of social and political bonds as well as places of enduring pain[5] (Alexander 2010). Toggia's (2008) account of mass detention and consistency in use across changing carceral regimes in Ethiopia and Branch's (2005) analysis of the colonial prison in Kenya are other examples of the central role prison histories have in the literature compared with the relative dearth of material on contemporary everyday practices behind the walls.[6]

The use of imprisonment

How much is prison used in Africa, how and for whom? Can we explain the variation across the continent and where will it take us? As we will emphasize below, the use of imprisonment by the state in Africa is a distinctly colonial legacy. During colonial rule, Africans experienced periods of mass incarceration a short century before the 'penal explosion' became a household term for prison practices in the USA and Europe. According to Bernault, the extraction of tax, the pervasive use of convict labour and the taming of resistance to white domination resulted in spiking prisoner populations that were much higher than in the West. From the 1930s to the 1950s African colonies had between 160 and 330 prisoners per 100,000 people, whereas the UK and France had prisoner population rates between 40 and 90 per 100,000 (Bernault 2007: 63). There were quite extreme cases: 'In Belgian Congo in the late 1930s annual detainees represented 10 per cent of the adult male population', Bernault writes (ibid.: 64). The end of colonial rule deflated this period of mass incarceration and the contemporary picture is generally that African states imprison people relatively less often than many other regions in the world. Incarceration rates do seem to be increasing across the continent, but in many cases the reach of the formal state apparatus is relatively limited so state incarceration rates are often relatively low. That is, the African state seldom has a monopoly on the power to deprive people of their liberty so official figures can be misleading. Moreover, authoritarian states often also detain people – especially political prisoners – illegally and incommunicado in so-called 'safe houses' or 'ungazetted' detention centres, where torture is rampant and records are non-existent. Such uses of imprisonment have long and entrenched histories in many authoritarian and militarized African regimes, and are likely to expand as African nations like Nigeria, Kenya and Uganda are also today caught up in their own localized 'wars on terror'.

Still, within the formal state sector prison in Africa is often the sanction of first rather than last resort. It is often the only formal option available (except fines) though some countries have begun to experiment with parole schemes and alternatives to custody. Our impression is that many prisoners are held for petty crimes such as 'frequenting' (loitering), implying a criminalization of poverty. Some African countries have long histories of incarcerating the political opposition or rights activists and an enduring colonial legislation to underpin such authoritarianism. New laws also increase the number of Africans in prison. Uganda is a case in point: a harsh anti-defilement law was recently put in place to protect girls under 18 years of age from sexual abuse. According to this law defilement became a capital offence, and Ugandan prisons were soon swamped by young men awaiting trial in the heavily congested high court – to some extent at least on dubious charges as consensual sexual relations between young men and women had gone sour. Along somewhat comparable lines, legislation that criminalizes sexual behaviour in Uganda is currently also putting homosexual, bisexual and transsexual people in prison amidst a global uproar. Generally, African jurisdictions have relatively severe sentences and according to Penal Reform International the available data indicate that the share of prisoners sentenced to ten years or more in Africa is significantly higher than the global average (PRI 2014: 8).

Data about the use of imprisonment in Africa are scarce, but the formidable source of information from the *World Prison Brief* of the International Centre for Prison Studies (ICPS) in the UK does offer some important points.[7] First of all, it is quite telling that two African countries are listed as the most and the least incarcerating nations in the world. The Seychelles has a prisoner population rate of 868 per 100,000 people (by far surpassing the US rate of 707) and the Central African Republic has a rate of 19 (one of the least incarcerating nations together with the Faroe Islands and Liechtenstein). Such numbers obviously pose more questions than answers, and raise concerns about generalization and reliability of quantitative data. In fact, much of the most striking information gleaned from the available data concerns the significant outliers. Rwanda is probably the most obvious example, which following the genocide in 1994 saw overpopulation on an unprecedented scale and a high degree of prisoner self-governance (Tertsakian 2008). Today, overpopulation has been reduced as new prison facilities have been built, but the prisoner population of 492 per 100,000 people remains the ninth highest in the world – even topping the Russian Federation's 471. South Africa also stands out, with a high prisoner population rate of 293, probably due to the South African exceptionalism described above.

Still, a few general and commonly agreed upon issues about the use of imprisonment can be gleaned from the available data. First of all – and as mentioned above – prison population rates are generally low. The prison population rate for the world is about 144 prisoners per 100,000 people. In Africa, the rates are generally lower, but again with considerable variation – the median rate for Western African countries is just below 50, whereas the median rate for Southern Africa is about 200.

Yet, overpopulation is quite high. Five of the ten most overcrowded prison systems in the world are found in Africa (Benin 364%, Comoros 343%, Zambia 279%, Sudan

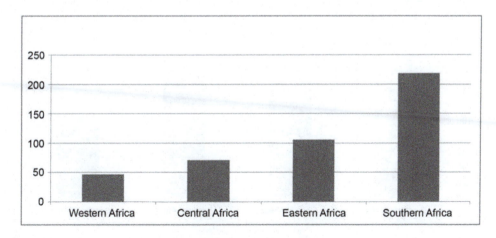

Figure 24.1 Prison population rate per 100,000 in Africa, 2014
(ICPS *World Prison Brief,* www.prisonstudies.org/world-prison-brief (accessed 8 August 2014))

255%, and Uganda 253%). On average, the overcrowding is somewhat less extreme than these five outliers, but still quite high – and again with considerable regional variations.

The number of pre-trial detainees is also high in African prisons. Again five of the ten countries in the world with most pre-trial detainees are African countries (Comoros 92%, Liberia 83%, Democratic Republic of the Congo 82%, Republic of the Congo (Congo Brazzaville) 75%, and Benin 75%). Excessive numbers of pre-trial detainees is a pervasive problem that has very negative multiplier effects on any prison system. On average the picture across the continent is worrying, but less alarming than the outliers, and according to the World Pre-trial Imprisonment List of the ICPS, the number of pre-trial detainees has fallen in more countries in Africa than it has grown. In comparison, the number of pre-trial detainees has grown in Europe and the Americas. Yet, the *length* of pre-trial detention in African jurisdictions is a serious issue. According to PRI, 19 of the 28 member states of the European Union have average pre-trial detention lengths of about 5.5 months. In Nigeria, to take one African example, the average is 3.7 years (PRI 2014: 6). The numbers considered thus far indicate that although sub-Saharan African countries generally have relatively small prisoner populations, these prisoners live in highly overcrowded prisons and are to a great extent not yet proven guilty of a crime.

Finally, the imprisonment of women is significantly less common in Africa than in most other regions. The median rate of women's imprisonment is only 3.1% in Africa, compared with close to 6% in Asia and 4.45% in the world in general. Still, the available data present some puzzling outliers. Why, for instance, do women represent as much as 8% of the extremely low prison population of the Central African Republic (as mentioned above, the lowest rate in the world of about 19 prisoners per 100,000 people)?

The figures above clearly point to Southern Africa – probably mostly South Africa – as incarcerating more, but at the same time also being less overcrowded and with fewer pre-trial detainees, likely due to better funding and higher levels of bureaucratization. The question is how should we explain these apparent patterns of incarceration across Africa? Should we simply correlate these figures with national crime rates (for instance

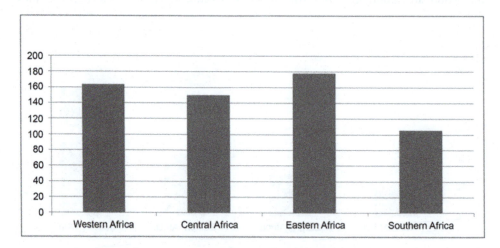

Figure 24.2 Occupancy level in African prisons, 2014 (%)
(ICPS *World Prison Brief*, www.prisonstudies.org/world-prison-brief (accessed 8 August 2014))

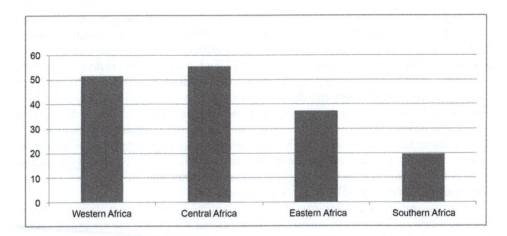

Figure 24.3 Pre-trial detainees in African prisons, 2014 (%)
(ICPS *World Prison Brief*, www.prisonstudies.org/world-prison-brief (accessed 8 August 2014))

from annual reports of the UN Office on Drugs and Crime)? Should we accept that a simple geographic divide explains differences in incarceration rates? Or might incarceration's legacy depend on whether countries were colonized by France, Portugal or Britain, or not colonized at all? Do contemporary prisons look different in one-party states compared with emerging democracies? How much impact do international development discourses that combine human rights, poverty reduction, rule of law and democratization under the umbrella of good governance have on prison populations? Are the uses of imprisonment different in peace time compared with times of open conflict? What impact has the proliferation of global penal norms had on prisons in Africa? These are some of the many puzzles facing scholars with an interest in international penal trends. From our point of view the jury is still out on how best to categorize, compare and make sense of the data. Clearly more reflection is needed on such matters. There is also a dearth of grand analysis of contemporary African penalities – akin to the works with which scholars like Garland or Wacquant have inspired American and European penology (Garland 2001; Wacquant 2008). We strongly encourage colleagues to take up this challenge. Our own contribution addresses these questions from a more bottom-up perspective through the notion of local 'prison climates', as we will show in the next section.

Prison conditions

Many prisons in Africa are operated against a background of severe infrastructural constraints, underprioritization and relative poverty. During political and societal transitions, be these from war to fragile peace or from dictatorship toward democracy, it is often the case that prison reform comes in a very distant last place on the list of what African governments and international donors choose to prioritize. Judicial, military and police reform typically gain more positive attention and funds. Conditions in prisons in Africa are often very poor. Basic amenities like food, soap, beds, blankets and medicine – and staff! – are inadequate and in some cases simply not available. Recreational facilities and meaningful and rehabilitative work opportunities are sparse. Instead, prisoners are often subjected to hard manual labour – either on prison farms or by being formally or informally rented out to private contractors by prison officers – to earn money and produce resources for the prison. Dilapidated, out-dated and overcrowded structures typically only offer very basic dormitory-like facilities, which often detract from the needs of special categories of prisoners and disallow the separation of convicted and accused prisoners. In order actually to act custodially and keep people locked up against their will in the context of such blatant infrastructural and human resource deficits, the prison systems that we know best have to rely heavily on informal modes of governance. An immediate consequence of this is that prison conditions are also significantly influenced by corruption, unlawful violence and the outsourcing of authority and privileges to strong or influential prisoners. We will return to this below.

Given the paucity of academic work the main source of information about conditions in African prisons is reports by international or national NGOs. Below we briefly review three more or less distinct genres of such 'grey literature' about prisons in Africa. Each represents differing forms of persuasion: persuasion through revelation; persuasion through documentation; and persuasion through diplomacy. This relatively cursory analysis is based on consideration of 11 reports concerning prisons in Africa published within the last decade: four from Human Rights Watch (HRW 2013, 2009, 2012, 2006), three from Amnesty International (AI 2012b, 2008, 2012a), three from the African Commission on Human and Peoples' Rights (ACHPR 2004b, 2012, 2004a), and one from the United Nations (Mendez 2014).

The reports from Human Rights Watch (HRW) emphasize torture and extreme violations. They vary in length (from 27–105 pages) and can be said to represent a genre of persuasion through revelation based on interviews and first-hand testimony. The reports' titles are indicative of their dramaturgical nature and exposé style: 'They Want a Confession'; 'Prison is Not for Me'; 'They Put Me in the Hole'; 'The Perverse Side of Things'. The first report focuses on 'serious human rights abuses, unlawful interrogation tactics, and poor detention conditions'; the second on 'violations of due process rights, patterns of wrongful deprivation of liberty, and the harsh, unacceptable prison conditions'; the third on 'disturbing pattern of human rights violations'; the fourth on 'how police brutally torture men and boys held in police custody.'

Amnesty International's reports resemble HRW's to a degree. They are entitled, 'Prisoners are bottom of the pile'; '"Locking up my rights": Arbitrary arrest, detention and treatment of detainees in Mozambique'; and 'Nigeria: Prisoners' rights systematically flouted'. They appeal to standards and norms in an attempt to responsibilize the state. There is a dominance of language highlighting inadequacy, unacceptability and failure to meet international standards. The reports are tentatively accusatory, focusing on shortcomings, gently suggesting, for example, that conditions 'may amount to torture or degrading treatment' and pointing out that states are culpable for deplorable conditions. If there is a difference compared with the HRW reports it is the slightly more finger-wagging rhetoric, but both speak from the position of the moral and legal high ground as they reveal negative truths about prison conditions and practices.

The reports of the African Commission's special rapporteur sound almost neutral in comparison, focusing on observed conditions and situations in prisons. Reports on Ethiopia and South Africa feature highly detailed descriptions of systems referred to as 'observations and findings', illustrated with tables and photos. Cases and examples of good practices are documented. The tone is conciliatory rather than condemnatory. They urge rather than demand action and include recommendations to government, civil society, the authorities and donors. In their own words, the purposes of country visits (two or so per year) are 'to draw the attention of prison officials to the numerous lapses in the criminal justice system in general and the treatment of persons deprived of their liberty in particular, and to advance appropriate measures for effective redress' (ACHPR 2004b: 4).

The final genre we consider here features persuasion through diplomacy or partnership. The report of the UN special rapporteur on torture follows a strict structure featuring sections on 'legal framework', 'assessment of situation', and 'conclusions and recommendations', and is representative of such a genre. The rapporteur 'hopes the Government will find his recommendations a useful tool for engaging in a constructive dialogue with all interlocutors to strengthen legal safeguards and improve the living conditions of those deprived of their liberty' (Mendez 2014: 1). The spirit is one of cooperation and partnership – a rather sharp contrast to the exposé style of the HRW and Amnesty reports.

A similar emphasis on documentation and diplomacy is found in another important body of grey literature, namely the monitoring reports from domestic oversight mechanisms. The monitoring of places of detention is typically invested in the mandates of national human rights institutions, ombudsmen and prison inspectorates – with the Judicial Inspectorate for Correctional Services in South Africa as the most well-known example. Domestic processes of constitutional reform and the implementation of the Optional Protocol to the UN Convention against Torture and Other Cruel, Inhuman or Degrading Treatment or Punishment[8] are step by step enabling the establishment of such independent state bodies. These institutions also produce knowledge about prison conditions – sometimes of quite high quality and professionalism (see for instance the reports of the Ugandan Human Rights Commission), but again, and as their mandates stipulate, from within a legalistic and standard-oriented perspective (see Ackerman 2013).

Grey literature is also produced by indigenous, grassroots NGOs which also sometimes take on a monitoring mandate. These reports are often less easily accessible and therefore less visible as sources of information. Our experience suggests that they vary in quality and scope and the extent to which they are revelatory, documentary or diplomatic. However, often they form an important and vital part of the food chain of knowledge informing more visible reports such as those discussed above.

Finally, the international NGO Penal Reform International (PRI) also represents a significant source of grey literature on prisons in Africa. Compared to HRW's and Amnesty's distinct watchdog profile, PRI typically develops more policy-oriented analysis and guidelines (often in direct relation to advocacy and training projects), but these reports are also prescriptive and directed towards the rolling out of 'best practice'.

From our point of view, the genres suggested above offer particular variations on the theme of 'the' prison in an African context which jointly produce a dominant representation or form. Many readers will recognize 'the African prison' in the following photofit description:

> The prison is overcrowded, ill-maintained, squalid and degrading. Abuse and ill-treatment are the norm. Inmates are not appropriately classified; disease (including TB, Hepatitis and HIV) is rampant; health facilities and provision is inadequate;

there is a massive overrepresentation of pre-trial detainees and little access to justice; vulnerable groups (women, children, LGBTs) are at extra risk; officers are corrupt and inept; basic human rights are violated; inhumanity and degradation abound …

This is the common result of applying an externally derived set of criteria to the prison in Africa. This dominant representation is an example of observers and commentators knowing everything that the African prison *is not*, rather than knowing or understanding the prison in Africa as it *is* (cf. Mbembe 2001).[9] An illustration of this tendency is found in Murray's discussion of the work of the special rapporteur on prisons under the African Commission on Human and Peoples' Rights (Murray 2008). In an emphatic critique, Murray laments that the outputs of this human rights watchdog are unsystematic and procedurally unclear. She writes: 'the approach to the [special rapporteur's] visits indicates that the findings are more a reflection of *what was seen* rather than a clear analysis of the compliance of the places visited with a set of identifiable standards' (ibid.: 207, our emphasis). From Murray's human rights perspective, prison practices have to be rigorously read and presented in human rights terms (which typically means in terms of their failure to live up to them – that is, as a lack) in order to speak to policy concerns and assist in the promotion and protection of prisoners' rights. Instead, we argue that a reflection of what is seen is of importance in itself if we want to fill the significant empirical and analytical gaps that characterize the study of prisons in Africa. We need to begin to understand these institutions in their own terms (Jefferson 2005: 502).

It feels necessary to add here – in order to prevent misconceptions – that our desire to understand prisons in Africa 'in their own terms' is not part of a quest to excuse or justify failure to comply with laws, norms and standards. Our argument is simply that analyses of prisons that only have their basis in external criteria of evaluation inevitably feature blind spots. Making local perspectives the point of departure for the study of prisons in Africa is not an apologetic exercise, but a wish to resist and challenge the tendency of powerful interventions to act, if not in the dark, then only in the light they themselves cast.

In our experience it is not the dramatic or spectacular prison events that stand out but the constant cruddy ordinariness of being forced into close confined proximity with persons not of one's own choosing under conditions of uncertainty. As we consider further below, prisons in Africa are often located at the sharp end of a continuum of law enforcement and judicial practices. They are the visceral end point of often opaque and difficult to negotiate procedures over which the detainee has little control and through which they have little support. Access to legal representation is the exception rather than rule across much of Africa. If you are poor you can neither bribe the police officer arresting you, nor the officer processing you at the station. Neither can you afford a lawyer. You may be held for days in police detention, possibly incommunicado. You may not be told the charges against you and if you are told, you might not understand their meaning or significance. Thus, the prisons we know in Africa are laced with experiences of not knowing and not being known about. Some prisoners are confused about why they are in prison at all; their families are not aware where they are; they do not know when they might ever get out. These uncertainties also permeate the institutional set-up and result in entanglement and fusion of roles and functions. In Sierra Leone, for instance, one of the most striking discoveries has been that prison staff and prisoners share experiential worlds. Both groups see their circumstances as punitive and unfair. Indeed, the complaints of prison staff are often more plaintive than those of prisoners.

Assessing climates

Such 'messy' findings have, in our cases at least, called for a more comprehensive entry point to the prison than simply paying attention to conditions. We have posited the notion of prison climate as one way of capturing both the everyday realities of prison life and the historical and societal position of a prison in any given context (Martin et al. 2014). Prison climate is both a concept and a phenomenon; it is a way of thinking about prison life attuned to everyday realities, societal context and practical norms and cognizant of the things that really matter to occupants of prisons, and it is something we can see, feel, sense and assess empirically.

An orientation to prison climate exploits the capacity of prison ethnography to zoom in and magnify specific details of prison practice and zoom out and capture panoramic vistas of penal practice across time and space. Ambitious perhaps, but not impossible.

How then do prisons in Africa look from this perspective? The picture remains incomplete. A recent edition of the *Prison Service Journal* offers a glimpse of prison worlds where the interdependency of guards and inmates, the diffusion of authority, and pragmatic, survival-oriented agency are common themes (Jefferson and Martin 2014). Based on studies from Rwanda, Ghana, Zambia, Ivory Coast, Uganda, Sierra Leone and Cameroon, this collection presents a sense of rather fluid, intense and mundane environments characterized by negotiation, contestation and ritual exchanges, amid struggles to survive. Informality trumps formality despite the importance of hierarchies. Uncertainty and insecurity dominate. Rules exist but are often circumvented as both prisoners and members of prison staff try to get safely through the day, week or month. Occasional crises in the form of escapes, or dramas in the form of the arrival of high-profile inmates, punctuate the humdrum everyday realities. Read together, this collection illustrates the ways in which prisons in these seven African countries are governed, the ways in which staff and inmates interact, and the way authority is distributed with particular focus on varying degrees of prisoner self-governance and the limits of human agency imposed by confined conditions.

Imprisonment within the wider criminal justice system

Prisons in Africa are embedded in wider criminal justice systems. This is no surprise, but it is highly important to think through this positioning when striving to understand prisons in Africa. The most obvious way to do this is to recognize the failure of police, courts and social services to deliver justice in many African countries. Prisons are literally at the receiving end of harsh and out-dated legislation, incompetent and politicized policing, and inefficient and corrupt judiciaries. With few (if any) alternatives to imprisonment, Africans end up and stay on in prisons unlawfully and unfairly and find it hard to access bail or get their cases processed. Thus, the high number of pre-trial detainees and the related scourge of overcrowding flow into African prisons from the upper tiers of a dysfunctional justice system.

To position problems of imprisonment in this way is relatively straightforward and legal reform or training of judges is therefore also often seen as a sensible and strategic justice sector reform intervention to improve prison conditions simply by getting people out of detention and relieving pressure on strained resources (be it infrastructure, personnel, food, medicine and so on). However, understanding the grounds for this apparent dysfunction and the ways that wider dynamics of state governance influence prisons in Africa is obviously more complicated and must include consideration of the position of the criminal justice system within history and within current geo-political discourses and unfolding circumstances. Therefore, below we briefly frame criminal justice in Africa in relation to colonialism and development aid.

First of all, it is crucial to recognize the distinct colonial and post-colonial histories of states in Africa and more especially the implications of this history on legal culture, law enforcement and punishment. Different forms of captivity (e.g. slavery and prisoners of war) were used in pre-colonial Africa, but these were rare means to sanction offences (Killingray 2003; Bernault 2003b). However, as the colonial project took form, administrators in Africa regarded prisons (together with paramilitary police forces) as fundamental to the establishment of colonial authority in Africa, and prisons mushroomed across the continent in the 19th century as one of the earliest colonial institutions (Killingray 2003: 97; Read 1969: 103). Most analysts read the birth of the colonial prison as directly stitched into the extraction of resources and the introduction of taxation and forced labour (Williams 1980; Tuck 2006). Yet, French and British colonialists presented the prison as part and parcel of the civilizing mission that they had established for themselves to impose order on the African 'chaos' and incorporate Africa into the modern capitalist world. The pre-colonial repertoire of punishments was unproductive from the colonialists' point of view. Torture and maiming, for instance, were considered barbaric and backward and thus outlawed. However, this filtering of indigenous African penality was not a matter of reduction and humanism. The colonial authorities rather found that the most commonly used sanction of pre-colonial justice, compensation, was too mild and lacked deterrent effect (Read 1969: 95–96). Instead, fines and prison were considered both modern and effective, and soon became 'the staple diet of sentencing courts in Eastern Africa' (ibid.: 107).

In practice, however, the colonial prison failed to live up to its ideals. Bernault argues strongly that the colonial prison blatantly failed to live up to metropolitan penal ideals and instead instigated the revival and maintenance of archaic violence and brutal, racialized exploitation (Bernault 2007: 68). Branch agrees that the colonial prison remained punitive, but from an East African context he emphasizes that the 'punitive nature of imprisonment in Kenya, as elsewhere in Britain's empire, had been somewhat blunted by a paucity of resources' (Branch 2005: 262). Amidst harsh deprivation, routinized violence and bouts of extreme brutality, everyday life in the colonial prison was allowed to gravitate towards a pragmatic negotiated order.[10] Relations between staff and prisoners were locally negotiated and detainees were seen to come and go more or less as they pleased. In 1935, the commissioner of prisons in Kenya consequently lamented that 'the deterrent effect of a period of imprisonment must be practically nil' and some 20 years later another senior colonial official exclaimed 'I would welcome anything which makes prison life less enjoyable for the Africans' (ibid.: 261).[11] Branch therefore characterizes prisons in colonial Kenya as 'African spaces' of chaotic reality with only a weak bureaucratic façade.

Bernault suggests that the pragmatic utility of a coercive penal agenda has served colonial and post-colonial politics equally well: 'African prisons today, reflect the exasperation of colonial modes of governance and social control', she writes, and 'these legacies are reinvented today in the context of a new political order (clientelism, personalisation of power, prebendal culture)' (Bernault 2003b: 33).

However, Bernault leaves us with rather sweeping statements about legacies of grand negative traits, which call for more nuanced views. It therefore seems more fruitful to look beyond the prisons literature out into broader debates about the colonial heritage of bureaucratic practice in Africa, which seeks to understand the gap between formal rules and actual delivery of public services from an empirical basis (Bierschenk and de Sardan 2014; Blundo and Le Meur 2009). This non-normative approach to 'everyday governance' argues that users and providers of public service in Africa draw on multiple repertoires of official rules and 'practical norms' (i.e. 'tacit, shared road rules' of bureaucratic practice (Olivier de Sardan 2008: 13)) to enable institutional reproduction and personal and professional survival. Thus, the argument is that the significant bending and breaking of formal rules and pragmatic manoeuvring among plural normative orders are deep, common, but also highly modern traits of bureaucratic governance that have a distinct colonial history and excessive character in most African countries. This also applies to prisons in Africa, and to understand their institutional set-up, the way they are governed and the way they change, we need to acknowledge the post-colonial bureaucratic territory they share with the wider justice sector in particular and the state in general.

The second and related dimension of positioning imprisonment in Africa in the wider justice system concerns the fact that prison reform is directly embedded in and influenced by development paradigms and actors. Most African states are challenged by poverty and involved in development cooperation as recipients of foreign aid. The resource deficits that characterize prisons in Africa are considerable and apparent. Seen in the context of generalized poverty, the plight of African prisoners remains severe and prison reform is thus also a feature of development interventions aimed to reach this 'vulnerable group', whose basic rights are so obviously violated. Prison reform processes in African contexts are typically weaved into grander security and/or justice sector reform programmes, where the influence of foreign donors and international norms, institutions and technologies has a very prominent role compared with, for instance, the UK. Thus, 'human rights', 'rule of law' and 'good governance' – the current zeitgeist of state building in the developing world – are explicated in new laws, policies and training curricula. A significant aspect of this aid environment is that civil society organizations are actively supported in these reform programmes, and national, international, faith-based and/or thematically oriented NGOs often take on quite prominent roles as monitors, trainers and service providers in and around prisons in Africa.

In sum, we simply argue that the contextualization of imprisonment in Africa needs to pay acute attention to colonial and post-colonial history and to the political economy of development aid. Prisons in Africa are subject to the diffusion of global penal norms. One route for this spread is via development discourse and practice that is exported into African state institutions through transnational flows of global governance (Sharma and Gupta 2006; Jefferson and Jensen 2009; Duffield and Hewitt 2009; Rajagopal 2006), or more mundanely, by the targeted actions of local decision makers and donors in response to international and national pressures. Formally, this export is meant to change the way these institutions are governed and the way they govern others. In our respective work we have highlighted the risks of 'imaginary reform' and unintended consequences of models of intervention that fail to take seriously local context, circumstances and logics of practice (Jefferson 2008). In our view, the positioning of imprisonment in the wider criminal justice system is more than a technical exercise of assessing formal mandates, roles and responsibilities. It is rather a question of understanding the able hands of African state officials that reach out for a variety of norms and technologies and seek to cobble together a local take on imprisonment that focuses less on formal prescriptions than on these local actors' efforts to make the institutions in which they strive to survive, work.

Conclusion

Despite our initial provisos about generalizations and dominant representations, we do believe that by suspending judgement and resisting dystopian visions of prisons in Africa it is possible to identify some key dilemmas and questions that could be explored more thoroughly in the future – it is hoped, also by more scholars from Africa. We have considered some major trends and themes already. Here we revisit some of these by way of a conclusion.

We have argued that prisons in Africa are overcrowded, challenged by poverty, underpinned by out-dated colonial laws and so on. We have also pointed out that prisons are not the only sites of confinement in Africa and there may be striking similarities to be drawn and a series of empirical questions that could be posed across sites of confinement. In Africa this would include detention centres, refugee camps, labour camps, witch camps, poor urban neighbourhoods, re-education camps, safe houses, non-gazetted prisons, the detention facilities of rebel armies and so on. We would add that exploring the use of imprisonment more comprehensively calls for more scholarship that does not simply take the functions and practices of prisons for granted. The endless demand to do good, where things are apparently so wrong, and the ceaseless calls to bring prisons in Africa up to standard, seem sometimes to drown out more profound questions about imprisonment and its role. In our experience discourses promoting prisons as places of correction rather than punishment are taking hold in jurisdictions in Africa, but there is little questioning of whether (or how) prisons in these particular contexts can achieve their revised stated aims.

Attention to historical trajectories has (for us at least) been crucial to understanding the complex processes of state formation and the excessive normative pluralism that characterizes prisons in Africa – and, very importantly, make them intensely modern. Similarly, we argue that the political economy of development aid and the appropriation of global norms and technologies have profound impact on prison settings in Africa.

Finally, and more generally, we have suggested quite strongly that positing African prisons as essentially failing might not be the best way to conceptualize them. Nor might it be the best way to encourage their transformation. Our argument is that activism would be better grounded if it took the complexity of prison climates in Africa as its point of departure – their persistence and endurance – rather than outrage at the extent to which prisons do not live up to norms. Suffering is a quality of everyday prison life in Africa. It demands a holistic, comprehensive and empirically informed understanding if responses are to be devised that meaningfully transform prisons or, more ambitiously, even reduce societies' commitment to them.

Notes

1 We'd like to express our thanks to the editors, Yvonne Jewkes, Ben Crewe and Jamie Bennett, for their comments and encouragement. We'd also like to thank our good colleagues from the Global Prisons Research Network (gprnetwork.org), whose joint work has inspired and

brought forward many of the perspectives in this chapter. Also a special thanks to our oft-neglected families who faithfully endure our many absences: thanks to Helle, Jakob, Aksel and Joakim; and to Lotte, Marie and Joshua.

2 We are indebted to Lorna Rhodes for this insight about the persistence and mutation of prisons.

3 Van Zyl Smit's work on prison law and practice can perhaps be seen as the forerunner of much subsequent scholarship (Van Zyl Smit 1992).

4 Lukas Muntingh's PhD thesis can be seen as continuing the tradition of socio-legal analysis of the post-1994 reform process (Muntingh 2012). Muntingh laments the failure of the prisons leadership from 1994–99 to show the necessary political imagination resulting in a more rather than less punitive criminal justice system.

5 Alexander has also written on the reform of Zimbabwe Prison Service whereby the foundation for the exercise of authority of 'professional' prison officers was subverted by a reorientation towards a militant ideology of liberation (Alexander 2013).

6 An alternative source of material on prisons is from prisoners' memoirs or poetry. These can also be found emerging in Africa (see Mapanje 2002, 2011), offering troubling hands-on, often visceral accounts of trials and tribulations (see also Aminatta Forna (2003) for an auto-biographical account of her quest to trace her father's history of detention and repression at the hands of the Sierra Leonean state).

7 Unless otherwise referenced, all quantitative data used in this section are taken from the ICPS *World Prison Brief*, www.prisonstudies.org/world-prison-brief (accessed 8 August 2014).

8 Ratification of the optional protocol entails the obligation to establish independent National Preventive Mechanisms with a mandate to monitor places of detention.

9 This is a version of the argument propounded by political philosopher Achille Mbembe about Western scholarship on Africa in general. He argues that Africa is typically treated only in terms of what it is not, as 'lack', or 'void' or even as simply 'primordial chaos' (Mbembe 2001).

10 The Mau Mau uprising broke this balance. Since corrective ideals and lawfulness had never taken root, punitiveness was the only and obvious register to draw from as detention became a central strategy to protect the colonial state against insurgency. According to Branch, the bla-tant atrocities in the Kenyan detention camps, 'the horror story of Britain's empire in the 1950s' (Branch 2005: 262), must be seen in relation to this particular history of the colonial prison.

11 It is well documented that this wish for making prison less enjoyable came through during the extreme detention and execution of Kenyans during the Mau Mau uprising in the 1950s (cf. Anderson 2005).

Bibliography

ACHPR (African Commission on Human and Peoples' Rights) (2004a) *Ethiopia: Mission on prisons and conditions of detention*, Banjul: African Commission on Human and Peoples' Rights.

ACHPR (African Commission on Human and Peoples' Rights) (2004b) *South Africa: Prisons and detention conditions*, Banjul: African Commission on Human and Peoples' Rights.

ACHPR (African Commission on Human and Peoples' Rights) (2012) *Report of the Special Rapporteur on Prisons and Conditions of Detention in Africa*, Banjul: African Commission on Human and Peoples' Rights.

Ackerman, M. (2013) *Survey of Detention Visiting Mechanisms in Africa*, Cape Town: Civil Society Prison Reform Initiative.

AI (Amnesty International) (2008) *Nigeria: Prisoners' Rights Systematically Flouted*, London: Amnesty International.

AI (Amnesty International) (2012a) *'Locking up my Rights': Arbitrary arrest, detention and treatment of detainees in Mozambique*, London: Amnesty International.

AI (Amnesty International) (2012b) *'Prisoners are Bottom of the Pile': The human rights of inmates in Ghana*, London: Amnesty International.

Akoensi, T.D. (2014) 'Governance through power sharing in Ghanaian prisons: A symbiotic relationship between officers and inmates', *Prison Service Journal*.

Alexander, J. (2010) 'The political imaginaries and social lives of political prisoners in post-2000 Zimbabwe', *Journal of Southern African Studies* 36: 483–503.

Alexander, J. (2013) 'Militarisation and state institutions: "Professionals" and "soldiers" inside the Zimbabwe Prison Service', *Journal of Southern African Studies* 39: 807–828.

Anderson, D. (2005) *Histories of the Hanged: The dirty war in Kenya and the end of empire*, New York: W.W. Norton & Company.

Ayete-Nyampong, L. (2013) *Entangled Realities and the Underlife of a Total Institution: An ethnography of correctional centers for juvenile and young offenders in Accra, Ghana*, PhD, Wageningen University.

Ayete-Nyampong, L. (2014) 'Entangled governance practices and the illusion of producing compliant inmates in correctional centres for juvenile and young offenders in Ghana', *Prison Service Journal*.

Barnett, T. and Whiteside, A. (2002) *AIDS in the Twenty-first Century: Disease and globalization*, New York: Palgrave Macmillan.

Bernault, F. (2003a) *A history of Prison and Confinement in Africa*, Portsmouth, NH: Heinemann.

Bernault, F. (2003b) 'The politics of enclosure in colonial and post-colonial Africa', in F. Bernault (ed.) *A History of Prison and Confinement in Africa*, Portsmouth, NH: Heinemann.

Bernault, F. (2007) 'The shadow of rule: Colonial power and modern punishment in Africa', in F.A.I.B. Dikötter (ed.) *Cultures of Confinement: A history of the prison in Africa, Asia and Latin America*, London: Hurst.

Bierschenk, T. and de Sardan, J.-P.O. (2014) *States at Work: Dynamics of African bureaucracies*, Boston, MA: Brill.

Blundo, G. and Le Meur, P.Y. (2009) 'An anthropology of everyday governance: Collective service delivery and subject-making', in G. Blundo and P. Le Meur (eds) *The governance of daily life in Africa*, Leiden: Brill.

Branch, D. (2005) 'Imprisonment and colonialism in Kenya, c.1930–1952: Escaping the carceral archipelago', *The International Journal of African Historical Studies* 38: 239–265.

Duffield, M. and Hewitt, V. (2009) *Empire, development & colonialism: The past in the present*, Suffolk: James Currey.

Egelund, A. (2014) 'Masculinity, sex and survival in Zambian prisons', *Prison Service Journal*.

Elkins, C. (2005) *Britain's Gulag: The brutal end of empire in Kenya*, London: Random House.

Forna, A. (2003) *The Devil that Danced on the Water: A daughter's quest*, London: Flamingo.

Gallinetti, J. (n.d.) *Civilian Oversight and South African Prisons: An examination of the independent visitor system. Law, democracy and development*, Cape Town: Faculty of Law, University of Western Cape.

Garland, D. (2001) *The Culture of Control: Crime and social order in contemporary society*, Oxford: Oxford University Press.

Gillespie, K. (2011) 'Containing the "wandering native": Racial jurisdiction and the liberal politics of prison reform in 1940s South Africa', *Journal of Southern African Studies* 37: 499–515.

Gregory, D. (2009) 'Vanishing points: Law, violence, and exception in the global war prison', in D. Gregory and A. Pred (eds) *Terror and the Postcolonial: A concise companion*, New York: Routledge.

HRW (Human Rights Watch) (2006) *'The Perverse Side of Things': Torture, inadequate detention conditions, and excessive use of force by Guinean security forces*, New York: Human Rights Watch.

HRW (Human Rights Watch) (2009) *'They Put me in the Hole': Military detention, torture, and lack of due process in Cabinda*, New York: Human Rights Watch.

HRW (Human Rights Watch) (2012) *'Prison is not for me': Arbitrary detention in South Sudan*, New York: Human Rights Watch.

HRW (Human Rights Watch) (2013) *'They Want a Confession': Torture and ill-treatment in Ethiopia's Maekelawi Police Station*, New York: Human Rights Watch.

Jefferson, A.M. (2005) 'Reforming Nigerian prisons: Rehabilitating a "deviant" state', *Br J Criminol* 45: 487–503.

Jefferson, A.M. (2007) 'Prison officer training and practice in Nigeria: Contention, contradiction and re-imagining reform strategies', *Punishment & Society* 9: 253.

Jefferson, A.M. (2008) 'Imaginary reform: Changing the postcolonial prison', in P. Carlen (ed.) *Imaginary penalities*, Portland, OR: Willan.

Jefferson, A.M., Feika, M.C. and Jalloh, A.S. (2014) 'Prison officers in Sierra Leone: Paradoxical puzzles', *Prison Service Journal*.

Jefferson, A.M. and Jensen, S. (2009) *State Violence and Human Rights: The role of state officials in the south*, Abingdon: Routledge Cavendish.

Jefferson, A.M. and Martin, T.M. (2014) 'Everyday prison governance in Africa', *Prison Service Journal*: 2–3.

Killingray, D. (2003) 'Punishment to fit the crime? Penal policy and practice in British colonial Africa', in F. Bernault (ed.) *A history of prison and confinement in Africa*, Portsmouth, NH: Heinemann.

Lindegaard, M. and Gear, S. (2014) 'Surviving South African prisons: Negotiating gang practices in order to be safe', *Focaal* 68: 35–54.

Mapanje, J. (2002) *Gathering Seaweed: African prison writing*, Oxford: Heinemann.

Mapanje, J. (2011) *And Crocodiles are Hungry at Night: Prison memoir*, London: James Currey Ltd.

Marcis, F.L. (2014) 'Everyday prison governance in Abidjan, Ivory Coast', *Prison Service Journal*.

Martin, T.M. (2014a) 'The importation of human rights by Ugandan prison staff', *Prison Service Journal*.

Martin, T.M. (2014b) 'Reasonable caning and the embrace of human rights in Ugandan prisons', *Focaal* 68: 68–82.

Martin, T.M., Jefferson, A.M. and Bandyopadhyay, M. (2014) 'Sensing prison climates: Governance, survival and transition', *Focaal* 68: 3–17.

Mbembe, A. (2001) *On the Postcolony*, Berkeley, CA: University of California Press.

Mendez, J.E. (2014) *Report of the Special Rapporteur on torture and other cruel, inhuman or degrading treatment or punishment: Mission to Ghana*, United Nations General Assembly.

Morelle, M. (2014) 'Power, control and money in prison: The informal governance of the Yaoundé Central Prison', *Prison Service Journal*.

Muntingh, L. (2012) *An Analytical Study of South African Prison Reform after 1994*, PhD, University of Western Cape.

Murray, R. (2008) 'The African Commission's approach to prisons', in J. Sarkin (ed.) *Human rights in African prisons*, Cape Town: HSRC Press.

Olivier de Sardan, J.-P. (2008) 'Researching the practical norms of real governance in Africa', *Africa, Power & Politics* (December).

PRI (2014) *The Use and Practice of Imprisonment: Current trends and future challenges*, London: Penal Reform International.

Rajagopal, B. (2006) 'Counter-hegemonic international law: Rethinking human rights and development as a Third World strategy', *Third World Quarterly* 27(148–169): 767–783.

Read, J.S. (1969) 'Kenya, Tanzania and Uganda', in A. Milner (ed.) *African penal system*, London: Routledge & Kegan Paul.

Sale, A. (2014) *Coping with, and Responding to, Prison Overcrowding: A study of Nigeria's prisons*, PhD, Bangor University.

Sarkin, J. (ed.) (2008) *Human Rights in African Prisons*, Cape Town: HSRC Press.

Sharma, A. and Gupta, A. (2006) 'Introduction', in A.A.G.A. Sharma (ed.) *The anthropology of the state: A reader*, Oxford: Blackwell Publishing.

Singh, S. (2007) 'Being a criminology ethnographer in a South African prison: A search for dynamics and prevalence of HIV/AIDS in the Westville Prison, Durban, South Africa', *Journal of Social Science* 15: 71–82.

Steinberg, J. (2004) *The Number: One Man's Search for Identity in the Cape Underworld and Prison Gangs*, Cape Town: Jonathon Ball Publications.

Tertsakian, C. (2008) *Le Château: The lives of prisoners in Rwanda*, London: Taylor & Francis.

Tertsakian, C. (2014) 'Some prisons are prisons, and others are like hell. Prison life in Rwanda in the ten years after the genocide', *Prison Service Journal.*

Toggia, P.S. (2008) 'The state of emergency: Police carceral regimes in modern Ethiopia', *Journal of Developing Societies* 24: 107–124.

Tuck, M.W. (2006) '"The rupee disease": Taxation, authority, and social conditions in early colonial Uganda', *The International Journal of African Historical Studies* 39: 221–245.

Van Zyl Smit, D. (1992) *South African Prison Law and Practice*, Durban: Butterworth Publishers.

Wacquant, L. (2008) *Urban Outcasts*, Cambridge: Polity Press.

Williams, D. (1980) 'The role of prisons in Tanzania – an historical perspective', *Crime and Social Justice* (Summer) 13: 27–38.

Chapter 25

Asian prisons

Colonial pasts, neo-liberal futures and subversive sites

Mahuya Bandyopadhyay

Introduction

If there is anything that may be marked as a common theme in writing about the nature of Asian prisons, it is, paradoxically, the variance in their character, spirit and practices of incarceration. Yet, in thinking and writing about Asian prisons, one is undoubtedly captivated by the transformations, potential, implicit or real, that most of these prisons are on the verge of witnessing. These transformations, I will argue, lie most often in a curious interface with their colonial pasts and contemporary neo-liberal contexts. The other significant commonality is located in the very sparse literature and information on the subject of prisons in Asia. A final theme of commonality is the nature of concealments about the prison as an institution, and about the practices and impending policies around incarceration, that most Asian contexts represent in varying degrees. One can infer, speculate and attempt to articulate the horrors of these prisons through the nature of their conspiracies of silence, neglect and censorship. The legitimation of this deadly triumvirate is often drawn from the dominant political cultures of these Asian countries.

This chapter reconstructs, from available secondary literature, albeit in a rather fragmented manner, the nature of prisons in Asia. The author's location and work in a prison in India is used as a significant register to juxtapose comparatively the available literature along with a view of the field.[1] Even though the material collected for this essay followed the geographical map, the content will not do so, owing to the very irregular data that are available for different countries. Instead the essay will map the nature of prison climates through a discussion of practices, socialities and events in different prisons in Asia. While I attempt to draw out instances to support my arguments from as many Asian countries as possible, this is not an exhaustive review of prison conditions in Asia. Another caveat that I must introduce at the outset is that as the chapter unravels commonalities between different prisons in Asia, it may appear to gloss over their differences and particularities through the very use of the term 'Asian prisons'. So the use of 'Asian prisons' here is a heuristic device; it does not suggest all-pervasive common ground.

Two related concepts guide my reading and understanding and, subsequently, this presentation of Asian prisons: the concept of 'field', drawn from Bourdieu's work (Bourdieu 1983)[2] and the notion of prison climates (Jefferson et al. 2014). The 'field' implies the political field, the multitude of relations of power, dominance and resistance that shape issues of governance in any context. The larger political field in the Asian countries has seen particular prison configurations emerge. To work with a notion of prison climates in order to draw a picture of Asian prisons will provide a way of decentring and deconstructing the prison by showing the multiple contexts in which it is appropriated by different groups, spaces and in different sorts of power dynamics.

Conceptual underpinnings

'Prison climate may commonly denote a set of general and prevailing conditions deeply characteristic of a particular site or system. Prison climate is a composite category, encompassing material conditions, values, relationships, and the political and moral economies – including the (ir)rationalities – that sustain them' (Jefferson et al. 2014: 6). Prison climate is clearly a concept laden with ethnographic meaning and implications. It recognizes the value of ethnographic work in narrating and understanding prisons through 'local explanations'. I use this concept to write about prisons in Asia, drawing on its potential to elicit ethnographic insights as I write about Asian prisons from the rather unfavourable vantage point of a 'book view'.[3] A prison climate is embedded in material conditions and physical environments and its experience by different actors is distinctive. In narrating the multiple distinctive and local dynamics of prison life, the 'artificiality' inherent in the notion of prison climate may be countered. Further 'climate' is particularly enabling in this context of writing about Asian prisons as it can reveal how local prison conditions are embedded in national and regional contexts, in larger, global discursive arenas such as human rights, neo-liberal agendas, increasing securitization and the tensions these create in everyday prison lives. The idea of prison climate is mirrored in Bourdieu's conception of the 'field'. A field is an assemblage of relations, interactions and material conditions around the flows of power and its resistance, the access to resources, control over them and the negotiations that ensue to moderate access.

There are two other critical links that I work with in anchoring this rather fragmented and variegated discussion on prisons in Asia – the historical, general, yet geographically unique and spatio-culturally grounded colonial encounter and the contemporary concern with global terrorism, diffuse in its inherent global connections and simultaneously rooted in the mundane everyday aspects of people's lives. Implicit in my discussion of Asian prisons is the idea that both these encounters with colonialism and terrorism have framed the prison as an organization, the discourse of punishment and dealing with the disposable in the global South. The term 'global South' is derived from the North–South divide, signifying the binary between rich and poor, developed and developing, first and third world nations. The term global is added to suggest that the South is not merely a strict geographical categorization, but is based on economic inequalities, with some 'cartographic continuities' (see Rigg 2007: 3–4; Brandt 1980).

Very broadly, the chapter addresses two interlinked themes: the continuities and breaks with colonial administration of prisons, and prisons as subversive sites, not just in the sense of manoeuvring and manipulating prison rules for prisoner gains and agency, but also in the composition of prison populations. Prison demographics thus indicate larger political and administrative issues in governing populations, framing a politics of disposability, from a state-centric perspective, and that of resistance, from a citizen- and people-centric standpoint.

In exploring Asian prisons as subversive sites, I hope to be able to engage with questions of emergent and potential changes in these prison systems, while tracing the continuities or discontinuities of such changes from their socio-historical trajectories. I reflect on prison practices, their connections to colonial histories and contemporary politics in different prisons in Asia, attempting to collate stories, information and data from as many countries as possible. However, given the limitations of the data, my own location in the global South (accessibility to literature that does exist is also compromised) and those of a volume such as this, I have been unable to reflect on prison systems in all the Asian countries. Even though I began with the caveat of tracing commonalities and the challenges of presenting anything comprehensive about Asian prisons, I must admit that in my reading on Asian prisons, I was struck by the recurrent themes of the rapidly growing prisoner population, deep infrastructural inadequacies, slow judicial processes, larger numbers of pre-trial or remand prisoners than convicts, the inability of many to offer money for the required bail bonds, which resolutely indicates the class background of the imprisoned, and the growing detention of young boys in most countries.

Chapter outline

The chapter is divided into three sections, dealing with aspects of prison administration and prisoners' lives: continuities with colonial rules, laws and practices; composition of prisoner population and classificatory systems for effective management; body disciplining, forced labour and violation of human rights. Each of these sections is intended as a way of elucidating the negotiated character of prison management; negotiated by prisoners and the administration. In the concluding section, I reflect on this negotiated character to argue that these prisons need not be understood merely as modern institutions, replicating a Western modernity and its concomitant notion of the well-ordered prison. Rather they could well be conceived as subversive sites; as subversions to colonial rule, to everyday prison practice and therefore to the notions of social order. More centrally, they represent subversions of state practice, effects, and of neo-liberal agendas. Through this, the picture of the well-ordered prison[4] is severely disrupted. Simultaneously, prison governance practices are increasingly replicated through the increasing securitization, surveillance, pervasiveness of panoptic structures, and the unpredictability of everyday life, blurring the otherwise sharply known boundaries between prison and non-prison environments.

Continuities with colonial rules, laws and practices

The colonial prison was the site for demonstrating 'the important function of ... superiority and inviolability of imperial power' (Singh 1998: 5). In asserting colonial power and superiority, administrators often used cultural specificities as a justification for opposing modern and reformative modes of management of aberrant and imprisoned populations. Feasibility and expenses involved were other factors that served as obstacles to initiating change in prison administration and infrastructure. In India, for instance, issues related to caste sensibilities, considered to be one such socio-cultural typicality, were detrimental to a rational approach to organizational practice in prison (Arnold 1994: 171; Yang 1987: 33). Rather, repression, physical violence and a system of other punishments, such as solitary confinement for prison offences, were accepted as the most effective ways of managing prison populations. Nevertheless, in most of these countries with a colonial past, the modernist break in prison management is seen as located in the colonial encounter. Colonization brought about modernization in institutions and a Western style of administration was introduced. Basically, the institutions of confinement came to be modelled along the lines of the well-ordered prison. The history of the prison too was written in terms of the replicability of the model of the well-ordered prison. Contrastingly, Zinoman (2001) wrote of the 'colonial Bastille' in Vietnam as an ill-disciplined prison that contributed substantially to the success of the anti-colonial project. The communal architecture, haphazard classification systems, forced labour regimes, poorly trained and ethnically divided surveillance staff, inadequate healthcare, provisioning and sanitation, he argues, were enabling features of the colonial prison, allowing for an anti-colonial movement (ibid.: 7). All these features of governance and management of prison populations were used effectively as sites for strategizing resistance to colonial rule.

Let us consider, for instance, the colonial practice of management of the prison population through gangs.[5] The prisoners, employed as convict warders and night watchmen, enabled much of this exercise of strict control over other prisoners in a purely physical manner. Officials and other staff members avoided the 'dirty work' of dealing with the prisoners directly. Such fusion of functions enabled subversions of prison rules; their allowance and disallowance was often the prerogative of the prisoners who were in control. The convict warders were responsible for reporting any violations, as they discharged their duties of control and surveillance of everyday activities of prisoners. Many subversions went unnoticed, unreported, drawing them into a larger repertoire of resistance to prison rules specifically, and colonial administrative practice more generally. The practice of fusion of functions thus contributed to two kinds of disruptions. First, it acted as a break in a classic and Goffmanian understanding of prison management: the strict separation of controller and controlled. Second, it compromised the picture of the well-ordered and controlled prison. Unpredictability, personal relationships and closeness, and situational exigencies shaped everyday prison practice. McNair (1899), in writing about prisons in Singapore and South-East Asia generally, characterized this system as 'making prisoners their own warders'. When the labour of free warders was not available and the system witnessed many vacancies and dismissals, 'an attempt was then made to enlist the services of well-behaved convicts to oversee their fellow-prisoners'. However, this system was branded objectionable as men would find it difficult to exercise authority over those people with whom they were intimately connected (McNair 1899: 18). The system of convict warders was in fact tantamount to a carrot and stick policy: effective controlling of prisoners would ensure greater freedoms for the convict warders (Sherman 2009: 5). Disciplining, thus, involved creating docile but labouring bodies, in return for varying degrees of freedom. So convicts' bodies were disciplined as docile and useful bodies.[6]

Creating discipline through docility and docility through labour were related strategies of colonial prisons. Not surprisingly, this idea persists. It coincides with the vehement and legal shunning of traditional modes of disciplining and punishment, such as violating the convicts' bodies through harsh punishments, mutilation and torture. With such a shift, the nature of deterrence changed. In India, around 1870, a law was passed that forbade punishment by mutilation of body parts, substituting it with hard labour. Similarly, the Reformatory Schools Act of 1897, which directed that youthful offenders should be sent to a reformatory school and not a prison, was another landmark legislation that was instrumental in altering the character of the punishment process. The restrictions on whipping and imposition of fetters and handcuffs as punishment for prison offences are also significant in this context. This was brought about primarily after the recommendations of the *Report of the Indian Jails Committee 1919–20*. However, the Prisons Act of 1894 remains largely unchanged and is still the basic governing document in many of the Indian states. This is also true of its immediate neighbours – Bangladesh, Pakistan and Sri Lanka. In Sri Lanka, for instance, the colonial government introduced the first prison ordinance in 1844. A related significant enactment was the ordinance for the 'safe custody of convicts employed upon public works' in 1853. Around this time the colonial state was instrumental in establishing many prisons, including the Welikada and Hultfsdorp prisons. The Prisons ordinance of 1869 was the first comprehensive legislation that marked the establishment of a uniform prison system in the country. A significant shift in the post-colonial prison system in Sri Lanka is attributed to the adoption of the 'United Nations Standard Minimum Rules for the Treatment of Prisoners' in 1957. This is, in fact, perceived as a transformative, modernizing shift in prison practice in the member nations – erstwhile colonies and the global South – as through this the different prison administrations aligned themselves to a global human rights paradigm. However, this apparently paradigmatic shift in prison management was possibly not all that radical as many of its provisions were already incorporated in the existing prison laws (Dharmadasa n.d.).

The legal foundations of the Indonesian penitentiary were laid in the colonial era, with the Indonesian Criminal Code, which is based on the Dutch 'Wetboek van Strafrecht voor Nederlandsch Indie' of 1918 and the Dutch prison regulations of 1917. These regulations governing the administration of prisons contain provisions for disciplining prisoners such as 'flogging twenty times with rattan if there is no punishment cell or if all cells are occupied'. The government has only introduced piecemeal changes in these regulations, while acknowledging the need for more humane conditions in the treatment of prisoners. There are two significant changes in criminal justice reform in Indonesia. The first is the enactment of the revised Criminal Procedure Code (*Kitab Undang-Undang Hukum Acara Pidana* or KUHAP) in 1981, which outlines a number of protections for arrested persons, including the right to a lawyer from the moment of arrest, time limits on pre-trial detention, and the right of families to be notified immediately of a suspect's arrest. However, prisoners charged under the Anti-Subversion law are outside the purview of such progressive legislation. Moreover, not all the protective norms laid out in KUHAP are followed through. The second aspect is the apparent spirit of reintegration with which the prison system functions: reintegration of prisoners into the community by creating awareness among prisoners about their wrongs, and by enabling them to be active participants in their own development towards turning themselves into responsible citizens (Roth 2006: 135).[7]

Despite such changes and acceptance of global standards, the basic governing document in most of these post-colonial nations did not change. This created a discordant situation in prison management as the basic governing document relied on deterrent principles. In India, for instance, if 'the jail officials were to follow the Prisons Act of 1894, ... almost every prisoner will be required to be punished daily' (Datir 1978: 71). For Datir, the move towards a reformative goal was made with the acceptance of rehabilitation and reform as the primary objectives of the prison, at least on paper. Before Independence, the reformative function was considered secondary. The post-colonial state made reform a primary objective and this marked an apparent break from colonial practice.

Similarly in American-ruled Philippines, a progressive rhetoric of reform and rehabilitation was used. In the Philippines, however, the senior prison officials were enthusiastic about treating prisoners scientifically and believed in the gains of rigorous scientific enquiry in reforming criminals. Prison conditions in Manila improved substantially during American rule, with many senior officials treating the prison as a laboratory for reform. Two practices introduced by American rule in the prison system in Manila have left their mark on the modernizing of prisons: the prisoners' court, and the provision of 'instructive and reformative amusements' for prisoners.

In contemporary Philippines there are seven national prison facilities: New Billibid prison, the correctional institution for women, the Davao prison and penal farm, Iwahig, San Ramon and Sablayan prisons and penal farms, and the Leyte regional prison. The Philippines also has a prison population rate amongst the highest in Asia. Based on an estimated national population of 98.13 million at August 2013 (from UN figures), its population rate is pinned at 113, twice as much as the South Asian countries, for instance. It is worth noting that the Philippines has the largest number of penal farms, possibly inspired by the successful colonial experiment at the Iwahig penal colony set up in the early 20th century. The penal colony was designed to be a self-governing republic, run by the convicts themselves. The colonial logic of control of large numbers of subversive elements while making labour and a 'life of usefulness' the foundational pillars of the treatment and punishment process in this penal colony is amply clear. Its functioning was marked by escapes, disease and mutinies (Brown 2007). Despite stories of such failures, the Iwahig penal farm stands today as a remarkable testimony to the progressive ambitions of the Philippine prison administration. No doubt such progressive ambitions have not necessarily impacted the overall prison system and in that sense the penal farms may still be seen as isolated experiments, for the prisons in the Philippines are otherwise marked by the supposedly usual problems of the global South – a rapidly growing prison population, and consequent congestion of as much as 249%, use of violent force as a form of control, rioting and large escapes, threatening both the sanctity of the institution as well as larger issues of security.

In many of the countries that witnessed colonial rule, changes in the prison structure, especially the shift from harsh and inhumane conditions of prisons and punishment to more humane ways of the treatment of criminals, were attributed to the encounter with Western modernity and the colonial attempt to modernize the prison along the lines of the well-ordered Western prison. Japan marks a departure, as it does not have a history of being colonized; rather it was the colonizer in Taiwan. In Japan too, however, the shift from the violent Tokugawa punishment system (which involved public floggings, burnings and other forms of judicial torture) to the modern reformative ideals of prison management, is linked to the encounter with Western modernity during the Meiji regime. Botsman (2005) argues that the cultural and historical specificities, the values of Western modernity and the logics of development and progress were partly instrumental in the changing penal system in Japan. Botsman (2005) makes two other interesting points regarding the encounter with the West and the making of modern institutions. First, the introduction of the notion of incarceration for reform made it possible for the regime to inflict suffering on a larger body of people (ibid.: 203). Second, the obvious association of Western modernity with humaneness needs to be questioned. The most disagreeable aspects of the Meiji regime could be linked to the fact that prisons were modelled along the line of French prisons. The model of the Western prison was rather seductive, and was also considered replicable.

For countries such as Kyrgyzstan and Kazakhstan, it was not the interface with a colonial power but the larger political field that shaped their penal institutions

(Kupatadze 2014). These countries echoed many practices of the Soviet era. Both record very high prison population rates, with Kazakhstan at 275 and Kyrgyzstan at 182 (International Crisis Group Report 2006, 2009). While the Kyrgyz prison system is administered by the General Directorate for the Implementation of Punishments (GUIN), in Kazakhstan, prisons are administered by the Committee for the Criminal Correction System. Suspects, when first arrested, are detained in a Temporary Remand Isolator (Russian acronym, IVS), usually in a police building or compound. During investigation, suspects are shifted to Investigatory Isolators (Russian acronym, SIZO), and housed there till trial is completed. Convicted offenders are sent to prisons or correctional colonies. If convicted they are sent to prisons or, more often, correctional colonies – Soviet-era camp-style prisons where prisoners live in barracks each with 40 to 100 beds. There are in all six SIZOs and 11 correctional colonies in Kyrgyzstan. Kazakhstan has 20 SIZOs and 73 correctional colonies. In these countries as in other Asian nations, prisons have been considered fertile ground for Islamists to carry out political activism. As plans for prison reform have not really made any headway in these Central Asian countries, prisons have slipped into a morass of corruption, violations and mismanagement.

Composition of prison population and classificatory systems

In this section I focus on three related issues of prison demographics and its implications, which are typical to Asian prisons. Overcrowding, implying a much larger number of prisoners than the official sanctioned capacity, a higher number of pre-trial detainees, generally spending substantial time in the prison, and the practice of classificatory systems for better management of prison populations are key descriptors of demographic aspects in the prisons of Asia. I draw on examples from some countries to highlight these descriptors and their implications for the ways in which they relate to and militate against notions of the colonial prison and the well-ordered Western prison.

Of all the documented and declared prisons, detention centres and prisoner camps in the countries of Asia, India possibly has the largest number, being pegged at 1,391 such institutions (International Centre for Prison Studies – ICPS data). Some of its immediate neighbours – Pakistan, Bangladesh and Sri Lanka – have recorded comparatively lower numbers of institutions with 97, 68 and 61, respectively. China has 700 such recognized institutions and 30 juvenile centres along with many unaccounted for detention camps. The only other country that comes close is the Philippines, with 1,137 carceral institutions.

The number of prisons in some other countries such as Japan, Iran, Indonesia and Afghanistan ranges from 180 to 440 prisons. Bhutan, Cambodia, Hong Kong and the Maldives are among the countries that have fewer carceral institutions, with an average of about 20. The prison population rate, being the number of people incarcerated per 100,000 of the national population, is another significant indicator of the levels of incarceration and the state of the criminal justice systems. Lower prison population rates, however, need not necessarily signify lower levels of incarceration. The figure of prison population rates must be read along with the number of institutions, the possible numbers of undocumented sites of confinement and illegal detentions, and also the documented pre-trial or remand prisoners. The prison population rate of Afghanistan is calculated at 83, based on an estimated national population of 35.05 million at the end of 2013 (from UN figures).

According to Walmsley (2013), China, along with the USA and Russia, has half of the world's prison population. China has about 1.65 million sentenced prisoners and there are more than 650,000 in 'detention centres'. With the inclusion of these figures, the overall Chinese total would be over 2.3 million. According to current calculation of a prison population rate in China, it stands at 124, and this rests on an estimated national population of 1.37 billion at mid-2013 (from UN figures). The rate would probably actually be much higher as this calculation is based on sentenced prisoners in Ministry of Justice prisons only. According to the calculations of the ICPS, in China the total prison population of 2,350,000 would raise the prison population rate to 172 per 100,000. China's neighbour, India, despite its large number of institutions, has a relatively low prison population rate, at 33, based on an estimated national population of 1,259.8 million at the end of 2013 (from UN figures). Bangladesh records a rate slightly higher than India, at 44, based on an estimated national population of 159.55 million at January 2015 (from UN figures). Japan's rate is 50, and this is drawn on an estimated national population of 127.2 million at the end of 2013 (from Japanese government statistics bureau figures). Japan's erstwhile colony, Taiwan, records a high prison population rate at 274 and this is hinged on an estimated national population of 23.42 million at the end of October 2014 (from Council for Economic Planning, Taiwan, figures). Thailand has the highest prison population rate in Asia, estimated at 483. This figure is based on an estimated national population of 67.32 million at January 2015 (from UN figures).[8]

What do these numbers mean? While size and demographics in these countries are obvious explanations for the number of institutions, the larger imperatives of governance, of finding a space and a solution for the 'disposable' population, of ensuring programmes directed at the disposable, and the imperatives related to the growth of religious radicalization and the global context of terrorism are also responsible for the number of institutions in Asia. The numbers also signify the spread and pervasiveness of imprisonment both as a method of punishment as well as a strategy to constrain and control the unwanted and 'disposable' individuals in society. Moreover, such statistical data also stand testimony to the continuities in the repressive nature of the state, through the shifting contours of colonial, post-colonial and so-called neo-liberal contexts of governance.

Many of the countries, such as Bangladesh, India, the Philippines, Nepal, Cambodia and Pakistan, have a high percentage of pre-trial or remand prisoners. In India, the total number of jail inmates as per a government report in 2013 is 411,992 with 95.6% constituting the male prisoner population and 67.6% are pre-trial or remand prisoners. The judicial processes in many of the South Asian countries are slow, with the courts unable to cope with a disproportionately large number of cases with their relatively restricted resources. The large numbers are possibly also attributable to the new contexts of criminality, framed in terms of global terrorism, the international drug mafia and growing concerns with internal security. Almost all the countries have registered an increase in prison populations in the last decade, with a few exceptions such as the Maldives, Kyrgyzstan and Hong Kong.

In Hong Kong, even though the total number of prisoners is substantially lower than other countries in Asia, it has a much higher imprisonment rate in comparison with the rest of Asia. The other significant detail in the imprisoned population in Hong Kong is the high proportion of female migrants (Walmsley 2006). This prison statistic is motivated largely by the routine use of imprisonment as a strategy for migration control. The migratory movements in the People's Republic of China are largely internal, from the rural to urban areas. According to the 2005 census, 147.35 million people in China were categorized as mobile population and this figure does not take into account the undocumented internal migrants. The major cities typically have one-quarter or one-third of their total population as migrant workers (Bakken 1998; Lee 2007). Detention is a key strategy through which state apparatuses deal with such mobilities.

The increasing numbers of pre-trial detainees and the excruciatingly slow judicial process in some of the Asian countries are considered the key drivers not only of the large prison populations, but also of their overcrowding and attendant poor living conditions. Certain contaminations in the conventional ordering of living space are 'normal' within prisons. One instance of this is the location of the toilet facilities in close proximity to living space. It is through such contaminations that carceral spaces are created as unique and designed to punish. However, apart from the 'normal' limits of such contaminations, built into the prisons' structural and architectural realms, Asian prisons also display, through everyday practice, many such contaminations, such as lack of proper sanitation, filthy living spaces, and lack of basic items in the living spaces, such as bedding, fans and so on. All these are assaults on the prisoners' bodies. Incarceration, then, comes to be embodied very differently in these prisons from their counterpart, the well-ordered, modern Western prison. I am not in any way suggesting the infallibility of that model; on the contrary, I wish to point to its limitations in understanding the many local variations with which the well-ordered prison has been accepted in different Asian countries. In the face of such poor living conditions, the Asian prison was also a site of everyday discontent, which was expressed not just as a way of registering protest with the prison practices, but also a way of connecting to the modern and global human rights-based perspective, with which prisons are now sought to be governed.

A significant way of managing this dissent was the classification of prisoners and their differential treatment based on such classification. In Sri Lanka, overcrowding is estimated at an astounding 250%. The rate of overcrowding for pre-trial prisoners in relation to the authorized accommodation for this category of prisoners is 600%. Such severe space shortage means that prisoners are forced to take turns sleeping at night. Sleep deprivation and forcing inmates to stand for hours on end are common practices of torture used in the many camps and illegal detention facilities in many of the Asian countries. The dangers of overcrowding spill over into other realms, such as health and hygiene, and impact everyday lives of prisoners and their in-prison relationships (Dharmadasa n.d.).

In India, prisoners are typically classified as (i) civil prisoners, (ii) criminal prisoners, (iii) prisoners under trial, (iv) convicted persons, (v) habitual offenders, (vi) non-habitual offenders, (vii) political prisoners, and (viii) detenus.[9] Further, each of these categories is divided by sex and into division I and division II prisoners, suggesting class background and educational status. The principle of separation of prisoners was generally laid down by colonial law and continued in the post-colonial prison. Female prisoners were to be accommodated in a correctional home for female prisoners or in the female ward of a correctional home, with further segregation as follows: (i) female prisoners classified as habitual offenders were to be segregated from female non-habitual offenders; (ii) female prisoners under trial must be segregated from female convicts; (iii) female prisoners convicted of or charged with any sexual or other offence involving grave moral depravity are segregated from all other types of female prisoners. A division I prisoner typically enjoys better facilities in prison, owing to her/his higher status in society. Thus a division I prisoner may be provided with better accommodation, and allowed more items of personal use. Such classification of prisoners in India is very similar to the Prisons Act of 1894. It appears to be strictly functional and does not hold any notion of discrimination or privilege. It corresponds to the larger aims of safety, security and control within prison walls. While this is a formal principle of managing the prisoner community, it is not always put into practice. As a staff member from my fieldwork in a prison in India has pointed out:

> We all agree that habitual criminals, hardened criminals should be kept separate from the under trial prisoners or even the first-time offenders. Or else as is happening now, a person may come in here as a petty thief and go out of jail as a dacoit.[10] Friendships are made and plans for further criminal activities are hatched within the four walls of this jail. Small criminals go out of here to become big *dadas* and *mastans*.[11] But what can we do? We try our best to maintain the principle of separation but there are so many prisoners … [this] creates more problems of violence, more fighting among the prisoners.

This classification and consequent separation of prisoners defines the nature of interaction between prisoners. Greater interaction is possible among those prisoners who inhabit the same space within the prison. Moreover, the prisoners under trial, the convicts and the prisoners awaiting execution have access to different facilities. This often leads to the formation of groups. Prisoners who share the same kind of privileges form a group and closer relationships develop within these group formations. The long-term convict prisoners, because of the years spent in the prison and their familiarity with the system and its people, have access to many facilities, otherwise inaccessible in the prison system. For instance, they are allowed a 'raw diet', a ration of food for the week, which they can cook themselves. The raw diet is given as a privilege and there are occasions when it is withdrawn. This enables and encourages community cooking and eating as groups of prisoners pool their raw diet, cook and eat together. Sometimes, they may have an under-trial prisoner cooking for them and, in return for this service, the under-trial prisoner can eat a little better food than what is normally served in the prison. Late lock-up, more private office 'interviews' with family and relatives, power to use the money they earn from their work within the prison to buy essential items, even cigarettes, are some of the privileges the convict prisoners are allowed within the framework of the legal system. However, these facilities are always positioned as privileges, allowing the authorities to withdraw any or all of these as and when they deem fit. The system of privileges sets off a convict class of prisoners from an under-trial or remand group of prisoners in a classical 'haves' and 'have nots' categorization.

There is a clear administrative justification in organizing prisoners into gangs, classifying them in groups based on their status within the criminal justice system and with the use of socio-economic criteria, marking a continuity with colonial rules. These practices ensure benefits for both prisoners and staff members. For the prison staff, it fosters an enabling environment as the task of surveillance is diffused, rather than being concentrated in the hands of a few officials. It also inculcates a spirit of self-discipline, closely monitored by the prisoner hierarchy that is fostered by the classificatory systems. However, the more general implication of such classificatory systems is that they produce and sustain a 'culture of lenience' (Bandyopadhyay 2010). This culture of lenience implies that prisoners are, sometimes, able to manipulate the system towards the fulfilment of personal gain. It also introduces unpredictability in the application of prison rules. When prison rules are subject to such capriciousness, tyranny is located in the arbitrariness of everyday practice, rather than in the rule itself.

In many prisons, this culture of lenience morphs into a web of corrupt everyday practices that define and order prison life. Everyday corruption is, in fact, a structuring element of many Asian prisons. It precludes the possibility of following rules strictly. Simultaneously, it opens up spaces and contexts of resistance and subversion, yet allowing for arbitrariness and the potential for random assertions of control, intimidation and violence. Almost everything is on sale in these prisons. In my fieldwork experience in prisons in India, items that were provided to prisoners would be sold at prices much lower than market rates, to the warders. For instance, women prisoners who had their young children staying with them in prison would get a packet of milk every day for their children. This was sold to the warders at a throwaway price, and both prisoners and warders benefited from such arrangements. The web of corruption, complex in its workings and pragmatic rules, was also significant in building and sustaining the fused roles of and relationships between warders/officials and prisoners. Fusion of functions, which I have highlighted earlier as a characteristic of many post-colonial prisons in Asia, carried over from the colonial practice of using prisoners as controllers, creating informers among them, and forming a system of privileges for the effective management of prison populations. Virtually everything is for sale in the prison. Large bribes will get prisoners transferred to the more comfortable conditions of prison hospitals, or to other prisons, or to get frequent furloughs. Smaller bribes will ensure the safe passage of contraband, from drugs to banned political literature, into prisons. Prison personnel often rely on prisoners for earning extra money and run errands for them to supplement their meagre salaries.

In Thailand, while there was recognition of the need for classification as a way of ensuring the appropriate treatment of criminals and preventing possible contamination and corruptibility of one type of prisoner/criminal by another, budgetary constraints made it difficult for rigid principles of segregation to be followed. However, in practice, convicted prisoners were divided into classes such as excellent, very good, good, moderate, bad, very bad. This classification formed the basis of their rights, privileges and the kinds of work they were assigned. This classification was declared in the Penitentiary Act, first enacted 1915, during the reign of King Rama VI and later again in 1936, in order to abolish the previous laws and frame modern measures of prison administration.[12]

The Penitentiary Act gave the minister the power to discriminate between classes of prisoners and to specify conditions for transferring from one kind or class to another by way of promotion or retrogression as well as attributing different treatment to prisoners. All new convicts started out by being placed automatically in the moderate class. If a prisoner violated a legitimate rule, he/she could possibly suffer a retrogression of class, or a deferment of promotion. On the contrary, in reward for good conduct, a prisoner could gain more chances to have regular and contact visits, permission to use their own clothes sometimes and even promotion to a new class. This example from Thailand shows how the principle of segregation was conveniently moulded, not just in practice, but also expressed as such in the rules, owing to the local exigencies of prison administration.

Body disciplining, forced labour and violation of human rights

Through the arbitrariness, corrupt everyday practices and the fusion of functions in prison life, a deeply entangled prison world is assembled. I have argued so far that this entangled prison climate, typical to many prisons in Asia, opens up prison spaces for prisoners and staff, while simultaneously creating locked-in, oppressive structures, inherently damaging for the practice of human rights and the assertion of prisoners' sense of self. In this section, I articulate how prisons in Asia effectively accomplish the latter, disciplining the prisoner's body through surveillance, physical labour and the control of time, the subtle tactics of ensuring self-disciplining and through the more direct horrific violations of the human body, reminiscent of the spectacle of bodily torture that Foucault described in tracing the history of modern methods of punishment (Foucault 1977). The latter are crucial in the production of the images of prison as the worst kinds of torture institutions.

Nowak (2009), in describing his experiences as UN special rapporteur on torture, argues that torture, though pervasive, takes place behind closed doors and is the 'smoking gun' – hard to find. There were innumerable cases where he had encountered torture, had walked into interrogation rooms where it was clear to him that torture had just taken place, even though it was denied by the detainee himself. He recounts that in his fact-finding missions to Nepal and Jordan, he presented such overwhelming evidence of torture that the respective police officers were forced to admit its practice. His narratives of torture were thus carefully built through the evidence on the body of the detainee, the opinion of the forensic experts and, wherever possible, the actions and statements of the people involved – the interrogators and the tortured detainees.

I highlight a few instances of such bodily harm in various Asian countries. In Burma, for instance, many political prisoners freed in a general amnesty in 2011, spoke of the horrors of prison life – trial without defence, solitary confinement and regular beatings in prison, and prison practice being defined not by rules but by the person in charge. In a journalist's report, Kawvida, a Buddhist monk who spent four years in prison, said: 'Prison conditions changed depending on the officer in charge … They have no rules. One officer was very cruel and refused to allow my relatives who had come from about 500 miles away to visit me twice' (Hla Tun 2011: 1).

In India, a young tribal woman, a teacher, was arrested for being a courier between Maoists and a large corporate group. Soni Sori was repeatedly sexually assaulted while in custody at the police station. In her many letters she complained of torture, the denial of sustenance and the fear of loss of life. In one letter to the Supreme Court of India she wrote: 'Giving electric shocks, stripping me naked, shoving stones inside me – is this going to solve the Naxal problem' (sonisori.wordpress.com). Soni Sori has become the representative voice for the many human rights violations that the state has unleashed on the people of some states, such as Chhattisgarh, and the terrifying narrative of bodily harm that is used in carceral spaces.[13]

The case of Soni Sori and many others like her, jailed for protesting against state policy, for seeking rights to livelihood and other basic rights, highlights the way in which state power and authority operate, as if acting independently in the interests of internal security, progress and development. A 'disposable' population is marked out, incarcerated, tortured and/or killed. Somewhat contrarily, in Afghanistan, the state may be encountered as being clearly complicit with 'global' forces, designed to achieve similar ends. Prisons become the main conduits through which the politics of 'disposability' is articulated. The prison becomes the symbol as well as the message of disposability. In Afghanistan, the controversial military detention centre, Bagram, referred to as the 'Gitmo[14] no one talks about' (Elliot 2011), has allegedly seen a threefold increase in its population since the Bush regime. Illegal detentions, torture in custody to elicit confessions, convictions without evidence, detention of women on charges of 'moral crimes', and the holding of prisoners in inhuman living conditions are common in Afghan prisons. According to a report based on a UN survey, different methods of torture, such as electric shocks, twisting of genitals, suspension from wrists or feet, were used.

In a survey of prison camp experiences in North Korea the authors found that the conditions considered characteristic of the 'infamous gulag[15] of political penal-labour colonies' are in fact pervasive, present across the penal system, in large penitentiaries, lower-level jails and facilities for labour training (Nolan and Haggard 2009). This survey also shows that there is evidence that 'the authorities disproportionately incarcerate politically-suspect populations: those among the wavering classes, those involved in economic activities beyond direct state control, and those with higher education. However, the strategy of intimidation is not simply related to detention and incarceration, but what happens to inmates once imprisoned' (ibid.: 16).[16]

These instances reflect the routine, random and yet planned ways in which prison administrations in particular and the state in general use bodily harm as a way of regulating compliance and ensuring order and discipline within their institutions. They challenge the Foucauldian idea of imprisonment, the confinement and control of the 'soul' as being at the heart of modern systems of punishment. In fact, these strategies seem to be inadequate for modern prison systems, and are always interlocked in a deadly combination with torturing the body, either through submitting the body to a lack of basic infrastructure, or through direct violations, such as beatings, sexual violence and extreme tests of physical endurance.

The more subtle forms of control are focused on disciplining the body through control of time and labour. Both physical labour and time create value. The prison in China is marked out for its practices of disciplining and management through labour. In China, the use of indeterminate sentencing and forced agricultural labour were the twin plans on which the project of reform through labour was based. As a result of this, a large number of people, unaccounted for, ended up in labour camps, and were subjected to forced labour until the party considered them re-educated (Dikötter 2002a, 2002b). Forced labour, executions and 'black jails' are all terms from the outside – the international community and human rights groups – that are used to describe conditions in the prisons of China. The black jails persist despite the fact that the Chinese government abolished the laws that permitted the detention of non-residents and vagrants. These black jails typically housed petitioners against the government and its local bodies. Detention in black jails is a way of protecting government officials from scrutiny, of identifying dissenting voices among citizens, and rendering them 'disposable' through illegal, indeterminate and violent extra-legal detentions.

In India, one of the largest prisons, Tihar Jail, considered within the country as an exemplar of reform, has a brand of goods that it now sells. Prison labour is cheap, but more fundamentally it is captive. In Burma, the use of prison labour marks a significant point of continuity between pre-colonial and colonial prison administrations. The use of convicts as jailors and often for the positions involving gruesome and dehumanizing tasks was a common practice in colonial prisons and often tends to continue in the post-colonial Asian prisons. In a similar vein, the convict warder in many prisons in India was a position used both as an informer, as a mode of surveillance, and as a tool for punishment against infractions of prison rules. The convict warders, the use of convicts as jailors and in other aspects of prison administration, implies a fusion of functions, and subsequently, a deeply entangled prison climate. These entanglements of power often arose from the exigencies of colonial rule, administrative convenience, and the need to understand and form categories. Arnold (1994), using Foucault's notion of discursive power, articulated the ways in which colonial prisons (especially with reference to his work on India) were used to regulate the native populace, both through actual disciplining of bodies, and also through the generation of knowledge and categories of understanding, further cemented through administrative practices. Prisons in most of the newly colonized countries were documented to be evolving from otherwise indiscriminate structures, yet marked in the barrenness of violence, abuse and denial of humane treatment. Colonial power, contrarily, made determined moves to disassociate prisons from their absurdly barbaric representations, while establishing the custodial sentence within a Pentonville-style[17] modern prison as the only legitimate mode of punishment. The modern prison in Asian nations was, thus, a remnant of colonial rule, one that was accepted in the new post-colonial nations along with its physical structure, modelled on the panopticon[18] and its administrative practices. In fact, in countries such as India and Bangladesh, the Prisons Act of the British Empire continues to be the basis of prison administration even today. While the common condemnation for this is the absurdity of being governed by imperial rules despite being citizens of a free nation, such continuity is also indicative of the rather insignificant positioning of prisons and punishment systems in nation-building projects. The advances made in modernizing prison systems by colonial powers had seemingly succeeded in establishing a radical break from prisons of the pre-colonial era while forging connectedness through similarities with the trope of the well-ordered Western prison. In housing the 'disposable', the prison as an organization assumed a marginal, almost disposable positioning in relation to larger programmes of institution building in the newly independent nations. This sense of disposability persists in the contemporary Asian prisons. Any critical reflection on prison conditions seems to be largely driven by reports of human rights violations, overcrowding, and inhumane living conditions undertaken by external forces – international organizations, human rights groups and, more generally, an international human rights protocol. The latter tends to shape the discourse within which prisons of the global South are viewed, represented and understood. The image shifts that seem to characterize our understanding of prisons in this part of the world – namely the barbaric prison, well-ordered prison, post-colonial reformed prison – are in fact not really discrete entities or characterizations. They are intermeshed with each other.

Concluding comments

Almost all the Asian countries, with the exception of Japan, Thailand, Bhutan and China, are marked by their colonized past. Japan was a colonizer and had colonized Korea and Taiwan. Even though Bhutan was never formally under colonial rule, the British exerted substantial control. Parts of China have been under colonial influence; however, the Chinese nation has not been under colonial rule in the same way as the other Asian nations. The colonized pasts of these Asian countries thus have an indelible impact on the practices of prison administration and, equally significantly, on the ways in which citizens are tagged as 'criminal', 'suspects' and subsequently, 'disposable'. The criminal justice systems in most of these countries have been characterized by the paradox of continuity with colonial laws along with the need to establish a break from their colonial pasts, by remaking and thinking anew the nature, composition, functions and organization of key institutions. Any decolonization project thus not only implied a reordering of formal relations of ruling and power, but also an overhaul of key institutions to reflect and inscribe ideas of nationhood and national pride, independence, freedom and indigeneity on these institutions. At the same time, the pressures of modernity and the will to modernize were paramount. The dominant, even hegemonic, tropes of modern institutions were Western and those belonging to the colonial powers.

In attempting to unravel this paradox through a discussion of prison practices in Asian countries, I used the broad themes of continuance with colonial rules of prison administration and the persistence of discriminations practised by colonial administrations, often under different garbs – severe human rights violations and a return to repressive body disciplining in punishment processes. Both of these aspects are encapsulated within a global context of terrorism in a post-9/11 world.[19] This has implications for the composition of prison populations and the nature of prison management. In India, for instance, the arbitrary jailing of young Muslim men as suspected terrorists is common practice. In fact, the prison population in India and other countries in South Asia constituted largely those under trial, with many who serve time in prison for years more than their punishment requires.

Finally, I have presented the nature of Asian prisons as institutions that serve to further peripheralize and abandon certain marginalized groups in society. While it carries on this task of removing people at the margins and confining them, the prison also, I argue, takes on a peripheralized identity. Paradoxically, in the context of the reconfigured politics involving terrorism, global economic connections, and the continued and possibly heightened need for cheap labour, the prison's significance as an institution of control and maintenance of order stands to increase many times over. The new prisons in the neo-liberal regimes potentially are spaces of captive labour, implicating these institutions in new logics of management and administration and qualitatively different repressive tactics.

The study and understanding of modern prisons, since the publication of the landmark book *Discipline and Punish*, has been expressed in Foucauldian terms to suggest the diffuseness of power in new modes and technologies of surveillance and the dissolution of a focus on punishing the body. However, as documentation of everyday life and practices in prisons across Asia reveals, there appears to be a return to the focus on the corporeal body, as discipline, punishments and notions of order are increasingly inscribed on the body. On the one hand, the technologies of surveillance and the panoptic order coincide with the extreme forms of violations of bodily integrity and rights. On the other, many kinds of contamination, disruptions of order and everyday situations of chaos permeate some of these prison environments, challenging the picture of the well-ordered prison. Another theme is significant in the notion of the well-ordered prison – the aspect of reform and rehabilitation. The well-ordered Western prison acquires this epithet on the basis of maintenance of human rights, and a concern with reform, which find expression in grand images through policy documents, government reports and changes in governance practices through legislation, or in the negotiations in everyday practices. The notions of reform, rehabilitation and human rights have thus travelled, been adapted to, and reworked in the post-colonial prisons.

In many of the Asian countries, in the throes of rapid social change and in the midst of concerted efforts to cope with globalization, prisons become the space for the dissenting voices. The prison itself thus becomes a site of dissent and seeks to create, albeit implicitly, a larger subversive political field. The entangled interactions within prison, the fusion of functions and the subversive practices within and outside the prison, uncovered through the unravelling of the suppressed voices (such as those of Soni Sori), represent multiple layers of subversion. Prisoners and prisons tend to challenge the repressive character of the prisons and, by extension, the State. They do this by engaging critically with the everyday, through regular attempts at escapes, riots and reporting of human rights violations. In assimilating the specific cultural idiosyncrasies of their contexts, prisons in Asia have gone beyond the rhetoric of being remnants of colonial institutions. Nor can they be seen as fully embracing modernity in the carceral complex. In these senses, the prison in Asia also stands as an emerging critique of the neo-liberalism and the hegemonic narrative of global terrorism.

Notes

1 See Bandyopadhyay 2010. Here the author gives a detailed ethnographic account of everyday life in a prison in India.
2 In Bourdieu's (1983) understanding a field is constituted by the organizing laws and practices as well as the continuous struggle for appropriation of different types of capital by the participants in a particular field. In this sense, it is both ordered and dynamic.
3 Srinivas (1976, 1979), one of the pioneers in sociology in India, made a significant departure in the study of Indian society by diverting significantly from the Indological approach, also known as the 'book view', implying a picture of society that emerged from classical Hindu and that provided by colonial ethnography. Field view, or the use of anthropological methods and fieldwork to understand the structure of Indian society, contested the earlier dominant 'book view'.
4 McGowen (1995) in a collection of essays on the practice of punishment in Western society writes of the 'well-ordered prison' of the 19th century as presenting a sharp contrast to the prison of the earlier century. The modern prison was 'quiet and orderly' with clearly demarcated groups of prisoners and jailers, identical cells for prisoners, no conversation or pleasure and a general sense of dreariness. While the well-ordered prison was 'drab and functional, it was also clean and healthy' (ibid.: 79).
5 Research in Western prisons has consistently focused on gangs as a way of regulating prison life. For a recent account of how prison gangs function as mechanisms of prison governance in America, see Skarbek 2014.
6 Anderson (2012) in her work on 'Subaltern Lives' discusses the implications of convict transportation on colonial practices around labour, incarceration and disciplining the body. The issues of new forms of enslavement and indenture, the use of convicted felons for public works as well as for the management and running of prisons were significant elements of colonial practices. Clearly the complex spheres of work, incarceration and punishment, transportation and the nature of prison practices are embedded in this discussion (ibid.: 43). Also see Wintin and Brown (2005) for a discussion on the use of convict warders in colonial Burma, a practice that continues in modern prisons. They argue that convict warders were 'men of considerable power' and other 'convict staff – long-serving and trusted inmates who were appointed night watchmen, overseers, or convict warders – were essential in the running of colonial Burma's prisons' (ibid.: 5).
7 Also see Human Rights Watch Report 1990, *Prison Conditions in Indonesia* for an overview of the legal framework of prisons in Indonesia, www.hrw.org/reports/pdfs/i/indonesia/indonesi908.pdf.

8 These prison statistics have been taken from the International Centre for Prison Studies online database (www.prisonstudies.org). The research, publication and the collation of various reports and fact-finding exercises undertaken by this organization attempts to address the silences around prison governance in many of the countries in the world.

9 A *detenu* means any person lodged in custody. In the Indian prison system, this term continues to be used along with the terms on trial or remand prisoners. There are instances where the term *detenus* is used as a synonym for political prisoners. See for instance, Raj Jai 1996: 99.

10 The word *dacoit* means brigand, or a member of a gang that ambushes and robs people in the forests and mountains. In common parlance, it came to mean planned and armed robbery in gangs. See for instance Van Woerkens 1995.

11 Both terms mean goons or gang leaders.

12 For a discussion of prisoners' rights and an outline of the premises within which the Thai prison system functioned see www.internationalpenalandpenitentiaryfoundation.org/Site/documents/Stavern/30_Stavern_Report%20Thailand.pdf. This report was written by specialists from the Department of Corrections and narrates a brief history of the prison system in Thailand, along with a description of how prisons and punishment are administered in contemporary Thailand.

13 Also see sanhati.com for information on the Soni Sori case and for documentation on the movement to ensure justice for Soni Sori and others like her. Similarly, Arun Ferreira, a human rights activist, wrote in *Colours of the Cage: A Prison Memoir*, about his five-year experience of imprisonment and torture after being arrested on charges of being a Naxalite. The term Naxalite has reference to the town of Naxalbari in West Bengal, which was the seat of a peasant uprising against local landlords in 1967, and is now used to refer to several Maoist-oriented and militant insurgent and separatist groups that operate in India.

14 The Guantanamo Bay Naval Base, located at Guantanamo Bay, Cuba, has since 2002 contained a military prison for prisoners captured during the 'war on terror' from places such as Iraq and Afghanistan. Allegations of human rights violations and torture in this US military prison have been rife in the aftermath of 9/11. See Slahi (2015) for an account of the horrors of the Guantanamo Bay prison. This is commonly referred to as GTMO or 'Gitmo'.

15 Gulag is a commonly used term for the Stalinist prison labour camps of the former Soviet Union. Literally, gulag is the Russian-language acronym for 'chief administration of corrective labour camps'. This term has since Stalin's regime come to signify the acutely repressive system of slave labour characterized by illegal arrests and detention, destruction of families, transportation of prisoner bodies, and many early and unnecessary deaths (Hawk 2003: 7).

16 Also see Hawk (2003) for an uncompromising and raw account of the political prisoner camps, extra-judicial detention and the forced prison labour practices of the Democratic People's Republic of Korea (North Korea).

17 For a sociological study of Pentonville prison, which became a prototype of a modern prison, see Morris and Morris (2013).

18 Jeremy Bentham (1995) designed a panopticon structure for penal institutions, in which the prisoner cells and guard watchtowers were arranged in a way that the guard could watch the inmates at all times. However, since such surveillance was not actually possible, the panopticon would make the inmates unsure whether they were being watched or not. The structure would create a sense of being under constant surveillance.

19 See Lokaneeta (2012) for an incisive analysis of how the 'war on terror' and the escalation of torture of prisoners created a domino effect in other countries such as in India. She challenges the notion that there has been a decline in the incidence of torture in contemporary liberal democracies, showing in fact that torture is integral to modern jurisprudence.

Bibliography

Anderson, C. (2012) *Subaltern Lives: Biographies of colonialism in the Indian Ocean world, 1790–1920*, Cambridge: Cambridge University Press.

Arnold, D. (1994) 'The colonial prison: power knowledge and penology in nineteenth century India', in D. Arnold and D. Hardiman (eds) *Subaltern Studies VIII: Essays in Honour of Ranajit Guha*, New Delhi: Oxford University Press.

Bakken, B. (1998) *Migration in China*, Copenhagen: NIAS Press.

Bandyopadhyay, M. (2010) *Everyday Life in a Prison: Confinement, surveillance, resistance*, New Delhi: Orient Blackswan.

Bentham, J. (1995) *The Panopticon Writings*, ed. and introduction M. Bozovic, London: Verso.

Botsman, D.V. (2005) *Punishment and Power in the Making of Modern Japan*, Princeton, NJ: Princeton University Press.

Bourdieu, P. (1983) *The Field of Cultural Production*, Cambridge: Polity Press.

Brandt, W. (1980) *North–South: A programme for survival*, London: Pan.

Brown, I. (2007) 'South East Asia: Reform and the colonial prison', in F. Dikötter and I. Brown (eds) *Cultures of Confinement: A history of the prison in Africa, Asia and Latin America*, New York: Cornell University Press, 221–269.

Datir, R.N. (1978) *Prison as a Social System*, Bombay: Popular Prakashan.

Dharmadasa, H.G. (n.d.) 'A general overview of the prison system in Sri Lanka since independence', www.lawandsocietytrust.org/PDF/resource/prison_system.pdf (accessed 30 March 2015).

Dikötter, F. (2002a) *Crime, Punishment and the Prison in Modern China*, New York: Columbia University Press.

Dikötter, F. (2002b) 'The Promise of Repentance: Prison reform in modern China', *British Journal of Criminology* 42: 240–249.

Elliot, J. (2011) 'The Gitmo no one talks about', www.salon.com/2011/06/04/bagram_obama_gitmo/ (accessed 30 March 2015).

Ferreira, A. (2014) *Colours of the Cage: A prison memoir*, New Delhi: Aleph Book Company.

Foucault, M. (1977) *Discipline and Punish: The birth of the prison*, New York: Vintage Books.

Goffman, E. (1962) *Asylums: Essays on the social situations of mental patients and other inmates*, Chicago, IL: Aldine Publishing Company.

Hawk, D. (2003) *The Hidden Gulag*, Washington, DC: US Committee for Human Rights in North Korea.

Hla Tun, A. (2011) 'Insight: Brutal prisons complicate Myanmar's reform', *Reuters*, 8 November: 1–4, www.reuters.com/article/2011/11/08/us-myanmar-prisoners-idUSTRE7A70GG20111108.

Indian Jails Committee (1919–20) *Report of the Indian Jails Committee*, Simla: Government of India Publications.

International Crisis Group (2006) 'Kyrgyzstan's Prison System Nightmare', *Asia Report* No.118, 16 August 2006, www.crisisgroup.org/~/media/Files/asia/centralasia/kyrgyzstan/118_kyrgyzstans_prison_system_nightmare.pdf (accessed 1 September 2015).

International Crisis Group (2009) 'Central Asia: Islamists in prison', update briefing, *Asia Briefing* No.97, Bishkek/Brussels, www.crisisgroup.org/~/media/Files/asia/central asia/b97%20Central %20Asia%20Islamists%20in%20Prison.pdf (accessed 1 September 2015).

Jefferson, A., Martin, T. and Bandyopadhyay, M. (2014) 'Sensing Prison Climates: Governance, survival and transition', *Focaal* 68: 3–17.

Kupatadze, A. (2014) 'Prisons, politics and organised crime: The case of Kyrgyzstan', *Trends in Organised Crime* 17(3): 141–160.

Lee, M. (2007) 'Women's imprisonment as a mechanism of migration control in Hong Kong', *British Journal of Criminology* 47(6): 847–860.

Lokaneeta, J. (2012) *Transnational Torture: Law, violence and state power in the United States and India*, New Delhi: Orient BlackSwan.

McGowen, R. (1995) 'The well-ordered prison', in N. Morris and D. Rothman (eds) *The Oxford History of the Prison: The practice of punishment in Western society*, New York: Oxford University Press, 79–110.

McNair, J.F.A. (1899) *Prisoners their Own Warders: A Record of the Convict Prison at Singapore in the Straits Settlements Established 1825, Discontinued 1873, Together with a Cursory History of the Convict Establishments at Bencoolen, Penang and Malacca from the Year 1797*, Westminster: Archibald Constable and Co., www.gutenberg.org/files/26974/26974-h/26974-h.htm (accessed 25 March 2015).

Morris, T. and Morris, P. (2013 [1963]) *Pentonville: A sociological study of an English prison*, London: Routledge & Kegan Paul.

Nolan, M. and Haggard, S. (2009) *Repression and Punishment in North Korea: Survey evidence of prison camp experiences*, MPRA Paper No. 17705: 1–39, East West Centre Working Papers, mpra.ub. uni-muenchen.de/17705/pdf.

Nowak, M. (2009) 'Fact-finding on torture and ill-treatment and conditions of detention', *Journal of Human Rights Practice* 1(1): 101–119.

Raj Jai, J. (1996) *Emergency Excesses: A daylight robbery of human rights and JP, the saviour*, New Delhi: Regency Publications.

Rhodes, L.A. (2001) 'Toward an anthropology of prisons', *Annual Review of Anthropology* 30: 65–87.

Rigg, J. (2007) *An Everyday Geography of the Global South*, New York: Routledge.

Roth, M. (2006) *Prisons and Prison Systems: A Global Encyclopedia*, New Haven. CT: Greenwood.

Sherman, T.C. (2009) 'Tensions of colonial punishment: Perspectives on recent developments in the study of coercive networks in Asia, Africa and the Caribbean', *History Compass* 7(3): 659–677.

Singh, U. (1998) *Political Prisoners in India*, Delhi: Oxford University Press.

Skarbek, D. (2014) *The Social Order of the Underworld: How prison gangs govern the American penal system*, New York: Oxford University Press.

Slahi, M.O. (2015) *Guantanamo Diary*, London: Little, Brown and Co.

Srinivas, M.N. (1976) *The Remembered Village*, Delhi: Oxford University Press.

Srinivas, M.N. (1979) 'The fieldworker and the field: A village in Karnataka', in M.N. Srinivas, A. M. Shah and E.A. Ramaswamy (eds) *The Field Worker and the Field: Problems and Challenges in Sociological Investigation*, Delhi: Oxford University Press.

Van Woerkens, M. (1995) *The Strangled Traveller: Colonial Imaginings and the Thugs of India*, Chicago, IL: University of Chicago Press.

Walmsley, R. (2006) *World Female Imprisonment List*, London: International Centre for Prison Studies Core Publications.

Walmsley, R. (2013) *World Prison Population List*, London: International Centre for Prison Studies Core Publications.

Walmsley, R. (2014) *World Pre-trial/Remand Imprisonment List*, London: International Centre for Prison Studies Core Publications.

Wintin, T.T. and Brown, I. (2005) 'Colonial Burma's prison: Continuity with its pre-colonial past?', *IIAS Newsletter* 19(5), www.iias.nl/sites/default/files/IIAS_NL39_05.pdf (accessed 30 March 2015).

Yang, A.A. (1987) 'Disciplining "natives": Prisons and prisoners in early nineteenth century India', *Journal of South Asian Studies* 10(2): 29–45.

Yang, A.A. (2004) 'Indian convict workers in Southeast Asia in the late eighteenth and early nineteenth centuries', *Journal of World History* 14(2): 179–208.

Zinoman, P. (2001) *The Colonial Bastille: A history of imprisonment in Vietnam, 1862–1940*, Berkeley: University of California Press.

Chapter 26

Latin American prisons

Sacha Darke and Maria Lúcia Karam

As with other areas of criminology (e.g. Aas 2012; Cain 2000; Lee and Laidler 2013) and social science (e.g. Connell 2006; Santos 2007; Tuhiwai Smith 1999), socio-legal, historical, ethnographic and first-hand examinations of prisons beyond North America and Western Europe have recently begun to emerge in the English language. Anglophone scholars are also increasingly engaging with academic and biographical accounts of prisons in the transitional and developing world which have not been translated into English. This chapter is co-authored by criminologists from the United Kingdom and Brazil; the first named author is one of just a handful of Northern researchers to have familiarized themselves with Latin American prisons literature and conducted in-situ research in Latin American prisons. The second named author similarly joins a relatively small club of Latin American prison researchers to have published in English. The authors have previously collaborated in publishing two articles on Brazilian prisons (Darke 2014a; Darke and Karam 2012). Here we broaden our object of analysis and explore what we perceive to be the key features of prisons and prison life in Latin America as a whole. Alongside special journal editions recently produced by the Global Prisons Research Network (Focaal 2014), Cheliotis (South Atlantic Quarterly 2014), and Hathazy and Müller (Crime, Law and Social Change 2014), we hope to make a significant contribution to reducing the gap in academic knowledge of Latin American prisons in the Northern world. Mindful of our target audience, wherever possible we cite the work of Latin American prison scholars that has been published or translated into English. As far as we are aware, besides Unger and Magaloni (Ungar 2003; Ungar and Magaloni 2009), we are the first social scientists to write such a regional analysis in any language.

Despite the extraordinary task of identifying commonalities between prisons across the 20 nations that make up the region, we do not wish to provide a purely descriptive account. In the conclusion we also take the opportunity to develop a number of insights into the utility of Northern theories in explaining (and potentially changing or learning from) justice systems in other parts of the world. In the context of globalization, increasing policy exchange and international activism, it is all the more important to explore the historical and cultural contexts in which justice systems have been shaped in different countries and regions. Cohen (1982) explained that North American and Western European penology has not only largely developed in ignorance of the socio-economic structures of other parts of the world, but the centralized, professionalized and specialized Northern justice systems upon which it is based emerged during a specific (early 19th-century) period of industrialization, urbanization, democratization and progressive modernization, conditions that vary enormously from one place to another.

The irony, Cohen emphasized, is that the crime control models that came to dominate 19th- and 20th-century Northern justice systems are ever more exported across the globe just as the practices are increasingly questioned at home. He gives as an example the promotion of therapeutic interventions in prison. However, there is little evidence of any international prison reform initiatives having had any real impact in Latin America (Macaulay 2013). As Aguirre and Salvatore have highlighted in a series of Latin American historical studies (Aguirre 2005, 2007; Salvatore and Aguirre 1996; Salvatore et al. 2001), prison modernizers have routinely met resistance at all political levels, from a lack of state resources or control over local practices, to a culturally ingrained authoritarian tradition that not only permeates relationships between elites and lower classes, but is reproduced by the latter 'in a seemingly endless chain of abusive and despotic behaviour' (Aguirre 2007: 9). Alongside our more general aim to provide an overview of prisons and prison life, in this chapter we draw particular attention to two paradigms of globalized crime control that quite clearly have, in contrast to the international human rights/professional therapy agenda, particular resonance in Latin America: those of criminal justice militarization and, quite the opposite of rehabilitation, securitization of the prison environment. In these two regards, Latin America is, and always has been, a world leader. In the case of criminal justice militarization, it is becoming even more so in the context of the 'war on drugs'.

In the first half of the chapter we chart the extraordinary rise in Latin American prison populations over the past two decades, as well as deteriorating prison conditions, and question the extent to which the region's prison systems continue to adhere to international human rights norms (if they had indeed ever adhered to these norms). We then turn our attention to the daily lives of prison inmates and staff in the second half of the chapter. Here our focus shifts onto the self-governing nature of Latin American prisons.

However, this is neither the time nor the place to attempt a systematic account of the socio-economic conditions underpinning prison conditions and the use of prison in Latin America. In place of the theoretically impossible task of developing universal, culture-free social theories (Karstedt 2001) and conceptions of human rights (Santos 2007), such a piece of work would need to focus on how global ideas are, 'appropriated and transformed by very distinct local styles of expression dependent on the political, economic, social and cultural variables of particular institutions and social groups' (Dikötter 2007: 7). In addition to exploring cultural specificities in and within individual countries, a complete study of Latin American prisons would need to cover a range of interrelated historical and contemporary, global and regional factors. These would include such issues as the legacies of colonialism (e.g. Aguirre and Salvatore 2001), slavery (Aguirre 2007) and military dictatorship (de Azevedo 2006), post-colonial state building (Hay 2001), the dominance of individualist positivist sciences and social Darwinism in Latin American criminology (Del Olmo 1981, 1999), the spread of neo-liberal penality (Müller 2012; Wacquant 2003), the threat to state sovereignty posed by the illicit drugs trade (Garces 2014a), political and judicial practices and procedures (Macaulay 2013), political indifference (Ungar 2003) and incapacity (Ungar and Magaloni 2009), popular justice/cultural distrust of law (Caldeira 2000), fear of violence (Bergman and Whitehead 2009), machismo (Karstedt 2001), and Christianity, including the recent rise of evangelicalism (Dias 2005). Our understanding of Latin American prisons is informed by each of these ideas, and we return to a number of them in this chapter. In the future we hope to consolidate these works in an effort to develop a more comprehensive criminology of Latin American prisons.

The expanding power of punishment

A continuous expansion of the power of punishment has been noticeable worldwide from the last decades of the 20th century, bringing increased diversification in its enforcement. Criminal justice systems have gone beyond the walls of prisons. Community-based sanctions, home detention, electronic monitoring devices and other penal measures have widened the net of social control and discipline. However, these new technologies of punishment have not dispensed with the deprivation of liberty. On the contrary, the expansion of the limits of the criminal justice system has run in parallel with the growth of imprisonment. Despite the recognized failure of the stated functions of the deprivation of liberty and the introduction of alternative sanctions, imprisonment not only subsists, but is growing and becoming tougher on the prisoner. Alternative sanctions have brought an increased number of people under penal control without any meaningful reduction in the number of people behind bars.

Indeed, more than 10.2 million people are known to be held in penal institutions throughout the world. In the past 15 years the estimated world prison population has increased by some 25–30% (while the world population has risen by 20%). The world prison population rate has risen from 136 per 100,000 of the world population to the current rate of 144 (Walmsley 2013).

In Latin America the continuous expansion of the power of punishment has been nourished mainly by drug prohibition policies. Drug prohibition refers to the criminalization of conduct that, besides being extensively practised throughout the world, facilitates the creation of fantasies and the launching of moralizing crusades. Since the 1970s, the production, supply and consumption of the selected drugs that were made illicit have been presented as something extraordinarily dangerous, uncontrollable by regular means and needing confrontation by more rigorous, exceptional and emergency measures, conceptualized under a war-like framework (Karam 2009). A 'war on drugs' was declared in 1971 by former president Richard Nixon in the USA, and soon spread throughout the American continent. The 'war on drugs' has intensively focused on Latin American production and supply countries, thus impacting heavily on the region's penal systems. Drug trafficking is now the third (and in some cases the second) leading category of offences by which inmates are charged and sentenced: Brazil – 26.9% of the prison population in 2012 (Brazil. Ministério da Justiça 2012); Peru – 24% in 2013 (Peru. Ministerio de Justicia y Derechos Humanos 2013); Bolivia – 30% in 2009 (TNI/WOLA 2010); Colombia – 17% in 2009 (ibid.). In Ecuador, until the amnesty given to small-scale drug couriers in 2008, 34% of Ecuadorian inmates were imprisoned on drug charges (ibid.).

It is worth noting that the late 20th century also marked another remarkable change in many Latin American countries: the transition from dictatorships to democracy, the most publicized cases being Brazil, Argentina, Uruguay and Chile. However, the democratizing shift paradoxically did not have any progressive impact on the enforcement of penal law. Criminal justice militarization helped to ensure that Latin American despotism survived re-democratization, moulding a 'cool authoritarianism' (Zaffaroni 2006) which has maintained the formal structures of democracy while reinforcing the police state within its boundaries (Zaffaroni et al. 2000).[1] In Brazil, for instance, the new democratic 1988 Constitution rescued and reaffirmed fundamental rights, but provided that exceptionally stringent laws should be adopted to prosecute and punish torture, terrorism and other crimes defined as 'heinous', including the trafficking of drugs. This provision opened the ground for the proliferation of hyper-criminalizing, infra-constitutional norms, in turn enabling the growth of prisons.[2]

According to the latest official statistics (Brazil. Ministério da Justiça 2012), in December 2012 Brazil had the fourth largest prison population in the world: 548,003 individuals were incarcerated, corresponding to a rate of 287.31 prison inmates per 100,000 national population. In two decades the Brazilian prison population has more than tripled: in 1995, there were 148,760 inmates in penal custody (92 per 100,000 national population). Recent research indicates that the prison population had reached 567,655 by May 2014 (Brazil. Conselho Nacional de Justiça 2014). A further 147,937 individuals are held under home detention (ibid.), effectively giving Brazil the third largest prison population in the world: 715,665 individuals, corresponding to a rate of 358 per 100,000. The Brazilian case serves as a major illustration of the above-mentioned trend of growing imprisonment running in parallel with the use of alternative sanctions: the increase in the Brazilian prison population has taken place at the same time as a growing number of individuals were submitted to other kinds of penal control. By the end of 2009, 671,078 individuals were serving alternative sanctions. In 2002 this number amounted to just 102,403 (Brazil. Ministério da Justiça 2012). Similar trends can be found in Peru. The prison population rose from 15,718 inmates in 1995 (69 per 100,000 national population) to 67,891 in January 2014 (220 per 100,000). Another 17,118 individuals were serving alternative sanctions in December 2013 (International Centre for Prison Studies 2014; Peru. Ministerio de Justicia y Derechos Humanos 2013).

Almost all other Latin American countries' prison population rates are likewise higher than the world rate: Uruguay (281); French Guyana (278); Chile (266); Colombia (245); Mexico (210); Suriname (186); Venezuela (161); Ecuador (149). In some Central American countries even higher rates are found: Belize (476); El Salvador (422); Panama (411); Costa Rica (314) (Walmsley 2013). Like Brazil, nearly every Latin American country has seen a doubling or tripling of its prison population over 20 years. The largest increases have been in Colombia and Costa Rica, whose prison populations rose from 30,304 and 3,490, respectively, in 1995 (Müller 2012) to 117,231 (June 2014) in Colombia, and 14,963 (July 2012) in Costa Rica (International Centre for Prison Studies 2014).

A large number of Latin American prisoners are held in pre-trial detention and other forms of remand imprisonment. In Brazil, at the end of 2012, 41% of the 548,003 individuals in penal institutions were pre-trial detainees or remand prisoners (Brazil. Ministério da Justiça 2012). Again, similar rates can be found in other Latin American countries: Peru (54%) (Peru. Ministerio de Justicia y Derechos Humanos 2013); Ecuador (64%); Honduras (62%); Colombia (35%); El Salvador (29%) (IACHR 2011). In some Latin American countries, for instance Argentina, Brazil and Guatemala, it is quite normal for detainees to wait several years for their trial (ibid.; International Bar Association 2010). The high rates of pre-trial detention indicate that the principles inscribed in international declarations of human rights and democratic constitutions, especially the presumption of innocence,[3] have not been respected. According to these norms, any individual charged with a criminal offence should be granted the right to be seen and treated as innocent: a conviction should not take effect until a person has been sentenced through a regularly pronounced, definitive decision (a decision imposed in accordance with the due process of law, which is not subjected to any further revision). The presumption of innocence implies that pre-trial detention and other forms of remand imprisonment are exceptional measures that can only be imposed on the rare occasion they are necessary to ensure the normal evolvement of judicial proceedings. However, as the above-mentioned high rates indicate, incarceration before a definitive conviction has become the rule rather than the exception in many parts of Latin America. This is even more true when it comes to drug-related offences. In many Latin American countries legislation unlawfully establishes mandatory pre-trial detention for drug offences charges. Although the Brazilian Supreme Court declared the unconstitutionality of such a provision of the Brazilian drug law, research carried out in Rio de Janeiro found that almost all defendants (98%) facing drug offences charges remained in prison during the whole evolvement of judicial proceedings (Lemgruber et al. 2013).

Latin American prisons have long been renowned for their inhumane living conditions. This situation has deteriorated further with overcrowding, which has been a natural consequence of the growth of prison populations. Despite the frenetic construction of new prisons in Brazil (the number of prison units almost doubled from 798 in 2005 to 1,478 in 2012), penal institutions have invariably operated over capacity: in December 2012, the 548,003 Brazilian inmates were squeezed into 310,687 available spaces (Brazil. Ministério da Justiça 2012). Brazilian Law 7210/84, which regulates the operation of prisons, establishes that both convicted and remand prisoners should stay in an individual cell measuring at least $6m^2$. This seems to be a law 'for the British to see', a phrase first used when the traffic of slaves was 'officially' abolished in 1831 at the request of Britain, but the law was not actually applied (slavery was finally abolished in 1888). Individual cells only exist in Brazil in maximum security state units or in supermax-style federal prisons, in which a relatively small number of 'dangerous' inmates are held in solitary confinement, under a special regime known as differentiated disciplinary regime.

Similar conditions are found in other Latin American countries, such as Ecuador (13,237 inmates for 9,403 spaces available); Peru (44,760 inmates for 24,894 spaces available); Uruguay (8,785 inmates for 6,413 spaces available); and Chile (53,673 inmates for 35,212 spaces available) (IACHR 2011). Even these figures underestimate the full scale of the problem. Across the region, prisoners are regularly held three to four per 'individual' cell, or in multi-occupancy dormitories, where conditions of under $1m^2$ per person are commonplace. Alongside the excessive and extended use of pre-trial detention, these features of Latin American prisons attract widespread criticism from human rights organizations, including the Inter-American Commission on Human Rights (IACHR). Not only are overcrowding and densely shared accommodation identified as major sources of poor hygienic conditions, the spread of illness, inactivity and friction between and among prisoners and staff, and removal of individuals' rights to privacy, but they also reduce opportunities for rehabilitation-orientated activities such as work and study. The International Covenant on Civil and Political Rights, as well as several democratic constitutions, expressly establishes that punishment – especially the deprivation of liberty – shall have as its aim the re-education and/or social reinsertion of convicts.[4]

Of course, the pains of imprisonment are not restricted to Latin America. By its very nature, imprisonment implies restrictions such as limitation of space, impossibility of going to a different place, to meet and to be together with one's family and other loved ones, segregation, distance from the social environment, and loss of contact with the normal experiences of life. In addition, prisoners across the world experience lack of air, sun and light, precarious sanitary conditions, lack of hygiene, and frequently low-quality food. These physical pains disseminate disease, especially contagious diseases which affect inmates in a much higher proportion than those registered among free populations. In comparison with their North American and Western European counterparts, Latin American prisoners are often able to maintain relatively close contact with their families, who are typically granted the right to weekly visits of up to four hours, albeit often following humiliating entry procedures, including body cavity examinations (Garces et al. 2013). Ironically, prisoners' access to their families has increased with overcrowding, as prison administrators have become more dependent on them to make up for shortfalls in state provision, including medicines (IACHR 2011). In Brazil, for instance, an estimated 86% of male prisoners receive family visits (Brasil. Câmara dos Deputados 2008). However, in all other ways the extraordinary levels of overcrowding experienced by Latin American prisoners worsen both the psychological and physical effects of confinement. The aggravating effect that overcrowding has on prisoners' physical deterioration is reflected, for example, in excessively high levels of tuberculosis and HIV/AIDS (ibid.). In Peru, more than 10% of the prison population is infected with HIV, while TB incidence is as high as 30%. These TB incidence rates are 20 to 23 times higher than in the general Peruvian population (Comisión Episcopal de Acción Social 2013).

Prison life

In their analysis of the rise of Latin America's largest prison gang, the PCC (Primeiro Comando do Capital – First Command of the Capital) in São Paulo, Brazil, Sérgio Adorno, Camila Dias and Fernando Salla (Dias and Salla 2013; Adorno and Salla 2007; Salla 2006) make the point that in recent decades prison staff have lost much of their authority over inmates as their numbers have failed to keep up with the rising prison population. In 1994, when São Paulo's prison population stood at 31,842, the state employed 14,702 prison staff. By 2006, when over a few days in early May the PCC orchestrated rebellions in 74 of the state's 144 prison units, the prison population had quadrupled (to 125,523) but prison staff numbers had risen by just two thirds (to 25,172). Moreover, prison officers made up three-quarters of total prison staff. Once staff sickness and shift patterns are taken into account, it had become quite usual for prisons with populations of over 500 inmates to operate with just two or three officers on duty at any time. Today this situation has deteriorated further. In December 2011 the official inmate–staff ratio in São Paulo stood at 7.5:1. In comparison, the official inmate–staff ratio is under 5:1 in the USA. In England and Wales it is 1.5:1; in Sweden 1:1.

The grave shortage of prison staff in São Paulo is replicated across Brazil and most of Latin America (Birkbeck 2011; Macaulay 2013; Salla et al. 2009; Ungar and Magaloni 2009). To make matters worse, the few officers that are employed to watch over prisoners are generally poorly paid and trained. Among the most extreme examples of staff shortage cited are a prison in Venezuela that in 2006 employed eight staff to guard 1,448 inmates (IACHR 2011), and a prison in Brazil with a population of over 4,000 that during a visit in 2008 was found to have just five officers on duty (Brasil. Câmara dos Deputados 2008). This has enormous implications for prison governance. As Salla et al. (2009: 23) put it, 'unskilled professionals in small numbers cannot control minimally the daily routines in a prison and provide a safe place for ... prisoners'. Across Latin America, prison managers barely have the personnel to secure the perimeter walls of their establishments, let alone ensure, for instance, that inmates are supervised in workshops or classes, or that an adequate level of goods and services flows to and from the wings. Further, in the majority of prisons, officers rarely enter the cell blocks except at unlock and lockup (IACHR 2011). As staff numbers have failed to keep up with the prisoner population, inmates have gradually been left more to their own devices, in free and unsupervised association, and expected to govern themselves, much in the same way as many of the region's poor, urban areas are becoming 'no-go zones' for the police (Koonings and Kruijt 2007).

While scandalous by Northern standards, these developments are not exceptional in Latin America. As we noted in the introduction, since their inception the region's prison systems have been less concerned with correcting than securing offenders, most of whom enter prison with extremely low levels of formal education (for instance, 63% of Brazilian, 67% of Colombian and 74% of Argentine inmates have attended no more than elementary school; Argentina. Ministerio de Justicia y Derechos Humanos 2014; Brazil. Ministério da Justiça 2012; Colombia. Ministerio de Justicia y del Derecho 2014) or employment in the formal economy (in Brazil, three quarters of prisoners were not in employment when they entered; Brazil. DEPEN 2012). As Zaffaroni (1991: 221–236) points out, Latin American justice systems operate like an epidemic, preferentially affecting those who have low defences. Their narrow focus on managing the poor has become increasingly prevalent in the contemporary neo-liberal, global era of rising social disparities and falling social security. To borrow from Wacquant's analysis of 'the penalization of poverty in Brazil', the region's prisons are 'more akin to concentration camps for the dispossessed, or public enterprises for the industrial storage of social refuse, than to judicial institutions serving any identifiable penological function' (Wacquant 2003: 200; cf. Ungar and Magaloni 2009).

What is striking about Latin American prisons, however, is not only that they are on average more inhumane, under-resourced or exclusionary than prisons in Western Europe or North America, but that under conditions of severe human and material deprivation they continue to exhibit complex social orders. Like other researchers, our starting point is to treat Latin American prisons as zones of containment and abandonment. Where we depart from much of the existing literature concerns the view, sometimes more assumed than substantiated, that Latin American prisons are necessarily places of extraordinary disorder. Conscious of the dangers of playing down the plight of Latin American inmates, we simply observe that for the majority of prisoners life goes on with some degree of everyday normality: meals are distributed, rubbish is collected, families visit at the weekend, minor illnesses get treated, disputes are usually avoided or settled – hardly a life that could be considered good, but certainly one that is worth conceptualizing in its own terms rather than dismissing it as unstructured and ungoverned, or otherwise as pre-modern and exceptional and beyond the comprehension of outsiders or comparison to other regions of the world. Ethnographic, biographical and autobiographical accounts of those who have been incarcerated in, researched, worked or regularly visited Latin American prisons (e.g. Biondi 2010; Carrillo Leal 2001; Carter 2014; Darke 2014a, 2014c; Lima 1991; MacNeil 2006; Mendes 2001; Varella 1999, 2012; Young 2003) testify to a reality in which inmates are often able to create and maintain professional and interpersonal relationships, and carve out a meaningful existence in even the most hostile and desperate of settings. The point is that, just as systems of 'parallel power' and survival 'know how' have filled the gap left by ineffective state governance in the region's *favelas* and *barrios* (Koonings and Kruijt 2007), most Latin American prisons continue to operate under a normative, if thin (normally requiring inmates to do little more than to be humble and respect one another) and volatile order (as witnessed, for instance, in the occasional outbreak of violent rebellion). Further, relations between inmates and staff are not always that much worse than in prisons in the North. Of importance here, the daily lives of Latin American inmates and staff have become increasingly entwined as they become more and more dependent on each other. Inmates rely on the dwindling number of staff to remain motivated to ensure, for instance, that meal and visiting times run smoothly, while, as previously mentioned, staff become more reliant on the cooperation of inmates for day-to-day prison order.

Whether by design or default, such informal prison dynamics shape the prison environment across Latin America and the rest of the postcolonial world (Garces et al. 2013). To make sense of these apparent contradictions, we focus attention on the situational adjustments by which prisoners and staff counter the inhumane conditions in which they find themselves living and working. These include, in particular, the ways in which prisoners participate in administering the institutions in which they are incarcerated, alongside and (especially in the cellblocks) in place of prison staff; and the positions assumed by prisoners' families, as previously mentioned, and also the voluntary sector in making up for shortages in state provision, for example providing material goods such as food, cooking equipment, clothing, bedding and toiletries, as well as legal, medical and religious services. In São Paulo, for example, 19,608 prisoners (almost 9% of the state's prison population) were officially employed as *apoios* (helpers; trusty prisoners) in December 2011. Already high by North American or Western European standards, this figure nevertheless excludes many thousands of prisoners who work informally on the wings, under the direction of inmate leaders, usually with the implicit or explicit support of prison staff. In a detailed account of prisoner participation in São Paulo's (since deactivated) Carandiru prison, Latin America's largest ever penal establishment, Varella (1999) describes how in the 1990s the administration relied on some 1,700 of the prison's 7,000 inmates to perform various prison tasks: 1,000 of these prisoners were formally employed as trusties, working among other things as cooks, cleaners, porters, orderlies and office clerks. A further 700 or so worked informally in the cellblocks. In addition to performing domestic tasks, the latter *faxina* (cleaners) also enforced inmate codes. At the weekend, the prison would be filled by over 2,000 visitors. Varella, himself a doctor, worked voluntarily at the prison for more than ten years.

Again, these features of prison life are mirrored across the remainder of Brazil and Latin America. In the case of trusty prisoners, prison ethnographer Guttiérez Rivera (2010) describes how Honduran prison administrators have made up for staff shortages by appointing inmate *rondinés* (patrollers) to monitor and report on other prisoners. Similarly, Garces (2010) describes how during his fieldwork visits to a penitentiary in Ecuador, where just 30 officers were typically on duty to take care of 4,000 prisoners, he was regularly escorted to the cellblocks by inmate *guias* (guides). Prison guards have also been reported as recruiting *polipresos* (inmate police) to maintain order in Venezuelan prisons (Birkbeck 2011). In at least one prison these trusty prisoners are selected among former police officers (El Impulso 2014). In studies of a police lockup in Rio de Janeiro and a number of voluntary sector, community prisons in Minas Gerais, Brazil, one of the current authors explored the positions of inmate *colaboradores* (collaborators) and *auxiliares de plantão* (assistant caretakers) in, for instance, controlling access to cellblocks and individual dormitories (Darke 2014b, 2014c). At the lockup prisoners referred to the director and his two most senior *colaboradores*, both former police officers, as forming the prison's *administração* (administration).

Among numerous accounts in the Latin American prisons literature of the roles played by inmate leaders and inmate councils in governing the interior of cellblocks and cells/dormitories are those of: the *directivas* (directors) of San Pedro prison, Bolivia (Skarbek 2010; Young 2003), the *cabos/delegados de pabellón* (heads/dormitory delegates) and *jefes de patio o pasillo* (heads of patio or corridor)/*gremio* (management) of Venezuela (Birkbeck 2011; MacNeil 2006), the *nueva mafia* (new mafia) and 'coordinators' of Honduras (Carter 2014), and the *delegados* (delegates) of Lurigancho prison, Peru (Veeken 2000). IACHR (2011) also cites numerous examples of such inmate self-governance from a number of UN and Organization of American States national human rights reports, including the *comités de orden y disciplina* (committees of order and discipline) of Guatemala, the 'cellblock bosses' of Mexico, the 'internal chiefs' of Colombia, the *capataces* (foremen) of Paraguay, and the *limpiezas* (cleaners) of Argentina (Salla et al. 2009). The current co-author's fieldwork also explored the means by which inmate *representantes* (representatives) and *comissões* (commissions) at the lockup and *conselhos de sinceridade e solidariedade* (sincerity and solidarity councils) at the community prisons organized prison routines, adjudicated and administered punishments. At the lockup inmate *representantes* were referred to as forming the *ligação* (link) between prisoners, staff and their *colaboradores* (cf. Guttiérez Rivera 2010). As the international trend away from correctional towards securitized prison environments increases, it appears that Latin American prisons are likely to become yet more self-governing, resulting in what Garces et al. (2013) describe as the 'informalization of prison governance'.

Last, it is important to note the recent intensification of inmate organization associated with the rise of organized criminal gangs such as the PCC in Brazil, already mentioned, and the *Maras* in central American countries such as El Salvador, Guatemala, Honduras and Nicaragua (Carter 2014; Guttiérez Rivera 2010; Lessing 2014; Rocha 2013). Latin American gangs increasingly operate across prison systems and between prisons and poor, urban communities, and are known to have corrupted local officials, lawyers and accountants, and even to have gained informal concessions from state officials (Dias and Salla 2013; Lessing 2014). As such, they are associated with a strengthening and monopolizing of inmate positions of authority, and with it the right to define the use of 'legitimate' violence. Whilst it would be a mistake to regard organized criminal gangs as egalitarian, or as 'pacifying' Latin America's prison systems (Dias and Darke 2015), it is equally important not to underestimate the role they play, or at least have the potential to play, in increasing levels of mutual protection and support among prison inmates. As Latin American prison gangs have expanded and settled (or more often imposed) territorial disputes, at least three trajectories towards a minimizing of social violence can be identified. First, there is a tendency towards the production of tight-knit communities of 'unified *barrios*' (Guttiérez Rivera 2010). Second, if prison gangs are to retain power in the long term there is a corresponding need for them to integrate the wider population of ordinary prisoners, so as to foster 'legitimate community status' (ibid.). On the one hand, this may involve increased animosity towards those identified as common enemies, for instance sex offenders or members of competing gangs. However, these prisoners are invariably held in separate cell blocks, if not prisons, and barring occasional outbreaks of prison-wide rebellion present few opportunities for violence. To sustain control over inmates in their own cell blocks, on the other hand, prison gangs depend on the creation of relationships of solidarity and trust. Finally, as prison gangs consolidate power they almost inevitably develop vertical, hierarchical structures, including systems of informal social control and conflict resolution. In São Paulo, for instance, prisoners have been banned from resorting to violence without permission; gang hierarchies have also abolished the use of hard drugs and the carrying of knives (Dias and Salla 2013).

Conclusion

In observing that mass incarceration, state abandonment and self-governance are defining features of Latin American prison systems, and are becoming more so in the contemporary context of criminal justice militarization and securitization of the prison environment, we summarize and conclude this chapter with a call for the development of nuanced understandings of the extent to which the classic sociology of prison life literature can be applied beyond the North, in particular theories on panopticism and the pains of imprisonment and total institutions associated with the work of Foucault, Sykes and Goffman.

Starting with panopticism, as the first named author has explained elsewhere (Darke 2014c), there is a clear disjuncture between Northern analysis of the development of prison as a correctional institution and prison realities in the South, including Latin America. Foucault (1977) demonstrated how prisons were originally designed to be 'complete institutions' which aimed to transform inmates through segregation, continuous observation, discipline and training. Not only was solitary confinement almost unheard of in Latin American prisons before the recent, but limited importation of the supermax model of immobilization (De Jesus Filho 2013; Garces 2014a; O'Day and O'Connor 2013), but we have seen prison staff also have little direct involvement in day-to-day activities in the cell blocks. Nor, as King (2007: 115) emphasizes in a comparison of Russian and Brazilian prisons, 'are members of staff under the gaze of their superiors'. A key characteristic of Latin American and other Southern prisons literature is the effort to explain, on the contrary, the continuation of imperial prison practices of corporal punishments and social defence. Latin American prisons achieve certain levels of situational control, and this is largely administered by/through inmate trusties and cell/dormitory and cellblock leaders. However, today, as in the past, with the exception of a number of penitentiaries in Argentina (Aguirre 2007) and voluntary sector community prison units in Brazil (Darke 2014c; Macaulay 2014), it is difficult to dispute Birkbeck's (2011) conclusion that Latin American prisons remain less institutions of imprisonment, in the sense that their regimes are geared at least in some part towards changing inmates, than institutions of internment (cf. Aguirre 2007; Macaulay 2013; Salla et al. 2009). Where more radical Northern scholars question the extent that prisons continue to be, or indeed have ever been, institutions of rehabilitation, there is a much clearer consensus among Southern scholars, including Latin American scholars, that prisons have never aimed to do more than punish and incapacitate offenders, irrespective of the hopes and expectations of the prison reformers that introduced them.

Similarly problematic in our experience is the view that there is an inverse relationship between poor prison conditions and relations among inmates and staff. Here it is important to acknowledge the communal nature of prison life in Latin America – that is, the ways in which inmates' and (to a lesser extent) staff's lives are shaped as much by personal relations produced through everyday encounters (for instance, in multi-occupancy cells and dormitories, during free association, and in negotiations between inmate leaders, trusties and prison staff), collective struggles and reciprocal exchanges as individual indignities (Garces et al. 2013). These shared experiences of abandonment form an essential part of what Aguirre (2005: 144) describes as 'the customary order of the prison' to develop, moreover quasi-legitimate orders based on shared interests in safety and certainty, and common welfare needs.[5] It can be argued that the organic practices that arise from these everyday encounters help offset some of the destabilizing features of prison life first outlined by Sykes (1958). As Aguirre (2007) emphasizes, in Latin America it is more productive to analyse inmates' relationships with prison staff in terms of strategies of survival than through a dichotomy between resistance and accommodation. Under conditions of forced reciprocity (Darke 2013; Darke and Karam 2012), material deprivations in Latin American prisons are as likely to strengthen as hinder the development of inmate solidarity, while relations between inmates and staff are likely to be defined as much by negotiation as normative distance.

Finally, and closely related, we join Birkbeck (2011) in drawing attention to the questionable universal applicability of Goffman's (1961) concept of the total institution, with its focus on separation between inmates and staff, prisons and communities. In place of detachment, we have seen that a situated account of the encompassing character of institutional life in Latin American prisons points towards a need to consider the effects of fused (staff–inmate) functions (resulting from the roles played by prisoners working alongside or in the place of prison staff) and entangled (staff–inmate and prison–community) relations. First, the barriers between prisons and communities are generally more permeable than in Western Europe or North America. Not only do prisoners generally have greater contact with their families, but with the growing phenomenon of gang culture, prison and community life are becoming increasingly linked. Latin American prisons, it seems, are not insulated from the community, and as a result need to be analysed as parallel social universes, as microcosms of society. Second, power in Latin American prisons emerges from hierarchies of inmate as well as staff authority. When staff–inmate interactions become essential aspects of prison life, prisoners do not need to rely on the corruption of individual officers to gain control over their experiences of incarceration. As Indian prisons anthropologist Bandyopadhyay (2010: 176 and 178) explains, 'deficiencies in the exercise of total power are to be located in the "interactional space" that binds prisoners and staff [...] [interwoven] relationships, strategies to maintain these relations, communication networks, rules of engagement ...' In circumstances in which staffing levels are so low that officers are simply not able to run their institutions without the support of inmates, defects in the power of prison officers may amount to more than aberrations: bureaucratic power may be far from total, and inmate power and ability to circumvent the processes of mortification may be more norm than exception.

Notes

1 Zaffaroni et al. develop a deep analysis of the tension between democratic principles and the practices that reflect the police state surviving within democratic states. The authors stress that, as history demonstrates, there is no actual democratic state (historically determined) that is pure or perfect. There are only historically determined democratic states that control and restrain, in a better or worse way, those practices reflecting the police state surviving within them.

2 For a comparative analysis of the introduction of extraordinary penal penalties in the post-dictatorship era in Argentina, Brazil and Chile, see Salla et al. (2009).

3 Universal Declaration of Human Rights – Article 11(1): 'Everyone charged with a penal offence has the right to be presumed innocent until proved guilty according to law in a public trial at which he has had all the guarantees necessary for his defence.' International Covenant on Civil and Political Rights, Article 14(2): 'Everyone charged with a criminal offence shall have the right to be presumed innocent until proved guilty according to law.'

4 Article 10.3 of the International Covenant on Civil and Political Rights states: 'the penitentiary system shall comprise treatment of prisoners the essential aim of which shall be their reformation and social rehabilitation [...]'

5 For analysis of the conditions required for legitimate prison governance, see Bottoms and Tankebe (2012).

Bibliography

Aas, K.F. (2012) '"The earth is one but the world is not": Criminological theory and its geopolitical divisions', *Theoretical Criminology* 16(1): 5–20.

Adorno, S. and Salla, F. (2007) 'Criminalidade organizada nas prisões e os ataques do PCC', *Estudos Avançados* 21(61): 7–29.

Aguirre, C. (2005) *The Criminals of Lima and their Worlds: The prison experience, 1850–1935*, Durham, NC: Duke University Press.

Aguirre, C. (2007) 'Prisons and prisoners in modernising Latin America', in F. Dikötter and I. Brown (eds) *Cultures of Confinement: A history of the prison in Africa, Asia, and Latin America*, Ithaca, NY: Cornell University Press.

Aguirre, C. and Salvatore, R.D. (2001) 'Writing the history of law, crime, and punishment in Latin America', in R.D. Salvatore, C. Aguirre and G.M. Joseph (eds) *Crime and Punishment in Latin America*, Durham, NC: Duke University Press.

Argentina. Ministerio de Justicia y Derechos Humanos (2012) 'Sistema nacionalde estadísticas sobre ejecución de la pena', www.jus.gob.ar/media/1125932/informe_sneep_argentina_2012.pdf (accessed 14 August 2014).

Argentina. Ministerio de Justicia y Derechos Humanos (2014) 'Sistema Argentino de información jurídica', www.infojus.gov.ar/home;jsessionid=1jpppvnx9etpvtfdkezykoga9?0 (accessed 10 August 2014).

Bandyopadhyay, M. (2010) *Everyday Life in a Prison: Confinement, surveillance, resistance*, New Delhi: Orient BlackSwan.

Bergman, M. and Whitehead, L. (eds) (2009) *Criminality, Public Security, and the Challenge to Democracy in Latin America*, Notre Dame, IN: University of Notre Dame.

Biondi, K. (2010) *Junto e Misturado: Uma Etnografia do PCC*, São Paulo: Teirciero Nome.

Birkbeck, C. (2011) 'Imprisonment and internment: Comparing penal institutions North and South', *Punishment and Society* 13(3): 307–332.

Bottoms, A. and Tankebe, J. (2012) 'Beyond procedural justice: A dialogic approach to legitimacy in criminal justice', *Journal of Criminal Law and Criminology* 102(1): 119–170.

Brazil. Câmara dos Deputados (2008) 'CPI do sistema carcerário', bd.camara.leg.br/bd/bitstream/handle/bdcamara/2701/cpi_sistema_carcerario.pdf?sequence=5 (accessed 10 August 2014).

Brazil. Conselho Nacional de Justiça (2014) 'Novo diagnóstico de pessoas presas no Brasil', www.cnj.jus.br/images/imprensa/Pessoas_presas_no_Brasil_1.pdf (accessed 10 August 2014).

Brazil. Ministério da Justiça (2012) 'Departamento nacional penitenciário', portal.mj.gov.br (accessed 10 August 2014).

Cain, M. (2000) 'Orientalism, occidentalism and the sociology of crime', *British Journal of Criminology* 40: 239–260.

Caldeira, T.P.R. (2000) *City of Walls: Crime, Segregation and Citizenship in São Paulo*, Berkeley: University of California Press.

Carrillo Leal, W. (2001) 'From my prison cell: Time and space in prison in Colombia, an ethnographic approach', trans. D. Mond, *Latin American Perspectives* 28(1): 149–164.

Carter, J.H. (2014) 'Gothic sovereignty: Gangs and criminal community in a Honduran prison', *South Atlantic Quarterly* 113(3): 475–502.

Cohen, S. (1982) 'Western crime control models in the third world: Benign or malignant', *Research in Law, Deviance and Social Control* 5: 85–119.

Colombia. Ministerio de Justicia y del Derecho (2014) 'Instituto nacional penitenciario y carcelario', www.inpec.gov.co/portal/page/portal/Inpec (accessed 10 August 2014).

Comisión Episcopal de AcciónSocial (2013) 'Las personas privadas de libertad en el Perú: Un análisis y reflexión desde la labor de pastoral de cárceles – Informe 2012', www.ceas.org.pe/p ublicaciones/0000007_INFORME%20CARCELES%202012.pdf (accessed 14 August 2014).

Connell, R. (2006) *Southern Theory: The global dynamics of knowledge in social sciences*, Cambridge: Polity.

Crime, Law and Social Change (2014) 'The rebirth of the prison in Latin America: Variations, changes and continuities', 62(5).

Darke, S. (2013) 'Inmate governance in Brazilian prisons', *Howard Journal of Criminal Justice* 52(3): 272–284.

Darke, S. (2014a) 'Comunidades prisionais autoadministradas: O fenômeno APAC', trans. M.L. Karam, *Revista Brasileira de Ciências Criminais* 107: 257–276.

Darke, S. (2014b) 'Managing without guards in a Brazilian police lockup', *Focaal* 68(1): 55–67.

Darke, S. (2014c) 'Recoverers helping recoverers: Discipline and peer-facilitated rehabilitation in Brazilian faith-based prisons', in S. Badcock et al. (eds) *Transnational Penal Cultures*, London: Routledge.

Darke, S. and Karam, M.L. (2012) 'Administrando o cotidiano da prisão no Brasil', *Discursos Sediciosos* 17(19/20): 405–423.

De Azevedo, R. (2006) 'Crime and criminal justice in Latin America', *Sociologias* 2: 1517–1522.

De Jesus Filho, J. (2013) 'The rise of the supermax in Brazil', in J.I. Ross (ed.) *The Globalization of Supermax Prisons*, New Brunswick, NJ: Rutgers University Press.

Del Olmo, R. (1981) *America Latina y su Criminologia*, delegación Coyoacán: Siglo xxi.

Del Olmo, R. (1999) 'The development of criminology in Latin America', *Social Justice* 26(2): 19–45.

Dias, C.C.N. (2005) 'Evangélicos no cárcere: Representação de um papel desacreditado', *Debates do NER* 6(8): 39–55.

Dias, C.C.N. and Darke, S. (2015, in press) 'From dispersed to monopolized violence: Expansion and consolidation of the Primeiro Comando da Capital (PCC)'s hegemony in São Paulo's prisons', *Crime, Law and Social Change*.

Dias, C.C.N. and Salla, F. (2013) 'Organized crime in Brazilian prisons: The example of the PCC', *International Journal of Criminology and Sociology* 2: 397–408.

Dikötter, F. (2007) 'The prison in the world', in F. Dikötter and I. Brown (eds) *Cultures of Confinement: A History of the Prison in Africa, Asia, and Latin America*, Ithaca, NY: Cornell University Press.

El Impulso (2014) 'En Comandancia de PoliLara: Denuncian Maltrato de "Polipresos" (Fotos)', elimp ulso.com/articulo/en-comandancia-de-polilara-denuncian-maltrato-de-polipresos-fotos (accessed 21 August 2014).

Focaal (2014) 'Sensing prison climates: Governance, survival and transition', 68.

Foucault, M. (1977) *Discipline and Punish: The birth of the prison*, London: Penguin.

Garces, C. (2010) 'The cross politics of Ecuador's penal state', *Cultural Anthropology* 25(3): 459–496.

Garces, C. (2014a) 'Denuding surveillance at the carceral boundary', *South Atlantic Quarterly* 113(3): 447–473.

Garces, C. (2014b) 'Ecuador's "black site": On prison securitization and its zones of legal silence', *Focaal* 68: 18–35.

Garces, C., Martin, T. and Darke, S. (2013) 'Informal prison dynamics in Africa and Latin America', *Criminal Justice Matters* 91(1): 26–27.

Goffman, E. (1961) 'On the characteristics of total institutions', in D. Cressey (ed.) *The Prison: Studies in Institutional Organization and Change*, New York: Holt, Rinehart and Winston.

Guttiérez Rivera, L. (2010) 'Discipline and punish? Youth gangs' response to "zero tolerance" policies in Honduras', *Bulletin of Latin American Research* 29(4): 492–504.

Hay, D. (2001) 'Law and society in contemporary perspective', in R.D. Salvatore, C. Aguirre and G.M. Joseph (eds) *Crime and Punishment in Latin America*, Durham, NC: Duke University Press.

IACHR (Inter-American Commission on Human Rights) (2011) 'Report on the human rights of persons deprived of liberty in the Americas', www.oas.org/en/iachr/pdl/docs/pdf/PPL2011eng. pdf (accessed 10 August 2014).

International Bar Association (2010) '1 in 5: The crisis in Brazil's prisons and criminal justice system', www.ibanet.org/Article/Detail.aspx?ArticleUid=9a841b12-4a44-41db-a4bd-4433e694e2ba (accessed 10 August 2014).

International Centre for Prison Studies (2014) *World Prison Brief*, www.prisonstudies.org/world-p rison-brief (accessed 10 August 2014).

Karam, M.L. (2009) *Proibições, Riscos, Danos e Enganos: As Drogas Tornadas Ilícitas*, Rio de Janeiro: Lumen Juris.

Karstedt, S. (2001) 'Comparing cultures, comparing crime: Challenges, prospects and problems for a global criminology', *Crime, Law and Social Change* 36(3): 285–308.

King, R. (2007) 'Imprisonment: Some international comparisons and the need to revisit panopticism', in Y. Jewkes (ed.) *Handbook on Prisons*, London: Willan.

Koonings, K. and Kruijt, D. (eds) (2007) *Fractured Cities: Social Exclusion, Urban Violence and Contested Spaces in Latin America*, London: Zed Books.

Lee, M. and Laidler, K.J. (2013) 'Doing criminology from the periphery: Crime and punishment in Asia', *Theoretical Criminology* 17(2): 141–157.

Lemgruber, J., Fernandes, M., Cano, I. and Musumeci, L. (2013) *Usos e Abusos da Prisão Provisória no Rio de Janeiro*, Rio de Janeiro: Associação pela Reforma Prisional (ARP) e Centro de Estudos de Segurança e Cidadania (CESEC).

Lessing, B. (2014) 'How to build a criminal empire from behind bars: Prison gangs and projection of power', www.iza.org/conference_files/riskonomics2014/lessing_b9947.pdf (accessed 10 August 2014).

Lima, W.S. (1991) *Quatrocentos Contra Um: Uma História do Camando Vermelho*, Rio de Janeiro: Iser.

Macaulay, F. (2013) 'Modes of prison administration, control and governmentality in Latin America: Adoption, adaptation and hybridity', *Conflict, Security and Development* 13(4): 361–392.

Macaulay, F. (2014) 'Whose prisoners are these anyway? Church, state and society partnerships and co-production of offender resocialization', in S. Badcock et al. (eds) *Transnational Penal Cultures*, London: Routledge.

MacNeil, D. (2006) *Journey to Hell: Inside the world's most violent prison system*, Preston: Milo.

Mendes, L.A. (2001) *Memórias de um Sobrevivente*, São Paulo: Companhia de Bolso.

Müller, M. (2012) 'The rise of the penal state in Latin America', *Contemporary Justice Review* 15(1): 57–76.

O'Day, P. and O'Connor, T. (2013) 'Supermaxes south of the border', in J.I. Ross (ed.) *The Globalization of Supermax Prisons*, New Brunswick, NJ: Rutgers University Press.

Peru. Ministerio de Justicia y Derechos Humanos (2013) 'Informe estadístico penitenciario – Diciembre 2013 (INPE)', www.scribd.com/doc/208235707/informe-Noviembre-2013-inpe (accessed 15 August 2014).

Rocha, J.L.R. (2013) 'Gangs and maras', *International Association of Youth and Family Judges and Magistrates Chronicle*, January: 47–51.

Salla, F. (2006) 'As rebeliões nas prisões: Novos significados a partir da experiência Brasileira', *Sociologias* 8(16): 274–307.

Salla, F., Ballesteros, P.R., Espinoza, O., Martínez, F., Litvachky, P. and Museri, A. (2009) 'Democracy, human rights and prison conditions in South America', www.udhr60.ch/report/detention_salla 0609.pdf (accessed 10 August 2014).

Salvatore, R.D. and Aguirre, C. (eds) (1996) *The Birth of the Penitentiary in Latin America*, Austin: University of Texas Press.

Salvatore, R.D., Aguirre, C. and Joseph, G.M. (eds) (2001) *Crime and Punishment in Latin America*, Durham, NC: Duke University Press.

Santos, B.S. (ed.) (2007) *Another Knowledge is Possible: Beyond northern epistemologies*, London: Verso.

Skarbek, D. (2010) 'Self-governance in San Pedro prison', *Independent Review* 14(2): 569–585.

South Atlantic Quarterly (2014) 'Prison realities: Views from around the world', 113(3).

Sykes, G.M. (1958) *The Society of Captives: A study of a maximum security prison*, Princeton, NJ: Princeton University Press.

TNI/WOLA (2010) 'Systems overload: Drug laws and prisons in Latin America', www.wola.org/sites/default/files/downloadable/Drug%20Policy/2011/TNIWOLA-Systems_Overload-def.pdf (accessed 15 August 2014).

Tuhiwai Smith, L. (1999) *Decolonizing Methodologies: Research and indigenous peoples*, London: Zed Books.

Ungar, M. (2003) 'Prisons and politics in contemporary Latin America', *Human Rights Quarterly* 25(4): 909–934.

Ungar, M. and Magaloni, A.L. (2009) 'Latin America's prisons: A crisis of criminal policy and democratic rule', in M. Bergman and L. Whitehead (eds) *Criminality, Public Security, and the Challenge to Democracy in Latin America*, Notre Dame, IN: University of Notre Dame.

Varella, D. (1999) *Estação Carandiru*, São Paulo: Companhia das Letras (trans. (2012) A. Entrekin, as *Lockdown: Inside Brazil's Most Dangerous Prison*, London: Simon & Schuster).

Varella, D. (2012) *Carcereiros*, São Paulo: Companhia das Letras.

Veeken, H. (2000) 'Lurigancho prison: Lima's "high school" for criminality', *British Medical Journal* 320: 173–175.

Wacquant, L. (2003) 'Towards a dictatorship over the poor: Notes on the penalization of poverty in Brazil', *Punishment and Society* 5(2): 197–205.

Walmsley, R. (2013) *World Prison Population List*, tenth edn, International Centre for Prison Studies, www.prisonstudies.org/sites/prisonstudies.org/files/resources/downloads/wppl_10.pdf (accessed 10 August 2014).

Young, R. (2003) *Marching Powder*, London: Sidgwick & Jackson.

Zaffaroni, E.R. (1991) 'El sistema penal en los países de América Latina', in J.M. de Araújo (ed.) *Sistema Penal para o Terceiro Milenio*, Rio de Janeiro: Revan.

Zaffaroni, E.R. (2006) *El Enemigo en el Derecho Penal*, Madrid: Dykinson.

Zaffaroni, E.R., Alagia, A. and Slokar, A. (2000) *Derecho Penal – Parte General*, Buenos Aires: Ediar.

Part IV

The penal spectrum

High security prisons in England and Wales

Principles and practice

Alison Liebling

> To speak about the problems of order and control in prisons today raises questions of power, of unintended consequences, of the impact of modern managerial techniques, and of the relationship between social structure and personal agency that prison studies has not yet confronted adequately, but which are the very stuff of social theory.
>
> (Sparks et al. 1996: 62)

> What works in a maximum security prison can work anywhere.
>
> (Johnson 2005: v)

High security prisons embody and express the coercive power of the state in its most extreme form. They represent 'deep incarceration' (Sparks 2002: 557; and see the quotes from Sparks et al. (1996), and Johnson (2005), above), combining the most severe form of punishment with significant added control for prisoners regarded as the most dangerous. In England and Wales, high security prisons were, unusually, designed and administered with much official concern for combining security with the concept of 'humanity', despite the difficulties this aspiration brings about in practice, and this concern has lasted for half a century (see Liebling 2002). The deep and accentuated tensions between the accomplishment of security on the one hand, and legitimate order on the other, have been regularly revisited in policy and practice reviews (e.g. Home Office 1979, 1984, 1987; Ditchfield 1990). In a spirit of continuing to aspire to enlightened practice, several aspects of their operation have been the subject of sustained and officially orchestrated empirical research (e.g. Jepson and Elliott 1991; Sparks et al. 1996; Liebling and Price 1999; Liebling et al. 2012; Clare and Bottomley 2001), as well as some 'unofficial' research (Cohen and Taylor 1972). High security prisons almost always add additional provisions to their basic structure, which take the shape of 'prisons within prisons', for the most defiant. As Richard Sparks has observed in relation to the Scottish experience:

> Inside prisons, situations of intractable conflict between certain prisoners and correctional authorities arise. The choices available to either party in escaping the sometimes desperate consequences of these battles are usually severely limited. One effect ... can be the creation of a yet deeper level of incarceration for the most recalcitrant.
>
> (Sparks 2002: 556)

Policy evolution in the high security estate reflects various routes into, as well as 'notable attempts to discover routes out' of, this scenario. It reflects different although sustained attempts to balance competing values 'in a minefield' (former director of the high security estate, personal communication, 2015). The outcomes of failure in either direction (too much freedom and choice for a challenging and sometimes disturbed population, or too much coercion and security for human beings to endure) have been dramatic, whether leading to escapes, major disturbances or other catastrophes. The tensions between punishment and rehabilitation, or between constraint and human dignity and personal development, have been less formally or regularly addressed than the tensions between security and order, but they constitute a major concern for prisoners. High security prisons are inherently places of internal contradiction (Rhodes 2004). Close empirical scrutiny of life and experience in them helps to clarify the meaning of the term humanity and makes clear the limits to its accomplishment in prison. As Bob Johnson argues above, they paradoxically provide a particularly stringent test for humanitarian ideas or penal aspirations.

The origins and evolution of high security prisons in England and Wales[1]

> A purpose built prison is required at the earliest possible date to house those prisoners who must in no circumstances be allowed to get out, whether because of the security considerations affecting spies, or because their violent behaviour is such that members of the public or the police would be in danger of their lives if they were to get out. I call these prisoners category A ... There are obvious advantages to building [this prison] on an Island ... I have come to the conclusion that the Home Office proposal to build a new maximum security prison on the Isle of Wight is, weighing all the various considerations, the right one.
>
> (Home Office 1966: 56–7)

On 24 October 1966 the Earl Mountbatten of Burma was asked to conduct an Inquiry into prison escapes and security by the Right Honourable Roy Jenkins, secretary of state for the Home Department. The events to precipitate this request were the escapes of George Blake, a spy serving 42 years, on 3 May 1961 from Wormwood Scrubs, of Charles Wilson from Birmingham prison on 12 August 1964, and of Ronald Biggs and three others from Wandsworth prison on 8 July 1965. Other escapes, from a court escort, and from D Hall, Wormwood Scrubs, were also taken into account. Blake was five and a half years into his sentence, and his case was considered by the Lord Chief Justice as 'one of the worst that can be envisaged in peace times' (Home Office 1966: 7). In facilitating the escapes, the role of rope ladders, doors left open, easily broken bars and windows, the vulnerability of prison officers to financial bribes, and the 'daring and resource of determined escapers' (ibid.: 54) were included as matters of concern. The suspension of the death penalty and 'the unprecedentedly long fixed sentences' imposed by the courts made it hard for prisoners to contemplate their sentences:

> The whole philosophy of prison administration and punishment has depended on the fact that even a man sentenced to life imprisonment had a reasonable hope that if he mended his ways he would be allowed to return to free society.
>
> (Home Office 1966: 54)

There were 'clear weaknesses in physical security and in administration at prison level and at the Home Office' (Home Office 1966: 2) and there was 'no really secure prison in existence in this country' (ibid.: 4). The original 19th-century prison had been built on the assumption that prisoners would be locked in their cells most of the time:

> In effect, imprisonment was solitary confinement and all security depended on this fact.
> (Home Office 1966: 53)

Mountbatten recognized that 'The policy of giving very long sentences up to and including the full life of a prisoner introduces a new type of imprisonment, bringing with it human problems that have to be faced' (Home Office 1966: 5). This included family contact. Penal reform had brought about new security challenges:

> Prison governors are now expected to treat the prisoners in their care with humanity and do their best to devise a regime which will prepare them for living an honest life at the end of their sentence, but at the same time they are expected to prevent them from escaping. A constructive liberal prison regime and secure prisons are not necessarily incompatible, but conflict will arise if an attempt is made to conduct a liberal regime in buildings designed in accordance with the 19th century philosophy of prison treatment.
> (Home Office 1966: 53)

Security could be improved 'without imposing a harsh and inhumane regime' (Home Office 1966: 4), but this would require keeping a limit on the numbers of prisoners sentenced to custody. Mountbatten argued:

> I consider that the modern policy of humane liberal treatment aimed at rehabilitating prisoners rather than merely exacting punishment is right, and that escapes should be prevented by far better perimeter security.
> (Home Office 1966: 4)

The Mountbatten report recommended a new system of security categorization, from A (for prisoners whose escape would be highly dangerous to the public) to D (for prisoners who could be housed in open prisons without danger). He fully supported the setting up of open prisons, provided 'care is taken in the selection of prisoners for open conditions' (Home Office 1966: 55). Category A prisoners, on the other hand, of whom there were likely to be around 120, should be housed in a single 'escape proof' maximum security prison. He said: 'Proper machinery must be set up to ensure that prisoners are allocated to the correct category' (ibid.: 4).

Escapes were a 'justifiable cause of public anxiety' (Home Office 1966: 55). Some of the escapees had used firearms, and most were, by the nature of their crimes, capable of extreme violence. The consequences of any particular prisoner's escape should also be taken into account in their categorization.

Mountbatten suggested that staff working in this prison should be given additional pay, and their tour of duty should be short, because of the burden of the work, but also to minimize opportunities for prisoners 'well supplied with funds' to bring 'improper pressure' on staff. He proposed that the allocation of prisoners be kept under continuous review and 'subjected to careful research' (Home Office 1966: 59). Every effort should be made to prepare such prisoners gradually for release, by transferring them between categories, and into a hostel towards the end of their sentence (ibid.: 59).

In the Prison Service in general, more staff were needed, to reflect the increased range of activities on offer in prisons, and an additional rank (of senior officer) should be introduced, to raise morale. He said:

> Unless prison officers are recognised as men and women fulfilling an essential task for the safety and well being of the law abiding public, no amount of leadership can give them that sense of pride and responsibility without which a really high morale cannot be built up.
>
> (Home Office 1966: 6)

Promotion should be based on merit and ability rather than time served. A careful eye should be kept on pay and conditions, in order that 'they are adequate to attract sufficient men and women of good quality' (Home Office 1966: 59). There should be more emphasis on security in training, and a small number of specialist security staff should be directly responsible to the governor. Mountbatten also recommended that specialists in training and rehabilitation should be developed, and that all specialists should receive extra pay. There should be some 'enhancement of the prestige of the Prison Service as a career' (ibid.: 60).

A 'liberal and constructive' and even 'permissive' regime, including regular home leaves, could 'reduce the temptation to escape' (Home Office 1966: 5, 88). Anticipating many decades of research, and many later inquiry reports, he argued:

> The closer the relationship between prisoners and staff, and the more the majority of prisoners accept the fairness of their treatment, the easier it will be to detect the symptoms of unrest which often indicate the planning of an escape attempt.
>
> (Home Office 1966: 86)

Most of Mountbatten's recommendations were implemented. The exception was his proposed single high security prison on the Isle of Wight. In February 1967, in response to the Mountbatten report, the home secretary asked the Advisory Council on the Penal System to consider what kind of regime should be developed for long-term prisoners detained in conditions of maximum security, and to make recommendations. There might be 'wider and more fundamental issues' to consider (Radzinowicz 1999: 303). The report to follow, written by the first director of the Cambridge Institute of Criminology, Professor Leon Radzinowicz, was to establish the principles on which long-term prisoners in conditions of maximum security prisons were to be treated.

From a proposed 'vectis' to the dispersal system

> The manner in which the Prison Service of this country meets the challenge of containing long-term prisoners in conditions that combine security and humanity will have a lasting effect on the Service as a whole.
>
> (ACPS 1968: 3)

During the course of its inquiry the sub-committee, under the chairmanship of Professor Leon Radzinowicz, became increasingly doubtful about the possibility of establishing a satisfactory regime within a fortress-type prison in which all maximum security prisoners would be concentrated.[2] Such a concentration of the most dangerous prisoners in one place would lead to negative labelling, a 'nothing to lose' ethos, a shortage of options for the difficult to place, a form of certainty in the process of classification that was not justified in practice, and the destructive atmosphere of a single segregation unit. It might also lead to a negative reputation for the prison service abroad. Instead, a liberal regime within a secure perimeter would allow good governance of the prison, support the interests of staff, and encourage prisoners to lead a 'good and useful life' in the future. This recommendation came with a call for an increase in the 'co-efficient of security in our closed prisons', as well as an acknowledgement that dispersal would never be a 'problem free' option, and that special efforts would have to be made to 'supply the needs, administrative and humanitarian' of this 'penitentiary configuration' (Radzinowicz 1999: 307). The sub-committee concluded that the setting up of a small prison for a restricted category of long-sentence prisoners in conditions of near absolute security was not the right solution to 'what are admittedly very difficult problems', and it recommended that these prisoners should instead be dispersed among three or four larger prisons with strengthened perimeter security. The risks of inflation to numbers on Category A would have to be continually addressed. Penal policy should not be implemented in an atmosphere of 'panic' or 'frustration' (Radzinowicz 1999: 309). As Radzinowicz writes in his memoirs, the committee, 'a group of people of unusual distinction, experience and ripeness of judgment', 'reached the dispersal conclusion ... still with anguish in their hearts and minds' (Radzinowicz 1999: 320–321).

The necessary ingredients of this liberal and constructive regime were activity, a reasonable atmosphere and good facilities. The aim was to change the attitudes and behaviour of prisoners, and to achieve this via the governor and staff of the prison, armed with the new knowledges of sociology and psychiatry. A man in prison did not cease to be 'the father of his children' or a human being:

> If our society is concerned, as it is, and as it must be, with the worth of all individual men and women, and if it believes that in the last resort what men have in common is more important than their differences, then it cannot treat as less than human those men it finds necessary to send to prison. This means that the community must provide for the prison service the necessary resources to enable men to be contained for long periods in conditions that combine security with humanity.
>
> (Home Office 1968: 77)

The principles of self-respect, choice, variety, movement, and the earning of additional privileges through work and cooperative behaviour were essential to the organization of a long-term prison. The report argued that there should be constructive relationships between prisoners and staff and regular individualized reviews of progress. The prisons were envisaged as having a population of about 400 prisoners each. The Advisory Council assumed that a minority of disruptive or unstable ('control problem') prisoners would have to be contained in a separate segregation unit within a larger prison. This resource should be used 'intelligently' and the prisoners within it should be subject to regular review.

Some variation between the regimes of these maximum security prisons was expected, and was to be encouraged, if only to experiment with solutions to the inevitable problems posed by long-term imprisonment. A continuing programme of research should be carried out on the effects of different types of regimes on different types of prisoners, the effects of long-term imprisonment more generally, and the effects on staff of changes in the administration of such prisons. Staff and prisoners should be fully involved in such research, so that its impact on the establishments could be made as valuable as possible.

The report argued that the governors of such maximum security prisoners should have plenty of experience, and should show concern for and understanding of the complexities of human nature, without 'sentimentality'. Staff should have the opportunity to discuss difficulties and frustrations on their wings, and should 'try to reach a better understanding of the causes of friction and of the behaviour of difficult prisoners' (Radzinowicz 1999: 34), with the assistance of specialists. Prison officers should 'be able to attend university courses, such as the short courses now held in Criminology', and they should be able to see related work done elsewhere and abroad. Communications within the establishment must be good, as prisoners could quickly exploit divisions between staff groups.

The humane regime envisaged was dependent on two essential prerequisites: an increased ratio of staff to prisoners over other prisons (to about one uniformed officer for three prisoners) and the establishment of separate segregation units for the persistently disruptive. The essential principles on which the high security estate was established, then, were that prisoners requiring the highest conditions of security would be 'absorbed' into the general population, and that as a result of this practice, the regime should be liberal and humane (see King and Elliott 1977: 325–326; Bottoms and Light 1987). It was intended that no more than 15% of each establishment's population would be Category A. Both of these elements were linked to rehabilitative ideals (Sparks et al. 1996: 104). As a director of the high security estate argued, 'we could have taken a different route … we chose to negotiate order with powerful groups of prisoners who were determined to get their way. This was the courageous option, but our [negotiation] practices were not always defensible' (personal communication, 2015). In the *Report of their Inquiry into the United Kingdom Prison Services in 1978–9*, the May Committee observed that this question of dispersal versus concentration was 'one of the most difficult they had to consider' (Home Office 1979). In the end, for reasons of both principle and pragmatism (the design constraints of existing prisons, and the effects of more controlled approaches on staff), the May Committee agreed with the Radzinowicz Committee that dispersal was the 'least worst' option. This question has been revisited on several occasions (see e.g., Home Office 1995; King 1997) and is still the subject of political as well as operational disagreement.

Dispersal prisons aimed to provide some highly valued freedoms, a high level of security, and some control, or order, via a delicate combination of relationships, incentives and activities ('dynamic security', Dunbar 1985). The trouble was, in the words of senior managers, 'prisoners used these freedoms against us, or against each other … they were embattled states' (personal communication). They did not live up to expectations. Four prisons were initially identified for use as dispersal prisons, and their security levels were upgraded accordingly. Others were identified, where upgrading was more difficult to achieve. Long Lartin, and Albany, for example, had been Category C establishments, which may have influenced the types of relationship established in them. King and

Elliott describe the transformation in purpose as they were added to the estate, and the introduction of the new grade of senior officer, in their detailed study of Albany (King and Elliott 1977). Frankland was the first purpose-built dispersal prison, and opened in 1983.

Of the original eight (Albany, Gartree, Hull, Parkhurst, Wakefield, D Hall Wormwood Scrubs, Long Lartin and Frankland), five experienced major losses of control causing substantial structural and other damage between 1969 and 1983: Parkhurst in 1969 and 1979, Albany in 1972 and 1983, Hull in 1976 and 1979, Gartree in 1972 and 1978, and Wormwood Scrubs in 1979 and 1983. Much has been written about these events, their handling and their aftermath (e.g. King and Elliott 1977; Home Office 1977, 1984; Thomas and Pooley 1980; Bottoms and Light 1987; Adams 1992; Sparks et al. 1996). The first of these riots, at Parkhurst in 1969, was precipitated by a new Home Office instruction requiring official approval, with ID, of visitors. Seven prison officers were taken hostage, and 33 prison officers and 22 prisoners were injured. Nine prisoners were 'subsequently committed for trial on charges arising' from these events. Seven were 'sentenced to various terms of further imprisonment as a result' (Home Office 1984: 63). Some incidents led to terms of imprisonment for staff. Powerful feelings of injustice and rage were expressed when either prisoners or staff were 'found not guilty' due to insufficient evidence or lack of corroboration at subsequent court hearings (such as in the case of Wormwood Scrubs 1979; see Home Office 1984). Such major disturbances left scars. Scores were sometimes settled in establishments at later dates (King and Elliott 1977: 282–286). Questions of the accountability of power, or the culture and orientation of staff, tended to be silenced in conceptualizations of disorder based on the pathologies of 'bad apple' prisoners.

It was significant that these disturbances took place not 'in the crowded and highly disadvantaged conditions of local prisons, but in the comparatively relaxed and privileged regimes of the dispersal prison' (Ditchfield 1990: iii). There had been significant reductions in the quality of life for many prisoners as a result of the introduction of the dispersal policy, and as a result of the early breakdowns in order. Why were they so 'susceptible to major breakdowns in control'? (Home Office 1984: 7). The explanations offered included the increased opportunities for trouble, rising expectations among prisoners, decreasing incentives (for example, restrictions on the availability of parole) and the types of prisoners concerned. King and Elliott add to this list the rise of sophisticated cliques, the mixing of short-term with long-term prisoners, the growth of campaigning in social and political life outside, and the arrival of prisoners from special wings elsewhere (see further below), who were no longer treated as special (King and Elliott 1977). The designation of a number of prisoners as Category A in itself had unintended effects. Staff, official commentators and the press were sometimes melodramatic in their descriptions of the 'toughest and most hardened criminals' housed in high security establishments (King and Elliott 1977: 283). This was despite the fact that inside them, officers described 'a friendlier relationship between staff and prisoners ... than at any other prison where I have served' (ibid.: 283). Being Category A could be both status enhancing and soul destroying. Routes off Category A were opaque and infrequently accessed (see e.g., Price 2000). Not being Category A in a high security prison (which applied to 85% or more of the prisoners in the high security estate throughout its early years) could be unnecessarily restrictive and deeply frustrating. Prisoners battled for power, but also for their understanding of the concept of humanity: this required *hope*, and possibilities for *growth* (Home Office 1983; Bottoms 1990), as well as reasonable administrative standards (see Morgan and Richardson 1987).

A disproportionate number of those prisoners categorized as Category A saw themselves (but were never recognized) as political prisoners or were prisoners categorized as 'terrorists' throughout the 1970s and 1980s. These prisoners had 'a special place in the culture of the prison' (Borland et al. 1995: 376), were organized and relatively powerful, and often led negotiations with the authorities about the terms and conditions of their imprisonment (on behalf of all prisoners) during the more peaceful, post-Control Review Committee (CRC) years (Home Office 1989). Disapproval of their offences (particularly by staff) was balanced by some respect (especially among prisoners) for their political status and mode of doing time ('they are straight and can be counted on': prisoner, in Borland et al. 1995: 377). As one senior manager said:

> They had an interesting standing amongst other prisoners in spite of the mainland bombing campaign. They were trusted because they were seen as being motivated by a deeply held cause as opposed to having a selfish streak which meant even the best regarded fellow criminal might inform on you if there was sufficient self interest. They were often articulate and well used to organising protest. It was of course in the interest of their cause to disrupt prisons, to highlight the injustices of the English authorities and if possible to provoke over reaction which could be used to generate useful propaganda.
>
> (Former director of the high security estate, personal communication, 2015)

Other long-term prisoners in high security establishments were 'professional' criminals with significant external resources. Both of these (and other) groups were educated and well informed, and used increasingly available legal avenues to challenge and resist the authority of their captors, as a political tactic (see McEvoy 2001) and as a strategy for countering power as the courts began to intervene in the management and organization of, for example, disciplinary hearings (*R. v Board of Visitors ex parte St Germain 1979*). The 'prison struggle' (dissidents and rebels versus 'the state') was played out – first overtly in the high security estate – with disputes over what books might be read, the status and treatment of 'disruptive' prisoners, and the introduction of control units to isolate and manage the most 'dangerous' in the 1970s. Intimidation of staff, or families of staff, was not unusual (but was more lethal and common in Northern Ireland), and long-term campaigns to 'push staff back' and improve conditions were relatively successful throughout this period, up to the Woodcock Report of 1994. Literal 'work-to-rule' practices by disgruntled prison officers could lead to further resentment and resistance among powerful groups of prisoners who fought hard to maximize their living or regime standards. Campaigning organizations outside were visible, credible and supportive at the time (Ryan 1993). At this stage the 'dissidents' (and most of the 'rebels') were white and spoke the same language as the British (Adams 1992: 142). This was to change at the turn of the century.

After the establishment of the CRC, there was greater emphasis on the structure of regimes, and on securing the consent of prisoners to more constructive regimes. As the peace process approached resolution, the terms of debate modified. IRA prisoners still often led the negotiations relating to the introduction of new policies and practices in high security prisons – for example, in the implementation of incentives and earned privileges (see Liebling 2002) – but the negotiations were relatively cooperative. The Joint Declaration on Peace, and the continuing moves to agreement in 1993–94, led to the eventual release or repatriation of most IRA prisoners, and their decline in the high security population, although not before five had escaped from Whitemoor prison in 1994, having 'conditioned' staff to relax many day-to-day security practices (see Home Office 1994; and further below).

The power struggle between staff and prisoners was not all one way. Many of the prisoners who challenged staff were reasonable and well informed. Tensions arose between flexibility on the one hand, which could stray into collusion and laxity, and strict rule enforcement on the other (see Crewe et al. 2014). The relationships that formed between staff and prisoners were long, and sometimes deeply personal. Individual prisoners were known by governors, and some of those with policy responsibility in headquarters. They were certainly well known by prison staff. Individual officers might spend many months talking individual prisoners out of segregation units, back onto mainstream wings, where they might 'fail', only to do the rounds again, somewhere else. Case conferences would be held, at which the handling of exceptionally challenging (and also notorious) prisoners was discussed, and options considered. Segregation unit staff would take pride in settling a prisoner who refused to locate on mainstream wings in previous establishments, by whatever means they could find. These investments were often disappointed. Disruptive or violent prisoners found it hard to shake off their reputations in the system, among their peers as well as in the eyes of officials.

The only two dispersals not to have a major riot over this period were Long Lartin and Wakefield. Their apparently successful approach to control needed to be understood, and developed elsewhere. It was the liberal and negotiated model – enhancing choice, self-respect, responsibility and good relationships, as well as 'sending the right signals' (building incentives and regular reviews into sentences) – that seemed to work (see further Sparks et al. 1996). Proceedings of a Cropwood Conference exploring 'Problems of Long-Term Imprisonment' in 1986 called for efforts to articulate and measure these important differences in 'institutional ethos' and their effects (Rutherford 1987: 65). In practice, and as a result of a dramatic series of escapes in the mid-1990s, the advantages of the 'liberal' model faced considerable challenge. I shall return to these events and some important contemporary developments later. First, no account of high security prisons is complete without mention of the small and special, including segregation, units that support them.

Small and special units

Complementary to the dispersal system, and fundamental to its relative openness, has been a strategy of small units intended to remove those prisoners who threatened or took advantage of its relative freedom (the 'disruptive minority', Home Office 1984: 56). A number of prisoners were spending long periods in segregation units due to their 'unsuitability' for mainstream prison conditions, or were moved about from 'seg to seg' on what became known colloquially as 'the ghost train' (see Sparks et al. 1996). The pre-emptive act of taking out (relocating in other prisons' segregation units) suspected 'disruptive' or 'subversive' individuals to avert trouble (on Rule 43) could either lower the temperature or fuel the fire, depending on the accuracy of intelligence, the degree and direction of support among other prisoners, how sparingly it was used, and the approach or procedures adopted.

Two 'control units', operating a strict regime, were set up initially, at Wakefield (opening in 1974 but closing in 1975) and a planned unit at Wormwood Scrubs (which never opened), but these were controversial and never held more than four prisoners. Their negative effects (on prisoners' resistance and hatred of the prison authorities) out-lasted their tenure, as the intentionally austere regime was bitterly and legally challenged, and the stage system became 'an obstacle course' (Home Office 1984: 17). In an imagi-native and developmental response to their failure, and to the problems faced by dispersal prisons more generally, a more constructive number of CRC 'special units' were devel-oped instead, to provide relief and to address the behavioural challenges posed by the most 'difficult and disruptive' prisoners. If the mainstream system was based on progres-sion, it 'sent the right signals to prisoners' in terms of rewarding compliant behaviour in meaningful ways, and was consistent and 'psychologically credible', then fewer control problem prisoners would emerge (Home Office 1984: 16–17).

The units were conceptualized or designed (operationally rather than architecturally) to provide a variety of experimental regimes in order to individualize the management of such prisoners (they were physically developed on selected wings of existing, traditionally designed prisons). They were based on four important principles: they should not be puni-tive; none should be regarded as a place of last resort; the different units should com-plement each other and should not be an ad hoc collection of aims and regimes; and the Prison Service should be completely open about the establishment of these units and the way they operated (Home Office 1984: 66–70). 'Outside academics' should 'participate in their planning and evaluation' (ibid.: para. 135).

A Research and Advisory Group on the Long-Term Prison System was established to advise on their development and organize and oversee a research strategy (see Home Office 1987; Bottoms 1991). Three units were established: C Wing at Parkhurst (which had psychiatric support and was intended for prisoners who had a history of 'both trou-blesome behaviour and psychiatric illness or abnormality'; Home Office 1987: 7), Lin-coln (which had a more psychological specialist team advising staff, more staff engagement and more structure), and Hull (which was the least structured, based broadly on 'social learning' and educational principles). The units experienced many troubles (including 'teething troubles', one escape, violence, POA resistance and high levels of stress among staff) and some success (including reductions in violence among violence-prone prisoners). Evaluations suggested that their effects on some individuals, whilst in them, was positive (Walmsley 1991; Bottomley 1994). In some units, at some times, transformations took place (Davies 1994; Cook and Wilkinson 1998) and prisoners wrote publicly about the help they had received (for example, from psychiatrist Bob Johnson at Parkhurst; see Johnson 2005). However, they became controversial and politically unpopular as some prisoners 'bedded in', refusing to be located elsewhere in the system, and levels of material privileges were felt to be inappropriately high given the nature of the population in them (Liebling 2001). Given the lengthy admissions procedures, and the criteria developed for admission, few dispersal prison governors regarded them as a resource to help them resolve what they experienced as immediate operational difficulties with individual prisoners. They housed relatively small numbers, and were expensive to run. There were still far too many prisoners doing the rounds of segregation units on the 'Continuous Assessment Scheme' (or 'ghost train').

The CRC special units and the Continuous Assessment Scheme were replaced in 1998 by Close Supervision Centres (CSCs), which were designed to overcome some of the limitations of their predecessors: that is, to relieve more of the pressure on the mainstream, and to encourage such prisoners to behave in less disruptive ways without encouraging illegitimate gains in power, or such élite status (HM Prison Service 1996). In other words, they had to gain legitimacy 'with ministers and the public as well as with prisoners' (senior manager, personal communication, 2000). This system still operates at the time of writing, although they have undergone several reviews of their operating practice, clinical provision, and underlying philosophy. The current operating instruction states:

> CSCs were established in recognition of the need for a more controlled environment in which dangerous, disturbed and disruptive prisoners could be managed through a robust care and management approach, to enable them to develop a more settled and acceptable pattern of behaviour.

The CSC system consists of a series of small units within four prisons. First, new-generation design HMP Woodhill: this is the entry point to the system, where prisoners are assessed during a four-month period as to their suitability for CSC. Second, HMP Wakefield: a segregated regime for prisoners posing an exceptional risk. Third, HMP Whitemoor: this unit offers a more open regime for those with a prospect of being reintegrated into mainstream custody. Fourth, HMP Sutton, whose CSC opened in 2013 (see below). All the prisons in the high security estate have CSC-designated cells within segregation units for the temporary confinement of prisoners subject to Prison Rule 46 (as detailed within the CSC Operating Manual and in accordance with Prison Rule 4).

These centres house 52 prisoners in total and were originally based on a graduated progression from very restricted conditions to more general conditions involving activities and intervention. Unlike the CRC units, in practice, they did not require the consent of those selected (although individual prisoners challenged their selection vigorously; see *Regina v Secretary of State for Home Department ex parte Mehmet and O'Connor 1999*). The basic, segregation and standard regimes in themselves were also seriously resisted by the first intake of prisoners (see Clare and Bottomley 2001; HMCIP 2000; Liebling 2001). The first three years of the operation of the new close supervision centres were regarded by some as deploying a 'cruel and excessive' form of penal discipline (see HMCIP 2000). They were criticized by campaigning organizations and were variously termed 'the British Alcatraz' (*The Telegraph*), and 'torture units' (Bristol ABC 2012).

Improved selection and oversight mechanisms, as well as cultural changes and increased provision of 'treatments' or violence prevention and other courses, were introduced in 2001. Thematic inspections carried out in 2006 and 2009 continued to raise concerns about 'sensory deprivation' (HMCIP 2006) and about an apparent lowering of the threshold for selection (HMCIP 2009). Improvements were made to staff engagement, to the provision of mental healthcare, to progressive routes out, and to the operating philosophy and practice of the CSCs around 'violence reduction' in the light of these reports. Prisoners in them continue to challenge and campaign against their practices (e.g. Bristol ABC 2012).

In 2011 all 'specialist units' within the high security estate (the CSCs, High Security Units (HSUs) and Special Security Units (SSUs), the Protected Witness Units (PWUs) and the Detainee Units (DUs)) were brought under a single instruction and management strategy. According to the specification document, the decision to relocate a prisoner to any of these specialist units is based on one or more of the following aims: to provide an opportunity for the prisoner to address their psychological and mental health needs; address their disruptive and anti-social behaviour; address offending behaviour; 'to provide long term containment for those prisoners whose actions pose a significant threat to the safety of themselves, others, and/or the good order and discipline of an establishment'; to 'disrupt' an individual prisoner's activities 'which pose a significant risk to others or the good order of the establishment' (based on substantial intelligence); and 'to prepare for a return to an ordinary location' (NOMS 2014: n.p.).

The overall aim of the CSC system is 'to remove the most significantly disruptive and dangerous prisoners from ordinary locations and manage them within a small and highly supervised unit'. Referrals are made 'following a single serious incident or when attempts to manage an individual through standard strategies (for example, PSO 1810 Maintaining Order in Prisons) have failed due to their behaviour'. Referrals are also made 'if the prisoner's response to management under the Managing Challenging Behaviour Strategy has been negative'. Prisoners located within CSCs 'often have a range of complex and diverse psychological, psychiatric, or security needs'.

In 2013 a newly opened CSC at Full Sutton prison was exploring a 'new psycho-social operational model', with additional funding and training support from the Department of Health Personality Disorder (PD) pathway. In 2015 a thematic Inspection by HM chief inspector of prisons (HMCIP) reported more positively on the treatment of prisoners than at any other time in their history and development (HMCIP 2015), but still called for better and more transparent progression pathways for prisoners housed in them.

Contemporary problems of high security imprisonment

> Is this a liberal regime within a secure perimeter? I'd say it's a *controlled* regime within a secure perimeter. I don't like the word 'liberal' ... I wouldn't say we are governing prisons with the prisoners' *consent*, but with their *approval*, if you can see what I mean. They are *informed*, rather than *consulted*. We are not taking them for mugs, but we're not allowing them to run the place.
>
> (Senior manager, PSHQ, in Liebling 2002: 128)

Hull, Albany, Gartree, Wormwood Scrubs and Parkhurst were all gradually removed from the high security estate as a result of architectural and other weaknesses, and following a series of escapes, from Gartree (famously by helicopter) in 1987, and Whitemoor and Parkhurst in 1994 and 1995. Full Sutton and Whitemoor were added to the list of dispersal prisons in 1988 and 1991, respectively, bringing the total number of high security prisons to five (plus three 'core locals', or prisons holding unsentenced prisoners with category A accommodation).[3]

Several important events changed the landscape in high security prisons during the 1990s and subsequently, only brief accounts of which are included here (for further detail, see Sparks et al. 1996; Lewis 1997; Liebling 2001, 2002, 2014; and Drake 2011, 2012). Most important in relation to subsequent events, a dramatic series of escapes from both Whitemoor and Parkhurst in 1994 and 1995, respectively, changed the terms and conditions of high security imprisonment significantly, redrawing the boundaries again, turning the tide very much away from the 'liberal regime within a secure perimeter' model, and exposing its dangers. Whilst staff assumed the perimeter security was fool-proof and relaxed their treatment of prisoners in the interests of good order, well orga-nized prisoners plotted their escape, accumulating the means to do so over a number of years. Six exceptional-risk prisoners, five of them members of the IRA, escaped from Whitemoor's SSU, using firearms and injuring a prison officer in the process. They were quickly captured, but the political and policy consequences were major. The investiga-tion found that one prisoner had accumulated 84 boxes of property, a small amount of semtex and a bicycle (Home Office 1994). Prison staff, some of whom had been inti-midated by powerful prisoners into underenforcing security practices, had been 'playing scrabble' whilst the men worked their way out of the apparently impenetrable building. Five months later, three prisoners escaped from Parkhurst prison, from a hole cut in the wire perimeter fence. Two of the three were Category A prisoners. Long and detailed planning had taken place, and prisoners had been able to exploit small but important loopholes in everyday practices. The report of the inquiry described 'a chapter of errors at every level and a naivety which defies belief'. The scathing and emotive Woodcock and Learmont Reports (Home Office 1994, 1995), led by police and army personnel, led to the sacking of the then private sector chief executive of the Prison Service Agency, Derek Lewis, following an intense political battle which also threatened the position of the then Home Secretary Michael Howard (see Lewis 1997), and a renewed political interest in the details of life in high security prisons, which has only intensified since. In his gripping account of these events and their aftermath, Lewis describes 'a profound ministerial misunderstanding of the way organisations work and staff are motivated' (Lewis 1997: 173).

That these escapes occurred just a few years after the disturbances at Strangeways and other prisons (these prisons were not dispersals but local prisons) and the inquiry by Lord Justice Woolf establishing fairness and 'legitimate expectations' as foundations for decent prison practice, was especially unfortunate. Lord Woolf had emphasized justice and security in his landmark report, but in high security prisons the emphasis on 'justice and care' outlined in a White Paper that followed had misled staff into believing that backing off from some of the more aggravating security practices might be justifiable in the interests of maintaining 'good relationships' with challenging prisoners: an understandable but fatal error (see Liebling, with Arnold 2004; Home Office 1991). It was also the case that Long Lartin's 'liberal regime' had permitted some uncontrolled dynamics between pris-oners to foment, resulting in considerable backstage violence, and in the late 1990s, its first murder (another followed in 2013).[4] Problems of control dominated attention in the newly established high security prisons, and were being addressed, but at the cost of attention to internal security practices. Balancing the tensions between security, order and justice in high security prisons was extremely difficult, yet urgent (Liebling 1997). Senior operators, and prison staff, had to find a way between coercion and consensus that was both effective and politically acceptable (see further King 1991, 1997). This could only be achieved through relationships and 'dynamic security' (Dunbar 1985).

High security prisons were tightened up from 1995 onwards (as were other parts of the estate), with some variation between them remaining, but with a newly established Directorate of High Security Prisons leading a retaking of power by staff and senior managers, as well as a dramatic increase in the security resources and practices in high security prisons, which reduced the freedoms and privileges of prisoners considerably. Some prisoners reported improvements in the legitimacy of regimes over this period as they became more consistent, and quiet, well-behaved prisoners were rewarded with additional privileges and (if all worked to plan) earlier release (see Liebling and Price 1999; Liebling 2002). However, many saw drastic and painful reductions in their living and social conditions (Liebling 1999). Much of the 'guarded trust' which had existed between staff and prisoners in traditional high security prisons was removed from mainstream prison landings as fears of 'conditioning' and 'manipulation' began to dominate. Auditing and detailed specification of practices were introduced throughout the prison system. A new era of 'security first' and risk management, new generations of prison staff trained 'post-Woodcock', a changing senior management approach (which was more performance-oriented and audit-focused), and a less sympathetic political climate making the apparent 'pampering' of prisoners unacceptable, changed the tone as well as the purpose of high security prisons, away from 'fostering choice and responsibility' towards secure containment (Liebling et al. 2012).

These developments had some positive effects, once the dust had settled, including increased order and safety, increased perceived legitimacy in some prisons, and increasing professional confidence among staff, but the early years of the CSC, and the changing political mood, posed threats. Officers had often acted to bridge the gap between their human instincts and 'the rules' in long-term prisons, to good effect, but this kind of practice (also characteristic of some styles of policing, in the interests of the higher goal of social order) was now perceived as dangerous. The days of 'negotiated order' (Liebling 2002) were over.

From that point onwards, the 'ideology' of security resolved some of the tensions inherent in maximum security prisons, by settling them in favour of security (Drake 2012). Staff felt they had been complicit in the escapes (ibid.: 62–3), a legacy which has lasted, and had consequences since, but the organizational response, encouraged by the tone and language of the Learmont Report, was to cast prisoners as 'the enemies of security' (Drake 2012: 65) rather than as complex, challenging humans with possible futures. The 'pursuit of security' in social and political life (Zedner 2003, 2009) and the dominance of risk thinking in criminal justice policy and practice (Hannah-Moffat 2005) introduced a new harshness to life and management in some high security prisons, which made terms like 'liberal humanitarian' newly unsayable. The politics of sentencing and imprisonment also took a turn for the worse in most Western countries over this period (e.g. Ruggiero and Ryan 2013; Lacey 2008; Wacquant 2009; Garland 2001; Simon 2009) but perhaps especially in England and Wales (e.g. Newburn and Rock 2006; Tonry 2010; Gamble 2009; Pantazis and Pemberton 2009).

New problems of legitimacy soon appeared, and were most clearly illustrated in a 'return ethnography' carried out at Whitemoor high security prison in 2009–10 (Liebling et al. 2012). Lengthening and unexpected sentences (for example, for prisoners convicted on 'joint enterprise' charges[5]), more complex routes out, via psychological risk assessments and ascribed offending behaviour courses that were rarely available, increasing proportions of black, mixed race and other minority group prisoners finding themselves in high security prisons and, post-9/11, a new generation of al-Qaeda-inspired prisoners convicted of carrying out or planning offences against the Terrorism Act, created a new demographic to the long-term prison system, and a new set of dynamics. Fears of extremism and 'radicalization' added to the increased fears of conditioning and manipulation of staff described above, this time by a less familiar or 'recognizable' population of prisoners. The impact of these new management concerns was felt by staff who were less confident in their handling of a changing population of prisoners who made complex religious demands (Liebling 2014). Social dynamics began to emerge in which faith identities and power became fused, creating new possibilities for disaffected prisoners. Some black and mixed race prisoners, who had been formerly Christian or with no history of religious observance, for example, converted to Islam in prison and began to fight for recognition of their needs. A complex set of new moral and religious challenges were exploited by some groups of prisoners, whilst constituting legitimate concerns for others. Muslim prisoners came under intense scrutiny as everyday religious practices became confounded with extremism – concerns that were reflected in increasing quantities of permanent registrations of concern in Security Information Reports (Liebling et al. 2012). Prison chaplaincies, once the location of open dialogue, became sites of struggle and confusion as prison imams were brought into 'the war on terror'.

Islam has become the fastest growing religion in prisons in many jurisdictions, particularly among black, Hispanic and mixed race groups (see Hamm 2013), but selective and distorted versions of the faith have created tensions among prisoners, leading to fierce rivalry and violence among competing groups, and distress among the devoutly religious. There are many complex reasons for the attractions of 'Prison Islam', as Hamm and others have argued. The 'reinvention of black manhood' in prison, for example, involves new unities across many cultures (Hamm 2013: 45), offering an outlet and collective identity for the excluded and alienated. A post-9/11 fear of extremism in prison, as well as a rise in Islamophobia, adds considerable potency to these trends (see Liebling and Arnold 2012; Liebling et al. n.d., in progress). Senior managers in the high security estate have responded to these developments with some imagination and much concern, but the politics of handling the risks has been reminiscent of Derek Lewis's darker days (see Liebling 2015).

Conclusion

The tensions and difficulties discussed above – of managing those diagnosed as dangerous without inflaming their violence, of combining security with humanity, of maintaining control, of accurately identifying and legitimately removing apparently problem prisoners who may pose threats to a liberal order for the rest, of subjecting other, lower security category prisoners to dispersal conditions, of negotiating power, and of policing complex social dynamics within the population – remain major challenges for those managing the high security estate, and for prisoners living in high security prisons, who are dangerously susceptible to 'mis-' or 'over-' labelling. These problems have increased as new social dynamics, longer and more complex sentences, some new social and political fears, and political restrictions on the provision of activities constituting 'humanity' or offering personal development bite deeply into the original official aspirations for high security regimes (Liebling 2011). Concerns about 'the risks of radicalization' in high security prisons in particular, where a number of offenders convicted of acts of terrorist violence are housed and may have influence, have raised new questions about the possible disadvantages of a dispersal policy. It remains the case that policy in relation to high security prisons shapes the tone of, and practices in, all penal establishments.

At the time of writing, an independently funded study of the location and building of trust in high security prisons was close to completion (Liebling et al. n.d.), and energetic dialogue on improving the culture and practices of high security prisons was under way with officials and senior practitioners. As is so often the case in high security prisons, some promising new practices were being implemented: the introduction of Enabling Environments and Psychologically Informed Planned Environments for the personality disordered; a revised categorization review process including oral hearings for prisoners who are post-tariff; greater interest in the experiences of Category A prisoners, of both the effects of the label and the system of assessment (e.g. Wordie 2014); and a renewed emphasis on offering support for prisoners' 'progression'. These and other initiatives, often passionately led by committed individuals, illustrate the persistence of hope and humanitarian aspirations in the context of increasingly coercive control and, in particular, drastically lengthening sentences. It has been a major theme of official discourse on the treatment of long-term prisoners in high security since their inception that 'a viable life', hope and the preservation of dignity are important principles to adhere to in policy and practice. This morality has come under increasing threat, despite the best efforts of some individuals working within, and others outside, the prison system (see Liebling 2013). These 'places of contradiction' require continuing challenge and scrutiny. Their legitimacy in the eyes of different audiences, who have very different expectations (e.g. staff, prisoners, ministers and the public), is continually contested (Bottoms and Tankebe 2013; and Sparks 1994). The terminology of control, order and relationships that is used to organize and manage them should also be subjected to continuing sociological analysis and empirical examination (as Peter Young argued in 1987), as should the level and type of violence involving both staff and prisoners in them, and any successful or innovative practices enabling more rather than less safety, dignity and humanity to be accomplished in these unlikely settings. The form, size and operation of high security prisons tell us much that matters about the nature of our society as well as the state of our prisons.

Notes

1 In this chapter, for reasons of space, I focus exclusively on England and Wales. Scotland and Northern Ireland each have distinctive histories and practices, worthy of chapters in their own right. For now, I refer the reader to Sparks 2002, Bottomley et al. 1994, Coyle 1987a, and Toch 2014 in the case of Scotland; and McEvoy 2001 in the case of Northern Ireland. Outstanding work on supermax prisons in the USA is also readily available, notably Shalev 2009; Haney 2003, 2008; Haney and Lynch 2007; Rhodes 2004; King 1999; and Dolovich 2011.
2 Other jurisdictions have tended to favour concentration. Some scholars support this option on the grounds that fewer prisoners are subject to its practices; see Coyle 1987b.
3 Full Sutton replicates the much criticized design of Frankland (see NAO 1985), although new accommodation was added to Frankland in the early 1990s, in 2003 and 2009, which has better sight lines and open galleries. Whitemoor was designed 'before the impact of new generation architecture was fully felt' (Borland et al. 1995: 373) but likewise, has had new accommodation added which allows more space and light (as well as oversight) into the wings. It was originally assumed that 'new generation architecture' would allow greater flexibility within high security prisons, perhaps altering the balance of the arguments for concentration in the future.
4 Murders of prisoners by other prisoners have also occurred at Frankland (2011) and Full Sutton (2005, 2011). See Freer 2012.
5 The principle underlying the common law notion of Joint Enterprise is that when a 'gang' assaults a victim, those members who do not physically participate, but lend encouragement to the crime, are as guilty as the chief perpetrator and will receive a similar sentence. It is not a new offence but has become more widely used. See Liebling 2011; Crewe et al. 2015.

Bibliography

ACPS (Advisory Council on the Penal System) (1968) *The Regime for Long-term Prisoners in Conditions of Maximum Security* (The Radzinowicz Report), London: HMSO.

Adams, R. (1992) *Prison Riots in Britain and the USA*, New York: Palgrave Macmillan.

Borland, J., King, R. and McDermott, K. (1995) 'The Irish in prison: A tighter nick for "The Micks"', *The British Journal of Sociology* 46(3) (September): 371–394.

Bottomley, K. (1994) *CRC Special Units: A general assessment*, Report to the Home Office, Hull: University of Hull.

Bottomley, K., Liebling, A. and Sparks, R. (1994) *An Evaluation of Barlinnie and Shotts Units*, Scottish Prison Service Occasional Paper No. 7, Edinburgh: Scottish Prison Service.

Bottoms, A.E. (1990) 'The aims of imprisonment', in D. Garland (ed.) *Justice, Guilt and Forgiveness in the Penal System*, Edinburgh: University of Edinburgh Centre for Theology and Public Issues.

Bottoms, A.E. (1991) 'The control of long-term prisoners in England: Beyond the control review committee report', in A. Keith Bottomley and W. Hay (eds) *Special Units for Difficult Prisoners*, Hull: University of Hull, 1–15.

Bottoms, A.E. and Light, R. (1987) *Problems of Long-term Imprisonment*, Aldershot: Gower.

Bottoms, A.E. and Tankebe, J. (2013) '"Voice Within": Power-holders' perspectives on authority and legitimacy', in J. Tankebe and A. Liebling (eds) *Legitimacy and Criminal Justice: An International Exploration*, Oxford: Oxford University Press.

Bristol ABC (2012) 'Close supervision centres – Torture units in the UK: Voices from prisons within prisons', bristolabc.files.wordpress.com/2012/04/cscs-torture-units-in-the-uk-screen2.pdf.

Clare, E. and Bottomley, K. (assisted by Grounds, A., Hammond, C., Liebling, A. and Taylor, C.) (2001) *An Evaluation of Close Supervision Centres*, Home Office Research Study 219, London: Home Office.

Cohen, S. and Taylor, L. (1972) *Psychological Survival: The experience of long-term imprisonment*, Harmondsworth: Penguin.

Cook, F. and Wilkinson, M. (1998) *Hard Cell*, Liverpool: The Bluecoat Press.

Coyle, A. (1987a) 'The Scottish experience with smaller units', in A.E. Bottoms and R. Light (eds) *Problems of Long-term Imprisonment*, Aldershot: Gower.

Coyle, A. (1987b) 'The management of dangerous and difficult prisoners', *Howard Journal* 26(2): 139–152.

Crewe, B., Liebling, A. and Hulley, S. (2014) 'Heavy/light, absent/present: Rethinking the "weight" of imprisonment', *British Journal of Sociology* 65(3): 387–410.

Crewe, B., Liebling, A., Padfield, N. and Virgo, G. (2015) 'Joint enterprise: The implications of an unfair and unclear law', *The Criminal Law Review* 4: 252–269.

Davies, N. (1994) 'The mad word of Parkhurst prison', *The Guardian*.

Ditchfield, J. (1990) *Control in Prisons*, London: HMSO.

Dolovich, S. (2011) 'Exclusion and control in the carceral state', *Berkeley Journal of Criminal Law* 16(2): 259–339.

Drake, D. (2011) 'The "dangerous other" in maximum-security prisons', *Criminology and Criminal Justice* 11(4) (September): 367–382.

Drake, D. (2012) *Prisons, Punishment and the Pursuit of Security*, Basingstoke: Palgrave Macmillan.

Dunbar, I. (1985) *A Sense of Direction*, London: Home Office.

Freer, E. (2012) *Prison Homicides in England and Wales: Is it safe inside?* unpublished MPhil thesis, University of Cambridge.

Gamble, A. (2009) *Spectre at the Feast: Capitalist crisis and the politics of recession*, New York: Palgrave Macmillan.

Garland, D. (2001) *The Culture of Control*, Oxford: Oxford University Press.

Hamm, M. (2013) *The Spectacular Few Prisoner Radicalization and the Evolving Terrorist Threat*, New York: New York University Press.

Haney, C. (2003) 'Mental health issues in long-term solitary and "supermax" confinement', *Crime & Delinquency* 49: 124–156.

Haney, C. (2008) 'A culture of harm: Taming the dynamics of cruelty in supermax prisons', *Criminal Justice and Behavior* 35: 956–984.

Haney, C. and Lynch, M. (2007) 'Regulating prisons of the future: psychological analysis of supermax and solitary confinement', *New York Review of Law and Social Change* 23: 477–570.

Hannah-Moffat, K. and Maurutto, P. (2005) 'Assembling risk and the restructuring of penal control', *British Journal of Criminology* 45: 1–17.

HMCIP (2000) *Inspection of Close Supervision Centres: A thematic review, August–September 1999*, London: Home Office.

HMCIP (2006) *Extreme Custody: A Thematic Inspection of Close Supervision Centres and High Security Segregation*, London: Home Office.

HMCIP (2009) *Report on an Unannounced Inspection of HMP Woodhill*, London: Home Office.

HMCIP (2015) *Inspection of the Close Supervision Centres System*, London: Home Office.

HM Prison Service (1996) *Management of Disruptive Prisoners: CRC Review Final Report* (The Spurr Report), unpublished.

Home Office (1966) *Report of the Inquiry into Prison Escapes and Security* (The Mountbatten Report), Cmnd 3175, London: HMSO.

Home Office (1977) *Report of an Inquiry by the Chief Inspector of the Prison Service into the Causes and Circumstances of the Events at HM Prison Hull*, London: HMSO.

Home Office (1979) *Committee of Inquiry into the United Kingdom Prison Service – The May Inquiry*, Cmnd 7673, London: HMSO.

Home Office (1983) *Working Party on Regimes for Dangerously Disruptive Prisoners Report*, London: Home Office Prison Department, Chaplain-General's Office.

Home Office (1984) *Managing the Long-Term Prison System: The report of the control review committee*, Cmd. 3175, London: HMSO.

Home Office (1987) *Special Units for Long-Term Prisoners: Regimes, management and research. A report by the Research and Advisory Group on the long-term prison system*, London: HMSO.

Home Office (1991) *Prison Disturbances 1990* (The Woolf Report), London: HMSO.

Home Office (1994) *Report of the Enquiry into the Escape of Six Prisoners from the Special Security Unit at Whitemoor Prison* (The Woodcock Report), London: HMSO.

Home Office (1995) *Review of Prison Service Security in England and Wales and the Escape from Parkhurst Prison on Tuesday 3rd January 1995* (The Learmont Report), London: HMSO.

Jepson, N. and Elliott, K. (1991) *An Evaluative Report on Hull Prison Special Unit*, Leeds: Leeds University.

Johnson, B. (2005) *Emotional Health: What emotions are and how they cause social and mental diseases*, Ventnor: Trust Consent Publishing.

King, R. (1991) 'Maximum security custody in Britain and the USA: A study of Gartree and Oak Park Heights', *British Journal of Criminology* 31(2): 126–152.

King, R. (1997) 'Can supermax help solve security and control problems?', in A. Liebling (ed.) *Security, Justice and Order in Prison: Developing Perspectives*, Cambridge: Institute of Criminology.

King, R. (1999) 'The rise and rise of supermax: An American solution in search of a problem?', *Punishment and Society: The International Journal of Penology* 1(2): 163–186.

King, R. and Elliott, K. (1977) *Albany: Birth of a prison – end of an era*, London: Routledge & Kegan Paul.

Lacey, N. (2008) *The Prisoners' Dilemma: Political economy and punishment in contemporary democracies*, Cambridge: Cambridge University Press.

Lewis, D. (1997) *Hidden Agendas. Politics, Law and Disorder*, London: Hamish Hamilton.

Liebling, A. (ed.) (1997) *Security, Justice and Order in Prison: Proceedings of a Cropwood Conference*, Cambridge: Institute of Criminology, University of Cambridge.

Liebling, A. (1999) 'Doing research in prison: Breaking the silence', *Theoretical Criminology* 4(3): 333–357.

Liebling, A. (2001) 'Policy and practice in the management of disruptive prisoners: Incentives and earned privileges, the Spurr Report and close supervision centres', in E. Clare and A.K. Bottomley (assisted by A. Grounds, C. Hammond, A. Liebling and C. Taylor) (eds) *An Evaluation of Close Supervision Centres*, Home Office Research Study 219, London: Home Office, 115–164.

Liebling, A. (2002) 'A "liberal regime within a secure perimeter"? Dispersal prisons and penal practice in the late twentieth century', in M. Tonry and A.E. Bottoms (eds) *Ideology, Crime and Justice: A Symposium in Honour of Sir Leon Radzinowicz*, Cambridge Criminal Justice Series, Cambridge: Institute of Criminology, 97–150.

Liebling, A. (2011) 'Moral performance, inhuman and degrading treatment, and prison pain', *Punishment and Society* 13(5): 530–550.

Liebling, A. (2013) '"Legitimacy under pressure" in high security prisons', in J. Tankebe and A. Liebling (eds) *Legitimacy and Criminal Justice: An International Exploration*, Oxford: Oxford University Press, 206–226.

Liebling, A. (2014) 'Moral and philosophical problems of long-term imprisonment', *Studies in Christian Ethics* 27(3): 258–269.

Liebling, A. (2015) 'Description at the edge? I-it/I-thou relations and action in prisons research', *International Journal for Crime, Justice and Social Democracy* 4(1): 18–32.

Liebling, A. and Price, D. (1999) *An Exploration of Staff-Prisoner Relationships at HMP Whitemoor*, Prison Service Research Report, No. 6, London: HMPS.

Liebling, A., Armstrong, R., Bramwell, R. and Williams, R. (n.d., in progress) 'Locating trust in a climate of fear: Religion, moral status, prisoner leadership, and risk in maximum security prisons', *ESRC Award* ES/L003120/1.

Liebling, A., with Arnold, H. (2004) *Prisons and their Moral Performance: A study of values, quality and prison life*, Oxford: Clarendon Studies in Criminology, Oxford University Press.

Liebling, A. and Arnold, H. (2012) 'Social relationships between prisoners in a maximum security prison: Violence, faith, and the declining nature of trust', *Journal of Criminal Justice* 40(5): 413–424.

Liebling, A., Arnold, H. and Straub, C. (2012) *An Exploration of Staff-Prisoner Relationships at HMP Whitemoor: Twelve Years On*, London: National Offender Management Service.

McEvoy, K. (2001) *Paramilitary Imprisonment in Northern Ireland: Resistance, management and release*, Oxford: Oxford University Press.

Morgan, R. and Richardson, G. (1987) 'Civil liberties, the law and the long-term prisoners', in A.E. Bottoms and R. Light (ed.) *Problems of Long-term Imprisonment*, Aldershot: Gower, 158–180.

NAO (National Audit Office) (1985) *Home Office and Property Services Agency: Programme for the Provision of Prison Places*, HC 135, Report by the Controller and Auditor-General, London: HM Stationery Office.

Newburn, T. and Rock, P. (eds) (2006) *The Politics of Crime Control: Essays in honour of David Downes*, Clarendon Studies in Criminology, Oxford: Oxford University Press.

NOMS (National Offender Management Service) (2014) *Service Specification for Specialist Units: Service Specification*, p. 5. www.gov.uk/government/uploads/system/uploads/attachment_data/file/278905/2014-01-15_Specialist_Units_HSE_Specification_P1.0.pdf.

Pantazis, C. and Pemberton, S. (2009) 'From the "old" to the "new" suspect community examining the impacts of recent UK counter-terrorist legislation', *The British Journal of Criminology* 49: 646–666.

Price, D. (2000) *Security Categorisation in the English Prison System*, unpublished PhD thesis, University of Cambridge.

Radzinowicz, L. (1999) *Adventures in Criminology*, London: Routledge.

Rhodes, L. (2004) *Total Confinement: Madness and reason in the maximum security prison*, Berkeley: University of California Press.

Ruggiero, V. and Ryan, M. (2013) *Punishment in Europe: A critical anatomy of penal systems*, London: Palgrave.

Rutherford, A. (1987) 'The control review committee report – discussant', in A.E. Bottoms and R. Light (eds) *Problems of Long-term Imprisonment*, Aldershot: Gower.

Ryan, M. (1993) *Penal Policy and Political Culture: Four essays on policy and process*, Hook: Waterside Press.

Shalev, S. (2009) *Supermax: Controlling risk through solitary confinement*, Cullumpton: Willan.

Simon, J. (2009) *Governing Through Crime. How the war on crime transformed American democracy and created a culture of fear*, Oxford: Oxford University Press.

Sparks, R. (1994) 'Can prisons be legitimate? Penal politics, privatization, and the timeliness of an old idea', *British Journal of Criminology, Prisons in Context* 34, Special Issue, ed. R.D. King and M. Maguire: 14–28.

Sparks, R. (2002) 'Out of the digger: The warrior's honour and the guilty observer', *Ethnography* 3(4): 556–581.

Sparks, R., Bottoms, A.E. and Hay, W. (1996) *Prisons and the Problem of Order*, Oxford: Clarendon Press.

Thomas, J.E. and Pooley, R. (1980) *The Exploding Prison: Prison riots and the case of Hull*, London: Junction.

Toch, H. (2014) *Organizational Change Through Individual Empowerment: Applying social psychology in prisons and policing*, Washington, DC: American Psychological Association.

Tonry, M. (2010) 'The costly consequences of populist posturing: ASBOs, victims, "rebalancing" and diminution in support for civil liberties', *Punishment and Society* 12(4): 387–413.

Wacquant, L. (2009) *Prison of Poverty*, Minneapolis: University of Minnesota Press.

Walmsley, R. (1991) *Managing Difficult Prisoners: The Parkhurst Special Unit*, Home Office Research Study 122, London: HMSO.

Williams v Home Office (1981) *All England Law Reports* [1981] 1 ALL ER: 1211–1248.

Woolcock, N. (2003) 'A solitary life in the "British Alcatraz"', *The Telegraph*. www.telegraph.co.uk/news/uknews/1432506/A-solitary-life-in-the-British-Alcatraz.html.

Wordie, C.L. (2014) *How do Category A Prisoners Experience their Time in Custody? An Interpretative Phenomenological Analysis*, Research thesis.

Young, P. (1987) 'The concept of social control and its relevance to the prisons debate', in A.E. Bottoms and R. Light (eds) *Problems of Long-term Imprisonment*, Aldershot: Gower.

Zedner, L. (2003) 'Too much security?' *International Journal of the Sociology of Law* 31(3): 155–184.

Zedner, L. (2009) *Security*, Routledge Key Ideas in Criminology Series, New York: Routledge.

Chapter 28

Therapeutic communities

Alisa Stevens

For over 50 years, the penal spectrum has accommodated a highly distinctive, if not always accurately understood or adequately appreciated, outlier: the therapeutic community (TC). A seemingly incongruous alliance, the prison-based TC conjoins the antithetical interests and instincts of the therapeutic and the penal to pursue a treatment and custodial model which radically challenges hegemonic conceptions of correctional rehabilitation and imprisonment. The relationship, though, is unequal and so the integrity and ideals of the TC are sometimes eroded by the dominant concerns or constraints of the prison. This chapter therefore explores how the TC's rehabilitative regime is experienced by 'residents', as prisoners in TCs are called, before considering some of the difficulties that arise from situating therapeutic communities within correctional settings. First, though, some background on these 'special kind' of prisons and the prisoners in whose treatment they specialize.

Prison-based TCs and their residents

A democratic therapeutic community[1] – habitually shortened to TC – is a psychosocial method and programme of treatment for people whose long-standing mental health, emotional and interpersonal problems are causing them distress and preventing them from leading full, and fulfilling, lives. The origins of the modern TC movement are attributed in particular to two psychiatrists, Tom Main and Maxwell Jones. Their desire to provide more humane and effective in-patient care to traumatized Second World War soldiers led them to scrutinize the residential setting and its social structure for its psychodynamic significance and therapeutic climate. The philosophy and treatment modality that has since evolved rests upon the creation of a tolerant, supportive milieu and dynamic 'culture of enquiry'. The residential or day patient lives as part of a community whose 'total resources … are self-consciously pooled in furthering treatment' (Jones 1968: 85) and participates in psychotherapy, until such time as he or she is able to (re-)establish a 'stable life in a real role in the real world' (Main 1996: 80).

TC principles and practices were imported into English prisons in 1962 with the opening of 'a penal institution of a special kind' for 'abnormal and unusual types of criminal' (East and Hubert 1939: 159, para. 172) and 'the psychopath' (Snell 1962: 791): Grendon 'psychiatric prison' in Buckinghamshire. By modelling its regime upon the therapeutic community, albeit one adjusted from the outset 'to meet the requirements of a secure institution' (Pickering 1970: 11), Grendon was able to formulate a distinctly 'different' 'TC way' (Stevens 2013a) of imprisonment and offender rehabilitation. This rejects or revises enduring features of 'normal' prison social life and culture (discussed below), and replaces 'mainstream' time-limited and manualized cognitive-behavioural interventions with open-ended and non-directive psychodynamic psychotherapy. The overt delivery of this therapy occurs through the morning groups: thrice-weekly 'small groups' comprising eight to ten residents and facilitated by one or more psychotherapists, forensic psychologists or therapeutically trained prison officers; and bi-weekly community meetings involving all members, which fulfil a dual therapeutic and executive function.

Unusually for prisons, though entirely in keeping with the TC's enquiring and transparent culture, it was always intended that this 'special' institution should serve 'as a centre for criminological research' (East and Hubert 1939: 159, para. 172), and indeed Grendon now boasts an unrivalled back catalogue of diverse, methodologically rigorous, internally and externally authored research 'outputs'. These have repeatedly evidenced that long-staying residents record statistically meaningful and clinically significant improvements in various indicators of healthy psychological, attitudinal and interpersonal functioning and behaviours, including decreased psychoticism, anxiety, impulsivity and hostility, and enhanced self-esteem, self-efficacy and emotional self-management (Gunn et al. 1978; Newton 1998; Shuker and Newton 2008; Birtchnell et al. 2009). By contrast, convincing evidence of the TC's effectiveness in reducing reconviction has proven more elusive, with only a small number of studies completed, and some inconclusive results. However, in a four-year post-treatment follow-up, Marshall (1997) found that Grendon graduates who remained in treatment for 18 months demonstrated a reduction in reconviction rates of around one-fifth to one-quarter – a finding replicated at seven years by Taylor (2000). Both studies established that by comparing Grendon's men with a carefully matched control group of prisoners who had been accepted for, but not admitted to, the establishment, the graduates' rates of reconviction were lower than might have been expected, had they not received treatment at Grendon.

This emerging research base, combined with quantitative identification of the unmet need among prisoners for TC treatment (Gunn et al. 1991; Maden et al. 1994), and the renaissance of rehabilitation enabled by the 'something works' literature, has allowed for the development of wholly or partially self-contained TC wings or units within 'ordinary' prisons. These are typically separated from their 'host' establishment by high fences, and their residents reintegrate with the 'regular' prison population for activities such as work, education and gym, and for access to healthcare, chapel and visits. Sixteen TCs in five medium security adult prisons now exist – which sounds impressive until one considers that these TCs collectively accommodate less than 1% of the prison population.

Of these, Grendon (long 'uncoupled' from its psychiatric label) remains the only British prison exclusively to consist of therapeutic communities, with 238 places for men across five semi-autonomous communities and an induction and assessment unit, each with its own dedicated multi-disciplinary staff group. One community is reserved for vulnerable and sexual offenders,[2] while another, known as 'TC Plus', offers an adapted regime[3] for people whose low IQ (typically, between 60 and 80 on the Wechsler Adult Intelligence Scale) or other learning disability would normally preclude their participation.

The purpose-built therapeutic facility within the contracted-out HMP Dovegate in Staffordshire opened in 2001. With 200 places across five communities, one of which is a TC Plus, and an assessment unit, Dovegate most closely resembles Grendon in its capacity, and in its capability to add to the research literature. Notably, the winning bid to design, construct, manage and finance Dovegate included ring-fenced funding for externally conducted evaluative research, the contract for which was awarded to a team of psychologists led by Professor Jennifer Brown, then of the University of Surrey. This has yielded, for example, findings of similar, statistically meaningful psychological and behavioural treatment gains to those evidenced at Grendon, and a reconviction rate of 48% after an average period in the community of 19 months which, as the researchers noted, is significantly lower than rates recorded in national samples (Neville et al. 2007; Brown et al. 2014).

The longest established TC unit has been located at HMP Gartree in Leicestershire since 1993. Known as GTC, it accepts 25 internal referrals from this prison's population of early stage indeterminate sentenced prisoners, along with 12 places in its TC Plus. For ten years from 2003, a 40-bed TC operated at HMP Blundeston, before that prison's unanticipated closure. After being briefly accommodated at HMP Norwich, this community transferred in 2014 to HMP Warren Hill, Suffolk. Finally, the sole resource for long-term women prisoners seeking TC treatment has been based at HMP Send, in Surrey, since 2004. This 24-bed community is currently located on a wing shared with other prisoners, and while community and therapy rooms are designated for the TC's sole use, residents do not have sole use of residential landings.

Prisoners must apply for admittance to the TC, and can leave and return to 'mainstream' prisons – or what in TCs is disparagingly referred to as 'the system' – at any time. A substantial number do, finding the emotionally invasive demands of group therapy unpalatable, and aspects of the intentionally counter-culture nature of the regime unacceptable: 39% of residents received at Grendon between 1995 and 2010 left prematurely, either by choice or compunction, within 12 months. Those who choose to persevere commit to a minimum residency of 18 months (or three years for TC Plus), although in practice, most residents who successfully complete therapy[4] stay well in excess of two years. This requirement, arising from the research findings about the optimum treatment 'dosage', means that almost half of the entire sentenced prison population is not serving 'long enough' to benefit from TC treatment.[5]

The type of prisoners in whom TCs specialize, then, are high risk offenders serving substantial, often indeterminate, sentences for crimes of extreme interpersonal violence, and who may have been highly disruptive and/or violent in other prisons. Grendon in particular has gained an international reputation for its treatment of psychopathic and personality disordered offenders: people whose embedded and enduring ways of experiencing their world may cause substantial subjective distress and impaired social functioning. Although its residents are not routinely assessed for these disorders, previous surveys of new arrivals found that 26% of Grendon's men displayed traits associated with prototypical psychopathy (Hobson and Shine 1998), and 88% met the criteria for at least one personality disorder (Birtchnell and Shine 2000). Corresponding figures for the general male prison population are almost 8% (Coid et al. 2009) and 64% (Singleton et al. 1998), respectively.

This specialism has made TCs an obvious contributor to the developing national 'offender personality disorder pathway' (OPDP) programme. Responding to recommendations contained in the Bradley Report (2009), this strategy promises each offender who is identified as personality disordered an individualized sequence of interventions, or 'pathway plan', drawing, as appropriate, from a range of criminal justice and health services, co-commissioned by the National Offender Management Service (NOMS) and NHS England. The inclusion of TCs in the OPDP should therefore increase the number of applications they receive and embed TCs strategically within the envisaged coordinated, 'end-to-end' offender management of personality disordered offenders (NOMS and NHS England 2014a, 2014b).

The OPDP programme is also significant for TCs because it finally evidences some joined-up thinking (rather than establishment-specific initiatives[6]) about the onward movement needs of prisoners, by incorporating into the pathway 'Progression PIPEs'. These 'psychologically informed planned environments' respect the essential values of TCs and other 'enabling environments' and provide prisoners who have successfully completed some form of intensive treatment with a 'step-down' facility within which to apply what they have learned. The establishment of PIPEs therefore implicitly acknowledges that the long-standing practice of 'testing' the durability of change by immediately 'resettling' TC graduates within the anti-therapeutic milieu of the 'mainstream' prison risks stalling, if not reversing, treatment gains; both they and society are better served by transferring them to a structured, supportive unit within which to consolidate that change. Progression PIPEs are already established at HMPs Send, Gartree and Warren Hill, where they offer an obvious follow-on resource for their residents, and are or will shortly be available to men and women at a number of closed prisons and approved premises (NOMS and NHS England 2014a, 2014b).

Prisoners who elect for TC treatment can therefore fairly, if rather brutally, be described as 'damaged, disturbed and dangerous' (Shine and Newton 2000) individuals, with multiple, complex needs. They are not, by the nature of their offence, sentence and psyche, 'normal' offenders, and hence they need a treatment intervention that goes beyond the 'normal' – beyond the straightforward logic of the cognitive-behavioural 'courses' most long-term prisoners 'do' and into the subterranean intricacies of psychodynamic psychotherapy. The democratic TC has been an accredited offending behaviour programme since 2004, meaning that it has provided the Correctional Services Accreditation and Advisory Panel (CSAAP) with robust evidence of the theoretical basis for its model of change and programme design and hence of its potential to reduce reoffending. The experience of this treatment is the focus of the next section and is illustrated by verbatim excerpts from interviews the author conducted with residents from Grendon, Gartree and Send (Stevens 2013a).[7]

The prison-based TC as 'a rehabilitative changing house'

> This is the hardest time you will ever do, because you have to confront who you are and what you've done. There's no hiding from it, in that group room. It's painful, so *fucking painful*. But you've got to go through it so you can change.[8]
>
> (Ian, Grendon)

A treatment intervention as multifaceted as the democratic therapeutic community invites a variety of multi-disciplinary explanations about how it 'works' to effect personal change (notably, Genders and Player 1995; Morris 2004; Miller et al. 2006; Stevens 2013a). For the purposes of this chapter, the discussion that follows focuses upon key therapeutic factors which contribute to a psychodynamic model of change generally (Yalom 1995) and the fundamental principles and ideal-typical characteristics of TCs specifically (Rapoport 1960; Haigh 1999). Its structure is informed by Haigh's (1999) depiction of 'five universal qualities', presented as a developmental sequence through which the TC member progresses.

Attachment: joining and belonging

To the psychodynamic way of thinking, offending occurs 'when an individual falls out of relationship' with oneself, other people and wider society (Cullen and Mackenzie 2011: 228). Prisoners who migrate towards TCs are typically people whose psychogenesis and psychological and emotional development was corrupted or derailed by catastrophic formative experiences, personally or vicariously, of abandonment and abuse. Surveys of Grendon's men, for example, have found that around two-thirds reported experiencing severe physical abuse, and 40% sexual abuse, during childhood; and approaching three-quarters experienced the loss of or separation from their natural or surrogate parents for at least one year before the age of 16 (Shine and Newton 2000; Newberry 2009). Such traumatic early experiences ingrain 'internal working models' (cognitive maps and affective schemas) which persistently define how one perceives oneself and prospectively shape how one interacts socially with, and what one expects from, others (Bowlby 1988). Accordingly, one of the TC's key tasks is to provide a 'corrective emotional experience' (Alexander, cited in Yalom 1995: 24) by creating reparative relationships, between residents and with staff, which challenge these self-defeating core beliefs.

This goal of cultivating capacity for secure, healthy attachments begins with the experience of 'a really friendly welcome' (Shelley, Send), and is developed through immediately apparent institutional idiosyncrasies. The unusually very small size, and long-term stability, of the communities ensures that all residents are regularly seen by and become well known to all wing staff, and all wing staff are regularly seen by and become well known to all residents. Both address each other informally, by their first (or pre-ferred) name, which 'put[s] you on a level ... As people, not just screws and cons' (Steve, GTC). Also in contrast to most 'mainstream' men's establishments, residents can eat together in their community's dining room, while the 'open door' policy of the wing office empowers residents to 'pop in' throughout the day to chat, read newspapers or just 'hang out' *while* officers complete routine tasks. Collectively, these shared resources and sociable practices engender a 'family-like' (Richie, GTC), 'relaxed vibe' (Francis, GTC), 'so completely different to the system' (Clive, Grendon), and undermine the relevance and power of the 'inmate code', the idealized model of prisoner behaviour and solidarity-inspiring value system which advocates, among other things, cautiously limited, even actively antagonistic, social relations between the 'them and us' of 'screws and cons'.

Containment: feeling safe

A seemingly paradoxical feature of the TC is that its 'permissiveness' (Rapoport 1960) co-exists within clearly defined limits and consistently maintained, ritualized structures. These give community members confidence that the forensic TC is both able to contain high risk, personality disordered offenders in secure conditions and to manage the emotional revelations that emerge during psychotherapy and the interpersonal volatility inherent to communal living. For example, the morning groups run to strictly enforced boundaries: latecomers are refused admittance and discussions end promptly at the scheduled time. It is also not normally possible for residents to change their allocated community or small group. Moreover, all communities prohibit recourse to violence, alcohol and drugs, and sexual relationships. While this is also (nominally) the case in all prisons, in TCs the reasoning relates not just to the maintenance of 'good order or discipline', but to the need to enable residents to express their opinions without fear of peer rejection or physical retaliation, and to guard against illicit activities or exclusionary cliques which would inhibit therapeutic engagement and create secretive dependencies.

Yet, important source material for group therapy results from residents behaving naturally, without self-editing verbal responses or trying to disguise emotional reactions, and from periodically 'pushing boundaries'. Consequently, as Shane (Grendon) put it, 'making mistakes isn't seen as a bad thing here. [The staff] want you to fuck up really, because it will make you look at yourself and talk about your issues'.

Communication: 'opening up' to change

The creation of this safe 'holding' frame within which to participate in psychotherapy, and the relative stability and dependability of one's small group, creates an environment conducive to 'opening up' about one's life and problems. Guided by the staff facilitators, each resident gradually recounts his or her entire personal and offending history, and shares the internal world associated with that history. All aspects of the resident's life – every formative relationship and significant developmental experience, personal triumph and trauma, ill-judged decision, emotionally motivated choice and maladjusted coping mechanism – are explored, interrogated and deconstructed, in explicit, meticulous detail and in front of the unflinching, knowing gaze of one's small group.

Group therapy produces group dynamics that resemble and reproduce familial dynamics (Yalom 1995). As basic trust and secure attachment deepens, the resident returns discursively to the 'unfinished business' of relationships that 'went wrong' in early life, re-enacts them symbolically in the benign and conflictual attachments that emerge in the TC, and then tries to 'put right' these relationships by experimenting with new ways of relating and experiencing emotional intimacy. Disciplinary and clinical staff, as authority figures, are especially well placed to appreciate the impact of pathogenic parenting through their scrutiny of transference, and to remedy the harms caused through their re-educative modelling of attachment as reliable, responsive and attentive (Stevens 2013b). However, 'senior' (therapeutically advanced, well-respected) residents can also represent older and wiser siblings, who exercise positive peer influence, demonstrate productive engagement in psychotherapy, and advance reconsideration about which behaviours, attitudes and values command respect in the TC. In particular, for residents who may be more accustomed to, and more comfortable with, concealing their feelings behind 'hard man' 'masks' and the associated 'façades of being macho' (Muktar, Grendon), the evident willingness and learned ability of senior male residents to experience, absorb and communicate 'unmanly' and 'messy' emotions of vulnerability and distress, *in front of other men*, can be highly revelatory, both about what 'opening up' necessarily entails, and the cathartic benefits that ultimately accrue.

The culture of enquiry in TCs, then, goes beyond exploration of the past to examination of the present. Within the psychodynamic tradition, all the individual's conscious and unconscious (that is, not directly in one's field of awareness, until verbalized) thoughts, feelings, drives, wishes and actions are purposeful. Everything that happens in the TC – seemingly inconsequential incidents and interactions as much as dramatic rule infractions and the concomitant crises – is therefore diagnostically and therapeutically informative and so must be 'taken to the group' for dissection, elaboration and interpretation. In this pursuit of uncovering and elucidating 'the *true meaning* behind your behaviour' (Charles, Grendon), residents are particularly encouraged to 'make links' (or in psychologist speak, to discern functionally analogous 'offence paralleling') between the socially harmful ways they responded to problems or related to people in the past and continue to do so in the 'here and now' of the TC. The following example illustrates how residents' anti-social and clinically relevant behavioural patterns may emerge, be identified and analysed:

> – I went to the pod[9] and asked for a juice, and I took it bad when [the pod worker] said no ... I threatened him because I was pissed off ... So I got grouped[10] and had to talk about why the juice was so important to me [laughs]. And then [name of senior resident] started asking me loads of questions and I ended up talking about my index offence.
> – *How did you go from talking about juice to rape?*
> – Er, he said my problem was entitlement; that I feel like I'm entitled to what I want and don't think about how my behaviours make other people feel.
> – *Right. So that's how you make links between ...*
> – Between little things that you do that are a bit wrong and the big things you do that are very wrong. It's not easy but [name of senior resident], he's a sensible fella, he's got good insight into therapy, and him and me have similar issues, so I did take on board what he said.
>
> (Eddie, Grendon)

As Eddie's account suggests, to disclose one's problems to 'sensible', empathetic peers with 'similar issues' brings bilateral benefits. To find that one is able to impart information and offer advice that is valued by others boosts self-esteem, while the shame of one's past and despair of existential isolation is lessened by the realization that one's seemingly unique problems are shared with and understood by others. Such reassuring realization of 'universality' (Yalom 1995) not only instils therapeutically important hope for change, but gives residents more confidence to trust each other with their 'guilty secrets, hidden things, nasty things about me, that I'm ashamed of, that I've never told no one' (Alan, Grendon), and more capacity to access the repressed emotions which, psychodynamic theory argues, unconsciously motivate dysfunctional behaviour:

> I hadn't felt no feelings about things that had happened to me before but here, hearing other people's stories, just to know you're not the only one that's gone there or done that, it does help ... Just hearing the other girls talk about things what they've been through, and their feelings about it, makes it easier for me to feel my feelings and get support with them feelings.
>
> (Caroline, Send)

At best, this reciprocal sharing of intimate details of one's life and internal world fosters 'more genuine, more mature friendships ... [of] true emotion and affection' (Raymond, GTC), which bear little comparison with the strategic alliances, defensive partnerships and superficial bonds centred on 'taking drugs and having the screws over' (Don, Grendon) which prevail in the system. Moreover, and especially at Grendon with its four offence-integrated communities, 'proper' friendships may be forged between non-sexual and sexual offenders. This is noteworthy because in mainstream prisons, sexual offenders are routinely spatially and culturally constructed as 'the other': exiled in 'vulnerable prisoners' units' or 'sex offender only' prisons; rejected by 'normal' prisoners 'as a breed apart; like they're from a totally different planet to the rest of us' (Ravi, Grendon); and consigned to the lowest rung of the inmate-code-approved hierarchy of offending, which assigns status, or stigma, to certain crimes. Yet, when residents, regardless of offence, live alongside each other and collaborate in each other's therapy, this tends to reveal that, first, a sexual offender is 'not a monster; he's just like anyone else' (Wesley, Grendon), and second, that 'similar issues' with, for example, attachment deficits and emotional regulation, resonate across offending 'types'. Men who exclusively offend sexually, and hence are not generally mired in 'criminal values', are also able to contribute valuable insights and beneficial therapeutic challenges to those 'regular cons' who are. This helps the latter to confront the reality of, take responsibility for, and focus upon 'what *you've* done and the pain *you've* caused' (Chris, Grendon), rather than fixating upon the unacceptability of others' crimes. Such 'de-othering', re-evaluation of the utility of the hierarchy and concomitant acceptance of the 'very uncomfortable truth' that 'we've all done wrong and created victims' (Tony, Grendon), therefore, further erodes the applicability to the TC of 'system thinking', and further evidences the 'ways' in which the TC advantageously creates a radically different penal culture and ethos.

Involvement: increasing commitment

Community meetings embody most completely the TC's democratic, or to be more precise, democratized (Rapoport 1960), nature and its communitarian social order. Each community creates its own written constitution and selects, from among its residents, a chair and vice-chair who preside over these meetings and liaise between staff and residents, and representatives ('reps') who carry out a succession of tasks for the community's benefit. Each community member is entitled to raise in these meetings problems or grievances that potentially jeopardize the peaceful functioning, efficient management and rehabilitative purpose of the community, to share decision making and problem solving with staff, and to vote, through a public show of hands, upon one's preferred outcomes. (Staff, however, retain an exceptional right of veto.) Additionally, immediately after each small group session and periodically during community meetings, a summary of the therapeutic material discussed in each group is presented in order to advance residents' reciprocal involvement in each other's treatment and progress.

This culture of delegated authority and active participatory citizenship or 'communalism' (Rapoport 1960) solidifies residents' sense of ownership of, and proprietorial concern for, their community and its members, and prompts them to embrace the opportunities the TC presents for individual and collective responsibility. Notably, the more demanding 'rep jobs' require residents to adopt pro-social identities, and through their reiterative practice, prompt them to re-examine any self-limiting or self-sabotaging beliefs they hold about who they 'naturally' are and of what they are capable:

I never really believed I could be anything better; it's very hard to think highly of yourself when you're a drug addict and committing crimes, you know? ... [My rep job] showed me that I've got a good head on my shoulders and it can be put to good use; I am capable of *more*; I can be someone totally different, basically – that's what this place gives you.

(Nate, Grendon)

If a rep job is not performed satisfactorily, however, 'things are messed up for everyone, so that teaches you something about responsibility you won't get elsewhere' (Muktar, Grendon). To fail to be a good TC citizen, or to break one of the TC's cardinal rules, is therefore to offend not against the amorphous prison service, but against one's peers and one's community-formulated and community-endorsed values and customs. The response is not ordinarily or only a 'nicking' (adjudication), but being held accountable to one's small group and the sanctions it imposes:

And I don't know anyone who wouldn't rather take the nicking than explain themselves to their group! It's about learning the consequences of what we do, and owning that responsibility, and having respect for others.

(Tim, Grendon)

While 'mistakes' are 'permissively' tolerated, then, they do not pass without comment or consequence. Group members are frequently more willing to accept critical observations from 'real world' peers than paid professionals (Yalom 1995), but such 'reality confrontation' (Rapoport 1960) may be particularly effective in forensic settings because, as prisoners assert, 'you can't con a con': other offenders are both more credible discussants about offending and more attuned to self-deception, minimization and obfuscation.

Agency: empowered to change

The most serious failures of containment, communication or involvement – when residents have 'broken and betrayed the way we do things here' (Michael, Grendon) – are referred for discussion in the community meetings. Residents may voluntarily put themselves 'on the agenda' but more often, allegations of wrong-doing emanate from their peers: in other words, what would constitute the intolerable (criminal and inmate) code violation of 'grassing' (informing) in the system is legitimized in the TC as beneficial 'feedback to help someone with his behaviours and to keep the community safe' (Steve, GTC). If the 'offending' is egregious or persistent, a 'commitment vote' may be held, in which residents indicate to staff whether they believe it warrants the transgressor's expulsion.

The TC is therefore just as invested as the 'normal' prison in inculcating self-control and promoting social control, but it seeks to achieve this as much as possible through the 'bottom-up' self-governance and conscious agency of residents, rather than the 'top-down' infliction of authority and discipline; through social incentives rather than situational deterrents. This experience of a morally defensible and legitimate penal regime generates (for the most part) normative compliance (Sparks and Bottoms 1995) and helps to explain the TC's usually very safe (and, against comparable prisons, much safer) environment (Newton 2010). In developing a passionate enthusiasm for 'our TC rules, what we've decided on' (Adele, Send) and doing 'what's best for the community' (Raymond, GTC), residents acquire an acute appreciation of the moral and relational interdependency of human beings and the benefits of collaborative working and social cohesion. Moreover, as agentic actors, TC residents experience their responsibilities as self-esteem enhancing and dependency reducing, and assume a repertoire of attributes and roles – empathetic auxiliary therapist, perceptive peer supporter and mentor, responsible decision maker and rule enforcer – seldom associated with prisoners.

The process of personal change in the TC can therefore be summarized as the successful progression through a series of discernible and sequential stages, or a 'therapeutic career' (Genders and Player 1995: 149–150), in which residents incrementally acquire the self-knowledge and self-determination to change. Perhaps this sounds too easy, too neat, for making 'structural' reforms to one's personality and worldview is rarely straightforward or linear. Periods of ambivalence and resistance, of reversals and plateaux, are commonplace and, moreover, to be expected: emotionally revisiting 'the dark places of your life, your sadness, your upset' (Josephine, Send), excavating sublimated traumas and unresolved ontological conflicts against which the resident has been desperately psychically defended for many years, and exposing the horrific realities of one's criminal actions, shorn of comforting minimizations and imperfect rationalizations, is an excruciating process of self-evisceration.

Yet, for those who can endure, and once they feel part of and safe within 'a rehabilitative changing house' (Johnny, Grendon), the combination of communal living and psychotherapeutic exploration encourages residents to develop insight into what motivates their behaviour and to resolve troubling inner conflicts; learn from the critical but constructive challenges of their peers; derive hope from witnessing senior residents overcome similar, and perhaps once seemingly intractable, problems; and imitate pro-social and altruistic behaviours (Yalom 1995). It is therefore the community in its totality – those participating in and facilitating psychotherapy, the deliberately designed social milieu and determinedly affirmative social climate, the structure of the day, its range of activities and the social attachments that are formed and the group dynamics that transpire – which constitutes 'the primary therapeutic instrument' (Roberts 1997: 4).

The prison-based TC as 'still a prison'

> Sometimes we talk about coming together to do extra things together as a community, but it doesn't fit with the prison's timetable, so the prison won't allow it. Or like the garden at the back, we done it and we're supposed to maintain it but there's never any staff available to be out there with us, so it's not done ... For the prison, security is final; it's more important than anything else, like therapy or rehabilitation. So this is still a prison; it's the prison that's important, it's the prison we belong to, and we're always aware of that.
>
> (Sarah, Send)

From its creation, Grendon has had to reconcile being 'an integral part of the prison service' (Snell 1962: 790) with a 'character ... [that] must be essentially therapeutic' (ibid.: 791). Cardinal characteristics of the TC – personal autonomy, mutual collaboration, transparent decision making, some tolerance of 'mistakes' – have always been modified, in favour of the demands of the prison (Genders and Player 1995; Cullen 1997). Inevitably so, since the 'therapeutic prison' appears to be an oxymoron: 'a psychosocial environment which holds, and heals and empowers' (Haigh 1999: 247) is an unlikely cohabitee of a repressive, coercive institution whose primary association is with punishment and whose primary purpose is incapacitation.

In the TC practitioner literature, this dialectic has been constructed around the pragmatic need to 'broker' a healthy balance, and manage the internecine tensions, between therapy and security, care and control, the clinical and the penal (Morris 2001; Bennett 2006). Both elements are always essential if the establishment's twin purposes are to be achieved, but neither should consistently dominate or excessively intrude to the detriment of the other. A range of practical difficulties has also been commonly observed (Rawlings 1998). For example, and as Sarah (above) intimated, TC-specific activities have to be scheduled within and around a centrally determined 'core day', and even simple requests that require some (additional) staff time can be regarded as an unwarranted demand or unnecessary complication. For this reason, the TC units are particularly susceptible to being viewed by their 'host' institution as a 'resource heavy' 'parasite' (Woodward 2007: 223) or 'a foreign body, or transplant, in the human body' (Lewis 1997: 8), incurring the risk – sometimes realized[11] – of 'the same process of "rejection"' (ibid.).

An additional way to problematize the issues arising from operating a TC within a prison is to appreciate that the contemporary prison-based TC aspires to satisfy two masters: the Community of Communities (C of C) and the NOMS.

Founded in 2002, the C of C is part of the Royal College of Psychiatrists' Centre for Quality Improvement and works with partner organizations to identify, share and support TC best practice. This is chiefly achieved through agreeing a detailed set of core service standards and ideals by which member TCs – which include all the prison-based TCs – should operate. The achievement and retention of C of C membership has significant implications for the prison-based TC. By aligning itself with a professional body entirely independent of NOMS, the TC is beneficially imbued with an authority and legitimacy that resides in the values and expectations of the quasi-medical and therapeutic, rather than the penal. Moreover, compliance with C of C standards is audited through regular peer and self-review (see Paget et al. 2014). This effectively ensures that the regime one encounters in TC prisons is remarkably similar in style, if not discursive substance, to those in non-forensic settings. Failing the C of C audit could result in the TC losing its status as a CSAAP-approved offending behaviour programme, and thus should confer a powerful instrumental impetus to maintain therapeutic standards.

NOMS is also, and more explicitly, a performance-oriented organization. Since the advent of the public management agenda in the 1990s, all prisons have been monitored, assessed and held accountable for their attainment of a wide-ranging and quantifiable assortment of (national) 'key performance indicators', (local) 'targets' and 'standards'. The C of C therapeutic audit exists alongside this NOMS-produced managerial and operational audit, and accordingly prison-based TCs are uniquely subject to two different assessments, from two very different assessors, each with their own ideas about what constitutes, and how to measure, acceptable 'performance'.

Moreover, NOMS, as an executive agency of the Ministry of Justice, is subject to politically determined, ideologically driven policymaking. Periodically, as in the present era of (post-global financial crisis, post-recession) 'austerity', this results in the imposition of exceptionally severe, year-on-year financial cutbacks and budgetary constraints ('efficiency savings'). If prisons that operate one or a collective of therapeutic communities consequently find themselves required to choose which elements of their operation to 'streamline' or sacrifice, it is the therapeutic function, and not the custodial, which suffers. Ultimately, the TC's performance as a prison matters more than its performance as a TC, because a TC that fails as a prison may close (or be contracted out to the private sector), but one that fails as a TC can still function as a prison.

This doomsday scenario has happily not befallen the current cohort of prison-based TCs. What has become evident, however, is that while a contraction in available resources and corresponding curtailment of the core day adversely affects all prisons, the consequences for TCs are especially severe. This is because, as noted above, it is the community in its entirety that is the method of change: the whole *is* the sum of (*as well as* greater than) its parts. The TC is therefore more than usually sensitive to any impairment to the implementation of its treatment model and day-to-day functioning of its regime that degrades the therapeutic ethos and disturbs the TC dynamic. Reduced time out of cell, for example, represents more than the expendable luxury of association; it impacts upon residents' ability to nurture attachments, experience communalism, profit from 'living-learning experiences' (Jones 1968: 108), and expose offence-paralleling behaviours. Even seemingly minor modifications to the regime can therefore impede the optimal operation of the all-encompassing, '24/7' TC and, eventually, over time, erode the 'culture of enquiry' and secure attachments upon which the entire edifice of safe, sustainable and hence successful forensic psychotherapy rests.

These two issues – performance measures of the TC and the prison that may conflict, and the current 'challenging' fiscal climate for prisons – have been highlighted as problematic in successive recent reports from HM Chief Inspector of Prisons (HMCIP) and in academic studies.

For example, TCs are expected to maintain high levels of occupancy, and retain residents through to completion. As Shefer (2012) cautions, performance targets for programme completion rates erroneously assume that staff are able to increase the number of prisoners who are capable of completing the programme successfully. Skilled staff can run programmes as intended, but they cannot ensure that the prisoner intellectually or emotionally commits to it or insist that he or she persists with it. While this is also true for 'mainstream' correctional interventions, the messy, painful nature of psychotherapy virtually guarantees substantial attrition. Indeed, if the integrity and rigour of the programme is to be sustained, there should be highly selective admission and robust expulsion policies.

To maintain high therapeutic standards, by expelling those unsuited to the regime or under-recruiting, however, risks the unintended consequence of being forced to accept 'lodgers' – prisoners who are housed in the TC simply to prevent the unacceptability of serviceable cells remaining unoccupied in an otherwise overcrowded penal estate. A supplementary complication arises when residents who are ready for a progressive move, or who have been voted out or taken themselves 'out of therapy', are unable to relocate speedily to another prison, because of the logistical difficulties of transferring prisoners to establishments with minimal spare capacity. At best, the presence of such prisoners dilutes the therapeutic environment but does not disrupt it, or transforms what should be a participatory rehabilitative programme into 'a period of stagnation … [and] a relatively benign form of asylum' (Genders and Player 2010: 442). If, however, lodgers and ex-residents have no respect for the TC regime, its rules of abstinence and behavioural expectations, they can undermine the therapeutic progress of residents, damage morale and destabilize the community (ibid.; Shefer 2010).

At the privately run Dovegate, this universal pressure to 'fill beds' is compounded by the commercial imperative to maintain the contracted occupancy figure (initially of 194, then 190, out of the 200 TC beds available). Cullen and Mackenzie (2011), who detailed with exceptional candour the multiple difficulties Dovegate TC endured during its first decade of 'struggle, achievement, dissent and, more recently, revival' (ibid.: 226), described how this target 'hung like a Sword of Damocles over the heads of successive directors of therapy' (ibid.: 73) and led to the professionally unethical selection of unsuitable residents, and the lengthy retention of therapeutically inactive prisoners, in order 'to keep the numbers up' (ibid.: 202; HMCIP 2006, 2008). In 2008, the numbers of lodgers and out of therapy prisoners across all Dovegate communities reached 32%, and in one community, over 50%. These (and other) problems 'seriously undermined' Dovegate TC (HMCIP 2008: 5), and were only remedied following a significant reorganization of the regime (Cullen and Mackenzie 2011; Brown et al. 2014).

Grendon's regime was also observed to deteriorate rapidly. In 2007, the HMCIP had some concerns about the effects of 'financial savings' on the regime, but was still able to conclude that 'the health – and importance – of the prison is not in doubt' (HMCIP 2007: 5). By 2009, however, the 'cumulative financial efficiencies had begun to erode Grendon's capacity to deliver a therapeutic regime at all' (HMCIP 2009: 6). The continued reduction in the numbers of uniformed and clinical staff, combined with the preference for detailing officers to 'key performance' operational duties, sometimes resulted in the cancellation of therapy groups – which are, of course, equally 'key' to the TC. A backlog of residents' therapy reports had accumulated, and the availability of therapeutic supervision for staff decreased. Chief Inspector of Prisons added ominously that further proposed budgetary reductions, which 'appeared to take little notice of Grendon's unique role ... threatened the viability of the entire therapeutic regime' (ibid.: 5; see also Genders and Player 2010).

It was following this decline in Grendon's therapeutic performance that the only homicide to have been perpetrated in any prison-based TC occurred at Grendon in August 2010, when Robert Coello (a sexual offender) was murdered by fellow resident Lee Foye on an offence-integrated wing that had been re-opened (after refurbishment) less than nine months previously. The subsequent Prisons and Probation Ombudsman (2013: 3) investigation noted 'the context of wider institutional factors' within which this otherwise unforeseeable tragedy occurred. Grendon had been under pressure to open the community prematurely, with some therapeutically inexperienced and inadequately trained staff; to fill its spaces more quickly than initially anticipated, with some residents for whom assessment and induction protocols had been circumvented or, as for Mr Foye, truncated; and had operated, for lengthy periods of time, without a full quota of experienced clinical staff and without consistent facilitators for the therapy groups, thereby compromising the attainment of the categorical principles of secure attachment and communication of information discussed earlier. This hastiness in the planning for and commencement of a new community was dictated by the managerial imperative of maximizing occupational capacity, and the deficiencies in practice that became apparent were not remedied due to resourcing constraints. Although an atypical and extreme example, the murder of Mr Coello therefore indicates the potentially calamitous consequences that can follow when operational pressures and targets from *the prison* impinge upon the therapeutic integrity and clinically justifiable practice of *the TC*.

Concluding comments

The democratic therapeutic community prison represents the apex of liberal and enlightened thinking about the need to rehabilitate, rather than merely incarcerate, serious offenders. As an accredited intervention, the TC combines a clear-eyed correctional focus upon risk and reducing reoffending with a compassionate concern to relieve psychological distress and cultivate self-worth among people who were, to misquote Shine and Newton (2000), damaged and disturbed by others long before they became damaging and disturbing to others. As an exemplar of humane imprisonment, embodied through a range of symbolic, social and situational factors that enable and promote an alternative penal environment and culture, the TC is ideologically problematic for both sides of the penological coin. The values and practices it embodies expose the futile vindictiveness of hegemonic discourses of unchangeable 'deviancy' and retributive punishment, and unsettle conventional, narrow conceptions of what the prison is, does and should normatively strive to achieve. Equally, though, the TC repudiates reductionist representations of 'the prison' as a monolithic dispenser of psychological pains and harms, whose atavistic culture inevitably reduces and harms those who live (and work) within its walls.

Despite – or because of – these achievements, Grendon, the most lauded, most researched prison in the criminological global North, has seen its template for strengths-based rehabilitation and penal decency emulated in only a handful of TC units within 'mainstream' English establishments, and has failed to exert a wider benign influence upon a penal system that lacks the political will and penological imagination to engage with the progressive possibilities it enshrines. Thus 'the system' has consistently ignored not only the rebuke Grendon represents, but the promise it contains. Perhaps one should not be surprised: psychodynamically, anything that appears threatening is liable to be disowned, denied and 'split off'. As a numerically marginal entity, TCs are easily marginalized.

More positively, the history and evolution of Grendon over five decades attests to the prison-based TC's remarkable resilience in rising above and learning from intermittent, intrinsically arising and externally created crises. The emerging OPDP programme, by enfolding TCs within an apparently well-resourced, interdepartmental and integrated service, also allows some cautious optimism about the TC's immediate future and continuing ability to merge, however uncomfortably at times, the specialist therapeutic with the generic custodial. Perhaps then, after a recent 'winter of despair' for therapeutic communities, a 'spring of hope' and renewal beckons for this most 'special kind' of prison.

Notes

1 This chapter discusses, and hence implies reference solely to, English prison-based democratic TCs. One of the difficulties in defining TCs is that a number of similar-but-different TC programmes function around the world. In the USA, 'therapeutic community' refers to a structured and stratified programme for offenders with problematic drug misuse. This 'hierarchical', 'concept-based' or 'addictions' model transferred with some modifications to Europe, and has been available within a handful of 'mainstream' English prisons since 1996. The prisons

and forensic psychiatric hospitals of assorted European and Australasian countries have also adopted some features and principles of democratic TCs in various 'social therapeutic' and hybrid TC/cognitive-behavioural programmes.

2 Offenders convicted of sexual offences also reside on Grendon's other therapy wings, and consistently comprise around 20% of its total population. At Dovegate TC, the numbers of sexual offenders have ranged from 9% in 2006 to 3% in 2013 (HMCIP 2006, 2014).

3 'TC Plus' (or TC+) treatment is more therapist initiated and directed, and proceeds at a slower pace. Greater emphasis is placed on non-verbal, creative (psychodrama, art, music) therapies, as a way of articulating one's experiences and emotions, and pictorial imagery and emoticons replace some written material. The first TC Plus opened at Dovegate in January 2013.

4 'Completion' is a destination that is therapeutically difficult to define, but involves achieving one's therapy targets including demonstrably reducing one's risk, possibly resulting in re-categorization.

5 In June 2014, of the sentenced prison population, 18% were serving an indeterminate sentence, and 38% a determinate sentence of more than four years (Ministry of Justice 2014).

6 During the 1970s, Grendon established an 'outpost' in a room in Toynbee Hall, London, where ex-residents could meet prison officers for 'discussion and counselling' (Lynn 1973: 256), and from 1993 to 1995, operated a small pre-release and pre-transfer unit for category D residents whose discharge from prison was imminent (Healey 2000). Today, eligible Grendon graduates can transfer directly to an adjacent open prison, providing the possibility of sporadic follow-up, and the TC units often provide similarly informal 'after care' to former residents while they remain within the host establishment.

7 Given its much greater population size, the majority of the 60 participants resided at Grendon. Interviewees were tape recorded with their consent. All names are pseudonyms.

8 Some quotes appeared in Stevens 2013a, reproduced with permission from Taylor & Francis.

9 'The pod': small kitchen on each community.

10 'Grouped': the referral to a resident's small group of an issue for discussion.

11 In sometimes controversial circumstances and for contested reasons, three separate TC units for young offenders have closed, in addition to the 'social community' of the Barlinnie Special Unit and the Max Glatt Centre TC within Wormwood Scrubs.

Bibliography

Bennett, P. (2006) 'Governing a humane prison', in D. Jones (ed.) *Humane Prisons*, Abingdon: Radcliffe.

Birtchnell, J. and Shine, J. (2000) 'Personality disorders and the interpersonal octagon', *British Journal of Medical Psychology* 73(4): 433–448.

Birtchnell, J., Shuker, R., Newberry, M. and Duggan, C. (2009) 'An assessment of change in negative relating in two male forensic therapy samples using the Person's Relating to Others Questionnaire (PROQ)', *Journal of Forensic Psychiatry and Psychology* 20(3): 387–407.

Bowlby, J. (1988) *A Secure Base: Clinical Applications of Attachment Theory*, London: Routledge.

Bradley, K. (2009) *The Bradley Report: Lord Bradley's review of people with mental health problems or learning disabilities in the criminal justice system*, London: Department of Health.

Brown, J., Miller, S., Northey, S. and O'Neill, D. (2014) *What Works in Therapeutic Prisons: Evaluating psychological change in Dovegate Therapeutic Community*, Basingstoke: Palgrave Macmillan.

Coid, J., Yang, M., Ullrich, S., Roberts, A., et al. (2009) 'Psychopathy among prisoners in England and Wales', *International Journal of Law and Psychiatry* 32: 134–141.

Cullen, E. (1997) 'Can a prison be a therapeutic community: The Grendon template', in E. Cullen, L. Jones and R. Woodward (eds) *Therapeutic Communities for Offenders*, Chichester: Wiley.

Cullen, E. and Mackenzie, J. (2011) *Dovegate: A therapeutic community in a private prison and developments in therapeutic work with personality disordered offenders*, Hook: Waterside Press.

East, W. and Hubert, W. (1939) *The Psychological Treatment of Crime*, London: HM Stationery Office.

Genders, E. and Player, E. (1995) *Grendon: A study of a therapeutic prison*, Oxford: Clarendon Press.

Genders, E. and Player, E. (2010) 'Therapy in prison: Revisiting Grendon 20 years on', *Howard Journal of Criminal Justice* 49(5): 431–450.

Gunn, J., Maden, T. and Swinton, M. (1991) 'Treatment needs of prisoners with psychiatric disorders', *British Medical Journal* 303(6798): 338–341.

Gunn, J., Robertson, G., Dell, S. and Way, C. (1978) *Psychiatric Aspects of Imprisonment*, London: Academic Press.

Haigh, R. (1999) 'The quintessence of a therapeutic community: Five universal qualities', in P. Campling and R. Haigh (eds) *Therapeutic Communities: Past, present, and future*, London: Jessica Kingsley.

Healey, B. (2000) *Grendon Prison: The history of a therapeutic experiment 1939–2000*, Wotton-under-Edge: HMP Leyhill.

HMCIP (HM Chief Inspector of Prisons) (2006) *Report on an Unannounced Short Follow-up Inspection of HMP Dovegate Therapeutic Community, 29–31 August 2006*, London: HM Inspectorate of Prisons.

HMCIP (HM Chief Inspector of Prisons) (2007) *Report on an Unannounced Short Follow-up Inspection of HMP Grendon, 31 October–2 November 2006*, London: HM Inspectorate of Prisons.

HMCIP (HM Chief Inspector of Prisons) (2008) *Report on an Announced Inspection of HMP Dovegate Therapeutic Community, 16–20 June 2008*, London: HM Inspectorate of Prisons.

HMCIP (HM Chief Inspector of Prisons) (2009) *Report on an Announced Inspection of HM Prison Grendon, 2–6 March 2009*, London: HM Inspectorate of Prisons.

HMCIP (HM Chief Inspector of Prisons) (2014) *Report on an Unannounced Inspection of HMP Dovegate Therapeutic Community, 23 October–2 November 2013*, London: HM Inspectorate of Prisons.

Hobson, J. and Shine, J. (1998) 'Measurement of psychopathy in a UK prison population referred for long-term psychotherapy', *British Journal of Criminology* 38(3): 504–515.

Jones, M. (1968) *Social Psychiatry in Practice: The Idea of the Therapeutic Community*, Harmondsworth: Penguin.

Lewis, P. (1997) 'Sustaining therapeutic communities: The Grendon experience', *Prison Service Journal* 111: 8–12.

Lynn, P. (1973) 'A visitor's impression of Grendon psychiatric prison', *Australian and New Zealand Journal of Criminology* 6(4): 254–256.

Maden, T., Swinton, M. and Gunn, J. (1994) 'Therapeutic community treatment: A survey of unmet need among sentenced prisoners', *Therapeutic Communities* 15(4): 229–236.

Main, T. (1996) 'The hospital as a therapeutic institution', *Therapeutic Communities* 17(2): 77–80 (originally published (1946) in *Bulletin of the Menninger Clinic* 10: 66–68).

Marshall, P. (1997) *A Reconviction Study of HMP Grendon Therapeutic Community*, London: Home Office Research and Statistics Directorate.

Miller, S., Sees, C. and Brown, J. (2006) 'Key aspects of psychological change in residents of a prison therapeutic community: A focus group approach', *Howard Journal of Criminal Justice* 45(2): 116–128.

Ministry of Justice (2014) *Offender Management Statistics Bulletin, 31 July 2014*, London: Ministry of Justice.

Morris, M. (2001) 'Grendon Underwood: A psychotherapeutic prison', in J. Williams Saunders (ed.) *Life within Hidden Worlds: Psychotherapy in Prisons*, London: Karnac.

Morris, M. (2004) *Dangerous and Severe – Process, Programme and Person: Grendon's Work*, London: Jessica Kingsley.

Neville, L., Miller, S. and Fritzon, K. (2007) 'Understanding change in a therapeutic community: An action systems approach', *Journal of Forensic Psychiatry and Psychology* 18(2): 181–203.

Newberry, M. (2009) *Changes in the Profile of Prisoners at HMP Grendon*, unpublished report, HMP Grendon.

Newton, M. (1998) 'Changes in measures of personality, hostility and locus of control during residence in a prison therapeutic community', *Legal and Criminological Psychology* 3(2): 209–223.

Newton, M. (2010) 'Changes in prison offending among residents of a prison-based therapeutic community', in R. Shuker and E. Sullivan (eds) *Grendon and the Emergence of Forensic Therapeutic Communities: Developments in research and practice*, Chichester: Wiley-Blackwell.

NOMS and NHS England (2014a) *Brochure of Women Offender Personality Disorder Services*, London: NOMS and NHS England.

NOMS and NHS England (2014b) *Brochure of Offender Personality Disorder Services for Men at High Risk of Harm to Others*, London: NOMS and NHS England.

Paget, S., Thorne, J., Fildes, N. and Rashid, S. (eds) (2014) *Service Standards for Therapeutic Communities*, eighth edn, London: Community of Communities, Royal College of Psychiatrists.

Pickering, I. (1970) 'Foreword', in T. Parker, *The Frying Pan: A prison and its prisoners*, London: Hutchinson.

Prisons and Probation Ombudsman (2013) *Investigation into the Death of a Man at Hospital in August 2010, while a Prisoner at HMP Grendon*, London: Prisons and Probation Ombudsman.

Rapoport, R. (1960) *Community as Doctor: New Perspectives on a Therapeutic Community*, London: Tavistock Publications.

Rawlings, B. (1998) 'The therapeutic community in the prison: Problems in maintaining therapeutic integrity', *Therapeutic Communities* 19(4): 281–294.

Roberts, J. (1997) 'How to recognise a therapeutic community', *Prison Service Journal* 111: 4–7.

Shefer, G. (2010) *Doing Rehabilitation in the Contemporary Prison: The case of one-wing therapeutic communities*, unpublished PhD thesis, Institute of Criminology, University of Cambridge.

Shefer, G. (2012) 'The impact of performance management culture on prison-based therapeutic communities', *European Journal of Criminology* 9(4): 407–424.

Shine, J. and Newton, M. (2000) 'Damaged, disturbed and dangerous: A profile of receptions to Grendon therapeutic prison 1995–2000', in J. Shine (ed.) *A Compilation of Grendon Research*, Grendon Underwood: HMP Grendon.

Shuker, R. and Newton, M. (2008) 'Treatment outcome following intervention in a prison-based therapeutic community: A study of the relationship between reduction in criminogenic risk and improved psychological well-being', *British Journal of Forensic Practice* 10(3): 33–44.

Singleton, N., Meltzer, H. and Gatward, R. (1998) *Psychiatric Morbidity among Prisoners in England and Wales*, London: The Stationery Office.

Snell, H. (1962) 'H.M. Prison, Grendon', *British Medical Journal* 2(5307): 789–792.

Sparks, R. and Bottoms, A. (1995) 'Legitimacy and order in prisons', *British Journal of Sociology* 46 (1): 45–62.

Stevens, A. (2013a) *Offender Rehabilitation and Therapeutic Communities: Enabling change the TC way*, Abingdon: Routledge.

Stevens, A. (2013b) 'The "meanings" of female staff in male therapeutic community prisons: Gender as symbolism and specialism', *Howard Journal of Criminal Justice* 52(5): 479–497.

Taylor, R. (2000) *A Seven Year Reconviction Study of HMP Grendon Therapeutic Community*, London: Home Office Research, Development and Statistics Directorate.

Woodward, R. (2007) 'Symbiosis: Therapeutic communities within non-therapeutic community organizations', in M. Parker (ed.) *Dynamic Security: The democratic therapeutic community in prison*, London: Jessica Kingsley.

Yalom, I. (1995) *The Theory and Practice of Group Psychotherapy*, fourth edn, New York: Basic Books.

Chapter 29

Older age, harder time

Ageing and imprisonment

Natalie Mann[1]

The past two decades have seen an unprecedented rise in the number of male prisoners aged 60 years and over (Mann 2012). With approximately 102 prisoners aged 80 years and over, and five aged over 90 years, this age group now represents the fastest growing population in prisons in England and Wales (Justice Select Committee 2013). This astonishing rise, which has dramatically altered the 'make-up' of the prison population, is a result of a number of factors, including a general increase in life expectancy, an increase in individuals committing crime later in life and, more recently, the targeted pursuit of the historic sexual offender. This chapter draws on studies of ageing prisoners conducted over the last two decades and on my own recent research (Mann 2012), which was conducted in three very different establishments in England. In-depth interviews were carried out with ten prison officers and 40 prisoners, aged 55 to 81 years of age, about their experiences of ageing and imprisonment.

The 'greying' of America's prisons, and its associated problems, first sparked academic debate in the UK over a decade ago (Wahidin 2000, 2003, 2004; Frazer 2003; PRT and The Centre for Policy on Ageing 2003; Gidley 2004). However, despite warnings from criminologists and reform groups alike, it was not until very recently that the issue of ageing prisoners made it on to the UK government agenda. As such, the Prison Service in England and Wales was poorly prepared for the rapid rise in the number of older prisoners, and the increased presence of frail, disabled and infirm individuals within prison establishments across the country has resulted in an extremely complex management challenge. These older offenders constitute a diverse section of the prison population and their heterogeneity necessitates specialist requirements which struggle to be met by a Prison Service that has had to cut £650 million from its £3.4 billion budget by 2015 (PRT 2014).

As this chapter will examine, our prisons are struggling to cope with the emergence of this new population whose characteristics and needs differ greatly from those of the average prisoner. As a form of punishment, imprisonment both physically and administratively fails to provide for the ageing and, as the research I have carried out has revealed, in addition to the general 'pains of imprisonment' discussed by Sykes (1958), the ageing prison population is subject to specific pains which result from an unsuitable environment, inadequate healthcare and a lack of meaningful activity. These are the 'hidden injuries' discussed by Crawley and Sparks (2005c: 350), and arguably it is these additional pains which result in ageing prisoners doing 'harder time' than their younger counterparts.

The emergence of an ageing prison population

As early as the 1980s, US criminologists were researching the new phenomenon of 'elderly criminals' (Malinchak 1980; Newman et al. 1984). While many thought they were detecting the emergence of a new social problem where ageing individuals would commit a disproportionate amount of crime (see Rothman et al. 2000), wider social issues such as an increase in life expectancy and better access to healthcare quickly began to dominate discussion and debate. Although no 'elderly crime wave' occurred, each year we are imprisoning a greater number of older men. While they still constitute a relatively small proportion of prisoners within the system, it is the multitude of associated problems which has led to recognition of their importance as a highly 'significant minority' (Wahidin 2005).

Although the UK's ageing prison population continued to rise under the Conservative–Liberal Democrat coalition government of 2010–15, it was in fact the policies of New Labour that did much to damage the effectiveness of the penal system and increase the number of ageing men in prison. In an attempt to redress the balance of the justice system in favour of the victims of crime, the New Labour government implemented a number of legislative changes during their 13-year reign, which served to widen the net and inflate sentence lengths. Such changes include the introduction of the mandatory life sentence for those convicted of a second serious sexual assault under the Crime Sentences Act 1997 (Maguire et al. 1997), 'extended post-release supervision, and registration and surveillance within the community' (Matravers and Hughes 2003: 53–54), and the introduction of indeterminate sentences for public protection (IPP).

These key legislative changes undoubtedly had a marked impact on the prison system in the UK; however, it was Labour's commitment to the pursuit of the historic sexual offender which resulted in the dramatic increase in the number of ageing men being sentenced to imprisonment. As Crawley and Sparks explain:

> One important factor ... seems to be the very much greater readiness (and technical capacity) of police and prosecutors to pursue and secure convictions against sex offenders, including those charged with 'historic' offences (many elderly men in prison are serving sentences for crimes allegedly committed two, three or even four decades ago.
> (Crawley and Sparks 2005a: 1)

This trend, which has gained momentum in the wake of the Jimmy Savile inquiry and the launch of the police Operation Yewtree, demonstrates recognition by policymakers that sex crime can produce severe physical and psychological damage, even decades after the offence was committed. However, as Crawley and Sparks (2006) discuss, the imprisoning of elderly men, for crimes they committed possibly 40 years ago, can create many problems, and if we are to address the rising number of ageing people being received into prison, then it is up to those involved in the sentencing of 'historic' sexual offenders to resist the huge amount of pressure to incarcerate that is placed on them by the public and the media (Hough et al. 2003).

The consequences of aged imprisonment

Many prisons in England and Wales were built in the Victorian era and, as such, clearly incorporate the ideals and objectives of Jeremy Bentham's (1791) panopticon, epitomizing the balance between surveillance and control. Unsurprisingly, such archaic designs result in an environment which many of the older prison population find extremely challenging. This is perhaps best illustrated by Crawley and Sparks, who state:

> Their very fabric (the stairs and steps and walkways, the distances, the gates, the football pitches and gymnasia; the serveries and queues; the communal showers; the incessant background noise) is, in general, constructed in blithe unconsciousness of the needs and sensibilities of the old.
>
> (Crawley and Sparks 2005c: 350)

Prison by its very nature epitomizes Giddens's concept of 'material constraints' (Giddens 1984: 174); by restricting the actions of the individuals whom it seeks to punish, prison also limits the agency of the prisoner. However, for those who are elderly, disabled or infirm, their options for agency are further limited by the often unmanageable prison environment, which results in their increased passivity. Prison life, for this group of men, is characterized by daily breaches of their fundamental human rights, as I will explain below.

This current situation is exacerbated by an ever increasing prison population which continues to place significant strain on already overstretched resources. With exceptionally high levels of overcrowding and a 28% fall in the number of prison staff, the Prison Reform Trust (PRT) has very recently warned of worsening safety, and fewer opportunities for rehabilitation (PRT 2014). This warning was reinforced by HM Chief Inspector of Prisons Nick Hardwick, who spoke of a 'political and policy failure' in prisons (BBC 2014), a statement compounded by the latest Ministry of Justice statistics which show that the prison estate is currently holding 9,242 more prisoners than it was designed for (PRT 2014).

With continuing cuts to the Prison Service, resources stretched to the limit, no indication of policy level changes that will address the increasing number of people being sentenced to imprisonment, and the announcement by the director of public prosecutions that the Crown Prosecution Service will engage in a new drive to pursue convictions of child sex offenders (CPS 2013), prison life will continue to become more damaging for the individuals it is meant to assist. Those who will suffer the most are the significant minority of older men who pose very little control problem for staff, but whose rights and unique problems are so frequently neglected (HMCIP 2004).

Deterioration and decline

Ageing brings with it increased incidents of deterioration and morbidity but these issues become magnified in an environment as unsuitable and unaccommodating as a prison. Deterioration, as Cohen and Taylor (1972) discovered, can be a grave concern to ageing or long-term prisoners and this was something noted by the men in my study. Many were acutely aware of their physical and mental decline, but unlike those in Cohen and Taylor's study, they accepted degeneration as an inevitable part of prison life. One life sentence prisoner, Eric, explained why he thought prison often increases the speed of ageing:

> It's the lack of activities, the lack of making your own decisions. Everything is done for you here, you're told when to lock up, when to stop work, when to go to bed,

you don't have to think for yourself ... even now I can't think of words or I can't think of names; it's going up there [his mind].

A frequently cited issue that older prisoners face is the complete lack of policy-level regime differentiation (Wahidin 2004; HMCIP 2004; Mann 2012; Ministry of Justice 2014). In the majority of establishments, older men are subject to the same regime as the younger prisoners, despite being more than twice the age of the average prisoner, which currently stands at 27 years (PRT 2013). Neil, a life sentence prisoner, highlighted this issue:

There's this 'one size fits all' approach where we're expected to perform as well as a 26 year old both physically in work and in all other aspects of prison life ... we still have to compete; we've gotta be there by the right time, no allowances made for lateness, never mind we might be a bit infirm, some have disabilities, no excuses accepted, we're expected to perform as the younger men do.

Neil's observation resonates strongly with Crawley and Sparks's (2005c: 352) concept of 'institutional thoughtlessness' which encompasses all 'the resulting acts and omissions that impinge negatively on older prisoners'. Far from providing equality of treatment, the perception of prisoners as a homogeneous group can actually 'constitute grossly unfair treatment' (Crawley and Sparks 2005a: 5).

The ageing prison population is a highly heterogeneous one, which is characterized by an extensive assortment of life stories and marked differences in the effects of ageing. While some older offenders are able to manage the built environment of the prison, others are not; for those ageing men who cannot make their way around unaided, walk reasonable distances or manage stairs, a life in prison very quickly becomes both challenging and isolating (HMCIP 2004; Mann 2012; Ministry of Justice 2014). One 79-year-old, Tony, explained to me how he was confined to his cell because of physical disabilities and the need for a wheelchair:

The chair don't even come out of me cell; I have to get up on me crutches and that, then somebody has to fold me chair up and put it out of the cell. The doors aren't wide enough, so I don't get to come out and see the other lads, so I'm stuck in there ... The cell door is shut all the time.

For this prisoner, a poorly designed and unaccommodating prison, coupled with a cell on the first floor, meant that he was completely reliant on prison staff for assistance and was serving his sentence in total isolation. This is not only a clear breach of the Disability Discrimination Act 2005 and the Equalities Act 2010 (Ministry of Justice 2014), but also a breach of his fundamental human rights. Such experiences are common among the ageing prison population, as supported by the findings of the recent Select Committee on ageing prisoners, who state:

The difficulties that older prisoners face in the physical environment have been exacerbated by social care that is described variously as variable, sparse and non-existent; there has been a deplorable absence of basic personal social care, for example for prisoners with serious mobility problems.

(Justice Select Committee 2013: 3)

Constraints created by poor health and disability are inevitable during old age, but when coupled with the material constraints of the prison environment, the result is a highly passive population who have had all but the most basic opportunities for agency, such as deciding when to go to the toilet, taken from them. However, for some, even this most basic of functions is experienced in increasingly distressing ways, as the Prison Reform Trust highlights:

> One older prisoner who had bladder trouble told the Prison Reform Trust that when he mentioned wetting his bedclothes to an officer he laughed, and that the younger men and officers started teasing him about his body smell and the stench in his cell.
>
> (Day 2014: n.p.)

This example resonates strongly with many research findings over recent years (PRT and The Centre for Policy on Ageing 2003; Wahidin 2003, 2004; Crawley and Sparks 2005c; Wahidin and Aday 2005; Mann 2012); it is also a clear example of the changing face of imprisonment and consequently the changing nature of the role of the prison officer.

Social care

The rapid and highly significant increase in ageing prisoners, both in absolute terms and as a proportion of the overall prison population (Justice Select Committee 2013), has had a marked effect on the duties and responsibilities of the prison officer. Traditionally, officers were responsible for the security, supervision, training and rehabilitation of people committed to prison by the courts (Crawley 2004). However, with increased incidents of the health and social issues that accompany ageing, such as incontinence, dementia and even palliative care, those officers who manage the ageing prison population have, in effect, become primary carers (Age UK 2011), dealing with a whole plethora of issues for which they have received little or no training.

In recent years, there has also been marked confusion amongst the Prison Service, local authorities and local NHS trusts over who is actually responsible for the social care needs of older prisoners, a situation the Ministry of Justice (2014: 53) referred to as 'disgraceful'. As they explain, prisoners with unidentified or unsupported care requirements are often unable to become fully integrated into the prison system and thus miss out on opportunities for meaningful activity that can be vital to the progression of their sentence, their rehabilitation and their life post-incarceration.

Although the new Care Bill, which came into effect from April 2015, states that responsibility lies with the local authority within which the prisoner is resident, its implementation will undoubtedly create further hurdles for the Prison Service. As the Justice Select Committee (2013) notes, initial estimates indicate that approximately 3,500 prisoners will be eligible for care and support services in prison, under the criteria of the Care Act 2014. However, apart from the very brief and ambiguous statement that 'prisoners must pay full or part of the costs if they are in a position to do so' (Department of Health 2014), there has been very little discussion or clarification on how local authorities with large prison populations are meant to fund such services. However positive the potential impact of the Care Act 2014 may be on older prisoners, the financial and practical burdens of necessary ongoing needs assessments and the difficulties associated with identifying what is a medical responsibility and what is a social care responsibility mean that the future of the Prison Service remains firmly tied to the costly and heterogeneous needs of its ageing population.

Healthcare

It is commonly accepted that prisoners who have grown old in prison, or have spent lengthy periods of time in prison during old age, have a physiological age approximately ten years in advance of their chronological age (Aday 2003; Ministry of Justice 2014). It is also agreed that the psychological strains of prison life and the relative inactivity of older prisoners further accelerates the ageing process. With this in mind, it becomes clear that prison healthcare is in greater demand now than at any other time in history.

The health complaints of the ageing prison population unsurprisingly reflect the morbidity of the ageing population in the free world and include such things as heart problems, diabetes, cancer, hypertension, and mental health problems, such as depression and anxiety disorders (Fazel et al. 2001; PRT and The Centre for Policy on Ageing 2003; Justice Select Committee 2013). However, despite the frequent occurrence of these common complaints, the health problems of this section of the prison population very often go unmet. Nearly two decades ago, Ornduff (1996) highlighted how prison overcrowding had led to problems of inadequate healthcare and poor treatment for prisoners, and this problem has been exacerbated by the increase in the ageing prison population over the last two decades. The fact that healthcare for older prisoners costs three times more than that of younger prisoners (Wahidin 2013), coupled with the ongoing cut-backs which have been felt by the majority of prisons in England and Wales, means that the Prison Service has neither the funding nor the resources to employ the preventative model of healthcare that currently exists in outside society.

The discussions I had with older prisoners regarding healthcare were characterized by stories of wrongly prescribed medication, degeneration caused by infrequent check-ups, and the premature deaths of fellow prisoners attributed to a lack of concern by healthcare staff. The following account provided by 67-year-old Alf represents a typical response:

> I suffer from some health complaints which ought to require treatment but what healthcare is there? … If it was a 50% possibility that you were going to die, I'd say it was a 100% likely in here!

Prison healthcare has long been an issue of debate and criticism, with some suggesting that the medical discourse in prison is used as another form of power over prisoners (Sim 1990). Many men spoke to me about the inadequate accessibility of the healthcare department in terms of its opening hours and its location (often upstairs). This was also supported by the testimony of one officer, who explained:

> Here it's rubbish, really crap. From 5 o'clock onwards we don't have no healthcare available until 7.30 the next morning, so that's not very good … We've got nurses who have got no idea about how to deal with prisoners.

This officer clearly felt that the current healthcare arrangements were unsuitable for an increasingly large ageing population, but he also alluded to an issue documented by Sim (2002), who discusses how the position of healthcare workers in prison has long been characterized by a 'culture clash' between the need for care and the need for security and control. Not simply healthcare professionals, then, these individuals are 'integral to the control and disciplinary apparatus of the modern prison' (ibid.: 315). This complex balancing act can result in a lower standard of care for prisoners, as 55-year-old Jimmy explained to me:

> The healthcare staff in general have been trained to think that we're all liars, we're all thieves, all the women think we're paedophiles or rapists and so it makes it hard for them to care about us.

The medical discourse of the prison exercises power over the prisoners in multiple ways and the fact that ageing prisoners require five times as many healthcare visits as their counterparts in free society (Chiu 2010) means that it is this age group that most frequently feels its harmful effects. Making prisoners queue for lengthy periods in what can very often be a hostile and dangerous environment, cancelling specialist hospital appointments without warning or explanation, and chaining prisoners to officers on transfers to outside hospitals (Wahidin 2003; Mann 2012; Justice Select Committee 2013), the prison visibly signifies that prisoners are undeserving of usual standards of care. This point is underlined by Wahidin, who, discussing an ageing female prisoner who was denied access to a healthcare specialist, states:

> ... her defiance, her agency and her insistence on the continued relevance of the outside status and resources, was punished by the institution and the deliverers of care, leaving her feeling infantilised and less than human.
>
> (Wahidin 2004: 135)

Characterized by inaccessibility, lengthy waiting times and a lower standard of care, prison medical services are struggling to cope with the increasing demand, as 55-year-old Hughie told me:

> The healthcare's over-stretched, the staff on the wings don't have time, the old men cannot physically access the healthcare and really you'd have to be in immediate danger of dying before anything was done.

Meaningful activity

In order for the ageing prison population to overcome the potential for deterioration and decline, it is essential that, like older people in free society, they remain active both socially and physically (Bond et al. 1993; Reuter 2012). Meaningful prison activity is therefore not only key in the prevention of boredom and isolation of older prisoners, but also plays an essential part in the ongoing battle against inactivity and deteriorating health. For the general prison population, prison activity such as education and employment are often undertaken as a means of combatting the boredom of daily life. With the disappearance of all that filled their lives in free society, the unmarked time of the prison day can be extremely challenging and is considered by some as an additional form of punishment (Cohen and Taylor 1972). By stripping each prisoner of his/her liberty, incarceration also strips the prisoner of the activities, people, events and appointments which so effectively filled their time on the outside.

However, whilst the younger men access appropriate education, a range of employment and training opportunities and gym-based physical activities, the older prisoners are often engaged in monotonous and irrelevant training, education and employment or, at worst, left to 'stagnate' in their cell (Johnson and Toch 1982; Aday 1994). The Prison Reform Trust has noted a grave lack of differentiation in prison activities, particularly within the area of education and training, which, as they explain, tends to focus on 'returning the offender to mainstream society' (PRT and The Centre for Policy on Ageing 2003: 33) and is often of little use to the ageing population – a sentiment echoed by the Justice Select Committee (2013). Standing firmly outside the Prison Service's remit on rehabilitation and its use as a means of providing the skills necessary to lead useful and active lives on release, the ageing prison population often finds itself unemployed and unengaged, a frustrating reality for those who have worked their entire lives.

For many older men, the opportunities are simply too rare, or fail to occupy them in their role, as 69-year-old Tony explained:

> I was doing the stamps here [tearing the postage stamps off the mail] … there aren't no stamps in there for me to do, so I can't just sit there and do nothing … I can't get up and down the stairs, so I can't get a job out here [level 2 – IT and cleaning].

Ageing prisoners also find very little relief in prison education, which is often as inappropriate as the training on offer. This was highlighted by one long-serving prison officer who explained how, rather than teaching the men simple woodwork, or delivering dedicated over-50s education classes, which would develop new skills and aid the sociability and activity of the older men, staff were instead telling them to 'go over to education and read nursery rhymes' (Mann 2012: 56).

Such problems have been exacerbated by prison overcrowding and cuts to the budget. As one officer summarized: 'Activities in jail is all geared towards the young because they're the ones who need to burn off energy … when you've only got a finite amount of resources, you have got to strike the best balance' (Mann 2012: 61). Recognizing that prison drastically fails to meet the needs of the growing ageing prison population, a number of prisons in the UK have utilized the services of, or low-level funding from, organizations such as Age UK or RECOOP (Resettlement and Care for Older Ex-offenders and Prisoners), in order to run 'age-tailored' programmes such as over-50s clubs, nostalgia groups and specialized gym sessions (Mann 2012; Justice Select Committee 2013). By taking a more inclusive approach to ageing prisoners, it is these establishment-based schemes that have led the way and provided examples of best practice.

Masculinity

Rendered less physical and less active, with increased health problems and disengagement from the discourse of employment, it can become very difficult for older males to find a role within a society that places so much importance on 'manhood' and youthfulness

(Gilleard and Higgs 2000). However, for ageing male prisoners, these issues are often magnified by the 'hyper-masculine' nature of the prison environment.

The relatively low number of females present within male prisons inevitably creates an overly masculine organization with an inherent culture of toughness and aggression (Carrabine and Longhurst 1998). Although female officers and other staff are present in much greater numbers than in previous eras, the relative lack of women can become problematic for the demonstration of masculinity among prisoners (Jewkes 2002). Without the usual opportunities for assertions of manliness, prisoners tend to engage in a Goffmanesque construction of masculinity through the use of bravado and performance. However, other more radical methods of 'proving' one's masculinity, such as body building, fighting and predatory sexual behaviour, are also used.

Jewkes (2002) suggests that the perceived toughness of a prisoner's regime and entrenched status hierarchies can be further indicators of masculinity and power. For many ageing prisoners, the nature of their offence (frequently child sex offences), or the physical and mental deterioration that they frequently experience, means they are often segregated from the wider prison population, either through the use of Rule 43 and Vulnerable Prisoners Units or through the use of specialized prison wings. Life within such units is often considered easier than life in the mainstream prison, casting further doubt on the masculine credentials and status of this age group.

Unable to take part in the performance of masculinity, assigned a lowly position in the tacit prison hierarchy (Sim 1994) because of the perception that all older prisoners are sex offenders, and with female prison staff directly threatening their 'hegemonic masculinity' (Arber et al. 2003), ageing prisoners have had to adapt and develop their own tactics for the maintenance of masculinity. One such method is the development of father–daughter-style relationships with female prison officers. By engaging in fatherly type interaction, these men are able to recapture some level of masculinity as well as establish the 'surrogate familial relationships', which Crewe (2006) discusses as an important feature of prison subculture. One life sentence prisoner, affectionately known as 'Pops', explained this to me:

> The female staff tend to see me as a fatherly figure and they do chat a little bit more, it's nice to have a chat, they seem to have more time to ask about things like your family and they ask about my Mum and that, they spend that little bit of time to ask if you're okay which the men don't do.

Another method for maintaining masculinity is to engage in the total denial and rejection of the femininity of the female officers, as 65-year-old Duncan demonstrates:

> Something I've noticed is that all prison officers seem to have something wrong with them and although it's not always obvious what it is in the male ones, with the female officers it's very obvious what's wrong with them, usually they're well over weight and not very attractive and one wonders whether that's one of the reasons why they came to work in here.

By setting the female members of staff apart from other 'normal' women, Duncan had reduced the negative effects on his status as a man and had also undermined the legitimacy of the female staff's authority (see also Crewe 2006).

Adaptation and survival

Despite experiencing many more issues than the younger prison population and arguably doing their 'time' in a harder way (Mann 2012), many ageing prisoners have demonstrated an ability to be highly resourceful when it comes to adaptation and survival within prison.

One of the key aspects of the older men's ability to cope with what can be considered as a 'catastrophic' change in the life course (Crawley and Sparks 2005a) is through their 'habitus' (Bourdieu 1977), or to use Stones's (2005) more malleable version, their general dispositional internal structure. For a large number of older prisoners in my study, experiences such as the horrors of world war and the difficulties of rationing provided them with a shared experience which greatly aided their ability to manage prison life. By drawing on a habitus characterized by deprivation and suffering, many of the men were able to cope with prison life much more successfully. This is an issue that Crawley and Sparks term 'attempts at mastery', which, for them, involves a 'review of past coping and survival'. By drawing on the memories of past experiences, such as 'the brutalizing environments of military life ... or ... a childhood of institutional care' (Crawley and Sparks 2006: 69), older prisoners seem to be able to cope much more successfully with prison life.

For others, their habitus required some adaptation in order to suit the new environment of the prison. One successful example of this was a 55-year-old prisoner who had internalized the structure of the prison so significantly that he was considered an expert on matters relating to prison service procedure. For this individual, the adaptation of his general disposition had allowed him to find a role within the prison community and, as such, he was enjoying a newly acquired form of power (Mann 2012).

Older prisoners pose very few discipline problems and also tend to have a very stabilizing effect on younger prisoners. They are more likely to have an inherent respect for authority and engage in more inventive and much less aggressive forms of resistance. It is these characteristics that are undoubtedly responsible for the popularity of the older prisoners (excluding sex offenders) among prison staff, who often refer to them as 'old school boys' or 'real characters' (Mann 2012). The relationship between staff and older prisoners is very often characterized by mutual respect and, as such, any rejection of the prison structure tends to come in more innovative forms of 'working the system' as opposed to the more vocal resistance in which younger prisoners tend to engage. This was highlighted by one officer, who explained:

> They're much better to deal with, they're old school and so they accept what you tell them ... They're characters. They know how to play the system ... and not try and play the system by shouting about things 'til they get their own way. The old ones are more crafty, they get your respect, they earn your respect and that's how they get their privileges.

The future of the ageing prison population

In the absence of any national strategy for older prisoners, the burden of their unique needs and specialized requirements has been shouldered by innovative and dedicated members of prison service staff and non-governmental agencies, such as Age Concern, the Prison Reform Trust and NACRO. This was something Chief Inspector of Prisons Anne Owers found in her follow-up report to the 2004 thematic review, 'No Problems – Old and Quiet'. She concluded:

> There is still far too much reliance on the unsupported initiative of particularly committed officers, and too great an assumption that the care of older prisoners, including their social care, is a matter for health services and not for the whole prison.
> (HMCIP 2008: 5)

Although the ad hoc arrangements made by prison staff have provided a number of positive changes for the older prisoners who are resident at these establishments, it could be argued that by resourcefully 'managing' the problem, these prisons have prevented the problem from reaching the crisis point needed in order to place the issue onto the government agenda. However, small but significant steps were taken in 2013, when a Justice Select Committee (2013) on Older Prisoners heard evidence from academics, non-governmental agencies, prisoners and prisoners' families. This review of the ageing prison population not only brought attention to the current situation but also provided a catalyst for potential change. In the government response to the review, Lord Chancellor and Secretary of State for Justice Chris Grayling concluded that in conjunction with the National Offender Management Service (NOMS), 'real change' would be implemented by 2015 (Ministry of Justice 2014).

The government response to the report highlighted a number of key areas in which it felt development was needed. The first of these was the suitability of the prison regime (Ministry of Justice 2014). In light of the many older prisoners who reside in establishments that are completely inappropriate, the government has promised to develop a process for conducting an assessment of current accommodation for prisoners with specific needs and has stated that NOMS will, as far as is practicable, begin to ensure that older prisoners are not allocated to establishments that cannot accommodate their specialized needs. The use of day centres and other practices which positively bring together the older prison population will be developed, along with greater regime adaptation and an examination of the examples of best practice highlighted by the report (ibid.).

The health and social care of prisoners will also be reviewed so that opportunities for video link hospital appointments might be developed in order to overcome the problems of missed or cancelled appointments due to staff shortages (Wahidin 2003; Mann 2012; Justice Select Committee 2013). The continuity of care received by older prisoners on release will be addressed via the development of a new IT system, which will allow patient information to be transferred smoothly from NOMS to NHS England, and NOMS will develop clear guidelines on how the prison officer's role will envelop the provision of care and support for older prisoners (Ministry of Justice 2014).

The government response acknowledged many of the issues raised in the Select Committee report. However, while it appears that some steps will be taken to ensure more positive developments in the key areas that directly affect older prisoners, the response has fallen short of agreeing to a national strategy for older prisoners, instead suggesting that '[t]he needs of older prisoners should be addressed by prisons as part of a wider approach to supporting all those with health and social care needs' (Ministry of Justice 2014: 4). Many of the changes proposed in the government response, such as the ongoing assessment of needs, the responsibility for the provision of a minimum standard of social care and more consistent delivery of healthcare provision, would have been implemented under the 2014 Care Act, regardless. If positive change for older prisoners is evident in the near future, it will undoubtedly be born of the Care Act 2014 rather than the outcome of the Select Committee review.

Conclusion

An ever increasing number of ageing individuals are being convicted in our courts and, of these, a large percentage are being sentenced for historic sexual offences (Office for National Statistics 2013). While highly publicized police operations such as Yewtree will continue to empower victims and encourage the reporting of such offences, there is an increasing danger that these ageing men, along with many others, will spend their remaining years in an environment that is inappropriate for them, which fails to address their offending behaviour (PRT 2014) and which, for some, is completely disproportionate to the current risk they pose to society.

The unaccommodating nature of the prison in terms of its layout, facilities and general regime all highlight the unsuitability of the prison both as a punishment for older offenders and as a site for ageing. While implementations for 'real change' may be well intended, the substantial and large-scale changes necessary to prevent an 'older prisoner crisis' are unlikely to be implemented at a time when the Criminal Justice System is having to make continual cuts to its budget (PRT 2014). In addition to the general 'pains of imprisonment' discussed by Sykes (1958) and Johnson and Toch (1982), the ageing prison population will, for the foreseeable future, continue to be subjected to specific pains that result from a penal system simply unable to cope with their specialized needs.

In a time when there are currently more non-custodial forms of punishment available than at any other point in history, the potential for 'real change' lies within sentencing. There needs to be a committed and highly publicized drive for the use of community-based punishments in order to overcome the perception of them as an 'easy option' for offenders. By addressing public opinion on this issue, sentencers will be under less pressure to enforce custodial sentences on those offenders whose crimes or current risk are not serious enough to warrant imprisonment, or for whom imprisonment would be a fundamental breach of their human rights (see Hough et al. 2003).

The nearly 10,000 prisoners aged 55 years and over that we now have in England and Wales (Ministry of Justice 2014) are draining an already overstretched and pressurized Prison Service. With their healthcare costs alone rising to three times more than that of the average prisoner (Wahidin and Aday 2005), it seems obvious that incarceration is not the most economic or effective way of punishing this group of offenders. Prison officers have been expected to become carers rather than custodians, providing social care, palliative care and even mental healthcare, often without necessary training and support (Age UK 2011). Such net widening, in terms of the role and responsibilities that prison staff are expected to fulfil, is costly, ineffective and raises a fundamental question regarding the necessity of having such ageing individuals serving sentences in prison.

Note

1 Excerpted by permission of the publishers from *Doing Harder Time?* by Natalie Mann (Farnham: Ashgate, 2012), copyright © 2012.

Bibliography

Aday, R. (1994) 'Golden years behind bars', *Federal Probation* 58(2) (June): 47–54.

Aday, R. (2003) *Aging Prisoners*, Westport, CT: Praeger Publishers.

Age UK (2011) 'Supporting older people in prison: Ideas for practice', www.ageuk.org.uk/docum ents/en-gb/for-professionals/government-and-society/older%20prisoners%20guide_pro.pdf?dtrk= true (accessed 7 November 2012).

Arber, S., Davidson, K. and Ginn, J. (2003) *Gender and Ageing: Changing Roles and Relationships*, Berkshire: Open University Press.

BBC (2014) 'Prisons inspector accuses minister of prisons "failure"', www.bbc.co.uk/news/ uk-27847007 (accessed 15 January 2015).

Bond, J., Coleman, P. and Peace, S. (1993) *Ageing in Society: An Introduction to Social Gerontology*, London: Sage Publications.

Bourdieu, P. (1977) *Outline of a Theory of Practice*, Cambridge: Cambridge University Press.

Carrabine, E. and Longhurst, B. (1998) 'Gender and prison organisation: Some comments on masculinities and prison management', *Howard Journal of Criminal Justice* 37(2): 161–176.

Chiu, T. (2010) *It's About Time: Aging Prisoners, Increasing Costs, and Geriatric Release*, Vera Institute of Justice, www.vera.org/sites/default/files/resources/downloads/Its-about-time-aging-priso ners-increasing-costs-and-geriatric-release.pdf (accessed 15 January 2015).

Cohen, S. and Taylor, L. (1972) *Psychological Survival: The Experience of Long Term Imprisonment*, Middlesex: Penguin Books Ltd.

CPS (Crown Prosecution Service) (2013) 'The criminal justice response to child sexual abuse: Time for a national consensus', www.cps.gov.uk/news/articles/the_criminal_justice_response_ to_child_sexual_abuse_-_time_for_a_national_consensus/ (accessed 8 July 2014).

Crawley, E. (2004) *Doing Prison Work: The public and private lives of prison officers*, Cullumpton: Willan.

Crawley, E. and Sparks, R. (2005a) 'Surviving the prison experience? Imprisonment and elderly men', *Prison Service Journal* 160, www.hmprisonservice.gov.uk/resourcecentre/prisonservice journal/index.asp?id=3833,3124,11,3148,0,0 (accessed 12 April 2006).

Crawley, E. and Sparks, R. (2005b) 'Older men in prison: Survival, coping and identity', in A. Liebling and S. Maruna (eds) *The Effects of Imprisonment*, Cullumpton: Willan.

Crawley, E. and Sparks, R. (2005c) 'Hidden injuries? Researching the experiences of older men in English prisons', *The Howard Journal of Criminal Justice* 44(4): 345–356.

Crawley, E. and Sparks, R. (2006) 'Is there life after imprisonment? How elderly men talk about imprisonment and release', *Criminology and Criminal Justice* 6(1): 63–82.

Crewe, B. (2006) 'Male prisoners' orientations towards female officers in an English prison', *Punishment and Society* 8: 395–421.

Day, M. (2014) 'Prison for old people can be double punishment', www.nottinghampost.com/ Mark-Day-Prison-old-people-double-punishment/story-20876215-detail/story.html#ixzz3OV paLygk (accessed 10 January 2015).

Department of Health (2014) 'Care Act guidance factsheet 12: Prisoners and people resident in approved premises', www.gov.uk/government/publications/care-act-2014-part-1-factsheets/ca re-act-factsheets-2#factsheet-12-prisoners-and-people-in-resident-in-approved-premises (accessed 15 January 2015).

Fazel, S., Hope, T., O'Donnell, I., Piper, M. and Jacoby, R. (2001) 'Health of elderly male pris-oners: Worse than the general population, worse than younger prisoners', *Age Ageing* 30: 403–407.

Frazer, L. (2003) *Ageing Inside*, Bristol: School for Policy Studies, University of Bristol.

Giddens, A. (1984) *The Constitution of Society: Outline of the Theory of Structuration*, Cambridge: Polity Press.

Gidley, S. (2004) *Pensioner Prisoners, A Report by Sandra Gidley MP, Liberal Democrat Spokesperson for Older People*.

Gilleard, C. and Higgs, P. (2000) *Cultures of Ageing: Self, citizen and the body*, Essex: Prentice Hall.

Goffman, E. (1961) *Asylums*, Victoria, Australia: Penguin Books.

HMCIP (HM Chief Inspector of Prisons) (2004) *No Problems – Old and Quiet: Older prisoners in England and Wales: a thematic review*, London: Home Office.

HMCIP (HM Chief Inspector of Prisons) (2008) *Follow up Report on the Thematic Review 'No Problems – Old and Quiet': Older prisoners in England and Wales*, London: HMCIP.

Hough, M., Jacobson, J. and Millie, A. (2003) *The Decision to Imprison: Key Findings*, London: Prison Reform Trust.

Jewkes, Y. (2002) *Captive Audience*, Cullumpton: Willan.

Johnson, R. and Toch, H. (1982) *The Pains of Imprisonment*, London: Sage Publications Ltd.

Justice Select Committee (2013) 'Older prisoners', www.parliament.uk/documents/commons-committees/Justice/Older-prisoners.pdf (accessed 23 January 2015).

Maguire, M., Morgan, R. and Reiner, R. (1997) *The Oxford Handbook of Criminology*, second edn, Oxford: Clarendon Press.

Malinchak, A. (1980) *Crime and Gerontology*, Upper Saddle River, NJ: Prentice Hall.

Mann, N. (2012) *Doing Harder Time? The Experiences of an Ageing Male Prison Population in England and Wales*, Aldershot: Ashgate Publishing.

Matravers, A. and Hughes, G.V. (2003) 'Unprincipled sentencing? The policy approach to dangerous sex offenders', in M. Tonry (ed.) *Confronting Crime: Crime control policy under New Labour*, Cullumpton: Willan.

Ministry of Justice (2014) 'Government response to the Justice Committee's fifth report of session 2013–2014 "older prisoners"', www.gov.uk/government/uploads/system/uploads/attachment_data/file/256609/response-older-prisoners.pdf (accessed 23 January 2015).

Morag, M. and Fallon, P. (2007) 'Health professionals in prisons', in J. Bennett, B. Crewe and A. Wahidin (eds) *Understanding Prison Staff*, London: Routledge.

Newman, E., Newman, D. and Gewirtz, M. (1984) *Elderly Criminals*, Cambridge: Oelgeschlager, Gunn and Hain.

Office for National Statistics (2013) 'Crime statistics', period ending June 2013, www.ons.gov.uk/ons/rel/crime-stats/crime-statistics/period-ending-june-2013/index.html (accessed 3 July 2014).

Ornduff, J. (1996) 'Releasing the elderly inmate', *Elder Law Journal* 4 (September): 173–200.

PRT (Prison Reform Trust) (2011) 'Bromley Briefings prison factfile autumn', www.prisonreformtrust.org.uk/Portals/0/Documents/Factfile%20autumn%202013.pdf (accessed 13 March 2012).

PRT (Prison Reform Trust) (2013) 'Bromley Briefings Prison Factfile Autumn 2013', www.prisonreformtrust.org.uk/Portals/0/Documents/Factfile%20autumn%202013.pdf (accessed 3 September 2015).

PRT (Prison Reform Trust) (2014) 'Bromley Briefings prison factfile autumn', www.prisonreformtrust.org.uk/Portals/0/Documents/Bromley%20Briefings/Factfile%20Autumn%202014.pdf (accessed 15 January 2015).

PRT (Prison Reform Trust) and The Centre for Policy on Ageing (2003) *Growing Old in Prison: A scoping study on older prisoners*, Northburgh, London: PRT.

Reuter, I. (2012) 'Aging, physical activity, and disease prevention', *Journal of Aging Research*, dx.doi.org/10.1155/2012/373294 (accessed 23 January 2015).

Rothman, M.B., Dunlop, B.D. and Entzel, P. (2000) *Elders, Crime, and the Criminal Justice System: Myths, perceptions and reality in the 21st century*, New York: Springer.

Sim, J. (1990) *Medical Power in Prisons: The Prison Medical Service in England 1774–1989*, Milton Keynes: Open University Press.

Sim, J. (1994) 'Tougher than the rest? Men in prison', in T. Newburn and E.A. Stanko (eds) *Just Boys Doing Business? Men, Masculinities and Crime*, London: Routledge.

Sim, J. (2002) 'The future of prison health care: A critical analysis', *Critical Social Policy* 22: 300–323.

Stones, R. (2005) *Structuration Theory*, New York: Palgrave Macmillan.

Sykes, G. (1958) *The Society of Captives*, Princeton, NJ: Princeton University Press.

Wahidin, A. (2000) 'Life behind the shadows: Women's experiences of prison in later life', in R. Horn and S. Warner (eds) *Issues in Forensic Psychology: Positive directions for women in secure environments*, Leicester: The British Psychological Society, 24–35.

Wahidin, A. (2003) 'Doing hard time: Older women in prison', *Prison Service Journal* 145: 25–29.

Wahidin, A. (2004) *Older Women in the Criminal Justice System*, London: Jessica Kingsley Publishers.

Wahidin, A. (2005) 'We are a significant minority: Elderly women in English prisons', *British Journal of Criminology*, www.britsoccrim.org/volume6/001.pdf (accessed 7 February 2008).

Wahidin, A. (2013) *Written Submission for the Justice Select Committee on Older Prisoners*, www.publications.parliament.uk/pa/cm201314/cmselect/cmjust/writev/olderprisoners/m05.pdf (accessed 10 January 2015).

Wahidin, A. and Aday, R. (2005) 'The needs of older men and women in the criminal justice system: An international perspective', *Prison Service Journal* 160, www.hmprisonservice.gov.uk/resourcecentre/prisonservicejournal/index.asp?id=3835,3124,11,3148,0,0 (accessed 12 April 2006).

Chapter 30

Young people and prison

Rob Allen

Introduction

The imprisonment of young people is one of the more contested issues in penal policy, with a seemingly constant debate about both the extent to which young people should be locked up and the form that such incarceration should take. This is particularly true in respect of children under the age of 18 for whom it is widely agreed that custody should be an option of last resort and implemented in secure facilities distinct and separate from adult prisons (HM Government 2014). Controversy about the imprisonment of children flows partly from what has proven to be the ineffectiveness of custody for this age group: of under 18s released from custody in England and Wales in 2011–12, 69.3% were known to reoffend within a year, a rate which has stayed fairly stable over recent years (YJB 2014: 50). While international comparisons are difficult to make, rates of recidivism both in the UK and elsewhere tend to be highest among the youngest detainees.

Concern about the damaging impact that deprivation of liberty can have on childhood development also makes the use of custody for under 18s a contentious measure, particularly for practitioners who are under a duty to protect and promote the welfare of children. At best, secure establishments might provide a safe, structured and caring environment, which could help address the years of neglect, abuse and educational failure that characterize the upbringing of many of the most serious and persistent young offenders. This would require an approach that genuinely meets the needs of individual children in small-scale living units, with intensive preparation for release and continuing care once back in the community.

At worst, closed institutions can be a frightening interlude in young lives already impoverished by neglect and punishment. Even smaller secure establishments often struggle to overcome the hostility and alienation felt by many of the children detained against their will. After all, detention facilities of whatever kind represent an abnormal living experience, which can impair the normal course of adolescent development. Whatever the intentions of the law, policymakers and staff, concentrating highly delinquent young people in a closed environment risks reinforcing rather than weakening the attitudes that the justice system is seeking to challenge. The common use of physical restraint in custodial establishments may further contribute to an 'us and them' attitude towards authority. The incidence of self-harm and even deaths – 16 boys died in juvenile custody in England and Wales between 2000 and 2014 – illustrates the vulnerability of many young people behind bars. It is perhaps not surprising that two leading experts have concluded that in respect of children under 18, 'interventions that are ineffective or more problematically that violate international human rights obligations, are known to be damaging and harmful and/or aggravate the very issues that they seek to resolve should be abolished. This applies ... in particular to imprisonment' (Muncie and Goldson 2012: 351).

Albeit less fierce, there is a debate, too, about the best form of custodial establishments for young adult offenders aged 18–21 who, at the time of writing in England and Wales, are required to serve custodial sentences in specialist Young Offender Institutions (YOIs). Reoffending rates for this age group are also high. Based on proven reoffending data for prisoners released in the 12 months ending September 2011, 18–20 year olds have a reoffending rate of 56.1% compared with a rate of 45.6% for prisoners aged 21 and over (MoJ 2013). However, there is a normative component to the debate about young adults too. Then Chief Inspector of Prisons Lord Ramsbotham, in a 1997 thematic review of young prisoners, considered that it would be wrong to ignore the particular needs of those aged 18 to 21 by regarding them as adult prisoners: 'For many the process of maturation will still be taking place beyond the age of 18 and they still require help and direction to become adults. The inability to withstand peer pressure is a particular feature of this age group. Others will be vulnerable and, if mixed with adults, might well be preyed upon' (HMIP 1997: para. 8.16).

Since then, despite a growing recognition and acceptance of the distinctive needs of the young adult age group, they have been largely neglected in policymaking (Allen 2013). However, a series of highly critical reports about YOIs from the chief inspector of prisons during 2013 and 2014 has called into question the desirability of accommodating this age group separately from adults in prison. In his report on Glen Parva, the chief inspector concluded that the large young offender institution 'is a model of custody that does not work' (HMIP 2014: 5). Yet, his immediate predecessor had warned that 'what will not work is simply to decant young adults into the mainstream adult prison population' (HMIP 2006: 5). It has been a great deal easier to identify unsuccessful approaches to the custodial care of the young adult age group than to develop institutional arrangements that are safe and effective.

The Conservative–Liberal Democrat coalition government (2010–15) proposed important changes in the custodial arrangements for both under 18s and young adults in England and Wales. The Criminal Justice and Courts Act 2015 contains provisions for a new model of youth custody for 12–17 year olds called secure colleges which will aim to place education at the heart of regimes in order to improve outcomes. A pathfinder college for 320 is being developed in the East Midlands, in what looks like the latest in a long line of closed establishments that have promised – but generally failed – to deliver better results for juvenile offenders than those that have gone before. There is a good deal of concern that the large size of the first secure college will militate against individualized treatment that young people in this age group require (Standing Committee on Youth Justice et al. 2014). The coalition government also published proposals to reform the management of 18–21 year olds in custody on the basis that the current use of YOIs is no longer appropriate or effective (MoJ 2013). Plans to accommodate all young adults in institutions mixed with adults, however, were deferred pending the outcome of an independent review into self-inflicted deaths in prison by 18–24 year olds, which was due to report in 2015. The need for such a review illustrates one of the many drawbacks of custodial treatment for this age group.

While the progress of both of these initiatives is uncertain, they are symptomatic of the complex and turbulent history of institutional approaches to offending by young people.

As Hagell and Hazel (2001) have shown, such a history needs to be understood at the macro level of ideological swings in policy about how delinquent young people should be treated, but also at the micro level of developments within institutions themselves and the criminal justice and social work systems in which they are located.

The aim of this chapter is threefold. The first is to describe the current structure, performance and recent history of custodial institutions for young people in England and Wales. The second is to discuss one of the key questions that recurs when dealing with this age group in custody: maintaining the safety of young people in prisons. The chapter concludes with brief reflections on possible developments in the field.

Background

There has been a specialist approach to young offenders in prison custody since the 19th century. Naval ships in the Thames estuary in the 1820s gave way to a boys' prison at Parkhurst on the Isle of Wight, established in 1838. Following a heavy dose of what was to become a standard criticism of such institutions as a training ground for young criminals, it closed 30 years later. The Gladstone Committee at the end of the century confirmed the need to keep young people apart from older and more experienced convicts, and the Borstal system was developed shortly afterwards. This aimed to provide an educational approach based on the structure of public schools for young offenders up to the age of 21 and subsequently 23.[1] With faith in rehabilitation declining, in 1982, indeterminate sentences of borstal training were replaced by fixed-term punishment in Youth Custody Centres. An altogether harsher philosophy was enshrined through the introduction of junior and senior Detention Centres in 1948, where the infamous short sharp shock regimes were briefly implemented in the early 1980s.

Since 1988, all prison service establishments for under 21s have been designated Young Offender Institutions. YOIs have somewhat uneasily sought to combine the conflicting philosophies of their predecessor institutions. After 2000, when the Youth Justice Board assumed responsibility for commissioning and purchasing secure places for under 18s remanded and sentenced to custody, specific YOIs or parts of YOIs have been designated for this age group. The majority of YOI places, however, accommodate 18–21 year olds.

Outside the prison system, the 19th-century Reformatory and Industrial Schools were combined into Approved Schools in 1933. From 1969, these were renamed Community Homes with Education, with responsibility transferring to local government from the Home Office. Although for the most part open establishments, some developed closed units for unruly pupils and those who absconded. Three large secure facilities were established at Kingswood, Redhill and Redbank. The ineffectiveness and costs of residential institutions for young people have led many of these units to close over the last 40 years. There remained 17 Secure Children's Homes (SCHs) open at the end of March 2014 in England and Wales, providing a total of 298 beds; 166 of these beds in ten establishments were commissioned by the Youth Justice Board to accommodate particularly young or vulnerable children on remand or serving sentences. The total capacity of SCHs has fallen by more than 50 since 2003 and by 150 since 1993 (Department for Education 2014).

Alongside the SCHs, two centrally run Youth Treatment Centres were established in the 1970s to accommodate the most serious and disturbed young offenders. St Charles was closed by the Department of Health in 1995 and Glenthorne seven years later, as they were deemed surplus to requirements. In the meantime, a new type of closed facility, the Secure Training Centre (STC), had been introduced to respond to what were seen as the specific needs of persistent young offenders aged 12–14 who emerged as a growing problem in the early 1990s. While outside the prison system, STCs were designed exclusively for sentenced young people and run, controversially, by the private sector. Four of these STCs were in operation at the time of writing. Although their role and scope were quickly expanded after they opened, their future is now in doubt, since the proposed new secure colleges are intended to allow the government 'to close expensive STC provision and a number of places in SCHs, as well as YOIs' (MoJ 2014: para. 5).

While, since 2000, the YJB has been able to give some leadership and coherence to a defined secure estate for under 18s, such a focus has been lacking in respect of young adults. The murder of 19-year-old Zahid Mubarek by his racist cell mate in Feltham in 2000 did briefly focus public attention on the shortcomings and levels of violence within YOIs, but the Labour government developed a somewhat contradictory approach to the problem. On the one hand, they legislated to abolish the sentence of Detention in a Young Offender Institution (DYOI), so that all defendants aged 18 or over receiving a custodial sentence would be sentenced to imprisonment and lose the protections afforded by a separate sentence served in specialist establishments. On the other hand, the 2001 Labour Party election manifesto promised to build on its youth justice reforms, 'to improve the standard of custodial accommodation and offending programmes for 18- to 20-year-old offenders' (Labour Party 2001: 32).

In the event, neither the legislation to abandon DYOI nor the manifesto commitment to improve it were implemented. YOIs were retained and efforts were made to implement the mainly operational recommendations from the public inquiry into Mubarek's death which reported in 2006. However, what resources were available were directed at improving the parts of the YOI estate used for under 18s. Young adults remained 'a neglected and under-resourced age group' (HMIP 2010: 7). Until the coalition government published their proposals for *Transforming the Management of Young Adult Offenders* in 2013, no definitive answer had been given to the question raised by the Mubarek inquiry as to 'whether the advantages of holding young offenders on the same wing as adult prisoners outweigh the disadvantages, and whether the practice should be extended' (HMIP 2014a: para. 4.51).

Routes into custody

While the process is today simpler than it once was, there is complexity and frequent change too in the ways in which young people find themselves placed in custodial institutions. For younger defendants the use of pre-trial detention has for many years been more restricted than for adults. Following the Legal Aid, Sentencing and Punishment of Offenders Act 2012, all children remanded into custody must be treated as looked after by the local authority designated by the court, including 17 year olds who were hitherto treated as adults for remand purposes.

There are two basic kinds of custodial sentence for under 18s: the Detention and Training Order (DTO), which can last for a specified period of between four months and two years; and longer-term detention for young people convicted of the gravest crimes and deemed a danger to the public. Half of the DTO is served in custody, half under supervision in the community. Under the provisions of the Crime and Disorder Act (1998), the YJB's role in relation to the secure estate is not only to commission and pay for secure places for children and young people remanded or sentenced to custody, but also to decide where in that estate individual young people should be placed. In doing this, the YJB Placement Service takes account of the individual risks and circumstances of the young person, as assessed by the responsible youth offending team (YOT), any special needs a young person may have, availability of places, and discussions with staff at prospective secure estate establishments regarding the current mix of young people in their establishments.

For 18–21 year olds, the routes into custody are more straightforward. Remand arrangements are basically the same as for adults, but under the current legal framework these young adults cannot, once convicted, be sentenced to imprisonment. Instead, the vast majority of young adults in prison establishments are subject to the criminal sentence of DYOI or – in the most serious cases – custody for life. The DYOI sentence, however short, is always followed by a period of supervision in the community on release. Placement decisions are made by the Prison Service.

Since 2008, the number of young people in custody has fallen, in the case of under 18s dramatically so. The number of children under 18 in closed establishments in England and Wales declined by 60% from about 3,000 in the first half of 2008 to about 1,100 in the first part of 2014. This unexpected fall represents the largest reduction in custody for children since the 1980s (Allen 2011; Bateman 2012). The sharp fall does not reflect a broader trend in the use of imprisonment, which has stayed relatively stable for adults over the same period, but has been largely brought about by a reduction in the number of children being sentenced to DTOs, with particularly marked declines in the numbers of younger children and girls. The number of young adults in prison has also fallen over this period, although not to the same extent as with the under 18s. There were 6,272 18–20 year olds in custody in June 2013 compared with 8,825 five years before – a reduction of 29%.

The custodial estate for under 18s

YOIs, which form part of the prison service, accommodate the majority of under 18s remanded in or sentenced to custody: 67% in June 2014. SCHs, largely run by local authorities (and which also accommodate children in need of protection), take less than 10% of those in penal custody; and secure training centres (STCs), run by private companies, detained about 24% of the juvenile custody population in June 2014.

A recent change to the law enables the secretary of state to specify additional forms of accommodation where young people serving a DTO may be placed, but the provision has yet to be implemented. A similar power exists in relation to the placement of under 18s subject to longer terms of detention. There are small numbers of young people held in secure accommodation in the health system whose costs are met by the NHS, but the vast majority of those under 18 in custody are held in YOIs, SCHs and STCs, and of these, more than two thirds are in YOIs. Generally speaking, SCHs and STCs accommodate the younger and more vulnerable young people and since 2013 all of the girls and young women under 18.

Under 18 YOIs

At the time of writing in August 2014, there are six YOIs taking boys under the age of 18 in England and Wales. Three are exclusively used for under 18s, with capacities of 259 at Wetherby, 160 at Werrington and 126 at Cookham Wood (HC Deb 2014: col. 544W). Of the other three YOIs, Feltham and Hindley accommodate under 18s on the same site, but separately from young adults, while at Parc, the privately run prison in south Wales, the juvenile unit for 64 boys is situated in what is primarily an adult Category C establishment. Following the fall in the custodial population from 2008 onwards, three YOIs taking young women under 18 were decommissioned in 2013; girls are now accommodated in SCHs or STCs. Under 18s can occasionally be moved to the adult estate through a process known in the system as 'starring up'. Fewer than ten under 18s were moved each year between 2010 and 2012 and none in 2013 (HC Deb 2014: col. 644W). YOIs tend to be larger than either STCs or SCHs and have a lower staff ratio of one staff member to every ten boys. It has been reported that this will be further reduced to 1:12 (Allen 2013a). YOI places cost on average around £65,000 per year (MoJ 2014).

All YOI's are subject to specific legislation in the form of the Young Offender Institution Rules 2000, although most of these are very similar to the adult prison rules. They make it clear that the aim of a young offender institution is to help offenders to prepare for their return to the outside community and that this should be achieved in three ways: first, by providing activities, including education, training and work designed to assist offenders to acquire or develop personal responsibility, self-discipline, physical fitness, interests and skills, and to obtain suitable employment after release; second, by fostering links between the offender and the outside community; and third, by cooperating with the services responsible for the offender's supervision after release.

A *Prison Service Instruction* (2012/08) sets out further specific requirements for the care and management of young people in prison establishments. Despite its title, its scope is limited to under 18s (and the small number of 18 year olds who are held in an under 18 establishment finishing off a sentence imposed while subject to the youth justice system). The instruction states that:

> Underpinning the entire PSI [Prison Service Instruction] is the belief that custody should not just be about containment, and that regimes should have a positive influence by recognising that young people do change, that adults matter to young people and that young people need the right balance between care and control.
>
> (Prison Service 2008: 4)

The recent history of under 18 YOIs has been a mixed one. In 2001, the then director-general of the Prison Service, responding to a series of critical assessments by the Howard League, expressed the view that 'there was not a prison service anywhere in the world that could better British standards of care for this frequently volatile and unpredictable age group' (Narey, quoted in *Youth Justice* 2001b: 51), but until the YJB started to commission places, and for some time thereafter, those standards were in truth poor. The years after 2000 saw increased funding and infrastructure improvements together with attempts to improve regimes. Some specific units – the Keppel Unit at Wetherby for vulnerable young men – have succeeded in providing good levels of care. However, the

Prison Service has remained resistant to change. Only after prolonged negotiations was it agreed that staff in under 18 YOIs would give up the normal prison 'black and whites' in favour of less militaristic uniform. The POA waged a campaign for staff to carry batons inside the residential units and only after another long dispute did the Prison Service in 2014 agree to end routine strip searching of all young trainees – a practice that had been used with much more discrimination in other parts of the secure estate (Puffett 2014).

The 2012–13 annual report of the chief inspector of prisons (HMIP 2013: 56) describes 'a reasonably good picture' in under 18 YOIs, but surveys of young people found that almost a third said they had not felt safe in the establishment at some time, and one in ten said they did not feel safe at the time of the survey (Kennedy 2013). More than one in five said they had been bullied by other young people or victimized by staff. A consistent finding over the years has been that young men from black and minority ethnic backgrounds have more negative perceptions than young men from white backgrounds across almost all areas of their treatment and conditions.

As with the prison service as a whole, education in under 18 YOIs is provided under contract. At the time of writing, education providers in public sector YOIs are contracted to deliver 15 hours a week of education, though on average each young person receives only 12 hours a week. This is supplemented by an additional ten hours of constructive activity delivered by the National Offender Management Service (NOMS). When the existing education contracts expired in 2014, the Ministry of Justice and YJB were planning to commission a substantially increased number of hours of education each week; a more holistic and integrated approach, with education providers delivering a wide range of academic, vocational and developmental activity; and a new approach to the arrangement of the 'core day' in YOIs, minimizing the number of interruptions to young people's time in education. A head teacher will oversee all education provision and contribute to the overall management of the establishment. Many young people in custody are not enthusiastic about taking courses in literacy and numeracy, being more focused on entering the world of work (Hurry et al. 2010). Being realistic about the motivations of young people and using techniques most likely to inspire them will be essential if this latest initiative is to fare better than previous ones.

STCs

The origins of the STCs lie in the period after the 1992 election, when new Home Secretary Kenneth Clarke wanted to reintroduce Approved Schools in order to deal with a perceived problem of highly persistent young offenders whom the courts were seen as powerless to detain. In February 1993, the febrile climate on youth crime (after the murder of two-year-old James Bulger by two boys, aged ten and eleven) led the government to accelerate plans for a new custodial sentence for 12–14 year olds, the Secure Training Order (STO), which would be served half in custody and half in the community. It would be served in five new privately run STCs, each of which would hold 40 young offenders. The plans were opposed by the Labour Party, which argued instead for an expansion of local authority secure accommodation. Delays in finding suitable sites, selecting providers and finalizing what were novel private financing contract arrangements meant that the first STC had not opened by the time of the 1997 election. However, faced with the prospect of buying out expensive contracts, the new Labour government abandoned their opposition and continued with the programme. Medway, the first STC, opened in April 1998 under a 15-year contract. Hassockfield in County Durham and Rainsbrook in the Midlands opened for a similar period in 1999. The fourth and final STC, Oakhill, opened in Milton Keynes in 2004 – this time an 80-space establishment on a 25-year contract.

Labour did dispense with the specific sentence of the STO and once the YJB assumed responsibility for purchasing and commissioning secure places in 2000, STC places were used not only for the specific persistent offenders for whom they had been designed but the full range of remanded and sentenced young people up to 18. In 2002, Medway and Rainsbrook each expanded to accommodate a total of 76 boys and girls, and in 2006, Rainsbrook opened a purpose-built mother-and-baby unit to care for detained young mothers and their babies, as well as those in the final stages of pregnancy. Hassockfield was also expanded to accommodate a total of 58. In 2013 and 2014, the contracts for the first three STCs were each extended for short periods while the government developed their policy for secure colleges, the first of which was not planned to be ready until 2017 at the earliest.

STCs are much better resourced than YOIs, with an annual cost per place of £178,000 and a ratio at best of two staff to five trainees. The centres are governed by specific rules which were introduced in the Crime and Disorder Act 1998. Their history has been a chequered one. An evaluation of the first two years of Medway found that staff were confused about the purpose of the centre and ill-prepared to deal with the trainees (Hagell et al. 2000). The study found that two-thirds of trainees committed criminal offences leading to arrest before the STO expired, half of these within the first four weeks after release. The tragic deaths of two boys, Gareth Myatt and Adam Rickwood (the latter just 14 years old), in STCs in 2004 focused attention on the use and practice of physical restraint (which was a factor in both deaths) and on the culture and performance of STCs more widely. Oakhill STC experienced problems when it first opened, operating at reduced capacity until its performance improved. However, since 2008, inspection reports on STCs have generally been positive. From the 40 reports published between 2008 and 2014, the overall effectiveness of STCs has been found to be outstanding on 12 occasions, good on 21 occasions, satisfactory on five occasions and inadequate on two.

SCHs

In 2013–14, the YJB contracted with ten SCHs to provide places for remanded and sentenced children. SCHs are run by local authorities and are subject to licensing and inspection by the Department for Education. The largest is Aycliffe in County Durham where the YJB purchases 24 of the 42 beds; the smallest is Aldine House in Sheffield where four of the eight places are reserved for alleged and convicted young offenders. SCHs have the highest staff ratios of the under 18 establishments, with up to three staff to every four children. They are the most expensive of the three establishment types, costing an average of £212,000 per place per year.

SCHs play an important role in providing secure care for children who are not necessarily offenders but who need to be locked up for their own protection – often children who run away from other placements. Local authority demand for welfare places has fallen in recent years, contributing to the closure of several units. The declining availability of places in secure children's homes has meant that the young people placed in them are likely to be a long way from home. The YJB's target that at least 90% of young people in secure settings should be within 50 miles of home was discontinued in 2009. In a study in 2010, inspectors met many young people who were more than 200 miles away from their families (Ofsted 2010). Distant placements restricted the number of visits by families and increased the young people's unhappiness and sense of vulnerability. Distance also limited the extent to which families could be directly involved in planning and reviews. The main reasons for this situation were the lack of local placements and the concentration of specialist resources in a small number of centres.

The custodial estate for 18–21 year olds

The secure estate for 18–21 year olds is a good deal more elastic than that for under 18s. For one thing, young adults remanded in custody can be placed in adult prisons and while those sentenced to DYOI must be held in YOIs, increasing numbers of establishments have been designated both as prisons and YOIs. While the YOI rules apply to 18–20 year olds wherever they are held, evidence from inspection reports suggests that a distinctive approach to young adults is sometimes difficult to achieve in a predominantly adult establishment.

As at 30 June 2013, there were 6,272 18–20 year olds in the YOI estate, of whom 188 were female (MoJ 2013). At this time there were 2,831 young adults still being held in single-use dedicated YOIs (all male), and 3,270 young adults held in dual-designated institutions, including all young adult women. An additional 27 young adult males were held in adult prisons for security and safety reasons. Furthermore, 101 young adults were held in under 18 YOIs (usually because a decision was made that they should remain there to finish the custodial part of their sentence), and 43 were held in Immigration Removal Centres. A further 492 young people who were aged 21–24 were held in single-use YOIs in the same period. In July 2013, young adults were being held in 54 institutions, of which only seven were single-use institutions that were dedicated to 18–20 year olds. The remaining 47 institutions, including all 12 holding young adult women, are dual designated as both prisons and YOIs. At the end of June 2013, over half of all young adults, including all women, were held in dual-designated institutions.

Dedicated YOIs

The Prison Service website is admirably frank when it says that 'Prison life for a young offender held in a Young Offender Institution (or YOI) isn't that different to prison life for adult prisoners' (MoJ n.d.). There is a different system of categorization in YOIs and certain distinctive aspects to the regime. All YOIs are supposed to provide a personal officer scheme and according to the Ministry of Justice, 'recreation and interaction with other young offenders is encouraged and most YOIs provide at least one hour per day. At the weekends there are more opportunities for activities such as voluntary work, sports and leisure activities such as arts and crafts' (ibid.).

The cost per place in the young adult YOIs in 2012–13 was more than the average for the prison service as a whole but much less than the cost of under 18 establishments. In terms of overall resource expenditure a place in a closed YOI was £40,858 compared with £57,429 for the juvenile YOIs and an overall average across the estate of £36,808 (MoJ 2013a).

There is no Prison Service instruction or order setting out a distinctive approach to young adults. Prison Service Order (PSO) 4800 (MoJ 2008) on women prisoners does contain guidance about how prison establishments should meet the needs of young women, arising perhaps from the fact that young adult women are all held in combined establishments. The PSO points out the need to address vulnerabilities such as high levels of self-harm, mental health needs and victimization from their peer group. The PSO also says that younger prisoners will tend to need more supervision and organization in their leisure time and that they should be consulted (at least once a year) to determine their need for particular activities, regimes and programmes. Younger women may need particular supervision and encouragement to use their spare time constructively and to avoid boredom, and may need particular help in overcoming barriers to learning.

The detailed criteria used by HM Inspectorate of Prisons to assess establishments do include some specific requirements in respect of the young adult age group (HMIP 2012). Staff are expected to be aware of the distinct needs of young adults, recognizing and responding to their levels of maturity on an individual basis. Staff should also undertake comprehensive risk assessments to ensure young adults are and feel safe from other prisoners, and where necessary a multidisciplinary care plan should be produced, kept up to date and reviewed regularly. Particular attention should be paid to supporting young people transferring from the juvenile estate at the age of 18.

In practice, many dedicated YOIs have struggled to provide a safe and decent environment for young adults, let alone achieve any more ambitious objectives. Indeed, HMIP's recent inspection findings indicate that safety and activity outcomes for young adults in dedicated YOIs are in many areas worse than for comparable prisons holding adult male prisoners. This appears to contrast with the findings of a thematic review of young adult males carried out in 2006 which found that young adults benefited substantially from being in dedicated units provided that their specific needs were identified and regularly reviewed, provision was tailored to need and staff were trained and provided with clear and comprehensive guidance in dealing with this particular age group (HMIP 2006).

An example of a consistently poor YOI is provided by Brinsford. In 2000, when it held both under 18s and 18–20s, prison inspectors described it as a stain on the prison system, showing a breath-taking neglect and lack of understanding of young prisoners' needs. Bullying was rife and a significant factor in at least two of five suicides that had occurred over an eight-month period. While the following year, marked improvements were found with a totally changed atmosphere, by 2005 inspectors found Brinsford once again struggling to provide appropriate levels of safety, respect and even basic cleanliness. Little positive change was noted in a series of negative inspections culminating two years later; despite the critical 2005 report, managers had failed to remedy many of the deficits in safety and respect that inspectors considered were within their control. In 2009 Brinsford was unable to provide a sufficiently safe and purposeful environment for young adults and in 2011 this was still the case. In 2012 inspectors made significant criticisms of safety, the quality of the environment and the prison's disappointing approach to resettlement. The 2013 report found that hardly any previous concerns had been addressed effectively and that in almost all respects the prison had deteriorated markedly. The chief inspector described these as the worst overall findings the inspectorate had identified in a single prison during his four-year tenure.[2] The findings, together with the significant shortcomings at Feltham, Aylesbury and Glen Parva Young Offender Institutions, led him to the conclusion that large YOIs were not a sustainable way forward. Clearly, detaining large numbers of volatile young men presents considerable challenges for the prison system, placing strain on management and front-line staff alike. It is not clear that abolishing separate establishments is necessarily the lesson to be drawn. There is a case for developing an approach that more genuinely seeks to meet the needs of the age group, although the costs of doing so are likely to prove prohibitive, in the current climate at least.

Dual-designation establishments

While successive governments have so far baulked at scrapping the separate sentence of DYOI and the specialist institutions in which it is served, young adults are increasingly held alongside adults, both on remand and under sentence. Unless and until the law changes, the government has assured Parliament that whatever their location, young adults have separate sleeping accommodation, although in dual-designation establishments the majority of facilities are shared (HC Deb 2011: col. 173W).

The 2013 consultation paper *Transforming Management of Young Adults in Custody* highlights several reasons for the increased use of dual-designated institutions in recent years (MoJ 2013). It is unarguable that they provide a wider range of locations where young adults can be held so that they can stay closer to home. It is also true that allocating young adult males to dual-designated institutions reduces the need to transfer them to adult prisons when they reach 21. Two of the other reasons are more contested: first, that dual-designation establishments provide better access to programmes and interventions than dedicated YOIs; and second, that they are less volatile and more stable.

In the absence of a body of research on YOIs, the findings of inspection reports of various kinds are the main source of data. In its response to the consultation, HMIP reported that young adults perceive worse treatment and outcomes when integrated into the adult estate (whether on split sites, on separate wings, or fully integrated). There are a number of reasons why this might be so. For example, the Independent Monitoring Board at Portland YOI, which became a combined establishment in 2011, reported adult prisoners placing coercive pressures of various kinds on youngsters (Portland IMB 2012: para. 21). At Rochester, HMIP reported that organized fights, involving adult prisoners betting on young adults, had occurred during 2012 (HMIP 2013a). At HMP/YOI Moorland, by contrast, some prisoners told the Inspectorate that groups of young offenders were bullying older men (HMIP 2013b). More common is likely to have been the experience at Winchester, where there had been inadequate consideration given to the needs and the impact of the introduction of young adults to the prison population. This had proved challenging to the staff, with insufficient attempts across the prison to identify this group's specific needs and to address these challenges constructively (HMIP 2014b).

The picture is more positive in respect of young adult women, all of whom are placed in combined establishments. PSO 4800 describes how many older prisoners take on the role of the parent to young prisoners but points to the risks involved in mixing age groups: 'young women may be vulnerable to exploitation by other prisoners – both adults and other YOs' (MoJ 2008: 41). At Holloway, however, HMIP found that the small number of young adults were integrated with the adult population and staff knew who they were: 'They received some reasonable support and most they spoke to felt well looked after' (HMIP 2013c: 13). Less reassuring is the experience of young men at HMP/YOI Isis, which seeks to provide a distinctive regime for a broader category of young offenders – those aged 18–30. Two inspection reports have found high levels of violence and the imposition of an emergency regime as a result of staff shortages (HMIP 2012a, 2014c).

Placing young adults both reasonably close to home and in establishments that meet their developmental needs is a difficult circle to square. It is not made easier by the fact that custody for young adults lacks an overall strategy and, unlike the under 18s, there is no body like the YJB to drive policy and practice development. Without this, there is a danger that the pressures of population management will prevail over the needs of young people.

Violence and safety in the custodial estate

When naval vessels were used in the 1820s, there were reports of boys so terrorized by bullying that they deliberately harmed themselves in order to be transferred to the prison hospital on shore (Hagell and Hazel 2001). While there are a number of challenges perpetually facing many of the custodial establishments that accommodate young people, the most important has always been keeping people safe, whether they are prisoners, staff or visitors. Whatever the configuration of closed institutions, young people are always likely to face high risks of violence from each other, from staff and from themselves.

Research suggests that both physical and verbal bullying behaviour is more prevalent among younger prisoners than adults (Ireland 2002). The concept is taken to mean the use of physical, psychological and verbal aggression to intimidate others to submit to the will of another and/or cause emotional upset (Butler 2008). However, there is less agreement about what specific behaviours constitute bullying and it has been argued that a gap exists between how bullying is understood by academics and how it is experienced by prisoners (Edgar et al. 2003). That it is a serious problem is not, however, in dispute. In 2012–13, for example, HMIP reported that bullying was evident at all the boys' YOIs they inspected in that period, and there continued to be high numbers of fights (HMIP 2013). An inspection at Feltham found that many young people told inspectors they were frightened and had little confidence in staff to keep them safe. Gang-related graffiti was endemic. There was an average of almost two fights or assaults every day: 'Some of these were very serious and involved groups of young people in very violent, pre-meditated attacks on a single individual with a risk of very serious injury resulting' (HMIP 2013d: 5).

Violence among juveniles is not limited to YOIs. Some 20% of young people reported in STCs that they had felt unsafe in their centre at some point, ranging from 30% at one centre to 8% at another; 19% said that they had been victimized by other young people and 13% said they had been victimized by staff (Elwood 2013). Violence is a serious problem in the young adult estate too. At Glen Parva, in 2014, while the atmosphere was not tense, almost half of the young men held told inspectors that they had felt unsafe in the establishment at some time, and about one in five said they felt unsafe at the time of the inspection. According to the inspectors, they were right to be concerned.

Recorded levels of assaults on other prisoners and staff had risen by about a quarter over the previous year and the inspectors were not assured that all incidents were recorded. They saw and heard evidence of prisoners charging 'rent' for cells with the threat of violence if this was not paid (HMIP 2014).

High levels of violence impact on everything that can be done in an establishment. In the majority of YOIs involved in a recent study of education in prison, violent behaviour and conflict between gangs were a problem, especially where youngsters were being held from the local area. This impinged on the education offer that could be made: some types of courses were restricted because of the danger presented by using particular resources that could be used as weapons, and in other cases learners could not be put into the same group as other learners if they had issues around gang membership (Hurry et al. 2012).

Violence reduction is an important priority in many establishments but all too often this appears to be achieved through reducing the hours that young people spend out of their cells and through the disciplinary system. In 2010–11, the Inspectorate found some establishments for young adults were over-reliant on using formal disciplinary procedures and under-used the more flexible minor reports system. Across the prison estate, 11% of prisoners reported having spent a night in the segregation unit. This was highest for young adults (23%), higher even than those in high security prisons (22%). In HMIP surveys, 18% of young adults said they had been physically restrained by staff in the previous six months, compared with no more than 7% in local, training, high security and open prisons (HMIP 2011).

An alternative approach was recommended by Sir David Ramsbotham when he inspected Stoke Heath in 2000, finding that there had been 717 injuries in eight months. His call was for much more in the way of physical exercise in fresh air: 'Don't lock them up all the time but provide them with a full purposeful and active regime' (*Youth Justice* 2001a: 58). A more recent study has suggested that sport can play a much greater role with this age group in reducing the high reoffending rate among young adult men (Meek 2014).

As in all prisons, there are many causes of violence among young offenders, ranging from pre-existing animosities, gang affiliations to unpaid debts. At HMP Thameside, for example, which opened in 2012, inspectors found problematic gang issues between young adult gangs in south-east London, with prisoners routinely trying to settle scores or debts from the community. Attempts have been made in some establishments to apply the lessons learned about how to manage self-harm and suicide, to incidents of violence. Restorative responses have also been piloted, although there seems considerable scope for developing more in the way of problem-solving approaches. The current chief inspector has noted that at Feltham, 'the reduction of violence and making the prison safer would need an improvement of staff-prisoner relationships and the provision of more meaningful and challenging activity' (HMIP 2013f: 6). Such improvements are likely to be needed in other YOIs too.

Use of force by staff

Responding to acts of violence may of course require staff themselves to use force. However, there are strong reasons for seeking to limit and regulate the use of force and to authorize appropriate methods. In the under 18 estate, the deaths in 2004 of Gareth

Myatt while being restrained and Adam Rickwood not long afterwards while being restrained led to the immediate prohibition of two restraint techniques and somewhat later to an independent review, conducted by two former directors of Social Services Departments (Smallridge and Williamson 2008). The report of the review made 58 recommendations relating to the use of physical restraint across the secure estate for children and young people. These included the development of one new system of restraint to replace those in use in STCs and under 18 YOIs, and the creation of a Restraint Advisory Board (RAB) to oversee its implementation. The new system, called Minimising and Managing Physical Restraint (MMPR), was being piloted at the time of writing, with a training programme for staff in the STC and under-18 YOI estate due to be completed in 2015.

Controversially, the independent review concluded that 'a degree of pain compliance may be necessary in exceptional circumstances', and MMPR allows pain-inducing techniques in both YOI and STC settings. In contrast, guidance from the Department for Education has made clear that any techniques designed to inflict pain are to be avoided in SCHs (Department for Education 2011). Following an assessment by the RAB, the guidelines in the MMPR manual on use of pain induction make clear that the only permissible circumstances in which pain can be deliberately induced are when there is an immediate danger of serious physical harm (to the child and/or another person) which exceptionally necessitates use of pain, all other options having been exhausted and/or due to the nature of the physical threat (for example, removal of a dangerous weapon). In 2013, the United Nations Committee against Torture was concerned that the UK was still using techniques of restraint that aim to inflict deliberate pain on children, recommending that the State party ban the use of any technique designed to inflict pain on children (United Nations 2013).

Alongside the development of policy relating to techniques of restraint there has also been controversy relating to the circumstances in which it can lawfully be used. In 2008 the Court of Appeal ruled that the use of force in order to ensure good order and discipline was unlawful in STCs because it amounted to inhuman or degrading treatment.

Restricting the use of force is also important for young adults. When inspectors went to Feltham B in 2013, they were shocked at what seemed to be the unprecedented use of extendable batons by staff, which had been drawn 108 times during 2012 and used 25 times. This was beyond anything the inspectors had seen in other establishments, and suggested that use had become normalized to an extent at odds with the Prison Service's own instructions (HMIP 2013f).

Self-harm and suicide

Investigations have shown that bullying and violence can be linked with self-harm and suicide. The Prison and Probation Ombudsman (PPO) looked at bullying and violence in self-inflicted deaths of prisoners of all ages and noted that it was especially common in deaths in YOIs (PPO 2011). A fifth (20%) of the 18–24 year olds in the PPO's young adult sample were recorded as having experienced bullying from other prisoners in the month before their death, compared with 13% of other prisoners (PPO 2014).

The study found that frequently, young adults were, by turns, both the aggressor and the victim. Perhaps understandably, both staff and the policies that guide anti-bullying can struggle with how best to manage this apparent contradiction. Similar concerns were highlighted in a review of self-inflicted deaths of children. The children's behaviour was often challenging: damaging their cells, disobeying orders and being aggressive towards staff. However, these acts were too often considered only as security concerns and, even for one child who was being monitored under suicide and self-harm prevention procedures, with little consideration that the challenging behaviour might also indicate underlying emotional distress.

Conclusions

Hagell and Hazel (2001) have identified eight recurring themes in the history of secure establishments for young people since the early 19th century. Two relate to the political and policy context in which such establishments operate, and the remaining six to what happens within institutions themselves. Arguably, the period since 2000 has not seen much in the way of macro swings in policy in relation to the use of custody for young people. The Street Crime Initiative in 2002 and the urban disorders of 2011 led to short-term rises in the use of custody, but there has been little in the way of high political or public interest in the creation of new kinds of secure establishment that led to the introduction of secure units following the Carlton Approved School riots in 1959, Youth Treatment Centres following the grave crimes committed by Mary Bell in the late 1960s, or the secure training centres after the murder of James Bulger in 1993. What seems to have played a greater role in the last ten years has been concern about costs, the reducing demand for places (since 2008 at least) and concerns with poor reconviction rates – the last of which is one of Hagell and Hazel's micro themes, which has in recent years perhaps been elevated to the macro level.

The proposed Secure College looks to maintain the educational focus of STCs and SCHs but at much lower cost. While the (to many minds) dangerously large population envisaged for the pathfinder college could certainly produce economies of scale, it is not at all clear that the kinds of savings envisaged will be deliverable. After all, STCs were intended to fall somewhere between YOIs and SCHs in cost terms, but ended up being a lot closer to the latter – notwithstanding the alleged efficiencies of private sector providers. It remains to be seen whether the first of Hagell and Hazel's micro themes – initial high demand for places in a honeymoon period – comes to pass in the Secure College. Indeed there was some doubt whether the project would continue if the Labour Party were to take office in 2015, having taken the view that the £85 million set aside for the project would 'be better spent on existing youth prisons rather than on a vanity bricks-and-mortar project for Chris Grayling' (Labour Party 2014). However, just as with STCs in the 1990s, much seemed to depend on the cost of withdrawing from the programme to a new government with limited funds.[3]

Two of Hagell and Hazel's themes that are readily apparent in recent years have manifested themselves in a more complex form than in the past. Hagell and Hazel identify a process by which institutions shift their regimes away from the punitive towards more of a treatment orientation. The overall impact of the YJB on the secure estate has been to encourage more of a treatment orientation. The introduction of a (limited) social work presence in YOIs has added some therapeutic capacity in these establishments, but the YOI rules and prison culture have proven highly resistant to change at the institutional level. The plans to bolster education in YOIs could help to bring about a further shift in culture but radical transformation seems unlikely.

Shifts in the other direction have been modest, largely rhetorical and driven by politics rather than practice. In 2013, the Ministry of Justice introduced a more restrictive system of incentives and earned privileges which applied to young adults (but not under 18s) and a policy of 'lights out' at 10.30pm for under 18s but not young adults.

The proposals to move young adults into adult prisons could be seen to illustrate a theme, relating to problems with behaviour within institutions and consequent changes of criteria for admission. There is no doubt that YOIs have struggled to provide a safe environment for young adults, but whether that justifies their demise is not clear. Many of those who responded to the government's consultation doubted that the distinctive needs and developing maturity of young adults would be met in combined institutions, and felt rather that those needs were being sacrificed for the convenience of the prison system as a whole. The major restructuring of the overall estate through the designation of Resettlement prisons makes the status quo in respect of YOIs even more difficult to sustain.

There is no doubt about the salience of the remaining two recurring themes in custodial institutions. The first relates to management difficulties including the high turnover of and lack of training and experience among staff. These problems have been heightened in the Prison Service institutions through the need to reduce staff numbers since 2010. Glen Parva, the young adult establishment where the inspectors reported a disturbing decline in performance in their 2014 report, saw prison officer grades falling from 250 in 2010 to 160 in 2013, according to the Howard League (2014). It may be that the loss of experience rather than just the numbers has had an impact. The greenness of the staff is suggested by the Independent Monitoring Board's report that there was to be 'training in recognition of cannabis following false suspicions caused by new leather furniture. The smell of the new furniture was mistaken for cannabis' (Glen Parva IMB 2013: 18).

Budget reductions will have had other impacts. Leather furniture notwithstanding, the latest Inspectorate report found that many cells lacked basic amenities such as curtains, a toilet seat, chairs and lockable cabinets. Failing to provide such basics is unlikely to enhance the prison's legitimacy in the eyes of the young men or to encourage respect for property or the people around them. At worst, the overcrowding, lack of activity and daily violence that may arise from further cuts in staffing may violate the human rights of prisoners as well as damage their well-being. Concern about welfare and human rights is the final theme observed by Hagell and Hazel – one where developments have been mixed. There has been some progress in regulating the use and practice of restraint and strip searching (for juveniles at least), but less in relation to separation in solitary confinement, which is widely used for young people.

Despite the general disdain for human rights, particularly of those in prison, it is mildly encouraging that the future of YOIs seems likely to depend on the recommendations of the Independent Review of Deaths in Custody, which was established after a long campaign by Inquest and others. For under 18s, the Secure College plans are meeting strong resistance in the House of Lords on many grounds, not least of which is the impact on the rights and welfare of the children who may be detained there. That resistance, too, is fuelled by the strength and quality of civil society interest and involvement in the issues relating to young people in prison. In that at least, the UK can be proud of its record.

At the time of writing, the ways in which young people in England and Wales are detained look to be at a crossroads. Controversial plans for Secure Colleges reached the statute book in February 2015. The governance of youth justice may also face important changes. The coalition government backed away from their initial proposal to abolish the Youth Justice Board, instead reining it in so that to many it seems little more than a department of the Ministry of Justice.

Whatever the forms that are eventually taken by the custodial establishments and their systems of management and accountability, the many problematic questions arising from locking up young people are unlikely to be resolved. The recent fall in the number of under 18s in custody has been more prolonged than many thought possible. Any heightening of public and political concern about young people and crime could and most likely will at some point lead to a policy reversal resulting in a rising population in custody. How such concern is handled – politically and institutionally – could provide the next major driver of change in the custodial system for young people.

Within that system, what emerges from the often unhappy experience of individual establishments for young people is how hard they are to manage. This may result from poor physical infrastructure which can restrict the opportunities available for young people (to undertake vocational training work or sports) and make necessary levels of surveillance, supervision and separation difficult to achieve. It may be a consequence of systems of assessment and regime provision that do not fully reflect the developing maturity of young people – a process which may last well into a young person's twenties. Problems may also arise either if there are insufficient staff to meet the demands of young people or if prison officers and other personnel are inadequately trained or experienced to work effectively with young people. Staff–prisoner relationships are key in all prisons, but some of the characteristics of young people – impulsiveness, inability to consider the consequences of their actions or manage their emotions – place particular strains on those charged with looking after them on a day-to-day basis.

Such strains are likely to be greater when the use of custody is reserved – as it should be – for the most serious and persistent young offenders. One result of the welcome fall in the number of under 18s in custody since 2008 has been that those who continue to be detained tend to be the most challenging and to have the greatest needs. There is a strong argument that some of the savings achieved by reducing numbers should be used to improve the experience of those who are locked up.

Notes

1 Through the medium of a four-part reality television series in 2015, criminologist David Wilson campaigned to 'Bring back Borstal', but he appears to have overestimated the success that the institutions enjoyed in the 1930s and ignored very significant differences between those who experienced them and today's young people in custody (Allen 2015a, 2015b).
2 In a subsequent report in 2015, the inspectorate found that Brinsford had systematically addressed their earlier recommendations and was 'transformed'.
3 In fact the Conservative administration that took office in May 2015 abandoned the Secure College on the basis that it would not be right to house one-third of the entire youth offender population in one setting.

Bibliography

Allen, R. (2011) *Last Resort: Exploring the Reduction in Child Imprisonment 2008–2011*, London: Prison Reform Trust.
Allen, R. (2013a) *Young Adults in Custody: The way forward*, London: Barrow Cadbury Trust.

Allen, R. (2013b) 'Paying for justice prison and probation in an age of austerity', *British Journal of Community Justice* 11(1): 5–18.

Allen, R. (2015a) 'Bring back borstal: serious policy or punishment porn?', reformingprisons.blogsp ot.co.uk/2015/01/bring-back-borstal-serious-policy-or.html.

Allen, R. (2015b) 'Don't bring back borstal; but we can learn something from it', reformingp risons.blogspot.co.uk/2015/01/dont-bring-back-borstal-but-we-can.html.

Bateman, T. (2012) 'Who pulled the plug? Towards an explanation of the fall in child imprisonment', *Youth Justice* 12(1): 36–52.

Butler, M. (2008) 'Bullying', in Y. Jewkes and J. Bennett (eds) *Dictionary of Prisons and Punishment*, Cullompton: Willan.

Department for Education (2011) *Children Act 1989 Guidance and Regulations Volume 5: Children's Homes March 2011*, www.education.gov.uk/publications/standard/publicationDetail/Page1/ DFE-00024-2011.

Department for Education (2014) *Children Accommodated in Secure Children's Homes at 31 March 2014: England and Wales.*

Edgar, K., O'Donnell, I. and Martin, C. (2003) *Prison Violence: The dynamics of conflict, fear and power*, Cullompton: Willan.

Elwood, C. (2013) *Children and Young People in Custody 2012–2013: An Analysis of 12–18-year-olds' Perceptions of their Experience in Secure Training Centres*, London: HM Inspectorate of Prisons and Youth Justice Board.

Glen Parva IMB (2013) *Annual Report.*

Hagell, A. and Hazel, N. (2001) 'Macro and micro patterns in the development of secure custodial institutions for serious and persistent young offenders in England and Wales', *Youth Justice* 1(1): 3–16.

Hagell, A., Hazel, N. and Shaw, C. (2000) *Evaluation of Medway STC*, London: Home Office.

HC Deb (2011) 7 June, c.173W.

HC Deb (2014) 18 June, c.644W.

HM Government (2014) 'Fifth Periodic Report to the UN Committee on the Rights of the Child', www.gov.uk/government/policies/creating-a-fairer-and-more-equal-society/supporting-pa ges/the-united-nations-convention-on-the-rights-of-the-child-uncrc (accessed 26 August 2014).

HMIP (1997) *Young Prisoners: A thematic review by HM Chief Inspector of Prisons for England and Wales*, October.

HMIP (2006) *Young Adult Male Prisoners: A short thematic report*, October.

HMIP (2010) *HM Chief Inspector of Prisons for England and Wales Annual Report 2008–2009*, C 323.

HMIP (2011) *HM Chief Inspector of Prisons for England and Wales Annual Report 2010–2011.*

HMIP (2012a) *Expectations Criteria for Assessing the Treatment of Prisoners and Conditions in Prisons*, vol. 4.

HMIP (2012b) *Isis Report on an Announced Inspection of HMP/YOI Isis 12–16 September 2011 by HM Chief Inspector of Prisons.*

HMIP (2013a) *Report on an Announced Full Follow-up Inspection of HMP Rochester 21–25 January 2013.*

HMIP (2013b) *Report on an Unannounced Full Follow-up Inspection of HMP/YOI Moorland 3–7 December 2012.*

HMIP (2013c) *Report on an Unannounced Inspection of HMP Holloway by HM Chief Inspector of Prisons 28 May–7 June 2013.*

HMIP (2013d) *Report on an Unannounced Inspection of HMP/YOI Feltham (Feltham A – Children and Young People) 21–25 January 2013.*

HMIP (2013e) *Report on an Unannounced Inspection of HMP Thameside 14–17 January 2013 by HM Chief Inspector of Prisons.*

HMIP (2013f) *Report on an Unannounced Full Follow-up Inspection of HMP/YOI Feltham (Feltham B – Young Adults) 18–22 March 2013 by HM Chief Inspector of Prisons.*

HMIP (2014a) *Report on an Unannounced Inspection of HMYOI Glen Parva by HM Chief Inspector of Prisons, 31 March–11 April 2014.*

HMIP (2014b) *Report of a Review of the Implementation of the Zahid Mubarek Inquiry Recommendations.*

HMIP (2014c) *Report on an Announced Inspection of HMP Winchester by HM Chief Inspector of Prisons 17–21 February 2014.*

HMIP (2014d) *Report on an Unannounced Inspection of HMP/YOI Isis by HM Chief Inspector of Prisons 17–28 February 2014.*

HMIP (2015) *Report on an Announced Inspection of MHYOI Brinsford by HM Chief Inspection of Prisons 16–20 February.*

Howard League (2014) *Breaking Point: Understaffing and Overcrowding in Prisons.*

Hurry, J., Brazier, L. and Wilson, A. (2010) *Improving the Literacy and Numeracy of Young People in Custody and the Community*, London: NRDC IOE.

Hurry, J., Rogers, L., Simonot, M. and Wilson, A. (2012) *Inside Education: The Aspirations and Realities of Prison Education for Under 25s in the London Area.*

Ireland, J.L. (2002) *Bullying Among Prisoners: Evidence, research and intervention strategies*, Abingdon: Brunner Routledge.

Justice Studio (2014) *They Helped Me, they Supported Me. Achieving outcomes and value for money in secure children's homes*, London.

Kennedy, E. (2013) *Children and Young People in Custody 2012–2013: An analysis of 15–18-year-olds' perceptions of their experiences in young offender institutions*, London: HM Inspectorate of Prisons and Youth Justice Board.

Labour Party (2001) *Ambitions for Britain.*

Labour Party (2014) 'Secure College Announcement Response Sadiq Khan', press.labour.org.uk/post/88269796419/secure-college-announcement-response-sadiq-khan.

Meek, R. (2014) *Sport in Prison: Exploring the role of physical activity in correctional settings*, Abingdon: Routledge.

MoJ (Ministry of Justice) (2008) *PSO 4800 Women Prisoners*, London: Ministry of Justice.

MoJ (Ministry of Justice) (2012) *Government Response to the Restraint Advisory Board*, London: Ministry of Justice.

MoJ (Ministry of Justice) (2013a) *Transforming Management of Young Adults in Custody*, CM 8733, London: Ministry of Justice.

MoJ (Ministry of Justice) (2013b) 'Costs per place and costs per prisoner by individual prison establishment 2012–2013', www.gov.uk/government/publications/prison-and-probation-trusts-performance-statistics-201213.

MoJ (Ministry of Justice) (2014) 'Factsheet Secure Colleges', www.gov.uk/government/uploads/system/uploads/attachment_data/file/322165/fact-sheet-secure-colleges.pdf.

MoJ (Ministry of Justice) (n.d.) www.justice.gov.uk/offenders/types-of-offender/young-adult-offenders.

Muncie, J. and Goldson, B. (2012) 'Youth Justice: In a Child's Best Interests?' in J. Simon and R. Sparks (eds) *The Sage Handbook of Punishment and Society*, London: Sage.

Ofsted (2010) *Admission and Discharge from Secure Accommodation*, No. 090228.

Portland IMB (2012) *Annual Report.*

PPO (2011) *Learning from PPO Investigations: Violence reduction, bullying and safety*, www.ppo.gov.uk/other-reports-and-publications.htm.

PPO (2013) *Learning Lessons Bulletin: Fatal Investigations Issues 3: Learning from PPO investigations into three recent deaths of children in custody.*

PPO (2014) *Learning Lessons Bulletin: Fatal incident investigations 6: young adult prisoners.*

Prison Service (2008) *Prison Service Instruction (2012/08).*

Puffett, N. (2014) 'Strip Searching of Young Offenders in Custody to End', *Children and Young People Now*, www.cypnow.co.uk/cyp/news/1143648/strip-searching-offenders-custody.

Smallridge, P. and Williamson, A. (2008) *Independent Review of Restraint in Juvenile Secure Settings.*

Standing Committee on Youth Justice et al. (2014) *Secure Colleges and the Criminal Justice and Courts Bill (Part 2 and Schedules 3 & 4), Submission to the Public Bill Committee*, March, scyj.org.uk/wp-content/uploads/2014/03/CRAE-HL-SCYJ-Criminal-Justice-and-Courts-Bill-Public-Bill-Committee-Submission.pdf.

United Nations (2013) *Concluding Observations on the Fifth Periodic Report of the United Kingdom of Great Britain and Northern Ireland, adopted by the Committee at its Fiftieth Session (6–31 May 2013)*, CAT/C/GBR/CO/5.

YJB (Youth Justice Board) (2014) *Youth Justice Statistics 2012/13 England and Wales*, London: Youth Justice Board/Ministry of Justice.

Youth Justice (2001a) 1(2).

Youth Justice (2001b) 1(3).

Chapter 31

Doing gendered time

The harms of women's incarceration

Linda Moore and Phil Scraton

Contextualizing the punishment of women

Depriving individuals of freedom, confining them to a place and regime in which all relational decision making, movement and interaction is determined by their captors, constitutes the penultimate authority of the state, exceeded only by execution. In most Western democracies indeterminate sentences served in prisons or unlimited detention in mental institutions are the extreme point of severity on the carceral continuum; a 'life sentence' is literal. At the milder end of the continuum prisoners are held for hours or days awaiting bail or imprisoned for non-payment of fines. Prison sentences are state-imposed sanctions, their measurement in time indicating the perceived and established seriousness of 'crimes' committed. Young (1981: 255–256) states, in applying a 'rational calculus' the penal reformer Jeremy Bentham formalized a legal code through which 'punishment made to bear directly on the individual' is 'predictable and proportionate to the offence'. Morrison (1995:74) considers Bentham's intention was to utilize punishment as an 'efficient and economic means of preventing crime', inflicting 'an amount of pain in excess of the pleasure ... derived from the criminal act'.

Cavadino and Dignan (2007) propose that historical analysis of prison-as-punishment reveals tensions between *retributivism* (which according to the reformer John Howard constituted a 'just measure of pain') and *reductivism* (combining incapacitation, deterrence and rehabilitation). Incapacitation to protect others, and deterrence as a warning to others, are presented in penal policy and public discourse to justify regimes of confinement. In contrast, rehabilitation emphasizes reform of the individual. Yet, deeply institutionalized operational policies and routines of prisons and reformatories, out of sight and mind of citizens on whose behalf they function, generate a 'series of abasements, degradations, humiliations and profanations of self' (Goffman 1968: 24). In his defining text on asylums Goffman raised a persistent dichotomy: the capacity of punitive regimes to deliver rehabilitative change.

The forced removal of an individual's familiar and family context and its replacement by a regime that imposes rigid conformity, controls inter-personal relationships and denies legitimacy to personal identity is, as Leder (2004) notes, both infantilizing and disempowering. The prison, whether located in remote countryside or inner-city, operates its own distinctive world of 'normative commitments and ritual compulsions' in which 'order', contact and movement are routinized (Carrabine 2005: 910). Davis (1990: 52) argues that the routines and interactions of imprisonment are imposed 'by the governing penal hierarchy', yet negotiated and challenged by 'prisoner culture'. She proposes that all prisoners 'invent and continually invoke various and sundry defences ... a resistance of desperation' (ibid.: 53), within a 'deeply gendered character of punishment' reflecting and consolidating 'the gendered structure' of the outside world (Davis 2003: 61). She argues that 'prison's presumed goals of rehabilitation' are not gender neutral and 'have been thoroughly displaced by incapacitation as the *major* objective of imprisonment' (ibid.: 72–73, emphasis added).

Historically, however, criminological research and criminal justice policymaking neglected the regulation, punishment and incarceration of women and girl 'offenders'. As Smart (1976: 177) stated in her pioneering text, this reflected a prevalent view that women and girls were 'too insignificant to be worthy of consideration' as the 'deviant, the criminal ... is always male'. Rather, they were assumed 'abnormal either biologically or psychologically'. Considered doubly deviant – breaking criminal laws while betraying female respectability and conformity – their treatment affirmed their 'inferior social position' (ibid.: 144). Thus women who offended were stigmatized as unnatural and unwomanly, categorized in official and popular discourse as 'mad' or 'bad' – or both. Processed through the criminal courts, they were assessed as dutiful wives, mothers or daughters. In her ground-breaking research into women's imprisonment in Scotland, Pat Carlen (1983: 155) concluded that the 'principles of definition and penal organisation which co-ordinate a woman's prison-worthiness are largely negative'. Thus women offenders' personal lives are redefined by the criminal justice system as 'maternal failure and dereliction of duty ... outwith family, sociability, femininity and adulthood'.

In the 1990s there was an 'unprecedented explosion in women's prison populations worldwide' (Sudbury 2005a: xiv), reflecting a growth in authoritarian legislation and harsh sentencing practices (McIvor and Burman 2011). It stimulated research exploring women's offending, their experiences of imprisonment and their marginalization from services that prioritized male prisoners. In turn, this inspired the development of gender-specific policies and community-based alternatives to prison. Yet strategies geared to providing women-centred initiatives have not reduced women's imprisonment and women continue to endure inappropriate regimes in which their rights are routinely breached (Moore and Scraton 2014).

This chapter considers the rise and consolidation of women's imprisonment in UK jurisdictions, drawing brief comparison with other advanced democratic states. In addressing prison-as-punishment it raises the inherent tensions between retributivism/ incapacitation and reformism/rehabilitation. It focuses on the complex needs and vulnerabilities of women and girl prisoners, the gendered harm experienced within penal regimes and the recent development and limitations of gender-specific policies and practices. The 'responsibilization' of women based on assessment of 'risk' is critiqued within the context of structural disadvantage and discrimination. This connects to the debate regarding women's agency, particularly inhibitions on women's self-determination inside and outside prison, and punitive responses to acts of resistance. The chapter's conclusion focuses on the decarceration and abolition of women's imprisonment via alternatives to custody.

The rise and consolidation of women's imprisonment

Historically, women categorized as deviant or criminal were considered 'more depraved and morally corrupt' than men and were subjected to intensive social controls (Welch

2011). In early modern England, physical and shaming punishments were inflicted for offences including witchcraft, adultery, disobedience to spouse or parents, sexual deviance, for gossiping or being 'scolds'. The regulation of women's moral and sexual behaviour intensified during the Industrial Revolution. Houses of Correction and Bridewells were established as places of punishment for the 'idle poor' and petty offenders, and within these institutions women were vulnerable to sexual exploitation (Zedner 1998). Throughout the late 18th and 19th centuries, women captives were subjected to sexual violence perpetrated by male convicts and sailors during and after penal transportation from Britain and Ireland to the colonies of Australia and North America.

Medlicott (2007: 246) considers the history of women's imprisonment 'shadowy', their needs subsumed by male institutional policies and practices. Prior to the 18th century, women and men were incarcerated together in filthy, chaotic and unsafe conditions. Spierenburg (1998: 55) records the 'triumphant rise' of the prison, emphasizing discipline, punishment and the creation of what Foucault (1975) terms 'docile bodies'. The growth of imprisonment in Europe, Australia and North America led to demands for penal reform, including the separation of men and women and the supervision of 'fallen women' by women warders. Yet gender separation left women marginalized as a small minority subjected to discriminatory and oppressive regimes (Rafter 1985). Reformatories, which developed in the USA in the late 19th century, were designed to provide women prisoners with milder disciplinary interventions than men. In practice, however, such regimes were oppressive, reserved primarily for white women considered 'worthy of redemptive efforts', as black women and girls were banished to the severity of plantation prisons (ibid.: 155).

England and Wales

Berman (2012: 18) notes that at the turn of the 20th century 2,976 women were imprisoned in England and Wales, comprising 17% of the overall prison population, yet by 1930 this figure had declined to 735, just under 7% of the total. The consolidation of London's main prison for women, Holloway, encapsulates the contemporary history of women's imprisonment. Opened in 1852 as a mixed institution, in 1902 it became a women-only prison. In the early 19th century, the imprisonment of suffragettes demanding women's franchise raised the public profile of women prisoners' treatment, particularly the force-feeding of hunger strikers. In 1927 Mary Size was appointed as Holloway's first woman deputy governor and initiated a reform programme prioritizing healthcare. Yet she experienced strong resistance from prison officers who opposed positive involvement with prisoners (Size 1957).

Throughout the 20th century the imprisonment of women was relatively rare, although bolstered by other institutions of 'coercive confinement' for 'deviant' women (O'Sullivan and O'Donnell 2012). In contrast to men, the small women's prison population reflected lower offending and reoffending rates, less serious or violent offences and strong informal social controls (Carlen 2002). Increasingly, women were imprisoned in discrete women's prisons rather than small units within men's prisons. As Garland (1985) notes, the professional development of the probation service and social work extended the web of surveillance, regulation and punishment into communities.

By the mid-20th century the prevailing ideology was that most 'deviant' or 'criminal' women required psychiatric or therapeutic treatment, a view underpinning the 1967 redevelopment of Holloway as a secure hospital for women prisoners (Carlen and Worrall 2004). Throughout the 1960s women averaged just 2.5% of the total prison population (Berman and Dar 2013: 8). This led the Home Office to predict that by 'the end of the century ... penological progress will result in ever fewer or no women at all being given prison sentences' (cited in Carlen 1983: 23). Emphasis on welfarism and rehabilitation, however, became 'routinely subordinated to other penal goals, particularly retribution, incapacitation, and the management of risk' (Garland 2001: 8). When Holloway's redevelopment was completed, its regime was punitive (Rock 1996) and an inspection report published in 1985 recorded overcrowding, lengthy lock-ups, filthy conditions and high incidence of mental ill-health, self-harm and violence (Home Office 1985, cited in Scott and Codd 2010).

Coincidentally, a Conservative government Green Paper, *Custody in the Community*, proposed greater use of community sentences and supervision. Yet, the expectation that this heralded a period of positive reform was 'misplaced' (Carlen and Worrall 2004: 13). Financial recession, high rates of unemployment and welfare cuts, coupled with 'folk-devilling' (Cohen 2011) single mothers and social benefits claimants, products of Thatcherism's austerity agenda, fuelled a political climate in which severe sentencing and punitive prison conditions were demanded. In 1995 'new punitivity' was exposed when the chief inspector of prisons walked out of Holloway mid-inspection protesting against appalling conditions and lack of purposeful activity (Ramsbotham 2003). This prompted a thematic inspection of women's imprisonment (HMCIP 1997).

Elected in 1997, the 'New Labour' government introduced a raft of criminalizing legislation contributing to an unprecedented increase in the prison population. Between June 1993 and June 2012 the total prison population in England and Wales increased from 41,800 to over 86,000 (MoJ 2013a: 1). Proportionately, the rise in the women's prison population – 173% – was greater: from 1,577 in 1992 to 4,299 in 2002 (Home Office 2003). This led to government consultation to develop a Strategy for Women Offenders, and to the initiation of a multi-agency Women's Offending Reduction Programme (Home Office 2004). New legislation (the Single Equality Act 2006, and Equality Act 2010) imposed a duty on public bodies to give 'due regard' to the elimination of discrimination and promotion of equal opportunities, focusing on policies and practices. This had implications for women's imprisonment.

Baroness Jean Corston conducted a review of vulnerable women in the criminal justice system in England and Wales. It was a consequence of public concerns and campaigns following prison suicides, particularly the deaths of six women in HMP Styal between 2002 and 2003. Predictably, Corston (2007: i) found that most women prisoners were serving short sentences for minor offences, bringing 'chaos and disruption to their lives and families, without any realistic chance of addressing the causes of their criminality'. She advocated a 'women-centred' approach, seeking 'better ways to keep out of prison those women who pose no threat to society' while improving conditions for a minority for whom a custodial response was deemed appropriate.

Corston proposed the replacement, 'within 10 years', of existing women's prisons with 'suitable, geographically dispersed, small, multi-functional custodial centres'. She recommended that centres be removed from Prison Service management and located within a new Commission for Women responsive to women who 'offend or are at risk of offending' (ibid.: 86). Other recommendations included the reduction of strip-searching to an 'absolute minimum compatible with security', and less use of imprisonment for foreign national women (ibid.: 5). The Labour government (MoJ 2007) accepted most of Corston's recommendations, announcing significant financial support for community projects for women inspired by existing initiatives. The response to Corston's most significant proposal, to build replacement small units, was limited to a commitment to review the women's custodial estate (ibid.).

In July 2010, a thematic inspection across the prison estate (HMIP 2010) found that many women were imprisoned far from their homes, creating a significant barrier to family contact. Limited in number, each prison accommodated a complex mix of prisoners: remand; short, medium, long and indeterminate sentences; mothers and babies; young and older women. While the inspection reported relationships between prisoners and staff as generally positive, some prisons had an over-representation of male staff. There were examples of purpose-built accommodation but in some prisons women lived in cramped dormitories. Locked confinement to cells was excessive and most regimes failed the expectation of ten hours out-of-cell time each day. Support for substance users had improved but some prisons failed to provide prescribed medication on induction and the inspection noted a lack of staff experienced in dealing with women presenting with dual-diagnosis (mental ill health and addictions). Resettlement support often was inadequate as was the failure to identify women's needs, or to establish effective links to local community, training and employment services.

The Conservative–Liberal Democrat coalition government's *Programme for Government* committed to better public protection and a 'rehabilitation revolution' via the privatization of offender supervision with payment by results (The Coalition Government 2010: 23). This was progressed in a Green Paper, *Breaking the Cycle*, proposing that regimes should operate through 'the tough discipline of regular working hours' alongside 'tougher … more intensive' community sentences offering 'pay back' to the community (MoJ 2010: 9, 14).

A follow-up review of women's imprisonment (All Party Parliamentary Group on Women in the Penal System 2011) welcomed developments including: publication of gender-specific standards for women's prisons and the Gender Equality Scheme; reduction in full-body strip searching; and investment in community alternatives for women. The review also noted the emphasis on gender-specific training for staff and volunteers. Yet, not all Corston's recommendations had been progressed and the 'scale of the problem' remained 'significant' (ibid.: 9).

In its *Strategic Objectives for Female Offenders* (MoJ 2013b: 4) the Ministry of Justice established four priorities: provision of 'credible, robust sentencing options in the community'; gender-specific services to meet women's needs; adapting custodial provision to rehabilitate and support women through maintaining family links, while punishing 'properly' and protecting the public; and promoting 'better life management by female offenders' (MoJ 2013c). To realize these objectives the Advisory Board for Female Offenders was established, chaired by the minister of state for justice and civil liberties.

A review of the women's penal estate in England recommended both the closure of open prisons for women and the establishment of 'strategic prison hubs' with open units situated close to urban areas, thus maximizing work opportunities (Robinson 2013: 3). In response to Corston's recommendation to establish locally based custodial units, the review noted that providing adequate services, including healthcare, might prove difficult in small institutions.

Following reorganization, the women's penal estate in England consists of 12 prisons (including HMP Peterborough which holds men and women), each of which is designated a resettlement institution. In September 2012, 247 women in English prisons had home addresses in Wales (Soroptimist International 2013: 8), yet there are no women's prisons in Wales. The review of the women's penal estate (Robinson 2013) recommended all women prisoners from Wales should be accommodated in either HMP Eastwood Park or HMP Styal.

Recent statistics confirm that women's offending remains markedly less serious, violent and frequent than male offending. Women before the courts are more usually first-time offenders. Following conviction they are more likely to receive community sentences on imprisonment under 12 months (MoJ 2012). Despite Corston's recommendations, and custodial alternatives including 55 projects supporting women who offend, there has been minimal reduction in women's imprisonment. In June 2014 it was 3,929, 4.6% of the prison population (Soroptimist International 2013).

Gelsthorpe and Morris (2002) argue that the real and proportionate increase in the imprisonment of women in England and Wales is not attributable to more serious or persistent offending but a consequence of the criminalizing impact of deepening social and economic exclusion. Custodial remand has increased, coupled with harsher sentencing practices (HMIP 2005; Hedderman 2010) and a disproportionate rise in foreign national women imprisoned for drug-related offences (PRT 2012). Further, as Sudbury (2005b: 169) notes, although African-Caribbean women constitute just 1% of the general population, they are 24% of all women in prison, where they are 'confined to the more physically demanding work ... verbally abused ... their needs and concerns systematically ignored by guards'. This proportion has remained constant. In 2014 those self-identifying as 'black and minority ethnic' comprised 25.9% of the overall prison population, 20% of the women prison population, with a discernible increase in Muslim women prisoners (MoJ 2014: 8).

Describing the high female prison population as an 'unintended consequence of other policies', Hedderman (2012: 4) warns that community alternatives, although important, will not alter sentencing practices and could have a 'net-widening' effect. Restrictions on custodial sentences for breaching community orders and for first-time, non-violent offences would be more effective. Player (2013: 2), however, identifies barriers to progressive, rights-based policies for women who offend within a criminal justice system 'dominated by the management of risk and the concept of less eligibility'.

Scotland

The Scotland Act (1998) created a devolved government incorporating responsibility for criminal justice. Between the late 1960s and early 1990s, Scotland's criminal justice system did not follow the punitive direction taken in England and Wales (McAra 2008). From the mid-1990s, however, there developed a 'retreat from welfarist principles' and a significant rise in imprisonment rates, and the public discourse on offending became even 'more punitive in tone' (ibid.: 490).

Scotland's only women's prison and young offenders' unit, Cornton Vale, opened in 1975. Women are also held in Edinburgh and Greenock prisons, and within prison integration units in Inverness and Aberdeen. Following a previous spate of custody deaths in Cornton Vale, further public concern was raised by the deaths of eight women between 1995 and 1998. They were investigated by the longest running Fatal Accident Inquiry in Scotland's legal history, which led to a review of community disposals and custody by the chief inspector of prisons and the chief inspector of social work (Scottish Office 1998). The review recommended a significant reduction in the imprisonment of women. Subsequently a Ministerial Group on Women's Offending (Scottish Executive 2002) was established with a remit to 'reduce significantly the number of women in custody in Scotland'. In 2003 the 218 Service opened in Glasgow as an alternative to custody, offering 'a specialist facility for women involved in the Criminal Justice System'. Intended to provide a 'safe environment' to address 'underlying causes of offending behaviour', it prioritizes women's reintegration into the community (Beglan 2013: 153–154). Despite positive evaluations (Loucks et al. 2006; Easton and Matthews 2010), the provision of diversionary alternatives had no impact on the use of imprisonment. From 1999 to 2009, the average daily women's prison population rose from 210 to 413, although most convictions were for relatively minor offences (McIvor and Burman 2011: 18).

Reviewing the role and impact of imprisonment, the Scottish Prisons Commission (2008) contrasted a future based on prison building, overcrowding, demoralized staff and crisis management with an alternative vision of reduced imprisonment, sentencing based on community 'payback', and use of electronic monitoring to reduce custodial remands. Regarding women, concerns about conditions in Cornton Vale persisted. An inspection in 2009 described a prison in 'crisis' (cited in HMIP 2011: para. 2.8), neither 'providing the care and attention that Scotland's vulnerable women prisoners needed' nor offering 'sufficient purposeful activity and rehabilitative work' (ibid.: para. 2.4). A follow-up inspection reported the treatment of women as 'not sufficiently good' (ibid.: para. 2.8), concluding that in a 'perfect world Cornton Vale would be re-built and would have staff comprehensively trained in the very specific role of working with women offenders … [within] a regime and interventions tailored to the needs of this complex population' (ibid.: para. 2.17).

Several years later, the Commission on Women Offenders (2012: 5) also condemned Cornton Vale as 'not fit for purpose', with overcrowding, high levels of self-harm, unmet mental health needs, lack of purposeful activity, inadequate resettlement services and ineffective leadership. The commission recommended greater provision of community-based support and effective mental health services and Cornton Vale's replacement by a smaller 'specialist prison' for women on long sentences, together with a purpose-built mother and baby unit and family friendly facilities (ibid.: 10). The Scottish government accepted most of the commission's recommendations and committed to funding new Women's Justice Centres in Glasgow, Edinburgh, Dundee and Aberdeen. Plans were also progressed to build HMP Inverclyde, Greenock as a national prison with a capacity of 350, along with new regional units for women prisoners at HMP Edinburgh and HMP Grampian, Peterhead. Following widespread criticism, however, the Inverclyde initiative was dropped in January 2015 (Alderson 2015).

Northern Ireland

The criminal justice system in Northern Ireland has been affected profoundly by more than three decades of conflict in which over 3,700 people were killed, many thousands injured and displaced in the context of a long history of sectarian politics. Thirty prison officers were killed by paramilitaries. In 1998 the Good Friday/Belfast Agreement established a framework for devolution of powers to an elected Assembly. Eventually, in 2010, justice and policing were devolved. Throughout the conflict prisoners with Republican or Loyalist political affiliations constituted a high proportion of convicted prisoners. They resisted prison regimes shaped by sectarianism as the overwhelming majority of prison officers were male, recruited from Protestant/Unionist/Loyalist communities.

Women were imprisoned in 18th-century Armagh gaol until 1986. The prison held internees, remand and convicted Republican and Loyalist prisoners alongside so-called 'ordinary' offenders. Confined to their cells without access to appropriate sanitation, During the 1980s, republican women mounted a 'dirty protest' smearing excrement and menstrual blood on walls, and a hunger strike in 1980. Forcible strip searching was condemned by international human rights organizations and 'came to epitomise, for many, the resolve of the security services to have women submit to the process of criminalisation and surveillance by taking control of women's nakedness' (Pickering 2002: 181).

Armagh's closed in 1986 and all women prisoners were transferred to Mourne House, a discrete unit within the new high-security Maghaberry male prison. Following the Good Friday/Belfast Agreement, the majority of politically affiliated prisoners were granted early release. Soon after, Mourne House was severely criticized by the Inspectorate for inappropriate high security conditions, over-representation of male governors and guards, inadequate facilities and inadequate care of self-harming and suicidal women. A Northern Ireland Human Rights Commission (NIHRC) investigation confirmed a deteriorating regime, the neglect of women's needs, the punishment through isolation of vulnerable women, and staff disinterest and hostility (Scraton and Moore 2005). Three women died in custody, resulting in severe criticism by inquest juries and the coroner (see Moore and Scraton 2014).

Mourne House closed in 2004. The Inspectorate, the NIHRC and international bodies recommended its replacement by a small women's prison. These recommendations were ignored and women prisoners were transferred to Ash House, a unit within Hydebank Wood (male) Young Offenders' Centre. Inspectorate reports and NIHRC research (Scraton and Moore 2007) criticized the limitations placed on women's movement, work and educational opportunities. In sharing transport and healthcare facilities women endured persistent verbal abuse.

Following devolution of justice and policing the Department of Justice commissioned a review of prison conditions including assessing compliance of women's imprisonment with international human rights standards. The independent Prison Review Team (PRT) concluded that the prison system in Northern Ireland had been shaped by conflict, was dominated by a 'culture of denial and compromise' (PRT 2011: 6) and inherently resistant to change. It recommended immediate implementation of a 'change strategy' prioritizing early retirement of guards and recruitment to achieve balance in religion, gender and age. The PRT (ibid.: 68) criticized women's imprisonment for fine default, describing the practice as 'criminalizing poverty', and the excessive use of custodial remand. It recommended a decarceration strategy offering community alternatives and, echoing Corston, the replacement of Ash House with a discrete unit to accommodate 'the small number of women requiring custody'. It would operate as a 'therapeutic' facility, integrated with 'services and support in the community' (ibid.: 70).

In 2004, on daily average, 24 women prisoners were held in Mourne House (Scraton and Moore 2005). A decade later, this had markedly increased to 68, almost one-third unsentenced and eight serving life sentences (NIPS 2014). The strategy document, *Reducing Offending Among Women* (DoJ 2013: 4), prioritizes the development of a statutory, community and voluntary sector partnership to 'deliver interventions that address the complex issues underlying offending behaviour among women'. It includes a commitment to decarceration. While the Probation Service-run Inspire Women's project has offered significant support to women offenders, there was no reduction in women's imprisonment.

Wider context

According to Walmsley (2012), at any one time globally over 625,000 women and girls are imprisoned, approximately 100,000 in Europe. Typically, they comprise between 2% and 9% of the overall prison population. In some states, including Bahrain, Hong Kong-China and the Maldives, the proportion of women prisoners is significantly higher. Yet women's imprisonment 'is growing in all five continents' (Walmsley 2012: 1). There has been a marked increase in the USA, where approximately one-third of the world's women prisoners are incarcerated, 70% of whom are black or Latina (Tapia 2010: 3). According to Law (2009: 165), between 1970 and 2000 this increase was 2,800% as a direct consequence of hardening drug laws and punitive welfare policies combining 'to push poor women, particularly women of color, closer to prison'. This trend has extended to Canada and Latin America where, in some states, particularly Argentina, Costa Rica and Peru, the majority of women are detained for drug-related offences (Fleetwood 2014).

Neve and Pate (2005) link increases in women's imprisonment to neo-liberalism and austerity politics arguing that women's offending relates directly to social and economic deprivation. Sudbury (2010: 12) identifies four key factors: a 'war on the poor' in which 'women's survival strategies' are criminalized; the 'war on drugs' which criminalizes addictions; the criminalization of migration; and the consolidation of the prison-industrial complex as a profit-making enterprise. She argues that a 'global lockdown' has exacerbated overcrowding, poor conditions and persistent rights violations within prisons (Sudbury 2005a). The legacy of colonialism weighs heavy on indigenous people who experience disproportionately high rates of imprisonment, particularly in Canada and Australia where aboriginal women are significantly over-represented (Stubbs 2012).

Exploring the 'troubling relationship' between 'race', control and punishment in US prisons, Bosworth and Flavin (2007: 2) consider that the over-representation of black and Hispanic prisoners (Davis also includes Native Americans) is but a 'starting-point' in interrogating the 'four sociohistorical processes – colonialism, slavery, immigration and globalisation'. Within these processes 'structural and cultural factors' shaped contemporary 'public sentiment and criminal justice policy'. Thus, 'it is the poorest, most marginalised, least powerful and most vulnerable people who are imprisoned and detained in disproportionate numbers' within 'societies divided by "race", class, gender and age' (Scraton and McCulloch 2009: 15).

While women's imprisonment in Western democratic states increasingly has received attention, there is minimal research emerging from 'the majority of jurisdictions, especially in Asia, the Middle East, Africa and Latin America' (PRI 2014: 5). However, punishment and stigmatization of women judged to have breached sexual and moral norms persists, particularly in states where legislation is underpinned by religious codes (UNODC 2014). Women imprisoned for 'crimes against morality', such as adultery or illegal abortion, risk abandonment by their families and are unsupported in prison and following release (UNODC 2014: 17). Some Scandinavian states, including Sweden, Finland and Denmark, have avoided the expansion of women's imprisonment. In Sweden, for example, electronic tagging has been used as an alternative. In Denmark's Tinge high security prison men and women prisoners are accommodated in small units (Fair 2009).

Gendered penal experiences and gender-specific reform

As discussed above, published research and policy statements demonstrate that women prisoners have complex inter-connected needs manifested in life-threatening physical and mental ill health, addiction, low self-esteem, and self-harm and suicide (HMCIP 1997; HMIP 2005). The HM Inspectorate of Prisons for England and Wales notes that within prisons inspected during 2013–14, '59% of women said they were in prison for the first time, and 30% said they felt depressed or suicidal on arrival' (HMCIP 2014: 57). Entering prison, over half were mothers, almost a quarter had a disability and one-third had addiction problems. Further, the lives of women processed through the criminal justice system are characterized by poverty, debt, homelessness, unemployment and education deficits (SEU 2002; Cabinet Office Social Exclusion Unit and Ministry of Justice 2009). As Corston (2007: 3) found, exploitation and violence within relationships 'feature strongly in women's pathways into crime'. Often they are coerced into offending by men and suffer physical and emotional abuse. Despite widespread acknowledgement of their vulnerabilities, the language of criminalization persists within official discourse; they are judged as having 'attitudinal issues' or 'pro-criminal views' (Cabinet Office Social Exclusion Unit and Ministry of Justice 2009: 11).

Hawton et al. (2014) note that self-harm rates among women prisoners are over ten times higher than for male prisoners. Up to a quarter self-harm each year, and their suicide rate is 20 times higher than in the general population. Factors contributing to women's deaths in prison include isolation through extended lock-ups; separation from family, particularly children; unaddressed bullying; inadequate healthcare and addiction services; lack of staff training; and poor communications (INQUEST 2013). Sandler and Coles (2008: 69) note that 'racist bullying' and institutionalized racism within prison regimes are often the context in which black women in custody take their own lives. Women with mental health difficulties regularly conceal their anxieties to avoid placement in isolation under oppressive surveillance (Moore and Scraton 2014). Despite the introduction of initiatives aimed at reducing self-harm and suicide, these issues remain a 'permanent and enduring feature of prison life' (INQUEST 2013: para. 10).

Women's prison experiences remain significantly gendered, with limited services and opportunities compared with men (Carlen 1983; Moore and Scraton 2014). As noted in the introduction, their pains of imprisonment are intensely gender-related (Carlen 2002). Fundamental care needs, such as access to sanitary protection, are regulated (Smith 2009) and often they are vulnerable to sexual abuse and assault, including exploitation by male guards. Security practices also can constitute violations. For example, strip searches are experienced as 'sexual coercion, reinforc[ing] women's sense of powerlessness and undermin[ing] self-esteem and self-worth' (McCulloch and George 2009: 121–122; also Scraton and Moore 2005, 2007).

The institutionalized failure to recognize and respond to women prisoners' specific needs regarding reproductive health, menstruation, ante-natal and post-natal care and menopause not only threatens physical health but damages mental health. Subjugating 'needs' to a discourse of 'risk' results in the most vulnerable women, often those with the greatest mental health difficulties, being labelled and treated as dangerous, and punished through lock-down and isolation. Yet women prisoners also resist punitive regimes and practices using open and hidden strategies. The price paid for non-conformity, however, invariably results in harsh discipline and punishment of body and mind and, occasionally, suicide (Moore and Scraton 2014). Released from prison, needs unidentified and unmet, still suffering stigma, institutionalization and trauma, they are 'highly vulnerable to the "revolving door syndrome" of relapse, crime and imprisonment' (Plugge et al. 2006: 62).

Within prison and detention in many jurisdictions foreign national women are over-represented yet appropriate services remain under-developed including translation services or appropriate support in maintaining contact with family and friends. Transgender women experience discrimination, violence and rape in male prisons and, whether in male or female prisons, are often isolated through segregation, ostensibly for their own safety (Arkles 2009). Wahidin (2004: 69) notes that older women experience 'roleless-ness, powerlessness and embarrassment', condemning them to the 'periphery of prison life'. Girl prisoners (under 18) when imprisoned with adult women typically have no access to age-appropriate regimes or services (Fair 2009).

Pregnancy creates significant physical and emotional challenges for women prisoners. It is also 'not uncommon' for women prisoners to experience simultaneously confirmation of pregnancy and HIV diagnosis (UNODC and WHO 2009: 4). Imprisoned mothers suffer the stresses and trauma of separation from their children. The impact of separation is particularly marked when children have been born in prison and are taken from mothers. Enforced separation has profound long-term implications for children, with most unable to remain in their family home, cared for by family members or placed in alternative care.

The impact of incarceration, together with existing vulnerabilities, continues beyond release. Institutionalized into prison 'routine and discipline', women regularly experience difficulties adapting to 'the most mundane of tasks' (Eaton 1993: 18–19). Up to a third lose their previous accommodation (Corston 2007) and are allocated to unsuitable, unsafe hostels, sometimes shared with men. As Carlen observes, they are 'repeatedly released back into those same circumstances of poverty and malign neglect which catapulted them into jail in the first place … put back into their class and cultural milieu … put back in their place' (in Carlton and Segrave 2013). Carlton and Segrave (2011: 560) also note that the trauma of imprisonment is a significant barrier to resettlement, leading to 'loneliness, boredom, coping with disappointment' and suicide.

Responding to spiralling rates of women's imprisonment, and compelling evidence of the harms of incarceration, gender-specific initiatives have developed across jurisdictions (Malloch and McIvor 2013). Gender-specific programmes operate on the premise that services should take account of the context of women's lives and their relationships and social networks (Bloom and Covington 2008). Barry and McIvor (2008: 6) suggest that such interventions should be 'more informal, less structured and supportive of needs other than offending behaviour'. In 2010 the United Nations Rules for the Treatment of

Women Prisoners and Non-custodial Measures for Women Offenders (the Bangkok Rules) set international standards establishing women prisoners' right to gender-sensitive treatment alongside an expectation that states would provide alternatives to prison.

Yet prisons have proven resistant to change. In Canada, for example, the creation of the Okimaw Ohci Healing Lodge provided 'an opportunity for Aboriginal women to reconnect with cultural and spiritual traditions while serving a federal prison sentence', offering the 'opportunity to access support and "time" to collect the fragments of a life' (Malloch 2013: 79, 86). Despite their disproportionate presence in prison, however, few Aboriginal women accessed the Lodge, the majority subjected to non-adaptive regimes within federal prisons. More broadly, Pollack (2008) has found a persistent emphasis on discipline and punishment in women-centred initiatives. Hannah-Moffat (2001) warns that, even if well intentioned, gender-specific regimes reinvent the prison, reflecting an ultimately flawed project.

Reflections on resistance, decarceration and abolition

Women prisoners as victims, survivors or resisters of institutions raises the relationship between the prison as a powerful, confining institution and the prisoner as the dis-empowered, disciplined subject; between structure and agency. Feminist scholars stress that 'even under the most violent and oppressive conditions women can resist their violent oppressors' and 'contest and evade the rules that grind them down' (Carlen and Worrall 2004: 88). Such manifestations of personal and collective agency have been evident most clearly in consciously constructed resistance strategies adopted by poli-tically affiliated prisoners. More typically, women prisoners adopt 'strategies, ploys and disruptions – formal and informal, individual and collective – to negotiate and chal-lenge authority to which they are subjected', yet the prison is a 'powerful institution' and 'the forces deployed against resisting women are significant' (Moore and Scraton 2014: 37, 41).

Tightly drawn limitations on prisoners' agency are evident from the moment their freedom is withdrawn. Prisons are total institutions, their regimes, routines and disciplinary procedures operate within tightly defined parameters established by prison managers and administered by prison guards. While prisoners often negotiate and occasionally resist institutionalized power, their removal from association and reallocation to segregated lock-down is the most profound denial of prisoner agency. As this chapter shows, the 'crisis' identified in women's incarceration has become so enduring it is more appro-priately represented as malaise. This is evident in escalating prison populations, increases in mental illness as a consequence of imprisonment and the desperation of self-harm and custody-related deaths, each of which has been formally recognized by damning inspections.

Hedderman (2010: 487) notes the persistent rise in women's incarceration despite their 'involvement in crime [being] only a little more prevalent', reflecting only marginal increases in the 'seriousness of their offending'. As discussed above, the harm caused by women's incarceration regularly extends to children, and often involves the loss of home, education, training and employment, and stigma for both the prisoner and her family. Imprisonment is an expensive form of punishment yet outcomes are poor in preventing reoffending, or 'reintegrating' women into communities. Inevitably this has generated significant debate focusing on alternatives.

Reviews have advocated increased investment in community-based, women-centred initiatives as a necessary prelude to decarceration. Such initiatives have been demonstrably effective in supporting women (cf. Easton and Matthews 2010, 2011; Loucks et al. 2006), yet there has been minimal reduction in women's imprisonment. Carlen's (2002) warning of 'carceral clawback' was prophetic as penal institutions adjust to incorporate recommended reforms, rebranding as educational and therapeutic spaces.

Yet decarceration has been adopted within statutory and non-statutory agencies' policy agendas articulated within official strategies for dealing with 'women offenders'. Community 'alternatives', however, while often providing significant support, may be 'punitive in their own right' and can 'extend women's involvement with the penal system' (Malloch and McIvor 2013: 7). Lawsten (2013: 111) concludes from the US experience that 'community corrections are thought to be an alternative to prison' yet, in reality, 'are an expansion of punishment and confinement' which do 'nothing to address the human rights of marginalized women'. The process of decarceration, therefore, involves not only reevaluating the purpose, function and future of prisons, but also challenging community-based sentences underpinned by the politics and ideology of punishment and surveillance.

While the success of decarceration depends on significant changes in sentencing policy, it also requires the development of a radical perspective and language that engages with the realities and contexts of violence, 'crime' and 'deviance'. As Sudbury (2005a: xii) states, 'official language is often adopted by criminologists, who use the terms "inmates", "offenders", and "correctional institutions" as if these were natural and uncontested'. In his earlier work, Christie (1981: 13) notes how language provides a 'good means of disguising the character of our activities', thus reconstructing the reality of incarceration via a 'shield of words'. The 'person to be punished' is recast as a 'client', the 'prisoner' an 'inmate', a 'cell', a 'room', 'solitary confinement', a 'single-room treatment' and so on. This reflects the reconstitution and new professionalism of penal reform, as 'a clear, hygienic operation', yet the 'targets for penal action are just as they used to be: scared, ashamed, unhappy'.

Decarceration was central to Corston's (2007) report in which she recommended the removal of responsibility for women's custody units from the prison service. Beyond decarceration, however, others advocate abolition. It is three decades since Carlen (1990) argued persuasively that women's imprisonment is 'a prime candidate for abolition'. More recently, Scott and Codd (2010: 165) propose that women are among the groups of people who 'should be deliberately excluded from imprisonment'. As Kilroy et al. (2013: 156) argue, the 'locked gates of a prison compound the litany of injustices criminalized women are already facing in the community'. Thus, it is necessary to move beyond penal reformism and 'challenge imprisonment as a response to gendered and racialized realities such as poverty, immigration, homelessness, mental health difficulties, violence against women and addictions' (Pollack 2008: 32).

In the USA Angela Davis, herself a former political prisoner, argues that while penal reformism occasionally results in improved conditions, it reinforces 'the stultifying idea that nothing lies beyond the prison' (Davis 2003: 13). Challenging prison expansionism, she proposes that 'alternatives to custody' should not be one-dimensional but be advanced as a 'constellation' of community-based initiatives generating a 'continuum' of appropriate interventions. Prisons, therefore, should not be considered in a vacuum but within the prevailing climate of criminalization, regulation and punishment, and their abolition progressed alongside the 'revitalisation of education at all levels', a health system that offers appropriate and effective mental health interventions, and 'a justice system based on reparation and reconciliation rather than retribution and vengeance' (ibid.: 107).

Concluding comment

This chapter clearly illustrates the political and ideological tensions regarding justifications for penal expansionism, particularly the incarceration of women and girls. As stated elsewhere, the 'unmet needs' of women prisoners 'persist against a backdrop of violence and restraint, strip searching and the systemic denial of bodily integrity, self-harm, segregation, appalling physical and mental health care ... punitive detox programmes, restricted contact with families and children, bereavement, inadequate preparation for release and poorly trained guards' (Moore and Scraton 2014: 233). As noted in the introduction, these privations are perpetuated within a political ideology originating in the enduring principles of retribution and reductivism – the powerful, populist assumption being that whatever the offence, the prisoner's pain 'pays back' her gain, her incapacitation serving as a deterrent to others, thereby leading to crime reduction. It is demonstrably flawed and the primary objective – to punish the 'deviant', the 'criminal' – undermines any stated commitment to rehabilitation or resettlement.

The history of penal reformism is one of compromise and accommodation. Campaigns for discrete and comfortable living conditions for all prisoners, gender-appropriate policies, regimes and programmes, access to families in supportive environments, and human rights compliance are important and immediate objectives for reform that undoubtedly would improve the lives of prisoners and their visitors. Reform, however, should not be confused with fundamental change. The process of criminalization restricts solutions to criminal justice disposals. In societies where social exclusion and political marginalization are directly related to economic deprivation, in which women bear the brunt of poverty and gendered violence, they are impelled by their material circumstances 'into conflict with the law' (Neve and Pate 2005: 4). While not all women's offending behaviour has a direct economic correlation, its prevalence is self-evident in prisons within advanced capitalist states. Inside women's prisons there is a significant over-representation of women and girls from the most marginalized communities, whose offences reflect the structural inequalities that circumscribe their daily lives and opportunities.

Bibliography

Alderson, R. (2015) 'New £75m women's prison scrapped, confirms Scottish minister', BBC News Scotland, 26 January, www.bbc.co.uk/news/uk-scotland-scotland-politics-30958609 (accessed 15 February 2015).

All Party Parliamentary Group on Women in the Penal System (Chaired by Baroness Corston) (2011) *Second Report on Women with Particular Vulnerabilities in the Criminal Justice System.*

Arkles, G. (2009) 'Safety and solidarity across gender lines: Rethinking segregation of transgender people in detention', *Temple Political and Civil Rights Law Review* 18(2): 515–560.

Barry, M. and McIvor, G. (2008) *Chaotic Lives: A profile of women offenders in the criminal justice system in Lothian and Borders*, Peebles: Lothian and Borders Community Justice Authority.

Beglan, M. (2013) 'The 218 experience', in M. Malloch and G. McIvor (eds) *Women, Punishment and Social Justice: Human rights and penal practices*, London: Routledge.

Berman, G. (2012) *Prison Population Statistics*, London: House of Commons Library.

Berman, G. and Dar, A. (2013) *Prison Population Statistics*, London: House of Commons Library.

Bloom, B. and Covington, S. (2008) 'Addressing the mental health needs of women offenders', in R. Gido and L. Dalley (eds) *Women's Mental Health Issues Across the Criminal Justice System*, Columbus, OH: Prentice Hall.

Bosworth, M. and Flavin, J. (2007) 'Introduction: Race, control, and punishment: From colonialism to the global war on crime', in M. Bosworth and J. Flavin (eds) *Race, Gender and Punishment*, New Brunswick, NJ: Rutgers University Press.

Cabinet Office Social Exclusion Unit and Ministry of Justice (2009) *Short Study on Women Offenders, May 2009*, London: CO & Ministry of Justice.

Carlen, P. (1983) *Women's Imprisonment: A Study in Social Control*, London: Routledge & Kegan Paul.

Carlen, P. (1990) *Alternatives to Women's Imprisonment*, Milton Keynes: Open University.

Carlen, P. (ed.) (2002) *Women and Punishment: The struggle for justice*, Cullompton: Willan.

Carlen, P. and Worrall, A. (2004) *Analysing Women's Imprisonment*, Cullompton: Willan.

Carlton, B. and Segrave, M. (2011) 'Women's survival post-imprisonment: Connecting imprisonment with pains past and present', *Punishment and Society* 13(5): 551–570.

Carlton, B. and Segrave, M. (eds) (2013) *Women Exiting Prison: Critical Essays on Gender, Post-release Support and Survival*, London: Routledge.

Carrabine, E. (2005) 'Prison riots, social order and the problem of legitimacy', *British Journal of Criminology* 45(6): 896–913.

Cavadino, P. and Dignan, M. (2007) *The Penal System: An introduction*, London: Sage.

Christie, N. (1981) *Limits to Pain*, Oxford: Martin Robertson.

The Coalition Government (2010) *The Coalition: Our programme for government*, London: HM Government.

Cohen, S. (2011) *Folk Devils and Moral Panics: The creation of the mods and rockers*, Abingdon: Routledge Classics.

Commission on Women Offenders (2012) *Final Report April 2012*, Edinburgh: Scottish Government.

Corston, J. (2007) *Review of Women with Particular Vulnerabilities in the Criminal Justice System*, London: Home Office.

Davis, A. (1990) *Women, Race and Class*, London: The Women's Press.

Davis, A. (2003) *Are Prisons Obsolete?* New York: Seven Stories.

DoJ (Department of Justice) (2013) *Reducing Offending Among Women 2013–2016*, Belfast: DOJ.

DoJ (Department of Justice) (2014) *The Northern Ireland Prison Population: Receptions 2009–2012, Research and Statistical Bulletin 10/2014*, Belfast: DOJ.

Easton, H. and Matthews, R. (2010) *Evaluation of the 218 Service: Examining implementation and outcomes*, Edinburgh: Scottish Government Social Research.

Easton, H. and Matthews, R. (2011) *Evaluation of the Inspire Women's Project*, London: London South Bank University.

Eaton, M. (1993) *Women after Prison*. Buckingham: Open University Press.

Fair, H. (2009) 'International review of women's prisons', *Prison Service Journal* 184: 3–8.

Fleetwood, J. (2014) *Drug Mules: Women in the international cocaine trade*, Basingstoke: Palgrave Macmillan.

Foucault, M. (1975) *Discipline and Punish: The birth of the prison*, New York: Random House.

Garland, D. (1985) *Punishment and Welfare: A history of penal strategies*, Aldershot: Gower.

Garland, D. (2001) *The Culture of Control: Crime and social order in contemporary society*, Oxford: Oxford University Press.

Gelsthorpe, L. and Morris, A. (2002) 'Women's imprisonment in England and Wales', *Criminal Justice* 2(3): 277–301.

Goffman, E. (1968) *Asylums: Essays on the social situation of mental patients and other inmates*, Harmondsworth: Penguin.

Hannah-Moffat, K. (2001) *Punishment in Disguise: Penal governance and federal imprisonment of women in Canada*, Toronto: University of Toronto Press.

Hawton, K., Linsell, L., Adeniji, T., Sariaslan, A. and Fazel, S. (2014) 'Self-harm in prisons in England and Wales: An epidemiological study of prevalence, risk factors, clustering, and subsequent suicide', *The Lancet* 383(9923): 1147–1154.

Hedderman, C. (2010) 'Government policy on women offenders: Labour's legacy and the coalition's challenge', *Punishment and Society* 12(4): 485–500.

Hedderman, C. (2012) *Empty Cells or Empty Words?: Government policy on reducing the number of women going to prison*, London: Criminal Justice Alliance.

HMCIP (HM Chief Inspector of Prisons) (1997) *Women in Prison: A thematic review*, London: HMCIP.

HMCIP (HM Chief Inspector of Prisons) (2014) *Annual Report for 2013–2014*, London: HMCIP.

HMIP (HM Inspectorate of Prisons) (2005) *Women in Prison*, London: Ministry of Justice.

HMIP (HM Inspectorate of Prisons) (2010) *Women in Prison: A short thematic review*, London: HMIP.

HMIP (HM Inspectorate of Prisons) (Scotland) (2011) *HMP and YOI Cornton Vale Follow up Inspection 1–4 February 2011*, London.

Home Office (2003) *Women and the Criminal Justice System Report*, London: Home Office.

Home Office (2004) *Women's Offending Reduction Programme*, London: Home Office.

INQUEST (2013) *Preventing the Deaths of Women in Prison: The need for an alternative approach*, London: INQUEST.

Kilroy, D., Barton, P., Quixley, S., George, A. and Russell, E. (2013) 'Decentring the prison: Abolitionist approaches to working with criminalized women', in B. Carlton and M. Segrave (eds) *Women Exiting Prison: Critical Essays on gender, post-release support and survival*, London: Routledge.

Law, V. (2009) *Resistance Behind Bars: The struggles of incarcerated women*, Oakland: OM Press.

Lawsten, J. (2013) 'Prisons, gender responsive strategies and community sanctions: The expansion of punishment in the United States', in M. Malloch and G. McIvor (eds) *Women, Punishment and Social Justice: Human rights and penal practices*, Abingdon: Routledge.

Leder, D. (2004) 'Imprisoned bodies: The life-world of the incarcerated', *Social Justice* 31(1–2): 51–66.

Loucks, N., Malloch, M., McIvor, G. and Gelsthorpe, L. (2006) *Evaluation of the 218 Centre*, Crime and Criminal Justice, Social Research, Scottish Executive Justice Department.

McAra, L. (2008) 'Crime, criminology and criminal justice in Scotland', *European Journal of Criminology* 5(4) (October): 481–504.

McCulloch, J. and George, A. (2009) 'Naked power: Strip searching women in prison', in P. Scraton and J. McCulloch (eds) *The Violence of Incarceration*, Abingdon: Routledge.

McIvor, G. and Burman, M. (2011) *Understanding the Drivers of Female Imprisonment in Scotland*, Report No. 02.2011, Universities of Stirling and Glasgow, Scottish Centre for Crime and Justice Research.

Malloch, M. (2013) 'A healing place? Okimaw Ohci and a Canadian approach to Aboriginal women', in M. Malloch and G. McIvor (eds) *Women, Punishment and Social Justice: Human rights and penal practices*, Abingdon: Routledge.

Malloch, M. and McIvor, G. (eds) (2013) *Women, Punishment and Social Justice: Human rights and penal practices*, Abingdon: Routledge.

Medlicott, D. (2007) 'Women in prison', in Y. Jewkes (ed.) *Handbook on Prisons*, Cullompton: Willan.

MoJ (Ministry of Justice) (2007) *The Government's Response to the Report by Baroness Corston of a Review of Women with Particular Vulnerabilities in the Criminal Justice System*, London: Ministry of Justice.

MoJ (Ministry of Justice) (2010) *Breaking the Cycle: Effective punishment, rehabilitation and sentencing of offenders*, London: Ministry of Justice.

MoJ (Ministry of Justice) (2013a) *Story of the Prison Population: 1993–2013 England and Wales, January 2013*, London: Ministry of Justice.

MoJ (Ministry of Justice) (2013b) *Strategic Objectives for Female Offenders*, London: Ministry of Justice.

MoJ (Ministry of Justice) (2013c) *Transforming Rehabilitation: A Strategy for Reform*, London: Ministry of Justice.

MoJ (Ministry of Justice) (2014) *Statistics on Women and the Criminal Justice 2013*, London: Ministry of Justice.

Moore, L. and Scraton, P. (2014) *The Incarceration of Women: Punishing bodies, breaking spirits*, Basingstoke: Palgrave Macmillan.

Morrison, W. (1995) *Theoretical Criminology from Modernity to Post-modernism*, London: Cavendish Publishing.

Neve, L. and Pate, K. (2005) 'Challenging the criminalization of women who resist', in J. Sudbury (ed.) *Global Lockdown: Race, Gender and the Prison Industrial Complex*, London: Routledge.

NIPS (Northern Ireland Prison Service) (2014) 'Analysis of NIPS prison population from 01/04/2013 to 30/06/2014', www.dojni.gov.uk/index/ni-prison-service/nips-population-statistics-2/population-statistics-june-2014.pdf (accessed 15 November 2014).

O'Sullivan, E. and O'Donnell, I. (2012) *Coercive Confinement in Ireland: Patients, prisoners and penitents*, Manchester: Manchester University Press.

Pickering, S. (2002) *Women, Policing and Resistance in Northern Ireland*, Belfast: Beyond the Pale.

Player, E. (2013) 'Women in the criminal justice system: The triumph of inertia', *Criminology and Criminal Justice* 14(3): 276–297 (1–22, online version).

Plugge, E., Douglas, N. and Fitzpatrick, R. (2006) *The Health of Women in Prison: Study findings*, Oxford: Oxford University Press.

Pollack, S. (2008) *Locked In and Locked Out: Imprisoning women in the shrinking and punitive welfare state*, Waterloo: Wilfred Laurier University.

PRI (Prison Reform International) (2008) *Women in Prison: Incarcerated in a man's world*, Penal Reform Briefing No. 3 2008(1), London: PRI.

PRI (Prison Reform International) (2014) *Who are Women Prisoners? Survey results from Jordan and Tunisia*, London: PRI.

PRT (Prison Reform Trust) (2012) *Women in Prison, August 2012*, London: PRT.

PRT (Prison Reform Trust) (2014) *Prison – The Facts: Bromley briefings summer 2014*, London: PRT.

PRT (Prison Review Team) (2011) *Review of the Northern Ireland Prison System: Conditions, management and oversight of all prisons. Final Report. October 2011*, Belfast: PRT.

Rafter, N. (1985) *Women in State Prisons, 1800–1935*, Boston, MA: Northeastern University Press.

Ramsbotham, D. (2003) *Prisongate: The shocking state of Britain's prisons and the need for visionary change*, London: Simon and Schuster.

Robinson, C. (2013) *Review of Women's Custodial Estate*, London: National Offender Management Service.

Rock, P. (1996) *Reconstructing a Women's Prison: The Holloway redevelopment project, 1968–88*, Oxford: Clarendon Press.

Sandler, M. and Coles, D. (2008) *Dying on the Inside: Examining women's needs in prison*, London: INQUEST.

Scott, D. and Codd, H. (2010) *Controversial Issues in Prisons*, Maidenhead: Open University Press.

Scottish Executive (2002) *A Better Way: The report of the Ministerial Group on Women's Offending*, Edinburgh: The Stationery Office.

Scottish Office (1998) *Women Offenders – A Safer Way? A review of community disposals and the use of custody for women offenders in Scotland*, Edinburgh: Social Work Services and Prisons Inspectorates for Scotland.

Scottish Prisons Commission (2008) *Scotland's Choice: Report of the Scottish prisons commission*, Edinburgh: Scottish Government.

Scottish Prison Service (2012) *Women in Custody: A Consultation.*

Scraton, P. and McCulloch, J. (2009) 'The violence of incarceration: Introduction', in P. Scraton and J. McCulloch (eds) *The Violence of Incarceration*, London: Routledge.

Scraton, P. and Moore, L. (2005) *The Hurt Inside*, Belfast: Northern Ireland Human Rights Commission.

Scraton, P. and Moore, L. (2007) *The Prison Within*, Belfast: Northern Ireland Human Rights Commission.

SEU (2002) *Reducing Offending by Ex-Prisoners*, London: Social Exclusion Unit.

Size, M. (1957) *Prisons I Have Known*, London: George Allen and Unwin.

Smart, C. (1976) *Women, Crime and Criminology*, London: Routledge & Kegan Paul.

Smith, C. (2009) 'A period in custody: Menstruation and the imprisoned body', *Internet Journal of Criminology*: 1–25.

Social Exclusion Unit (2002) *Reducing Re-offending by Ex-prisoners*, London: SEU.

Soroptimist International (2013) *Transforming Lives: Reducing Women's Imprisonment*, Stockport: Soroptimist International.

Spierenburg, P. (1998) 'The body and the state: Early modern Europe', in N. Mossir and D. Rothman (eds) *The Oxford History of the Prison: The Practice of Punishment in Western Society*, Oxford: Oxford University Press.

Stubbs, J. (2012) 'Indigenous women and penal politics', in K. Carrington et al. (eds) *Crime, Justice and Social Democracy: International Perspectives*, Houndmills: Palgrave Macmillan.

Sudbury, J. (2005a) 'Introduction: Feminist critiques, transnational landscapes, abolitionist visions', in J. Sudbury (ed.) *Global Lockdown: Race, Gender, and the Prison-Industrial Complex*, London: Routledge.

Sudbury, J. (2005b) '"Mules", "yardies", and other folk devils: Mapping cross-border imprisonment in Britain', in J. Sudbury (ed.) *Global Lockdown: Race, Gender, and the Prison-Industrial Complex*, London: Routledge.

Sudbury, J. (2010) 'Unpacking the crisis: Women of color, globalization and the prison-industrial complex', in R. Solinger, P. Johnson, M. Raimon, T. Reynolds and R. Tapia (eds) *Interrupted Life: Experiences of Incarcerated Women in the United States*, Berkeley, Los Angeles and London: University of California Press.

Sykes, G. (1958) *The Society of Captives: A Study of a Maximum Security Prison*, Princeton, NJ: Princeton University Press.

Tapia, R. (2010) 'Introduction: Certain failures: Representing the experiences of incarcerated women in the United States', in R. Solinger, P. Johnson, M. Raimon, T. Reynolds and R. Tapia (eds) *Interrupted Life: Experiences of Incarcerated Women in the United States*, Berkeley, Los Angeles and London: University of California Press.

Tombs, J. and Jagger, E. (2006) 'Denying responsibility: Sentencers' accounts of their decisions to imprison', *British Journal of Criminology* 46: 803–821.

UNODC (United Nations Office on Drugs and Crime) (2014) *Handbook on Women and Imprisonment*, second edn, Vienna: UNODC.

UNODC (United Nations Office on Drugs and Crime) and WHO (World Health Organization) (2009) *Women's Health in Prison: Correcting Gender Inequity in Prison Health*, Vienna: UNODC.

Wahidin, A. (2004) *Older Women in the Criminal Justice System: Running Out of Time*, London: Jessica Kingsley Publishers.

Walmsley, R. (2012) *World Female Prison Population List*, second edn, Essex: International Centre for Prison Studies, University of Essex.

Welch, M. (2011) *Corrections: A Critical Approach*, third edn, London and New York: Routledge.

Worrall, A. and Gelsthorpe, L. (2009) 'What works with women offenders: The past 30 years', *Probation Journal* 56: 329–346.

Young, J. (1981) 'Thinking seriously about crime: Some models of criminology', in M. Fitzgerald, G. McLennan and J. Pawson (eds) *Crime and Society: Readings in History and Theory*, London: Routledge & Kegan Paul/The Open University Press.

Zedner, L. (1998) 'Wayward sisters: The prison for women', in N. Morris and D. Rothman (eds) *The Oxford History of the Prison: The Practice of Punishment in Western Society*, Oxford: Oxford University Press.

Chapter 32

Race, ethnicity, multiculture and prison life

Rod Earle[1]

The persistence, and in some instances intensification, of racial disparities in many Western prison populations challenges prison's central position in any system of justice. On either side of the Atlantic, the US and the UK prison populations stand out against their neighbours in terms of scale and in terms of racial disparity. As several commentators have pointed out (Lacey 2010; Newburn 2010), the exceptional size of the US penal population dwarfs every other, but the notoriety of its racial configuration and the sheer scale of the American carceral archipelago overshadows the fact that ethnic disproportionality on this side of the Atlantic in UK prisons is even greater than it is in the USA (Phillips 2012; Daems 2008). In this chapter I briefly outline Loic Wacquant's exploration of the racialized dynamics of imprisonment. Drawing on the work of Stuart Hall, the chapter will critically interrogate how race and ethnicity are theorized, and consider whether or how such theorization may be implicated in sustaining the disparities it exposes. Using Crewe's (2009), and Phillips and Earle's[2] (see Phillips 2012) ethnographic studies of English prisons, the chapter will examine how attending to the specificities of human diversity and difference may reveal dilemmas and opportunities to unpick the enduring harms of racism that are so thoroughly laced through Western penal systems.

Brute facts and complex structures: the racialized dynamics of imprisonment

> Three brute facts stand out and give a measure of the grotesquely disproportionate impact of mass incarceration of African-Americans. First the ethnic composition of the prison population in the United States has been virtually inverted in the last half century going from about 70% (Anglo) White to less than 30% today ... Next, ... the White-Black incarceration gap has grown rapidly in the past quarter-century, jumping from 1 [white] for 5 [black] in 1985 to about 1 for 8 today ... Lastly, the lifelong cumulative probability of 'doing time' in a state or federal penitentiary based on the imprisonment rates of the early 90s is 4% for whites, 16% for Latinos and a staggering 29% for blacks.
>
> (Wacquant 2002a: 43)

Loic Wacquant (*inter alia*, Wacquant 2007, 2009a, 2009b) provides an extensive analysis of prison's place in the transformations occurring in modern life. He characterizes these neo-liberal transformations as 'epochal' – i.e. of world-historical proportions that are equivalent in scale to the shifts (in the West) from feudalism to capitalism. According to Wacquant, the penal state represents a newly ambidextrous state arising from the 'dynamic coupling' of 'the maternal and nurturing social arm of the welfare state' with its more conventionally paternal 'virile and controlling arm'. This transition from the feminized 'nanny state' of the Fordist-Keynesian era to the strict 'daddy state' of neo-liberalism is characterized by Wacquant (2009a: 290) as 'the re-masculinization of the state'. In the process, the velvet gloves that once concealed the iron fist of the state are discarded: the state 'mans-up' and gets down to the increasingly urgent business of pacifying the marginal and dispossessed populations of a rampant neo-liberal world order, mainly by putting them in prison. The prison, according to Wacquant, is central to the neo-liberal project, an essential element of its statecraft. In this respect, he echoes Sykes's (1958: 8) cautionary remarks that: 'The prison is not an autonomous system of power, rather it is an instrument of the state, shaped by its social environment, and we must keep this simple truth in mind if we are to understand the prison'.

Wacquant (2010: 79) also insists that the ethnic transformation of the US prison population is both more dramatic and more complex than most penal commentators allow for. Driving the transformation are class dynamics: '[C]lass, not race, is the first filter of selection for incarceration ... inmates are first and foremost poor people', but whereas this has been a historical constant, the newly expanded dimensions of US penal enclosure are constituted by the additional force of racism. As a result, a 'double selection' occurs that scoops those who are poor and black from the ghetto to the prison, and back again.

In some respects, Wacquant's analysis of race and class is not so distant from that offered of the UK in the early 1980s by Stuart Hall (1980). Hall also stressed that the mutually reinforcing intersections of race and class did not necessarily cancel their relative autonomy. However, Hall calls attention to the historical 'specificity of those social formations which exhibit distinctive or ethnic characteristics' (ibid.: 308) and helpfully refines the Althusserian terminology of 'articulation' as:

> a metaphor used to indicate relations of *linkage and affectivity* between different levels of all sorts of things ... [T]hese things need to be linked, because though connected they are not the same. The unity which they form is thus not that of an identity, where one structure perfectly recapitulates or reproduces or even 'expresses' another; or where each is reducible to the other ... The unity formed by this combination or articulation, is always, necessarily, a 'complex structure': a structure in which things are related, as much through their differences as through their similarities ... It also means – since the combination is a structure (an articulated combination) and not a random association – that there will be structured relations between its parts, i.e., relations of dominance and subordination. Hence, in Althusser's cryptic phrase, a 'complex unity, structured in dominance'.
>
> (Hall 1980: 325, emphasis added)

The persistence of ethnic disproportionality in prisons in the USA and the UK (see respectively Alexander 2012; Phillips 2012), as well as other jurisdictions, provides Wacquant with an abundance of 'brute facts', but the articulation of race and class continues to frustrate theoretical explanation. It is a feature of 'complex unity, structured in dominance' which resists intelligibility.

Wacquant's recognition that race is thoroughly imbricated in Western state politics and social life places him close to Hall's (1992) and Gilroy's (2004, 2005) post-colonial approach. However, the complexity of this contemporary conjuncture, and Wacquant's difficulty in generating a consistent and coherent theoretical synthesis accommodating class, race and gender, has twice resulted in the withdrawal from the publisher of the final instalment of his trilogy: *Urban Outcasts* (2007), *Punishing the Poor* (2009a) and *Deadly Symbiosis: Race and the Rise of the Penal State* (in press). The controversies and complexities of analysing the different historical legacies of race thinking and statecraft on both sides of the north Atlantic are enormous and frequently problematic, as Wacquant (2013: 8) concedes with his candid admission: 'These difficulties explain why I have twice taken this book back from my publisher [Polity] to revise it top to bottom'.

The tensions identified by Hall in the early days of neo-liberal ascendancy between the crude economic determinism that sees only the rational individual, and the vapidity of postmodern 'sociological pluralism' (Hall 1980: 336), remain as vivid as ever. Hall's account of 'societies structured in dominance' also provides a series of advisory indicators that bear repetition, not least because his death in 2014 means he is no longer in a position to do so himself. Hall is adamant that the 'rigorous application' (ibid.: 336) of the 'premise of historical specificity' (ibid.: 336) must be applied when addressing the racialized characteristics of social formations. As such, racism cannot be 'dealt with as a general feature of human societies' (ibid.: 336) that recur with similar functional characteristics, but rather must be understood in terms of 'historically specific racisms' (ibid.; see also Goldberg 2009). This begins with an 'assumption of difference, of specificity rather than of a unitary, transhistorical or universal "structure"' (Hall 1980: 336). It is vital, argues Hall, to 'distinguish those social features which fix the different positions of social groups and classes on the basis of racial ascription (biologically or socially defined) from other systems which have a similar social function' (ibid.: 337). He reiterates his warning against 'extrapolating a common and universal structure to racism, which remains essentially the same, outside of its specific historical location. It is only as the different racisms are historically specified – in their difference – that they can be properly understood' (ibid.: 337). The place and the time of race are as key to Hall's analysis as the permutations of class. As he memorably concluded, '"race" is the modality through which class is lived, the medium through which class relations are experienced, the form in which it is appropriated and "fought through"' (ibid.: 342).

The US carceral nightmare and the contortions of race within it have taken on dazzling proportions (Jewkes 2013). Nearly half the world's prison population is located in the USA. Black people account for approximately 13% of the general population (US Census Bureau 2005), but of the 1.54 million people imprisoned in 2008 for over a year in federal and state prisons, 38% were black, and 20% were Hispanic (Sabol et al. 2009). As Phillips (2012: 12–13) is careful to observe, the sheer awesome scale of imprisonment rates in the USA dwarfs those of every other country but it should not be allowed to erase the scale of ethnic disproportionality that persists in the UK, a disproportionality that exceeds the US pattern. Using the most recent available comparative data, Phillips notes that the black:white ethnic ratio in the USA is 7.7:1 for men and 6:1 for women, while the combined figure in England and Wales is 8.5:1. These 'brute facts' rarely surface in the extensive academic prison literature that has flourished alongside the more modest expansion of prison populations in the UK.

Wacquant is congratulated and celebrated for bringing a wider sociological range to conventional criminological analysis that sometimes struggles to move beyond a narrow focus on penality (Squires and Lea 2013). However, many of his specific claims about the reach and novel character of neo-liberal penality are deeply contested (see, *inter alia*, Daems 2008; Lacey 2010; Cheliotis and Xenakis 2010; Nelken 2010; Newburn 2010). Vivid, illuminating and eloquent as his work is in tracing historical and empirical connections from slavery, the Jim Crow system and the US urban ghettos, generalizing his account across the Atlantic, Wacquant has struggled to accommodate the diversity of penal experience, the specificities of ethnicity and differences of historical and local conditions. For Stuart Hall (1980: 342) the imperative has always been to analyse specific re-workings of race that account for its contradictory forms, and accommodate the vagaries of resistance to it. As he warned in 1980, '[a]ny attempt to delineate the politics and ideologies of racism which omit these continuing features of struggle and contradictions win an apparent adequacy of explanation only by operating a disabling reductionism'.

US and them: eclipses and ellipsis

Each of Wacquant's energizing contributions to penal scholarship has established itself as a landmark publication, prompting academic symposia to be convened and special issues of journals to be compiled. As he embarked on this trajectory in 2002, he wrote a compelling account of his brief visit to Los Angeles County Jail. Published in the journal *Ethnography*, it conveys his sense of horror and outrage at what he witnessed there, and his concern that as carceral populations have inflated in the USA, they have been accompanied by an alarming deflation in qualitative studies of prisoners' lives. With many of the foundational texts of prison sociology emerging from the rich traditions of ethnographic and qualitative research in the USA of the 1950s and 1960s, this decline is cruelly ironic.

Detailed and descriptively rich accounts provided by sociologists and anthropologists offer the means to identify 'linkages between the prison and its surrounding institutions on the ground, as they actually exist and operate, rather than from afar and above' (Wacquant 2002b: 387). However, while the 'curious eclipse of prison ethnography' may be casting a disabling shadow over North America, it has not prevented Wacquant from extending his analysis and moving beyond it. As Wacquant acknowledges, the last decade in the UK has hosted a thriving prison research community, and one that is keen to qualify and critique the reach and purchase of his analytical project. However, it is surprising given the central and recurring position of race in Wacquant's literature, and the rising levels of ethnic disproportionality in UK prison populations, that a detailed and sustained engagement with race and ethnicity in England and other UK jurisdictions has been more the exception than the rule in these responses.

A contrasting UK penal perspective on the ways in which a 21st-century neo-liberal State is becoming almost obsessively involved in the micromanagement of everyday life can be found in Crewe's (2009) detailed study of prisoner society. More modest in scope than Wacquant, Crewe's prison ethnography provides an exceptionally thorough, rich and vivid account of men's lives in an English prison. He reports relations between black prisoners and other groups as being 'neither tense nor entirely harmonious' (ibid.: 354), but declines to provide a contextualizing theoretical framework for the discussion of ethnicity or the salience of race, around which the otherwise insightful account of friendship and social relations between prisoners might be placed. In Crewe's (ibid.: 365) study, 'racial, religious and ethnic relations were subtexts rather than organising features of the social world' of Wellingborough Prison. He distinguishes this low-key state of ethnicity in the prison's social relations from the more determining role it appears to occupy in

North America. 'The fragile calm' (ibid.: 354) that Crewe reports between prisoners implicitly indicates an alternative state of ethnic affairs. White prisoners referred to this with 'hyperbolic' allusion to 'race wars' simmering below the surface: 'There is always an undercurrent of racism in prison', according to one of Crewe's (ibid.: 354) white respondents. As others have reported (Genders and Player 1989; Edgar and Martin 2004), 'the spectre of race' (Crewe 2009: 355) haunts the 'constrained conviviality' of prison life (Earle and Phillips 2009). The easing and tightening of social relations along the axis of ethnicity flexes with the violence of race. That race is never entirely exorcised, that its presence is simultaneously peripheral and central, ephemeral and material, challenges our theoretical constructs.

Crewe's broader argument is that the conventionally steep hierarchies of prison authority that once generated lateral solidarities among prisoners have been largely superseded by a more pervasive and diffuse 'neo-paternalism'. Within these restructured relations ethnic difference sometimes appeared to operate as a proxy for explicit resistance to institutional control because prisoners found they could exploit its unsettling presence. Ethnic difference troubled management, individual prison officers (mostly white) and white prisoners. This troubling presence was further emphasized by widespread talk among prisoners and prison officers of 'the race card'.

'The race card' has become a popular but oblique vernacular for what Phillips (2008) refers to as the 'difficult terrain' of negotiating race in late modern contexts. Though it first started to appear in the anti-racist literature of the 1980s (Miles 1993), 'the race card' is now a well-established signifier, a form of short-hand, to a particular 'subtext' that has emerged in British political life since the term 'institutional racism' was used by Lord Macpherson in his report on the police investigation of the murder of the black teenager Stephen Lawrence. 'The race card' corresponds to, and has become synonymous with, what Lentin and Titley (2010) describe as 'the crises of multiculturalism'.

Rather than investing further in the wider politics of race and against the trend of Wacquant's grand theoretical sweep, Crewe's account provides nuanced perspectives on the micropolitics of prison orders that are continually in flux; maintained, resisted and reconciled around the respective, but relatively narrower, agendas, interests and biographies of prisoners, prison officers and particular prison regimes. Crewe's (2009) focus is on the 'internal dynamics' of the reinvention of prison, those features that are 'shaped but not fully determined by [the] macro-social change' (ibid.: 20) that preoccupies Wacquant. Concentrating on prisoner adaptation to new forms of 'soft power', Crewe resists generalization: 'There is no simple model of prisonization'; 'This is just one study and just one prison'. Ethnicity and racism are present and acknowledged, but their articulation, *their relation of linkage and affectivity*, to wider society is restrained.

Race and prison multicultures

For a more detailed exploration of the place ethnicity and race occupy in the contemporary penal landscape of the UK it is necessary to turn to Phillips's (2012) ethnographic study of the multicultural prison. Phillips fully situates her study in the transformations of institutional and political management that occurred during the New Labour government (1997–2010). The Macpherson Report's (1999) identification of 'institutional racism' propelled a remarkable series of reforms to anti-discrimination legislation and policy (see Ahmed 2007; and Wrench 2005, for a critical commentary). Macpherson's exposure of institutional racism, and the report's adoption of a terminology first coined by the American Black Panthers in the 1960s, put racism and anti-racism firmly on the agenda.

Widely recognized as a significant watershed, the Labour government's acceptance of Macpherson's report resulted in the ground-breaking Race Relations Amendment Act 2000, which established a positive legal duty to 'promote good relations between people of different racial groups'. The impetus provided by Macpherson was further propelled by wider exposure of the racist treatment of Claude Johnson, a black prison officer in HMP Brixton. A series of positive findings in Johnson's favour by employment tribunals in 1995, 1996 and 2000 combined with reports of racist brutality in three prisons to prompt the Commission for Racial Equality (CRE) into mounting a formal investigation into Her Majesty's Prison Service (HMPS). As it launched its inquiry in 2000, a young British Pakistani prisoner, Zahid Mubarek, was battered to death by his white cell mate in a racially motivated attack in Feltham Young Offender Institution (YOI). A public inquiry into Zahid Mubarek's murder, led by Lord Keith, reported in 2006, while the CRE findings were published in two long reports with damning conclusions (CRE 2003a, 2003b; see also Keith 2006). They documented 14 areas of specific failure, which included poor institutional practices that negatively affected minority ethnic prisoners' treatment, access to goods, services and facilities, and experiences of the complaints system.

In response, HMPS, in conjunction with the CRE, developed a detailed action plan to respond to these widespread, large-scale problems. It was underpinned by an approach to managing race equality through high-level management structures, a Prison Service Standard on race equality, and the development of a comprehensive ethnic monitoring tool, the Systematic Monitoring and Analysing of Race Equality Template (SMART) (NOMS 2008). The SMART system allows for the continuous monitoring of decision making and service delivery. With this system in place, any disproportionate variance by ethnic group in any monitored prison procedure signals the possibilities of discrimination. This variance is highlighted in a consequential gravity scale (green/orange/red), which must be then subject to further investigation.

The profiles accorded to these, and other, legislative and cultural manifestations of the movement towards equality, or against discrimination and prejudice, are quite commonly caricatured in popular culture and elsewhere, as being aspects of 'political correctness', i.e. a managerial mantra devoid of proper meaning and ripe for ridicule. The 'race card' alluded to by Crewe's respondents refers both to this sense of active deployment and to the genuine power play that defines race's presence in social relations (for examples, see Phillips and Earle 2012).

As Phillips's (2012) insightful summary of the pre-existing research literature on race and prison makes clear, despite the persistence of disparities, disproportionalities and negative experience, very little of the research literature addresses the lived realities of race, racism and ethnicities among prisoners themselves:

> The primary focus of race equality research and policy has been to produce more positive and less discriminatory vertical relations between prison officers and prisoners which are of course of profound importance but less attention has been paid to horizontal relations in the prison milieu.
>
> (Phillips 2012: 46)

The experiential dimensions of what Goodman (2008: 740) calls the woeful neglect of 'the construction of race in carceral facilities' provides Phillips with the opening for her examination of the 'ways ethnic identities [are] articulated in prison social relations in England'.

Racism and cosmopenalism beyond the boundaries of the English metropol

At the time of Phillips's study in two men's prisons in Kent, south-east England (2006– 08), 27% of male prisoners in England and Wales were of minority ethnic origin and 15% were foreign nationals (Ministry of Justice 2007). HMP Maidstone and HMYOI Rochester were selected to reflect this because they had an ethnically mixed population of prisoners from both urban and semi-rural settings. Each of the prisons held approximately 400 men, mostly convicted in the Greater London area courts. In these London courts, minority ethnic men were heavily over-represented (Phillips 2012). The two prisons also received men from courts, or other prisons, in the neighbouring counties of Kent, Essex and Sussex, where white ethnicities predominate.

Phillips (2012) reveals a complex and contradictory picture of social relations among prisoners in which ethnic differences were frequently seen as quite an ordinary and unremarkable aspect of men's lives, both inside and outside the prison. Black and minority ethnic men tended to have more established senses of ethnic identity, sometimes expressed through styles of hair care, idioms of speech, modes of greeting, social interaction and ways of wearing prison-issue clothes. Trousers, for example, worn beltless and low over the backside represented an ironic transatlantic echo of young men's street fashions that draw from the iconography of US prison dress codes (the enforced removal of trouser belts to prevent them from being used in prison suicides resulted in such low-slung, apparently ill-fitting habits of dress). Some white prisoners also felt comfortable with such stylings, but for others they seemed defiant of convention and were resented. However, many white and ethnic minority prisoners preferred to ignore ethnic differences and focus on a sense of 'common humanity' in which differences of skin colour and culture were dismissed in favour of a kind of dissolute, egalitarian prison humanism.

Some prisoners talked about ethnicity and race relations as being like an ill-fitting category into which they were invited to place themselves, mainly for the purposes of being counted. Adam, for example, described feeling 'forced to fit into an ethnic group', while seeing himself as white Scottish and most definitely not white British. Similarly, Nathan, a white British Maidstone prisoner insisted that, 'I'm a person, you know what I mean, I'm not a fucking sheep, I'm not a breed of sheep, I'm a person'. He went on to admit regularly refusing to identify his ethnic origin, feeling that the world had gone 'PC [politically correct] mad'. Barry, another white prisoner in Maidstone, also resented the prison's monitoring of his ethnicity by emphasizing the contradiction in society urging its members to be colour-blind while also investing so heavily in recording prisoners' 'ethnic codes' (see Earle 2014 for a more detailed account of Barry's perspectives).

When asked directly about inter-ethnic interaction, many of the men in prison described a process of informal separation and clustering, although it was usually emphasized that this loose gathering was not heavily marked or stressed by aggravation and antagonism. As in Crewe's study, a common first reaction to the research project's interest in ethnicity and social relations between prisoners was for prisoners to remark on the banality of ethnic grouping in the prison: 'The Asians keep to themselves, the blacks to themselves and the whites too. Just simple. I don't know why but that is how it is' (unrecorded conversation, field note, RE – August 2006).[3] Although prisoners initially referred to the existence of loose separation, involving 'black', 'white', 'Asian', Muslim and foreign national groupings, the fieldwork and in-depth interviews indicated that these groupings and associations between prisoners were not rigidly fixed and were only rarely actively exclusive. Hence, while prisoner groupings appeared to have a low-key ethnic component, this was just part of the story, a part that receded when it was discussed more extensively in interview.

A notable finding of Phillips's study is the extent to which overt or explicit racism was suppressed within the prisoner's social relations. While there appeared to be a general acceptance of the simple facts of ethnic diversity and grouping, the opposite was the case in respect of overt racism. Racism of this kind was widely regarded as totally unacceptable. Prisoners acting in an explicitly racist manner risked considerably more than disapproval from other inmates, both black and white. Prisoners referred to an informal code in which racist behaviour could expect to be met with violent retaliation. For example, the researchers were told of some specific examples where such action had been taken, usually, but not always, by black prisoners, and there appeared to be widespread acceptance of the legitimacy of this kind of behaviour. This suggested a consensus against explicit racism, and the legitimacy of punishment for any inmate identified as 'being a racist' (see Earle and Phillips 2015). This consensus went so far as to be included and exploited, instrumentally, in the informal sanctions inmates used against each other. Michael at HMYOI Rochester told Phillips: 'Say I wanted you kicked in. I'd say to a black feller, "Look he's a racist, him, he's telling me you're a monkey and all that", and you'd get your head kicked in'.

The stigmatization of racism had acquired a kind of dual currency within the prison, part of both its informal and formal structures of social control. While the prison administration's SMART system monitored and coded officer decisions and prison procedures, prisoners themselves operated a variety of constraints against explicit racism. Prisoners' policing of racism co-existed with the high-profile diversity policy of the prison but was quite distinct from it.

Hiding in the white

However, this did not mean that the prisons in Phillips's study were free of tension, fear or anxiety around the questions of race and ethnicity. In the privacy of interviews with the white researcher (myself), white inmates divulged more traditional narratives of white superiority. Some, for example, expressed their irritation with the linguistic styles and expressive vernaculars of minority ethnic inmates, objecting to the way spoken English was changing to include the phrasing and terminology of minority ethnic communities, such as the Jamaican patois greeting 'Wha' Gwaan' or 'Hey, Blood'.

For white prisoners, racism remained a potent but less fully available resource, because the sanctions against it (both informal and formal) meant that it was indulged mainly in private. Public expressions of racist sentiments or slang were used sparingly and rarely in 'mixed company'. Nevertheless, Phillips (2012) provides further evidence of the common use of racist language and of the existence of racist hostility (see Wilson 2003).

White prisoners gave voice to suppressed sentiments of racialized antagonism by using terms such as 'the niggers', 'black pricks', 'Pakis', in several interviews conducted by the white interviewer. Moreover, the comments of some white foreign nationals, who passed as 'white' but did not necessarily share the British national vision of racial superiority, were particularly illuminating. One white foreign national prisoner commented to Phillips, who is mixed race:

> There are a few prisoners, there are some English that live around Kent, around here, they're saying they don't like refugees, like black people, stuff like that. They don't really like us. I am white and when I'm with them I can see, they say like 'Oh fuck the black fucking …', you know, 'look at the niggers', stuff like that.

In many of the accounts of white British prisoners, ethnicity was regarded as something suspiciously prescriptive, and was actively disavowed. This is consistent with much of the empirical and theoretical work on the perceived normative character of whiteness where white ethnicities are invisible, denied or regarded as devoid of ethnic content (Nayak 2005; Garner 2007). White British ethnicities had an evacuated, vacant quality. It was as if whiteness could only be aligned with images of Empire, sources of privilege and positions of superiority, and were thus particularly ill fitting in the prison. The powers of whiteness to which they turned in private, behind prison doors and in white company, were those of an exclusive, nostalgic national belonging and the desire to exclude. In prison, as elsewhere, these besieged and resentful white British ethnicities stand in stark contrast to 'culture-rich' black and Asian ethnicities (see Ray et al. 2004; Gilroy 2005; Earle and Phillips 2015).

Many responses from white British national prisoners to questions about ethnicity in Phillips's study were consistent with Nayak's (2003: 173) view of whiteness as '*the ethnicity that is not one*'. The prison context, where there are powerful explicit and implicit institutional efforts to mould conforming and compliant identities, intensifies the ways in which talk of ethnicity conveys a sense of being constructed by others, of being objectified and being seen as 'something' rather than 'someone'. Slowly, however, as the parameters of whiteness enter the structured domain of ethnicity, white people are beginning to encounter this exteriority, sense the implications of visibility and better appreciate the epistemic violence of race (Macey 1999).

As in Crewe's (2009) study of a Midlands prison, although there appeared to be a durable, consensual and stable 'surface' equanimity amongst an ethnically diverse prisoner population, this was relatively thin, concealing the persistence of submerged racialized tensions. One of the most common ways white prisoners vented these tensions and anxieties was through the vocabulary of racialized victimization, arguing that they suffered as a consequence of both the prejudice of black inmates and the existence of double standards in the recognition of what constituted 'racism'. Indeed, the idea of 'reverse racism' was not uncommon among white prisoners. As Barry put it in Phillips's (2012: 119) study:

> the West Indians are a minority obviously, but they're one of the bigger minorities, they are very strong, they're not afraid to have a fight because they pull the race card straight away. If you hit a black guy, you'll get shipped off the wing because you've assaulted him in a racist manner. That's the way it always goes. It's reverse racism.

The idea of reverse racism operates an understanding of racism as if it were an unfortunate symmetry that can be simply flipped from one way round to another. It is a conceptualization of racism ridiculed to comic effect by the Melbourne-based comedian Aamer Rahman in a routine that became an Internet viral phenomenon in 2014.[4] In it he describes how some people say his jokes about white people are a kind of racism, 'reverse racism'. Aamer explains that for him to be a reverse racist, he would need 'a time machine to go back in time before Europe colonized the world' so that he could convince the leaders of Africa, Asia, the Middle East and South America to invade and colonize Europe, steal their land and resources, set up a trans-Asian slave trade to export white people to work on rice plantations in China, ruin Europe and establish a system that 'privileged black and brown people at every conceivable political and economic opportunity'. Then, if he were to get on stage and say, 'Hey, what's the deal with white people? Why can't they dance?', he would be demonstrating reverse racism. The point is that the historical legacies of racism have constructed enduring cultural and resource hierarchies on a planetary scale. The reduction of these structural hierarchies and their historical dimensions to a whimsical symmetry of personal affect where white people are made to feel uncomfortable, is literally laughable, but widespread, as Aamer's comic routine extols to good effect.

In prison white men's ambivalence towards a racializing discourse comes across strongly in both Crewe's (2009) and Phillips's (2012) research. It may be based on a genuine uncertainty about its potential benefits and anxiety about a way of talking about 'race' that puts them in a picture where they do not feel they belong. Foucault (1979) argues that visibility is often 'a trap', the opening of a new disciplinary discourse by the identification of a categorical object, and being seen as 'white' is challenging for prisoners when the traditional comforts of whiteness are invisibility; privilege, not discipline.

Statecraft, racecraft, whiteness and multiculturalism

In both Crewe's and Phillips's prisons the struggle over multiculture is a struggle over the meanings of difference and their futures, as it is elsewhere in society. Since the landmark Macpherson Inquiry, and CRE reports that followed the murder of Zahid Mubarek (CRE 2003a, 2003b), the whole criminal justice system, and specifically HMPS, has been at the forefront of a certain kind of multiculturalism (Earle 2011). This struggle requires sustained critical scrutiny because of the symbolic importance of the institutions of criminal justice in the politics of race (Gilroy 1987; Solomos 1993) and their unprecedented power to impact so heavily on people's lives.

Phillips describes in meticulous detail how multicultural realities generate complex and fluctuating patterns of racialization. In the multicultural prison 'race' was everywhere and nowhere, something and nothing. It could surface in any institutional interaction and also had a spectral presence in less formal relations between people, where it flitted into and out of view. In this context, prison administrators expend considerable efforts to address the stubborn persistence of both empirical and anecdotal evidence of racial disparities, racial prejudice and discrimination in formal and informal interactions between prison officers and prisoners, and between prisoners themselves.

This explicit management of multicultural realities is characterized, and sometimes dismissed, as 'multiculturalism', a set of policies and procedures designed to challenge prejudice and discrimination, but Phillips's study provides insights into what it means to prisoners. It explores the daily negotiation of ethnic difference as a form of micro-politics where everyday and mostly unavoidable social contact among a diverse population is routine. Phillips's study reveals a politics in which there is a strange kind of reversal of the sociological wisdom 'that if men define situations as real, they are real in their effects' (Thomas and Thomas 1928: 572; see Merton 1995). Many prisoners and prison officers defined race as unreal so as to deny the reality of its effects, but the results haunted them.

Almost nobody believes in 'race', or at least explicitly states that they do, but middle-class white people are more likely to think of 'race' in abstract terms as a kind of intellectual unicorn that has now wandered off-stage into some kind of harmless never-land. In this post-racial schema 'race' does not exist, so neither does its history or any material effects. This disavowal of the existence of race is a recurring and defining feature of contemporary white identities (Garner 2007). Frankenberg (1993) analyses the way white people adopt a kind of wilful 'colour-blindness' by asserting themselves to be oblivious of 'race'. This 'blindness' is less an issue of chromatic discernment than a desire for virtue. As Frankenberg (ibid.: 145) points out, for a white person 'to be caught in the act of seeing race [is] to be caught being prejudiced'. Ironically, being 'free' of the stain of racism involves presenting oneself as 'whiter than white', spotless. It is such unhelpful polarization that is the stock-in-trade of racism, and sometimes, anti-racism.

For people whose experience of racism has been more direct, the effects of 'race' are continuous and continuing, changing and shifting but most definitely real and present, despite the exaggerated reports of its apparent demise. The disproportionate number of black people in prison, or excluded from schools, or employment and their under-representation in positions of power and influence attest to the dynamics of exclusion. This enigma of the persistent presence of the effects of 'race' without 'race' presents a considerable intellectual and political challenge. It is a challenge the multicultural prison reflects in its efforts to accommodate diverse and diversifying people that are not pulled behind its wire fences at random. In the multicultural prison, questions of Britain's cultural identities are played out with vigour and force, condensed as they are by the heavily managed proximities of prison life. Prisons rehearse, in simplistic miniature, the mechanics of statecraft whether it be the fair allocation of resources, the defence of borders or the organization of space and movement. In governing the unruly bodies and artificial spaces of the multicultural prison, prison officers and prisoners are locked into a very human encounter with the legacies and actualities of 'race'; not as a fixed and timeless biological essence, but as a struggle with a history, a present and a future.

The irrelevance of the social scientific truth that there are no races may be glimpsed by reference to feminist theory. Feminist theory distinguishes the ahistorical biological fact of anatomical difference, sex, from the social historicity of gender. Feminist theory, however, does not insist that because gender is socially constructed it is meaningless, but invests heavily in its experiential and ontological dimensions. Feminist critique has traced the way power differentials shape gender rather than cancel it. In this context, the oft-repeated statement that races do not exist, what Lentin and Titley (2010) refer to as 'the primary recited truth' of a bogus multiculturalism, can be recognized as an invitation to see the privileges of whiteness vanish in a post-racial puff of smoke.

The alibi of biological sex that feminism contests so productively and effectively has no semantic equivalence in phenotype when it comes to race. As the biologism of race has been historicized and discredited it has been substituted with what Anthias (2013: 324) refers to as 'the culturalization of social relationships'. Nowhere is this more obvious, in prison and elsewhere, than in the way ideas about essentialist identities and radical, irreconcilable otherness appear to be settling on Muslim populations, rendering them at a collective and personal level, 'the new blacks' (Earle and Phillips 2013).

Muslim is the new black

A Muslim presence in both Crewe's and Phillips's studies was widely recognized as significant and was prone to stereotypical simplification. Jed, for example, a white British prisoner in Maidstone with no declared religious affiliation, was convinced that 'Muslims are the most powerful group apart from officers'. Another insisted that Muslims could 'manipulate things for their own ends'. The image of a unitary, cohesive and separate block of Muslim prisoners tended to be expressed more vehemently by non-Muslims and prisoners of the white majority. The image did not correspond to the interview and observational data in Phillips's study, which indicated diverse Muslim identities and religious observance that varied considerably according to age and ethnicity. For some prisoners, the replacement of one racialized 'other' with another was almost self-evident. A young white British prisoner at Rochester glossed his account with elements of a 'harmony discourse' where blacks and whites could get along fine now, whereas relations between 'Muslims and white people' in the prison simply reflected the new divisions outside it (see Earle and Phillips 2009, 2013; HMIP 2010):

> I think it's sort of where black and whites, they get on fine. I'm saying controversial things here, but black and white people get on a lot better than Muslims and white people, because obviously what's happening all over the world and in the news, people see it, they can't get away from it. They see it in the newspapers when they read them, on the TV, everywhere, so gradually there's a big divide coming down between them.

Liebling et al.'s (2011) study of an English maximum security prison for men revealed prison staff to be struggling to accommodate and manage a growing proportion of Muslim prisoners. Complex tensions were generated by overlapping issues of political extremism, religious fundamentalism, 'radicalization' and conversion to Islam. Liebling et al. report on how the whole prison and all prisoners had been affected by these developments, and the challenge they pose to the prison's 'moral performance'. Islamic identities provided prisoners with resources and hope of a better life, but on terms that challenged the prison's aspirations for both rehabilitation and peaceful containment.

In the USA, Islam has historical permutations that connect it with the civil rights movement, black nationalism and prison life. The extent and distinctive character of concern about Islam in the USA can be gauged from a 2010 poll that revealed nearly a quarter of Americans continue to believe that their president, Barack Obama, is a Muslim, and that this proportion rises to 40% among registered Republicans, and more than 60% among self-disclosed Tea Party members (Aslan 2011; see also Parlett 2014).

Decades of Islamic outreach work in US prisons have not only shaped prison law and policy through proactive litigation in defence of prisoners' rights, but they have offered sustained solace and comfort to prisoners. Hamm (2009) criticizes the prevailing rhetoric around 'radicalization' for reducing the complex presence of Islam in America's prisons to a single, simple threat. Islam *is* the fastest growing faith tradition in US prisons

(Pew 2012), but the relationship between this growth and political violence is deeply contested. As elsewhere, Islamic traditions of peace and non-violence with a long-standing and empirically supported record of prisoner rehabilitation are suppressed under the weight of misinformed fears about the growth of Islam (Aslan 2011).

The resurgence of Islam in the West, and for the West, is not a myth and nor is it reducible to the simplistic appeals of fundamentalism. By challenging contemporary trends against essentialism and toward relativism, Islam appears to threaten the intellectual and cultural elites of Western society. Because the perceived threat thus extends upwards beyond the usual suspects and 'disposable' populations of the working class, the cultural racism of Islamophobia is particularly venomous and constitutes a uniquely challenging configuration (Modood 1997; Said 1995; Werbner 2012). Islam, in the racist imaginary, questions the very identity of Europe and the pre-eminent position of the Enlightenment in global history. Rampant Islam, thus represented, is colonialism's worst nightmare because it has the same global ambitions but has stolen its hopes and contests its grip on history (Sayyidd 2003). It is colonialism's mirror image and all the more ter-rifying for being so fearfully repressed (cf. Fanon 2001). In contemporary manifestations 'the Muslim' has come to symbolize 'aggressive religiosity' and the 'threat of death', which were once the exclusive preserve of 'the black' in the racial imaginary (Goldberg 2009).

The recognition among prisoners, both black and white, of the correspondence between the new racisms and the old has profound implications for those concerned about the living conditions of black and minority ethnic prisoners, and the multicultural societies that so disproportionately fill their prisons with such people. It suggests that taking the concept of ethnicity further, and making it do work other than racism's, remains work undone. According to Hall (1992: 257), it is work that will define the 21st century and involves 'retheorizing the concept of difference'.

Prisoners in Phillips's and Crewe's studies often testified to the alchemical, ambivalent qualities of 'race' and their feel for its crafting (Fields and Fields 2012). They find some resources to resist the pull of 'race' in prisoners' traditional refusal to be reduced to a mere number, or to be held as less than human. In prison there is a discernible affinity between the work that prison does and the work that 'race' does which prompts this resistance: both rely on exclusion, inferiorization, subordination and exploitation (Anthias and Yuval-Davis 1993), and prison, as Foucault (1979) points out, always 'continues a work begun elsewhere'.

Prisoners, ghosts and the return of the uncivil dead: spectres of race

> Racist implications linger, silenced but assumed, always already returned and haunting. Buried but alive.
>
> (Goldberg 2009: 152)

> How do you recognise a ghost? By the fact that it does not recognise itself in a mirror.
>
> (Derrida 1994: ii)

Prison, as is widely acknowledged, imposes a form of civil death (Gordon 2010). Where the death penalty is not in use, it is the ultimate sanction, and a form of punishment that takes a life out of civil circulation in precise increments and proportions. The imprisoned are intended to haunt society by their non-presence. They are buried but alive.

In 2014 26% of the adult prison population of England and Wales (21,769 people) was from an ethnic minority, i.e. approximately one in four, in contrast to their proportion in the general population of one in ten (Prison Reform Trust 2014). In England and Wales just over two-thirds of the children in custody were from black and minority ethnic backgrounds (ibid.). Meanwhile, for every African-Caribbean male undergraduate at a Russell Group university,[5] there are three African-Caribbean men aged 18–24 in prison. In this age group, 7% of the prison population is made up of African-Caribbean men, but they constitute only 0.1% of the undergraduate population of Russell Group universities (Sviensson 2012). The uplift provided by a university degree in terms of future earnings and social status is widely recognized. The lockdown that a prison sentence provides in terms of social and spatial mobility is also widely recognized in the research literature, if somewhat less well appreciated outside academic criminology. With the former you emerge with a qualification to rise up the social hierarchy (or – more likely – secure your already elevated position in it); from the latter you receive a prison record that permanently qualifies your right to belong, to work and to travel. You leave prison with negative credentials pre-loaded with stigma, fear and ignorance. The under-representation of black and other ethnic minorities in the elite university system should be a scandal in its own right; their massive over-representation in the prison system a source of outrage.

Hall (1989: 133) noted that the least remarked upon source of neo-liberalism's strength as a political project is the powerful, enduring and effective influence of cultural racism. In his subsequent work Hall identified 'new ethnicities' as disruptive to the essentializing tendencies of cultural racism. For Hall the implications of embracing new ethnicities are profound because it potentially involves exchanging the bogus guarantees of biology and the alibi of national culture for the uncertain contingencies of attachment 'to particular communities, localities, territories, languages, religions or cultures'. The 'new ethnicities' paradigm is no simple replacement discourse that falls off an academic shelf and into place in cultural life. It is not a set of nice ideas about diversity; it is a struggle 'for position' in, and for, a more equitable and egalitarian future that involves everyone, rather than one that secures the position of those who have risen to the top. It demands that majority and privileged populations 'recognise that what they have to say comes out of particular histories and cultures' (ibid.: 133). Aamer Rahman's imaginary time machine is not there to sweep us back in history and reverse racism; there is only time's arrow arcing forwards, inviting us to bend it, as Martin Luther King said, towards justice and freedom.

Arjun Appadurai (2006) argues that as ethnic minorities have secured a post-colonial presence in Western nation-states, those states have developed greater ambivalence towards them. With the accelerating momentum of globalization and increasing flows of migration, their minority-ness becomes more qualified, threateningly suggestive of majority-ness. Under these circumstances 'the prison' starts to look like an emblematic form of the nation-state, a state in highly managed miniature (Bauman 1993). In Phillips's (2012) study of the modern multicultural prison, the strategies of the powerful – the institutionalization of ethnicity which seeks to mark out and monitor trajectories of prejudice in individual and collective actions – meet the tactics of the weak, the reluctance of ordinary people to be labelled by remote authorities. Both are intensified by felt histories of class and race. The resistance generates a brittle conviviality: fraught and constrained, creative and conflicted because prison, for prisoners, is a kind of involuntary and coercive commune where ideas about sociality, race and identity are inevitably played out through the lives of those sent there for punishment.

Condemned, symbolically, to life without life, the structured constraints of prison life show some of what is hidden in wider society. As Gordon (2008) suggests, when the dead speak to the living, the experience is a haunting one, giving notice that something is missing. Prisons reveal the ghostly and unsettling presence of racialized injustice and should prick our conscience. As both Toni Morrison (1987) and Jacques Derrida (1994) suggest, talking to the ghost rather than denying it is there is a good place to begin. Wacquant's warning about the dangers of an ethnographic eclipse in prison research are answered by Crewe's and Phillips's detailed studies that endow the field with resources to address the 'complex unities structured in dominance' to which Hall attends. Wacquant's (*op. cit.*) insistence on the salience of race to penal inflation and neo-liberal expansion trips up on the diversity and specificity of the New Times described by Hall (1989), but his active resistance to the growing silence around race is significant. The desire to bury race without proper decommissioning creates unruly and frightening ghosts. It flourishes in the absence of any serious militancy concerning racial injustice and it neglects the new politics of ethnicity that Stuart Hall (ibid.) advocated, a politics aligned 'with that immense process of historical relativisation which is just beginning to make the British, at least, feel just marginally marginal' (Hall 1987: 46). It is well past time to join that beginning, but never too late.

Notes

1 The author acknowledges helpful discussion with Coretta Phillips in developing this chapter and the constructive comments of Ben Crewe on various drafts.
2 I have published articles with Phillips on this study and was the co-investigator.
3 As the second researcher on the project, I refer here to my field notes.
4 See www.youtube.com/watch?v=LsbbmdGrcI0&feature=kp.
5 The Russell Group of universities in the UK is an association set up in 1994 to represent the interests of universities 'which are committed to maintaining the very best research, an outstanding teaching and learning experience and unrivalled links with business and the public sector' (RG website, 2014). There are currently 24 universities included in the Russell Group.

Bibliography

Ahmed, S. (2007) 'The language of diversity', *Ethnic and Racial Studies* 30: 235–256.
Alexander, M. (2012) *The New Jim Crow: Mass incarceration in the age of colourblindness*, New York: The New Press.
Anthias, F. (2013) 'Moving beyond the Janus face of integration and diversity discourses: Towards an intersectional framing', *The Sociological Review* 61: 323–343.
Anthias, F. and Yuval-Davis, N. (1993) *Racialized Boundaries: Race, nation, gender, colour and class and the anti-racist struggle*, London: Routledge.
Appadurai, A. (2006) *Fear of Small Numbers: An essay on the geography of anger*, Durham, NC: Duke University Press.
Aslan, R. (2011) *No God But God: The origins, evolution and future of Islam*, London: Arrow.
Bauman, Z. (1993) *Postmodern Ethics*, Cambridge: Polity Press.

Cheliotis, L.K. and Xenakis, S. (2010) 'What's neoliberalism got to do with it? Towards a political economy of punishment in Greece', *Criminology and Criminal Justice* 10(4): 353–373.

CRE (Commission for Racial Equality) (2003a) *A Formal Investigation by the Commission for Racial Equality into HM Prison Service of England and Wales – Part 1: The murder of Zahid Mubarek*, London: Commission for Racial Equality.

CRE (Commission for Racial Equality) (2003b) *A Formal Investigation by the Commission for Racial Equality into HM Prison Service of England and Wales – Part 2: Racial equality in prisons*, London: Commission for Racial Equality.

Crewe, B. (2009) *The Prisoner Society: Power, Adaption and Social Life in an English Prison*, Oxford: Oxford University Press.

Daems, T. (2008) *Making Sense of Penal Change*, Oxford: Oxford University Press.

De Certeau, M. (1984) *The Practice of Everyday Life*, Berkeley: University of California Press.

Derrida, J. (1994) *Spectres of Marx: The state of the debt, the work of mourning and the new international*, New York: Routledge.

Drake, D., Earle, R. and Sloan, J. (2015, forthcoming) *The International Handbook of Prison Ethnography*, Basingstoke: Palgrave.

Earle, R. (2011) 'Ethnicity, multiculture and racism in a young offenders' institution', *The Prison Service Journal* 197: 32–38.

Earle, R. (2014) 'Inside white – racism, social relations and ethnicity in an English prison', in C. Phillips and C. Webster (eds) *New Directions in Race, Ethnicity and Crime*, London: Routledge.

Earle, R. and Phillips, C. (2009) 'Con-viviality and beyond: Identity dynamics in a young men's prison', in M. Wetherall (ed.) *Identity in the 21st Century: New Trends in Changing Times*, Basingstoke: Palgrave.

Earle, R. and Phillips, C. (2013) '"Muslim is the new black": New ethnicities and new essentialisms in the prison', *Race and Justice* 3(2): 114–129.

Earle, R. and Phillips, C. (2015) 'Prison ethnography at the threshold of race, reflexivity and difference', in D. Drake, R. Earle and J. Sloan (eds) *The International Handbook of Prison Ethnography*, Basingstoke: Palgrave.

Edgar, K. and Martin, C. (2004) *Perceptions of Race and Conflict: Perspectives of minority ethnic prisoners and of prison officers*, RDS Online Report11/04, London: Home Office.

Fanon, F. (2001 [1963]) *The Wretched of the Earth*, London: Penguin Books.

Fields, K. and Fields, B. (2012) *Racecraft: The soul of inequality in American life*, London: Verso.

Foucault, M. (1979) *Discipline and Punish: The birth of the prison*, Harmondsworth: Penguin.

Frankenberg, R. (1993) *White Women, Race Matters: The social construction of whiteness*, Minneapolis: University of Minnesota Press.

Garner, S. (2007) *Whiteness: An introduction*, London: Routledge.

Genders, E. and Player, E. (1989) *Race Relations in Prison*, Oxford: Clarendon Press.

Gilroy, P. (1987) *There Ain't no Black in the Union Jack*, London: Routledge.

Gilroy, P. (2000) *Between Camps: Nations, culture and the allure of race*, London: Allen Lane.

Gilroy, P. (2004) *After Empire – Melancholia or Convivial Culture*, Abingdon: Routledge.

Gilroy, P. (2005) 'Multiculture, double consciousness and the "war on terror"', *Patterns of Prejudice* 39(4): 431–443.

Goldberg, T. (2009) *The Threat of Race: Reflection on racial neoliberalism*, Oxford: Willey-Blackwell.

Goodman, P. (2008) '"It's just black, white or Hispanic?": An observational study of racialising moves in California's segregated prison reception centres', *Law and Society Review* 42(4): 735–770.

Gordon, A. (2008) *Ghostly Matters: Haunting and the sociological imagination*, Minneapolis, MN: University of Minnesota Press.

Gordon, A. (2010) 'The prisoner's curse', in H. Gray and M. Gomez-Barris (eds) *Toward a Sociology of the Trace*, Minneapolis, MN: University of Minnesota Press.

Hall, S. (1980) 'Race, articulation, and societies structured in dominance', in *Sociological Theories: Race and Colonialism*, Paris: UNESCO, 305–345.

Hall, S. (1987) 'Minimal selves', in H. Bhaba and L. Appignanesi (eds) *Identity: The Real Me*, London: Institute for Contemporary Arts.

Hall, S. (1989) 'The meaning of new times', in S. Hall and M. Jacques (eds) *New Times – The Changing Face of Politics in the 1990s*, London: Lawrence and Wishart.

Hall, S. (1992) 'New ethnicities', in J. Donald and A. Rattansi (eds) *'Race', Culture and Difference*, London: Sage.

Hall, S. (2003) '"In Europe but not of Europe": Europe and its myths', in L. Paserini (ed.) *Figures d'Europe: Images and Myths of Europe*, Brussels: Peter Lang.

Hamm, M. (2009) 'Prison Islam in the age of terror', *British Journal of Criminology* 49(5): 667–685.

HMIP (Her Majesty's Inspectorate of Prisons) (2010) *Muslim Prisoners' Experiences: A Thematic Review*, London: HMIP.

Jewkes, Y. (2013) 'What has prison ethnography to offer in an age of mass incarceration', *Criminal Justice Matters* 91(1).

Keith, B. (2006) *Report of the Zahid Mubarek Inquiry, HC 1082-I*, London: HMSO.

Lacey, N. (2010) 'Differentiating among penal states', *British Journal of Sociology* 61(4): 778–794.

Lentin, A. and Titley, G. (2010) *The Crises of Multiculturalism – Racism in a Neo-liberal Age*, London: Zed Press.

Liebling, A., Arnold, H. and Straub, C. (2011) *An Exploration of Staff–Prisoner Relationships at HMP Whitemoor: 12 Years On*, London: Ministry of Justice.

Macey, D. (1999) 'Fanon, phenomonology, race', *Radical Philosophy* 95: 8–14.

Macpherson, W. (1999) *The Stephen Lawrence Inquiry, Report of an Inquiry by Sir William Macpherson of Cluny, Cm 4262-1*, London: Home Office.

Merton, R. (1995) 'The Thomas theorem and the Matthew effect', *Social Forces* 74(2): 379–424.

Miles, R. (1993) *Racism after 'Race Relations'*, London: Routledge.

Ministry of Justice (2007) *Statistics on Race and the Criminal Justice System 2006*, London: Ministry of Justice.

Modood, T. (1997) 'Introduction: The politics of multiculturalism in the New Europe', in T. Modood and P. Werber (eds) *The Politics of Multiculturalism in the New Europe: Racism, Identity and Community*, London: Zed Books, 261–267.

Morrison, T. (1987) *Beloved*, London: Chatto and Windus.

Nayak, A. (2003) *Race, Place and Globalization: Youth cultures in a changing world*, Oxford: Berg.

Nayak, A. (2005) 'White lives', in K. Murji and J. Solomos (eds) *Racialization: Studies in theory and practice*, Oxford: Oxford University Press, 141–162.

Nelken, D. (2010) 'Denouncing the penal state', *Criminology and Criminal Justice* 10(4): 331–340.

Newburn, T. (2010) 'Diffusion, differentiation and resistance in comparative penality', *Criminology and Criminal Justice* 10(4): 341–352.

NOMS (National Offender Management Service) (2008) *Race Review 2008: Implementing race equality in prisons – five years on*, London: NOMS.

Parlett, M. (2014) *Demonizing a President: The 'foreignization' of Barack Obama*, Oxford: Praeger.

Pew Research Centre (2012) *Religion in Prisons: A 50-state survey of prison chaplains*, Washington, DC: Pew Research Centre.

Phillips, C. (2008) 'Negotiating identities: Ethnicity and social relations in a young offenders' institution', *Theoretical Criminology* 12(3): 313–331.

Phillips, C. (2012) *The Multicultural Prison: Ethnicity, masculinity and social relations among prisoners*, Oxford: Oxford University Press.

Phillips, C. and Earle, R. (2012) 'Cultural diversity, ethnicity and race relations in prison', in B. Crewe and J. Bennett (eds) *The Prisoner*, London: Routledge.

Prison Reform Trust (2014) *Bromley Briefings Prison Factfile, Summer 2014*, London: PRT.

Ray, L., Smith, D.A. and Wastell, L. (2004) 'Shame, rage and racist violence', *British Journal of Criminology* 44(3): 350–368.

Sabol, W.J., West, H.C. and Cooper, M. (2009) *Correctional Populations in the United States, 2008*, Washington, DC: US Department of Justice.

Said, E.W. (1995 [1978]) *Orientalism*, London: Penguin Books.

Sayyidd, S. (2003) *A Fundamental Fear: Eurocentrism and the Emergence of Islam*, London: Zed Books.

Solomos, J. (1993) 'Constructions of black criminality: Racialisation and criminalisation in perspective', in D. Cook and B. Hudson (eds) *Racism and Criminology*, London: Sage.

Squires, P. and Lea, J. (eds) (2013) *Criminalisation and Advanced Marginality: Critically Exploring the Work of Loic Wacquant*, Bristol: Policy Press.

Sviensson, K.P. (2012) 'Introduction', in K.P. Sveinson (ed.) *Criminal Justice v Racial Justice: Minority Ethnic Overrepresentation in the Criminal Justice System*, London: Runnymede Trust.

Sykes, G. (1958) *The Society of Captives: A Study of a Maximum Security Prison*, Princeton, NJ: Princeton University Press.

Thomas, W.I. and Thomas, D.S. (1928) *The Child in America: Behavior Problems and Programs*, Boston, MA: Knopf.

US Census Bureau (2005) 'Population profile of the United States: Dynamic version – race and Hispanic origin in 2005', www.census.gov/population/pop-profile/dynamic/RACEHO.pdf.

Wacquant, L. (2002a) 'From slavery to mass incarceration: Rethinking the "race question" in the US', *New Left Review* 13(1): 41–60.

Wacquant, L. (2002b) 'The curious eclipse of prison ethnography in the age of mass incarceration', *Ethnography* 3(4): 371–398.

Wacquant, L. (2007) *Urban Outcasts: A comparative sociology of advanced marginality*, Cambridge: Polity.

Wacquant, L. (2009a) *Punishing the Poor*, Durham, NC: Duke University Press.

Wacquant, L. (2009b) *Prisons of Poverty*, Minneapolis, MN: University of Minnesota Press.

Wacquant, L. (2010) 'Class, race & hyperincarceration in revanchist America', *Daedalus* (Summer): 74.

Wacquant, L. (2013) 'Marginality, ethnicity and penality in the neoliberal city: An analytic cartography', loicwacquant.net/assets/Papers/MARGINALITYETHNICITYPENALITY-Article-ERS.pdf (accessed 22 January 2014).

Wacquant, L. (forthcoming) *Deadly Symbiosis: Race and the rise of the penal state*, Cambridge: Polity.

Werbner, P. (2012) 'Folk devils and racist imaginaries in a global prism: Islamophobia and anti-Semitism in the twenty-first century', *Ethnic and Racial Studies* 36: 450–467.

Wilson, D. (2003) '"Keeping quiet" or "going nuts": Some emerging strategies used by young black people in custody at a time of childhood being re-constructed', *Howard Journal of Criminal Justice* 42(5): 411–425.

Wrench, J. (2005) 'Diversity management can be bad for you', *Race & Class* 46: 73–84.

Chapter 33

The prisoner

Inside and out

Jason Warr

> The Prisoner looks to liberty as an immediate return to all his ancient energy, quickened into more vital forces by long disuse. When he goes out, he finds he still has to suffer. His punishment, as far as its effects go, lasts intellectually and physically, just as it lasts socially. He still has to pay. One gets no receipt for the past when one walks out into the beautiful air.
>
> (Oscar Wilde – *Letter to Frank Harris*, in Conrad 2006: 174)

There is a peculiarity to prisons in England and Wales. They occupy a space in the collective conscience of politicians, the public and academics to varying degrees, yet this is an abstract space, a space with little or no corporeal content. Without first-hand experience the information that people have about prison, its practices and effects, is filtered through agenda-shaped and value-laden media representations and political rhetoric which rarely, if ever, correspond to the reality of prisoners' lived experience (Warr 2012). This chapter aims to redress this dissonance, focusing upon classic penological themes and utilizing a mix of first-hand experiences and academic literature. What follows is a discussion of how imprisonment can affect the individual psychologically, emotionally and physically throughout their carceral life and beyond. Starting at the point of arrest and initial imprisonment and tracing through to release and reintegration, I will explore how an individual's sense of self and placement is teleologically altered by the 'institution'.

The purpose of this chapter is to move the discussion on the pains of imprisonment beyond the focal point of the prison, and to explore how these pains may be generated before entrance to the institution, as well as how they may pertain beyond the physical boundaries of the walls. As the quote above from Oscar Wilde notes, the 'suffering' of the prisoner does not cease at the point of release. These 'pains' can, and do, pursue the prisoner into their outside life and can be as burdensome there as they are whilst the prisoner is inside. Any exploration of the prisoner and the pains we, as a society, subject them to must take note of this reality and elucidate what the consequences of this may be.

This chapter is informed by both my own history as an academic and as a former prisoner as well as work conducted on behalf of a third sector organization during a number of projects based in various prisons and with former prisoners in the community. With regard to the prison-based projects, my function was as an objective Prison Council facilitator employed to engage, formally and informally, both staff and prisoners and to collate their collective experiences of the prison and report them to the prison's management in a structured and solution-focused manner. In addition, though not there primarily to conduct academic research, I was to both observe and report on the prison, via written monthly and annual reports, to the governor/director regarding issues and problems noted within their establishments. These reports combined the experiences of myself and colleagues, quantitative data collected on issues raised/actioned, and experiences and accounts of prisoners and staff gathered during our interactions. Informed consent was sought for any and all quotes, case studies or instances reported.

The pains of imprisonment: genesis

Goffman (1961) speaks of 'mortifications' and Sykes (1958) refers to 'deprivations' and the 'pains of imprisonment'. These descriptives convey the process by which the individual is shaped by the prison or total institution. These are the traditional discourses utilized to examine how a person becomes a prisoner, a process inherent to the institution in which a person is incarcerated. The process of becoming a prisoner is presumed to commence, and be exemplified by, the reception process, where the first assaults on the person take place and 'entry shock' is initially experienced (Zamble and Porporino 1988). However, the process of mortification and the first psychological assault on the individual, their sense of self, their identity and their subjective narrative occurs not in the prison but at the point of arrest. It is here that examination of the inner and outer worlds of the prisoner shall begin.

> I was sat in the front, I saw a blur then SMASH the window came in … glass everywhere, in my face, in my ear. I could hear shouting but couldn't make it out coz all I was aware of was this fucking barrel about an inch from my eye. At first I thought we were getting merc'ed, innit, but nah the police. 'GET OUT, GET OUT' they shouted. I had my seatbelt on so couldn't … fuck sure wasn't reaching down to undo the seatbelt! My brethren vanished as he was dragged out the motor. I looked at the copper and said I'm undoing the seatbelt … I showed him as I moved in slowmo. BLAM, cunt bucked me upside my head! Next thing I know I'm between pavement and car, hands cuffed behind me, boot on my neck, and someone saying 'Who's the big man now?'[1]

> I remember them knocking on the door … as soon as I got the latch off they were through the door and rushing through the hallway. I was knocked out the way. A police woman, who was very kind to me, said I had to go with her. She was very gentle … I didn't really know what was going on. Obviously I knew my boyfriend dealt drugs but I never thought, I never … They bundled him away in a van then one of them came out with the bags. There was loads … that's when the nice police woman handcuffed me and arrested me for possession with intent to supply too.

For many, the point of arrest is shocking and, even if anticipated, discombobulating. The point of arrest represents both a drastic change in circumstance and a stark shift in the power relationship between state and individual. While the first example's extremity – the experience of one young offender convicted of armed robbery – contrasts with the second account, the elements of intrusion (into what were considered safe spaces), the display of power by state representatives and the forced acknowledgement of the self as a powerless individual are concomitant in both. Goffman (1961: 24) notes that upon entrance to a closed institution the individual begins a process of moral shift and 'disculturation' (movement away from the moral identity embodied in society) which is catalysed by a series of 'abasements, degradations, humiliations and profanations'. The individual is 'systematically' (if, perhaps, unintentionally) 'mortified', which ultimately results in 'civil death'. These practices have two purposes: reinforcement of the institution's power and authority, and the erosion of the public self. If one considers the process of arrest – cuffing, searching, forced transportation, finger printing, strip searching, removal of belts and laces, interrogation, placement in a cell, dictated regime, food, surveillance, etc. – the course of abasements and mortifications of the 'prisoner' acquire a continuous aspect. A process that begins at the point of arrest is reinforced in the police station, again in the reception of the prison, and at multiple points thereafter.

Prison reception rituals have been represented in numerous films and programmes and may be familiar to many. The stripping of the novel prisoner, the scrubbing, the delousing, the cavity search, the parade, the issuing of a bed pack, are all components that relate to the USA and media representations. They do not reflect the experience of the many in England and Wales. The rituals of abasement and moral decortication, the stripping of one's previous moral identity (and narrative) and the processes of prisonization (socialization into prison norms; Clemmer 1940; Thomas 1973) to which the prisoner in the UK is subject are no less destructive to the self. This is one of the most pernicious aspects of the modern prison experience and can result in a profound normative conflict and an entrenched ontological insecurity.

New, and intentionally punitory, policies introduced in 2013 have seen this aspect of the induction ritual become even more profound for new receptions. The new, and punitively weighted, incentive and earned privilege (IEP) system has been reconstructed in order to make induction into a prison more intensely impactful. The new initiate is no longer able to access the same privileges as longer-serving peers, undermining a decade or more of effective 'first night' practice. Instead they are to be placed on the new 'reception' level which limits access to their own clothing, the prison regime, time out of cell, funds necessary to maintain family contact and other materials and goods that would ease the transition to prison life. It is too early to say whether or not this new approach will constitute a new mortification in and of itself, but it will inevitably lead to a more painful and – given identification as a 'newbie' to the wider population – problematic entrance, exacerbating the pains associated with entering the closed world of the prison.[2]

The traditional pains of imprisonment

Sykes (1958) identified five core deprivations which he argued marked carceral life: the deprivations of liberty, security, autonomy, goods and services, and heterosexual relationships. These have formed the basis of much prison research but are worth revisiting in order to understand their nature and impact on the lived experience of prisoners. For the purposes of this chapter, the focus will be on the first three of these deprivations: liberty, security and autonomy. The popular media have long evoked the image of the prison as a place of ease and luxury as opposed to the places of stress, psychological turmoil and trauma that they are (Mason 2006). As a consequence, the deprivation of liberty, the loss of freedom, is no longer understood as a pain. The hegemonic ideology infecting criminal justice discourse reverses the age-old notion that prison is the punishment, not a place where punishment is enacted (Tonry 2004). This reflects a wider shift in the notion of freedoms which can be seen in the prosperous (and predominantly neoliberal) West where participation in consumerism is, erroneously, regarded as synonymous with personal freedom (Perez and Esposito 2010). Freedom has a much more pressing and immediate meaning for prisoners who no longer have sovereignty over their own bodies (Gunn 2010), who cannot walk where they want, when they want, cannot eat when they want, speak to whom they want, read what they want, watch they want, buy what they want, wear what they want, sleep where they want, wash when they want and even, in certain circumstances, go to the toilet when they want. It is the constraint of these acts (and countless others) that reinforces in a most invasive manner both what freedom means and how devastating to the self is its loss. As one former prisoner noted:

> It's the first time you try to do something mundane that is forbidden that the 'prison' hits you in the nuts. Its like that, that ... what's gone, your freedom, when you notice it its like being hit in the nuts ... constantly.

For the prisoner, it is the micro intrusions into their quotidian reality, more than the situational control measures (locks, gates, bars, walls, cameras), that reinforce the carceral reality to which they are subject. Another prisoner noted that he could 'get used to the walls' but could not become accustomed to not being able 'to do' the things he used to and not being able to 'go outside when you want'. For this prisoner, who described himself as an 'outdoorsy' person, the real pain of the loss of liberty was not being able to be outside. He noted that he would normally have spent most of his time outside – he worked out of doors and would even camp out at least once a week, but now he only got to be outside when he 'walked between the wing and the workshop, or to visits or healthcare'. He explained that he had not been outside after dark for four years and that he was struggling to 'get his head round that'. This reflected the experience of another interviewee, who described that after 11 years he had moved to open conditions and was able to sit outside with a friend of an evening. He related:

> that first day I sat out the back of the main housing unit, at 8 p.m., there was a local power cut so the lights in the area were all out, no light pollution, and stared into a cloudless night sky. There were stars. For the first time in over a decade, in fact since I was 17, I could see the stars. Right there, right then I felt the weight of those years as a prisoner ... like, right in your guts ... but could also begin to feel what getting out may be like.

Many describe the loss of freedom as a 'hollow' feeling or, more poetically, 'a cancer of the soul', something that hits at 'the core of you', and these emotive descriptions give weight to the sense that the deprivation of freedom is a profoundly experienced assault on the self.

Every minute of being is managed by the prison, the more evident this control of liberty, the 'deeper' one can be said to be within the prison (King and McDermott 1995) and the 'tighter' the range of burdens experienced (Crewe 2011). Being constrained, or even 'smothered' as one prisoner phrased it, by the institution, its routines and the manner in which the experience of time is mediated impacts the prisoner in a profound way. These very real pains impact on every aspect of self, identity, internal and emotional personhood, and social and performed character (Jewkes 2002). These 'pains' are not experienced in any linear or conjunctive fashion; they are a perpetual aspect of prison life. They do not affect certain aspects of a prisoner's self or identity in isolation but as a whole and all the time.

It is argued here that it is the micro-interactions between prisoner and prison that exemplify the pains felt by the deprivation of liberty. There may also be a sense in which the situational aspects of imprisonment intrude into the consciousness of the prisoner, reinforcing the relationship between themselves and the institution in a way that transcends their mere physicality. Herrity (2014) notes that although frequently included in prisoner accounts (for example, see Hassine 1996), there is a distinct lacuna of academic understanding with regard to the manner in which the acoustic elements of these measures, and their addition to the overwhelming sound ecology of a prison, reinforce and impose the institution onto prisoners' psychological reality.

The deprivation of security is often recognized as the most obvious of the 'pains' of imprisonment because prisons are perceived as 'dangerous'. Sykes (1958) argues that one of the most acute pains is an enforced proximity to fellow prisoners who pose, by their very circumstance, a danger. It has been argued elsewhere (Crewe et al. 2014; Warr 2014) that traditional understanding of the brutality of the prison environment has been somewhat misread. Although the episodic outbreaks of violence or disorder that mark the prison environment can pose a physical threat to the individual, it is the state of *diffidence*, constant and 'consumptive wariness', that can be a profound pain to the individual. Every interaction, conversation, bodily movement, glance, laugh, smile and even yawn must be monitored by the individual to ensure it is not causing offence, being taken out of context or rendering the prisoner vulnerable in the eyes of peers:

> Big Man t'ing [seriously] Fam[3] ... mans have to watch everyone and everything, innit? If next man is gassing [winding] up someone on the landing and calling him a pussy hole you gotta watch that he don't see you as a pussy hole he can come tax [rob]. Coz if he does then he's gonna come test innit? Like that 24/7. Man's gotta come strong, innit fam?

> I just found it ... wearying. Having to be on the lookout all the time, careful what you say and to whom. It was exhausting ... exhausting.

It is in this sense that Bentham's panopticon, with the intent that the 'persons to be inspected should always feel themselves as if under inspection' (Bentham 1791: 24), has gained some reality. What marks the modern prison are these varying levels of interspection and intraspection by those occupying the spaces within the confines of the walls. Prisons are places where everything you do is watched by others (as you watch them in turn), but that censorious gaze is also focused inwards, at the self. This leads to adaptive behaviours that, in terms of the prison at least, can be seen as anti-social (or maladaptive). Due to these deprivations in security, prisoners, to borrow Goffman's (1959) dramaturgical language, learn to manage their 'front stage' behaviours in ways that may obfuscate their 'back stage' realities from their peers as well as the authorities. Crewe

(2009) highlighted one aspect of this when discussing the 'soft power' of the institution, the means by which people can be 'killed off' on file, and prisoner responses to that. He noted that prisoners, especially those serving indeterminate or parole-governed sentences, would attempt to manage/control how they were perceived and what was officially recorded about them. This may become more widespread given that the new IEP scheme, implemented in November 2013, limits the opportunities to gain privileged statuses, thus making perception management necessary for a greater portion of the population.

How prisoners cope with the episodic but high levels of violence (physical, emotional, psychological and indeed sexual) that they experience or witness within prison[4] is another aspect of these behaviours. For myself, and other former prisoners, one of the mechanisms was the divorcing of empathy from sympathy (Warr 2012). When in a highly hostile and frequently violent environment, the invocation of sympathy towards others can become wearying and a 'deep' pain. When your own well-being becomes paramount, the misery of others must be 'managed' so as not to cause you further injury. As these prisoners noted:

> You may see some yout' getting banged in his face every day. You may feel sorry for him ... to begin with. But when 'bang' it happens again and 'bang' it happens again ... you can't keep feeling sorry for him, or some next br'er [brother]. You gotta ignore that shit, innit? Learn to deal with yours and fuck them ...

> You would hear [some of the women] screaming of a night time. I couldn't deal with their pain on top of my own ... and I had a lot of my own ... so you learn to ... I don't know ... not feel. You just block it out ... otherwise you won't survive.

Here, the interviewees' references are to the need to manage empathetic feelings to such a degree that they no longer result in vicarious trauma. They 'learn' to separate the evocation of sympathy from their empathetic response to witnessing someone's suffering. This emotional work, or labour, is designed to protect them, a defensive means of guarding against the emotional vicissitudes of the environment. However, these behaviours, though understandable adaptations, can be interpreted by authorities in negative ways. They can be seen as evidence of both callousness/'shallow affect' and, when occurring alongside self-censoring and front-stage management, of an overly controlled personality.

There is also a wider sense in which the deprivation of security goes beyond the mere physical or psychosocial threat thus far discussed. The security of ontology and sense of place, which in many carceral settings and for many prisoners is also an aspect where pain is experienced, must too be noted. I shall discuss later the newer pains of indeterminacy and the deprivations of certainty faced by specific populations, but there are also issues with regard to the bureaucracy of prisons and how the retreat of front line power has evinced new pains that relate to the navigation of a prison sentence and a subsequent loss of ontological security.

Giddens (1991) notes there is a distinction between the security felt when in structured and predictable (i.e. navigable) circumstances and the insecurity that is evoked when those boundaries are eroded or absent. Placed in environments, such as prisons, where the rules and regulations that govern and control an individual's existence are assured, there can be ontological security – the individual can be confident in the nature of their reality. Where those rules are opaque or transgressed without recourse, and their trustworthiness and reliability are shadowed in doubt, people become ontologically insecure – they no longer have confidence in their reality. Both Warr (2007) and Crewe (2009) have argued that the primary power that was once held by the uniformed staff body has now retreated away from the wing to senior managers who are located away from the centrality of prison life. This has resulted in levels of bureaucracy which can stymie effective decision-making processes – all the more so given the deleterious effect that benchmarking, budget cuts and staff reductions have had on the operations of many prisons.

This situation has resulted in many prisons becoming less navigable than would once have been true. As one prisoner stated, '[you] used to know where you stood, but now? Don't even know if we getting unlocked, let out for work or if there be association, nothing ...' Whilst another noted that in their prison it was no good submitting applications, as you would not hear anything back, and when they chased a 'Guv' about it, they were told to 'put in another fucking application'. This position was supported by a uniformed staff member of long standing who noted that they now could not do much 'for the lads' as they had to 'pass everything on'. As a consequence, in many circumstances, the bureaucratic legitimacy or administrative organization (Carrabine 2005) of the prison has been eroded. If a prisoner's attempts to access some element of the regime are denied, either through the disempowerment of the uniformed body or the inefficiencies of the bureaucratic system, then trust in the system begins to wane. If this situation begins to affect a large percentage of the prisoner population, then not only are trust and faith in the system diminished, but so too is the sense of personal placement and ontological security. The more difficult the prison is to navigate or abide within, then the more difficult it is to feel safe and secure within the environment, and this can exacerbate the other pains that the prison inflicts upon the prisoner.

This was evident in one of the prisons in which I operated that had undergone a number of major shifts of both management and remit over a period of 30 months. It had been subject to a budget reduction of £3 million, which resulted in significant loss of front line staff. The prisoner population had drastically altered, and there had been three core-day regime changes and two alterations to staff shift patterns. The impact of the rapid programme of changes introduced by the Ministry of Justice (MoJ) as well as policy implications introduced by the 'hubs and spokes' agreement between the National Offender Management Service (NOMS) and the UK Border Agency (UKBA) (MoJ and UKBA 2009; Kaufman 2013) added to these operational challenges. Accumulatively, this had a disastrous effect on the running of the prison. Core deliverables were not being met, there were systemic failures in communication, increases in instances of self-harm and interpersonal violence, and a number of deaths in custody. All contributed to high levels of distress amongst prisoners. The bureaucracy of the prison had become the 'institutional black hole into which problems could be cast' (Crewe 2009: 112), and was grindingly slow and impersonal (often with blanket responses being issued). Prisoners' activities, IEP statuses and risk levels were changed or altered with little or no information being supplied. Finally, nearly all aspects of the prison had adopted a default 'no' response to most prisoner requests. This resulted in a significant proportion of the population feeling alienated, in despair and with no hope that they could either navigate or securely exist within the prison. As one prisoner noted:

> Nothing, they give nothing. You ask for what PSO [Prison Service Orders] say you should have, they say 'You right, PSO say that, put in application' so you put in application ... Nothing. You put in next application. Nothing. Put in next ... then they say no. No longer you trust them to keep to rules. No longer can we trust prison. No trust ... no hope. There is no hope here.

Legitimacy (see Sparks 1996; Loader and Sparks 2013) was falling, the prison had become difficult to navigate and exist within (Liebling et al. 2005), and trust was non-existent. Unsurprisingly, a bout of concerted disorder followed.

Trust is an essential element of the prison emotional landscape, but is little understood. Minimal trust is afforded to prisoners as they are seen as a wilfully untrustworthy group (Melvin et al. 1985). This attitude of the powerful allows them to deny, in the sense that Cohen (2001) explicates as a form of interpretive denial, the impact that their practice has on the prisoner. However. trust necessarily flows in both directions: the prison and its staff must also be trusted by the prisoners in their care. This relationship is a delicate matter, something often forgotten by ministers and Ministry of Justice officials. This 'relationship' is really earmarked by the manner in which trust, and its role in interactions and relationships within the prison, either flows or is constrained. However, the question of trust goes beyond that of the authorities and manifestly impacts on every interaction and relationship within the prison; its absence can form a particular and acute pain for a prisoner related to the deprivation of security.

The deprivation of autonomy is potentially the most destructive of the pains of imprisonment as it confers a direct assault on one's sense of self and erodes any positive notion of the self. Haney (2001) notes that imprisonment, with its attendant impositions of identity (de)valuing, strips the notion of 'adult' from the prisoner and can be infantilizing. Whilst the prisoner is expected to take 'responsibility' for their past, present and future actions (in order to reduce perceived risk), they have little or no power to do so. Prisoners are forced constantly to confront their lack of power, their lack of ability to affect decision-making parameters via their reliance on official others. Whilst Haney notes that this is an acute pain in and of itself, especially for those who never manage to adjust to this loss, he further argues that there are a number of consequences to this infantilization which represent additional pains: first, the destruction of a sense of self-value which can result in a prisoner accepting or believing that any ill directed towards them is deserved because of their (offender) stigmata; second, robbing the prisoner of decision-making faculties which can result in a passivity towards authority. These factors result in what I shall refer to as a reduced penological imagination – the ability to discern the structure of a prison, the manner in which its power is manifest, the dominating operational mechanics and how these affect wing life and the complexities of the prison's social landscape. This imagination loss also leads to an inability to 'imagine' efficacious forms of resistance, which may result in resistant behaviours that are ill conceived or reactive in nature and which do little more than reaffirm the power and control of the prison authorities.

Deprivation of autonomy is evident in even the minor interactions between the adjunct (the prison and its agents) and the subaltern (the prisoner). However, it is when events occur outside the institution that the prisoner is really confronted by their powerlessness, and the deprivation of autonomy truly becomes a 'pain'. The Irish poet Joseph Campbell equates the state of being imprisoned as like being chess pieces 'taken, Swept from the chessboard' ('Chesspieces' by Campbell 1923, cited in Crotty 2010: 611), which captures the powerlessness of prisoners as they are unable to affect any outcome in the world outside whilst they are 'taken'. They must await a new game (release) before they can become actors again. It is this aspect that can cause a great deal of pain for the prisoner, as one elderly prisoner related:

> it was when my wife died. I know she wanted to be sent off in a particular church, where her mum was buried, but there was no one to organise it. I was in here. What could I do? I ain't got no money or nothing. The prison were good ... but ... that's when it hit home you know? I could do fuck all. Never forgive myself for that ...

For me, the lack of autonomy was brought home by what happened to a very close friend. K had started out as a pen pal, introduced to me through a fellow prisoner. After a number of years, she began to visit on a regular basis. She met my family. We grew close. One day I sat on the wing waiting for my visit to be called. At first my fellow cons were bantering that she had 'blown me out', for they knew she was always never more than a few minutes late. The wing staff made repeated calls to visits as they too knew she would have contacted the prison if she could not make it. Nothing. I tried to call her from the prison phones. No answer. I phoned my mum to see if she had heard from K. Nothing. The banter stopped. One of the most painful aspects of prison life is when a visitor fails to materialize. The inability to locate them, establish reason or to gain any reassurance is a terrible stress for the prisoner. Your imagination runs to the worst possible scenarios – car crashes, death, rejection. Here the deprivation of autonomy (as well as liberty) becomes keen, is felt most profoundly. You cannot do anything.

After nearly a month of no contact I was notified that K had booked a visit. I knew something was wrong, but the relief I felt was intoxicating, until I saw her. K was always smartly dressed in expensive clothing with immaculate hair and make-up. This day, K was in baggy jeans and jumper. Hair tied back. No make-up. I barely recognized her. When I went to give her a hug she flinched away from me so hard she nearly fell. I knew. We sat down and she said nothing for 20 minutes. Eventually she told me. She told me that she had been raped – raped by a friend of a friend after he had drugged her on a night out and left her dazed, abused and naked in a house full of strangers. She told me she only remembered flashes, snippets, impressions. She told me that she had not told anyone else; had not reported it to the police. She said the only reason she had told me was because I was safe to tell – I could not do anything, I was in prison. She told me because she could completely control what I heard and what response she had from me. If I gave her anything but the cold analysis and the comfort she gained from talking about it without emotion, she could walk away.

When you enter a prison, you enter a pseudo-static state, a state of 'abeyance' (Mathiesen 1990). Those you love and care for, whom you need and rely upon, do not. As Fishman (1990) points out, the lives of partners and families continue: they have trials and tribulations, successes and traumas. However, the prisoner feels as if they only play a minimal role in those events. They are not actors in those events, nor can they be. In terms of the events of the outside world, the prisoner experience is that of a voyeur peeking over the walls at the lives that play out on the other side. They can only impact on those people's lives from afar and at a time removed. In one sense, this is how pernicious the deprivation of liberty and autonomy is – for the prisoner, the outside world retreats to an abstract, only to be perceived, barely, via memory and secondary sources (letters, media, film, music). This becomes, with every example, with every reinforcement, with every realization an acute and inescapable pain for the prisoner.

In terms of the deprivation of autonomy the prisoner suffers a decortication of their moral identity and self. Herein lies an emotional, or even psychological, danger – if the outside world is so retreated or abstracted how do you engage with it emotionally or in any pro-social and healthy way? I was in Wormwood Scrubs when 9/11 occurred. My abiding memory was the laughter of the prisoners and the horror of the staff. For the prisoners, many of whom were long termers or lifers, it did not feel real, there was no emotion attached to it, it was an amusement much like anything else on TV. For the staff, the reaction of the prisoners was a source of horror and evidence of their deviance.

A further problem of the outside world having become an abstracted entity is in the planning for release. As noted, the responsibilization agenda is contraindicated with the deprivation of autonomy. This results in the 'side-effect' of putting prisoners in a position whereby they must take responsibility for their actions and their rehabilitation but have no means of doing so; and are then punished for this 'irresponsibility' by the various disciplinary discourses to which they are subject. Nowhere is this Catch-22 more evident than when it comes to lifers and their need to make plans for a future beyond the prison. During the long expanse of time that a lifer can spend in prison, the outside world can change dramatically. However, having no substantive interaction with the world at large when in closed conditions, this 'planning' can be problematic and result in unrealistic or fantastical plans and objectives. To believe that the prison aids the prisoner in truly preparing for the outside world is to believe a myth or an 'imagined' penal reality (Carlen 2008). When conjoined with other consequences or adaptive behaviours, this can pose a significant problem for the lifer or long-term prisoner.

The new pains of imprisonment

The prison is a mutable entity that is subject to the vicissitudes of time, political influence and shifts in penal discourse. With every shift comes the potential for new deprivations and pains. Developments in penal policy and wider society have brought a number of pains of imprisonment into sharper focus. Increased technologies of surveillance, expanded economies of scale (40% of the population are now housed in prisons that hold 1,000+ prisoners; PRT 2014), creeping self-governance or self-punishment (see Crewe 2011), the lack of access to newer technologies and information sources, and the pains related to separation and censure suffered by new mothers (see Rowe 2012), are amongst those concerns informing contemporary penology. However, this section will focus on the deprivation of certainty.

For certain populations, the problem of navigability is an inherent aspect of their sentence. Those serving indeterminate sentences and the expanding number of foreign national prisoners experience an additional 'pain': the deprivation of certainty. Mason (1990) argues that the indeterminate sentence, once seen as the 'backbone' of therapeutic sentences, actually became, in the USA, a new and unusually cruel form of punishment.

Others (e.g. Jewkes 2005; Crewe 2011; Addicott 2011; Rose 2012) have argued that indeterminate sentences, especially the indeterminate sentence for public protection (IPP), and life sentences in the context of England and Wales, can be viewed through the same lens. There are currently around 12,500 people (19% of the prison population) serving indeterminate sentences in England and Wales (PRT 2014).

Indeterminate sentences in England and Wales are in effect 99 years long but will entail a minimum punitive aspect (tariff). A prisoner must complete this tariff before being considered for release by the Parole Board. The key consideration for the indeterminately sentenced prisoner is that the amount of time they will eventually serve in prison is unknown. As noted, prisoners are transformed into risk subjects whose risk must be 'managed', but this is especially so for indeterminately sentenced prisoners. Release is difficult to achieve and time in custody often exceeds their minimum tariff (at the end of March 2014, 69% of IPP prisoners were post-tariff) (see PRT 2014). Addicott (2011) identifies a number of acute pains that characterize the deprivation of certainty for indeterminately sentenced prisoners, including: feelings of being lost within the system; unknown (and potentially unknowable) barriers to release; not being able to settle into the sentence and feeling constantly on 'remand'; an absence of accurate and usable information regarding the sentence and securing release; and the interminability of the sentence – not being able to see or predict an end. Although Addicott was researching IPP prisoners, the same factors pertain to all indeterminate- and life-sentenced prisoners. One 'lifer', having started as a juvenile, had served eight years of his 18-year tariff, and described his situation as follows:

> It's like you're supposed to be making progress all the time ... and the prison makes you do that, jump through all those hoops ... but 1. You don't know if you're making progress cause the goal posts keep on shifting and 2. When you think about it you ain't actually going anywhere. Its not real progress. Its illusionary progress. Do this, do that ... and for what? I still got another 10–15 years to do. Don't matter what I do now ... I'm still in prison. There ain't no fucking progress, just running to stand still. Drives you fucking mad ...

This sense of being on a Penrose staircase (Penrose and Penrose 1958; also Escher 1960), of going round and round but not getting anywhere, is a common theme even amongst those early in their indeterminate 'career'. In a Young Offender Institution, where 40% of the population were serving indeterminate sentences, a number of aggravating factors were identified. These issues related to knowledge of sentence, the perceived legitimacy of their sentence and the erosion of the lifer officer scheme. It became evident that amongst the group I was working with were a number of IPP prisoners who were not aware of the indeterminate nature of their sentence. In one instance we had to inform the prisoner a matter of weeks before his first parole hearing (which he had thought was his release date) of the likelihood of a parole 'knockback'. This resulted in a form of 'shock', similar to that experienced on first entry to the prison, as they struggled to readjust and come to terms with the actual nature of their sentence.

In terms of legitimacy there were two issues: first, many IPP prisoners felt that receiving what is in effect a life sentence, for relatively minor but repeat offences, was overly harsh and unwarranted. Second, many of those convicted of Joint Enterprise little understood their conviction, and as such questioned the legitimacy of their sentence.

Under the common law principle of Joint Enterprise (JE) individuals can be 'parasitically' guilty if their presence at, or in the precursory events leading to, an offence is seen as adding either assistance or encouragement to the primary actor or if they were able to 'foresee' the likelihood of the offence resulting from some agreed criminal action (Krebs 2010). For these 'lifers', convicted of homicide under the JE principle, not only did the sentence feel unjust but so too the mechanisms by which they were risk assessed. They were counted as murderers though they had often not physically taken anyone's life. Both IPP prisoners and those convicted under the principle of JE often found it difficult to reconcile their offending behaviours with the sentences that they subsequently received. This disjunction undermined both their sense of self as social actors and their ontological security, thus entrenching further this sense of deprived certainty. A consequence of this could be, as the prisoner attempts to maintain some stability in their perceived reality, for IPP prisoners to deny the seriousness of their offending and for JE convicted prisoners to deny the offence for which they were convicted. This could pose problems in terms of progression through the system as well as in terms of the new IEP scheme, where their 'denial' could prevent them gaining privileges and work. As one young prisoner stated:

> it's peak [rubbish] fam … me nah do nothing, me nah bore [stabbed] the brae [brother] but me were there when da t'ing kick off innit. Me, was on way to [bed], but buck up on [meet] da mans [friends] them on da bus. We all get off on the ends [home area] … BAM it's off. Next thing man's got blood on him and splitting … didn't even see what, who, where nothing … them wrap [arrest] us all up fam … we all get guilty. I tell these pussyhole guvs that I was just there, that it was nah me who bore the yout' but them just say 'in denial' and BAM … they nah give me nothing, nah enhanced, nah good job, nothing. Can't get nothing.

The last issue related to the erosion of the lifer officer scheme. Once, every lifer was assigned a trained personal 'lifer' officer who would understand the administration of the sentence, the means of navigating the parole process and the specific needs of their wards. There was also a wider support network of lifer governors and clerks who would maintain the institutional knowledge base of lifer issues and developments. The system was not perfect but it worked, after a fashion; however, in the mid-2000s, after the explosion in numbers of indeterminate prisoners it was felt that the system was too burdened and specialist, and was thus scrapped. Consequently, the ever growing numbers of indeterminately sentenced prisoners have largely lost specialized support. There has been an institutional loss of knowledge, and the rapid changes in legislation and parole protocols, whilst disseminated, are rarely explained. This has led to a situation where such sentences are barely navigable and many indeterminate-sentenced prisoners feel abandoned in a system that denies them certainty. This boundless form of incarceration, with its nebulous progressions and unknowable parameters, is experienced as a deep and pervasive pain.

However, it is not just lifers/IPPs who now have to cope with the deprivation of certainty; foreign nationals who have to prove or resolve their immigration status now face similar issues. Simon (1998) argued that the political shift occurring in the USA in the 1980s would result in the targeting and imprisoning of refugees as a tool of political utility. Bosworth and Kaufman (2011) argue that although 'prescient' in many ways, it is not the refugee who has become the focus of this US and UK politico-carceral shift but instead 'alien others': the 'undocumented worker' and the designated 'non-citizen'. Since the UK Borders Act of 2007 came into effect, every non-European Economic Area prisoner with a sentence of more than 12 months and every European Economic Area prisoner with a sentence of 24 months or more is designated as a non-citizen and is, as a matter of Home Office priority, earmarked for expulsion. There are somewhere in the region of 10,700 prisoners who are classified as foreign nationals (PRT 2014). The above authors argue that these specialized populations are subject to new matrices of political, carceral and ethical practices that both place them beyond the gaze of much contemporary criminological inquiry and render them especially vulnerable. To quote one such prisoner:

> No longer am I prisoner. My sentence finish. But still these UKBA bastards keep me here. I can not go home. Can not go to family. They say they send me to [country of origin]. What I do there? Where I go, live? I been here 17 years. I work. I pay tax. Now I get into trouble. Now they want to send me back. I have children here. Life is here. They issue IS91[5] so I am fighting but I am stuck here. I not know for how long. I not know what happen. My family not know what happen. I am not prisoner, this no longer prison. This internment!

This sense of being 'interred' was common and was iterated by many of those consulted; they felt as if they were in a liminal stage, not quite in prison but not quite in immigration detention either. This resulted in a number of frustrations. As with the indeterminate prisoners, there was a lack of information, the prison had become unnavigable, many felt lost, there was little or no chance of progression and there was no predictability with regard to their carceral future. However, as the above quote indicates, there were unique factors that relate to foreign national prisoners specifically: remaining in prison past the end of the sentence and not knowing how long that period would be; the prospect of removal from the country if appeals were unsuccessful; the potential loss of family life; and an uncertain ability to resettle beyond the prison. The problem faced by these prisoners is that, as Bosworth (2011) notes, the UKBA and prison authorities expect the foreign national prisoner to be simply and easily 'removed', either at the end of the sentence or under Repatriation Agreements, or through mechanisms like the Facilitated/Early Returns Scheme, without any fuss or bother. Yet many will 'not go quietly'. They are often people who have built a life here and who wish to remain. As another prisoner stated:

> I was to go home but then two days before they give IS91. Now ... I am staying. I thought this was sorted. I spoke to my children last night and they ask me why I not home. What can I say to them? I try bail but court decline ... say no because not all papers done. I give them but they say they not got. I feel hopeless now. No one cares. No one cares that my children ... about my wife ... No one care that I am depressed now. They make you not to want to live ... never during sentence I feel like this but now ...?

There is no succour for these prisoners, as this trauma is neither expected nor catered for. The process 'imagined' by the UKBA and the prison does not match the reality, but there is little accounting for this dissonance. This can result in an extreme assault on the prisoner's ability to cope – especially if, as with the person here, they had completed their sentence and were expecting to be released. To have that snatched away at the last minute can result in a profound pain and a degree of psychological trauma.

Thus far, this chapter has concentrated on the incarcerated prisoner, but of course most prisoners will be released back into the communities from where they were drawn. Although the prisoner may long once again to be an active chess piece, the reality is that getting 'out' can often be just as painful as being 'in'. In terms of practicality, there are the issues of securing housing, finances and re-establishing relationships/networks and mechanisms of support. All can pose real and lasting problems for the prisoner which can hamper successful reintegration. However, what must also be overcome are the pernicious effects of incarceration. In order to reintegrate successfully those adaptations, those learned behaviours, that enabled the prisoner to survive the prison environment, must be shed. As noted elsewhere (Warr 2012), the first challenge is to recognize the damage and harms that prison has caused and to then learn ways to overcome them.

For some this process begins in open conditions and will involve release on temporary licence (ROTL). Working outside the prison, having visits in the community, being able to attend family functions, spending time 'on the out' all aid this process of identifying the harms caused by being inside and allow the prisoner to work on them prior to release. This can include re-establishing relationships, overcoming the deprivation of hetero-social skills, learning to cope with new technologies, once again moving beyond the parasitic lifestyle that prisoners are forced into, and beginning to utilize the goods and services that they have previously been denied. It may even involve something mundane like learning to smile in response to people again. Time out of the prison can be fundamental to this process. Yet the incumbent justice secretary has ordered this tool to be granted to fewer individuals in the future. Of course, not every prisoner has the opportunity to go to open conditions and get used to the outside world via ROTL; for many, release comes with little preparation. For these individuals, released with £48 in their pocket, if they do not have the benefit of a family or support network, then the outside world can be a place of chaos and turmoil.

If going to prison represents a 'civil death' (Goffman 1961), then release should represent a 'civil rebirth', but unfortunately it does not. As Mathiesen (1990) notes, societies are 'absolved of responsibility' in this regard and thus do not fund or resource, or even truly support, this 'return'. Instead, he argues that all the resources are channelled into the 'pomp and circumstance' of the procedures that strip the prisoner of their moral worth and rehabilitation (whatever its form) is, to a certain degree, starved or 'neutralized'. Proponents of probation will no doubt argue that its function is to aid and support this 'return', escape from moral abeyance, but unfortunately this has long ceased to be its function. Probation has moved well beyond a remit of 'befriend, advise and assist' (Mair and Burke 2012), to one of public protection, risk supervision and management. In this context, and in the manner noted by Hannah-Moffatt (2005), the needs of the probationer are, once more, translated into risks that are to be managed, not necessarily resolved. As this lifer explained:

> When the parole board ordered my release I thought 'that's it, it's over'. But it wasn't, not by a long shot. I've had to put up with probation ever since. I'm still on weekly reporting and it's ... well it's pointless. They don't do nothing. I needed

help with housing and benefits and they started talking about me not coping and that being a risk. Well okay that may be a risk … but then fucking help me with that shit, you know? What did they do? They gave me a number to call, a fucking number! Not for housing association or nothing, a charity that gives advice. That's it. That's all the help I got from them, all they could do.

Another former prisoner noted a similar issue:

all good if you're a smack head [heroin addict], then they got time for ya. Bend over for ya then. Get you support and help and what have ya. But if you're stuck and can't get work and that, then what? Nothing. Fuck all. Nada. Useless mate, know what I mean? I couldn't get a job for love nor money mate, tried everything and everywhere. Ain't proud. Can't afford to be at my age but … couldn't even get an interview. Me … felt like a proper leper, know what I mean? So I asked my probation officer for help … all she could say was 'we could get you on a fork lift truck driving course'. I laughed right in her face, I did that course 15 odd years ago. There weren't any fork lift driving jobs around then and there's even fucking less now!

This brings me to the final issue that faces the prisoner once out in the community: the problem of getting a job, having to declare the criminal offence and stigma. Stigma can take many forms and can result in a number of harms for differing people. There can be cultural 'shames' associated with having been in prison – for instance one Bangladeshi woman explained that, after being released from a fraud conviction, her family had refused to house her, give her access to her children or give her any aid at all. She was also shunned by others in what she had once considered a close-knit community. In the end she had to move away and try to start a life over again in a new town, away from a Bangladeshi community, where she and her past were not known. For others, stigma can relate to forming relationships. Echoing the findings of Lebel (2012a, 2012b), one former prisoner who had been convicted of kidnap, torture and robbery and had spent 13 years in prison explained that when meeting people for the first time, the fear of them rejecting him due to his 'past' resulted in him avoiding many interactions and from starting any conversation. This individual's perception of the type of stigma that their past conferred on them, and the subsequent discrimination they felt they would be subject to, did not allow them to construct any form of 'redemptive script' (Maruna 2001) which paralyzed them in terms of social reintegration. As such, he was now lonely and disengaged from those around him and felt that he had no future.

There are particular areas, however, where the impact of prison stigmata is all-pervasive – one such is employment. In virtually all circumstances in official and bureaucratic life, there is now a requirement to declare an offence (insurance, bank loans, mortgages, etc.). Nowhere is this more evident than when it comes to applying for jobs. This poses some real problems for the former prisoner, as it is a factor that can deter the employer from even considering the application – but to decline to declare it can also have negative consequences. That is even if the application makes it to the employer for consideration. In some instances, online job application software will, as a default setting, automatically side-line applications if the criminal convictions box has been ticked. HR departments and employers may not even be aware that this is happening unless they have had cause to check the default settings. As Loeffler (2013) explains, post-release unemployment is a substantive problem where interaction with the criminal justice system can radically impact on a person's life course and narrow their opportunities for employment.

A further barrier to employment can be the Disclosure and Barring procedures which have been established to protect vulnerable populations from those who may predate them in some way. The contemporary practice of criminal conviction checks came into effect with the Police Act of 1997 and then later with the creation of the Criminal Records Bureau (CRB) in 2002 (Mustafa et al. 2013). The CRB was later merged with the Independent Safeguarding Authority to become the Disclosure and Barring Service (DBS) (MoJ 2014). Whilst few would argue against organizations working with vulnerable populations having the right to vet potential staff, or that some individuals should not be allowed to work with vulnerable groups, sometimes the protocols can act as a needless barrier. Two recent examples are people barred from holding Police and Crime Commissioners positions due to juvenile convictions dating back many decades (Travis 2012). A further example is a lifer with an Enhanced DBS working for a third sector organization within criminal justice who, when accepted for a new job, was made to wait for more than four months, without recourse, for the police to complete their checks.

Attempting to make a new life after prison is hard, but these examples show that in some regards a former prisoner cannot move beyond their conviction. McNeill et al. (2014) note this as a particular issue and one which needs to be addressed if we are to move towards a more effective criminal justice system. However, currently the shedding of the 'offender' or 'prisoner' label is difficult as they are particularly adhesive. Even if employers do not access the DBS, there is still the problem of Google and information held on the Internet. There are sites dedicated to naming people with convictions and any Internet search holds the potential to reveal a former prisoner's past. Their tarnished moral identity is forever and is inescapable – a point made in the film *The Dark Knight Rises* (Nolan 2012) by the character Selina Kyle:

> There's no fresh start in today's world. Any twelve-year-old with a cell phone could find out what you did. Everything we do is collated and quantified. Everything sticks.

Conclusion

I have in this chapter tried to explicate some of the pains that are associated with contemporary imprisonment and those issues that can haunt the prisoner once beyond the wall. Whether it is having to learn how to adjust to the loss of liberty and the constraint of mundane activity, surviving the decortication of your moral and social self, having the institution, and its ever present oculus, intrude into every aspect of your being, having to hide your trauma from front stage performances, having to suppress emotional and sympathetic responses to the brutality that you witness, being forced into a parasitic lifestyle and relying on the graces of family, friends and official others, having to invent stimulation to hold back the crushing boredom, being consumptively wary, or surviving any of the other flagitious impositions, the prison is harmful and that harm continues far beyond the ending of the period of incarceration. All are assaults on the self and impact on the manner in which an individual perceives themselves and their place in the world.

Notes

1   All quoted material is taken from field notes and permission to utilize it was sought and agreed at the time. No identifiers are included in order to maintain anonymity. Where prisoners have been quoted, permission was sought and obtained from the establishments at the time the projects were running for use in reports and academic publications.
2   It is worth noting that a report released by the Prison and Probation Ombudsman in April 2014 noted that there has been an increase in self-inflicted deaths in custody in the period since these changes were introduced, but no direct correlation has been drawn.
3   'Fam' is an informal mode of address utilized by young urban men which denotes friendship or association. In use it is similar to the term 'mate'.
4   See for instance the video sent out of HMP Elmley that was reported in the *Daily Mirror*, www. mirror.co.uk/news/uk-news/video-brutality-uk-prisons-exposed-3603883.
5   The IS91 is an authorization to detain a prisoner under Immigration powers and will be issued by the Home Office.

Bibliography

Addicott, P. (2011) *An Exploratory Study of Frustrations, Compliance and Resistance Among Prisoners Serving Indeterminate Sentences*, MSt dissertation, Institute of Criminology, University of Cambridge.

Bentham, J. (1791) *Panopticon, or The Inspection House*, London: T. Payne, Mews Gate.

Bosworth, M. (2011) 'Deportation, Detention and Foreign National Prisoners in England and Wales', *Citizenship Studies* 15(5): 583–595.

Bosworth, M. and Kaufman, E. (2011) 'Foreigners in a Carceral Age: Immigration and Imprisonment in the United States', *Stanford Law & Policy Review* 22(2): 429–454.

Campbell, J. (1923) *'As I was Among Captives': Joseph Campbell's prison diary* (ed. Eilean Ni Chuilleanain 2001), Cork: Cork University Press.

Carlen, P. (2008) 'Imaginary penalities and risk crazed governance', in P. Carlen (ed.) *Imaginary Penalities*, Cullompton: Willan.

Carrabine, E. (2005) 'Prison Riots, Social Order and the Problem of Legitimacy', *British Journal of Criminology* 45: 896–913.

Clemmer, D. (1940) *The Prison Community*, Hanover, MA: Christopher Publishing House.

Cohen, S. (2001) *States of Denial: Knowing about atrocities and suffering*, Cambridge: Polity Press.

Cohen, S. and Taylor, L. (2006) 'Time and deterioration' in Y. Jewkes and H. Johnston (eds) *Prison Readings: A critical introduction to prisons and imprisonment*, Cullompton: Willan.

Conrad, T. (2006) *Oscar Wilde in Quotation: 3,100 Insults, Anecdotes and Aphorisms, Topically Arranged with Attributions*, Jefferson, NC: McFarland & Co. Inc.

Crewe, B. (2009) *The Prisoner Society: Power, adaptation and social life in an English prison*, Clarendon Studies in Criminology, Oxford: Oxford University Press.

Crewe, B. (2011) 'Depth, weight, tightness: revisiting the pains of imprisonment', *Punishment & Society* 13(5): 509–529.

Crewe, B., Warr, J., Bennett, P. and Smith, A. (2014) 'The Emotional Geography of Prison Life', *Theoretical Criminology* 18(1): 56–74.

Crotty, P. (ed.) (2010) *The Penguin Book of Irish Poetry*, London: Penguin Books.

Escher, M.C. (1960) 'Ascending and Descending', www.mcescher.com/gallery/lithograph/ascending-and-descending/.

Fishman, L.T. (1990) *Women at the Wall: A study of prisoners' wives doing time on the outside*, Albany: State University of New York Press.

Giddens, A. (1991) *Modernity and Self Identity: Self and society in the late modern age*, London: Polity.

Goffman, E. (1959) *The Presentation of Self in Everyday Life*, London: Penguin.

Goffman, E. (1961) *Asylums: Essays on the social situation of mental patients and other inmates*, London: Penguin Books Ltd.

Gunn, B. (2010) 'Ben's prison blog – lifer on the loose: my body isn't mine', blog entry, Friday 5 November 2010, prisonerben.blogspot.co.uk/2010/11/my-body-isnt-mine.html (accessed 15 May 2014).

Haney, C. (2001) 'The psychological impact of incarceration: implications for post-prison adjustment', in *National Policy Conference – From Prison to Home: The effect of incarceration and re-entry on children, families and communities*, 30–31 January 2002, Washington, DCUS Department of Health and Human Services, The Urban Institute.

Hannah-Moffatt, K. (2005) 'Criminogenic needs and the transformative risk subject: Hybridizations of Risk/Need in Penality', *Punishment & Society* 7(1): 29–51.

Hassine, V. (1996) *Life without Parole: Living in prison today*, Los Angeles, CA: Roxbury Publishing.

Herrity, K.Z. (2014) *The Significance of Music to the Prison Experience*, BSc, Royal Holloway, University of London.

Jewkes, Y. (2002) *Captive Audience: Media, masculinity and power in prisons*, Cullompton: Willan.

Jewkes, Y. (2005) 'Loss, liminality and the life sentence: managing identity through a disrupted lifecourse', in A. Liebling and S. Maruna (eds) *The Effects of Imprisonment*, Cullompton: Willan, 366–388.

Kaufman, E. (2013) 'Hubs and spokes: the transformation of the British prison', in K.F. Aas and M. Bosworth (eds) *The Borders of Punishment: Migration, citizenship and social exclusion*, Oxford: Oxford University Press.

King, R. and McDermott, K. (1995) *The State of our Prisons*, Oxford: Clarendon Press.

Krebs, B. (2010) 'Joint criminal enterprise', *The Modern Law Review* 73(4): 578–604.

Lebel, T. (2012a) 'Invisible stripes? Formerly incarcerated persons' perceptions of stigma', *Deviant Behavior* 33(2): 89–107.

Lebel, T. (2012b) '"If one doesn't get you another will": formerly incarcerated persons' perceptions of discrimination', *The Prison Journal* 92(1): 63–87.

Liebling, A. and Arnold, H. (2004) *Prisons and their Moral Performance: A study of values, quality and prison life*, Clarendon Studies in Criminology, Oxford: Oxford University Press.

Liebling, A., Durie, L., Stiles, A. and Tait, S. (2005) 'Revisiting prison suicide: the role of fairness and distress', in A. Liebling and S. Maruna (eds) *The Effects of Imprisonment*, Cullompton: Willan.

Loader, I. and Sparks, R. (2013) 'Unfinished business: legitimacy, crime control and democratic politics', in J. Tankebe and A. Liebling (eds) *Legitimacy and Criminal Justice: An international exploration*, Oxford: Oxford University Press.

Loeffler, C.E. (2013) 'Does imprisonment slter the life course? Evidence on crime and employment from a natural experiment', *Criminology* 51(1): 137–166.

McNeill, F., Farrall, S., Ligthowler, C. and Maruna, S. (2014) 'Desistance and supervision', in G. Bruinsma and D. Weisburd (eds) *Encyclopaedia of Criminology and Criminal Justice*, New York: Springer, 958–967.

Mair, G. and Burke, L. (2012) *Redemption, Rehabilitation and Risk Management: A history of probation*, London: Routledge.

Maruna, S. (2001) *Making Good: How ex-convicts reform and rebuild their lives*, Washington, DC: The American Psychological Society.

Mason, G.L. (1990) 'Indeterminate sentencing: cruel and unusual punishment, or just plain cruel?' *New England Journal on Criminal and Civil Confinement* 16(1): 89–120.

Mason, P. (2006) 'Lies, distortion and what doesn't work: monitoring prison stories in the British media', *Crime Media Culture* 2(3): 251–267.

Mathiesen, T. (1990) *Prison on Trial*, London: Sage Publications Ltd.

Melvin, K.B., Gramling, L.K. and Gardner, W.M. (1985) 'A scale to measure attitudes towards prisoners', *Criminal Justice and Behaviour* 12(2): 241–253.

MoJ (Ministry of Justice) (2013) *Criminal Justice Statistics: Quarterly Update to March 2013*, London: Ministry of Justice.

MoJ (Ministry of Justice) (2014) 'Disclosure and barring service: overview', www.gov.uk/disclosure-barring-service-check/overview (accessed 20 June 2014).

MoJ (Ministry of Justice) and UKBA (UK Border Agency) (2009) *Service Level Agreement to Support the Effective and Speedy Removal of Foreign National Prisoners*, 1 May, London: Ministry of Justice.

Morris, J.A. and Feldman, D.C. (1996) 'The dimensions, antecedents and consequences of emotional labour', *Academy of Management Review* 21(4): 986–1010.

Mustafa, N., Kingston, P. and Beeston, D. (2013) 'An exploration of the historical background of criminal record checking in the United Kingdom: from the eighteenth to the twenty-first century', *European Journal on Criminal Policy and Research* 19(1): 15–30.

Nolan, C. (dir) (2012) *The Dark Knight Rises*, film, Warner Bros. Legendary Pictures.

Penrose, L.S. and Penrose, R. (1958) 'Impossible objects: a special type of visual illusion', *British Journal of Psychology* 49(1): 31–33.

Perez, F. and Esposito, L. (2010) 'The global addiction and human rights: insatiable consumerism, neoliberalism and harm reduction', *Perspectives on Global Development and Technology* 9(1): 84–100.

PRT (Prison Reform Trust) (2014) 'Prison: the facts – Bromley Briefings summer 2014', www.prisonreformtrust.org.uk/Portals/0/Documents/Prison%20the%20facts%20May%202014.pdf (accessed 5 June 2014).

Rose, C. (2012) 'RIP the IPP: a look back at the sentence of imprisonment for public protection', *Journal of Criminal Law* 76(4): 303–313.

Rowe, A. (2012) 'Women prisoners', in B. Crewe and J. Bennett (eds) *The Prisoner*, Abingdon: Routledge.

Simon, J. (1998) 'Refugees in a carceral age: the rebirth of immigration prisons in the United States', *Public Culture* 10(3): 577–607.

Sparks, R., Bottoms, A.E. and Hay, W. (1996), *Prisons and the Problem of Order*, Oxford: Oxford University Press.

Sykes, G.M. (1958) *The Society of Captives – A Study of a Maximum Security Prison*, Princeton, NJ: Princeton University Press.

Thomas, C.W. (1973), 'Prisonization or resocialization? A study of external factors associated with the impact of imprisonment', *Journal of Research in Crime and Delinquency* 10(1): 13–21.

Tonry, M. (2004) *Punishment and Politics: Evidence and emulation in the making of English crime control policy*, Cullompton: Willan.

Travis, A. (2012) 'Second police commissioner candidate withdraws over juvenile conviction', *The Guardian*, www.theguardian.com/uk/2012/aug/10/police-commissioner-candidate-withdraw-conviction (accessed 20 June 2014).

Walker, S. and Worrall, A. (2006) 'Life as a woman: the gendered pains of indeterminate imprisonment', in Y. Jewkes and H. Johnston (eds) *Prison Readings: A critical introduction to prisons and imprisonment*, Cullompton: Willan.

Warr, J. (2007) 'Personal reflections on prison staff', in J. Bennett, B. Crewe and A. Wahidin (eds) *Understanding Prison Staff*, Cullompton: Willan, 17–29.

Warr, J. (2012) 'Afterword', in B. Crewe and J. Bennett (eds) *The Prisoner*, Abingdon: Routledge.

Warr, J. (2014) 'Does prison size matter?', *Prison Service Journal* 211: 25–30.

Zamble, E. and Porporino, F.J. (1988) *Coping, Behavior and Adaptation in Prison Inmates*, Dordrecht: Springer-Verlag Publishers.

Part V

Beyond the prison

Chapter 34

Prisons and desistance

Fergus McNeill and Marguerite Schinkel

Introduction

Since the 'birth of the prison' (Foucault 1975), penal policymakers, administrators and practitioners have been preoccupied with the potential of the prison as an architecture and a technology for producing change in prisoners. Views about how best to design penal institutions, regimes and practices have certainly changed a great deal over the years and continue to vary in different jurisdictions; examples of different approaches include pursuing reform or rehabilitation through religious instruction and practice, or political re-education, or psychological interventions, or through the discipline and 'dignity' of labour. At other times and places, optimism about the reformative potential of imprisonment has withered or waned to the extent that even advocates of imprisonment aimed merely for 'humane containment'.

Although the development of criminology, and in particular the evolution of theory and research about rehabilitation, has been an important factor in constructing and reconstructing penal regimes (see Rotman 1990), research about how and why people come to stop offending (and stay stopped) has rarely been used either to reimagine or to critique imprisonment, despite the fact that 'desistance' research also has a relatively long history. That said, what we might term the popularization of the concept of desistance, and its emergence into criminal justice discourses and practices, is a very recent phenomenon. It is, in fact, a 21st-century phenomenon. A superficial reading of these developments would probably point to the significance of an increasing body of literature (and other materials) in which several authors have made conspicuous and consistent efforts to interpret and apply desistance theory and research for and with criminal justice policymakers and practitioners – and with those who have lived experience of punishment and rehabilitation, both in prisons and in the community. A more critical perspective might want to dig a little deeper – looking at the ways in which desistance research has been used both to resist and to support penal reform efforts of diverse and even contradictory sorts, ranging from the marketization of probation (in England and Wales), to the promotion of penal reductionism, to the reframing and/or displacement of punitive and risk discourses and practices, to the recognition and prioritization of 'user voice' in criminal justice.

Although this chapter cannot aim to provide a comprehensive and critical account of relationships between prisons and desistance, we hope that it can serve to enliven such discussion. To that end, the structure of this chapter is as follows. After a very brief account of some of the core themes in desistance research, we turn first to arguments about the implications of this evidence for penal *policy* in general, before going on to examine its implications for penal *practice*. We then move to examine more specifically the complex relationships between imprisonment and desistance, drawing primarily on the doctoral research of one of the authors (Schinkel). We go on to examine briefly two recent attempts to 'apply' desistance theory and research in redesigning the prison systems in Northern Ireland and in Scotland. In the concluding section, we consider some of the challenges and contradictions that remain for desistance research and for prison reform.

Desistance from crime

Defining desistance is far from straightforward, but most discussions begin with the idea of the cessation of offending behaviour. However, since it is impossible to know the moment at which any behaviour ceases permanently, scholars have increasingly come to conceptualize and to study desistance as a process (see, for example, Bottoms et al. 2004; Maruna 2001; Farrall 2002; Laub and Sampson 2003). More specifically, we can think of desistance as a process of human development in social context; one that involves moving *away* from offending and *into* compliance with law and social norms. Maruna and Farrall (2004) draw an important distinction between *primary* and *secondary* desistance; the former relates merely to behaviour, the latter implies a related shift in identity. They posit that shifts in identity and self-concept matter in securing longer-term, sustained changes in behaviour as opposed to mere lulls in offending. Though the importance of this distinction has been debated by some (e.g. Bottoms et al. 2004), secondary desistance and with it substantive or committed compliance to the law (see Robinson and McNeill 2008) is likely to be important for people who have been heavily involved in offending and/or heavily criminalized. 'Spoiled identities' need to be shed if change is to be secured.

We suspect it may also make sense to develop the concept of *tertiary* desistance – referring not just to shifts in behaviour or identity but to shifts in one's sense of belonging to a (moral) community. Our argument, based on developing research evidence (for example, Laub and Sampson 2003; Bottoms and Shapland 2011; Weaver 2013), is that since identity is socially constructed and negotiated, securing long-term change depends not just on how one sees oneself but also on how one is seen by others, and on how one sees one's place in society. Putting it more simply, desistance is a social and political process as much as a personal one.

In fact, the links between behaviour, identity and belonging are implicit in the main explanatory theories of desistance. These are commonly divided into ontogenic theories which stress the importance of age and maturation; sociogenic theories which stress the importance of social bond and ties; and narrative theories which stress the importance of subjective changes in identity (Maruna 2001). Recently, in an important review of desistance research, Bottoms (2014) has suggested a fourth set of explanatory factors that are situational in character (see also Farrall et al. 2014). Drawing on his expertise in socio-spatial criminology, as well as on desistance research, Bottoms points out that various aspects of our social environments and of our situated 'routine activities' also provide important influences on our behaviour, for better or worse. While our environments and activities are closely connected to our social bonds or ties (for example, bonds within intimate relationships and to families, work and faith communities), they deserve attention in their own right.

Given that desistance research itself is diverse and varied, and that there is so much debate within the field (for example, about the relative contribution of structural and subjective factors to the process), it makes little sense to talk about critical perspectives on desistance research per se. That said, some critical criminologists (e.g. Baldry 2010) have been wary both about whether desistance research might not represent another responsibilizing discourse (and therefore a discursive resource for associated oppressive practices) and about the over-generalization of theories of desistance across diverse populations. This second observation has been recognized and has begun to be addressed seriously by desistance researchers themselves (e.g. Calverley 2012; Farrall et al. 2014; Glynn 2014; Sharpe 2012; Weaver and McNeill 2010). The issue of responsibilization is more complex. While it is true that some desistance theorists have offered rational choice explanations of the process, most are highly critical of such perspectives. Even those desistance researchers who have come to stress the role of personal agency in desistance processes (e.g. Giordano et al. 2002; Maruna 2001; Farrall and Calverley 2006) tend to stress an interactionist perspective in which social structural factors continue to be seen as important.

Desistance and penal policy and practice

As well as seeking to advance explanations for or understandings of desistance, many criminologists have recently engaged with practitioners, 'ex-offenders' and others in the shared task of exploring the implications of this research for policy and practice, and in particular for how we approach the challenges of punishment and rehabilitation (McNeill 2003, 2006, 2009, 2012a; McNeill and Weaver 2007, 2010). Desistance research has particular policy salience to the extent that policy is concerned with reducing reoffending and its associated economic, human and social costs. Rather than simply observing or understanding desistance, the question becomes: 'Can we enable desistance through criminal sanctions, or do they tend to frustrate it?' In a series of publications (e.g. McNeill and Weaver 2010), recommendations for penal policies and practices have tended to centre on the following themes:

- For people who have been involved in persistent offending – and who have been persistently criminalized and penalized – desistance is a complex and difficult process, so we need to be realistic about these difficulties, and to expect and manage lapses and relapses.
- Since the process is different for different people (even if there are many common threads), interventions need to be properly individualized and tailored to the circumstances of the individual and to their subjective apprehension of resources and opportunities for positive change.
- Since desistance is relational, interventions need to work on, with and through professional and social relationships (and not just through individualized programmes). Developing social capital (meaning networks of reciprocal relationships) is crucial to supporting desistance.
- Since desistance often involves developing hope for the future, interventions need to work to nurture hope and motivation. Since hope seems to be connected to developing a sense of 'agency' (meaning the capacity to govern one's life), interventions

should seek to identify and mobilize personal strengths and self-determination, encouraging the acquisition of a sense of agency.

• The language of policy and practice matters; to the extent that it entrenches criminalized identities, it may frustrate desistance. We need to mind our language, as well as ensuring that we recognize and celebrate progress, so as to reinforce the development or redevelopment of positive identities.

In the recent chapter already referred to above, Bottoms (2014) suggests that we need to add to this list interventions that attend to the routine activities and social environments of offenders. In other words, we need to provide practical supports and activities that enable and sustain change.

More broadly, some desistance researchers have begun to argue that over the last 20 years our approaches to punishment and rehabilitation have become too narrowly focused on supporting personal change, not as a result of the influence of desistance research (which the trend predates), but rather because of the conjunction of narrow conceptions of evidence-based practice and the managerialization of criminal justice since the late 1980s. One of us has argued in previous papers (McNeill 2012a, 2014) that this has led to neglect of three other forms of rehabilitation – moral, social and judicial. The central argument is that no amount of personal change can secure desistance if change is not recognized and supported by the community ('social rehabilitation'), by the law and by the state ('judicial rehabilitation'). Without these forms of informal and formal recognition, legitimate opportunities (for example, for participation in the labour market or in social life) will not become available and return to offending may be made more likely. In some cases, the failure in state punishment to attend directly to the need for moral rehabilitation (the settling of debts between the offender, victim and community) may undermine social rehabilitation. Restorative justice may have something to offer here. More generally, my position is that these four forms of rehabilitation are often interdependent, and that failing to attend to all four reduces the likelihood of successful desistance.

More recently still, one of us has begun to argue that penal policy and practice needs to reconsider how it frames its goals (McNeill n.d., forthcoming). Studying and supporting desistance eventually forces us to address the complex question not of what people desist *from*, but what they desist *to*. In other words, if desistance is a process or a journey, we are eventually compelled to seek to understand and articulate its destination. The concepts of citizenship, integration and solidarity may have much to offer in addressing this question; perhaps a positively framed set of goals for criminal sanctions operationalizing these concepts (and a positive set of metrics for judging their successes) may help us move beyond an increasingly fruitless preoccupation with risk and reoffending.

'Offender management' and desistance

Initial discussions in the UK of whether and how criminal sanctions might support desistance from crime were focused on probation practice (Rex 1999; Farrall 2002; McNeill 2003, 2006). In the dissemination of these studies, most probation staff in England and Wales (and their colleagues in similar roles in other jurisdictions) were pleased to discover a body of evidence that seemed to affirm: (i) that the social context of offending and desistance matters profoundly; (ii) that offending behaviour programmes may be necessary but are not a sufficient means of supporting desistance; and (iii) that the (moral) character and quality of the relationships between supervisors and supervised are critical in supporting change.

These reactions are entirely understandable; vindication of these forms of 'practice wisdom' had been a long time coming for practitioners, many of whom felt that their professionalism had been assailed since the mid-1990s both by punitive penal policies and by a hollowed out and managerialized bastardization of 'what works' research (McNeill 2012b). Indeed, some of the associated literature has consciously and conspicuously deployed evidence from desistance studies as a resource for resisting the twin forces of punitiveness and managerialization (see, for example, McNeill 2006).

It is perhaps not surprising, then, that Probation Trusts in England and Wales have been enthusiastic readers and users of desistance research. Again, there are contextual factors at play here. The development of the National Offender Management Service's 'Offender Engagement Programme' drew on both desistance and 'what works' research to refocus development efforts on enhancing the effectiveness of one-to-one supervision – a neglected practice (Burnett and McNeill 2005) which, after all, reaches far more people than offending behaviour programmes. The relevant national standards were also revised and significantly relaxed, so as to allow practitioners much more discretion, and this seemed to generate a thirst both for new knowledge (to guide discretion) and for new tools and approaches. For example, the recent special edition of *Scottish Justice Matters* on desistance[1] includes a short article on one such development (see Goodwin et al. 2013). That said, the ongoing marketization and privatization of English probation now seems likely to undermine recent progress in that jurisdiction (on which see the special edition of the *British Journal of Community Justice*[2]).

The special issue of *Scottish Justice Matters* also contains a paper (McNeill et al. 2013) that summarizes the results of the ESRC-funded 'Desistance Knowledge Exchange' project.[3] That project was a UK-wide attempt to generate a dialogue between people with convictions, service users, their families and supporters, practitioners, policymakers and academics about how best to reform supervision in order to better support desistance. Space prohibits a full discussion of the process and its outcomes here, but the ten 'provocative propositions' that emerged were radical and wide-ranging, and extended far beyond the initial focus on practice models for supervision:

1 'There is a need for meaningful service user involvement in the design, delivery, assessment, and improvement of policies and provision across the criminal justice system; and for clear career routes for former service users that recognise and value the skills that people with convictions possess …

2 There is a dire need to reduce the prison population, first and foremost in order to free up resources to invest in efforts more likely to support desistance …

3 A rethink of criminal justice social work/probation is necessary to make it more "holistic" and "humanised", more focused on the service user's strengths and needs, and more flexible and open to creative work …

4 In the future, CJSW/probation offices and officers need to become better connected with local communities with greater community involvement in all of their work …

5 A wider circle of society should be encouraged to take responsibility for helping people stop offending …

6   Interventions ought to focus less on risk and more readily on the positives, and what people have achieved *and can achieve* in the future ...
7   Community supervision needs to work to challenge inequality and promote fairness, equalising life chances and contributing to social justice ...
8   Redraft the Rehabilitation of Offenders Act 1974 to encourage and recognise rehabilitation much earlier, and not stand in the way of desistance in the name of "rehabilitation" ...
9   The public needs more accurate information about the lives of those in the criminal justice system and in particular on the process of leaving crime behind ...
10   Finally – but perhaps foremost in the tenor of the discussions – the criminal justice system needs to become more acquainted with hope and less transfixed with risk, pessimism and failure ...'

(McNeill et al. 2013: 4–5)

Clearly some of these proposals have some bearing on how and when we use imprisonment as a sanction and about how we organize and run prisons. We turn next to these questions.

Imprisonment and desistance

Most desistance researchers argue that prisons reflect an inherently problematic context in which to seek to support desistance. Reflecting on the four main theoretical perspectives discussed above, it is not difficult to argue, for example: (i) that the experience of imprisonment often deprives people of responsibility and may delay maturation (Liebling and Maruna 2004); (ii) that imprisonment often damages positive social ties and weakens bonds between prisoners and society; (iii) that imprisonment tends to cement spoiled identities rather than nurturing positive ones; and (iv) that the routine activities of life in prison, even if rendered 'purposeful', are detached from the desistance-supporting routines that need to be established in the community. Indeed, there is some evidence that compared with community sanctions, imprisonment in general may be somewhat criminogenic (Joliffe and Hedderman 2012). For these reasons, desistance researchers and penal reform groups have found common cause in arguing for reduced reliance on custody as a sanction (e.g. McNeill and Weaver 2007; Hough et al. 2012).

Nonetheless, as we noted at the outset, while imprisonment may have certain common features that militate against supporting desistance, ever since the inception of the penitentiary, people involved in designing and implementing prison regimes have (admittedly to varying degrees in different times and places) been attracted to the idea that institutions may, under certain circumstances, exercise some 'reformative' effect. Just as probation workers have been attracted by desistance research's counter-narrative to a narrow emphasis on psychological programmes, so contemporary prison managers and staff may have been attracted by a body of evidence that seems capable of informing how prison regimes (in the widest sense) might be more constructively reconfigured. Whereas the impact of 'what works' research (on risk assessment processes and offending behaviour programmes) has tended to be limited to the work of those in 'offender management units' (or their equivalents), the broader purview of desistance research lends it relevance across all roles and tasks. Moreover, where prisons (like probation trusts) have come to be judged increasingly on their contribution to reducing reoffending rates, it is obviously in the interests of prison managers to seek to improve processes of rehabilitation and reintegration.

Despite the problems noted at the outset of this section, some desistance studies seem to provide good news for these would-be reformers (of prisons and prisoners), suggesting that imprisonment sometimes does play a positive role in the narratives of people who have desisted. For example, Giordano et al. (2002) reported that some of their interviewees found in imprisonment the 'hook for change' that they needed to change their life around. Similarly, in Aresti et al.'s (2010) research 'defining moments' happened within the prison, where reflecting on the length of time they had to serve, and on the impact on their sense of self of the prison environment, prisoners re-evaluated their lives and their plans for the future. Indeed, the impact of having time to think in prison on the motivation to desist has figured in many descriptions of the lived experience of imprisonment (see for example, Ashkar and Kenny 2008; Barry 2006; Comfort 2008; Farrall and Calverley 2006). However, drawing on research in the USA, Comfort (2008) has suggested that ex-prisoners may be casting their prison sentence in a positive light in order to rescue some meaning from the experience, rather than having found the experience truly rehabilitative. Indeed, in the absence of any meaningful rehabilitative input, she has called this type of portrayal of imprisonment '"as if" rehabilitation'.

On the other hand, Sampson and Laub's (2005) research suggests that imprisonment might have some value in bringing about desistance by 'knifing off' prisoners from their usual lives. While this has many deleterious consequences, such as severing family ties, the loss of housing and jobs and the risk of institutionalization, it also means that, temporarily, the 'habitual offender' is not offending and is cut off from their usual identities and opportunities on the outside, which may create the space to form new ambitions and hopes. Significantly in this context, Sampson and Laub (2005) included time spent in reform schools (alongside marriage, work, military service and moving to a new place) as one of their possible 'turning points' – when their changed *circumstances* meant people came to re-evaluate their behaviour.

In recent research examining the meaning of long-term imprisonment in Scotland,[4] one of the authors found that while 'knifing off' the outside world was reflected in the prisoners' accounts, it was only a specific group of prisoners who ascribed transformative power to their prison sentence when they were interviewed just before release (Schinkel 2014). For those who had not been imprisoned before (especially when their sentence was for a first offence), imprisonment was a temporary dip in an otherwise positive life story. They fully (and realistically) expected to return to their previous positive lives after their release. Those with more serious histories of offending, but with significant resources on the outside (such as savings, family support or their own accommodation) expected these resources would help them to turn their life around. They attributed their wish to desist to having matured and become more risk-averse. By contrast, the most disadvantaged group of prisoners, those who had spent most of their adult life (and often their teenage years) in institutions and prisons, were more or less resigned to further imprisonment, and therefore did not need to explain a change in their life course. However, those who wanted to desist, but had a significant criminal record and few resources, often positioned their most recent sentence as transformative.

The aspects of imprisonment this group of prisoners credited with their transformation varied. Some felt they had made the most of the various opportunities on offer (thereby in effect transforming themselves) or benefited from time to think. Others positioned themselves as much more passive in the transformation process, instead crediting the interventions of staff, or the impact of cognitive behavioural offending behaviour programmes. Not all of their accounts therefore could be seen as descriptions of 'as if' rehabilitation.[5] On the other hand, it was clear that they imbued their imprisonment with transformative power because they had no other way to explain their future desistance. With few resources, there was nothing else to stand between them and their histories of significant offending *but* their imprisonment.

Despite, or perhaps given, the obstacles they faced upon release (having no clear prospects of suitable and stable accommodation or employment and no significant support from others), their accounts resembled 'redemption narratives' (Maruna 2001) in some ways. In order to maintain the belief that they would be able to desist in less than promising circumstances, these men ascribed 'super-agency' to their future selves (like Maruna's 'desisters') – seeing their future selves as having the power to overcome even seemingly insurmountable obstacles. In contrast, other prisoners who faced similar obstacles told more half-hearted stories about their future desistance, saying that their sentence had changed them, but later contradicting themselves and outlining the reasons why they were likely to reoffend. This might mean that those who managed to maintain coherence were more committed to their transformation through imprisonment, and therefore more likely to desist.

Sadly, however, interviews with (other) men on licence after serving long-term sentences showed that these men were unlikely to achieve what we have called 'tertiary desistance', where people have desisted in the eyes of others and are re-accepted into the community. The majority of these men described living a bleak existence. They attributed this to their isolation, to feeling under surveillance and to withdrawing from social participation – this being the only way for them to avoid further offending (see Shapland and Bottoms 2011, on diachronic self-control). They also spoke of their inability to secure a new identity and routine. The men felt most keenly the lack of employment, which their criminal records and the economic downturn had made almost impossible to secure. Their inability to move forward towards the lives they wanted (of employment, their own house and a stable relationship) meant that many of the men on licence were stuck in a kind of half-life that looked like desistance (at least in the primary sense that they were not offending), but they did not feel their lives were meaningful or that they were socially integrated. Their inability to achieve 'early goals' (Aresti 2010) meant that they lost any sense of progression and their prison-based hopes had been displaced by uncertainty about how their story would work out. For these men 'tertiary' desistance was essential to secure their happy endings (and perhaps to maintain primary and secondary desistance), but it was proving exceptionally hard to secure.

These findings go some way towards identifying what is needed from prison regimes to facilitate desistance – at least for long-term prisoners. While those with resources or minimal histories of offending will likely be able to desist despite the negative consequences of imprisonment, other groups need more support not only to develop any hope of desistance, but also to have solid ground on which to base these hopes. Crucially, interventions in the prison need to be tailored to the individual but also to reach beyond the prison gates, having positive consequences for sustaining or renewing a life outside. Ideally, obstacles upon release, such as a lack of accommodation, employment and support, need to be tackled before release. These sorts of practical help might engender greater hope in those who are less committed to a future of desistance while also making desistance more achievable for those who desire it.

Implementing desistance research in prisons

The first significant practical attempt to map out the implications of desistance research for the organization of a whole prison system was that of the recent Prisons Review Team (PRT) in Northern Ireland. The PRT was established by Minister of Justice David Ford, and was chaired by Dame Anne Owers (former chief inspector of prisons in England and Wales); it reported in 2011 after a lengthy examination of the conditions, management and oversight of prisons in Northern Ireland. One of the authors (McNeill) was a member of the review team, which also included a former chief executive of the National Offender Management Service for England and Wales, a human rights lawyer and a retired senior police officer.

As well as being influenced by desistance research, the Owers Report (2011) drew on recent work on legitimacy and criminal justice (Crawford and Hucklesby 2012), and in particular on the work of the Prisons Research Centre at the University of Cambridge on moral performance in prisons (Liebling 2004, 2011). One of the key findings of the Cambridge team, from their analysis of the results of the measuring of the quality of prison life (MQPL) survey in numerous prisons, concerns a domain of the survey that deals with 'personal development'. Since this domain concerns 'help with the development of potential', it comes closest to measuring the extent to which prisoners surveyed consider the prisons they inhabit to be sites in which progress towards desistance is possible.

The MQPL results suggest that very few prisons score well on this domain. However, in these few prisons the surveys reveal statistically significant positive correlations between personal development and the moral quality of the prison regime as measured in several other domains (listed here in order of significance):

- Help and assistance ('support and encouragement for problems, including drugs, healthcare and progression');
- Humanity ('an environment characterised by kind regard and concern for the person');
- Staff professionalism ('staff confidence and competence in the use of authority');
- Bureaucratic legitimacy ('the transparency and responsivity of the prison/prison system and its moral recognition of the individual');
- Organization and consistency ('the clarity, predictability and reliability of the prison').

(Liebling 2011)

In other words, personal development (towards desistance) seems to be more possible in some prisons than others, and specifically it seems more possible in prisons where the regimes are characterized both by the availability of practical help, and by relationships and processes that are legitimate and consistent.

Set alongside the findings of desistance research discussed above, these MQPL findings were influential in framing the recommendations in the Owers Report (2011). Some of those recommendations are specific to the Northern Irish context and its peculiar post-conflict challenges, but many have wider relevance. Chapter one of the report discusses the purposes and values of prison systems, chapter two is entitled 'Desistance: the Wider Picture', and chapter three examines the potential characteristics of 'Prisons Supporting Change'. The link between these chapters is the argument that prisons need to be places that respect human rights not merely by preventing abuse, but also by providing opportunities for human development. That said, chapter two of the Owers Report (2011) recognizes the risks of seeking to construct prisons as positive places, noting that more productive investments in services and communities outside prisons are ultimately more likely to support crime reduction. However, the report argues that unless prisons support change, they cannot benefit society or prisoners and that supporting change requires partnership with organizations, services and families outside. The authors are careful to recognize that supporting desistance is not just about personal change; as we have noted above, it is a social process and one that requires social change too.

Chapter three goes on to elaborate the seven fundamental characteristics of 'Prisons Supporting Change', arguing that such prisons require:

- *A whole prison approach*: meaning that design of the whole system, the roles of all staff and the articulation of all processes should reflect the central commitment to promoting change.
- *Fair and reasonable treatment*: recognizing that, in the light of human rights standards and of research on both moral performance (Liebling 2004) and desistance from crime, a commitment to the proper treatment of prisoners (and staff) is both morally necessary and practically required if change is to be supported.
- *Strong and meaningful relationships between staff and prisoners*: reflecting the evidence both from research that the quality and character of relationships between staff and prisoners (and prisons and families and outside services) is critical to supporting change.
- *Effective staff development, appraisal and discipline systems*: meaning that these systems need to work to develop and sustain a staff culture that promotes and supports change.
- *Prisoner motivation and achievement*: requiring prisoner progression processes to reward change efforts and not mere 'compliance'.
- *Practical help to promote a crime-free life outside*: ensuring that the right range of services and supports are available to tackle obstacles to change.
- *Supporting the development of a non-criminal identity*: suggesting the need for constructive, creative and reparative opportunities, and for a culture that recognizes and celebrates achievement.

Though there had been some prior discussion of desistance research and about the Owers review with senior managers and governors in the Scottish Prison Service (SPS), the arrival of Colin McConnell as the new chief executive in May 2012 heralded the beginning of a major and still ongoing reform effort. Significantly, McConnell brought with him the experience of having led the Northern Irish service during the Owers review.

As its title suggests, the report of the SPS Organisational Review,[6] *Unlocking Potential, Transforming Lives* (SPS 2013), reflects and elaborates many of the themes of the Owers review and in many respects goes much further, engaging seriously not just with desistance research, but also with the 'assets-based approach' popularized in the public health field by Sir Harry Burns, former chief medical officer of Scotland.

The review report runs to some 250 pages, 47 of which mention desistance. Space and time preclude any attempt here at a critical review of the way that desistance research is used in the report. In any event, as with any report, the more interesting question is whether and to what extent its recommendations will be implemented in ways that really change social and penal institutions, cultures and practices. It is much too soon to make that judgement about the SPS. The change programme will take many years. However, perhaps the most striking aspects of the report are to be found in the way that the 'vision' and 'mission' of the service are reconceived. The vision is of 'Helping to build a safer Scotland – Unlocking Potential – Transforming Lives' (SPS 2013: 5). The mission is 'Providing services that help to transform the lives of people in our care so they can fulfill their potential and become responsible citizens' (SPS 2013: 5).

The vision statement is interesting in several respects; it seems modest in recognizing that SPS can *help* build a safer Scotland, but by implication cannot do so alone; it implies a belief in the value of prisoners and in their potential; and it sets a very aspirational goal (transforming lives). The mission focuses on what the SPS will do to fulfil that aspiration. Our central observation on this statement (and a similar statement in the Scottish government's Reducing Reoffending Programme 2) is that although the focus on citizenship (rather than offending) is welcome, the emphasis remains on enabling transformation of the *individual* citizen (i.e. to fulfil his or her *responsibilities*) and less on addressing social and structural barriers to enjoying citizenship *rights*. The imbalance is most powerfully illustrated in the Scottish government's stubborn refusal to allow prisoners to vote in the recent independence referendum; for us, this was a totemic exemplar of this frustratingly asymmetric use of discourses of citizenship. That said, both the new SPS vision statement and the section of the report that deals with partnership at least suggest an appreciation of the need to work with *communities* as well as *agencies* in supporting change. In some respects, it seems too much to expect an internal prison service review to seek to argue for wider socio-structural changes – but if prison managers and practitioners really want to support desistance then perhaps this is precisely what they must do.

Conclusions: desistance and prisons

One of us (McNeill) was fortunate to have the opportunity to share and discuss a draft version of this chapter (written prior to the contribution of the second author and without reference to her work) with a reading group in a Scottish prison. The group comprised mainly people serving long prison sentences, along with some education staff, prison staff and visiting criminologists. The discussion was revealing, not just in relation to desistance theory but also in relation to the prospects of constructive reform to prison regimes.

In the former connection, the reading group members stressed differences in prison experiences and life trajectories of people who have been involved in persistent offending (but who are typically serving short sentences) and people who have been involved in serious offending, perhaps on a one-off basis (but nonetheless serving long sentences). As Schinkel's (2014) study reveals, not everyone in the latter group has a spoiled identity and not everyone requires a narrative of transformation. That said, some of those in the group (particularly those who had a longer criminal record and long-term involvement with the care and justice systems) did recognize, from their own experiences, many aspects of the desistance process described above – and it is fair to say that all members of the group recognized the relevance of desistance research for most prisoners with significant offending histories.

Unsurprisingly, however, the main focus of the discussion was not so much on desistance research itself, as on its implications for reconstructing processes of rehabilitation in prisons. Partly, the discussion centred on the prospects for significant reform of the Scottish prisons system – in line with the aspirations of the organizational review discussed above. Members of the group had different views on this. Some recognized signs of change – even in the changing discourse of the service; others were more sceptical – pointing to what they considered regressive developments, for example around delayed progression to the open estate and less support for compassionate and other forms of home leave. Many members of the group expressed concerns about the effects of risk discourses and practices on their experiences of imprisonment and rehabilitation, expressing frustration at the double bind presented by regimes that permitted progression only when it was judged that risk had reduced, but offered limited opportunities to prisoners to undertake work to reduce risk (see also Crewe 2009).

A prison staff member in the group reflected honestly on the inherent contradictions between the (new and less familiar) pressures to trust and support prisoners to change, and the (old but enduring) pressures to maintain security. As he put it, it is hard to act as a supporter of change, expressing belief in the capacity of prisoners to progress, whilst at the same time carrying out a cell search or a mandatory drug test – both of which are routine practices that communicate *distrust*. No one in the group was in any doubt about how far the service and the staff will have to travel in order to develop not just processes and practices but also occupational and organizational cultures that are capable of supporting change.

These contradictions neatly sum up the paradoxes implied by seeking to construe prisons as 'desistance-supporting' places. Prisons can and should aim to be *capacity-building* places; indeed, their ultimate contributions to public safety and ex-prisoner reintegration cannot be secured unless they can become such places (Owers Report 2011). Liebling's (2011) research suggests that, under certain conditions, prisons can support personal development but that it is both rare and difficult for them to do so. In a sense, this is unsurprising. Prisons are inherently *incapacitating* places. Whilst the sentence of imprisonment may be intended in part to communicate to someone that they need to reflect upon and then to develop themselves, the realities of imprisonment often mitigate against such a project. To be sure, imprisonment requires adaptation – but that adaptation is typically focused on surviving the experience, not on preparing for life *after* it. As Schinkel's (2014) research (and many previous prison sociologies) make clear, these two forms of adaptation – to punishment and to life after punishment – may push and pull in opposite directions. Perhaps it is only in prison regimes that minimize the need for adaptation to life inside, that adaptation for life after punishment becomes possible.

However, if we conceive of desistance as being about processes of human growth and development (within their social contexts), then there is an even more fundamental problem with imprisonment. Imprisonment is not an act of nurture; it is an act of violence – at least insofar as it is always and everywhere underwritten by the state's claim to an entitlement to use physical force in the process of punishment. In the dishonouring of those punished – and in the insistence on their submission to processes of classification – prisons are also places of 'symbolic violence' (Bourdieu and Wacquant 1992). Imprisonment defines, categorizes and dominates its subjects (or at least it seeks to do so). It is hard to see how the power dynamics in play in these processes can be easily rendered compatible with the implications of desistance research, for example around growth, hope, agency and self-determination. Again, it seems reasonable to suggest that it is only in those prisons where these forms of violence are minimized that change can be supported.

In this context, one of the criminologist members of the reading group pointed out that there is a fundamental problem with desistance research: it implicitly accepts that crime is the problem or the phenomenon to be reduced or managed. Even if by insisting on the links between behaviour change and wider processes of social integration, desistance research has been useful in confronting penality with its own failure to support the process it often claims to support, it colludes in framing the debate in terms of reducing reoffending – and it defines the 'desister' with reference to his or her prior offending (which is, of course, an act of symbolic violence in itself). Perhaps, therefore, the more fundamental challenge is that we need to reverse the polarity of the crime–punishment nexus and start with the question of how and why we might *punish* less, or at least punish less violently. If we did that, we suspect we might find that desisting from punishment is one of the best ways of supporting desistance from crime.

Notes

1 See: scottishjusticematters.com/the-journal/december-2013-desistance-issue/ (accessed 23 July 2014).
2 See: www.cjp.org.uk/bjcj/volume-11-issue-2-3/ (accessed 23 July 2014).
3 See: blogs.iriss.org.uk/discoveringdesistance/ (accessed 24 July 2014).
4 For this study, 27 narrative interviews about their perceptions of the legitimacy and purpose of their sentence were conducted with six men at the start of their sentence, 12 men at the end of their sentences, and nine men on licence after release.
5 However, all other prisoners saw the prison as failing in its aim to rehabilitate because individual input and attention were limited; cognitive behavioural courses were often described as a cynical exercise to reassure politicians and their electorate that rehabilitation was happening.
6 For the record, I should note that I served in an advisory capacity as a member of the Review's Project Steering Group.

Bibliography

Aresti, A. (2010) *'Doing Time after Time': A hermeneutic phenomenological understanding of reformed ex-prisoners' experiences of selfchange and identity negotiation*, PhD, Birkbeck: University of London.

Aresti, A., Eatough, V. and Brooks-Gordon, B. (2010) 'Doing time after time: an interpretative phenomenological analysis of reformed ex-prisoners' experiences of self-change, identity and career opportunities', *Psychology, Crime & Law* 16(3): 169–190.

Ashkar, P.J. and Kenny, D.T. (2008) 'Views from the inside: young offenders' subjective experiences of incarceration', *International Journal of Offender Therapy and Comparative Criminology* 52(5): 584–597.

Barry, M. (2006) 'Dispensing [with?] justice: young people's views of the criminal justice system', in K. Gorman, M. Gregory, M. Hayles and N. Parton (eds) *Constructive Work with Offenders*, London: Jessica Kingsley, 177–192.

Bottoms, A. (2014) 'Desistance from crime', in Z. Ashmore and R. Shuker (eds) *Forensic Practice in the Community*, London: Routledge.

Bottoms, A. and Shapland, J. (2011) 'Steps towards desistance among male young adult recidivists', in S. Farrall, M. Hough, S. Maruna and R. Sparks (eds) *Escape Routes: Contemporary Perspectives on Life after Punishment*, London: Routledge.

Bottoms, A., Shapland, J., Costello, A., Holmes, D. and Muir, G. (2004) 'Towards desistance: theoretical underpinnings for an empirical study', *The Howard Journal* 43(4): 368–389.

Bourdieu, P. and Wacquant, L. (1992) *An Invitation to Reflexive Sociology*, Chicago, IL: The University of Chicago Press.

Burnett, R. and McNeill, F. (2005) 'The place of the officer-offender relationship in assisting offenders to desist from crime', *Probation Journal* 52(3): 221–242.

Calverley, A. (2012) *Cultures of Desistance: Rehabilitation, reintegration and ethnic minorities*, International Series on Rehabilitation and Desistance, London: Routledge.

Comfort, M. (2008) 'The best seven years I could'a done: the reconstruction of imprisonment as rehabilitation', in P. Carlen (ed.) *Imaginary Penalities*, Cullompton: Willan, 252–274.

Crawford, A. and Hucklesby, A. (eds) (2012) *Legitimacy and Compliance in Criminal Justice*, London: Routledge.

Crewe, B. (2009) *The Prisoner Society: Power, adaptation and social life in an English prison*, Oxford: Oxford University Press.

Farrall, S. (2002) *Rethinking What Works with Offenders: Probation, social context and desistance from crime*, Cullompton: Willan.

Farrall, S. and Calverley, A. (2006) *Understanding Desistance from Crime*, Maidenhead: Open University Press.

Farrall, S., Hunter, B., Sharpe, G. and Calverley, A. (2014) *Criminal Careers in Transition: The social context of desistance from crime*, Clarendon Studies in Criminology, Oxford: Oxford University Press.

Foucault, M. (1975 [English trans. 1977]) *Discipline & Punish*, London: Allen Lane.

Giordano, P.C., Cernkovich, S.A. and Rudolph, J.L. (2002) 'Gender, crime, and desistance: toward a theory of cognitive transformation', *American Journal of Sociology* 107(4): 990–1064.

Glynn, M. (2014) *Black Men, Invisibility and Crime: Towards a critical race theory of desistance*, International Series on Rehabilitation and Desistance, London: Routledge.

Goodwin, R., Tuncer, J. and Nickeas, J. (2013) 'The Wirral Desistance Project: seeing beyond the risk agenda in probation practice', *Scottish Justice Matters* (December): 7–8.

Hough, M., Farrall, S. and McNeill, F. (2012) *Intelligent Justice: Balancing the effects of community sentences and custody*, London: Howard League for Penal Reform.

Joliffe, D. and Hedderman, C. (2012) 'Investigating the impact of custody on reoffending using propensity score matching', *Crime and Delinquency* (6 December), DOI: 0011128712466007.

Laub, J. and Sampson, R. (2003) *Shared Beginnings, Divergent Lives: Delinquent boys to age seventy*, Cambridge, MA: Harvard University Press.

Liebling, A. (2011) 'Is there a role for the prison in desistance? Personal development, human flourishing and the unequal pains of imprisonment', presentation at a European Union Project Strengthening Transnational Approaches to Reducing Re-offending (STARR) Conference on 'What Works in Reducing Re-offending', Sofia, Bulgaria, 8–10 June 2011.

Liebling, A. with Arnold, H. (2004) *Prisons and their Moral Performance: A study of values, quality and prison life*, Clarendon Studies in Criminology, Oxford: Oxford University Press.

Liebling, A. and Maruna, S. (eds) (2005) *The Effects of Imprisonment*, Cullompton: Willan.

McNeill, F. (2003) 'Desistance based practice', in W.-H. Chui and M. Nellis (eds) *Moving Probation Forward: Evidence, arguments and practice*, Harlow: Pearson Education, 146–162.

McNeill, F. (2006) 'A desistance paradigm for offender management', *Criminology and Criminal Justice* 6(1): 39–62.

McNeill, F. (2009) *Towards Effective Practice in Offender Supervision*, Glasgow: Scottish Centre for Crime and Justice Research, www.sccjr.ac.uk/documents/McNeil_Towards.pdf.

McNeill, F. (2012a) 'Four forms of "offender" rehabilitation: towards an interdisciplinary perspective', *Legal and Criminological Psychology* 17(1): 18–36 (pre-publication final draft available at: www.blogs.iriss.org.uk/discoveringdesistance/useful-resources/http//blogs.iriss.org.uk/discoveringdesistance/files/2011/09/McNeill-2012-Four-forms-of-offender-rehabilitation.pdf).

McNeill, F. (2012b) 'Counterblast: a copernican correction for community sentences', *Howard Journal of Criminal Justice* 51(1): 94–99.

McNeill, F. (2014) 'Punishment as rehabilitation', in G. Bruinsma and D. Weisburd (eds) *Encyclopedia of Criminology and Criminal Justice*, DOI 10.1007/978-1-4614-5690-2, (a final draft version of this paper is available open access online at blogs.iriss.org.uk/discoveringdesistance/files/2012/06/McNeill-When-PisR.pdf): 4195–4206.

McNeill, F. (forthcoming) 'Positive criminology, positive criminal justice?', in N. Ronei and D. Segev (eds) *Positive Criminology*, London: Routledge.

McNeill, F., Farrall, S., Lightowler, C. and Maruna, S. (2013) 'Discovering desistance: reconfiguring criminal justice?', *Scottish Justice Matters* (December): 3–6.

McNeill, F. and Weaver, B. (2007) *Giving Up Crime: Directions for policy*, Edinburgh: Scottish Consortium on Crime and Criminal Justice.

McNeill, F. and Weaver, B. (2010) *Changing Lives? Desistance research and offender management*, Glasgow: Scottish Centre for Crime and Justice Research, blogs.iriss.org.uk/discoveringdesistance/files/2012/12/Changing-Lives.pdf.

Maruna, S. (2001) *Making Good*, Washington, DC: American Psychological Association.

Maruna, S. and Farrall, S. (2004) 'Desistance from crime: a theoretical reformulation', *Kvlner Zeitschrift fur Soziologie und Sozialpsychologie* 43: 171–194.

Owers Report (2011) *Review of the Northern Ireland Prison Service*, Belfast: Prison Review Team.

Priechenfried, K. (2010) 'Aftercare and transition work "through the gate"', presented at the EQUAL Conference, Budapest, ec.europa.eu/education/grundtvig/doc/conf11/wa8/priechenfried.pdf.

Rex, S. (1999) 'Desistance from offending: experiences of probation', *Howard Journal of Criminal Justice* 38(4): 366–383.

Robinson, G. and McNeill, F. (2008) 'Exploring the dynamics of compliance with community penalties', *Theoretical Criminology* 12(4): 431–449.

Rotman, E. (1990) *Beyond Punishment. A new view of the rehabilitation of criminal offenders*, New York: Greenwood Press.

Sampson, R.J. and Laub, J.H. (2005) 'A life-course view of the development of crime', *The ANNALS of the American Academy of Political and Social Science* 602(1): 12–45.

Schinkel, M. (2014) *Being Imprisoned: Punishment, adaptation and desistance*, Houndmills: Palgrave MacMillan.

Shapland, J. and Bottoms, A. (2011) 'Reflections on social values, offending and desistance among young adult recidivists', *Punishment & Society* 13(3): 256–282.

Sharpe, G. (2012) *Offending Girls: Young Women and Youth Justice*, Abingdon: Routledge.

SPS (Scottish Prison Service) (2013) *Unlocking Potential, Transforming Lives. Report of the Scottish Prison Service Organisational Review*, Edinburgh: Scottish Prison Service.

Weaver, B. (2013) *The Story of the Del: From delinquency to desistance*, PhD thesis, Glasgow: University of Strathclyde.

Weaver, B. and McNeill, F. (2010) 'Travelling hopefully: desistance research and probation practice', in J. Brayford, F. Cowe and J. Deering (eds) *What Else Works? Creative Work with Offenders*, Cullompton: Willan.

Chapter 35

Social injustice and collateral damage

The families and children of prisoners

Rachel Condry, Anna Kotova and Shona Minson[1]

Introduction

By virtue of their relationship to a prisoner, prisoners' families are denied a number of rights and entitlements. As has long been documented, prisoners' families are drawn into the criminal justice process and become subject to a number of harms as a result. In this chapter, we explore the experiences of the families of prisoners and argue that their circumstances need to be seen as more than just the by-product of criminal justice processes and that the inequities they experience should be addressed in their own right, if a society is to claim to be just. As Lacey (2013) has argued we cannot deliver criminal justice without attending to problems of social justice. The chapter argues that the families of those who are punished need to be included in this endeavour and explores how this might operate. These issues are then examined in the context of two ongoing research studies, one which examines the children of prisoners, and another which focuses on the partners of long-term prisoners.

So why is the impact of imprisonment on the families of prisoners a question of social justice, and what exactly do we mean by social justice? Theories of social justice have a long history and vary in their conceptions of what a just society should look like. The aim of achieving social justice is claimed by parties from across the political spectrum and given varying interpretations to suit their rhetoric. As Cook (2006: 4) has said, it is a concept laden with common-sense meanings and as Craig et al. (2008: 1) have argued, social justice is something of which everybody is in favour, almost by definition. Furthermore, there is no single straightforward definition and each attempt to pin it down leads to further questions. For example, if it is about the distribution of resources, then how can we measure or define those resources? If it is about systematic inequality in society, then on what basis do we judge that inequality?

In this chapter we take a broad conception of social justice, drawing particularly upon the work of Iris Marion Young (1990) and the application of her analysis in the context of parental incarceration by Joyce Arditti (2012). Prior to Young's work, many theories of social justice had focused primarily on the inequitable distribution of resources in society. While acknowledging the importance of distribution of material goods, Young argues that the scope of justice is wider than this and stresses the importance of the institutional context that produces and reproduces disadvantage. Young (1990: 15) defines social justice as 'the elimination of institutional domination and oppression'. She proposes what she describes as:

an enabling conception of justice. Justice should refer not only to distribution, but also to the institutional conditions necessary for the development and exercise of individual capacities and collective communication and cooperation. Under this conception of justice, injustice refers primarily to two forms of disabling constraints, oppression and domination. While these constraints include distributive patterns, they also involve matters which cannot easily be assimilated to the logic of distribution: decisionmaking procedures, division of labor, and culture.

(Young 1990: 39)

Young further defines oppression as consisting 'in systematic institutional processes which prevent some people from learning and using satisfying and expansive skills in socially recognized settings, or institutionalized social processes which inhibit people's ability to play and communicate with others or to express their feelings and perspective on social life in contexts where others can listen' (Young 1990: 38). Domination, in Young's analysis, 'consists in institutional conditions which inhibit or prevent people from participating in determining their actions or the conditions of their actions. Persons live within structures of domination if other persons or groups can determine without reciprocation the conditions of their actions. Thorough social and political democracy is the opposite of domination' (ibid.: 38).

Prison is an institutional structure of oppression and domination. By definition, prisons restrict the liberty of those imprisoned, and their freedom of expression, access to resources, self-determination and democratic participation. The degree to which this is so and the varying levels of, for example, disenfranchisement, are beyond the focus of our analysis but are addressed by other chapters in this Handbook. Our focus here is on the ways in which imprisonment as an institution imposes systematic disadvantage, oppression and domination on not only prisoners, but on the families of those who are imprisoned.

In her US analysis, Arditti (2012) has argued that the context of parental incarceration has four key characteristics: 'the demographic characteristics of incarcerated parents and their children'; 'cumulative disadvantage'; 'institutional practices'; and what she calls 'sociopolitical: stigma and disenfranchisement' (see also Codd 2008; and Comfort 2008: Appendix 2). We think these categories provide a useful guide for exploring the broader context of the impact of imprisonment on all family members. In particular, they allow us to consider the circumstances of families before, during and after imprisonment, and to explore exactly what it is that prison *does* to the family. Using Arditti's distinction as a guide, we develop each category in turn and consider how they play out in the more general context of the impact of imprisonment on the family.

Demographic characteristics and patterns of pre-existing disadvantage

Prisoners and their families are more likely to come from backgrounds with systematic patterns of pre-existing disadvantage. In the USA, imprisonment has a well-documented drastic impact on members of minority ethnic groups, and particularly African Americans. In the UK, a disproportionate number of prisoners are also drawn from ethnic minority groups – about a quarter of all prisoners (Berman and Dar 2013). This is a large proportion when compared with one in 11 of the general population in 2009 (Prison Reform Trust 2014b). We can assume that many of these ethnic minority prisoners will have families who are also from ethnic minority groups. Ethnicity has an impact on the likelihood of being drawn into the criminal justice system, but also on treatment within it (see Cheliotis and Liebling 2006; and Bowling and Phillips 2007). The consequences of imprisonment for prisoners' families might therefore be exacerbated by their ethnic background. For example, they may not only go through all the hardships experienced by prisoners' families in general, but may also have to endure racist abuse when visiting prison (Light and Campbell 2007) or experience a misunderstanding of cultural or religious needs.

Imprisonment also has a disproportionate impact on the economically disadvantaged. We know that the prison population in the UK is more likely to come from backgrounds of poverty, interrupted education and other problems (Social Exclusion Unit 2002). Although systematic data have not been collected on the backgrounds of prisoners' families in the UK, studies from both the USA and the UK suggest they are more likely to have lower socio-economic status and be contending with a range of associated problems (see Condry 2007; Comfort 2008; Wakefield and Wildeman 2014).

Patterns of gender disadvantage are also important to understanding the experiences of prisoners' families. Those family members who support prisoners are usually women – wives, girlfriends, mothers and sisters (Condry 2007; see also Christian 2005; and Comfort 2008 for the US context). These women will already be contending with patterns of gender oppression. Worldwide, women represent a disproportionate number of the world's poor – this 'feminization of poverty' also includes deprivations of opportunities and capabilities (Nussbaum 2011). Society often takes women's care work for prisoners (and care work in general) for granted as a 'natural' female role or duty (Aungles 1993), rarely recognizing that this work may be financially, emotionally and socially burdensome. Women are subject to a prevailing conception of natural caregiving and responsibility for other families (see Condry 2007), which permeates society in general and criminal justice in particular. For example, it is startling that women in the UK may lose their social housing if their sons and/or male partners act antisocially, even when these women have done nothing wrong themselves (Hunter and Nixon 2001). The underlying rationale seems to be that it is a woman's duty to control 'her' men and the domestic domain (see Hunter and Nixon 2001).

These patterns of pre-existing disadvantage are complex and interrelated and will intersect in particular ways for individual prisoners' families. Other patterns of oppression might also be important, such as discrimination based upon sexuality or disability. Although it is important to recognize these common broader patterns of pre-existing disadvantage, the families of prisoners will come from a wide variety of backgrounds and will experience the intersection of disadvantage and the impact of imprisonment in different ways, a point to which we will return.

Cumulative disadvantage

Furthermore, imprisonment itself can compound and magnify patterns of economic, social, educational, health and mental health disadvantage and create new problems for families. Taking economic difficulties as an example, imprisonment is strongly correlated with a fall in the income of the prisoner's partner (Smith et al. 2007). Supporting a prisoner can be expensive and might include spending significant amounts of money to send parcels to prisoners, write letters, visit, and sending money. Prisoners earn very low wages and often rely upon family members to supply clothing or money to buy toiletries or food items within prison. Supporting a prisoner can be very demanding in terms of time and energy, and impact upon the reserves of a family member's social and personal resources. Worries about the prisoner and his or her welfare and feelings of loss can further compound pre-existing mental health problems and create new anxieties for the family.

Institutional practices

Existing research on prisoners' families has found that punishment extends beyond prison walls and reaches into every facet of these families' lives. The restrictive institutional practices of the prison extend 'punishment beyond the legal offender' (Comfort 2007) to the prisoner's family members. Prisoners' families 'experience restricted rights, diminished resources, social marginalisation, and other consequences of penal confinement' (Comfort 2007: 7). Through her research in the USA, Comfort found that prison visitors would have to adjust their choice of clothing according to somewhat arbitrary prison regulations, and that a huge amount of time would be absorbed by the hours spent visiting and waiting to go on a visit. The women in Comfort's study were themselves fundamentally changed by their interaction with the prison, assuming the status of quasi-inmates as they came under its rules and discipline, and as the boundary between home and prison became blurred. In the UK context, Condry (2007) described how some prisoners' partners arranged their daily lives around supporting their imprisoned loved one, which included waiting for phone calls, going on visits and writing frequent letters. Comfort (2007, 2008) has described this as 'secondary prisonization': 'a weakened but still compelling version of the elaborate regulations, concentrated surveillance, and corporeal confinement governing the lives of ensnared felons' (Comfort 2009: 2). The ways in which prisons are organized and the channels through which relatives interact with the prison work together to produce an institutional burden of punishment for these families.

Socio-political: stigma and disenfranchisement

Prisoners families are subject to a range of exclusionary and stigmatizing practices. Some of these stem from the exclusionary nature of imprisonment itself and the treatment of the prisoner as 'other'. Dehumanizing practices might include the way prisoners are spoken to and addressed, the deprivation of basic necessities, limits on their interaction with their families, restrictions on voting and political participation both during and after imprisonment, and curtailing of employment opportunities on release, all of which have implications for the 'negative othering' of prisoners and their families. Furthermore, the families of prisoners might be directly stigmatized themselves because of their relationship with a prisoner.

Condry's study of the relatives of serious offenders found that family members felt they were perceived to be the same as the offender because of their close association – 'tarred with the same brush' – or because of a genetic connection that could provoke very primitive ideas of bad blood. Mothers in her study, for example, often spoke of their horror that someone born of their body had committed a heinous offence, and sons worried whether they might inherit some of their offending fathers' traits. Family members felt they were blamed directly for things they had or had not done that were seen to contribute to the offence (Condry 2007). Explanations that locate the source of deviant behaviour within the family have a long history and are woven through political, media and lay discourse, and expert and therapeutic analyses. The families in Condry's study felt they were constantly faced with the belief that serious offenders were somehow 'made' by their families. The consequences of being blamed and stigmatized could be severe. Friendships were lost, a mother was spat at in the street, another had eggs thrown at her windows and abuse from neighbours, and another received abusive phone calls. One wife had all the windows of her house broken, and another was taunted in the street: 'you murderer's wife' (Condry 2007).

Social injustice and prisoners' families

Crucially, this meshing of disadvantage produces and reproduces social injustice at the level of the individual member of a prisoner's family, and at the level of a prisoner's family group, but also at the level of society. These sustained and reproduced patterns of inequality and disadvantage – for hundreds of thousands of prisoners' family members in the UK and for several million in the USA – have a profound impact upon the social fabric and organization of society both in the current context and in the future.

More recently, attention has turned to this wider societal impact. One powerful book, Wakefield and Wildeman's (2014) *Children of the Prison Boom*, demonstrates clearly the devastating impact of mass incarceration for generations of children in the USA and provides striking evidence of the impact this has on inequality in American society. For example, the authors show that children with an incarcerated parent are more likely to experience multiple difficulties including mental health and behavioural problems, the risk of being homeless, and even the chance that they will die before they reach the age of one. African Americans born around 1990 had a one in four risk of parental imprisonment by their 14th birthday, compared with a risk of one in 30 for white children. For those African American children whose fathers dropped out of high school there was a better than even chance of having a father imprisoned at 50.5%; to put this in further context, black children are more likely to have a parent imprisoned by their first birthday than white children are before their 14th birthday. The authors argue that this is storing up deeply rooted patterns of inequality for the future of American society. This level of entrenched inequality and social injustice needs a more fundamental response and cannot be addressed by family-friendly prison programmes which tinker at the edge of this devastating impact.

We therefore need to understand fully the harm inflicted by criminal justice processes upon society's already disadvantaged groups, of which the families of prisoners are one such example. At the same time, it is important to keep in mind that the category of 'prisoners' families' contains a range of different kin relationships; variations in demographics such as age, gender, ethnicity and social class; variation in sentence type and previous experience of imprisonment; and a wide range of different life experiences outside prison. Although we can discern common patterns in the impact of imprisonment on family members, it is important also to recognize their heterogeneity. We now turn to two ongoing research studies that focus upon specific groups to explore how patterns of social disadvantage play out in different contexts.

Children of imprisoned parents

That millions of children each year become separated from their parents looks, at first glance, more like something caused by war or perhaps natural disaster than a product of a carefully planned and well thought out policy on crime and imprisonment in a modern democratic nation.

(Scharff-Smith 2014: 10)

The past decade has seen an increased recognition amongst academics, governments and non-governmental organizations (NGOs) that significant numbers of children are affected each year by parental imprisonment, and that parental imprisonment can, and does, affect children in very significant ways. There is a growing body of work internationally, focusing attention on this population, some of the most recently published books on the subject being those by Scharff-Smith (2014), Wakefield and Wildeman (2014), and Arditti (2012). In England and Wales it has been estimated that around 200,000 children each year experience the imprisonment of a parent (Ministry of Justice 2012). This number is likely to be an underestimate as no data pertaining to children of prisoners are collected routinely, and the prison population has continued to increase over the past few years.

In the UK since 2013 the Department of Education has funded a programme (I-Hop – information hub on offenders' families with children – managed jointly by voluntary sector organizations Barnardo's and Partners of Prisoners Service), which provides information to those working with or encountering children of prisoners. I-Hop is working with higher education establishments to ensure that the particular needs of these children are covered in the training of teachers, social workers and health professionals. The issue has recently been brought before Parliament in the form of proposed amendments to Bills, which would place a statutory duty on the courts to enquire at remand or sentencing about the welfare of any children who will be affected by the imprisonment of their parent. At the time of writing the proposals had not been accepted.

A number of factors may have influenced interest in this population. First and foremost, the increasing number of children affected each year by parental imprisonment, and the realization that this may fundamentally impact upon society both now and in the future (Wakefield and Wildeman 2014) is of concern. Children's rights in this context have been subject to academic attention in recent years (Scharff-Smith 2014; Scharff-Smith and Gampell 2011; Minson and Condry 2015), and the Court of Appeal gave guidance in 2001 that the Article Eight right of a child to family life must be balanced with other factors when a custodial sentence is being considered for a parent (*R (on the application of P and Q) v Secretary of State for the Home Department*, 2001). There has also been a flow of research into the experiences of children of imprisoned parents which has countered assumptions that have been made in the past about these children.

Such assumptions may have facilitated seeming disregard for the children of imprisoned parents. For example, the assumption that criminally involved parents are bad parents, and therefore their removal through imprisonment benefits, or does not harm, their children, may well have affected the behaviours and decision making of police, sentencers, media and the wider community. Recent research (Wakefield and Wildeman 2014) refutes that particular assumption and it may be helpful for the reader to consider those arguments at this stage.

The central tenet of the rebuttals is that research evidence demonstrates that the negative impact on a child of their parent's imprisonment is not dependent on the quality of the relationship prior to the imprisonment, save for the caveat that there must have been a degree of connection to family life prior to imprisonment. For example, 'cascading effects' such as stress in the home, financial loss and stigma, will affect all children who lose a parent from the home, not just those who had a good relationship with their parent prior to the imprisonment. Their research also demonstrates that even when a parent is 'inconsistently involved' with their children, the child still experiences a negative loss when the parent is imprisoned. They also contend that as more people are imprisoned for non-violent offences, 'the contemporary prison, then, may be more likely to house inconsistent or irresponsible parents but perhaps less likely to house harmful ones' (Wakefield and Wildeman 2014: 46).

If it is accepted that children are, in general, negatively affected by the imprisonment of their parent, then it is arguable that the state is failing in its duty under Article Two of the United Nations Convention on the Rights of the Child 1989, to protect children from discrimination or punishment which they suffer as a consequence of the status or activities of their parents.

The next section of the chapter uses Minson's ongoing research[2] on the impact of maternal imprisonment to provide an illustration of some of the disadvantages children face in England and Wales as a consequence of their mothers' imprisonment, when viewed through the social justice lens of Arditti's (2012) four-point analysis.

Focus on the children of imprisoned women

Demographic characteristics and patterns of pre-existing disadvantage

By looking at the characteristics of the female prison population in England, 66% of whom are mothers of children under the age of 18 (Liebling and Maruna 2005: 159), and 33% of whom are lone parents (Social Exclusion Unit 2002: 137), it is possible to gain some insight into the lives of children prior to their mothers' imprisonment. Some 46% of women in prison report having suffered domestic violence (Prison Reform Trust 2014a: 4), 25% were looked after in care as children and 53% report having experienced emotional, physical or sexual abuse as a child (Ministry of Justice 2012). They are five times more likely than women in the general population to have a mental health concern (Plugge et al. 2006, in Prison Reform Trust 2013: 34), and 41% have attempted suicide at some time (Ministry of Justice 2013). It is widely recognized that they are a population of particularly vulnerable women. It is possible therefore that their children have experienced an unsettled childhood even prior to incarceration. The following excerpts from interviews illustrate this.

The grandmother and carer of a 16-year-old boy, who had been in her care full time since the age of four, spoke about his early childhood experiences prior to his mother's imprisonment:

> He [my grandson] used to tell us quite vividly how he remembered the police coming round and him hiding in cupboards or standing on the balcony or climbing over the edge of the balcony when the police used to appear, and this was all from when he was just one or two.
>
> … their Dad was there just comatose and [my grandsons] were just crawling around in all this filth and scraping chocolate and cheese off the floor to try and survive, so we brought them back and we had to soak them in a bath to get rid of their own faeces for about an hour.

The carer of a four-year-old boy spoke of how he was affected when he moved to live with her following the imprisonment of his mother:

> I think like him having a routine and going to nursery and coming back when he's supposed to, things like that, it helped him.

Cumulative disadvantage

The primary disadvantage suffered by a child when their parent is imprisoned is the loss of that parent. Experts liken it to bereavement, but it is often made more difficult for the children by a number of issues. First, there is such stigma surrounding imprisonment that children are not always told the truth about their parents' whereabouts, thus adding to their confusion about the situation. Second, prison sentences are not set to a fixed date, as release can be influenced by a number of factors, and therefore until someone is actually released from prison there is always some uncertainty regarding the end date of the sentence. It is difficult for children to maintain contact with the imprisoned parent, particularly when it is their mother in prison, as research figures indicate that when a mother is imprisoned only 9% are cared for by their father during their mother's absence (Corston 2007), indicating that many children may end up in extended family or friendship care, or in local authority care. Many women in prison do not receive visits from their children because those caring for them are unable or unwilling to bring them, or because the mothers do not wish their children to see them under those circumstances. The average distance women in prison are held from their home is 60 miles (Women in Prison 2013). An 11-year-old girl whose mother had been in prison for ten years was asked about the frequency of visits:

> – So how often do you get to see your Mum?
> – Not much. I think we've been like once or twice in the last couple of years. We used to go see her quite a bit but she moved further away and then she moved even further away.
> – So where is she now?
> – I don't exactly know. I only know we can't go and see her 'cos we can't afford it.

Telephone contact is expensive and limited and relies upon the mother having sufficient money to pay for calls. It is difficult for children to be limited to set times for communication, as illustrated by an interview with a 16-year-old boy whose mother had been in prison for three years:

> There's certain days when you wake up and you're like, I could really do with talking to my Mum and because of the situation you can't.

Only 5% of children remain in the family home when their mother is imprisoned (Caddle and Crisp 1997), the remainder moving to live with other relatives, friends or into local authority care. Such moves can then also necessitate a change of school and separation from siblings and friends. All of these changes occur at a time when the child is already experiencing significant loss.

Institutional practices

The notion of punishment extending beyond the legal offender to his or her legally innocent family members has been clearly articulated by Megan Comfort (2007, 2008), and it applies to children of prisoners in many of the same ways as it applies to adults. If children attend prison visits they will be subjected to the rigorous security checks and visitor restrictions, which can feel very oppressive to children. Although it has recently been found to be the right of a child to have visits in a way that is not frightening for them, this is not always the case (*Hoyrech v Poland*, ECHR 17.04.2012). The restrictions on contact with prisoners, e.g. by telephone calls, impose a level of 'prisonization' on a child, whose need to have contact with their parent at particular times is not facilitated by prison regimes and suffers due to the high cost of telephone calls from prison. An 11-year-old whose mother was serving a life sentence, and who has been cared for by her grandmother since her mother's imprisonment, explained:

Stigma and exclusionary practices

> Marginalisation is perhaps the most dangerous form of oppression. A whole category of people is expelled from useful participation in social life and thus potentially subjected to severe material deprivation and even extermination. The material deprivation marginalisation often causes is certainly unjust.
>
> (Young 2011: 53)

Whether real or imagined, the perception of children whose parents are imprisoned is that there is shame attached to the status of their parent. When a 16-year-old boy whose parents have both been in prison was asked what advice he would give another child in his situation, he said without hesitation:

> Lie – well not lie, just don't tell the full story. Just change it.

Another 16-year-old boy whose mother had been in prison for four years was asked whether his friends knew about her imprisonment:

> Some of them do. Like my really close friends do, but to others I say my Mum's on holiday. I didn't want to make it really public.

The interviewer asked why he did not tell people and he replied:

> It's not like to me I'm really ashamed of it, but it's not any of their business to know why she's in prison or if she's in prison or not. So yeah.

It seems that such feelings, whether expressed as stigma, shame or privacy, may in some instances cause children to self-exclude from situations and relationships, causing them to become marginalized. Parental imprisonment is a taboo subject, and the boy above disclosed that in the four years his mother had been in prison he had not been asked by anyone how he felt about the situation. So from the ages of 13–16, no one was willing to broach the subject with him.

At a recent international conference on children of imprisoned parents (COPE 2014), a Norwegian worker reported that the children she worked with felt that their dignity and respect had been removed by their parents' imprisonment. It was only when the Norwegian Children's Ombudsman sought their views that they felt that those things were theirs again (Holden at COPE, ibid.)

Moving forward

> Young's political philosophy established a much needed framework for thinking about justice under conditions of modern mass politics, where citizens seek liberty and egalitarian community in contexts where they are for the most part strangers to one another.
>
> (Allen, in Young 2011: x)

Within our society it seems unlikely that any arguments would be made for treating the children of prisoners in a different or lesser way to any other child, yet perhaps because they are pushed through disadvantage and stigma to the margins of our society, they are 'strangers' to us and it is for that reason that their systemic disadvantage has been ignored.

It can only be hoped that as the body of research on these children grows there will be a number of changes in the way that they are viewed and treated. First, a recognition that although for some children there is benefit in the removal of a parent from the family through imprisonment, for the majority of children there is no benefit, and there is in fact negative loss. Second, no longer should the impact on children of parental imprisonment be regarded as anticipated and acceptable collateral damage. The idea that because a parent committed a crime the state has no need to consider their dependent children in sentencing should no longer form any part of judicial or community thinking. It is encouraging that an analysis of Court of Appeal transcripts has indicated that there is a willingness to recognize the need to look at the sentencing of primary carers within a more holistic framework, but this needs to become standard practice across the court system, with a starting position of non-custodial sentencing options being the preferred outcome when a parent, in particular a primary carer, is to be sentenced (Minson and Condry 2014). In cases where imprisonment is the only possible outcome, a greater awareness of the impact of different sentence lengths on children would assist the courts in making decisions. It would also make a great difference to children and those who care for them during the course of the imprisonment if sentences of imprisonment had definite end dates, which would not be altered save for grave circumstances. There is a lack of social justice in the impact of prison on unimprisoned children which needs to be addressed in a more deliberate manner.

Female partners of long-term male prisoners

A large proportion of male prisoners in the UK have partners, with a 2012 study reporting that 8% have partners to whom they are married, and 24% are in an unmarried partnership (Williams et al. 2012). Over 90% of male prisoners say that their children are cared for by their partners (Home Office 2004), therefore even if the prisoner is separated from his partner, his access to his children is likely to be mediated through her. The impact of imprisonment on the child may also be mediated or exacerbated by the impact on the carer (see Murray 2005). Lowenstein (1986: 86) found that the extent to which a mother is able to cope with a father's imprisonment has a significant impact on how well the child copes.

A growing body of academic work, both in the UK (e.g. Condry 2007; Codd 2003, 2010; May 2000) and the USA (e.g. Comfort 2007, 2008; Fishman 1990; Girshick 1996) has explored the impact imprisonment has on partners of male prisoners, to uncover the wide range of consequences affecting this group when their husband or boyfriend is imprisoned. These consequences can be emotional and centre on loss: financial, such as when a breadwinner is removed from the family home, for example; social, such as the loss of friendships or taunting by others in the community; and the exposure to petty humiliations and deprivations when visiting a prison. Condry (2007) posits that a long sentence may exacerbate these problems and deprivations, but there has been little research in the UK into the impact of long-term imprisonment itself on partners of prisoners.

There is, in the UK, very little structured support for prisoners' partners and it is notable that there is no single governmental authority responsible for addressing the needs of prisoners' families generally (Action for Prisoners Families 2013). Front-line support that does exist is usually provided by small organizations with limited resources. Adult partners of prisoners do not garner the same level of support or sympathy as the children of prisoners, being viewed as having chosen, to some degree, their circumstances.

An ongoing UK study into the impact of long-term imprisonment on female partners of male prisoners in the UK[3] can be used to illustrate some of the injustices and dis-advantages these partners face. We know very little about the social backgrounds of female partners of long-term male prisoners, though we may assume that they are likely to experience the patterns of social disadvantage described above. Prisoners' families are notoriously difficult to access for research purposes and narrowing the field to those partners 'standing by' and supporting prisoners through long-term sentences of ten years or more increases this difficulty considerably. In this ongoing research, participants have been sourced widely through voluntary organizations, social media and newsletters such as *Inside Time*. Those who responded to requests and eventually agreed to interview have tended to have fewer pre-existing disadvantages and to be of a higher socio-economic status (with some exceptions) than that reported in other prisoners' families research. This might be due to a number of factors, but it is likely to be heavily influenced by the willingness to volunteer for and participate in research.

What is interesting for the purposes of this chapter is that coming from less difficult circumstances prior to imprisonment does not provide protection or insulation from the social injustices that follow. Following Arditti's framework, these partners particularly experienced cumulative disadvantage centring upon financial and health difficulties; dis-advantage that developed from the institutional practices and the extension of punishment to them as partners; and practices of social exclusion and 'othering'.

Cumulative disadvantage

Partners in this study reported a range of difficulties stemming from the imprisonment of their partner. These included the emotional consequences of separation and loss, the difficulties of sustaining a relationship through such a prolonged period of separation, and particularly financial consequences and an impact on their own health.

A wife, whose husband had been sentenced to 15 years, reported having a relatively comfortable lifestyle prior to imprisonment, but that this changed immediately following her husband's arrest and imprisonment:

> my mother supports me, it's the only way I'm living in my house, she pays my mortgage. And that's the only way I survive at the moment, and I've got friends and family that help me with food and that.
>
> (Wife, sentence 15 years)

Another participant was unable to continue her job as a result of her long-term relationship with a life sentence prisoner. This had devastating financial consequences:

> I've lost my job, I've lost my career, I'm losing my house ... [because] I can't pay the mortgage ... No job.
>
> (Partner, life sentence)

While another participant had lost a crucial source of financial support following her fiancé's 11-year sentence:

> I'm now on benefits ... – If he was with me, he'd be supporting me [financially].
>
> (Fiancée, sentence 11 years)

Overall, the financial impact of long-term imprisonment was severe and compounded by the cost of supporting the prisoner through the sentence.

Partners of long-term prisoners in this study also reported health difficulties which had either emerged or worsened following imprisonment. Some of these were stress, anxiety and mental health-related, others were physical, and yet others were harder to disentangle. A wife said her GP had 'sent me for counselling, because I couldn't cope with the injustice of it', and went on to say that she had 'developed stress asthma' (Wife, sentence 15 years).

A fiancée reported the worsening of a health condition thought to be stress-related, which she put down to her partner's imprisonment:

> Since he's been gone, I've developed inflammatory arthritis, so I'm on medication and I can't work now because my wrists and shoulders pack up. It's a nightmare.
>
> I don't think the arthritis would have kicked in [if my fiancé had not gone to prison]. He reckons it's stress-related. I wouldn't be surprised. I'm sure I'm depressed, I know some evenings I just sit there and cry.
>
> (Fiancée, sentence 11 years)

The difficulties reported by these partners are likely to be increased by the length of the prison sentence.

Institutional practices

Comfort (2009: 2) has defined 'secondary prisonization' of prisoners' partners as 'a weakened but still compelling version of the elaborate regulations, concentrated surveillance, and corporeal confinement governing the lives of ensnared felons'. Prisoners' partners may get heavily entangled within the criminal justice system and the many ways in which it supervises and controls individuals – and this is likely to be all the more onerous when a long sentence is involved. A partner of a life sentence prisoner described this as 'constantly hitting barriers where the Prison Service wishes you didn't exist'. She went on to explain how she felt the prison system treated families unfairly:

> But when you're dealing one-to-one with a system that says – go and wait outside in the rain for an hour, no you can't stand in this little bit that's dry. We want you [to] stand there in the rain. And that's what they do to us.

A wife whose husband had been sentenced to 20 years continued this theme of inconsiderate treatment of families by the prison:

> It doesn't take Einstein to work out that you don't change a system so that everybody has to book by phone and then close the booking line for a week.
> You've got to be prepared to fight for everything. And you have to keep finding this inner strength from somewhere ...
>
> (Wife, sentence 22 years)

She then went on to say how this was particularly hard across a long sentence and that the prospect of doing it for a long time, with no release date on the horizon, was difficult.

A partner of a life sentence prisoner drew attention to the ways in which the lives of supporting partners become enmeshed with the prison and its routines:

> The prison shapes our lives as well, very much so, because we work round their bang-up times. And you get a day where they don't fit into the routine we're in, because we're so institutionalised by it, and it's panic. Absolute panic [when he does not call for some reason].
>
> (Partner, life sentence)

When asked whether bearing with these difficulties gets any easier with time, most women admitted that although they got to know the ins and outs of the prison system over time, the emotional burden did not improve. The frustrations and deprivations – such as lack of privacy – still affected them. To cope, some adopted, to quote one participant, a 'sod you' attitude. The partners in this study had chosen to continue to support the prisoner and therefore had to accept the controls and deprivations associated with maintaining a relationship with someone with a long sentence.

Social stigma and 'negative othering'

Partners reported being stigmatized and experiencing negative treatment in the prison itself (both from some prison officers and from fellow visitors, in the cases of partners of men convicted of sex offences especially). A participant said, 'We're treated so badly [by the Prison Service] ... we're treated absolutely appallingly'. She reported constantly wondering 'how am I gonna be treated this week [by the Prison Service]? What sort of rubbish am I going to have to contend with with these people?' (Partner, life sentence). In her words, the weight of these thoughts, over the years, had built up into a 'horrendous' emotional burden.

Some women were also stigmatized in the community, describing incidents of people crossing the street so as to avoid them and dog's mess being thrown through letterboxes. Others were simply cautious whom they told about their partner's imprisonment, fearing potential stigma and negative reactions. One participant described herself as 'wearing a mask 24/7'.

The experience of stigmatizing and exclusionary practices in the community was common to a number of partners:

> I've got quite a few friends that don't speak to me any more ... – I've been trying to get a couple of jobs even as a carer, and the stigma that's attached ... it's just like – you're a liability.
>
> (Partner, life sentence)

> I'm disowned [by the family], as well as [my husband]. And [my husband's son] is getting married this year, so, you know, obviously, [my husband] is not going to the wedding, and I haven't been invited either. So I'm clubbed along with [my husband], when, you know, the rest of his family are all preparing for a wedding! So, it's hurtful ...
>
> (Wife, life sentence)

> It came in the paper, of course, in the local paper... So you're wondering: who knows? Who doesn't know? You've no idea how it is, going out the front door, and make that effort to walk to the bus stop, and get the bus ... And thinking: who knows? ... somebody had graffitied on the front of my house. So that was awful.
>
> (Wife, IPP)

This ongoing research indicates that long sentences have a continuing negative impact on partners of prisoners, even those for whom pre-existing disadvantage was not so evident. The practical, emotional and social consequences are both negative and lasting, and the burdens do not necessarily get easier as the years go by. In fact, a few participants indicated that new problems arise as time passes, such as fears about dying while the partner is still in prison, or health issues as both the prisoner and the partner get older.

Reducing social injustice for prisoners' families

What can be done to improve the circumstances of prisoners' families and to reduce the impact of imprisonment upon the legally innocent? As we have suggested in this chapter, there needs to be a broader focus on social inequality and social injustice which addresses the complex difficulties facing prisoners' families, and it needs to see the family members of prisoners as citizens in their own right, not just as prison visitors who only become visible when they walk through the prison gate.

There are fundamental issues that go beyond the family of the prisoner to the impact of punishment broadly and imprisonment specifically on groups in society who are already contending with layers of intersecting social disadvantage. The extension of this impact to families and communities is profound and needs to be understood and recognized as interwoven with firmly entrenched patterns of ethnic, gender and socio-economic disadvantage. There needs to be a clear recognition of how imprisonment impacts upon families that are already subject to a range of restricted central capabilities and freedoms (Nussbaum 2000), which are then compounded as they are drawn into the criminal justice system. Selection into prison both reflects existing stratification processes and generates ongoing inequalities in its own right (see Wakefield and Uggen 2010 for a review).

As Lacey and Pickard (2013) argue, this need not be so. Systems of punishment could adopt an approach that holds offenders accountable and responsible as is more common in a clinical model, without resorting to harsh and stigmatizing measures. Exclusionary practices include depriving prisoners of the opportunity for meaningful work, restitution, education and therapeutic opportunities and such measures as restriction on employment, voting or access to welfare benefits on release (Lacey and Pickard 2013), all of which have significant implications for families. Prisoners and those who come into the prison to visit them are also entitled to dignified, respectful and humane treatment, which is not always forthcoming in an under-resourced and poorly valued prison system.

The detrimental impact of imprisonment on legally innocent family members might also be taken into account at sentencing, where non-custodial measures could be used instead. This is more likely to hold sway where the family members concerned are recognized as dependent on the defendant, such as in the case of children, or adult relatives who require care. However, we might think carefully about a wider definition of 'dependency' and the detrimental effect on the family.

There is already a general consensus amongst both researchers and the judiciary that short sentences are not effective as punishment or to reduce reoffending. In circumstances where a short sentence could be considered, it is becoming more consistently the practice that the court will consider non-custodial alternatives. However, in more serious cases there is still a reluctance, influenced by sentencing guidelines, to use non-custodial alternatives as the means of punishment.

The impact on children should be considered when a parent is before the court. Case law has set out that even when sentencing a parent for more serious crimes, the court should consider a child's right to family life. In the case of R *(on the application of P and Q) v Secretary of State for the Home Department* (2001) it was determined that a criminal conviction does not remove that right from the child or the parent. In any case to which Article Eight of the Human Rights Act 1998 applies (the right to family life), the court should ask three questions: (i) is there an interference with family life?; (ii) is the interference in accordance with law and in pursuit of a legitimate aim?; and (iii) is the interference proportionate given the balance between various factors? (R v *Petherick*, 2012).

That case, and others which followed (R v *Dartford Magistrates Court* 2011; and R v *Petherick* 2012), established the principle that when state intervention disrupts a right, there must be compelling justification for the disruption. The courts stated that the more serious the intervention, the more compelling the justification must be, and interventions cannot be much more serious than the act of separating a mother from a very young child.

In England and Wales the courts already have the power to suspend custodial sentences that are up to two years in length, and they have the power to defer sentence in order to allow a defendant the opportunity to prove a willingness to engage with non-custodial alternatives. It may be the case that in order to take family impact into account, no new sentencing options need to be created, but rather those that already exist could be used with a greater frequency and flexibility than is currently the norm.

A number of other countries have already engaged with this issue, in particular with regard to the children of prisoners. In South Africa the 2007 case of *M v State* explored the reasons for taking children's rights into account when sentencing defendants with dependent children:

> the purpose of emphasizing the duty of the sentencing court to acknowledge the interests of the children, then, is not to permit errant parents unreasonably to avoid appropriate punishment. Rather it is to protect the innocent children as much as is reasonably possible in the circumstances from avoidable harm.

The case identified the two competing interests that sentencing judges must endeavour to balance: the integrity of family care, and the duty on the state to punish criminal misconduct. Such balancing should 'promote uniformity of principle, consistency of treatment and individualization of outcome'. The problems that the children in that case would suffer if their mother were imprisoned were listed, and it is a clear articulation of the breadth of issues that a judge should consider in relation to dependants:

> loss of their source of maternal and emotional support; loss of their home and familiar neighbourhood; disruption in school routines, possible problems in transporting to and from school; impact on their healthy developmental process; and separation of the siblings.

In that landmark decision the court allowed the appeal, and suspended the remaining 45 months of a four-year sentence.

Since that decision a number of other cases have demonstrated that it is now established in South African law that the rights of children of defendants must be considered fully by the court. This has led courts to use innovative sentences such as weekend imprisonment for a defendant convicted of murder, which enabled him to care for, educate and financially provide for the children Monday to Friday, whilst also punishing him with imprisonment (*S v Ntikedzeni* (CC 26/2010) [2011] AZLMPHC 2).

Other countries are more aware of child dependants than the UK and the USA. In Italy, for example, women with children under a certain age serve their sentence under a home curfew rather than in a prison, to enable them to continue to care for their children. Measures such as this could be extended to take account of the exclusionary impact of imprisonment on the family.

Finally, when imprisonment is inevitable, we can note some very practical measures that have improved the experience of family members visiting the prison and supporting a prisoner. These include measures to improve the experience of visiting including supportive visitors' centres, family days and attention to the impact of rules and regulations upon visitors, as well as measures to improve family contact such as reducing the cost of telephone calls. Family-focused prison programmes that allow prisoners to improve, for example, their parenting skills, are beneficial, and perhaps consideration should be given to more consistent home leave or conjugal visits – though the latter never occur in the UK.

We suggest that family-friendly prison policies and measures to improve contact between prisoners and their families are important and have immediate practical benefit, but that a full understanding of the experience of prisoners' families requires a social justice perspective. It may be that many of the 'collateral consequences' of imprisonment on family members are not really collateral at all, but rather an in-built part of a system of imprisonment that is exclusionary and stigmatizing, and fundamentally entwined with social inequality.

Cases

R (on the application of P and Q) v Secretary of State for the Home Department, EWCA Civ 1151.
M v The State, Constitutional Court of South Africa, CCT 53/06 [2007] ZACC 18.
S v Ntikedzeni (CC 26/2010) [2011] AZLMPHC 2 (31 August 2011).

Notes

1 Our thanks to the Sir Halley Stewart Trust for funding Anna Kotova's doctoral project. All views expressed in this chapter are those of the authors, and not necessarily those of the Trust. Shona Minson would like to acknowledge the ESRC for funding her doctoral studentship.
2 The interview material referenced in this section is taken from Shona Minson's ongoing PhD study considering the impact upon children of maternal imprisonment. Participants were recruited via prisoner support organizations, social media and snowball sampling. The interviews were conducted in person and were semi-structured in format.
3 This is Anna Kotova's ongoing PhD study, as part of which 26 (at the time of writing) wives, girlfriends and fiancées of men serving a determinate sentence of ten years or more, or an IPP or life sentence, have been interviewed. Participants were recruited via social media, voluntary organizations that support families of prisoners, snowball sampling, and written pieces in voluntary organizations' newsletters and *Inside Time*. The interviews were in person and semi-structured, and explored the experiences of supporting a prisoner through a long sentence.

Bibliography

Action for Prisoners' Families (2013) 'Facts and figures about prisoners' families', www.prison ersfamilies.org.uk/uploadedFiles/2010_Publications_And_Resources/Facts_and_figures_about_p risoners_families_June2013.pdf (accessed 3 November 2014).

Arditti, J. (2012) *Parental Incarceration and the Family: Psychological and social effects of imprisonment on children, parents and caregivers*, New York: NYU Press.

Aungles, A. (1993) 'Prisons – penal policies: the hidden contracts', in P. Easteal and S. McKillop (eds) *Women and the Law: Proceedings of a conference Held 24–26 September 1991*, Canberra: Australian Institute of Criminology.

Berman, G. and Dar, A. (2013) 'Prison population statistics', Commons Library Standard Note, www.parliament.uk/briefing-papers/sn04334 (accessed October 2013).

Bowling, B. and Phillips, C. (2007) 'Ethnicities, racism, crime, and criminal justice', in M. Maguire, R. Morgan and R. Reiner (eds) *Handbook of Criminology*, Oxford: Oxford University Press.

Caddle, D. and Crisp, D. (1997) *Mothers in Prison*, HO Research and Statistics Directorate Findings No. 38, London: The Stationery Office.

Cheliotis, L.K. and Liebling, A. (2006) 'Race matters in British prisons: towards a research agenda', *British Journal of Criminology* 46(2): 286–317.

Christian, J. (2005) 'Riding the bus: barriers to prison visitation and family management Strategies', *Journal of Contemporary Criminal Justice* 21(1): 31–48.

Codd, H. (2002) '"The ties that bind": feminist perspectives on self-help groups for Prisoners' partners', *The Howard Journal* 41(4): 334–347.

Codd, H. (2003) 'Women inside and out: prisoners' partners, women in prison and the struggle for Identity', *Internet Journal of Criminology*: 1–24.

Codd, H.L. (2008) *In the Shadow of Prison: Families, imprisonment and criminal justice*, Cullompton: Willan.

Comfort, M. (2007) 'Punishment beyond the legal offender', *Annual Review of Law and Social Science* 3: 271–296.

Comfort, M. (2008) *Doing Time Together: Love and family in the shadow of the prison*, Chicago, IL: University of Chicago Press.

Comfort, M. (2009) '"We share everything we can the best way we can": Sustaining Romance Across Prison Walls', *Transatlantica* 1.

Condry, R. (2007) *Families Shamed: The consequences of crime for relatives of serious offenders*, Cullompton: Willan.

Cook, D. (2006) *Criminal and Social Justice*, Thousand Oaks, CA: Sage Publications.

COPE (2014) *Children of Prisoners*, Europe Annual Conference, Edinburgh.

Corston, J. (2007) *The Corston Report: A review of women with particular vulnerabilities in the criminal justice dystem*, London: Home Office.

Craig, G., Burchardt, T. and Gordon, D. (2008) *Social Justice and Public Policy*, Bristol: Policy Press.

Eisler, R. and Otis, K. (2014) *Unpaid and Undervalued Care Work Keeps Women on the Brink* (The Shriver Report), shriverreport.org/unpaid-and-undervalued-care-work-keeps-women-on-the-brink/#_edn1 (accessed 3 November 2014).

Fishman, L.T. (1990) *Women at the Wall: A study of prisoners' wives doing time on the outside*, New York: State University of New York Press.

Girshick, L. (1996) *Soledad Women: Wives of prisoners speak out*, Westport, CT: Praeger Publishers.

Holden, K. (2014) *FPP, Organisation for Families and Friends of Prisoners*, Norway.

Home Office (2004) *Women's Offending Reduction Programme Action Plan*, London: Home Office.

Hunter, C. and Nixon, J. (2001) 'Taking the blame and losing the home: women and anti-social behaviour', *Journal of Social Welfare and Family Law* 23(4): 395–410.

Lacey, N. (2013) 'Rethinking justice: penal policy beyond punishment', *Howard League for Penal Reform* podcast, www.howardleague.org/conference-podcasts/ (accessed November 2014).

Lacey, N. and Pickard, H. (2013) 'From the consulting room to the court room? Taking the clinical model of responsibility Without Blame into the Legal Realm', *Oxford Journal of Legal Studies* 33: 1–29.

Liebling, A. and Maruna, S. (2005) *The Effects of Imprisonment*, Cullompton: Willan.

Light, R. and Campbell, B. (2007) 'Prisoners' families: still forgotten victims?', *Journal of Social Welfare and Family Law* 28(3–4): 297–308.

Lowenstein, A. (1986) 'Temporary single parenthood – the case of prisoners' families', *Family Relations* 35(1): 79–85.

May, H. (2000) '"Murderers' relatives": managing stigma, negotiating identity', *Journal of Contemporary Ethnography* 29(2): 198–221.

Ministry of Justice (2012) *Prisoners' Childhood and Family Backgrounds*, London: Ministry of Justice.

Ministry of Justice (2013) *Gender Differences in Substance Misuse and Mental Health Among Prisoners*, London: The Stationery Office.

Minson, S. and Condry, R. (2015) 'The visibility of children whose mothers are being sentenced for criminal offences in England and Wales' *Law in Context* 32: 28–45.

Murray, J. (2005) 'The effects of imprisonment on families and children of prisoners', in A. Liebling and S. Maruna (eds) *The Effects of Imprisonment*, Cullompton: Willan.

Nussbaum, M. (2000) *Women and Human Development: The capabilities approach*, Cambridge: Cambridge University Press.

Nussbaum, M. (2011) *Creating Capabilities: The hum dev approach*, Cambridge, MA: Harvard University Press.

Plugge, E., Douglas, N. and Fitzpatrick, R. (2006) *The Health of Women in Prison Study Findings*, Oxford: Department of Public Health, University of Oxford.

Prison Reform Trust (2013) *Bromley Briefings Prison Factfile: Autumn 2013*, www.prisonreformtrust. org.uk/Portals/0/Documents/Women's%20Justice%20Taskforce%20Report.pdf.

Prison Reform Trust (2014a) *Bromley Briefings Prison Factfile: Summer 2014*, London: Prison Reform Trust.

Prison Reform Trust (2014b) 'Projects and research: race', Prison Reform Trust website, www. prisonreformtrust.org.uk/ProjectsResearch/Race (accessed November 2014).

Scharff-Smith, P. (2014) *When the Innocent are Punished*, Basingstoke: Palgrave Macmillan.

Scharff-Smith, P. and Gampell, L. (ed.) (2011) *Children of Imprisoned Parents*, Copenhagen: Danish Institute of Human Rights.

Smith, R., Grimshaw, R., Romeo, R. and Knapp, M. (2007) 'Poverty and disadvantage among prisoners' families', Joseph Rowntree Foundation, www.jrf.org.uk/system/files/2003-poverty-p risoners-families.pdf (accessed November 2014).

Social Exclusion Unit (2002) *Reducing Reoffending by Ex-prisoners*, London: Social Exclusion Unit.

Wakefield, S. and Uggen, C. (2010) 'Incarceration and stratification', *Annual Review of Sociology* 36: 387–406.

Wakefield, S. and Wildeman, C. (2014) *Children of the Prison Boom: Mass incarceration and the future of American inequality*, New York: Oxford University Press.

Williams, K., Papadopoulou, V. and Booth, N. (2012) *Prisoners' Childhood and Family Backgrounds – Results from the Surveying Prisoner Crime Reduction (SPCR) Longitudinal Cohort Study of Prisoners*, Ministry of Justice Research Series 4/12, www.gov.uk/government/uploads/system/uploads/atta chment_data/file/278837/prisoners-childhood-family-backgrounds.pdf (accessed 3 November 2014).

Women in Prison (2013) *State of the Estate – Women in Prison's Report on the Women's Custodial Estate 2011–2012*, London: Women in Prison.

Young, M. (2011 [1990]) *Justice and the Politics of Difference*, with new foreword by D. Allen, Princeton, NJ: Princeton University Press.

Chapter 36

Inspecting the prison

Nick Hardwick

In 1773, John Howard, who might fairly be called the first prison inspector, was appointed the sheriff of Bedfordshire. Part of his duties included responsibility for the county gaol and, contrary to the usual practice of the time, he did not pay someone else to carry out this task for him but went to look for himself. Visiting the prison for the first time, he was appalled by what he found and decided to see what happened elsewhere:

> Looking into the prisons, I beheld scenes of calamity, which I grew daily more anxious to alleviate. In order therefore to gain a more perfect knowledge of the particulars and extent of it, by various and accurate observation, I visited most of the County-gaols in England.[1]

For the next 17 years until his death in 1790, Howard raced across England, Ireland and Europe, visiting prisons, demanding entry, talking to prisoners and railing in his reports against what he found.

In his great work *The State of Prisons*, published in 1777, Howard described what he did and why he did it:

> I have described no prison but from my own examination at the several dates set down before the number of prisoners. At each visit I entered every room, cell and dungeon with a memorandum book in my hand, in which I noted particulars on the spot. My description will to some readers appear too minute; but I choose rather to relate circumstances, than to characterize them in general terms. By these, the legislature will be better acquainted with the real state of gaols; and magistrates will be able to judge whether the prisons over which they preside, and to which they commit offenders, be fit for the purpose they are designed to answer. I might add that a variety of descriptions may possibly suggest something useful in the plans of such prisons as may hereafter be erected; since whatever may appear worth copying may be extracted from any.[2]

It is, a little disconcertingly perhaps, not so very different from what HM Inspectorate of Prisons does today: criss-crossing the country visiting prisons and other custodial institutions, demanding access, visiting every cell, notebook in hand (no laptops allowed on the wings), talking to prisoners, and describing exactly what we find in the hope that it will influence the prison authorities and the legislature both to ensure existing establishments are fit for purpose and to learn from existing practice in developing the prison system of the future. I hope too that our inspections replicate the urgency and concern about injustice that comes through so powerfully in Howard's writing.

Writing for the *Criminal Law Review* in 2013, Stephen Shute vividly describes how the inspection system developed over the 250 years or so since John Howard's day.[3] Of course, the character, competence and outlook of those involved and the resources available to them were critical to the stance and effectiveness of the inspection bodies. However, the most significant issue, and a controversy that surrounds the inspectorate still, is the extent to which prison inspections should be part of the political and operational management of the prison service or independent from it.

How the inspectorate is positioned on that 'management-independent' spectrum is a reflection of both the wider political and social context of a particular time, and a response to specific events within the prison system. In this chapter I want to describe how the inspection system has moved backwards and forwards across that spectrum throughout its history and how we are trying to position it now in response to the wider political climate and specific challenges that confront the prison system in England and Wales today.

Shute describes how a system of statutory prison inspection was initially established in Ireland in the first quarter of the 19th century and was championed in England first by John Howard and later by the prison reformer, Elizabeth Fry. Various Parliamentary committees proposed the establishment of a prisons inspectorate under the political control of ministers. Eventually, the Gaol Act of 1835 empowered one of His Majesty's principal secretaries of state to:

> nominate and appoint a sufficient Number of fit and proper Persons, not exceeding Five, to visit and inspect, either singly or together, every Gaol, Bridewell, House of Correction, Penitentiary, or other Prison or Place kept or used for the confinement of Prisoners, in any Part of the Kingdom of Great Britain.[4]

Although the newly appointed inspectors enjoyed the confidence of ministers, Shute argues that a lack of powers and resources and the fact that each acted in a semi-autonomous way undermined their ability to influence locally managed prisons.

Fundamental reform was not achieved until the Prison Act 1877 which brought local prisons into a national system under the control of a Prison Commission and subsumed the inspection system into the Commission. This was the system that broadly stayed in place to the 1960s. Prisons remain a national service and to this day that distinguishes the prison inspectorate from the other major inspectorates that inspect local services.

Shute argues that the more 'managerial' inspection system established by the 1877 Act was more effective than the more 'independent' system that preceded it for three main reasons. First, it operated with the power of prison management behind it. Second, it was much better resourced than its predecessors. Third, it championed more liberal thinking than had gone before – although that, surely, depended on there being the political support to do so.

The escape from Wormwood Scrubs of the notorious spy George Blake in 1966 led to the Mountbatten Inquiry which sought to make prison processes much more consistent and advocated the further integration of prison management and inspection processes to achieve this. This initially led in 1967 to the creation of an inspector-general post that did combine both functions, but in 1969 the inspectorate was reconstituted as a separate team – albeit with decent resources – headed since 1971 by a chief inspector and reporting to the Prisons Board rather than directly to ministers. This marked a low point in the inspectorate's independence although it is worth noting here that the preoccupation of the time was on security and escapes. These are not central to the current inspectorate's role and the team that carries out security audits, still a key part of an overall judgement about the performance of a prison, is still rightly a function of the Prison Service itself.

However, high-profile escapes continued and, together with growing concerns about riots, industrial relations tensions and poor physical conditions, culminated in 1979 in the May Committee's inquiry into the Prison Service, which recommended the establishment of a more robustly independent inspectorate although there was no intention that it should be free from ministerial control. The Home Office submission to the inquiry was dubious about the idea of an independent inspectorate. May responded as follows:

> We accept that in both theory and practice no inspection can be independent of Parliament, and thus generally cannot be independent of government: we also accept that in theory and practice no inspection carried out by a member of the Home Office can be independent of that government department nor thus of a prison service which also forms part of it. Nevertheless we have no doubt that the prison service would benefit from and public sentiment requires that as many aspects of government, which includes the prison service, should be opened up to as wide an audience as possible. We therefore think that there should be a system of inspection of the prison service which although not 'independent' of it in either of the senses canvassed in the Home Office paper, should nevertheless be distanced from it as far as possible.[5]

The current core statutory basis of Chief Inspector of Prisons was established by the Criminal Justice Act 1982. The Act sets out the Chief Inspector's role and functions in just a few short paragraphs. They are to:

- inspect or arrange for the inspection of prisons in England and Wales and report to the secretary of state on them;
- in particular, report to the secretary of state on the treatment of prisoners and conditions in prisons;
- report on matters connected with prisons in England and Wales and prisoners in them referred to the Inspectorate by the secretary of state; and
- submit an annual report to be laid before Parliament.

These duties were extended to immigration centres, short-term holding facilities and escort arrangements throughout the UK by the Immigration, Asylum and Nationality Act 2006. The Police and Justice Act 2006 added to the 1982 Act by setting out the chief inspector's further powers and duties to consult the relevant secretaries of state on his or her inspection programme and inspection framework, and to cooperate and consult with other criminal justice Inspectorates and other bodies. Under these powers HMIP has inspected police custody jointly with HM Inspectorate of Constabulary (HMIC) since 2007. The Public Bodies Act 2011 abolished the courts inspectorate and enabled its powers to inspect court custody to be transferred to HMIP. By invitation the inspectorate also inspects prisons in Northern Ireland, military detention in the UK, and custody in the Isle of Man, the Channel Islands and some other overseas territories with close links to the UK. There is a separate prisons inspectorate in Scotland.

Although the Inspectorate's remit has been extended by successive legislation, its core duties and powers have remained largely unchanged since the early 1980s. These duties and powers are broadly drawn and it has been left to each of the six chief inspectors who so far have held the office in its modern form to interpret how they should be applied and, in particular, to determine their relationship with ministers (since 2007 principally in the Ministry of Justice – MoJ) and Prison Service management (since 2004, the National Offender Management Service – NOMS).

The first chief inspector, William Pearce, died in office in 1981. He was succeeded from 1982 to 1987 by Sir James Hennessy, a career diplomat, who established the Inspectorate's credibility with ministers and carried out a major inquiry into an escape of IRA prisoners from the Maze Prison in Northern Ireland. Hennessy's successors put more distance between themselves and both ministers and the Prison Service. Judge Stephen Tumim, who followed from 1987 to 1995, quickly earned himself a reputation as a critic of the system and spoke out against slopping out (with success), poor mental health provision and the enforced idleness in prisons (with less success). He was not always popular with the successive Conservative home secretaries he served under and in 1995, no doubt hoping for a chief inspector with more congenial views, the Rt Hon.Michael Howard MP, the Home Sectretary at the time, replaced him with the ex-army General Sir David (now Lord) Ramsbotham. If Michael Howard expected a quieter life, he was badly mistaken. Ramsbotham led what inspectors still describe in hushed tones as 'the age of heroic inspection'. Early in his tenure, Ramsbotham stormed out of Holloway prison, so appalled was he by the conditions he found, and subsequently he rampaged (there is no other word for it) around the prison estate demanding improvement in the 'squalor, poor management, appalling industrial relations and allegations of brutality'[6] he found.

Partly in response to the concerns Ramsbotham identified, yet another committee was established to inquire into prison management. Lord Lamming's 2000 report, *Modernising the Management of the Prison Service*, also considered the role of the Inspectorate. You sense both frustration and wariness in his remarks. He noted that prison governors did not know the standards against which they were being judged and hinted that the process was arbitrary. In the introduction to his report, Lamming wrote:

> In our view a strong and independent Inspectorate is essential to ensuring that good standards of performance are in practice across the Prison Service. During the past five years the Chief Inspector and his staff have been working to produce an 'Expectations' document. Although we welcome this work, in our view the very title 'Expectations' suggests something which is hoped for rather than required. There should be created a set of standards based upon the philosophy and practice of a healthy prison. The process and methodology of inspections needs to be further developed. In our view the work of the Inspectorate is of such importance that it needs to be in a position to evaluate the performance of prisons against an agreed set of standards using a well-defined methodology which will allow comparisons to be made on unit costs and quality of service delivered. The findings of the Inspectorate should be 'evidence based' and not rely too much upon the personal operational experience of individual inspectors or the Chief Inspector. The 'Standards' against

which the Service is to be evaluated should be built on the solid foundation of legislation, policy and agreed standards of good practice, and should cover all aspects of the prison's operation, including security. Inspections should as far as possible be an objective process and performance measured in ways which highlight differences and allow for informed comparisons to be made.[7]

Ramsbotham brushed the report aside but the later development of the Inspectorate's work did address many of Lamming's concerns about its own performance.

In 2001, the Rt Hon. Jack Straw MP, the then home secretary, replaced Ramsbotham with Anne (now Dame) Owers, the former head of the human rights non-governmental organization (NGO), Justice. Owers's style was very different from Ramsbotham's – more restrained and more forensic – but she too won plaudits for the effectiveness and independence of her work. Owers also had to fight off attempts to abolish HMIP through its merger with other criminal justice inspectorates, a move promoted on the grounds of efficiency and opposed on the basis it would muffle the prison Inspectorate's independent voice. Owers and her supporters won. I replaced Anne Owers in 2010. They were all hard acts to follow.

A critical development in Owers's tenure as chief inspector, and a decisive argument against abolition, was the development of a specific human rights focus for the Inspectorate's work arising from the UK's ratification of the Optional Protocol to the United Nations Convention against Torture and Other Cruel, Inhuman or Degrading Treatment or Punishment (OPCAT) in December 2003.

OPCAT is an unusual human rights instrument. Most others focus on redress and accountability after human rights abuses have occurred. OPCAT aims to prevent such abuses occurring. The UK was one of the principal advocates amongst states for the creation of OPCAT and you see echoes of the UK inspection process in its drafting. The two great insights OPCAT provides are, first, the recognition of the particular vulnerability of prisoners and, second, the role regular independent visits can play in *preventing* abuse. The purpose of independent inspection visits is not primarily to detect human rights abuses, but to prevent such abuses from happening.

At a national level, OPCAT requires state parties to:

> set up, designate or maintain at the domestic level one or several visiting bodies for the prevention of torture, inhuman or degrading treatment or punishment ... These visits shall be undertaken with a view to strengthening, if necessary, the protection of these persons against torture and other cruel, inhuman or degrading treatment or punishment.[8]

These visiting bodies are known as the National Preventive Mechanism (NPM). Unusually, the UK designated 20 existing bodies as its NPM in 2009. HMIP is one of those bodies and coordinates the UK NPM as a whole.

At a minimum, OPCAT requires that NPMs are functionally independent, with diverse, expert personnel and sufficient resources. They must have the powers to go where they want, speak to whom they want and see what they want – and then use the information they gather to influence policy and practice at national and local levels.

At an international level, OPCAT creates the Sub-committee on Prevention of Torture (SPT), which supports the development of NPMs and may also carry out visits, although it has not yet done so in the UK. The Committee Against Torture to which the SPT reports will also carry out periodic reviews of the UK's compliance with OPCAT. As a member of the Council of Europe, the UK is also subject to visits by the European Committee for the Prevention of Torture and Inhuman and Degrading Treatment or Punishment (CPT).

In the Inspectorate's experience there are five reasons why the independent, preventative inspection of prison and other forms of custody is necessary:

- *The power imbalance between the detainee and their jailor.* This is manifest not just in the physical sense that prison officers can restrain a prisoner and use force against them but also in the sense that the prisoner is dependent on the prison officer for every aspect of their daily lives: access to showers, clean underwear or toilet paper, for instance; contact with their families; information about their sentence; safety from bullying by other prisoners, opening the door … and if staff cannot be bothered or are not available to help with these things, there is nothing an individual prisoner can do.
- *The closed nature of prisons and other places of detention.* The public, media and most authorities can only find out what happens inside the walls with the agreement of prison managers and in very controlled conditions. Sometimes it takes a very long time to find out what has been going on – as the accounts that are now emerging of abuses in children's homes, detention centres and other institutions decades ago remind us.
- *The supposed lack of credibility of prisoners and other detainees.* Even if prisoners do complain, who will believe them? We ask prisoners about their experience of the complaints system in our inspection surveys (see below). In 2012/13 13% of the prisoners we surveyed said it was not easy to make a complaint, 17% said they had been prevented from doing so, and of those who had made a complaint, 62% told us it had not been sorted out fairly.[9] Prisoners can turn to the local Independent Monitoring Board (IMB), but 17% told us it was very difficult to see the IMB and 34% did not know what the IMB was.[10] Prisoners do have access to the Prison and Probation Ombudsman, although this is inevitably a complex and slow process, but they cannot now get legal aid for issues relating to their treatment and conditions.
- *The normative effects of custody.* Prison staff and governors simply stop seeing things or they get used to things they should not – as perhaps we all do in our own places of work. Dirt is the big example of this. On many occasions we have fed back to governors about how dirty a prison is. Invariably they are shocked and deny it. So we take them to show them and we take photos – then they see it.
- *The virtual prison.* The virtual prison is what, in a memorable phrase, Anne Owers called the prison the governor thinks he or she is running, which is often very different from the real prison that is happening down on the wings. The governor will often confidently tell us how many prisoners are in activity and how much time out of cell they get, but when we check, we find prisoners consistently unlocked late and locked up early. Activities are closed because of staff shortages and when we get to the workshops, not much is going on. Some wing cleaning 'jobs' involve just a few minutes desultory sweeping. The hive of industry over which the governor thinks he or she presides does not exist.

The way in which the Inspectorate works today draws on the history I have described, aims to meet the obligations that arise from OPCAT and strikes its own balance on the 'management-independent' spectrum that is relevant to the political, social and operational context in which the Inspectorate operates today.

The inspectorate now has a budget of c. £4.5 million, mainly from the MoJ and Home Office, and has a team of 75 full-time and sessional staff. Over the last few years the number of inspectors who are seconded prison governors has reduced and now stands at about seven of the total. We have an office away from the main MoJ and Prison Service Headquarters and an independent website.

Our inspection process is set out in our *Inspection Framework*.[11] We have the same access to private as to public prisons. We carry out about 100 inspections a year and about half of these are of prisons and juvenile establishments in England and Wales. That means we can inspect each establishment on average once every three years but the frequency of inspections is risk-based and so we inspect a small number of establishments annually and there may be gaps of up to five years in the inspections of a few others. We select what prison to inspect on the basis of the establishment type and size (we inspect all juvenile establishments annually, for instance), time since the last inspection, our previous findings, significant changes to the prison or its leadership, intelligence such as IMB reports, serious incidents reported, how long it is since a new prison opened and the NOMS' own prison rating score.

Almost all inspections are now unannounced and take place over about seven working days. A small advance team of inspectors and social researchers arrives in the first week and phones from the car park, tells the prison they are outside, require access and that they should get keys ready. While some inspectors go immediately to look at the most critical areas of the prison such as the segregation block and take a view of cleanliness and activity levels, researchers carry out the prisoner survey and the inspection coordinator begins preparation with the prison for the full team to arrive the following week. We still announce a few inspections in advance where the previous report has been particularly poor and we want to give the establishment a clear deadline by which we expect to see improvement.

The full team will typically consist of a team leader, four core inspectors, a specialist healthcare inspector and a specialist substance misuse inspector. The HMIP team will be joined by inspectors from Ofsted, HMI Probation and the Royal Pharmaceutical Society who will work under the direction of the HMIP team leader but produce reports according to their own statutory requirements as well as contributing to the overall HMIP report.

Our starting point is to report 'on the treatment of prisoners and the conditions in prisons', as set out in our legislation. We interpret that to mean that we report on outcomes for prisoners, not the management of the prison. So if the prison is overcrowded, for instance, we will be critical of that and it will affect our overall judgement, although that may not be under the control of the governor of the prison. We make our judgements against four tests of a 'healthy prison':

- Safety: prisoners, particularly the most vulnerable, are held safely.
- Respect: prisoners are treated with respect for their human dignity.
- Purposeful activity: prisoners are able, and expected, to engage in activity that is likely to benefit them.

- Resettlement: prisoners are prepared for their release back into the community and effectively helped to reduce the likelihood of reoffending.

Each test set out is underpinned by 'Expectations'[12] or inspection criteria that are all referenced against relevant international human rights standards and norms. We are now on the fourth edition since Ramsbotham's efforts to produce the first set, as described by Lord Lamming in the extract above. This edition aims to be more focused on outcomes and less on process than those that preceded it, in part to acknowledge that in times of reduced budgets, while outcomes should not decline, governors may need to be more flexible in how they achieve them. Nevertheless, each expectation is supported by a set of indicators which describe the processes that inspectors would normally expect to find in place if the expectation is being met – but if prisons can demonstrate they are meeting the expectation in other ways, that is perfectly acceptable. There are separate expectations for men's and women's prisons and for other types of custody.

The 'expectations' do, as Lamming wished, provide prisons with transparent standards against which the Inspectorate will judge them. However, while ministers and others are consulted on them, they are not agreed with ministers. They are based on international standards, not current government policy. In some critical ways they run contrary to ministerial policy – they take a more critical view of overcrowding and physical conditions than ministers do, they did not support the recent toughening of the incentives and earned privileges scheme that ministers introduced, and they explicitly contradict the new approved restraint policy introduced into juvenile establishments which permits pain-compliance techniques. Nevertheless, these examples are exceptions; typically the expectations have endorsement from ministers, prison and other stakeholders as descriptions of best practice.

We make our judgements about whether each expectation has been met by triangulating five main sources of evidence.

If you want to know what is going on in prisons, ask prisoners. The prisoner voice is at the centre of our methodology. So first, we carry out a detailed survey of a statistically representative sample of prisoners about all aspects of prison life. We randomly select the sample and hand out and collect the forms, providing help for those with difficulty reading or understanding English. We have been carrying out the surveys for many years now and this enables us to compare results of a single prison with the last time we inspected and similar prisons. The survey rarely provides clear answers but it does indicate very clearly the areas the inspection team should focus on and the questions it should be asking.

Second, we will follow up the survey results with discussions with randomly selected groups of prisoners following a broad template. We will also talk to a very large proportion of the population individually and in private throughout the inspection. We are conscious that some prisoners may be reluctant to speak to us because of fear of repercussions after we have gone. Indeed, there have been rare instances when we are aware this has happened. We try to protect the confidentiality of those who have spoken to us and have a protocol with IMBs that they will follow up any accounts of victimization that later emerge.

Third, we speak to managers and staff. We increasingly now organize groups of staff in the same way we do prisoners, with useful results. We speak to other visitors to the prison and in particular the local IMB. IMBs should be a crucial source of information about the prison and as part of the NPM, an important part of the prevention of mistreatment. The involvement of community lay monitors is a strength of the UK NPM, but the poor performance of a few risks undermining the credibility of them all and this needs to be addressed.

Fourth, we look at the prison's own policies, records and data, checking the data are correct and comparing them with similar establishments. We will, for instance, look at the prison's data about the number of violent incidents and then compare those against adjudication records, healthcare data, wing logs, and what prisoners and staff tell us.

Finally, we simply observe what is going on. Inspectors are discouraged from going through a tick-box process but follow their noses if they see something that concerns them. Inspectors can go where they want, speak to whoever they want in private, look at what they want.

The team meets daily throughout the inspection to compare notes and pull together the various strands of evidence. Team members regularly feed back to those in charge of the areas they are inspecting and the team leader meets with the governor at the end of each day to feed back emerging findings. Any push-back from the governor can be checked the next day. At the end of the inspection there should be no disagreements about matters of fact, even if there is not agreement about the judgements that follow.

On the penultimate day of the inspection, the team will be joined by the Chief or Deputy Chief inspector. After looking round the prison themselves, they will meet with the whole team to review the evidence and to make an overall judgement about outcomes under each healthy prison test. Each inspection will follow up recommendations made at the previous inspection and progress in achieving these will be important to the overall judgements made. Outcomes are described with a corresponding numeric score as: 'Good' (4), 'Reasonably good' (3), 'Not sufficiently good' (2), or 'Poor' (1). On the final morning, the main findings will be formally fed back to the governor with an audience he or she invites. The governor will receive a detailed feedback note at that time, so there is no doubt about the main findings which they can start work on straight away.

A detailed draft report and recommendations should be ready two months after the inspection. The prison has an opportunity to comment on matters of factual accuracy at this point, these will be considered and the final report will be published, entirely at the chief inspector's discretion, about four months after the inspection. Reports are press released and published on the Inspectorate's website. Prisons are required to produce an action plan in response to the reports recommendations and this is submitted to the inspectorate and published on its website. The action plan is reviewed and progress against recommendations assessed at the next inspection when the process repeats.

Jamie Bennett, currently the experienced governor of Grendon Therapeutic Community prison and Spring Hill open prison was invited to attend an inspection as a 'critical friend' in 2012. His observations offered a perceptive (and pleasing) assessment of the inspection process from the governor's point of view.[13] Bennett positions the prison inspection process against the 'explosion' of audit and the stranglehold of managerialism, drawing a distinction between *managerial* accountability (a box-ticking exercise to check how well the organizations are doing against the various targets and expectations set for, and often by, their management), and *public* accountability (the provision of independent, authoritative assessments of the strengths and shortcomings of public services).[14]

Bennett acknowledges that the expectations, numeric scores and more systematic methodology move some way towards managerialism but he argues that by providing a form of public accountability through independent inspection, there is a distinctive and important contribution offered:

> Forms of audit and inspection are not merely detached and isolated evaluations and measurement, but play a role in the generation of values and modes of thinking and being ... inspection has an important role in resisting the values of managerialism and in maintaining space for humane values in prisons.[15]

He highlights in particular the importance of inspectors employing a 'variable assemblage' of methodologies in order to understand outcomes for *prisoners*, rather than resorting to an overly rigid application of measures which frequently result in detachment or disengagement from the realities of everyday experiences. Inspectors are, he says, craftsman-like and creative in the way they approach their work, but of necessity given the 'complexity of the task at hand and the contested nature of imprisonment'.[16] The culture of the inspection teams constitutes a 'community of practice'; a distinctive occupational culture incorporating (among other things):

- a focus on 'outcomes for prisoners';
- engagement with inspectees;
- independence;
- conservative appearance (suits, ties, muted colours);
- visible hard work (meals taken at work, long hours);
- team work and collegiality; and
- a distinct boundary between inspecting and managing (feedback and feedback style marks this boundary).

It may be that Bennett is too generous in his assessment of the Inspectorate's independence and eschewing of managerialism. I have already noted that the expectations and numeric final 'scores' owe something to this approach and go some way to meet the concerns of those like Lamming. In addition, prisons are expected to produce an action plan setting out whether they accept each recommendation, and if so, how they will meet it. Perhaps inevitably this often has the feel of a tick-box exercise. We have tried to address this by setting out main recommendations with the 'concern' they are intended to address so that the issue becomes if the concern has been resolved and not if the recommendation has been followed – but it is slow going.

Inspection scores are combined with other audit findings and management information to inform the NOMS 'prison rating system' against which all prisons are ranked. The inspection score is an important element of this, with a consequence that some prison managers are only interested in the number rather than the findings that support it. However, incorporation of our findings into management judgements of this kind does give weight and credibility amongst governors to the Inspectorate's work. Some of our expectations stray beyond prisoner outcomes to issues of prison security and public safety. We will not ignore obvious security breaches, and our assessments of offender management processes give as much weight to public as to prisoner outcomes. In my view, we could not credibly do otherwise. To value the approach of the Inspectorate is not to say that audit and management is not necessary too. Indeed, it is the internal safety and other process audits and external value for money audits by the National Audit

Office that give the Inspectorate space to carry out its role without neglecting the other legitimate concerns of those who have considered the work of the Inspectorate in its various incarnations.

As well as inspections of individual establishments, the Inspectorate also carries out cross-cutting thematic inspections and uses its inspection findings to respond to consultations on proposed legislation and other matters. This work is inherently more 'managerial' in nature as it often involves explicit comments on national systems and resources. However, it is an important part of the OPCAT prevention mandate which specifically states that NPMs should have powers to 'submit proposals and observations concerning existing or draft legislation'.[17]

Ministers have also occasionally exercised their powers to refer matters to the Inspectorate and require it to report on them.[18] The report on a succession of serious release on temporary licence (ROTL) failures in 2013, which was published in full following the conclusion of relevant court cases in 2015, is an example of this.[19]

As I have argued above, historically where the Inspectorate sits on a management-independence spectrum is a reflection of both the wider political and social context of a particular time and a response to specific events within the prison system, although of course the character, competence and outlook of those involved and the resources available to them are critical to the stance and effectiveness of the Inspectorate.

So how the Inspectorate might develop over the coming years depends very much on an assessment of those factors. There is not the space to develop the point here, but after a succession of major scandals — the police, media, MPs, health services — most would surely agree we are in an age where trust in major institutions is in sharp decline.

All the major inspectorates with which the Inspectorate works — the Care Quality Commission (CQC), HMIC, Ofsted — have, to a greater or lesser extent, come in for criticism for being insufficiently independent of the bodies they inspect and rigorous in their approach. All have changed as a result. Ofsted, for instance, has four tests against which it judges whether the performance of a school is 'outstanding', 'good', 'requires improvement', or is 'inadequate', and other inspectorates seek or have a similar system. For the time being at least, the era of 'light touch' inspection is over. Schools, hospitals, old people's homes and police forces are now being inspected by a system that in some ways is very similar to the prison inspection system. However, these other inspectorates have or seek greater powers to enforce the standards they inspect against. Ofsted may place a school in 'special measures', the CQC registers providers and can remove registration from providers that do not meet 'the government's' standards of quality and safety, and in August 2014 HMIC consulted on proposals which would enable it to take enforcement action against forces that did not meet required standards.

All of these other inspectorates have been given much greater resources and seem to enjoy political support for the direction in which they are trying to influence the bodies they inspect. They appear to meet Shute's test of effectiveness — independent of the bodies they inspect and independent in their judgements but operating within a framework set by the ministers to whom they are accountable. I do not suggest that relationship is wrong — the politicians are elected, they do not have operational control over the inspected services and it seems right to me that there should be an effective mechanism for ensuring these services meet standards they have approved.

The position of prisons is different, however. By and large, health trusts, police forces and schools are local services accountable to local elected bodies or boards. Prisons, on the other hand, are part of a national service and prison governors have a direct, hierarchical line management or contractual relationship to national operational leadership, who are in turn accountable to ministers. Ministers exercise operational control of prisons – the introduction of an early 'lights out' time across all juvenile establishments being one recent example. Furthermore, the UK has signed up to running its prisons in accordance with international human rights standards and a national and international system for checking that it has done so. Of course there is a good deal of ambiguity in all these relationships but I would argue that on the whole, most other inspectorates are part of the mechanism by which the executive – government – ensures the quality and effectiveness of locally delivered and managed services, whereas HMIP, perhaps like the Equality and Human Rights Commission or the Parliamentary and Health Service Ombudsman, is part of the mechanism by which the work of government itself is made accountable to international, Parliamentary and wider public scrutiny. In September 2015 there were indications that the current Justice Secretary, Michael Gove, was considering making some prisons accountable to local structures and reducing the central grip. That might change the argument but for the time being at least it seems to me that there is an argument for the prisons Inspectorate having a greater degree of independence from ministers than other inspectorates. However, is that, as Stephen Shute might argue, at the cost of effectiveness?

The Inspectorate can claim to have driven, or at least been part of, some pretty big changes in its modern history. For instance, Tumim successfully championed the end of slopping out; Ramsbotham's influential thematic, 'Suicide is everyone's concern', led to measures which significantly reduced the number of suicides in prisons (at least until recently); Owers had a key role in persuading the then Labour government not to proceed with plans to build 'Titan' prisons.

It is for others to judge how effective we have been recently, but I think, for instance, that we can claim some of the credit for the improvements there have been in women's prisons which are reflected in the decrease in the number of self-harm incidents and self-inflicted deaths – although these still remain disproportionately high, and too many women are locked up too far from home in excessively large establishments.

Our own stakeholder surveys suggest that 60% of practitioners, 88% of service managers and 70% of other stakeholders though the inspectorate was very or quite influential.[20] However, the Inspectorate does not have regulatory powers; just powers of persuasion. While we can point to the fact that the proportion of our recommendations that are at least partially accepted and partially implemented has remained consistent for many years at about 97% and 66%, respectively, and we can point to satisfying improvements in prisons like Brinsford and Lincoln which were undoubtedly heavily influenced by our inspection findings, we have been unable to prevent a deterioration in standards over the last year or so.

Prisons are full to bursting. There are two measure of prison capacity. 'Operational capacity' is the total number of prisoners that an establishment can hold without serious risk to good order, security and the proper running of the planned regime; 'Certified Normal Accommodation (CNA)' represents the good, decent standard of accommodation that the prison service aspires to provide all prisoners. Any prisoner places provided above CNA are referred to as crowding place. Any cell or establishment with an occupancy/population above CNA is referred to as crowded.

At the end of March 2015 the prison population stood at 85,681, 97.7% of the usable operational capacity – although a slight improvement on twelve months before when the system was operating at 99.1% of capacity.   However, looking at the CNA, the decent standard, local prisons and Category C training prisons for which inspection reports were published in 2014/15 were operating at 143% and 113% of CNA respectively.[21]

Overcrowding is not principally a matter of prisoners being doubled up with an unscreened toilet in cells that the Victorians designed for one – although that is highly undesirable – but a population that outstrips the facilities and activities available and the ability of reduced staff to keep prisoners safe. The population is not spread evenly and in prisons where the pressures are particularly acute, the problem has had to be managed by filling the prison above its recognized capacity, locking out and moving prisoners out on overcrowding drafts, even when they are in the middle of offending behaviour or training programmes.

The adult prison population is not getting any easier to manage either. The proportion of men serving long sentences for serious offences has grown. In 1993, 45% of the prison population were serving sentences of four years or more; by 2013 that figure had grown to 54%. On one side you have angry young men – and on the other, the fastest growing section of the prison population is those aged 60 or over. Prisons are fast becoming a large provider of care for the frail elderly. As I write in September 2015, prisons are struggling to deal with a surge in the availability of new psychoactive substances, specifically synthetic cannabis known as 'Spice' or Mamba', driven to large extent with by organised crime and leading to spiralling debt and associated violence.

These pressures have happened at a time when headquarters managers and prison governors struggled to manage a period of very significant change. The impact of budget reductions has been very significant. The NOMS budget as a whole (including probation) reduced by £898 million over the four years from 2011/12 to 2014/15 or 24% on its 2010/11 baseline. Public sector prisons alone delivered saving of £71million 2013/14. NOMS headquarters will make savings of 37% (£91 million) across the current spending review period.[22] This has been achieved by the closure of some smaller, older prisons such as HMP Shepton Mallet and their replacement with larger, modern facilities such as HMP Oakwood and expanded capacity at some existing prisons, wholesale management restructuring through the 'Fair and Sustainable' process, and overall reductions in staffing levels through the 'benchmarking' process. Regional offices and many national support and policy functions have been stripped out.

The challenge here has not just been the funding and staffing levels that remain once the reductions have been made, but the distractions created by the process of change itself. Managers are preoccupied with budgets and new targets, staff are worried about their jobs and as small, old prisons are replaced with large, modern, new ones, there has been a significant loss of experienced staff.

Budget cuts and population growth are not the only changes that have to be managed at the current time. Prisons also have to manage a significant policy agenda. The 'Transforming Rehabilitation' strategy is intended to place a much greater emphasis on rehabilitation outcomes and gives commercial Community Rehabilitation Companies (CRCs) responsibility for delivering the 'through-the-gate' services and supervision that are intended to produce better outcomes. It is too early to assess the success. It is too early to assess the success of otherwise of the CRCs but they are part of a pattern in which the management of prisons has become increasingly fragmented – health services commissioned by the NHS and delivered by NHS trusts, learning and skills delivered by colleges and other specialist providers and commissioned regionally, many support services contacted out and now resettlement functions too. There are benefits to having specialists delivering these services but management and governance structures are terribly confused. The inspectorate had tried not to exacerbate that fragmentation – all our recommendations in a prison inspection are made to the governor (director in a private prison) or NOMS centrally rather that the head of any commissioned service. If a governor does not feel responsible for the services in his or her prison – well, they should.

Of less long-term strategic importance but of more immediate concern to prisoners, a series of measures to toughen up prison regimes are currently causing a great deal of frustration which has to be carefully managed. Changes to the Incentives and Earned Privileges scheme make it more difficult for prisoners to reach the top level of the scheme and restrict what they may have sent in or keep in their cells. ROTL is rightly being managed with greater care – but this too is a cause of frustration as approvals are delayed or refused.

The pressures on secure training centres and juvenile Young Offender Institutions (YOIs) holding children under 18 (and a small number of 18 year olds) have been different from those in adult prisons. The number of children under 18 in any form of custody has fallen dramatically from a high point of 3,200 in October 2002 to 1,707 in June 2012 to 986 in June 2015 – a drop of 35% over those last three years alone.[23] The fall is very welcome but creates two challenges. First, children are now held in a smaller number of establishments and so may be held further away from home. Second, there is little doubt that the children who remain are both very vulnerable and very challenging. The self-inflicted deaths of three children within a few weeks of each other from 2011 and 2012 were stark reminders of that vulnerability. At the same time, inspections have consistently found YOIs struggling to manage very violent, bullying behaviour with frequent examples of group attacks on a single victim. What we found at HM YOI Feltham in January 2013 was not untypical and YOI inspections since have painted a similar picture:

> We had serious concerns about the safety of young people held at Feltham A. Many told us they were frightened at the time of the inspection, and that they had little confidence in staff to keep them safe. Gang-related graffiti was endemic. There was an average of almost two fights or assaults every day. Some of these were very serious and involved groups of young people in very violent, pre-meditated attacks on a single individual with a risk of very serious injury resulting.[24]

The number of young adults in custody has also fallen. Between April 2013 and June 2015 the number of 18 to 20 year olds in prison dropped by 22% from 6,504 to 5,050.[25] The Young Adult YOIs we inspect are amongst the worst establishments we inspect. Policy for this age group was in flux in the summer of 2015, with plans on hold to move most young adults into adult prisons, pending a review into the deaths of young adults in custody by Lord Harris.[26] Nevertheless, many young adults are already in adult prisons and as we found at HMP Winchester in 2014, proving difficult to manage.

In March 2013, the Public Accounts Committee recognized NOMS' success in meeting its financial targets despite the challenges it faced but warned of the risks. The chair of the committee, the Rt Hon. Margaret Hodge MP, said:

> There is also a risk that reduced numbers will result in staff being taken off offender management programmes to cover duty on prison wings. This means that training and rehabilitation activities could suffer, even though we know these reduce re-

offending after release. The Agency needs to seriously consider the long-term consequences of short term cuts. We are also concerned about the impact of reduced staff numbers on safety and decency in prisons. Assaults on staff, self-harm and escapes from contractor escorts have all increased, and more prisoners are reporting that they don't feel safe.[27]

There is now compelling evidence that those chickens are coming home to roost. Inspection findings that were already a cause for concern in 2013/14 have declined sharply since then. Since about the beginning of 2014 there has been a sharp decline in the number of establishments providing 'good' or 'reasonably good' outcomes for each healthy prison test. Safety in only just over half (52%) the prisons we inspected was good or reasonably good compared with three-quarters ten years previously in 2005/06. In only about a third of prisons (36%) was purposeful activity reasonably good or good, down from 48% in the same period. Resettlement outcomes fell from 68% to 57%. Only respect outcomes held up with 64% good or reasonably good.[28] It might be argued that these findings are not typical or that our judgements have become harsher. However, the data that NOMS itself produces tell us a similar story.

Of most concern, the number of self-inflicted deaths has shown a recent sharp increase. The number of self-inflicted deaths rose from 52 in the year ending March 2013 to 88 in the year ending March 2014 – an increase of 69%. Over the same period, the number of assaults increased from 14,083 to 15,033 – an increase of almost 7%. The number of serious assaults increased by 30% from 1,303 to 1,699 in 2013. The number of self-harm incidents rose from 22,722 to 23,478.[29] Improvements in the female estate and reductions in the number of children and young adults in custody mean that the overall figures above disguise much worse data for adult male prisoners.

The question therefore becomes whether the Inspectorate in its modern form, with its independence hard won from the Prison Service and ministers by Tumin, Ramsbotham and Owers, is the right vehicle to respond to the deteriorating outcomes that are currently being revealed or whether, as in some earlier incarnations, an inspectorate that more clearly had the support of ministers would have greater powers to enforce its recommendations. From almost the very birth of the idea of an independent prison inspectorate 200 years ago, successive drafters of legislation and inquiry heads have sought to respond to concerns about the state of our prisons by giving the Inspectorate management teeth – but just as surely, over time, those who have led the Inspectorate or its predecessor bodies have sought to loosen the constraints such powers inevitably bring.

In February 2015, the National Audit Office addressed the impact of the criminal justice and home affairs inspectorate's[30] impact and independence directly. The report was generally positive about the work and productivity of HMI Prisons and recognised:

> The act of inspection has a direct cultural impact on sector performance. Inspected bodies pointed to the burden of inspection. However, they recognised the profound cultural effect on behaviour of the act of inspection and knowing the inspector would, or could, visit. Having inspection standards, such as HMI Prisons has, that the sector knows, has an impact, as often managers will aim to meet these standards before they are inspected. [31]

Nevertheless, the report recommended the inspectorates should do more to maximise their impact and that relationships with sponsor departments should be clarified. When the House of Commons Public Accounts Committee considered the NAO report a few weeks later they found that the independence of the inspectorates risked being undermined by the role of Secretaries of State in setting their budgets and appointing Chief Inspectors and suggested the Cabinet Office should review arrangements. The committee agreed that the inspectorates needed to do more to demonstrate their impact.[32]

The issue of the process of appointing Chief Inspectors was thrown into sharp relief by concerns about the process for appointing the new Chief Inspector of Prisons in the spring of 2015. In its report on 'Prisons: planning and policies' published on 18 March 2015,[33] the committee went further than the PAC and concluded, echoing an earlier recommendation of the Public Administration Committee,[34] that the Chief Inspector of Prison should report directly to Parliament. Two days after this report was published, the Justice Committee rushed out another report, 'Appointment of HM Chief Inspector of Prisons, matters of concern'. This report describes concerns the committee had raised with the then Justice Secretary, the Rt Hon. Chris Grayling MP, after it had come to their attention that two members of panel conducting the appointment process for the new Chief Inspector were active members of the Conservative Party. Mr Grayling replied that he had decided not to appoint the panels' preferred candidate. The selection process was to be rerun.

The new government elected in the May 2015 rejected all the recommendation to review the independence of the prisons inspectorate and the process of recruiting a new Chief Inspector of Prisons began.

In the summer of 2015, the intentions of the new Justice Secretary for the prison system were unclear. Nevertheless, in his first speech to the Prisoners Learning Alliance in July 2015 he said he wanted to give governors more autonomy, particularly with regard to education:

> At the moment I fear that one of the biggest brakes on progress in our prisons is the lack of operational autonomy and genuine independence enjoyed by Governors. Whether in state or private prisons, there are very tight, centrally-set, criteria on how every aspect of prison life should be managed. Yet we know from other public services - from the success of foundation hospitals and academy schools - that operational freedom for good professionals drives innovation and improvement. So we should explore how to give Governors greater freedom - and one of the areas ripest for innovation must be prison education.[35]

The Prime Minister developed a similar theme speaking two months later:

> We also need to devolve power – like we have in education. At the moment, prison governors have almost no control over what is taught in their prison and who teaches it, nor the right financial freedoms to provide meaningful work for their prisoners.
>
> We need to give prison governors that control – and we are also looking at how we can incentivise and reward them for delivering the right outcomes.
>
> Going even further, we could also invite bids for new prisons from those charities and others who wish to work with specific types of offender. I especially want to see improvement in the youth justice system.[36]

We will see.

The question of the prison inspectorate's future role remains unresolved. Perhaps a more devolved prison system might mean a desire for a more light touch inspection regime or perhaps, if prisons are less directly managed from the centre, it might mean a more regulatory system is required. It is clear in any case that the current government does not want to put further distance between Ministers and the inspectorate. Budget pressures on the prison system are unlikely to lead to a reduction in the deteriorating outcomes and violence that is blighting so many prisons at present and the same budget pressures on the inspectorate mean that it will do well to continue to provide a timely and comprehensive account of what is happening. It will be an even bigger challenge to demonstrate greater impact in these circumstances.

In my view, the core role of modern prison inspectors should continue to be, as in John Howard's day, criss-crossing the country, demanding entry into prisons, visiting cells, notebook in hand, recording and reporting what they find, unrestricted by political requirements – but developed on the basis of the Inspectorate's experience over the years. Just as John Howard hoped for his reports that 'whatever may appear worth copying may be extracted from any', so I think we need to find ways of further developing that function and ensuring the lessons from the Inspectorate's work contribute more to improvement. However, great care should be taken to ensure that greater influence does not come at the expense of independence. Once the inspectorate becomes even in part accountable for the performance of the prison service, its ability to report independently and credibly on that performance will be diminished. Prisons need the light that inspection can shine on them today no less than in John Howard's day. That light should not be dimmed.

Notes

1 J. Howard (1777) *The State of Prisons*, Warrington, 1, quoted in T. West (2011) *The Curious Mr Howard*, Waterside Press, 173.
2 Ibid., 129.
3 S. Shute (2013) 'Serving their Political Masters: The Development of Criminal Justice Inspection in England and Wales – Prisons and Police', pre-publication text submitted to *The Criminal Law Review*.
4 5&6 Will. IV, c.38, 1835, quoted in Shute, *op. cit.*
5 Committee of Inquiry into the United Kingdom Prison Services (1979) *Report*, HMSO, 95.
6 W.H. Lamming (2000) *Modernising the Management of the Prison Service: An Independent Report by the Targeted Performance Initiate Working Group*, Home Office, 22.
7 Ibid., 4.
8 Optional Protocol to the Convention Against Torture and Other Cruel, Inhuman or Degrading Treatment or Punishment, Articles 3 and 4.
9 HMI Prisons (2013) *Submission to the Joint Committee on Human Rights – The Implications for Access to Justice of the Government's Proposed Legal Aid Reforms*, www.justiceinspectorates.gov.uk/prisons/wp-content/uploads/sites/4/2014/02/legal-aid-consultation-hmip-response.pdf.
10 Ibid.
11 HMI Prisons (2014) *Inspection Framework*, www.justiceinspectorates.gov.uk/prisons/wp-content/uploads/sites/4/2014/04/1.-INSPECTION-FRAMEWORK-April-2014-02.pdf.
12 HMI Prisons (2012)*Expectations: Criteria for Assessing the Treatment of Prisoners and Conditions in Prisons*, vol. 4, www.justiceinspectorates.gov.uk/prisons/wp-content/uploads/sites/4/2014/02/adult-expectations-2012.pdf.
13 For the full interview see J. Bennett (2014) 'Resisting the Audit Explosion: The Art of Prison Inspection', *The Howard Journal of Criminal Justice*.
14 Raine (2008: 100), quoted in Bennett, *op. cit.*

15 Bennett, *op. cit.*
16 Bennett, *op. cit.*
17 Optional Protocol to the Convention Against Torture and Other Cruel, Inhuman or Degrading Treatment or Punishment, Article 19c.
18 *Hansard* 10 March 2014, column 4WS.
19 HMI Prisons (2014) *Release on Temporary Licence (ROTL) failures,* www.justiceinspectorates.gov.uk/hmiprisons/wp-content/uploads/sites/4/2015/07/ROTL-unredacted-WEB-amended-16-July-2015.pdf.
20 HMI Prisons (2014) *HM Inspectorate of Prisons Stakeholder Survey 2014; Summary of main findings,* www.justiceinspectorates.gov.uk/hmiprisons/wp-content/uploads/sites/4/2015/02/Stakeholder-Survey-2014-FINAL-Summary-report.pdf.
21 HMI Prisons (2015)*Annual Report 2014–15,* www.justiceinspectorates.gov.uk/hmiprisons/wp-content/uploads/sites/4/2015/07/HMIP-AR_2014-15_TSO_Final1.pdf.
22 National Offender Management Service (2013) *Annual Report and Accounts 2012–2013,* House of Commons.
23 Youth Justice Board, *Monthly Youth Custody Report June 2014,* 2014.
24 HMI Prisons (2013) *Report on an unannounced inspection of HMP/YOI Feltham (Feltham A – children and young people),* 5.
25 Ministry of Justice (2014) *Offender management statistics quarterly – January-March 2015, Prison Population 2015: Table A1.1 Prison population by type of custody, age group and sex.*
26 *The Harris Review: Changing Prisons, Saving Lives: Report of the Independent Review into self-inflicted Deaths in Custody of 18-24 year olds* HMSO, 2015.
27 Public Accounts Committee (2013) *MPs Release Report on Restructuring the Offender Management Service,* House of Commons, www.parliament.uk/business/committees/committees-a-z/commons-select/public-accounts-committee/news/restructuring-noms/.
28 HMI Prisons, *Annual Report 2014–15, op. cit.*
29 Ministry of Justice Statistics Bulletin (2015) *Safety in Custody Statistics England and Wales Deaths in prison custody to June 2015; Assaults and Self-harm to March 2015,* Ministry of Justice.
30 HMI Prisons, HMI Constabulary, HMI Probation, HM Crown Prosecution Service Inspectorate, the Independent Chief Inspector of Borders and Immigration.
31 House of Commons (2015) *The Comptroller and Auditor General, Inspection: A comparative study.*
32 House of Commons (2015) *House of Commons Committee of Public Accounts, Inspection in home affairs and justice, Fifty-third report of Sesion 2014–15.*
33 House of Commons (2015) *House of Commons Justice Committee, Prisons: policies and planning.*
34 House of Commons (2014) *House of Commons Public Administration Select Committee, Who's accountable? Relationships between Government and arms-length bodies.*
35 Gove, Michael (2015) *The treasure in the heart of man – making prisons work,* www.gov.uk/government/speeches/the-treasure-in-the-heart-of-man-making-prisons-work.
36 Cameron, David (2015) *My vision for a smarter state,* www.gov.uk/government/speeches/prime-minister-my-vision-for-a-smarter-state.

Chapter 37

Researching the prison

Yvonne Jewkes and Serena Wright

Introduction

Researching the prison can be a challenging, fascinating, fatiguing, exhilarating, exhausting, tedious, poignant business. Frequently all these emotions – and more – are experienced by the researcher in quick succession. Many of us are drawn to the prison out of a sense of curiosity about a world that is hidden to most, a fascination with human nature and what the human spirit can endure and, in some cases, out of a strong personal sense of (in)justice, or perhaps a conflicted relationship with power and authority (Liebling 1999). However, while we might have strong motivations driving our research activities in prisons, the process of gaining access, dealing with gatekeepers and entering prison for the first time can be daunting, and not a little frustrating. This chapter aims to 'unpack' this process, and in doing so make more transparent the development of research within the carceral, and engage with the practical and emotional experience of studying the prison, and those who live or work within its walls. It does this specifically with the potential first-time prisons researcher in mind, and in doing so has three main concerns. First, to provide a brief potted history of some of the 'classic' sociological studies of prisons, prisoners and prison staff, against a backdrop of the political and policy contexts in which they were conducted. Second, to take the reader through the process of doing research in prisons – frequently summarized as 'getting in, getting on and getting out'. Third, and finally, to describe the emotional dimensions of researching the prison; what it *feels* like to observe and, to some degree, participate in the everyday, interior world of the prison. In this final section, we will also offer some personal reflections on our own experiences of researching the prison.

Prison ethnographies: a brief history

Early optimism and enthusiasm for research

While the birth of the prison is usually dated to the early 19th century, prisons research is commonly thought of as emerging – and quickly flourishing – in the mid-20th century. In its early phase, research focused on broad concerns such as prisoner values, coping and adaptation strategies (e.g. Sykes 1958; Giallombardo 1966; Cohen and Taylor 1972; Heffernan 1972; Toch 1977). Rehabilitative thinking underpinned penal policy at this time and the dominance of the welfarist model resulted in criminal justice being influenced by a raft of professional 'experts', including social workers, psychologists, health professionals and academics. Surprisingly, from a current perspective, some US states, including California, Minnesota and Wisconsin, rivalled countries such as the Nether-lands and Sweden for innovation in rehabilitative programmes (Rothman 1980). This optimistic period in penal policy provided an extraordinarily supportive context for prison studies, especially in the USA, although scholars in the UK and parts of Europe also took advantage of the relatively open access afforded to researchers. Sociologists were considered a central part of the ambition to forge a more humane and successful prison system and, in that climate, ethnographic or semi-ethnographic research thrived (Crewe 2008).

Donald Clemmer's *The Prison Community* (1940), written while Clemmer was a prison officer at the Southern Illinois Penitentiary, was a landmark text because it introduced the idea that prisoners adhere to an 'inmate code' which helps them to survive their sen-tence, subsequently summarized by Sykes and Messinger (1960) as a five-fold set of rules: 'never rat [grass] on a con'; 'play it cool and do your own time'; don't exploit or steal from other prisoners; don't show weakness – 'be tough; be a man'; and 'be sharp' – don't ever side with prison officers and authorities.

However, Esther Heffernan's (1972) subsequent study of life at the Women's Refor-matory in Occoquan, Virginia, USA challenged the relevance of such frameworks – and specifically of 'prisonization' and the 'inmate social structure' – to women in prison. Although not an 'insider' herself, the importance of introducing Heffernan's study here is two-fold: first, it underscores the importance of studies that explore the *gendered* experi-ence of imprisonment; and second, it provides a practical example of the old adage, 'It is not *what* you know, but *who* you know', in terms of gaining research access to prisons (Heffernan was acquainted with Donald Clemmer, who by this time was in a position to grant such access, in his role as District of Columbia's director of prisons).

Back in the male estate, and prior to the publication of his article with Messinger, Gresham Sykes had written what is frequently described as the most influential book within 20th-century prison studies, while employed as a prison officer. At around the time that Sykes was carrying out the research for *Society of Captives* (1958), John Irwin was serving a five-year sentence in Soledad Prison, California, an experience that would provide the empirical basis for his 1962 article with Donald Cressey challenging Sykes's assumptions about the origins of prisoner culture and the 'deprivations' entailed by incarceration (Irwin and Cressey 1962, cited in Crewe and Jewkes 2012). Erving Goff-man's early career as an assistant at the National Institute for Mental Health in Bethesda, Maryland, allowed him to conduct the participant observation that informed his stu-dies of *Asylums* (Goffman 1961), a text which also significantly influenced prison studies. Through this work, Goffman popularized the term 'total institution' and alerted scholars to the particular trauma – the 'civil death' – that many inmates experience on reception to a closed institution (Goffman 1961: 25).

Returning to the women's penal estate, another important study of the purpose and nature of women's carceral experience from an 'insider' perspective was Joanna Kelley's *When the Gates Shut* (1967), based on her experiences as governor of Holloway Prison (1959–66). This study of one English prison represented a distinctive break from the US-dominated prison studies of the time, and followed the publication *Prisons I Have Known* (1957) by reformist Mary Size who had been (the first female) deputy governor of HMP Holloway, and the first governor of HMP Askham Grange. An even earlier example of practitioner engagement in examining women's carceral experiences can be found in

Cicely McCall's *They Always Come Back*, authored in her capacity as a qualified psychiatrist social worker 'interested in prison conditions' (McCall 1938: xv).

In short, in this formative period of prison studies – and particularly in the USA – researchers and practitioners operated in close alliance, and knowledge about the prison's inner world was seen as crucial for the rational governance of prisons (Crewe 2008). However, 'insiders' were not always authorized by prison managers. Adopting a much less orthodox approach, two young sociology lecturers in England, Stan Cohen and Laurie Taylor (1972), decided to exploit the opportunity provided by an invitation to give weekly classes in social science to long-term prisoners in the special security wing at HMP Durham by conducting covert research. Their project, carried out in Durham's E Wing between 1968 and 1971, represented a 'collaborative' research study (that is, a collaboration between themselves and their students, who included some of the UK's most notorious criminals) on how people survive in extreme and adverse situations. In doing so, Cohen and Taylor defied all rules of research access and the study of total institutions to conduct what is still one of the best, most authentic and insightful studies of long-term imprisonment (Liebling et al. n.d., forthcoming). In a more transparent, yet perhaps equally (for the time) unorthodox study, Pat Carlen (et al. 1985) 'explode[d] the myth that women's prisons are caring places organized for the succour of the weak' by collaborating with four female offenders – Jenny Hicks, Diana Christina, Josie O'Dwyer and the late Chris Tchaikovsky (who would later go on to found Women in Prison, a charity providing support to women who were both current and ex-prisoners).

These sociological studies were individually and collectively ground-breaking. Up to this point, psychologists had largely concluded that imprisonment was not especially harmful. Using methods such as structured questionnaires and psychometric tests, they determined that the effects of imprisonment were negligible and that there was no causal relationship between length of time spent in prison and deterioration of mental faculties (Banister et al. 1973; Bukstel and Kilmann 1980), reporting that prisoners cope surprisingly well with confinement after an initial period of distress or disorientation (Zamble and Porporino 1988). At worst, a prison sentence was thought to be experienced as a period of stasis or 'deep freeze' (ibid.), although Bukstel and Kilmann (1980: 478) went so far as to state that those prisoners on death row find confinement 'quite stressful'. For Alison Liebling (1999), this kind of bland understatement illustrates the failure of psychological research to ask the right questions, or to account for those prisoners who have not survived (or who have *almost* not survived) the prison experience, allowing psychologists to perpetuate the popular myth that many inmates cope better with institutional life than with 'freedom'.

In contrast, the new generation of scholars who emerged from the sociological tradition in the mid-20th century consistently argued that prison is a painful, debilitating and stigmatizing experience which requires the prisoner (particularly those serving very long and/or indeterminate sentences) to develop certain modes of coping and adaptation in order to survive (Crewe et al. 2014). In addition, these researchers highlighted the collateral effects of imprisonment, noting that adverse impacts are experienced not only by prisoners, but by their partners, children, family and the community at large (see e.g., Comfort 2007; Condry 2007; Smith 2014). Post-release offending, drug misuse, mental illness and suicide are all disproportionately high among prison inmates, and have devastating consequences not only for the individual in custody, but also for their family and for society (see Chapter 35, this volume). For women in prison, who are frequently the primary carers for children and other family members, these effects can be 'catastrophic' (Corston 2007: i), although it was not until much later – at the end of the 20th and into the first decade of the 21st centuries – that studies began documenting the 'particular vulnerabilities' (Corston 2007) of women in prison; that is, the adverse and disproportionate impact of incarceration on women and the 'collateral consequences' (Dodge and Pogrebin 2011) of this on their post-release lives (e.g. Gelsthorpe 2004; Baldry 2010; Cobbina 2010; Carlton and Segrave 2011, 2013; Cobbina and Bender 2012; Celinska 2013). Concerns with the importance and necessity of 'gender-responsive' structures within women's prisons continue to be raised in both the USA and the UK (e.g. Covington and Bloom 2006; Corston 2007). However, well-documented studies examining these issues elsewhere in the world remain comparatively (and problematically) few, although more critical voices (e.g. Hannah-Moffat) identify a range of problems with the state re-appropriation of gender responsivity, and the conflation of risk and need within the carceral nexus. In the main, however, the broader field of prisons research has remained characterized by a 'haunting silence' on such matters (Hannah-Moffat 2006: 189).

Dramatic rises in imprisonment and official suspicion towards researchers

In the decades that followed the first wave of classic sociological prison studies, a rapid de-coupling of prison research and prison management occurred, along with a general decline in empirically grounded studies of prison life, particularly in the USA (Crewe 2008). As the 1970s progressed, the rehabilitation model was subjected to increasing criticism. 'Treatment' came to be seen as an expression of the state's excessive intervention and repressive disciplinary tendencies. Critics opposed the use of indeterminate sentencing – whereby prisoners would be treated for as long as it took to make them 'better' – and, by the mid-1970s, the rehabilitative ideal was finally sunk by the doctrine that 'nothing works' (Martinson 1974). This had a swift and profound impact on 'expert' knowledge, policy and practice. Across many penal estates in the English-speaking world, educational and psychological programmes were starved of funds and closed, and there essentially followed a long period when prisons became little more than 'warehouses', subjecting prisoners to regimes of 'coerced and regimented idleness' in which 'productiveness' and 'purpose' had little or no place (Robertson 1997: 1004).

Overcrowded, deprived of any kind of meaningful occupation, frustrated by promised reforms which never materialized, and angered by perceived absences of penal legitimacy – issues from which Tartaro (2012) suggests contemporary prison administrators have failed to learn – rioting broke out across a series of US prisons, culminating in the infamous riot at Attica Penitentiary, NY, in 1971 during which 39 individuals, including ten staff, died (Useem and Kimball 1991). Meanwhile, in the UK, a series of 'violent disturbances' took hold in the early 1970s, first at HMP Albany and HMP Gartree (Player and Jenkins 1994); the issues underpinning these – particularly overcrowding – were not resolved, however, and in 1990, prisoners rioted at HMP Strangeways in Manchester, England. In the period immediately preceding the Strangeways riot, key issues included inadequate sanitary facilities (typically 15–20 prisoners were forced to share just one wash bucket each morning), mass overcrowding (the prison was at 170% capacity at the time of the riot), and there were few opportunities for 'meaningful' activity amongst the population (Tartaro 2012).

In the wake of these (and other similar) riots, a duty of care was placed on prison administrators in both the USA and the UK to improve conditions; however, nothing was done to address the funding shortfall which had, in part, contributed to the over-crowding that was so central to the above-named riots in the first place. When private firms started actively lobbying to be granted contracts to manage correctional facilities, the time seemed right – given rising imprisonment rates and an increasingly punitive public mood – to admit that prisons were no longer required to rehabilitate or train inmates, but simply to incapacitate them, and to hand them over to private sector man-agement (see Chapter 9, this volume). Crime became associated with moral depravity and a new 'war on drugs' propelled a strategy of mass incarceration (Garland 2001). While this era of hyper-incarceration was problematic for many (particularly impover-ished) social communities in the USA (Pattillo et al. 2004), it was those from African American backgrounds who were most disproportionately affected; indeed, Street (2003: 34) went so far as to suggest that 'echoes of slavery' haunted the new 'incarceration state' in light of its disparate impact on America's black citizens. Jacobs's (1977) ground-breaking ethnographic study at Stateville Penitentiary, Illinois ('the world's toughest prison') similarly highlighted the growing centrality of problematic race relations to the male carceral estate. Furthermore, black drug-using (or drug-selling) women were so excessively incarcerated that one commentator has argued that the 'war against drugs' would more accurately be described as 'a war against black women' (Bush-Baskette 1999).

Against this backdrop, sociologically informed prison research declined. The move towards warehousing prisoners (albeit that this occurred later in the UK than in the USA) meant that, in both countries, practitioners had less to gain from understanding prisoners' values and adaptations, and more to lose from allowing researchers inside their establishments. As policy and legislation increasingly emphasized the suffering experi-enced by victims (accompanied by decline in a focus on rehabilitating offenders in favour of retribution as the main goal of punishment), research on the prison and the prisoner increasingly came to be viewed as less important than other aspects of criminal justice. In addition, low levels of government funding for research, the difficulties of combining full-time academic positions with the commitment required to do sustained research in closed institutions, and – as we will discuss further below – the stringency of university ethics committees and access procedures combined to diminish the salience of empirical prison research. In the UK, would-be prisons researchers continued to feel the impact of Cohen and Taylor's clandestine approach, which resulted in an enduring offi-cial suspicion and hostility towards subsequent academics seeking access and, although it was not impossible for scholars to gain entry to the interior world of the prison, it became a great deal more difficult. In addition, over the last decade or so, access has become controlled and sanctioned by prison psychologists, whose priorities and terms of reference are not always compatible with more sociological, critical and theoretical research.

The net result of these processes meant that it became less common for prison researchers to seek or be granted access to prisons, and the interests of many researchers consequently shifted to the sentencing policies behind the rapid rises in the prison population (Crewe 2008). Wacquant (2002: 385) observed that, at the very time when the prison population was rising suddenly and dramatically, prison ethnography became 'not merely an endangered species but a virtually extinct one'.

Recent trends in prison research

Wacquant's observations about the 'eclipse' of empirical prison studies were made in the context of prison research in the USA. In the UK and Europe, notwithstanding the situation described above, the picture has been somewhat mixed. Indeed, after the research drought of the post-Cohen and Taylor era, the 1990s and 2000s witnessed a revival of prison studies, which corresponded with a period of significant change and growth in the prison estates of the UK. Within the context of continually increasing prisoner numbers, a new prison building programme, a strongly interventionist political agenda preoccupied by security, risk and dangerousness, and a concomitant hardening of penal sensibilities, many scholars have found cause to describe the interior world of the prison from the perspective of those who experience it at first hand: prisoners and, though to a much lesser extent, prison staff. Most recent prison ethnographies have thus emphasized what it means to be human in a highly controlled and securitized custodial environment (see, for example, Crewe 2009; Rhodes 2004; Piacentini 2004; Drake 2012; Crewe et al. 2014).

Other reasons for the sudden rejuvenation of sociological prison research in the 1990s and 2000s are speculative, but among them must surely be the rapid burgeoning of university-taught criminology degrees and newly qualified students whose interest in prisons and penology led them to pursue a career in academic research. In particular, the establishment of the Prisons Research Centre (PRC) at the Institute of Criminology, University of Cambridge, has produced a new generation of prison scholars, many of whom have conducted ethnographic fieldwork within prisons in the UK and elsewhere. It might be considered disingenuous if we were not to point out at this juncture that the authors of this chapter have both benefited from the *relatively* privileged (though by no means unproblematic) access that being associated with this Centre affords. We are also aware of the criticism that is sometimes directed at it, by those who feel that the blessings bestowed on the PRC by those with the power to grant or deny access to prisons operate at the expense of prison researchers *not* based at Cambridge. Certainly, studies commissioned and/or supported by the National Offender Management Service (NOMS) or the Ministry of Justice – as some of those carried out at the PRC are – do not face the same level of difficulties in terms of access, but theoretically this *could* lead to problems arising at the stage of publication if results are deemed politically sensitive or unpleasing. There are always dangers that any prison research can become hostage to political fortune, that gatekeepers can restrict access, that only a narrow research agenda may be pursued, or that findings may be harnessed for political and managerial purposes that might differ from those of researchers and research subjects (Crewe 2008). It must also be emphasized that much of the work carried out by members of the PRC is funded by Research Councils UK and other research councils, and that both the Centre, and the Institute that houses it, have a long and distinguished tradition of 'critical' research that has informed understandings about the pains of imprisonment, the harms inflicted by long-term confinement, manifestations of prisoner distress, and so on. Of course, important and innovative research on the prison is by no means limited to the Cambridge PRC, as the contributions to this volume clearly illustrate.

Nonetheless, while links between policymakers and *some* academics remain strong, many researchers are finding that the changing political structure administering criminal justice (the establishment of NOMS, the creation of a new Ministry of Justice, the introduction of competition in the prison sector and the privatization of the Probation

Service, among the changes) has created new difficulties and previously unanticipated obstacles in prisons research. Unprecedented political intervention in the day-to-day running of prisons, swingeing budget cuts, and a high level of largely hostile scrutiny by the popular media, means that persuading prison managers to allow researchers across the threshold of their establishment has, very recently, become a great deal trickier. In a nutshell, in such politically sensitive times, and in the era of key performance indicators, performance management and the ever-present threat of being privatized (or of being returned to the public sector, in the case of private prisons), many governors simply do not want a spotlight to be shone into the darker recesses of their establishments and, equally importantly, increasingly lack the resources to welcome researchers through their doors. It may be, then, that the eclipse of prison ethnography witnessed in the USA described by Wacquant (2002) has begun to take hold in the carceral establishments and prisons sociology of the UK. The myriad reasons for this advent are explored further in the next section.

Negotiating access and conducting the study: the nuts and bolts of doing prison research

As intimated in the previous section, since the heady days of Sykes, Irwin and Cressey, Jacobs, and Cohen and Taylor, it has become a great deal more difficult to do prison research. Indeed, even since the first edition of this *Handbook* was published in 2007, prison ethnographers have been met with new challenges which can make it very diffi-cult to gain access to prisons, especially for postgraduate students. In this part of the chapter, we will draw on our own experiences and data to illustrate some of the pleasures and pitfalls of researching the prison.

'Getting in': managing gatekeepers, maintaining ethical obligations

There are two particular barriers to doing prisons research in the 21st century that did not exist to anything like the same degree even a decade ago. First, there now exists a lengthy gatekeeping process which the potential prisons researcher must successfully negotiate if they are to engage with imprisoned populations. Researchers must complete a lengthy application to the NOMS and the Ministry of Justice, via IRAS (the Integrated Research Application System) – an online system designed to 'streamline' the process of requesting permission to conduct research within specific organizations in addition to NOMS (e.g. the National Health Service, the Social Care Research Ethics Committee). As any prisons researcher will be able to tell you, such systems rarely seem designed for appraising the merits of qualitative, person-centred ethnographic research. Moreover, successfully negotiating these arduous government-level gatekeeping processes may prove ultimately fruitless, since approval gained through IRAS does *not* guarantee entry into a prison to conduct the planned study; this final say on access remains the prerogative of the governing governor of the chosen establishment. Indeed, both authors have had the bitter-sweet experience of gaining approval by the national bodies, only for their research plans to be scuppered at the local level (further discussion of the various levels of gatekeeping involved in prisons research, and tips for the neophyte carceral researcher in successfully negotiating these, can be found in Sloan and Wright 2015).

Second, universities and other research institutions have become much more pre-scriptive in their ethical guidelines, which in some areas now reduce ethical judgements to mechanical practices – e.g. 'Has every participant signed a consent form?', 'Has every participant received an information sheet?' This frequently occurs with little thought given to whether or not prisoners can actually *make sense* of them. Of course, ethical standards are important, but they can impose a 'one size fits all' framework on research. This can serve both to suffocate the study of particularly 'risky' populations (cf. Arm-strong et al. 2014), and risk making a mockery of the collection of 'informed' consent, particularly within incarcerated populations where low rates of literacy and high rates of mental illness co-exist in abundance. This is similarly the case in relation to standard promises of 'confidentiality' and 'anonymity', which are *particularly* difficult to maintain within the prison environs – for instance, the fact that prison staff may have to bring prisoners to and from interviews undermines promises of 'anonymity', as does approaching individuals on the wing to discuss possible recruitment. This might also cause particular problems for those prisoners seeking to hide the true nature of their offence, who may find themselves the centre of unwanted attention should the focus of the research be discovered, thus raising questions relating to ethical obligations not to cause harm to participants/potential participants. With regards to 'confidentiality' within the interview situation, most consent forms and information sheets state that where interviewees disclose an intention to harm others or themselves, or to commit further crimes, this will be relayed to prison staff. This seemingly black-and-white issue dissolves into shades of grey when interviewees disclose offences perhaps previously unknown to the criminal justice system, or breaches of prison security (for example, having a mobile phone, securing narcotics through a prison staff member), where the need to maintain good relations with prisoners is balanced against loyalties to gatekeepers.

There are further problems with the necessity of explicitly *informed* consent being granted by prisoner participants in research. It is not always practical to request this, as research in prison frequently takes unexpected turns. It is quite common, for example, for prisoners to view university researchers with suspicion, to be guarded in what they say, or to think that they are obliged to talk to you because it might enhance their chances of winning favour with the staff, governor, or even the Sentencing Review or Parole Boards. The motif of researcher as spy is common in the prison research literature (Jewkes 2002), so the idea of informed consent, as demanded by university ethics com-mittees and professional bodies such as the British Society of Criminology, is hardly practicable in reality – many participants would just back off if an ethics pro-forma were thrust upon them at the outset. However, as interviews proceed, and as rapport is established and trust is won, a different atmosphere can be created in which prisoners realize, ironically, that they have a captive audience; someone who is sympathetic to their plight, non-judgemental about their offending behaviour, and – specifically in the case of indeterminately sentenced prisoners – powerless to negatively affect their chances of release.

With this realization, many participants end up using interviews to talk about the most intimate aspects of their lives, but unexpectedly and unpredictably so, as in this example from one of our own doctoral research interviews:

SW: I mean, like do [prison officers] give you any sort of emotional support in here?

LOUISE: [laughs, derisively] Na. They, they're just all key happy mate, they just like to lock 'em in, d'ya know what I mean, an' they go home at the end of the day. [sighs] So, I dunno — some of 'em I just ain't got the time of day for.

SW: Are there any sort of positive, er positives, or any that you sort of do get on with?

LOUISE: Sometimes yeah like, yeah, pffft [pauses] But I don't, 'cos goin' back when I was in [prison name], um, I was workin' in the gardens [pause] and erm [longer pause this time] I got, er — Oh I'm gonna tell you it [lets breath out], I got, er, I got sexually abused by a member of staff.

The choice to disclose is, as Hollway and Jefferson (2000) note, made moment by moment in a largely unconscious response to the quality of the relationship in that instant. It is thus an ongoing, free-flowing, dynamic negotiation of informed consent in which power is not invested solely in the researcher. When genuine rapport is established, the research participant may feel that they can talk relatively freely and disclose information that they are not generally able to in their everyday lives. Many prisoners find that the experience of being interviewed by an academic researcher — independent of any of the authorities whom they perceive as responsible for their confinement — is therapeutic, cathartic and often pleasurable, as these excerpts from interviews illustrate:

> I'm really glad I've talked to you. I wasn't sure at first — sorry if I seemed a bit narky, but I didn't know who you were. I feel much better for our chat. I wouldn't mind seeing you again tomorrow if you wanted.
>
> (YJ interview)

> I haven't talked for this long to anyone in all the months I've been in here. Not even my personal officer. I don't talk to any of 'them' if I can help it — I refuse to talk to psychologists and all the welfare people they send my way. I've really enjoyed myself today though.
>
> (YJ interview)

> I wanted to do this, wanted to tell you, and then hopefully in time you can help, can help PPO [Prolific and other Priority Offender] people — you know, I can see that you're passionate about this … and you don't get a lot of people like you out there … And it is nice to know that there's actual people out there tryin' to help us.
>
> (SW interview)

That individuals in prison feel particularly disenfranchised and lack a voice in which to communicate their experiences to the world, often leads to acknowledgement and appreciation of researchers whose intentions they believe to be genuine. While care must be taken by the researcher not to give the false impression that they possess skills or qualifications, e.g. in psychotherapy or counselling, this kind of feedback illustrates, as Elliott (2005: 137) comments, that incarcerated individuals often 'benefit from being given the chance to reflect on and talk about their lives with a good listener'.

'Getting on': carrying keys (and Dictaphones), conducting the research, creating rapport

As Crewe (2008) notes, many accounts of doing prison research suggest that it is 'intense, unpredictable and emotionally taxing', yet often fail to note that it is 'rarely dangerous', with both prisoners *and* prison staff being 'generally welcoming' to the researchers in their midst. This has certainly been our own experience – as discussed further in the final section of this chapter – and in terms of 'getting on' with prisons research, generating rapport within the prison environment has often been the *least* problematic issue to consider, in light of the myriad practical considerations and dilemmas involved.

Central among these is the thorny issue of carrying keys, a concern that is both practical *and* political. As King (2000: 303) states, doing prisons research is 'inevitably going to be disruptive' to the regime, both in terms of demands on prisoner *and* staff time. In regard to the latter, carrying keys can be a way of reducing the institutional burden one may feel they represent by transporting themselves from place to place across the prison site. This can avoid the sort of situation described by King (2000) during his fieldwork in Colorado State Penitentiary (whereby the escort duties involved across the study period were estimated at the equivalent cost of one officer's wages for three weeks!). Indeed, Roberts (2011: 189) reports that her research was only possible *because* she 'accept[ed] responsibility for carrying keys'. On the other hand, *refusing* to take keys – not as an issue of responsibility, but as one of political statement – is one way that prison researchers have sought to 'minimize their differential access to power and resources' in relation to prisoner respondents (Jewkes 2012: 67). It is of course worth remembering that such decision making may be taken out of the hands of the researcher as the option of carrying keys may be denied in the first instance, particularly where the security level of the prison is high and/or the security clearance level of the researcher is low.

If access to keys is both desired and approved, physically obtaining them will usually involve some degree of security training by prison staff, which explains such matters as: which keys are used when, and how; best practice for conducting oneself safely in the prison; and identifying and managing attempted coercion or corruption by prisoners. In our recent experience, such sessions ranged widely from the formal to the (very) informal, lasting anything between 30 minutes and two hours, with heavy emphasis placed on the corruptive potential of *all* prisoners. In almost every establishment SW visited in her most recent work, this security training included being warned not to take anything *out* of the establishment if asked by a prisoner ('Even if they missed the last post and it's Granny's birthday tomorrow', was the oft-repeated – but never yet encountered – refrain), nor to bring anything *in* (theoretically, this ranged from smuggling drugs and mobile phones, to offering a prisoner a biscuit – it seemed somewhat contrary to point out that the authorities ought to be *more* concerned with their own wing staff, whom prisoners frequently identified as their key supplier of the former). Such talks also emphasized the inherently manipulative and corruptive nature of every single prisoner, with one female officer at a high-security male estate even warning that when talking with us, prisoners would 'already be thinking about where to bury the body'.

Another security issue arises when researchers wish to take Dictaphones inside the prison. This is most likely to arise with those engaging in qualitative, often ethnographic research – the 'favoured' design of the prison researcher (Crewe 2008) – which involves deep, narrative and life history-centred interviews. Patton (2002: 380) argues that such studies 'come to naught if you fail to capture the actual words of the person being interviewed', highlighting the importance of verbatim data to the integrity of such projects. While security teams are often reluctant to allow such prohibited items into the prison, their fears can usually be assuaged once the case is put clearly to them in these terms, and assurances made in relation to the capability of the researcher(s) to competently manage the protection both of the interview data *and* of the unit itself.

Once the researcher has successfully negotiated these practical obstacles, there are yet further political hurdles to consider. To consider this experience within a dramaturgical framework, we would argue that one is *always* in 'front-stage' (cf. Goffman 1969) when 'getting on' with research inside the carceral arena. To be front-stage requires an individual to 'give the appearance that his activity in the region maintains and embodies certain standards' (Goffman 1969: 110). Certainly this is important in the prison environs, where researchers are concerned to present a particular (and often different) identity to both prisoners *and* staff, while similarly having their identity(ies) constructed and reconstructed by these same two groups. So, for example, Sloan and Wright (2015) describe how their presentation caused them to be variously mistaken for undergraduate students, social workers, bereavement counsellors, psychologists, and even senior management team members during the course of their respective doctoral studies, and how these misperceptions structured the ways in which prisoners and staff responded to them. Smith and Wincup (2000) – similarly discussing their respective doctoral research projects – identify their relative youth and femaleness as 'more enabling than constraining' in the successful completion of their studies. Such issues of identity are often bound up with assumptions related to dress, confidence and the tone of one's conversation, underpinned by considerations of gender, race, social class, nationality and age. Phillips, for example, talks about the ways in which staff routinely disregarded her (as a black/mixed race woman, and the principal investigator) when engaged with the research team in favour of her white, male – yet junior – colleagues, and that her 'loxed hair' elicited a palpable hostility from some white prison staff (Phillips and Earle 2010). Hayman (2006: 11), meanwhile, draws attention to the various pros and cons of being a 'Euro' and non-Canadian researcher 'venturing into Aboriginal [prison] territory', which undoubtedly fed into the way in which she was perceived by prisoners and staff.

Further issues of identity politics arise in terms of researchers' apparent – or actual – alliance with either staff or prisoners. Liebling (2001) argues that it is possible – and indeed, important – to consider the story of the research from *all* sides. In some instances, however, maintaining neutrality may be 'almost impossible' (Crewe 2008). Intense divisions may exist between 'cons' and 'screws', as well as between different prisoner factions – while often perceived to be more of an issue in the deeply raced and gang-based realities of US prisons (cf. Jacobs 1977), it is worth noting that religious and racial tensions (particularly within the context of pro- and anti-Muslim sentiment) has begun to infiltrate high-security prisons in England (cf. Liebling et al. 2011).

Relatedly, 'getting on' with prisons research – specifically that which involves interviewing – requires the generation of a degree of *rapport* with those being interviewed. 'Rapport' does not mean 'bonding'; it usually involves respect for a person and for what they are saying, and signals to both parties that on *this* occasion, conditions are right for disclosing thoughts and feelings (Lindlof 1995). Rapport is thus a quality of a communication event, not of a relationship (ibid.). As noted above – and as suggested by Crewe (2008) – prisoner engagement may be 'less likely' in higher security establishments, although King (2000) suggests that in the main, the suspicions and concerns of prisoners can be assuaged by researchers who 'put the time in', and who display a genuine interest in relaying prisoner issues from the inside to the outside world. Gender can also affect the interaction between potential interviewees and researchers in a number of ways and it is worth addressing these separately (if somewhat briefly)

Gender and 'getting on' in prisons research

In her doctoral thesis, YJ reflects on the ways in which being ascribed with a formal form of address by prisoners – i.e. being called 'Miss', usually reserved for prison officers and psychologists – potentially restricted the development of rapport with these individuals. This represented a markedly different situation from the rapport and relationships established with those using her first name as a mode of address. Indeed, with regard to the latter, she found that the 'rapport' which developed was often underpinned with 'mild flirtation' and 'courtship rituals', and occasionally transcended into 'genuine, if very transitory, friendship[s]' (Jewkes 2000; cf. Jewkes 2002).

SW similarly found that being female and relatively young was helpful in developing rapport in her doctoral research with women in prison, who were often of a similar age. She also found that disclosing her previous work experience – as a drugs/alcohol support worker, and an independent domestic and sexual violence advocate (IDVA/ISVA) – helped to assuage the women's fears of being misunderstood when discussing experiences in this vein. However, her current research project – with long-term *male* prisoners – has seen her age and gender (i.e. a woman in her late twenties) interact in a completely different manner, with some prisoners openly stating that they only agreed to take part in the research 'so I could sit alone in a room with you!' It is worth bearing in mind that it is here that the power differentials between researcher and the researched can be *reversed* when the latter is male and the former is female, as SW found when a male prisoner exposed himself to her during a conversation on a prison wing, while at a different establishment a female colleague was invited from a cell window to 'show us ya gash!' Such experiences are surely not uncommon in the field of prison research, even if they – and our visceral responses to them – are generally absent from our written-up accounts. Among the rare exceptions are Julie Mills (2004), who described feeling overwhelmed and terrified when greeted in prison by a large group of men who shouted, wolf whistled and subjected her to sexual innuendo, and Hanne Tournel's disclosures about obscene comments directed at her by unseen prisoners in a prison in Belgium:

> Suddenly a lot of shouting started … 'Hey slut', 'Hey delicious whore', 'I will show you how to please a woman', etc. … although the staring and name-calling had become a daily occurrence, I had never expected such vulgar and insulting communication for which I wasn't prepared at all.
>
> (Claes et al. 2013: 66)

The examples above reveal the potentially unpleasant side of prison studies for the female researcher (in male prisons, at least), and highlight the gender power asymmetry of being constantly under 'the male gaze' (cf. Mulvey 1975). Female ethnographers are arguably more likely to be assigned different identities or 'labels' by male respondents based on marital status, physical appearance and sexual dynamics, as well as notions of professional status, social power, ethnicity, class, gender and age (although see Crewe 2014; and Ugelvik 2012 for critiques arguing that men are not immune to such treatment). Again, academic scholars rarely write about these issues, although Coretta Phillips has noted that aspects of shared identity with a male prisoner respondent (primarily, ethnicity) were cancelled out by positioning her as a sexualized gender subject and insistence on regarding the interview as 'more of a date' (Phillips and Earle 2010: 367).

However, there is another side to gender dynamics in prisons. Following her doctoral research, YJ wrote about the fact that the majority of prisoners she interviewed – most of whom were serving very long sentences and were mid-life or older – were unfailingly candid and honest in their responses, and offered information of a deeply personal nature. They also often tempered their language and demonstrated a degree of old-fashioned, gentlemanly courtesy not usually found any more in general life. She relates an occasion when a prisoner who described himself as a 'romantic' and a 'musician' followed up an interview by returning with a guitar under each arm, intent on serenading her (Jewkes 2002). It was a poignant moment, immediately followed by the awkwardness of him being manhandled back to his cell by two prison officers, but it does illustrate that 'rapport' between researcher and participant can, in some cases, be superseded by a genuine and meaningful connection (ibid.). Such moments highlight the emotional texture of prison ethnography, which is an unavoidable dimension of research in this setting, but one that has only recently been acknowledged by scholars (although see Liebling 1999, 2001). The next section will discuss this emerging literature and will include our own reflections on the emotional experience of interviewing in prisons.

Managing the emotional dimensions of prisons research (aka 'getting out')

> Prison research is not easy. There are too many realities that press the role of the researcher to the limits of personal and professional integrity. A prison *is* a total institution, and its demands are total.
>
> (Heffernan 1972: ix)

The totality of the total institution, even as a research site, has been discussed by Jewkes (2014), who argues that the fact that prisons are so spatially and temporally defined – and in the most limiting, constraining ways imaginable – makes prison ethnography unlike any other qualitative enterprise. Despite only experiencing a tiny fraction of the restrictive binds of carceral space and time felt by prisoners, researchers nonetheless cannot help but be touched, if not deeply affected, by the cultural isolation and emotional intensity of confinement, even though they are largely experiencing it at one step removed and in relatively short doses. Moreover, prisons are *intensely* human environments, giving rise to *acute* difficulties, dilemmas, complexities and contradictions. The tendency of in-depth interviews to involve the discussion of deeply personal and emotional experiences presents particular ethical issues, likened by Lieblich (1996: 177) to 'opening a Pandora's box' of distress and pain for the interviewee.

Both of us have, on many occasions, opened that box. The women in SW's study on persistent offending/repeat criminalization across the female life course disclosed in interviews their experiences of domestic abuse, physical and sexual assault (both in childhood and adulthood), family bereavements, and the effects of lifelong substance abuse. In some cases, these disclosures had a tangible impact on the women – some would break down and cry, or become visibly angry. SW managed this by pausing the interview, asking if they would like a break/to step outside, or whether they wanted to end the interview. When concluding the interview, she always made sure to ask how they were feeling, openly discussing any impact that the session might have had, and offering to arrange follow-on support from staff if desired. In rather different circumstances, during a study conducted by YJ, a male participant started telling her about his history of self-harming. As he recounted his damaged childhood and life since the age of 12 in custodial institutions, he became very upset and started to show her all the scars on his arms where, over many years, he had cut himself. At that moment, a prison officer burst into the room and announced abruptly, 'That's it. Time up. Let's get you back to your cell'. YJ's field notes relate not only how mortifying this was, but how culpable she felt: 'a can of worms had been opened and there was no time to even try and put them back, to bring the interview back to something normal. I was horrified.' She followed it up with wing staff, explaining that the man may have been left in a vulnerable state, and was able to speak with his personal officer the following morning. However, such practical interventions aside, SW and YJ were both similarly 'tormented' by the acknowledgment of their role in causing the distress (cf. Lieblich 1996).

These incidents further illustrate that the research process frequently does not permit us as much contact time with individuals as we would like and forces us to rely on prison staff to 'do the right thing' while we are in, or when we leave, the field. SW recalls how, on the first day of interviews on a project, alone on a wing while her first interviewee was being collected, she was called over to a door by a woman with blood streaming down her face. She had clearly self-harmed, and was crying, asking SW to inform someone in the office. SW was torn between leaving her, and doing as she asked. She tried to reassure the woman, and rushed to the office to relay what she had seen, but was met with a lacklustre, disinterested response from staff – 'Oh, was that X? She's always doing that, don't worry' – which was somehow *equally* disturbing as that which she had witnessed. SW then had to go to her first prisoner interview – which she felt needed to 'go right', as it would set the tone of the whole research project – with that experience weighing heavily on her mind. Such incidents inevitably impact on one's ability to be fully 'in the room' while conducting interviews and, indeed, may troublingly stay with the researcher for many years. For the researcher, then, 'getting out' of the prison is far more of an emotional and psychological challenge than a physical one.

The unpredictable nature of the prison environment can also act in other ways to unsettle the research process. YJ recalls how in an early interview, she was shown into the designated room by a prison officer who said, 'you know where the alarm button is', as he waved non-specifically in no particular direction while backing hastily out of the room. She did not, and it weighed on her mind as she conducted the interview, to the detriment of its quality. On an occasion in which SW was interviewing, a fight broke out on the landing, immediately outside the room. The interviewee was visibly shaken and verbalized her concerns that the aggressors might come into the room which – until very recently having previously been a store room – was not, SW suddenly realized, equipped with an alarm bell. This also impacted heavily on the quality of the data generated from the interview, as it completely unsettled the interviewee, and interrupted the rapport and 'flow' that had been established pre-incident.

While these kinds of incidents are not uncommon in prison fieldwork, it is important not to 'overstate' the potential for negative impact in life story/biographical interviewing

(Elliott 2005: 137), or to suggest that the prison is an unremittingly painful or dangerous environment. Many of us are driven towards prison research out of compassion and empathy with respondents or, indeed, perhaps by the 'sneaky thrills' (Katz 1988) of entering a world closed to most people. Prisons can be 'stimulating, exhilarating, and curiously life-affirming environments in which to do qualitative research, and ... a positive and powerful stimulus in the formulation of knowledge' (Jewkes 2012: 69).

Concluding thoughts

What it means to 'do' prisons research is a highly individualized enterprise, and one which is shaped in large degrees by historical, socio-political and personal concerns. The importance of conducting empirically grounded prisons research lies in its ability to expose the human and lived experience of living (and working) in the total institution of the carceral; to 'speak truth to power', and – to some extent – temporarily bring down the walls that separate 'us' from 'them'.

Of course, this is no simple task. The gatekeepers of our incarcerated populations are numerous, and gaining research access to the prison is no mean feat. It is a task dominated by deeply bureaucratic processes, and ones that can be weighted heavily against qualitative and experiential research, particularly that which has no immediate 'value' to the establishment. It is possible to surmount these obstacles: the tradition of rich ethnographic studies of the prison experience attests to this. However, this is a process that is perceived by many working in prisons research as becoming increasingly difficult, particularly for the neophyte or doctoral researcher who may lack the contacts to exploit for these purposes (i.e. 'It's not *what* you know ...' etc.). We hope that the issues we have covered here may support such individuals in their endeavours, as well as preparing the first-time prisons researcher with a degree of insight as to what they might expect behind the walls of the carceral.

Conducting research in prisons not only acts to reveal the human experience of being behind bars, but – with the right attitude, interview technique and rapport – can also offer incarcerated individuals an opportunity to step out of their daily routine; one in which they may speak with relative freedom, without fear of judgement or reprisal. In our experience, such opportunities are welcomed, and are increasingly important as the prison population continues to rise inexorably across the Western world.

Bibliography

Armstrong, R., Gelsthorpe, L. and Crewe, B. (2014) 'From paper ethics to real-world research: Supervising ethical reflexivity when taking risks in research with "the risky"', in K. Lumsden and A. Winter (eds) *Reflexivity in criminological research: Experiences with the powerful and the powerless*, Houndmills: Palgrave Macmillan, 207–219.

Baldry, E. (2010) 'Women in transition: From prison to...', *Current Issues in Criminal Justice*, 22(2): 253–267.

Banister, P.A., Smith, F.V., Heskin, K.J. and Bolton, N. (1973) 'Psychological correlates of long-term imprisonment I: Cognitive variables', *British Journal of Criminology* 13: 312–323.

Bukstel, L.H. and Kilmann, P.R. (1980) 'Psychological effects of imprisonment on confined individuals', *Psychological Bulletin* 88(2): 469–493.

Bush-Baskette, S. (1999) 'The war on drugs: A war against women?', in S. Cook and S. Davies (ed.) *Harsh punishment: International experiences of women's imprisonment*, Boston, MA: Northeastern University Press, 211–229.

Carlen, P., Christina, D., Hicks, J., O'Dwyer, J.C. and Tchaikovsky, C. (1985) *Criminal women*, Oxford: Blackwell.

Carlton, B. and Segrave, M. (2011) 'Women's survival post-imprisonment: Connecting imprisonment with pains past and present', *Punishment & Society* 13(5): 551–570.

Carlton, B. and Segrave, M. (2013) *Women Exiting Prison: Critical essays on gender, post-release support and survival*, Abingdon: Routledge.

Celinska, K. (2013) 'The role of family in the lives of incarcerated women', *Prison Service Journal* 207: 23–26.

Claes, B., Lippens, V., Kennes, P. and Tournel, H. (2013) 'Gender and prison ethnography: Some fieldwork implications', in K. Beyens, J. Christiaens, B. Claes, H. Tournel and H. Tubex (eds) *The pains of doing criminological research*, Brussels: VUB Press.

Clemmer, D. (1958 [1940]) *The Prison Community*, New York: Holt, Rinehart & Winston.

Cobbina, J.E. (2010) 'Reintegration success and failure: Factors impacting reintegration among incarcerated and formerly incarcerated women', *Journal of Offender Rehabilitation* 49(3): 210–232.

Cobbina, J.E. and Bender, K.A. (2012) 'Predicting the future: Incarcerated women's views of reentry success', *Journal of Offender Rehabilitation* 51(5): 275–294.

Cohen, S. and Taylor, L. (1972) *Psychological Survival*, Harmondsworth: Penguin.

Comfort, M. (2007) 'Punishment beyond the legal offender', *Annual Review of Law and Social Science* 3: 271–296.

Condry, R. (2007) *Families Shamed: The consequences of crime for relatives of serious offenders*, Cullompton: Willan.

Corston, J. (2007) *The Corston Report. A report by Baroness Jean Corston of a review of women with particular vulnerabilities in the criminal justice system: The need for a distinct, radically different, visibly-led, strategic, proportionate, holistic, woman-centred, integrated approach*, London: HMSO.

Covington, S.S. and Bloom, B.E. (2006) 'Gender responsive treatment and services in correctional settings', *Women & Therapy* 29: 9–33.

Crewe, B. (2008) 'Research in prisons', in Y. Jewkes and J. Bennett (eds) *Dictionary of prisons and punishment*, Cullompton: Willan.

Crewe, B. (2009) *The Prisoner Society: Power, adaptation and social life in an English prison*, Oxford: Oxford University Press.

Crewe, B. (2014) 'Not looking hard enough: Masculinity, emotion, and prison research', *Qualitative Inquiry* 20(4): 392–403.

Crewe, B., Hulley, S. and Wright, S. (2014) 'Experiencing long-term imprisonment from young adulthood: Identity, adaptation and penal legitimacy', 14th Annual Conference of the European Society of Criminology, Prague.

Crewe, B. and Jewkes, Y. (2012) 'Introduction to special issue of Punishment & Society: Pains of imprisonment revisited', *Punishment & Society* 13(5).

Dodge, M. and Pogrebin, M.R. (2011) 'Collateral costs of imprisonment for women: Complications of reintegration', *The Prison Journal* 81(1): 42–54.

Drake, D. (2012) *Prisons, Punishment and the Pursuit of Security*, Basingstoke: Palgrave Macmillan.

Elliott, J. (2005) *Using Narrative in Social Research: Qualitative and quantitative approaches*, London: Sage Publications.

Garland, D. (2001) *Mass Imprisonment: Social causes and consequences*, London: Sage Publications.

Gelsthorpe, L. (2004) '"Making it on the out": The resettlement needs of women offenders', *Criminal Justice Matters* 56(1): 34–41.

Giallombardo, R. (1966) *Society of Women: A study of a women's prison*, New York: John Wiley.

Goffman, E. (1961) *Asylums: Essays on the social situation of mental patients and other inmates*, Harmondsworth: Penguin.

Goffman, E. (1969 [1959]) *The Presentation of Self in Everyday Life*, Harmondsworth: Penguin.

Hannah-Moffat, K. (2006) 'Pandora's box: Risk/need and gender-responsive corrections', *Criminology & Public Policy* 5(1): 183–192.

Hayman, S. (2006) *Imprisoning our Sisters: The new federal women's prisons in Canada*, Montreal: McGill-Queen's University Press.

Heffernan, E. (1972) *Making it in Prison: The square, the cool, and the life*, New York: Wiley.

Hollway, W. and Jefferson, T. (2000) *Doing qualitative research differently: Free association, narrative and the interview method*, London: Sage Publications.

Jacobs, J. (1977) *Stateville: The penitentiary in mass society*, Chicago, IL: University of Chicago Press.

Jewkes, Y. (2000) *Captive Audiences: Media, masculinity and power in prisons*, unpublished PhD thesis, University of Cambridge.

Jewkes, Y. (2002) *Captive Audience: Media, masculinity and power in prisons*, Cullompton: Willan.

Jewkes, Y. (2012) 'Autoethnography and emotion as intellectual resources: Doing prison research differently', *Qualitative Inquiry* 18(1): 63–75.

Jewkes, Y. (2014) 'An introduction to "doing prison research differently"', *Qualitative Inquiry* 20(4): 387–391.

Katz, J. (1988) *Seductions of Crime*, New York: Basic Books.

Kelley, J. (1967) *When the Gates Shut*, London: Longford.

King, R. (2000) 'Doing research in prisons', in R. King and E. Wincup (eds) *Doing research on crime and justice*, Oxford: Oxford University Press, 285–312.

Lieblich, A. (1996) 'Some unforeseen outcomes of conducting narrative research with people of one's own culture', in R. Josselson (ed.) *Ethics and process in the narrative study of lives*, Thousand Oaks, CA: Sage Publications.

Liebling, A. (1999) 'Doing research in prison: breaking the silence?' *Theoretical Criminology* 3(2): 147–173.

Liebling, A. (2001) 'Whose side are we on? Theory, practice and allegiances in prisons research', *British Journal of Criminology* 41(3): 472–484.

Liebling, A., Arnold, H. and Straub, C. (2011) *An Exploration of Staff-prisoner Relationships at HMP Whitemoor: 12 years on. Revised final report*, London: Ministry of Justice/National Offender Management Service.

Liebling, A., Arnold, H. and Straub, C. (n.d., forthcoming) 'Prisons research beyond the conventional: Dialogue, "creating miracles", and staying sane in a maximum security prison', in D. Drake, R. Earle and J. Sloan (eds) *International Handbook on Prison Ethnography*, London: Routledge.

Lindlof, T.R. (1995) *Qualitative Communication Research Methods*, Thousand Oaks, CA: Sage Publications.

McCall, C. (1938) *They Always Come Back*, London: Methuen & Company Limited.

Martinson, R. (1974) 'What works? Questions and answers about prison reform', *The Public Interest* 35: 22–54.

Mills, J. (2004) '"There's a lot in those keys isn't there?" The experience of a female researcher researching rape in a male prison', in G. Mesko, M. Pagon and B. Dobovsek (eds) *Policing in Central and Eastern Europe: Dilemmas of contemporary*, Maribor, Slovenia: University of Maribor, www.ncjrs.gov/pdffiles1/nij/Mesko/208040.pdf (accessed 18 January 2015).

Mulvey, L. (1975) 'Visual pleasure and narrative cinema', *Screen* 16(3): 6–18.

Pattillo, M., Western, B. and Weiman, D. (2004) *Imprisoning America: The social effects of mass incarceration*, New York: Russell Sage Foundation.

Patton, M.Q. (2002) *Qualitative Research and Evaluation Methods*, third edn, Thousand Oaks, CA: Sage Publications.

Phillips, C. and Earle, R. (2010) 'Reading difference differently? Identity, epistemology, and prison ethnography, *British Journal of Criminology* 50(2): 360–378.

Piacentini, L. (2004) 'Penal identities in Russian prison colonies', *Punishment & Society* 6(2): 131–147.

Player, E. and Jenkins, M. (1994) 'Introduction', in E. Player and M. Jenkins, *Prisons after Woolf: Reform through riot*, London: Routledge.

Rhodes, L. (2004) *Total Confinement: Madness and reason in the maximum security prison*, Berkeley: University of California Press.

Roberts, S. (2011) 'Doing research with imprisoned adult male child sexual abusers: Reflecting on the challenges', *Child Abuse Review* 20(3): 187–196.

Robertson, J.E. (1997) 'Houses of the dead: Warehouse prisons, paradigm change, and the Supreme Court', *Houston Law Review* 34: 1003–1064.

Rothman, D.J. (1980) *Conscience and Convenience: The asylum and its alternatives in progressive America*, Boston, MA: Little, Brown.

Size, M. (1957) *Prisons I have Known*, London: George Allen & Unwin.

Sloan, J. and Wright, S. (2015) 'Going in green: Reflections on the challenges of "Getting in, getting on, and getting out" for doctoral prisons researchers', in D. Drake, R. Earle and J. Sloan (eds) *The International Handbook of Prison Ethnography*, Houndmills: Palgrave Macmillan.

Smith, C. and Wincup, E. (2000) 'Breaking in: Researching criminal justice institutions as women', in R. King and E. Wincup (eds) *Doing Research on Crime and Justice*, Oxford: Oxford University Press, 331–350.

Smith, P.S. (2014) *When the Innocent are Punished: The children of imprisoned parents*, Houndmills: Palgrave Macmillan.

Street, P. (2003) 'Color blind', in T. Herivel and P. Wright (eds) *Prison nation: The warehousing of America's poor*, New York: Routledge, 30–40.

Sykes, G. (1958) *Society of Captives: A study of a maximum security prison*, Princeton, NJ: Princeton University Press.

Sykes, G.M. and Messinger, S.L. (1960) 'The inmate social system', in R.A. Cloward, D.R. Cressey, G.H. Grosser, R.H. McCleery and L.E. Ohlin (eds) *Theoretical Studies in Social Organization of the Prison (Pamphlet No. 15)*, New York: Social Science Research Council, 5–19.

Tartaro, C. (2012) 'Missed opportunities: Learning from the mistakes at Attica', *Contemporary Justice Review: Issues in Criminal, Social, and Restorative Justice* 15(3): 339–358.

Toch, H. (1977) *Living in Prison: The ecology of survival*, New York: Macmillan.

Ugelvik, T. (2012) 'Prisoners and their victims: Techniques of neutralization, techniques of the self', *Ethnography* 13(3): 259–277.

Useem, B. and Kimball, P. (1991) *States of Siege: U.S. prison riots 1971–1986*, New York: Oxford University Press.

Wacquant, L. (2002) 'The curious eclipse of prison ethnography in the age of mass incarceration', *Ethnography* 3(4): 371–397.

Wright, S. (2015) *'Persistent' and 'Prolific' Offending across the Life-course as Experienced by Women: Chronic recidivism and frustrated desistance*, unpublished PhD thesis, University of Surrey.

Zamble, E. and Porporino, F.J. (1988) *Coping, Behavior, and Adaptation in Prison Inmates*, New York: Springer-Verlag Publishing.

Chapter 38

Representing the prison

Eamonn Carrabine

This chapter examines some of the diverse ways in which imprisonment has been represented in the visual arts. Metaphors of incarceration played a major role shaping philosophical understandings of the ancient world: Socrates regarded the body as a prison in which the spirit is enchained, expressing a conceptual divide between flesh and soul, while other thinkers maintained that 'the *kosmos* (the orderly universe) itself is a kind of prison (*desmoterion*) for human beings' (Peters 1998: 8). These images are ones that would be later appropriated by many Christian texts, but here suffering in captivity comes to be equated with spiritual growth and purification. The imaginary origins of Western civilization are to be found in tales of banishment, confinement, exile, torture and suffering. It has even been claimed that the 'history of society ... is the history of how we incarcerate our fellow creatures', yet paradoxically the 'prison cell is also the space of dream and poetry, of meditation and religious fervour' (Ruggiero 2003: 194). This strange contradiction has held a powerful attraction to cultural traditions, where the prison image haunts and sustains dynamic mediations on the human condition.

The chapter inevitably only scratches the surface of what is a vast subject and begins with a discussion of how imprisonment was understood in the medieval world, before turning to the early modern period when prisons of all manner of descriptions are becoming a prominent feature of urban life. While the 18th century came to be known as the 'age of reason', it was also an age that delighted in horror, as well as reform and these diverse forms of penal representation informed how new institutional spaces should discipline the poor. From the middle of the 19th century there has been a growing concern with documenting the wretched conditions endured in the slum quarters of Victorian cities and life in prison was a particularly fertile subject for artists, illustrators and photographers. The final section examines how this documentary tradition is flourishing today, across a number of contemporary projects, which are committed to shedding fresh light on imprisonment.

Early penal imaginaries

Although contemporary prisons have very little in common with those that figured in ancient and medieval worlds, it is also important to recognize that up until the 18th century imprisonment was only one, and by no means the most important, element in systems of punishment. The main purposes of the medieval prison were custodial and coercive, with the sentences likely to have been corporal or capital, and it was not uncommon 'for a person to be sentenced and hanged or flogged on the same day' (McConville 1998: 118). The view that justice in the Middle Ages was equated with extreme cruelty is a longstanding one, where the insistence is that gruesome torture and spectacular executions were an integral part of everyday medieval life (see Puppi 1991, for a graphic catalogue of such images). Such characterizations are examples of what Umberto Eco has dubbed 'shaggy medievalism' (cited in Mills 2005: 8), where the epoch is understood to be so dominated by violence, plague, famine and death that it is no surprise that the culture displays 'a profound fascination with flowing blood, torn flesh and fragmented body parts'. However, this emphasis on medieval alterity, in which the monstrous otherness of the times is accentuated, has been challenged by some recent writers who have instead sought to provide a more nuanced interpretation of premodern experience.

The idea that a prison sentence, both as a form of penitence and a test of faith, could bring one closer to God is one that emerged during the early persecutions of Christians under Roman rule. Likewise, the Jewish Bible is full of prison imagery where 'vivid expressions of human helplessness and terror' mix with the 'language of confinement and release, of captives ransomed by God, of refuge and sanctuary, and of exile and return' (Peters 1998: 13). From such sources there developed an early imaginary of the prison emphasizing martyrdom, in which physical suffering is transformed into divine grace. The most famous example is Boethius's *On the Consolations of Philosophy*, written in the early sixth century while a prisoner of the Ostrogoths in Italy, which describes his mental tribulations during captivity, torture and eventual execution. Among the lessons he imparts while contemplating his fate is that even the most terrible ordeals offer opportunities to enrich the mind and soul.

Boethius's text was a major influence on medieval and Renaissance Christianity and helped instil the virtues of religious piety through contemplation and penance. In this way the prison came to be understood as a cloister and it is no accident that the carceral metaphors of early monastic spirituality were so intertwined and helped promote the ascetic life. The close association between imprisonment and purgation was further reinforced in the 13th century when doctrinal changes established Purgatory as a distinct place in the netherworld landscape and revitalized interest in the hereafter, where God is cast for the first time as a 'potentially benevolent jailer' (Geltner 2008: 86).

However, it was the image of the dungeon that was the most widespread when priests spoke of Hell, the place of eternal damnation for the wicked. It has been shown how the penal realities of the 12th and 13th centuries gave shape to popular understandings of the punishments that awaited sinners in the underworld (Baschet 1993). Dante's *Inferno*, composed around 1310, is the most well-known piece of apocalyptic literature produced in these times. He provides a 'vision of hell as a deep pit, dark and smelly, its inmates suffering extremes of either heat or cold, with every additional form of torture inflicted upon them', to suggest that the worst that could happen in this world was just a foretaste of what was to come in the next (Dunbabin 2002: 169). The likening of prison to Hell (Jewkes 2014, 2015) gains considerable traction from the 14th century onwards. In Padua and Verona, prison wards become called 'the Inferno', the Flint Tower at the Tower of London was nicknamed 'Lytle Hell', and by 1310 'Helle' was the name of the king's debtors' prison at Westminster (Geltner 2008: 92).

In looking back, an immediately striking feature of medieval imprisonment is the sheer variety of prisons in existence combined with the range of people who held the right to keep prisons. The structures themselves, too, ranged from castles, or more often a hut in the castle yard, to rooms in gatehouses, parts of monasteries, houses and civic buildings. At this time a 'prison' was often a makeshift arrangement, and most were small, with only a room set aside for the purpose. From the outset separate places were reserved for different kinds of offenders: felons and serious malefactors were often held in underground chambers, while debtors, foreigners and higher classes of prisoner were segregated from them (Johnston 2000: 7). Prisons were essentially local places and while there was no dominant, shared view of incarceration, the evidence suggests that the 'prison was not a place of shame', but instead it 'became another public site for celebrating or protesting against the regime, for promoting charity, and for negotiating or challenging the social order' (Geltner 2008: 99). In other words, early modern penal imaginaries varied, sometimes quite widely, and imprisonment (as we now understand it) only slowly emerges as a conceptually distinct element within the broader category of captivity.

Nevertheless, it is clear that by 1300, the link between the prison and criminal law was becoming more conspicuous across Europe (Dunbabin 2002: 3). Yet it is important to note that the association of prisons with an Earthly Hell is likely to have been a late-medieval innovation, and one quickly gaining widespread currency in the art and literature of the time; similarly in the medieval Muslim world, 'representations of hell offered a powerful discourse that helped the underprivileged to come to grips with the reality of punishment and suffering in *this* world' (Lange 2008: 15, emphasis in original). In both cases the relationships between state punishment and divine retribution deserve more attention than I can give here, but they do suggest that the perceived centrality of spectacular forms of punishment in medieval culture operated at the level of 'discourse and fantasy', where what is recorded in these chronicles is not so much evidence of how the law worked in practice, but how it should ideologically (Mills 2005: 16). Such an interpretation helps explain the paradox of why recent studies of crime and punishment reveal that judicial violence was exercised much more selectively and leniently across many regions of late medieval Europe than is commonly understood (Dean 2001), yet the images and texts of the times give the overriding impression of a culture punctuated with blood-curdling penal spectacles. Here the depiction of pain and suffering offers a 'powerful emblem of intersubjective experience' (Merback 1999: 20), so that the images of extreme violence do not exactly reflect the realities of medieval life, but rather helped to dramatize them. As Javier Moscoso (2012: 12) puts it, they 'do not show us history, but emotions' constituting and organizing sensibilities.

The rise of the prison

This section concentrates on the period 1500 to 1800, which historians would describe as 'early modern', and distinguishes it from the medieval era that preceded it in many ways. Among the most important are the declining power of the Church and corresponding growth in the rationalizing authority of law, science and state. As feudal systems of existence began to break down, with the advent of mercantile capitalism, large numbers of people migrated from rural areas to burgeoning towns and cities. In response there emerged a range of secular institutions (which are the precursors of modern imprisonment) across Europe, which sought to confine the growing numbers of poor, homeless and dispossessed citizens. From the 1500s onwards bridewells, workhouses and transportation to colonies came to complement conventional forms of corporal and capital punishment, as a means of distinguishing the 'deserving' from the 'undeserving' poor and fuelling colonial expansion. In Elizabethan England houses of correction were established not to punish criminals, but to force vagrants and the idle to work under regimes of hard labour. By the early 17th century it has been estimated that as many as 170 houses had opened across the country (McGowen 1998: 75). The model was soon picked up in the Netherlands, Germany and Scandinavia, as an alternative to galley servitude then prevailing in the Mediterranean states. Both developments are indicative of new attitudes towards poverty, which insisted that those who refused to work should be forced to do so in forms of 'punitive bondage' (Spierenburg 1998: 60).

Throughout much of the early modern period imprisonment was still only one element in systems of punishment. The majority of those held continued to be either debtors or awaiting criminal trial, and most prisons were not purposely built for confinement. They 'remained largely crude structures with one or two chambers', and while large prisons did exist and were designed by architects, the exteriors 'reflected current ideas of how a grand public building should look', yet behind the façade, 'prison spaces were quite ordinary, usually consisting of a group of cells, often arranged in no systematic pattern, or simply disposed around interior courtyards' (Johnston 2000: 33). The Amsterdam rasphouse provides a striking example of this practice (see Figure 38.1). The exterior foreground details the elaborate, ornamental buildings, which speak to 'the civic spirit of the Dutch urban elites', while the inner courtyard is modelled on the confiscated Catholic convent from which it was rebuilt into a prison workhouse (Spierenburg 2005: 32).

Figure 38.1 Het Rasp-Huys

Bird's-eye view of the house of correction and its environment. On the foreground the Heiligeweg (Holy Road) number 1 up to and including number 21, and on the left the Kalverstraat. From 'Historische Beschryving der Stadt Amsterdam', by O. Dapper. Printmaker: Jacob van Meurs (1619–1680). Date: 1663. Etching.

(Amsterdam City Archives, www.isgeschiedenis.nl/nieuws/rasphuis-voorloper-van-de-moderne-gevangenis/)

By now prisons of various descriptions are becoming a feature of urban life and to take the example of London, which Daniel Defoe (1986 [1724–26]: 321–322) thought contained more prisons 'than any City in Europe' in the 1720s during his tour of Britain, there is detailed an extensive carceral network that is worth examining in more detail. After listing some 27 'public gaols', he identifies a host of 'private houses of confinement' that are 'little purgatories, between prison and liberty'. The most numerous of these were 119 'Spunging Houses' for debtors, followed by 15 'private mad houses' and an assortment of 'houses' reserved for political prisoners, who were frequently dispersed among the different institutions to nullify the threat of insurrection and opposition (Harding et al. 1985: 85). It is difficult now to comprehend the extent to which imprisonment figured in the life of the city. An indication of their significance can be gleaned from the way the 'body politic demanded that prisons be rebuilt before the churches' after the Great Fire of London in 1666, and they were the 'only new City buildings to be awarded parliamentary subsidy' (White 2009: 71).

Among the most important were Newgate, rebuilt in 1667, which had long been the most famous municipal prison, based on the site of an ancient Roman gatehouse, which had held criminal felons since the 12th century. Likewise, the moated medieval Fleet prison was rebuilt after the fire and remained one of the three main gaols for debtors in London alongside the Marshalsea and the King's Bench. The 'New-Bridewell' listed by Defoe had replaced the earlier palace (known as Saint Bride's well) destroyed by the fire, which had been set up for correcting the idle and bawdy through hard labour. By this time Bridewell had become the generic term for a House of Correction punishing a range of miscreants (mostly apprentices, servants, prostitutes and vagabonds), with the exception of felons, who were detained in public gaols. Although there were separate institutions for distinctive kinds of offender (debtors, felons and misdemeanants), the divisions were not fixed and firm. There were also many mixed prisons where the different categories mingled together, but the decisive factor of prison life for all prisoners remained its cost. Fees varied, but they were payable on admission and release, and at every point in between – such that life inside remained largely unchanged since the medieval period. Every kind of provision and privilege could be bought for a price, irons could be lightened or evaded for a fee, and food and alcohol were available, resulting in a lucrative trade in goods and services for the gaoler who could profit from whatever commercial opportunities they could facilitate.

Consequently, it has been concluded that the 'fundamental cruelty of seventeenth- and eighteenth-century imprisonment was therefore the cruelty of extortion' (Evans 1982: 23). It is such cruelty that Moses Pitt's (1691) The Cry of the Oppressed condemned in his account of debtor's prison conditions and illustrated with various images depicting gaolers exploiting and abusing prisoners in the Fleet. That such outrage was directed at those who profited from it in the first instance, rather than the overall system, is a theme repeated regularly in the decades that followed. The revelation of abuses occasionally prompted the authorities to intervene and one of the more significant attempts to reform conditions came at the end of the 1720s. The immediate trigger leading James Oglethorpe to question the state of the gaols in Parliament was the death of his friend Robert Castel in the Fleet in November 1728. Castel had been a promising architect, but had been committed to the Fleet for debt and, unable to pay the gaoler's fee for better quarters, was taken to a 'sponging house' (so called because they squeezed the prisoner's money out of him) where 'the Small-Pox then raged' (cited in White 2009: 76). Castel contracted the disease and died within a month. The Gaol's Committee Oglethorpe established quickly set about highlighting widespread abuses in their report on conditions in Marshalsea and the Fleet, achieving enduring celebrity in the process but little in the way of concrete change.

A broadsheet from 1729 entitled 'The Representations' is an indication of the way the nascent press reported the revelations of cruelty to their audience (see Figure 38.2). Combining images and text, the document highlights the maltreatment prisoners experienced. Plate (a) depicts the Marshalsea's airless sick room, where prisoners are stacked in three tiers and starving to death. The Committee reported that prisoners were dying on almost a daily basis, yet contrary to the law of the kingdom, no coroner's inquest had been convened for a Marshalsea death in years. Also highlighted is the case of a carpenter, Thomas Bliss, who had 'almost starved to death' and been tortured with the implements in plate (b), which included 'the sheers', heavy irons forcing his legs wide apart (g), thumbscrews (h), and fitted with an 'Iron Scull-Cap' (i) that 'was screwed so close that it forced the Blood out of his Ears and Nose'. As is typical of press accounts from this period the tone ambiguously hovers between sensationalism and condemnation, but there is no doubt that the coverage will have drawn attention to the scandalous treatment prisoners experienced in the Marshalsea.

A further example of how the cruelty was exposed to public view can be seen in William Hogarth's painting of the Committee at work (Figure 38.3). Hogarth was commissioned by one of the Committee's members to paint the examination of the notorious gaoler Thomas Bambridge at the Fleet. The scene vividly contrasts a half-starved prisoner, in rags, bent before the reputable members, while various instruments of torture surround him. Standing in the left-hand corner is the shifty Bambridge being questioned, but our attention is clearly directed to the helpless captive at the centre of the picture, and in doing so the picture has a striking moral tale to tell. It anticipates two of Hogarth's most famous sequences, A Harlot's Progress (1730/32) and A Rake's Progress (1734/35), which chart the demise of naïve protagonists caught up in corrupt social institutions. In the former series of engravings the contradictions surrounding prostitution and sex trafficking are explored through the plight of a vulnerable country girl tricked into the occupation and her journey through the brothels of Covent Garden, before ending up in a Bridewell forced to beat hemp, and eventually dying of venereal disease. The brutalizing forces of city life are also portrayed in the rake's riches-to-rags story, wasting away his inherited wealth on high and low living as he then descends through London's spaces of confinement – from imprisonment in a debtor's prison, to the madness of Bedlam.

The juxtaposition between respectable and criminal is a persistent theme in Hogarth's work, often speaking to the power of ruthless economic and sexual forces destroying human beings and exploiting social relations. These political points are most often made through satire and elsewhere I have explained how biting criticisms of institutions were frequently made in the 18th century through ridicule (Carrabine 2011, 2012a). Indeed, many literary and visual sources highlighted the failings of the legal system and mocked the rituals of punishment. The work that most revels in the many contradictions governing representations of crime, justice and punishment during this era is John Gay's hugely successful musical drama The Beggar's Opera (1728). Set in the criminal underworld rather than royal palaces, it gleefully parodies the generic conventions of the then fashionable Italian opera. The ploy of associating Newgate society with larger political

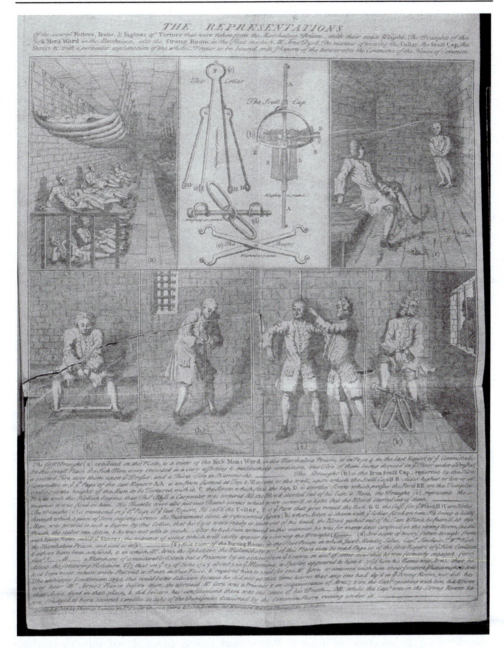

Figure 38.2 The Representations of the several Fetters, Irons, & Ingines of Torture that were taken from the Marshalsea Prison
(© The British Library Board, 10350.g.12, no.26)

Figure 38.3 The Gaols Committee of the House of Commons (includes Henry Howard, 4th Earl of Carlisle; John Perceval, 1st Earl of Egmont; Sir Andrew Fountaine; Sir Archibald Grant, 2nd Bt; William Hucks; James Edward Oglethorpe; Arthur Onslow; Edward Stables; Sir James Thornhill)
(Artist: William Hogarth, Sitter: Henry Howard, 4th Earl of Carlisle. Project title: Representing the Prison. Credit line: © National Portrait Gallery, London)

corruption exposed contradictions at the heart of the social order. Hogarth painted the play many times, and the prison scene depicted borrows from a Baroque tradition of theatrical stage design that was to have a major influence on the Gothic imagination emerging much later in the century.

Here the influence of Giambattista Piranesi's labyrinthine images of prisons, which drew on the operatic set tradition but transformed the conventions into macabre fantasy structures, has been especially profound. In a series of etchings contained in his *Carceri d'Invenzione*, initially published in 1750, Piranesi's dark vision has had an immeasurable impact on cultural sensibilities. In his own day, he had achieved acclaim for his images of the decaying architecture of ancient Rome and it was the scale of this 'melancholy dilapidation' (Scott 1975: 20) that also informed the awesome imagery contained in the *Carceri*. Piranesi's nightmare settings bear little relation to actually existing prison buildings, but they do herald a new aesthetic combining both terror and beauty to sublime effect. The reason they have such a menacing energy is that they are neither protest nor satire, but places where the imagination can lose itself. While the 18th century came to be known as the 'age of reason', it was also an age that delighted in horror – especially as the century came to a close, whether these be the 'cruel fantasies of the Marquis de Sade conceived in prison and projected into further enclosed spaces, the setting of Gothic novels in dungeons, vaults, and oubliettes' (Brombert 1978: 4), they highlight a growing cultural fascination with the mythology of confinement.

These diverse forms of penal representation were also coming to inform prison design. It has been noted how many prison exteriors drew on these forbidding elements, while the interior practices remained mostly intact (see Chapter 7). The old contract system based on gaolers' fees stubbornly resisted change, while new prison designs 'outwardly assumed a fearful, awesome, sublimely intimidating aspect – imagery envisioned in the graphic arts by Piranesi and in architecture by George Dance's 1768 design for London Newgate' (Bender (1984: 58). At the same time, the famous prison reformer John Howard denounced the interior design of the New Newgate as 'hopelessly old-fashioned' (cited in Bender 1987: 243), which he and others thought was cramped, airless and unhealthy. The rebuilt Newgate was the last and grandest prison to be constructed before the full impact of late 18th-century reform was realized. Up until this point it is hard to escape the conclusion that while prison abuses were well known, the political will to tackle them was largely missing throughout much of this period. However, between the demolition of old Newgate in 1767, which was still essentially a medieval gatehouse, and the completion of the 'Model Prison' at Pentonville in 1842, nearly every gaol and house of correction in England had been demolished and rebuilt according to new principles of confinement.

Penitentiary visions

Throughout the 18th century the cultural and ideological importance of the law ensured that it remained at the forefront of public debate. These discussions took many forms, sometimes overlapping, sometimes conflicting, yet always providing commentary – ranging from the burgeoning newspapers, satirical journals and political pamphlets, through to other literary sources like poems, novels and plays. In the English context such sources could deliver quite damning critiques of government and justice through stories of crime and punishment. This literature is important as it is closely allied to the rise of the liberal public sphere from the early 18th century. The 'public sphere' was much more than a purely discursive realm, but was grounded in a network of social spaces and institutions that regulated manners and promoted urbane conduct. Satire was crucial as it enabled a form of political opposition that highlighted the cultural tensions between the civilized and barbaric in metropolitan life, so that accompanying the development of a refined public sphere were numerous attempts at 'social hygiene' seeking to regulate the unruly and the vulgar.

It is in this context that John Howard's (1777) *The State of the Prisons* can be situated, a book that did much to popularize prison reform by detailing just how bad conditions were in English prisons when compared with those on the Continent (see Chapter 36). Howard (1777: 5) was offended by the indiscriminate mixing of men and women, the lack of segregation between the tried and untried, the open sale of alcohol, gambling and generally filthy conditions, where diseases like typhus were rife, rules disregarded and prisoners whiling away their time in 'sloth, profaneness and debauchery'. Ultimately, the unruly prison was morally degenerate and the squalid antithesis of Christian benevolence. Yet Howard's work helped create the impression that the prison was the natural form of punishment, and that 'a proper prison regime already existed, only somewhere else'

(McGowen 1998: 79). Influenced by religious piety and Enlightenment reason, Howard and his fellow reformers advocated the benefits of classification, isolation and sanitation.

However, there was no single victory of the penitentiary idea. Reformers were divided over the kind of work prisoners should do and the role of solitary confinement. It was in this climate that the utilitarian philosopher Jeremy Bentham pitched his famous panopticon prison design in 1787. The innovative idea was that inspection would be continuous from a central watchtower, but the inmates could not know whether they were being watched in their peripheral cells because of a series of blinds shielding the inner tower. Bentham's elaborate machinery was set to 'grinding rogues honest' and he readily acknowledged that it was an omniscient 'way of obtaining power, power of mind over mind' and thus a potent magnification of his own philosophy – though Burke drew a far less flattering comparison of 'the spider in his web' (cited in Evans 1982: 198–199). Critics not only worried over the tyranny exemplified in the design, but disliked Bentham's insistence that the panopticon could be run as a profitable commercial business, and it was this latter objection that ultimately led to the rejection of his plans. Nevertheless, significant elements of his design have informed subsequent prisons. Notable examples include Millbank (1816) and Pentonville (1842) in England, while Joliet (1858) in Illinois became a model for prisons in the USA and the Isle of Pines prison built in Cuba in the 1920s is closely structured on panoptic principles.

Bentham (1787: 40) also thought that the panopticon was 'applicable to any sort of establishment, in which persons of any description are to be kept under inspection' and this included 'prisons, houses of industry, work-houses, poor-houses, manufactories, mad-houses, lazarettos, hospitals and schools'. Recently it has been speculated that the design of the panopticon was influenced by the Rotunda at Ranelagh House (Smith 2009: 106–107). This large, circular wooden hall was the centrepiece of the gardens and lasted from 1742 until 1803. Canaletto painted the interior in 1754 and captured how this enormous public space provided opportunities for assembly, courtship, display and promenade. The pleasure gardens were located in Chelsea, then just outside London, and were an immensely popular and fashionable venue, hosting dances, concerts and masquerades. The central octagonal bandstand is surrounded by two tiers of 52 private boxes and the diameter was said to be greater than the Coliseum in Rome. Bentham will no doubt have been aware of this architectural wonder, and its reputation in 'polite society' as a place to be seen, and it is possible that the fusion of theatre and spectacle here informed his own thinking on the power of public visibility.

Revisionist historians like Foucault (1977) and Ignatieff (1978) have highlighted how the penitentiary offered a vision of social order set to discipline the urban poor and contain the social disruptions unleashed by the Industrial Revolution. Although these accounts are not as popular as they once were, it is clear that the focus of punishment fundamentally changed in quite a short space of time. By the middle of the 19th century the characteristic features of the modern prison were in place and almost the entire range of Georgian criminal sentences – the pillory, the whipping post, the gallows and the convict ship – had disappeared from public view by the 1860s. There is no doubt that the new institution was involved in the ideological legitimation of industrial society and the extension of disciplinary techniques that sought to transform criminal bodies and problem populations.

It is clear that Pentonville provided a blueprint for an entire generation of Victorian prisons and consequently it is worth concentrating on how the institution was represented, not least since it also incorporated ideas from American penitentiaries where two great rival penal philosophies had come to fruition. These were known as the 'separate' and 'silent' systems respectively, and the radial design of Pentonville achieved the complete separation of prisoners, while silence was so rigidly enforced that a visitor in 1864 felt compelled to look into several cell spy-holes to make sure prisoners were actually there (Evans 1982: 349; and see Chapter 2 this volume). Convicts spent almost their whole time isolated in their cells, while solitary confinement was maintained in the chapel through the use of individual cubicles preventing communication (see Figure 38.4) and at all other times prisoners wore face masks with eye holes preserving anonymity. In Henry Mayhew and John Binny's account of their visit to Pentonville in 1862, they are particularly struck by this practice and they describe how:

> the eyes alone of the individual appearing through the two holes cut in the front, and seeming almost like phosphoric lights shining through the sockets of a skull. This gives to the prisoners a half-spectral look ... the costume of the men seems like the outward vestment to some wandering soul rather than that of a human being; for the eyes, glistening through the apertures in the mask, give one the notion of a spirit peeping out behind it.
>
> (Mayhew and Binny 1968 [1862]: 141)

Mayhew and Binny's study of *The Criminal Prisons of London and Scenes of Prison Life* is a rich source of descriptions of Victorian imprisonment, not least since it contains many drawings taken from the then novel medium of photography. It is also indicative of the

THE CHAPEL, ON THE "SEPARATE SYSTEM," IN PENTONVILLE PRISON, DURING DIVINE SERVICE.

Figure 38.4 The Chapel, Pentonville, 1862
(Mary Evans Picture Library)

new ways in which journalists, missionaries, novelists, reformers and others began analytically to document the wretched conditions endured by the urban poor through a mass of detailed observation.

Few thought of themselves as social scientists, but they were pioneering social science methods as they went along in their sporadic forays into the 'unknown continents' of the industrial city. Mayhew's earlier work on *London Labour and the London Poor* (1851–62) pioneered this approach, which was a mix of oral history, ethnographic detail and social statistics, with a deliberate emphasis on sensational reportage. Before undertaking his exploration of urban lowlife he had co-founded the satirical *Punch* magazine in the 1840s and it has been noted how it was in these years that he met the talented illustrators whom he employed to work from daguerreotypes to produce the images in his later publications (Taithe 1996). This is one of the first examples of the photograph being used as documentation, where the authenticity is stressed and the image is mobilized as a reliable witness, to show people places they would not otherwise have been able to see. The new kind of graphic journalism that Mayhew helped to establish lay strong claims to 'objectivity' and the illustrations were said to speak the 'truth' without bias and devoid of sectional interest. Such an ideology was fundamental to the expanding middle class, where the term 'middle' itself was important, implying an impartial role independent of either the aristocracy or working class (Fox 1988).

If satire was the defining form of cultural opposition in the 18th century, then it is the language of realism that became the dominant way of representing imprisonment in the 19th century. As the century progresses, distinctions are increasingly made between realistic detail (realism as method), realism as an ontological disposition towards reality (the search for a larger reality beyond surface details) and realistic subject matter (Williams 1988: 257). An influential example is the engraving by Gustave Doré of the Newgate exercise yard, (Figure 38.5), taken from the 1872 book *London: A Pilgrimage*, written by the journalist and playwright Blanchard Jerrold, who suggested to the famous illustrator that they work together to produce a portrait of the city. This image, like others in the book, rendered social hardships in harsh but realistic ways, and achieved acclaim for the frankness of the investigative 'slumming' displayed across the text.

A number of more contemporary art historians have addressed the issue of realism and rhetoric in Doré's engravings, and concluded that they cannot be used as documentary in any strict sense, because of the 'overt Romanticism and Gothic extravagance of the images (dramatic use of light and dark, tunnelling perspectives, dwarfed figures, massed crowds, and so forth)' so as to then recast the artist as an 'exceptional individual able to offer a more penetrating realism outside the evasive conventions by which Victorian artists typically displaced social divisions' (Pollock 1988: 26). In the picture no attempt is made to sentimentalize the scene, which is one of the usual ways social antagonisms were tamed. Instead, the circle of trudging convicts suggests that criminality might be confined, classified and observed by a single warder in this yard, the fact that one prisoner is depicted as looking up and out, directly at the viewer and seems to be questioning the act of looking itself. Consequently, it has been argued that the 'return of the gaze', here and in many of the drawings from the East End that follow, 'provocatively disrupts the relations of viewing and surveillance' (Pollock 1988: 36), registering a sense of defiance that must have generated unease for some readers, and excitement in others.

The image was later reworked by Vincent Van Gogh in his famous painting *The Round of Prisoners*, which depicts prisoners walking in a futile circle in an exercise yard,

Figure 38.5 Newgate Prison
(Artist: Gustave Doré. Mary Evans Picture Library)

and was painted during a self-admitted stay at the asylum in Saint-Rémy in 1890, when he produced a number of paintings that were copies of works by other artists. Yet in this picture Van Gogh is not overly concerned with providing an accurate representation of prison life, but through the evocative colours and exaggerated forms, the haunting image has something more telling to say on the experience. The illustration will be immediately recognizable to some readers as a detail from it has been used on the cover of the Penguin edition of Michel Foucault's *Discipline and Punish* for many years, as it powerfully alludes to the deadening monotony of the disciplinary society detailed in his book. During his year-long voluntary confinement Van Gogh also painted several scenes from within the asylum grounds and his famous painting *Starry Night* was the view from his sanatorium room window at night.

Likewise, the drawings and paintings produced by the provocative Austrian Expressionist artist Egon Schiele during his imprisonment at Neulengbach in 1912 are a remarkable rendering of the despair felt behind bars. Some deliberately recall Van Gogh's interiors of the asylum and deal with the prisoner's immediate surroundings, while others turn inwards to produce emaciated self-portraits and continue Schiele's narcissistic preoccupation with his own tormented image. Taken together, they constitute a striking visual record balancing the stark sterility of the setting with an intense angst. Among the sequence are his watercolour 'The Single Orange Was The Only Light', which contrasts the solitary fruit against the drab blanket in his cell, while his 'I Feel Not Punished But Cleansed!' is a sarcastic comment on the corridor outside his cell, and the brutally distorted self-portraits powerfully convey inner turmoil.

Although Van Gogh disrupted artistic conventions of realist representation through expressive exaggerations of colour, line and form, these are taken to raw extremes in Schiele and their work can be understood as part of a broader cultural movement developing towards the end of the 19th century which sought to convey the fragmentary nature of social life in the modern era. In doing so, artists lost interest in presenting the 'illusion of reality' and part of this is due to the invention of photography, which could now almost instantly 'produce "perfectly realistic" images every time' (Howells and Negreiros 2012: 170) in monochrome. Instead, artists became preoccupied with introducing fresh and radical ways of capturing light, mood and space in their art. These innovations remain important and helped to define the European avant-garde, but I now want to turn from the world of fine art to the medium of photography, as from the outset the status of the technology rested on its ability to capture an objective record of events that painting could never achieve. The relationship between photography and reality has prompted much debate, and these arguments are important as they enable a more nuanced understanding of how imprisonment has been represented by the camera.

Documentary and imprisonment

The documentary tradition in photography can be traced back to the 19th century, when the approach was associated with particular kinds of social investigation dedicated to prompting social change by exposing injustice. Some of the earliest practitioners travelled into 'the abyss' to document those dark, dangerous and ungovernable places in which the urban poor lived and were carrying on the investigative journalism pioneered by Henry Mayhew and his contemporaries. Here the photograph was regarded as a neutral representation of reality, an authentic, objective and truthful record of the scene, where the crusading photographer used the camera to reveal a world hidden from middle-class view in an effort to shape public reform. By the 1930s, when this form of socially concerned photography flourished in newspapers and magazines, a distinctive eye-witness style had become firmly established.

Not all were enamoured with this movement. The celebrated landscape photographer Ansel Adams complained at the time that 'What you've got are not photographers. They're a bunch of sociologists with cameras' (cited in Marien 2002: 280) in response to a major project documenting poverty in the Great Depression. Among them were Dorothea Lange, Margaret Bourke-White, Walker Evans and Arthur Rothstein, who are some of the most influential photographers of the 20th century. This is one of the central tensions running through the entire documentary project, where we 'are invited to accept that these are "honest" images drawn from life, but are the product of extra-ordinarily gifted photographers' (Price 2009: 99). The images are not simply a visual record, passively recounting facts, but are skilfully composed documents presenting sub-jects as objects of pity and imposing their own aesthetic understanding of how despair should look. An important shift occurred in the decades following the Second World War when it became clear that a new generation of documentary photographers were less preoccupied with offering up monumental images of America and more interested in new kinds of cultural landscape and subject matter.

In the post-war period the 'new' documentarists began exploring more 'subjective' approaches to image making, which reopened important questions about photography's complex relationship with reality (Carrabine 2012b). This shift marked a move away from social reform onto a renewed focus on the more personal, aesthetic qualities of photographic vision. A key representative here is Robert Frank, who in a series of road trips across North America in the 1950s, captured the bleak, neurotic restlessness of the decade by recasting the icons of post-war austerity as profoundly alienating, while his loose, casual, gritty style of composition proved both controversial and influential. Among those following this new approach to capturing social landscapes were Garry Winogrand, who is frequently quoted as explaining, 'I photograph to find out what the world looks like photographed' (cited in Emerling 2012: 28), a definition succinctly characterizing the complex, visual ambiguities he and others explored in their work during the 1960s.

It is in this context that Danny Lyon's study of imprisonment should be situated. His *Conversations with the Dead* (1971) depicts prison life in Texas State Prisons in the late 1960s and is regarded as his most powerful work, containing an 'often visceral exposé of the relentless cruelty of the American penal system' (O'Hagan 2014). Alongside photo-graphs of the dehumanizing conditions, it also includes text taken from prison records, convict letters and inmate artwork. Lyon had also worked in the civil rights movement, and the book can be seen as contributing to that activism, while also continuing his interest in outlaw biker subcultures from earlier in the decade (Lyon 1967). His approach has much in common with the 'new documentary' movement then rising to promi-nence, which involved an immersion in the social world that was being documented and is indicative of a more subjective style that came to redefine the practice. In his attention to layout, design and sequencing he helped establish the genre of the art photography book, where the dynamic of the series was 'dramatized by the photographer's unique perspective on how to order the images' through 'rhythm, connections, and contra-dictions of form and subject' (Marien 2011: 354). Figure 38.6 is one of the striking

Figure 38.6 PAR55771 – USA. Huntsville, Texas. 1968
Ellis is a prison farm for the convicts considered to be the most dangerous or unmanageable.
Building shakedown.
(Danny Lyon/Magnum Photos)

images from the work, where the disjuncture between the supremely confident, non-chalant almost, guards and the naked line of prisoners leaves no one in any doubt over where the power lies and where our sympathies belong.

During the 1970s and 1980s the very practice of documentary critique came under sustained critique, when the movement was charged with exploiting the other and the 'truth claims' were debunked as stage-managed fictions. Under these, and other criticisms, documentary fell out of fashion, but more recently there has been a resurgence of interest in the genre. Contemporary practitioners seem to be less troubled by terms like 'truth', 'evidence' and 'reality', which is not to say they are blind to the way photographs are constructed, but are more attuned to them as 'carefully fabricated cultural objects' (Price 2009: 107).

It is clear that the subject is thriving. The website and blog at www.prisonphotography. org lists some 120 professional practitioners at work, so what follows concentrates on only a handful of projects, but I hope to show some of the diversity of approaches visually documenting imprisonment, as well as the continuities.

One example of a contemporary photographer working in similar ways to Danny Lyon is the South African photographer Mikhael Subotzky. In his work he has focused on the small town of Beaufort West, which lies at the halfway point along South Africa's great highway – the N1, running from Cape Town to Johannesburg. Here its prison is situated in the middle of town, on an island in the highway, or what is called in the UK a roundabout, and his work concentrates on the inside and outside of South Africa's prisons. In doing so it combines the directness of social documentary with a questioning of the nature of the photographic medium itself. The work explores the structures of narrative and representation by examining the relationship between socially concerned storytelling and the formal poetics of image making. In the essay that accompanies the photobook, Jonny Steinberg (2008: 75) notes how almost 'every photograph carries a suggestion of theatre'. In a recent interview he has explained how:

> Initially I thought of the work in traditional documentary terms whereby I sought to make visible that which is hidden – an aspiration that I think is particularly relevant to state institutions such as prisons. However, as I spent time in situation, I began to think of the work more broadly and contemplatively ... having read some academic writing on South African penal history, and Foucault. I tried out different types of images, set up workshops with prisoners, and then expanded the project in the Umjiegwana series to look at the lives of ex-prisoners. At this point the work became much more personal as I established and built up relationships with a group of disparate people who inhabited the same city as me, but very different worlds.
> (From jmcolberg.com/weblog/extended/archives/a_conversation_with_mikhael_subotzky/ (accessed 6 May 2014))

Although a long passage, it does highlight how Subotzky attempted to immerse himself in the social worlds he is depicting and is clearly an attempt to shift away from the traditional objectifying practices of documentary towards a more subjective exploration of identity, difference and the power of representation itself.

A somewhat different example of a visual study of prison as a cultural site is Bruce Jackson's (2009) *Pictures from a Drawer*, which uses around 200 discarded prison identification photographs, likely dating from 1915 up to 1940, given to him in 1975 to provide a remarkable account of prisons, portraiture and US social history. As Jackson argues, the function of these photos was not portraiture, but rather to 'fold a person into the controlled space of a dossier'. Here, freed from their prison 'jackets' and printed at sizes far larger than their originals, these one-time ID photos have now become portraits. Jackson's restoration transforms what were small bureaucratic artefacts into moving images of real men and women. As he suggests, these photographs are second only to 'coroners' photographs of the newly dead, prisoner identification portraits are perhaps the least merciful, the most disinterested, the most democratic, and the most anonymous portraits of all' (Jackson 2009: 11). Neither the sitters nor the photographers who took them have any interest in the photographs they are making, and they strive only for the literal. Unlike arrest identification photographs, or 'mugshots' as they are known, in which the people having their picture taken in the police station face an uncertain future, in prisoner identification photographs all possibility is foreclosed, the individuals sitting for them have already been through gaol, through trial and have been unambiguously removed from ordinary life.

While Jackson constructs his work from 'found' images, Luigi Gariglio's (2007) *Portraits in Prisons* was over ten years in the making and is a series of prisoner portraits from countries on the periphery of Europe. Interspersed among the frank, stark and highly detailed pictures of mostly despondent faces are a few unpopulated images of bare prison spaces and letters written by prisoners, so that the three elements – portrait, place, text – are fragmented, to disconcerting effect. Nevertheless, care is taken from the outset to

Figure 38.7 LON92615 – South Africa. Beaufort West. 2006
Beaufort West Prison is contained in a traffic circle in the centre of the N1 highway which
connects Cape Town and Johannesburg.
(Mikhael Subotzky/Magnum Photos)

explain how much effort went into building up trust with his subjects and how, in each
case, the prisoners chose where they were to be photographed, and crucially no organizing taxonomy is imposed on the images. Most of the photographs are of 'vulnerable,
lonely men and women, thrown into relief by their chosen background' (Visser 2007: 8),
but these are most emphatically portraits, not candid shots or documentary images
commenting on the deeper terms of human existence. Instead, they speak poignantly to
the intimate codes of portraiture, where we are asked to present rather than reveal a face
for public consumption. Many leading 20th-century portrait photographers have
questioned the very basis on which someone can ever 'be "known" or "expressed" in
terms of a photographic image' (Clarke 1997: 115) and something of this uncertainty is
registered across the book.

By moving from portraiture to the still life genre we can further see how contemporary photographers are attempting to say something visually new about imprisonment. One example is Jürgen Chill's (2007) study of German prison cells, which are
largely unexplored as living spaces. His distinctive approach deploys a central overhead
view of what initially looks like a budget hotel room, or a university hall of residence,

but it slowly becomes apparent that we are looking into a different kind of institutional space. Chill has explained that his method was to 'talk to prisoners to get to know them a little and explain his project. Then, and only with their permission, he took a series of overhead photographs' that were then digitally collaged back in his studio to create the final image with a single view (from Confined website, issuu.com/mikecarney/docs/confined_singles). On one level the photographs provide an intimate insight into how dehumanized spaces are individualized by prisoners, but on another the absence of the inhabitants themselves speaks to the largely anonymous lives prisoners lead.

Other contemporary documentary projects that confront criminological issues include Richard Ross's (2012) *Juvenile in Justice*, which combines powerful imagery with excerpts from life stories the young people in custody shared with him (for further details see the website, www.juvenile-in-justice.com). The work builds on his earlier *Architecture of Authority* (Ross 2007), a book capturing carceral spaces ranging from the innocuous to the notorious, but in such a way that the oppressive structures look strangely inviting and even seductive to unsettling effect. The pictures encountered include a Montessori pre-school environment through diverse civic spaces (including a Swedish courtroom, the Iraqi National Assembly hall, the United Nations) to more ominous manifestations of authority: an interrogation room at Guantánamo, segregation cells at Abu Ghraib, and finally, a capital-punishment death chamber.

These are only a handful of examples that seek to convey the pains of confinement in visually striking ways. Although the documentary genre can be condemned and dismissed for its morbid fascination with human suffering, it also offers new ways of seeing social practices. They are visual texts telling a story about confinement in ways that words, on their own, cannot do. Despite all the contradictions running through the tradition, the desire to bear witness to the suffering and violence of the age remains paramount, and requires of us to learn new ways of seeing, especially in those places where seeing is not simple and is often hidden from view.

Bibliography

Baschet, J. (1993) *Les justice de l'au delà: les representations de l'enfer en France et en Italie (XII–XV siècle)*, Rome: École Française de Rome.

Bender, J. (1984) 'The Novel and the Rise of the Penitentiary: Narrative and Ideology in Defoe, Gay, Hogarth, and Fielding', *Stanford Literature Review* (Spring): 55–84.

Bender, J. (1987) *Imagining the Penitentiary: Fiction and architecture of mind in eighteenth-century England*, Chicago, IL: University of Chicago Press.

Brombert, V. (1978) *The Romantic Prison: The French tradition*, Princeton, NJ: Princeton University Press.

Carrabine, E. (2008) *Crime, Culture and the Media*, Cambridge: Polity.

Carrabine, E. (2011) 'The Iconography of Punishment: Execution Prints and the Death Penalty', *Howard Journal* 50(5): 452–464.

Carrabine, E. (2012a) 'Telling prison stories: the spectacle of punishment and the criminological imagination', in L. Cheliotis (ed.) *The Arts of Imprisonment*, Aldershot: Ashgate.

Carrabine, E. (2012b) 'Just Images: aesthetics, ethics and visual criminology', *British Journal of Criminology* 52(3): 463–489.

Clarke, G. (1997) *The Photograph*, Oxford: Oxford University Press.

Defoe, D. (1986 [1724–26]) *A Tour Through the Whole Island of Great Britain*, London: Penguin.

Dunbabin, J. (2002) *Captivity and Imprisonment in Medieval Europe, 1000–1300*, Basingstoke: Macmillan.

Emerling, J. (2012) *Photography: History and theory*, London: Routledge.

Evans, R. (1982) *The Fabrication of Virtue: English prison architecture, 1750–1840*, Cambridge: Cambridge University Press.

Foucault, M. (1977) *Discipline and Punish: The birth of the prison*, Harmondsworth: Penguin.

Fox, C. (1988) *Graphic Journalism in England During the 1830s and 1840s*, London: Garland.

Gariglio, L. (2007) *Portraits in Prisons*, Rome: Contrabooks.

Geltner, G. (2008) *The Medieval Prison: A social history*, Princeton, NJ: Princeton University Press.

Harding, C., Hines, B., Ireland, R. and Rawlings, P. (1985) *Imprisonment in England and Wales: A concise history*, London: Croom Helm.

Howard, J. (1777) *The State of the Prisons*, Warrington: William Eyres.

Howells, R. and Negreiros, J. (2012) *Visual Culture*, Cambridge: Polity.

Ignatieff, M. (1978) *A Just Measure of Pain: The penitentiary in the Industrial Revolution, 1750–1850*, London: Macmillan.

Jackson, B. (2009) *Pictures from a Drawer: Prison and the art of portraiture*, Philadelphia, PA: Temple University Press.

Jerrold, B. and Doré, G. (2005 [1872]) *London: A pilgrimage*, London: Anthem.

Jewkes, Y. (2014) 'Punishment in Black and White: Penal "Hell-holes", Popular Media and Mass Incarceration', *Atlantic Journal of Communication* special issue on 'Reframing Race and Justice in the Age of Mass Incarceration' 22(1): 42–60.

Jewkes, Y. (2015) 'Fear-suffused Hell-holes: The Architecture of Extreme Punishment', in K. Reiter and A. Koenig (eds) *Extraordinary Punishment: An empirical look at administrative black holes in the United States, the United Kingdom, and Canada*, London: Palgrave

Johnston, N. (2000) *Forms of Constraint: A history of prison architecture*, Chicago, IL: University of Illinois Press.

Lange, C. (2008) *Justice, Punishment and the Medieval Muslim Imagination*, Cambridge: Cambridge University Press.

McConville, S. (1998) 'The Victorian Prison: England, 1865–1965', in N. Morris and D. Rothman (eds) *The Oxford History of the Prison*, Oxford: Oxford University Press.

McGowen, R. (1995) 'The well ordered prison: England, 1780–1865', in N. Morris and D. Rothman (eds) *The Oxford History of the Prison*, Oxford: Oxford University Press.

Marien, M. (2010) *Photography: A cultural history*, London: Laurence King.

Mayhew, H. (1861–62) *London Labour and the London Poor*, London: Griffin, Bohn and Company.

Mayhew, H. and J. Binny (1968 [1862]) *The Criminal Prisons of London and Scenes of Prison Life*, London: Frank Cass.

Merback, M. (1999) *The Thief, the Cross and the Wheel: Pain and the spectacle of punishment in Medieval and Renaissance Europe*, London: Reaktion.

Mills, R. (2005) *Suspended Animation: Pain, pleasure and punishment in medieval culture*, London: Reaktion.

Moscoso, J. (2012) *Pain: A cultural history*, Basingstoke: Palgrave.

O'Hagan, S. (2014) 'Danny Lyon's Inside Shots', *The Observer*, 20 April, www.theguardian.com/arta nddesign/2014/apr/20/danny-lyon-photographer-outlaw-bikers (accessed 30 September 2014).

Peters, E. (1998) 'Prisons before prison', in N. Morris and D. Rothman (eds) *The Oxford History of the Prison*, Oxford: Oxford University Press.

Pitt, M. (1691) *The Cry of the Oppressed*, London: Pitt.

Pollock, G. (1988) 'Vicarious excitements', *New Formations* 4 (Spring): 25–50.

Price, D. (2009) 'Surveyors and surveyed: photography out and about', in L. Wells (ed.) *Photography: A Critical Introduction*, London: Routledge.

Puppi, L. (1991) *Torment in Art: Pain, violence and martyrdom*, New York: Rizzoli.

Ruggiero, V. (2003) *Crime in Literature: Sociology of Deviance and Fiction*, London: Verso.

Scott, R. (1975) *Piranesi*, London: St Martins Press.

Smith, P. (2009) *Punishment and Culture*, Chicago, IL: University of Chicago Press.

Sontag, S. (1977) *On Photography*, London: Penguin.

Spierenburg, P. (1998) 'The Body and the State: Early Modern Europe', in N. Morris and D. Rothman (eds) *The Oxford History of the Prison*, Oxford: Oxford University Press.

Spierenburg, P. (2005) 'Origins of the prison', in C. Elmsley (ed.) *The Persistent Prison: Problems, images and alternatives*, London: Francis Boutle Publishers.

Steinberg, J. (2008) 'Essay', in M. Subotzky (ed.) *Beaufort West*, London: Chris Boot.

Taithe, B. (1996) *The Essential Mayhew: Representing and communicating the poor*, London: Rivers Oram Press.

Visser, H. (2007) 'Portraits, spaces, texts', in L. Gariglio (ed.) *Portraits in Prisons*, Rome: Contrabooks.

White, J. (2009) 'Pain and degradation in Georgian London: life in the Marshalsea Prison', *History Workshop Journal* 68: 69–98.

Williams, R. (1988) *Keywords: A vocabulary of culture and society*, London: Fontana.

Chapter 39

Imprisonment in a global world

Rethinking penal power

Mary Bosworth, Inês Hasselberg and Sarah Turnbull

Introduction

Traditionally, scholars in prison studies have considered penal institutions to be bounded by the nation-state. In countries without the death penalty, the prison is the most extreme expression of state power and coercion on those within sovereign borders. The prison is, in short, an institution inherently bound to the territory in which it is situated. When a wider view is taken, it is typically comparative, often hinging on relative rates of imprisonment. Thus, we can find with ease lists of global prison populations, and accounts in which countries are grouped together based on their penal practices – usually their perceived punitiveness, as represented by the imprisonment rate – are also widespread (Cavadino and Dignan 1997; Lacey 2008; Pratt 2009; Pratt and Eriksson 2013).

Such literature is useful, providing important statistical information and macro-level analysis. However, due to the emphasis on overall rates of imprisonment or rankings of punitiveness, these studies do little to challenge the basic assumption that prisons are nation-specific. Instead, countries are arranged alongside one another. Only when these lists provide a more detailed breakdown of the imprisoned populations can more critical issues emerge. Countries do not simply differ on their overall rates of incarceration, but also in terms of the race, gender and citizenship of their prison populations. There is also variation among countries in the use of sentences of imprisonment to 'unmake' citizens, stripping foreign-born residents of their right to remain, thereby producing deportable populations (De Genova 2002; Gibney 2013).

By concentrating on these matters, we start to generate new questions. Specifically, what are we to make of the enormous differences between countries in the numbers of foreign national prisoners? What are the implications of the fact that European countries – typically considered less punitive than the USA – often have very high numbers of 'foreigners'[1] within their penal establishments (Barker 2012), whereas in the USA, a world leader of incarceration, the proportion of non-citizens is considerably lower (Melossi 2012)? How can we understand the racialized and gendered nature of this incarceration? What are its connections to past and current practices of colonialism, imperialism and unequal global relations of power (Bosworth and Kaufman 2011)?

If we move the frame of analysis from the prison to its population, other questions emerge. What are foreigners incarcerated for? What happens to them post-sentence? Why, in the UK for instance, are foreign national women so disproportionately incarcerated? What, if any, are the links between the foreigners behind bars and those in the wider community? In what ways is the incarceration of non-citizens related to broader practices of criminalizing and illegalizing non-Western migrants and racialized minorities?

These are the kinds of questions that animate this chapter. In answering them, we draw on insights from ethnographic field research in foreign national prisons and immigration detention centres as well as official statistics and reports. All form part of a larger project[2] in which we are involved, examining the intersections of local, national and global power in these sites. Through our discussion, we reveal that the contemporary prison stretches far beyond its walls, not only reaching into the community in which it is based (Beckett and Murakawa 2012), but across the world (Sudbury 2005a). In so doing, the prison joins with other, putatively non-penal institutions and practices like immigration detention and deportation in the service of border control and regulation of foreigners on national soil (Bosworth 2008; Bosworth and Guild 2008; Fekete and Webber 2010; Collyer 2012).

Such issues are timely, especially as the number of foreign nationals in prison has in recent years accelerated in most countries, even in the USA, propelled by harsher legislation and by the growing intersections between immigration and criminal law (Stumpf 2006; Bosworth and Guild 2008; Aliverti 2013). As their numbers have expanded, in many countries, like the UK and USA, immigration detention centres have emerged as important institutions to facilitate the containment and expulsion of this population. Although not designed to punish, detention centres closely resemble prisons in their architectural design and staffing (Martin and Mitchelson 2009; Bosworth 2014). For those who move from one to another, the distinction between the two is often lost (Kaufman and Bosworth 2013). Still further, states may seek to circumvent detention altogether by removing foreign prisoners during their sentences. Whereas some countries already have signed prisoner transfer agreements to accept their citizens, others have been reluctant to take this population home. In their bid to persuade them to do so, the 'Northern penal state' extends its governance over citizens of the global South (Aas 2013).

Thinking about imprisonment in a global context not only challenges accepted criminological views of the boundaries of the prison, but also raises a series of methodological and intellectual tasks. What vocabulary should we use to interrogate immigration detention centres, for instance, which mimic the prison but are administrative and thus not restrained by criminal law? How can we appreciate the relationships between incarceration and deportation without following ex-prisoners back to their countries of origin? Although this chapter cannot hope to answer all of these questions equally, by raising them, it suggests we should revisit key concepts and approaches in our understanding of the prison as an institution, which has been a principal focus of criminological scholarship for so long.

Foreign national prisoners: an overview

Until recently, criminologists paid little attention to the nationality of prisoners. Outside the work of a few (see, for example, Bhui 2004; Sudbury 2005a; Kruttschnitt et al. 2013; Kaufman 2015), prison researchers were not interested in where people were from, but rather their experiences of incarceration. Statistical accounts of imprisonment have been similarly slow to reveal the nationalities of those confined. Instead, prison populations were typically presented as aggregates, or, when more detail was required, were broken down into type of offence, gender, age and sentence length.

These days, while the former claim remains broadly true – that prison researchers usually overlook nationality – states around the world offer considerable detail about the national origins of prisoners. Statistics in England and Wales, for instance, tell us not only what proportion of the prison population are foreign-born, but indicate the countries from which they originate. According to the most recent figures, 12% of the overall prison population are foreign nationals, with Poland, the Republic of Ireland, Jamaica, Romania and Pakistan as the five most common nations of origin (Ministry of Justice 2014).

Similar details can be found elsewhere. In their comparison, we witness a broad range. In Europe, scholars have documented an increasingly punitive turn towards foreigners (Wacquant 1999; De Giorgi 2010; Barker 2012; Light 2015). Italy, for example, reports 32.7% of its prison population as foreign-born (International Centre for Prison Studies 2015a; see also Colombo 2013), while in Switzerland the proportion attains the heights of 73% (International Centre for Prison Studies 2015b). Within the USA, similar variance, albeit one that never reaches these totals, appears across states and the federal system. In 2012, 28,959 foreign citizens were imprisoned in the US federal prison system, while California housed 15,079. That same year, Alaska, Idaho and Oklahoma reported no foreign nationals at all (Carson and Golinelli 2013: Appendix, Table 8).[3]

Nearly a decade ago, Hindpal Singh Bhui (2007) enumerated a series of challenges for the foreign-born in English prisons. Foreigners were more isolated than British citizen prisoners, facing language and cultural barriers, and experiencing difficulties in obtaining information about life in prison and the overall criminal justice system. Foreign national prisoners also encountered additional barriers in maintaining contact with their families, some of whom had uncertain immigration status in the UK, while others had remained in the country of origin (Bhui 2007). In addition to untreated mental illnesses, as Borrill and Taylor (2009) discovered, these barriers rendered this segment of the prison population particularly vulnerable to suicide and self-harm.

As legislation in the UK and other Western nations has been redrafted to broaden eligibility for deportation and hasten the removal of those deemed 'foreign', the nationality of prisoners has become increasingly important to how prisons operate, and the manner in which imprisonment is experienced. In the UK, for instance, since the passage of the UK Borders Act in 2007, foreign citizens convicted of any criminal offence may be removed from the country. For those sentenced to more than 12 months' imprisonment, deportation is mandatory unless there are compelling human rights barriers, while those with shorter prison sentences can be considered for such treatment. Consequently, penal establishments now have the added responsibility of determining citizenship, notifying immigration authorities and holding under immigration powers an increasing number of foreign nationals upon the end of their sentences.

These sorts of developments, which exist elsewhere as well, have had myriad effects. In recent years, in the UK and Norway, for example, the penal estate has been restructured explicitly to facilitate the deportation of foreign national prisoners (Kaufman 2013, 2015; Ugelvik 2013). Both countries have built facilities exclusive to foreign national prisoners, justified, in part, by the recognition of the challenges identified by Bhui (2007) above. For proponents, distinct prisons for foreign nationals are better able to provide cultural support and offer classes in English as a second language, while simultaneously facilitating and expediting the work of immigration enforcement in removing those considered deportable. Critics, however, argue that segregating prisoners according to nationality actually undermines the quality of care and support provided to foreign nationals by preventing full access to the same range of rehabilitation and reintegration initiatives available to citizen prisoners (Bailey 2009; Webber 2009; CLINKS 2010; Bosworth 2011a; Immigration Law Practitioners' Association 2011; Kaufman 2014).

Current research findings regarding nationality in prison

Recent scholarship has improved our understanding of the importance of nationality in prison by highlighting the interconnections between gender, race and citizenship in shaping prisoners' identities and their experiences of confinement and release. It has also demonstrated the relevance of such matters for how prisons operate.

In an extensive ethnographic account, Emma Kaufman (2012, 2015) has shown that the current emphasis on identifying foreigners in British penal institutions has changed how race, identity and national belonging are experienced in prison. The lived and legal conceptions of citizenship and belonging are at play as efforts to identify foreign nationals draw heavily on racialized assumptions of foreignness and Britishness. In contrast, prisoners themselves – particularly those who have lived in the UK for long periods of time – present more nuanced understandings of race and belonging. For many, identification as a foreigner and consequent actions by prison and immigration staff (and other prisoners) marks the beginning of their lived experience as outsiders in the UK. Kaufman (2014: 136) also examines how men articulate sexist and homophobic views to assert belonging. The 'pains of imprisonment' (Sykes 1958), in other words, are not only gendered but also shaped by prisoners' mobility, identity and nationality (Kaufman 2014).

In Norway, research by Thomas Ugelvik (2014) on ethnic minority prisoners concentrates on how imprisoned fathers make sense of their separation from their families through masculine and ethnic identities. In setting their ideals of fatherhood against Norwegian values – in particular, those pertaining to gender equality – and expressing narratives of violence against state officials and institutions, incarcerated men use fatherhood as a resource to challenge an unwelcomed prison status. Those who are transferred to foreign national prisons struggle to make such claims due to their geographical distance from their family. Scarce visits not only affect their emotional well-being and sense of self, but also hinder men's chances of appealing deportation on the European Convention on Human Rights (ECHR) Article 8 grounds (i.e. right to respect for private and family life) as it becomes more difficult to establish family life.[4]

Several studies have documented how prison life for foreign national prisoners is marked by concerns about deportation and an uncertain future (Kaufman 2012; Phillips 2012; Boe 2016). In France, Carolina Boe (2016) has found such matters produce significant behavioural changes in prisoners of the so-called '1.5 generation' (i.e. those who migrated as children) from marginalized neighbourhoods. Heavily dependent on prison staff and probation officers to strengthen their chances of avoiding deportation, these young prisoners became 'model prisoners', taking up prison activities, engaging in their sentencing plans and obeying prison staff. Whatever the performative nature of such behaviours, the result is that foreign national prisoners from these neighbourhoods become disciplined bodies in an otherwise difficult to manage prison population whose behaviours are dominated by neighbourhood alliances and a general tendency to oppose prison and probation staff.

In an English prison exclusive to foreign national prisoners, Inês Hasselberg (2015) found a similar environment. In this prison, as in France, prisoners attributed the low levels of conflict and violence to the pressures of keeping their records clean either to contest their deportation or to apply for assisted voluntary departure schemes. Like Boe's participants, the men at HM Prison (HMP) Huntercombe felt they had few options to register their concerns or contest their control within the prison (Hasselberg 2015).

Although prisoners' interactions with staff tend to be shaped by matters of citizenship, relations between prisoners are not necessarily so affected. In her examination of a multicultural prison in the UK, Coretta Phillips (2012) depicts a convivial exchange of cuisine and practices among incarcerated men, in which nationality is subsumed by ethnicity and regional orientation. Wherever they had been born, men from London, for instance, tended to share certain beliefs, expectations and practices. Other than for those who could not speak English, nationality was not a barrier to friendships and alliances.

In HMP Huntercombe, which is exclusive to foreign-born prisoners, nationality can hardly be overlooked. Despite the diversity of national backgrounds, prisoners at HMP Huntercombe felt defined less in relation to their own nationality than to that which they did not have: that is, that of their British citizenship. As they progressed through their sentences, rather than feeling Jamaican, Polish or Brazilian, they felt, or were made to feel, non-British. This is not to say that nationality had no impact on social groupings and characterizations. Prisoners and their social behaviours were stereotyped (both by staff and by prisoners themselves) in terms of nationality: the 'Jamaicans' were loud, the 'Lithuanians' macho, the 'Pakistanis' great cooks and so on. Such labels were fluid, heterogeneous and crossed by other markers such as age, language and religion. Groups of 'Jamaicans', for instance, included prisoners from all Caribbean countries and Rastafarians from other nationalities (Hasselberg 2015). Similar to Phillips's (2012) discussion of the multicultural prison, and despite the overbearing importance of nationality in a prison exclusive to foreign prisoners, Hasselberg (2015) found an environment where religion, age, language and cultural background were more influential in prisoners' social relations than the actual countries of their citizenship.

Foreign national women in prison face particular vulnerabilities and have specific needs. Their pathways to prison also differ from those of men. In the UK, a large proportion of foreign women are imprisoned upon arrival in the country while couriering drugs, while many others are convicted of immigration offences after escaping from conditions of sexual or domestic abuse. It is often through coercion, intimidation or misinformation that women find themselves as drug mules or victims of human trafficking (Prison Reform Trust 2012). Many are the primary care givers of children who remain in the country of origin. As Julia Sudbury (2005b) has shown, it is necessary to extend the analysis of the prison, and the imprisonment of women in particular, beyond the borders of the nation to consider those transnational processes that result in the disproportionate numbers of racialized women in the prisons of the global North.

Just as the consideration of citizenship points to the need for a new geographical and temporal scale of analysis in order to make sense of how people end up in prison and their behaviours within it, the focus on nationality reveals the need for a broader understanding of penal power in order to make sense of the contemporary expansion of sites of incarceration. At present, a sentence of imprisonment for foreign citizens not only may result in deportation, but in an additional period of confinement before they are forcibly removed. Such confinement, under immigration act powers, both mimics and departs from a prison sentence, unveiling new and familiar forms of state power.

Immigration detention centres: extending penality

Western states have had the power to detain people for immigration purposes for many decades (see Bashford and Strange 2002; Bosworth 2014: Chapter 1; Silverman and Nethery 2015). In comparison with the numbers of foreigners in prison and those living without immigration status in the community, however, the detention estate is, and always has been, small. At present, for instance, in the UK, there are ten immigration detention centres, with combined space for approximately 3,200 people.[5] In the USA, too, where 2.4 million men, women and children languish behind bars in prisons and jails, the immigration detention estate constitutes 34,000 bed spaces in over 250 facilities across the country (Hernández 2014; Haines and Kalhan 2015). Greece and Italy, which host hundreds of thousands of newly arrived irregular migrants each year, have a likewise limited number of secure bed spaces available. Most undocumented migrants everywhere live among us.

Notwithstanding its limited effect, in light of the numbers of people on the move, confinement is being utilized in an increasing number of countries as a part of a concerted effort to restrict migration, or, at least, to be seen to be attempting to restrict migration and facilitate the expulsion of unwanted foreigners (Welch 1996; Simon 1998; Wacquant 2008; Flynn 2014). This practice is deeply politicized. Apart from the level and vociferousness of the debate, and unlike the extensive body of literature on prisons in most countries, we have little evidence about daily life in detention (although see Bosworth 2012, 2013, 2014; Hall 2010, 2012; Turnbull 2015).

From the small extant body of research on immigration detention centres, we can discern a number of important overlaps with the prison, from the make-up of the population, to those guarding and governing the institutions, to their architectural designs and the rules and regulations that bind them (see Bosworth 2007, 2011a, 2014; Bosworth and Turnbull 2015). In most Western nations, detention centres are quasi-penal institutions that hold foreign nationals in order to facilitate immigration-related aims, such as deportation or removal, identification and the prevention of absconding. Although not technically a punishment (but see Hernández 2014; Bosworth and Turnbull 2015), detention centres share many of the same architectural features, activities and staffing as prisons. Architecturally, detention centres often occupy the spaces of former custodial institutions or are purpose-built to resemble penal environments. These centres are typically located behind layers of razor wire and locked gates, and mimic prison security measures (e.g. pat-downs, CCTV surveillance, room searches). Additionally, there is often significant cross-over in staffing between detention centres and prisons, with some staff working in both types of institution, and with detention centre staff receiving similar training to prison officers (Bosworth 2014). In countries where the privatization of correctional institutions is common, such as the USA and UK, detention centres may be operated under contract by the same companies that are hired to run prisons and provide other criminal justice services (e.g. tagging, escorting). In the UK, this includes Serco and G4S, whereas in the USA, the Corrections Corporation of America is active in both sectors.

The spreading of rationales and techniques from penal institutions to immigration detention centres presents particular challenges for individuals who are detained for administrative purposes. Unlike those imprisoned for a criminal offence, detainees are not technically punished by their detention, although the denial of liberty through detention and related practices (e.g. being handcuffed during escort) tends to be experienced as highly punitive. Administrative detainees also have fewer legal rights and protections than those afforded to citizens who are accused or convicted of criminal offences (O'Nions 2008; Bosworth 2011b). For many foreign national ex-prisoners, immigration detention is often the next stop after the completion of their custodial and/or community-based sentences – confinement that is experienced as a double punishment (Bosworth and Kaufman 2011).

The reliance on penal rationales, techniques and logics of security in the realm of immigration detention suggests that the prison provides a ready-made, convenient model through which detention and the broader field of border control operates (Simon 1998; Coleman and Kocher 2011). The involvement of the private sector in immigration detention has also contributed to the growth in the use of detention for immigration matters (Bacon 2005; Doty and Wheatley 2013). In the USA, a 'bed mandate' for immigration detention means that at any given time, there must be 34,000 foreigners detained (Gilman 2013) – a troubling policy decision linked to the power of private prison lobbies (Doty and Wheatley 2013; Hernández 2014).

In the UK, for many foreign national ex-prisoners, immigration removal centres (IRCs) constitute their second place of confinement. These ex-prisoners may be held in IRCs pending their deportation and/or as they appeal their deportation orders. They may be moved from prison to detention at the end of their custodial sentences. They may be detained while serving the non-custodial portion of their sentences (e.g. probation). Or they may be put into detention after the completion of their sentences, such as when they are signing on at immigration reporting centres.

Whereas the UK had previously held some asylum seekers in prison while considering their claims, as well as others found in violation of immigration law, such practices had largely been ad hoc. After criticism from the European Committee for the Prevention of Torture and Inhuman or Degrading Treatment or Punishment, the UK government agreed in 2001 to stop holding those seeking refuge in this way. However, rather than manage everyone in the community, the government set about expanding its small immigration detention estate, constructing new facilities and redeploying others from past use as prisons or military establishments (see Bosworth 2014: Chapter 1).

Immigration detention centres differ from prisons in important ways. In many countries, the period of detention is indefinite, with detainees unaware of how long they will be confined (Broeders 2010; Silverman and Nethery 2015). Detention centres house people with a range of linguistic, cultural, ethnic and religious profiles – a multiplicity that poses challenges for staff and detainees alike – for a variety of reasons. They may have breached the terms of their visas; they may be foreign national ex-prisoners with deportation orders; they may be asylum seekers with in-process or failed applications; they may be individuals who overstayed their visas. The confinement of asylum seekers is especially controversial as those fleeing persecution are viewed as most undeserving of immigration detention (Welch and Schuster 2005). Conversely, while ex-prisoners may receive less popular sympathy, staff often find them easier to manage and recognize (Bosworth 2014).

In Western countries, the race, gender and citizenship of those subject to immigration detention point to important connections between imprisonment and patterns of migration in a globalized, postcolonial world. In the UK, for example, the nationalities of the majority of detainees are of former British colonies (e.g. Bangladesh, India, Pakistan and Nigeria) (Home Office 2015). In the USA, the detainee population is also highly racialized, reflecting patterns of immigration enforcement tied to the criminalization of Latino/a migrants (Hernandez 2008). Of the total number of those detained, Mexican nationals comprise 67% of the population, followed by Guatemalans (9%), Hondurans (6.3%) and Salvadoreans (5.5%) (Simanski and Sapp 2012).

Outsourcing imprisonment

In addition to the imprisonment of foreign nationals and the expanding practice of immigration detention, sovereign states are, increasingly, building facilities outside their own national borders altogether. Whereas some, like Guantánamo Bay, have received considerable media, political and academic attention, others are less well known. None has been particularly well integrated into the literature on prisons.

In 2014, after decades of political machinations, the UK finally signed a prisoner-transfer agreement with Nigeria (British High Commission Abuja 2014). That same year, Jamaica refused to ratify an earlier agreement on prisoner transfers (Boyle 2014). While the former means that Nigerian nationals serving prison terms in Britain can be forcefully returned to Nigeria to serve their sentences, the latter reveals the difficulty in insisting on such schemes.

Prisoner transfer agreements are not, in themselves, all that unusual (Van Zyl Smit and Mulgrew 2012; Mulgrew 2011). In many cases, prisoners may request to serve their sentences in their home countries. In addition to such voluntary arrangements, a growing number of countries have agreed to take back their citizens without their consent (Mulgrew 2011).

In a bid to persuade nations like Nigeria and Jamaica, whose citizens make up a significant part of those foreigners serving sentences in prisons in England and Wales, the British government set up in 2008 the Returns and Reintegration Fund (RRF). A joint venture between immigration enforcement within the Home Office (then known as the UK Border Agency), the Ministry of Justice, Department for International Development (DFID) and the Foreign and Commonwealth Office (FCO), this fund is used for a variety of purposes, including, but not limited to, training and equipping criminal justice and migration officials in other countries, and providing housing and education programmes for deportees. In Nigeria, the RRF helped fund the design and building of an entire new wing in Kirikiri prison in Lagos to meet European Union human rights standards. In Jamaica, the RRF pays for a variety of programmes for deportees, as well as prison training courses in home economics (for young women) and animal husbandry (for men).

At the same time as media agencies reported with outrage the payments to the Nigerian government for constructing the new prison wing and its failure to persuade Jamaica to take back its citizens, the UK government has been sharing sovereignty with France with little fanfare. In 2013, HM Chief Inspector of Prisons published a co-authored report with France's Controleur général des lieux privation liberté (HMCIP and CGLPL) into their joint inspection of the two short-term holding facilities for migrants at Calais and Coquelles (HMIP and CGLPL 2013). The following year, a second report was issued on a similar site at Dunkirk (HMCIP and CGLPL 2014). These centres, which in Calais are staffed by UK private security guards and may hold detainees for up to five days (although typically individuals are housed in such places for only a matter of hours), line France's north coast (see HMCIP and CGLPL 2014).

In these institutions, women and men from outside European territory are first subject to the power of the British state, which has been farmed out to the private sector, under the so-called 'juxtaposed border control' with France. It is only in their custody, however, that they are subject to British control. On leaving the facilities, detainees are handed over to the French border police, Police Aux Frontières (PAF), who may elect to detain them further in a French detention facility, expel them from French territory, or release them onto the streets. The 'primary aim of control' in these border sites, the most recent report on the holding facility at Dunkirk makes clear, 'is to prevent irregular migrants entering the UK to claim asylum' (HMCIP and CGLPL 2014: 5).

Such examples, from Lagos to the French coastline, reveal an increasing policy trend, located at the intersection of criminal justice and migration control, in which the penal state radiates well beyond the confines of the nation via agreements made in relation to other policy matters and through a range of government departments. The juxtaposed controls, for instance, tell us as much about free trade within Europe as they do about the regulation of the movement of people. So the involvement of the FCO and DFID not only integrates the prison into humanitarian aid, but reveals the dependency of the penal state on these other aspects of governance and government outside the nation-state.

Through these forms of outsourced imprisonment, we bear witness to a vibrant yet volatile form of state penal power. In Nigeria, for instance, it seems the British state has (re)asserted its authority, while in Jamaica it has been far less successful. The arrangements with the French state have been criticized by the local population, who wonder why their government prevents from departing those who evidently wish to leave. The extension of penal power in these ways underscores the use of prison and related practices in the pursuit of border control.

Conclusion: rethinking imprisonment in a globalized world

The incarceration of foreign citizens is of particular relevance in the context of national and regional security agendas in which foreigners have been increasingly conceptualized as risky, and as national immigration policies continue to tighten, making it harder for individuals to arrive legally and easier for the state to remove them. In the incarceration of foreign nationals in prisons, detention centres and outsourced penal institutions, we have shown that these processes have implications for the character of the prison, as well as for how incarceration is experienced and justified. These processes also impact how we study imprisonment.

According to Katja Aas (2013: 21), criminologists must revisit the 'established partition between the domestic and the international', attending to the ways in which punishment extends outwards, across borders. While she advocates a new 'scalar' analysis of the Northern penal state, there are important practical and methodological challenges to taking a global perspective. How might we learn, in the UK, about policies in France or Nigeria? How can we speak to those who are not fluent in our tongue? Are women and men, seeking to avoid deportation or removal, more or less likely to participate in scholarly research? Can we trust their accounts or understand them?

Studying incarcerated populations also presents important challenges of access and ethics. For one thing, prisons and detention centres are often difficult institutions to gain entry to for research purposes. The vulnerability of imprisoned populations also raises important ethical concerns related to informed consent and confidentiality, among others.

In the case of foreign nationals in prisons and detention centres, such concerns are compounded by the realization that this segment of the population has often experienced trauma before migrating and/or during their migration journeys. Furthermore, all have been thoroughly and repeatedly interrogated by a variety of individuals: government agents, solicitors, barristers, immigration judges and so on. Research means asking imprisoned individuals to submit to another questioning session, to retell their stories yet another time.

Just as a global frame requires attention to conceptual matters that have often been overlooked, it may also necessitate creative methodological interventions. For those awaiting deportation or removal, the conditions and relationships inside places of confinement, which have traditionally been the focus of institutional studies, may be of less significance. Rather than directing all of our attention to their present incarceration, how might we build in attention to their pasts and their futures? For a population where communication may be complicated by language barriers, are there other techniques of gathering data?

In our own work, we have been experimenting with visual methods and social media. Handing out cameras to detainees as they leave detention, we seek to gather information about their lives after detention. To integrate migration studies into our analyses, we gather information about the mobility of those in prison, seeking to map where they came from and why. Email, Skype, Facebook and Twitter provide novel means of maintaining contact, which exist alongside, rather than usurping, more familiar ethnographic methods of participant observation. It is important to bear in mind that foreign nationals are increasingly immobilized through restrictive immigration policies, whether as a direct result of such policies (when placed in prison or immigration detention), or as a response to them (when developing their own evasion strategies to avoid detection and deportation). As such, a creative use of different research methods is vital to an examination of the reach of penal power in the service of border control.

In short, under conditions of globalization, as people are increasingly on the move, and as some countries enact legal provisions to strip citizenship from certain segments of their domestic populations, it is important to consider how the issue of nationality plays out in the prison context, both in terms of the impact on how imprisonment is experienced and the effects that citizenship (or the lack thereof) has on what comes after. In so doing, certain key criminological concepts come into question. What exactly is punishment when a criminal conviction includes more than one kind of incarceration? Where is punishment located when a prison sentence may lead to deportation? Who is administering the penalty and to what end? What is the relationship between the private and public sectors? What about that between the British state and the sending country? As more criminologists attend to the growing intersections of criminal and immigration law, and acknowledge the importance of race, gender and citizenship to our understanding of penal power, these are the sorts of questions that lend support to a broader view of the prison and its changing characteristics.

Notes

1 In using the terms 'foreigner' and 'foreign national', we are cognizant that these terms are socially produced and contested labels tied to complex issues of identity and belonging.
2 See www.bordercriminologies.law.ox.ac.uk for further information.
3 In fact, in the USA it is difficult to be sure about the rates of foreigners in state prison systems due to variance in how nationality is recorded. In Missouri, for instance, nationality is based on

self-reported place of birth while in California rates include only those held by the Immigration and Customs Enforcement (ICE) (Carson and Golinelli 2013: Appendix, Table 8).
4 In the UK, deportation may be appealed at the Immigration Tribunal on human rights grounds only. Article 8 and Article 3 of the ECHR are thus the main grounds to contest deportation and fight for the right to stay in the country. Under the Conservative–Liberal Democrat coalition government of 2010–15, considerable effort was expended by the Home Secretary Theresa May to limit the access of foreign offenders to these protections.
5 This number increases by one-third if we include the number of beds available in the prison system for immigration purposes only.

Bibliography

Aas, K.F. (2013) 'The ordered and the bordered society: Migration control, citizenship, and the northern penal state', in K.F. Aas and M. Bosworth (eds) *The Borders of Punishment: Migration, Citizenship, and Social Exclusion*, Oxford: Oxford University Press, 21–39.

Aliverti, A. (2013) *Crimes of Mobility: Criminal law and regulation of mobility*, Abingdon: Routledge.

Bacon, C. (2005) 'The evolution of immigration detention in the UK: The involvement of private prison companies', Refugee Studies Centre Working Paper, www.rsc.ox.ac.uk/publications/the-evolution-of-immigration-detention-in-the-uk-the-involvement-of-private-prison-companies (accessed 10 September 2015).

Bailey, R. (2009) 'Up against the wall: Bare life and resistance in Australian immigration detention', *Law and Critique* 20(2): 113–132.

Barker, V. (2012) 'Global mobility and penal order: Criminalizing migration, a view from Europe', *Sociology Compass* 6(2): 113–121.

Bashford, A. and Strange, C. (2002) 'Asylum-seekers and national histories of detention', *Australian Journal of Politics and History* 48(4): 509–527.

Beckett, K. and Murakawa, N. (2012) 'Mapping the shadow carceral state: Toward an institutionally capacious approach to punishment', *Theoretical Criminology* 16(2): 221–244.

Bhui, H.S. (2004) *Going the Distance: Developing effective policy and practice with foreign national prisoners*, London: Prison Reform Trust.

Bhui, H.S. (2007) 'Alien experience: Foreign national prisoners after the deportation crisis', *Probation Journal* 54(4): 368–382.

Boe, C. (2016) 'From banlieue youth to undocumented migrant: illegalized foreign-nationals in penal institutions and public space', *Criminology & Criminal Justice*.

Borrill, J. and Taylor, D.A. (2009) 'Suicides by foreign national prisoners in England and Wales 2007: Mental health and cultural issues', *The Journal of Forensic Psychiatry & Psychology* 20(6): 886–905.

Bosworth, M. (2007) 'Immigration detention in Britain', in M. Lee (ed.) *Human Trafficking*, Cullompton: Willan, 159–177.

Bosworth, M. (2008) 'Border control and the limits of the sovereign state', *Social & Legal Studies* 17(2): 199–215.

Bosworth, M. (2011a) 'Deportation, detention and foreign-national prisoners in England and Wales', *Citizenship Studies* 15(5): 583–595.

Bosworth, M. (2011b) 'Human rights and immigration detention', in M.-B. Dembour and T. Kelly (eds) *Are Human Rights for Migrants? Critical Reflections on the Status of Irregular Migrants in Europe and the United States*, Abingdon: Routledge, 165–183.

Bosworth, M. (2012) 'Subjectivity and identity in detention: Punishment and society in a global age', *Theoretical Criminology* 16(2): 123–140.

Bosworth, M. (2013) 'Can immigration detention be legitimate? Understanding confinement in a global world', in K. Aas and M. Bosworth (eds) *The Borders of Punishment: Migration, Citizenship, and Social Exclusion*, Oxford: Oxford University Press, 149–165.

Bosworth, M. (2014) *Inside Immigration Detention*, Oxford: Oxford University Press.

Bosworth, M. and Guild, M. (2008) 'Governing through migration control: Security and citizenship in Britain', *British Journal of Criminology* 48(6): 703–719.

Bosworth, M. and Kaufman, E. (2011) 'Foreigners in a carceral age: Immigration and imprisonment in the United States', *Stanford Law & Policy Review* 22(2): 429–454.

Bosworth, M. and Turnbull, S. (2015) 'Immigration detention and the expansion of penal power in the United Kingdom', in K. Reiter and A. Koenig (eds) *Extraordinary Punishment: Comparative Studies in Detention, Incarceration and Solitary Confinement*, London: Palgrave Macmillan, 50–67.

Boyle, S. (2014) 'Jamaica snubs prisoner transfer deal: Hundreds to stay in UK costing taxpayer £27 million per year after their government refuses to take them back', *Daily Mail*, 2 April, www. dailymail.co.uk/news/article-2594776/Jamaica-snubs-prisoner-transfer-deal-Hundreds-stay-UK-costi ng-taxpayer-27million-year-government-refuses-back.html (accessed 10 September 2015).

British High Commission Abuja (2014) 'News article: UK – Nigeria Sign Compulsory Prisoner Transfer Agreement', 10 January, www.gov.uk/government/world-location-news/uk-nigeria -sign-compulsory-prisoner-transfer-agreement (accessed 10 September 2015).

Broeders, D. (2010) 'Return to sender: Administrative detention of irregular migrants in Germany and the Netherlands', *Punishment & Society* 12(2): 169–186.

Carson, E.A. and Golinelli, D. (2013) *Prisoners in 2012: Trends in admissions and releases, 1991–2012*, Washington, DC: US Department of Justice, www.bjs.gov/content/pub/pdf/p12tar9112.pdf (accessed 10 September 2015).

Cavadino, M. and Dignan, J. (1997) *Penal Systems: A comparative approach*, London: Sage Publications Ltd.

CLINKS (2010) 'NOMS' hub and spoke arrangements for foreign national prisoners', *CLINKS Members Briefing*, Worcester: CLINKS, www.clinks.org/sites/default/files/Members%20Briefing %20-%20Foreign%20National%20Prisoners.pdf (accessed 10 September 2015).

Coleman, M. and Kocher, A. (2011) 'Detention, deportation, devolution and immigrant incapacitation in the US, post 9/11', *The Geographical Journal* 177(3): 228–237.

Collyer, M. (2012) 'Deportation and the micropolitics of exclusion: The rise of removals from the UK to Sri Lanka', *Geopolitics* 17(2): 276–292.

Colombo, A. (2013) 'Foreigners and immigrants in Italy's penal and administrative detention systems', *European Journal of Criminology* 10(6): 746–759.

De Genova, N.P. (2002) 'Migrant "illegality" and deportability in everyday life', *Annual Review of Anthropology* 31(1): 419–447.

De Giorgi, A. (2010) 'Immigration control, post-Fordism, and less eligibility: A materialist critique of the criminalization of immigration across Europe', *Punishment & Society* 12(2): 147–167.

Doty, R.L. and Wheatley, E.S. (2013) 'Private detention and the immigration industrial complex', *International Political Sociology* 7(4): 426–443.

Fekete, L. and Webber, F. (2010) 'Foreign nationals, enemy penology and the criminal justice system', *Race & Class* 51(4): 1–25.

Flynn, M. (2014) *How and Why Immigration Detention Crossed the Globe*, Working Paper No. 8, Global Detention Project Working Paper Series, Geneva: Global Detention Project, www.globa ldetentionproject.org/publications/working-papers/diffusion.html (accessed 10 September 2015).

Gibney, M. (2013) 'Deportation, crime, and the changing character of membership in the United Kingdom', in K. Aas and M. Bosworth (eds) *The Borders of Punishment: Migration, Citizenship, and Social Exclusion*, Oxford: Oxford University Press, 218–236.

Gilman, D. (2013) 'Realizing liberty: The use of international human rights law to realign immigration detention in the United States', *Fordham International Law Journal* 36(2): 243–333.

Haines, C.E. and Kalhan, A. (2015) 'Detention of asylum seekers en masse: Immigration detention in the United States', in A. Nethery and S.J. Silverman (eds) *Immigration Detention: The Migration of a Policy and its Human Impact*, London: Routledge, 69–78.

Hall, A. (2010) '"These people could be anyone": Fear, contempt (and empathy) in a British immigration removal centre', *Journal of Ethnic and Migration Studies* 36(6): 881–898.

Hall, A. (2010) *Border Watch: Cultures of immigration, detention and control*, London: Pluto Press.

Hasselberg, I. (2015) *The Postcolonial Prison*, unpublished working paper. Centre for Criminology, University of Oxford..

Hernández, C.C.G. (2014) 'Immigration detention as punishment', *UCLA Law Review* 61(5): 1346–1414.

Hernandez, D.M. (2008) 'Pursuant to deportation: Latinos and immigrant detention', *Latino Studies* 6(1–2): 35–63.

HM Chief Inspector of Prisons and Contrôleur Général des Lieux de Privation de Liberté (2013) *Report on Unannounced Joint Inspections of Coquelles and Calais Non-residential Short-term Holding Facilities, 6–7 November 2012*, London: HM Inspectorate of Prisons, www.justiceinspectorates.gov.uk/p risons/wp-content/uploads/sites/4/2014/03/calais-coquelles-2012.pdf (accessed 10 September 2015).

HM Chief Inspector of Prisons and Contrôleur Général des Lieux de Privation de Liberté (2014) *Report on an Unannounced Inspection of the Short-term Holding Facility at Dunkerque*, London: HM Inspectorate of Prisons, www.justiceinspectorates.gov.uk/hmiprisons/wp-content/uploads/sites/4/2014/06/2014-Dunkerque-Web.pdf (accessed 10 September 2015).

Home Office (2015) *Immigration Statistics, January to March 2015*, London: Home Office, www.gov.uk/government/statistics/immigration-statistics-january-to-march-2015 (accessed 10 September 2015).

Immigration Law Practitioners' Association (2011) *ILPA Response to the Ministry of Justice Consultation: Breaking the Cycle: Effective Punishment, Rehabilitation and Sentencing of Offenders*, London: Immigration Law Practitioners' Association, www.ilpa.org.uk/resources.php/4114/minis try-of-justice-consultation-breaking-the-cycle-effective-punishment-rehabilitation-and-sentenci (accessed 10 September 2015).

International Centre for Prison Studies (2014a) *World Prison Brief: Italy*, www.prisonstudies.org/country/italy (accessed 10 September 2015).

International Centre for Prison Studies (2014b) *World Prison Brief: Switzerland*, www.prisonstudies.org/country/switzerland (accessed 10 September 2015).

Kaufman, E. (2012) 'Finding foreigners: Race and the politics of memory in British prisons', *Population, Space and Place* 18(6): 701–714.

Kaufman, E. (2015) *Punish and Expel: Border Control, Nationalism, and the New Purpose of the Prison*, Oxford: Oxford University Press.

Kaufman, E. (2013) 'Hubs and spokes: The transformation of the British prison', in K.F. Aas and M. Bosworth (eds) *The Borders of Punishment: Migration, citizenship, and social exclusion*, Oxford: Oxford University Press, 166–182.

Kaufman, E. (2014) 'Gender at the border: Nationalism and the new logic of punishment', *Punishment & Society* 16(2): 135–151.

Kaufman, E. and Bosworth, M. (2013) 'Prison and national identity: Citizenship, punishment and the sovereign state', in D. Scott (ed.) *Why Prison?*, Cambridge: Cambridge University Press, 170–188.

Kruttschnitt, C., Dirkzwager, A. and Kennedy, L. (2013) 'Strangers in a strange land: Coping with imprisonment as a racial or ethnic foreign national inmate', *The British Journal of Sociology* 64(3): 478–500.

Lacey, N. (2008) *The Prisoners' Dilemma*, Cambridge: Cambridge University Press.

Light, M.T. (2015) 'The punishment consequences of lacking national membership in Germany, 1998–2010', *Social Forces* (Advance Access doi: 10.1093/sf/sov084).

Martin, L.L. and Mitchelson, M.L. (2009) 'Geographies of detention and imprisonment: Interrogating spatial practices of confinement, discipline, law, and state power', *Geography Compass* 3(1): 459–477.

Melossi, D. (2012) 'The processes of criminalization of migrants and the borders of "Fortress Europe"', in S. Pickering and J. McCulloch (eds) *Borders and Crime: Pre-crime, mobility and serious harm in an age of globalization*, London: Palgrave Macmillan, 17–34.

Ministry of Justice (2014) *Offender Management Statistics (Quarterly): October–December 2013 and Annual*, London: Ministry of Justice, www.gov.uk/government/publications/offender-managem ent-statistics-quarterly-october-december-2013-and-annual (accessed 10 September 2015).

Mulgrew, R. (2011) 'The international movement of prisoners', *Criminal Law Forum* 22(1): 103–143.

O'Nions, H. (2008) 'No right to liberty: The detention of asylum seekers for administrative convenience', *European Journal of Migration and Law* 10: 149–185.

Phillips, C. (2012) *The Multicultural Prison: Ethnicity, masculinity, and social relations among prisoners*, Oxford: Oxford University Press.

Pratt, J. (2009) *Penal Populism*, London: Routledge.

Pratt, J. and Eriksson, A. (2013) *Contrasts in Punishment: An explanation of anglophone excess and nordic exceptionalism*, London: Routledge.

Prison Reform Trust (2012) *No Way Out: A briefing paper on foreign national women in prison in England and Wales*, London: Prison Reform Trust, www.prisonreformtrust.org.uk/Portals/0/ Documents/NoWayOut.pdf (accessed 10 September 2015).

Silverman, S.J. and Nethery, A. (2015) 'Understanding immigration detention and its human impact', in S.J. Silverman and A. Nethery (eds) *Immigration Detention: The migration of a policy and its human impact*, London: Routledge, 1–12.

Simanski, J. and Sapp, L.M. (2012) *Immigration Enforcement Actions: 2011*, Washington, DC: Office of Immigration Statistics, www.dhs.gov/sites/default/files/publications/immigration-statistics/ enforcement_ar_2011.pdf (accessed 10 September 2015).

Simon, J. (1998) 'Refugees in a carceral age: The rebirth of immigration prisons in the United States', *Public Culture* 10(2): 577–607.

Stumpf, J. (2006) 'The crimmigration crisis: Immigrants, crime, and sovereign power', *American University Law Review* 56(2): 367–419.

Sudbury, J. (ed.) (2005a) *Global Lockdown: Race, gender, and the prison-industrial complex*, London: Routledge.

Sudbury, J. (2005b) '"Mules", "yardies", and other folk devils', in J. Sudbury (ed.) *Global Lockdown: Race, gender, and the prison-industrial complex*, New York: Routledge, 167–183.

Sykes, G. (1958) *The Society of Captives: A study of a maximum security prison*, Princeton, NJ: Princeton University Press.

Turnbull, S. (2015) '"Stuck in the middle": Waiting and uncertainty in immigration detention', *Time & Society* (Advanced Access doi: 10.1177/0961463X15604518).

Ugelvik, T. (2013) 'Seeing like a welfare state: Immigration control, statecraft, and a prison with double vision', in K.F. Aas and M. Bosworth (eds) *The Borders of Punishment: Migration, Citizenship, and Social Exclusion*, Oxford: Oxford University Press, 183–198.

Ugelvik, T. (2014) 'Paternal pains of imprisonment: Incarcerated fathers, ethnic minority masculinity and resistance narratives', *Punishment & Society* 16(2): 152–168.

Van Zyl Smit, D. and Mulgrew, R. (2012) *Handbook on the International Transfer of Sentenced Prisoners*, New York: United Nations.

Wacquant, L. (1999) '"Suitable enemies": Foreigners and immigrants in the prisons of Europe', *Punishment & Society* 1(2): 215–222.

Wacquant, L. (2008) 'Extirpate and expel: On the penal management of postcolonial migrants in the European Union', *Race/Ethnicity* 2(1): 46–52.

Webber, F. (2009) 'Segregating foreign national prisoners', Institute of Race Relations, www.irr. org.uk/news/segregating-foreign-national-prisoners/ (accessed 10 September 2015).

Welch, M. (1996) 'The immigration crisis: Detention as an emerging mechanism of social control', *Social Justice* 23(3): 169–184.

Welch, M. and Schuster, L. (2005) 'Detention of asylum seekers in the US, UK, France, Germany, and Italy: A critical view of the globalizing culture of control', *Criminal Justice* 5(4): 331–355.

Chapter 40

Campaigning for and campaigning against prisons

Excavating and reaffirming the case for prison abolition

Mick Ryan and Joe Sim[1]

Introduction

Since the formation of Radical Alternatives to Prison (RAP) in 1970, and the publication of Mathiesen's *The Politics of Abolition* in 1974, abolitionism has had a significant ideological and material impact on the nature and direction of penal policy. Over the last four decades, abolitionists have consistently opposed the state's 'truth' that prisons were concerned with benevolent reform. Instead, they presented an alternative discourse – namely, that 'prisons were primarily places of punishment and/or containment … Abolitionists put politics back into penal reform, identifying the prison as just one of a series of disciplinary institutions at the disposal of the State to order and discipline the working classes' (Ryan and Ward 2013: 9–10). This discourse disrupted the cosy relationship between liberal prison reform groups and the state by dragging a number of these insider groups onto more radical terrain. Furthermore, the abolitionist interventions directly contributed to the abolition of the prison medical service, challenged state-defined 'truth' around deaths in custody and generated radical, alternative policies for the families of those who had died in the state's 'care' (Sim 1994a).

At the heart of these interventions was (and is) one simple contention: the prison was a place of terror, punishment and humiliating vilification for the confined. Additionally, abolitionists exploited the contradictions in bourgeois law in order to develop an alternative legal framework that challenged the unfettered discretion of prison staff which underpinned the formal and informal culture of punishment that was (and remains) institutionalized in the everyday life of the prison (Sim 2009).

Where are we now?

When we began working on the first version of this chapter (in Jewkes 2007), we noted that the rate of imprisonment in England and Wales was 142 per 100,000 of the population. This propensity to imprison, while still not matching that of the USA, was nonetheless on a definite upward curve. In 2013, the Ministry of Justice confirmed the extent of this prolonged drive. Between June 1993 and June 2012, the prison population rose by 41,800 to reach 86,000 (MoJ 2013a). In August 2014, the population stood at 85,795 (Howard League for Penal Reform 2014). This increase was due to: more offenders being sentenced to immediate imprisonment; the average time served in prison increasing from 8.1 to 9.5 months for those serving determinate sentences; the decline in the parole rate; and the increase in recalling those released on licence.

This sustained growth in prison numbers, drawn, as ever, from the economically and politically powerless and increasingly racialized and feminized, has been ideologically legitimated by politicians, the judiciary and the media who, with the wider population, have become locked into a deep-rooted fear surrounding a risk-filled present and a melancholic trepidation about an uncertain future (Garland 2001; Young 1999). At the same time, offenders have been confronted with alternatives to custody, built on 'punishment in the community'. These developments have been reinforced by the emergence of new, semi-penal institutions to detain, and sometimes destroy, those labelled as potentially disorderly and socially problematic. Taken together, the institutional and non-institutional have created an edifice of punishment which appears unshakeable in the ongoing conflict to restore law, maintain order and reduce risk to communities beleaguered by feral atavists who are either unwilling or unable to 'responsibilize' themselves and participate in the multifarious benefits offered by globalized consumer capitalism. Importantly, and while being clear that official statistics should be used with great caution, these developments have taken place in a political context where, across a range of Western countries, crime rates have been stable or actively decreasing.

Accompanying this expansion has been the explicit neo-liberal demand that penal services should be delivered economically, if necessary by reorganizing them into competitive, efficient free market entities. In other words, state agencies, and their private partners, should engage in the normalization of the socially excluded, working through a range of heavily promoted offender behaviour programmes specifically designed to responsibilize them (Cooper and Sim 2013). Yet, in spite of such claims, and the boast by the Conservative–Liberal Democrat coalition government, elected in 2010, that it was in the business of 'breaking the cycle' of reoffending (MoJ 2010), recidivism rates remain stubbornly and predictably high (MoJ 2013b). In this chapter we consider these developments within the compass of abolitionism, and its impact in England and Wales.

Penal reform in the post-war period

One of the distinguishing features of the British system of government after 1945 was its highly centralized nature. All roads led to Whitehall, where elected politicians worked with permanent civil servants and accredited outside experts, to map out the contours of the new welfare state. Nowhere was this more evident than in the Home Office which, in the early 1960s, consolidated its already iron grip on the system by incorporating the Prison Commission – the mid-Victorian quango ostensibly in charge of prisons – into its fiefdom. Those operatives who actually ran the prison system – for example, prison officers, medical officers and governors – were rarely asked for their opinions on major issues of policy during these years. When they were consulted, their views were mostly ignored (Thomas 1972).

Given the highly centralized nature of policymaking, it was inevitable that those campaigning around prisons should direct their attention towards Whitehall. The leading campaigners were mostly found in the Howard League for Penal Reform whose small, London-based, professionally educated membership had inside *access* to senior civil servants. Through close personal contacts (and family ties) with the powerful, its overlapping membership on Home Office advisory bodies, and its own, and not inconsiderable, body of legal expertise, the League played an important, though invisible, role in shaping post-war penal policy (Ryan 1978; Loader 2006).

The orientation of policy, at least in theory, was directed more towards prisoner welfare than punishment (although, given the harsh disciplinary ethos of prison officer culture, how much welfare there was in practice is debatable). The Labour Party, in particular, argued that many of those who came into contact with the criminal justice system had been victims of unbridled market forces, and were therefore more in need of social support than punishment. However, this view was tempered by a cross-bench distrust in Parliament of 'do-gooders' who sought to extend this liberal sentiment to the 'undeserving' rather than the 'deserving poor'. The consequence of this was a modest programme of reform which confidently reaffirmed the centrality of the prison as a vehicle for disciplining and reforming the poor and the powerless (Ryan 1983).

This 'top-down' model, built around a welfare consensus, was, as we have already suggested, not uncommon. Across government, in the immediate post-war decades, it was grudgingly accepted that the 'men from the Ministry' probably knew best, and buttressed by a highly restrictive Official Secrets Act, and latterly by the threat (and use) of the insidious libel laws, politicians and civil servants were able to create the framework of the modern welfare state without the level of public scrutiny that we would now take for granted. Elite policymaking was compounded by the conviction among the 'great and the good' that penal reform was unpopular with the public and that the more they became involved in making policy, the more repressive that policy would become. Public opinion, therefore, became something to be actively 'managed' or 'circumvented' rather than persuaded, while prisoners' opinions remained non-existent.

This picture of the post-war penal lobby as a small coterie of privileged, well-connected, self-satisfied reformers, who did little to engage with the public to secure significant changes in the prison system, is not a flattering one. Perhaps it does less than justice to those reformers who collaborated across the political divide in an effort to push penal reform up the political agenda at a time when other social priorities, like health and education, were clearly more pressing. Nonetheless, while the 1948 Criminal Justice Act was not quite the dinosaur it has been painted, there was little on the agenda of post-war penal reform to challenge the potential of the prison as a force for dealing with those who had fallen outside the progressive social democratic consensus. Indeed, all that was required was just a little more knowledge – as promised in the 1964 document, *Crime: A Challenge to Us All* – and the prison could fulfil its disciplinary and reforming promise.

The fragmenting consensus

This cosy world of penal reform was severely disrupted in the late 1960s. Partly prompted by Britain's perceived economic decline, the top-down approach through which policy was constructed and delivered was challenged by a new generation of political activists seeking to secure more radical change by campaigning from below and bypassing the traditional machinery of central government. Instead of relying on civil servants, co-opted Whitehall experts and establishment pressure groups at the centre, these activist groups facilitated the development of new and *alternative realities* generated by those at the receiving end of the disciplinary network: prisoners themselves, those with mental health issues, benefit claimants and drug users – in other words, those who had been marginalized by the very process that was theoretically supposed to be offering them a road back to some kind of non-deviant normality. The emergence of radical groups such as the Preservation of the Rights of Prisoners (PROP), with its call for the unionization of prisoners *and* direct action to defend prisoners' interests, RAP and Release was significant not only because they sought to empower those opposing state control on a routine basis but also because their message often had a wider political resonance (Fitzgerald 1977; Ryan 1978).

Many of those involved in these groups questioned the historic compromise between capital and labour that underpinned the post-war welfare consensus, viewing much of the disciplinary network, not least prisons, as serving the interests of capital rather than empowering those on the margins (Ryan 1978). This was unsettling for the liberal, metropolitan elite who had dominated the movement for prison reform through groups such as the Howard League and the National Association for the Care and Resettlement of Offenders (NACRO). More particularly, and arguably more challenging for these organizations, was the growing belief among radical groups that prisons were incapable of being reformed, and that the only strategy was to work for their abolition. While the tactics to achieve this goal were a matter of much debate (Mathiesen 1974), discussions about the theory and practice of abolitionism began to be seriously considered both in the UK and in Western Europe (van Swaaningen 1997). These discussions were responding to a penal and criminal justice system whose commitment to welfare and rehabilitation was increasingly regarded as an ideological sham behind which lay a punitive system of discipline that contributed, however tangentially, to the unequal distribution of power in a deeply divided, and increasingly fragmented, social order.

The consequence of these critical interventions, underpinned at an academic level by the sociologically driven and critically orientated National Deviancy Conference, meant that by the early 1980s there was an enlarged, diverse and fractured policy network in England and Wales around imprisonment, with some lobby groups still campaigning for prison reform, while other groups campaigned against prisons, arguing instead for alternatives to custody at every turn, even envisaging in some cases *A World Without Prisons* (Dodge 1979).

Importantly, all social movements contain elements of contradiction and overlap, and these movements are not static. Therefore, arguably, the emergence of these new, more critical groups had a counter-hegemonic impact on the more traditional lobby, to some extent radicalizing them. During the 1970s, the liberals at the Howard League engaged with radicals at RAP to debate the strategic possibilities around abolition, while NACRO sought to promote a range of voluntary alternatives to prison. Furthermore, the official May Report (1979) questioned whether, on the basis of the government's own evidence, the objective of the prison system could still be said to be 'reform', opting instead for 'humane containment', while the Criminal Justice Act (1972) legislated for Community Service Orders which soon won great favour among liberal magistrates and judges, though arguably sometimes for the wrong reasons (Home Office 1975). The prison system was also affected by these wider debates. It was destabilized by the national strike by prisoners in 1972; by the uncompromising response of the Prison Officers Association (POA) to the strike; by the vigorous campaign against the notorious Control Units in 1974 (Fitzgerald 1977); and by the demonstration at Hull prison in 1976. The state's brutal and racist response to the demonstration, exposed by PROP in a public inquiry instigated by the organization, and the legal challenges mounted on behalf of prisoners against the disciplinary hearings that took place after the demonstration, also presented a serious challenge to the state's ability to construct an objective 'truth' around prisons under the blanket of secrecy that had prevailed since the early 20th century (Fitzgerald and Sim 1979).

However, despite the impact of these developments, they did not seriously undermine the central role of the modern prison (Fitzgerald 1977; Fitzgerald and Sim 1979). Radical critiques of the institution *had* penetrated public discourse, ensuring that its central disciplinary purposes were no longer entirely uncontested in the penal lobby, and some genuine radical alternatives to custody were pioneered (Dronfield 1980). Nonetheless, the prison retained its position as *the* symbolic, disciplinary institution at the centre of what was becoming an ever larger, and increasingly complex, penal network (Cohen 1985). Penal policy also remained firmly under state control, run by civil servants who were theoretically accountable to Parliament through elected ministers. In practice, the power to punish remained largely in the hands of a hidden and unaccountable group – prison officers – whose discretionary capacity for often-violent interventions in the lives of the confined remained undiminished.

We shall return to the question of the impact of the radical prisoners' rights movement below. However, before considering this issue, the chapter turns to the question of reform at this time, as it is central to the abolitionist critique of the traditional penal lobby.

Abolitionism, reform and the state

Abolitionists, while recognizing that *some* reforms at *some* historical moments may have enhanced the position of the confined, have consistently maintained that prison reformers have, however unintentionally, helped to reproduce the dominant discourses that the prison is the *natural* response to crime and deviance. For Angela Davis:

> As important as some reforms may be – the elimination of sexual abuse and medical neglect in women's prisons, for example – frameworks that rely exclusively on reforms help to produce the stultifying idea that nothing lies beyond the prison.
>
> (Davis 2003: 20)

This should not be surprising, as from its very inception in the late 18th century, the liberal penal reform movement was built on a process of mystification that legitimated 'the further consolidation of carceral power' (Ignatieff 1978: 220). Ignatieff's work appeared at a rich moment for abolitionist thinkers – among them, Mathiesen (1974, 1980), Foucault (1975), Ryan (1978), Fitzgerald and Sim (1979) – who raised critical questions about the politics of liberal reform, its relationship to the state and its role in the consolidation of penal power. Reform was not outside the prison, it was 'isomorphic, despite its "idealism", with the disciplinary functioning of the prison' (Foucault 1979: 271). In other words, liberal reform was caught in an ideological contradiction where humanizing prisoners was undercut by the drive towards 'disciplining their bodies and reconstructing their minds' (Sim 1990: 73). This critique was tied into a broader condemnation of the role of prison in maintaining a deeply divided social order. If the prison worked at all, it worked in the reproduction of that order, rather than for the salvation of the confined.

This critical work had impacted on those campaigning around the prison in the 1970s and 1980s. However, it appeared at a significant, historical moment with the electoral success of the New Right. Beginning with the first Thatcher government in May 1979, the state's authoritarian response to crime and disorder hegemonically cemented this ruling bloc, and the wider population, into a politics of 'regressive modernisation', dragging the society forwards by taking 'us backwards' (Hall 1988: 164). For prisons, the consequences of this development were profound. By the early 1980s, the government had committed itself to the biggest prison-building programme since mid-Victorian times; sentences for some offences, already long, were substantially increased, while attaining parole was made more difficult (Ryan and Sim 1984). Leon Brittan, the home secretary, also announced that there were to be no limitations on the size of the overall prison population and that the government was committed to ensuring that prison places would be available for those whom the courts thought should be locked up. The emphasis on punishment, and its intensification behind the prison walls, was reinforced in the early 1980s – a time of high unemployment, bitter strikes and inner-city disturbances – by a number of Parliamentary debates concerning the restoration of the death penalty, and the popular demand that life sentences should mean life (Sim 2009).

At this time, key liberal campaign groups were further incorporated into the state's expanding penal/disciplinary network. In 1987/88 alone, NACRO's income (mostly derived from the government for retraining and resettling offenders) reached a staggering £79 million (Wilson 2001). Less compliant lobby groups were mostly marginalized. Granted, the emergence of the Prison Reform Trust in 1981 went some way towards compensating for the Howard League, whose certainties had been challenged by the debate over reform versus abolition, but its reform agenda as a self-confessed creature of the liberal establishment was timid (ibid.). In truth, neither the Howard League nor the Prison Reform Trust had any real appreciation of the weight of the ideological shift that was taking place. However, it quickly became apparent to groups like RAP that Conservative politicians were more interested in listening to populist, red-top editors than to self-proclaimed government experts or the traditional penal lobby's 'pissing liberals' (Gilmour, cited in Sim 2000: 322).

RAP's response to the intensification in state authoritarianism was to return to reform and its relationship to abolitionism. For Tony Ward, the editor of RAP's journal, *The Abolitionist*, while many reforms were simply 'a sugar coating on a toxic pill', it was also important to 'gain support for reforms of the penal system which while making it more humane will also *show up its inherent limitations and contradictions*' (cited in Sim 1994a: 269, emphasis in the original). This meant that it was possible to call for the immediate abolition of the secrecy that dominated the prison system, and for the abolition of the prison medical service (which eventually did happen), while simultaneously defending institutions such as the Barlinnie Special Unit as a model of progressive confinement. Thus, while liberals and abolitionists shared a number of medium-term goals regarding reform, liberals failed to share:

> our political outlook: RAP's fundamental purpose is, through research and propaganda, to educate the public about the true nature, as we see it, of imprisonment and the criminal law; to challenge the prevailing attitudes to crime and delinquency; and to counter the ideology of law-and-order which increasingly helps to legitimate an increasingly powerful State machine.
>
> (cited in Sim 1994a: 269–270)

Unlike many in the traditional penal lobby, RAP also recognized that crime was a social construction in that acts and activities which were labelled as criminal – particularly those classified as violent and dangerous – depended on who had the power to label them as such. This position was not without its theoretical problems and was further refined and, indeed, critiqued through the work of feminist activists such as Jill Box-Grainger, who forced the organization to consider the impact of sexual violence on women 'and [their] demands to be protected from oppressive and gratuitous street and domestic violence' (Box-Grainger 1982: 21). For Ryan and Ward, this and other developments raised crucial issues about the nature of power itself:

> No longer did the world appear to be neatly divided between the 'powerful' and the 'powerless', nor were 'crimes of the powerful' the sole prerogative of the ruling class, once the concept was extended to take account of the power of men over women, of white people over black and of adults over children. RAP was one of the first groups in the lobby to engage seriously with the issue of child sexual abuse.
>
> (cited in Sim 1994a: 273)

The early 1980s also saw the emergence of two groups whose presence on the political landscape was to seriously challenge not only the traditional penal lobby's emphasis on piecemeal reform, but also, because of its acquiescent relationship to the state, its neglect of a range of key issues around prisons. First, the emergence of INQUEST in 1981 brought to public and political attention the disturbing issue of deaths in state custody (Ryan 1996a). Second, the emergence of *Women in Prison*, in 1983, focused on the desperate, invisible situation of women in prison (Carlen et al. 1985), an issue that had been effectively neglected by the traditional penal lobby, politicians and the mass media. As we noted above, these groups also had a significant, hegemonic impact on traditional reform groups by dragging them onto a more critical terrain so that they too began to address issues that had hitherto been ignored within their reformist discourse and agenda.

Refurbishing reform: Woolf, privatization and managerialism

During the 1980s the debates about abolition and reform were sharpened by the ongoing crisis in prisons manifested around overcrowding, prison officer militancy and the challenge to the legitimacy of the system through disturbances. This latest crisis reached its apotheosis in April 1990 with the 25-day demonstration at Strangeways. For liberals, the state's response to Strangeways in the form of the Woolf Report appeared to herald a significant shift in the politics of reform in that a senior judicial figure was calling for a reappraisal in the philosophy and practice of the penal system, and in the treatment of prisoners, to the point where 'justice' should be as central to penal policy as the twin pillars on which the prison system had traditionally rested, namely 'security' and 'control' (Woolf 1991).

Woolf's report 'transcended the divisions between politicians, penal reformers and media personnel and … united the different interests of these groups on the ideological terrain of penal reform' (Sim 1994b: 42). For abolitionists, Woolf's recipe for reform was problematic. Not only was his agenda quickly subverted and undermined by the Conservative government's ongoing law and order drive, exemplified by Michael Howard's defence of the prison, and his 'bleak doctrine of twentieth century less eligibility … compounded and reinforced by the emphasis on security and control' (Sim 2009: 61), but also the proposed reforms did little to challenge the prison's role as a punitive institution in a deeply divided society. Woolf's failure to confront the deeply embedded, punitive discourses within prison officer culture which continued to seriously undermine more enlightened policies and practices towards prisoners represented a further significant weakness in the report (Sim 1994a).

Woolf's agenda was also compromised by the struggle against private prisons which, for the Prison Reform Trust, the Howard League and NACRO, bordered on the unethical. Others, notably the POA, were less troubled by profit from punishment but saw privatization as a threat to their members' conditions of employment and, ultimately, their job security. More critical commentators argued that privatization would prove to be a vehicle for expanding the prison population. The private sector would, at some stage, offer to pick up the initial capital cost of building new prisons, thus enabling the Treasury to defer the full cost of its declared policy to provide even more prisons (Ryan and Ward 1989).

The fierce campaign against private prisons diverted resources away from the ongoing struggle to consolidate Woolf's liberal agenda. Yet the penal lobby could not have ignored this fight, not least because privatization was presented by some of its Conservative supporters as yet another, new vehicle for reform; the private sector would deliver what the state had demonstrably failed to achieve for over a century – namely, prisons that truly 'redeemed' their inmates (Ryan 1996b). However, the lobby was brushed aside on this issue, and it is arguable that the pace of prison privatization was only slowed by a directive from Europe – the European Transfer Undertaking Protection of Employment (TUPE). This directive maintained that where a public service was transferred into the private sector, existing workers' conditions of service had to be protected (Ryan 1996b). Despite limiting the market testing of existing prisons, contracting out the building and management of new prisons gathered momentum, and there was even a threat to privatize aspects of probation (Ryan and Ward 1990/91), a threat that was to become a reality in the first decades of the 21st century.

Additionally, the Conservative government sought to improve the accountability of the Prison Service through the implementation of new public management (NPM) techniques imported from the private sector. These techniques aimed to disaggregate the service, while simultaneously increasing state control over management through the introduction of key performance indicators involving auditing: the number of escapes; the number of prisoner disciplinary offences; and the time prisoners spent out of their cells (see Chapter 8, this volume). Like many other public sector workers and managers, prison staff came to be more worried by efficiency audits than about visits from the chief inspector of prisons. Indeed, when the Prison Service acquired agency status in April 1993, the director-general claimed that NPM techniques had done more to improve the performance of the service than any other innovation, including the arrival of private prisons (Ryan 2003). The persistent complaint by prison administrators that this improvement, if that is what it was, was being achieved in practice by taking away their freedom to manage the newly disaggregated prison system, was naively to miss the point. Neo-liberalism, as embodied in NPM, was about governing and controlling more, not less, as managers across the public sector were to learn to their cost as they scrambled to meet centrally imposed targets on limited resources.

Taken together, these changes propelled the Prison Service towards the new millennium. What had once been a highly centralized service, run by public servants on uniform lines, became a competitive, binary system in which a growing number of prisoners and prison managers/operatives worked under different conditions of employment for different rates of pay. Additionally, globalized, capitalist companies such as the Corrections Corporation of America and Wakenhut were among the first companies to move into the penal market place. This development meant that the normative discourse of campaigns around the prison became driven less by notions of reform, and more by questions about value for money. The discourse of reform instigated by Woolf was not entirely rejected, it was simply overlaid. Inevitably, too, the policy network became more complicated as auditors and inspectors became prominent, sometimes helping to shape normative goals that had once been the prerogative of liberal elites in the immediate post-war period.

In the early 1990s, the establishment of the liberal Penal Affairs Consortium can reasonably be interpreted as a rational response to this changing policy landscape. It was an attempt to create a concerted, united front in punitive times. However, internal differences over its reform agenda and the changing nature of British governance towards the millennium meant that it never regained the inside single track as a lobby group that had once been the privilege of the Howard League, nor did it ever stand much chance of stemming the hard-edged, populist thrust of Thatcherism, and its ideological successor Blairism, the issue to which we now turn.

New Labour and the reformed prison

Under New Labour, Woolf's liberal reforms were relegated still further. From 1997, Tony Blair and Gordon Brown's economic and political agenda was to pursue not only the privatization of public institutions but also their marketization through the demand that they remodel themselves to reflect the discipline of the marketplace. This meant 'erecting markets as the only measure of efficiency and value and destroying the very idea of "the public"' (Hall 2009: xviii). Marketization impacted on prisons at a number of different levels. First, private prisons were to remain. Second, the managerial reforms, which had dominated Conservative thinking, continued and, arguably, intensified in terms of auditing and setting targets for public services. Third, the prison and probation services were amalgamated to create a National Offender Management Service (NOMS). Suggested by an internal Home Office review (Home Office 2001), the amalgamation was designed to reduce reoffending rates by 10% through ensuring that the 'custody plus' sentences introduced by the Criminal Justice Act (2003) were more effectively managed and delivered.

A comprehensive regional structure was promised where markets would ensure the efficient allocation of service delivery across the whole penal apparatus, from prisons to punishment in the community. In these new, 'joined-up' times, it would not matter much whether penal services were delivered by the state, by for-profit organizations or by voluntary providers. The more important point was to guarantee contestability, to ensure that in-service provision value was added, and to conduct research in order to identify 'what works'. Some lobby groups, e.g. NACRO, clearly saw this blurring of the public/private boundary as providing further opportunities for the organization's growth, as it was already thinking deeply about how to engage with the new marketplace (NACRO 2004).

Thus, the goal of New Labour's penal policy, in theory, was to shift away from the less eligible, 19th-century bleakness of Michael Howard's philosophy of 'prison works', to the sleek, late 20th-century managerial smoothness of Jack Straw's 'working prison', built around:

> a combination of joined-up policies, partnerships and programmes. In official and expert discourses, the confined are constructed as socially excluded subjects whose reintegration will allow them to participate in the globalised marketplace, as opposed to individuals whose identities have been forged, and social subordination maintained, through the dialectics of class, gender, 'race', age and sexual divisions.
>
> (Sim 2005: 222–223)

Pat Carlen analysed this development utilizing the concept of 'carceral clawback' where reforms were (and are) constantly being incorporated and reincorporated into a system of penal power in which there is 'no serious attempt to develop strategies for a reduction in the use of imprisonment' (cited in Sim 2005: 223). New Labour's penal policy was, therefore, another link in a punitive and ideological chain which stretched back two centuries and continued to accept the 'natural' and inevitable existence of the prison. In that sense, to paraphrase Foucault, the New Labour prison *was* the reformed prison. As with their Conservative predecessors, the institution's extraordinary capacity to deliver punishment and pain remained invisible under New Labour.

The coalition: back to Bentham

Following the election of the Conservative–Liberal Democrat coalition government in May 2010, two key policy developments should be considered – developments articulated under the banner of reform. First, competition among service providers became institutionalized and intensified with more private sector involvement in the running of prisons, particularly in the provision of work opportunities and training, and the remodelling of the probation service. The existing 35 relatively new probation trusts were to be replaced by 21 government-backed Community Rehabilitation Companies (CRCs), which will oversee bids from private companies to run probation schemes such as the one pioneered at Peterborough (MoJ 2013c).

Those bidding for contracts were expected to include G4S and Serco, both under investigation by the Ministry of Justice for alleged fraud (*Independent*, 19 September 2013). In order to defray the expense (and risk) involved in this substantial extension of social control at a time of fiscal crisis, participating groups were to be subjected to a system of 'payment by results'. The government was confident that its new framework would provide the answer to disappointing rates of recidivism which among some probation categories were running at over 50% (MoJ 2013b). Yet there was no firm evidence to justify this optimism. Even a sympathetic reading of the government's policy document on 'transforming rehabilitation' (MoJ 2013c), which tracked the Peterborough initiative, suggested not only that there was still much work to be done, but also that massive uncertainties remained.

More broadly, within a month, the new system was described as being in 'chaos', a 'train crash' that 'posed a risk to public safety', including: the loss, freezing and wiping of thousands of case files due to computer failures; an increasing backlog of work for probation staff; 2,500 offenders having no allocated probation officer; and the files of high-risk sex offenders being sent to the CRCs rather than to the remaining rump of the

National Probation Service (*Independent*, 6 July 2014). By July 2014, it was reported that a number of the probation partnerships bidding for contracts had withdrawn because, they argued, they could not deliver a service that was safe, given the funds that had been made available. According to Harry Fletcher, 'the justification for the sell-off has evaporated. Probation is a rich money-cow, for the usual multinationals' (cited in *Private Eye*, 11–24 July 2014: 39).

The second policy development, as we discuss below, was that despite the change of government, punishment remained central to the everyday life of the prison. Indeed, it was further intensified both by the budget cuts demanded by the Treasury, and the policy changes made under the hard line taken by Minister of Justice Chris Grayling. Less eligibility, due to changes in the incentives and earned privileges scheme (IEPS), and to the parole system, coupled with the increase in the prison population, meant that life inside for many prisoners was becoming intolerable to the point where there were a 'series of rooftop protests' around the country (*Observer*, 29 June 2014).

For coalition ministers, the prison was a site which not only rehabilitated but was also a place where *hard work and discipline* were central to the daily life of the institution. So, after two decades of structural upheaval, underwritten by all three major parties, we were left with the same blind faith in the power of prisons to 'grind rogues honest', which was not much of an advance on what Bentham offered two centuries previously. Given the privatization agenda, and the commercial interests involved, the reformed and reforming prison was quite literally back in business.

Power, politics and abolitionism in the 21st century

As we noted above, Thomas Mathiesen's foundational text, *The Politics of Abolition*, was published in 1974. Forty years on, Mathiesen's analysis concerning the ideological and material role of the prison within an advanced capitalist society, the relationship between punishment, prisons and the capitalist state, and the need for reforms which negatively impact on the prison thereby inducing fundamental abolitionist change, remains as valid as ever and has, indeed, recently been revised and republished in a new edition (Mathiesen 2014). Over the last four decades, abolitionists have self-reflexively built on Mathiesen's theoretical insights. The role of the prison in the policing of class divisions has been augmented by different writers who have pointed to the institution's role in reproducing other social divisions, including: gender (Carlen 1990); race (Davis 2003); the intersectionality between the two (Russell and Carlton 2013); and sexuality (Mogul et al. 2011).

At the same time, different challenges to abolitionism have emerged. These challenges have arisen in the context of the brutal consolidation of neo-liberalism, the profound economic crisis that has gripped the neo-liberal project, and the terror and trauma induced by the toxic drumbeat of austerity whose corrosive impact on the poor and the powerless has been profound (Sim 2014a). Importantly, however, these challenges have also generated new sites and strategies of opposition regarding abolitionist praxis. Here we consider four of these challenges: the relationship between abolitionism, the prison, and newly emerging and allied forms of confinement and surveillance; the punishment of the contemporary 'rabble' in and through the penal/welfare complex; the consolidation of state power in the context of the privatization, commercialization and contracting out of a range of state services; and the ideological reassertion that a 'rehabilitation revolution' is taking place in prisons (Sim 2013).

The challenge of carceral expansion

Justin Piche and Mike Larsen (2010: 398–403) have argued that a range of authoritarian state strategies have materialized on the back of the economic, political and cultural impact of neo-liberalism, which presents theoretical, political and strategic challenges for abolitionists. These strategies include: the use of preventative detention; the extension of state practices of criminalization; the emphasis on risk, security and surveillance; the ongoing expansion of the prison-industrial complex and its links with the military-industrial complex; and the proliferation of new forms of detention such as immigration detention centres. These developments raise a series of questions about how confinement has been defined within abolitionist thought. Abolitionists need to expand the definition of 'what is to be abolished', to think about '*carceral* abolition' and 'address the use of confinement, and the systematic deprivation of liberty in spaces outside and adjacent to the penal system, as traditionally conceived' (Piche and Larsen 2010: 392, 398, emphasis in the original). This point has been reinforced by Gerlinda Smaus. For her, 'the abolitionist movement has to consider … detention camps as seriously as prisons' (Smaus 2007: 22–23).

Immigration detention centres provide a stark example – amongst many – of the new politics of confinement, and the social harms and damage they generate. Between 1989 and 2014, there were 21 deaths in immigration removal centres – 18 men and three women. Harmondsworth detention centre accounted for eight of these deaths. Five further deaths occurred between 2005 and 2014, shortly after individual detainees had been released (Athwal 2014). According to Women for Refugee Women, one in five of the women they surveyed had tried to kill themselves (Walter 2014). Additionally, the social harm inflicted on the families of the detained can be seen in the treatment of children who suffered a range of 'state sponsored cruelt[ies]' including psychological and physical harms, poor conditions, witnessing violence, and poor provision of medical care. For Burnett et al. (2010: frontispiece, 5) the implications of their analysis were clear: 'the detention of children must be abolished immediately'.

Importantly, however, as with the prison system, detainees resist. This resistance provides compelling evidence of the fragility, and lack of legitimacy, of the regimes in detention centres. They include: seeking legal remedies to make 'deportations and removals … difficult to enforce' (Gibney, cited in Bosworth and Slade 2014: 183); hunger strikes (27 between 1994 and 2011); escapes and attempted escapes (12, involving over 100 detainees, between 1994 and 2011); riots and other protests (24 in the same period); and demonstrations outside the institutions to show solidarity with the confined (nearly 50 between 1994 and 2011).[2]

The challenge of the penal/welfare complex

The second issue concerns the punitive intertwining of penal and welfare institutions, propelled by private and third sector interests. This development has resulted in an intensification in the criminalization and punishment of the poor and the dispossessed as the disciplinary logic of the penal/welfare state becomes increasingly and destructively calibrated (Wacquant 2009; Sim 2009, 2014a; Meiners 2011). Thus, the 'punishing existence of the poor' (Moloney, cited in Sim 2014a: 17), and their social construction as feckless parasites, has legitimated not only their voyeuristic surveillance but also their subjugation to a range of policy interventions which have led to a high rate of self-inflicted deaths (Sim 2014a). Their programming through these interventions is built on the cod-psychology articulated by a range of 'judges of normality' (Foucault 1979: 304), employed by private companies and contracted to the state who are remorseless in their intent to break welfare claimants down and re-moralize and rebuild their 'deviant' personalities so that they become acceptable drones in the service economy. Similar developments are occurring in prisons through the introduction of behaviourist programmes again designed to rebuild the 'deviant' personalities of those confined within an institution that continues to act as a 'warehouse' for 'the social dynamite and social wreckage' that neo-liberal capitalism inevitably and unscrupulously generates (Parenti 1999: 169).

For Wacquant, the authoritarian focus of penal and welfare institutions is built on 'deterrence, surveillance, stigma and graduated sanctions'. The goal is to 'modify [the] conduct' of the deviant (Wacquant 2009: 288). Thus:

> Welfare revamped as workfare and prison stripped of its rehabilitative pretension now form a single organisational mesh flung at the same clientele mired in the fissures and ditches of the dualizing metropolis.

More recently, the focus on conduct has been further overlaid by the discourse of vulnerability, at least for welfare claimants. This, in turn, not only reinforces 'the individualisation of social problems' but also, at least within the juvenile justice system, has meant that those who '"perform" their vulnerability more adeptly might be those who enjoy more sympathy in sentencing, or less punitive sanctions' (Brown 2014: 50).

Overall, the intensification in the link between punishment and welfare has become a key component in contemporary, neo-liberal state practices:

> welfare retrenchment and punishment expansion represent opposite trends in state spending but they rely on the same ideology. That ideology holds that the liberal welfare state corrodes personal responsibility, divorces work from reward, and lets crime go without punishment; consequently the lenient welfare regime attracts opportunistic immigrants and cultivates criminal values.
> (Bohrman and Murukara, cited in Meiners 2011: 21)

Individually, the pursuit of neo-liberal welfare and penal policies is toxic. Together, they are deadly. Importantly, however, this reconfiguration of the penal/welfare complex into new strategies of domination in the struggle to maintain a volatile and brittle neo-liberal social order also opens up different possibilities for forging new links between those groups resisting the reforms to the welfare state and those struggling around the consolidation of prisons and other institutions. Linking with radical welfare rights organizations, and developing strategies that reflect and embrace the oppositional concerns of these groups, provides one such example for 21st-century abolitionists to consider. In effect, this means supporting the attempts of both welfare claimants and the confined 'to reconstitute themselves not only as citizens with rights, but as *subjects of value* ... refus[ing] and revolt[ing] against the disenfranchising effects of their classification' (Tyler 2013: 214, emphasis in the original).

The challenge of state power and the marketization of punishment

Third, analysing the prison as a coercive and institutionally violent *state* institution has clearly demarcated abolitionists from their more liberal counterparts over the last four decades (Sim 2009). However, the consolidation of the neo-liberal state has raised further theoretical and strategic questions for abolitionists. Different writers, while utilizing a range of critical, conceptual frameworks to explain this consolidation, are united on a terrain which understands neo-liberal state power in the context of the ongoing policing, criminalization and confinement of the powerless, while the destructive and socially harmful activities of the powerful still remain effectively outside the scope of the state's gaze (Coleman et al. 2009; Wacquant 2009; Hall et al. 2013).

Therefore, following the theoretical and political trajectory of the last four decades, the relationship between the penal system and state power remains central to contemporary abolitionism, particularly in terms of the punitive regulation and degrading control inflicted on the socially marginalized, and their ongoing social construction as a risk and danger to the neo-liberal social order. As Wacquant has noted, 'the penal state has become a potent cultural engine in its own right, which spawns categories, classifications, and images of wider import and use in broad sectors of government action and social life' (Wacquant 2009: 288).

Furthermore, as noted above, since May 2010 there has been an intensification in the marketization of punishment through private and third sector involvement in prison building and management, which in turn has been extended to the provision of work opportunities and training, and the reconfiguration of the probation service. The introduction of cost-cutting private operators, international in their reach, through the creation of new and varied penal markets, stretching from prisons and immigrant detention centres to aftercare, presents significant theoretical, political and strategic challenges to abolitionists not least with respect to the further erosion of the fragile principle of democratic accountability, a principle which itself has been virtually non-existent since 1877 when the state assumed responsibility for the prison system.

Importantly, these developments can be understood not as the state *losing* its grip, but *adjusting* and *re-adjusting* its grip in the light of the wider neo-liberal economic imperatives, relentlessly pursued by international capital and parroted by different governments across the globe. In that sense, the state has not only *not* disappeared, but its power is being augmented and reinforced through its partnerships with third sector agencies, charities and private companies. In practice, the state is being strengthened, not weakened by these developments and is becoming *more*, not *less* integrated (Davies 2011).

At the same time, these new developments have created new possibilities for activist interventions. For Julia Sudbury, an effective challenge to the 'interlocking systems' of militarism, incarceration and globalization demands the establishment of broad-based, cross-movement coalitions in the USA and internationally:

> cross-fertilization between movements will encourage activists to address wider issues that are not always made visible in issue-based campaigns. For example, intensified

analysis of globalisation might encourage prison abolitionists to consider the need for anti-capitalist economic models as a prerequisite for a world without prisons.

(Sudbury 2004: 27)

The Reclaim Justice Network's intervention at the annual general meeting (AGM) of G4S, in June 2014, illustrates the emergence of new, activist possibilities. In becoming shareholders through owning one share, activists attended the AGM, thereby challenging the link between profit and pain. They publicized a number of issues: the company's involvement in the Middle East; deaths in custody; para-suicide and self-harm; the management of Oakwood prison and the profits being made from prisoners (personal communication from David Scott to Mick Ryan). For contemporary abolitionists, therefore, state power is not omniscient and omnipotent; the exercise of power is contradictory and contingent, open, as ever, to opposition and contestation.

The challenge of the 'rehabilitation revolution'

The final challenge concerns the government's recognition that there *are* problems with the prison. Crucially, however, government ministers assert that they can institute reforms to solve these problems. In particular, prisoner rehabilitation can be achieved, 'nudged forward' by new programmes developed by traditional state servants and a range of private service providers. In other words, 'rehabilitation is back on the state's agenda' (Sim 2014a: 17).

From an abolitionist perspective, there are problems with this assertion. Crucially, it ignores the fact that the prison remains a place of often-violent intimidation and degradation for many of the confined. Prisoners remain less eligible subjects in need of formal and informal punishment. In that sense, the institution is not about rehabilitating prisoners but subordinating them (Melossi 2008). For those at the sharp end of this process of subordination – that is, the ones who have 'nothing to expect but a hiding' – it is the 'hiding' itself which is:

> the *permanent* lesson that penitentiary institutions have been teaching, especially in those times when they are seen as giant entrance gates to the niceties of the social contract and their function resides – it is commonly assumed – in literally 'breaking in' the newcomers. This is not a function that should be underemphasised or go unnoticed. It is a powerful instrument of government which teaches discipline.
>
> (Melossi 2008: 242, emphasis in the original)

The retributive changes to the IEPS, discussed above, provide a powerful, contemporary example of the politics of less eligibility and the gap between rhetoric and reality in the coalition's penal policy. The rolling back of the state, due to the imposition of Treasury-inspired budget cuts, was also having a detrimental impact on the lives of prisoners (Day 2014: 24). Many complain about being required to work in prison industries for large profit-making companies and for a fraction of the minimum wage:

> We are ... forced to work for big profit companies for £7 a week at the same time as being ripped off by the privatised canteen and prison phone companies ... Our

written complaints are disregarded and our requests are ignored, and they expect a 6 week offending behaviour course to re-programme our thinking … It's a sick joke.

(Letter to *Inside Time*, No. 180, June 2014: 9)

At the same time, the prison remained a place where the vulnerable were traumatized, with often devastating consequences. In 2013, the suicide and murder rates, especially in male prisons, were at their highest for a number of years. There were four homicides, the highest since 1998 (*Guardian*, 20 January 2014). Between 1978 and 2013, 4,381 prisoners died in prison, 2,014 of these deaths self-inflicted (MoJ 2014a: table 1.1). There were 215 deaths in 2013, up 12% from 2012, of which 74 deaths were self-inflicted. Up to mid-June 2014, 92 deaths had occurred, 43 of which were self-inflicted.[3] Additionally, between 2004 and 2013, there were 237,269 incidents of self-harm, with women prisoners disproportionately self-harming. In 2013, the figure was 1,530 per 1,000 women, a figure which itself had dropped from a high of 2,991 per 1,000 in 2005 (MoJ 2014b: table 2.1).

There are two final issues to consider here. First, Carlen has pointed to the systemic, broader structures of power and powerlessness that remain ingrained in the wider society so that the economically marginalized and psychologically traumatized, who still comprise the majority of the prison population, are being released back to the same system that induces, reproduces and legitimates their powerlessness. For her:

> re-integration, re-settlement or re-entry are often used instead of re-habilitation. Yet all of these terms, with their English prefix 're', imply that the law breakers or ex-prisoners, who are to be 're-habilitated'/'re-integrated'/'re-settled' or 're-stored', previously occupied a social state or status to which it is desirable they should be returned. Not so. The majority of prisoners worldwide have, prior to their imprisonment, usually been so economically and/or socially disadvantaged that they have nothing to which they can be advantageously rehabilitated.
>
> (Carlen, cited in Cooper and Sim 2013: 202)

Second, the changes to IEPS have generated their own, internal contradictions. In June 2014, they were criticized by the chief inspector of prisons and the president of the Prison Governors' Association. According to the latter, they were leading to 'a tipping point of instability' (cited in McGraw 2014: 1). In other words, the very legitimacy of the system, with the spectre of serious disturbances, was again being contested. Given that there had been at least six demonstrations since November 2013, in Northumberland, Oakwood, Ashwell, Ranby, Maidstone and Rugby, this fear was not without foundation.

Taken together, these challenges pose significant theoretical, political and strategic questions for contemporary abolitionists. Crucially, however, they have not derailed the fundamental demand that penal institutions, in whatever form they take, should be abolished. In making these demands, and in confronting the ongoing terrors and traumas induced by institutional confinement, abolitionist interventions can be understood in the context of Stuart Hall's work. For Hall, nothing in the social world is 'inevitable'. Rather, everything is 'contestable, contingent and contradictory, and, above all, *winnable*' (Sim 2014b: 28, emphasis in the original). In that sense, a different, more utopian form of confinement is still winnable, given the debilitating contradictions inherent in contemporary structures of punishment.

Conclusion

> Abolitionism is a movement to end systemic violence, including the interpersonal vulner-abilities and displacements that keep the system going. In other words, the goal is to change how we interact with each other and the planet by putting people before profits, welfare before warfare, and life over death.
>
> (Berger 2014: vii–viii)

The abolitionist movement has many critics. It is criticized and caricatured for its appar-ent disregard for the victims of crime. It is also caricatured as an idealistic, naive social movement which would simply 'open the gates' and allow prisoners their freedom, irrespective of their crimes. Those abolitionists who see penal institutions as having an inbuilt tendency to reinforce deeply embedded and destructive social divisions are drawn as 'crude reductionists'. While this chapter has attempted to disprove such crass, and often offensive, caricatures, they have had an impact on the prisons debate in three distinct ways.

First, they have distracted attention away from the richness and subtlety in abolitionist thinking. Pat Carlen, for example, has outlined an abolitionist vision for women's prisons without degenerating into either idealism or naivety:

> To reduce the prison population we must first reduce the number of prisons; to reduce the number of prisons we must first abolish certain categories of imprison-ment. Women's imprisonment is, for several reasons, a prime candidate for aboli-tion. Those reasons can, first, be derived pragmatically from the characteristics of the female prison population and, then, be related more fundamentally to *possible* shifts in the social control of women and *desirable* shifts in the relationships between women and men … *I am suggesting that, for an experimental period of 5 years, imprison-ment should be abolished as a 'normal' punishment for women and that a maximum of only 100 custodial places should be retained for female offenders convicted or accused of abnormally serious crimes.*
>
> (Carlen 1990: 121, emphasis in the original)

Abolitionists have also confronted the caricature that they wish to open the prison doors and free all prisoners, irrespective of their crimes. Rather, they have recognized that some conventionally dangerous individuals need to be detained because of their pre-datory behaviour. However, it is the *nature* of that confinement which is at issue. This issue is particularly relevant regarding those who engage in violence against women. It remains strikingly relevant today given the nature and level of violence against women and the masculinized culture of most prisons, which does little to rehabilitate men in prison, but rather is more likely to reinforce their masculine sense of power (Sim 1994c).

Recent work focusing on institutions such as Grendon Underwood (Stevens 2013), and the need for a proactive and positive moral philosophy to underpin regimes for long-term prisoners (Drake 2014), has highlighted models of confinement and philoso-phical principles that could be extended throughout the criminal justice system without compromising public safety, and preventing future victimization. For abolitionists, this work poses one significant question: why have the philosophy and practices utilized in institutions like Grendon not been extended? Arguably, the answer lies in the fact that in providing a vision of an 'abolitionist alternative' (Davis 2003: 109), they challenge the regressive atavism inherent in contemporary political and popular law-and-order mentalities which construct long-term prisoners, in particular, as unchanging, irredeemable purveyors of evil. In holding a mirror up to the conventional prison system, they reflect its abject failure, as well as the hypocrisy of its defenders, to induce individual change, reduce victimization and protect the wider society (Sim 2014c).

Second, these caricatures distract attention away from the relationship between crime and social harm. In other words, while it is clear that there are individuals who have committed serious crimes, as conventionally defined by the criminal law, there are other activities the impact of which can be equally devastating for those who experience them but which are marginalized by the criminal justice system and, beyond that, the mass media:

> corporate crime, domestic violence and sexual assault and police crimes [are] all largely marginal to dominant legal, policy enforcement, and indeed academic agendas, yet at the same time [they create] widespread harm, not least among already disadvantaged and powerless peoples. There is little doubt, then, that the undue attention given to events, which are defined as crimes, distracts attention away from more serious harm. But it is not simply that a focus on crime *deflects* attention from other more socially pressing harms – in many respects it positively *excludes* them.
>
> (Hillyard and Tombs 2004: 13, emphasis in the original)

We are not saying anything new here. Crimes committed by the powerful have been analysed within criminology since Edwin Sutherland began writing a series of papers on white-collar crime over 70 years ago. Crucially, however, in 2015, the depredations committed by the powerful – individuals, organizations, institutions and states – still remain virtually ignored. The continuing failure to address these harms, particularly in the aftermath of the institutionalized criminality and mendacity that underpinned the 2008 economic crash, has reinforced the reductive and distorted theorization around dangerousness and social harm that lie at the heart of what Jock Young called 'establishment criminology' (Young 2013: xxix). Furthermore, this has led to a lamentable failure to consider what actions are punished and what actions are *not* punished in the toxic world of 21st-century capitalism. The fact remains that while:

> governments have tinkered with regulations … [and] have rapped various individuals over the knuckles … they remain as supine in the face of the financial services sector, as they have ever been. Only in Ireland and Iceland have individuals actually been jailed. Most of the bankers who oversaw wrongdoing remain in situ.
>
> (Kampfner 2014: 37)

Thus, the prison continues to reproduce a vision of modernity based on delivering injustice, nationally and internationally, to the criminalized powerless:

The century just concluded perhaps saw the greatest amount of inter-human slaughter, rape, and destruction of property of any century; in partial recognition of which we even created a new crime, genocide, but in the face of which extremely few persons were ever punished.

(Morrison 2005: 290)[4]

Third, caricaturing abolitionism distracts attention away from the destructive impact of confinement on the detained, their families and communities. In that sense, Foucault's denunciation of the modern prison, and its abject failure to achieve its stated goals even at the precise moment of its birth, remains pointedly and poignantly relevant. As Foucault noted, 'word for word, from one century to the other, the same fundamental propositions are repeated. They appear in each new, hard-won, finally accepted formulation of a reform that has always been lacking' (Foucault 1979: 270). His insight suggests that the prison crisis is also a crisis of liberalism in that liberalism offers very little beyond the endless, debilitating cycle of crisis–reform–crisis.

Abolitionism is not simply a political and theoretical movement but is also a *moral* philosophy. In that sense, the inevitable question that is always asked of abolitionists – is a world without prisons defensible and realizable? – can be turned around. Instead, it is the liberal defenders of reform who should be asked to justify *their* position. Can they imagine continuing with prisons, and other institutions, given their malignant capacity for destroying rather than rebuilding lives? Should we not be thinking about their capacity for pain-inducing punishment, which, rather than delivering individual redemption, generates physical and psychological trauma and little by way of public protection? Asking these questions means that it is the prison reform industry that needs to make the case for retaining penal institutions in their present form. With over 200 years of futile history behind it, the bankrupt nature of that reformist defence remains undiminished.

Notes

1   This chapter is dedicated to the memory of Barbara Hudson.
2   See network23.org/antiraids/2014/05/08/notes-for-a-brief-history-of-resistance-in-uk-detention -centres/ (accessed 18 June 2014).
3   See www.inquest.org.uk/statistics/deaths-in-prison (accessed 18 June 2014).
4   Thanks to Barbara Hudson for pointing out this reference to us.

Bibliography

Athwal, H. (2014) *Deaths in Immigration Detention: 1989–2014*, London: Institute of Race Relations.

Berger, D. (2014) *The Struggle Within: Prisons, political prisoners and mass movements in the United States*, Montreal: Kersplebedeb Publishing and Distribution.

Bosworth, M. and Slade, G. (2014) 'In search of recognition: Gender and staff-detainee relations in a British immigration removal centre', *Punishment and Society* 16(2): 169–186.

Box-Grainger, J. (1982) 'RAP-a new strategy?' *The Abolitionist* 12: 14–19.

Brown, K. (2014) 'Beyond protection: "The vulnerable" in the age of austerity', in M. Harrison and T. Sanders (eds) *Social Policies and Social Control*, Bristol: Policy Press.

Burnett, J., Carter, J., Evershed, J., Kohli, M.B., Powell, C. and de Wilde, G. (2010) *'State Sponsored Cruelty': Children in Immigration Centres*, London: Medical Justice.

Carlen, P. (1990) *Alternatives to Women's Imprisonment*, Milton Keynes: Open University Press.

Carlen, P., Hicks, J., O'Dwyer, J., Christina, D. and Tchaikovsky, C. (1985) *Criminal Women*, Cambridge: Polity.

Cohen, S. (1985) *Visions of Social Control*, Cambridge: Polity.

Coleman, R., Sim, J., Tombs, S. and Whyte, D. (2009) 'Introduction: State, power crime', in R. Coleman, J. Sim, S. Tombs and D. Whyte (eds) *State Power Crime*, London: Sage.

Cooper, V. and Sim, J. (2013) 'Punishing the detritus and the damned: penal and semi-penal institutions in Liverpool and the North West', in D. Scott (ed.) *Why Prison?* Cambridge: Cambridge University Press.

Davies, J. (2011) *Challenging Governance Theory*, Bristol: Policy Press.

Davis, A. (2003) *Are Prisons Obsolete?* New York: Seven Sisters Press.

Day, M. (2014) 'Punishment without purpose', *Inside Time* 180 (June): 24.

Dodge, C. (1979) *A World Without Prisons*, Lahnam, MD: Lexington Books.

Drake, D. (2014) *Prisons, Punishment and the Pursuit of Security*, Basingstoke: Palgrave Macmillan.

Dronfield, L. (1980) *Outside Chance*, London: RAP.

Fitzgerald, M. (1977) *Prisoners in Revolt*, Harmondsworth: Penguin.

Fitzgerald, M. and Sim, J. (1979) *British Prisons*, Blackwell: Oxford.

Foucault, M. (1975) *Discipline and Punish*, Paris: Gallimard.

Foucault, M. (1979) *Discipline and Punish*, Harmondsworth: Penguin.

Garland, D. (2001) *The Culture of Control*, Oxford: Oxford University Press.

Hall, S. (1988) *The Hard Road to Renewal*, London: Verso.

Hall, S. (2009) 'Preface', in R. Coleman, J. Sim, S. Tombs and D. Whyte (eds) *State Power Crime*, London: Sage.

Hall, S., Critcher, C., Jefferson, T., Clarke, J. and Roberts, B. (2013) 'Preface to the second edition', in S. Hall, C. Critcher, T. Jefferson, J. Clarke and B. Roberts (eds) *Policing the Crisis*, Basingstoke: Palgrave Macmillan.

Hillyard, P. and Tombs, S. (2004) 'Beyond criminology?' in *Beyond Criminology: Taking harm seriously*, London: Pluto.

Home Office (1975) *Community Service Orders*, London: HMSO.

Home Office (2001) *Making Punishment Work*, London: Home Office Communications Directorate.

Howard League for Penal Reform (2014) *Weekly Prison Watch*, London: Howard League for Penal Reform.

Ignatieff, M. (1978) *A Just Measure of Pain*, Basingstoke: Macmillan.

Jewkes, Y. (2007) *Handbook on Prisons*, London: Routledge.

Kampfner, J. (2014) 'Spivs, crooks and rogues who took us all for billions', *The Observer*, 20 July: 37.

Loader, I. (2006) 'Fall of the "platonic guardians": Liberalism, criminology and political responses to crime in England and Wales', *British Journal of Criminology* 44(4): 561–586.

McGraw, E. (2014) '"Tipping point" of instability', *Inside Time* 180 (June): 1.

Mathiesen, T. (1974) *The Politics of Abolition*, London: Martin Robertson.

Mathiesen, T. (1980) *Law, Society and Political Action*, London: Academic Press.

Mathiesen, T. (2014) *The Politics of Abolition Revisited*, London: Routledge.

May, The Hon. Mr Justice (1979) *Report of the Committee of Inquiry into the United Kingdom Prison Services*, Cmnd 7673, London: HMSO.

Meiners, E.R. (2011) 'Building an abolition democracy; or, The fight against public fear, private benefits and prison expansion', in S.J. Hartnett (ed.) *Challenging the Prison Industrial Complex*, Urbana: University of Illinois Press.

Melossi, D. (2008) *Controlling Crime, Controlling Society: Thinking about Crime in Europe and America*, Cambridge: Polity Press.

MoJ (Ministry of Justice) (2010) *Breaking the Cycle: Effective Punishment, Rehabilitation and the Sentencing of Offenders*, Cmnd 7972, London: HMSO.

MoJ (Ministry of Justice) (2013a) *The Story of the Prison Population 1993–2012 England and Wales*, London: Ministry of Justice.

MoJ (Ministry of Justice) (2013b) *Proven Reoffending Statistics October 2010–September 2011*, London: Ministry of Justice.

MoJ (Ministry of Justice) (2013c) *Transforming Rehabilitation: A Survey of the Evidence on Reducing Offending*, London: Ministry of Justice.

MoJ (Ministry of Justice) (2014a) *Safety in Custody: Deaths in Prison Custody*, London: Ministry of Justice.

MoJ (Ministry of Justice) (2014b) *Safety in Custody: Self-harm in Prison*, London: Ministry of Justice.

Mogul, J.L., Ritchie, A.J. and Whitlock, K. (2011) *Queer (In)Justice: The criminalization of LGBT people in the United States*, Boston, MA: Beacon Press.

Morrison, W. (2005) 'Rethinking narratives of global change in penal context', in J. Pratt, D. Brown, M. Brown, S. Hallsworth and W. Morrison (eds) *The New Punitiveness*, Cullompton: Willan.

NACRO (2004) *NOMS – Will it Work?* London: NACRO.

Parenti, C. (1999) *Lockdown America*, London: Verso.

Piche, J. and Larsen, M. (2010) 'The moving targets of penal abolitionism: ICOPA, past, present and future', *Contemporary Justice Review: Issues in Criminal, Social and Restorative Justice* 13(4): 391–410.

Russell, E. and Carlton, B. (2013) 'Pathways, race and gender responsive reform: Through an abolitionist lens', *Theoretical Criminology* 17(4): 474–492.

Ryan, M. (1978) *The Acceptable Pressure Group*, Farnborough: Teakfield.

Ryan, M. (1983) *The Politics of Penal Reform*, Longman: Harlow.

Ryan, M. (1996a) *Lobbying from Below: INQUEST in Defence of Civil Liberties*, London: UCL Press.

Ryan, M. (1996b) 'Private prisons; contexts; performance and issues', *European Journal on Criminal Policy and Research* 4(3): 92–107.

Ryan, M. (2003) *Penal Policy and Political Culture in England and Wales*, Winchester: Waterside Press.

Ryan, M. and Sim, J. (1984) 'Decoding Leon Brittan', *The Abolitionist* 16: 3–7.

Ryan, M. and Ward, T. (1989) *Privatization and the Penal System*, Milton Keynes: Open University Press.

Ryan, M. and Ward, T. (1990/91) 'Restructuring, resistance and privatisation in the non-custodial sector', *Critical Social Policy* 10(3): 54–67.

Ryan, M. and Ward, T. (2013) 'Prison abolition in the UK: They dare not speak its name', unpublished paper, available from the authors.

Sim, J. (1990) *Medical Power in Prisons*, Milton Keynes: Open University Press.

Sim, J. (1994a) 'The abolitionist approach: A British perspective', in A. Duff, S. Marshall, R.E. Dobash and R.P. Dobash (eds) *Penal Theory and Practice: Tradition and innovation in criminal justice*, Manchester: Manchester University Press.

Sim, J. (1994b) 'Reforming the penal wasteland? A critical review of the Woolf Report', in E. Player and M. Jenkins (eds) *Prisons After Woolf: Reform through riot*, London: Routledge.

Sim, J. (1994c) 'Tougher than the rest? Men in prison', in T. Newburn and E. Stanko (eds) *Just Boys Doing Business*, London: Routledge.

Sim, J. (2000) 'Against the punitive wind', in P. Gilroy, L. Grossberg and A. McRobbie (eds) *Without Guarantees*, London: Verso.

Sim, J. (2005) 'At the centre of the new professional gaze: Women, medicine and confinement', in W. Chan, D. Chunn and R. Menzies (eds) *Women, Madness and the Law: A feminist reader*, London: Glasshouse Press.

Sim, J. (2009) *Punishment and Prisons: Power and the carceral state*, London: Sage.

Sim, J. (2013) *Exploring 'the Edges of What is Possible': Abolitionist Activism and Neoliberal Austerity*, Paper presented at the States of Confinement Conference, Liverpool John Moores University, March.

Sim, J. (2014a) '"Welcome to the machine": Poverty and punishment in austere times', *Prison Service Journal* 123 (May): 17–23.

Sim, J. (2014b) 'For Stuart Hall', *Criminal Justice Matters* 96 (June): 28.

Sim, J. (2014c) 'Review of Stevens, A. (2013) *Offender Rehabilitation and Therapeutic Communities: Enabling Change the TC Way*', *British Journal of Criminology*, doi: 10.1093/bjc/azu029 (first published online 2 June 2014).

Smaus, G. (2007) 'Comments from Gerlinda Smaus (2.10.2007)', in J. Feest and B. Paul (eds) *Does Abolitionism Have a Future? Documentation of an Email Exchange among Abolitionists*, www.sozialwiss. uni-hamburg.de/publish/IKS/KrimInstituteVereinigungenZs/Zusatzmaterial_print.html (accessed 16 April 2014).

Smith, M. and Tilley, N. (eds) (2005) *Crime Science*, Cullompton: Willan.

Stevens, A. (2013) *Offender Rehabilitation and Offender Communities*, London: Routledge.

Sudbury, J. (2004) 'A world without prisons? Resisting militarism, globalized punishment and empire', *Social Justice* 31(1–2): 9–30.

Thomas, J.E. (1972) *The English Prison Officer Since 1850*, London: Routledge & Kegan Paul.

Travis, A. (2005) 'Probation hurtles towards Labour's big market test', *The Guardian*, 19 October: 6.

Tyler, I. (2013) *Revolting Subjects*, London: Zed Books.

Van Swaaningen, R. (1997) *Critical Criminology: Visions from Europe*, London: Sage.

Wacquant, L. (2009) *Punishing the Poor*, Durham, NC: Duke University Press.

Walter, N. (2014) 'Raped in Congo, locked up in UK', *The Guardian*, 10 June: 12–13.

Wilson, C. (2001) 'Networking and the lobby for penal reform in policy networks', in M. Ryan, S. Savage and D. Wall (eds) *Criminal Justice*, London: Palgrave.

Woolf, L.J. (1991) *Prison Disturbances April 1990: Report of an Inquiry by the Rt Hon. Lord Justice Woolf (Parts I and II) and His Honour Stephen Tumim (Part II)* (The Woolf Report), London: HMSO.

Young, J. (1999) *The Exclusive Society*, London: Sage.

Young, J. (2013) 'Introduction to 40th anniversary edition', in I. Taylor, P. Walton and J. Young (eds) *The New Criminology*, London: Routledge.

Index

Page numbers in **bold** refer to figures, page numbers in *italic* refer to tables.

A Human Rights Approach to Prison Management (ICPS) 335–6
A Universal Declaration of Human Responsibilities (Inter-Action Council) 325
Aas, K. 134, 706
abolitionism 712–30; 21st century 722–8; aims 728–30; authoritarian response 716–7; and carceral expansion 723; caricatures of 728–30; challenges to 722–8; Conservative–Liberal Democrat coalition government policy 721; critics 728; current context 713; New Labour's penal policy 720–1; and new public management (NPM) 719–20; penal lobby 716–8; penal reform 713–4, 716; and the penal/welfare complex 723–5; prisoners' rights movement 714–6; and privatization 719; radical alternatives to custody 716; and the rehabilitation revolution 726–8; and the state 716–8; state power and the market-ization of punishment 725–6; thinkers 716; and women 718; and the Woolf Report 718–9
Abu Ghraib prison, Iraq 20, 21
action function 48
actuarial penology 321
Adams, Ansel 691
Addicott, P. 596
additional strain 224
Adey, P. 121, 122
administrative segregation 175
Advisory Board for Female Offenders 553
Afghanistan 447, 452–3
Africa: abuses 424; colonial rule 426, 434, 435; corruption 430; criminal justice 433–6; development 423, 435; diversity 424; gang system 425; history 423; HIV/AIDS 425; imprisonment 426–9, **427**, **428**, **429**, 433–6, 436; imprisonment rates 426; infrastructural constraints 429–30; legal systems 432;

literature 423–4, 424–6, 430–1; overcrowding 427–8, 433, 436; pre-trial detainees 428, **429**, 433; prison climate 433, 436; prison conditions 429–32; prison occupancy level **428;** prison population 427, **427**; prison reform 435; prisons 423–36; sentences 426–7; similarity and difference 423; torture 430, 431, 434; women prisoners 428
African Commission on Human and Peoples' Rights 16, 328, 430–1, 432
Age UK 521
ageing prisoners 514–25; adaptation and survival 523; age-tailored programmes 521; consequences of 515–6; continuity of care 524; costs 519; deterioration and decline 516–8; emergence of 515; and female staff 522; the future 523–5; health complaints 519; healthcare 519–20, 524; heterogeneity 514, 517; historic sexual offenders 515, 525; human rights 525; and masculinity 521–2; meaningful activity 520–1; physiological age 519; population 514, 525; primary carers 518; regimes 517; sentences 515; social care 518–9, 524; status 522; USA 514, 515
Aguirre, C. 461, 470
aims, imprisonment 39–52, 56, 115, 607, 618; antecedents 39–41; consensus 45–7; constriction of ambition 47–8; debate about 40, 50–2; delivery 49; deprivation of liberty 45; fragmentation 50–2; and hope 46; international comparisons 42–3; managerial approaches 44–5, 48; minimalist statement 39, 52; null effect 45, 46–7; official formulations 42–5; performance manage-ment 39; politics of 60–2; public protection 43; re-education 42; rehabilitation 41, 46–7; risk reduction 39, 46–7; social control 49–50;

social functions 48–50; targets 44; time dimension 45–6
alcohol abuse *see* drugs and drug abuse
Alexander, J. 425–6
American Correctional Association 287–8
American Jail Association 362
Amnesty International 325, 430
Amsterdam rasphouse, the 680, **680**
Andersen, S.N. 395–6
Anthias, F. 578–9
Appadurai, A. 581
Appleby, L. 197
Approved Schools 531, 535
architecture 16, 32, 40, 95, 116; *see also* prison design
Arditti, J. 622, 623, 627, 628
Argentina 462, 463, 469, 557
Arizona Department of Corrections 156
Arnold, D. 454
Arnold, H. 265, 266, 268
Asia: colonial rule 442, 443–5, 454–5; commonality 441; corruption 451; culture of lenience 450–1; deterrence 444; disposability 452–3; gang system 444; human rights 452–4, 455–6; labour 444–5, 446, 453; literature 441; neo-liberalism 455, 456; overcrowding 449; prison administration 443–7; prison climate 441–2, 442; prison conditions 449; prison population 447–9, 455; prisoner classification 449–52; prisons 441–56; staff 450–1; torture 452–3; transformations 441; women prisoners 449
Assessment, Care in Custody and Teamwork procedure (ACCT) 226
asylum seekers 704
ATG 289–90, 291
Auburn system, the 40
austerity 57
Australasia 403; imprisonment rate *404*, 404–12, *405*, *406*, *407*, *412*; mental health 416–7; overcrowding 413–4; prison conditions 413–4; prison population 403; prisons 403–17; rehabilitation 414–6
Australia 25; Aboriginal Customary Law 346; custodial contracts 161; imprisonment rate *404*, 404–5, *405*, *406*, *407*, 407–9; indigenous prisoners 340, 346–51, 353, *407*, 407–8, 408–9; inter-jurisdictional differences 409; mental health problems 416–7; not-for-profit NGO sector 162; overcrowding 413; prison infrastructure 152; prison population 151, 403, 404, 405, *406*; private prisons 149, 150, 153, 159, 161, 162; recidivism 160; rehabilitation 414–5
sentences *405*; sex offenders 251–2;

unsentenced prisoners 405, *405*; women prisoners *406*, 408–9
Austria 7, 104
autonomy, deprivation of 593–5

Bailey, W.C. 366
Bales, W.D. 286
Ballatt, J. 199
Ban Ki-moon 324
Bandyopadhyay, M. 470
Bangladesh 445, 447, 448, 454
Barker, V. 103, 104, 376
Barlow, D. 318
Barnett, G.D. 248
Barnett-Page, C. 268
Barry, M. 559
Bataille, G. 385
Beckett, K. 315, 321
Behring Breivik, Anders 392
Belgium 96, 190
Bennett, J. 649–50
Bentham, Jeremy 29, 41, 71, 149, 312–3, 515, 549, 590, 686, 722
Berman, G. 551
Bernault, F. 426, 434–5
Best, D. 214
Bhui, Hindpal Singh 700
Big House era 87–8
Binny, J. 687
Birkbeck, C. 470
Birmingham, L. 191
black prisoners 86, 88, 108–9
Blackstone, E.A. 156
Blackstone, William 29
Blagden, N. 253, 255
Blagg, H. 408
Blair, Tony 21
Blake, George 478, 642–3
Blakey, D. 213
Bloody Code, the 28
Blunkett, David 15
Boe, C. 701
Boethius, *On the Consolations of Philosophy* 678
Bolivia 462
Book, H.E. 275
Boone, M. 377–8
Borders Act 2007 700
Borrill, J. 700
borstal system 15–6, 34, 531
Bosworth, M. 557, 597–8
Botsman 446
Bottoms, A. 608, 610
Bottoms, A.E. 233–4, 271, 505
bounded institutions 1
Bourdieu, P. 441
Bowers, W.J. 365

Bowery, M. 159
Box, S. 315–6, 318
Box-Grainger, J. 718
Bradley Report 189–90, 198
Branch, D. 426
Brazil 103; inmate self-governance 468; militarization 462; pre-trial detainees 463, 464; prison conditions 464; prison population 462, 463, 465; prison staff shortages 465; prison violence 12; prisons 469; private prisons 154, 159–60
Breaking the Cycle Green Paper 553
Brecheen, Robert 371
bridewells 27–8, 679
British Academy 13, 22
British Journal of Criminology 117
Brittan, Leon 717
Brixton Prison 7, 21, 25–6
Brombert, V. 685
Brooker, C. 191
Broom, Romell 368
Brown, Jennifer 499
Brown, R. 299
Bruhn, A. 398
brutalization theory 365–6
Bryans, S. 133, 135, 266
Bucklew, Russell 370
Bukstel, L.H. 661
Bulgaria 379–80
bullying 58, 230, 535, 540, 542–3, 558
bureaucracy 592–3
Burke, Edmund 686
Burma 452
Burman, M. 550
Burnett, J. 723
Burns, Sir Harry 617
Burvil, P.W. 233
Byers, Patrick Albert, Jr. 298

Cain, T. 403
California: imprisonment rates 65–6; and solitary confinement 178; women's prisons 92
Cambodia 17
Cambridge, University of, Prisons Research Centre (PRC) 664
Cambridge Institute of Criminology 226
Cameron, David 57, 656
Campbell, Joseph 594
Campling, P. 199
Canada: aims, imprisonment 43, 44, 49; Corrections and Conditional Release Act 344; indigenous prisoners 340, 343–6, 353, 560; mental healthcare provision 190; prison population 345; private prisons 150; sex

offenders 252, 259; women's imprisonment 557
Canaletto 686
Caniglia, J. 298
Canter 117
capacity-building 618
capital punishment 28–9, 60; abolition 370; botched executions 360, 367–71; brutalization effect 365–6; deterrence 364–5; review 371; USA 359–60, 364–71; value 367; wrongful conviction 366–7
capitalism 107, 134, 136, 360–4, 729
carceral clawback 721
carceral expansion 723
carceral geography 114, 120–2
carceral space 114, 118, 120, 124, 126
Care Act 2014 518, 525
Care Bill 2015 518
Caring for the Suicidal in Custody strategy 225
Carlen, P. 74, 138, 550, 559, 560, 661, 721, 727, 728
Carlton, B. 559
Carnarvon Committee 26
Carrabine, E. 86, 549
Castel, Robert 681–2
Category A prisoners 479, 481, 482, 483–4, 492
Cavadino, M. 106
Cavadino, P. 549
cell phones 295–9, 301; access 298–9; confiscations 296–7; countermeasures 297–8
Central African Republic 427
change, political will for 17–9
chaplains 9, 40
Cheliotis, L. 135, 138, 383
Chicago 82–3
Chief Inspector of Prisons 643–4, 656
children: cumulative disadvantage 629; impact of parent's imprisonment 627–8; of imprisoned parents 626–31, 636–7; of imprisoned women 628–30; imprisonment of 529, 654; institutional practices and 630; prisonization 630; rights 627, 636–7; stigma 629, 630–1. *see also* young offenders
Chile 462, 463
Chill, Jürgen 694–5
China 454; aims, imprisonment 42; forced labour 453; migrants 448–9; prison conditions 464; prison population 447, 448; prisons 453
Christie, N. 360, 377, 561
Churchill, Winston 34, 51, 56
Ciavarella, Mark A., Jr. 363–4
civil death 580–2, 588
Claes, B. 670
Clark, V. 160

Clarke, G. 694
Clarke, Kenneth 535
Clemmer, D. 79, 81, 84, 87–8, 90, 234, 660
Close Supervision Centres (CSCs) 486–7, 488, 490
Cochran, J.K. 366
Codd, H. 561
Coello, Robert 509–10
cognitive behaviourism 41
Cohen, Madeline 369
Cohen, S. 32, 86, 321, 460–1, 516–7, 552, 593, 661, 663
Coid, J. 231
Coles, D. 558
Colombia 103, 462, 463
Comfort, M. 613, 625, 630, 634
Commission on Women Offenders 555
communication technologies: access 285, 287, 287–8, 298–9, 299–301; background considerations 284–6, 284–301; benefits 286, 291–2, 295; cell phones 295–9, 301; control and oversight 291, 293–4, 296; costs 289, 290, 293–4, 296; email 289–92; OffNet 290; OMail 289–92, 295–6; potential 301; price gouging 296; and recidivism 285–6; risk and risk management 285; state use 287–8; study 286–9; telemedicine services 292; ubiquity of 284; video conferencing 292–5, 296; video visitations 288
Community Homes with Education 531
Community of Communities (C of C) 507
Community Rehabilitation Companies 653, 721–2
community service 378
comparative cost analysis, private prisons 156
comparative criminology 114
Conahan, Michael T. 363–4
Condry, R. 625, 625–6, 632
conformity 85
contract prisons. see private prisons
contracting out 82–3
control, culture of 84
Control and Restraint 270
control measures, situational 94–5, 95
control problem prisoners 481
Control Review Committee (CRC) 484
Convention Against Torture and Other Cruel, Inhuman or Degrading Treatment or Punishment 118
conversion 85
convict prisons 25–6
convict subculture 81
Cook, D. 622
coping mechanisms 208; prison officers 277–9; violence 591

correctional effectiveness, private prisons 157–60
Correctional Institution Environment Scale (CIES) 118
Correctional Service Canada (CSC) 343
Correctional Services Accreditation and Advisory Panel (CSAAP) 500
Corrections Corporation of America 150, 157–8, 703, 720
corrections industry 360–1; corruption 363–4; economic dynamics 362–3; financial infrastructure 362; juvenile detention 363–4; opportunities 361–2; USA 361–3
correspondence, prisoners 290–1
Corston, Jean 552–3, 561, 662
Council of Europe 7, 16, 17, 104, 376; European Prison Rules 64
Courtenay, W.H. 209
Coyle, A. 3, 336
Craig, G. 622
Crawford, William 31
Crawley, E. 270, 514, 515, 516, 517, 523
Crawley, E.M. 273, 274, 277
Crawley, P. 270
'Creating Choices' (Task Force on Federally Sentenced Women) 344
Cressey, D.R. 81, 82, 309, 310, 660
Crewe, B. 208, 210, 252, 253, 522, 568, 571–2, 576, 579–80, 582, 590–1, 592, 668, 669
crime: causes 310–1; control 83, 103–5, 106; definition 309; and punishment 309–10, 314; rates 28, 65, 104, 106; reduction 104–5; social construction 717–8; trends 102; Victorian response to 25, 26
Crime: A Challenge to Us All 714
Crime and Disorder Act 1998 533, 536
Crime Sentences At 1997 515
crimes against morality 558
criminal classes 26
criminal conviction checks 601
Criminal Justice Act 1948 714
Criminal Justice Act 1967 9
Criminal Justice Act 1982 643
Criminal Justice Act 1991 122
Criminal Justice Act 2003 15, 720
Criminal Justice and Courts Act 2015 530
Criminal Justice and Public Order Act 1994 122
Criminal Justice Bill, 1990 122
criminal justice management 133
Criminal Justice Mental Health Teams 189–90
criminal justice policy 110
criminal justice social workers 9
criminal justice system 109; expansion of 462; and prison design 114

Criminal Law Amendment Act 1885 33
Criminal Law Review 642
Criminal Records Bureau (CRB) 601
criminalization 110, 378, 361, 558, 562
criminology 607; criticisms of materialistic 314–6; scope of 309, 310–1
Critchley, S. 278
Cropwood Conference, 1986 485
Cullen, E. 501
Cunneen, C. 195, 403, 408
Currie, E. 101, 111
custodial contracts 161
Custody in the Community Green Paper 552

Daily Chronicle 33
daily routine 8
Dance, George 685
Dangerous and Severe Personality Disorder (DSPD) 197–8, 198
Dante, *Inferno* 678
Davis, A. 549–50, 561–2, 716
Davis, A. Y. 107–8, 108, 110
Davison, R. 117, 126
Davitt, Michael 46
Day, M. 518
De Giorgi, A. 107, 312, 314, 317
de Tocqueville, A. 57
de Viggiani, N. 195
De Zuleuta 237
deaths in custody 58
debtor's prisons 681
decarceration 33, 115, 125, 560–1
decency 140
decent but austere mantra 57
deep incarceration 477
Defoe, Daniel 681
degradation 10
dehumanization 625
delegitimating experiences 233–4
Denmark 7, 125; imprisonment rates 104; key statistical figures 390, *390*; prison population 14; prison size 391; prisons 388, 395, 398; women's imprisonment 558
Dennis, J.A. 257, 259
dependency 69
deportation 699, 700, 702–3
deprersonalisation 80
deprivation theory 81
Derrida, J. 582
Design, Construct, Manage and Finance (DCMF) contracts 122–3
desistance 607–19; definition 608; Desistance Knowledge Exchange project propositions 611–2; hook for change 613; and identity 608; and imprisonment 612–5; interventions 609–10, 614–5; literature 611; need for

support 610; and offender management 610–2; and penal policy and practice 609–10; personal development 615; primary 608; relevance 617; research 607, 609, 612, 617, 619; research implementation 615–7; secondary 608; support 616; tertiary 608, 614; theories of 609
Desistance Knowledge Exchange project 611–2
Detention and Training Order (DTO) 532–3
deterrence 32–3, 104, 171, 311–2; Asia 444–5; capital punishment 364–5; and solitary confinement 178–9
deterrence theory 365
Dickens, Charles 16, 24, 26
differential criminalization 378
Dignan, J. 106
Dignan, M. 549
DiIulio, J. 133
Dikötter, F. 461
disability 362–3
Disability Discrimination Act 2005 517
discipline 311
disciplinary prison, the 32
discipline officers 8
Disclosure and Barring procedures 601
dispersal prisons 482–5
dispersal system 480–5
Ditchfield, J. 483
diverting function 48
dividing practices, and mental healthcare provision 198–9
Dodge, C., *A World Without Prisons* 715
Dollinger, B. 378
domination 77, 78, 623
Dominican Republic, Nuevo Modelo prisons 18–9
Donohue, J. 365
Doob, A.N. 49
Doré, Gustave, Newgate prison 688, **689**
Dostoyevsky, Fyodor 56
Douglas, M. 72
Douzinas, C. 324, 325
Drory, A. 272
Drug Strategy 211
drugs and drug abuse 83, 205–18; causes 205–6; criminalization of 361; dealers 209, 210; demand reduction 212–3; dependency 206; discouragement 210; drug categories 205; drug users 205; economic incentives and rewards 210; effects 206; experiences 206; explanations 208–10; holistic approach 217; and imprisonment 207; Integrated Drug Treatment System 212; Latin America 462; mandatory drug testing (MDT) 213–4; mindscaping 208–9; NOMS drug strategy 210–1; Norway 396; novel psychoactive

substances (NPS) 215–6; Patel Report 211, 212; pharmaceutical interventions 212; placebo effect 206; prescription medicines 216–7; prevalence 206–7, 213–4; psychological factors 206; psychosocial interventions 212–3; recovery 211; recovery capital 214–5, 217; recovery durability 217–8; responses to 210–4; self-medication 208; social network 209; and status 90; status model 209; *Supply Reduction Good Practice Guide* (NOMS) 213; supply restriction 213–4; time management 208–9; treatment programmes 207, 212–3, 214–5, 396; war on drugs 62

Du Cane, Edmund 27, 33

Duff, A. 180

duty of care 271, 273

Duwe, G. 160

dynamic security 124

Earle, R. 568

early release 9, 13, 25

East, W. 498

Ecenbarger, W. 363, 364

Eckholm, E. 368, 369

Eco, Umberto 678

economic cycles, and punishment 317–20, **319**

economic insecurity 60

economic marginalization 360–1

economic structures 110

economic-punishment nexus 371; corrections industry 361–3; corruption 363–4; juvenile detention 363–4; production of prisoners 360–1; USA 359, 360–4

economy 44, 47

Ecuador 462, 463, 464

Ede, Chuter 35

Eden, William 29

Education, Department of 627

effectiveness 47

efficiency 44, 47, 155, 156

Ehrlich, I. 364

Eligon, J. 370

Elizabethan England 679–80

Elliott, J. 667

Elliott, K. 482–3, 483

email 289–92

emotional geographies 124

emotional intelligence 273–7, *276*

emotions, in prison work 274–5

enabling environments 236

Enabling Environments and Psychologically Informed Planned Environments 492

England and Wales: aims, imprisonment 42, 49; women's imprisonment 551–4

English Prisons Today 34

entry shock 587–8

environmental modification 118

environmental psychology 117–8

Equalities Act 2010 517

Eriksson, A. 389

Erlanger, S. 369

ethical standards 20

Ethiopia 426, 430–1

ethnic codes 574

ethnic-minority prisoners 82, 623–4

ethnographies 659–65

European Committee for the Prevention of Torture

European Committee for the Prevention of Torture and Inhuman and Degrading Treatment or Punishment (CPT) 7, 328, 335, 398, 646, 704

European Convention on Human Rights (ECHR) 7, 701

European Court of Human Rights 7, 57, 64, 325, 328, 380, 383

European Monitoring Centre for Drugs and Drug Addiction 215–6

European Prison Rules, Council of Europe 64

European prisons 375–85, 382–3; Bulgaria 379–80; cultures of punishment 383–5; east 379–81; Finland 375–6; Germany 378; Greece 383; Italy 381–2; the Netherlands 377–8; Nordic exceptionalism 375–7; north 375–7; Norway 375–6, 377; Poland 380–1; punitive harshness 375; Russian Federation 381; south 381–3; Sweden 375–7; west 377–9

European Union (EU), prison population 331

Evans, R. 681

exercise 8

expurgatory function 48

Extended Determinate Sentences 15

Exworthy, T. 195

families, prisoners': access 632; children 626–31, 636–7; cumulative disadvantage 624–5, 629, 632–3; demographic characteristics 623–4; ethnic minority prisoners 624; female partners 631–5; financial impact 633; gender disadvantage 624; health difficulties 633; institutional practices and 625, 630, 634; negative othering 634–5; pre-existing disadvantage 624; secondary prisonization 625, 634; social injustice 622–38, 626; social injustice reduction 635–8; stigma 625–6, 629, 630–1, 634–5, 636; support 632; women 625

Farrall, S. 608

Fazel, S. 188

Feeley, M. 71, 321

Feinberg, J. 170–1
Feltham Young Offenders' Institution 12–3,
    58, 119
feminist theory 578
Fenner Brockway, A. 34
Fieser, E. 18
*Final Report of the Royal Commission into A
    boriginal Deaths in Custody* (Royal Commission
    into Aboriginal Deaths in Custody) 407
fines 378
Finland 19; aims, imprisonment 43, 44, 49;
    imprisonment rates 104, 375, 376; key
    statistical figures *390*; prison conditions 115;
    prison population 332; prisons 375–6, 388;
    women's imprisonment 558
Finnis, J. 173
First World War 34–5
Fishman, L.T. 594
Fitzgerald, M. 716
Flavin, J. 557
Fletcher, H. 722
force, use of 9–10
foreign national prisoners 698–707; asylum
    seekers 704; challenges facing 700; deportation
    699, 700, 702–3; detainee population 705;
    diversity 702; human rights 701; identification
    701; immigration detention centres 699,
    703–5; international comparisons 700;
    interrogation 707; juxtaposed border control
    706; Norway 396–7; outsourcing
    imprisonment 705–6; overview 699–701;
    pains of imprisonment 597–9, 701; prison
    life 701–2, 707; prison population 700;
    prisoner-transfer agreements 705; questions
    698–9; relevance 706; segregation 700–1;
    studies 701–3; USA 698, 699, 700, 705;
    vulnerability 700, 706–7; women 554, 559,
    702, 723
Foucault, M. 32, 83, 93, 95, 311, 469, 551,
    576–7, 580, 607, 686, 716, 724, 730;
    Discipline and Punish 311, 312–3, 455, 690
Fountain, J. 210
Fox, Lionel 35
fragmentation 653–4
France 316; foreign national prisoners 701;
    imprisonment rates 104, 378–9; prisons
    378–9; *prisons semi-privées* 150, 153–4;
    sentences 379; suicide 228
Frank, Robert 691
Frankenberg, R. 578
Free Market ideology 152
freedom, loss of 589–90
free-market economic reforms 68
free-riders 70
Fridhov, I.M. 395
Frost, Natasha 1

Fry, Elizabeth 30, 32, 642
Fulham Refuge 26
funding 51

G4S 110, 161, 721, 726
Gaes, G.G. 156
Gallo, E. 379
Galtung, J. 395
gang system 82–3, 88, 91
Gaol Act 1835 642
Gaol Fees Abolition Act 1815 29–30
Gaols Act 1823 30
Gaol's Committee 682, 684, **684**
Garces, C. 467
Gariglio, L. 693
Garland, David 33–4, 44, 49, 55, 61, 83, 84,
    107, 314, 384, 551
Gartner, R. 92
Gay, John, *The Beggar's Opera* 682
Gear, S. 425
Gearty, C. 337
Gelsthorpe, L. 554
Geltner, G. 678, 679
Genders, E. 506
Geo Group 110
George, A. 559
Germany: imprisonment rates 378; prison
    population 14; prisons 378; private prisons
    153–4
Giddens, A. 64, 136, 137, 268, 516, 591–2
Gilbert, M.J. 266
Gilligan, J. 105
Gilroy, L. 156
Gilroy, P. 569–70
Giordano, P.C. 613
Gladstone, Herbert 33
Gladstone Committee 33, 56, 531
Global Prisons Research Network 460
global South, the 442
globalization 64, 132, 133–6, 136–8, 143, 460,
    707
Godefroy, T. 316
Goffman, E. 85–6, 207, 470, 587, 588, 590,
    669; *Asylums* 80–1, 549, 660
Goldney, R.D. 233
Goldson, B. 530
Gonnella, P. 381
Gordon, A. 582
Gordon, A. F. 107–8
Gossop, M. 205, 206
Gourevitch, P. 20
Gove, Michael 652
governing through crime thesis 106
governors: high security prisons 482; ideal types
    133
Granheim, P.K. 397

Grassian, S. 177
Grayling, Chris 524, 656, 722
Greece 383, 703
Greenberg, David 315
Greenland 340, 351–3, 353
Gregory, D. 424
Gulag system 381
Gunn, J. 195
Guttiérez Rivera, L. 467

Hagell, A. 543–4
Haggard, S. 453
Haigh,R 507
Hakim, S. 156
Hale, C. 315–6, 318
Hall, S. 569, 570, 571, 580, 581, 586–602,
    717, 727
Hamm, M. 491, 579
Hampton, J. 174
Hancock, L. 125
Haney, C. 177, 237, 593
Hankoff, L.D. 228
Hannah-Moffatt, K. 231, 560, 599–600
Hanson, R.K. 249, 257, 259
Harding, R.W. 153
Hardwick, Nick 11
harm reduction 62
Harris Review 238
Hart, H.L.A. 171
Hasselberg, I. 702
Hassine, V. 91, 120
Haugen, S. 396
Hawkins, G. 65–6
Hawkins, G.J. 364
Hawton, K. 558
Hay, W. 265, 268–9
Hayman, S. 669
Hazel, N. 543–4
Health and Social Care Act 2012 211
Health in Prisons Programme, World Health
    Organization 195–6
health promotion 196
healthcare 193, 425; ageing prisoners 519–20,
    524
healthy prisons 195–6
Heath, Mark 369
Hedderman, C. 554, 560
Hedges, C. 109
Heffernan, E. 660
Hennessy, Sir Jam 644
Herrity, K.Z. 590
high security prisons 477–92; aspirations 477,
    481; Category A prisoners 479, 482; Close
    Supervision Centres (CSCs) 486–7, 488,
    490; contemporary problems 488–91;
    Continuous Assessment Scheme 486; control

units 486; demographic changes 490–1;
    dispersal system 480–5; dynamic security
    489; escapes 488–90; governors 482; history
    and development 478–80; institutional ethos
    485; IRA prisoners 484–5; legitimacy 492;
    losses of control 483–5; Managing Challenging
    Behaviour Strategy 488; policy evolution
    478; population 481; prison officers 480,
    482; psychiatric support 486; regimes 480,
    480–2, 489–90; segregation units 482, 485,
    485–6, 487; small units 485–6; special units
    486–8; staff 479, 482; staff to prisoners ratio
    482; tensions 477–8, 484–5, 491; and trust
    491–2
Hillyard, P. 729
historic sexual offenders 515, 525
historical contexts: 1895–1945 32–6;
    experience of change 3, 7–22; importance
    1; lessons 15–20; reform, 1770s–1850s
    27–32
history and development 24–36; 1895–1945
    32–6; First World War 34–5; prison
    inspection 642–4; private prisons 149–50;
    punishment 312–3; reform, 1770s–1850s
    27–32; Second World War 34–6; Victorian
    period 24, 25–7
HIV/AIDS 425, 465, 559
Hla Tun, A. 452
HM Inspectorate of Prisons 9, 216, 225, 641–57;
    accountability 649–50, 651–2, 657;
    assessment 649–50; budget 647, 653, 657;
    Chief Inspector of Prisons 643, 656;
    community of practice 650; draft report and
    recommendations 649; effectiveness 651,
    652; Expectations 648; Feltham Young
    Offenders' Institution report 12–3; future
    challenges 652–7; history and development
    642–4; and human rights 645; independence
    651, 655; Inspection Framework 647;
    inspection process 647–50; inspection score
    650; inspection teams 647; judgement
    criteria 647–8; judgements 649;
    management-independent spectrum 642,
    651; methodologies 650; National Audit
    Office report 655–6; National Preventive
    Mechanism (NPM) 645–6, 649; observation
    649; occupational culture 650; prison policy
    inspection 649; prisoner survey and
    discussions 648; reasons for independent
    646; role 644–5, 657; staff 647; staff
    discussions 648; stakeholder surveys 652;
    team meetings 649; thematic inspections
    651; visits 641–2
HM Prison Service Orders 119
Hobhouse, Stephen 34
Hodge, Margaret 654–5

Hogarth, William, *The Gaols Committee* 682, 684, **684**
Holford Committee 30
Holleran, D. 104–5
Hollway, W. 667
Home Office Control Review Committee 267
homosexuality 83, 91
Hong Kong 448–9
hope 46, 483, 609, 614
Hopgood, S. 324–5
Hough, M. 208, 209
houses of correction 27–8
Howard, John 29, 30, 32, 57, 641, 642, 657, 685–6
Howard, Michael 644, 718
Howard, P.D. 248
Howard League for Penal Reform 713, 715, 717, 719
Huber, A. 327–8
Hubert, W. 498
Hudson, B. 109
Hughes, G.V. 515
hulks 26
human rights 74, 324–37; ageing prisoners 525; Asia 452–4; foreign national prisoners 701; the future 336–7; global perspective 328–32; international standards compliance 335–6; legal framework 327–8, 337; and overcrowding 330, 332–5; and prison inspection 645; pushback against 324–5; regional instruments 328; responsibility 326; rise of 324; and sentences 334–5; universalization of 325; women 556; young offenders 544
Human Rights and Prisons (UNODC) 335–6
Human Rights Watch 325, 430
humane containment 46
humour, prison officers 277–9
Hungary 335
hyper-masculinity 91–2, 522

Iceland 121, 125, 388, 390, *390*
ICPS International Prison News Digest 329–30, 332
identity 87, 90; assertions of 85; and desistance 608; loss of 593, 595; prison officers 269; prisoners 79, 124; rebuilding 80; and solitary confinement 177–8; spoiled 608
Ievins, A. 252, 253
Ignatieff, M. 32, 686, 716
I-Hop 627
immigration detention centres 699, 703–5, 723
immigration removal centres 704
importation model 394
importation-deprivation debate 81–2
imported vulnerability 187, 207

imprisonment: additional strain 224; Africa 433–6, 436; aims 39–52, 60–2, 115, 607, 618; antecedents 39–41; boundary cases 60; Bulgaria 379; of children 529, 654; civil death 580–2; comparative differences 62–3; continuum 549; contracting out 82–3; coping mechanisms 86; core deprivations 589–95; and crime reduction 104–5; criminological studies 311–4; debate about 24; decent but austere 57; depoliticization 60; and desistance 612–5; and drugs and drug abuse 207; and economic cycles **319**; Finland 375, 376; France 378–9; Germany 378; global context 698–9; goals 549–50; Greece 383; increased use of 21–2; influence of politics on 55–6; Italy 381; and the labour market 314–5; legitimacy 59; literary and cinematic traditions 59; medieval period 677–9; the Netherlands 377; Norway 375, *390*, 391; pains of 79, 586–602, 701; and penal philosophy 115; Poland 380; politics of 55–75; properties of 79; and punishment 317–20; racialized dynamics of 568, 568–71; reliance on 107; Russian Federation 381; social costs 105; social functions 48–50; sociology of 77–97; Spain 383; spread of 1; the state and 63–4; statistics 104; Sweden 375, *390*, 391; Sykes's analysis 77–80; treatment of prisoners 56; trends 102–3; Uganda 426–7; use of and social problems 107–9, 110–1; Victorian period 686–8, **687**, **689**, 690; votes in 55; women 87, 549–62
imprisonment rates 332–3, 391; Africa 426; Australasia *404*, 404–12, *405*, *406*, *407*, *412*; Australia *404*, 404–5, *405*, *406*, *407*, 407–9; Austria 104; Bulgaria 379; California 65–6; Denmark 104; Finland 104, 375, 376; France 104, 378–9; Germany 378; Greece 383; Italy 381; Latin America 103; Netherlands 104' 377; New Zealand 104, 410–1; Nordic model 388; Norway 375, *390*, 391; Poland 380; and prison expansionism *102*, 102–3; private prisons 150; Russian Federation 381; Spain 383; Sweden 375, *390*, 391; United States of America 65–6, 83, *102*, *103*, 104, 316–7, **319**, 319–20, 359
incapacitation 61–2, 105
incentives and earned privileges (IEP) scheme 94, 95, 589, 654, 722, 726–7
The Independent 11, 13
Independent Monitoring Boards (IMBs) 9
indeterminate sentences 15, 595–7
indeterminate sentences for public protection (IPP) 515
India 451; caste sensibilities 443; deterrence 444–5; forced labour 453–4; pre-trial

detainees 448; prison administration 445; prison population 447, 448, 455; prisoner classification 449–50; remand prisoners 14; torture 452
indigenous prisoners 340–54; abuse 343; Australia 340, 346–51, 353, *407*, 407–8, 408–9; Canada 340, 343–6, 353, 560; cultural obligations 345, 347; cultural values and norms 342; gang affiliations 345, 351, 353; Greenland 340, 351–3, 353; New Zealand 340, 349–51, 353, 410–1; Norway 399; prison population 340, 341, 343, 344, 345, 346, 349, 353, 407, *407*, 410; and private prisons 342–3; religious freedoms 342–3; respect 344, 354; sentences 343; spirituality 343; traditional items 342; United States of America 340; USA 340–3, 353; women 344–5, 346, 350–1, 408–9, 410, 560
indigenous theory 81
Indonesia 445
Industrial Revolution 686
industrialization 311, 313, 424, 460
inequality 21, 385
informal economy, the 91
information exchange, penal politics 64–5
inmate code, the 78–80, 90
inmate culture 80–3
inmate equality 88
inmate leaders 78, 95–6
INQUEST 718
Inspection Framework, HM Inspectorate of Prisons 647
institutional memory, lack of 15
Integrated Drug Treatment System 212
Integrated Research Application System (IRAS) 665
intelligent kindness 199
Inter-Action Council 325
Inter-American Commission on Human Rights 328, 464
Inter-American Court of Human Rights 328
inter-ethnic interaction 574–5
International Bill of Human Rights 327
International Centre for Prison Studies (ICPS) 328–32, 335–6, 352
International Committee of the Red Cross (ICRC) 190
International Covenant on Civil and Political Rights (ICCPR) 327, 332, 464
International Covenant on Economic, Social and Cultural Rights (ICESCR) 327
International Criminal Court 328
International Penitentiary Congress 40–1
International Prison Chaplains' Association 376
Internet, the 215, 287
interpersonal power 90

Iraq, Abu Ghraib prison 20, 21
Ireland 42, 49
Irwin, J. 81, 82, 88, 660
Islam 44, 490–1, 579–80
isolation 284
Israel 154
Italy 316, **319**, 319–20, 381–2, 700, 703

Jack, R. 231
Jackson, Bruce 693
Jacobs, J. 663
Jacobs, Jesse 366–7
Jacobs, J.M. 124
Jamaica 705, 706
James, P. 210
Jankovic, I. 314
Japan 446, 447, 448, 454
Jefferson, A,. 107
Jefferson, T. 667
Jeffreys, Derek 21
Jenkins, Roy 13, 478
Jewkes, Y. 16, 116, 125, 284, 285, 287, 522, 670, 671, 672, 673
Johnsen, B. 397
Johnson, B. 477, 478, 486
Johnson, Claude 573
Johnson, R. 88, 284, 285, 286, 301, 525
Johnston, H. 284, 287
Johnston, N. 116, 680
Joint Enterprise (JE) individuals 596–7
Jones, M. 497, 508
Jowitt, A. 403
J-Pay 289
Justice, Ministry of 16, 246, 553, 592
juvenile detention, USA 363–4
juxtaposed border control 706

Kampfner, J. 729
Katz, J. 673
Kauffman, K. 270
Kaufman, E. 597–8, 701
Kazakhstan 446–7
Keene, J. 208
Kelley, J. 660
Kennedy, P. 136, 137
Kenny, H. 156
Kenya 426, 434
key performance targets 139–40, 143
Khantzian, E.J. 208
Kiesel, Ryan 369
Kilcommins, S. 48
Kilmann, P.R. 661
King, R. 469, 482–3, 483, 668, 670
Kirchheimer, O. 32, 311, 311–2, 314–5, 316–7
Kondratieff, N. 317
Kraftl, P. 121, 122

Kretschmann, A. 378
Krisberg, B. 73
Kruttschnitt, C. 92
Kupers, T. 177
Kyrgyzstan 446–7

labour 25, 33, 444–5, 446, 453–4, 726–7
labour colonies 381
labour market, and punishment 314–5, 316
Lacey, N. 317, 622, 636
Laffargue, B. 316
Lamming, Lord 644–5, 648
Land, K. 365
Lange, C. 679
Långström, N. 257, 259
Lappi-Seppälä, T. 104, 332
Larsen, M. 723
Latin America: colonial rule 461; composition
    460; cultural specificities 461; defining
    features 469; drug prohibition policies 462;
    expansion of punishment 462–5; gangs
    468–9; imprisonment rates 103; inmate
    self-governance 468; militarization 461, 462,
    469; overcrowding 464–5; pre-trial detainees
    463–4; prison conditions 464–5; prison life
    465–9, 469–70; prison population 462, 463,
    465; prison reform 461; prison social orders
    466–7; prison staff shortages 465–6; prison
    violence 12; prisons 460–70; securitization
    461, 469; situational control 469;
    socio-economic conditions 461; solitary
    confinement 469; staff–prisoner relationships
    467–8, 469–70; trusty prisoners 467–8;
    women's imprisonment 557
Laub, J. 613
Laudet, A.B. 214
Law, V. 557
Lawrence, Stephen 572
Lawsten 561
leadership 19–20, 132–3
Learmont Report 490
Lebel, T. 600
Leder, D. 549
Legal Aid, Sentencing and Punishment of
    Offenders Act 2012 532
Leighton, P. 107, 110
Lentin, A. 572, 578
letter writing 290–1
Lewis, D. 139
Lewis, G. 197
Lewis, O.F. 169
liberty, deprivation of 45
Lieblich, A. 671
Liebling, A. 84, 89, 207, 226–7, 266, 267, 268,
    489, 490, 579, 615, 618, 661, 669
life imprisonment 15, 52, 515

life without parole (LWOP) 52
Lindegaard, M. 425
Lines, R. 195
literary and cinematic traditions 59
Lithuania 190
local prisons 25, 26–7, 31
Lockett, Clayton 368–9, 370–1
Loeffler, C.E. 601
Lombardo, L.X. 266
London 681–2
Lösel, F. 257, 259
Louis, E. 296
Lowenstein, A. 632
Ludlow, A. 232
Lundahl, B.W. 155
Lushington, Sir Godfrey 56
Lynch, Timothy 13–4
Lyon, Danny 691–2, **692**

Maahs, J. 155–6, 158
McAra, L. 554
McCall, C. 661
McConnell, Colin 616
McConville, S. 27, 72–3, 677
McCulloch, J. 557, 559
McEvoy, K. 93
Machiavelli, N. 182
McIvor, G. 550, 559
Mackenzie, J. 501
McNair, J.F.A. 444
McNeill, F. 617–8
Macpherson Report 572–3
McWatters, M. 118
Magaloni, A.L. 460
Main, Tom 497
Makarios, M.D. 158
Malta 7
Manage & Maintain (M&M) contracts 122
management and managerialism 131–44;
    accountability 135; competition 134;
    criminal justice 133; division of labour 135;
    dualities 138; ethos 135; and globalization
    133–6, 136–8; growth of managerialism 132;
    human resource management techniques
    134; key performance targets 139–40, 143;
    under late modernity 136–8; occupational
    culture 132–3; organizational structure and
    practices 137–8; perspectives 131–6; practice
    138–9; and quality of prison life 140–2,
    143; resistance to 135; rise of 133–6;
    self-regulation 134
Managing Challenging Behaviour Strategy 488
Manard, John 298
mandatory drug testing (MDT) 213–4
mandatory life sentence 515
Mandel, E. 317

Mandela, Nelson 51, 324, 325, 424
Mann, N. 521, 523
Mann, R.E. 250, 252–3, 255, 259, 260
Mannheim, Hermann, *The Dilemma of Penal Reform* 57–8
Manson, Charles 298
Maori traditional practices 64–5
marketization 720, 725–6
Marshall, P. 498
Marshall, W.L. 255, 256
Martinson, R. 662
Maruna, S. 608
masculinity: and ageing prisoners 521–2; culture of 91–2, 132, 140
mass incarceration 285
Massachusetts Institute for Technology's (MIT) 287
Mathiesen, T. 48, 82, 86, 376, 384, 395, 599, 716; *The Politics of Abolition* 712, 722
Matravers, A. 515
Matza, D. 310
May, C. 206
May, Theresa 63, 115, 116
May Committee 482, 643, 715
Mayhew, H. 687
meals 8, 8–9
meaningful activity 520–1
Mears, D.P. 179, 286
measuring the quality of prison life' (MQPL) 140–2, 143, 159, 397, 615
medieval period, imprisonment 677–9
Medlicott, D. 188, 551
Melossi, D. 32, 311, 313–4, 316, 318–9, 319, 320, 321, 726
Mendez, J.E. 431
Mental Health Act 1983 198
Mental Health Act 2007 198
mental health in-reach teams (MHIRTs) 190, 192–5, 197
mental health problems 187–99; and age 189; American prisons 188; Australasia 416–7; causes 187; critical issues 192–8; Dangerous Severe Personality Disorder 197–8; definition 187; depressive illness 189; diagnosis 193; diversion 189–90; equivalence of care 190–1, 192–5; gender differences 188–9; and health 10; healthcare provision 189–90, 190–2; identification 191; imported vulnerability 187; levels 187, 188–9; literature 187–8, 188–9; offender pathway 189–90; personality disorder 197–8; risk management 196–7; severe mental illness (SMI) 188; and solitary confinement 179, 180; stress 187; women 558; young offenders 189

mental healthcare provision: access 191–2, 193; community mental healthcare 192; community provision 195; critical issues 192–8; diversion 189–90; and dividing practices 198–9; equivalence of care 190–1, 192–5; and ethnicity 192; in-reach services 191; intelligent kindness 199; models 190–1; pressure 194; primary mental healthcare 193; risk management 196–7; staff 194
Merback, M. 679
Merriman, P. 124
Merton, R. 85–6
Messinger, S. 79
Messinger, S.L. 660
Mexico 103, 463
migrants 381–2, 448–9, 705–6
militarization 461, 462–3, 469
Mills, J. 670
mindscaping 208–9
Minimising and Managing Physical Restraint (MMPR) 542
Minke, L.K. 395
minority groups 109
Minson, S. 628
mission statements 42–4, 47–8, 52
Moczydlowski, Pavel 19
mode of calculation, changes in 61–2
Modernising the Management of the Prison Service 644–5
Moore, A. 156
Moore, L. 556, 560, 562
Moore, M. 172
Morin, K.M. 125
Morreall, J. 278
Morris, A. 554
Morris, E. 20
Morrison, T. 582
Morrison, W. 549, 729
Morrison, William D. 33
Moscoso, J. 679
Mountbatten, Earl Louis 478–80
Mubarek, Zahid 58, 532, 573
Müller, M. 460
multicultural prison, the 572–5
multiculturalism 88–9, 577–9
Muncie, J. 530
Murder (Abolition of the Death Penalty) Act 1965 9
Murder Act 1752 28
murder rates 727
Murphy, J. 172
Murray, R. 432
Muslim prisoners 89, 579–80
mutilation 444
Myatt, Gareth 536, 541–2

National Association for the Care and
Resettlement of Offenders (NACRO) 715,
717, 719
National Audit Office (UK) 158, 650–1, 655–6
National Council for Independent Monitoring
Boards 11
National Deviancy Conference 715
National Health Service (NHS) 190–1, 211,
500
National Offender Management Service
(NOMS) 11, 14, 210–1, 500, 507–8, 524,
535, 592, 611, 653, 654–5, 664, 720; *Supply
Reduction Good Practice Guide* 213
National Partnership Agreement 211
National Preventive Mechanism (NPM) 645–6,
649
National Prison Association (USA) 40
Native Americans 340–3
Nayak, A. 575–6
negative othering 634–5
Nelken, D. 67
neo-conservatism 67
neo-liberalism 67, 83, 152, 196, 196–7, 317,
337, 398, 455, 456, 557, 569, 581, 713, 722
Neroth, P. 376
Netherlands, the, imprisonment rates 104, 377;
prison design 118; prison population 14;
prisons 377–8; private prisons 153–4
networking, sex offenders 251–2
Neve, L. 557, 562
new criminology 310
New Labour 515, 552–3, 572–3, 720–1
new penology 71
new public management (NPM) 719
new punitiveness 120, 121, 152, 326, 413, 552;
rise of 116
New Right 65, 67–70, 152
New York Daily News 296
The New York Times 1
New York Times 370
New Zealand 64–5; aims, imprisonment 43,
49; biculturalism 411; imprisonment rates
104, 410–1; indigenous prisoners 340,
349–51, 353, 410–1; Māori Focus Units
340, 350, 351; mental health problems
416–7; mental healthcare provision 189,
190, 192; overcrowding 413; Pacific Islander
Units 340, 351; prison population 410;
private prisons 150, 154; punitive turn 410;
Regional Prison Project 350–1;
rehabilitation 414–5
Newgate Prison 301, 681, 685, 688, **689**
Newsnight (TV program) 11
Newton, C. 91
Newton, M. 500, 510
Nielson, M. 277

Nigeria 107, 424, 426, 705, 706
no-frills prisons 57
Nolan, M. 453
NOMS 159
non-custodial sentences 33
Nordic exceptionalism 67, 115–6, 121–2, 125,
388–90
Nordic model: imprisonment rates 388; key
statistical figures *390*, 390–2; pre-trial
detention 398; prison conditions 388, 389;
prison officers 397–8; prison population *390*,
390; prison size 391; prisons 388–99;
recidivism 395–6; regimes 397; rehabilitation
395; sentences 392–3; studies 394–8, 399;
welfare schemes 393–4
North Korea 453
Northern Ireland 21, 93, 555–7, 615–6
Northern Ireland Human Rights Commission
556
Norway 82, 96, 125; children 631; drugs and
drug abuse 396; foreign national prisoners
396–7, 700, 701; importation model 394;
imprisonment rates 375, *390*, 391;
indigenous prisoners 399; key statistical
figures *390*, 390–2; measuring the quality of
prison life' (MQPL) 397; pre-trial detention
398; preventive detention order ('*forvaring*')
392; prison officers 397; prison population
390, *390*; prison size 389, 391; prisons
375–6, 377, 388–99; probation offices 392;
recidivism 395–6; regimes 397; reintegration
guarantee 394; sentences 391, 392, 392–3;
solitary confinement 398; studies 394–8,
399; welfare schemes 393–4, 396; young
offenders 391
not-for-profit NGO sector 162
novel psychoactive substances (NPS) 215–6
Nowak, M. 452
NSW Department of Corrective Services 159
Nuevo Modelo prisons 18–9
null effect 45, 46–7
Nussbaum, M. 624

OASys Sexual Predictor (OSP) 248–9
Obama, Barack 370–1
occupational cultures 132, 132–3
occupational therapy 193
O'Donnell, I. 49–50
Offender Engagement Programme 611
offender management, and desistance 610–2
offender personality disorder pathway (OPDP)
programme 499–500
Oglethorpe, James 681–2
O'Hagan, S 691
OMail 289–92, 295–6
O'Malley, P. 135

OOIIO Architecture 121
open prisons 35
opportunity theory 209
oppression 623
order 93–6
order, maintenance of 78
Organization for Security and Co-operation in Europe 17
Organization of American States 16
Ornduff, J. 519
O'Sullivan, E. 49–50
overcrowding 11, 151–2, 652–3; Africa 427–8, 433, 436; Asia 449; Australasia 413–4; and human rights 330, 332–5; Latin America 464–5; local circumstances 333
Owers, A. 267, 524, 615, 645, 646, 652
Owers Report 615–6, 618

Pacific islands: imprisonment rates 411–2, *412*; mental health problems 416; prison conditions 413–4; prison population 411, *412*; rehabilitation 415–6
pains of imprisonment 586–602; civil death 588; deprivation of autonomy 593–5; deprivation of certainty 595–9; deprivation of security 590–3; disculturation 588; entry shock 587–8; foreign national prisoners 597–9, 701; loss of freedom 589–90; micro intrusions 589–90; moral shift 588; new 595–601; reception rituals 589; release and reintegration 599–601; traditional 589–95; and trust 593; violence 591
Pakistan 445, 447
panopticon model 16, 29, 41, 71, 590, 686
Parenti, C. 724
Parhar, K.K. 257
Parkhurst Prison 26, 31
parole, eligibility 9
parole board hearings, video conferencing 292, 294–5
Pate, K. 557, 562
Patel Report 211, 212
Paterson, Alexander 15–6, 34
Patton, M.Q. 668–9
Pavarini, M. 32, 311, 313–4
Pearce, William 644
Penal Affairs Consortium 720
penal climate 66
penal culture 111
penal expansionism 111
penal modernism, crisis of 61
penal philosophy, and prison design 114–6, 124, 126
penal politics 55–75; aims, imprisonment 56, 60–2; comparative differences 62–3; debate antecedents 56–7; decent but austere mantra

57; diversity 71; and globalization 64; influence 55–6; information exchange 64–5; issues 55–6; New Right and 65, 67–70; prison population 62–7; of punishment 58, 61, 62; risk calculation 61–2, 70–2; and risk management 61–2; risk representation 72–3; scope 59; treatment of prisoners 56; votes in 55
penal probity 74
penal range 61
Penal Reform International (PRI) 427, 431
penal servitude 25
Penal Servitude Act 1853 40
Penal Servitude Act 1857 40
Penal Servitude Act 1864 26
Penal Servitude Commission 26
penal severity 106
penal solitude 41
penal trends 64
penal-welfare 33–4
penal/welfare complex 723–5
Penfold, C. 213, 214
Penitentiary Act 1779 29
Pennsylvania system, the 40
penological imagination 593
penological modernism 55
Pentonville Prison 16, 25, 30, 31, 685, 686–7, **687**
performance management 39, 143
performance measurement 135, 136, 138, 143; key performance targets 139–40; performance indicators 47, 158; and quality of prison life 140–2
permissiveness 70
Perrone, D. 156
personality disorder 197–8
Peru: pre-trial detainees 463; prison conditions 464; prison population 462, 463; women's imprisonment 557
Peters, E. 678
Petersilia, J. 285–6
Philippines, the 445–6, 447
Phillips, C. 568, 572, 572–4, 574, 575–6, 576–7, 579–80, 581–2, 669, 671, 702
physical force 94–5
physical restraint, young offenders 536, 541–2
Piacentini, L. 381
Piche, J. 723
Pickard, H. 636
Pickering, S. 556
Pierce, G. 365
Piketty, T. 385
Piranesi, Giambattista 684, 685
Pitt, Moses, *The Cry of the Oppressed* 681
Pizzaro, J.M. 179
Plain Dealer, The 297–8

Platek, M. 380
Player, E. 506
Plugge, E. 559
Poland 19–20, 315, 380–1
Police Act 1997 601
political correctness 573, 574
political economy: criticisms of 314–6;
    economic cycles 317–20, **319**; post-Fordist
    society 320–1; of punishment 309–21,
    360–1
political prisoners 21, 484
political will, for change 17–9
Pollack, S. 560, 561
Pollock, G. 688
populist punitiveness 74–5
positive custody 46
poverty 108, 624
power: imbalance 95; interpersonal 90;
    legitimate 95; prison officers 268; prisoners
    93; relations 85
power-draining function 48
Powers, G. 177
Pratt, J. 390, 397, 403, 410
Pratt, S. 388–9
Pratt, T.C. 155–6, 156
pre-trial detainees: Africa 428, 429, 433; Latin
    America 463–4; Nordic model 398; prison
    population 447, 448–9
Preservation of the Rights of Prisoners (PROP)
    714–5, 715
Price, D. 266, 267, 691
Priestley, P. 41, 249, 250–1, 252
Prieur, A. 394
Prins, S.J. 192
Prison Act 1877 27, 642
prison adaptation and socialization 84–7
prison building programme 333–4
prison churn rate 207
prison climate 433, 436, 441–2
Prison Commission 27, 35, 713
prison conditions 1, 8–12; Africa 429–32; Latin
    America 464–5; Nordic model 388, 389
prison culture 87–93
prison design 114–27; agenda 126–7; American
    117, 118, 120, 125; building process 123–4;
    carceral geography 120–2; carceral space
    114; and criminal justice system 114; cultural
    symbolism 116; immigration detention
    centres 703; lived environment 118; Nordic
    exceptionalism 121–2, 125; and penal
    philosophy 114–6, 124, 126; policy context
    114, 118–20; privatization 118–9, 122–3;
    process 122–4; and punishment 116;
    research 117–8, 126; supermax prisons
    175–6; and surveillance technologies 124–5,
    126; symbolic role 121; value for money

119; women's prison 121; *see also*
    architecture
prison disturbances, United States of America
    77
prison expansionism 101–11; and crime control
    103–5; drivers 106–7; and imprisonment
    rates *102*, 102–3; persistence of prisons
    106–7; social and economic structures
    107–10, 111
Prison Governors' Association 727
prison industrial complex 110
prison inspection 9, 641–57, 652–7, 657;
    accountability 649–50, 651–2; budget 647,
    653, 657; Chief Inspector of Prisons 643,
    656; community of practice 650; draft report
    and recommendations 649; effectiveness
    651, 652; Expectations 648; future challenges
    652–7; history and development 642–4; and
    human rights 645; independence 655;
    international 7–8; judgement criteria 647–8;
    judgements 649; management-independent
    spectrum 642, 651; National Audit Office
    (UK) 650–1; National Preventive Mechanism
    (NPM) 645–6, 649; observation 649; policy
    inspection 649; prisoner survey and discussions
    648; process 647–50; reasons for independent
    646; role 644–5, 657; staff discussions 648–9;
    stakeholder surveys 652; teams 647; thematic
    inspections 651; visits 641–2
Prison Islam 491
prison life: foreign national prisoners 701–2,
    707; Latin America 465–9, 469–70; quality
    of 140–2, 143, 159, 397, 615
prison managers: accountability 135; agency
    134, 137–8; American 133; diversity 132–3;
    ethos 135; and globalization 133–6, 136–8;
    ideal types 133; insularity 132; key
    performance targets 139–40, 143; under late
    modernity 136–8; as local practitioners
    132–3; occupational culture 132–3;
    perspectives 131–6; prison managerialism
    142–4; and quality of prison life 140–2, 143;
    role 131; self-regulation 134; use of
    discretion 135
prison officers 78, 265–80; ambitions 272;
    coping mechanisms 277–9; culture 277–9,
    280; custodial tasks 266; duty of care 271,
    273; emotional effects on 274–5; emotional
    intelligence 273–7, *276*; empathy 273; good
    273–7; high security prisons 480, 482;
    humour 277–9; identity 269; insularity 132,
    270; interpersonal interactions 266–7;
    literature coverage 265; machismo 132;
    morale 480; motivation 269, 271–2; Nordic
    model 397–8; occupational culture 132–3;
    occupational socialization 269–71;

peacekeeping 268; power 268; promotion 480; purpose 271–2; qualities 273; recruitment process 269; and rehabilitation 267; rehabilitative orientation 272; as role model 267–8; roles 266–9, 272; and security 271–2; solidarity. 270; training 269–70, 389; trust 279–80; typical 269; women 522; work 266–9; working personality 132

Prison Officers Association 10, 719

Prison Policy Institute (PPI) 291, 294

prison population 8, 652–3, 699; absolute size 65; Africa 427, **427**; Asia 447–9; Australasia 403; Australia 151, 403, 404; Bolivia 462; Brazil 462, 463, 465; Canada 345; Chile 463; China 447, 448; Colombia 462, 463; Denmark 14; and economic cycles 317–20, **319**; Ecuador 462, 463; ethnic origin 574–5, 581; European Union (EU) 331; Finland 332; foreign national prisoners 700; Germany 14; global perspective 330–2; Hong Kong 448–9; Iceland 390; increase in 1, 11, 13–4, 73, 74, 101, 103, 110, 120, 330–2, 361–2, 384, 712–3, 719; India 447, 448, 455; indigenous prisoners 340, 341, 343, 344, 345, 346, 349, 353, *407*, 407; international comparisons 17; Japan 447; Latin America 462, 463, 465; Mexico 463; the Netherlands 14; New Zealand 410; Nordic model 390, *390*; Norway *390*, 390; penal politics 62–7; Peru 462, 463; the Philippines 446; pre-trial detainees 331–2, 447, 448–9; and privatization 151; racial disparities 568; reduction in 33; Russia 17; Second World War 35; sex offenders 246–7; Uruguay 463; USA 1, 13–4, 151, 332, 570; Venezuela 463; women 13, 331, *406*, 408–9, 551, 552, 555, 557, 628; world 101, 462, 557, 698

Prison Rating System (PRS) 158–9

Prison Reform Trust 717, 719

prison representations 59, 677–95; 18h century 685–6; 1500 to 1800 679–82, **680**, **681**, **682**, 683–5; documentary 690–5, **692**, **694**; graphic journalism 688; medieval period 677–9; photography 688, 690, 690–5, **692**, **694**; portraits 693–4; realism 688, **689**; still life genre 694–5; truth claims **692**; Victorian 686–90, **687**, **689**; young offenders 695

prison research 96–7, 659–73; access 664, 665, 665–7, 673; agenda 664; anonymity 666; carrying keys 668; collaborative 661; conduct 668–70; confidentiality 666; contact time 672; Dictaphones 668–9; distress 672; emotional dimensions 671–3; ethical obligations 666–7; ethnographies 659–65; formative period 659–61; funding 664;

gatekeeping process 665; gender issues 670–1; identity politics 669; importance 673; informed consent 666; interviews 666–7, 671, 672; methods 661; motivations 659; neutrality 669; prisoner engagement 669–70; psychological 661; qualitative 668–9; rapport 669–70, 671; recent trends 664–5; security issues 668–9; suspicion and hostility 663; women 661–2

Prison Service Instruction (2012/08) 534

Prison Service Journal 433

Prison Service Order (PSO) 4800 538

prison stigmata 600–1

prison work 266–9; emotions in 274–5

prisoner classification 479; Asia 449–52

prisoner community 87–8

prisoner distress: measure 234; and suicide 233–4, *235*, 236, **236**, 237, 237–8

prisoners 14–5; aging 514–25; compromises with 78; correspondence 290–1; criminological studies 311; daily routine 8; hierarchy 87, 89–90, 91, 95–6, 522; identity 79, 124; isolation 284; lack of sympathy for 55; leadership 96; living conditions 119; moral reform 30–1; null effect on 45, 46–7; numbers 13–4; political 21; power 93; production of 360–1; real men 79–80; on remand 9, 14–5; rights 56, 74; rights organizations 50–1; safety 46; self-respect 39; serving indeterminate sentences 15; socialization 84–7; status 81, 87, 89–90, 522; submission 94; Sykes's analysis 78; treatment of 56; types 79, 85–6; unsentenced 9; value system 78–80; victimization 46; Victorian period women 25–6; voting rights 57–8, 66, 617; vulnerable 33; women 13, 25–6

Prisoners Learning Alliance 656

prisoners' rights movement 50–1, 714–6

prisoner-transfer agreements 705

prisonization 84–5, 630; secondary 625, 634

prisons: Africa 423–-36; Argentina 469; Asia 441–56; Australasia 403–17; Brazil 469; Bulgaria 379–80; China 453; continental European 375–85; and crime control 103–5; definition 1; Denmark 388, 395, 398; distinctive qualities 77; Ethiopia 426, 430–1; Finland 375–6, 388; France 378–9; gang system 444; Germany 378; Greece 383; Iceland 388; incapacitation function 105; Italy 381–2; Kenya 426; Latin America 460–70; literary and cinematic traditions 59; the Netherlands 377–8; Nigeria 424; Nordic model 388–99; Norway 375–6, 377, 388–99; and the outside world 83–4; persistence of 106–7; physicality 58–9;

Poland 380–1; political economy of 312–4; political justification for 103; post-Fordist society 320–1; private sector construction 152; privatization 83; purpose 103, 105; role 77, 83, 101, 107, 722; Russian Federation 381; Sierra Leone 424; soft power 591; South Africa 424, 425, 430–1; Spain 382–3; Sweden 375–7, 388, 397; Sykes's analysis 77–80; symbolic role 105; treatment-oriented 82; Uganda 424; Vietnam 444; women's 553, 554, 554–5, 556; Zimbabwe 425–6
Prisons Act 1835 31
Prisons Act 1839 31
Prisons Act 1865 26–7
Prisons Act 1898 33
Prisons Act 1952 35–6
Prisons and Probation Ombudsman 238
Prisons Research Centre (PRC), University of Cambridge 665
Prisons Review Team (PRT) 615
private finance initiatives (PFI) 122, 152–5
private prisons 110, 149–62; American 149, 150, 155–6, 157–8, 162; Australia 149, 150, 153, 159, 161, 162; Brazil 154, 159–60; Canada 150; comparative cost analysis 156; contracts 161–2; corporate structure review 161; correctional effectiveness 157–60; cost efficiency 152–3, 155–7; definition 149; efficiency comparisons 155, 156; France 150, 153–4; the future 162; Germany 153–4; historical 149; history and development 149–50; incarceration rates 150; and indigenous prisoners 342–3; Israel 154; issues 161–2; literature 149; the Netherlands 153–4; New Zealand 150, 154; not-for-profit NGO sector 162; operational savings 153; outcomes 155–61; political influences 152–5; profit 149–50, 154; recidivism 160; semi-privée 153–4; service delivery reform 153; South Africa 150, 154; spread of 153–4; state involvement 149, 150, 161; support services 153–4; United Kingdom 150, 153, 156–7, 158–9
privatization 51, 83, 110, 719; catalysts of 151–2; history and development 149–50; and overcrowding 151–2; overview 150; political influences 152–5; prison design 118–9, 122–3; and prison population 151; support services 153–4
probation 34, 378, 380, 599–600, 607
probation officers 9
probation offices 392
probation trusts 721
Progression PIPEs 500
Prosser, Barry, death of 9–10
psychodynamic theory 503

Public Accounts Committee 654–5, 656
public protection 3, 43, 68–9
public spending, priorities 1
public–private partnerships 122, 152–5
punishment 57, 78, 94; actuarial calculus 384; aims 62; alternative sanctions 462; approaches to 310–4; budgetary pressure 385; and consent 173–4; costs 385; and crime 309–10, 314; and crime control 61; cultural turn 316–7; definition 170–1, 309–10; and deprivation 170; deterrence 311–2; and economic cycles 317–20, **319**; expansion of 462–5; expressive function 171–2; fairness 172–4; function 385; Garland on 314; history and development 312–3; justification 171–2; and the labour market 314–5, 316; marketization 725–6; medieval period 677; methods 170; more vs. better 63; New Right and 67–70; Nordic model 388–99; political economy 309–21, 360–1; politics of 58, 61, 62; post-Fordist society 320–1; preventative 384; and prison design 116; quality 311; quantity 311; retributive 169, 171, 172–4, 182; severity hypothesis 315; sociology of 49, 309, 310; the state and 63–4; threat of 311–2; and trust 384; Victorian period 25; and welfare 723–5; Wilde on 52
punishment-as-crime-control 49
punishment-as-moral-problem 49
punitive bondage 680
Putnum, R. 291

race, racism and racial disparities 88–9, 568–82; biologism 578–9; black:white ethnic ratio 570; civil death 580–2; and class 569; controversies and complexities 570; double selection 569; dynamics of imprisonment 568, 568–71; ethnic codes 574; ethnic differences 574; inter-ethnic interaction 574–5; literature 573–4; Muslim prisoners 579–80; negotiating 571–2; new ethnicities 581; prison ethnographies 571–2; prison multicultures 572–4; prison population 568; race equality 573; reverse racism 576–7; social relations 574; white prisoners and 575–7; and whiteness 576–7
Race Relations Amendment Act 2000 573
Radical Alternatives to Prison (RAP) 712, 715, 717
radicalization 489–90, 491, 579
radio 286
Radzinowicz, L 480, 481
Rahman, Aamer 577
Ramsbotham, David 541, 644–5, 652
Ramsey, M. 206

Rapoport, R. 504, 505
rational choice models 94
Read, J.S. 434
reception rituals 589
recidivism 27, 33, 44, 713; and communication technologies 285–6; Nordic model 395–6; Norway 395–6; private prisons 160; sex offenders 255, 261
Reclaim Justice Network 726
RECOOP (Resettlement and Care for Older Ex-offenders and Prisoners) 521
recovery capital, drugs and drug abuse 214–5, 217
recreation 9
redistributive social policy 69
reductionism 607
reductivism 549
re-education 42, 607
Reform 158–9
reform, 1770s–1850s 27–32
Reformatory and Industrial Schools 531
reformatory prison project 26
Regional Prison Project, New Zealand 350–1
regressive modernisation 717
rehabilitation 41, 46–7, 84, 105, 169, 171, 375–6, 378, 607, 613, 662; Australasia 414–6; forms 610; Nordic model 395; Pacific islands 415–6; and prison officers 267; risk assessments 415; sex offenders 253, 260; women 415
rehabilitation revolution, the 726–8
Reiman, J. 107, 110
Reiner, R. 268
release and reintegration 599–601, 613, 614
release on temporary licence (ROTL) 599, 654
religious freedoms 340–3, 342–3
remand prisoners 9, 14–5
rendition 325
reoffending rates 247, 247; sex offenders 247–9, 248, 261
Repatriation Agreements 598
Research and Advisory Group on the Long-Term Prison System 486
Research Councils UK 664
resistance 93, 95–6
resources 49
responsibility 69
responsibilization 609
restorative justice 64–5, 610
Restraint Advisory Board (RAB) 542
retreatism 85
retribution 169, 171, 172, 182; fairness 172–4, 179, 180–1; and solitary confinement 179–81
retributivism 549
Returns and Reintegration Fund (RRF) 705

reverse racism 576–7
rewards 78, 94
Rickwood, Adam 536, 542
RICS 119
Ridgeway, J. 52
riots 95–6, 483–5, 662–3
Risk, Need and Responsivity (RNR) principles 257, 259, 261
risk and risk management 61–2, 70–1, 196–7, 199; climate 68; communication technologies 285; reduction 39, 46–7; representation 72–3; suicide 224, 228, 234, 236; women 552
risk assessments 197, 199, 415, 538
risk calculations 61–2, 70–2
Risk Matrix 2000 248–9
ritual humiliation 90
Robert, P. 379
Roberts, S. 668
Robertson, J.E. 662
Robinson, C. 554
Rock, P. 231
Ross, Richard 695
Roxell, L. 252
Royal Commission into Aboriginal Deaths in Custody (1987–1991) 346, 407
Rua, M. 396
Ruggiero, V. 677
Rule 43 Units 250, 250–4
Rusche, G. 32, 311, 311–2, 314–5, 316–7
Russell, Whitworth 31
Russian Federation 16–7, 68, 381
Rutherford, A. 133
Rwanda 427
Ryan, M. 712, 716, 718
Ryan, Rod 362

Sabo, D. 209
Safer Custody Group 225–6
Safer Locals Programme 226
Salla, F. 465
Salter, A. 256
Salvatore, R.D. 461
Samaritans, The 225
Sampson, A. 249–50, 251, 253–4
Sampson, R. 613
Sandler, M. 558
sanitation 10–1, 58
Santana, Roberto 18
Saving Lives: Our Healthier Nation White Paper 225
Scharff Smith, P. 177, 287–8, 291, 627
Schiele, Egon 690
Schinkel, M. 617
Schmucker, M. 257, 259
Schumpeter, J. 317, 320

Schwaebe, C. 254, 259
Schwartz, J. 369
Scotland 42, 49, 66, 554–5, 613, 616–8
Scotland Act 1998 554
Scott, D. 106–7, 266, 561
Scottish Justice Matters 611
Scraton, P. 556, 557, 560, 562
Scull, A. 32, 311
Second World War 34–6
secondary prisonization 625, 634
Secure Children's Homes (SCHs) 531, 533, 534, 536–7
secure containment 105
Secure Training Centre (STC) 532, 533, 534, 535–6, 540–1
securitization 461, 469
security, deprivation of 590–3
security categorization 479
security industry 110
Security Information Reports 491
Securus Technology 293–4
Seddon, T. 195, 198
Seewald, K. 188
Segal, G.F. 156
Segrave, M. 559
segregation 485–6; foreign national prisoners 700–1; sex offenders 250–4, 260; *see also* solitary confinement
segregation units 175, 176
Select Committee on ageing prisoners 517, 524
Select Committee on Home Affairs, 1987 122
self-harm: rates 727; and suicide 232–3; women 92, 188, 231, 552, 558, 727; young offenders 529, 542–3
sentences 515; ageing prisoners 515; Australia *405*; boundary cases 60; continuum 549; controversy 60; Detention and Training Order (DTO) 532–3; Detention in a Young Offender Institution (DYOI) 532, 533; France 379; and human rights 334–5; indeterminate 15, 595–7; indigenous prisoners 343; lengths 334–5; life without parole (LWOP) 52; non-custodial 33; Norway 391, 392, 392–3; Secure Training Order (STO) 535; sex offenders 246–7; solitary confinement 177; women 553
separate system, the 30–1, 40, 41
Serco 110, 161, 721
service delivery reform, private prisons 153
Severson, K. 299
sex offenders 89, 246–61; abuse 249–50; American 254; Australia 251–2; Canada 252, 259; denial 254, 254–6; 'Don't Ask – Can't Tell' principle 260; imprisonment experience 246, 249–56; integrated units 254; networking 251–2; paradox 249, 260;

policymaking 246; prison population 246–7; recidivism 255, 261; rehabilitation 253, 260; reoffending rates *247*, 247–9, *248*, 261; scapegoating 249; segregation 250–4, 260; sentences 246–7; staff treatment 252–3; survival strategy 254; Sweden 252; treatment programmes 256–61, *258*, 260–1
Sexual Offences Act 2003 246
sexual subculture 91
sexual victimization 46
Seychelles, the 427
Shalev, S. 179
shame 600
Shamir, B. 272
Shammas, V.L. 125, 397
Shank, A. 368
Sherwan, D. 210
Shine, J. 500, 510
Shute, S. 642, 651
Sierra Leone 107, 424, 432
silent system, the 30–1, 40, 41
Sim, J. 194, 712, 716, 718, 726
Simon, J. 71, 106–7, 317, 320, 321, 597
Singapore 444
Single Equality Act 2006 552
Size, M. 660–1
Skanska 123
Skarbek, D. 91
Skardhamar, T. 396
Sloan, J. 669
slopping out 8, 10–1
Smallbone, S. 251, 252
Smart, C. 550
Smaus, G. 723
Smith, A. 363, 364
Smith, P.S. 398
Smulls, Herbert 370
Snell, H. 506
Snowball, L. 408
social care, ageing prisoners 518–9, 524
social contract theory 173–4
social control 49–50, 83, 360
Social Exclusion Unit 207
social functions 48–50
social justice 622–3
social networks, drugs and drug abuse 209
social relations 87–93
social structures 107–10, 111
socialization 84–7; prison officers 269–71
Socrates 677
Sodexo 161
soft power 591
solitary confinement 41, 169; conditions 175–6; definition 175; and deterrence 178–9; discipline 176; duration 174, 177; environmental uniformity 176; and fairness

179, 180–1; the future 181–2; inmates 176; justification 180–1; Latin America 469; and mental illness 179, 180; Norway 398; numbers in 175; psychological impact 177; and retribution 179–81; and the self 177–8; sentences 177; turn to 174–5; young offenders 541

Soltis, Kathleen 368

Sori, Soni 452

South Africa 17, 68; children's rights 637; Judicial Inspectorate for Correctional Services 431; prison population 427; prisons 424, 425, 430–1; private prisons 150, 154

Soviet Union 7

Spain 382–3

Sparks, R. 57, 95, 138, 208, 233–4, 265, 266, 269, 477, 505, 514, 515, 516, 517, 523

Spierenburg, P. 680

Spohn, C. 104–5

Spunging Houses 681

Sri Lanka 445, 447, 449

staff: decline in numbers 516; ethical standards 20; high security prisons 479, 482; inspection 648–9; Latin American shortages 465–6; training 8, 336; treatment of sex offenders 252–3; women 522

staff–prisoner relationships 132, 467–8, 469–70

Starr, P. 385

state, the: and imprisonment 63–4; legitimacy 70; moral test 324; power 725–6; responsibility 161; role of 61, 67–70; sovereign obligations 150; Wacquant on 568–9

state building 107

Stein, S.J. 275

Steinberg, J. 425, 693

Stengel, E. 233

Stevens, Terrence 362–3

Stevenson, B. 108–9

Stone, Michael 197–8, 523

Story of the Prison Population 2003–2012 (Ministry of Justice) 246

Strategic Objectives for Female Offenders (MoJ) 553

Straw, Jack 645, 721

Street Crime Initiative 543

Sub-committee on Prevention of Torture (SPT) 645–6

Subotzky, Mikhael 692–3, **694**

subversion 85

Sudbury, J. 554, 557, 561, 702, 725

suicide 224–38, 655; attempted 227, 233; causes 226–9, 230, 234; collective responsibility 225; combined models 226, 234; definition 232; deprivation models 226; early studies 227; importation models 226; individual vulnerability factors 226–8, 227; methods

228; models 238, **238**; motivation 229; policy background 225–6; prevention 224, 227, 236, 238; prisoner distress 233–4, 235, **236**, 236, 237–8; prisoner profiles 231–2; and psychiatric history 228, 232; rates 226, 230, 234, 235, 236, 238, 727; reporting 232; risk 224, 228, 234, 236; and self-harm 232–3; situational vulnerability factors 228–9; statistical information 232; studies 233; timing 228; women 558, 559; women prisoners 188, 228, 230–1; young offenders 229–30, 529, 542–3

Suicide is Everyone's Concern (HMCIP) 225

supermax confinement 169–83; the future 181–2; philosophical background 170–4; solitary confinement 169, 174–82

supermax prisons 94, 95, 96, 175; prison design 175–6

Supply Reduction Good Practice Guide (NOMS) 213

surplus population 360–1

surveillance technologies 124–5, 126

Sutherland, E. 309, 311, 729

Sutton, J.R. 106

Swann, R. 210

Sweden: aims, imprisonment 43, 44, 49; imprisonment rates 375, 390, 391; key statistical figures 390, 390; prison officers 397–8; Prison Treatment Act 376; prisons 375–7, 388, 397; sex offenders 252; women's imprisonment 558

Switzerland 700

Sykes, G. 514, 525, 569, 587, 589, 590, 660; The Society of Captives 77, 77–80, 80, 81, 82, 84, 87, 90, 93–4, 96, 117, 179

Sykes, G.M. 470

symbolic function 48

symbolic violence 619

Systematic Monitoring and Analysing of Race Equality Template 573

Tabler, Richard Lee 298

Tafero, Jessie Joseph 368

Taiwan 446, 448

Tanner, W. 160

targets 44, 47, 139–40

Tartaro, C. 662

Taylor, D.A. 700

Taylor, L. 86, 516–7, 661, 663

Taylor, R. 498

telemedicine services 292

television 286–7

Telle, K. 396

Thailand 448, 451

Tham 376

Thatcher, Margaret 67–8, 716

therapeutic communities 497–510; accreditation 500; achievements 510; agency 505–6; aims 497; application process 499; and attachment 501; budgetary constraints 507–8; commitment 499; and communication 502–4; and containment 501–2; criminological research 498; culture of enquiry 502–4; de-othering 504; developmental sequence 500–6; effectiveness 498; expulsions 508–9; friendships 503–4; group therapy 502–3; involvement 504–5; limits 501–2; meetings 504; occupancy levels 508, 509; offender personality disorder pathway (OPDP) programme 499–500; origins 497; oversight 507–8; participatory citizenship 504–5; permissiveness 501; places 498–9; principles and practices 497–8; process of personal change 500–6; Progression PIPEs 500; relationship with prison 506–10; rep jobs 504–5; residents 499, 500; resilience 510; size 501; therapeutic performance 508–10; therapy and security balance 507; women 556
therapeutic prisons 3, 90
thief culture 81
time, loss of 45–6, 209
time envy 285
time management 208–9
Titley, G. 572, 578
Toch, H. 525
Toggia, P.S. 426
toilet facilities 10–1
Tombs, S. 729
Tompkins, C.N.E. 209
Tonry, M. 65, 70
torture 325, 336, 430, 431, 434, 452–3, 678
total institutions 80–1, 470, 660
Tournel, H. 670
training, prison officers and staff 8, 269–70, 336, 389
Transforming Management of Young Adults in Custody 539
Transforming Rehabilitation strategy 653
Transforming the Management of Young Adult Offenders 532
transparency 9
transportation 25, 26, 28, 29, 40, 679
Transportation Act 1718 29
Transue, Hillary 363
treatment programmes; drug abuse 207, 212–3, 214–5, 396; sex offenders 256–61, 258, 260–1
treatment-oriented prisons 82
tribal prisons 341, 343
Trotter, C. 267–8
trust 125, 279–80, 384, 491–2, 593, 618

Tumim, Stephen 644, 652
Turkey 7, 21
Tyler, I. 724–5

Uganda 17, 424, 426–8
Ugelvik, T. 395, 701
UK Border Agency 592, 598
UN Centre for Human Rights 17
unemployment 314–5, 316
Ungar, M. 460
United Kingdom: private prisons 150, 153, 156–7, 158–9; recidivism 160
United Nations Basic Principles for the Treatment of Prisoners 192
United Nations Convention against Torture and Other Cruel, Inhuman or Degrading Treatment or Punishment, Optional Protocol 7–8, 645
United Nations Convention on the Rights of the Child 628
United Nations Office on Drugs and Crime 215, 216
United Nations Rules for the Treatment of Women Prisoners and Non-custodial Measures for Women Offenders 559–60
United Nations (UN) 16, 645; Latin American Institute 18
United Nations (UN) 42, 327
United States of America 96, 359–71; ageing prisoners 514, 515; aims, imprisonment 43, 44, 49; black prisoners 86, 108–9; botched executions 360, 367–71; capital punishment 60, 359–60, 364–71; communicative technology 284–301; community corrections 561; corrections industry 361–3; drug trade 361; economic cycles 318, 319, 319–20; economic-punishment nexus 359, 360–4, 371; ethnic minority prisoners 623–4; Federal Bureau of Prisons 156, 158; foreign national prisoners 698, 699, 700, 705; history and development 30–1; and human rights 325; immigration detention centres 699, 703, 704, 705; imprisonment rates 65–6, 83, 102, 103, 104, 316–7, 319, 319–20, 359; indigenous prisoners 340, 340–3, 353; Jim Crow system 571; juvenile detention 363–4; the Marion lockdown 174–5; mass incarceration 285; mental health problems 188; mental healthcare provision 191–2; Muslim prisoners 579–80; National Prison Association 40; Native Americans 340–3; new punitiveness 121; not-for-profit NGO sector 162; paradoxes 359, 371; penal severity 61; prison design 117, 118, 120, 125; prison disturbances 77; prison expansion 73; prison managers 133; prison

population 1, 13–4, 151, 332, 570; prison population ethnic disproportionality 570; prison privatization 83; prison research 660, 662, 663, 664, 665; private prisons 110, 149, 150, 155–6, 157–8, 162; production of prisoners 360–1; punitiveness 359; racial disparities 568, 569, 570, 571; recidivism 160; role of the state 68; sentencing policy 335; separate system 30–1; sex offenders 254; silent system 30–1; social injustice 626; state variations 359; supermax confinement 169–83; Tribal Law and Order Act 341; tribal legal structures 341; tribal prisons 341; victims' rights movement 169; women's imprisonment 557

Universal Declaration of Human Rights (UDHR) 327
unlawful killing 9–10
Unlocking Potential, Transforming Lives (SPS) 616
unsentenced prisoners 9
urbanization 313, 424, 460, 679
Urbina, I. 368
Uruguay 462, 463, 464
US Supreme Court 67

value system, prisoners 78–80
Van Gogh, Vincent 688, 690
van Swaaningen, R. 377–8
Van Zyl Smit, D. 64, 425
Vanneste, C. 319
Venezuela 12, 463, 465
vengeance 365
Verhovek, S.H. 367
victimization 46, 230
victims' rights movement 169
Victorian period 24, 25–7; reform, 1770s–1850s 27–32
video conferencing 292–5, 296
video visitations 288, 292–5, 296
Vietnam 444
violence: causes 179–80; coping mechanisms 591; levels of 12–3; and status 90; symbolic 619
virtual prisons 646
Von Hofer, H. 376
voting rights, prisoners 57–8, 66, 617
Vulnerable Prisoner Unit (VPU) 250, 250–4

Wacquant, L. 83, 96, 107, 108, 316, 394–5, 398, 466, 568, 568–71, 571, 582, 663, 664, 665, 724, 725–6
wages 726–7
Wahidin, A. 515, 519
Wakefield, S. 626, 627–8
Wakeling, H.C. 248
Walker, S. 364–5

Walmsley, R. 101, 331–2, 448, 557
war on drugs 62, 461, 462
war on terror 325
Ward, T. 227, 712, 718
warehouse prisons 96
warehousing 321
Warr, J. 592
Washington Post 294
Weatherburn, D. 408
Webster, C.M 49
Weekes, J.R. 212, 252
Welch, M. 550–1
welfare consensus 714
welfare officers 9
welfare provision regimes 48–9
welfare state 67–8
welfare-oriented exceptionalism 388–99
well-being 236, **237**
Wener, R.E 114, 122, 126
Western, B. 315, 321
Wheeler, S. 84–5
White, Tavon 298
White, W.L. 217–8
Widdecombe, Ann 10–1
Wild, N.J. 252
Wilde, Oscar 33, 52, 586
Wildeman, C. 626, 627–8
Wilkins 361
Wilson, D. 34, 132–3
Wilson, T.D. 260
Winberg, Birgitta 376
Winogrand, Garry 691
Wolfers, J. 365
women: and abolitionism 718; Africa 428; agency 560; Asia 449; Australian prison population *406*, 408–9; bullying 558; children of imprisoned 628–30; crimes against morality 558; criminalization 558, 562; custodial alternatives 554, 560–2; decarceration 560–1; doubly deviant 550, 550–1; enforced separation 559; England and Wales 551–4; foreign national prisoners 554, 559, 702, 723; gender-specific reform 559–60; HIV/AIDS 559; human rights 556; impact of imprisonment upon 231; imprisonment 87, 549–62; indigenous prisoners 344–5, 346, 350–1, 408–9, 410, 560; international comparisons 557–8; mental health problems 188–9, 558; Northern Ireland 555–7; offending behaviour 408; partners of long-term male prisoners 631–5; poverty 624; pregnancy 559; prison adaptations 92–3; prison culture 92–3; prison experiences 558–9; prison officers 522; prison population 13, 331, *406*, 408–9, 551, 552, 555, 557, 628; prison

research 660, 660–1; prisoners 428; rehabilitation 415; reproductive health 559; resistance 560; rise and consolidation of imprisonment 550–7; risk management 552; role 624; Scotland 554–5; secondary prisonization 625; self-harm 92, 188, 231, 552, 558, 727; sentences 553; social control 83; specific needs 558–9; staff 522; stigmatization of 558, 634–5; suicide 188, 228, 230–1, 558, 559; therapeutic communities 556; Victorian period prisoners 25–6; young offenders 533, 536, 537, 539–40

Women for Refugee Women 723
Women in Prison 718
Women's Offending Reduction Programme 552
women's prisons: conditions 11; culture 92–3; design 121
Wood, Joseph R. III 368
Woodcock Report 484
Woolf, Lord Justice 10–1, 333, 489
Woolf Report 718–9
work and work parties 8–9; shortage of 11
work camps 347
workhouses 312, 679
World Health Organization 187, 190, 225; Health in Prisons Programme 195–6
World Pre-Trial/Remand Imprisonment List 331–2
World Prison Brief 330, 427
World Prison Population List 1, 101, 330–1
World Research Group 362
Worrall, A. 560
Wortley, R. 119
Wortley, R.K. 251, 252
Wright, S. 669, 670, 671–2
Wynne, J.M. 252

Xenakis, S. 383

Yalom, I. 505, 506
Young, I.M. 622–3
Young, J. 549, 729
young adults 532, 533, 537, 538, 539–40, 544, 654

Young Offender Institutions (YOIs) 90, 530, 531, 532, 533–5, 537–9, 540, 541, 543–4, 654
young offenders 529–45; borstal system 15–6, 34, 531; budget reductions 544; bullying 535, 540, 542–3; care and management requirements 534; costs 534, 536, 537–8, 543; debate about 529–30; Detention and Training Order (DTO) 532–3; Detention in a Young Offender Institution (DYOI) sentence 532, 533; dual-designation establishments 539–40; education 535; entry shock 587–8; gangs 541; girls 533, 536; history and development 531–2; human rights 544; indeterminate sentences 596; mental health problems 189; Norway 391; numbers in custody 533, 654; physical restraint 536, 541–2; placements 537; prison representations 695; prison violence 12–3; racism 535; reoffending rates 530; risk assessments 538; routes into custody 532–3; Secure Children's Homes (SCHs) 531, 533, 534, 536–7; Secure College 543, 544–5; Secure Training Centre (STC) 532, 533, 534, 535–6, 540–1; Secure Training Order (STO) 535; self-harm 529, 542–3; solitary confinement 541; staff 538, 544; strains 545; suicide 229–30, 529, 542–3; USA 363–4; victimization 540; violence against 529, 540–1; vulnerability 529; women 533, 537, 539–40; young adults 532, 533, 537, 538, 539–40, 544, 654; Young Offender Institutions (YOIs) 530, 531, 532, 533–5, 537–9, 540, 541, 543–4, 654; Youth Custody Centres 531; Youth Treatment Centres 531–2
Youth Custody Centres 531
Youth Justice Board 531, 532, 533, 537
Youth Treatment Centres 531–2

Zaffaroni 466
Zedner, L. 490
Zijderveld, C. 278
Zimbabwe 425–6
Zimring, F. 65–6
Zimring, F.E. 364
Zinoman, P. 444
Zivot, Joel 369